Financial & Managerial Accounting

TENTH EDITION

Belverd E. Needles, Jr., Ph.D., C.P.A., C.M.A.
DePaul University

Marian Powers, Ph.D.
Northwestern University

Susan V. Crosson, M.S. Accounting, C.P.A.
Emory University

SOUTH-WESTERN
CENGAGE Learning

Australia • Brazil • Japan • Korea • Mexico • Singapore • Spain • United Kingdom • United States

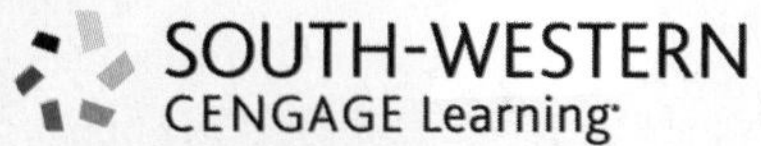

Financial & Managerial Accounting, 10e
International Edition

Belverd Needles, Marian Powers, Susan Crosson

Senior Vice President, LRS/Acquisitions & Solutions Planning: Jack W. Calhoun

Editorial Director, Business & Economics: Erin Joyner

Editor-in-Chief: Rob Dewey

Executive Editor: Sharon Oblinger

Development Editor: Krista Kellman

Editorial Assistant: A.J. Smiley

Sr. Brand Manager: Kristen Hurd

Sr. Market Development Manager: Natalie Livingston

Sr. Marketing Communications Manager: Sarah Greber

Marketing Coordinator: Eileen Corcoran

Sr. Content Project Manager: Scott Dillon

Media Editor: Lysa Kosins

Manufacturing Planner: Doug Wilke

Production Service: Cenveo Publisher Services

Sr. Art Director: Stacy Jenkins Shirley

Internal Designer: Craig Ramsdell

Cover Designer: Patti Hudepohl

Cover Images:

Black and white image: Getty Images/ Rubberball

Color image: Shutterstock Images/ Maxx-Studio

Rights Acquisition Director: Audrey Pettengill

Library of Congress Control Number: 2012955354

International Edition
ISBN-13: 978-1-133-95900-7
ISBN-10: 1-133-95900-8

Asia
www.cengageasia.com
tel: (65) 6410 1200

Australia/New Zealand
www.cengage.com.au
tel: (61) 3 9685 4111

Brazil
www.cengage.com.br
tel: (55) 11 3665 9900

India
www.cengage.co.in
tel: (91) 11 4364 1111

Latin America
www.cengage.com.mx
tel: (52) 55 1500 6000

UK/Europe/Middle East/Africa
www.cengage.co.uk
tel: (44) 0 1264 332 424

Represented in Canada by Nelson Education, Ltd.
www.nelson.com
tel: (416) 752 9100 / (800) 668 0671

Cengage Learning is a leading provider of customized learning solutions with office locations around the globe, including Singapore, the United Kingdom, Australia, Mexico, Brazil, and Japan. Locate your local office at: **www.cengage.com/global**

For product information and free companion resources:
www.cengage.com/international
Visit your local office: **www.cengage.com/global**
Visit our corporate website: **www.cengage.com**

Printed in the United States of America
1 2 3 4 5 6 7 18 17 16 15 14 13

BRIEF CONTENTS

CONTENTS

CHAPTER 5 Accounting for Merchandising Operations 240

CHAPTER 6 Inventories 286

CHAPTER 7 Cash and Internal Control 326

CHAPTER 8 Receivables 362

CHAPTER 9 Long-Term Assets 396

CHAPTER 10 Current Liabilities and Fair Value Accounting 440

CHAPTER 13 The Statement of Cash Flows 594

SUPPLEMENT TO CHAPTER 13 THE DIRECT METHOD OF PREPARING THE STATEMENT OF CASH FLOWS 643

CHAPTER 14 Financial Statement Analysis 652

CHAPTER 15 Managerial Accounting and Cost Concepts 709

CHAPTER 16 Costing Systems: Job Order Costing 753

CHAPTER 17 Costing Systems: Process Costing 793

CHAPTER 18 Value-Based Systems: Activity-Based Costing and Lean Accounting 831

CHAPTER 22 Standard Costing and Variance Analysis 997

CHAPTER 23 Short-Run Decision Analysis 1039

CHAPTER 24 Capital Investment Analysis 1073

LATEST RESEARCH ON STUDENT LEARNING

We talked to over 150 instructors and discovered that current textbooks did not effectively:

- Help students logically process information
- Build on what students already know in a carefully guided sequence
- Reinforce core accounting concepts throughout the chapters
- Help students see how the pieces of accounting fit together

The Needles/Powers/Crosson series addresses these challenges by creating a better solution for you. This includes new features and a brand new structure for enhanced learning.

We have worked hard to create a textbook that mirrors the way you learn!

© Martin Marraud/Getty Images

A LOGICAL METHODOLOGY TO BUILDING KNOWLEDGE: THE THREE SECTION APPROACH

Needles/Powers/Crosson continuously evolves to meet the needs of today's learner. As a result of our research, the chapters in Needles/Powers/Crosson have been organized into a **Three Section Approach**, which helps students more easily digest the content.

ThreeSection APPROACH

1. The first section is **Concepts** and focuses on the overarching accounting concepts that require consistent reiteration throughout the course.
2. With a clear understanding of the concepts, you can proceed to the second section, **Accounting Applications**. Here, you can practice the application of accounting procedures with features like "Apply It!" and a new transaction analysis model, which breaks down the transaction in a simple, visual format.
3. Finally, move to section three, **Business Applications**. This section illustrates how the concepts and procedures are used to make business decisions. Real company examples are used throughout the chapter to show the relevance of accounting.

"I think this new chapter structure would be much easier for students to read and comprehend."

Shannon Ogden
Black River Technical College

TriLevel Problems within CengageNOW mirror the Three Section Approach and connect the sections—Concepts, Accounting Applications, and Business Applications. In this way, the problems teach you to think holistically about an accounting issue.

Breaking Down the Three Section Approach

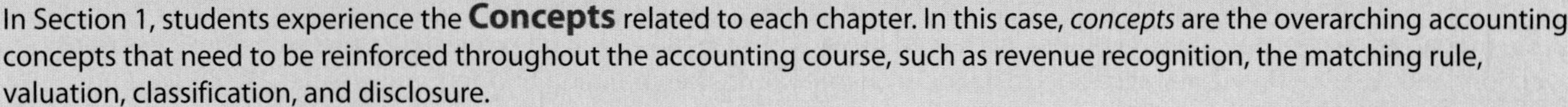

In Section 1, students experience the **Concepts** related to each chapter. In this case, *concepts* are the overarching accounting concepts that need to be reinforced throughout the accounting course, such as revenue recognition, the matching rule, valuation, classification, and disclosure.

Every chapter's Section 1 reinforces these key concepts so that once students understand the concepts, they can apply them to every aspect of the accounting system—from measuring to processing to communicating information about a business. This is a clear and logical way to present accounting.

SECTION 1 — **CONCEPTS**

CONCEPTS
- Accrual accounting (matching principle)
- Valuation
- Disclosure

RELEVANT LEARNING OBJECTIVE

LO 1 Define receivables, and explain the allowance method for valuation of receivables as an application of accrual accounting.

LO 1 Concepts Underlying Notes and Accounts Receivable

The most common receivables are *accounts receivable* and *notes receivable*. The *allowance method* is used to apply *accrual accounting* to the *valuation* of accounts receivable. Proper *disclosure* in the financial statements and the notes to them is important for users of the statements to interpret them.

Accounts Receivable

Accounts receivable are short-term financial assets that arise from sales on credit and are often called **trade credit**. Terms of trade credit usually range from 5 to 60 days, depending on industry practice, and may allow customers to pay in installments. Credit sales or loans not made in the ordinary course of business, such as those made to employees, officers, or owners, should appear separately under asset titles like Receivables from Employees. Exhibit 1 shows the level of accounts receivable in selected industries.

"It does a very good job in explaining each concept and reinforcing each one by giving specific examples."

Paul Jaijairam
Bronx Community College

SECTION 2: ACCOUNTING APPLICATIONS

In Section 2, students learn the accounting procedures and the technical **application** of concepts. Students can apply the fundamental concepts they have already learned in Section 1. Section 2 includes things like recording business transactions and creating financial statements in financial chapters, and then building budgets and creating schedules and reports in the managerial chapters.

SECTION 2 ACCOUNTING APPLICATIONS

ACCOUNTING APPLICATIONS

- Estimate uncollectible accounts and uncollectible accounts expense using
  - Percentage of net sales method
  - Accounts receivable aging method
- Write off uncollectible accounts
- Make common calculations for notes receivable

RELEVANT LEARNING OBJECTIVES

LO 2 Apply the allowance method of accounting for uncollectible accounts.

LO 3 Make common calculations for Notes Receivable.

LO 2 Uncollectible Accounts

The allowance account is necessary because the specific uncollectible accounts will not be identified until later. It is not like another contra account, Accumulated Depreciation, whose purpose is to show how much of the plant and equipment cost has been allocated as an expense to previous periods.

If management takes an optimistic view and projects a small loss from uncollectible accounts, the resulting net accounts receivable will be larger than if management takes a pessimistic view. The net income will also be larger under the optimistic view because the estimated expense will be smaller. The company's accountant makes an estimate based on past experience and current economic conditions. For example, losses from uncollectible accounts are normally expected to be greater in a recession than during a period of economic growth. The final decision on the amount of the expense will depend on objective information, such as the accountant's analyses, and on certain qualitative factors, such as how investors, bankers, creditors, and others view the performance of the debtor company. Regardless of the qualitative considerations, the estimated losses from uncollectible accounts should be realistic.

Two common methods of estimating uncollectible accounts expense are the percentage of net sales method and the accounts receivable aging method.

Percentage of Net Sales Method

The basis for the **percentage of net sales method** is the amount of this year's *net sales* that will not be collected. The answer determines the amount of uncollectible accounts expense for the year.

Uncollectible Accounts: The Percentage of Net Sales Method

Transaction The following balances represent Varta Company's ending figures for 2014:

"Section 2 walks through the accounting procedures very well. I like the use of a visual plus the narrative to explain the procedures."

Gerald Childs
Waukesha County Technical College

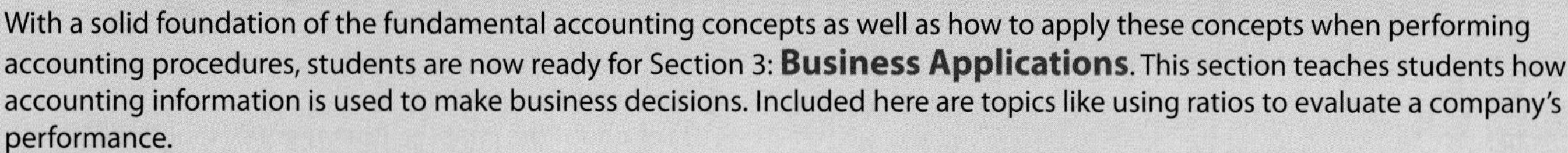

With a solid foundation of the fundamental accounting concepts as well as how to apply these concepts when performing accounting procedures, students are now ready for Section 3: **Business Applications**. This section teaches students how accounting information is used to make business decisions. Included here are topics like using ratios to evaluate a company's performance.

SECTION 3 BUSINESS APPLICATIONS

BUSINESS APPLICATIONS

- Receivables turnover
- Days' sales uncollected
- Financing receivables
  - Factoring of accounts receivable
  - Securitization of accounts receivable
  - Discounting of accounts receivable
- Ethics

RELEVANT LEARNING OBJECTIVE

LO 4 Show how to evaluate the level of receivables, and identify alternative means of financing receivables.

LO 4 Evaluating the Level of Accounts Receivable and Ethical Ramifications

Receivables are an important asset for any company that sells on credit. For them, it is critical to manage the level of receivables. Two common measures of the effect of a company's credit policies are receivables turnover and days' sales uncollected. Further, many companies manage their receivables by using various means to finance them. Finally, the judgments in estimating uncollectible accounts are a temptation for unethical behavior.

Receivables Turnover

The **receivables turnover** shows how many times, on average, a company turned its receivables into cash during a period. It reflects the relative size of a company's accounts receivable and the success of its credit and collection policies. It may also be affected by external factors, such as seasonal conditions and interest rates.

The receivables turnover is computed by dividing net sales by the average accounts receivable (net of allowances). Theoretically, the numerator should be net credit sales; but since the amount of net credit sales is rarely available in public reports, investors use total net sales. Using data from **HP**'s annual report (presented at the beginning of the chapter), we can compute the company's receivables turnover in 2011 as follows (dollar amounts are in millions).

RATIO

Receivables Turnover: How Many Times Did the Company Collect Its Accounts Receivable During an Accounting Period?

$$\text{Receivables Turnover} = \frac{\text{Net Sales}}{\text{Average Accounts Receivable}}$$

$$\frac{\$127{,}245}{(\$18{,}224 + \$18{,}481)/2} = \frac{\$127{,}245}{\$18{,}352.50} = 6.9 \text{ times*}$$

* Rounded

"This is a nice and useful touch to help students tie everything together. The theory can be dry at times, so this recap helps engage the students' attention again."

Dennis Mullen
City College of San Francisco

EXAMPLES, ACTIVITIES, AND PRACTICE

Business Perspective

A Whirlwind Inventory Turnover—How Does Dell Do It?

Dell Computer Corporation turns its inventory over every 10 days. How can it do this when other computer companies have inventory on hand for 60 days or even longer? Technology and good inventory management are a big part of the answer.

Dell's speed from order to delivery sets the standard for the computer industry. Consider that a computer ordered by 9 A.M. can be delivered the next day by 9 P.M. How can Dell do this when it does not start ordering components and assembling computers until a customer places an order? First, Dell's suppliers keep components warehoused just minutes from Dell's factories, making efficient, just-in-time operations possible. Dell also saves time by sending an e-mail message for some finished products to a shipper, such as **United Parcel Service**, and the shipper picks up the product from a supplier and schedules it to arrive with the PC. In addition to contributing to a high inventory turnover, this practice saves Dell in freight costs. Dell is showing the world how to run a business in the cyber age by selling more than $39 million worth of computers a day on its website.[7]

© Alija / iStockphoto.com

Business Perspective

Throughout the chapter, **Business Perspective** features keep students engaged by providing real business context and examples from well-known companies, including **Google**, **CVS**, **Boeing**, **Ford Motor Company**, **Microsoft**, **L.L. Bean**, and **The Walt Disney Company**.

RECEIVABLES

Business Insight

Hewlett-Packard (HP) Company

Hewlett-Packard Company (HP) is one of the largest and best-known companies in the computer industry. It sells its computers, printers, and related products to individual consumers, small and large businesses, and government, health, and educational organizations. Like any company that sells on credit, HP must give its customers time to pay for their purchases while at the same time retaining enough cash to pay its suppliers. As you can see from HP's Financial Highlights, cash and accounts receivable have made up over 50 percent of the company's current assets in recent years.[1] HP must therefore plan and control its cash flows very carefully.

HP'S FINANCIAL HIGHLIGHTS (in millions)

	2011	2010	2009
Cash	$ 8,043	$ 10,929	$ 13,279
Accounts receivable, net	18,224	18,481	16,537
Total current assets	51,021	54,184	52,539
Net revenue	127,245	126,033	114,552

1. **CONCEPT** ▶ How does HP apply accrual accounting to its receivables, and how does it properly disclose their value?
2. **ACCOUNTING APPLICATION** ▶ How can HP estimate the value of its receivables?
3. **BUSINESS APPLICATION** ▶ How can HP evaluate the effectiveness of its credit policies and the level of its accounts receivable?

A Look Back At: Hewlett-Packard Company

Aldo Murillo/iStockphoto.com

Hewlett-Packard Company

The beginning of this chapter focused on **Hewlett-Packard Company**. Complete the following requirements in order to answer the questions posed at the beginning of the chapter.

Section 1: Concepts
How does HP apply accrual accounting to its receivables, and how does it properly disclose their value?

Section 2: Accounting Applications
How can HP estimate the value of its receivables?

Section 3: Business Applications
How can HP evaluate the effectiveness of its credit policies and the level of its accounts receivable?

Business Insight and A Look Back At ▲

Each chapter opens with a **Business Insight** that shows how a small company would use accounting information to make decisions. The Business Insight poses three questions—each of which will be answered in one of the three sections of the chapter. At the end of each chapter, **A Look Back At** revisits the Business Insight company to tie the three sections together.

Apply It! and Try It! ▶

Apply It! activities throughout the chapter illustrate and solve a short exercise and then reference end-of-chapter assignments where students can go to **Try It!** This provides students with an example to reference as they are working to complete homework, making getting started less intimidating.

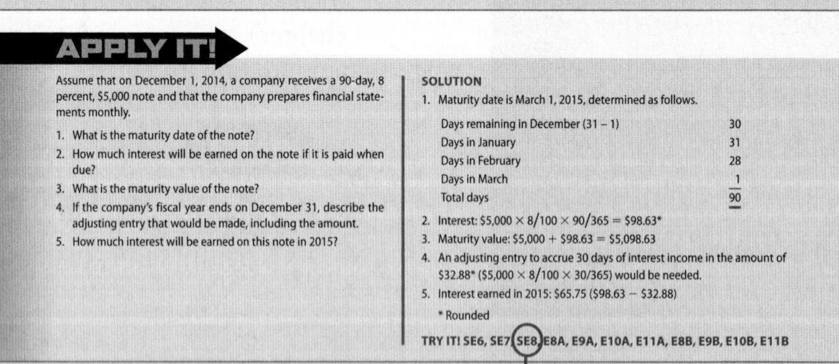

APPLY IT!

Assume that on December 1, 2014, a company receives a 90-day, 8 percent, $5,000 note and that the company prepares financial statements monthly.

1. What is the maturity date of the note?
2. How much interest will be earned on the note if it is paid when due?
3. What is the maturity value of the note?
4. If the company's fiscal year ends on December 31, describe the adjusting entry that would be made, including the amount.
5. How much interest will be earned on this note in 2015?

SOLUTION

1. Maturity date is March 1, 2015, determined as follows.

Days remaining in December (31 – 1)	30
Days in January	31
Days in February	28
Days in March	1
Total days	90

2. Interest: $5,000 × 8/100 × 90/365 = $98.63*
3. Maturity value: $5,000 + $98.63 = $5,098.63
4. An adjusting entry to accrue 30 days of interest income in the amount of $32.88* ($5,000 × 8/100 × 30/365) would be needed.
5. Interest earned in 2015: $65.75 ($98.63 − $32.88)

* Rounded

TRY IT! SE6, SE7, SE8, E8A, E9A, E10A, E11A, E8B, E9B, E10B, E11B

Notes Receivable Calculations

SE8. On August 25, Intercontinental Company received a 90-day, 9 percent note in settlement of an account receivable in the amount of $20,000. Determine the maturity date, amount of interest on the note, and maturity value. (Round to the nearest cent.)

Business Transaction Model ▶

A new business transaction model for all financial accounting chapters involving transactions visually guides students step-by-step through accounting for business transactions as follows:

- Statement of the transaction
- Analysis of the effect on the accounts
- Application of double-entry accounting in T accounts
- Illustration of the journal entry (linked to the T account showing the relationships between the methods and featuring accounting equations)
- Comments that offer supporting explanations regarding the significance of the transaction (often looping back to the concepts covered in Section 1)

Prepayment of Expenses in Cash

Transaction On July 3, Blue Design Studio, Inc., rents an office for and pays $3,200 for two months' rent in advance.

Analysis The journal entry to record the prepayment of office rent in cash

▲ *increases* the asset account *Prepaid Rent* with a debit

▼ *decreases* the asset account *Cash* with a credit

Application of Double Entry

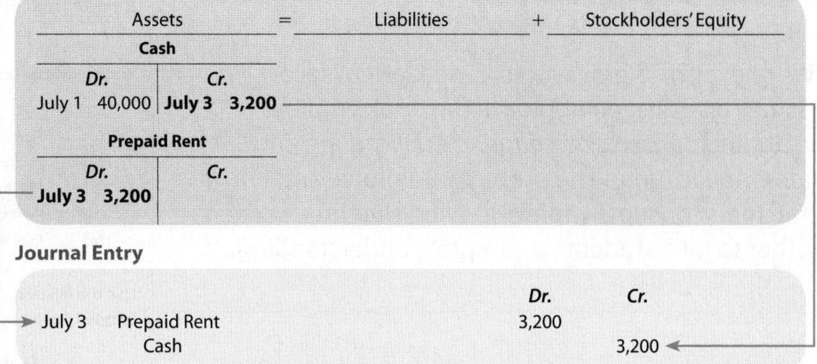

Assets = Liabilities + Stockholders' Equity
Cash
Dr. Cr.
July 1 40,000 | July 3 3,200
Prepaid Rent
Dr. Cr.
July 3 3,200
Journal Entry
Dr. Cr.
July 3 Prepaid Rent 3,200
Cash 3,200

Comment A prepaid expense is *classified* as an asset because the expenditure will benefit future operations. This transaction does not affect the totals of assets or liabilities and stockholders' equity because it simply trades one asset for another asset. If the company had paid only July's rent, the stockholders' equity account *Rent Expense* would be *recognized* and debited because the total benefit of the expenditure would be used up in the current month.

RATIO

Profit Margin: How Much Income Does Each Dollar of Sales Generate?

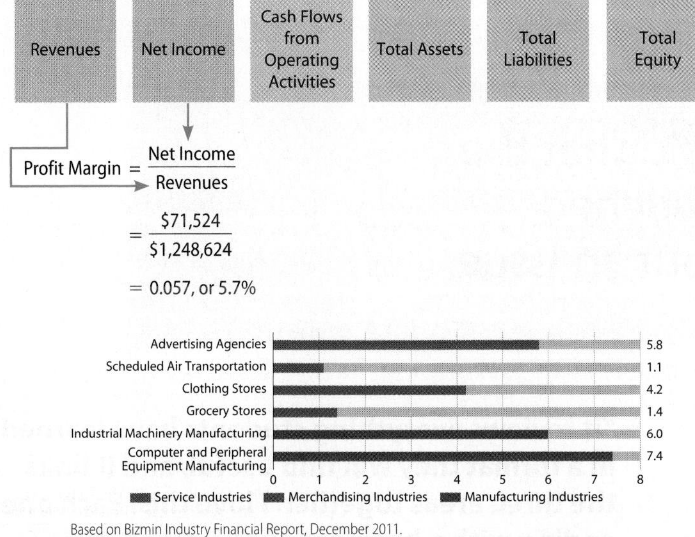

Based on Bizmin Industry Financial Report, December 2011.

◀ Ratio Analysis Model

A new framework for teaching how to analyze company information and make informed decisions simplifies ratio analysis as follows:

- Key question regarding company performance (which the ratio answers)
- Elements of the financial statements that are needed to compute the ratio (focusing on revenue and net income from the income statement, cash flows from operating activities from the statement of cash flows, and total assets, total liabilities, and total equity from the balance sheet)
- Formula for the ratio (which links to the related elements of the financial statements)
- Computation/example
- Graph of industry averages
- Comments that explain what the ratio means (whether it's good or bad)

TRILEVEL PROBLEM: TYING IT ALL TOGETHER!

NEW TriLevel Problems within CengageNOW follow the same Three Section Approach the book employs by including *Concepts, Accounting Applications*, and *Business Applications*. The problems reinforce and apply overarching concepts while also tying the three sections together to give students a complete understanding.

Transaction Analysis

The process of assigning business transactions to accounts is called [Select].

One of the most important classification issues in accounting is the difference between an asset and
their cost is classified as an [Select]. If the items will be used in the future, they are classified as

Travis Services is an office cleaning company. Consider Travis Services' transactions during its first mo

(a)	Received cash from Stanley Travis, in exchange for stock, $18,680.
(b)	Performed services for a client on account, $6,530.
(c)	Purchased equipment with cash, $12,920.
(d)	Performed services for a customer who paid cash, $7,150.
(e)	Purchased supplies with cash, $3,480.

Use the following T accounts to record these transactions. You will need to record the transactions in
bottom) on the debit or credit side of the T account, whichever is appropriate.

Cash — Accounts Receivable — Supplies

Equipment — Fees Earned — Common Stock

As supplies are used, Travis Services debits Supplies Expense and credits Supplies.

Stanley Travis would like to charge Supplies Expense when the supplies are purchased. He wants to

a. "Great idea. By increasing expenses Travis Services income is lowered and that translates to lo
b. "Accounting rules dictate that purchases that are consumed in future periods be classified as a
purposes."

"Any time the students are engaged in the learning process and have to actively participate, I think they enhance their retention of the material. The ability to relate this to an actual company (whether real or not) allows students to see this information in practice."

Chuck Smith
Iowa Western Community College

96% of instructors surveyed said that the TriLevel Problem adequately coached students through thinking about an issue.

"The [TriLevel Problem] links procedure to the creation and use of information, and closes that loop between what students are doing and why it is useful."

Andy Williams
Edmonds Community College

"It reviews everything students have learned in a format they will find useful, and it links the three areas together. I love this. Each one ending with a business application."

Joan Ryan
Clackamas Community College

NEW CENGAGENOW FEATURES HELP STUDENTS MAKE CONNECTIONS

NEW Blueprint Problems ▶

In CengageNOW, these problems cover primary learning objectives and help students understand the fundamental accounting concepts and their associated building blocks—not just memorize the formulas or journal entries required for a single concept. *Blueprint Problems* include rich feedback and explanations, providing students with an excellent learning resource.

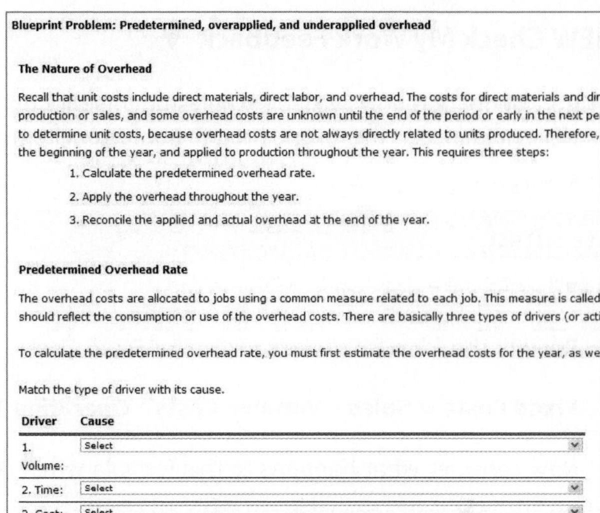

Blueprint Problem: Predetermined, overapplied, and underapplied overhead

The Nature of Overhead

Recall that unit costs include direct materials, direct labor, and overhead. The costs for direct materials and dir production or sales, and some overhead costs are unknown until the end of the period or early in the next per to determine unit costs, because overhead costs are not always directly related to units produced. Therefore, the beginning of the year, and applied to production throughout the year. This requires three steps:

1. Calculate the predetermined overhead rate.
2. Apply the overhead throughout the year.
3. Reconcile the applied and actual overhead at the end of the year.

Predetermined Overhead Rate

The overhead costs are allocated to jobs using a common measure related to each job. This measure is called should reflect the consumption or use of the overhead costs. There are basically three types of drivers (or acti

To calculate the predetermined overhead rate, you must first estimate the overhead costs for the year, as wel

Match the type of driver with its cause.

Driver	Cause
1. Volume:	Select
2. Time:	Select
3. Cost:	Select

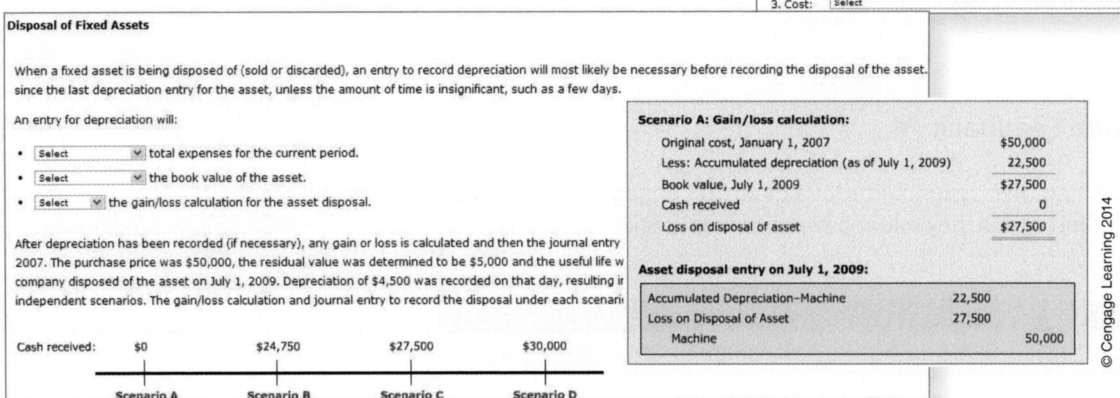

Disposal of Fixed Assets

When a fixed asset is being disposed of (sold or discarded), an entry to record depreciation will most likely be necessary before recording the disposal of the asset. since the last depreciation entry for the asset, unless the amount of time is insignificant, such as a few days.

An entry for depreciation will:

- Select total expenses for the current period.
- Select the book value of the asset.
- Select the gain/loss calculation for the asset disposal.

After depreciation has been recorded (if necessary), any gain or loss is calculated and then the journal entry 2007. The purchase price was $50,000, the residual value was determined to be $5,000 and the useful life w company disposed of the asset on July 1, 2009. Depreciation of $4,500 was recorded on that day, resulting ir independent scenarios. The gain/loss calculation and journal entry to record the disposal under each scenari

Cash received:	$0	$24,750	$27,500	$30,000
	Scenario A	Scenario B	Scenario C	Scenario D

Scenario A: Gain/loss calculation:

Original cost, January 1, 2007	$50,000
Less: Accumulated depreciation (as of July 1, 2009)	22,500
Book value, July 1, 2009	$27,500
Cash received	0
Loss on disposal of asset	$27,500

Asset disposal entry on July 1, 2009:

Accumulated Depreciation-Machine	22,500	
Loss on Disposal of Asset	27,500	
Machine		50,000

NEW Blueprint Connections ▲

Blueprint Connections in CengageNOW build upon concepts covered and introduced within the *Blueprint Problems*. These scenario-based exercises help reinforce students' knowledge of the concept.

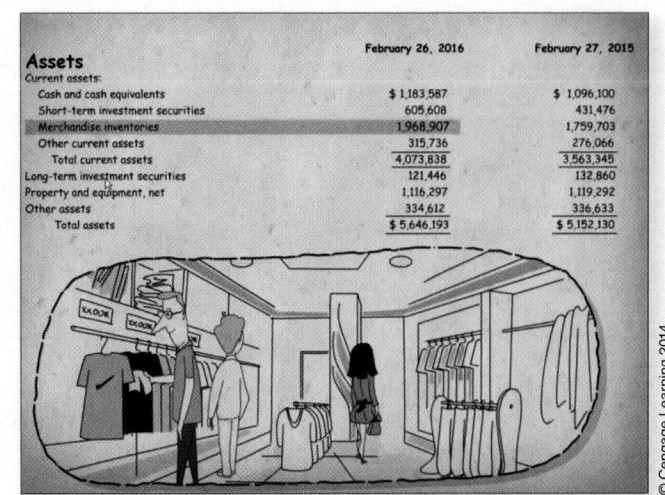

NEW Animated Activities ▶

Animated Activities in CengageNOW are videos that guide students through selected core topics using a realistic company example to illustrate how the concepts relate to the everyday activities of a business.

Assets	February 26, 2016	February 27, 2015
Current assets:		
Cash and cash equivalents	$ 1,183,587	$ 1,096,100
Short-term investment securities	605,608	431,476
Merchandise inventories	1,968,907	1,759,703
Other current assets	315,736	276,066
Total current assets	4,073,838	3,563,345
Long-term investment securities	121,446	132,860
Property and equipment, net	1,116,297	1,119,292
Other assets	334,612	336,633
Total assets	$ 5,646,193	$ 5,152,130

NEW CENGAGENOW FEATURES HELP STUDENTS MAKE CONNECTIONS

NEW Check My Work Feedback ▼

Written feedback is now available when students click on "Check My Work" in CengageNOW to provide students with valuable guidance as they work through homework items.

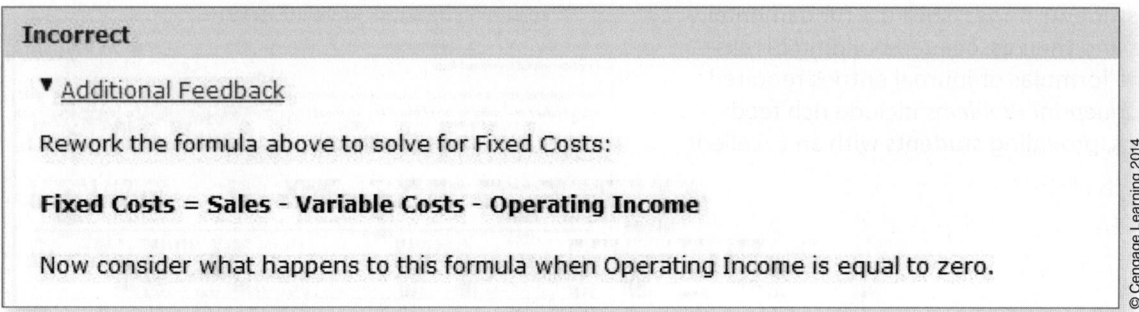

NEW Post-submission Feedback ▼

After students have submitted their assignments for a grade in CengageNOW, they can go back and see the correct answers to better understand where they might have gotten off track.

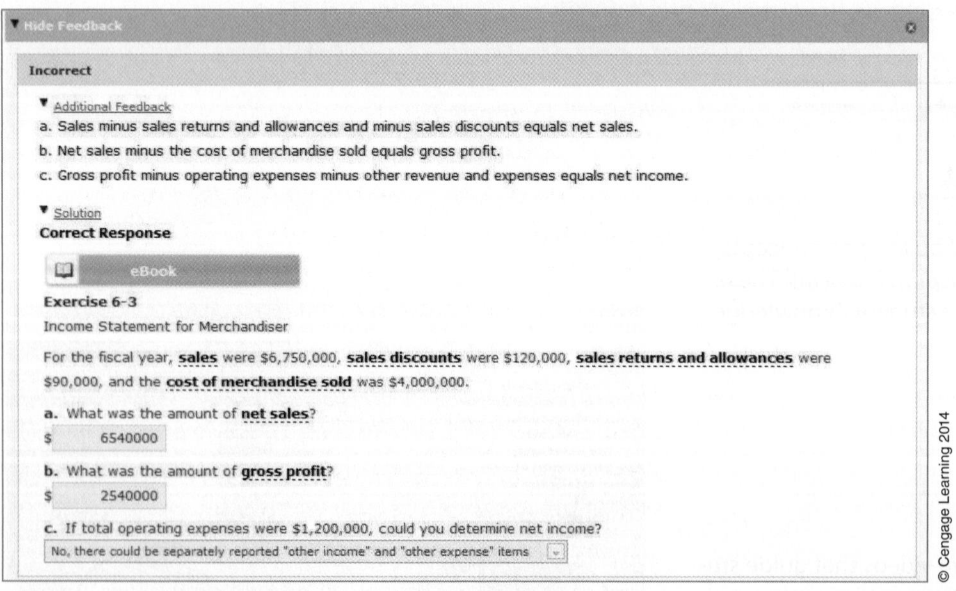

NEW Apply It Demos

These demonstration videos in CengageNOW will help students complete end-of-chapter questions from Section 2.

ACKNOWLEDGMENTS

In developing and refining the tenth edition of *Financial and Managerial Accounting*, we wanted to ensure that we were creating a textbook that truly reflected the way we teach accounting. To do so, we asked for feedback from over 150 professors, other professional colleagues, and students. We want to recognize those who made special contributions to our efforts in preparing this edition through their reviews, suggestions, and participation in surveys, interviews, and focus groups. We cannot begin to say how grateful we are for the feedback from the many instructors who have generously shared their responses and teaching experiences with us.

John G. Ahmad, *Northern Virginia Community College*
Robert Almon, *South Texas College*
Elizabeth Ammann, *Lindenwood University*
Paul Andrew, *SUNY, Morrisville*
Ryan Andrew, *Columbia College Chicago*
Sidney Askew, *Borough of Manhattan Community College*
Joe Atallah, *Irvine Valley College*
Shele Bannon, *Queensborough Community College*
Michael Barendse, *Grossmont College*
Beverly R. Beatty, *Anne Arundel Community College*
Robert Beebe, *Morrisville State College*
Teri Bernstein, *Santa Monica College*
Cynthia Bird, *Tidewater Community College*
David B. Bojarsky, *California State University*
Linda Bolduc, *Mount Wachusett Community College*
John Bongorno, *Cuyahoga Community College*
Anna Boulware, *St. Charles Community College*
Amy Bourne, *Oregon State University*
Thomas Branton, *Alvin Community College*
Billy Brewster, *University of Texas at Arlington*
Nina E. Brown, *Tarrant County College*
Tracy L. Bundy, *University of Louisiana at Lafayette*
Jacqueline Burke, *Hofstra University*
Marci L. Butterfield, *University of Utah*
Charles Caliendo, *University of Minnesota*
Gerald Childs, *Waukesha County Technical College*
James J. Chimenti, *Jamestown Community College*
Alice Chu, *Golden West College*
Sandra Cohen, *Columbia College*
Lisa Cole, *Johnson County Community College*
Debora Constable, *Georgia Perimeter College*
Barry Cooper, *Borough of Manhattan Community College*
Cheryl Copeland, *California State University, Fresno*
Susan Cordes, *Johnson County Community College*
Meg Costello, *Oakland Community College*
Richard Culp, *Ball State University*
Sue Cunningham, *Rowan Cabarrus Community College*
Robin D'Agati, *Palm Beach State College*
Emmanuel Danso, *Palm Beach State College*
Robert Derstine, *Kutztown University*
Michael Dole, *Marquette University*
Jap Efendi, *University of Texas at Arlington*
Dustin Emhart, *North Georgia Technical College*
Denise M. English, *Boise State University*
Michael Farina, *Cerritos College*
J. Thomas Franco, *Wayne County Community College*
Dean Gray, *Reedley College*
Timothy Green, *North Georgia Technical College*
Timothy Griffin, *Hillsborough Community College*
Teri Grimmer, *Portland Community College*
Michael J. Gurevitz, *Montgomery College*
Qian Hao, *Wilkes University*
Sara Harris, *Arapahoe Community College*
Syed Hasan, *George Mason University*
Wendy Heltzer, *DePaul University*
Merrily Hoffman, *San Jacinto College*
Shanelle Hopkins, *Carroll Community College*
David Hossain, *California State University, Los Angeles*
Phillip Imel, *NOVA Community College, Annadale*
ThankGod O. Imo, *Tompkins Cortland Community College*
Paul Jaijairam, *Bronx Community College*
Gene Johnson, *Clark College*
Howard A. Kanter, *DePaul University*
Irene Kim, *George Washington University*
Christopher Kinney, *Mount Wachusett Community College*
Gordon Klein, *University of California, Los Angeles*
Shirly A. Kleiner, *Johnson County Community College*
Leon Korte, *University of South Dakota*

Lynn Krausse, *Bakersfield College*
Les Kren, *University of Wisconsin, Milwaukee*
Donnie Kristof-Nelson, *Edmonds Community College*
Christopher Kwak, *De Anza College*
Richard Lau, *California State University, Los Angeles*
Suzanne R. Laudadio, *Durham Technical Community College*
George Leonard, *St. Petersburg College*
Lydia Leporte, *Tidewater Community College*
Hui Lin, *DePaul University*
Joseph Lipari, *Montclair State*
Xiang Liu, *California State University, San Bernardino*
Angelo Luciano, *Columbia College*
Susan Lueders, *DePaul University*
Cathy Lumbattis, *Southern Illinois University*
Sakthi Mahenthiran, *Butler University*
Eileen Marutzky, *DePaul University*
Robert Maxwell, *College of the Canyons*
Mark McCarthy, *DePaul University*
Clarice McCoy, *Brookhaven College*
Terra McGhee, *University of Texas at Arlington*
Florence McGovern, *Bergen Community College*
Cheryl McKay, *Monroe County Community College*
John McQuilkin, *Roger Williams University*
Jeanette Milius, *Iowa Western Community College*
Jeanne K. Miller, *Cypress College*
Rita Mintz, *Calhoun Community College*
Jill Mitchell, *Northern Virginia Community College, Annandale*
Odell Moon, *Victor Valley College*
Kathleen Moreno, *Abraham Baldwin Agricultural College*
Walter Moss, *Cuyahoga Community College*
Dennis Mullen, *City College of San Francisco*
Elizabeth A. Murphy, *DePaul University*
Penny Nunn, *Henderson Community College*
Christopher O'Byrne, *Cuyamaca College*
Shannon Ogden, *Black River Technical College*
Glenn Pate, *Palm Beach State College*
Sy Pearlman, *California State University, Long Beach*
Rama Ramamurthy, *College of William & Mary*
Lawrence A. Roman, *Cuyahoga Community College*
Gregg Romans, *Ivy Tech Community College*
Joan Ryan, *Clackamas Community College*
Donna B. Sanders, *Guilford Technical Community College*
Regina Schultz, *Mount Wachusett Community College*
Jay Semmel, *Broward College*
Andreas Simon, *California Polytechnic State University*
Jaye Simpson, *Tarrant County College*
Alice Sineath, *Forsyth Technical Community College*
Kimberly Sipes, *Kentucky State University*
Chuck Smith, *Iowa Western Community College*
Robert K. Smolin, *Citrus College*
Jennifer Sneed, *Arkansas State University, Newport*
Lyle Stelter, *Dakota County Technical College*
Rhonda Stone, *Black River Technical College*
Gracelyn Stuart-Tuggle, *Palm Beach State College – Boca Raton*
Linda Tarrago, *Hillsborough Community College*
Steve Teeter, *Utah Valley University*
Don Trippeer, *SUNY Oneonta*
Robert Urell, *Irvine Valley College*
La Vonda Ramey, *Schoolcraft College*
Patricia Walczak, *Lansing Community College*
Scott Wandler, *University of New Orleans*
Chris Widmer, *Tidewater Community College*
Andy Williams, *Edmonds Community College*
Wanda Wong, *Chabot College*
Ronald Zhao, *Monmouth University*
Teri Zuccaro, *Clarke University*

We also wish to express deep appreciation to colleagues at DePaul University, who have been extremely supportive and encouraging.

Finally, very important to the quality of this book are our Developmental Editor, Krista Kellman; Executive Editor, Sharon Oblinger; and Senior Brand Manager, Kristen Hurd.

ABOUT THE AUTHORS

Belverd E. Needles, Jr., received B.B.A. and M.B.A. degrees from Texas Tech University and his Ph.D. degree from the University of Illinois at Urbana-Champaign. He teaches financial accounting, managerial accounting, and auditing at DePaul University, where he is an internationally recognized expert in international accounting and education. He has published in leading journals and is the author or editor of more than 20 books and monographs. His current research relates to international financial reporting, performance measurement, and corporate governance of high-performance companies in the United States, Europe, India, and Australia. His textbooks are used throughout the world and have received many awards, including (in 2008) the McGuffey Award from the Text and Academic Authors Association. Active in many academic and professional organizations, he is immediate past Vice-President-Education of the American Accounting Association. He has received the Distinguished Alumni Award from Texas Tech University, the Illinois CPA Society Outstanding Educator Award and its Life-Time Achievement Award, the Joseph A. Silvoso Faculty Award of Merit from the Federation of Schools of Accountancy, the Ledger & Quill Award of Merit, and the Ledger & Quill Teaching Excellence Award. He was named Educator of the Year by the American Institute of CPAs, Accountant of the Year for Education by the national honorary society Beta Alpha Psi, and Outstanding International Accounting Educator by the American Accounting Association. He has received the Excellence in Teaching Award from DePaul University.

Marian Powers received her B.S. degree from Chicago State University and her Ph.D. degree from University of Illinois at Urbana-Champaign. In addition to the Kellogg School of Management at Northwestern University, she has taught financial accounting at the University of Illinois, Chicago, and at the Lake Forest Graduate School of Management. Internationally recognized as a dynamic teacher in executive education, she specializes in teaching nonfinancial managers how to read and understand internal and external financial reports, including the impact of international financial reporting standards (IFRS). Her current research relates to international financial reporting, performance measurement, and corporate governance of high-performance companies in the United States, Europe, India, and Australia. Her research has been published in leading journals. Her textbooks, coauthored with Belverd E. Needles, Jr., are used throughout the world and have received many awards, including the Textbook Excellence Award and the McGuffey Award from the Text and Academic Authors Association. She has also coauthored three interactive multimedia software products. She currently serves on the Board of the CPA Endowment Fund of Illinois and is immediate past-chair of the Board of Governors of the Winnetka Community House. She is a member of International Association of Accounting Education and Research, and Illinois CPA Society. She has served on the Board of Directors of the Illinois CPA Society, the Educational Foundation of Women in Accounting, and both the national as well as Chicago chapters of ASWA.

Susan V. Crosson received her B.B.A. degree in economics and accounting from Southern Methodist University and her M.S. degree in accounting from Texas Tech University. She is currently teaching in the Goizueta Business School at Emory University in Atlanta, Georgia. Until recently, she was the Accounting Faculty Lead and Professor at Santa Fe College in Gainesville, Florida. She has also been on the faculty of the University of Florida; Washington University in St. Louis; University of Oklahoma; Johnson County Community College in Kansas; and Kansas City Kansas Community College. She is internationally known for her YouTube accounting videos as an innovative application of pedagogical strategies. In recognition of her professional and academic activities, she was a recipient of the Outstanding Service Award from the American Accounting Association (AAA), an Institute of Management Accountants' Faculty Development Grant to blend technology into the classroom, the Florida Association of Community Colleges Professor of the Year Award for Instructional Excellence, and the University of Oklahoma's Halliburton Education Award for Excellence. Currently, she serves as President of the Teaching, Learning, and Curriculum section of the AAA. Recently, she served as a Supply Chain Leader for The Commission on Accounting Higher Education, which published *"Pathways to a Profession," Charting a National Strategy for the Next Generation of Accountants.* She has also served on various committees for the AICPA, Florida Institute of CPAs, and the Florida Association of Accounting Educators.

Financial & Managerial Accounting

TENTH EDITION

CHAPTER 1

LEARNING OBJECTIVES

LO 1 Define *accounting*, explain the concepts underlying accounting measurement, explain the three forms of business entities, and describe the characteristics of a corporation.

LO 2 Define *financial position*, and state the accounting equation.

LO 3 Identify the four basic financial statements and their interrelationships.

LO 4 Explain how generally accepted accounting principles (GAAP) and international financial reporting standards (IFRS) relate to financial statements and the independent CPA's report, and identify the organizations that influence GAAP.

LO 5 Identify the users of accounting information, and identify business goals, activities, and performance measures.

LO 6 Explain the importance of ethics in financial reporting.

Pat Canova/Alamy

USES OF ACCOUNTING INFORMATION AND THE FINANCIAL STATEMENTS

Business Insight
CVS Caremark

CVS Caremark operates a chain of more than 7,300 stores. Its pharmacies fill more than 1 billion prescriptions each year. Over the last five years, CVS has opened or purchased 2,600 new stores and more than doubled its sales and profits. This performance places it among the fastest-growing retail companies.

Why is CVS considered successful? Customers give the company high marks because of the quality of the products that it sells and the large selection of good service that its stores offer. Investment firms and others with a stake in CVS evaluate the company's success in financial terms.

Whether a company is large or small, the same financial measures are used to evaluate its management and to compare it with other companies. In this chapter, as you learn more about accounting and the business environment, you will become familiar with these financial measures.

CVS's Financial Highlights (In millions)

	2011	2010	2009
Net revenues	107,100	95,778	98,215
Net earnings	3,457	3,424	3,696
Total assets	64,543	62,169	61,641
Stockholders' equity	38,051	37,700	35,768

Note: Most companies list the most recent year of information in the first column, as shown here.

1. **CONCEPT** ▶ What is accounting, and what are the concepts that underlie it?
2. **ACCOUNTING APPLICATION** ▶ What financial statements does CVS need to present to its investors to evaluate its performance?
3. **BUSINESS APPLICATION** ▶ What are two principal financial goals investors will be able to determine by reviewing CVS's financial statements?

SECTION 1

CONCEPTS

CONCEPTS

- Accounting measurement
- Business transactions
- Money measure
- Separate entity
- Assets
- Liabilities
- Stockholders' equity

RELEVANT LEARNING OBJECTIVES

LO1 Define *accounting*, explain the concepts underlying accounting measurement, explain the three forms of business entities, and describe the characteristics of a corporation.

LO2 Define *financial position*, and state the accounting equation.

LO1 Concepts Underlying Accounting Measurement

Accounting is an information system that measures, processes, and communicates financial information about a business.[1] Accountants focus on the needs for financial information, whether the decision makers are inside or outside a business or other economic entity. An **economic entity** is a unit that exists independently, such as a business, hospital, or a governmental body. Accountants supply the information decision makers need to make "reasoned choices among alternative uses of scarce resources in the conduct of business and economic activities."[2] As shown in Exhibit 1, accounting is a link between business activities and decision makers.

- Accounting measures business activities by recording data about them for future use.
- The data are stored until needed and then processed to become useful information.
- The information is communicated through reports to decision makers.
- Based on information from accounting, decision makers take actions that affect subsequent business activities.

In other words, data about business activities are the input to the accounting system, and useful information for decision makers is the output.

Exhibit 1
Accounting as an Information System

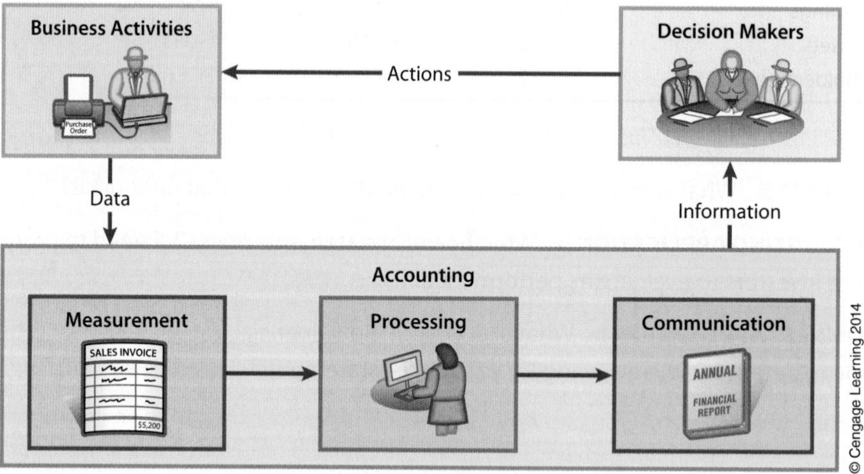

Financial and Managerial Accounting

Accounting's role of measuring, processing, and communicating financial information is usually divided into financial accounting and managerial accounting. Although the functions of financial accounting and managerial accounting overlap, they can be distinguished by the principal users of their information.

Financial Accounting External decision makers use **financial accounting** to evaluate how well the business has achieved its goals. These reports, called **financial statements**, are a central feature of accounting. **CVS**, whose stock is traded on the New York Stock Exchange, sends its financial statements to its owners (called *stockholders*), its banks and other creditors, and government regulators. Financial statements report on a business's financial performance and are used extensively both inside and outside a business to evaluate its financial success.

It is important to distinguish accounting from bookkeeping and management information systems.

- **Bookkeeping** is the process of recording financial transactions and keeping financial records. It is mechanical and repetitive, yet an important part of accounting that is usually handled by computers.
- **Management information systems (MIS)** consist of the interconnected subsystems, including accounting, that provide the information needed to run a business.

Managerial Accounting Internal decision makers use information provided by **managerial accounting** about operating, investing, and financing activities. Managers and employees need information about how they have done in the past and what they can expect in the future. For example, **Gap, Inc.**, a retail clothing business, needs an operating report that tells how much was sold at each store and what costs were incurred, and it needs a budget that projects each store's sales and costs for the next year.

Accounting Measurement

To make an *accounting measurement*, the accountant must answer four basic questions:

- What is measured?
- When should the measurement be made?
- What value should be placed on what is measured?
- How should what is measured be classified?

Accountants debate the answers to these questions constantly, and the answers change as new knowledge and practice require. But the basis of today's accounting practice rests on a number of widely accepted concepts and conventions. We begin by focusing on the first question: What is measured? We discuss the other three questions in the next chapter.

Business Transactions **Business transactions** are economic events that affect a business's financial position. Businesses can have hundreds or even thousands of transactions every day. These transactions are the raw material of accounting reports.

A transaction can be an exchange of value (a purchase, sale, payment, collection, or loan) between two or more parties. A transaction also can be an economic event that does not involve an exchange. Some examples of nonexchange transactions are losses from fire, flood, explosion, and theft; physical wear and tear on machinery and equipment; and the day-by-day accumulation of interest.

To be recorded, a transaction must relate directly to a business entity. Suppose a customer buys toothpaste from **CVS** but buys shampoo from a competing store because CVS is out of shampoo. The transaction in which the toothpaste was sold is entered in CVS's records. However, the purchase of the shampoo is not entered in CVS's records because, even though it indirectly affects CVS economically (by losing a sale), it does not involve a direct exchange of value between CVS and the customer.

Money Measure All business transactions are recorded in terms of money. This concept is called **money measure**. Of course, nonfinancial information may also be recorded, but a business's transactions and activities are measured through the recording of monetary amounts. Money is the only factor common to all business transactions, and thus it is the only unit of measure capable of producing financial data that can be compared. The monetary unit a business uses depends on the country in which the business resides. For example, in the United States, the basic unit of money is the dollar.

In China, it is the yuan; in Japan, the yen; in the European Union (EU), the euro; and in the United Kingdom, the pound. In international transactions, exchange rates must be used to translate from one currency to another. An **exchange rate** is the value of one currency in terms of another. For example, a British person purchasing goods from a U.S. company like **CVS** and paying in U.S. dollars must exchange British pounds for U.S. dollars before making payment. In effect, currencies are goods that can be bought and sold.

Exhibit 2 illustrates the exchange rates for several currencies in dollars. It shows the exchange rate for British pounds as $1.59 per pound on a particular date. Like the prices of many goods, currency prices change daily according to supply and demand. For example, a year and a half earlier, the exchange rate for British pounds was $1.63.

Exhibit 2
Examples of Foreign Exchange Rates

Country	Price in $U.S.	Country	Price in $U.S.
Australia (dollar)	1.07	Hong Kong (dollar)	0.13
Brazil (real)	0.58	Japan (yen)	0.012
Britain (pound)	1.59	Mexico (peso)	0.08
Canada (dollar)	1.00	Russia (ruble)	0.03
European Union (euro)	1.32	Singapore (dollar)	0.79

Source: The Wall Street Journal, February 18, 2012.

***STUDY NOTE:** For accounting purposes, a business is always separate and distinct from its owners, creditors, and customers.*

Separate Entity For accounting purposes, a business organization is a **separate entity**, distinct not only from its creditors and customers but also from its owners. It should have its own set of financial records, and its records and reports should refer only to its own affairs.

For example, Just Because Flowers Company should have a bank account separate from the account of Molly Dar, the owner. Molly Dar may own a home, a car, and other property, and she may have personal debts; but these are not the resources or debts of Just Because Flowers. Molly Dar may own another business, say a stationery shop. If she does, she should have a completely separate set of records for each business.

Forms of Business Organization

The three basic forms of business organization recognized as separate entities are the sole proprietorship, the partnership, and the corporation.

Sole Proprietorship A **sole proprietorship** is a business owned by one person. The owner takes all the profits or losses of the business and is liable for all its obligations. As Exhibit 3 shows, sole proprietorships represent the largest number of businesses in the United States, but typically they are the smallest in size.

***STUDY NOTE:** A key disadvantage of a partnership is the unlimited liability of its owners. Unlimited liability can be avoided by organizing the business as a corporation or, in some states, by forming what is known as a limited liability partnership (LLP).*

Partnership A **partnership** is like a sole proprietorship in most ways, but it has two or more owners. The partners share the profits and losses of the business according to a prearranged formula. Generally, any partner can obligate the business to another party, and the personal resources of each partner can be called on to pay the obligations. A partnership must be dissolved if the ownership changes, as when a partner leaves or dies. If the business is to continue as a partnership after this occurs, a new partnership must be formed.

Corporation Both the sole proprietorship and the partnership are convenient ways of separating the owners' commercial activities from their personal activities. Legally,

Oleg V. Ivanov/Shutterstock.com

Ron Jon Surf Shop was founded in New Jersey in 1959. The corporation now includes nine store locations, a surf school, and a resort including a restaurant.

however, there is no economic separation between the owners and the businesses. A **corporation**, on the other hand, is a business unit chartered by the state and legally separate from its owners (the stockholders). The **stockholders**, whose ownership is represented by shares of stock, do not directly control the corporation's operations. Instead, they elect a board of directors to run the corporation for their benefit. In exchange for their limited involvement in the corporation's operations, stockholders enjoy **limited liability**; that is, their risk of loss is limited to the amount they paid for their shares. Thus, stockholders are often willing to invest in risky, but potentially profitable, activities. Also, because stockholders can sell their shares without dissolving the corporation, the life of a corporation is unlimited and not subject to the whims or health of a proprietor or a partner.

The characteristics of corporations make them very efficient in amassing capital, which enables them to grow extremely large. As Exhibit 3 shows, even though corporations are fewer in number than sole proprietorships and partnerships, they contribute much more to the U.S. economy in monetary terms. For example, in 2011, **ExxonMobil** generated more revenues than all but 28 of the world's countries.[3]

Exhibit 3
Number and Receipts (Revenues) of U.S. Proprietorships, Partnerships, and Corporations

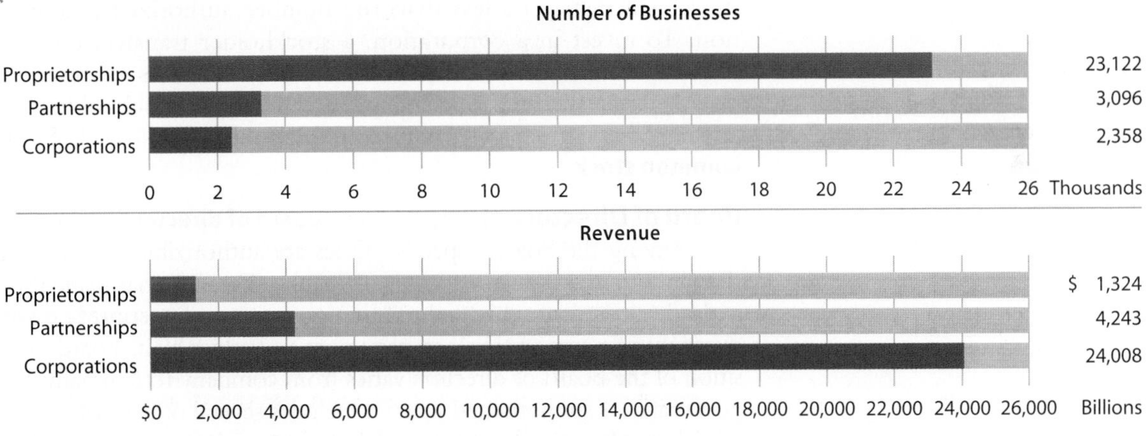

Source: U.S. Treasury Department, Internal Revenue Service, *Statistics of Income Bulletin*, Winter 2012.

© Alija / iStockphoto.com

Business Perspective
Are Most Corporations Big or Small Businesses?

Most people think of corporations as large national or global companies whose shares of stock are held by thousands of people and institutions. Indeed, corporations can be huge and have many stockholders. However, of the approximately 4 million corporations in the United States, only about 15,000 have stock that is publicly bought and sold. The vast majority of corporations are small businesses privately held by a few stockholders. Illinois alone has more than 250,000 corporations. Thus, the study of corporations is just as relevant to small businesses as it is to large ones.

Formation and Organization of a Corporation

To form a corporation, most states require individuals, called *incorporators*, to sign an application and file it with the proper state official. This application contains the **articles of incorporation**. If approved by the state, these articles, which form the company charter, become a contract between the state and the incorporators. The company is then authorized to do business as a corporation.

The authority to manage a corporation is delegated by its stockholders to a board of directors and by the board of directors to the corporation's officers. That is, the stockholders elect a board of directors, which sets corporate policies and chooses the corporation's officers, who in turn carry out the corporate policies in their management of the business, as shown in Exhibit 4.

Exhibit 4
The Corporate Organization

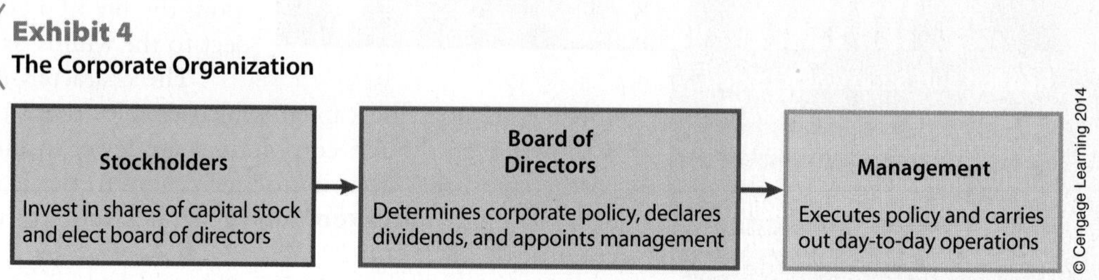
Stockholders
Invest in shares of capital stock and elect board of directors
Board of Directors
Determines corporate policy, declares dividends, and appoints management
Management
Executes policy and carries out day-to-day operations
© Cengage Learning 2014

Stockholders A unit of ownership in a corporation is called a **share of stock**. The articles of incorporation state the maximum number of shares that a corporation is authorized to issue. The number of shares held by stockholders is the outstanding stock, which may be less than the number authorized in the articles of incorporation. To invest in a corporation, a stockholder transfers cash or other resources to the corporation. In return, the stockholder receives shares of stock representing a proportionate share of ownership. Afterward, the stockholder may transfer the shares at will. Corporations may have more than one kind of stock, but here we refer only to **common stock**.

Board of Directors A corporation's **board of directors** decides on major business policies. Among the board's specific duties are authorizing contracts, setting executive salaries, and arranging major loans with banks. The financial scandals at **Enron**, **WorldCom**, and other companies highlighted the importance of **corporate governance**, which is the oversight of a corporation's management and ethics by its board of directors. The composition of the board of directors varies from company to company, but generally corporate governance is strengthened when it includes several officers of the corporation and several outsiders. The outsiders are called *independent directors* because they do not directly participate in managing the business.

To strengthen corporate governance, the Sarbanes-Oxley Act requires boards of directors to establish an **audit committee** made up of the independent directors who have financial expertise. The purpose of this provision is to ensure that boards of directors are objective in evaluating management's performance. The audit committee is also responsible for engaging the corporation's independent auditors and reviewing their work. Another of the committee's functions is to ensure that adequate systems exist to safeguard the corporation's resources and that accounting records are reliable. In short, the audit committee is the front line of defense against fraudulent financial reporting.

Management Management, appointed by the board of directors to carry out corporate policies and run day-to-day operations, consists of the operating officers—generally the president, or chief executive officer; vice presidents; chief financial officer; and chief operating officer. Besides being responsible for running the business, management has the duty of reporting the financial results of its administration to the board of directors and the stockholders. Though management must, at a minimum, make a comprehensive annual report, it generally reports more often. The annual reports of large public corporations are available to the public. Excerpts from many of them appear throughout this book.

APPLY IT!

Match each description with the appropriate term.

1. Owners have limited liability
2. Requires an exchange of value between two or more parties
3. Owned by only one person
4. Multiple co-owners
5. An amount associated with a business transaction
6. Management appointed by board of directors
7. Distinct from customers, lenders, and owners
8. Biggest segment of the economy

a. Business transactions
b. Corporation(s)
c. Money measure
d. Partnership
e. Sole proprietorship
f. Separate entity

SOLUTION

1. b; 2. a; 3. e; 4. d; 5. c; 6. b; 7. f; 8. b

TRY IT! SE1, SE2, E1A, E2A, E3A, E12A, E1B, E2B, E3B, E12B

LO2 Concepts Underlying Financial Position

Financial position refers to a company's economic resources, such as cash, inventory, and buildings, and the claims against those resources at a particular time. Another term for claims is *equities.*

Every corporation has two types of equities: creditors' equities, such as bank loans, and stockholders' equity. The sum of these equities equals a company's resources:

$$\text{Economic Resources} = \text{Creditors' Equities} + \text{Stockholders' Equity}$$

In accounting terminology, economic resources are called *assets* and creditors' equities are called *liabilities.* So the equation can be written like this:

$$\text{Assets} = \text{Liabilities} + \text{Stockholders' Equity}$$

This equation is known as the **accounting equation (A = L + SE)**. The two sides of the equation must always be equal, or "in balance," as shown in Exhibit 5. To evaluate the financial effects of business activities, it is important to understand their effects on this equation.

Exhibit 5
The Accounting Equation

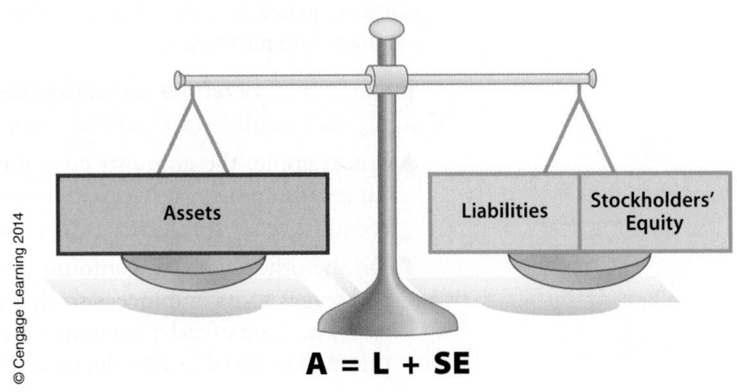

Assets

Assets are the economic resources that are expected to benefit the company's future operations. Certain kinds of assets—for example, cash and money that customers owe to the company (called *accounts receivable*)—are monetary items. Other assets—inventories (goods held for sale), land, buildings, and equipment—are nonmonetary, physical items. Still other assets—the rights granted by patents, trademarks, and copyrights—are nonphysical.

Liabilities

Liabilities are a business's present obligations to pay cash, transfer assets, or provide services to other entities in the future. Among these obligations are amounts owed to suppliers for goods or services bought on credit (called *accounts payable*), borrowed money (e.g., money owed on bank loans), salaries and wages owed to employees, taxes owed to the government, and services to be performed.

Liabilities are claims recognized by law. That is, the law gives creditors the right to force the sale of a company's assets if the company fails to pay its debts. Creditors have rights over owners and must be paid before the owners receive anything, even if the payment of debt uses up all the assets.

Stockholders' Equity

Stockholders' equity (or *shareholders' equity*) represents the claims by the owners of a corporation (the stockholders) to the assets of the business. Theoretically, stockholders' equity is what would be left if all liabilities were paid, and it is sometimes said to equal **net assets** (or *net worth*). By rearranging the accounting equation, we can define stockholders' equity this way:

$$\text{Stockholders' Equity} = \text{Assets} - \text{Liabilities}$$

Stockholders' equity has two parts, contributed capital and retained earnings:

$$\text{Stockholders' Equity} = \text{Contributed Capital} + \text{Retained Earnings}$$

- **Contributed capital** is the amount that stockholders invest in the business. Typically, contributed capital is divided between par value and additional paid-in capital. **Par value** is an amount per share that when multiplied by the number of common shares becomes the corporation's common stock amount. It is the minimum amount that can be reported as contributed (invested) capital. When the value received is greater than par value, the amount over par value is called **additional paid-in capital**.[4]
- **Retained earnings** are earnings of the corporation since its inception, less any losses, dividends, or transfers to contributed capital. Retained earnings are reinvested in the business. They are not a pool of funds to be distributed to the stockholders; instead, they represent the stockholders' claim to assets resulting from profitable operations.

STUDY NOTE: *The retained earnings is affected by the business's revenues and expenses and any dividends paid by the corporation.*

Simply stated, **revenues** and **expenses** are the increases and decreases in stockholders' equity that result from operating a business.

▲ For example, the amounts customers pay (or agree to pay in the future) to **CVS** for its prescription services are revenues for CVS. As a result, CVS' assets (cash or accounts receivable) increase, as does its stockholders' equity in those assets.

▼ On the other hand, the amount CVS must pay out (or agree to pay out) for rent and wages to its employees so that it can provide its services are expenses. In this case, the assets (cash) decrease or the liabilities (accounts payable) increase, and the stockholders' equity decreases.

Generally, a company is successful if its revenues exceed its expenses.

▲ When revenues exceed expenses, the difference is called **net income**.

▼ When expenses exceed revenues, the difference is called **net loss**.

In summary, retained earnings is the accumulated net income (revenues − expenses) minus dividends over the life of the business.

Dividends are distributions of resources, generally in the form of cash, to stockholders, and only the board of directors has the authority to declare them. Paying dividends is one way of rewarding stockholders for their investment when the corporation has been successful in earning a profit. (The other way is through an increase in the market value of the stock.) Although there is usually a delay of two or three weeks between the time the board declares a dividend and the date of the actual payment, we assume in the early chapters of this book that declaration and payment are made on the same day.

APPLY IT!

Stevenson Company had assets of $140,000 and liabilities of $60,000 at the beginning of the year, and assets of $200,000 and liabilities of $70,000 at the end of the year. During the year, $20,000 was invested in the business, and dividends of $24,000 were paid. What amount of net income did the company earn during the year?

Beginning of the year

Assets	=	Liabilities	+	Stockholders' Equity		
$140,000	=	$60,000	+			$ 80,000
				Investment	+	20,000
				Dividends	−	24,000
				Net income		?
$200,000	=	$70,000	+			**$130,000**

SOLUTION

Net income = $54,000

Start by finding the stockholders' equity at the beginning of the year: $140,000 − $60,000 = $80,000

Find the stockholders' equity at the end of the year: $200,000 − $70,000 = $130,000

Then, determine net income by calculating how the transactions during the year led to the stockholders' equity amount at the end of the year: $80,000 + $20,000 − $24,000 + net income = $130,000; net income = $54,000

TRY IT! SE3, SE4, SE5, SE6, E4A, E5A, E4B, E5B

SECTION 2 ACCOUNTING APPLICATIONS

ACCOUNTING APPLICATIONS

- Describe the income statement
- Describe the statement of retained earnings
- Describe the balance sheet
- Describe the statement of cash flows

RELEVANT LEARNING OBJECTIVES

LO 3 Identify the four basic financial statements and their interrelationships.

LO 4 Explain how generally accepted accounting principles (GAAP) and international financial reporting standards (IFRS) relate to financial statements and the independent CPA's report, and identify the organizations that influence GAAP.

LO 3 Financial Statements

Financial statements are the primary means of communicating accounting information about a business to those who have an interest in the business. These statements model the business enterprise in financial terms. As is true of all models, however, financial statements are not perfect pictures of the real thing. Four major financial statements are used to communicate accounting information: the income statement, the statement of retained earnings, the balance sheet, and the statement of cash flows. Exhibit 6 presents an overview of these four financial statements and their interrelationships. The following sections examine them in more detail.

Income Statement

The **income statement** summarizes the revenues earned and expenses incurred by a business over an accounting period. Many people consider it the most important financial report because it shows whether a business achieved its profitability goal—that is, whether it earned an acceptable income. Exhibit 7 shows that Roland Consultancy had revenues of $14,000. From this amount, total expenses of $3,900 and income taxes expense of $1,700 were deducted to arrive at net income of $8,400. To show the period to which the statement applies, it is dated "For the Month Ended December 31, 2014."

Statement of Retained Earnings

The **statement of retained earnings** shows the changes in retained earnings over an accounting period. In Exhibit 8, beginning retained earnings is zero because Roland Consultancy began operations in this period. During the month, the company earned an income (as shown on the income statement) of $8,400. Dividends of $2,400 are deducted from this amount, leaving an ending balance of $6,000.

Balance Sheet

The purpose of a **balance sheet** is to show the financial position of a business on a certain date, usually the end of the month or year. For this reason, it often is called the *statement of financial position*. It's important to note that the date on the balance sheet is a single date, whereas the dates on the other three statements cover a period of time, such as a month, quarter, or year. The balance sheet presents a view of the business as the holder of resources, or assets, that are equal to the claims against those assets. The claims consist of the company's liabilities and the stockholders' equity. Exhibit 9 shows that Roland Consultancy has several categories of assets, which total $208,400. These assets equal the total liabilities of $2,400 plus the stockholders' equity of $206,000. Notice that the amount of the retained earnings account on the balance sheet comes from the ending balance on the statement of retained earnings.

Exhibit 6
Financial Statement Relationships

Income Statement
For Year Ended 12/31/14

Revenues
– Costs and expenses

Net income (loss)

Statement of Retained Earnings
For Year Ended 12/31/14

Retained earnings, 12/31/13
+ Net income (loss)
– Dividends

Retained earnings, 12/31/14

Balance Sheet
12/31/14

Assets	**Liabilities**
Cash	Accounts payable
Receivables	Wages payable
Inventory	etc.
Building	Total Liabilities
Equipment	**Stockholders' Equity**
etc.	Common stock
	Retained earnings
	Total stockholders' equity

Total Assets = Total Liabilities + Equity

Statement of Cash Flows
For Year Ended 12/31/14

Cash from (used by) *operating* activities
Cash from (used by) *investing* activities
Cash from (used by) *financing* activities

Increase (decrease) in cash
Cash, 12/31/13

Cash, 12/31/14

Exhibit 7
Income Statement for Roland Consultancy

Roland Consultancy
Income Statement
For the Month Ended December 31, 2014

Revenues:		
Consulting fees earned		$14,000
Expenses:		
Wages expense	$1,600	
Utilities expense	1,200	
Equipment rental expense	1,100	
Total expenses		3,900
Income before taxes		$10,100
Income tax expense		1,700
Net income		$ 8,400

Exhibit 8
Statement of Retained Earnings for Roland Consultancy

Roland Consultancy
Statement of Retained Earnings
For the Month Ended December 31, 2014

Retained earnings, December 1, 2014	$ 0
Net income for the month	8,400
Subtotal	$8,400
Less dividends	2,400
Retained earnings, December 31, 2014	$6,000

Exhibit 9
Balance Sheet for Roland Consultancy

Roland Consultancy
Balance Sheet
December 31, 2014

Assets		**Liabilities**		
Cash	$ 62,400	Accounts payable		$ 2,400
		Stockholders' Equity		
Accounts receivable	4,000			
Supplies	2,000	Common stock	$ 200,000	
Land	40,000	Retained earnings	6,000	
Buildings	100,000	Total stockholders' equity		206,000
Total assets	$208,400	Total liabilities and stockholders' equity		$208,400

Statement of Cash Flows

STUDY NOTE: *The statement of cash flows explains the change in cash in terms of operating, investing, and financing activities over an accounting period. This information cannot be determined in examination of the other financial statements.*

Whereas the income statement focuses on a company's profitability, the **statement of cash flows** focuses on *liquidity*, that is, balancing the inflows and outflows of cash to enable it to operate and pay its bills when they are due. **Cash flows** are the inflows and outflows of cash into and out of a business. Net cash flows are the difference between the inflows and outflows.

As you can see in Exhibit 10, the statement of cash flows is organized according to three major business activities:

- **Cash flows from operating activities:** The first section of Exhibit 10 shows the cash produced by business operations. Roland's operating activities produced net cash flows of $4,800 (liquidity) compared to net income of $8,400 (profitability). The company used cash to increase accounts receivable and supplies. However, by borrowing funds, it increased accounts payable. This is not a good trend, which Roland should try to reverse in future months.
- **Cash flows from investing activities:** Roland used cash to expand by purchasing land and a building.
- **Cash flows from financing activities:** Roland obtained most of its cash from the stockholders, and paid a small cash dividend.

Overall, Roland had a net increase in cash of $62,400, due in large part to the investment by the stockholders. In future months, Roland must generate more cash through operations.

Exhibit 10
Statement of Cash Flows for Roland Consultancy

Roland Consultancy
Statement of Cash Flows
For the Month Ended December 31, 2014

Cash flows from operating activities:		
Net income		$ 8,400
Adjustments to reconcile net income to net cash flows from operating activities:		
(Increase) in accounts receivable	$ (4,000)	
(Increase) in supplies	(2,000)	
Increase in accounts payable	2,400	(3,600)
Net cash flows from operating activities		$ 4,800
Cash flows from investing activities:		
Purchase of land	$ (40,000)	
Purchase of building	(100,000)	
Net cash flows used by investing activities		(140,000)
Cash flows from financing activities:		
Issuance of common stock	$ 200,000	
Payment of dividends	(2,400)	
Net cash flows from financing activities		197,600
Net increase (decrease) in cash		$ 62,400
Cash at beginning of month		0
Cash at end of month		$ 62,400

Note: Parentheses indicate a cash outflow.

The statement of cash flows is related directly to the other three financial statements. Notice that net income comes from the income statement and that dividends come from the statement of retained earnings. The other items in the statement represent changes in the balance sheet accounts: accounts receivable, supplies, accounts payable, land, and buildings.

Relationships Among the Financial Statements

***STUDY NOTE:** Notice the sequence in which these statements are prepared: income statement, statement of retained earnings, balance sheet, and finally, the statement of cash flows.*

Exhibit 11 illustrates the relationships among the four financial statements for Roland Consultancy. Notice the similarity of the headings at the top of each statement. Each identifies the company and the kind of statement. The income statement, the statement of retained earnings, and the statement of cash flows indicate the period to which they apply; the balance sheet gives the specific date to which it applies.

Exhibit 11
Income Statement, Statement of Retained Earnings, Balance Sheet, and Statement of Cash Flows for Roland Consultancy

Roland Consultancy
Statement of Cash Flows
For the Month Ended December 31, 2014

Cash flows from operating activities:		
Net income		$ 8,400
Adjustments to reconcile net income to net cash flows from operating activities:		
(Increase) in accounts receivable	$ (4,000)	
(Increase) in supplies	(2,000)	
Increase in accounts payable	2,400	(3,600)
Net cash flows from operating activities		$ 4,800
Cash flows from investing activities:		
Purchase of land	$ (40,000)	
Purchase of building	(100,000)	
Net cash flows used by investing activities		(140,000)
Cash flows from financing activities:		
Issuance of common stock	$ 200,000	
Payment of dividends	(2,400)	
Net cash flows from financing activities		197,600
Net increase (decrease) in cash		$ 62,400
Cash at beginning of month		0
Cash at end of month		$ 62,400

Roland Consultancy
Income Statement
For the Month Ended December 31, 2014

Revenues:		
Consulting fees		$14,000
Expenses:		
Equipment rental expense	$2,800	
Wages expense	1,600	
Utilities expense	1,200	
Total expenses		5,600
Net income		$ 8,400

Roland Consultancy
Statement of Retained Earnings
For the Month Ended December 31, 2014

Retained earnings, December 1, 2014	$ 0
Net income for the month	8,400
Subtotal	$8,400
Less dividends	2,400
Retained earnings, December 31, 2014	$6,000

Roland Consultancy
Balance Sheet
December 31, 2014

Assets		Liabilities	
Cash	$ 62,400	Accounts payable	$ 2,400
Accounts receivable	4,000	Total liabilities	$ 2,400
Supplies	2,000	**Stockholders' Equity**	
Land	40,000	Common stock	$200,000
Buildings	100,000	Retained earnings	6,000
		Total stockholders' equity	$206,000
Total assets	$208,400	Total liabilities and stockholders' equity	$208,400

APPLY IT!

Complete the following financial statements by determining the amounts that correspond to the letters. (Assume no new investments by stockholders.)

Income Statement

Revenues	$2,775
Expenses	(a)
Net income	$ (b)

Statement of Retained Earnings

Beginning balance	$7,250
Net income	(c)
Less dividends	500
Ending balance	$7,500

Balance Sheet

Total assets	$ (d)
Total liabilities	$4,000
Common stock	1,000
Retained earnings	(e)
Total liabilities and stockholders' equity	$ (f)

SOLUTION

Net income links the income statement and the statement of retained earnings. The ending balance of retained earnings links the statement of retained earnings and the balance sheet.

Thus, start with (c), which must equal $750 ($7,500 − $7,250 + $500 = $750). Then, (b) equals (c), or $750. Thus, (a) must equal $2,025 ($2,775 − $750 = $2,025). Because (e) must be $7,500, which is the ending balance in the statement of retained earnings, (f) must equal $12,500 ($4,000 + $1,000 + $7,500 = $12,500). Finally, (d) must equal (f), or $12,500.

TRY IT! SE7, SE8, E6A, E7A, E8A, E9A, E10A, E11A, E6B, E7B, E8B, E9B, E10B, E11B

LO4 Generally Accepted Accounting Principles

To ensure that financial statements are understandable to their users, a set of **generally accepted accounting principles (GAAP)** has been developed to provide guidelines for financial accounting. "Generally accepted accounting principles encompass the conventions, rules, and procedures necessary to define accepted accounting practice at a particular time."[5] In other words, GAAP arises from wide agreement on the theory and practice of accounting at a particular time. These "principles" evolve to meet the needs of decision makers, and they change as circumstances change or as better methods are developed.

In this book, we present accounting practice, or GAAP, as it is today, and we try to explain the reasons or theory on which the practice is based. Accounting is a discipline that is always growing, changing, and improving. However, it may take years for new accounting discoveries to be implemented. As a result, you may encounter practices that seem contradictory. In some cases, we point out new directions in accounting.

GAAP and the Independent CPA's Report

Many companies of all sizes have their financial statements audited by an independent **certified public accountant (CPA)**. *Independent* means that the CPA is not an employee of the company being audited and has no financial or other compromising ties to it. CPAs are licensed by all states to protect the public by ensuring the quality of professional service. The firms listed in Exhibit 12 employ about 25 percent of all CPAs.

Exhibit 12
Large International Certified Public Accounting Firms

Firm	Home Office	Some Major Clients
Deloitte & Touche	New York	General Motors, Procter & Gamble
Ernst & Young	New York	Coca-Cola, McDonald's
KPMG	New York	General Electric, Xerox
PricewaterhouseCoopers	New York	ExxonMobil, IBM, Ford

An **audit** is an examination of a company's financial statements and the accounting systems, controls, and records that produced them. The purpose of the audit is to ascertain that the financial statements have been prepared in accordance with generally accepted accounting principles. If the independent CPA is satisfied that this standard has been met, his or her report contains the following language:

> *In our opinion, the financial statements . . . present fairly, in all material respects . . . in conformity with generally accepted accounting principles . . .*

This wording emphasizes that accounting and auditing are not exact sciences. The auditor can render only an opinion about whether the financial statements *present fairly* or conform *in all material respects* to GAAP. The auditor's report does not preclude minor or immaterial errors in the financial statements. However, a favorable report from the auditor does imply that, on the whole, investors and creditors can rely on the financial statements. In other words, the audit lends credibility to a set of financial statements. Auditors offer opinions, based on testing, about the fairness of the presentation of a company's financial information, but they cannot attest to the absolute accuracy of such information.

Historically, auditors have enjoyed a strong reputation for competence and independence. The independent audit has been an important factor in the worldwide growth of financial markets.

Organizations That Issue Accounting Standards

Two organizations issue accounting standards that are used in the United States: the FASB and the IASB.

- The **Financial Accounting Standards Board (FASB)** has been designated by the Securities and Exchange Commission (SEC) to issue *Statements of Financial Accounting Standards.* The FASB organizes these statements including any amendments, interpretations, or other references to them into a topical U.S. GAAP compendium called an American Standard Codification (ASC). This codification, which is available through the FASB website, makes it easy to find all references to a particular topic, such as revenues, in one place.

- The **International Accounting Standards Board (IASB),** which issues **international financial reporting standards (IFRS)**, is becoming increasingly important because of the acceptance of its standards in many financial markets throughout the world. The SEC now allows foreign companies to use these standards in the United States rather than having to convert their statements to U.S. GAAP. The SEC is also presently considering allowing U.S. public companies to use IFRS.

Other Organizations That Influence GAAP

Many other organizations directly or indirectly influence GAAP:

- The **Public Company Accounting Oversight Board (PCAOB),** a governmental body created by the Sarbanes-Oxley Act, has wide powers to determine the standards that auditors must follow. The PCAOB regulates audits of public companies registered with the SEC.
- The **American Institute of Certified Public Accountants (AICPA),** a professional association, influences accounting practice through the activities of its senior

International Perspective

IFRS The Arrival of International Financial Reporting Standards in the United States

Over the next few years, international financial reporting standards (IFRS) will become much more important in the United States and globally. The International Accounting Standards Board (IASB) has been working with the Financial Accounting Standards Board (FASB) and similar boards in other nations to achieve identical or nearly identical standards worldwide under what is called the convergence project. IFRS are now required in many parts of the world, including Europe, Canada, and parts of Asia. The Securities and Exchange Commission (SEC) allows foreign registrants in the United States to use IFRS. This is a major development because in the past, the SEC required foreign registrants to explain how the standards used in their statements differed from U.S. standards. This change affects approximately 10 percent of all public U.S. companies. In addition, the SEC may in the near future allow U.S. companies to use IFRS.[6]

technical committees. In addition to endorsing standards issued by the FASB, the AICPA has determined that standards issued by the IASB are also of high quality and are thus acceptable for use in the United States.* The AICPA is the primary professional organization of certified public accountants.

- The **Securities and Exchange Commission (SEC)**, a governmental agency, has the legal power to set and enforce accounting practices for companies whose securities are offered for sale to the general public.
- The **Governmental Accounting Standards Board (GASB)**, a separate but related body to the FASB, issues accounting standards for state and local governments.
- The **Internal Revenue Service (IRS)** interprets and enforces the tax laws that specify the rules for determining taxable income. In some cases, the rules conflict with good accounting practice, but they are nonetheless important.

Professional Conduct

The code of professional ethics of the American Institute of Certified Public Accountants (and adopted, with variations, by each state) governs the conduct of CPAs. Fundamental to this code is the responsibility of CPAs to clients, creditors, investors, and anyone else who relies on their work. The code requires CPAs to act with:

- **Integrity**: Be honest and candid and subordinate personal gain to service and the public trust.
- **Objectivity**: Be impartial and intellectually honest.
- **Independence**: Avoid all relationships that impair or appear to impair objectivity.

Research shows that these are the attributes that business decision makers and the investing public most closely associate with CPAs.[7] The accountant must also exercise **due care** in all activities, carrying out professional responsibilities with competence and diligence. For example, an accountant must not accept a job for which he or she is not qualified, even at the risk of losing a client to another firm, and careless work is unacceptable. These broad principles are supported by more specific rules that public accountants must follow. For instance, with certain exceptions, client information must be kept strictly confidential. Accountants who violate the rules can be disciplined or even suspended from practice.

The **Institute of Management Accountants (IMA)**, the primary professional association of managerial accountants, also has a code of professional conduct. It emphasizes that managerial accountants have a responsibility:

- To be competent in their jobs
- To keep information confidential except when authorized or legally required to disclose it
- To maintain integrity and avoid conflicts of interest
- To communicate information objectively and without bias[8]

APPLY IT!

Match the common acronym with its description.

1. GAAP	a. Sets U.S. accounting standards
2. IFRS	b. Audits financial statements
3. CPA	c. Established by the Sarbanes-Oxley Act
4. FASB	d. Sets international accounting standards
5. IASB	e. Established by the FASB
6. PCAOB	f. Established by the IASB
7. AICPA	g. Influences accounting standards through member CPAs
8. SEC	h. Receives audited financial statements of public companies

SOLUTION

1. e; 2. f; 3. b; 4. a; 5. d; 6. c; 7. g; 8. h

TRY IT! E12A, E13A, E14A, E12B, E13B, E14B

*Established in January 2007, the Private Company Financial Reporting Committee of the AICPA is charged with amending FASB accounting standards so that they better suit the needs of private companies, especially as they relate to the cost or benefit of implementing certain standards. A Blue-Ribbon Committee established by the FASB, AICPA, and other organizations is currently studying this issue. Its recommendations could ultimately result in two sets of standards, one for private companies and one for public companies.

SECTION 3 BUSINESS APPLICATIONS

SINESS APPLICATIONS
- Profitability
- Liquidity
- Ethics

LEVANT
ARNING OBJECTIVES

5 Identify the users of accounting information, d identify business goals, ivities, and performance asures.

6 Explain the importance of ethics in financial orting.

LO5 Decision Makers: The Users of Accounting Information

As shown in Exhibit 13, the people who use accounting information to make decisions fall into three categories: managers (internal users of accounting information), outsiders who have a direct financial interest in the business, and outsiders who have an indirect financial interest. These categories apply to governmental and not-for-profit organizations as well as to profit-oriented ventures.

Exhibit 13
The Users of Accounting Information

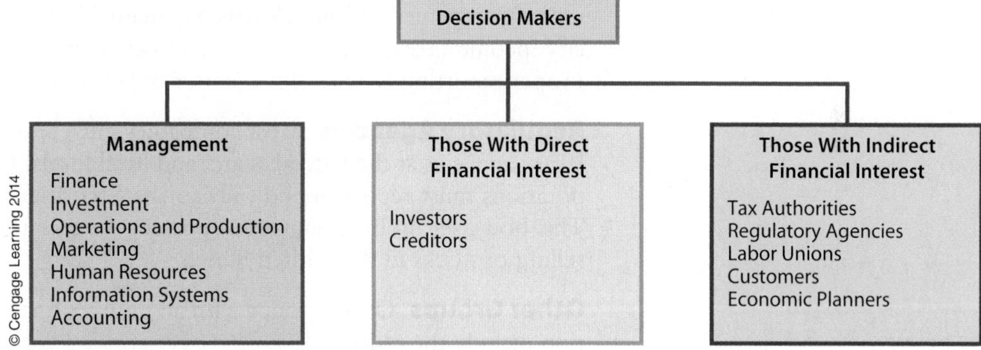

Management

Management is responsible for ensuring that a company meets its goals of profitability and liquidity. All companies pursue these goals by engaging in operating, investing, and financing activities. Making decisions about these activities is the basic function of managers; and to make good decisions, they must have timely and valid accounting information.

For example, to make good decisions, managers at **CVS** and other companies need answers to such questions as:

- What were the company's earnings during the past quarter?
- Is the rate of return to the owners adequate?
- Does the company have enough cash?
- Which products or services are most profitable?

Users with a Direct Financial Interest

Most companies periodically publish financial statements that report their success in meeting the goals of profitability and liquidity. These statements, discussed earlier, show what has happened in the past and are important indicators of what will happen in the future. Many people outside a company, particularly investors and creditors and potential investors and creditors, study these statements carefully.

STUDY NOTE: The primary external users of accounting information are investors and creditors.

Investors **Investors**, like the stockholders who have invested in **CVS**, have a direct financial interest in the success of their companies. They depend on financial statements to evaluate how their businesses have performed. A thorough study of a company's financial statements helps potential investors judge the prospects for a profitable investment.

Creditors **Creditors**, those who lend money or deliver goods and services before being paid, are interested mainly in whether a company will have the cash to pay interest charges and to repay the debt on time. They study a company's cash flow to determine its liquidity; they also look at its profitability. Banks, finance companies, mortgage companies, securities firms, insurance firms, suppliers, and other lenders must analyze a company's financial position before they make a loan.

Users with an Indirect Financial Interest

In recent years, governmental and public groups have become one of the largest and most important users of accounting information. These groups include tax authorities and regulatory agencies.

Tax Authorities Government at every level is financed through the collection of taxes. Companies and individuals pay many kinds of taxes, including federal, state, and city income taxes; Social Security and other payroll taxes; excise taxes; and sales taxes. Proper reporting is generally a matter of law and can be very complicated.

Regulatory Agencies Most companies must report periodically to one or more regulatory agencies at the federal, state, and local levels. For example, all publicly traded corporations must report periodically to the Securities and Exchange Commission (SEC). This body, set up by Congress to protect the public, regulates the issuing, buying, and selling of stocks in the United States.

Other Groups Other groups with an indirect financial interest in accounting information include the following:

- **Labor unions:** As they prepare for contract negotiations with a company, labor unions study the company's financial statements. A company's income and expenses often play an important role in these negotiations.
- **Advisors of investors and creditors:** Financial analysts, brokers, underwriters, lawyers, economists, and the financial press all have an indirect interest in the financial performance and prospects of a business.
- **Consumer groups, customers, and the general public:** The public has become more concerned about financing and earnings as well as about the effects that corporations have on inflation, the environment, social issues, and the quality of life.
- **Economic planners:** The President's Council of Economic Advisers and the Federal Reserve Board use aggregated accounting information to set and evaluate economic policies and programs.

Governmental and Not-for-Profit Organizations

More than 30 percent of the U.S. economy is generated by governmental and not-for-profit organizations (hospitals, universities, professional organizations, and charities). The managers of these diverse entities need accounting information and knowledge of how to use it. Their functions include raising funds from investors (including owners), creditors, taxpayers, and donors and deploying scarce resources. They must also plan how to pay for operations and to repay creditors on a timely basis. In addition, they have an obligation to report their financial performance to legislators, boards, and donors, as well as to deal with tax authorities, regulators, and labor unions. Although most of the examples in this text focus on business enterprises, the same basic principles apply to governmental and not-for-profit organizations.

Business Goals and Activities

A **business** is an economic unit that aims to sell goods and services at prices that will provide an adequate return to its owners. The list that follows contains the names of some well-known businesses and the principal goods or services that they sell.

Wal-Mart Corp.	Comprehensive discount goods
Reebok International Ltd.	Athletic footwear and clothing
Best Buy Co.	Consumer electronics, personal computers
Wendy's International, Inc.	Food service
Starbucks Corp.	Coffee and related service
Southwest Airlines Co.	Passenger airline service

These businesses have similar goals and engage in similar activities, as shown in Exhibit 14.

Exhibit 14
Business Goals and Activities

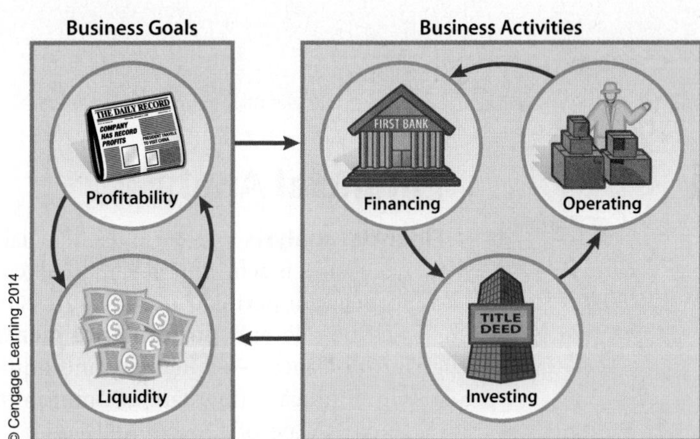

The two major goals of all businesses are profitability and liquidity.

- **Profitability** is the ability to earn enough income to attract and hold investment capital.
- **Liquidity** is the ability to have enough cash to pay debts when they are due.

To succeed and even survive, a company must meet both goals. For example, **Toyota** may sell many cars at a price that earns a profit, but if its customers do not pay quickly enough to enable Toyota to pay its suppliers and employees, the company may not meet the goal of liquidity, which could force it into bankruptcy.

All businesses pursue their goals by engaging in operating, investing, and financing activities.

- **Operating activities** include buying, producing, and selling goods and services; hiring managers and other employees; and paying taxes.
- **Investing activities** involve spending a company's capital in ways that will help it achieve its goals. They include buying resources for operating the business, such as land, buildings, and equipment, and selling those resources when they are no longer needed.
- **Financing activities** involve obtaining adequate funds to begin operating the business and to continue operating it. They include obtaining capital from creditors, such as banks and suppliers, and from the company's stockholders. They also include repaying creditors and paying a return to the stockholders.

Business Perspective
What Does CVS Have to Say About Itself?

CVS, a major drug store chain, describes the company's progress in meeting its major business objectives as follows:

- **Liquidity:** "We generated $4.6 billion in free cash for the year, exceeding our goal, and returned more than $3.5 billion to our shareholders in the form of dividends and share repurchases."
- **Profitability:** "2011 was a year of great accomplishment for CVS Caremark. We executed successfully on a number of key initiatives across the Company and reported solid financial results, delivering on our promises. Our retail business continued to post strong top- and bottom-line results, and our PBM enjoyed strong revenue growth, another very successful selling season, and great progress on several important initiatives."[9]

CVS's main business activities are shown at the right.

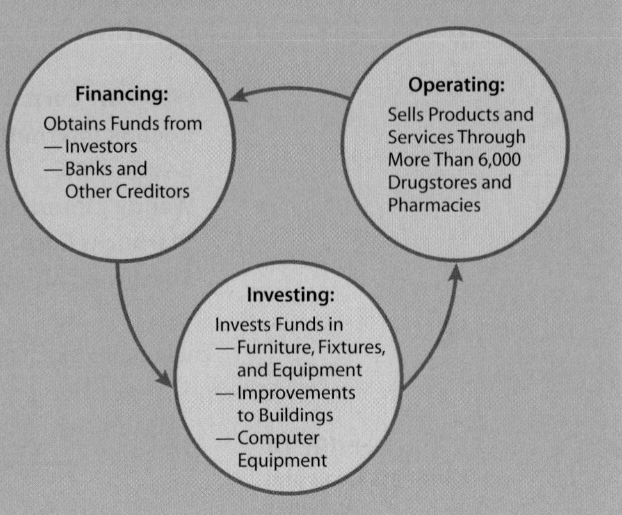

Financial Analysis

Financial analysis is the use of financial statements to determine that a business is well managed and is achieving its goals. The effectiveness of financial analysis depends on the use of relevant performance measures and financial ratios.

To be relevant, **performance measures** must be well aligned with the two major goals of business—profitability and liquidity. Profitability is commonly measured in net income, and cash flows are a common measure of liquidity. For example, in 2011, **CVS** had net income of $3,457 million and cash flows from operating activities of $5,856 million. These figures indicate that CVS was both profitable and liquid. In 2008, however, **General Motors** curtailed spending on new auto and truck models because its earnings were negative and, even worse, its cash flows were negative. Its cash flow problem led to its bankruptcy and a government bailout in 2009. Clearly, General Motors was not meeting either its profitability or liquidity goals.

Financial ratios show how the elements of financial statements relate to each other. They allow for comparisons from one period to another and from one company to another. For example, to assess **CVS**'s profitability, it would be helpful to consider the ratio of its earnings to total assets, and for liquidity, the ratio of its cash flows to total assets.

APPLY IT!

Match the terms that follow with the definitions or the type of user of accounting information (some answers may be used more than once).

1. Managerial accounting
2. Management
3. Financial accounting
4. Investing activities
5. Regulatory agencies
6. Financing activities
7. Profitability
8. Tax authorities
9. Investors
10. Liquidity
11. Creditors
12. Operating activities

a. A business goal
b. Engaged in by all businesses
c. Financial information developed for external users
d. Internal user
e. Direct external user
f. Indirect external user
g. Accounting information used by management

SOLUTION

1. g; 2. d; 3. c; 4. b; 5. f; 6. b; 7. a; 8. f; 9. e; 10. a; 11. e; 12. b

TRY IT! SE9, E13A, E13B

LO6 Ethical Financial Reporting

Ethics is a code of conduct that applies to everyday life. It addresses the question of whether actions are right or wrong. Actions—whether ethical or unethical, right or wrong—are the product of individual decisions. Thus, when an organization uses false advertising, cheats customers, pollutes the environment, or treats employees unfairly, the management and other employees have made a conscious decision to act in this manner.

Ethics is especially important in preparing financial reports because users of these reports must depend on the good faith of the people involved in their preparation. Users have no other assurance that the reports are accurate and fully disclose all relevant facts.

The intentional preparation of misleading financial statements is called **fraudulent financial reporting**.[10] It can result from:

- Distortion of records (e.g., the manipulation of inventory records)
- Falsified transactions (e.g., fictitious sales)
- Misapplication of various accounting principles

There are a number of motives for fraudulent reporting—for instance, to cover up financial weakness to obtain a higher price when a company is sold; to meet the expectations of investors, owners, and financial analysts; or to obtain a loan. The incentive can also be personal gain, such as additional compensation, promotion, or avoidance of penalties for poor performance.

Whatever the motive for fraudulent financial reporting, it can have dire consequences, as the accounting scandals at **Enron Corporation** and **WorldCom** in 2001 and 2002, respectively, attest. Unethical financial reporting and accounting practices at those two major corporations caused thousands of people to lose their jobs, their investment incomes, and their pensions. They also resulted in prison sentences and fines for the corporate executives who were involved.

In response to these scandals, the **Sarbanes-Oxley Act** of 2002 regulates financial reporting of public companies and their auditors. This legislation requires chief executives and chief financial officers of all publicly traded U.S. companies to swear that, based on their knowledge, their quarterly statements and annual reports filed with the Securities and Exchange Commission (SEC) are accurate and complete. Violation can result in criminal penalties.

Management expresses its duty to ensure that financial reports are not false or misleading in the management report that appears in the company's annual report. For example, in its management report, **Target Corporation** makes the following statement:

> *Management is responsible for the consistency, integrity, and presentation of the information in the Annual Report.*[11]

However, it is accountants, not management, who physically prepare and audit financial reports. They must apply accounting concepts in such a way as to present a fair view of a company's operations and financial position and to avoid misleading the readers of their reports. Accountants have a responsibility—not only to the profession but also to employers, clients, and society as a whole—to ensure that their reports provide accurate, reliable information. The historically high regard for the accounting profession is evidence that most accountants have upheld the ethics of the profession.

APPLY IT!

Match each definition with the appropriate terms that follow.

1. The intentional preparation of misleading financial statements.
2. A code of conduct that applies to everyday life.
3. Regulates financial reporting of public companies and their auditors.
4. Has a duty to ensure that financial reports are not false or misleading.

a. Ethics
b. Fraudulent financial reporting
c. Management
d. Sarbanes-Oxley Act

SOLUTION

1. b; 2. a; 3. d; 4. c

TRY IT! SE10, E15A, E15B

A Look Back At: CVS Caremark

Pat Canova/Alamy

CVS Caremark

The beginning of this chapter focused on **CVS Caremark**. Complete the following requirements in order to answer the questions posed at the beginning of the chapter.

Section 1: Concepts
What is accounting, and what are the concepts that underlie it?

Section 2: Accounting Applications
What financial statements does CVS need to present to its investors to evaluate its performance?

Section 3: Business Applications
What are two principal financial goals investors will be able to determine by reviewing CVS's financial statements?

SOLUTION · SOLUTION · SOLUTION

SOLUTION

Section 1: Concepts
Accounting is an information system that measures, processes, and communicates financial information about a business useful to internal and external decision makers. Accounting achieves its objectives by *measuring* the effects of *business transactions* on *separate entities* in terms of *money measures*. It summarizes the results in financial statements based on the equation: *Assets = Liabilities + Stockholders' Equity* (A = L + SE).

Section 2: Accounting Applications
CVS needs to provide its investors with an income statement, statement of retained earnings, balance sheet, and statement of cash flows. (These statements appear in the Supplement to Chapter 1.)

Section 3: Business Applications
Investors will find the financial statements useful in evaluating CVS's profitability and liquidity.

Review Problem

On January 1, 2014, Jenny Mullin, an experienced fitness coach, started a business called Keep-Fit Center, Inc., which offers classes and private instruction in aerobics, yoga, and Pilates. Use the financial statement items and amounts listed below from the records of Keep-Fit Center, Inc., for the month ended April 30, 2014, and prepare (1) an income statement, (2) a statement of retained earnings, and (3) a balance sheet. For examples of the statements, refer to Exhibits 7, 8, and 9.

Accounts payable	$ 19,000	Property, plant, and equipment	$189,000
Accounts receivable	104,000	Rent expense	91,000
Cash	111,000	Retained earnings, April 1, 2014	163,000
Common stock	100,000	Salaries expense	172,000
Dividends	10,000	Salaries payable	78,000
Fees revenue	375,000	Supplies	2,000
Income taxes expense	21,000	Supplies expense	6,000
Marketing expense	18,000	Utilities expense	11,000

SOLUTION

1.

	A	B	C	D	E
1			**Keep-Fit Center, Inc.**		
2			**Income Statement**		
3			**For the Month Ended April 30, 2014**		
4	**Revenues:**				
5		Fees revenues			$375,000
6	**Expenses:**				
7		Marketing expense		$ 18,000	
8		Rent expense		91,000	
9		Salaries expense		172,000	
10		Supplies expense		6,000	
11		Utilities expense		11,000	
12	Total expenses				298,000
13	Income before income taxes				$ 77,000
14	Income taxes expense				21,000
15	Net income				$ 56,000

2.

	A	B	C	D	E
1			**Keep-Fit Center, Inc.**		
2			**Statement of Retained Earnings**		
3			**For the Month Ended April 30, 2014**		
4	Retained earnings, April 1, 2014				$163,000
5	Net income for the month				56,000
6	Subtotal				$219,000
7	Less dividends				10,000
8	Retained earnings, April 30, 2014				$209,000

3.

	A	B	C	D	E
1			**Keep-Fit Center, Inc.**		
2			**Balance Sheet**		
3			**April 30, 2014**		
4	**Assets**		**Liabilities**		
5	Cash	$111,000	Accounts payable	$19,000	
6	Accounts receivable	104,000	Salaries payable	78,000	
7	Supplies	2,000	Total liabilities		$ 97,000
8	Property, plant, and equipment	189,000			
9			**Stockholders' Equity**		
10		—	Common stock	$100,000	
11			Retained earnings	209,000	
12			Total stockholders' equity		309,000
13	Total assets	$406,000	Total liabilities and stockholders' equity		$406,000

Chapter Review

Define *accounting*, explain the concepts underlying accounting measurement, explain the three forms of business entities, and describe the characteristics of a corporation. **LO 1**

Accounting is an information system that measures, processes, and communicates financial information about a business. It provides the information necessary to make choices among alternative uses of scarce resources in the conduct of business and economic activities.

Managerial accounting focuses on the preparation of information primarily for internal use by management. Financial accounting is concerned with the development and use of reports that are communicated to those outside the business as well as to management.

The accountant must determine what is measured, when the measurement should be made, what value should be placed on what is measured, and how to classify what is measured. The objects of accounting measurement are business transactions. Financial accounting uses a money measure to gauge the impact of these transactions on a business entity.

The three basic forms of business organization are the sole proprietorship, the partnership, and the corporation. A sole proprietorship is a business owned by one person. A partnership is like a sole proprietorship in most ways, but it has two or more owners. A corporation is a business unit chartered by the state and legally separate from its owners (the stockholders). A corporation's ownership is represented by shares of stock. The stockholders own the corporation and elect the board of directors. The board of directors is responsible for the overall direction of the corporation for the benefit of the stockholders. Thus, the board is responsible for determining corporate policies and appointing corporate officers, or top managers, to operate the business in accordance with the policies that it sets. The board is also responsible for corporate governance, the oversight of a corporation's management and ethics. The audit committee, which is appointed by the board and is made up of independent directors, is an important factor in corporate governance.

Define *financial position*, and state the accounting equation. **LO 2**

Financial position refers to a company's economic resources and the claims against those resources at a particular time. The accounting equation shows financial position as Assets = Liabilities + Stockholders' Equity. Business transactions affect financial position by decreasing or increasing assets, liabilities, and stockholders' equity in such a way that the accounting equation is always in balance.

Identify the four basic financial statements and their interrelationships. **LO 3**

The four basic financial statements are the income statement, the statement of retained earnings, the balance sheet, and the statement of cash flows. They are the primary means by which accountants communicate the financial condition and activities of a business to those who have an interest in the business.

Explain how generally accepted accounting principles (GAAP) and international financial reporting standards (IFRS) relate to financial statements and the independent CPA's report, and identify the organizations that influence GAAP. **LO 4**

Acceptable accounting practice consists of the conventions, rules, and procedures that make up generally accepted accounting principles. GAAP are essential to the preparation and interpretation of financial statements and the independent CPA's report. Foreign companies registered in the United States may use international financial reporting standards (IFRS).

Among the organizations that influence the formulation of GAAP are the Public Company Accounting Oversight Board, the Financial Accounting Standards Board, the American Institute of Certified Public Accountants, the Securities and Exchange Commission, and the Internal Revenue Service.

All accountants are required to follow a code of professional ethics. Accountants must act with integrity, objectivity, and independence, and exercise due care in all their activities.

Identify the users of accounting information, and identify business goals, activities, and performance measures. LO 5

Accounting provides information to managers of all institutions and to individuals with a direct financial interest in those institutions, including present or potential investors and creditors. Accounting information is also important to those with an indirect financial interest in the business—tax authorities, regulatory agencies, and economic planners.

A business is an economic entity that engages in operating, investing, and financing activities to achieve goals of profitability and liquidity.

Explain the importance of ethics in financial reporting. 

Ethical financial reporting is important to the well-being of a company. Fraudulent financial reports can have serious consequences for many people.

Key Terms

accounting 4 (LO1)
accounting equation (A = L + SE) 9 (LO2)
additional paid-in capital 10 (LO2)
American Institute of Certified Public Accountants (AICPA) 17 (LO4)
articles of incorporation 8 (LO1)
assets 10 (LO2)
audit 17 (LO4)
audit committee 8 (LO1)
balance sheet 12 (LO3)
board of directors 8 (LO1)
bookkeeping 5 (LO1)
business 21 (LO5)
business transactions 5 (LO1)
cash flows 14 (LO3)
certified public accountant (CPA) 16 (LO4)
common stock 8 (LO1)
contributed capital 10 (LO2)
corporate governance 8 (LO1)
corporation 7 (LO1)
creditors 20 (LO5)
dividends 11 (LO2)
due care 18 (LO4)
economic entity 4 (LO1)
ethics 23 (LO6)
exchange rate 6 (LO1)
expenses 10 (LO2)
financial accounting 4 (LO1)
Financial Accounting Standards Board (FASB) 17 (LO4)
financial analysis 22 (LO5)
financial position 9 (LO2)
financial ratios 22 (LO5)
financial statements 4 (LO1)
financing activities 21 (LO5)
fraudulent financial reporting 23 (LO6)
generally accepted accounting principles (GAAP) 16 (LO4)
Governmental Accounting Standards Board (GASB) 18 (LO4)
income statement 12 (LO3)
independence 18 (LO4)
Institute of Management Accountants (IMA) 18 (LO4)
integrity 18 (LO4)
Internal Revenue Service (IRS) 18 (LO4)
International Accounting Standards Board (IASB) 17 (LO4)
international financial reporting standards (IFRS) 17 (LO4)
investing activities 21 (LO5)
investors 20 (LO5)
liabilities 10 (LO2)
limited liability 7 (LO1)
liquidity 21 (LO5)
management 19 (LO5)
management information systems (MIS) 5 (LO1)
managerial accounting 5 (LO1)
money measure 5 (LO1)
net assets 10 (LO2)
net income 11 (LO2)
net loss 11 (LO2)
objectivity 18 (LO4)
operating activities 21 (LO5)
par value 10 (LO2)
partnership 6 (LO1)
performance measures 22 (LO5)
profitability 21 (LO5)
Public Company Accounting Oversight Board (PCAOB) 17 (LO4)
retained earnings 10 (LO2)
revenues 10 (LO2)
Sarbanes-Oxley Act 23 (LO6)
Securities and Exchange Commission (SEC) 18 (LO4)
separate entity 6 (LO1)
share of stock 8 (LO1)
sole proprietorship 6 (LO1)
statement of cash flows 14 (LO3)
statement of retained earnings 12 (LO3)
stockholders 7 (LO1)
stockholders' equity 10 (LO2)

Chapter Assignments

DISCUSSION QUESTIONS

LO 1 **DQ1.** What makes accounting a valuable discipline?

LO 1 **DQ2. CONCEPT ▶** Are all economic events business transactions?

LO 1 **DQ3.** Sole proprietorships, partnerships, and corporations differ legally; how and why does accounting treat them alike?

LO 2 **DQ4.** How are expenses and dividends similar, and how are they different?

LO 4 **DQ5.** How do generally accepted accounting principles (GAAP) differ from the laws of mathematics?

LO 5 **DQ6.** Why do managers in governmental and not-for-profit organizations need to understand financial information as much as managers in profit-seeking businesses?

LO 5 **DQ7.** In what ways are **CVS** and **Southwest Airlines** comparable? Not comparable?

LO 6 **DQ8. BUSINESS APPLICATION ▶** What are some unethical ways in which a business may do its accounting or prepare its financial statements?

SHORT EXERCISES

LO 1 Accounting Concepts

SE1. CONCEPT ▶ Indicate whether each of the following words or phrases relates most closely to (a) a business transaction, (b) a separate entity, or (c) a money measure:

1. Partnership
2. U.S. dollar
3. Payment of an expense
4. Sole proprietorship
5. Sale of an asset

LO 1 Forms of Business Organization

SE2. Match the descriptions that follow with the appropriate forms of business organization.

1. Most numerous
2. Commands most revenues
3. Has two or more co-owners
4. Has stockholders
5. Is owned by only one person
6. Has a board of directors

a. Sole proprietorship
b. Partnership
c. Corporation

LO 2 The Accounting Equation

SE3. Determine the amount missing from each accounting equation that follows.

	Assets	=	Liabilities	+	Stockholders' Equity
1.	?		$100,000		$140,000
2.	$312,000		$168,000		?
3.	$584,000		?		$384,000

LO 2 The Accounting Equation

SE4. Use the accounting equation to answer each question that follows.

1. Ambria Company's assets are $240,000, and its liabilities are $90,000. What is the amount of its stockholders' equity?
2. Dao Company's liabilities equal one-fifth of the total assets. The stockholders' equity is $40,000. What is the amount of the liabilities?

LO 2 **The Accounting Equation**

SE5. Use the accounting equation to answer each question that follows.

1. At the beginning of the year, Palette Company's assets were $90,000, and its stockholders' equity was $50,000. During the year, assets increased by $30,000 and liabilities increased by $5,000. What was the stockholders' equity at the end of the year?
2. At the beginning of the year, Carmines Company had liabilities of $100,000 and stockholders' equity of $96,000. If assets increased by $40,000 and liabilities decreased by $30,000, what was the stockholders' equity at the end of the year?

LO 2 **The Accounting Equation and Net Income**

SE6. Vivaldi Company had assets of $280,000 and liabilities of $120,000 at the beginning of the year, and assets of $400,000 and liabilities of $140,000 at the end of the year. During the year, an additional $40,000 of common stock was issued, and the company paid dividends of $48,000. What amount of net income did the company earn during the year?

LO 3 **Preparation and Completion of a Balance Sheet**

SE7. Use the following accounts and balances to prepare a balance sheet with the accounts in proper order for Manteno Company at June 30, 2014, using Exhibit 9 as a model:

Accounts Receivable	$3,200	Building	$44,000
Wages Payable	1,400	Common Stock	48,000
Retained Earnings	9,400	Cash	?

LO 3 **Preparation of Financial Statements**

SE8. Randall Company engaged in activities during the first year of its operations that resulted in the following: service revenue, $4,800; expenses, $2,450; and dividends, $410. In addition, the year-end balances of selected accounts were as follows: Cash, $1,890; Other Assets, $1,000; Accounts Payable, $450; and Common Stock, $500. Prepare Randall's income statement, statement of retained earnings, and balance sheet (assume the year ends on December 31, 2014). (*Hint:* You must solve for the ending balance of retained earnings.)

LO 5 **Accounting and Business Enterprises**

SE9. Match the terms that follow with the appropriate definitions.

1. Accounting
2. Profitability
3. Liquidity
4. Financing activities
5. Investing activities
6. Operating activities
7. Financial accounting
8. Managerial accounting
9. Ethics
10. Fraudulent financial reporting

a. The process of producing accounting information for the internal use of a company's management
b. Having enough cash available to pay debts when they are due
c. Activities of management engaged to obtain adequate funds for beginning and continuing to operate a business
d. The process of generating and communicating accounting information in the form of financial statements to decision makers outside the organization
e. Activities of management engaged to spend capital in ways that are productive and will help a business achieve its objectives
f. The ability to earn enough income to attract and hold investment capital
g. An information system that measures, processes, and communicates financial information about an identifiable economic entity
h. The intentional preparation of misleading financial statements
i. Activities of management engaged to operate the business
j. A code of conduct that addresses whether actions are right or wrong

LO 6

Ethics and Accounting

SE10. BUSINESS APPLICATION ▶ Match the following descriptions with the appropriate terms.

1. Preparation of financial statements that mislead the public
2. An important underpinning of financial reporting
3. A law that strengthened financial reporting of public companies and their auditors
4. Have a duty to prepare financial reports that are not false or misleading

a. Ethics
b. Fraudulent financial reporting
c. Accountants
d. Sarbanes-Oxley Act

EXERCISES: SET A

LO 1

Business Transactions

E1A. CONCEPT ▶ Austin Corporation operates a minimart. Which of Austin's actions described below are business transactions? Explain why any other actions are not considered business transactions.

1. Austin reduces the price of a gallon of milk in order to match the price offered by a competitor.
2. Austin pays a high school student cash for cleaning up the driveway behind the market.
3. Austin fills an employee's car with gasoline in payment for the employee restocking the vending machines and the snack food shelves.
4. Austin pays interest to a stockholder on a loan made to the business three years ago.

LO 1

Accounting Concepts

E2A. CONCEPT ▶ Financial accounting uses money measures to gauge the impact of business transactions on a separate business entity. Indicate whether each of the following words or phrases relates most closely to (a) a business transaction, (b) a separate entity, or (c) a money measure:

1. U.S. dollars
2. Indian rupees
3. Partnership
4. Receipt of cash
5. Sole proprietorship
6. Corporation
7. Sales of products
8. Sale of common stock
9. Japanese yen
10. Purchase of supplies

LO 1

Money Measure

E3A. CONCEPT ▶ You have been asked to compare the sales and assets of four companies that make computer chips to determine which company is the largest in each category. You have gathered the following data, but they cannot be used for direct comparison because each company's sales and assets are in its own currency:

Company (Currency)	Sales	Assets
Abril Chip (U.S. dollar)	2,000,000	1,300,000
Dao (Hong Kong dollar)	5,000,000	2,400,000
Aiko (Japanese yen)	350,000,000	250,000,000
Orca (euro)	3,000,000	3,900,000

Assuming that the exchange rates in Exhibit 2 are current and appropriate, convert all the figures to U.S. dollars (multiply amount by exchange rate) and determine which company is the largest in sales and which is the largest in assets.

LO 2 **The Accounting Equation**

E4A. Use the accounting equation to answer each question that follows. Show any calculations you make.

1. Oshkosh Company's assets are $400,000, and its stockholders' equity is $155,000. What is the amount of its liabilities?
2. Salvatore Company's liabilities and stockholders' equity are $72,000 and $79,500, respectively. What is the amount of the assets?
3. Radisson Company's liabilities equal one-third of the total assets, and stockholders' equity is $160,000. What is the amount of its liabilities?
4. At the beginning of the year, Sun Company's assets were $275,000, and its stockholders' equity was $150,000. During the year, assets increased $75,000 and liabilities decreased $22,500. What is the stockholders' equity at the end of the year?

LO 2 **Stockholders' Equity and the Accounting Equation**

E5A. Daiichi Company's total assets and liabilities at the beginning and end of the year follow.

	Assets	Liabilities
Beginning of the year	$175,000	$ 68,750
End of the year	275,000	162,500

Determine Daiichi's net income or loss for the year under each of the following alternatives:

1. No common stock was issued, and no dividends were paid during the year.
2. No common stock was issued, but Daiichi paid $27,500 in dividends during the year.
3. Common stock of $16,250 was issued, but no dividends were paid during the year.
4. Common stock of $12,500 was issued, and Daiichi paid dividends of $27,500 during the year.

LO 3 **Identification of Accounts**

E6A.

1. Indicate whether each of the following accounts is an asset (A), a liability (L), or a part of stockholders' equity (SE):
   a. Building
   b. Salaries Payable
   c. Accounts Receivable
   d. Common Stock
   e. Cash
   f. Accounts Payable
   g. Equipment
2. Indicate whether each account that follows would be shown on the income statement (IS), the statement of retained earnings (RE), or the balance sheet (BS).
   a. Commissions Earned
   b. Automobile
   c. Utilities Expense
   d. Land
   e. Supplies Expense
   f. Accounts Payable
   g. Dividends

LO 3 **Preparation of a Balance Sheet**

E7A. Listed in random order are some of Oxford Services Company's account balances as of December 31, 2014.

Accounts Payable	$ 50,000	Accounts Receivable	$62,500
Building	112,500	Cash	25,000
Common Stock	125,000	Equipment	50,000
Retained Earnings	87,500		
Supplies	12,500		

Place the balances in proper order and prepare a balance sheet similar to the one in Exhibit 9.

LO 3 **Preparation and Integration of Financial Statements**

E8A. Dukakis Company had the following accounts and balances during 2014: Service Revenue, $13,200; Rent Expense, $1,200; Wages Expense, $8,340; Advertising Expense, $1,350; Utilities Expense, $900; and Dividends, $700. In addition, the year-end balances of selected accounts were as follows: Cash, $1,550; Accounts Receivable, $750; Supplies, $100; Land, $1,000; Accounts Payable, $450; and Common Stock, $1,240. The beginning Retained Earnings balance was $1,000.

Prepare Dukakis's income statement, statement of retained earnings, and balance sheet (assume the year ends on December 31, 2014). (*Hint*: You must first solve for the net income and the ending balance of retained earnings for 2014.)

LO 3 **Statement of Cash Flows**

E9A. Arlington Service Company began the year 2014 with cash of $55,900. In addition to earning a net income of $32,500 and distributing a cash dividend of $19,500, Arlington Service borrowed $78,000 from the bank and purchased equipment with $117,000 of cash. Also, accounts receivable increased by $7,800, and accounts payable increased by $11,700.

Determine the amount of cash on hand at December 31, 2014, by preparing a statement of cash flows similar to the one in Exhibit 10.

LO 3 **Statement of Retained Earnings**

E10A. ACCOUNTING CONNECTION ▶ Information from Mrs. Shah's Cookies' statement of retained earnings for 2014 follows.

Dividends	$ 0
Net income	?
Retained earnings, January 31, 2014	159,490
Retained earnings, January 31, 2013	102,403

Prepare Mrs. Shah's Cookies' statement of retained earnings. You will need to solve for the amount of net income. What is retained earnings? Why might the board of directors decide not to pay any dividends?

LO 3 **Preparation and Integration of Financial Statements**

E11A. Complete the financial statements that follow by determining the amounts that correspond to the letters.

Income Statement	
Revenues	$11,100
Expenses	(a)
Net income	$ (b)
Statement of Retained Earnings	
Beginning balance	$29,000
Net income	(c)
Less dividends	2,000
Ending balance	$30,000
Balance Sheet	
Total assets	$ (d)
Total liabilities	$16,000
Stockholders' equity:	
Common stock	$50,000
Retained earnings	(e)
Total liabilities and stockholders' equity	$ (f)

LO 1, 4 **Users of Accounting Information and Forms of Business Organization**

E12A. Avalon Pharmacy has recently been formed to develop a new type of drug treatment for cancer. Previously a partnership, Avalon has now become a corporation. Describe the various groups that will have an interest in Avalon's financial statements. What is the difference between a partnership and a corporation? What advantages does the corporate form have over the partnership form of business organization?

LO 4, 5 **The Nature of Accounting**

E13A. Match the terms that follow with the appropriate descriptions.

1. Communication
2. Business transactions
3. Investors
4. Financial Accounting Standards Board (FASB)
5. Creditors
6. Management
7. Bookkeeping
8. Securities and Exchange Commission (SEC)
9. Money measure
10. Sarbanes-Oxley Act
11. Financial statements
12. Management information system

a. The recording of all business transactions in terms of money
b. A process by which information is exchanged between individuals through a common system of symbols, signs, or behavior
c. The process of identifying and assigning values to business transactions
d. Legislation requiring CEOs and CFOs to swear that any reports they file with the SEC are accurate and complete
e. Show how well a company is meeting the goals of profitability and liquidity
f. Collectively, the people who have overall responsibility for operating a business and meeting its goals
g. People who commit money to earn a financial return
h. The interconnected subsystems that provide the information needed to run a business
i. The most important body for developing and issuing rules on accounting practice, called *Statements of Financial Accounting Standards*
j. An agency set up by Congress to protect the public by regulating the issuing, buying, and selling of stocks
k. Economic events that affect a business's financial position
l. People or businesses to whom money is due

LO 4 **Accounting Abbreviations**

E14A. Identify the accounting meaning of each of the following abbreviations: CPA, IRS, PCAOB, GAAP, FASB, SEC, GASB, IASB, IMA, and AICPA.

LO 6 **Ethics and Accounting**

E15A. BUSINESS APPLICATION ▶ Match the descriptions that follow with the appropriate terms.

1. Responsible for the ethical preparation of financial statements
2. Preparation of financial statements that mislead the public
3. Underlies both management's and accountants' actions in preparing financial statements
4. A law related to regulation of financial reporting of public companies and their auditors following the Enron scandal
5. Has overall responsibility for ensuring that financial reports are not false or misleading

a. Accountants
b. Ethics
c. Fraudulent financial reporting
d. Management
e. Sarbanes-Oxley Act

EXERCISES: SET B

Visit the textbook companion web site at www.cengagebrain.com to access the Exercise Set B for this chapter.

PROBLEMS

LO 3, 5

Preparation and Interpretation of Financial Statements

P1. A list of financial statement items follows.

Utilities expense	Accounts payable
Building	Rent expense
Common stock	Dividends
Net income	Fees earned
Land	Cash
Equipment	Supplies
Revenues	Wages expense
Accounts receivable	

REQUIRED

1. Indicate whether each item is found on the income statement (IS), statement of retained earnings (RE), and/or balance sheet (BS).
2. **BUSINESS APPLICATION ▶** Which statement is most closely associated with the goal of profitability?

LO 3

✔ 1(f): Total liabilities and stockholders' equity: $6,600

Integration of Financial Statements

P2. The following three independent sets of financial statements have several amounts missing:

Income Statement	**Set A**	**Set B**	**Set C**
Revenues	$1,100	$ (g)	$ 240
Expenses	(a)	5,200	(m)
Net income	$ (b)	$ (h)	$ 80
Statement of Retained Earnings			
Beginning balance	$2,900	$24,400	$ 340
Net income	(c)	1,600	(n)
Less dividends	200	(i)	(o)
Ending balance	$3,000	$ (j)	$ (p)
Balance Sheet			
Total assets	$ (d)	$31,000	$ (q)
Total liabilities	$1,600	$ 5,000	(r)
Stockholders' equity			
Common stock	$2,000	$10,000	$ 100
Retained earnings	(e)	(k)	280
Total liabilities and stockholders' equity	$ (f)	$ (l)	$ 380

REQUIRED

1. Complete each set of financial statements by determining the missing amounts that correspond to the letters.
2. **ACCOUNTING CONNECTION ▶** Why is it necessary to prepare the income statement prior to the balance sheet?

LO 3, 5

SPREADSHEET

✔ 1: Net income: $52,200
✔ 1: Total assets: $122,800

Preparation and Interpretation of Financial Statements

P3. Fuel Designs' financial accounts follow. The company has just completed its tenth year of operations ended December 31, 2014.

Accounts Payable	$ 3,600	Income Taxes Expense	$27,000
Accounts Receivable	4,500	Income Taxes Payable	13,000
Cash	57,700	Marketing Expense	20,100
Commission Sales Revenue	400,000	Office Rent Expense	36,000
Commissions Expense	225,000	Retained Earnings, December 31, 2013	35,300
Commissions Payable	22,700	Supplies	700
Common Stock	29,000	Supplies Expense	2,600
Dividends	33,000	Telephone and Computer Expenses	5,100
Equipment	59,900	Wages Expense	32,000

REQUIRED

1. Prepare Fuel Designs' income statement, statement of retained earnings, and balance sheet. There was no common stock issued during the year.
2. **ACCOUNTING CONNECTION ▶** The company is considering expansion. What other financial statement would be useful to the company in assessing whether the its operations are generating sufficient funds to support the expenses? Why would it be useful?

LO **3, 5**

Preparation and Interpretation of Financial Statements

✓ 1: Net income: $2,040
✓ 1: Total assets: $28,300

P4. The accounts of Frequent Ad, an agency that develops marketing materials for print, radio, and television, follow. The agency's first year of operations just ended on January 31, 2014.

Accounts Payable	$ 19,400	Income Taxes Payable	$ 560
Accounts Receivable	24,900	Marketing Expense	6,800
Advertising Service Revenue	165,200	Office Rent Expense	13,500
Cash	1,800	Salaries Expense	86,000
Common Stock	5,000	Salaries Payable	1,300
Dividends	0	Supplies	1,600
Equipment Rental Expense	37,200	Supplies Expense	19,100
Income Taxes Expense	560		

REQUIRED

1. Prepare Frequent Ad's income statement, statement of retained earnings, and balance sheet.
2. **BUSINESS APPLICATION ▶** Review the financial statements and comment on the financial challenges Frequent Ad faces.

LO **3, 4, 5**

Use and Interpretation of Financial Statements

P5. Athena Riding Club's financial statements follow.

Athena Riding Club
Income Statement
For the Month Ended November 30, 2014

Revenues:		
Riding lesson revenue	$4,650	
Locker rental revenue	1,450	
Total revenues		$6,100
Expenses:		
Salaries expense	$1,125	
Feed expense	750	
Utilities expense	450	
Total expenses		2,325
Income before income taxes		$3,775
Income taxes expense		725
Net income		$3,050

Athena Riding Club
Statement of Retained Earnings
For the Month Ended November 30, 2014

Retained earnings, October 31, 2014	$35,475
Net income for the month	3,050
Subtotal	$38,525
Less dividends	2,400
Retained earnings, November 30, 2014	$36,125

Athena Riding Club
Balance Sheet
November 30, 2014

Assets		**Liabilities**	
Cash	$ 5,975	Accounts payable	$11,250
Accounts receivable	900	**Stockholders' Equity**	
Supplies	750	Common stock	$ 6,000
Land	15,750	Retained earnings	36,125
Building	22,500	Total stockholders' equity	$42,125
Horses	7,500		
Total assets	$53,375	Total liabilities and stockholders' equity	$53,375

Athena Riding Club
Statement of Cash Flows
For the Month Ended November 30, 2014

Cash flows from operating activities:		
Net income		$3,050
Adjustments to reconcile net income to net cash flows from operating activities:		
Increase in accounts receivable	$ (400)	
Increase in supplies	(550)	
Increase in accounts payable	400	(550)
Net cash flows from operating activities		$2,500
Cash flows from investing activities:		
Purchase of horses	$(2,000)	
Sale of horses	1,000	
Net cash flows from investing activities		(1,000)
Cash flows from financing activities:		
Issuance of common stock	$ 6,000	
Dividends paid	(2,400)	
Net cash flows from financing activities		3,600
Net increase in cash		$5,100
Cash at beginning of month		875
Cash at end of month		$5,975

REQUIRED

1. **ACCOUNTING CONNECTION ▶** Explain how Athena Riding Club's four statements relate to each other.
2. **BUSINESS APPLICATION ▶** Which statements are most closely associated with the goals of liquidity and profitability? Why?
3. **BUSINESS APPLICATION ▶** If you were the CEO of this business, how would you evaluate the company's performance? Give specific examples.
4. **ACCOUNTING CONNECTION ▶** If you were a banker considering Athena Riding Club for a loan, why might you want the company to be audited by an independent CPA? What would the audit tell you?

ALTERNATE PROBLEMS

LO 3, 5

Preparation and Interpretation of Financial Statements

P6. A list of financial statement items follows.

Wages expense	Accounts payable
Equipment	Rent expense
Equipment rental expense	Dividends
Net income	Fees earned
Land	Cash
Retained earnings	Supplies
Revenues	Utilities expense
Accounts receivable	

REQUIRED

1. Indicate whether each item is found on the income statement (IS), statement of retained earnings (RE), and/or balance sheet (BS).
2. **BUSINESS APPLICATION ▶** Which statement is most closely associated with the goal of profitability?

LO 3

✔ 1(f): Total liabilities and stockholders' equity: $10,880

Integration of Financial Statements

P7. Three independent sets of financial statements with several amounts missing follow.

Income Statement	**Set A**	**Set B**	**Set C**
Revenues	$2,400	$ (g)	$ 480
Expenses	(a)	10,000	(m)
Net income	$ (b)	$ (h)	$ 296
Statement of Retained Earnings			
Beginning balance	$5,800	$48,800	$ 480
Net income	(c)	3,200	(n)
Less dividends	400	(i)	(o)
Ending balance	$6,180	$ (j)	$ (p)
Balance Sheet			
Total assets	$ (d)	$60,000	$ (q)
Total liabilities	$3,200	$10,000	$ (r)
Stockholders' equity:			
Common stock	$1,500	$10,000	$ 120
Retained earnings	(e)	(k)	560
Total liabilities and stockholders' equity	$ (f)	$ (l)	$1,160

REQUIRED

1. Complete each set of financial statements by determining the amounts that correspond to the letters.
2. **ACCOUNTING CONNECTION ▶** In what order is it necessary to prepare the financial statements and why?

LO 3, 5

SPREADSHEET

✔ 1: Net income: $72,150
✔ 1: Total assets: $125,650

Preparation and Interpretation of Financial Statements

P8. Sears Labs' financial accounts follow. The company has just completed its third year of operations ended November 30, 2014.

Accounts Payable	$ 7,400	Marketing Expense	$19,700
Accounts Receivable	9,100	Office Rent Expense	18,200
Cash	115,750	Retained Earnings, November 30, 2013	55,400
Common Stock	15,000	Salaries Expense	96,000
Design Service Revenue	248,000	Salaries Payable	2,700
Dividends	40,000	Supplies	800
Income Taxes Expense	38,850	Supplies Expense	3,100
Income Taxes Payable	13,000		

REQUIRED

1. Prepare Sears Labs' income statement, statement of retained earnings, and balance sheet.
2. **BUSINESS APPLICATION ▶** Evaluate the company's ability to meet its bills when they come due.

LO **1, 3**

✔ 1: Net income: $17,800
✔ 1: Total assets: $52,200

Preparation and Interpretation of Financial Statements

P9. Bachino's Pizza's accounts follow. The company has just completed its first year of operations ended September 30, 2014.

Accounts Payable	$ 21,000	Income Taxes Expense	$ 6,000
Accounts Receivable	26,400	Income Taxes Payable	6,000
Cash	15,600	Marketing Expense	3,000
Common Stock	8,000	Pizza Revenue	164,000
Dividends	2,000	Salaries Expense	112,000
Delivery Truck Rent Expense	14,400	Salaries Payable	1,400
Equipment	9,400	Supplies	800
Equipment Rental Expense	2,600	Supplies Expense	8,200

REQUIRED

1. Prepare Bachino's Pizza's income statement, statement of retained earnings, and balance sheet.
2. Why would Bachino's Pizza's owner set his business up as a corporation and not a sole proprietorship? Discuss how profits and obligations are shared in the two forms of business organizations.

LO **3, 4, 5**

Use and Interpretation of Financial Statements

P10. Aqua Swimming Club's financial statements follow.

Aqua Swimming Club
Income Statement
For the Month Ended November 30, 2014

Revenues:		
Swimming lesson revenue	$4,650	
Locker rental revenue	1,275	
Total revenues		$5,925
Expenses:		
Salaries expense	$1,125	
Supplies expense	750	
Utilities expense	450	
Total expenses		2,325
Income before income taxes expense		$3,600
Income taxes expense		700
Net income		$2,900

Aqua Swimming Club
Statement of Retained Earnings
For the Month Ended November 30, 2014

Retained earnings, October 31, 2014	$34,975
Net income for the month	2,900
Subtotal	$37,875
Less dividends	2,500
Retained earnings, November 30, 2014	$35,375

Aqua Swimming Club
Balance Sheet
November 30, 2014

Assets		**Liabilities**	
Cash	$ 6,325	Accounts payable	$13,350
Accounts receivable	900	**Stockholders' Equity**	
Supplies	750	Common stock	$ 5,000
Land	15,750	Retained earnings	35,375
Building	22,500		
Equipment	7,500		
Total assets	$53,725	Total liabilities and stockholders' equity	$53,725

Aqua Swimming Club
Statement of Cash Flows
For the Month Ended November 30, 2014

Cash flows from operating activities:		
Net income		$2,900
Adjustments to reconcile net income to net cash flows from operating activities:		
Increase in accounts receivable	$ (400)	
Increase in supplies	(550)	
Increase in accounts payable	400	(550)
Net cash flows from operating activities		$2,350
Cash flows from investing activities:		
Sale of equipment	$ 2,000	
Purchase of equipment	(1,000)	
Net cash flows from investing activities		1,000
Cash flows from financing activities:		
Issuance of common stock	$ 5,000	
Dividends paid	(2,500)	
Net cash flows from financing activities		2,500
Net increase in cash		$5,850
Cash at beginning of month		475
Cash at end of month		$6,325

REQUIRED

1. **ACCOUNTING CONNECTION ▶** Explain how Aqua Swimming Club's four statements relate to each other.
2. **BUSINESS APPLICATION ▶** Which statements are most closely associated with the goals of liquidity and profitability? Why?
3. **BUSINESS APPLICATION ▶** If you were the CEO of this business, how would you evaluate the company's performance? Give specific examples.
4. **ACCOUNTING CONNECTION ▶** If you were a banker considering Aqua Swimming Club for a loan, why might you want the company to be audited by an independent CPA? What would the audit tell you?

CASES

LO 5 **Conceptual Understanding: Business Activities and Management Functions**

C1. Costco Wholesale Corporation is America's largest membership retail company. According to its letter to stockholders:

> *For the first time [in 2011], four of our locations had more than $300 million in annual sales, including one which had more than $400 million in sales. This rate of top line revenue per building stands out in the retail industry and results from our ongoing focus on value – that winning combination of quality and price on every item we sell that, we believe, sets Costco apart from many of its competitors.*[12]

To achieve its strategy, Costco must organize its management by functions that relate to the principal activities of a business. Discuss the three basic activities Costco will engage in to achieve its goals, and suggest some examples of each. What is the role of Costco's management? What functions must its management perform to carry out these activities?

LO 2 **Conceptual Understanding: Concept of an Asset**

C2. CONCEPT ▶ Southwest Airlines Co. is one of the most successful airlines in the United States. One of its annual reports contained this statement:

> *We are a company of People, not Planes. That is what distinguishes us from other airlines and other companies. At Southwest Airlines, People are our most important asset.*[13]

Are employees considered assets in the financial statements? Why or why not? Discuss in what sense Southwest considers its employees to be assets.

LO 4 **Conceptual Understanding: Generally Accepted Accounting Principles**

C3. Fidelity Investments Company is a well-known mutual fund investment company. It makes investments worth billions of dollars in companies listed on the New York Stock Exchange and other stock markets. Generally accepted accounting principles (GAAP) are very important for Fidelity's investment analysts. What are generally accepted accounting principles? Why are financial statements that have been prepared in accordance with GAAP and audited by an independent CPA useful for Fidelity's investment analysts? What organizations influence GAAP? Explain how they do so.

LO 3 **Interpreting Financial Reports: Analysis of Four Basic Financial Statements**

C4. Refer to the **CVS** annual report in the Supplement to Chapter 1 to answer the questions below. Keep in mind that every company, while following basic principles, adapts financial statements and terminology to its own special needs. Therefore, the complexity of CVS's financial statements and the terminology in them will differ somewhat from the financial statements in the text.

1. What names does CVS give to its four basic financial statements? (Note that the word *consolidated* in the names of the financial statements means that these statements combine those of several companies owned by CVS.)
2. Prove that the accounting equation works for CVS on December 31, 2011, by finding the amounts for the following equation: Assets = Liabilities + Stockholders' Equity.
3. What were the total revenues of CVS for the year ended December 31, 2011?
4. Was CVS profitable in the year ended December 31, 2011? How much was net income (loss) in that year, and did it increase or decrease from the year ended December 31, 2010?
5. Did the company's cash and cash equivalents increase from December 31, 2010 to December 31, 2011? If so, by how much? In what two places in the statements can this number be found or computed?
6. Did cash flows from operating activities, cash flows from investing activities, and cash flows from financing activities increase or decrease from years 2010 to 2011?
7. Who is the auditor for the company? Why is the auditor's report that accompanies the financial statements important?

LO 5 **Comparison Analysis: Performance Measures and Financial Statements**

C5. BUSINESS APPLICATION ▶ Refer to the **CVS** annual report and the financial statements of **Southwest Airlines Co.** in the Supplement to Chapter 1 to answer the questions that follow.

1. Which company is larger in terms of assets and in terms of revenues? What do you think is the best way to measure the size of a company?
2. Which company is more profitable in terms of net income? What is the trend of profitability over the past three years for both companies?
3. Which company has more cash? Which increased its cash the most in the last year? Which has more liquidity as measured by cash flows from operating activities?

LO 6 **Ethical Dilemma: Professional Situations**

C6. BUSINESS APPLICATION ▶ Discuss the ethical choices in the situations below. In each instance, describe the ethical dilemma, determine the alternative courses of action, and tell what you would do.

1. You are the payroll accountant for a small business. A friend asks you how much another employee is paid per hour.
2. As an accountant for the branch office of a wholesale supplier, you discover that several of the receipts the branch manager has submitted for reimbursement as selling expenses actually stem from nights out with his spouse.
3. You are an accountant in the purchasing department of a construction company. When you arrive home from work on December 22, you find a large ham in a box marked "Happy Holidays—It's a pleasure to work with you." The gift is from a supplier who has bid on a contract your employer plans to award next week.
4. As an auditor with one year's experience at a local CPA firm, you are expected to complete a certain part of an audit in 20 hours. Because of your lack of experience, you know you cannot finish the job within that time. Rather than admit this, you are thinking about working late to finish the job and not telling anyone.
5. You are a tax accountant at a local CPA firm. You help your neighbor fill out her tax return, and she pays you $200 in cash. Because there is no record of this transaction, you are considering not reporting it on your tax return.
6. The accounting firm for which you work as a CPA has just won a new client, a firm in which you own 200 shares of stock that you received as an inheritance from your grandmother. Because it is only a small number of shares and you think the company will be very successful, you are considering not disclosing the investment.

Continuing Case: Annual Report Project

C7. Choose a company in which you are interested, and obtain its most recent annual report online at the company's website. Click on *Investor Relations*; then, select *Annual Report* or *SEC Form 10-K*. (*Hint:* When performing a search, use "*company name* investor relations" to avoid the customer-oriented home page.)

1. Identify the company by writing a summary that includes the following elements:
   - Name of the chief executive officer
   - Location of the home office
   - Ending date of latest fiscal year
   - Description of the company's principal products or services
   - Main geographic area of activity
   - Name of the company's independent accountants (auditors). In your own words, explain what the accountants said about the company's financial statements.
2. Identify the company's four financial statements. What differences, if any, do you see in the titles given to the statements as compared to those used in the chapter? Trace the interrelationships of the statements.
3. Show that the accounting equation (Assets = Liabilities + Stockholders' Equity) is in balance for the most recent year.

Comparison Analysis: Performance Measures and Financial Statements

C5. BUSINESS APPLICATION ▶ Refer to the **CVS** annual report and the financial statements of **Southwest Airlines Co.** in the Supplement to Chapter 1 to answer the questions that follow.

1. Which company is larger in terms of assets and in terms of revenues? What do you think is the best way to measure the size of a company?
2. Which company is more profitable in terms of net income? What is the trend of profitability over the past three years for both companies?
3. Which company has more cash? Which increased its cash the most in the last year? Which has more liquidity as measured by cash flows from operating activities?

Ethical Dilemma: Professional Situations

C6. BUSINESS APPLICATION ▶ Discuss the ethical choices in the situations below. In each instance, describe the ethical dilemma, determine the alternative courses of action, and tell what you would do.

1. You are the payroll accountant for a small business. A friend asks you how much another employee is paid per hour.
2. As an accountant for the branch office of a wholesale supplier, you discover that several of the invoices the branch manager has submitted for reimbursement as selling expenses actually are for a personal trip with his spouse.
3. You are an accountant in the purchasing department of a construction company. When you arrive home from work on December 22, you find a large ham in a box marked, "Happy Holidays—It's a pleasure to work with you." The gift is from a supplier who has bid on a contract your employer plans to award next week.
4. As an auditor with one year's experience at a local CPA firm, you are expected to complete a certain part of an audit in 20 hours. Because of your lack of experience, you know you cannot finish the job within that time. Rather than admit this, you are thinking about working late to finish the job and not telling anyone.
5. You are a tax accountant at a local CPA firm. You help your neighbor fill out her tax return, and she pays you $200 in cash. Because there is no record of this transaction, you are considering not reporting it on your tax return.
6. The accounting firm for which you work as a CPA has just won a new client, a firm in which you own 200 shares of stock that you received as an inheritance from your grandmother. Because it is only a small number of shares and you think the company will be very successful, you are considering not disclosing the investment.

Continuing Case: Annual Report Project

C7. Choose a company in which you are interested, and obtain its most recent annual report online at the company's website. Click on *Investor Relations*; then select *Annual Report*. [illegible]

1. Identify the company by writing a summary that includes the following elements:
   a. Name of the chief executive officer
   b. Location of the home office
   c. Ending date of latest fiscal year
   d. Description of the company's principal products or services
   e. Main geographic area of activity
   f. Name of the company's independent accountants (auditors). In your own words, explain what the accountants said about the company's financial statements.
2. Identify the company's four financial statements. What differences, if any, do you see in the titles given to the statements as compared to those used in the chapter? Trace the interrelationships of the statements.
3. Show that the accounting equation (Assets = Liabilities + Stockholders' Equity) is in balance for the most recent year.

SUPPLEMENT TO CHAPTER 1
How to Read an Annual Report

More than 4 million corporations are chartered in the United States. Most of them are small, family-owned businesses. They are called *private* or *closely held corporations* because their common stock is held by only a few people and is not for sale to the public. Larger companies usually find it desirable to raise investment funds from many investors by issuing common stock to the public. These companies are called *public companies.* Although they are fewer in number than private companies, their total economic impact is much greater.

Public companies must register their common stock with the Securities and Exchange Commission (SEC), which regulates the issuance and subsequent trading of the stock of public companies. Public companies are required to report their financial performance annually to their stockholders. This report, called an *annual report*, contains the company's annual financial statements and other pertinent data. It must also be filed with the SEC on a Form 10-K.

The general public may obtain an annual report by calling or writing the company or accessing the report online at the company's website. If a company has filed its 10-K electronically with the SEC, it can be accessed at http://www.sec.gov/edgar/searchedgar/webusers.htm. Many libraries also maintain files of annual reports or have them available on electronic media, such as *Compact Disclosure.*

This supplement describes the major components of the typical annual report. We have included many of these components in the annual report of **CVS Caremark Corporation**, one of the country's most successful retailers. Case assignments in many chapters refer to this annual report. For purposes of comparison, the supplement also includes the financial statements and summary of significant accounting policies of **Southwest Airlines Co.**, one of the largest and most successful airlines in the United States.

The Components of an Annual Report

In addition to listing the corporation's directors and officers, an annual report usually contains a letter to the shareholders (or *stockholders*), a multiyear summary of financial highlights, a description of the company, management's discussion and analysis of the company's operating results and financial condition, the financial statements, notes to the financial statements, a statement about management's responsibilities, and the auditors' report.

Letter to the Shareholders

Traditionally, an annual report begins with a letter in which the top officers of the corporation tell shareholders (or stockholders) about the company's performance and prospects. In **CVS**'s 2011 annual report, the chairman and chief executive officer wrote to the shareholders about the highlights of the past year, the key priorities for the new year, and other aspects of the business. He reported as follows: "By capitalizing on CVS Caremark's best-in-class businesses as well as the power of our combined entity, we are well-positioned to deliver on our goal of reinventing pharmacy for better health … and better shareholder value." CVS Caremark reported strong revenue and earnings and record free cash flow. Total revenue rose 11.8 percent to $107.1 billion, and generated $4.6 billion in free cash flow, a 39 percent increase over 2010's level.

Financial Highlights

The financial highlights section presents key statistics for at least a 5-year period but often for a 10-year period. It is often accompanied by graphs. **CVS**'s annual report, for example, gives critical figures for sales, operating profits, and other key measures. Note that the financial highlights section often includes nonfinancial data and graphs as well. For instance, CVS includes the number of its stores.

Description of the Company

An annual report contains a detailed description of the company's products and divisions. Although this section often contains glossy photographs and other image-building or marketing material, it may provide useful information about past results and future plans.

Management's Discussion and Analysis

In this section, management describes the company's financial condition and results of operations and explains the difference in results from one year to the next. For example, **CVS**'s management explains the effects of an acquisition and the length of its 2011 fiscal year on its net revenues as follows.

- Net revenues increased $11.3 billion and decreased $2.4 billion during 2011 and 2010, respectively.
- During 2011, the Longs Acquisition increased net revenues by $6.6 billion, compared to 2008.
- Three fewer days in the 2009 fiscal year negatively impacted net revenues by $671 million, compared to 2008.

This kind of detail is invaluable to understanding CVS's financial performance.

Financial Statements

All companies present the same four basic financial statements in their annual reports, but the names they use may vary. As you can see in Exhibits 1 through 4, **CVS** presents the following:

- Statements of income
- Balance sheets
- Statements of cash flows
- Statements of shareholders' equity (includes retained earnings)

(Note that the numbers given in the statements are in millions, but the last six digits are omitted. For example, $107,100,000,000 is shown as $107,100.) CVS's financial statement headings are preceded by the word *consolidated*. A corporation issues consolidated financial statements when it consists of more than one company and has combined the companies' data for reporting purposes.

CVS provides several years of data for each financial statement (two years for the balance sheet and three years for the others). Financial statements presented in this fashion are called *comparative financial statements*. Such statements are in accordance with generally accepted accounting principles and help readers assess the company's performance over several years.

CVS's fiscal year ends on the Saturday nearest the end of December (December 31, 2011 in the latest year). Retailers commonly end their fiscal years during a slow period, usually the end of January, which is in contrast to CVS's choosing the end of December.

Income Statements As shown in Exhibit 1, **CVS** uses a multistep form of the income statement in that results are shown in several steps. The steps are gross profit, operating profit, earnings before income tax provision, and net earnings. The company also shows net earnings available to common shareholders, and discloses basic earnings per share and diluted earnings per share. *Basic earnings per share* is used for most analysis. *Diluted earnings per share* assumes that all rights that could be exchanged for common shares,

Exhibit 1
CVS's Income Statements

Consolidated means that data from all companies owned by CVS are combined.

CVS Caremark Corporation
Consolidated Statements of Income

(In millions, except per share amounts)	Year Ended December 31, 2011	2010	2009
Net revenues	$ 107,100	$ 95,778	$ 98,215
Cost of revenues	86,539	75,559	77,857
Gross profit	20,561	20,219	20,358
Operating expenses	14,231	14,082	13,933
Operating profit	6,330	6,137	6,425
Interest expense, net	584	536	525
Income before income tax provision	5,746	5,601	5,900
Income tax provision	2,258	2,179	2,200
Income from continuing operations	3,488	3,422	3,700
Income (loss) from discontinued operations, net of tax	(31)	2	(4)
Net income	3,457	3,424	3,696
Net loss attributable to noncontrolling interest	4	3	—
Net income attributable to CVS Caremark	$ 3,461	$ 3,427	$ 3,696
Basic earnings per common share:			
Income from continuing operations attributable to CVS Caremark	$ 2.61	$ 2.51	$ 2.58
Loss from discontinued operations attributable to CVS Caremark	(0.02)	—	—
Net income attributable to CVS Caremark	$ 2.59	$ 2.51	$ 2.58
Weighted average common shares outstanding	1,338	1,367	1,434
Diluted earnings per common share:			
Income from continuing operations attributable to CVS Caremark	$ 2.59	$ 2.49	$ 2.55
Loss from discontinued operations attributable to CVS Caremark	(0.02)	—	—
Net income attributable to CVS Caremark	$ 2.57	$ 2.49	$ 2.55
Weighted average common shares outstanding	1,347	1,377	1,450
Dividends declared per common share	$ 0.500	$ 0.350	$ 0.305

See accompanying notes to consolidated financial statements.

such as stock options, are in fact exchanged. The weighted average number of shares of common stock, used in calculating the per share figures, are shown at the bottom of the income statement.

Balance Sheets **CVS** has a typical balance sheet for a retail company, as shown in Exhibit 2. In the assets and liabilities sections, the company separates out the current assets and the current liabilities. *Current assets* will become available as cash or will be used up in the next year. *Current liabilities* will have to be paid or satisfied in the next year. These groupings are useful in assessing a company's liquidity.

The shareholders' equity section includes a number of items. *Common stock* represents the number of shares outstanding at par value. *Capital surplus* (*additional paid-in capital*) represents amounts invested by stockholders in excess of the par value of the common stock. *Preferred stock* is capital stock that has certain features that distinguish it from common stock. *Treasury stock* represents shares of common stock the company repurchased.

Statements of Cash Flows Whereas the income statement reflects **CVS**'s profitability, the statement of cash flows reflects its liquidity. As shown in Exhibit 3, this statement provides information about a company's cash receipts, cash payments, and investing and financing activities during an accounting period.

Exhibit 2
CVS's Balance Sheets

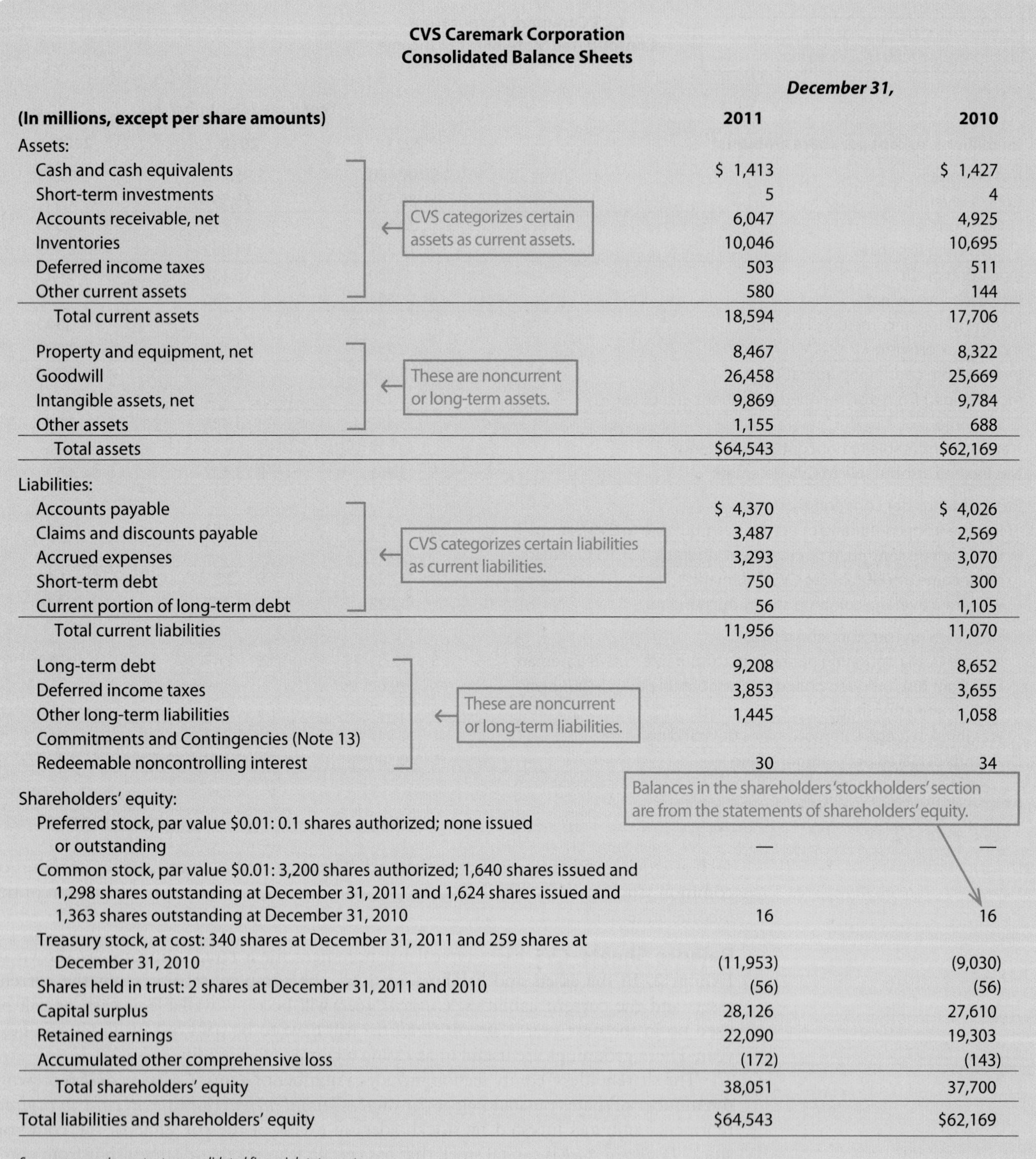

CVS Caremark Corporation
Consolidated Balance Sheets

(In millions, except per share amounts)	December 31, 2011	December 31, 2010
Assets:		
Cash and cash equivalents	$ 1,413	$ 1,427
Short-term investments	5	4
Accounts receivable, net	6,047	4,925
Inventories	10,046	10,695
Deferred income taxes	503	511
Other current assets	580	144
Total current assets	18,594	17,706
Property and equipment, net	8,467	8,322
Goodwill	26,458	25,669
Intangible assets, net	9,869	9,784
Other assets	1,155	688
Total assets	$64,543	$62,169
Liabilities:		
Accounts payable	$ 4,370	$ 4,026
Claims and discounts payable	3,487	2,569
Accrued expenses	3,293	3,070
Short-term debt	750	300
Current portion of long-term debt	56	1,105
Total current liabilities	11,956	11,070
Long-term debt	9,208	8,652
Deferred income taxes	3,853	3,655
Other long-term liabilities	1,445	1,058
Commitments and Contingencies (Note 13)		
Redeemable noncontrolling interest	30	34
Shareholders' equity:		
Preferred stock, par value $0.01: 0.1 shares authorized; none issued or outstanding	—	—
Common stock, par value $0.01: 3,200 shares authorized; 1,640 shares issued and 1,298 shares outstanding at December 31, 2011 and 1,624 shares issued and 1,363 shares outstanding at December 31, 2010	16	16
Treasury stock, at cost: 340 shares at December 31, 2011 and 259 shares at December 31, 2010	(11,953)	(9,030)
Shares held in trust: 2 shares at December 31, 2011 and 2010	(56)	(56)
Capital surplus	28,126	27,610
Retained earnings	22,090	19,303
Accumulated other comprehensive loss	(172)	(143)
Total shareholders' equity	38,051	37,700
Total liabilities and shareholders' equity	$64,543	$62,169

See accompanying notes to consolidated financial statements.

Exhibit 3
CVS's Statements of Cash Flows

Cash flows are shown for operating activities, investing activities, and financing activities.

CVS Caremark Corporation
Consolidated Statements of Cash Flows

(In millions)	2011	2010	2009
		Year Ended December 31,	
Cash flows from operating activities:			
Cash receipts from customers	$ 97,688	$ 94,503	$ 93,568
Cash paid for inventory and prescriptions dispensed by retail network pharmacies	(75,148)	(73,143)	(73,536)
Cash paid to other suppliers and employees	(13,635)	(13,778)	(13,121)
Interest received	4	4	5
Interest paid	(647)	(583)	(542)
Income taxes paid	(2,406)	(2,224)	(2,339)
Net cash provided by operating activities	5,856	4,779	4,035
Cash flows from investing activities:			
Purchases of property and equipment	(1,872)	(2,005)	(2,548)
Proceeds from sale-leaseback transactions	592	507	1,562
Proceeds from sale of property and equipment	4	34	23
Acquisitions (net of cash acquired) and other investments	(1,441)	(177)	(101)
Purchase of available-for-sale investments	(3)	—	(5)
Sale or maturity of available-for-sale investments	60	1	—
Proceeds from sale of subsidiary	250	—	—
Net cash used in investing activities	(2,410)	(1,640)	(1,069)
Cash flows from financing activities:			
Increase (decrease) in short-term debt	450	(15)	(2,729)
Proceeds from issuance of long-term debt	1,463	991	2,800
Repayments of long-term debt	(2,122)	(2,103)	(653)
Dividends paid	(674)	(479)	(439)
Derivative settlements	(19)	(5)	(3)
Proceeds from exercise of stock options	431	285	250
Excess tax benefits from stock-based compensation	21	28	19
Repurchase of common stock	(3,001)	(1,500)	(2,477)
Other	(9)	—	—
Net cash used in financing activities	(3,460)	(2,798)	(3,232)
Net increase (decrease) in cash and cash equivalents	(14)	341	(266)
Cash and cash equivalents at the beginning of the year	1,427	1,086	1,352
Cash and cash equivalents at the end of the year	$ 1,413	$ 1,427	$ 1,086
Reconciliation of net income to net cash provided by operating activities:			
Net income	$ 3,457	$ 3,424	$ 3,696
Adjustments required to reconcile net income to net cash provided by operating activities:			
Depreciation and amortization	1,568	1,469	1,389
Stock-based compensation	135	150	165
Gain on sale of subsidiary	(53)	—	—
Deferred income taxes and other noncash items	144	30	48
Change in operating assets and liabilities, net of effects from acquisitions:			
Accounts receivable, net	(748)	532	(86)
Inventories	607	(352)	(1,199)
Other current assets	(420)	(4)	48
Other assets	(49)	(210)	(2)
Accounts payable	1,128	(40)	4
Accrued expenses	85	(176)	(66)
Other long-term liabilities	2	(44)	38
Net cash provided by operating activities	$ 5,856	$ 4,779	$ 4,035

Cash and cash equivalents move to balance sheets.

This section explains the difference between net earnings and net cash provided by operating activities.

See accompanying notes to consolidated financial statements.

- The first major section of CVS's consolidated statements of cash flows shows cash flows from operating activities. It shows the cash received and paid for various items related to the company's operations.
- The second major section is cash flows from investing activities. The largest outflow in this category is additions for property and equipment. This figure demonstrates that CVS is a growing company.
- The third major section is cash flows from financing activities. CVS's largest cash inflows are for borrowing of long-term debt.

At the bottom of the statements of cash flows, you can see a reconciliation of net earnings to net cash provided by operating activities. This disclosure is important to the user because it relates the goal of profitability (net earnings) to liquidity (net cash provided). Most companies substitute this disclosure for the operating activities at the beginning of their statement of cash flows.

Statements of Shareholders' Equity Instead of a simple statement of retained earnings, **CVS** presents consolidated statements of shareholders' equity, as shown in Exhibit 4. These statements explain the changes in components of shareholders' equity (or stockholders' equity), including retained earnings.

Notes to the Financial Statements

To meet the requirements of *full disclosure*, a company must add notes to the financial statements to help users interpret some of the more complex items. The notes are an integral part of the financial statements. In recent years, the need for explanation and further details has become so great that the notes often take more space than the statements themselves. The notes to the financial statements include a summary of significant accounting policies, explanatory notes, and supplementary information.

Summary of Significant Accounting Policies Generally accepted accounting principles require that the financial statements include a *Summary of Significant Accounting Policies.* In most cases, this summary is presented in the first note to the financial statements or as a separate section just before the notes. In this summary, the company tells which generally accepted accounting principles it has followed in preparing the statements. For example, in **CVS**'s report, the company states the principles followed for revenue recognition for its Retail Pharmacy Segment:

> **Retail Pharmacy Segment.** *The RPS recognizes revenue from the sale of merchandise (other than prescription drugs) at the time the merchandise is purchased by the retail customer. Revenue from the sale of prescription drugs is recognized at the time the prescription is filled, which is or approximates when the retail customer picks up the prescription.*

Explanatory Notes Other notes explain some of the items in the financial statements. For example, **CVS** describes its commitments for future lease payments as follows.

> *Following is a summary of the future minimum lease payments under capital and operating leases as of December 31, 2011:*

(In millions)	Capital Leases	Operating Leases
2012	$ 20	$ 2,230
2013	20	2,143
2014	20	1,936
2015	20	1,880
2016	20	1,806
Thereafter	237	17,630
Total future lease payments	$337	$27,625

Information like this is very useful in determining the full scope of a company's liabilities and other commitments.

Exhibit 4
CVS's Statements of Shareholders' Equity

Each component of shareholders' equity is explained.

CVS Caremark Corporation
Consolidated Statements of Shareholders' Equity

(In millions)	Shares 2011	Shares 2010	Shares 2009	Dollars 2011	Dollars 2010	Dollars 2009
	Year Ended December 31,			Year Ended December 31,		
Preference stock:						
Beginning of year	—	—	4	$ —	$ —	$ 191
Conversion to common stock	—	—	(4)	—	—	(191)
End of year	—	—	—	$ —	$ —	$ —
Common stock:						
Beginning of year	1,624	1,612	1,603	$ 16	$ 16	$ 16
Stock options exercised and stock awards	16	12	9	—	—	—
End of year	1,640	1,624	1,612	$ 16	$ 16	$ 16
Treasury stock:						
Beginning of year	(259)	(219)	(165)	$ (9,030)	$ (7,610)	$ (5,812)
Purchase of treasury shares	(84)	(42)	(73)	(3,001)	(1,500)	(2,477)
Conversion of preference stock	—	—	17	—	—	583
Employee stock purchase plan issuances	3	2	2	78	80	96
End of year	(340)	(259)	(219)	$(11,953)	$ (9,030)	$ (7,610)
Shares held in trust:						
Beginning of year	(2)	(2)	(2)	$ (56)	$ (56)	$ (56)
End of year	(2)	(2)	(2)	$ (56)	$ (56)	$ (56)
Capital surplus:						
Beginning of year				$ 27,610	$ 27,198	$27,280
Stock option activity and stock awards				495	384	291
Tax benefit on stock options and stock awards				21	28	19
Conversion of preference stock				—	—	(392)
End of year				$ 28,126	$ 27,610	$ 27,198
Retained earnings:						
Beginning of year				$ 19,303	$ 16,355	$ 13,098
Net income attributable to CVS Caremark ← Net income is from the income statement.				3,461	3,427	3,696
Common stock dividends				(674)	(479)	(439)
End of year				$ 22,090	$ 19,303	$ 16,355
Accumulated other comprehensive loss:						
Beginning of year				$ (143)	$ (135)	$ (143)
Net cash flow hedges, net of income tax				(9)	(1)	1
Pension liability adjustment, net of income tax				(20)	(7)	7
End of year				$ (172)	$ (143)	$ (135)
Total shareholders' equity				$ 38,051	$ 37,700	$ 35,768
Comprehensive income:						
Net income				$ 3,457	$ 3,424	$ 3,696
Other comprehensive income:						
Net cash flow hedges, net of income tax				(9)	(1)	1
Pension liability adjustment, net of income tax				(20)	(7)	7
Comprehensive income				3,428	3,416	3,704
Comprehensive loss attributable to noncontrolling interest				4	3	—
Comprehensive income attributable to CVS Caremark				$ 3,432	$ 3,419	$ 3,704

See accompanying notes to consolidated financial statements.

Supplementary Information Notes In recent years, the FASB and the SEC have ruled that certain supplemental information must be presented with financial statements. Examples are the quarterly reports that most companies present to their stockholders and to the SEC. These quarterly reports, called *interim financial statements*, are in most cases reviewed but not audited by a company's independent CPA firm. In its annual report, **CVS** presents unaudited quarterly financial data from its 2011 quarterly statements. The quarterly data also include the high and low price for the company's common stock during each quarter.

Statements of Management's Responsibilities

Separate statements of management's responsibility for the financial statements and for internal control structure accompany the financial statements as required by the Sarbanes-Oxley Act of 2002. In its reports, **CVS**'s management acknowledges its responsibility for the consistency, integrity, and presentation of the financial information and for the system of internal controls.

Auditors' Reports

The *registered independent auditors' report* deals with the credibility of the financial statements. This report, prepared by independent certified public accountants, gives the accountants' opinion about how fairly the statements have been presented. Because management is responsible for preparing the financial statements, issuing statements that have not been independently audited would be like having a judge hear a case in which he or she was personally involved. The certified public accountants add the necessary credibility to management's figures for interested third parties. They report to the board of directors and the stockholders rather than to the company's management.

In form and language, most auditors' reports are like the one shown in Exhibit 5. Usually, such a report is short, but its language is very important. It normally has four parts, but it can have a fifth part if an explanation is needed.

1. The first paragraph identifies the financial statements that have been audited. It also identifies responsibilities. The company's management is responsible for the financial statements, and the auditor is responsible for expressing an opinion on the financial statements based on the audit.
2. The second paragraph, or *scope section*, states that the examination was made in accordance with standards of the Public Company Accounting Oversight Board (PCAOB). This paragraph also contains a brief description of the objectives and nature of the audit.
3. The third paragraph, or *opinion section*, states the results of the auditors' examination. The use of the word *opinion* is very important because the auditor does not certify or guarantee that the statements are absolutely correct. To do so would go beyond the truth, because many items, such as depreciation, are based on estimates. Instead, the auditors simply give an opinion about whether, overall, the financial statements "present fairly," in all material respects, the company's financial position, results of operations, and cash flows. This means that the statements are prepared in accordance with generally accepted accounting principles. If, in the auditors' opinion, the statements do not meet accepted standards, the auditors must explain why and to what extent.
4. The fourth paragraph states whether in the auditor's opinion, the company's internal controls are effective in accordance with the standards set by the Committee of Sponsoring Organizations (COSO).

Exhibit 5
Auditors' Report for CVS

Report of Independent Registered Public Accounting Firm
The Board of Directors and Shareholders
CVS Caremark Corporation

① We have audited the accompanying consolidated balance sheets of CVS Caremark Corporation as of December 31, 2011 and 2010, and the related consolidated statements of income, shareholders' equity, and cash flows for each of the three years in the period ended December 31, 2011. These financial statements are the responsibility of the Company's management. Our responsibility is to express an opinion on these financial statements based on our audits.

② We conducted our audits in accordance with the standards of the Public Company Accounting Oversight Board (United States). Those standards require that we plan and perform the audit to obtain reasonable assurance about whether the financial statements are free of material misstatement. An audit includes examining, on a test basis, evidence supporting the amounts and disclosures in the financial statements. An audit also includes assessing the accounting principles used and significant estimates made by management, as well as evaluating the overall financial statement presentation. We believe that our audits provide a reasonable basis for our opinion.

③ In our opinion, the financial statements referred to above present fairly, in all material respects, the consolidated financial position of CVS Caremark Corporation at December 31, 2011 and 2010, and the consolidated results of its operations and its cash flows for each of the three years in the period ended December 31, 2011, in conformity with U.S. generally accepted accounting principles.

④ We also have audited, in accordance with the standards of the Public Company Accounting Oversight Board (United States), CVS Caremark Corporation's internal control over financial reporting as of December 31, 2011, based on criteria established in *Internal Control – Integrated Framework* issued by the Committee of Sponsoring Organizations of the Treadway Commission and our report dated February 17, 2012 expressed an unqualified opinion thereon.

Ernst & Young LLP

Boston, Massachusetts
February 17, 2012

Excerpts from CVS Caremark Corporation's 2011 Annual Report

CVS Caremark is the largest pharmacy health care provider in the United States with integrated offerings across the entire spectrum of pharmacy care. Through our unique suite of assets, we are reinventing pharmacy to offer innovative solutions that help people on their path to better health. At the same time, we are highly focused on lowering overall health care costs for plan members and payors. CVS Caremark operates more than 7,300 CVS/pharmacy® stores; serves in excess of 60 million plan members as a leading pharmacy benefit manager (PBM); and cares for patients through the nation's largest retail health clinic system at our approximately 600 MinuteClinic® locations.

Financial Highlights

(in millions, except per share figures)	fiscal year 2011	fiscal year 2010	% change
Net revenues	**$ 107,100**	$ 95,778	11.8%
Operating profit	**$ 6,330**	$ 6,137	3.1%
Net income attributable to CVS Caremark	**$ 3,461**	$ 3,427	1.0%
Diluted EPS from continuing operations	**$ 2.59**	$ 2.49	4.0%
Stock price at year-end	**$ 40.78**	$ 34.77	17.3%
Market capitalization at year-end	**$ 52,937**	$ 47,426	11.6%

NET REVENUE
(in billions of dollars)

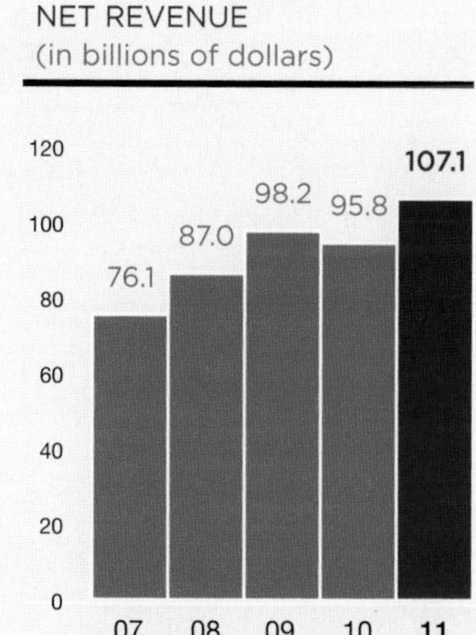

DILUTED EPS FROM CONTINUING OPERATIONS
(in dollars)

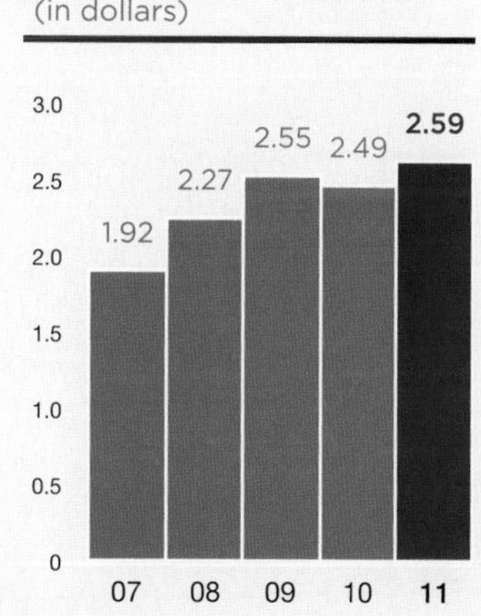

CASH DIVIDENDS
(in cents per common share)

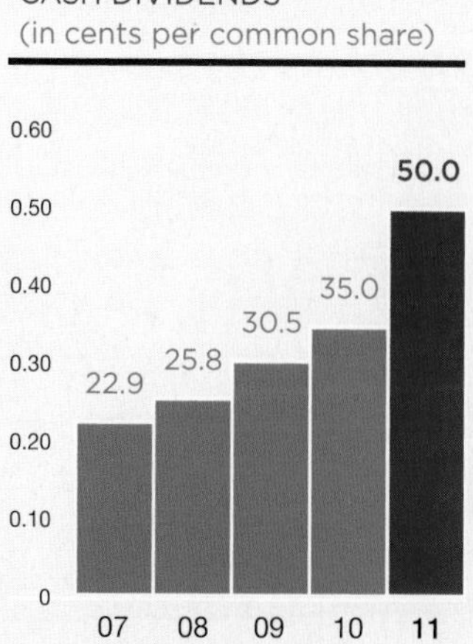

Consolidated Statements of Income

in millions, except per share amounts	Year Ended December 31, 2011	2010	2009
Net revenues	**$ 107,100**	$ 95,778	$ 98,215
Cost of revenues	**86,539**	75,559	77,857
Gross profit	**20,561**	20,219	20,358
Operating expenses	**14,231**	14,082	13,933
Operating profit	**6,330**	6,137	6,425
Interest expense, net	**584**	536	525
Income before income tax provision	**5,746**	5,601	5,900
Income tax provision	**2,258**	2,179	2,200
Income from continuing operations	**3,488**	3,422	3,700
Income (loss) from discontinued operations, net of tax	**(31)**	2	(4)
Net income	**3,457**	3,424	3,696
Net loss attributable to noncontrolling interest	**4**	3	—
Net income attributable to CVS Caremark	**$ 3,461**	$ 3,427	$ 3,696
Basic earnings per common share:			
Income from continuing operations attributable to CVS Caremark	**$ 2.61**	$ 2.51	$ 2.58
Loss from discontinued operations attributable to CVS Caremark	**(0.02)**	—	—
Net income attributable to CVS Caremark	**$ 2.59**	$ 2.51	$ 2.58
Weighted average common shares outstanding	**1,338**	1,367	1,434
Diluted earnings per common share:			
Income from continuing operations attributable to CVS Caremark	**$ 2.59**	$ 2.49	$ 2.55
Loss from discontinued operations attributable to CVS Caremark	**(0.02)**	—	—
Net income attributable to CVS Caremark	**$ 2.57**	$ 2.49	$ 2.55
Weighted average common shares outstanding	**1,347**	1,377	1,450
Dividends declared per common share	**$ 0.500**	$ 0.350	$ 0.305

See accompanying notes to consolidated financial statements.

Consolidated Balance Sheets

	December 31,	
in millions, except per share amounts	**2011**	2010
Assets:		
Cash and cash equivalents	**$ 1,413**	$ 1,427
Short-term investments	**5**	4
Accounts receivable, net	**6,047**	4,925
Inventories	**10,046**	10,695
Deferred income taxes	**503**	511
Other current assets	**580**	144
Total current assets	**18,594**	17,706
Property and equipment, net	**8,467**	8,322
Goodwill	**26,458**	25,669
Intangible assets, net	**9,869**	9,784
Other assets	**1,155**	688
Total assets	**$ 64,543**	$ 62,169
Liabilities:		
Accounts payable	**$ 4,370**	$ 4,026
Claims and discounts payable	**3,487**	2,569
Accrued expenses	**3,293**	3,070
Short-term debt	**750**	300
Current portion of long-term debt	**56**	1,105
Total current liabilities	**11,956**	11,070
Long-term debt	**9,208**	8,652
Deferred income taxes	**3,853**	3,655
Other long-term liabilities	**1,445**	1,058
Commitments and Contingencies (Note 13)		
Redeemable noncontrolling interest	**30**	34
Shareholders' equity:		
Preferred stock, par value $0.01: 0.1 shares authorized; none issued or outstanding	**—**	—
Common stock, par value $0.01: 3,200 shares authorized; 1,640 shares issued and 1,298 shares outstanding at December 31, 2011 and 1,624 shares issued and 1,363 shares outstanding at December 31, 2010	**16**	16
Treasury stock, at cost: 340 shares at December 31, 2011 and 259 shares at December 31, 2010	**(11,953)**	(9,030)
Shares held in trust: 2 shares at December 31, 2011 and 2010	**(56)**	(56)
Capital surplus	**28,126**	27,610
Retained earnings	**22,090**	19,303
Accumulated other comprehensive loss	**(172)**	(143)
Total shareholders' equity	**38,051**	37,700
Total liabilities and shareholders' equity	**$ 64,543**	$ 62,169

See accompanying notes to consolidated financial statements.

Consolidated Statements of Cash Flows

	Year Ended December 31,		
in millions	**2011**	2010	2009
Cash flows from operating activities:			
Cash receipts from customers	**$ 97,688**	$ 94,503	$ 93,568
Cash paid for inventory and prescriptions dispensed by retail network pharmacies	**(75,148)**	(73,143)	(73,536)
Cash paid to other suppliers and employees	**(13,635)**	(13,778)	(13,121)
Interest received	**4**	4	5
Interest paid	**(647)**	(583)	(542)
Income taxes paid	**(2,406)**	(2,224)	(2,339)
Net cash provided by operating activities	**5,856**	4,779	4,035
Cash flows from investing activities:			
Purchases of property and equipment	**(1,872)**	(2,005)	(2,548)
Proceeds from sale-leaseback transactions	**592**	507	1,562
Proceeds from sale of property and equipment	**4**	34	23
Acquisitions (net of cash acquired) and other investments	**(1,441)**	(177)	(101)
Purchase of available-for-sale investments	**(3)**	—	(5)
Sale or maturity of available-for-sale investments	**60**	1	—
Proceeds from sale of subsidiary	**250**	—	—
Net cash used in investing activities	**(2,410)**	(1,640)	(1,069)
Cash flows from financing activities:			
Increase (decrease) in short-term debt	**450**	(15)	(2,729)
Proceeds from issuance of long-term debt	**1,463**	991	2,800
Repayments of long-term debt	**(2,122)**	(2,103)	(653)
Dividends paid	**(674)**	(479)	(439)
Derivative settlements	**(19)**	(5)	(3)
Proceeds from exercise of stock options	**431**	285	250
Excess tax benefits from stock-based compensation	**21**	28	19
Repurchase of common stock	**(3,001)**	(1,500)	(2,477)
Other	**(9)**	—	—
Net cash used in financing activities	**(3,460)**	(2,798)	(3,232)
Net increase (decrease) in cash and cash equivalents	**(14)**	341	(266)
Cash and cash equivalents at the beginning of the year	**1,427**	1,086	1,352
Cash and cash equivalents at the end of the year	**$ 1,413**	$ 1,427	$ 1,086
Reconciliation of net income to net cash provided by operating activities:			
Net income	**$ 3,457**	$ 3,424	$ 3,696
Adjustments required to reconcile net income to net cash provided by operating activities:			
Depreciation and amortization	**1,568**	1,469	1,389
Stock-based compensation	**135**	150	165
Gain on sale of subsidiary	**(53)**	—	—
Deferred income taxes and other noncash items	**144**	30	48
Change in operating assets and liabilities, net of effects from acquisitions:			
Accounts receivable, net	**(748)**	532	(86)
Inventories	**607**	(352)	(1,199)
Other current assets	**(420)**	(4)	48
Other assets	**(49)**	(210)	(2)
Accounts payable	**1,128**	(40)	4
Accrued expenses	**85**	(176)	(66)
Other long-term liabilities	**2**	(44)	38
Net cash provided by operating activities	**$ 5,856**	$ 4,779	$ 4,035

See accompanying notes to consolidated financial statements.

Consolidated Statements of Shareholders' Equity

	Shares			Dollars		
	Year Ended December 31,			Year Ended December 31,		
in millions	**2011**	2010	2009	**2011**	2010	2009
Preference stock:						
Beginning of year	**–**	–	4	**$ –**	$ –	$ 191
Conversion to common stock	**–**	–	(4)	**–**	–	(191)
End of year	**–**	–	–	**$ –**	$ –	$ –
Common stock:						
Beginning of year	**1,624**	1,612	1,603	**$ 16**	$ 16	$ 16
Stock options exercised and stock awards	**16**	12	9	**–**	–	–
End of year	**1,640**	1,624	1,612	**$ 16**	$ 16	$ 16
Treasury stock:						
Beginning of year	**(259)**	(219)	(165)	**$ (9,030)**	$ (7,610)	$ (5,812)
Purchase of treasury shares	**(84)**	(42)	(73)	**(3,001)**	(1,500)	(2,477)
Conversion of preference stock	**–**	–	17	**–**	–	583
Employee stock purchase plan issuances	**3**	2	2	**78**	80	96
End of year	**(340)**	(259)	(219)	**$ (11,953)**	$ (9,030)	$ (7,610)
Shares held in trust:						
Beginning of year	**(2)**	(2)	(2)	**$ (56)**	$ (56)	$ (56)
End of year	**(2)**	(2)	(2)	**$ (56)**	$ (56)	$ (56)
Capital surplus:						
Beginning of year				**$ 27,610**	$ 27,198	$ 27,280
Stock option activity and stock awards				**495**	384	291
Tax benefit on stock options and stock awards				**21**	28	19
Conversion of preference stock				**–**	–	(392)
End of year				**$ 28,126**	$ 27,610	$ 27,198

See accompanying notes to consolidated financial statements.

Consolidated Statements of Shareholders' Equity

	Dollars		
	Year Ended December 31,		
in millions	**2011**	2010	2009
Retained earnings:			
Beginning of year	**$ 19,303**	$ 16,355	$ 13,098
Net income attributable to CVS Caremark	**3,461**	3,427	3,696
Common stock dividends	**(674)**	(479)	(439)
End of year	**$ 22,090**	$ 19,303	$ 16,355
Accumulated other comprehensive loss:			
Beginning of year	**$ (143)**	$ (135)	$ (143)
Net cash flow hedges, net of income tax	**(9)**	(1)	1
Pension liability adjustment, net of income tax	**(20)**	(7)	7
End of year	**$ (172)**	$ (143)	$ (135)
Total shareholders' equity	**$ 38,051**	$ 37,700	$ 35,768
Comprehensive income:			
Net income	**$ 3,457**	$ 3,424	$ 3,696
Other comprehensive income:			
Net cash flow hedges, net of income tax	**(9)**	(1)	1
Pension liability adjustment, net of income tax	**(20)**	(7)	7
Comprehensive income	**3,428**	3,416	3,704
Comprehensive loss attributable to noncontrolling interest	**4**	3	—
Comprehensive income attributable to CVS Caremark	**$ 3,432**	$ 3,419	$ 3,704

See accompanying notes to consolidated financial statements.

Notes to Consolidated Financial Statements

1 SIGNIFICANT ACCOUNTING POLICIES

Description of business – CVS Caremark Corporation and its subsidiaries (the "Company") is the largest pharmacy health care provider in the United States based upon revenues and prescriptions filled. The Company currently has three reportable business segments, Pharmacy Services, Retail Pharmacy and Corporate, which are described below.

Pharmacy Services Segment (the "PSS") – The PSS provides a full range of pharmacy benefit management services including mail order pharmacy services, specialty pharmacy services, plan design and administration, formulary management and claims processing. The Company's clients are primarily employers, insurance companies, unions, government employee groups, managed care organizations and other sponsors of health benefit plans and individuals throughout the United States.

As a pharmacy benefits manager, the PSS manages the dispensing of pharmaceuticals through the Company's mail order pharmacies and national network of approximately 65,000 retail pharmacies to eligible members in the benefits plans maintained by the Company's clients and utilizes its information systems to perform, among other things, safety checks, drug interaction screenings and brand to generic substitutions.

The PSS' specialty pharmacies support individuals that require complex and expensive drug therapies. The specialty pharmacy business includes mail order and retail specialty pharmacies that operate under the CVS Caremark® and CarePlus CVS/pharmacy® names.

The PSS also provides health management programs, which include integrated disease management for 28 conditions, through our strategic alliance with Alere, L.L.C. and the Company's Accordant® health management offering.

In addition, through the Company's SilverScript Insurance Company ("SilverScript"), Accendo Insurance Company ("Accendo") and Pennsylvania Life Insurance Company ("Pennsylvania Life") subsidiaries, the PSS is a national provider of drug benefits to eligible beneficiaries under the Federal Government's Medicare Part D program.

The PSS generates net revenues primarily by contracting with clients to provide prescription drugs to plan members. Prescription drugs are dispensed by the mail order pharmacies, specialty pharmacies and national network of retail pharmacies. Net revenues are also generated by providing additional services to clients, including administrative services such as claims processing and formulary management, as well as health care related services such as disease management.

The pharmacy services business operates under the CVS Caremark® Pharmacy Services, Caremark®, CVS Caremark®, CarePlus CVS/pharmacy®, CarePlus™, RxAmerica® and Accordant® names. As of December 31, 2011, the PSS operated 31 retail specialty pharmacy stores, 12 specialty mail order pharmacies and 4 mail service pharmacies located in 22 states, Puerto Rico and the District of Columbia.

Retail Pharmacy Segment (the "RPS") – The RPS sells prescription drugs and a wide assortment of general merchandise, including over-the-counter drugs, beauty products and cosmetics, photo finishing, seasonal merchandise, greeting cards and convenience foods, through the Company's CVS/pharmacy® and Longs Drugs® retail stores and online through CVS.com®.

The RPS also provides health care services through its MinuteClinic® health care clinics. MinuteClinics are staffed by nurse practitioners and physician assistants who utilize nationally recognized protocols to diagnose and treat minor health conditions, perform health screenings, monitor chronic conditions and deliver vaccinations.

As of December 31, 2011, the retail pharmacy business included 7,327 retail drugstores (of which 7,271 operated a pharmacy) located in 41 states the District of Columbia and Puerto Rico operating primarily under the CVS/pharmacy® name, the online retail website, CVS.com and 657 retail health care clinics operating under the MinuteClinic® name (of which 648 were located in CVS/pharmacy stores).

Corporate Segment – The Corporate segment provides management and administrative services to support the Company. The Corporate segment consists of certain aspects of the Company's executive management, corporate relations, legal, compliance, human resources, corporate information technology and finance departments.

Principles of Consolidation – The consolidated financial statements include the accounts of the Company and its majority owned subsidiaries. All intercompany balances and transactions have been eliminated.

Use of estimates – The preparation of financial statements in conformity with accounting principles generally accepted in the United States of America requires management to make estimates and assumptions that affect the reported amounts in the consolidated financial statements and accompanying notes. Actual results could differ from those estimates.

Fair Value Hierarchy – The Company utilizes the three-level valuation hierarchy for the recognition and disclosure of fair value measurements. The categorization of assets and liabilities within this hierarchy is based upon the lowest level of input that is significant to the measurement of fair value. The three levels of the hierarchy consist of the following:

- Level 1 – Inputs to the valuation methodology are unadjusted quoted prices in active markets for identical assets or liabilities that the Company has the ability to access at the measurement date.
- Level 2 – Inputs to the valuation methodology are quoted prices for similar assets and liabilities in active markets, quoted prices in markets that are not active or inputs that are observable for the asset or liability, either directly or indirectly, for substantially the full term of the instrument.
- Level 3 – Inputs to the valuation methodology are unobservable inputs based upon management's best estimate of inputs market participants could use in pricing the asset or liability at the measurement date, including assumptions about risk.

Cash and cash equivalents – Cash and cash equivalents consist of cash and temporary investments with maturities of three months or less when purchased. The Company invests in short-term money market funds, commercial paper, time deposits, as well as other debt securities that are classified as cash equivalents within the accompanying consolidated balance sheets, as these funds are highly liquid and readily convertible to known amounts of cash. These investments are classified within Level 1 of the fair value hierarchy because they are valued using quoted market prices.

Short-term investments – The Company's short-term investments consist of certificate of deposits with initial maturities of greater than three months when purchased. These investments, which were classified as available-for-sale within Level 1 of the fair value hierarchy, were carried at historical cost, which approximated fair value at December 31, 2011 and 2010.

Fair value of financial instruments – As of December 31, 2011, the Company's financial instruments include cash and cash equivalents, accounts receivable, accounts payable and short-term debt. Due to the short-term nature of these instruments, the Company's carrying value approximates fair value. The carrying amount and estimated fair value of total long-term debt was $9.3 billion and $10.8 billion, respectively, as of December 31, 2011. The fair value of long-term debt was estimated based on rates currently offered to the Company for debt with similar terms and maturities. The Company had outstanding letters of credit, which guaranteed foreign trade purchases, with a fair value of $6 million as of December 31, 2011 and 2010. There were no outstanding derivative financial instruments as of December 31, 2011 and 2010.

Accounts receivable – Accounts receivable are stated net of an allowance for doubtful accounts. The accounts receivable balance primarily includes trade amounts due from third party providers (e.g., pharmacy benefit managers, insurance companies and governmental agencies), clients and members, as well as vendors and manufacturers.

The activity in the allowance for doubtful trade accounts receivable is as follows:

	Year Ended December 31,		
in millions	**2011**	2010	2009
Beginning balance	**$ 182**	$ 224	$ 189
Additions charged to bad debt expense	**129**	73	135
Write-offs charged to allowance	**(122)**	(115)	(100)
Ending balance	**$ 189**	$ 182	$ 224

Notes to Consolidated Financial Statements

Inventories – Inventories are stated at the lower of cost or market on a first-in, first-out basis using the retail inventory method in the retail pharmacy stores, the weighted average cost method in the mail service and specialty pharmacies, and the cost method on a first-in, first-out basis in the distribution centers. Physical inventory counts are taken on a regular basis in each store and a continuous cycle count process is the primary procedure used to validate the inventory balances on hand in each distribution center and mail facility to ensure that the amounts reflected in the accompanying consolidated financial statements are properly stated. During the interim period between physical inventory counts, the Company accrues for anticipated physical inventory losses on a location-by-location basis based on historical results and current trends.

Property and equipment – Property, equipment and improvements to leased premises are depreciated using the straight-line method over the estimated useful lives of the assets, or when applicable, the term of the lease, whichever is shorter. Estimated useful lives generally range from 10 to 40 years for buildings, building improvements and leasehold improvements and 3 to 10 years for fixtures, equipment and internally developed software. Repair and maintenance costs are charged directly to expense as incurred. Major renewals or replacements that substantially extend the useful life of an asset are capitalized and depreciated. Application development stage costs for significant internally developed software projects are capitalized and depreciated.

The following are the components of property and equipment at December 31:

in millions	2011	2010
Land	$ 1,295	$ 1,247
Building and improvements	2,404	2,265
Fixtures and equipment	7,582	7,148
Leasehold improvements	3,021	2,866
Software	1,098	757
	15,400	14,283
Accumulated depreciation and amortization	(6,933)	(5,961)
	$ 8,467	$ 8,322

The gross amount of property and equipment under capital leases was $211 million and $191 million as of December 31, 2011 and 2010, respectively.

Goodwill – Goodwill and other indefinite-lived assets are not amortized, but are subject to impairment reviews annually, or more frequently if necessary. See Note 4 for additional information on goodwill.

Intangible assets – Purchased customer contracts and relationships are amortized on a straight-line basis over their estimated useful lives between 10 and 20 years. Purchased customer lists are amortized on a straight-line basis over their estimated useful lives of up to 10 years. Purchased leases are amortized on a straight-line basis over the remaining life of the lease. See Note 4 for additional information about intangible assets.

Impairment of long-lived assets – The Company groups and evaluates fixed and finite-lived intangible assets, excluding goodwill, for impairment at the lowest level at which individual cash flows can be identified. When evaluating assets for potential impairment, the Company first compares the carrying amount of the asset group to the estimated future cash flows associated with the asset group (undiscounted and without interest charges). If the estimated future cash flows used in this analysis are less than the carrying amount of the asset group, an impairment loss calculation is prepared. The impairment loss calculation compares the carrying amount of the asset group to the asset group's estimated future cash flows (discounted and with interest charges). If required, an impairment loss is recorded for the portion of the asset group's carrying value that exceeds the asset group's estimated future cash flows (discounted and with interest charges).

Redeemable noncontrolling interest – The Company has an approximately 60% ownership interest in Generation Health, Inc. ("Generation Health"), and consolidates Generation Health in its consolidated financial statements. The noncontrolling shareholders of Generation Health hold put rights for the remaining interest in Generation Health that if exercised would require the Company to purchase the remaining interest in Generation Health in 2015 for a minimum of $27 million and a maximum of $159 million, depending on certain financial metrics of Generation Health in 2014. Since the noncontrolling shareholders of Generation Health have a redemption feature as a result of the put rights, the Company has classified the redeemable noncontrolling interest in Generation Health in the mezzanine section of the consolidated balance sheet outside of shareholders' equity. The Company initially recorded the redeemable noncontrolling interest at a fair value of $37 million on the date of acquisition which was determined using inputs classified as Level 3 in the fair value hierarchy. At the end of each reporting period, if the estimated accreted redemption value exceeds the carrying value of the noncontrolling interest, the difference is recorded as a reduction of retained earnings. Any such reductions in retained earnings would also reduce income attributable to CVS Caremark in the Company's earnings per share calculations.

The following is a reconciliation of the changes in the redeemable noncontrolling interest:

in millions	2011	2010	2009
Beginning balance	$ 34	$ 37	$ —
Acquisition of Generation Health	—	—	37
Net loss attributable to noncontrolling interest	(4)	(3)	—
Ending balance	$ 30	$ 34	$ 37

Revenue Recognition

Pharmacy Services Segment – The PSS sells prescription drugs directly through its mail service pharmacies and indirectly through its retail pharmacy network. The PSS recognizes revenues from prescription drugs sold by its mail service pharmacies and under retail pharmacy network contracts where the PSS is the principal using the gross method at the contract prices negotiated with its clients. Net revenue from the PSS includes: (i) the portion of the price the client pays directly to the PSS, net of any volume-related or other discounts paid back to the client (see "Drug Discounts" later in this document), (ii) the price paid to the PSS ("Mail Co-Payments") or a third party pharmacy in the PSS' retail pharmacy network ("Retail Co-Payments") by individuals included in its clients' benefit plans, and (iii) administrative fees for retail pharmacy network contracts where the PSS is not the principal as discussed below.

The PSS recognizes revenue when: (i) persuasive evidence of an arrangement exists, (ii) delivery has occurred or services have been rendered, (iii) the seller's price to the buyer is fixed or determinable, and (iv) collectability is reasonably assured.

The Company has established the following revenue recognition policies for the PSS:

- Revenues generated from prescription drugs sold by mail service pharmacies are recognized when the prescription is shipped. At the time of shipment, the Company has performed substantially all of its obligations under its client contracts and does not experience a significant level of reshipments.
- Revenues generated from prescription drugs sold by third party pharmacies in the PSS' retail pharmacy network and associated administrative fees are recognized at the PSS' point-of-sale, which is when the claim is adjudicated by the PSS' online claims processing system.

The PSS determines whether it is the principal or agent for its retail pharmacy network transactions on a contract by contract basis. In the majority of its contracts, the PSS has determined it is the principal due to it: (i) being the primary obligor in the arrangement, (ii) having latitude in establishing the price, changing the product or performing part of the service, (iii) having discretion in supplier selection, (iv) having involvement in the determination of product or service specifications, and (v) having credit risk. The PSS' obligations under its client contracts for which revenues are reported using the gross method are separate and distinct from its obligations to the third party pharmacies included in its retail pharmacy

Notes to Consolidated Financial Statements

network contracts. Pursuant to these contracts, the PSS is contractually required to pay the third party pharmacies in its retail pharmacy network for products sold, regardless of whether the PSS is paid by its clients. The PSS' responsibilities under its client contracts typically include validating eligibility and coverage levels, communicating the prescription price and the co-payments due to the third party retail pharmacy, identifying possible adverse drug interactions for the pharmacist to address with the physician prior to dispensing, suggesting clinically appropriate generic alternatives where appropriate and approving the prescription for dispensing. Although the PSS does not have credit risk with respect to Retail Co-Payments, management believes that all of the other indicators of gross revenue reporting are present. For contracts under which the PSS acts as an agent, the PSS records revenues using the net method.

Drug Discounts – The PSS deducts from its revenues any rebates, inclusive of discounts and fees, earned by its clients. The PSS pays rebates to its clients in accordance with the terms of its client contracts, which are normally based on fixed rebates per prescription for specific products dispensed or a percentage of manufacturer discounts received for specific products dispensed. The liability for rebates due to the PSS' clients is included in "Claims and discounts payable" in the accompanying consolidated balance sheets.

Medicare Part D – The PSS participates in the Federal Government's Medicare Part D program as a Prescription Drug Plan ("PDP"). The PSS' net revenues include insurance premiums earned by the PDP, which are determined based on the PDP's annual bid and related contractual arrangements with the Centers for Medicare and Medicaid Services ("CMS"). The insurance premiums include a beneficiary premium, which is the responsibility of the PDP member, but is subsidized by CMS in the case of low-income members, and a direct premium paid by CMS. Premiums collected in advance are initially deferred in accrued expenses and are then recognized in net revenues over the period in which members are entitled to receive benefits.

In addition to these premiums, the PSS' net revenues include co-payments, coverage gap benefits, deductibles and co-insurance (collectively, the "Member Co-Payments") related to PDP members' actual prescription claims. In certain cases, CMS subsidizes a portion of these Member Co-Payments and pays the PSS an estimated prospective Member Co-Payment subsidy amount each month. The prospective Member Co-Payment subsidy amounts received from CMS are also included in the PSS' net revenues. The Company assumes no risk for these amounts, which represented 3.1%, 2.6% and 3.5% of consolidated net revenues in 2011, 2010 and 2009, respectively. If the prospective Member Co-Payment subsidies received differ from the amounts based on actual prescription claims, the difference is recorded in either accounts receivable or accrued expenses.

The PSS accounts for CMS obligations and Member Co-Payments (including the amounts subsidized by CMS) using the gross method consistent with its revenue recognition policies for Mail Co-Payments and Retail Co-Payments (discussed previously in this document). See Note 8 for additional information about Medicare Part D.

Retail Pharmacy Segment – The RPS recognizes revenue from the sale of merchandise (other than prescription drugs) at the time the merchandise is purchased by the retail customer. Revenue from the sale of prescription drugs is recognized at the time the prescription is filled, which is or approximates when the retail customer picks up the prescription. Customer returns are not material. Revenue generated from the performance of services in the RPS' health care clinics is recognized at the time the services are performed. See Note 14 for additional information about the revenues of the Company's business segments.

Cost of Revenues

Pharmacy Services Segment – The PSS' cost of revenues includes: (i) the cost of prescription drugs sold during the reporting period directly through its mail service pharmacies and indirectly through its retail pharmacy network, (ii) shipping and handling costs, and (iii) the operating costs of its mail service pharmacies and client service operations and related information technology support costs including depreciation and amortization. The cost of prescription drugs sold component of cost of revenues includes: (i) the cost of the prescription drugs purchased from manufacturers or distributors and shipped to members in clients' benefit plans from the PSS' mail service pharmacies, net of any volume-related or other discounts (see "Drug Discounts" previously in this document) and (ii) the cost of prescription drugs sold (including Retail Co-Payments) through the PSS' retail pharmacy network under contracts where it is the principal, net of any volume-related or other discounts.

Retail Pharmacy Segment – The RPS' cost of revenues includes: the cost of merchandise sold during the reporting period and the related purchasing costs, warehousing and delivery costs (including depreciation and amortization) and actual and estimated inventory losses. See Note 14 for additional information about the cost of revenues of the Company's business segments.

Vendor Allowances and Purchase Discounts

The Company accounts for vendor allowances and purchase discounts as follows:

Pharmacy Services Segment – The PSS receives purchase discounts on products purchased. The PSS' contractual arrangements with vendors, including manufacturers, wholesalers and retail pharmacies, normally provide for the PSS to receive purchase discounts from established list prices in one, or a combination of, the following forms: (i) a direct discount at the time of purchase, (ii) a discount for the prompt payment of invoices, or (iii) when products are purchased indirectly from a manufacturer (e.g., through a wholesaler or retail pharmacy), a discount (or rebate) paid subsequent to dispensing. These rebates are recognized when prescriptions are dispensed and are generally calculated and billed to manufacturers within 30 days of the end of each completed quarter. Historically, the effect of adjustments resulting from the reconciliation of rebates recognized to the amounts billed and collected has not been material to the PSS' results of operations. The PSS accounts for the effect of any such differences as a change in accounting estimate in the period the reconciliation is completed. The PSS also receives additional discounts under its wholesaler contract if it exceeds contractually defined annual purchase volumes. In addition, the PSS receives fees from pharmaceutical manufacturers for administrative services. Purchase discounts and administrative service fees are recorded as a reduction of "Cost of revenues".

Retail Pharmacy Segment – Vendor allowances received by the RPS reduce the carrying cost of inventory and are recognized in cost of revenues when the related inventory is sold, unless they are specifically identified as a reimbursement of incremental costs for promotional programs and/or other services provided. Amounts that are directly linked to advertising commitments are recognized as a reduction of advertising expense (included in operating expenses) when the related advertising commitment is satisfied. Any such allowances received in excess of the actual cost incurred also reduce the carrying cost of inventory. The total value of any upfront payments received from vendors that are linked to purchase commitments is initially deferred. The deferred amounts are then amortized to reduce cost of revenues over the life of the contract based upon purchase volume. The total value of any upfront payments received from vendors that are not linked to purchase commitments is also initially deferred. The deferred amounts are then amortized to reduce cost of revenues on a straight-line basis over the life of the related contract. The total amortization of these upfront payments was not material to the accompanying consolidated financial statements.

Insurance – The Company is self-insured for certain losses related to general liability, workers' compensation and auto liability. The Company obtains third party insurance coverage to limit exposure from these claims. The Company is also self-insured for certain losses related to health and medical liabilities. The Company's self-insurance accruals, which include reported claims and claims incurred but not reported, are calculated using standard insurance industry actuarial assumptions and the Company's historical claims experience.

Facility opening and closing costs – New facility opening costs, other than capital expenditures, are charged directly to expense when incurred. When the Company closes a facility, the present value of estimated unrecoverable costs, including the remaining lease obligation less estimated sublease income and the book value of abandoned property and equipment, are charged to expense. The long-term portion of the lease obligations associated with facility closings was $327 million and $368 million in 2011 and 2010, respectively.

Advertising costs – Advertising costs are expensed when the related advertising takes place. Advertising costs, net of vendor funding (included in operating expenses), were $211 million, $234 million and $317 million in 2011, 2010 and 2009, respectively.

Interest expense, net – Interest expense, net of capitalized interest, was $588 million, $539 million and $530 million, and interest income was $4 million, $3 million and $5 million in 2011, 2010 and 2009, respectively. Capitalized interest totaled $37 million, $47 million and $39 million in 2011, 2010 and 2009, respectively.

Shares held in trust – The Company maintains grantor trusts, which held approximately 2 million shares of its common stock at December 31, 2011 and 2010. These shares are designated for use under various employee compensation plans. Since the Company holds these shares, they are excluded from the computation of basic and diluted shares outstanding.

Notes to Consolidated Financial Statements

Accumulated other comprehensive loss – Accumulated other comprehensive loss consists of changes in the net actuarial gains and losses associated with pension and other postretirement benefit plans, and unrealized losses on derivatives. The amount included in accumulated other comprehensive loss related to the Company's pension and postretirement plans was $250 million pre-tax ($152 million after-tax) as of December 31, 2011 and $217 million pre-tax ($132 million after-tax) as of December 31, 2010. The net impact on cash flow hedges totaled $32 million pre-tax ($20 million after-tax) and $18 million pre-tax ($11 million after-tax) as of December 31, 2011 and 2010, respectively.

Stock-based compensation – Stock-based compensation expense is measured at the grant date based on the fair value of the award and is recognized as expense over the applicable requisite service period of the stock award (generally 3 to 5 years) using the straight-line method. Stock-based compensation costs are included in selling, general and administrative expenses.

Income taxes – The Company provides for federal and state income taxes currently payable, as well as for those deferred because of timing differences between reported income and expenses for financial statement purposes versus tax purposes. Federal and state tax credits are recorded as a reduction of income taxes. Deferred tax assets and liabilities are recognized for the future tax consequences attributable to differences between the carrying amount of assets and liabilities for financial reporting purposes and the amounts used for income tax purposes. Deferred tax assets and liabilities are measured using the enacted tax rates expected to apply to taxable income in the years in which those temporary differences are expected to be recoverable or settled. The effect of a change in tax rates is recognized as income or expense in the period of the change.

Earnings per common share – Basic earnings per common share is computed by dividing: (i) net earnings by (ii) the weighted average number of common shares outstanding during the year (the "Basic Shares").

Diluted earnings per common share is computed by dividing: (i) net earnings by (ii) Basic Shares plus the additional shares that would be issued assuming that all dilutive stock awards are exercised. Options to purchase 30.5 million, 34.3 million and 37.7 million shares of common stock were outstanding as of December 31, 2011, 2010 and 2009, respectively, but were not included in the calculation of diluted earnings per share because the options' exercise prices were greater than the average market price of the common shares and, therefore, the effect would be antidilutive.

16 QUARTERLY FINANCIAL INFORMATION (UNAUDITED)

in millions, except per share amounts	First Quarter[1]	Second Quarter[1]	Third Quarter	Fourth Quarter	Year
2011:					
Net revenues	$ 25,695	$ 26,414	$ 26,674	$ 28,317	$ 107,100
Gross profit	4,742	5,086	5,178	5,555	20,561
Operating profit	1,305	1,484	1,584	1,957	6,330
Income from continuing operations	709	813	867	1,099	3,488
Income (loss) from discontinued operations, net of tax	3	2	—	(36)	(31)
Net income	712	815	867	1,063	3,457
Net loss attributable to noncontrolling interest	1	1	1	1	4
Net income attributable to CVS Caremark	$ 713	$ 816	$ 868	$ 1,064	$ 3,461
Basic earnings per common share:					
Income from continuing operations attributable to CVS Caremark	$ 0.52	$ 0.60	$ 0.65	$ 0.84	$ 2.61
Loss from discontinued operations attributable to CVS Caremark	$ —	$ —	$ —	$ (0.03)	$ (0.02)
Net income attributable to CVS Caremark	$ 0.52	$ 0.60	$ 0.65	$ 0.82	$ 2.59
Diluted Earnings per common share:					
Income from continuing operations attributable to CVS Caremark	$ 0.52	$ 0.60	$ 0.65	$ 0.84	$ 2.59
Loss from discontinued operations attributable to CVS Caremark	$ —	$ —	$ —	$ (0.03)	$ (0.02)
Net income attributable to CVS Caremark	$ 0.52	$ 0.60	$ 0.65	$ 0.81	$ 2.57
Dividends per common share	$ 0.125	$ 0.125	$ 0.125	$ 0.125	$ 0.500
Stock price: (New York Stock Exchange)					
High	$ 35.95	$ 39.50	$ 38.82	$ 41.35	$ 41.35
Low	$ 32.08	$ 34.21	$ 31.30	$ 32.28	$ 31.30

(1) The results of operations previously filed have been revised to reflect the results of TheraCom as discontinued operations. See Note 3.

Notes to Consolidated Financial Statements

in millions, except per share amounts	First Quarter [(1)]	Second Quarter [(1)]	Third Quarter [(1)]	Fourth Quarter [(1)]	Year [(1)]
2010:					
Net revenues	$ 23,593	$ 23,885	$ 23,711	$ 24,589	$ 95,778
Gross profit	4,738	5,012	5,015	5,454	20,219
Operating profit	1,404	1,494	1,478	1,761	6,137
Income from continuing operations	768	819	815	1,020	3,422
Income (loss) from discontinued operations, net of tax	2	2	(7)	5	2
Net income	770	821	808	1,025	3,424
Net loss attributable to noncontrolling interest	1	—	1	1	3
Net income attributable to CVS Caremark	$ 771	$ 821	$ 809	$ 1,026	$ 3,427
Basic earnings per common share:					
Income from continuing operations attributable to CVS Caremark	$ 0.56	$ 0.60	$ 0.60	$ 0.75	$ 2.51
Income (loss) from discontinued operations attributable to CVS Caremark	$ —	$ —	$ (0.01)	$ —	$ —
Net income attributable to CVS Caremark	$ 0.56	$ 0.61	$ 0.59	$ 0.75	$ 2.51
Diluted Earnings per common share:					
Income from continuing operations attributable to CVS Caremark	$ 0.55	$ 0.60	$ 0.60	$ 0.74	$ 2.49
Income (loss) from discontinued operations attributable to CVS Caremark	$ —	$ —	$ (0.01)	$ —	$ —
Net income attributable to CVS Caremark	$ 0.55	$ 0.60	$ 0.59	$ 0.75	$ 2.49
Dividends per common share	$ 0.0875	$ 0.0875	$ 0.0875	$ 0.0875	$ 0.3500
Stock price: (New York Stock Exchange)					
High	$ 37.32	$ 37.82	$ 32.09	$ 35.46	$ 37.82
Low	$ 30.36	$ 29.22	$ 26.84	$ 29.45	$ 26.84

(1) The results of operations previously filed have been revised to reflect the results of TheraCom as discontinued operations. See Note 3.

Five-Year Financial Summary

in millions, except per share amounts	2011 [1]	2010 [1]	2009 [1]	2008 [1]	2007 [1][2]
Statement of operations data:					
Net revenues	$ 107,100	$ 95,778	$ 98,215	$ 87,005	$ 76,078
Gross profit	20,561	20,219	20,358	18,272	16,098
Operating expenses	14,231	14,082	13,933	12,237	11,309
Operating profit	6,330	6,137	6,425	6,035	4,789
Interest expense, net	584	536	525	509	435
Income tax provision[3]	2,258	2,179	2,200	2,189	1,720
Income from continuing operations	3,488	3,422	3,700	3,337	2,634
Income (loss) from discontinued operations, net of tax benefit[4]	(31)	2	(4)	(125)	3
Net income	3,457	3,424	3,696	3,212	2,637
Net loss attributable to noncontrolling interest[5]	4	3	—	—	—
Preference dividends, net of income tax benefit	—	—	—	(14)	(14)
Net income attributable to CVS Caremark	$ 3,461	$ 3,427	$ 3,696	$ 3,198	$ 2,623
Per common share data:					
Basic earnings per common share:					
Income from continuing operations attributable to CVS Caremark	$ 2.61	$ 2.51	$ 2.58	$ 2.32	$ 1.97
Loss from discontinued operations attributable to CVS Caremark	(0.02)	—	—	(0.09)	—
Net income attributable to CVS Caremark	$ 2.59	$ 2.51	$ 2.58	$ 2.23	$ 1.97
Diluted earnings per common share:					
Income from continuing operations attributable to CVS Caremark	$ 2.59	$ 2.49	$ 2.55	$ 2.27	$ 1.92
Loss from discontinued operations attributable to CVS Caremark	(0.02)	—	—	(0.09)	—
Net income attributable to CVS Caremark	$ 2.57	$ 2.49	$ 2.55	$ 2.18	$ 1.92
Cash dividends per common share	$ 0.50000	$ 0.35000	$ 0.30500	$ 0.25800	$ 0.22875
Balance sheet and other data:					
Total assets	$ 64,543	$ 62,169	$ 61,641	$ 60,960	$ 54,722
Long-term debt	$ 9,208	$ 8,652	$ 8,756	$ 8,057	$ 8,350
Total shareholders' equity	$ 38,051	$ 37,700	$ 35,768	$ 34,574	$ 31,322
Number of stores (at end of year)	7,388	7,248	7,095	6,997	6,301

(1) On December 23, 2008, our Board of Directors approved a change in our fiscal year-end from the Saturday nearest December 31 of each year to December 31 of each year to better reflect our position in the health care, rather than the retail, industry. The fiscal year change was effective beginning with the fourth quarter of fiscal 2008. As you review our operating performance, please consider that 2011, 2010 and 2009 include 365 days; fiscal 2008 includes 368 days, and fiscal 2007 includes 364 days.

(2) Effective March 22, 2007, Caremark Rx, Inc., was merged into a newly formed subsidiary of CVS Corporation, with Caremark Rx, L.L.C., continuing as the surviving entity (the "Caremark Merger"). Following the Caremark Merger, the name of the Company was changed to "CVS Caremark Corporation." By virtue of the Caremark Merger, each issued and outstanding share of Caremark common stock, par value $0.001 per share, was converted into the right to receive 1.67 shares of CVS Caremark's common stock, par value $0.01 per share. Cash was paid in lieu of fractional shares.

(3) Income tax provision includes the effect of the following: (i) in 2010, the recognition of $47 million of previously unrecognized tax benefits, including interest, relating to the expiration of various statutes of limitation and settlements with tax authorities and (ii) in 2009, the recognition of $167 million of previously unrecognized tax benefits, including interest, relating to the expiration of various statutes of limitation and settlements with tax authorities.

(4) As discussed in Note 3 to the consolidated financial statements, the results of the Theracom business are presented as discontinued operations and have been excluded from continuing operations for all periods presented.

In connection with certain business dispositions completed between 1991 and 1997, the Company retained guarantees on store lease obligations for a number of former subsidiaries, including Linens 'n Things which filed for bankruptcy in 2008. The Company's income (loss) from discontinued operations includes lease-related costs which the Company believes it will likely be required to satisfy pursuant to its Linens 'n Things lease guarantees.

Below is a summary of the results of discontinued operations:

			Fiscal Year		
in millions	2011	2010	2009	2008	2007
Income from operations of TheraCom	$ 18	$ 28	$ 13	$ 11	$ 5
Gain on disposal of TheraCom	53	—	—	—	—
Loss on disposal of Linens 'n Things	(7)	(24)	(19)	(214)	—
Income tax benefit (provision)	(95)	(2)	2	78	(2)
Income (loss) from discontinued operations, net of tax	$ (31)	$ 2	$ (4)	$ (125)	$ 3

(5) Represents the minority shareholders' portion of the net loss from our majority owned subsidiary, Generation Health, Inc., acquired in the fourth quarter of 2009.

Report of Independent Registered Public Accounting Firm

The Board of Directors and Shareholders
CVS Caremark Corporation

We have audited the accompanying consolidated balance sheets of CVS Caremark Corporation as of December 31, 2011 and 2010, and the related consolidated statements of income, shareholders' equity, and cash flows for each of the three years in the period ended December 31, 2011. These financial statements are the responsibility of the Company's management. Our responsibility is to express an opinion on these financial statements based on our audits.

We conducted our audits in accordance with the standards of the Public Company Accounting Oversight Board (United States). Those standards require that we plan and perform the audit to obtain reasonable assurance about whether the financial statements are free of material misstatement. An audit includes examining, on a test basis, evidence supporting the amounts and disclosures in the financial statements. An audit also includes assessing the accounting principles used and significant estimates made by management, as well as evaluating the overall financial statement presentation. We believe that our audits provide a reasonable basis for our opinion.

In our opinion, the financial statements referred to above present fairly, in all material respects, the consolidated financial position of CVS Caremark Corporation at December 31, 2011 and 2010, and the consolidated results of its operations and its cash flows for each of the three years in the period ended December 31, 2011, in conformity with U.S. generally accepted accounting principles.

We also have audited, in accordance with the standards of the Public Company Accounting Oversight Board (United States), CVS Caremark Corporation's internal control over financial reporting as of December 31, 2011, based on criteria established in *Internal Control – Integrated Framework* issued by the Committee of Sponsoring Organizations of the Treadway Commission and our report dated February 17, 2012 expressed an unqualified opinion thereon.

Ernst + Young LLP

Boston, Massachusetts
February 17, 2012

Excerpts from Southwest Airlines Co.'s 2011 Annual Report

Item 8. ***Financial Statements and Supplementary Data***

SOUTHWEST AIRLINES CO.

CONSOLIDATED BALANCE SHEET

(in millions, except share data)

	DECEMBER 31, 2011	DECEMBER 31, 2010
ASSETS		
Current assets:		
Cash and cash equivalents	$ 829	$ 1,261
Short-term investments	2,315	2,277
Accounts and other receivables	299	195
Inventories of parts and supplies, at cost	401	243
Deferred income taxes	263	214
Prepaid expenses and other current assets	238	89
Total current assets	4,345	4,279
Property and equipment, at cost:		
Flight equipment	15,542	13,991
Ground property and equipment	2,423	2,122
Deposits on flight equipment purchase contracts	456	230
	18,421	16,343
Less allowance for depreciation and amortization	6,294	5,765
	12,127	10,578
Goodwill	970	—
Other assets	626	606
	$18,068	$15,463
LIABILITIES AND STOCKHOLDERS' EQUITY		
Current liabilities:		
Accounts payable	$ 1,057	$ 739
Accrued liabilities	996	863
Air traffic liability	1,836	1,198
Current maturities of long-term debt	644	505
Total current liabilities	4,533	3,305
Long-term debt less current maturities	3,107	2,875
Deferred income taxes	2,566	2,493
Deferred gains from sale and leaseback of aircraft	75	88
Other noncurrent liabilities	910	465
Stockholders' equity:		
Common stock, $1.00 par value: 2,000,000,000 shares authorized; 807,611,634 shares issued in 2011 and 2010	808	808
Capital in excess of par value	1,222	1,183
Retained earnings	5,395	5,399
Accumulated other comprehensive loss	(224)	(262)
Treasury stock, at cost: 35,050,991 and 60,177,362 shares in 2011 and 2010 respectively	(324)	(891)
Total stockholders' equity	6,877	6,237
	$18,068	$15,463

See accompanying notes.

SOUTHWEST AIRLINES CO.

CONSOLIDATED STATEMENT OF INCOME

(in millions, except per share amounts)

	YEAR ENDED DECEMBER 31,		
	2011	2010	2009
OPERATING REVENUES:			
Passenger	$14,735	$11,489	$ 9,892
Freight	139	125	118
Other	784	490	340
Total operating revenues	15,658	12,104	10,350
OPERATING EXPENSES:			
Salaries, wages, and benefits	4,371	3,704	3,468
Fuel and oil	5,644	3,620	3,044
Maintenance materials and repairs	955	751	719
Aircraft rentals	308	180	186
Landing fees and other rentals	959	807	718
Depreciation and amortization	715	628	616
Acquisition and integration	134	8	—
Other operating expenses	1,879	1,418	1,337
Total operating expenses	14,965	11,116	10,088
OPERATING INCOME	693	988	262
OTHER EXPENSES (INCOME):			
Interest expense	194	167	186
Capitalized interest	(12)	(18)	(21)
Interest income	(10)	(12)	(13)
Other (gains) losses, net	198	106	(54)
Total other expenses	370	243	98
INCOME BEFORE INCOME TAXES	323	745	164
PROVISION FOR INCOME TAXES	145	286	65
NET INCOME	$ 178	$ 459	$ 99
NET INCOME PER SHARE, BASIC	$ .23	$ .62	$ .13
NET INCOME PER SHARE, DILUTED	$ .23	$ .61	$ .13
Cash dividends declared per common share	**$ .0180**	**$ .0180**	**$ .0180**

See accompanying notes.

SOUTHWEST AIRLINES CO.

CONSOLIDATED STATEMENT OF STOCKHOLDERS' EQUITY

(in millions, except per share amounts)	Common Stock	Capital in excess of par value	Retained earnings	Accumulated other comprehensive income (loss)	Treasury stock	Total
	YEAR ENDED DECEMBER 31, 2011, 2010, AND 2009					
Balance at December 31, 2008	$808	$1,215	$4,907	$(984)	$(1,005)	$4,941
Issuance of common and treasury stock pursuant to Employee stock plans	—	—	(22)	—	42	20
Net tax benefit (expense) of options exercised	—	(13)	—	—	—	(13)
Share-based compensation	—	14	—	—	—	14
Cash dividends, $.018 per share	—	—	(13)	—	—	(13)
Comprehensive income (loss):						
Net income	—	—	99	—	—	99
Unrealized gain on fuel derivative instruments	—	—	—	366	—	366
Other	—	—	—	40	—	40
Total comprehensive income						505
Balance at December 31, 2009	$808	$1,216	$4,971	$(578)	$ (963)	$5,454
Issuance of common and treasury stock pursuant to Employee stock plans	—	—	(18)	—	72	54
Net tax benefit (expense) of options exercised	—	(45)	—	—	—	(45)
Share-based compensation	—	12	—	—	—	12
Cash dividends, $.018 per share	—	—	(13)	—	—	(13)
Comprehensive income (loss):						
Net income	—	—	459	—	—	459
Unrealized gain on fuel derivative instruments	—	—	—	330	—	330
Other	—	—	—	(14)	—	(14)
Total comprehensive income						775
Balance at December 31, 2010	$808	$1,183	$5,399	$(262)	$ (891)	$6,237
Repurchase of common stock	—	—	—	—	(225)	(225)
Issuance of common and treasury stock pursuant to Employee stock plans	—	(3)	(14)	—	37	20
Issuance of stock to acquire AirTran	—	—	(127)	—	650	523
Issuance of stock for conversion of debt	—	34	(27)	—	105	112
Net tax benefit (expense) of options exercised	—	(5)	—	—	—	(5)
Share-based compensation	—	13	—	—	—	13
Cash dividends, $.018 per share	—	—	(14)	—	—	(14)
Comprehensive income (loss):						
Net income	—	—	178	—	—	178
Unrealized gain on fuel derivative instruments	—	—	—	67	—	67
Other	—	—	—	(29)	—	(29)
Total comprehensive income						216
Balance at December 31, 2011	$808	$1,222	$5,395	$(224)	$ (324)	$6,877

See accompanying notes.

SOUTHWEST AIRLINES CO.

CONSOLIDATED STATEMENT OF CASH FLOWS

(in millions)	YEAR ENDED DECEMBER 31, 2011	2010	2009
CASH FLOWS FROM OPERATING ACTIVITIES:			
Net income	$ 178	$ 459	$ 99
Adjustments to reconcile net income to cash provided by operating activities:			
Depreciation and amortization	715	628	616
Unrealized (gain) loss on fuel derivative instruments	90	139	14
Deferred income taxes	123	133	72
Amortization of deferred gains on sale and leaseback of aircraft	(13)	(14)	(12)
Changes in certain assets and liabilities (excluding the effects of acquired business):			
Accounts and other receivables	(26)	(26)	40
Other current assets	(196)	(8)	(27)
Accounts payable and accrued liabilities	253	193	59
Air traffic liability	262	153	81
Cash collateral received from (provided to) derivative counterparties	(195)	265	(90)
Other, net	194	(361)	133
Net cash provided by operating activities	1,385	1,561	985
CASH FLOWS FROM INVESTING ACTIVITIES:			
Payment to acquire AirTran, net of AirTran cash on hand	(35)	—	—
Payments for purchase of property and equipment, net	(968)	(493)	(585)
Purchases of short-term investments	(5,362)	(5,624)	(6,106)
Proceeds from sales of short-term investments	5,314	4,852	5,120
Other, net	—	—	2
Net cash used in investing activities	(1,051)	(1,265)	(1,569)
CASH FLOWS FROM FINANCING ACTIVITIES:			
Issuance of long-term debt	—	—	455
Proceeds from credit line borrowing	—	—	83
Proceeds from sale leaseback transactions	—	—	381
Proceeds from Employee stock plans	20	55	20
Proceeds from termination of interest rate derivative instrument	76	—	—
Payments of long-term debt and capital lease obligations	(540)	(155)	(86)
Payments of convertible debt obligations	(81)	—	—
Payment of revolving credit facility obligations	—	—	(400)
Payment of credit line borrowing obligations	—	(44)	(97)
Payments of cash dividends	(14)	(13)	(13)
Repurchase of common stock	(225)	—	—
Other, net	(2)	8	(13)
Net cash provided by (used in) financing activities	(766)	(149)	330
NET CHANGE IN CASH AND CASH EQUIVALENTS	(432)	147	(254)
CASH AND CASH EQUIVALENTS AT BEGINNING OF PERIOD	1,261	1,114	1,368
CASH AND CASH EQUIVALENTS AT END OF PERIOD	$ 829	$ 1,261	$ 1,114
CASH PAYMENTS FOR:			
Interest, net of amount capitalized	$ 185	$ 135	$ 152
Income taxes	$ 13	$ 274	$ 5
SUPPLEMENTAL DISCLOSURE OF NONCASH TRANSACTIONS:			
Fair value of equity consideration given to acquire AirTran	$ 523	$ —	$ —
Fair value of common stock issued for conversion of debt	$ 78	$ —	$ —

See accompanying notes.

NOTES TO CONSOLIDATED FINANCIAL STATEMENTS
DECEMBER 31, 2011

1. Summary of Significant Accounting Policies

Basis of Presentation

Southwest Airlines Co. (the "Company") operates Southwest Airlines, a major domestic airline that provides point-to-point, low-fare service. The Consolidated Financial Statements include the accounts of the Company and its wholly owned subsidiaries, which include AirTran Holdings, LLC. On May 2, 2011 (the "acquisition date"), the Company acquired all of the outstanding equity of AirTran Holdings, Inc. ("AirTran Holdings"), the former parent company of AirTran Airways, Inc. ("AirTran Airways"), in exchange for common stock of the Company and cash. Throughout these Notes, the Company makes reference to AirTran, which is meant to be inclusive of the following: (i) for periods prior to the acquisition date, AirTran Holdings and its subsidiaries, including, among others, AirTran Airways; and (ii) for periods on and after the acquisition date, AirTran Holdings, LLC, the successor to AirTran Holdings, and its subsidiaries, including among others, AirTran Airways. The accompanying Consolidated Financial Statements include the results of operations and cash flows for AirTran from May 2, 2011 through December 31, 2011. See Note 2. All significant inter-entity balances and transactions have been eliminated. The preparation of financial statements in conformity with generally accepted accounting principles in the United States (GAAP) requires management to make estimates and assumptions that affect the amounts reported in the financial statements and accompanying notes. Actual results could differ from these estimates.

Cash and cash equivalents

Cash in excess of that necessary for operating requirements is invested in short-term, highly liquid, income-producing investments. Investments with original maturities of three months or less when purchased are classified as cash and cash equivalents, which primarily consist of certificates of deposit, money market funds, and investment grade commercial paper issued by major corporations and financial institutions. Cash and cash equivalents are stated at cost, which approximates fair value.

As of December 31, 2011 and 2010, the Company had provided cash collateral deposits to its fuel hedge counterparties totaling $226 million and $125 million, respectively. As of December 31, 2010, the Company also held cash collateral deposits of $60 million from a counterparty. Cash collateral amounts provided or held associated with fuel derivative instruments are not restricted in any way and earn interest income at an agreed upon rate that approximates the rates earned on short-term securities issued by the U.S. Government. Depending on the fair value of the Company's fuel derivative instruments, the amounts of collateral deposits held or provided at any point in time can fluctuate significantly. See Note 10 for further information on these collateral deposits and fuel derivative instruments.

Short-term and noncurrent investments

Short-term investments consist of investments with original maturities of greater than three months but less than twelve months when purchased. These are primarily short-term securities issued by the U.S. Government and certificates of deposit issued by domestic banks. All of these investments are classified as available-for-sale securities and are stated at fair value, which approximates cost. For all short-term investments, at each reset period or upon reinvestment, the Company accounts for the transaction as Proceeds from sales of short-term investments for the security relinquished, and Purchases of short-investments for the security purchased, in the accompanying Consolidated Statement of Cash Flows. Unrealized gains and losses, net of tax, if any, are recognized in Accumulated other comprehensive income (loss) ("AOCI") in the accompanying Consolidated Balance Sheet. Realized net gains and losses on specific investments, if any, are reflected in Interest income in the accompanying Consolidated Statement of Income. Both unrealized and realized gains and/or losses associated with investments were immaterial for all years presented.

Noncurrent investments consist of investments with maturities of greater than twelve months. At December 31, 2011, these primarily consisted of the Company's auction rate security instruments that it expects will not be redeemed during 2012. See Note 11 for further information. Noncurrent investments are included as a component of Other assets in the Consolidated Balance Sheet.

Accounts and other receivables

Accounts and other receivables are carried at cost. They primarily consist of amounts due from credit card companies associated with sales of tickets for future travel, amounts due from business partners in the Company's frequent flyer program, and amounts due from counterparties associated with fuel derivative instruments that have settled. The allowance for doubtful accounts was immaterial at December 31, 2011, 2010, and 2009. In addition, the provision for doubtful accounts and write-offs for 2011, 2010, and 2009 were each immaterial.

Inventories

Inventories consist primarily of aircraft fuel, flight equipment expendable parts, materials, and supplies. All of these items are carried at average cost, less an allowance for obsolescence. These items are generally charged to expense when issued for use. The reserve for obsolescence was immaterial at December 31, 2011, 2010, and 2009. In addition, the Company's provision for obsolescence and write-offs for 2011, 2010, and 2009 were each immaterial.

Property and equipment

Property and equipment is stated at cost. Depreciation is provided by the straight-line method to estimated residual values over periods generally ranging from 23 to 30 years for flight equipment and 5 to 30 years for ground property and equipment once the asset is placed in service. Residual values estimated for aircraft generally range from 5 to 15 percent and for ground property and equipment generally range from 0 to 10 percent. Property under capital leases and related obligations are initially recorded at an amount equal to the present value of future minimum lease payments computed on the basis of the Company's incremental borrowing rate or, when known, the interest rate implicit in the lease. Amortization of property under capital leases is on a straight-line basis over the lease term and is included in Depreciation and amortization expense. Leasehold improvements generally are amortized on a straight-line basis over the shorter of the estimated useful life of the improvement or the remaining term of the lease.

The Company evaluates its long-lived assets used in operations for impairment when events and circumstances indicate that the undiscounted cash flows to be generated by that asset are less than the carrying amounts of the asset and may not be recoverable. Factors that would indicate potential impairment include, but are not limited to, significant decreases in the market value of the long-lived asset(s), a significant change in the long-lived asset's physical condition, and operating or cash flow losses associated with the use of the long-lived asset. If an asset is deemed to be impaired, an impairment loss is recorded for the excess of the asset book value in relation to its estimated fair value.

Aircraft and engine maintenance

The cost of scheduled inspections and repairs and routine maintenance costs for all aircraft and engines are charged to Maintenance materials and repairs expense as incurred. The Company has "power-by-the-hour" agreements related to its Boeing 737-700 engines and AirTran's Boeing 717-200 engines with external service providers. Under these agreements, which the Company has determined effectively transfer the risk associated with the maintenance on such engines to the counterparty, expense is recorded commensurate with each hour flown on an engine. The Company modified its engine maintenance contract for its Classic fleet (737-300/500s) during fourth quarter 2011 and although payments made under this contract are made under a "power-by-the-hour" basis, the risk-transfer concept under this agreement is no longer met, and the Company now records expense on a time and materials basis when an engine repair event takes place.

Modifications that significantly enhance the operating performance or extend the useful lives of aircraft or engines are capitalized and amortized over the remaining life of the asset.

Goodwill and intangible assets

Goodwill represents the excess of the consideration transferred over the fair value of AirTran's assets and liabilities on the acquisition date. See Note 2. Goodwill is not amortized, but it is evaluated for impairment at least annually, or more frequently if events or circumstances indicate impairment may exist. A fair value-based methodology is utilized in testing the carrying value to Goodwill, utilizing assumptions including: (1) a long-term projection of revenues and expenses; (2) estimated discounted future cash flows; (3) observable earnings multiples of publicly-traded airlines; (4) weighted-average cost of capital; and (5) expected tax rate. Factors used in the valuation of goodwill include, but are not limited to, management's plans for future operations, recent operating results and discounted projected future cash flows. These factors are considered Level 3 inputs within the fair value hierarchy. No goodwill impairment was noted during 2011.

Intangible assets primarily consist of acquired leasehold rights to certain airport owned gates at Chicago's Midway International Airport, take-off and landing slots at certain domestic slot-controlled airports, and certain intangible assets recognized from the AirTran acquisition. See Note 2 for further information on acquired identifiable intangible assets. The following table is a summary of the Company's intangible assets, weighted-average useful lives, and balance of accumulated amortization as of December 31, 2011:

	Gross carrying amount (in millions)	Weighted-average useful life (in years)	Accumulated amortization (in millions)
Customer relationships/marketing agreements	$ 39	4	$14
Trademarks/trade names	36	3	8
Domestic slots	63	23	4
Internally developed software	2	2	1
Noncompete agreements	5	2	1
Gate leasehold rights	60	19	22
Total	$205	14	$50

Estimated aggregate amortization expense for the five succeeding years and thereafter is as follows: 2012 – $25 million, 2013 – $19 million, 2014 – $15 million, 2015 – $13 million, 2016 – $10 million, 2017 and thereafter – $73 million.

Revenue recognition

Tickets sold are initially deferred as Air traffic liability. Passenger revenue is recognized when transportation is provided. Air traffic liability primarily represents tickets sold for future travel dates and estimated refunds and exchanges of tickets sold for past travel dates. The majority of the Company's tickets sold are nonrefundable. Tickets that are sold but not flown on the travel date (whether refundable or nonrefundable) can be reused for another flight, up to a year from the date of sale, or refunded (if the ticket is refundable). A small percentage of tickets (or partial tickets) expire unused. The Company estimates the amount of tickets that expire unused and recognizes such amounts in Passenger revenue once the scheduled flight date has passed. Amounts collected from passengers for ancillary services such as baggage and other fees are generally recognized as Other revenue when the service is provided, which is typically the flight date.

The Company is also required to collect certain taxes and fees from Customers on behalf of government agencies and remit these back to the applicable governmental entity on a periodic basis. These taxes and fees include U.S. federal transportation taxes, federal security charges, and airport passenger facility charges.

These items are collected from Customers at the time they purchase their tickets, but are not included in Passenger revenue. The Company records a liability upon collection from the Customer and relieves the liability when payments are remitted to the applicable governmental agency.

Frequent flyer programs

The Company records a liability for the estimated incremental cost of providing free travel under its (and AirTran's) frequent flyer program for all amounts earned from flight activity that are expected to be redeemed for future travel. The estimated incremental cost includes direct passenger costs such as fuel, food, and other operational costs, but does not include any contribution to overhead or profit.

Southwest and AirTran also sell frequent flyer points and/or credits and related services to companies participating in their respective frequent flyer programs. Funds received from the sale of these points and/or credits are accounted for using the residual method. Under this method, the Company has determined the portion of funds received that relate to free travel, currently estimated at 92 percent of the amount received under Southwest's Rapid Reward program and 100 percent of amounts received under AirTran's A+ Reward program as of December 31, 2011. These amounts are deferred and recognized as Passenger revenue when the ultimate free travel awards are flown or the amounts expire unused. The remainder of the amount received per points sold (the residual), which is assumed not to be associated with future travel, includes items such as access to the Company's frequent flyer program population for marketing/solicitation purposes on a monthly or quarterly basis, use of the Company's logo on co-branded credit cards, and other trademarks, designs, images, etc. of the Company for use in marketing materials. This residual portion is recognized in Other revenue in the period earned, which the Company has determined is the period in which it has fulfilled its obligation under the contract signed with the particular business partner, which is on a monthly or quarterly basis, upon sale, as the related marketing services are performed or provided.

Advertising

Advertising costs are charged to expense as incurred. Advertising and promotions expense for the years ended December 31, 2011, 2010, and 2009 was $237 million, $202 million, and $204 million, respectively, and was recorded as a component of Other operating expense in the accompanying Consolidated Statement of Income.

Share-based Employee compensation

The Company has share-based compensation plans covering several of its Employee groups, including plans covering the Company's Board of Directors. The Company accounts for share-based compensation based on its grant date fair value. See Note 15.

Financial derivative instruments

The Company accounts for financial derivative instruments at fair value and applies hedge accounting rules where appropriate. The Company utilizes various derivative instruments, including crude oil, unleaded gasoline, and heating oil-based derivatives, to attempt to reduce the risk of its exposure to jet fuel price increases. These instruments consist primarily of purchased call options, collar structures, call spreads, and fixed-price swap agreements, and upon proper qualification are accounted for as cash-flow hedges. The Company also has interest rate swap agreements to convert a portion of its fixed-rate debt to floating rates and, including instruments acquired from AirTran, has swap agreements that convert certain floating-rate debt to a fixed-rate. These interest rate hedges are appropriately designated as either fair value hedges or as cash flow hedges.

Since the majority of the Company's financial derivative instruments are not traded on a market exchange, the Company estimates their fair values. Depending on the type of instrument, the values are determined by the use of present value methods or option value models with assumptions about commodity prices based on those observed in underlying markets. Also, since there is not a reliable forward market for jet fuel, the Company must estimate the future prices of jet fuel in order to measure the effectiveness of the hedging instruments in offsetting changes to those prices. Forward jet fuel prices are estimated through utilization of a statistical-based regression equation with data from market forward prices of like commodities. This equation is then adjusted for certain items, such as transportation costs, that are stated in the Company's fuel purchasing contracts with its vendors.

For the effective portion of settled fuel hedges, the Company records the associated gains or losses as a component of Fuel and oil expense in the Consolidated Statement of Income. For amounts representing ineffectiveness, as defined, or changes in fair value of derivative instruments for which hedge accounting is not applied, the Company records any gains or losses as a component of Other (gains) losses, net, in the Consolidated Statement of Income. Amounts that are paid or received in connection with the purchase or sale of financial derivative instruments (i.e., premium costs of option contracts) are classified as a component of Other (gains) losses, net, in the Consolidated Statement of Income in the period in which the instrument settles or expires. All cash flows associated with purchasing and selling derivatives are classified as operating cash flows in the Consolidated Statement of Cash Flows, within Changes in certain assets and liabilities. See Note 10 for further information on hedge accounting and financial derivative instruments.

The Company classifies its cash collateral provided to or held from counterparties in a "net" presentation on the Consolidated Balance Sheet against the fair value of the derivative positions with those counterparties. See Note 10 for further information.

Software capitalization

The Company capitalizes certain internal and external costs related to the acquisition and development of internal use software during the application development stages of projects. The Company amortizes these costs using the straight-line method over the estimated useful life of the software, which ranges from five to fifteen years. Costs incurred during the preliminary project or the post-implementation/operation stages of the project are expensed as incurred.

Income taxes

The Company accounts for deferred income taxes utilizing an asset and liability method, whereby deferred tax assets and liabilities are recognized based on the tax effect of temporary differences between the financial statements and the tax basis of assets and liabilities, as measured by current enacted tax rates. The Company also evaluates the need for a valuation allowance to reduce deferred tax assets to estimated recoverable amounts.

The Company's policy for recording interest and penalties associated with uncertain tax positions is to record such items as a component of income before income taxes. Penalties are recorded in Other (gains) losses, net, and interest paid or received is recorded in Interest expense or Interest income, respectively, in the Consolidated Statement of Income. Amounts recorded for penalties and interest related to uncertain tax positions were immaterial for all years presented.

Concentration risk

Approximately 82 percent of the Company's fulltime equivalent Employees are unionized and are covered by collective bargaining agreements, including 82 percent of Southwest's Employees and 81 percent of AirTran's Employees. Historically, the Company has managed this risk by maintaining positive relationships with its Employees and its Employee's Representatives. Southwest's Ramp, Operations, Provisioning, and Freight Agents, Aircraft Appearance Technicians, and Dispatchers are under agreements that have become amendable and are in discussions on new agreements. In addition, Southwest's Pilots, Mechanics, and Customer Service

Agents and Customer Service Representatives are subject to agreements that become amendable during 2012, which represent approximately 29 percent of the Company's (including AirTran's) fulltime equivalent Employees.

The Company attempts to minimize its concentration risk with regards to its cash, cash equivalents, and its investment portfolio. This is accomplished by diversifying and limiting amounts among different counterparties, the type of investment, and the amount invested in any individual security or money market fund.

To manage risk associated with financial derivative instruments held, the Company selects and will periodically review counterparties based on credit ratings, limits its exposure to a single counterparty, and monitors the market position of the program and its relative market position with each counterparty. The Company also has agreements with counterparties containing early termination rights and/or bilateral collateral provisions whereby security is required if market risk exposure exceeds a specified threshold amount or credit ratings fall below certain levels. Collateral deposits provided to or held from counterparties serve to decrease, but not totally eliminate, the credit risk associated with the Company's hedging program. See Note 10 for further information.

The Company (including AirTran) currently operates an all-Boeing fleet, the majority of which are variations of the Boeing 737. If the Company were unable to acquire additional aircraft or associated aircraft parts from Boeing, or Boeing were unable or unwilling to make timely deliveries of aircraft or to provide adequate support for its products, the Company's operations would be materially adversely impacted. In addition, the Company would be materially adversely impacted in the event of a mechanical or regulatory issue associated with the Boeing 737 or Boeing 717 aircraft type, whether as a result of downtime for part or all of the Company's fleet or because of a negative perception by the flying public. The Company is also dependent on sole suppliers for aircraft engines and certain other aircraft parts and would, therefore, also be materially adversely impacted in the event of the unavailability of, or a mechanical or regulatory issue associated with, engines and other parts. The Company considers its relationship with Boeing and other suppliers to be excellent and believes the advantages of operating with a single aircraft supplier currently outweigh the risks of such a strategy.

The Company has historically entered into agreements with some of its co-brand, payment, and loyalty partners that contain exclusivity aspects which place certain confidential restrictions on the Company from entering into certain arrangements with other payment and loyalty partners. These arrangements generally extend for the terms of the partnerships, none of which currently extend beyond May 2017. The Company believes the financial benefits generated by the exclusivity aspects of these arrangements outweigh the risks involved with such agreements.

CHAPTER 2

LEARNING OBJECTIVES

LO1 Explain how the concepts of recognition, valuation, and classification apply to business transactions.

LO2 Explain the double-entry system and the usefulness of T accounts in analyzing business transactions.

LO3 Demonstrate how the double-entry system is applied to common business transactions.

LO4 Prepare a trial balance, and describe its value and limitations.

LO5 Record transactions in the general journal, and post transactions to the ledger.

LO6 Explain why ethical financial reporting depends on proper recording of business transactions.

LO7 Show how the timing of transactions affects cash flows and liquidity.

Source/Jupiter Images

MEASUREMENT CONCEPTS: RECORDING BUSINESS TRANSACTIONS

Business Insight
The Boeing Company

In December 2009, **Boeing** received an order from **Singapore Airlines** for eight of Boeing's 777-300 Extended Range jetliners. Valued at about $2.4 billion, the order was an important economic event for both Boeing and Singapore Airlines.[1]

Typically, it takes Boeing two years to manufacture a plane; but a series of delays have slowed production of the long-range 777-300s. Even for "firm" orders, such as the one from Singapore, Boeing cautions its customers that various factors, such as an economic downturn and a delay in receiving parts from suppliers, could result in the rescheduling or cancellation of orders.[2]

1. **CONCEPT ▶** How will the concepts of recognition, valuation, and classification help Boeing to record the transaction properly?
2. **ACCOUNTING APPLICATION ▶** Should Boeing record the order in its accounting records?
3. **BUSINESS APPLICATION ▶** How important are liquidity and cash flows to Boeing?

SECTION 1 CONCEPTS

CONCEPTS

- Recognition
- Valuation
- Classification

RELEVANT LEARNING OBJECTIVE

LO 1 Explain how the concepts of recognition, valuation, and classification apply to business transactions.

LO 1 Concepts Underlying Business Transactions

Business transactions are economic events that should be recorded in the accounting records. As illustrated in Exhibit 1, the concepts of *recognition*, *valuation*, and *classification* underlie all business transactions.

Exhibit 1
Concepts Underlying Business Transactions

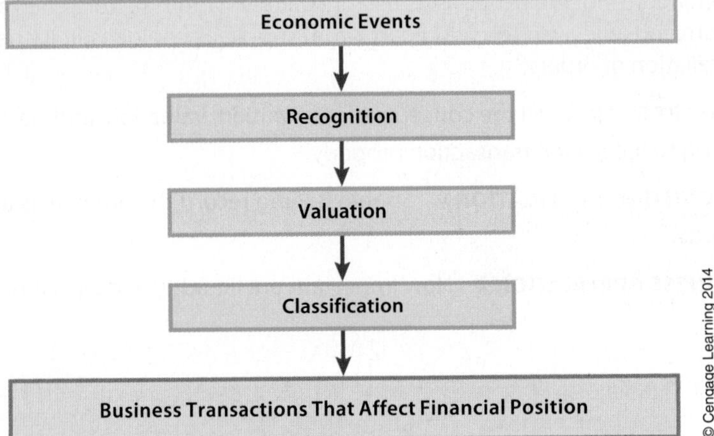

Recognition

Recognition refers to the decision as to *when* to record a business transaction. Usually, companies set specific recognition policies, such as recognizing revenue when title to goods passes or a service is provided. For example, the order of 8 jetliners described in the chapter opener was a very important economic event for both **Boeing** and **Singapore Airlines**, but the recognition point for these transactions for both the buyer and the seller is several years in the future—that is, when the planes are delivered and title to them transfers from Boeing to Singapore Airlines. The resolution of this issue

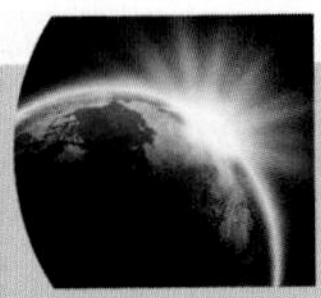

International Perspective

IFRS The Challenge of Fair Value Accounting

The measurement of fair value is a major success of the International Accounting Standards Board (IASB) and the Financial Accounting Standards Board (FASB) convergence project to merge U.S. GAAP with international financial reporting standards (IFRS).[3] After initially recording an asset at cost, fair value is the price at which an asset *could* be sold (or a liability settled) in a current transaction between independent parties. It is not the actual, or historical, price at which the asset was acquired or the liability assumed. Because it represents the price in a hypothetical transaction, fair value is often difficult to measure and subject to judgment. For example, when there is no ready market for an asset—as might be the case for used factory equipment—the potential selling price may not be easy to determine.

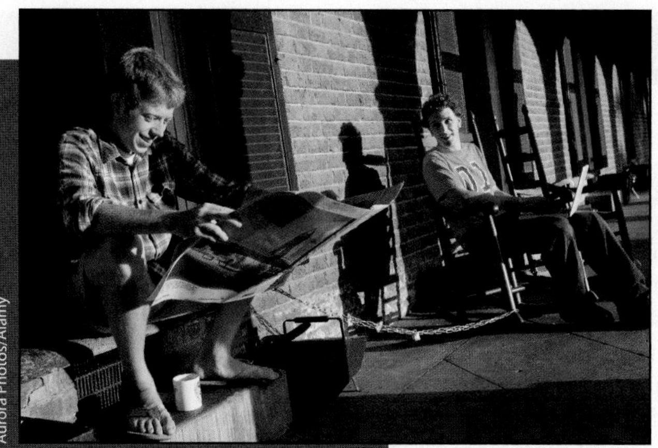

Aurora Photos/Alamy

Barter transactions, in which exchanges are made but no cash changes hands, can make valuation complicated. For example, if an office supply company provides a year's supply of computer paper to a local newspaper in exchange for an advertisement in the weekly paper, the value of the transaction equals the fair value of the items being traded.

is important because the date on which a transaction is recorded affects amounts in the financial statements.

Valuation

Valuation is the process of assigning a monetary amount to business transactions and the resulting assets and liabilities. Generally accepted accounting principles state that all business transactions should be valued at *fair value* when they occur. **Fair value** is the *exchange price* of an actual or potential business transaction between market participants.[4] Recording transactions at the exchange price at the point of recognition is called the **cost principle**. The cost, or exchange price, is used because it is verifiable. For example, when the aircraft is finally complete and **Boeing** delivers the planes to **Singapore Airlines**, the two entities will record the transaction in their respective records at the agreed-upon price.

Normally, the value of an asset remains at its initial fair value or cost until the asset is sold, expires, or is consumed. However, if a change in the fair value of the asset (or liability) occurs, an adjustment may be required. Different fair-value rules apply to different classes of assets. For example, a building or equipment remains at cost unless convincing evidence exists that the fair value is less than cost. In this case, a loss is recorded to reduce the value from its cost to fair value. Investments, on the other hand, are often accounted for at fair value, regardless of whether fair value is greater or less than cost.

Classification

Classification is the process of assigning all the transactions in which a business engages to appropriate categories, or accounts. Classification of debts can affect a company's ability to borrow money, and classification of purchases can affect its income. One of the most important classification issues in accounting is the difference between an expense and an asset, both represented by debits in the accounts. For example, it will take **Boeing** several years to manufacture 8 jetliners ordered by **Singapore Airlines**. Over those years, many classification issues will arise. A significant issue is how to classify the numerous costs that Boeing will incur in building the planes. As you will see, generally accepted accounting principles require that these costs be classified as assets until the sale is recorded at the time the planes are delivered. At that time, they will be reclassified as expenses. In this way, the costs will offset the revenues from the sale. It will then be possible to tell whether Boeing made a profit or loss on the transaction.

STUDY NOTE: *If* **CVS** *buys paper towels to resell to customers, the cost would be recorded as an asset in the Inventory account. If the paper towels are used for cleaning in the store today, the cost is an expense.*

As we explain later in the chapter, proper classification depends not only on correctly analyzing the effect of each transaction but also on maintaining a system of accounts that reflects that effect.

APPLY IT!

Three major issues underlie every accounting transaction: recognition, valuation, and classification. Match each of these issues to the statements that are most closely associated with the issue. A company:

1. Records a piece of equipment at the price paid for it.
2. Records the purchase of the equipment on the day on which it takes ownership.
3. Records the equipment as an asset because it will benefit future periods.

SOLUTION

1. valuation
2. recognition
3. classification

TRY IT! SE1, SE2, SE3, E1A, E3A, E1B, E3B

SECTION 2

ACCOUNTING APPLICATIONS

ACCOUNTING APPLICATIONS

- Record business transactions
- Prepare the trial balance

RELEVANT LEARNING OBJECTIVES

LO2 Explain the double-entry system and the usefulness of T accounts in analyzing business transactions.

LO3 Demonstrate how the double-entry system is applied to common business transactions.

LO4 Prepare a trial balance, and describe its value and limitations.

LO5 Record transactions in the general journal, and post transactions to the ledger.

LO2 Double-Entry System

Accounting is a very old discipline. Forms of it have been essential to commerce for more than 5,000 years. Accounting, in a version close to what we know today, gained widespread use in the 1400s, especially in Italy, where it was instrumental in the development of shipping, trade, construction, and other forms of commerce. This system of double-entry bookkeeping, i.e., *recording*, *valuing*, and *classifying* business transactions, was documented by the famous Italian mathematician, scholar, and philosopher Fra Luca Pacioli. In 1494, Pacioli published his most important work, *Summa de Arithmetica, Geometrica, Proportioni et Proportionalita*, which contained a detailed description of accounting as practiced in that age. This book became the most widely read book on mathematics in Italy and firmly established Pacioli as the "Father of Accounting." Goethe, the famous German poet and dramatist, referred to double-entry bookkeeping as "one of the finest discoveries of the human intellect."

What is the significance of the double-entry system? The system is based on the *principle of duality*, which means that every economic event has two aspects—such as effort and reward, sacrifice and benefit, source and use—that offset, or balance, each other. In the **double-entry system**, each transaction must be recorded with at least one debit and one credit, and the total amount of the debits must equal the total amount of the credits. All accounting systems, no matter how sophisticated, are based on the principle of duality.

Accounts

Accounts are the basic storage units for accounting data and are used to accumulate amounts from similar transactions. An accounting system has a separate account for each asset, each liability, and each component of stockholders' equity, including revenues and expenses. Managers must be able to refer to accounts so that they can study their company's financial history and plan for the future. A very small company may need only a few dozen accounts; a multinational corporation may need thousands.

An account title should describe what is recorded in the account. However, account titles can be rather confusing. For example, *Wages Expense* and *Salaries Expense* are both titles for labor expenses. Moreover, many account titles change over time as preferences and practices change.

Chart of Accounts

In a manual accounting system, each account is kept on a separate page or card. These pages or cards are placed together in a book or file called the **general ledger**. In computerized systems, accounts are maintained electronically. However, accountants still refer to the group of accounts as the *general ledger*, or simply the *ledger*.

To help identify accounts in the ledger and make them easy to find, the accountant often numbers them. A list of these numbers with the corresponding account titles is called a **chart of accounts**. A chart of accounts is a table of contents for the ledger. Typically, it lists accounts in the order in which they appear in the ledger, which is usually the order in which they appear in the financial statements. The numbering scheme allows some flexibility. A very simple chart of accounts appears in Exhibit 2. The first digit in the account number identifies the major financial statement *classification*—that is, an asset account begins with the digit 1, a liability account begins with a 2, and so forth. The second and third digits identify individual accounts. The gaps in the sequence of numbers allow the accountant to expand the number of accounts within the classification.

Exhibit 2
Chart of Accounts for a Small Business

Account Number	Account Name	Description
		Assets
111	Cash	Money and any medium of exchange (coins, currency, checks, money orders, and money on deposit in a bank)
112	Notes Receivable	Promissory notes (written promises to pay definite sums of money at fixed future dates) due from others
113	Accounts Receivable	Amounts due from others for revenues or sales on credit (sales on account)
116	Office Supplies	Prepaid expense; office supplies purchased and not used
117	Prepaid Rent	Prepaid expense; rent paid in advance and not used
118	Prepaid Insurance	Prepaid expense; insurance purchased and not expired
141	Land	Property owned for use in the business
142	Buildings	Structures owned for use in the business
143	Accumulated Depreciation—Buildings	Total of periodic allocation of the cost of buildings to expense; deducted from Buildings
146	Office Equipment	Office equipment owned for use in the business
147	Accumulated Depreciation—Office Equipment	Total of periodic allocation of the cost of office equipment to expense; deducted from Office Equipment
		Liabilities
211	Notes Payable	Promissory notes due to others
212	Accounts Payable	Amounts due to others for purchases on credit
213	Unearned Revenue	Unearned revenue; advance deposits for services to be provided in the future
214	Wages Payable	Amounts due to employees for wages earned and not paid
215	Income Taxes Payable	Amounts due to government for income taxes owed and not paid
		Stockholders' Equity
311	Common Stock	Stockholders' investments in a corporation for which they receive shares of stock
312	Retained Earnings	Stockholders' claims against company assets derived from profitable operations
313	Dividends	Distributions of assets (usually cash) that reduce retained earnings
314	Income Summary	Temporary account used at the end of the accounting period to summarize the revenues and expenses for the period
		Revenues
411	Service Revenue	Amounts earned from services
		Expenses
511	Wages Expense	Amounts earned by employees
512	Utilities Expense	Amounts for utilities, such as water, electricity, and gas, used
513	Telephone Expense	Amounts of telephone services used
514	Rent Expense	Amounts of property and building rent used
515	Insurance Expense	Amounts for insurance expired
517	Office Supplies Expense	Amounts for office supplies used
518	Depreciation Expense—Buildings	Amount of buildings' cost allocated to expense
520	Depreciation Expense—Office Equipment	Amount of office equipment cost allocated to expense
521	Income Taxes Expense	Amount of tax on income

The T Account

The T account is a good place to begin the study of the double-entry system. Such an account has the following three parts:

- a title, which identifies the asset, liability, or stockholders' equity account
- a left side, which is called the **debit** side
- a right side, which is called the **credit** side

The **T account**, so called because it resembles the letter *T*, is a tool used to analyze transactions and is not part of the accounting records. It looks like this:

Title of Account	
Debit (left) side	Credit (right) side

***STUDY NOTE:** It is important to realize that debit simply means "left side" and credit simply means "right side." Do not let preconceived ideas about what debit and credit mean affect your understanding.*

Any entry made on the left side of the account is a debit, and any entry made on the right side is a credit. The terms *debit* (abbreviated Dr., from the Latin *debere*) and *credit* (abbreviated Cr., from the Latin *credere*) are simply the accountant's words for "left" and "right" (*not* for "increase" or "decrease"). We present a more formal version of the T account, the ledger account form, later in this chapter.

The T Account Illustrated Suppose a company had several transactions during the month that involved the receipt or payment of cash. These transactions can be summarized in the Cash account by recording receipts on the left (debit) side of a T account and payments on the right (credit) side.

Cash

	Dr.	*Cr.*
	100,000	70,000
	3,000	400
		1,200
	103,000	71,600
Bal.	31,400	

The cash receipts on the left total $103,000. (The total is written in smaller, blue figures so that it cannot be confused with an actual debit entry.) The cash payments on the right side total $71,600. These totals are simply working totals, or **footings**. Footings, which are calculated at the end of each month, are an easy way to determine cash on hand. The difference between the total debit footing and the total credit footing is called the **account balance** (or *balance*). If the balance is a debit, it is written on the left side. If it is a credit, it is written on the right side. Notice that the Cash account has a debit balance of $31,400 ($103,000 − $71,600). This is the amount of cash the business has on hand at the end of the month.

Rules of Double-Entry Accounting

The double-entry system follows two rules:

- Every transaction affects at least two accounts.
- Total debits must equal total credits.

In other words, for every transaction, one or more accounts must be debited, or entered on the left side of a T account, and one or more accounts must be credited, or entered on the right side of a T account, and the total dollar amount of the debits must equal the total dollar amount of the credits.

Look again at the accounting equation:

Assets = Liabilities + Stockholders' Equity

▲ If a debit *increases* assets, then a credit must be used to *increase* liabilities or stockholders' equity because they are on opposite sides of the equal sign.

▼ Likewise, if a credit *decreases* assets, then a debit must be used to *decrease* liabilities or stockholders' equity.

These rules can be shown as follows.

Assets		=	Liabilities		+	Stockholders' Equity	
Debit for increases (+)	Credit for decreases (−)		Debit for decreases (−)	Credit for increases (+)		Debit for decreases (−)	Credit for increases (+)

One of the more difficult points is the application of double-entry rules to the components of stockholders' equity. Remember that dividends and expenses are deductions from stockholders' equity. Thus, transactions that *increase* dividends or expenses *decrease* stockholders' equity. Consider this expanded version of the accounting equation:

Stockholders' Equity

Assets = Liabilities + Common Stock + Retained Earnings − Dividends + Revenues − Expenses

Assets		=	Liabilities		+	Common Stock		+	Retained Earnings		−	Dividends		+	Revenues		−	Expenses	
+	−		−	+		−	+		−	+		+	−		−	+		+	−
(Dr.)	(Cr.)		(Dr.)	(Cr.)		(Dr.)	(Cr.)		(Dr.)	(Cr.)		(Dr.)	(Cr.)		(Dr.)	(Cr.)		(Dr.)	(Cr.)

STUDY NOTE: *To remember the normal balances and the rules of debit and credit, use the acronym ADE: Assets, Dividends, and Expenses are always increased by debits. All other accounts are increased by credits.*

Normal Balance

The **normal balance** of an account is its usual balance and is the side (debit or credit) that increases the account. Exhibit 3 summarizes the normal account balances of the major account categories.

Exhibit 3
Normal Account Balances of Major Account Categories

	Increases Recorded by		Normal Balance	
Account Category	**Debit**	**Credit**	**Debit**	**Credit**
Assets	×		×	
Liabilities		×		×
Stockholders' Equity:				
Common Stock		×		×
Retained Earnings		×		×
Dividends	×		×	
Revenues		×		×
Expenses	×		×	

Stockholders' Equity Accounts

Exhibit 4 illustrates how stockholders' equity accounts relate to each other and to the financial statements. The distinctions among these accounts are important for both legal purposes and financial reporting. Stockholders' equity accounts represent the legal claims of stockholders to the assets of the corporation. The Common Stock account represents the stockholders' claims arising from their investments in the business, and the Retained Earnings account represents stockholders' claims arising from profitable operations. Both are claims against the general assets of the company, not against specific assets. Dividends are deductions from stockholders' claims on retained earnings and are shown on the statement of retained earnings. Thus in summary, stockholders' equity is equal to the common stock purchased by the stockholders plus (or minus) income earned (or losses incurred) by the business minus dividends paid to the stockholders.

Exhibit 4
Relationships of Stockholders' Equity Accounts

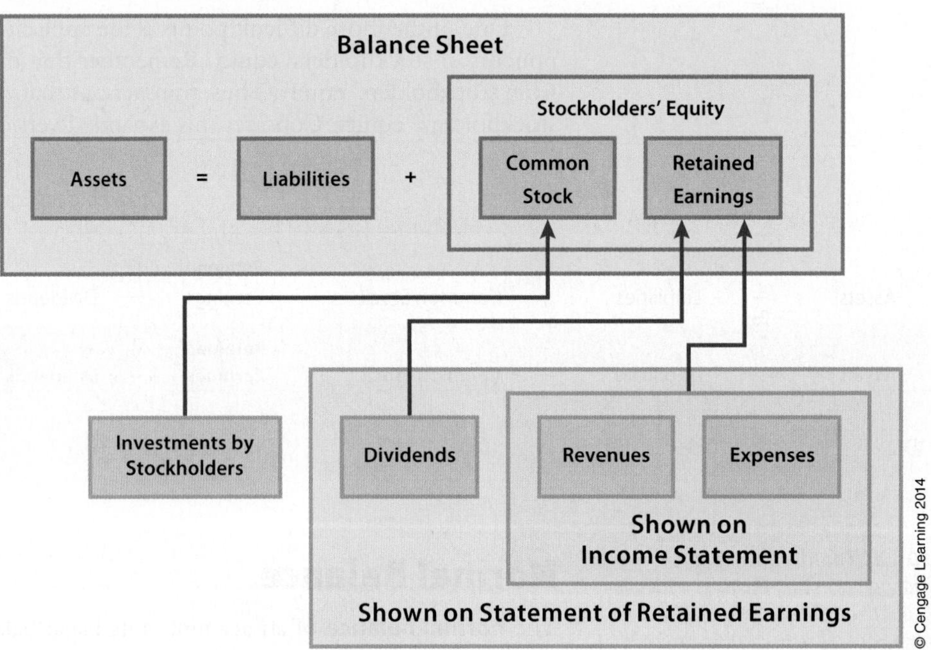

The Accounting Cycle

As Exhibit 5 shows, the **accounting cycle** is a series of steps that measure and communicate useful information to decision makers. These steps follow.

- **Step 1.** *Analyze* business transactions from source documents.
- **Step 2.** *Record* the transactions by entering them in the general journal.
- **Step 3.** *Post* the journal entries to the ledger, and prepare a trial balance.
- **Step 4.** *Adjust* the accounts, and prepare an adjusted trial balance.
- **Step 5.** *Prepare* financial statements.
- **Step 6.** *Close* the accounts, and prepare a post-closing trial balance.

Note that Steps 3, 4, and 6 entail preparation of trial balances, which are explained later in this chapter. The remainder of this chapter examines Steps 1–3 in detail.

Exhibit 5
Overview of the Accounting Cycle

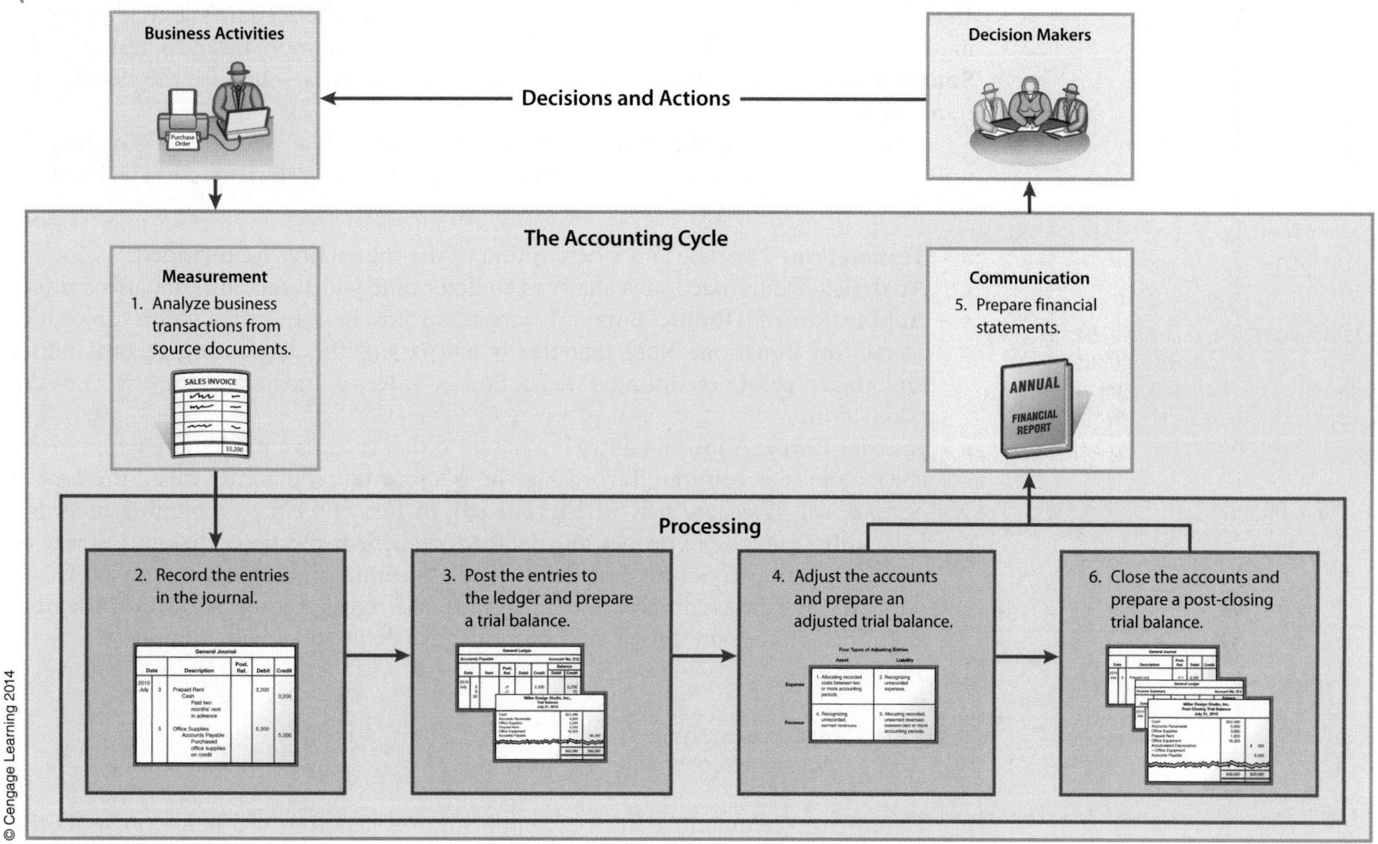

APPLY IT!

You are given the following list of accounts with dollar amounts:

Dividends	$ 75	Common Stock	$300
Accounts Payable	200	Fees Revenue	250
Wages Expense	150	Retained Earnings	100
Cash	625		

Insert the account title at the top of the corresponding T account that follows and enter the dollar amount as a normal balance in the account. Then show that the accounting equation is in balance.

Stockholders' Equity

Assets = **Liabilities** + **Common Stock** + **Retained Earnings** − **Dividends** + **Revenues** − **Expenses**

SOLUTION

Cash	Accounts Payable	Common Stock	Retained Earnings	Dividends	Fees Revenue	Wages Expense
625 (debit)	200 (credit)	300 (credit)	100 (credit)	75 (debit)	250 (credit)	150 (debit)

Assets = Liabilities + Stockholders' Equity
$625 = $200 + ($300 + $100 − $75 + $250 − $150)
$625 = $200 + $425
$625 = $625

TRY IT! SE1, SE4, E2A, E3A, E2B, E3B

LO3 Business Transaction Analysis

In the next few pages, we illustrate the first three steps of the accounting cycle by showing how to apply the double-entry system to some common business transactions. **Source documents**—invoices, receipts, checks, or contracts—support the details of a transaction.

Here, we focus on the transactions of a small firm, Blue Design Studio, Inc. To walk through every step of recording business transactions, each transaction will be broken into the following parts:

STUDY NOTE: *T accounts are used to understand and visualize the double-entry effects of a transaction on the accounting equation. They help in recording the journal entry.*

- **Transaction:** The date and a description of the transaction are provided.
- **Analysis:** The transaction is analyzed to determine which accounts are affected.
- **Application of Double-Entry:** T accounts show how the transaction affects the accounting equation. Note that this is *not* part of the accounting records but is undertaken before recording a transaction in order to understand the effects of the transaction.
- **Journal Entry:** A **journal entry** is a notation that records a single transaction in the chronological accounting record known as a **journal** (sometimes called the *book of original entry* because it is where transactions first enter the accounting records). Each entry must be in proper **journal form**, which, as illustrated below, is a way of recording a transaction with the date, debit account, and debit amount shown on one line, and the credit account (indented) and credit amount shown on the next line. The amounts are shown in their respective debit and credit columns.

		Dr.	Cr.
Date	Debit Account Name	Amount	
	Credit Account Name		Amount

- **Comment:** Comments that offer supporting explanations will help you apply the rules of double-entry accounting.

Stockholders' Investment to Form the Business

Transaction On July 1, stockholders invest $40,000 in Blue Design Studio, Inc.

Analysis The journal entry to record the stockholders' investment in the business

▲ *increases* the asset account *Cash* with a debit

▲ *increases* the stockholders' equity account *Common Stock* with a credit

Application of Double Entry

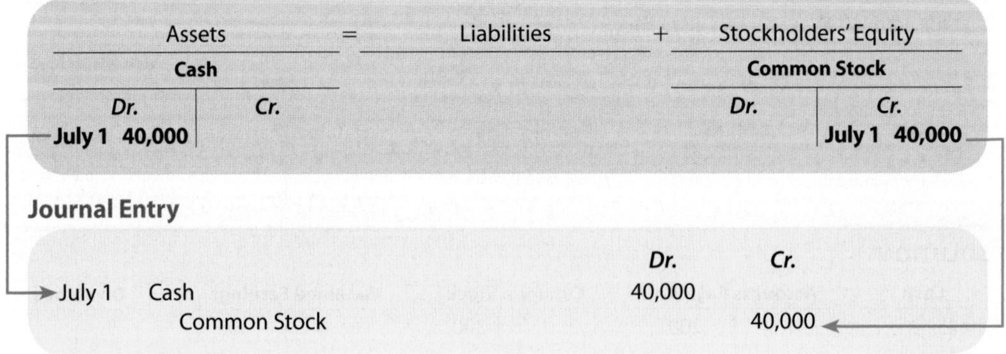

Journal Entry

		Dr.	Cr.
July 1	Cash	40,000	
	Common Stock		40,000

Comment If Joan Blue had invested assets other than cash in the business, the debit would be *classified* as the appropriate asset account (for example, Equipment).

Economic Event That Is Not a Business Transaction

Event On July 1, Blue Design Studio, Inc., orders $5,200 of office supplies.

Comment When an economic event is not a business transaction, it is not *recognized* and no entry is made. In this case, there is no confirmation that the supplies have been shipped or that title has passed.

Prepayment of Expenses in Cash

Transaction On July 3, Blue Design Studio, Inc., rents an office for and pays $3,200 for two months' rent in advance.

Analysis The journal entry to record the prepayment of office rent in cash

▲ *increases* the asset account *Prepaid Rent* with a debit

▼ *decreases* the asset account *Cash* with a credit

Application of Double Entry

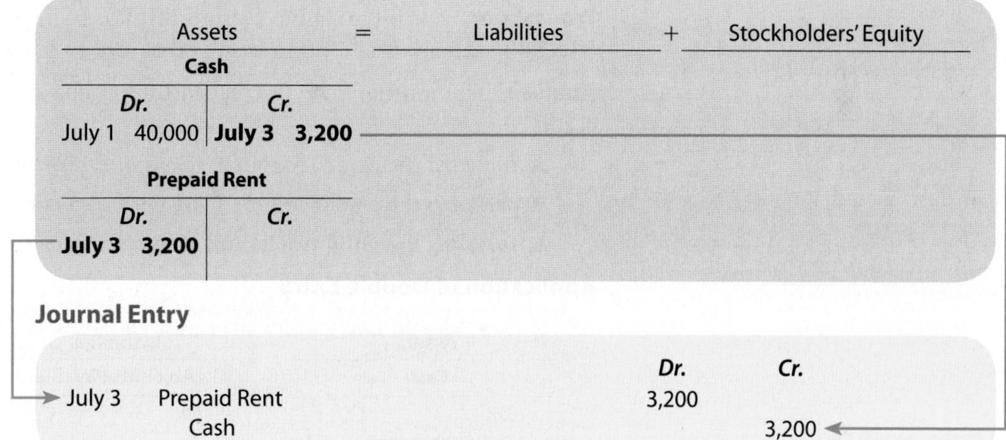

Journal Entry

		Dr.	Cr.
July 3	Prepaid Rent	3,200	
	Cash		3,200

Comment A prepaid expense is *classified* as an asset because the expenditure will benefit future operations. This transaction does not affect the totals of assets or liabilities and stockholders' equity because it simply trades one asset for another asset. If the company had paid only July's rent, the stockholders' equity account *Rent Expense* would be *recognized* and debited because the total benefit of the expenditure would be used up in the current month.

Purchase of an Asset on Credit

Transaction On July 5, Blue Design Studio, Inc., receives the office supplies ordered on July 2 and an invoice for $5,200.

Analysis The journal entry to record the purchase of office supplies on credit

▲ *increases* the asset account *Office Supplies* with a debit

▲ *increases* the liability account *Accounts Payable* with a credit

Application of Double Entry

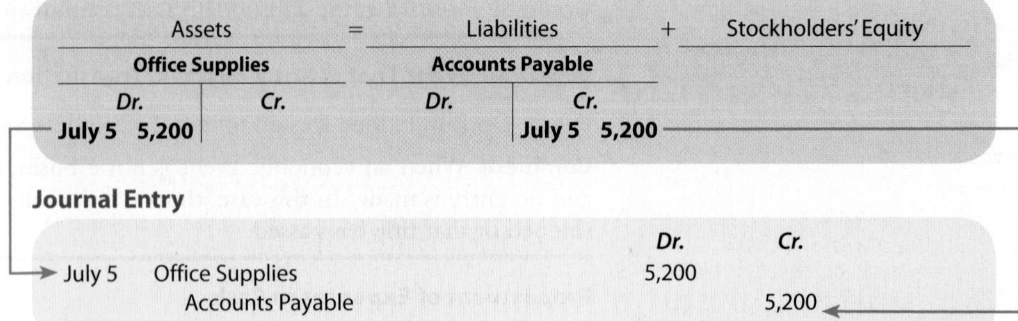

Comment Office supplies in this transaction are *classified* as an asset (prepaid expense) because they will not be used up in the current month and thus will benefit future periods. The credit is *classified* as Accounts Payable because there is a delay between the time of the purchase and the time of payment.

Purchase of an Asset Partly in Cash and Partly on Credit

Transaction On July 6, Blue Design Studio, Inc., purchases office equipment totaling $16,320 and pays $13,320 in cash and agrees to pay the rest next month.

Analysis The journal entry to record the purchase of office equipment in cash and on credit

▲ *increases* the asset account *Office Equipment* with a debit

▼ *decreases* the asset account *Cash* with a credit

▲ *increases* the liability account *Accounts Payable* with a credit

Application of Double Entry

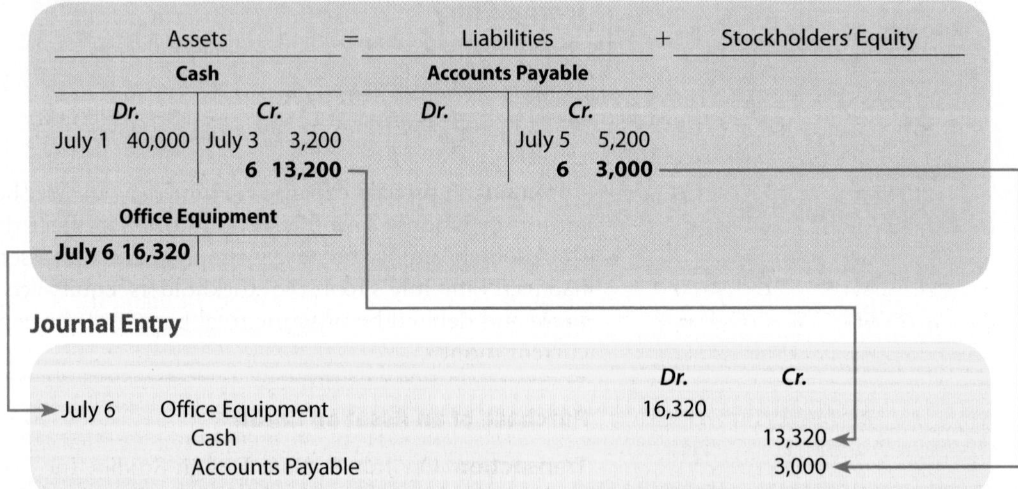

Comment As this transaction illustrates, assets may be paid for partly in cash and partly on credit. A journal entry in which more than two accounts are involved is called a **compound entry** because a portion of the entry is properly *classified* in two or more accounts.

Payment of a Liability

Transaction On July 9, Blue Design Studio, Inc., makes a partial payment of $2,600 for the amount owed for the office supplies received on July 5.

Analysis The journal entry to record the payment of a liability

▼ *decreases* the liability account *Accounts Payable* with a debit

▼ *decreases* the asset account *Cash* with a credit

Application of Double Entry

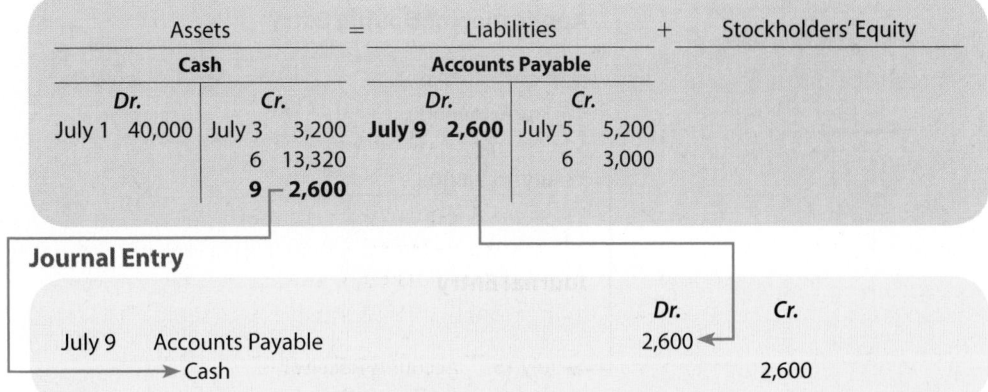

Comment Note that the office supplies, which were *recognized* and recorded when they were purchased on July 5, are not part of the July 9 transaction.

Revenue in Cash

Transaction On July 10, Blue Design Studio, Inc., performs a service for an investment advisor by designing a series of brochures and collects a $2,800 fee in cash.

Analysis The journal entry to record revenue received in cash

▲ *increases* the asset account *Cash* with a debit

▲ *increases* the stockholders' equity account *Design Revenue* with a credit

Application of Double Entry

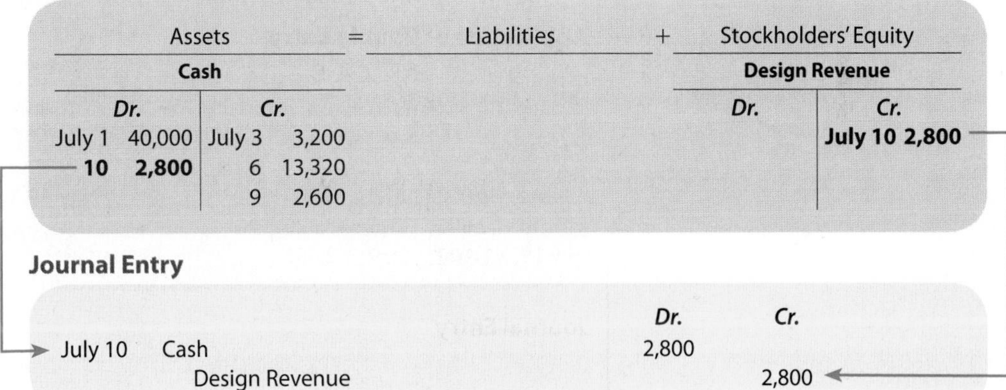

Comment For this transaction, revenue is *recognized* when the service is provided and the cash is received.

Revenue on Credit

Transaction On July 15, Blue Design Studio, Inc., performs a service for a department store by designing a TV commercial. The company bills for the $9,600 fee now but will collect it later.

Analysis The journal entry to record revenue billed to a customer

▲ *increases* the asset account *Accounts Receivable* with a debit

▲ *increases* the stockholders' equity account *Design Revenue* with a credit

Accounts Receivable is used to indicate the customer's obligation until it is paid.

Application of Double Entry

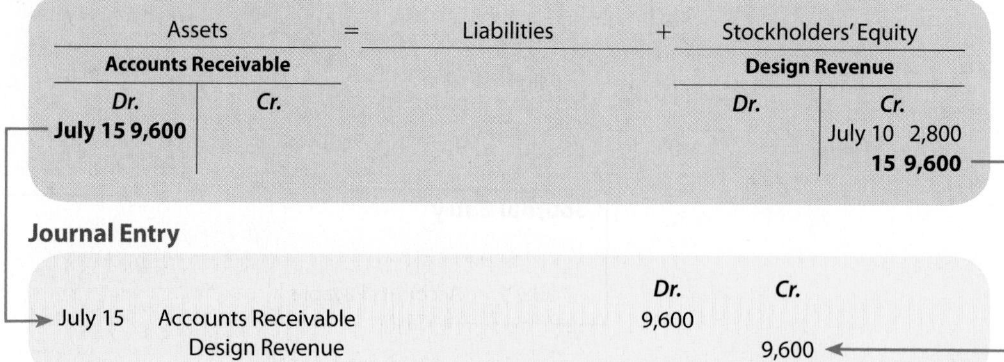

Journal Entry

		Dr.	Cr.
July 15	Accounts Receivable	9,600	
	Design Revenue		9,600

Comment In this case, there is a delay between the time revenue is earned and the time the cash is received. Revenues are *recognized* and recorded at the time they are earned and billed regardless of when cash is received.

Revenue Collected in Advance

Transaction On July 19, Blue Design Studio, Inc., accepts a $1,400 advance fee as a deposit on a series of brochures to be designed.

Analysis The journal entry to record revenue received in advance

▲ *increases* the asset account *Cash* with a debit

▲ *increases* the liability account *Unearned Design Revenue* with a credit

Application of Double Entry

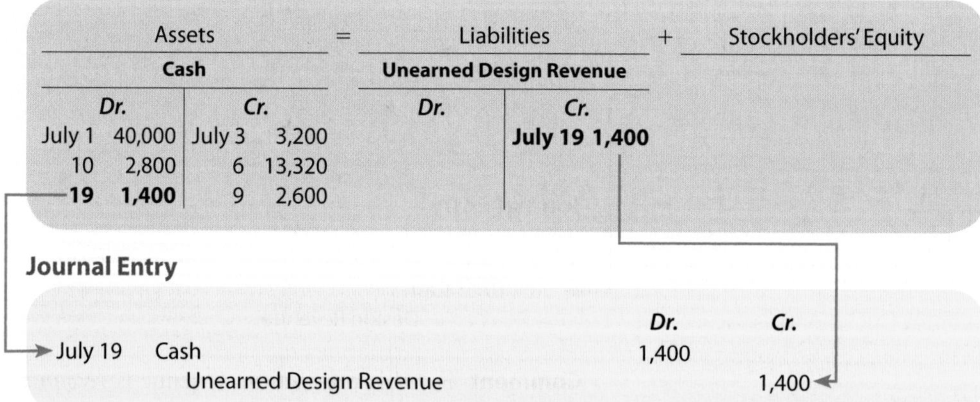

Journal Entry

		Dr.	Cr.
July 19	Cash	1,400	
	Unearned Design Revenue		1,400

Comment In this case, cash is received before the fees are earned. Unearned Design Revenue is *recognized* and *classified* as a liability because the firm must either provide the service or return the deposit.

Collection on Account

Transaction On July 22, Blue Design Studio, Inc., receives $5,000 cash from customer previously billed on July 15.

Analysis The journal entry to record the collection of an account receivable from a customer previously billed

▲ *increases* the asset account *Cash* with a debit

▼ *decreases* the asset account *Accounts Receivable* with a credit

Application of Double Entry

Assets	=	Liabilities	+	Stockholders' Equity

Cash

Dr.		Cr.	
July 1	40,000	July 3	3,200
10	2,800	6	13,200
19	1,400	9	2,600
22	**5,000**		

Accounts Receivable

Dr.		Cr.	
July 15	9,600	**July 22**	**5,000**

Journal Entry

		Dr.	Cr.
July 22	Cash	5,000	
	Accounts Receivable		5,000

Comment Note that the revenue related to this transaction was *recognized* and recorded on July 15. Thus, no revenue is recognized at this time.

Expense Paid in Cash

Transaction On July 26, Blue Design Studio, Inc., pays $4,800 for four weeks of employee wages.

Analysis The journal entry to record this cash expense

▲ *increases* the stockholders' equity account *Wages Expense* with a debit

▼ *decreases* the asset account *Cash* with a credit

Business Perspective

No Dollar Amount: How Can That Be?

Determining the value of a sale or purchase transaction isn't difficult when the value equals the amount of cash that changes hands. However, barter transactions, in which exchanges are made but no cash changes hands, can make valuation more complicated. Barter transactions are quite common in business today. Here are some examples:

- A consulting company provides its services to an auto dealer in exchange for the loan of a car for a year.
- An office supply company provides a year's supply of computer paper to a local weekly newspaper in exchange for an advertisement in 52 issues of the newspaper.
- Two Internet companies each provide an advertisement and link to the other's website on their own websites.

Determining the value of these transactions is a matter of determining the fair value of the items being traded.

Application of Double Entry

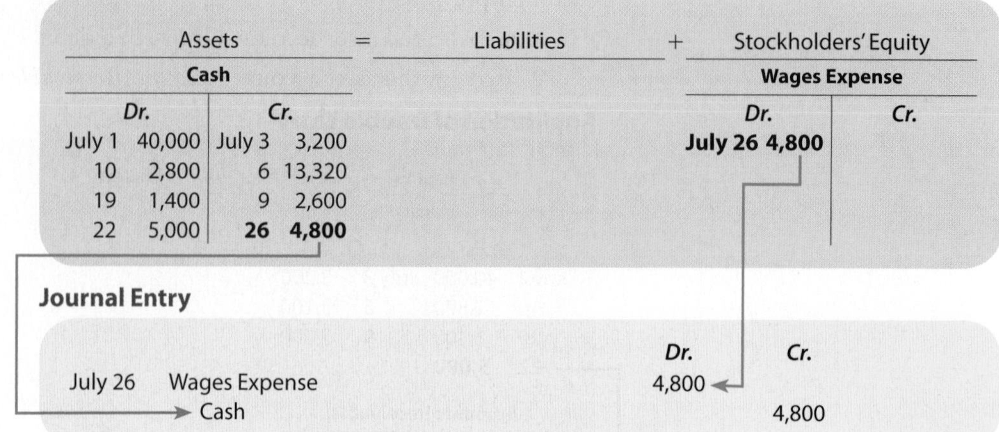

Comment Wages Expense will appear on the income statement as a deduction from revenues.

Expense to Be Paid Later

Transaction On July 30, Blue Design Studio, Inc., receives but does not pay the utility bill for $680 that is due next month.

Analysis The journal entry to record this cash expense

- ▲ *increases* the stockholders' equity account *Utilities Expense* with a debit
- ▲ *increases* the liability account *Accounts Payable* with a credit

Application of Double Entry

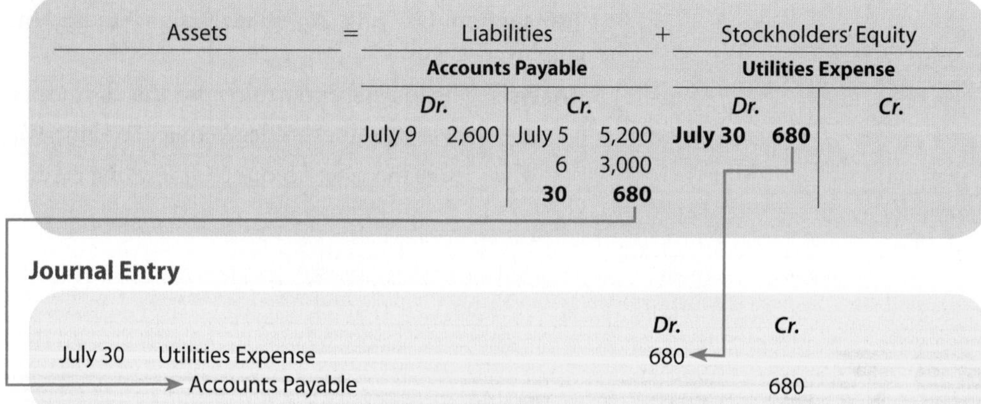

Comment The expense is *recognized* and recorded if the benefit has been received and the amount is owed, even if the cash is not to be paid until later.

Dividends

Transaction On July 31, the board of directors of Blue Design Studio, Inc., declares and pays a cash dividend of $2,800.

Analysis The journal entry to record a cash dividend

- ▲ *increases* the stockholders' equity account *Dividends* with a debit
- ▼ *decreases* the asset account *Cash* with a credit

Application of Double Entry

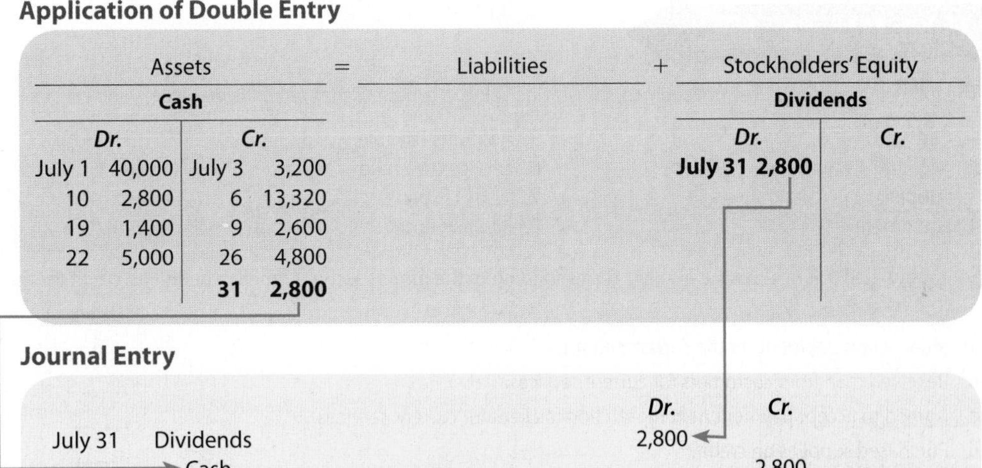

Assets = Liabilities + Stockholders' Equity

Cash

Dr.		Cr.	
July 1	40,000	July 3	3,200
10	2,800	6	13,320
19	1,400	9	2,600
22	5,000	26	4,800
		31	**2,800**

Dividends

Dr.		Cr.	
July 31	**2,800**		

Journal Entry

		Dr.	Cr.
July 31	Dividends	2,800	
	Cash		2,800

Comment Cash payments to stockholders are not *classified* as expenses but as dividends.

Summary of Transactions

Exhibit 6 uses the accounting equation to summarize the transactions of Blue Design Studio, Inc. Note that the income statement accounts appear under stockholders' equity and that the transactions in the Cash account will be reflected on the statement of cash flows.

Exhibit 6
Summary of Transactions of Blue Design Studio, Inc.

Assets = **Liabilities** + **Stockholders' Equity**

Assets

Cash

Dr.		Cr.	
July 1	40,000	July 3	3,200
10	2,800	6	13,320
19	1,400	9	2,600
22	5,000	26	4,800
		31	2,800
	49,200		**26,720**
Bal.	**22,480**		

This account links to the statement of cash flows.

Accounts Receivable

Dr.		Cr.	
July 15	9,600	July 22	5,000
Bal.	**4,600**		

Office Supplies

Dr.		Cr.	
July 5	5,200		

Prepaid Rent

Dr.		Cr.	
July 3	3,200		

Office Equipment

Dr.		Cr.	
July 6	16,320		

Liabilities

Accounts Payable

Dr.		Cr.	
July 9	2,600	July 5	5,200
		6	3,000
		30	680
	2,600		**8,880**
		Bal.	**6,280**

Unearned Design Revenue

Dr.		Cr.	
		July 19	1,400

Stockholders' Equity

Common Stock

Dr.		Cr.	
		July 1	40,000

Dividends

Dr.		Cr.	
July 31	2,800		

Design Revenue

Dr.		Cr.	
		July 10	2,800
		15	9,600
		Bal.	**12,400**

Wages Expense

Dr.		Cr.	
July 26	4,800		

Utilities Expense

Dr.		Cr.	
July 30	680		

These accounts link to the income statement.

Assets	=	**Liabilities**	+	**Stockholders' Equity**
$51,800	=	$7,680	+	$44,120

APPLY IT!

The following accounts are applicable to Kathy's Nail Salon, a company that provides manicures and pedicures:

1. Cash
2. Accounts Receivable
3. Supplies
4. Equipment
5. Accounts Payable
6. Services Revenue
7. Wages Expense
8. Rent Expense

For Kathy's Nail Salon, enter the number corresponding to the proper account for each debit and credit for the following transactions:

	Debit	Credit
a. Made a rent payment for the current month.	8	1
b. Received cash from customers for current services.	____	____
c. Agreed to accept payment next month from a client for current services.	____	____
d. Purchased supplies on credit.	____	____
e. Purchased a new chair and table for cash.	____	____
f. Made a payment on accounts payable.	____	____

SOLUTION

	Debit	Credit
a. Made a rent payment for the current month.	8	1
b. Received cash from customers for current services.	1	6
c. Agreed to accept payment next month from a client for current services.	2	6
d. Purchased supplies on credit.	3	5
e. Purchased a new chair and table for cash.	4	1
f. Made a payment on accounts payable.	5	1

TRY IT! SE2, SE5, SE6, E4A, E5A, E6A, E7A, E8A, E4B, E5B, E6B, E7B, E8B

LO4 The Trial Balance

The **trial balance**, prepared periodically, is a device used to ensure that the total of debits and credits in the accounts are equal, meaning that the accounts balance. Exhibit 7 shows a trial balance for Blue Design Studio, Inc. It was prepared from the accounts in Exhibit 6.

Exhibit 7
Trial Balance

Blue Design Studio, Inc.
Trial Balance
July 31, 2014

Cash	22,480	
Accounts Receivable	4,600	
Office Supplies	5,200	
Prepaid Rent	3,200	
Office Equipment	16,320	
Accounts Payable		6,280
Unearned Design Revenue		1,400
Common Stock		40,000
Dividends	2,800	
Design Revenue		12,400
Wages Expense	4,800	
Utilities Expense	680	
	60,080	60,080

Preparation and Use of a Trial Balance

Although a trial balance may be prepared at any time, it is usually prepared on the last day of the accounting period. The steps involved in preparing a trial balance follow.

- **Step 1.** List each account that has a balance, with debit balances in the left column and credit balances in the right column. Accounts are listed in the following order: assets, liabilities, stockholders' equity, dividends, revenues, and expenses.
- **Step 2.** Add each column.
- **Step 3.** Compare the totals of the columns.

Once in a while, a transaction leaves an account with a balance that isn't "normal." For example, when a company overdraws its bank account, its Cash account (an asset) will show a credit balance instead of a debit balance. The "abnormal" balance should be copied into the trial balance columns as it stands, as a debit or a credit.

The trial balance proves whether the accounts are in balance. *In balance* means that the total of all debits recorded equals the total of all credits recorded. But the trial balance does not prove that the transactions were analyzed correctly or recorded in the proper accounts. For example, the trial balance does not show that a debit should have been made in Office Supplies rather than in Office Equipment. And the trial balance does not detect whether transactions have been omitted, because equal debits and credits will have been omitted. Also, if an error of the same amount is made in both a debit and a credit, it will not be evident in the trial balance. The trial balance proves only that the debits and credits in the accounts are in balance.

Finding Trial Balance Errors

If the debit and credit balances in a trial balance are not equal, look for one or more of the following errors:

- A debit was entered in an account as a credit, or vice versa.
- The balance of an account was computed incorrectly.
- An error was made in carrying the account balance to the trial balance.
- The trial balance was summed incorrectly.

Other than simply adding the columns incorrectly, the two most common mistakes in preparing a trial balance are:

- Recording an account as a credit when it usually carries a debit balance, or vice versa. This mistake causes the trial balance to be out of balance by an amount divisible by 2.
- Transposing two digits when transferring an amount to the trial balance (for example, entering $23,459 as $23,549). This error causes the trial balance to be out of balance by an amount divisible by 9.

So, if a trial balance is out of balance and the addition of the columns is correct, determine the amount by which the trial balance is out of balance and divide it first by 2 and then by 9. If the amount is divisible by 2, look in the trial balance for an amount that is equal to the quotient. If you find such an amount, chances are it's in the wrong column. If the amount is divisible by 9, trace each amount back to the T account balance, checking carefully for a transposition error. If neither of these techniques is successful in identifying the error, first recompute the balance of each T account. Then, if you still have not found the error, retrace each posting to the journal or the T account.

APPLY IT!

Prepare a trial balance for Dras Company from the following list of accounts (in alphabetical order) as of March 31, 2014. Compute the balance of cash.

Accounts Payable	$ 9
Accounts Receivable	5
Building	10
Cash	?
Common Stock	13
Equipment	2
Land	6
Inventory	3
Retained Earnings	8

SOLUTION

Dras Company
Trial Balance
March 31, 2014

Cash	4	
Accounts Receivable	5	
Inventory	3	
Land	6	
Building	10	
Equipment	2	
Accounts Payable		9
Common Stock		13
Retained Earnings		8
Totals	30	30

TRY IT! SE7, E9A, E10A, E11A, E12A, E9B, E10B, E11B, E12B

LO 5 Recording and Posting Transactions

Earlier in the chapter, we described how transactions are analyzed according to the rules of double entry and how a trial balance is prepared. Recall in Exhibit 5, transaction analysis and preparation of a trial balance appear at several points in the process. Two intermediate steps are recording the entry in the general journal and posting the entry to the ledger. In this section, we demonstrate how these steps are accomplished in a manual accounting system.

General Journal

STUDY NOTE: *The journal is a chronological record of transactions.*

Although transactions can be entered directly into the ledger accounts, identifying individual transactions or finding errors is difficult because the debit is recorded in one account and the credit in another. The solution is to record all transactions chronologically in a journal, which, as we noted earlier, is where transactions first enter the accounting records. Later, the debit and credit portions of each transaction are transferred to the appropriate accounts in the ledger.

Most businesses have more than one kind of journal. The simplest and most flexible kind is the **general journal**. Businesses may also have several special-purpose journals, each for recording a common transaction, such as credit sales, credit purchases, cash receipts, and cash disbursements. At this point, we cover only the general journal. Exhibit 8, which displays two of the transactions of Blue Design Studio, Inc., shows the format for recording entries in a general journal.

Exhibit 8
The General Journal

A = L + SE
+ 3,200
− 3,200

A = L + SE
+ 5,200 + 5,200

General Journal **Page 1**

Date		Description	Post. Ref.	Debit	Credit
2014					
July	3	Prepaid Rent		3,200	
		Cash			3,200
		Paid two months' rent in advance			
	5	Office Supplies		5,200	
		Accounts Payable			5,200
		Purchase of office supplies on credit			

As you can see in Exhibit 8, the entries in a general journal include the following information about each transaction:

- **Date:** The year appears on the first line of the first column, the month on the next line of the first column, and the day in the second column opposite the month. For subsequent entries on the same page for the same month and year, the month and year can be omitted.
- **Accounts:** The names of the accounts debited and credited appear in the Description column. The names of the accounts that are debited are placed next to the left margin opposite the dates; on the line below, the names of the accounts credited are indented.
- **Amounts:** The debit amounts appear in the Debit column opposite the accounts that are debited, and the credit amounts appear in the Credit column opposite the accounts credited.
- **Explanation:** An explanation of each transaction appears in the Description column below the account names. An explanation should be brief but sufficient to identify the transaction.
- **Account numbers:** The account numbers appear in the Post. Ref. (posting reference) column, if they apply.

At the time the transactions are recorded, nothing is placed in the Post. Ref. column. Later, if the company uses account numbers to identify accounts in the ledger, the account numbers are filled in. They provide a convenient cross-reference from the general journal to the ledger and indicate that the entry has been *posted* to the ledger. If the accounts are not numbered, the accountant uses a checkmark (✓) to signify that the entry has been posted.

General Ledger

STUDY NOTE: *A T account is a means of quickly analyzing a set of transactions. It is simply an abbreviated version of a ledger account. Ledger accounts, which provide more information, are used in the accounting records.*

The general journal is used to record the details of each transaction. The general ledger is used to update each account.

The Ledger Account Form The T account is a simple, direct means of recording transactions. In practice, a somewhat more complicated form of the account is needed to record more information. The **ledger account form** is a form of the account that contains four columns for dollar amounts, as is illustrated in Exhibit 9.

Exhibit 9
Accounts Payable in the General Ledger

General Ledger

Accounts Payable — **Account No. 212**

Date		Item	Post. Ref.	Debit	Credit	Balance Debit	Balance Credit
2014							
July	5		J1		5,200		5,200
	6		J1		3,000		8,200
	9		J1	2,600			5,600
	30		J2		680		6,280

The account title and number appear at the top of the account form. As in the journal, the transaction date appears in the first two columns. The Item column is rarely used to identify transactions because explanations already appear in the journal. The Post. Ref. column is used to note the journal page on which the original entry for the transaction can be found. The dollar amount is entered in the appropriate Debit or

Credit column, and a new account balance is computed in the last two columns opposite each entry. The advantage of this account form over the T account is that the current balance of the account is readily available.

Posting After transactions have been entered in the journal, they must be transferred to the ledger. This process is called **posting**. Posting is usually done after several entries have been made—for example, at the end of each day or less frequently, depending on the number of transactions. As Exhibit 10 shows, each amount in the Debit column of the journal is transferred to the Debit column of the appropriate account in the ledger, and each amount in the Credit column of the journal is transferred to the Credit column of the appropriate account in the ledger.

Exhibit 10
Posting from the General Journal to the Ledger

A	=	L	+	SE
		+ 680		− 680

General Journal — **Page 2**

Date		Description	Post. Ref.	Debit	Credit
2014					
July	30	Utilities Expense	512	680	
		Accounts Payable	212		680
		Received bill from utility company			

General Ledger

Accounts Payable — **Account No. 212**

Date		Item	Post. Ref.	Debit	Credit	Balance Debit	Balance Credit
2014							
July	5		J1		5,200		5,200
	6		J1		3,000		8,200
	9		J1	2,600			5,600
	30		J2		680		6,280

General Ledger

Utilities Expense — **Account No. 512**

Date		Item	Post. Ref.	Debit	Credit	Balance Debit	Balance Credit
2014							
July	30		J2	680		680	

The steps in the posting process follow.

- **Step 1:** In the ledger, locate the debit account named in the journal entry.
- **Step 2:** Enter the date of the transaction in the ledger and, in the Post. Ref. column, the journal page number from which the entry comes.
- **Step 3:** In the Debit column of the ledger account, enter the amount of the debit as it appears in the journal.
- **Step 4:** Calculate the account balance and enter it in the appropriate Balance column.
- **Step 5:** Enter in the Post. Ref. column of the journal the account number to which the amount has been posted.

The same five steps are repeated in posting the credit side of the journal entry. As noted earlier, in addition to serving as an easy reference between the journal entry and the ledger account, the entry in the Post. Ref. column of the journal (Step 5) indicates that the entry has been posted to the ledger.

Some Notes on Presentation

Exhibit 11 offers some guidance on how to format financial statements, trial balances, journals, and ledgers in accordance with common accounting conventions.

Exhibit 11
Formatting Guidelines

BLUE DESIGN STUDIO, INC.'S FINANCIAL HIGHLIGHTS

Cash	$22,480
Accounts receivable	4,600
Office supplies	5,200
Prepaid rent	3,200
Office equipment	16,320
Total assets	$51,800

❶ A ruled line appears in financial reports before each subtotal and total to indicate that the amounts above are added or subtracted. It is common practice to use a double line under a final total to show that it has been verified.

❷ Dollar signs ($) are required in all financial statements and other schedules. On these reports, a dollar sign should be placed before the first amount in each column and before the first amount in a column following a ruled line. Dollar signs in the same column are aligned. Dollar signs are not used in journals and ledgers.

❸ On normal unruled paper, commas and decimal points are used when recording dollar amounts. On the paper used in journals and ledgers, commas and decimal points are unnecessary because ruled columns are provided to properly align dollars and cents. Commas, dollar signs, and decimal points are also unnecessary in electronic spreadsheets. In this book, because most problems and illustrations are in whole dollar amounts, the cents column usually is omitted. When accountants deal with whole dollars, they often use a dash in the cents column to indicate whole dollars rather than taking the time to write zeros.

❹ Account names are capitalized when referenced in text or listed in work documents like the journal or ledger. In financial statements, however, only the first word of an account name is capitalized.

APPLY IT!

Prepare journal entries to record the following transactions. Use the following account numbers—Cash, 111; Supplies, 114; and Accounts Payable, 212—to show in the Post Ref. columns that the entries have been posted:

June 4 Purchased supplies for $40 on credit.
8 Paid for the supplies purchased on June 4.

SOLUTION

Date		Description	Post. Ref.	Debit	Credit
June	4	Supplies	114	40	
		Accounts Payable	212		40
		Purchased supplies on credit			
	8	Accounts Payable	212	40	
		Cash	111		40
		Paid amount due for supplies			

TRY IT! SE8, SE9, SE10, E8A, E13A, E14A, E8B, E13B, E14B

Accounting uses a double-entry system to record business transactions based on source documents. Each transaction is recorded in a journal and then posted to the ledger. The final step of the transaction analysis is the preparation of the trial balance. As depicted in Exhibit 12, business transactions can affect all components of the accounting equation.

Exhibit 12
Transaction Effects on Accounting Equation

	Assets		= Liabilities	+ Stockholders' Equity				
Transaction	Cash	+ Other Assets		Common Stock	+ Retained Earnings	− Dividends	+ Revenues	− Expenses
1. Stockholders' cash investment	+			+				
2. Prepayment of expenses in cash	−	+						
3. Purchase of an asset on credit		+	+					
4. Purchase of an asset partly on credit and partly in cash	−	+	+					
5. Payment of liability	−		−					
6. Revenue received in cash	+						+	
7. Revenue on credit		+					+	
8. Revenue collected in advance	+		+					
9. Collection on account	+	−						
10. Expense paid in cash	−							+
11. Expense to be paid later			+					+
12. Cash dividend payment	−					+		

SECTION 3 BUSINESS APPLICATIONS

SINESS APPLICATIONS
Ethics
Cash flows
Liquidity

EVANT RNING OBJECTIVES

6 Explain why ethical financial reporting ends on proper recording usiness transactions.

7 Show how the timing of transactions affects h flows and liquidity.

LO6 Ethical Financial Reporting and Business Transactions

Financial statements result from the recording of business transactions. Users of these financial statements have a right to expect that all business transactions have been recorded and reflected properly in the statements. Thus, *recognition*, *valuation*, and *classification* as specified under generally accepted accounting principles are important factors in ethical financial reporting. These guidelines help managers meet their obligation to their company's stockholders and to their creditors. Many of the most egregious financial reporting frauds result from violations of these guidelines, as the following examples show:

- **Computer Associates** violated the guidelines for recognition when it kept its books open a few days after the end of a reporting period so revenues could be counted a quarter earlier than they should have been. In all, the company prematurely reported $3.3 billion in revenues from 363 software contracts. When the SEC ordered the company to stop the practice, Computer Associates' stock price dropped by 43 percent in a single day.
- Among its many other transgressions, **Enron Corporation** violated the guidelines for valuation when it transferred, to related companies, assets at far more than their actual value.
- By a simple violation of the guidelines for classification, **WorldCom** (now **MCI**, a component of **Verizon**) perpetrated the largest financial fraud in history. Over a period of several years, the company recorded as assets its expenditures that should have been classified as expenses, understating expenses and overstating income by more than $10 billion.

Recognition

The *recognition* issue can be particularly difficult to resolve. To illustrate some of the factors involved, suppose a company wants to purchase an office desk. The following events take place:

- **Event 1:** An employee sends a purchase request for the desk to the purchasing department.
- **Event 2:** The purchasing department sends a purchase order to the supplier.
- **Event 3:** The supplier ships the desk.
- **Event 4:** The company receives the desk.
- **Event 5:** The company receives the bill from the supplier.
- **Event 6:** The company pays the bill.

A transaction should be recorded when title to merchandise passes from the supplier to the purchaser and creates an obligation to pay. A purchase should usually not be recognized (recorded) before the title is transferred because, until that point, the vendor has not fulfilled its contractual obligation and the buyer has no liability. Thus, depending on the details of the shipping agreement for the desk, the transaction should be recognized (recorded) at the time of either Event 3 or 4. We generally use this guideline in this book. However, many small businesses that have simple accounting systems do not record a transaction until they receive a bill (Event 5) or pay it (Event 6), because these are the implied points of title transfer. The predetermined time at which a transaction should be recorded is the **recognition point**.

Business Perspective
Accounting Policies: Where Do You Find Them?

The Boeing Company, as noted in the chapter opener, takes orders for planes years in advance. Although it is an important economic event to both Boeing and the buyer, neither the buyer nor the seller would record the event as a transaction. So, how do you know when companies record sales or purchase transactions? The answer to this question and others about companies' accounting policies can be found in the Summary of Significant Accounting Policies in their annual reports. For example, in that section of its annual report, Boeing states: "We recognize sales for commercial airplane deliveries as each unit is completed and accepted by the customer."[5]

Although purchase requests and purchase orders (Events 1 and 2) are economic events, they do not affect a company's financial position, and they are not recognized in the accounting records. Even the most important economic events may not be recognized in the accounting records.

Here are some more examples of economic events that should and should not be recorded as business transactions:

Events That Are *Not* Recorded as Transactions	Events That *Are* Recorded as Transactions
• A customer inquires about the availability of a product	• A customer buys a product.
• A company hires a new employee.	• A company pays an employee for work performed.
• A company signs a contract to provide a service in the future.	• A company performs a service.

Consider an advertising agency that is planning a major advertising campaign for a client. Employees may work on the plan several hours a day for a number of weeks. They add value to the plan as they develop it. Should this added value be recognized as the plan is being developed or at the time it is completed? Usually, the increase in value is recorded at the time the plan is finished and the client is billed for it. However, the agency and the client may agree that the client will be billed at key points during its development. In that case, a transaction is recorded at each billing.

APPLY IT!

For each of the following ethical situations involving business transactions, indicate what accounting concept has been violated or whether there is no violation:

1. A sales transaction is recorded on the last day of the fiscal year because the customer indicates that she will be in next week to sign the agreement.
2. A purchase of an insurance policy is recorded as an asset (instead of as an expense) because it will be used in future periods.
3. A laser printer, in excellent condition, that is purchased at a garage sale for $50 is recorded at its estimated value of $150.

SOLUTION

1. Recognition concept: violated
2. Classification concept: no violation
3. Valuation concept: violated

TRY IT! SE3, SE11, E1A, E15A, E1B, E15B

LO 7 Cash Flows and the Timing of Transactions

To avoid financial distress, a company must be able to pay its bills on time. Because the timing of cash flows is critical to maintaining adequate liquidity to pay bills, managers and other users of financial information must understand the difference between transactions that generate immediate cash and those that do not. Consider the transactions of Blue Design Studio, Inc., shown in Exhibit 13. Most of them involve either an inflow or outflow of cash.

Blue's Cash account has more transactions than any of its other accounts. Look at the transactions of July 10, 15, and 22 in Exhibit 13:

- July 10: Blue received a design revenue payment in cash of $2,800.
- July 15: The firm billed a customer $9,600 for a service it had already performed.
- July 22: The firm received a partial payment of $5,000 from the customer, but it had not received the remaining $4,600 by the end of the month.

Because Blue incurred expenses in providing this service, it must pay careful attention to its cash flows and liquidity.

One way Blue can manage its expenditures is to rely on its creditors to give it time to pay. Compare the transactions of July 3, 5, and 9 in Exhibit 13.

- July 3: Blue prepaid rent of $3,200. That immediate cash outlay may have caused a strain on the business.
- July 5: The firm received an invoice for office supplies in the amount of $5,200. In this case, it took advantage of the opportunity to defer payment.
- July 9: The firm paid $2,600, but it deferred paying the remaining $2,600 until after the end of the month.

Of course, Blue expects to receive the rest of the cash from the customer that it billed on July 15, and it must eventually pay the rest of what it owes on the office supplies. In the meantime, the firm must perform a delicate balancing act with its cash flows to ensure that it achieves the goal of liquidity so that it can grow and be profitable.

Exhibit 13
Transactions of Blue Design Studio, Inc.

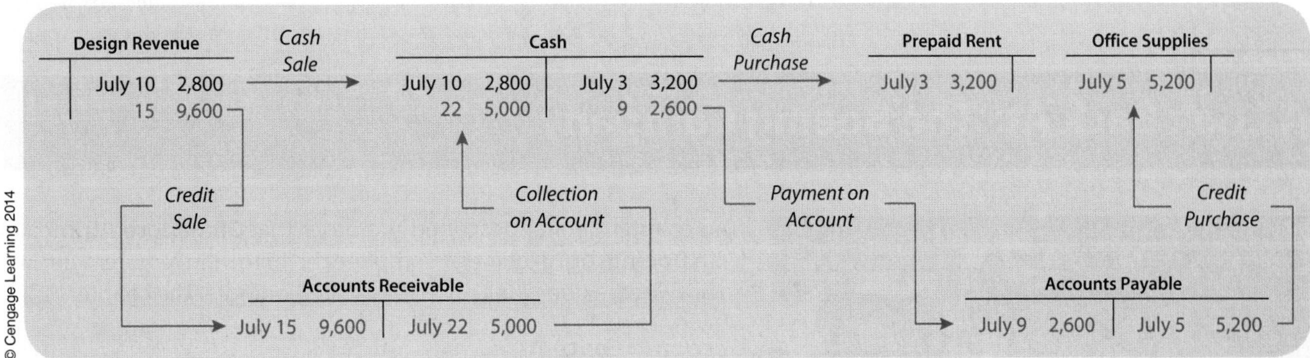

Large companies face the same challenge but often on a much greater scale. For example, it can take **Boeing** a number of years to plan and make the aircraft that customers order. At the end of 2011, Boeing had net orders of $103 billion and a backlog of orders totaling $356 billion.[6] Think of the cash outlays Boeing must make before it delivers the planes and collects payment for them. To maintain liquidity, Boeing's management must carefully plan the company's needs for cash.

APPLY IT!

A company engaged in the following transactions:

Oct. 1 Performed services for cash, $1,050.
2 Paid expenses in cash, $550.
3 Incurred expenses on credit, $750.
Oct. 4 Performed services on credit, $900.
5 Paid on account, $350.
6 Collected on account, $600.

Record these transactions using the T accounts below (remember to add the correct titles to the T accounts). Determine the cash balance after these transactions, the amount still to be received, and the amount still to be paid.

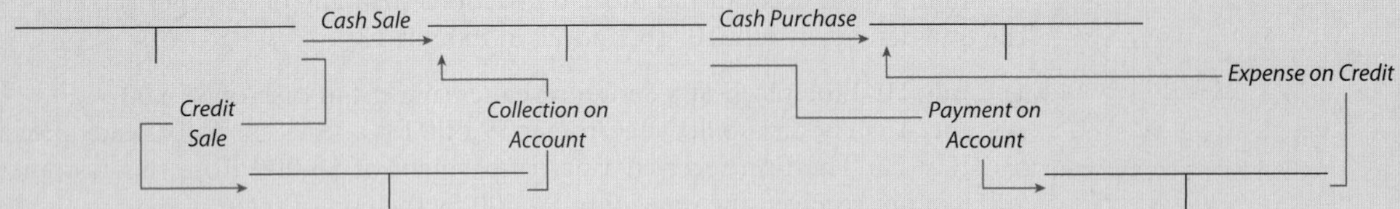

SOLUTION

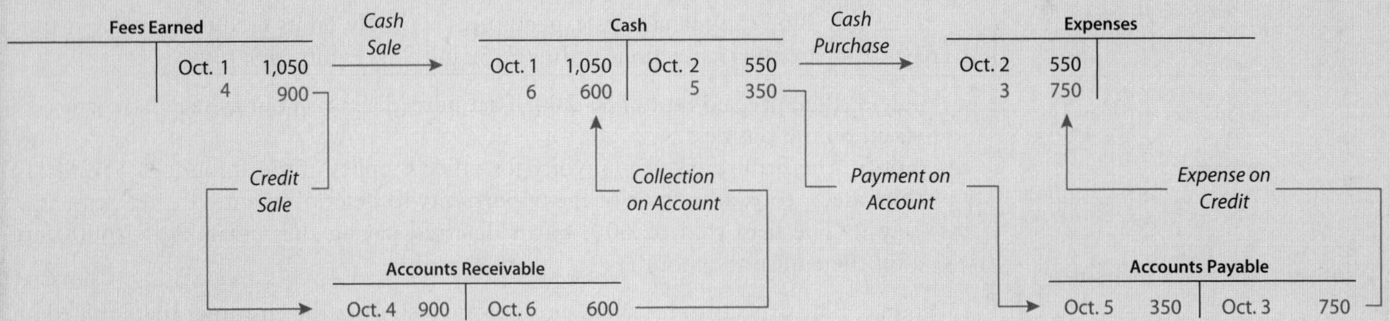

Cash balance after transactions: $1,050 + $600 – $550 – $350 = $750
Amount still to be received: $900 – $600 = $300
Amount still to be paid: $750 – $350 = $400

TRY IT! SE12, E16A, E16B

A Look Back At: The Boeing Company

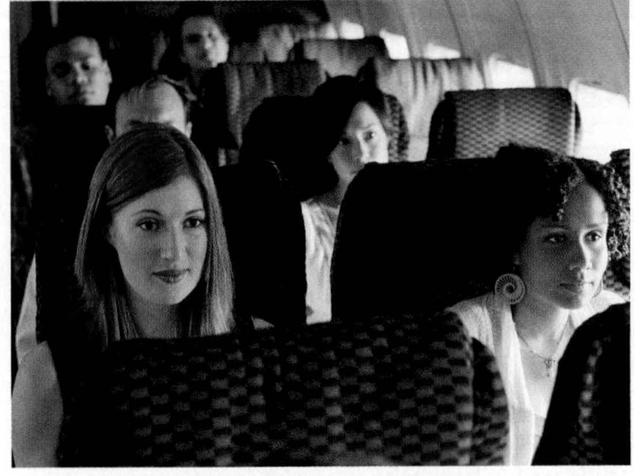
Image Source/Jupiter Images

The Boeing Company

The chapter opener described the order that **Singapore Airlines** placed with **Boeing** for 25 jetliners. Complete the following requirements in order to answer the questions posed at the beginning of the chapter.

Section 1: Concepts
How will the concepts of recognition, valuation, and classification help Boeing to record the transaction properly?

Section 2: Accounting Applications
Should Boeing record the order in its accounting records?

Section 3: Business Applications
How important are liquidity and cash flows to Boeing?

SOLUTION

Section 1: Concepts
Recognition helps decide when the transaction should be recorded, *valuation* refers to the value that is assigned to the transaction, and *classification* shows how to categorize the transaction (as an asset, expense, revenue, etc.).

Section 2: Accounting Applications
Despite its importance, the order did not constitute a business transaction, and neither the buyer nor the seller should have recognized it in its accounting records. At the time Singapore Airlines placed the order, Boeing had not yet built the planes. Until it delivers them and title to them shifts to United, Boeing cannot record any revenue.

Section 3: Business Applications
Because it takes almost two years to manufacture an airplane, Boeing must pay close attention to its liquidity and cash flows. It may incur costs for long periods without receiving any cash inflow. Even for "firm" orders like this one, Boeing cautions that "[c]hanges in the economic environment and the financial condition of the airline industry and our customers could result in customer requests to reschedule or cancel contractual orders."[7] In fact, in the period following the 9/11 attacks on the World Trade Center and the recent financial crisis, many airlines canceled or renegotiated orders they had placed with Boeing. The ongoing energy crisis is also causing airlines to rethink their orders. As a result, Boeing must plan carefully to provide sufficient liquidity to provide cash flows for its operations until the airplanes are built and delivered.

Review Problem

Paws and Hoofs Clinic, Inc., needs to record its business transactions in the accounting records. The company was engaged in the following economic events during May 2014:

May	1	Stockholders invested $20,000 in cash to form Paws and Hoofs Clinic, Inc.
	2	Made an agreement to provide $6,000 in services over the next year to Quarter Horse Stables.
	3	Paid $600 in advance for two months' rent of an office.
	9	Purchased medical supplies for $400 in cash.
	12	Purchased $4,000 of equipment on credit; made a 25 percent down payment.
	15	Provided veterinary services for a fee of $350 on credit.
	18	Made a payment of $500 on the equipment purchased on May 12.
	27	Paid a utility bill of $140.

1. Identify the company's business transactions, and prepare journal entries to record them.
2. Post the transactions to the following T accounts: Cash, Accounts Receivable, Medical Supplies, Prepaid Rent, Equipment, Accounts Payable, Common Stock; Veterinary Fees Earned, and Utilities Expense.
3. Prepare a trial balance for the month of May.
4. How does the transaction of May 15 relate to recognition and cash flows? How do the transactions of May 9 and May 27 relate to classification?

SOLUTION

1.

	A	B	C	D	E
1	May	1	Cash	20,000	
2			Common Stock		20,000
3			Issued $20,000 in stock		
4			to form Paws and Hoofs Clinic		
5		3	Prepaid Rent	600	
6			Cash		600
7			Paid two months' rent in advance		
8			for an office		
9		9	Medical Supplies	400	
10			Cash		400
11			Purchased medical supplies for cash		
12		12	Equipment	4,000	
13			Accounts Payable		3,000
14			Cash		1,000
15			Purchased equipment on credit,		
16			paying 25 percent down		
17		15	Accounts Receivable	350	
18			Veterinary Fees Earned		350
19			Fee on credit for veterinary services provided		
20		18	Accounts Payable	500	
21			Cash		500
22			Partial payment for equipment		
23			purchased May 12		
24		27	Utilities Expense	140	
25			Cash		140
26			Paid utility bill		
27					

Note: With regards to Paws and Hoofs' agreement to provide $6,000 in services over the next year to Quarter Horse Stables, making an agreement to provide services is an important economic event, but it is not recorded because it does not meet the recognition concept. No services have yet been performed and earned, thus Paws and Hoofs is not yet entitled to payment.

2.

	A	B	C	D	E	F	G	H	I	J	K	L	M
1	**Cash**							**Accounts Payable**					
2	May	1	20,000	May	3	600		May	18	500	May	12	3,000
3					9	400					*Bal.*		*2,500*
4					12	1,000							
5					18	500		**Common Stock**					
6					27	140					May	1	20,000
7			20,000			2,640							
8	*Bal.*		*17,360*					**Veterinary Fees Earned**					
9											May	15	350
10	**Accounts Receivable**												
11	May	15	350					**Utilities Expense**					
12								May	27	140			
13	**Medical Supplies**												
14	May	9	400										
15													
16	**Prepaid Rent**												
17	May	3	600										
18													
19	**Equipment**												
20	May	12	4,000										
21													

3.

	A	B	C
1	**Paws and Hoofs Clinic, Inc.**		
2	**Trial Balance**		
3	**May 31, 2014**		
4			
5	Cash	17,360	
6	Accounts Receivable	350	
7	Medical Supplies	400	
8	Prepaid Rent	600	
9	Equipment	4,000	
10	Accounts Payable		2,500
11	Common Stock		20,000
12	Veterinary Fees Earned		350
13	Utilities Expense	140	
14		22,850	22,850
15			

4. A business transaction can benefit a business even though no cash is received at the time of the transaction. For example, on May 15, Paws and Hoofs provided a service and thus a revenue is earned and recognized. Although both are recorded by debits, the supplies in the transaction of May 9 are classified as an asset because the supplies will be used and will benefit the future, whereas the utilities in the transaction of May 27 are classified as expenses because they benefit the current period.

Chapter Review

Explain how the concepts of recognition, valuation, and classification apply to business transactions. LO1

To measure a business transaction, you must determine when the transaction occurred (recognition), what value to place on the transaction (valuation), and how the components of the transaction should be categorized (classification). In general, recognition occurs when title passes, and a transaction is valued at the exchange price—the fair value or cost at the time the transaction is recognized. Classification refers to assigning transactions to the appropriate accounts.

Explain the double-entry system and the usefulness of T accounts in analyzing business transactions. LO2

In the double-entry system, each transaction must be recorded with at least one debit and one credit, and the total amount of the debits must equal the total amount of the credits. Each asset, liability, and component of stockholders' equity, including revenues and expenses, has a separate account, which is a device for storing transaction data. The chart of accounts is a list of account numbers and titles. It serves as a table of contents for the ledger. The T account is a useful tool for quickly analyzing the effects of transactions. It shows how increases and decreases in assets, liabilities, and stockholders' equity are recorded. The accounting cycle is a series of steps whose basic purpose is to produce financial statements for decision makers.

Demonstrate how the double-entry system is applied to common business transactions. LO3

The double-entry system is applied by analyzing transactions to determine which accounts are affected and by using T accounts to show how the transactions affect the accounting equation. The transactions may be recorded in journal form with the date, debit account, and debit amount shown on one line, and the credit account (indented) and credit amount on the next line. The amounts are shown in their respective debit and credit columns.

Prepare a trial balance, and describe its value and limitations. LO4

A trial balance is used to check that the debit and credit balances are equal. It is prepared by listing each account balance in the appropriate Debit or Credit column. The two columns are then added, and the totals are compared. The major limitation of a trial balance is that it does not guarantee that the transactions were analyzed correctly or recorded in the proper accounts.

Record transactions in the general journal, and post transactions to the ledger. LO5

The general journal is a chronological record of all transactions. It contains the date of each transaction, the titles of the accounts involved, the amounts debited and credited, and an explanation of each entry. After transactions have been entered in the general journal, they are posted to the ledger. Posting transfers the amounts in the Debit and Credit columns of the general journal to the Debit and Credit columns of the corresponding account in the ledger. After each entry is posted, a new balance is entered in the appropriate Balance column.

Explain why ethical financial reporting depends on proper recording of business transactions. LO6

GAAP provides guidance about the treatment of business transactions in terms of recognition, valuation, and classification. Failure to follow these guidelines is a major reason some companies issue fraudulent financial statements. Usually, a transaction should be recorded when title to merchandise passes from the supplier to the purchaser and creates an obligation to pay.

Show how the timing of transactions affects cash flows and liquidity. LO7

Some transactions generate immediate cash. For those that do not, there is a holding period in either Accounts Receivable or Accounts Payable before the cash is received or paid. The timing of cash flows is critical to a company's ability to maintain adequate liquidity so that it can pay its bills on time.

Key Terms

account balance 92 (LO2)
accounting cycle 94 (LO2)
accounts 90 (LO2)
business transactions 88 (LO1)
chart of accounts 90 (LO2)
classification 89 (LO1)
compound entry 98 (LO3)
cost principle 89 (LO1)
credit 92 (LO2)
debit 92 (LO2)
double-entry system 90 (LO2)
fair value 89 (LO1)
footings 92 (LO2)
general journal 106 (LO5)
general ledger 90 (LO2)
journal 96 (LO3)
journal entry 96 (LO3)
journal form 96 (LO3)
ledger account form 107 (LO5)
normal balance 93 (LO2)
posting 108 (LO5)
recognition 88 (LO1)
recognition point 111 (LO6)
source documents 96 (LO3)
T account 92 (LO2)
trial balance 104 (LO4)
valuation 89 (LO1)

Chapter Assignments

DISCUSSION QUESTIONS

LO 1 **DQ1.** A company incurs a cost for a part that is needed to repair a piece of equipment. Is the cost an asset or an expense? Explain.

LO 1, 6 **DQ2. CONCEPT ▶** Which is the most important issue in recording a transaction: recognition, valuation, or classification?

LO 2 **DQ3.** Which account would be most likely to have an account balance that is not normal?

LO 2 **DQ4.** How would the asset accounts in the chart of accounts for Blue Design Studio, Inc., differ if it were a retail company that sold promotional products instead of a service company?

LO 2, 3 **DQ5.** How are assets and expenses related, and why are the debit and credit effects for asset accounts and expense accounts the same?

LO 2, 3 **DQ6.** In what way are unearned revenues the opposite of prepaid expenses?

LO 6 **DQ7. CONCEPT ▶** What is an example of how a company could make false financial statements through a violation of the recognition concept?

LO 7 **DQ8. BUSINESS APPLICATION ▶** If a company's cash flows for expenses temporarily exceed its cash flows from revenues, how might it make up the difference so that it can maintain liquidity?

SHORT EXERCISES

LO 1, 2 **Classification of Accounts**

SE1. Tell whether each of the following accounts is an asset, a liability, a revenue, an expense, or none of these:

a. Accounts Payable
b. Supplies
c. Dividends
d. Fees Earned
e. Supplies Expense
f. Accounts Receivable
g. Unearned Revenue
h. Equipment

LO 1, 3

Recognition, Valuation, and Classification

SE2. CONCEPT ▶ Tell how the concepts of recognition, valuation, and classification apply to the transaction that follows.

Cash

Dr.		*Cr.*	
		June 1	1,000

Supplies

Dr.		*Cr.*	
June 1	1,000		

LO 1, 6

Recognition

SE3. CONCEPT ▶ Which of the following events would be recognized and entered in Hamak Corporation's accounting records? Why?

Jan. 10 Hamak places an order for office supplies.
Feb. 15 Hamak receives the office supplies and a bill for them.
Mar. 1 Hamak pays for the office supplies.

LO 2

Normal Balances

SE4. Tell whether the normal balance of each account in **SE1** is a debit or a credit.

LO 3

Transaction Analysis

SE5. Shawn Michael started a computer programming business, Michael's Programming Service, Inc. For each transaction that follows, indicate which account is debited and which account is credited.

May 2 Shawn Michael invested $10,000 in exchange for common stock.
5 Purchased a computer for $5,000 in cash.
7 Purchased supplies on credit for $600.
19 Received cash for programming services performed, $1,000.
22 Received cash for programming services to be performed, $1,200.
25 Paid the rent for May, $1,300.
31 Billed a customer for programming services performed, $500.

LO 3

Recording Transactions in T Accounts

SE6. Set up T accounts and record each transaction in **SE5**. Determine the balance of each account.

LO 4

Preparing a Trial Balance

SE7. From the T accounts created in **SE6**, prepare a trial balance dated May 31, 2014.

LO 5

Recording Transactions in the General Journal

SE8. Prepare a general journal form like the one in Exhibit 8, and label it Page 4. Record the following transactions in the journal:

Sept. 6 Billed a customer for services performed, $3,800.
16 Received partial payment from the customer billed on September 6, $1,800.

LO 5

Posting to the Ledger Accounts

SE9. Prepare three ledger account forms like the one in Exhibit 9 for the following accounts: Cash (111), Accounts Receivable (113), and Service Revenue (411). Post the transactions that are recorded in **SE8** to the ledger accounts for 2014, at the same time making the proper posting references.

LO 5

Recording Transactions in the General Journal

SE10. Record the transactions in **SE5** in the general journal for 2014.

LO 6

Identifying Ethical Transactions

SE11. CONCEPT ▶ For each of the following ethical situations involving business transactions, indicate what accounting concept has been violated or whether there is no violation:

1. A sales transaction is recorded on the first day of the fiscal year when payment was received even though the service for the customer was completed in the year before.
2. A laser printer in excellent condition purchased at a garage sale has an estimated value of $150, but is recorded at the $50 paid for it.
3. A purchase of truck fuel is recorded as an expense (instead of as an asset) because it will be used in the current period.

LO 7

Timing and Cash Flows

SE12. BUSINESS APPLICATION ▶ Use the T account for Cash below to record the portion of each of the following transactions, if any, that affect cash. How do these transactions affect the company's liquidity?

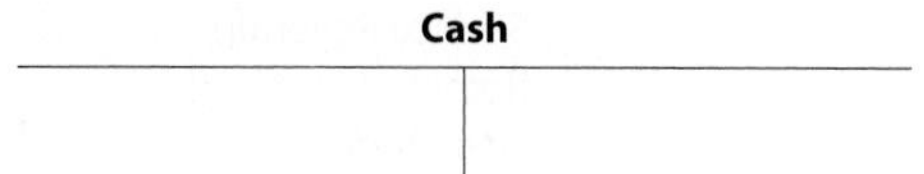

Jan.	2	Provided services for cash, $2,400.
	4	Paid expenses in cash, $1,400.
	8	Provided services on credit, $2,200.
	9	Incurred expenses on credit, $1,600.

EXERCISES: SET A

LO 1, 6

Recognition

E1A. CONCEPT ▶ Which of the following events would be recognized and recorded in Abril Corporation's accounting records on the date indicated?

Jan.	15	Abril offers to purchase a tract of land for $280,000. There is a high likelihood that the offer will be accepted.
Feb.	2	Abril receives notice that its rent will increase from $1,000 to $1,200 per month effective March 1.
Mar.	29	Abril receives its utility bill for the month of March. The bill is not due until April 9.
June	10	Abril places an order for new office equipment costing $42,000.
July	6	The office equipment Abril ordered on June 10 arrives. Payment is not due until August 1.

LO 1, 2

Classification of Accounts

E2A. CONCEPT ▶ The following ledger accounts are for Afocentric Service Corporation:

a. Supplies
b. Utilities Expense
c. Accounts Receivable
d. Common Stock
e. Land
f. Prepaid Rent
g. Accounts Payable
h. Investments in Securities
i. Service Revenue
j. Supplies Expense
k. Prepaid Insurance
l. Wages Expense
m. Fees Earned
n. Dividends
o. Wages Payable
p. Unearned Revenue
q. Office Equipment
r. Rent Payable
s. Notes Receivable
t. Interest Expense
u. Notes Payable
v. Cash
w. Interest Receivable
x. Rent Expense
y. Income Taxes Payable
z. Income Taxes Expense

(Continued)

Complete the following table, using X's to indicate each account's classification and normal balance (whether a debit or a credit increases the account).

	Type of Account						Normal Balance (increases balance)	
			Stockholders' Equity					
				Retained Earnings				
Item	**Asset**	**Liability**	**Common Stock**	**Dividends**	**Revenue**	**Expense**	**Debit**	**Credit**
a.	X						X	

LO 2

T Accounts, Normal Balance, and the Accounting Equation

E3A. You are given the following list of accounts with dollar amounts

Rent Expense	$ 900
Cash	3,450
Service Revenue	1,500
Retained Earnings	600
Dividends	750
Accounts Payable	1,200
Common Stock	1,800

Insert each account name at the top of its corresponding T account and enter the dollar amount as a normal balance in the account. Then show that the accounting equation is in balance.

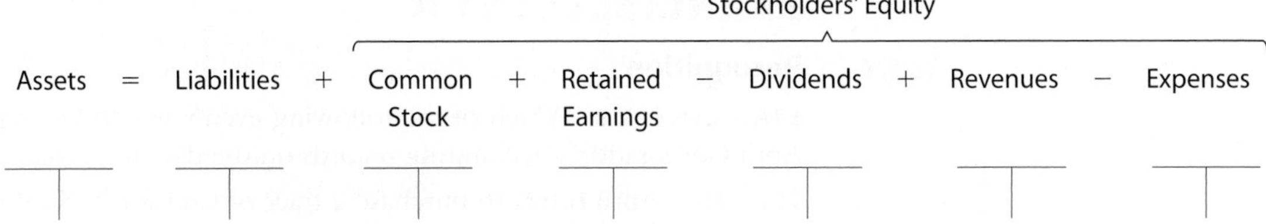

LO 3

Transaction Analysis

E4A. Analyze transactions **a–g**, using the example that follows.

a. Melissa Faubert established Faubert's Beauty Parlor, Inc., by incorporating and investing $2,400 in exchange for 240 shares of $10 par value common stock.
b. Paid two months' rent in advance, $1,680.
c. Purchased supplies on credit, $120.
d. Received cash for salon services, $600.
e. Paid for supplies purchased in **c**.
f. Paid utility bill, $72.
g. Declared and paid a dividend of $90.

Example

a. The asset account Cash was increased. Increases in assets are recorded by debits. Debit Cash $2,400. A component of stockholders' equity, Common Stock, was increased. Increases in Common Stock are recorded by credits. Credit Common Stock $2,400.

LO 3

Transaction Analysis

E5A. The accounts that follow are applicable to Harold's Car Service, Inc., a company that repairs cars.

1. Cash	5. Accounts Payable
2. Accounts Receivable	6. Repair Services Revenue
3. Supplies	7. Wages Expense
4. Equipment	8. Rent Expense

Harold's completed the following transactions:

	Debit	Credit
a. Paid for supplies purchased on credit last month.	5	1
b. Received cash from customers billed last month.	____	____
c. Made a payment on accounts payable.	____	____
d. Purchased supplies on credit.	____	____
e. Billed a client for repair services.	____	____
f. Made a rent payment for the current month.	____	____
g. Received cash from customers for repair services not yet billed.	____	____
h. Paid employee wages.	____	____
i. Ordered equipment.	____	____
j. Received and paid for the equipment ordered in **i**.	____	____

Analyze each transaction and show the accounts affected by entering the corresponding numbers in the appropriate debit or credit columns as shown in transaction **a.** Indicate no entry, if appropriate.

LO 3

Recording Transactions in T Accounts

E6A. Open the following T accounts: Cash; Repair Supplies; Repair Equipment; Accounts Payable; Common Stock; Dividends; Repair Fees Earned; Salaries Expense; and Rent Expense. Record the following transactions for the month of June directly in the T accounts; use the letters to identify the transactions in your T accounts. Determine the balance in each account.

a. Collin Ferdinand opened Ferdinand Repair Service, Inc., by investing $8,600 in cash and $3,200 in repair equipment in return for 11,800 shares of the company's $1 par value common stock.
b. Paid $800 for the current month's rent.
c. Purchased repair supplies on credit, $1,000.
d. Purchased additional repair equipment for cash, $600.
e. Paid salary to an employee, $900.
f. Paid $400 of amount purchased on credit in **c**.
g. Accepted cash for repairs completed, $3,720.
h. Declared and paid a dividend of $600.

LO 3

Analysis of Transactions

E7A. Explain each transaction (**a–h**) entered in the following T accounts:

Cash

	Debit		Credit
a.	10,000	b.	3,750
g.	375	e.	900
h.	225	f.	1,125

Accounts Receivable

	Debit		Credit
c.	2,000	g.	375

Equipment

	Debit		Credit
b.	3,750	h.	225
d.	2,250		

Accounts Payable

	Debit		Credit
f.	1,125	d.	2,250

Common Stock

	Debit		Credit
		a.	10,000

Service Revenue

	Debit		Credit
		c.	2,000

Wages Expense

	Debit		Credit
e.	900		

LO 3, 5

Analysis of Unfamiliar Transactions

E8A. Managers and accountants often encounter transactions with which they are unfamiliar. Use your analytical skills to analyze and prepare journal entries for the following transactions, which have not yet been discussed in the text.

May 1 Purchased merchandise inventory on account, $1,200.
2 Purchased marketable securities for cash, $2,800.
3 Returned part of merchandise inventory purchased for full credit, $250.
4 Sold merchandise inventory on account, $800 (record sale only).
5 Purchased land and a building for $300,000. Payment is $60,000 cash, and there is a 30-year mortgage for the remainder. The purchase price is allocated as follows: $100,000 to the land and $200,000 to the building.
6 Received an order for $12,000 in services to be provided. With the order was a deposit of $4,000.

LO 4

Trial Balance

E9A. After recording the transactions in **E6A**, prepare a trial balance in proper sequence for Ferdinand Repair Service, Inc., as of June 30, 2014.

LO 4

Preparing a Trial Balance

E10A. The list that follows presents Shah Corporation's accounts (in alphabetical order) as of March 31, 2014. The list does not include the amount of Accounts Payable.

Accounts Payable	?	Equipment	$ 7,200
Accounts Receivable	$ 1,800	Land	3,120
Building	20,400	Notes Payable	10,000
Cash	5,400	Prepaid Insurance	660
Common Stock	12,000	Retained Earnings	6,870

Prepare a trial balance with the proper heading (see Exhibit 7) and with the accounts listed in the chart of accounts sequence (see Exhibit 2). Compute the balance of Accounts Payable.

LO 4

Effects of Errors on a Trial Balance

E11A. ACCOUNTING CONNECTION ▶ Which of the following errors would cause a trial balance to have unequal totals? Explain your answers.

a. A payment to a creditor was recorded as a debit to Accounts Payable for $258 and as a credit to Cash for $204.
b. A payment of $300 to a creditor for an account payable was debited to Accounts Receivable and credited to Cash.
c. A purchase of office supplies of $840 was recorded as a debit to Office Supplies for $84 and as a credit to Cash for $84.
d. A purchase of equipment for $900 was recorded as a debit to Supplies for $900 and as a credit to Cash for $900.

LO 4

Correcting Errors in a Trial Balance

E12A. Hasson Services, Inc.'s trial balance at the end of July 2014 follows. It does not balance because of a number of errors. Hasson's accountant compared the amounts in the trial balance with the ledger, recomputed the account balances, and compared the postings. He found the following errors:

a. The balance of Cash was understated by $400.
b. A cash payment of $210 was credited to Cash for $120.
c. A debit of $60 to Accounts Receivable was not posted.
d. Supplies purchased for $30 were posted as a credit to Supplies.
e. A debit of $90 to Prepaid Insurance was not posted.
f. The Accounts Payable account had debits of $2,660 and credits of $4,590.
g. The Notes Payable account, with a credit balance of $1,200, was not included on the trial balance.
h. The debit balance of Dividends was listed in the trial balance as a credit.

i A $100 debit to Dividends was posted as a credit.
j. The actual balance of Utilities Expense, $130, was listed as $13 in the trial balance.

Hasson Services, Inc.
Trial Balance
July 31, 2014

	Debits	Credits
Cash	1,720	
Accounts Receivable	2,830	
Supplies	60	
Prepaid Insurance	90	
Equipment	3,700	
Accounts Payable		2,270
Common Stock		1,500
Retained Earnings		3,780
Dividends		350
Revenues		2,960
Salaries Expense	1,300	
Rent Expense	300	
Advertising Expense	170	
Utilities Expense	13	
	10,183	10,860

Prepare a corrected trial balance.

LO 5 **Recording Transactions in the General Journal**

E13A. Record the transactions in **E6A** in the general journal.

LO 5 **Recording Transactions in the General Journal and Posting to the Ledger Accounts**

E14A. Open a general journal form like the one in Exhibit 8, and label it Page 10. Then record the following transactions in the journal:

Dec. 14 Purchased equipment for $12,000, paying $4,000 as a cash down payment.
28 Paid $6,000 of the amount owed on the equipment.

Prepare three ledger account forms like the one shown in Exhibit 9. Use the following account numbers: Cash, 111; Office Equipment, 146; and Accounts Payable, 212. Then post the two transactions from the general journal to the ledger accounts, being sure to make proper posting references. Assume that the Cash account has a debit balance of $16,000 on the day prior to the first transaction.

LO 6 **Application of Recognition Point**

E15A. BUSINESS APPLICATION ▶ Affordable Flower Shop, Inc., uses a large amount of supplies in its business. The following table summarizes selected transaction data for supplies that Affordable purchased:

Order	Date Shipped	Date Received	Amount
A	June 26	July 5	$ 600
B	July 10	July 15	1,500
C	July 16	July 22	800
D	July 23	July 30	1,200
E	July 27	Aug. 1	1,500
F	Aug. 3	Aug. 7	1,000

Determine the total purchases of supplies for July alone under each of the following assumptions:

1. Affordable recognizes purchases when orders are shipped.
2. Affordable recognizes purchases when orders are received.

LO 7

Cash Flow Analysis

E16A. BUSINESS APPLICATION ▶ A company engaged in the following transactions:

Dec.	1	Performed services for cash, $1,500.
	1	Paid expenses in cash, $1,100.
	2	Performed services on credit, $1,800.
	3	Collected on account, $1,200.
	4	Incurred expenses on credit, $1,300.
	5	Paid on account, $700.

Enter the correct titles on the following T accounts and enter the above transactions in the accounts. Determine the cash balance after these transactions, the amount still to be received, and the amount still to be paid.

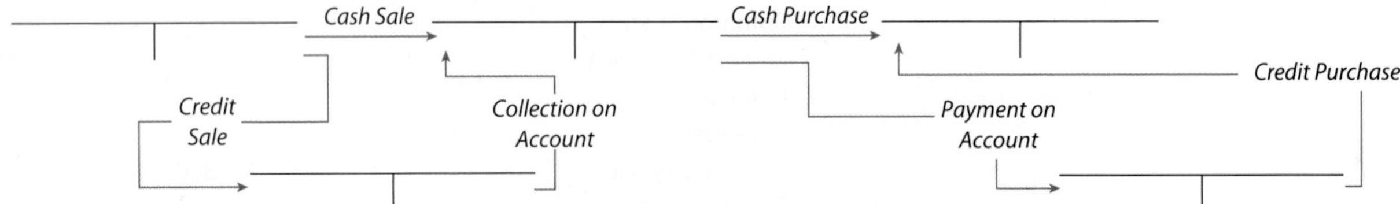

EXERCISES: SET B

Visit the textbook companion website at www.cengagebrain.com to access Exercise Set B for this chapter.

PROBLEMS

LO 2

T Accounts, Normal Balance, and the Accounting Equation

✔ Total Assets: $145,580

P1. Highland Design Corporation creates radio and television advertising for local businesses in the twin cities. The following alphabetical list shows Highland Design's account balances as of January 31, 2014:

Accounts Payable	$ 6,420	Equipment	?
Accounts Receivable	78,000	Loans Payable	$ 10,000
Cash	18,400	Rent Expense	11,880
Common Stock	30,000	Retained Earnings	44,000
Design Revenue	210,000	Telephone Expense	960
Dividends	36,000	Unearned Revenue	18,000
		Wages Expense	124,000

REQUIRED

Insert the account title at the top of its corresponding T account and enter the dollar amount as a normal balance in the account. Determine the balance of Equipment and then show that the accounting equation is in balance.

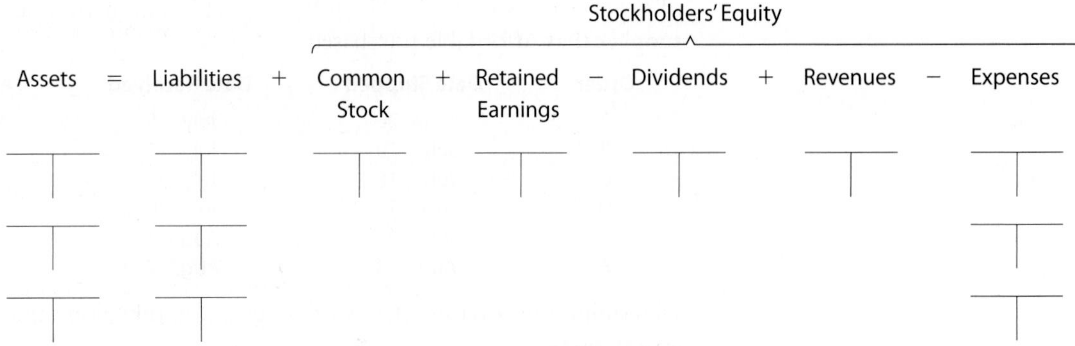

LO 3

Transaction Analysis

P2. The following accounts are applicable to George's Warehouse Sweeps, Inc.:

1. Cash
2. Accounts Receivable
3. Supplies
4. Prepaid Insurance
5. Equipment
6. Notes Payable
7. Accounts Payable
8. Common Stock
9. Retained Earnings
10. Dividends
11. Service Revenue
12. Rent Expense
13. Repair Expense

George's Warehouse Sweeps, Inc., completed the following transactions:

	Debit	Credit
a. Paid for supplies purchased on credit last month.	7	1
b. Received a bill for repairs.	___	___
c. Paid the current month's rent.	___	___
d. Purchased supplies on credit.	___	___
e. Received cash from customers for services performed but not yet billed.	___	___
f. Purchased equipment on account.	___	___
g. Billed customers for services performed.	___	___
h. Returned part of the equipment purchased in **f** for a credit.	___	___
i. Received payments from customers previously billed.	___	___
j. Paid the bill received in **b**.	___	___
k. Received an order for services to be performed.	___	___
l. Paid for repairs with cash.	___	___
m. Made a payment to reduce the principal of the note payable.	___	___
n. Declared and paid a dividend.	___	___

REQUIRED

Analyze each transaction and show the accounts affected by entering the corresponding numbers in the appropriate debit or credit column as shown in transaction **a.** Indicate no entry, if appropriate.

LO 3, 4, 7

SPREADSHEET

✔ Trial balance: $16,200

Transaction Analysis, T Accounts, and Trial Balance

P3. Jennifer Polk opened a school for administrative skills called Polk Office Training, Inc., and completed the following transactions:

a. Contributed the following assets to the business in exchange for 13,600 shares of $1 par value common stock:

Cash	$5,700
Computers	4,300
Office Equipment	3,600

b. Found a location for her business and paid the first month's rent, $260.
c. Paid for an advertisement announcing the opening of the school, $190.
d. Received applications from three students for a four-week secretarial program and two students for a ten-day keyboarding course. The students will be billed a total of $1,300.
e. Purchased supplies on credit, $330.
f. Billed the enrolled students, $1,740.
g. Purchased a second-hand computer, $480, and office equipment, $380, on credit.
h. Paid for the supplies purchased on credit in **e**, $330.
i. Paid cash to repair a broken computer, $40.
j. Received partial payment from students previously billed, $1,080.
k. Paid the utility bill for the current month, $90.
l. Paid an assistant one week's salary, $440.
m. Declared and paid a dividend of $200.

(Continued)

REQUIRED

1. Set up the following T accounts: Cash; Accounts Receivable; Supplies; Computers; Office Equipment; Accounts Payable; Common Stock; Dividends; Tuition Revenue; Salaries Expense; Utilities Expense; Rent Expense; Repair Expense; and Advertising Expense.
2. Record the transactions directly in the T accounts, using the transaction letter to identify each debit and credit.
3. Prepare a trial balance using today's date.
4. **BUSINESS APPLICATION ▶** Examine transactions **f** and **j**. What were the revenues, and how much cash was received from the revenues? What business issues might you see arising from the differences in these numbers?

LO **1, 3, 4**

✔ Trial balance: $21,080

Transaction Analysis, Journal Form, T Accounts, and Trial Balance

P4. Sid Patel bid for and won a concession to rent bicycles in the local park during the summer. During the month of April, Patel completed the following transactions for his bicycle rental business:

Apr.	2	Began business by placing $14,400 in a business checking account in the name of the corporation in exchange for 14,400 shares of $1 par value common stock.
	3	Purchased supplies on account for $300.
	4	Purchased 10 bicycles for $5,000, paying $2,400 down and agreeing to pay the rest in 30 days.
	5	Paid $5,800 in cash for a small shed to store the bicycles and to use for other operations.
	8	Paid $800 in cash for shipping and installation costs (considered an addition to the cost of the shed) to place the shed at the park entrance.
	9	Hired a part-time assistant to help out on weekends at $14 per hour.
	10	Paid a maintenance person $150 to clean the grounds.
	13	Received $1,940 in cash for rentals.
	17	Paid $300 for the supplies purchased on April 3.
	18	Paid a $110 repair bill on bicycles.
	23	Billed a company $220 for bicycle rentals for an employee outing.
	25	Paid the $200 fee for April to the Park District for the right to operate the bicycle concession.
	27	Received $1,920 in cash for rentals.
	29	Paid the assistant $480.
	30	Declared and paid a dividend of $400.

REQUIRED

1. Prepare journal entries to record these transactions.
2. Set up the following T accounts and post all the journal entries: Cash; Accounts Receivable; Supplies; Shed; Bicycles; Accounts Payable; Common Stock; Dividends; Rental Revenue; Wages Expense; Maintenance Expense; Repair Expense; and Concession Fee Expense.
3. Prepare a trial balance for Patel Rentals, Inc., as of April 30, 2014.
4. **CONCEPT ▶** Compare and contrast how the issues of recognition, valuation, and classification are settled in the transactions of April 3 and 10.

LO **3, 4, 5, 7**

CASH FLOW

SPREADSHEET

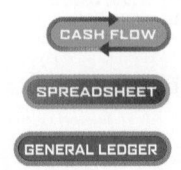

GENERAL LEDGER

✔ Trial balance: $30,900

Transaction Analysis, General Journal, Ledger Accounts, and Trial Balance

P5. Nordtown Corporation is a marketing firm. The corporation's trial balance on August 31, 2014, follows.

Nordtown Corporation
Trial Balance
August 31, 2014

Cash (111)	10,590	
Accounts Receivable (113)	5,500	
Office Supplies (116)	610	
Office Equipment (146)	4,200	
Accounts Payable (212)		2,600
Common Stock (311)		12,000
Retained Earnings (312)		6,300
	20,900	20,900

During the month of September, the company completed the following transactions:

Sept. 2 Paid rent for September, $650.
3 Received cash from customers on account, $2,300.
7 Ordered supplies, $380.
10 Billed customers for services provided, $2,800.
12 Made a payment on accounts payable, $1,300.
14 Received the supplies ordered on September 7 and agreed to pay for them in 30 days, $380.
17 Discovered some of the supplies were not as ordered and returned them for full credit, $80.
19 Received cash from a customer for services provided, $4,800.
24 Paid the utility bill for September, $250.
26 Received a bill, to be paid in October, for advertisements placed in the local newspaper during the month of September to promote Nordtown Company, $700.
29 Billed a customer for services provided, $2,700.
30 Paid salaries for September, $3,800.
30 Declared and paid a dividend of $800.

REQUIRED

1. Open accounts in the ledger for the accounts in the trial balance plus the following accounts: Dividends (313); Marketing Fees (411); Salaries Expense (511); Utilities Expense (512); Rent Expense (514); and Advertising Expense (516).
2. Enter the August 31, 2014, account balances from the trial balance.
3. Enter the September transactions in the general journal (page 22).
4. Post the journal entries to the ledger accounts. Be sure to make the appropriate posting references in the journal and ledger as you post.
5. Prepare a trial balance as of September 30, 2014.
6. **BUSINESS APPLICATION ▶** Examine the transactions for September 3, 10, 19, and 29. What were the revenues, and how much cash was received from the revenues? What business issues might you see arising from the differences in these numbers?

ALTERNATE PROBLEMS

LO 2

T Accounts, Normal Balance, and the Accounting Equation

✔ Total assets: $57,880

P6. Carlson Construction Corporation builds foundations for buildings and parking lots. The following alphabetical list shows Carlson's account balances as of April 30, 2014:

(Continued)

Accounts Payable	$ 3,900	Retained Earnings	$10,000
Accounts Receivable	10,120	Revenue Earned	17,400
Cash	?	Supplies	6,500
Common Stock	30,000	Supplies Expense	7,200
Dividends	7,000	Utilities Expense	420
Equipment	27,500	Wages Expense	8,800
Notes Payable	20,000		

REQUIRED

Insert the account at the top of its corresponding T account, and enter the dollar amount as a normal balance in the account. Determine the balance of cash and then show that the accounting equation is in balance.

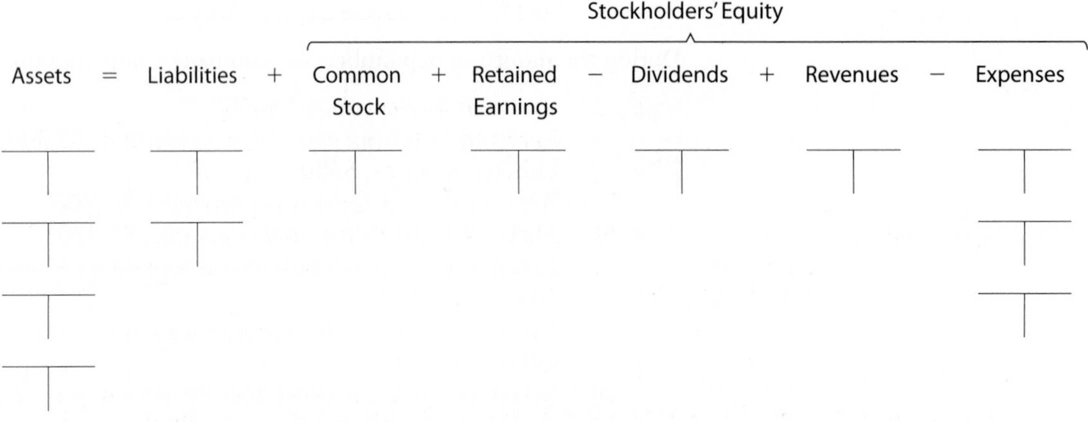

LO 3 **Transaction Analysis**

P7. The following accounts are applicable to Raymond's Chimney Sweeps, Inc.:

1. Cash
2. Accounts Receivable
3. Supplies
4. Prepaid Insurance
5. Equipment
6. Notes Payable
7. Accounts Payable
8. Common Stock
9. Retained Earnings
10. Dividends
11. Service Revenue
12. Rent Expense
13. Repair Expense

Raymond's Chimney Sweeps, Inc., completed the following transactions:

	Debit	Credit
a. Paid for supplies purchased on credit last month.	7	1
b. Billed customers for services performed.	___	___
c. Paid the current month's rent.	___	___
d. Purchased supplies on credit.	___	___
e. Received cash from customers for services performed but not yet billed.	___	___
f. Purchased equipment on account.	___	___
g. Received a bill for repairs.	___	___
h. Returned part of the equipment purchased in **f** for a credit.	___	___
i. Received payments from customers previously billed.	___	___
j. Paid the bill received in **g**.	___	___
k. Received an order for services to be performed.	___	___
l. Paid for repairs with cash.	___	___
m. Made a payment to reduce the principal of the note payable.	___	___
n. Declared and paid a dividend.	___	___

REQUIRED

Analyze each transaction and show the accounts affected by entering the corresponding numbers in the appropriate debit or credit column as shown in transaction **a**. Indicate no entry, if appropriate.

LO 3, 4, 7

Transaction Analysis, T Accounts, and Trial Balance

SPREADSHEET

✔ Trial balance: $32,400

P8. B. Turner opened a school for administrative skills called Blitz Secretarial Training, Inc., and completed the following transactions:

a. Turner contributed the following assets to the business in exchange for 27,200 shares of $1 par value common stock:

Cash	$11,400
Computers	8,600
Office Equipment	7,200

b. Found a location for his business and paid the first month's rent, $520.
c. Paid for an advertisement announcing the opening of the school, $380.
d. Received applications from three students for a four-week secretarial program and two students for a ten-day keyboarding course. The students will be billed a total of $2,600.
e. Purchased supplies on credit, $660.
f. Billed the enrolled students, $3,480.
g. Purchased a second-hand computer, $960, and office equipment, $760, on credit.
h. Paid for the supplies purchased on credit in **e**, $660.
i. Paid cash to repair a broken computer, $80.
j. Received partial payment from students previously billed, $2,160.
k. Paid the utility bill for the current month, $180.
l. Paid an assistant one week's salary, $880.
m. Declared and paid a dividend of $600.

REQUIRED

1. Set up the following T accounts: Cash; Accounts Receivable; Supplies; Computers; Office Equipment; Accounts Payable; Common Stock; Dividends; Tuition Revenue; Salaries Expense; Utilities Expense; Rent Expense; Repair Expense; and Advertising Expense.
2. Record the transactions directly in the T accounts, using the transaction letter to identify each debit and credit.
3. Prepare a trial balance using today's date.
4. **BUSINESS APPLICATION ▶** Examine transactions **f** and **j**. What were the revenues and how much cash was received from the revenues? What business issues might you see arising from the differences in these numbers?

LO 1, 3, 4

Transaction Analysis, T Accounts, and Trial Balances

✔ Trial balance: $37,600

P9. David Roberts began an upholstery cleaning business on August 1 and engaged in the following transactions during the month:

Aug.	1	Began business by depositing $30,000 in a bank account in the name of the corporation in exchange for 30,000 shares of $1 par value common stock.
	2	Ordered cleaning supplies, $6,000.
	3	Purchased cleaning equipment for cash, $5,600.
	4	Made two months' van lease payment in advance, $2,400.
	7	Received the cleaning supplies ordered on August 2 and agreed to pay half the amount in 10 days and the rest in 30 days.
	9	Paid for repairs on the van with cash, $2,160.
	12	Received cash for cleaning upholstery, $1,920.
	17	Paid half the amount owed on supplies received on August 7, $3,000.
	21	Billed customers for cleaning upholstery, $2,680.
	24	Paid cash for additional repairs on the van, $160.
	27	Received $1,200 from the customers billed on August 21.
	31	Declared and paid a dividend of $1,400.

REQUIRED

1. Set up the following T accounts: Cash; Accounts Receivable; Cleaning Supplies; Prepaid Lease; Cleaning Equipment; Accounts Payable; Common Stock; Dividends; Cleaning Revenue; and Repair Expense.

(Continued)

2. Record transactions directly in the T accounts. Identify each entry by date.
3. Prepare a trial balance for Roberts Upholstery Cleaning as of August 31, 2014.
4. **CONCEPT ▶** Compare and contrast how the issues of recognition, valuation, and classification are settled in the transactions of August 7 and 9.

LO 3, 4, 5, 7

Transaction Analysis, General Journal, Ledger Accounts, and Trial Balance

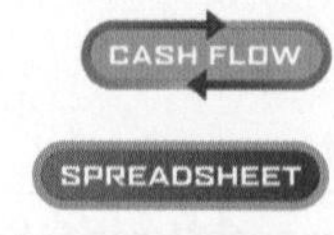

✔ Trial balance: $23,805

P10. Mount Prospect Nursery School Corporation provides baby-sitting and child-care programs. On January 31, 2014, the corporation had the following trial balance:

Mount Prospect Nursery School Corporation
Trial Balance
January 31, 2014

	Debits	Credits
Cash (111)	1,870	
Accounts Receivable (113)	1,700	
Equipment (141)	1,040	
Buses (143)	17,400	
Notes Payable (211)		15,000
Accounts Payable (212)		1,640
Common Stock (311)		4,000
Retained Earnings (312)		1,370
	22,010	22,010

During the month of February, the company completed the following transactions:

Feb. 2 Paid this month's rent, $270.
3 Received fees for this month's services, $650.
4 Purchased supplies on account, $85.
5 Reimbursed the bus driver for gas expenses, $40.
6 Ordered playground equipment, $1,000.
8 Made a payment on account, $170.
9 Received payments from customers on account, $1,200.
10 Billed customers who had not yet paid for this month's services, $700.
11 Paid for the supplies purchased on February 4.
13 Purchased and received playground equipment ordered on February 6 for cash, $1,000.
17 Purchased equipment on account, $290.
19 Paid this month's utility bill, $145.
22 Received payment for one month's services from customers previously billed, $500.
26 Paid part-time assistants for services, $460.
27 Purchased gas and oil for the bus on account, $325.
28 Declared and paid a dividend of $110.

REQUIRED

1. Open accounts in the ledger for the accounts in the trial balance plus the following ones: Supplies (115); Dividends (313); Service Revenue (411); Rent Expense (511); Gas and Oil Expense (512); Wages Expense (513); and Utilities Expense (514).
2. Enter the January 31, 2014, account balances from the trial balance.
3. Enter the above transactions in the general journal (pages 17 and 18).
4. Post the entries to the ledger accounts. Be sure to make the appropriate posting references in the journal and ledger as you post.
5. Prepare a trial balance as of February 28, 2014.
6. **BUSINESS APPLICATION ▶** Examine the transactions for February 3, 9, 10, and 22. What were the revenues, and how much cash was received from the revenues? What business issue might you see arising from the differences in these numbers?

CASES

LO 1, 3

Conceptual Understanding: Valuation and Classification of Business Transactions

C1. CONCEPT ▶ Tower Garden Center purchased two pre-owned trucks at a cash-only auction for 15 percent below current market value. The owners have asked you to record this purchase at current market value. You don't think that is correct. Write the owners a brief business memorandum in good form based on your knowledge of Chapter 2. Explain how the purchase of the pre-owned trucks will affect the balance sheet, include the entry to record the transaction, and explain why the amount must be at the price paid for the trucks.

LO 1, 3, 6

Conceptual Understanding: Recording of Rebates

C2. CONCEPT ▶ Is it revenue or a reduction of an expense? That is the question companies that receive manufacturer's rebates for purchasing a large quantity of product must answer. Food companies like **Sara Lee**, **Kraft Foods**, and **Nestlé** give supermarkets special manufacturer's rebates of up to 45 percent, depending on the quantities purchased. Some firms recorded these rebates as revenue, and others recorded them as a reduction of the cost until the SEC said that only one way is correct. What, then, is the correct way for supermarkets to record these rebates? Does your answer change net income?

LO 1, 2, 3

Interpreting Financial Statements: Interpreting a Bank's Financial Statements

C3. Mellon Bank is a large bank holding company. Selected accounts from the company's 2011 annual report are as follows (in millions):[8]

Cash and Due from Banks	$ 4,175
Loans to Customers	43,585
Securities Available for Sale	78,467
Deposits by Customers	219,094

1. Indicate whether each of these accounts is an asset, a liability, or a component of stockholders' equity on Mellon Bank's balance sheet.
2. Assume that you are in a position to do business with Mellon. Show how Mellon Bank's accountants would prepare the entry in T account form to record each of the following transactions:
   a. You sell securities in the amount of $2,000 to the bank.
   b. You deposit in the bank the $2,000 received from selling the securities.
   c. You borrow $5,000 from the bank.

LO 7

Interpreting Financial Statements: Cash Flows

C4. BUSINESS APPLICATION ▶ Having been promoted recently, you now have access to your firm's monthly financial statements. You notice that revenues are increasing rapidly and that income is at an all-time high. The balance sheet shows growth in receivables, and accounts payable have declined. However, the chief financial officer is concerned because the firm's cash flows from operating activities are decreasing. What are some reasons why a company with a positive net income may fall short of cash from its operating activities? What could be done to improve this situation?

Annual Report Case: Recognition, Valuation, and Classification

C5. CONCEPT ▶ Refer to the Summary of Significant Accounting Policies in the notes to the financial statements in the **CVS** annual report in the Supplement to Chapter 1.

1. How does the concept of recognition apply to advertising costs?
2. How does the concept of valuation apply to inventories?
3. How does the concept of classification apply to cash and cash equivalents?

LO 1, 6

Comparison Analysis: Revenue Recognition

C6. BUSINESS APPLICATION ▶ Refer to the financial statements of **CVS** and **Southwest Airlines Co.** in the Supplement to Chapter 1. What is the total revenue for CVS and Southwest on the respective income statements? How do you think the nature of each business will affect revenue recognition for prescriptions filled for CVS versus airline tickets for Southwest? When do you think cash is received and revenues are earned for each company?

LO 1, 6

Ethical Dilemma: Recognition Point and Ethical Considerations

C7. BUSINESS APPLICATION ▶ Robert Shah, a sales representative for Quality Office Supplies Corporation, will receive a substantial bonus if he meets his annual sales goal. The company's recognition point for sales is the day of shipment. On December 31, Shah realizes he needs sales of $2,000 to reach his sales goal and receive the bonus. He calls a purchaser for a local insurance company, whom he knows well, and asks him to buy $2,000 worth of copier paper today. The purchaser says, "But Robert, that's more than a year's supply for us." Shah says, "Buy it today. If you decide it's too much, you can return however much you want for full credit next month." The purchaser says, "Okay, ship it." The paper is shipped on December 31 and recorded as a sale. On January 15, the purchaser returns $1,750 worth of paper for full credit (approved by Shah) against the bill. Should the shipment on December 31 be recorded as a sale? Discuss the ethics of Shah's action.

Continuing Case: Annual Report Project

C8. CONCEPT ▶ Using the most recent annual report of the company you have chosen to study and that you have accessed online at the company's website, identify in the first note to the financial statements (usually labeled: Significant Accounting Policies) an accounting policy that illustrates each of the following:

1. Recognition
2. Valuation
3. Classification

CHAPTER 3

LEARNING OBJECTIVES

LO 1 Define *net income*, and explain the concepts underlying income measurement.

LO 2 Distinguish cash basis of accounting from accrual accounting, and explain how accrual accounting is accomplished.

LO 3 Identify four situations that require adjusting entries, and illustrate typical adjusting entries.

LO 4 Prepare financial statements from an adjusted trial balance.

LO 5 Explain the importance of ethical measurement of net income and the relation of net income to cash flows.

MEASURING BUSINESS INCOME: ADJUSTING THE ACCOUNTS

Business Insight

Netflix, Inc.

Netflix is the world's largest online entertainment subscription service. For a monthly fee, its subscribers have access to more than 90,000 DVD titles, which are shipped free of charge; with certain plans, they also have access to more than 5,000 movies online. At the end of any accounting period, Netflix has many transactions that will affect future periods. Two examples appear in the Financial Highlights that follow.[1]

- *Prepaid content* for the rights to movies in the future: Like prepaid expenses, these are paid in the period just ended but will benefit future periods. They are therefore recorded as current assets.
- *Accrued expenses:* These are expenses that the company has incurred but will not pay until a future period. They are therefore recorded as current liabilities.

If prepaid content and accrued expenses are not accounted for properly at the end of the period, Netflix's income will be misstated. Similar misstatements can occur when a company has received revenue that it has not yet earned or has earned revenue but not yet received it. If misstatements are made, investors will be misled about the company's financial performance.

Netflix's Financial Highlights:
Selected Balance Sheet Items (in thousands)

	2011	2010
Assets		
Prepaid content	$56,007	$62,217
Liabilities		
Accrued expenses	$63,693	$38,572

1. **CONCEPT ▶** Why are the concepts of continuity, periodicity, and accrual accounting necessary for Netflix to account for transactions that span accounting periods?

2. **ACCOUNTING APPLICATION ▶** How does Netflix apply accrual accounting to the measurement of net income?

3. **BUSINESS APPLICATION ▶** Which accounts on Netflix's income statement are potentially affected by adjusting entries? Which account on Netflix's balance sheet is never affected by an adjusting entry?

SECTION 1 CONCEPTS

CONCEPTS
- Net income
- Revenues
- Expenses
- Continuity
- Periodicity
- Accrual accounting (matching rule)
- Revenue recognition

RELEVANT LEARNING OBJECTIVES

LO 1 Define *net income*, and explain the concepts underlying income measurement.

LO 2 Distinguish cash basis of accounting from accrual accounting, and explain how accrual accounting is accomplished.

LO 1 Concepts Underlying Income Measurement

For a business to succeed or even survive, it must earn a profit. Profit, however, means different things to different people. Accountants prefer to use the term **net income** because it can be precisely defined as the *net increase in stockholders' equity that results from a company's operations.* Exhibit 1 illustrates the concepts underlying the measurement of net income.

Exhibit 1
Concepts Underlying Net Income

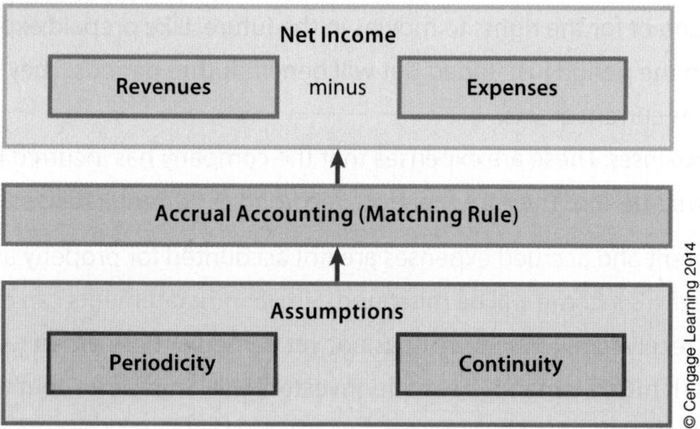

Net Income

Net income is accumulated in the Retained Earnings account and reported on the income statement. Management, stockholders, and others use it to assess a company's progress in meeting the goal of profitability. Readers of income statements need to understand net income and its strengths and weaknesses as an indicator of a company's performance.

In its simplest form, net income results when revenues exceed expenses:

$$\text{Net Income} = \text{Revenues} - \text{Expenses}$$

When expenses exceed revenues, a **net loss** occurs.

Revenues are *increases in stockholders' equity* resulting from selling goods, rendering services, or performing other business activities. When a business delivers a product or provides a service to a customer, it usually receives cash or a promise from customers to pay cash in the near future. In other words, revenue may be *earned* through the sale of goods or services, even though the cash may not be received until later. The promise to pay is recorded in either Accounts Receivable or Notes Receivable. The total of these accounts and the total cash received from customers in an accounting period are the company's revenues for that period.

Expenses are *decreases in stockholders' equity* resulting from the cost of selling goods or rendering services and the cost of the activities necessary to carry on a business, such as attracting and serving customers. Examples include salaries expense, rent expense, advertising expense, utilities expense, and depreciation (allocation of cost) of a building or office equipment. These expenses are often called the *cost of doing business* or *expired costs.* Note that the primary purpose of an expense is to generate revenue.

Not all increases in stockholders' equity arise from revenues, nor do all decreases in stockholders' equity arise from expenses. Stockholders' investments increase stockholders' equity but are not revenues, and dividends decrease stockholders' equity but are not expenses.

Income Measurement Assumptions

Users of financial reports should be aware that estimates and assumptions play a major role in the measurement of net income and other key indicators of performance. **Netflix**'s management acknowledges this in its annual report, as follows.

> *The preparation of financial statements in conformity with accounting principles generally accepted in the United States of America requires management to make estimates and assumptions that affect the reported amounts of assets and liabilities, disclosure of contingent assets and liabilities at the date of the financial statements, and the reported amounts of revenues and expenses during the reporting periods.*[2]

The major assumptions made in measuring business income are *continuity*, *periodicity*, and *accrual accounting (the matching rule)*.

Continuity Certain expense and revenue transactions are allocated over several accounting periods. Choosing the number of accounting periods raises the issue of *continuity*. What is the expected life of the business? Many businesses last less than five years, and in any given year, thousands of businesses go bankrupt. The majority of companies present annual financial statements on the assumption that the business will continue to operate indefinitely—that is, that the company is a **going concern**. The **continuity** assumption is as follows.

> *Unless there is evidence to the contrary, the accountant assumes that the business is a going concern and will continue to operate indefinitely.*

The continuity assumption allows the cost of certain assets to be held on the balance sheet until a future accounting period, when the cost will become an expense. When a firm is facing bankruptcy, the accountant may prepare financial statements based on the assumption that the firm will go out of business and sell all of its assets.

Periodicity Not all transactions can be easily assigned to specific periods. For example, when a company purchases a building, it must estimate the number of years the building will be in use. The portion of the cost of the building that is assigned to each period depends on this estimate and requires an assumption about **periodicity**. The assumption is as follows.

> *Although the lifetime of a business is uncertain, it is nonetheless useful to estimate the business's net income in terms of accounting periods.*

STUDY NOTE: *Accounting periods are of equal length so that one period can be compared with the next.*

Financial statements may be prepared for any time period, but generally, to make comparisons easier, the periods are of equal length. A 12-month accounting period is called a **fiscal year**; accounting periods of less than a year are called **interim periods**. The fiscal year of many organizations is the calendar year, January 1 to December 31. However, retailers and other companies often end their fiscal years during a slack season, so that the fiscal year corresponds to the yearly cycle of business activity. For example, **Toys "R" Us**' fiscal year ends in January, and **Apple Computer**'s ends in September.

Accrual Accounting (Matching Rule) Under **accrual accounting** (often referred to as *the matching rule*), net income is measured by assigning:

- Revenues to the accounting period in which the goods are sold or the services performed.
- Expenses to the accounting period in which they are used to produce revenue.

A direct relationship between expenses and revenues is often difficult to identify. When there is no direct means of connecting expenses and revenues, costs are allocated among the accounting periods that benefit from the costs. For example, a building's cost is expensed over the building's expected useful life, and interest on investments is recorded as income even though it may not have been received.

APPLY IT!

Match the assumptions or actions with the concepts that follow.

1. Increases in stockholders' equity resulting from selling goods, rendering services, or performing other business activities.
2. Increase in stockholders' equity that results from a company's operations.
3. Decreases in stockholders' equity resulting from the cost of selling goods, rendering services, and other business activities.

a. Net income
b. Revenues
c. Expenses

SOLUTION

1. b; 2. a; 3. c

TRY IT! SE1, E1A, E1B

LO2 Concepts Underlying Accrual Accounting

The **cash basis of accounting** is the practice of accounting for revenues in the period in which cash is received and for expenses in the period in which cash is paid. With this method, taxable income is calculated as the difference between cash receipts from revenues and cash payments for expenses. Although this method works well for some small businesses and many individuals, it does not fit the needs of most businesses.

In contrast, as noted above, in *accrual accounting*, revenues and expenses are recorded when they are earned or incurred rather than when they are received or paid. Adjusting the accounts is a technique used to accomplish accrual accounting.

Recognizing Revenues

As you may recall, the process of determining when revenue should be recorded is called **revenue recognition**. The Securities and Exchange Commission requires that all the following conditions be met before revenue is recognized:[3]

- Persuasive evidence of an arrangement exists.
- A product or service has been delivered.
- The seller's price to the buyer is fixed or determinable.
- Collectability is reasonably ensured.

For example, suppose Blue Design Studio, Inc., has created a brochure for a customer and that the transaction meets the SEC's four criteria:

- The company and the customer agree that the customer owes for the service.
- The service has been rendered.
- Both parties understand the price.
- There is a reasonable expectation that the customer will pay the bill.

When Blue bills the customer, it records the transaction as revenue by debiting Accounts Receivable and crediting Design Revenue. Note that revenue can be recorded because there is a reasonable expectation that cash will be received.

International Perspective

IFRS Revenue Recognition: Principles Versus Rules

Revenue recognition highlights the differences between international and U.S. accounting standards. Although U.S. standards are referred to as generally accepted accounting *principles*, the FASB has issued extensive *rules* (specific guidance) for revenue recognition in various situations and industries. The IASB, on the other hand, generally has a few broad IFRS for revenue recognition and leaves it to companies and their auditors to determine how to apply the broad *principle* in specific situations. The FASB and IASB are currently working together to converge on a single standard for revenue recognition; but it is a challenge, given the very different approaches.

to come

Recognizing Expenses

Expenses are recorded when all of the following conditions are met:

- There is an agreement to purchase goods or services.
- The goods have been delivered or the services rendered.
- A price has been established or can be determined.
- The goods or services have been used to produce revenue.

For example, when Blue Design Studio, Inc., receives its utility bill, it recognizes the expense as having been incurred and as having helped produce revenue. Blue records this transaction by debiting Utilities Expense and crediting Accounts Payable. Until the bill is paid, Accounts Payable serves as a holding account. Note that recognition of the expense does not depend on the payment of cash.

APPLY IT!

Four conditions must be met before revenue can be recognized. Identify which of these conditions applies to the following actions:

a. Determines that the firm has a good credit rating.
b. Agrees to a price for services before it performs them.
c. Performs services.
d. Signs a contract to perform services.

SOLUTION

a. Collectability is reasonably assured.
b. The seller's price to the buyer is fixed or determinable.
c. A product or service has been delivered.
d. Persuasive evidence of an arrangement exists.

TRY IT! SE1, E1A, E2A, E1B, E2B

SECTION 2

ACCOUNTING APPLICATIONS

ACCOUNTING APPLICATIONS
- Prepare adjusting entries
- Prepare financial statements from an adjusted trial balance

RELEVANT LEARNING OBJECTIVES

LO 3 Identify four situations that require adjusting entries, and illustrate typical adjusting entries.

LO 4 Prepare financial statements from an adjusted trial balance.

LO 3 The Adjustment Process

Accrual accounting also involves adjusting the accounts. Adjustments are necessary because the accounting period, by definition, ends on a particular day. The balance sheet must list all assets and liabilities as of the end of that day, and the income statement must contain all revenues and expenses applicable to the period ending on that day. Although operating a business is a continuous process, there must be a cutoff point for the periodic reports. Some transactions invariably span the cutoff point, and therefore, some accounts need adjustment.

In Exhibit 2, some of the accounts in Blue Design Studio, Inc.'s trial balance as of July 31 do not show the correct balances for preparing the financial statements. The trial balance lists prepaid rent of $3,200 for the months of July and August. So, on July 31, one-half of the $3,200 represents rent expense for July, and the remaining $1,600 represents an asset that will be used in August. An adjustment is needed to reflect the $1,600 balance in the Prepaid Rent account and the $1,600 rent expense. As you will see, several other accounts in Blue's trial balance do not reflect their correct balances. Like the Prepaid Rent account, they need to be adjusted.

Exhibit 2
Trial Balance for Blue Design Studio

Blue Design Studio, Inc.
Trial Balance
July 31, 2014

Cash	22,480	
Accounts Receivable	4,600	
Office Supplies	5,200	
Prepaid Rent	3,200	
Office Equipment	16,320	
Accounts Payable		6,280
Unearned Design Revenue		1,400
Common Stock		40,000
Dividends	2,800	
Design Revenue		12,400
Wages Expense	4,800	
Utilities Expense	680	
	60,080	60,080

When transactions span more than one accounting period, *accrual accounting* requires the use of **adjusting entries**. Exhibit 3 shows the four situations in which adjusting entries must be made. Each adjusting entry affects one balance sheet account and one income statement account. Note that adjusting entries provide information about past or future cash flows but never involve an entry to the Cash account.

Exhibit 3
The Four Types of Adjustments

Income Statement	Balance Sheet: Asset	Balance Sheet: Liability
Expense	1. Allocating recorded costs between two or more accounting periods.	2. Recognizing unrecorded expenses.
Revenue	4. Recognizing unrecorded, earned revenues.	3. Allocating recorded, unearned revenues between two or more accounting periods.

The four types of adjusting entries are as follows.

- **Type 1. Allocating recorded costs between two or more accounting periods.** Examples of these costs are prepayments of rent, insurance, and supplies and the depreciation of plant and equipment. The adjusting entry involves an asset account and an expense account.
- **Type 2. Recognizing unrecorded expenses.** Examples of these expenses are wages and interest that have been incurred but are not recorded during an accounting period. The adjusting entry involves an expense account and a liability account.
- **Type 3. Allocating recorded, unearned revenues between two or more accounting periods.** Examples include payments received in advance and deposits made for goods or services to be delivered or provided in the future. The adjusting entry involves a liability account and a revenue account.
- **Type 4. Recognizing unrecorded, earned revenues.** An example is revenue that a company has earned for providing a service but for which it has not billed or collected a fee by the end of the accounting period. The adjusting entry involves an asset account and a revenue account.

Adjusting entries are either deferrals or accruals.

- A **deferral** is the postponement of the *recognition* of an expense already paid (Type 1 adjustment) or of revenue received in advance (Type 3 adjustment). The cash payment or receipt is recorded before the adjusting entry is made.
- An **accrual** is the *recognition* of expense (Type 2 adjustment) or a revenue (Type 4 adjustment) that has arisen but not been recorded during the accounting period. The cash payment or receipt occurs in a future accounting period, after the adjusting entry has been made.

Type 1 Adjustment: Allocating Recorded Costs (Deferred Expenses)

Companies often make expenditures that benefit more than one period. These costs are debited to an asset account. At the end of an accounting period, the amount of the asset that has been used is transferred from the asset account to an expense account. Two important adjustments of this type are for prepaid expenses and the depreciation of plant and equipment.

Prepaid Expenses Companies customarily pay some expenses, including those for rent, supplies, and insurance, in advance. These costs are called **prepaid expenses**. By the end of an accounting period, a portion or all of the prepaid services or goods will have been used. The required adjusting entry reduces the asset and increases the expense, as shown in Exhibit 4. The amount of the adjustment equals the cost of the goods or services used or expired.

STUDY NOTE: *The expired portion of a prepayment is converted to an expense; the unexpired portion remains an asset.*

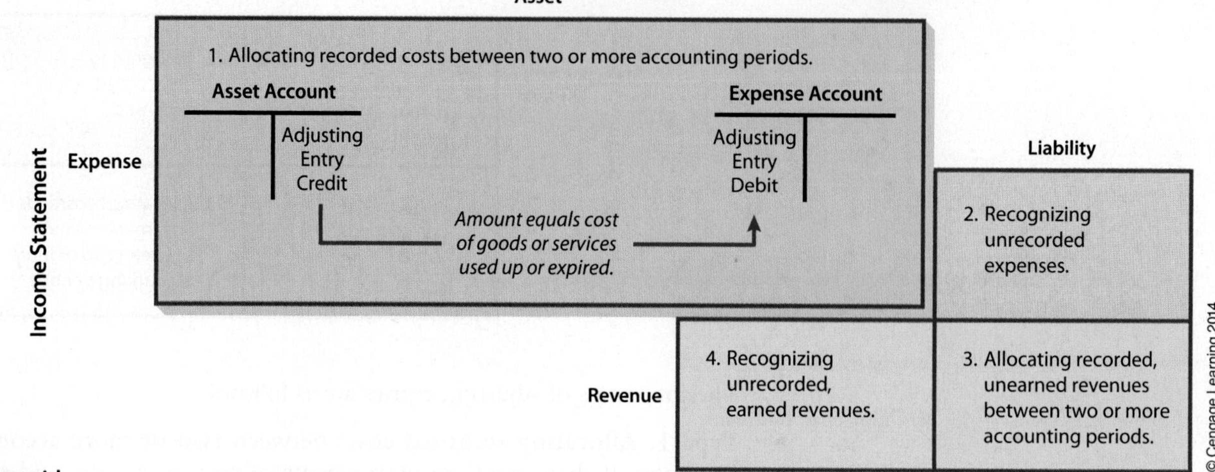

Exhibit 4
Adjustment for Prepaid (Deferred) Expenses

If adjusting entries for prepaid expenses are not made at the end of an accounting period, both the balance sheet and the income statement will present incorrect information. The company's assets will be overstated, and its expenses will be understated. Thus, stockholders' equity on the balance sheet and net income on the income statement will be overstated. Examples of adjusting entries for Blue Design Studio, Inc., follow.

Adjustment for Prepaid Rent

Transaction Blue Design Studio, Inc., paid two months' rent in advance at the beginning of July. The advance payment resulted in an asset—the right to occupy the office for two months. As each day in the month passed, part of the asset's cost expired and became an expense. By July 31, one-half of the asset's cost ($1,600) had expired.

Analysis The journal entry to record the expiration of prepaid rent

▼ *decreases* the asset account *Prepaid Rent* with a credit

▲ *increases* the expense account *Rent Expense* with a debit

Application of Double Entry

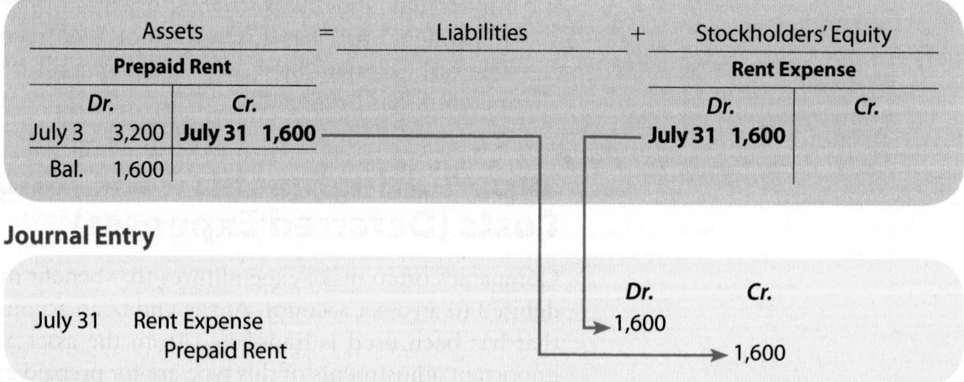

Assets				=	Liabilities	+	Stockholders' Equity	
Prepaid Rent							**Rent Expense**	
Dr.		*Cr.*					*Dr.*	*Cr.*
July 3	3,200	**July 31**	**1,600**				**July 31 1,600**	
Bal.	1,600							

Journal Entry

		Dr.	*Cr.*
July 31	Rent Expense	1,600	
	Prepaid Rent		1,600

Comment The Prepaid Rent account now has a balance of $1,600, which represents one month's rent that will be expensed during August.

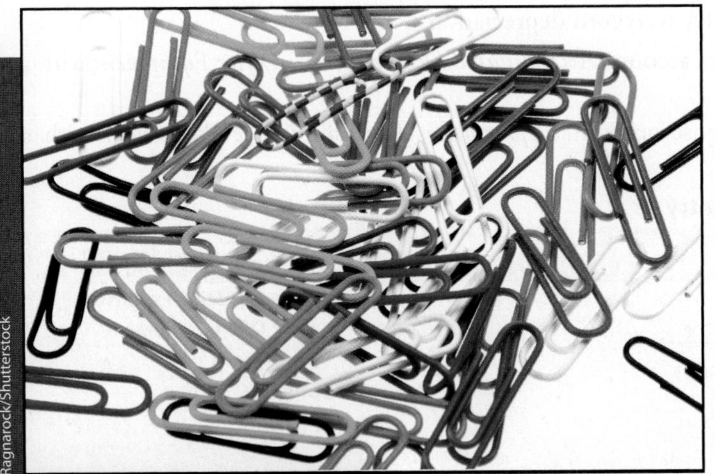

Ragnarock/Shutterstock

Think of accounting for supplies as using a storage cabinet in an office. Supplies are put in the cabinet when purchased (assets). Employees take some out and use them during the accounting period (expenses). At the end of the accounting period, the supplies left in the cabinet can be used in the next period (assets).

Adjustment for Supplies

Transaction Blue Design Studio, Inc., purchased $5,200 of office supplies in early July. At the end of July, an inventory shows that office supplies costing $3,660 are still on hand. This means that of the $5,200 of supplies originally purchased, $1,540 worth were used (became an expense) by July 31.

Analysis The journal entry to record the consumption of office supplies

▼ *decreases* the asset account *Office Supplies* with a credit

▲ *increases* the expense account *Office Supplies Expense* with a debit

Application of Double Entry

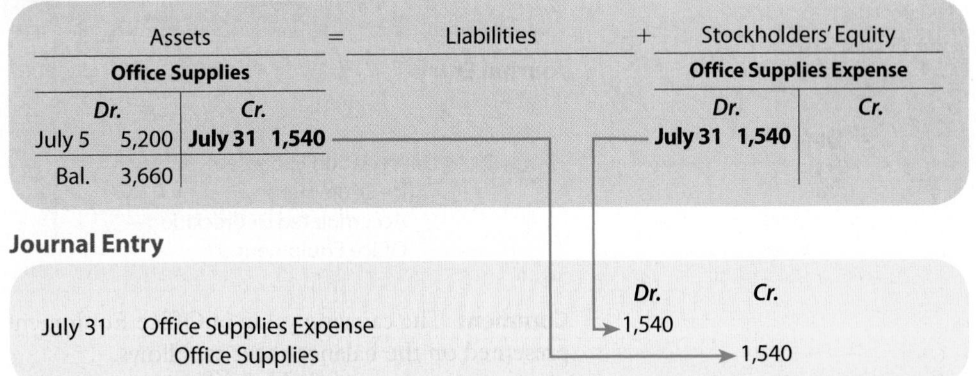

Comment The asset account Office Supplies now reflects the correct balance of $3,660 of supplies yet to be consumed.

STUDY NOTE: *In accounting, depreciation refers only to the allocation of an asset's cost, not to any decline in the asset's value.*

STUDY NOTE: *The difficulty in estimating an asset's useful life is further evidence that the net income figure is, at best, an estimate.*

Depreciation of Plant and Equipment When a company buys a long-term asset—such as a building, truck, computer, or store fixture—it is, in effect, prepaying for the usefulness of that asset for as long as it benefits the company. Because a long-term asset is a deferral of an expense, the accountant must allocate the cost of the asset over its estimated useful life. The amount allocated to any one accounting period is called **depreciation** (or *depreciation expense*).

It is often impossible to tell exactly how long an asset will last or how much of the asset has been used in any one period. For this reason, depreciation must be estimated. Accountants have developed a number of methods for estimating depreciation.[4]

To maintain historical costs, separate accounts are used to accumulate the depreciation on each long-term asset. These **Accumulated Depreciation** accounts are called *contra accounts.* A **contra account** is paired with a related account—in our example, an asset account. The balance of a contra account is shown on a financial statement as a deduction from its related account. The net amount is called the **carrying value** (or *book value*) of the asset. As time passes, the accumulated depreciation grows, and the carrying value of the asset declines.

Adjustment for Plant and Equipment

Transaction On July 31, Blue Design Studio, Inc., records $300 of depreciation of office equipment.

Analysis The journal entry to record depreciation

▲ *increases* the contra account *Accumulated Depreciation—Office Equipment* with a credit

▲ *increases* the expense account *Depreciation Expense—Office Equipment* with a debit

Application of Double Entry

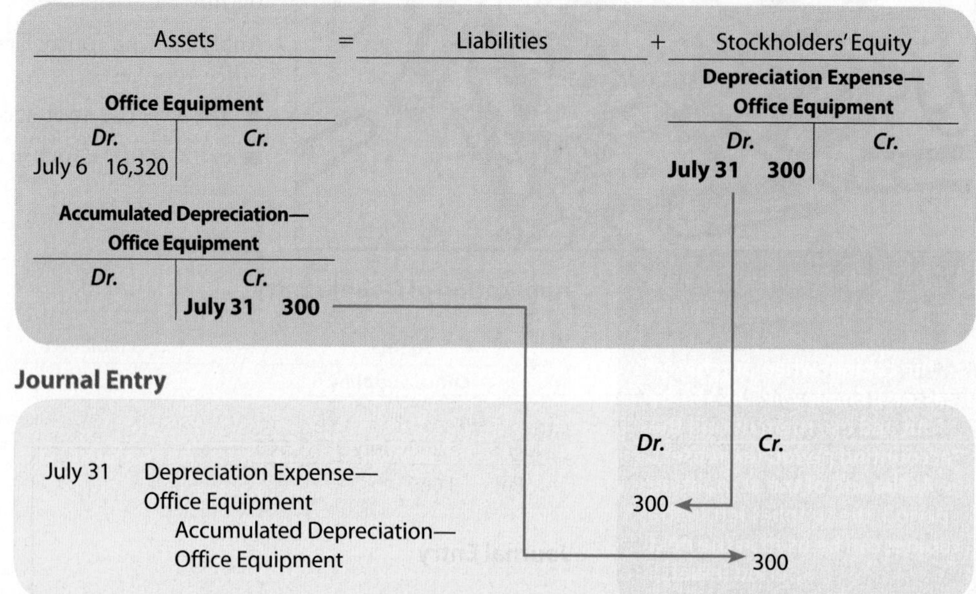

Comment The carrying value of Office Equipment is $16,020 ($16,320 – $300) and is presented on the balance sheet as follows.

Property, Plant, and Equipment		
Office equipment	$16,320	
Less accumulated depreciation	300	$16,020

Business Application **Netflix** has prepaid expenses and property and equipment similar to those in the examples we have presented. Among Netflix's prepaid expenses are payments to movie companies for rights to DVDs called Prepaid Content. By paying in advance, Netflix is able to negotiate lower prices. These fixed payments are debited to Prepaid Content. When the movies produce revenue, the prepaid amounts are transferred to expense through adjusting entries.[5]

Type 2 Adjustment: Recognizing Unrecorded Expenses (Accrued Expenses)

STUDY NOTE: *Remember that in accrual accounting, an expense must be recorded in the period in which it is incurred regardless of when payment is made.*

Usually, at the end of an accounting period, some expenses incurred during the period have not been recorded in the accounts. These expenses require adjusting entries. One such expense is interest on borrowed money. Each day, interest accumulates on the debt. As shown in Exhibit 5, an adjusting entry records the accumulated interest, which is an expense of the period, and the corresponding liability to pay the interest. Other common unrecorded expenses are wages and utilities. As the expense and the corresponding liability accumulate, they are said to *accrue*—hence the term **accrued expenses**.

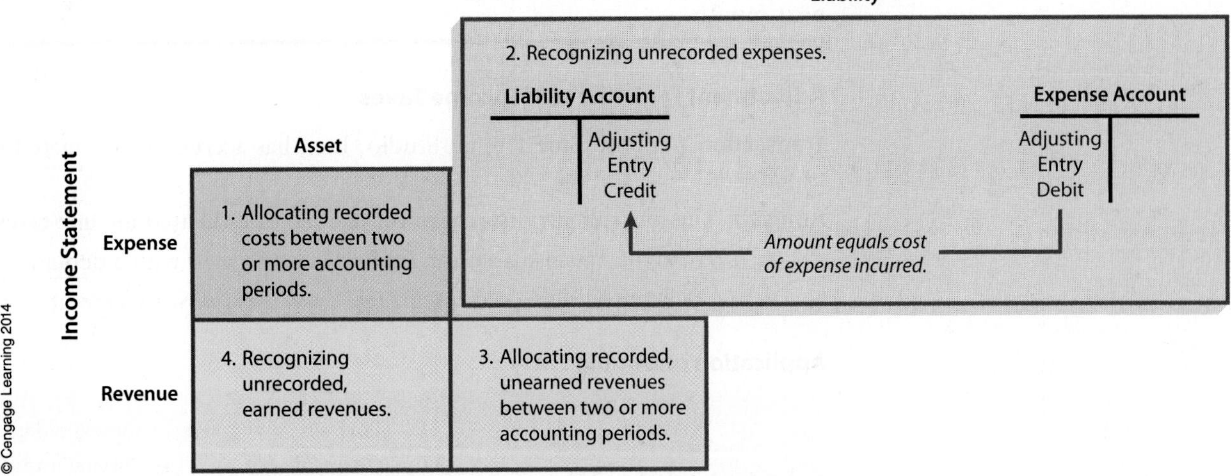

Exhibit 5
Adjustment for Unrecorded (Accrued) Expenses

Adjustment for Unrecorded (Accrued) Wages

Transaction Suppose Blue Design Studio, Inc., has two pay periods a month rather than one. In July, its pay periods end on the 12th and the 26th, as indicated in the calendar below.

July

Sun	M	T	W	Th	F	Sat
	1	2	3	4	5	6
7	8	9	10	11	**12**	13
14	15	16	17	18	19	20
21	22	23	24	25	**26**	27
28	**29**	**30**	**31**			

By the end of business on July 31, Blue's assistant will have worked three days (Monday, Tuesday, and Wednesday) beyond the last pay period. The employee has earned the wages for those days but will not be paid until the first payday in August. The wages for these three days are rightfully an expense for July, and the liabilities should reflect that the company owes the assistant for those days. Because the assistant's wage rate is $2,400 every two weeks, or $240 per day ($2,400 ÷ 10 working days), the expense is $720 ($240 × 3 days). On July 31, Blue would record the $720 accrual of unrecorded wages.

Analysis The journal entry to record the accrual of wages

▲ *increases* the expense account *Wages Expense* with a debit

▲ *increases* the liability account *Wages Payable* with a credit

Application of Double Entry

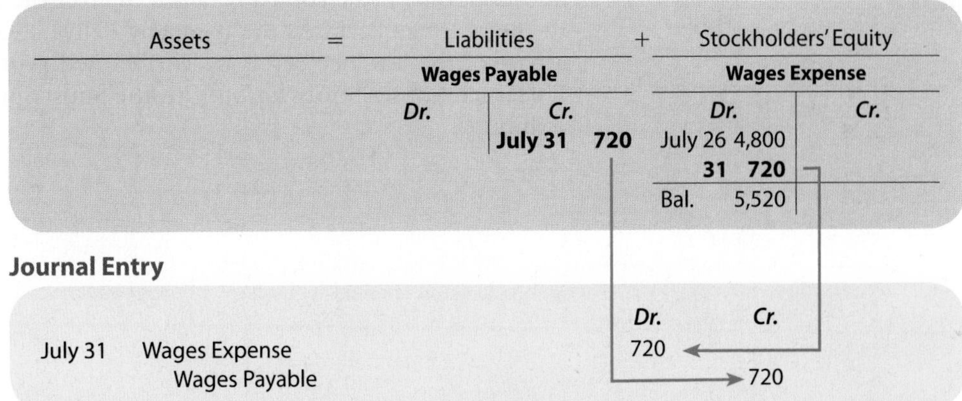

Assets = Liabilities + Stockholders' Equity
Wages Payable
Dr.
Cr.
July 31 720
Wages Expense
Dr.
Cr.
July 26 4,800
31 720
Bal. 5,520
Journal Entry
Dr.
Cr.
July 31 Wages Expense 720
Wages Payable 720

Comment Note that the increase in Wages Expense will *decrease* stockholders' equity and that total wages for the month are $5,520, of which $720 will be paid next month.

Adjustment for Estimated Income Taxes

Transaction Suppose Blue Design Studio, Inc., has accrued its estimated income taxes of $800.

Analysis The journal entry to record the accrual of estimated income taxes

- ▲ *increases* the expense account *Income Taxes Expense* with a debit
- ▲ *increases* the liability account *Income Taxes Payable* with a credit

Application of Double Entry

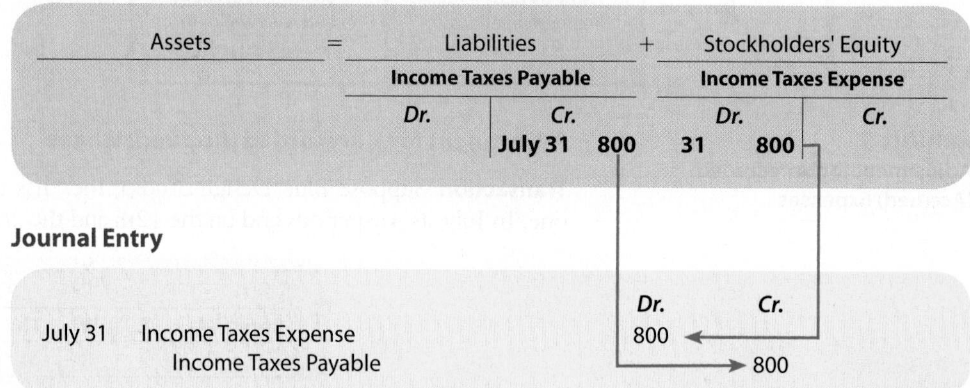

Journal Entry

		Dr.	Cr.
July 31	Income Taxes Expense	800	
	Income Taxes Payable		800

Comment Note that the increase in Income Taxes Expense will *decrease* stockholders' equity.

Business Application In 2011, **Netflix** had accrued expenses of $63,693,000. If the expenses had not been accrued, Netflix's liabilities would be significantly understated, as would the corresponding expenses on Netflix's income statement. The end result would be an overstatement of the company's earnings.

Type 3 Adjustment: Allocating Recorded, Unearned Revenues (Deferred Revenues)

STUDY NOTE: *Unearned revenue is a liability because there is an obligation to deliver goods or perform a service, or to return the payment. Once the goods have been delivered or the service performed, the liability is transferred to revenue.*

When a company receives revenues in advance, it has an obligation to deliver goods or perform services. **Unearned revenues** are therefore shown in a liability account.

For example, publishing companies usually receive cash in advance for magazine subscriptions. These receipts are recorded in a liability account, Unearned Subscriptions. If the company fails to deliver the magazines, subscribers are entitled to their money back. As the company delivers each issue of the magazine, it earns a part of the advance receipts. This earned portion must be transferred from the Unearned Subscriptions account to the Subscription Revenue account, as shown in Exhibit 6.

Exhibit 6
Adjustment for Unearned (Deferred) Revenues

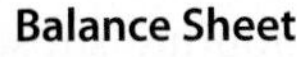

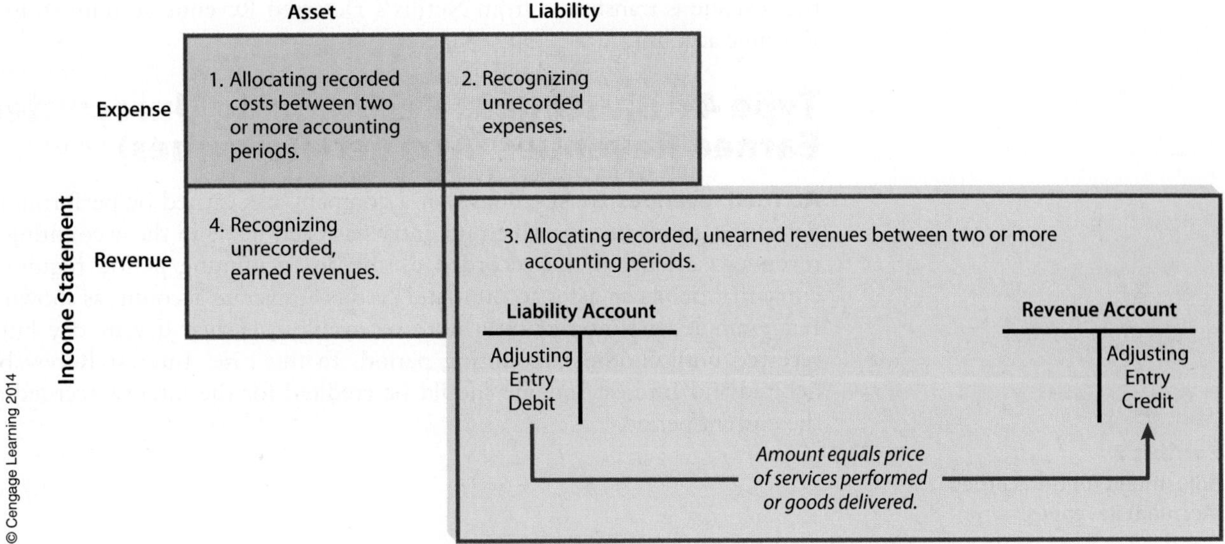

Adjustment for Unearned Revenue

Transaction During July, Blue Design Studio, Inc., received $1,400 from another firm as advance payment for a series of brochures. By the end of the month, it had completed $800 of work on the brochures, and the other firm had accepted the work. On July 31, Blue would record the performance of services for which $800 cash was received in advance.

Analysis The journal entry to record performing services for which cash was received in advance

▲ *increases* the revenue account *Design Revenue* with a credit

▼ *decreases* the liability account *Unearned Design Revenue* with a debit

Application of Double Entry

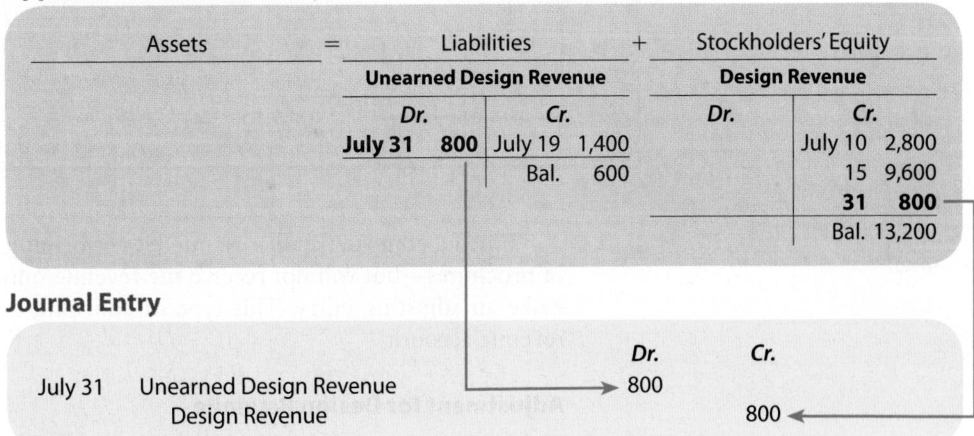

Assets	=	Liabilities		+	Stockholders' Equity	
		Unearned Design Revenue			**Design Revenue**	
		Dr.	*Cr.*		*Dr.*	*Cr.*
		July 31 800	July 19 1,400			July 10 2,800
			Bal. 600			15 9,600
						31 800
						Bal. 13,200

Journal Entry

		Dr.	Cr.
July 31	Unearned Design Revenue	800	
	Design Revenue		800

Comment Unearned Design Revenue now reflects the amount of work still to be performed, $600.

Business Application Netflix has a current liability account called Deferred (Unearned) Revenue. Deferred revenue consists of subscriptions (monthly payments) billed in advance to customers. Subscription revenues are pro-rated over each subscriber's monthly subscription period. As time passes and customers use the service, the revenue is transferred from Netflix's Deferred Revenue account to its Subscription Revenue account.

Type 4 Adjustment: Recognizing Unrecorded, Earned Revenues (Accrued Revenues)

Accrued revenues are revenues that a company has earned by performing a service or delivering goods but for which no entry has been made in the accounting records. Any revenues earned but not recorded during an accounting period require an adjusting entry that debits an asset account and credits a revenue account, as shown in Exhibit 7. For example, the interest on a note receivable is earned day by day but may not be received until another accounting period. In this case, Interest Receivable should be debited and Interest Income should be credited for the interest accrued at the end of the current period.

Exhibit 7
Adjustment for Unrecorded (Accrued) Revenues

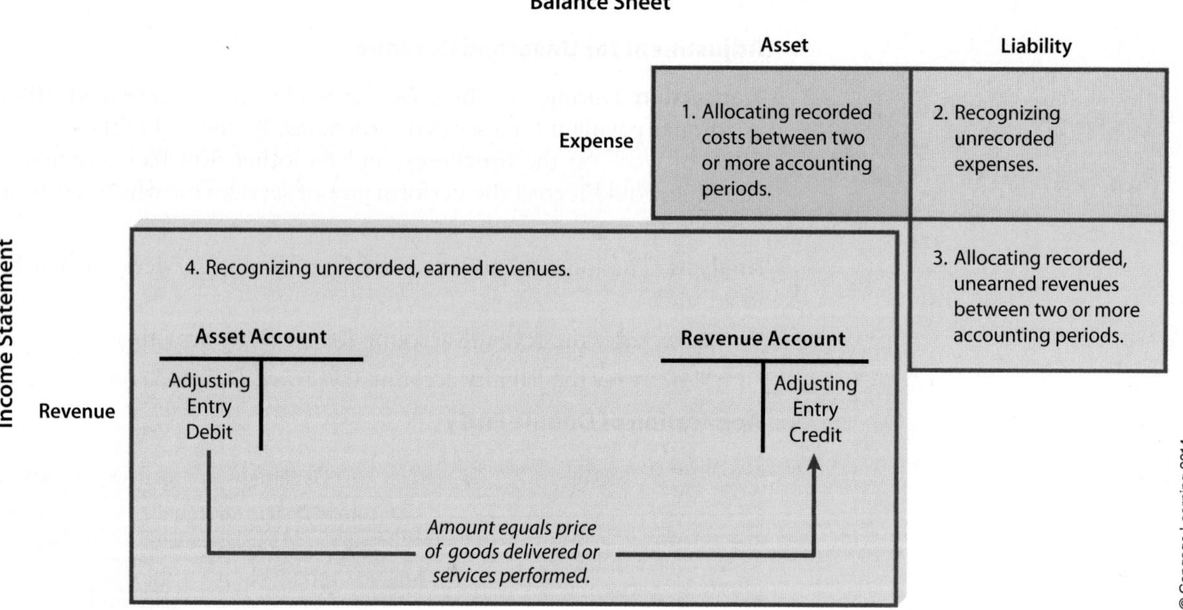

When a company earns revenue by performing a service—such as designing a series of brochures—but will not receive the revenue until a future accounting period, it must make an adjusting entry. This type of adjusting entry involves an asset account and a revenue account.

Adjustment for Design Revenue

Transaction During July, Blue Design Studio, Inc., agrees to create two advertisements for Maggio's Pizza Company and to finish the first advertisement by July 31. By the end of July, Blue has earned $400 for completing the first advertisement, but it will not bill Maggio's until the entire project has been completed. On July 31, Blue records the accrual of $400 of unrecorded revenue.

Analysis The journal entry to record the accrual of unrecorded revenue

▲*increases* the revenue account *Design Revenue* with a credit

▲*increases* the asset account *Accounts Receivable* with a debit

Application of Double Entry

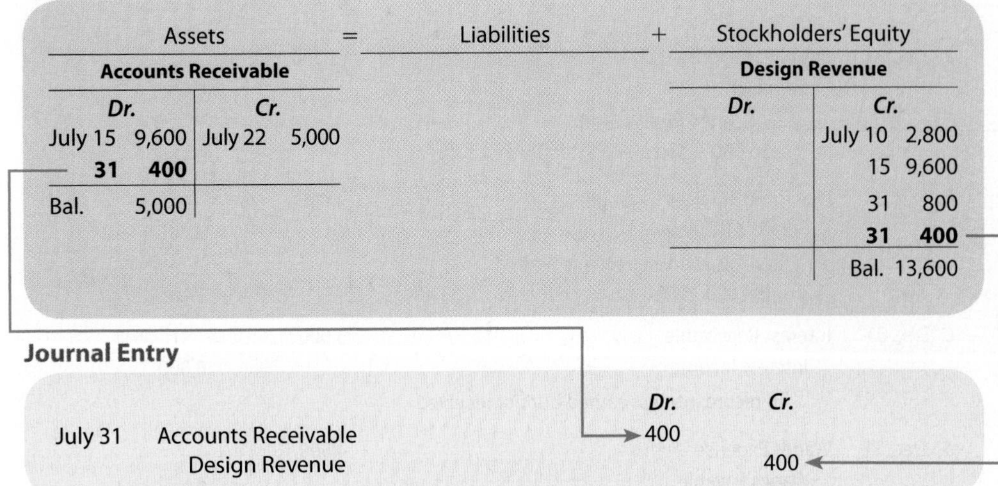

Comment Design Revenue now reflects the total revenue earned during July, $13,600. On the balance sheet, revenues that have been earned but not recorded are usually combined with accounts receivable.

Business Application Since **Netflix**'s subscribers pay their subscriptions in advance by credit card, Netflix does not need to bill customers for services provided but not paid. The company is in the enviable position of having no accounts receivable and thus a high degree of liquidity.

A Note About Business Transactions

Thus far, we have presented a full analysis of each journal entry and showed you the thought process behind each entry. Because you should now be fully aware of the effects of transactions on the accounting equation and the rules of debit and credit, we present simplified journal entries in the rest of the book.

APPLY IT!

On December 31, the end of the current fiscal year, the following information is available to assist Bora Company's accountants in making adjusting entries:

a. Bora's Supplies account shows a beginning balance of $6,000. Purchases during the year were $10,300. The end-of-year inventory reveals supplies on hand of $3,000.
b. On July 1, the company completed negotiations with a client and accepted an advance of $4,800 for services to be performed monthly for a year. The $4,800 was credited to Unearned Services Revenue.
c. Among the assets of the company is a note receivable in the amount of $100,000. On December 31, the accrued interest on this note amounted to $6,000.
d. On Saturday, January 3, the company, which is on a six-day workweek, will pay its regular employees their weekly wages of $9,000.

Required

1. Identify each adjustment as a Type 1, 2, 3, or 4 adjusting entry.
2. Prepare adjusting entries for each item listed.

SOLUTION

1. a. Type 1; b. Type 3; c. Type 4; d. Type 2

2.

		Dr.	Cr.
a. Dec. 31	Supplies Expense	13,300	
	Supplies		13,300
	To record supplies used ($6,000 + $10,300 – $3,000 = $13,300)		
b. Dec. 31	Unearned Services Revenue	2,400	
	Services Revenue		2,400
	To record service revenue earned [($4,800/12 months) × 6 months = $2,400]		
c. Dec. 31	Interest Receivable	6,000	
	Interest Income		6,000
	To record interest earned but not received		
d. Dec. 31	Wages Expense	4,500	
	Wages Payable		4,500
	To record wages incurred but not paid [($9,000/6 days) × 3 days = $4,500]		

TRY IT! SE2, SE3, SE4, SE5, SE6, E1A, E3A, E4A, E5A, E6A, E7A, E8A, E9A, E1B, E3B, E4B, E5B, E6B, E7B, E8B, E9B

LO4 Using the Adjusted Trial Balance to Prepare Financial Statements

After adjusting entries have been recorded and posted, an **adjusted trial balance** is prepared by listing all accounts and their balances. If the adjusting entries have been posted to the accounts correctly, the adjusted trial balance will have equal debit and credit totals. Exhibit 8 shows the adjusted trial balance for Blue Design Studio, Inc., and its relationship to the company's income statement, balance sheet, and statement of retained earnings. Some accounts in Exhibit 8, such as Cash and Accounts Payable, have the same balances as in the trial balance in Exhibit 2 because no adjusting entries affected them. The balances of other accounts, such as Office Supplies and Prepaid Rent, differ from those in the trial balance because adjusting entries did affect them. The adjusted trial balance also includes accounts that do not appear in the trial balance—for example, depreciation accounts and Wages Payable.

The adjusted trial balance facilitates the preparation of the income statement, the statement of retained earnings, and the balance sheet. As shown in Exhibit 8, the revenue and expense accounts are used to prepare the income statement, and the asset and liability accounts are used to prepare the balance sheet.

Notice that the net income from the income statement is combined with the Dividends account on the statement of retained earnings to give the net change in the Retained Earnings account. The balance of Retained Earnings at July 31 is used in preparing the balance sheet.

Exhibit 8
Relationship of the Adjusted Trial Balance to the Income Statement, Statement of Retained Earnings, and Balance Sheet

Blue Design Studio, Inc.
Adjusted Trial Balance
July 31, 2014

Cash	22,480	
Accounts Receivable	5,000	
Office Supplies	3,660	
Prepaid Rent	1,600	
Office Equipment	16,320	
Accumulated Depreciation—Office Equipment		300
Accounts Payable		6,280
Unearned Design Revenue		600
Wages Payable		720
Income Taxes Payable		800
Common Stock		40,000
Dividends	2,800	
Design Revenue		13,600
Wages Expense	5,520	
Utilities Expense	680	
Rent Expense	1,600	
Office Supplies Expense	1,540	
Depreciation Expense—Office Equipment	300	
Income Taxes Expense	800	
	62,300	62,300

Blue Design Studio, Inc.
Income Statement
For the Month Ended July 31, 2014

Revenues		
Design revenue		$13,600
Expenses		
Wages expense	$5,520	
Rent expense	1,600	
Office supplies expense	1,540	
Income taxes expense	800	
Utilities expense	680	
Depreciation expense—office equipment	300	
Total expenses		10,440
Net income		$ 3,160

Blue Design Studio, Inc.
Statement of Retained Earnings
For the Month Ended July 31, 2014

Retained earnings, July 1, 2014	—
Net income	$3,160
Subtotal	$3,160
Less dividends	2,800
Retained earnings, July 31, 2014	$ 360

Blue Design Studio, Inc.
Balance Sheet
July 31, 2014

Assets		
Cash		$22,480
Accounts receivable		5,000
Office supplies		3,660
Prepaid rent		1,600
Office equipment	$16,320	
Less accumulated depreciation	300	16,020
Total assets		$48,760
Liabilities		
Accounts payable		$ 6,280
Unearned design revenue		600
Wages payable		720
Income taxes payable		800
Total liabilities		$ 8,400
Stockholders' Equity		
Common stock	$40,000	
Retained earnings	360	
Total stockholders' equity		40,360
Total liabilities and stockholders' equity		$48,760

STUDY NOTE: *The net income figure from the income statement is needed to prepare the statement of retained earnings, and the bottom-line figure of that statement is needed to prepare the balance sheet. This dictates the order in which the statements are prepared.*

Adjusting Entries and the Financial Statements

Exhibit 9 shows that adjusting entries always affect at least one balance sheet account and one income statement account, but not the statement of cash flows.

Exhibit 9
Effects of Adjusting Entries on the Financial Statements

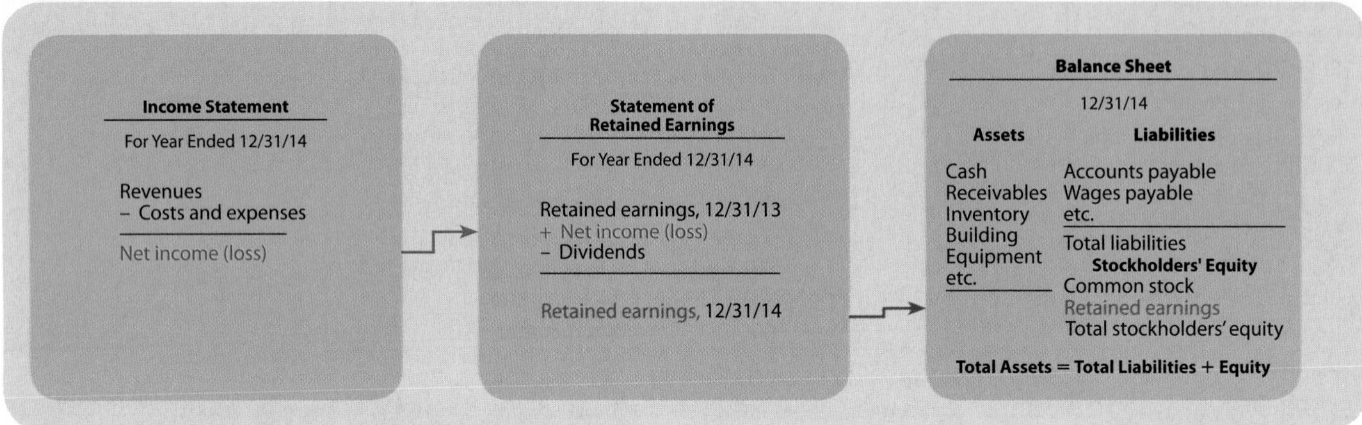

APPLY IT!

The adjusted trial balance for Carroll Corporation on December 31, 2014, contains the following accounts and balances: Common Stock, $180; Retained Earnings, $120 (as of December 1, 2014); Dividends, $100; Service Revenue, $1,000; Rent Expense, $250; Wages Expense, $400; Telephone Expense, $100; and Income Taxes Expense $50. Compute net income and prepare a statement of Retained Earnings for the month of December.

SOLUTION

Net income = Service Revenue − Rent Expense − Wages Expense − Telephone Expense − Income Taxes Expense
= $1,000 − $250 − $400 − $100 − $50
= $1,000 − $800
= $200

Carroll Corporation
Statement of Retained Earnings
For the Month Ended December 31, 2014

Retained earnings, December 1, 2014	$120
Net income	200
Subtotal	$320
Less dividends	100
Retained earnings, December 31, 2014	$220

TRY IT! SE7, SE8, E10A, E10B

SECTION 3 BUSINESS APPLICATIONS

SINESS PLICATIONS
- Ethics
- Cash flows
- Liquidity

LEVANT ARNING OBJECTIVE

5 Explain the importance of ethical easurement of net income d the relation of net ome to cash flows.

LO5 Net Income: Ethical Measurment and Cash Flows

In this section, we consider the ethical measurement of net income and the relation of accrual-based net income to cash flows.

Ethical Considerations for Business

Account adjustments take time to calculate and enter in the records. Also, adjusting entries do not affect cash flows in the current period because they never involve the Cash account. You might ask, "Why go to all the trouble of making them? Why worry about them?" For one thing, the SEC has identified issues related to *accrual accounting* and adjustments as an area of utmost importance because of the potential for abuse and misrepresentation.[6]

All adjustments are important because of their effect on profitability and liquidity. Adjusting entries affect net income, and they affect profitability comparisons from one period to the next. They also affect assets and liabilities on the balance sheet and thus provide information about a company's *future* cash inflows and outflows. This information is needed to assess the need for cash to pay ongoing obligations. The potential for abuse arises because judgment underlies the adjusting entries. When this judgment is misused, performance measures can be misleading.

Applying *accrual accounting* involves making assumptions. It also involves exercising judgment. Consider the assumptions and judgment involved in estimating the useful life of a building. The estimate should be based on realistic assumptions, but management has latitude in making that estimate, and its judgment will affect the final net income that is reported.

The manipulation of revenues and expenses to achieve a specific outcome is called **earnings management**. Research has shown that companies that manage their earnings are much more likely to exceed projected earnings targets by a little than to fall short by a little. Management may want to manage earnings to keep them from falling short in order to:

- Meet a previously announced goal and thus meet the expectations of the market.
- Keep the company's stock price from dropping.
- Meet a goal that will enable it to earn bonuses.
- Avoid embarrassment.

Earnings management, though not the best practice, is not always illegal. However, when the estimates involved in earnings management begin moving outside a reasonable range, the financial statements become misleading. For instance, net income is misleading when revenue is overstated by a significant amount or when expenses are understated by a significant amount. As noted earlier in the text, the preparation of financial statements that are intentionally misleading constitutes fraudulent financial reporting. Evidence of fraudulent financial reporting is often evidenced by lack of sufficient cash flows as explained in the next section.

Business Perspective
Adjusting Entries and Fraudulent Financial Reporting

© Alija / iStockphoto.com

Improper adjusting entries often play an important role in companies that fraudulently prepare the financial statements. The reason is that adjustments may easily be falsely prepared or ignored. The most common fraud technique involved improper *revenue recognition*, followed by the overstatement of existing assets or capitalization of expenses. Revenue may be overstated by simply debiting Accounts Receivable and crediting Revenue. Expenses may be understated by recording expenses as assets or keeping on the balance sheet assets that have been used up. The SEC investigated 347 alleged cases of public company fraudulent financial reporting from 1998 to 2007. Consistent with the high-profile frauds at **Enron**, **WorldCom**, etc., the dollar magnitude of fraudulent financial reporting soared in the last decade, with an average of nearly $400 million per case.[7]

Using Accrual-Based Information to Make Management Decisions

Management has the short-range goal of ensuring that it has sufficient cash to ensure the company's liquidity. Ultimately, cash must flow from income-producing activities for a company to be successful. To plan payments to creditors and assess the need for short-term borrowing, managers must know how to use accrual-based information to analyze cash flows.

Almost every revenue or expense account on the income statement has one or more related accounts on the balance sheet. For instance, Supplies Expense is related to Supplies, Wages Expense is related to Wages Payable, and Design Revenue is related to Unearned Design Revenue. As we have shown, these accounts are related by making adjusting entries, the purpose of which is to apply *accrual accounting* to the measurement of net income.

A company's cash inflows and cash outflows can also be determined by analyzing these relationships. For example, suppose that after receiving the financial statements in Exhibit 8, management wants to know how much cash was expended for office supplies. On the income statement, Office Supplies Expense is $1,540, and on the balance sheet, Office Supplies is $3,660. Because July was the company's first month of operation, there was no prior balance of office supplies, so the amount of cash expended for office supplies during the month was $5,200 ($1,540 + $3,660 = $5,200). Thus, the cash flow used in purchasing office supplies—$5,200—was much greater than the amount expensed in determining income—$1,540. Management can anticipate that the cash needed may be less than the amount expensed because the company will probably not have to buy office supplies in August. Understanding these cash flow effects enables management to better predict the business's need for cash.

The general rule for determining the cash flow received from any revenue or paid for any expense (except depreciation, which is a special case) is to determine the potential cash payments or cash receipts and deduct the amount not paid or not received. As shown in Exhibit 10, the application of the general rule varies with the type of asset or liability account.

Business Perspective
Are Misstatements of Earnings Always Overstatements?

© Alija / iStockphoto.com

Not all misstatements of earnings are overstatements. For instance, privately held companies, which do not have to be concerned about the effect of their earnings announcements on stockholders or investors, may understate income to reduce or avoid income taxes. In an unusual case involving a public company, the SEC cited and fined **Microsoft** for understating its income. Microsoft, a very successful company, accomplished this by overstating its unearned revenue on the balance sheet. The company's motive in trying to appear less successful than it actually was may have been that it was facing government charges of being a monopoly.[8]

Type of Account	*Potential Payment or Receipt Not Paid or Received*				*Result*
Prepaid Expense	Ending Balance	+ Expense for the Period	− Beginning Balance	=	Cash Payments for Expenses
Unearned Revenue	Ending Balance	+ Revenue for the Period	− Beginning Balance	=	Cash Receipts from Revenues
Accrued Payable	Beginning Balance	+ Expense for the Period	− Ending Balance	=	Cash Payments for Expenses
Accrued Receivable	Beginning Balance	+ Revenue for the Period	− Ending Balance	=	Cash Receipts from Revenues

Exhibit 10
Determination of Cash Flows from Accrual-Based Information

For instance, suppose that on May 31, the balance of Prepaid Insurance was $480, and that on June 30, the balance was $670. If the insurance expense during June was $120, the amount of cash expended on insurance during June can be computed as follows.

Prepaid Insurance at June 30	$670
Insurance Expense during June	120
Potential cash payments for insurance	$790
Less Prepaid Insurance at May 31	480
Cash payments for insurance during June	$310

The beginning balance is deducted because it was paid in a prior period. Note that the cash payments equal the expense plus the increase in the balance of the Prepaid Insurance account [$120 + ($670 − $480) = $310]. In this case, the cash paid was almost three times the amount of insurance expense. In future months, cash payments are likely to be less than the expense.

APPLY IT!

Supplies had a balance of $400 at the end of May and $360 at the end of June. Supplies Expense was $550 for the month of June. How much cash was paid for supplies during June?

SOLUTION

Supplies at June 30	$360
Supplies Expense during June	550
Potential cash payments for supplies	$910
Less Supplies at May 31	400
Cash payments for supplies during June	$510

TRY IT! SE9, SE10, E11A, E12A, E11B, E12B

A Look Back At: Netflix, Inc.

Jupiter Images/Photos.com

Netflix, Inc.

The beginning of this chapter focused on **Netflix, Inc.**, a company that has many transactions that span accounting periods. Complete the following requirements in order to answer the questions posed at the beginning of the chapter.

Section 1: Concepts

Why are the concepts of continuity, periodicity, and accrual accounting necessary for Netflix to account for transactions that span accounting periods?

Section 2: Accounting Applications

How does Netflix apply accrual accounting to the measurement of net income?

Section 3: Business Applications
Which accounts on Netflix's income statement are potentially affected by adjusting entries? Which account on Netflix's balance sheet is never affected by an adjusting entry?

SOLUTION

Section 1: Concepts
Nexflix applies the concept of *continuity* when its accountants assume that it will continue to operate indefinitely. The company applies the concept of *periodicity* by estimating its net income in terms of accounting periods. Netflix uses *accrual accounting* to measure net income by *recognizing revenues* when they are earned, and *recognizing expenses* when they are incurred.

Section 2: Accounting Applications
Netflix applies accrual accounting in measuring income by recognizing revenues when earned and expenses when incurred. This requires making adjusting entries at the end of the accounting period for deferrals of expenses and revenues on the balance sheet that must now be recognized on the income statement, and for accruals of revenues and expenses that must now be recognized on the income statement, with corresponding assets or liabilities on the balance sheet.

Section 3: Business Applications
All accounts on the income statement are potentially affected by adjusting entries. On the other hand, cash on the balance sheet is never affected by an adjusting entry.

Review Problem

Reliable Answering Service, Inc., takes telephone messages for doctors, lawyers, and other professionals and relays them immediately when they involve an emergency. Reliable's trial balance on December 31, 2014, follows.

	A	B	C	D	E
1			**Reliable Answering Service, Inc.**		
2			**Trial Balance**		
3			**December 31, 2014**		
4					
5	Cash			2,160	
6	Accounts Receivable			1,250	
7	Office Supplies			180	
8	Prepaid Insurance			240	
9	Office Equipment			3,400	
10	Accumulated Depreciation—Office Equipment				600
11	Accounts Payable				700
12	Unearned Revenue				460
13	Common Stock				2,000
14	Retained Earnings				2,870
15	Dividends			400	
16	Answering Service Revenue				2,900
17	Wages Expense			1,500	
18	Rent Expense			400	
19				9,530	9,530
20					

The following information is also available:

a. Insurance that expired during December amounted to $40.
b. Office supplies on hand on December 31 totaled $75.
c. Depreciation for December totaled $100.
d. Accrued wages on December 31 totaled $120.
e. Revenues earned for services performed in December but not billed by the end of the month totaled $300.
f. Revenues received in advance of services still to be performed totaled $300 at the end of the year.
g. Estimated income taxes for December amounted to $250.

Required

In order to understand how Reliable adjusts its revenues and expenses so that its net income is properly measured, complete the requirements that follow.

1. Determine the required adjusting entries, and record them in the general journal.
2. Post the entries to the T accounts. Open new T accounts as needed.
3. Prepare an adjusted trial balance.
4. Prepare an income statement, a statement of retained earnings, and a balance sheet for the month ended December 31, 2011.

SOLUTION

1.

		Dr.	Cr.
a. Dec. 31	Insurance Expense	40	
	Prepaid Insurance		40
	To record expired insurance		
b. Dec. 31	Office Supplies Expense	105	
	Office Supplies		105
	To record office supplies used ($180 − $75 = $105)		
c. Dec. 31	Depreciation Expense—Office Equipment	100	
	Accumulated Depreciation—Office Equipment		100
	To record depreciation expense		
d. Dec. 31	Wages Expense	120	
	Wages Payable		120
	To record wages incurred but not paid		
e. Dec. 31	Accounts Receivable	300	
	Answering Service Revenue		300
	To record revenues earned but not received		
f. Dec. 31	Unearned Revenues	160	
	Answering Service Revenue		160
	To record revenues earned by end of year ($460 − $300 = $160)		
g. Dec. 31	Income Taxes Expense	250	
	Income Taxes Payable		250
	To record estimated income taxes		

2.

	A	B	C	D	E	F	G	H	I	J	K	L	M	N
1		**Cash**					**Accounts Receivable**						**Office Supplies**	
2	Bal.	2,160				Bal.	1,250				Bal.	180	(b)	105
3						(e)	300				*Bal.*	*75*		
4						*Bal.*	*1,550*							
5													**Accumulated Depreciation—**	
6		**Prepaid Insurance**					**Office Equipment**						**Office Equipment**	
7	Bal.	240	(a)	40		Bal.	3,400						Bal.	600
8	*Bal.*	*200*											(c)	100
9													*Bal.*	*700*
10														
11		**Accounts Payable**					**Unearned Revenue**						**Wages Payable**	
12			Bal.	700		(f)	160	Bal.	460				(d)	120
13								*Bal.*	*300*					
14														
15		**Income Taxes Payable**					**Common Stock**						**Retained Earnings**	
16			(g)	250				Bal.	2,000				Bal.	2,870
17														
18							**Answering**							
19		**Dividends**					**Service Revenue**						**Wages Expense**	
20	Bal.	400						Bal.	2,900		Bal.	1,500		
21								(e)	300		(d)	120		
22		**Rent Expense**						(f)	160		*Bal.*	*1,620*		
23	Bal.	400						*Bal.*	*3,360*					
24														
25		**Insurance Expense**					**Office Supplies Expense**						**Depreciation Expense—**	
26	(a)	40				(b)	105						**Office Equipment**	
27											(c)	100		
28		**Income Taxes Expense**												
29	(g)	250												

3.

	A	B	C	D	E
1			**Reliable Answering Service, Inc.**		
2			**Adjusted Trial Balance**		
3			**December 31, 2014**		
4					
5	Cash			2,160	
6	Accounts Receivable			1,550	
7	Office Supplies			75	
8	Prepaid Insurance			200	
9	Office Equipment			3,400	
10	Accumulated Depreciation—Office Equipment				700
11	Accounts Payable				700
12	Income Taxes Payable				250
13	Income Taxes Expense			250	
14	Unearned Revenue				300
15	Wages Payable				120
16	Common Stock				2,000
17	Retained Earnings				2,870
18	Dividends			400	
19	Answering Service Revenue				3,360
20	Wages Expense			1,620	
21	Rent Expense			400	
22	Insurance Expense			40	
23	Office Supplies Expense			105	
24	Depreciation Expense—Office Equipment			100	
25				10,300	10,300

4.

	A	B	C	D	E
1			**Reliable Answering Service, Inc.**		
2			**Income Statement**		
3			**For the Month Ended December 31, 2014**		
4					
5	**Revenues:**				
6		Answering service revenue			$3,360
7					
8	**Expenses:**				
9		Wages expense		$1,620	
10		Rent expense		400	
11		Insurance expense		40	
12		Office supplies expense		105	
13		Depreciation expense—office equipment		100	
14		Income taxes expense		250	
15		Total expenses			2,515
16	**Net income**				$ 845
17					

	A	B	C	D	E
1			**Reliable Answering Service, Inc.**		
2			**Statement of Retained Earnings**		
3			**For the Month Ended December 31, 2014**		
4					
5	Retained earnings, November 30, 2014				$2,870
6	Net income				845
7	Subtotal				$3,715
8	Less dividends				400
9	Retained earnings, December 31, 2014				$3,315
10					

	A	B	C	D	E
1			**Reliable Answering Service, Inc.**		
2			**Balance Sheet**		
3			**December 31, 2014**		
4					
5			**Assets**		
6	Cash				$2,160
7	Accounts receivable				1,550
8	Office supplies				75
9	Prepaid insurance				200
10	Office equipment			$3,400	
11		Less accumulated depreciation		700	2,700
12	Total assets				$6,685
13					
14			**Liabilities**		
15	Accounts payable			$ 700	
16	Unearned revenue			300	
17	Wages payable			120	
18	Income taxes payable			250	
19	Total liabilities				$1,370
20					
21			**Stockholders' Equity**		
22	Common stock			$2,000	
23	Retained earnings			3,315	
24	Total stockholders' equity				5,315
25	Total liabilities and stockholders' equity				$6,685
26					

SOLUTION • SOLUTION • SOLUTION • SOLUTION • SOLUTION • SOLUTION • SOLUTION • SOLUTION • SOLUTION • SOLUTI

Chapter Review

Define *net income*, and explain the concepts underlying income measurement. LO 1

Net income is the net increase in stockholders' equity that results from a company's operations. Net income equals revenues minus expenses; when expenses exceed revenues, a net loss results. Revenues equal the price of goods sold or services rendered during a specific period. Expenses are the costs of goods and services used in the process of producing revenues.

The continuity assumption recognizes that, without evidence to the contrary, accountants must assume that a business will continue to operate indefinitely. The periodicity assumption recognizes that it is useful to estimate the business's net income in terms of accounting periods. Accrual accounting holds that revenues must be assigned to the period in which the goods are sold or the services performed, and expenses must be assigned to the period in which they are used to produce revenue.

Distinguish cash basis of accounting from accrual accounting, and explain how accrual accounting is accomplished. LO 2

The cash basis of accounting is based on cash received and cash paid. In contrast, accrual accounting consists of all the techniques accountants use to measure net income, which include recognizing revenues when they are earned, expenses when they are incurred, and adjusting the accounts.

Identify four situations that require adjusting entries, and illustrate typical adjusting entries. LO 3

Adjusting entries are required when (1) recorded costs must be allocated between two or more accounting periods; (2) unrecorded expenses exist; (3) recorded, unearned revenues must be allocated between two or more periods; and (4) unrecorded, earned revenues exist. The preparation of adjusting entries is summarized as follows.

Type of Adjusting Entry	Type of Account: Debited	Type of Account: Credited	Examples of Balance Sheet Accounts
1. Allocating recorded costs (previously paid, expired)	Expense	Asset (or contra-asset)	Prepaid rent Prepaid insurance Office supplies Accumulated depreciation—office equipment
2. Accrued expenses (incurred, not paid)	Expense	Liability	Interest payable Wages payable
3. Allocating recorded, unearned revenues (previously received, earned)	Liability	Revenue	Unearned revenue
4. Accrued revenues (earned, not received)	Asset	Revenue	Accounts receivable Interest receivable

Prepare financial statements from an adjusted trial balance. LO 4

An adjusted trial balance is prepared after adjusting entries have been posted to the accounts. Its purpose is to test whether total debits equal total credits after the adjusting entries have been posted and before the financial statements are prepared. The balances in the revenue and expense accounts in the adjusted trial balance are used to prepare the income statement. The balances in the asset and liability accounts in the adjusted trial balance and in the statement of retained earnings are used to prepare the balance sheet.

Explain the importance of ethical measurement of net income and the relation of net income to cash flows. LO 5

Because applying accrual accounting involves making assumptions and exercising judgment, it can lead to earnings management, which is the manipulation of revenues and expenses to achieve a specific outcome. When the estimates involved in earnings management move outside a reasonable range, financial statements become misleading. Financial statements that are intentionally misleading constitute fraudulent financial reporting.

To ensure a company's liquidity, managers must know how to use accrual-based information to analyze cash flows. The general rule for determining the cash flow received from any revenue or paid for any expense (except depreciation) is to determine the potential cash payments or cash receipts and deduct the amount not received or not paid.

Key Terms

accrual (143) LO3
accrual accounting (139) LO1
accrued expenses (146) LO3
accrued revenues (150) LO3
Accumulated Depreciation (145) LO3
adjusted trial balance (152) LO4
adjusting entries (142) LO3
carrying value (145) LO3
cash basis of accounting (140) LO2
continuity (139) LO1
contra account (145) LO3
deferral (143) LO3
depreciation (145) LO3
earnings management (155) LO5
expenses (138) LO1
fiscal year (139) LO1
going concern (139) LO1
interim periods (139) LO1
net income (138) LO1
net loss (138) LO1
periodicity (139) LO1
prepaid expenses (143) LO3
revenue recognition (140) LO2
revenues (138) LO1
unearned revenues (148) LO3

Chapter Assignments

DISCUSSION QUESTIONS

LO 1 **DQ1.** When a company has net income, what happens to its stockholders' equity, its assets, and/or its liabilities?

LO 3 **DQ2.** Will the carrying value of a long-term asset normally equal its market value?

LO 5 **DQ3.** If, at the end of the accounting period, you were looking at the T account for a prepaid expense like supplies, would you look for the amounts expended in cash on the debit or credit side? On which side would you find the amount expensed during the period?

LO 5 **DQ4. BUSINESS APPLICATION ▶** Is accrual accounting more closely related to a company's goal of profitability or liquidity?

LO 5 **DQ5. BUSINESS APPLICATION ▶** Would you expect net income to be a good measure of a company's liquidity? Why or why not?

LO 5 **DQ6. BUSINESS APPLICATION ▶** Can you think of some situations when earnings management is acceptable?

SHORT EXERCISES

LO 1, 2 **Accrual Accounting Concepts**

SE1. CONCEPT ▶ Match the concepts of accrual accounting that follow with the appropriate assumptions or actions.

1. Assumes expenses should be assigned to the accounting period in which they are used to produce revenues
2. Assumes a business will last indefinitely
3. Assumes revenues are earned at a point in time
4. Assumes net income that is measured for a short period of time, such as one quarter

a. Periodicity
b. Continuity
c. Accrual accounting
d. Revenue recognition

LO 3 **Adjustment for Prepaid Insurance**

SE2. The Prepaid Insurance account began the year with a balance of $460. During the year, insurance in the amount of $1,040 was purchased. At the end of the year (December 31), the amount of insurance still unexpired was $700. Prepare the year-end journal entry to record the adjustment for insurance expense for the year.

LO 3 **Adjustment for Supplies**

SE3. The Supplies account began the year with a balance of $380. During the year, supplies in the amount of $980 were purchased. At the end of the year (December 31), the inventory of supplies on hand was $440. Prepare the year-end journal entry to record the adjustment for supplies expense for the year.

LO 3 **Adjustment for Depreciation**

SE4. The depreciation expense on office equipment for the month of March is $100. This is the third month that the office equipment, which cost $1,900, has been owned. Prepare the adjusting entry to record depreciation for March and show the balance sheet presentation for office equipment and related accounts after the March 31 adjustment.

LO 3 **Adjustment for Accrued Wages**

SE5. Wages are paid each Saturday for a six-day workweek. Wages are currently $1,380 per week. Prepare the adjusting entry required on June 30, assuming July 1 falls on a Tuesday.

LO 3 **Adjustment for Unearned Revenue**

SE6. During the month of August, deposits in the amount of $1,100 were received for services to be performed. By the end of the month, services in the amount of $760 had been performed. Prepare the necessary adjustment for Service Revenue at the end of the month.

LO 4 **Preparation of an Income Statement and Statement of Retained Earnings from an Adjusted Trial Balance**

SE7. Shah Corporation's adjusted trial balance on December 31, 2014, contains the following accounts and balances: Retained Earnings, $8,600; Dividends, $350; Service Revenue, $2,600; Rent Expense, $400; Wages Expense, $900; Utilities Expense, $200; Telephone Expense, $50; and Income Taxes Expense, $350. Prepare an income statement and statement of retained earnings for the month of December.

LO 4 **Preparation of an Income Statement and Statement of Retained Earnings from an Adjusted Trial Balance**

SE8. Malesherbes Corporation's adjusted trial balance on June 30, 2014, contains the following accounts and balances: Retained Earnings, $12,750; Dividends, $580; Service Revenue, $6,300; Rent Expense, $900; Wages Expense, $1,050; Utilities Expense,

$300; Telephone Expense, $90; and Income Taxes Expense, $215. Prepare an income statement and statement of retained earnings for the month of June.

LO 4 **Determination of Cash Flows**

SE9. BUSINESS APPLICATION ▶ Unearned Revenue had a balance of $650 at the end of November and $450 at the end of December. Service Revenue was $2,550 for the month of December. How much cash was received for services provided during December?

LO 5 **Determination of Cash Flows**

SE10. BUSINESS APPLICATION ▶ Unearned Revenue had a balance of $1,120 at the end of November and $890 at the end of December. Service Revenue was $4,600 for the month of December. How much cash was received for services provided during December?

EXERCISES: SET A

LO 1, 2, 3 **Applications of Accounting Concepts Related to Accrual Accounting**

E1A. CONCEPT ▶ Carlos Company's accountant makes the assumptions or performs the activities listed below. Tell which of the following concepts of accrual accounting most directly relates to each assumption or action: (a) periodicity, (b) continuity, (c) accrual accounting, (d) revenue recognition, (e) deferral, and (f) accrual.

1. Recognizes the usefulness of financial statements prepared on a monthly basis even though they are based on estimates.
2. Prepares an income statement that shows the revenues earned and the expenses incurred during the accounting period.
3. In estimating the life of a building, assumes that the business will last indefinitely.
4. Postpones the recognition of a one-year insurance policy as an expense by initially recording the expenditure as an asset.
5. Records a sale when the customer is billed.
6. Recognizes, by making an adjusting entry, wages expense that has been incurred but not yet recorded.

LO 2 **Application of Conditions for Revenue Recognition**

E2A. CONCEPT ▶ Four conditions must be met before revenue should be recognized. In each of the following cases, tell which condition has *not* been met:

a. Company Alpha accepts a contract to perform services in the future for $4,000.
b. Company Beta ships products worth $6,000 to another company without an order from the other company but tells the company it can return the products if it does not sell them.
c. Company Centric performs $20,000 of services for a firm with financial problems.
d. Company Radiant agrees to work out a price later for services that it performs for another company.

LO 3 **Adjusting Entry for Unearned Revenue**

E3A. Stardust, Inc., publishes a monthly magazine featuring local restaurant reviews and upcoming social, cultural, and sporting events. Subscribers pay for subscriptions either one year or two years in advance. Cash received from subscribers is credited to an account called Magazine Subscriptions Received in Advance. On December 31, 2014, the end of the company's fiscal year, the balance of this account is $750,000. Expiration of subscriptions revenue is as follows.

During 2014	$150,000
During 2015	375,000
During 2016	225,000

Prepare the adjusting entry for December 31, 2014.

LO 3 **Adjusting Entries for Prepaid Insurance**

E4A. An examination of the Prepaid Insurance account shows a balance of $10,280 at the end of an accounting period, before adjustment. Prepare journal entries to record the insurance expense for the period under the following independent assumptions:

1. An examination of the insurance policies shows unexpired insurance that cost $4,935 at the end of the period.
2. An examination of the insurance policies shows insurance that cost $1,735 has expired during the period.

LO 3 **Adjusting Entries for Supplies: Missing Data**

E5A. Each of the following columns represents a Supplies account:

	a	b	c	d
Supplies on hand at June 1	$264	$217	$196	$?
Supplies purchased during the month	52	?	174	1,928
Supplies consumed during the month	194	972	?	1,632
Supplies on hand at June 30	?	436	56	1,118

1. Determine the amounts indicated by the question marks.
2. Make the adjusting entry for column **a**, assuming supplies purchased are debited to an asset account.

LO 3 **Adjusting Entry for Accrued Salaries**

E6A. Kiddle Incorporated has a five-day workweek and pays salaries of $70,000 each Friday.

1. Prepare the adjusting entry required on May 31, assuming that June 1 falls on a Wednesday.
2. Prepare the journal entry to pay the salaries on June 3, including the amount of salaries payable from requirement **1**.

LO 3 **Revenue and Expense Recognition**

E7A. Lacoma Company produces computer software that Kozuch, Inc., sells. Lacoma receives a royalty of 15 percent of sales. Kozuch pays royalties to Lacoma semiannually—on May 1 for sales made in July through December of the previous year and on November 1 for sales made in January through June of the current year. Royalty expense for Kozuch and royalty income for Lacoma in the amount of $12,000 were accrued on December 31, 2013. Cash in the amounts of $12,000 and $20,000 was paid and received on May 1 and November 1, 2014, respectively. Software sales during the July to December 2014 period totaled $300,000.

1. Calculate the amount of royalty expense for Kozuch and royalty income for Lacoma during 2014.
2. Record the adjusting entry that each company made on December 31, 2014.

LO 3 **Accounting for Revenue Received in Advance**

E8A. The law firm of Gayle, Peterson, & Gray received $72,000 on October 1 to represent a client in real estate negotiations over the next 12 months.

1. Prepare the journal entries required in the company's records on October 1 and at the end of the fiscal year, December 31.
2. **ACCOUNTING CONNECTION ▶** How would this transaction be reflected on the income statement and balance sheet on December 31?

LO 3 **Adjusting Entries**

E9A. Prepare year-end adjusting entries for each of the following:

1. Office Supplies has a balance of $168 on January 1. Purchases debited to Office Supplies during the year amount to $830. A year-end inventory reveals supplies of $570 on hand.

2. Depreciation of office equipment is estimated to be $4,260 for the year.
3. Property taxes for six months, estimated at $1,750, have accrued but have not been recorded.
4. Unrecorded interest income on U.S. government bonds is $1,700.
5. Unearned Revenue has a balance of $1,800. Services for $600 received in advance have now been performed.
6. Services totaling $400 have been performed; the customer has not yet been billed.

LO 4

Preparation of Financial Statements

E10A. Prepare the monthly income statement, monthly statement of retained earnings, and the balance sheet at August 31, 2014, for Kristina Cleaning Company, Inc., from the data provided in the adjusted trial balance that follows.

Kristina Cleaning Company, Inc.
Adjusted Trial Balance
August 31, 2014

Cash	4,590	
Accounts Receivable	2,592	
Prepaid Insurance	380	
Prepaid Rent	200	
Cleaning Supplies	152	
Cleaning Equipment	3,200	
Accumulated Depreciation—Cleaning Equipment		320
Truck	7,200	
Accumulated Depreciation—Truck		720
Accounts Payable		420
Wages Payable		80
Unearned Janitorial Revenue		920
Income Taxes Payable		700
Common Stock		4,000
Retained Earnings		11,034
Dividends	2,000	
Janitorial Revenue		14,620
Wages Expense	5,680	
Rent Expense	1,200	
Gas, Oil, and Other Truck Expenses	580	
Insurance Expense	380	
Supplies Expense	2,920	
Depreciation Expense—Cleaning Equipment	320	
Depreciation Expense—Truck	720	
Income Taxes Expense	700	
	32,814	32,814

LO 5

Determination of Cash Flows

E11A. BUSINESS APPLICATION ▶ After adjusting entries had been made, Infosys Company's balance sheets showed the following asset and liability amounts at the end of 2013 and 2014:

	2014	2013
Prepaid insurance	$1,200	$1,450
Wages payable	600	1,100
Unearned fees	2,100	950

(Continued)

The following amounts were taken from the 2014 income statement:

Insurance expense	$1,900
Wages expense	9,750
Fees earned	4,450

Calculate the amount of cash paid for insurance and wages and the amount of cash received for fees during 2014.

LO 5

Relationship of Expenses to Cash Paid

E12A. BUSINESS APPLICATION ▶ Wipro Company's income statement included the following expenses for 2014:

Rent expense	$ 78,000
Interest expense	11,700
Salaries expense	124,500

The related balance sheet account balances at year end for last year and this year follow.

	Last Year	This Year
Prepaid rent	—	$ 1,350
Interest payable	$1,800	—
Salaries payable	7,500	18,000

1. Compute the cash paid for rent during the year.
2. Compute the cash paid for interest during the year.
3. Compute the cash paid for salaries during the year.

EXERCISES: B SET

Visit the textbook companion web site at www.cengagebrain.com to access Exercise Set B for this chapter.

PROBLEMS

LO 3

Determining Adjustments

✔ d: Revenue balance: $9,150

P1. At the end of the first three months of operation, Kubose Answering Service, Inc.'s trial balance appears as follows. Kubose has hired an accountant to prepare financial statements to determine how well the company is doing after three months. Upon examining the accounting records, the accountant finds the following items of interest:

a. An inventory of office supplies reveals supplies on hand of $133.
b. The Prepaid Rent account includes the rent for the first three months plus a deposit for April's rent.
c. Depreciation on the equipment for the first three months is $208.
d. The balance of the Unearned Answering Service Revenue account represents a 12-month service contract paid in advance on February 1.
e. On March 31, accrued wages total $80.
f. Federal income taxes for the three months are estimated to be $980.

Kubose Answering Service, Inc.
Trial Balance
March 31, 2014

Cash	3,482	
Accounts Receivable	4,236	
Office Supplies	903	
Prepaid Rent	800	
Equipment	4,700	
Accounts Payable		2,673
Unearned Answering Service Revenue		888
Common Stock		5,933
Dividends	2,130	
Answering Service Revenue		9,002
Wages Expense	1,900	
Office Cleaning Expense	345	
	18,496	18,496

REQUIRED

All adjustments affect one balance sheet account and one income statement account. For each of these situations, show the accounts affected, the amount of the adjustment (using a + or – to indicate an increase or decrease), and the balance of the account after the adjustment in the following format:

Balance Sheet Account	Amount of Adjustment (+ or –)	Balance After Adjustment	Income Statement Account	Amount of Adjustment (+ or –)	Balance After Adjustment

LO 2, 3

✔ 1b: Debit to Insurance Expense: $6,874

Preparing Adjusting Entries

P2. On November 30, the end of the current fiscal year, the following information is available to assist Allerton Corporation's accountants in making adjusting entries:

a. Allerton's Supplies account shows a beginning balance of $2,350. Purchases during the year were $4,218. The end-of-year inventory reveals supplies on hand of $1,397.

b. The Prepaid Insurance account shows the following on November 30:

Beginning balance	$4,720
July 1	4,200
October 1	7,272

The beginning balance represents the unexpired portion of a one-year policy purchased in September of the previous year. The July 1 entry represents a new one-year policy, and the October 1 entry represents additional coverage in the form of a three-year policy.

c. The following table contains the cost and annual depreciation for buildings and equipment, all of which Allerton purchased before the current year:

Account	Cost	Annual Depreciation
Buildings	$298,000	$16,000
Equipment	374,000	40,000

d. On October 1, the company completed negotiations with a client and accepted an advance of $18,600 for services to be performed monthly for a year. The $18,600 was credited to Unearned Services Revenue.

(Continued)

e. The company calculated that, as of November 30, it had earned $7,000 on an $11,000 contract that would be completed and billed in January.
f. Among the liabilities of the company is a note payable in the amount of $300,000. On November 30, the accrued interest on this note amounted to $18,000.
g. On Saturday, December 2, the company, which is on a six-day workweek, will pay its regular employees their weekly wages of $15,000.
h. On November 29, the company completed negotiations and signed a contract to provide services to a new client at an annual rate of $23,000.
i. Management estimates income taxes for the year to be $22,000.

REQUIRED

1. Prepare adjusting entries for each item listed above.
2. **CONCEPT ▶** Explain how the conditions for revenue recognition are applied to transactions **e** and **h**.

LO **3, 4**

GENERAL LEDGER

✔ 3: Adjusted trial balance: $108,287

Determining Adjusting Entries, Posting to T Accounts, and Preparing an Adjusted Trial Balance

P3. Kinokawa Consultants Corporation's trial balance on December 31, 2014, follows.

Kinokawa Consultants Corporation
Trial Balance
December 31, 2014

Cash	12,786	
Accounts Receivable	24,840	
Office Supplies	991	
Prepaid Rent	1,400	
Office Equipment	6,700	
Accumulated Depreciation—Office Equipment		1,600
Accounts Payable		1,820
Notes Payable		10,000
Unearned Service Revenue		2,860
Common Stock		10,000
Retained Earnings		19,387
Dividends	15,000	
Service Revenue		58,500
Salaries Expense	33,000	
Utilities Expense	1,750	
Rent Expense	7,700	
	104,167	104,167

The following information is also available:

a. Ending inventory of office supplies, $86
b. Prepaid rent expired, $700
c. Depreciation of office equipment for the period, $600
d. Interest accrued on the note payable, $600
e. Salaries accrued at the end of the period, $200
f. Service revenue still unearned at the end of the period, $1,410
g. Service revenue earned but not billed, $600
h. Estimated federal income taxes for the period, $2,120

REQUIRED

1. Open T accounts for the accounts in the trial balance plus the following: Interest Payable; Salaries Payable; Income Taxes Payable; Office Supplies Expense; Depreciation Expense—Office Equipment; Interest Expense; and Income Taxes Expense. Enter the account balances.

2. Determine the adjusting entries and post them directly to the T accounts.
3. Prepare an adjusted trial balance.
4. **ACCOUNTING CONNECTION ▶** Which financial statements do each of the above adjustments affect? What financial statement is *not* affected by the adjustments?

LO **3, 4**

Determining Adjusting Entries and Tracing Their Effects to Financial Statements

✔4: Adjusted trial balance: $646,459

P4. Kitz Limo Service, Inc., was organized to provide limousine service between the airport and various suburban locations. It has just completed its second year of business. Its trial balance follows.

Kitz Limo Service, Inc.
Trial Balance
June 30, 2014

Cash (111)	9,812	
Accounts Receivable (113)	14,227	
Prepaid Rent (117)	12,000	
Prepaid Insurance (118)	4,900	
Prepaid Maintenance (119)	12,000	
Spare Parts (140)	11,310	
Limousines (148)	200,000	
Accumulated Depreciation—Limousines (149)		25,000
Notes Payable (211)		45,000
Unearned Passenger Service Revenue (212)		30,000
Common Stock (311)		30,000
Retained Earnings (312)		48,211
Dividends (313)	20,000	
Passenger Service Revenue (411)		428,498
Gas and Oil Expense (510)	89,300	
Salaries Expense (511)	206,360	
Advertising Expense (513)	26,800	
	606,709	606,709

The following information is also available:

a. To obtain space at the airport, Kitz paid two years' rent in advance when it began the business.
b. An examination of insurance policies reveals that $2,800 expired during the year.
c. To provide regular maintenance for the vehicles, Kitz deposited $12,000 with a local garage. An examination of maintenance invoices reveals charges of $10,944 against the deposit.
d. An inventory of spare parts shows $1,902 on hand.
e. Kitz depreciates all of its limousines at the rate of 12.5 percent per year. No limousines were purchased during the year. (Round to the nearest dollar.)
f. A payment of $1,500 for one full year's interest on notes payable is now due.
g. Unearned Passenger Service Revenue on June 30 includes $17,815 for tickets that employers purchased for use by their executives but which have not yet been redeemed.
h. Federal income taxes for the year are estimated to be $13,250.

REQUIRED

1. Determine the adjusting entries and enter them in the general journal (Page 14).
2. Open ledger accounts for the accounts in the trial balance plus the following: Interest Payable (213); Income Taxes Payable (214); Rent Expense (514); Insurance Expense (515); Spare Parts Expense (516); Depreciation Expense—Limousines (517); Maintenance Expense (518); Interest Expense (519); and Income Taxes Expense (520). Record the balances shown in the trial balance.

(Continued)

3. Post the adjusting entries from the general journal to the ledger accounts, showing proper references.
4. Prepare an adjusted trial balance, an income statement, a statement of retained earnings, and a balance sheet.
5. **ACCOUNTING CONNECTION ▶** What effect do the adjusting entries have on the income statement?

LO 3

Determining Adjustments

✔ e: Unearned Cleaning Revenue balance: $1,200

P5. At the end of its fiscal year, Berwyn Cleaners, Inc.'s trial balance is as follows.

Berwyn Cleaners, Inc.
Trial Balance
September 30, 2014

Cash	11,788	
Accounts Receivable	26,494	
Prepaid Insurance	3,400	
Cleaning Supplies	7,374	
Land	18,000	
Building	185,000	
Accumulated Depreciation—Building		45,600
Accounts Payable		20,400
Unearned Cleaning Revenue		1,600
Mortgage Payable		110,000
Common Stock		20,000
Retained Earnings		36,560
Dividends	10,000	
Cleaning Revenue		157,634
Wages Expense	101,330	
Cleaning Equipment Rental Expense	6,000	
Delivery Truck Expense	4,374	
Interest Expense	11,000	
Other Expenses	7,034	
	391,794	391,794

The following information is also available:

a. A study of the company's insurance policies shows that $680 is unexpired at the end of the year.
b. An inventory of cleaning supplies shows $1,244 on hand.
c. Estimated depreciation on the building for the year is $12,800.
d. Accrued interest on the mortgage payable is $1,000.
e. On September 1, the company signed a contract, effective immediately, with Hope County Hospital to dry clean, for a fixed monthly charge of $400, the uniforms used by doctors in surgery. The hospital paid for four months' service in advance.
f. Sales and delivery wages are paid on Saturday. The weekly payroll is $2,520. September 30 falls on a Thursday, and the company has a six-day pay week.
g. Federal income taxes for the three months are estimated to be $2,300.

REQUIRED

All adjustments affect one balance sheet account and one income statement account. For each of the above situations, show the accounts affected, the amount of the adjustment (using a + or − to indicate an increase or decrease), and the balance of the account after the adjustment in the following format:

Balance Sheet Account	Amount of Adjustment (+ or −)	Balance After Adjustment	Income Statement Account	Amount of Adjustment (+ or −)	Balance After Adjustment

LO 3, 4

GENERAL LEDGER

✓ 3: Adjusted trial balance: $126,092

Determining Adjusting Entries, Posting to T Accounts, and Preparing an Adjusted Trial Balance

P6. Brave Advisors Service, Inc.'s trial balance on December 31, 2014, is as follows.

Brave Advisors Service, Inc.
Trial Balance
December 31, 2014

Cash	16,500	
Accounts Receivable	8,250	
Office Supplies	2,662	
Prepaid Rent	1,320	
Office Equipment	9,240	
Accumulated Depreciation—Office Equipment		1,540
Accounts Payable		5,940
Notes Payable		11,000
Unearned Service Revenue		2,970
Common Stock		10,000
Retained Earnings		14,002
Dividends	22,000	
Service Revenue		72,600
Salaries Expense	49,400	
Rent Expense	4,400	
Utilities Expense	4,280	
	118,052	118,052

The following information is also available:

a. Ending inventory of office supplies, $264
b. Prepaid rent expired, $440
c. Depreciation of office equipment for the period, $660
d. Accrued interest expense at the end of the period, $550
e. Accrued salaries at the end of the period, $330
f. Service revenue still unearned at the end of the period, $1,166
g. Service revenue earned but unrecorded, $2,200
h. Estimated income taxes for the period, $4,300

REQUIRED

1. Open T accounts for the accounts in the trial balance plus the following: Interest Payable; Salaries Payable; Income Taxes Payable; Office Supplies Expense; Depreciation Expense—Office Equipment; Interest Expense; and Income Taxes Expense. Enter the balances shown on the trial balance.
2. Determine the adjusting entries and post them directly to the T accounts.
3. Prepare an adjusted trial balance.
4. **ACCOUNTING CONNECTION ▶** Which financial statements do each of the above adjustments affect? Which financial statement is *not* affected by the adjustments?

LO 2, 3

GENERAL LEDGER

✓ 1d: Debit to Supplies Expense: $4,195

Preparing Adjusting Entries

P7. On June 30, the end of the current fiscal year, the following information is available to BND Corporation's accountants for making adjusting entries:

a. Among the liabilities of the company is a mortgage payable in the amount of $240,000. On June 30, the accrued interest on this mortgage amounted to $12,000.
b. On Friday, July 2, the company, which is on a five-day workweek and pays employees weekly, will pay its regular salaried employees $19,200.

(Continued)

c. On June 29, the company completed negotiations and signed a contract to provide monthly services to a new client at an annual rate of $3,600.

d. The Supplies account shows a beginning balance of $1,615 and purchases during the year of $3,766. The end-of-year inventory reveals supplies on hand of $1,186.

e. The Prepaid Insurance account shows the following entries on June 30:

Beginning balance	$1,530
January 1	2,900
May 1	3,366

The beginning balance represents the unexpired portion of a one-year policy purchased in April of the previous year. The January 1 entry represents a new one-year policy, and the May 1 entry represents the additional coverage of a three-year policy. (Round to the nearest dollar.)

f. The following table contains the cost and annual depreciation for buildings and equipment, all of which were purchased before the current year:

Account	Cost	Annual Depreciation
Buildings	$185,000	$ 7,300
Equipment	218,000	21,800

g. On June 1, the company completed negotiations with another client and accepted an advance of $21,000 for services to be performed for a year. The $21,000 was credited to Unearned Service Revenue.

h. The company calculates that, as of June 30, it had earned $3,500 on a $7,500 contract that will be completed and billed in August.

i. Federal income taxes for the year are estimated to be $6,100.

REQUIRED

1. Prepare adjusting entries for each item listed above.
2. **CONCEPT ▶** Explain how the conditions for revenue recognition are applied to transactions **c** and **h**.

LO **3, 4**

Determining Adjusting Entries and Tracing Their Effects to Financial Statements

GENERAL LEDGER

✔ 3: Adjusted trial balance: $31,938

P8. Steven Tax Service, Inc.'s trial balance at the end of its second year of operation is as follows.

Steven Tax Service, Inc.
Trial Balance
December 31, 2014

Cash	2,268	
Accounts Receivable	1,031	
Prepaid Insurance	240	
Office Supplies	782	
Office Equipment	7,100	
Accumulated Depreciation—Office Equipment		770
Accounts Payable		635
Unearned Tax Fees		219
Common Stock		3,000
Retained Earnings		2,439
Dividends	6,000	
Tax Fees Revenue		21,926
Office Salaries Expense	8,300	
Advertising Expense	650	
Rent Expense	2,400	
Telephone Expense	218	
	28,989	28,989

The following information is also available:

a. Office supplies on hand, December 31, 2014, $227
b. Insurance still unexpired, $120
c. Estimated depreciation of office equipment, $770
d. Telephone expense for December, $19; the bill was received but not recorded.
e. The services for all unearned tax fees had been performed by the end of the year.
f. Estimated federal income taxes for the year, $2,160

REQUIRED

1. Open T accounts for the accounts in the trial balance plus the following: Income Taxes Payable; Office Supplies Expense; Insurance Expense; Depreciation Expense—Office Equipment; and Income Taxes Expense. Record the balances shown in the trial balance.
2. Determine the adjusting entries and post them directly to the T accounts.
3. Prepare an adjusted trial balance, an income statement, a statement of Retained Earnings, and a balance sheet.
4. **ACCOUNTING CONNECTION ▶** Why is it not necessary to show the effects of the above transactions on the statement of cash flows?

ALTERNATE PROBLEMS

LO 3

Determining Adjustments

✔ e: Wages Expense balance: $3,748

P9. At the end of the first three months of operation, Evergreen Repair, Inc.'s trial balance is as follows.

Evergreen Repair, Inc.
Trial Balance
March 31, 2014

Cash	7,983	
Accounts Receivable	5,872	
Office Supplies	970	
Prepaid Rent	1,500	
Equipment	5,200	
Accounts Payable		2,629
Unearned Repair Revenue		1,146
Common Stock		5,000
Retained Earnings		6,314
Dividends	1,800	
Repair Revenue		12,236
Wages Expense	3,580	
Office Cleaning Expense	420	
	27,325	27,325

Evergreen has hired an accountant to prepare financial statements to determine how well the company is doing after three months. Upon examining the accounting records, the accountant finds the following items of interest:

a. An inventory of office supplies reveals supplies on hand of $469.
b. The Prepaid Rent account includes the rent for the first three months plus a deposit for April's rent.
c. Depreciation on the equipment for the first three months is $560.
d. The balance of the Unearned Repair Revenue account represents a 12-month service contract paid in advance on February 1.
e. On March 31, accrued wages total $168.
f. Federal income taxes for the three months are estimated to be $1,250.

(Continued)

REQUIRED

All adjustments affect one balance sheet account and one income statement account. For each of these situations, show the accounts affected, the amount of the adjustment (using a + or − to indicate an increase or decrease), and the balance of the account after the adjustment in the following format:

Balance Sheet Account	Amount of Adjustment (+ or −)	Balance After Adjustment	Income Statement Account	Amount of Adjustment (+ or −)	Balance After Adjustment

LO **2, 3**

Preparing Adjusting Entries

GENERAL LEDGER

✔ 1d: Debit to Unearned Service Revenue: $10,667

P10. On March 31, the end of the current fiscal year, the following information is available to assist Zun Cleaning Corporation's accountants in making adjusting entries:

a. Zun's Supplies account shows a beginning balance of $5,962. Purchases during the year were $10,294. The end-of-year inventory reveals supplies on hand of $3,105.

b. The Prepaid Insurance account shows the following on March 31:

Beginning balance	$ 5,990
September 1	6,480
January 1	10,080

The beginning balance represents the unexpired portion of a one-year policy purchased in January of the previous year. The September 1 entry represents a new one-year policy, and the January 1 entry represents additional coverage in the form of a three-year policy.

c. The following table contains the cost and annual depreciation for buildings and equipment, all of which Zun purchased before the current year:

Account	Cost	Annual Depreciation
Buildings	$ 804,000	$34,000
Equipment	1,029,000	52,000

d. On December 1, the company completed negotiations with a client and accepted an advance of $32,000 for services to be performed monthly for a year. The $32,000 was credited to Unearned Services Revenue. (Round to the nearest dollar.)

e. The company calculated that, as of March 31, it had earned $9,200 on a $17,000 contract that would be completed and billed in January.

f. Among the liabilities of the company is a note payable in the amount of $600,000. On March 31, the accrued interest on this note amounted to $17,470.

g. On Saturday, April 3, the company, which is on a six-day workweek, will pay its regular employees their weekly wages of $22,000. (Round to the nearest dollar.)

h. On March 31, the company completed negotiations and signed a contract to provide services to a new client at an annual rate of $19,000, beginning April 1.

i. Federal income taxes for the year are estimated to be $31,000.

REQUIRED

1. Prepare adjusting entries for each item listed above.
2. **CONCEPT ▶** Explain how the conditions for revenue recognition are applied to transactions **e** and **h**.

LO 3, 4

Determining Adjusting Entries, Posting to T Accounts, and Preparing an Adjusted Trial Balance

✔ 3: Adjusted trial balance: $214,285

P11. Lee Technology Corporation's trial balance on December 31, 2014 is as follows.

Lee Technology Corporation
Trial Balance
December 31, 2014

Cash	35,572	
Accounts Receivable	59,680	
Office Supplies	2,443	
Prepaid Rent	2,400	
Office Equipment	14,300	
Accumulated Depreciation—Office Equipment		3,200
Accounts Payable		2,640
Notes Payable		15,000
Unearned Service Revenue		5,650
Common Stock		30,000
Retained Earnings		58,705
Dividends	15,000	
Service Revenue		89,000
Salaries Expense	58,000	
Utilities Expense	3,600	
Rent Expense	13,200	
	204,195	204,195

The following information is also available:

a. Ending inventory of office supplies, $538
b. Prepaid rent expired, $1,200
c. Depreciation of office equipment for the period, $800
d. Interest accrued on the note payable, $750
e. Salaries accrued at the end of the period, $800
f. Service revenue still unearned at the end of the period, $3,675
g. Service revenue earned but not billed, $1,800
h. Estimated federal income taxes for the period, $5,940

REQUIRED

1. Open T accounts for the accounts in the trial balance plus the following: Interest Payable; Salaries Payable; Income Taxes Payable; Office Supplies Expense; Depreciation Expense—Office Equipment; Interest Expense; and Income Taxes Expense. Enter the account balances.
2. Determine the adjusting entries and post them directly to the T accounts.
3. Prepare an adjusted trial balance.
4. **ACCOUNTING CONNECTION ▶** Which financial statements do each of the above adjustments affect? What financial statement is *not* affected by the adjustments?

LO 3, 4

Determining Adjusting Entries and Tracing Their Effects to Financial Statements

SPREADSHEET

✔ 4: Adjusted trial balance: $763,338

P12. USA Car Rental Service, Inc., was organized to provide car rental service at the airport. It has just completed its second year of business. Its trial balance follows.

(Continued)

USA Car Rental Service, Inc.
Trial Balance
June 30, 2014

Cash (111)	15,708	
Accounts Receivable (113)	19,830	
Prepaid Rent (117)	18,000	
Prepaid Insurance (118)	6,400	
Prepaid Maintenance (119)	13,620	
Spare Parts (140)	12,200	
Cars (148)	270,000	
Accumulated Depreciation—Cars (149)		35,000
Notes Payable (211)		78,000
Unearned Rental Service Revenue (212)		42,000
Common Stock (311)		25,000
Retained Earnings (312)		41,567
Dividends (313)	30,000	
Rental Service Revenue (411)		492,151
Gas and Oil Expense (510)	104,900	
Salaries Expense (511)	206,360	
Advertising Expense (513)	16,700	
	713,718	713,718

The following information is also available:

a. To obtain space at the airport, USA paid two years' rent in advance when it began the business.
b. An examination of insurance policies reveals that $2,000 expired during the year.
c. To provide regular maintenance for the vehicles, USA deposited $13,620 with a local garage. An examination of maintenance invoices reveals charges of $7,890 against the deposit.
d. An inventory of spare parts shows $2,170 on hand.
e. USA depreciates all of its cars at the rate of 12.5 percent per year. No cars were purchased during the year.
f. A payment of $2,000 for one full year's interest on notes payable is now due.
g. Unearned Rental Service Revenue on June 30 includes $20,325 for cars that customers prepaid but have not yet been rented.
h. Federal income taxes for the year are estimated to be $13,870.

REQUIRED

1. Determine the adjusting entries and enter them in the general journal (Page 14).
2. Open ledger accounts for the accounts in the trial balance plus the following: Interest Payable (213); Income Taxes Payable (214); Rent Expense (514); Insurance Expense (515); Spare Parts Expense (516); Depreciation Expense—Cars (517); Maintenance Expense (518); Interest Expense (519); and Income Taxes Expense (520). Record the balances shown in the trial balance.
3. Post the adjusting entries from the general journal to the ledger accounts, showing proper references.
4. Prepare an adjusted trial balance, an income statement, a statement of retained earnings, and a balance sheet.
5. **ACCOUNTING CONNECTION** ▶ What effect do the adjusting entries have on the income statement?

LO 2, 3

Determining Adjustments

✔ e: Upholstery Revenue balance: $158,034

P13. Gonzales Upholstery, Inc.'s trial balance at the end of its fiscal year follows.

Gonzales Upholstery, Inc.
Trial Balance
September 30, 2014

Cash	16,288	
Accounts Receivable	16,494	
Prepaid Insurance	1,900	
Upholstery Supplies	4,370	
Land	18,000	
Building	125,000	
Accumulated Depreciation—Building		26,300
Accounts Payable		17,400
Unearned Upholstery Revenue		1,600
Mortgage Payable		90,000
Common Stock		3,000
Retained Earnings		4,756
Dividends	10,000	
Upholstery Revenue		157,634
Wages Expense	81,930	
Upholstery Equipment Rental Expense	6,000	
Delivery Truck Expense	4,374	
Interest Expense	9,300	
Other Expenses	7,034	
	300,690	300,690

The following information is also available:

a. A study of the company's insurance policies shows that $380 is unexpired at the end of the year.
b. An inventory of upholstery supplies shows $1,040 on hand.
c. Estimated depreciation on the building for the year is $9,800.
d. Accrued interest on the mortgage payable is $960.
e. On September 1, the company signed a contract, effective immediately, with County Community Bank to repair and reupholster office furniture, for a fixed monthly charge of $400. The bank paid for four months' service in advance.
f. Sales and delivery wages are paid on Saturday. The weekly payroll is $1,530. September 30 falls on a Thursday, and the company has a six-day pay week.
g. Estimated federal income taxes for the period are $2,410.

REQUIRED

All adjustments affect one balance sheet account and one income statement account. For each of the above situations, show the accounts affected, the amount of the adjustment (using a + or − to indicate an increase or decrease), and the balance of the account after the adjustment in the following format:

Balance Sheet Account	Amount of Adjustment (+ or −)	Balance After Adjustment	Income Statement Account	Amount of Adjustment (+ or −)	Balance After Adjustment

LO 3

Determining Adjusting Entries, Posting to T Accounts, and Preparing an Adjusted Trial Balance

✔ 3: Adjusted trial balance: $134,131

P14. Scoop Consulting Service, Inc.'s trial balance on December 31, 2014, is as follows.

Scoop Consulting Service, Inc.
Trial Balance
December 31, 2014

Cash	19,250	
Accounts Receivable	7,360	
Office Supplies	2,861	
Prepaid Rent	1,820	
Office Equipment	9,240	
Accumulated Depreciation—Office Equipment		2,140
Accounts Payable		5,940
Notes Payable		11,000
Unearned Service Revenue		4,120
Common Stock		11,000
Retained Earnings		13,111
Dividends	22,000	
Service Revenue		76,200
Salaries Expense	51,300	
Rent Expense	5,400	
Utilities Expense	4,280	
	123,511	123,511

The following information is also available:

a. Ending inventory of office supplies, $564
b. Prepaid rent expired, $470
c. Depreciation of office equipment for the period, $820
d. Accrued interest expense at the end of the period, $730
e. Accrued salaries at the end of the period, $630
f. Service revenue still unearned at the end of the period, $2,722
g. Service revenue earned but unrecorded, $2,500
h. Estimated income taxes for the period, $5,940

REQUIRED

1. Open T accounts for the accounts in the trial balance plus the following: Interest Payable; Salaries Payable; Income Taxes Payable; Office Supplies Expense; Depreciation Expense—Office Equipment; Interest Expense; and Income Taxes Expense. Enter the balances shown on the trial balance.
2. Determine the adjusting entries and post them directly to the T accounts.
3. Prepare an adjusted trial balance.
4. **ACCOUNTING CONNECTION ▶** Which financial statements do each of the above adjustments affect? Which financial statement is *not* affected by the adjustments?

LO 2, 3

Preparing Adjusting Entries

GENERAL LEDGER

✔ 1e: Debit to Insurance Expense: $2,781

P15. On June 30, the end of the current fiscal year, the following information is available to Axel Corporation's accountants for making adjusting entries:

a. Among the liabilities of the company is a mortgage payable in the amount of $280,000. On June 30, the accrued interest on this mortgage amounted to $14,000.
b. On Friday, July 2, the company, which is on a five-day workweek and pays employees weekly, will pay its regular salaried employees $23,100.
c. On June 29, the company completed negotiations and signed a contract to provide monthly services to a new client at an annual rate of $6,645.

d. The Supplies account shows a beginning balance of $1,975 and purchases during the year of $2,846. The end-of-year inventory reveals supplies on hand of $1,984.
e. The Prepaid Insurance account shows the following entries on June 30:

Beginning balance	$1,333
January 1	2,544
May 1	3,168

The beginning balance represents the unexpired portion of a one-year policy purchased in April of the previous year. The January 1 entry represents a new one-year policy, and the May 1 entry represents the additional coverage of a three-year policy.

f. The following table contains the cost and annual depreciation for buildings and equipment, all of which were purchased before the current year:

Account	Cost	Annual Depreciation
Buildings	$235,000	$ 6,301
Equipment	198,000	11,520

g. On June 1, the company completed negotiations with another client and accepted an advance of $31,080 for services to be performed for a year. The $31,080 was credited to Unearned Service Revenue.
h. The company calculates that, as of June 30, it had earned $3,600 on a $9,600 contract that will be completed and billed in August.
i. Federal income taxes for the year are estimated to be $5,300.

REQUIRED

1. Prepare adjusting entries for each item listed above.
2. **CONCEPT** ▶ Explain how the conditions for revenue recognition are applied to transactions **c** and **h**.

LO **3, 4**

SPREADSHEET

✔ 3: Adjusted trial balance: $47,898

Determining Adjusting Entries and Tracing Their Effects to Financial Statements

P16. At the end of its second year of operation, Jacobs Financial Advisors, Inc., had the trial balance that follows.

Jacobs Financial Advisors, Inc.
Trial Balance
December 31, 2014

Cash	11,265	
Accounts Receivable	2,191	
Prepaid Insurance	520	
Office Supplies	682	
Office Equipment	7,980	
Accumulated Depreciation—Office Equipment		790
Accounts Payable		437
Unearned Tax Fees		519
Common Stock		2,400
Retained Earnings		3,074
Dividends	7,500	
Tax Fees Revenue		36,926
Office Salaries Expense	9,700	
Advertising Expense	650	
Rent Expense	3,200	
Telephone Expense	458	
	44,146	44,146

(Continued)

The following information is also available:

a. Office supplies on hand, December 31, 2014, $319
b. Insurance still unexpired, $180
c. Estimated depreciation of office equipment, $870
d. Telephone expense for December, $182; the bill was received but not recorded.
e. The services for all unearned tax fees had been performed by the end of the year.
f. Estimated federal income taxes for the year, $2,700

REQUIRED

1. Open T accounts for the accounts in the trial balance plus the following: Income Taxes Payable; Office Supplies Expense; Insurance Expense; Depreciation Expense—Office Equipment; and Income Taxes Expense. Record the balances shown in the trial balance.
2. Determine the adjusting entries and post them directly to the T accounts.
3. Prepare an adjusted trial balance, an income statement, a statement of retained earnings, and a balance sheet.
4. **ACCOUNTING CONNECTION ▶** Why is it not necessary to show the effects of the above transactions on the statement of cash flows?

CASES

LO 2, 3

Conceptual Understanding: Importance of Adjustments

C1. Never Flake Company provided a rust-prevention coating for the underside of new automobiles. The company advertised widely and offered its services through new-car dealers. When a dealer sold a new car, the salesperson attempted to sell the rust-prevention coating as an option. A key selling point was Never Flake's warranty, which stated that it would repair any damage due to rust at no charge for as long as the buyer owned the car.

For several years, Never Flake had been very successful, but in 2013, the company suddenly declared bankruptcy. Company officials said that the firm had only $5.5 million in assets against liabilities of $32.9 million. Most of the liabilities represented potential claims under the company's lifetime warranty. It seemed that owners were keeping their cars longer than they had previously. Therefore, more damage was being attributed to rust.

Discuss what accounting decisions could have helped Never Flake to survive under these circumstances.

LO 2, 3, 5

Conceptual Understanding: Earnings Management and Fraudulent Financial Reporting

C2. BUSINESS APPLICATION ▶ In recent years, the Securities and Exchange Commission (SEC) has been waging a public campaign against corporate accounting practices that manage or manipulate earnings to meet the expectations of Wall Street analysts. Corporations engage in such practices in the hope of avoiding shortfalls that might cause serious declines in their stock price.

For each of the following cases that the Securities and Exchange Commission challenged, explain why each was a violation of the accrual accounting:

a. **Lucent Technologies** sold telecommunications equipment to companies from which there was no reasonable expectation of payment because of the companies' poor financial condition.
b. **America Online (AOL)** recorded advertising as an asset rather than as an expense.
c. **Eclipsys** recorded software contracts as revenue even though it had not yet rendered the services.
d. **Xerox Corporation** recorded revenue from lease agreements at the time the leases were signed rather than over the lease term.
e. **KnowledgeWare** recorded revenue from sales of software even though it told customers they did not have to pay until they had the software.

LO 2, 3 **Interpreting Financial Reports: Application of Accrual Accounting**

C3. The **Lyric Opera of Chicago** is one of the largest and best-managed opera companies in the United States. Managing opera productions requires advance planning, including the development of scenery, costumes, and stage properties and the sale of tickets. To measure how well the company is operating in any given year, management must apply accrual accounting to these and other transactions. At year-end, April 30, 2011, Lyric Opera's balance sheet showed deferred production costs and other assets of $1,978,322 and deferred ticket and other revenue of $12,710,639.[9] What accounting policies and adjusting entries are applicable to these accounts? Why are they important to Lyric Opera's management?

LO 2, 3 **Interpreting Financial Reports: Analysis of an Asset Account**

C4. The Walt Disney Company is engaged in the financing, production, and distribution of motion pictures and television programming. In Disney's 2011 annual report, the balance sheet contains an asset called "film and television costs." Film and television costs, which consist of the costs associated with producing films and television programs less the amount expensed, were $4,357 million. The notes reveal that the amount of film and television costs expensed (amortized) during the year was $3,521 million. The amount spent for new film productions was $3,184 million.[10]

1. **CONCEPT ▶** What are film and television costs, and why would they be classified as an asset?
2. Prepare T accounts to record the amount the company spent on new film and television production during the year (assume all expenditures are paid for in cash).
3. Prepare an adjusting entry in T account form to record the expense for film and television productions.
4. **CONCEPT ▶** Suggest a method by which The Walt Disney Company might have determined the amount of the expense in **3** in accordance with the accrual accounting.

LO 3 **Annual Report Case: Analysis of Balance Sheet and Adjusting Entries**

C5. In the **CVS** annual report in the Supplement to Chapter 1, refer to the balance sheet and the Summary of Significant Accounting Policies in the notes to the financial statements.

1. Examine the accounts in the current assets, property and equipment, and current liabilities sections of CVS's balance sheet. Which are most likely to have had year-end adjusting entries? Describe the nature of the adjusting entries. For more information about the property and equipment section, refer to the notes to the financial statements.
2. Where is depreciation (and amortization) expense disclosed in CVS's financial statements?
3. CVS has a statement on the "Use of Estimates" in its Summary of Significant Accounting Policies. Read this statement, and tell how important estimates are in determining depreciation expense. What assumptions do accountants use in estimating depreciation?

LO 5 **Ethical Dilemma: Importance of Adjustments**

C6. BUSINESS APPLICATION ▶ Central Appliance Service, Inc., has achieved fast growth by selling service contracts on large appliances, such as washers, dryers, and refrigerators. For a fee, the company agrees to provide all parts and labor on an appliance after the regular warranty runs out. For example, by paying a fee of $200, a person who buys a dishwasher can add two years to the regular one-year warranty on the appliance. In 2014, the company sold service contracts in the amount of $1.8 million, all of which applied to future years. Management wanted all the sales recorded as revenues in 2014, contending that the amount of the contracts could be determined and the cash had been received. Do you agree with this logic? How would you record the cash receipts?

(Continued)

What assumptions do you think Central Appliance should make? Would you consider it unethical to follow management's recommendation? Who might be hurt or helped by this action?

Continuing Case: Annual Report Project

C7. Using the most recent annual report of the company you have chosen to study and that you have accessed online at the company's website, examine the current assets and current liabilities of your company. Identify accounts that would likely fall into one of the following two categories:

1. Deferral
2. Accrual

SUPPLEMENT TO CHAPTER 3
Closing Entries and the Work Sheet

Preparing Closing Entries

As you know, closing entries have two purposes:

- They clear the balances of all temporary accounts (revenue, expense, and Dividends accounts) so that they have zero balances at the beginning of the next accounting period.
- They summarize a period's revenues and expenses in the Income Summary account so that the net income or net loss for the period can be transferred as a total to Retained Earnings.

The steps involved in making closing entries follow.

- **Step 1.** Close the credit balances on the income statement accounts to the Income Summary account.
- **Step 2.** Close the debit balances on the income statement accounts to the Income Summary account.
- **Step 3.** Close the Income Summary account balance to the Retained Earnings account. (Although it is not necessary to use the Income Summary account when preparing closing entries, it does simplify the procedure.)
- **Step 4.** Close the Dividends account balance to the Retained Earnings account.

You will learn in later chapters that not all credit balance accounts are revenues and not all debit balance accounts are expenses. Therefore, we often use the term *credit balances* instead of *revenue accounts* and the term *debit balances* instead of *expense accounts.*

An adjusted trial balance provides all the data needed to record the closing entries. Exhibit 1 shows the relationships of the four kinds of closing entries to Blue Design Studio, Inc.'s adjusted trial balance.

Exhibit 1
Preparing Closing Entries from the Adjusted Trial Balance

Blue Design Studio, Inc.
Adjusted Trial Balance
July 31, 2014

Cash	22,480	
Accounts Receivable	5,000	
Office Supplies	3,660	
Prepaid Rent	1,600	
Office Equipment	16,320	
Accumulated Depreciation—Office Equipment		300
Accounts Payable		6,280
Unearned Design Revenue		600
Wages Payable		720
Income Taxes Payable		800
Common Stock		40,000
Dividends	2,800	
Design Revenue		13,600
Wages Expense	5,520	
Utilities Expense	680	
Rent Expense	1,600	
Office Supplies Expense	1,540	
Depreciation Expense—Office Equipment	300	
Income Taxes Expense	800	
	62,300	62,300

Exhibit 1
Preparing Closing Entries from the Adjusted Trial Balance (*Continued*)

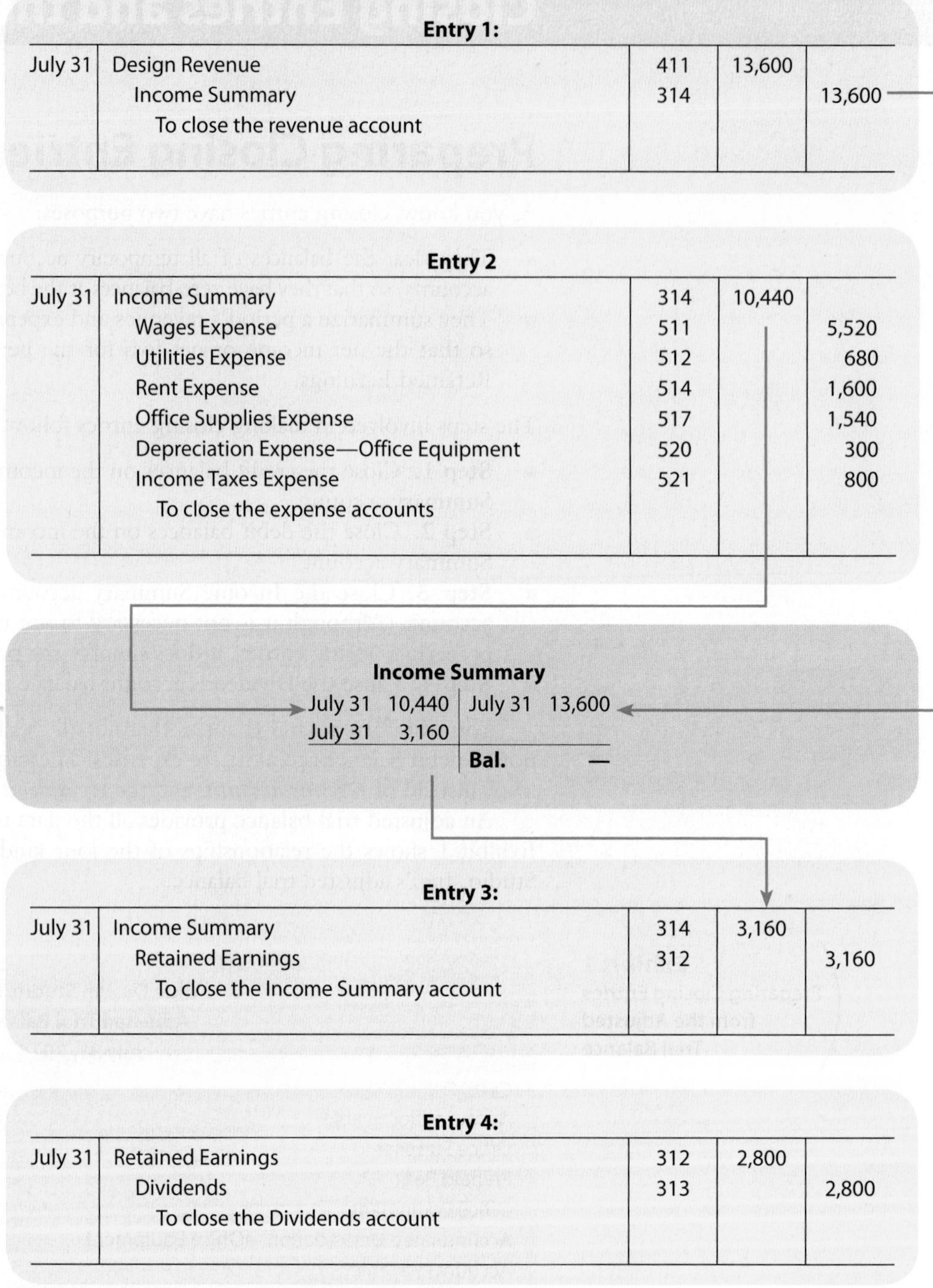

Entry 1:

July 31	Design Revenue	411	13,600	
	Income Summary	314		13,600
	To close the revenue account			

Entry 2

July 31	Income Summary	314	10,440	
	Wages Expense	511		5,520
	Utilities Expense	512		680
	Rent Expense	514		1,600
	Office Supplies Expense	517		1,540
	Depreciation Expense—Office Equipment	520		300
	Income Taxes Expense	521		800
	To close the expense accounts			

Income Summary

Debit		Credit	
July 31	10,440	July 31	13,600
July 31	3,160		
		Bal.	—

Entry 3:

July 31	Income Summary	314	3,160	
	Retained Earnings	312		3,160
	To close the Income Summary account			

Entry 4:

July 31	Retained Earnings	312	2,800	
	Dividends	313		2,800
	To close the Dividends account			

Step 1: Closing the Credit Balances

In the adjusted trial balance in Exhibit 1, Design Revenue shows a credit balance of $13,600 and is closed by debiting it for $13,600 and crediting the Income Summary account for the same amount.

Closing the Revenue Account

Account On July 31, Design Revenue of $13,600 credit balance is closed to Income Summary.

Analysis The journal entry to close Design Revenue

▼ *decreases Design Revenue* with a debit

▲ *increases Income Summary* with a credit

Application of Double Entry

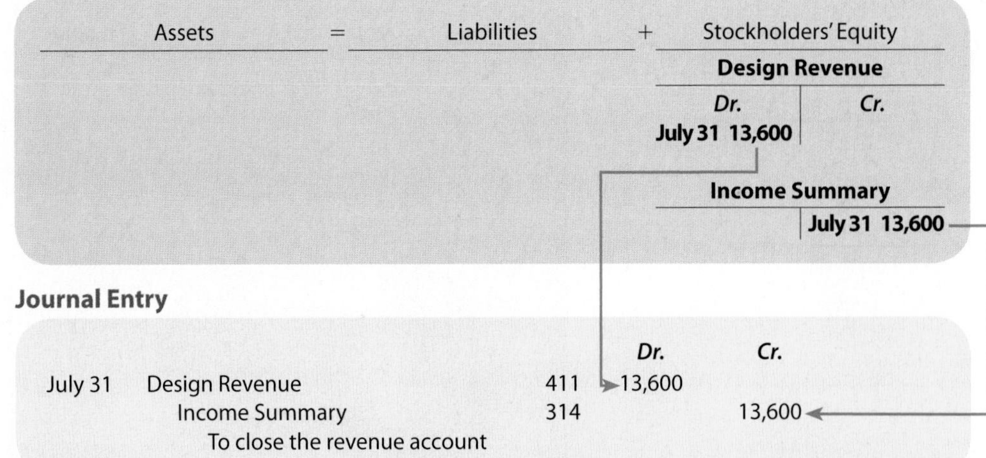

Assets = Liabilities + Stockholders' Equity
Design Revenue
Dr. Cr.
July 31 13,600
Income Summary
July 31 13,600

Journal Entry

			Dr.	Cr.
July 31	Design Revenue	411	13,600	
	Income Summary	314		13,600
	To close the revenue account			

Comment Design Revenue now has a zero balance in preparation for the next accounting period and Income Summary reflects revenue for the period. Exhibit 2 shows Design Revenue and Income Summary ledger accounts at this point in the closing process.

Exhibit 2
Posting the Closing Entry of a Credit Balance Account to the Income

Design Revenue — **Account No. 411**

Date		Item	Post. Ref.	Debit	Credit	Balance Debit	Balance Credit
July	10		J1		2,800		2,800
	15		J1		9,600		12,400
	31	Adj.	J3		800		13,200
	31	Adj.	J3		400		13,600
	31	Closing	J4	13,600			—

Income Summary — **Account No. 314**

Date		Item	Post. Ref.	Debit	Credit	Balance Debit	Balance Credit
July	31	Closing	J4		13,600		13,600

Step 2: Closing the Debit Balances

Several expense accounts show balances in the adjusted trial balance in Exhibit 1. A compound entry is needed to credit each of these expense accounts for its balance and to debit the Income Summary account for the total, as follows.

Closing the Expense Accounts

Accounts On July 31, expenses accounts shown in the trial balance in Exhibit 1 are closed to Income Summary.

Analysis The journal entry to close the expense accounts

- ▼ *decreases Income Summary* with a debit
- ▼ *decreases* the expense accounts with a credit

Application of Double Entry

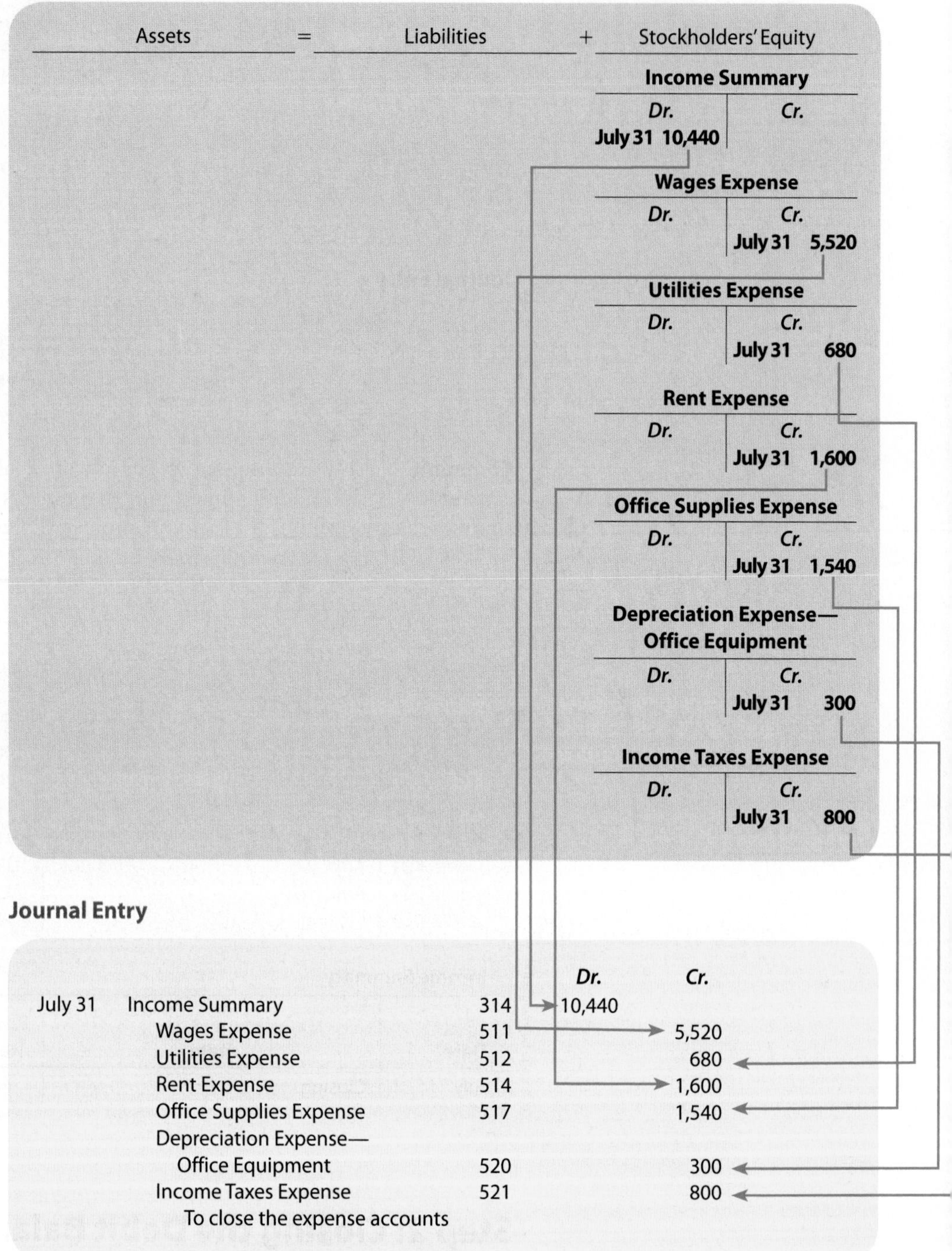

Assets = Liabilities + Stockholders' Equity
Income Summary
Dr. Cr.
July 31 10,440
Wages Expense
Dr. Cr.
July 31 5,520
Utilities Expense
Dr. Cr.
July 31 680
Rent Expense
Dr. Cr.
July 31 1,600
Office Supplies Expense
Dr. Cr.
July 31 1,540
Depreciation Expense—Office Equipment
Dr. Cr.
July 31 300
Income Taxes Expense
Dr. Cr.
July 31 800
Journal Entry
Dr. Cr.
July 31 Income Summary 314 10,440
Wages Expense 511 5,520
Utilities Expense 512 680
Rent Expense 514 1,600
Office Supplies Expense 517 1,540
Depreciation Expense—Office Equipment 520 300
Income Taxes Expense 521 800
To close the expense accounts

STUDY NOTE: The Income Summary account now reflects the account balance of the Design Revenue account before it was closed.

Comment All expense accounts now have zero balances in preparation for the next accounting period and Income Summary reflects revenue and expenses for the period. Exhibit 3 shows all expense ledger accounts and the Income Summary ledger account at this point in the accounting cycle.

Wages Expense — **Account No. 511**

Date		Item	Post. Ref.	Debit	Credit	Balance Debit	Balance Credit
July	26		J1	4,800		4,800	
	31	Adj.	J3	720		5,520	
	31	Closing	J4		5,520	—	

Office Supplies Expense — **Account No. 517**

Date		Item	Post. Ref.	Debit	Credit	Balance Debit	Balance Credit
July	31	Adj.	J3	1,540		1,540	
	31	Closing	J4		1,540	—	

Utilities Expense — **Account No. 512**

Date		Item	Post. Ref.	Debit	Credit	Balance Debit	Balance Credit
July	30		J2	680		680	
	31	Closing	J4		680	—	

Depreciation Expense—Office Equipment — **Account No. 520**

Date		Item	Post. Ref.	Debit	Credit	Balance Debit	Balance Credit
July	31	Adj.	J3	300		300	
	31	Closing	J4		300	—	

Rent Expense — **Account No. 514**

Date		Item	Post. Ref.	Debit	Credit	Balance Debit	Balance Credit
July	31	Adj.	J3	1,600		1,600	
	31	Closing	J4		1,600	—	

Income Taxes Expense — **Account No. 521**

Date		Item	Post. Ref.	Debit	Credit	Balance Debit	Balance Credit
July	31	Adj.	J3	800		800	
	31	Closing	J4		800	—	

Income Summary — **Account No. 314**

Date		Item	Post. Ref.	Debit	Credit	Balance Debit	Balance Credit
July	31	Closing	J4		13,600		13,600
	31	Closing	J4	10,440*			3,160

*Total of all credit closing entries to expense accounts is debited to the Income Summary account.

Exhibit 3
Posting the Closing Entry of Debit Balance Accounts to the Income Summary Account

Step 3: Closing the Income Summary Account Balance

A credit balance in the Income Summary account represents a net income (i.e., revenues exceed expenses), and a debit balance represents a net loss (i.e., expenses exceed revenues). The balance, whatever its nature, is closed to the Retained Earnings account, as follows.

Closing the Income Summary Account

Account On July 31, Income Summary account balance of $3,160 credit is closed to Retained Earnings.

Analysis The journal entry to close Income Summary

- ▼ *decreases Income Summary* with a debit
- ▲ *increases Retained Earnings* with a credit

Application of Double Entry

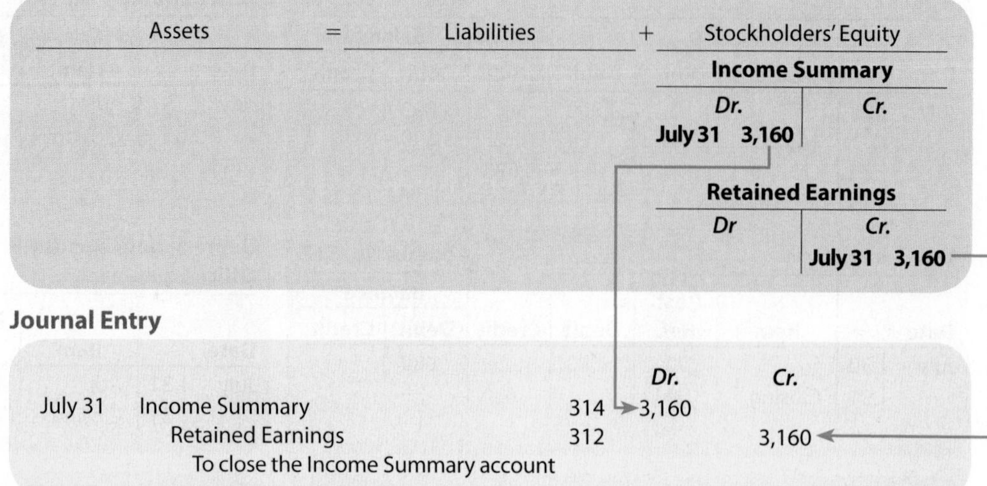

Journal Entry

			Dr.	Cr.
July 31	Income Summary	314	3,160	
	Retained Earnings	312		3,160
	To close the Income Summary account			

STUDY NOTE: *At this point, the credit balance of the Income Summary account ($3,160) represents net income—the key measure of performance. When a net loss occurs, debit the Retained Earnings account (to reduce it) and credit the Income Summary account (to close it).*

Comment Income Summary now has a zero balance in preparation for the next accounting period and Retained Earnings reflects the income for the period. Exhibit 4 shows Income Summary and Retained Earnings ledger accounts at this point in the closing process.

Exhibit 4
Posting the Closing Entry of the Income Summary Account Balance to the Retained Earnings Account

Income Summary — **Account No. 314**

Date		Item	Post. Ref.	Debit	Credit	Balance Debit	Balance Credit
July	31	Closing	J4		13,600		13,600
	31	Closing	J4	10,440			10,440
	31	Closing	J4	3,160			—

Retained Earnings — **Account No. 312**

Date		Item	Post. Ref.	Debit	Credit	Balance Debit	Balance Credit
July	31	Closing	J4		3,160		43,160

Step 4: Closing the Dividends Account Balance

The Dividends account shows the amount distributed to stockholders during an accounting period. The debit balance of the Dividends account is closed to the Retained Earnings account, as follows.

Closing the Dividends Account

Account On July 31, Dividends in the amount of a $2,800 debit is closed to Retained Earnings.

Analysis The journal entry to close Dividends

▼ *decreases Retained Earnings* with a debit
▼ *decreases Dividends* with a credit

Application of Double Entry

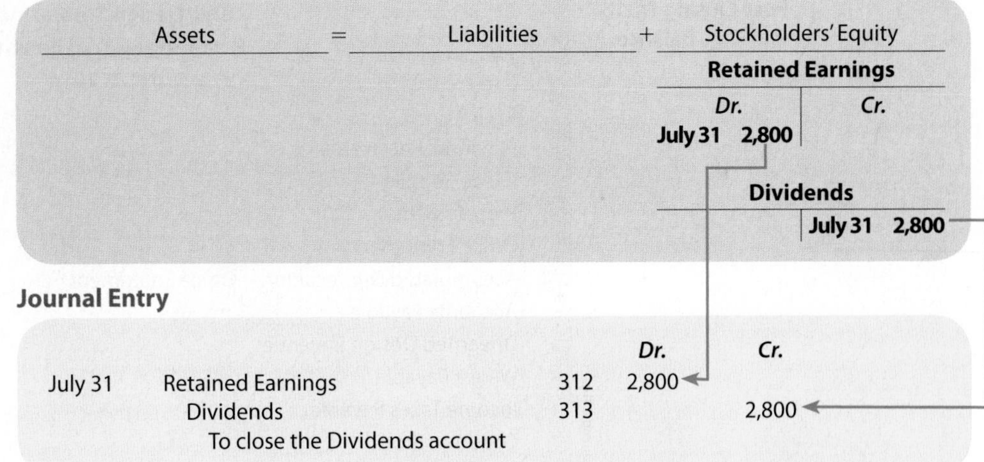

Assets = Liabilities + Stockholders' Equity
Retained Earnings
Dr. Cr.
July 31 2,800
Dividends
July 31 2,800
Journal Entry
Dr. Cr.
July 31 Retained Earnings 312 2,800
Dividends 313 2,800
To close the Dividends account

STUDY NOTE: Note that the Dividends account is closed to the Retained Earnings account, not to the Income Summary account.

Comment Dividends now has a zero balance in preparation for the next accounting period and Retained Earnings reflects the income minus the dividends for the period. Exhibit 5 shows Income Summary and Retained Earnings ledger accounts at this point in the closing process.

Exhibit 5
Posting the Closing Entry of the Dividends Account Balance to the Retained Earnings Account

Dividends — **Account No. 313**

Date		Item	Post. Ref.	Debit	Credit	Balance Debit	Balance Credit
July	31		J2	2,800		2,800	
	31	Closing	J4		2,800	—	

Retained Earnings — **Account No. 312**

Date		Item	Post. Ref.	Debit	Credit	Balance Debit	Balance Credit
July	31	Closing	J4		3,160		3,160
	31	Closing	J4	2,800			360

The Accounts After Closing

After all the steps in the closing process have been completed and all closing entries have been posted, everything is ready for the next accounting period. The revenue, expense, and dividends accounts (temporary accounts) have zero balances. The Retained Earnings account has been increased or decreased to reflect net income or net loss (net income in our example) and has been decreased for dividends. The balance sheet accounts (permanent accounts) show the correct balances, which are carried forward to the next period, as shown in the **post-closing trial balance** in Exhibit 6.

Exhibit 6
Post-Closing Trial Balance

Blue Design Studio, Inc.
Post-Closing Trial Balance
July 31, 2014

Cash	22,480	
Accounts Receivable	5,000	
Office Supplies	3,660	
Prepaid Rent	1,600	
Office Equipment	16,320	
Accumulated Depreciation—Office Equipment		300
Accounts Payable		6,280
Unearned Design Revenue		600
Wages Payable		720
Income Taxes Payable		800
Common Stock		40,000
Retained Earnings		360
	49,060	49,060

The Work Sheet: An Accountant's Tool

To organize data and important information, accountants use **working papers**. Because working papers provide evidence of past work, they also enable accountants to retrace their steps when they need to verify information in the financial statements.

STUDY NOTE: *The work sheet is not a financial statement, it is not required, and it is not made public.*

A **work sheet** is a special kind of working paper. It serves as a preliminary step in preparing financial statements. Using a work sheet lessens the possibility of omitting an adjustment and helps the accountant check the arithmetical accuracy of the accounts. The work sheet is never published and is rarely seen by management.

Because preparing a work sheet is a mechanical process, many accountants use a computer for this purpose. Some accountants use a spreadsheet program to prepare the work sheet. Others use a general ledger system to prepare financial statements from the adjusted trial balance.

Preparing the Work Sheet

A common form of work sheet has one column for account names and multiple columns with headings like the ones shown in Exhibit 7. A heading that includes the name of the company and the period of time covered (as on the income statement) identifies the work sheet. As Exhibit 7 shows, preparation of a work sheet involves five steps.

STUDY NOTE: *The Trial Balance columns of a work sheet take the place of a separate trial balance.*

Step 1. Enter and Total the Account Balances in the Trial Balance Columns The debit and credit balances of the accounts on the last day of an accounting period are copied from the ledger into the Trial Balance columns (the green columns in Exhibit 7). When accountants use a work sheet, they do not have to prepare a separate trial balance.

Step 2. Enter and Total the Adjustments in the Adjustments Columns The required adjustments are entered in the Adjustments columns of the work sheet (the purple columns in Exhibit 7). As each adjustment is entered, a letter is used to identify its debit and credit parts. For example, in Exhibit 7, the letter (a) identifies the adjustment made for the rent that Blue Design Studio, Inc., prepaid on July 3, which results in a debit to Rent Expense and a credit to Prepaid Rent. These identifying letters may be used to reference supporting computations or documentation for the related adjusting entries.

A trial balance includes only accounts that have balances. If an adjustment involves an account that does not appear in the trial balance, the new account is added below the accounts listed on the work sheet. For example, Rent Expense has been added to Exhibit 7. Accumulated depreciation accounts, which have a zero balance only in the initial period

Blue Design Studio, Inc.
Work Sheet
For the Month Ended July 31, 2014

	Trial Balance		Adjustments		Adjusted Trial Balance		Income Statement		Balance Sheet	
Account Name	**Debit**	**Credit**	**Debit**	**Credit**	**Debit**	**Credit**	**Debit**	**Credit**	**Debit**	**Credit**
Cash	22,480				22,480				22,480	
Accounts Receivable	4,600		(f) 400		5,000				5,000	
Office Supplies	5,200			(b) 1,540	3,660				3,660	
Prepaid Rent	3,200			(a) 1,600	1,600				1,600	
Office Equipment	16,320				16,320				16,320	
Accumulated Depreciation—Office Equipment				(c) 300		300				300
Accounts Payable		6,280				6,280				6,280
Unearned Design Revenue		1,400	(e) 800			600				600
Common Stock		40,000				40,000				40,000
Dividends	2,800				2,800				2,800	
Design Revenue		12,400		(e) 800 (f) 400		13,600		13,600		
Wages Expense	4,800		(d) 720		5,520		5,520			
Utilities Expense	680				680		680			
	60,080	60,080								
Rent Expense			(a) 1,600		1,600		1,600			
Office Supplies Expense			(b) 1,540		1,540		1,540			
Depreciation Expense—Office Equipment			(c) 300		300		300			
Wages Payable				(d) 720		720				720
Income Taxes Expense			(g) 800		800		800			
Income Taxes Payable				(g) 800		800				800
			6,160	6,160	62,300	62,300	10,440	13,600	51,860	48,700
Net Income							3,160			3,160
							13,600	13,600	51,860	51,860

Note: The columns of the work sheet are prepared in the following order: (1) Trial Balance, (2) Adjustments, (3) Adjusted Trial Balance, and (4) Income Statement and Balance Sheet columns. In the fifth step, the Income Statement and Balance Sheet columns are totaled.

Exhibit 7
The Work Sheet

of operation, are the sole exception to this rule. They are listed immediately after their associated asset accounts.

When all the adjustments have been made, the two Adjustments columns must be totaled. This procedure proves that the debits and credits of the adjustments are equal, and it generally reduces errors in the work sheet.

Step 3. Enter and Total the Adjusted Account Balances in the Adjusted Trial Balance Columns The adjusted trial balance in the work sheet is prepared by combining the amount of each account in the Trial Balance columns with the corresponding amount in the Adjustments columns and entering each result in the Adjusted Trial Balance columns (the beige columns in Exhibit 7).

Exhibit 7 contains examples of **crossfooting**, or adding and subtracting a group of numbers horizontally.

- The first line shows Cash with a debit balance of $22,480. Because there are no adjustments to the Cash account, $22,480 is entered in the debit column of the Adjusted Trial Balance columns.
- On the second line, Accounts Receivable shows a debit of $4,600 in the Trial Balance columns. Because there is a debit of $400 in the Adjustments columns, it is added to the $4,600 and carried over to the debit column of the Adjusted Trial Balance columns at $5,000.
- On the next line, Office Supplies shows a debit of $5,200 in the Trial Balance columns and a credit of $1,540 in the Adjustments columns. Subtracting $1,540 from $5,200 results in a $3,660 debit balance in the Adjusted Trial Balance columns.

This process is followed for all the accounts, including those added below the trial balance totals. The Adjusted Trial Balance columns are then *footed* (totaled) to check the accuracy of the crossfooting.

Step 4. Extend the Account Balances from the Adjusted Trial Balance Columns to the Income Statement or Balance Sheet Columns Each account in the adjusted trial balance is extended to its proper place as a debit or credit in either the Income Statement columns or the Balance Sheet columns (the blue columns in Exhibit 7). As shown in Exhibit 7, revenue and expense accounts are extended to the Income Statement columns, and asset, liability, Capital, and Dividends accounts are extended to the Balance Sheet columns.

To avoid overlooking an account, the accounts are extended line by line, beginning with the first line (Cash). For instance, the Cash debit balance of $22,480 is extended to the debit column of the Balance Sheet columns; then, the Accounts Receivable debit balance of $5,000 is extended to the debit column of the Balance Sheet columns; and so forth.

Step 5. Total the Income Statement Columns and the Balance Sheet Columns. Enter the Net Income or Net Loss in Both Pairs of Columns as a Balancing Figure, and Recompute the Column Totals. This last step, shown in the orange columns at the bottom of Exhibit 7, is necessary to compute net income or net loss and to prove the arithmetical accuracy of the work sheet.

Net income (or net loss) is equal to the difference between the total debits and credits of the Income Statement columns.

Revenues (Income Statement credit column total)	$13,600
Expenses (Income Statement debit column total)	(10,440)
Net Income	$ 3,160

In this case, revenues (credit column) exceed expenses (debit column). Thus, Blue Design Studio, Inc., has a net income of $3,160. The same difference occurs between the total debits and credits of the Balance Sheet columns.

The $3,160 is entered in the debit side of the Income Statement columns and in the credit side of the Balance Sheet columns to balance the columns. Remember that the excess of revenues over expenses (net income) increases stockholders' equity and that increases in stockholders' equity are recorded by credits.

When a net loss occurs, the opposite rule applies. The excess of expenses over revenues—net loss—is placed in the credit side of the Income Statement columns as a balancing figure. It is then placed in the debit side of the Balance Sheet columns because a net loss decreases stockholders' equity, and decreases in stockholders' equity are recorded by debits.

As a final check, the four columns are totaled again. If the Income Statement columns and the Balance Sheet columns do not balance, an account may have been extended or sorted to the wrong column, or an error may have been made in adding the columns. Of course, equal totals in the two pairs of columns are not absolute proof of accuracy. If an asset has been carried to the Income Statement debit column (or an expense has been carried to the Balance Sheet debit column) or a similar error with revenues or liabilities has been made, the work sheet will balance, but the net income figure will be wrong.

Exhibit 8
Adjustments from the Work Sheet Entered in the General Journal

General Journal **Page 3**

Date		Description	Post. Ref.	Debit	Credit
2014					
(a) July	31	Rent Expense	514	1,600	
		Prepaid Rent	117		1,600
		To recognize expiration of one month's rent			
(b)	31	Office Supplies Expense	517	1,540	
		Office Supplies	116		1,540
		To recognize office supplies used during the month			
(c)	31	Depreciation Expense—Office Equipment	520	300	
		Accumulated Depreciation—Office Equipment	147		300
		To record depreciation of office equipment for a month			
(d)	31	Wages Expense	511	720	
		Wages Payable	214		720
		To accrue unrecorded wages			
(e)	31	Unearned Design Revenue	213	800	
		Design Revenue	411		800
		To recognize payment for services not yet performed			
(f)	31	Accounts Receivable	113	400	
		Design Revenue	411		400
		To accrue design fees earned but unrecorded			
(g)	31	Income Taxes Expense	521	800	
		Income Taxes Payable	215		800
		To record accrued income taxes expense			

Key Terms

crossfooting 194
post-closing trial balance 191
work sheet 192
working papers 192

Assignments

SHORT EXERCISES

Closing Revenue Accounts

SE1. Assume that at the end of the accounting period there are credit balances of $3,400 in Patient Services Revenues and $1,800 in Laboratory Fees Revenues. Prepare the required closing entry. The accounting period ends December 31.

Closing Expense Accounts

SE2. Assume that debit balances at the end of the accounting period are $1,400 in Rent Expense, $1,100 in Wages Expense, and $500 in Other Expenses. Prepare the required closing entry. The accounting period ends December 31.

Closing the Income Summary Account

SE3. Assuming that total revenues were $5,200 and total expenses were $3,000, prepare the journal entry to close the Income Summary account to the Retained Earnings account. The accounting period ends December 31.

Closing the Dividends Account

SE4. Assuming that dividends during the accounting period were $800, prepare the journal entry to close the Dividends account to the Retained Earnings account. The accounting period ends December 31.

Posting Closing Entries

SE5. Show the effects of the transactions in **SE1, SE2, SE3,** and **SE4** by entering beginning balances in appropriate T accounts and recording the transactions. Assume that the Retained Earnings account had a beginning balance of $1,300.

EXERCISES: SET A

Preparation of Closing Entries

E1A. Hamilton Realty Company, Inc.'s income statement accounts at the end of its fiscal year, December 31, follow. Hamilton paid dividends of $5,000 during the year. Prepare the required closing entries.

Account Name	Debit	Credit
Commission Revenue		$25,620
Wages Expense	$8,110	
Rent Expense	1,200	
Supplies Expense	4,260	
Insurance Expense	915	
Depreciation Expense—Office Equipment	1,345	
Total Expenses		15,830
Net Income		$ 9,790

Completion of a Work Sheet

E2A. A highly simplified alphabetical list of trial balance accounts and their normal balances for the month ended March 31, 2014, follows.

Accounts Payable	8
Accounts Receivable	14
Accumulated Depreciation—Office Equipment	2
Cash	8
Common Stock	5
Dividends	12
Office Equipment	16
Prepaid Insurance	4
Retained Earnings	19
Service Revenue	46
Supplies	8
Unearned Revenues	6
Utilities Expense	4
Wages Expense	20

1. Prepare a work sheet, entering the trial balance accounts in the order in which they would normally appear and entering the balances in the correct debit or credit column.
2. Complete the work sheet using the following information: expired insurance, $2; estimated depreciation on office equipment, $2; accrued wages, $2; and unused supplies on hand, $2. In addition, $4 of the unearned revenues balance had been earned by the end of the month.

EXERCISES: SET B

Visit the textbook companion web site at www.cengagebrain.com to access Exercise Set B for this chapter.

PROBLEMS

Preparation of Closing Entries

P1. Salinas Trailer Rental, Inc., rents small trailers by the day for local moving jobs. Its adjusted trial balance at the end of the current fiscal year follows.

Salinas Trailer Rental, Inc.
Adjusted Trial Balance
June 30, 2014

Cash	1,384	
Accounts Receivable	1,944	
Supplies	238	
Prepaid Insurance	720	
Trailers	24,000	
Accumulated Depreciation—Trailers		14,400
Accounts Payable		542
Wages Payable		400
Common Stock		10,000
Retained Earnings		1,388
Dividends	14,400	
Trailer Rentals Revenue		91,092
Wages Expense	46,800	
Insurance Expense	1,440	
Supplies Expense	532	
Depreciation Expense—Trailers	4,800	
Other Expenses	21,564	
	117,822	117,822

REQUIRED

1. From the information given, record closing entries.
2. If closing entries were not prepared at the end of the accounting period, what problems would result in the next accounting period?

Preparation of a Work Sheet, Financial Statements, and Adjusting and Closing Entries

SPREADSHEET

✓ 2: Net income: $62,392
✓ 2: Total assets: $247,148

P2. At the end of the fiscal year, Siglo Delivery Service, Inc.'s trial balance appeared as follows.

Siglo Delivery Service, Inc.
Trial Balance
August 31, 2014

Cash	10,072	
Accounts Receivable	29,314	
Prepaid Insurance	5,340	
Delivery Supplies	14,700	
Office Supplies	2,460	
Land	15,000	
Building	196,000	
Accumulated Depreciation—Building		53,400
Trucks	103,800	
Accumulated Depreciation—Trucks		30,900
Office Equipment	15,900	
Accumulated Depreciation—Office Equipment		10,800
Accounts Payable		9,396
Unearned Lockbox Fees		8,340
Mortgage Payable		72,000
Common Stock		100,000
Retained Earnings		28,730
Dividends	30,000	
Delivery Service Revenue		283,470
Lockbox Fees Earned		28,800
Truck Drivers' Wages Expense	120,600	
Office Salaries Expense	44,400	
Gas, Oil, and Truck Repairs Expense	31,050	
Interest Expense	7,200	
	625,836	625,836

REQUIRED

1. Enter the trial balance amounts in the Trial Balance columns of a work sheet and complete the work sheet using the information that follows.

   a. Expired insurance, $3,060
   b. Inventory of unused delivery supplies, $1,430
   c. Inventory of unused office supplies, $186
   d. Estimated depreciation on the building, $14,400
   e. Estimated depreciation on the trucks, $15,450
   f. Estimated depreciation on the office equipment, $2,700
   g. The company credits the lockbox fees of customers who pay in advance to the Unearned Lockbox Fees account. Of the amount credited to this account during the year, $5,630 had been earned by August 31.
   h. Lockbox fees earned but unrecorded and uncollected at the end of the accounting period, $816
   i. Accrued but unpaid truck drivers' wages at the end of the year, $1,920

2. Prepare an income statement, a statement of retained earnings, and a balance sheet for the company.
3. Prepare adjusting and closing entries from the work sheet.
4. Can the work sheet be used as a substitute for the financial statements? Explain your answer.

The Complete Accounting Cycle Without a Work Sheet: Two Months *(second month optional)*

SPREADSHEET

✔5: May 31, 2014, net income: $962
✔5: May 31, 2014, total assets: $18,048
✔11: June 30, 2014, net income: $1,034
✔11: June 30, 2014, total assets: $18,408

P3. Stoker's Repair Services, Inc., engaged in the following transactions during the month of May in 2014:

May 1 Began business by issuing common stock for cash, $10,000.
1 Paid the rent for the store for current month, $850.
1 Paid the premium on a one-year insurance policy, $960.
2 Purchased repair equipment from Latin Company, $8,400. Terms were $1,200 down and $600 per month for one year. First payment is due June 1.
5 Purchased repair supplies from Tanaka Company on credit, $936.
8 Paid cash for an advertisement in a local newspaper, $120.
15 Received cash repair revenue for the first half of the month, $800.
21 Paid Tanaka Company on account, $450.
31 Received cash repair revenue for the last half of May, $1,950.
31 Paid a dividend, $600.

REQUIRED FOR MAY

1. Prepare journal entries to record the May transactions. Include the Post. Ref. column and fill in using the account numbers listed in requirement 2.
2. Open the following accounts: Cash (111); Prepaid Insurance (117); Repair Supplies (119); Repair Equipment (144); Accumulated Depreciation—Repair Equipment (145); Accounts Payable (212); Common Stock (311); Retained Earnings (312), Dividends (313); Income Summary (314); Repair Revenue (411); Store Rent Expense (511); Advertising Expense (512); Insurance Expense (513); Repair Supplies Expense (514); and Depreciation Expense—Repair Equipment (515). Post the May journal entries to the ledger accounts.
3. Using the following information, record adjusting entries in the general journal and post to the ledger accounts:
   a. One month's insurance has expired.
   b. The remaining inventory of unused repair supplies is $338.
   c. The estimated depreciation on repair equipment is $140.
4. From the accounts in the ledger, prepare an adjusted trial balance. (*Note:* Normally, a trial balance is prepared before adjustments but is omitted here to save time.)
5. From the adjusted trial balance, prepare an income statement, a statement of retained earnings, and a balance sheet for May.
6. Prepare and post closing entries.
7. Prepare a post-closing trial balance.
   (Optional)
   During June, Stoker's Repair Service, Inc., engaged in the following transactions:
   June 1 Paid the monthly rent, $850.
   1 Made the monthly payment to Latin Company, $600.
   6 Purchased additional repair supplies on credit from Tanaka Company, $1,726.
   15 Received cash repair revenue for the first half of the month, $1,828.
   20 Paid cash for an advertisement in the local newspaper, $120.
   23 Paid Tanaka Company on account, $1,200.
   30 Received cash repair revenue for the last half of the month, $1,634.
   30 Paid a dividend, $600.
8. Prepare and post journal entries to record the June transactions.

(Continued)

9. Using the following information, record adjusting entries in the general journal and post to the ledger accounts:
   a. One month's insurance has expired.
   b. The inventory of unused repair supplies is $826.
   c. The estimated depreciation on repair equipment is $140.
10. From the accounts in the ledger, prepare an adjusted trial balance.
11. From the adjusted trial balance, prepare the June income statement, statement of retained earnings, and balance sheet.
12. Prepare and post closing entries.
13. Prepare a post-closing trial balance.

CHAPTER 4

LEARNING OBJECTIVES

LO 1 Describe the objective of financial reporting, and identify the conceptual framework underlying accounting information.

LO 2 Identify and define the basic components of financial reporting, and prepare a classified balance sheet.

LO 3 Use classified financial statements to evaluate liquidity and profitability.

Directphoto.org/Alamy

FOUNDATIONS OF FINANCIAL REPORTING AND THE CLASSIFIED BALANCE SHEET

Business Insight
McDonald's Corporation

In its letter to stockholders, **McDonald's** focused on its goals of sales and earnings growth, return to stockholders, and its cash provided by operations.[1] In judging whether McDonald's or any other company has achieved its goals, investors, creditors, managers, and others analyze relationships between key numbers in the financial statements that appear in the company's annual report.

The company's annual report summarizes financial performance by condensing a tremendous amount of information into a few numbers that managers and external users of financial statements consider most important. As shown in the selected financial highlights that follow, McDonald's used key elements of the balance sheet in its 2011 annual report to summarize its financial strength.

McDonald's Financial Highlights Operating Results
(in millions, except earnings per share)

	2011	2010
Total revenues	$27,006	$24,075
Net income	5,503	7,473
Total assets	32,990	31,975
Total liabilities	18,600	17,341
Total stockholders' equity	14,390	14,634

1. **CONCEPT ▶** Why are relevance and faithful representation, as well as enhancing qualitative characteristics, important to understanding financial statements?
2. **ACCOUNTING APPLICATION ▶** How should the balance sheet be organized to provide relevant information for statement users?
3. **BUSINESS APPLICATION ▶** How does McDonald's perform on key profitability measures?

SECTION 1 CONCEPTS

CONCEPTS

- Relevance
  - Predictive value
  - Confirmative value
  - Materiality
- Faithful representation
  - Completeness
  - Neutrality
  - Free from material error
- Enhancing qualitative characteristics
  - Comparability
  - Verifiability
  - Timeliness
  - Understandability
- Accounting conventions
  - Consistency
  - Full disclosure
  - Conservatism

RELEVANT LEARNING OBJECTIVE

LO1 Describe the objective of financial reporting, and identify the conceptual framework underlying accounting information.

LO1 Concepts Underlying Financial Reporting

The FASB and the IASB are working toward convergence of U.S. generally accepted accounting principles (GAAP) with international financial reporting standards (IFRS). Their goal is "to increase the international comparability and the quality of standards used in the United States [which] is consistent with the FASB's obligation to its domestic constituents, who benefit from comparability across national borders."[2] An important part of this convergence project is agreement on the objective of financial reporting and conceptual framework underlying it. Exhibit 1 illustrates these factors, which we discuss in this section.

Exhibit 1
Concepts Underlying Financial Reporting

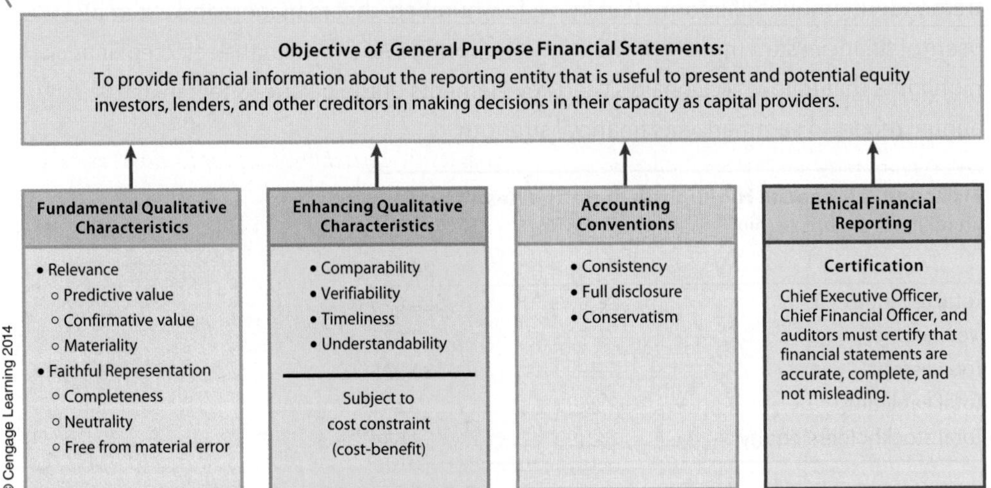

Objective of Financial Reporting

The Financial Accounting Standards Board (FASB) emphasizes the needs of current and potential investors (owners) and creditors while recognizing the needs of other users when it defines the objective of financial reporting as follows.[3]

> *To provide financial information about the reporting entity that is useful to present and potential equity investors, lenders, and other creditors in making decisions in their capacity as capital providers. Information that is decision-useful to capital providers may also be useful to other users of financial reporting who are not capital providers.*

To be useful for decision making, financial reporting must enable the user to:

- **Assess cash flow prospects.** The ultimate value of a business and its ability to pay dividends, interest, or otherwise provide returns to capital providers depends on its ability to generate future cash flows. Capital providers and other users, therefore, need information about the business's ability to generate cash flows.
- **Assess management's stewardship.** Capital providers and others need information about the business's resources (assets), claims against them (liabilities and owner's [stockholders'] equity), and changes in these resources and claims resulting from transactions (earnings and cash flows) and other economic events.

Financial reporting includes the financial statements (balance sheet, income statement, statement of owner's equity, and statement of cash flows) that are periodically presented to parties outside the business. Management's underlying assumptions and methods and estimates used in the financial statements are also important components of financial reporting. Because of a potential conflict of interest between managers, who must prepare the statements, and investors or creditors, who invest in or lend money to the business, financial statements usually are audited by outside accountants.

Qualitative Characteristics of Accounting Information

Introductory textbooks simplify basic accounting concepts to help students. All the problems can be solved, and all the numbers add up. In practice, however, accounting information is neither simple nor precise. The FASB emphasizes this fact in the following statement:

> *The information provided by financial reporting often results from approximate, rather than exact, measures. The measures commonly involve numerous estimates, classifications, summarizations, judgments, and allocations. The outcome of economic activity in a dynamic economy is uncertain and results from combinations of many factors. Thus, despite the aura of precision that may seem to surround financial reporting in general and financial statements in particular, with few exceptions the measures are approximations, which may be based on rules and conventions, rather than exact amounts.*[4]

The goal of generating accounting information is to provide data that different users need to make informed decisions for their unique situations. How this goal is achieved provides much of the interest and controversy in accounting. To facilitate interpretation of accounting information, the FASB has established standards, or **qualitative characteristics**, by which to judge the information.[5] The most fundamental of these characteristics are *relevance* and *faithful representation. Comparability, verifiability, timeliness,* and *understandability* are enhancing characteristics that assist in interpreting accounting information.

Relevance **Relevance** means that the information has a direct bearing on a decision. In other words, if the information were not available, a different decision would be made. To be relevant, information must have *predictive value*, *confirmative value*, or both. Further, it is subject to *materiality.*

- **Predictive value:** Information has **predictive value** if it helps capital providers make decisions about future actions. For example, the statement of cash flows can provide information as to whether the company has sufficient funds to expand or if it will need to raise funds from capital providers.
- **Confirmative value:** Information has **confirmative value** if it confirms or changes previous evaluations. For example, the income statement provides information as to whether or not a company met earnings expectations.
- **Materiality:** Information is **material** if its omission or misstatement could influence the user's economic decisions taken on the basis of the specific entity's financial statements. **Materiality** is related to both the nature of an item and its size or misstatement. Immaterial items are not relevant to the economic decision. The materiality of an item normally is determined by relating its dollar value to an element of the financial statements, such as net income or total assets. As a rule, when an item is worth 5 percent or more of net income, accountants treat it as material. However, materiality depends not only on the value of an item but also on its nature. For example, in a multimillion-dollar company, a mistake of $5,000 in recording an item may not be important, but the discovery of even a small bribe or theft can be very important. Moreover, many small errors can add up to a material amount.

The financial statements may provide information that is both predictive and confirmative. For example, the statement of cash flows not only helps to project future cash flows but also confirms expectations about various prior actions.

Business Perspective
How Much Is Material?

© Alija / iStockphoto.com

The materiality issue was long a pet peeve of the SEC, which contended that companies were increasingly abusing the convention to protect their stocks from taking a pounding when earnings did not reach their targets. Thus, the SEC issued a rule that includes both quantitative and qualitative guides. The traditional rule of thumb of 5 percent or more of net income is acceptable as an initial screening. However, companies cannot decline to book items in the interest of meeting earnings estimates, preserving a growing earnings trend, converting a loss to a profit, increasing management compensation, or hiding an illegal transaction, such as a bribe.[6]

Faithful Representation **Faithful representation** means that the financial information is *complete*, *neutral*, and *free from material error.*

- **Completeness: Complete information** provides all information necessary for a reliable decision.
- **Neutrality: Neutral information** is free from bias intended to achieve a certain result or to bring about a particular behavior.
- **Free from material error:** To be **free from material error** means information meets a minimum level of accuracy so it does not distort what is being reported. Free from material error does not mean that information is absolutely accurate because most financial information is based on estimates and judgments.

If major uncertainties about faithful representation exist, they should be *disclosed* in a note to the financial statements.

Enhancing Qualitative Characteristics Other qualitative characteristics that the FASB has established for interpreting accounting information include:

- **Comparability: Comparability** is the quality that enables users to identify similarities and differences between two sets of financial data.
- **Verifiability: Verifiability** is the quality that different knowledgeable and independent observers could reach consensus, although not necessarily complete agreement, that a particular depiction is a faithful representation.
- **Timeliness: Timeliness** is the quality that enables users to receive information in time to influence their decisions.
- **Understandability: Understandability** is the quality that enables users to comprehend the meaning of the information.

STUDY NOTE: *Theoretically, a $10 stapler is a long-term asset and should, therefore, be capitalized and depreciated over its useful life. However, the concepts of materiality and cost constraint allow the stapler to be expensed entirely in the year of purchase.*

These enhancing characteristics are subject to the **cost constraint** (or **cost-benefit**), which holds that the benefits to be gained from providing accounting information should be greater than the costs of providing it. Of course, minimum levels of relevance and faithful representation must be reached if accounting information is to be useful. Beyond the minimum levels, however, it is up to the FASB and the SEC, which stipulate the information that must be reported, and the accountant, who provides the information, to judge the costs and benefits in each case.

Accounting Conventions

For accounting information to be understandable, accountants must prepare financial statements in accordance with accepted practices, which include some concepts that are not formally part of the agreed-upon conceptual framework and which may conflict with it at times. Familiarity with the **accounting conventions**, or *constraints*, used in preparing financial statements enables the user to better understand accounting information. Among these accounting conventions are *consistency*, *full disclosure*, and *conservatism*.

Consistency **Consistency** requires that once a company has adopted an accounting procedure, it must use it from one period to the next unless a note to the financial statements informs users of a change. Generally accepted accounting principles specify what the note must contain:

> *The nature of and justification for a change in accounting principle and its effect on income should be disclosed in the financial statements of the period in which the change is made. The justification for the change should explain clearly why the newly adopted accounting principle is preferable.*[7]

For example, in the notes to its financial statements, **Goodyear Tire & Rubber Company** disclosed that it had changed its method of accounting for inventories because management felt it improved the matching of revenues and costs. Without such an acknowledgment, users of financial statements can assume that the treatment of a particular transaction, account, or item has not changed since the last period.

Full Disclosure (Transparency) **Full disclosure** (or *transparency*) requires that financial statements present all the information relevant to users' understanding of the statements. The statements must include any explanation needed to keep them from being misleading. For instance, the notes should disclose any change that a company has made in its accounting procedures.

A company must also disclose significant events arising after the balance sheet date. For example, suppose that a firm has purchased a piece of land for a future subdivision. Shortly after the end of its fiscal year, the firm is ordered to halt construction because the Environmental Protection Agency asserts that the land was once a toxic waste dump. This information, which obviously affects the users of the financial statements, must be disclosed in the statements for the fiscal year just ended.

Additional disclosures required by the FASB and other official bodies include the accounting procedures used in preparing the financial statements and important terms of a company's debt and commitments. Beyond the required disclosures, the application of the full-disclosure convention is based on the judgment of management and of the accountants who prepare the financial statements.

In recent years, independent auditors, the stock exchanges, and the SEC have made more demands for disclosure by publicly owned companies. As a result, more and better information about corporations is now available to investors and creditors than ever before.

STUDY NOTE: *The purpose of conservatism is not to produce the lowest net income and lowest asset value. It is a guideline for choosing among GAAP alternatives, and it should be used with care.*

Conservatism When accountants are uncertain about the judgments or estimates they must make, they look to the convention of **conservatism**. This convention holds that, when faced with choosing between two equally acceptable procedures or estimates, accountants should choose the one that is least likely to overstate assets and income. One of the most common applications of conservatism is the use of the *lower-of-cost-or-market method* in accounting for inventories. Under this method, if an item's market value is greater than its original cost, the more conservative cost figure is used. If the market value is below the original cost, the more conservative market value is used. The latter situation often occurs in the computer industry.

Business Perspective

When Is "Full Disclosure" Too Much?

Ernst & Young, a large accounting firm, reported that, over a 20-year period, the total number of pages in the annual reports of 25 large, well-known companies increased an average of 84 percent, and the number of pages of notes increased 325 percent—from 4 to 17 pages. Management's discussion and analysis increased 300 percent, from 3 pages to 12.[8] Because some people feel that "these documents are so daunting that people don't read them at all," the SEC allows companies to issue to the public "summary reports" in which the bulk of the notes can be reduced.

Summary reports are controversial because many analysts feel that the notes provide the detailed information necessary to understand complex business operations. One analyst remarked, "To banish the notes for fear they will turn off readers would be like eliminating fractions from math books on the theory that the average student prefers to work with whole numbers."[9] Detailed reports still must be filed with the SEC, but more and more companies are providing summary reports to the public.

Conservatism can be a useful tool, but if abused, it can lead to incorrect and misleading financial statements. For example, there is no uncertainty about how a long-term asset of material cost should be treated. As explained in Chapter 3, the cost of such an asset should be spread over the asset's useful life. When conservatism is used to justify expensing a long-term asset in the period of purchase, income and assets for the current period will be understated, and income in future periods will be overstated. Accountants, therefore, apply the conservatism convention only when they are uncertain about which accounting procedure or estimate to use.

Ethical Financial Reporting

As noted earlier, under the Sarbanes-Oxley Act, chief executive officers and chief financial officers of all publicly traded companies must certify that, to their knowledge, their quarterly and annual statements are accurate and complete. After this legislation passed, an investigation by the audit committee of **Dell**'s board of directors and management disclosed weaknesses in the company's controls and led to restatements of the financial statements for the prior four years. After extensive improvements in control and the restatements, the company's chief executive officer, Michael S. Dell, made the following certifying statement in the company's annual report to the SEC:

> *Based on my knowledge, the financial statements, and other financial information included in this report, fairly present in all material respects the financial condition, results of operations and cash flows . . . for the periods represented in this report.*[10]

Fraudulent financial reporting can have high costs for investors, lenders, employees, and customers. It can also have high costs for the people who condone, authorize, or prepare misleading reports—even those at the highest corporate levels. In March 2005, Bernard J. Ebbers, former CEO of **WorldCom**, was convicted of seven counts of filing false reports with the SEC and one count each of securities fraud and conspiracy.[11] In 2006, both Kenneth Lay, **Enron Corporation**'s former chairman, and Jeffrey Skilling, Enron's former CEO, were convicted on charges similar to the ones of which Ebbers was convicted.

International Perspective

IFRS What Is the Future of the Conservatism Convention?

Conservatism, which has been the bedrock of U.S. accounting practice for many decades, clearly conflicts with the agreed upon concept of *neutrality* in the conceptual framework. The practice under IFRS, for example, of writing up the value of an asset, such as inventory or equipment, that has increased in fair value and recording the increase as income violates the conservatism convention under U.S. GAAP. Thus, the convergence of IFRS with GAAP may well influence the way accountants in the United States prepare financial statements, but it will likely take a generation for this to change.

APPLY IT!

Match each concept that follows with the category in which it belongs.

a. Objective of accounting information
b. Underlies relevant financial information
c. Underlies faithful representation
d. Enhancing qualitative characteristics
e. Accounting convention

1. Consistency
2. Verifiability
3. Predictive value
4. Timeliness
5. Neutrality
6. Conservatism
7. Comparability
8. Completeness
9. Materiality
10. Confirmative value
11. Understandability
12. Furnishing information that is useful to capital providers

SOLUTION

1. e; 2. d; 3. b; 4. d; 5. c; 6. e; 7. d; 8. c; 9. b; 10. b; 11. d; 12. a

TRY IT! SE1, SE2, E1A, E2A, E1B, E2B

SECTION 2 ACCOUNTING APPLICATIONS

ACCOUNTING APPLICATIONS
- Identify components of a classified balance sheet
- Prepare a classified balance sheet

RELEVANT LEARNING OBJECTIVE

LO2 Identify and define the basic components of financial reporting, and prepare a classified balance sheet.

LO2 Classified Balance Sheet

As you know, a balance sheet presents a company's financial position at a particular time. The balance sheets presented thus far categorize accounts as assets, liabilities, and owner's equity. Because even a fairly small company can have hundreds of accounts, subcategories within the major categories can make financial statements much more useful. General-purpose external financial statements that are divided into subcategories are called **classified financial statements**. Exhibit 2 depicts the subcategories into which the principal elements of assets, liabilities, and stockholders' equity are broken down. This format enables owners and creditors to study and evaluate relationships among the subcategories.

Exhibit 2
Classified Balance Sheet

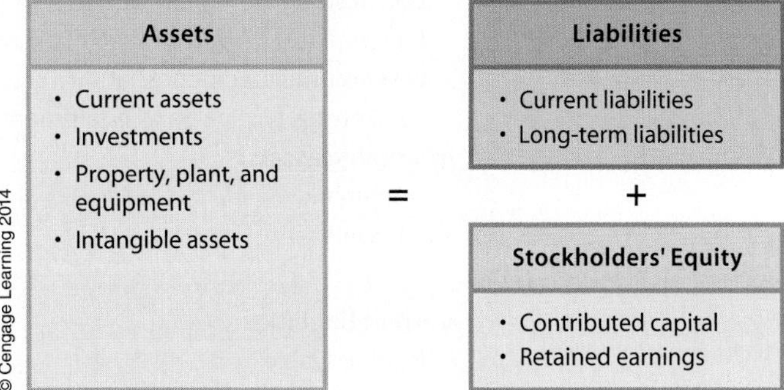

The subcategories of Bonali Company's classified balance sheet, shown in Exhibit 3, are those used by most U.S. corporations. The subcategories under stockholders' equity would, of course, be different if Bonali were a sole proprietorship or partnership rather than a corporation.

Assets

As shown in Exhibit 3, the classified balance sheet of a U.S. company typically divides assets into four categories: current assets; investments; property, plant, and equipment; and intangible assets. These categories are listed in the order of how easily they can be converted into cash. For example, current assets are usually more easily converted to cash than are property, plant, and equipment. For simplicity, some companies group investments, intangible assets, and other miscellaneous assets into a category called **other assets**.

Current Assets **Current assets** include cash and other assets that a company can reasonably expect to convert to cash, sell, or consume within one year or its normal operating cycle, whichever is longer. A company's **normal operating cycle** is the average time it needs to go from spending cash to receiving cash. For example, suppose a company uses cash to buy inventory and sells the inventory to a customer on credit. To classify the resulting receivable as a current asset, there must be a reasonable expectation that it will be collected in cash before the normal operating cycle ends.

As discussed, cash is a current asset. Short-term investments, notes and accounts receivable, and inventory that a company expects to convert to cash (by selling it) within

Exhibit 3
Classified Balance Sheet for Bonali Company

Bonali Company
Balance Sheet
December 31, 2014

		Assets	
Current assets:			
Cash		$ 41,440	
Short-term investments		28,000	
Notes receivable		32,000	
Accounts receivable		141,200	
Merchandise inventory		191,600	
Prepaid insurance		26,400	
Supplies		6,784	
Total current assets			$467,424
Investments:			
Land held for future use			50,000
Property, plant, and equipment:			
Land		$ 18,000	
Building	$ 82,600		
Less accumulated depreciation	34,560	48,040	
Equipment	$108,000		
Less accumulated depreciation	57,800	50,200	
Total property, plant, and equipment			116,240
Intangible assets:			
Trademark			2,000
Total assets			$635,664
		Liabilities	
Current liabilities:			
Notes payable		$ 60,000	
Accounts payable		102,732	
Salaries payable		8,000	
Total current liabilities			$170,732
Long-term liabilities:			
Mortgage payable			71,200
Total liabilities			$241,932
		Stockholders' Equity	
Common stock, $10 par value, 20,000 shares authorized, issued, and outstanding		$200,000	
Additional paid-in capital		40,000	
Total contributed capital		$240,000	
Retained earnings		153,732	
Total stockholders' equity			393,732
Total liabilities and stockholders' equity			$635,664

Business Perspective
Normal Operating Cycles Can Be Long

The normal operating cycle for most companies is less than one year, but there are exceptions. For example, because of the length of time it takes **The Boeing Company** to build aircraft, its normal operating cycle exceeds one year. The inventory used in building the planes is nonetheless considered a current asset because the planes will be sold within the normal operating cycle. Another example is a company that sells on an installment basis. The payments for a television set or a refrigerator can extend over 24 or 36 months, but these receivables are still considered current assets.

the next year or the normal operating cycle are also current assets. On the balance sheet, they are listed in order of how easily they can be converted to cash.

Prepaid expenses, such as rent and insurance paid in advance, and supplies bought for use rather than for sale should be classified as current assets. These assets are current in the sense that if they had not been paid for earlier, they would require a current outlay of cash.

STUDY NOTE: *Investments classified as current must be readily marketable—i.e., management must expect to sell them within the next year or within the current operating cycle.*

Investments **Investments** include assets, usually long-term, that are not used in normal business operations and that management does not plan to convert to cash within the next year. Examples of items in this category include the following:

- Securities held for long-term investment
- Long-term notes receivable
- Land held for future use
- Plant or equipment not used in the business
- Special funds established to pay off a debt or buy a building
- Large permanent investments (those a company does not intend to sell) made in another company for the purpose of controlling that company

Property, Plant, and Equipment **Property, plant, and equipment** (also called *operating assets*, *fixed assets*, *tangible assets*, *long-lived assets*, or *plant assets*) include tangible long-term assets used in a business's day-to-day operations. They represent a place to operate (land and buildings) and the equipment used to produce, sell, and deliver goods or services. Through depreciation, the costs of these assets (except the cost of land) are spread over the periods they benefit. Past depreciation is recorded in the Accumulated Depreciation accounts and deducted from their related asset accounts on the balance sheet.

To reduce clutter on the balance sheet, property, plant, and equipment accounts and related accumulated depreciation accounts are often combined—for example:

Property, plant, and equipment (net)	$116,240

The company provides the details in a note to the financial statements.

The property, plant, and equipment category also includes natural resources owned by the company, such as forest lands, oil and gas properties, and coal mines, if they are used in the regular course of business. If they are not, they are listed in the investments category.

Intangible Assets **Intangible assets** are long-term assets with no physical substance. Their value stems from the rights or privileges accruing to their owners. Examples include patents, copyrights, franchises, and trademarks. These assets are recorded at cost, which is spread over the expected life of the right or privilege. **Goodwill**, which arises in an acquisition of another company, is another intangible asset that is recorded at cost, but the cost is not allocated (amortized) over future periods. Goodwill is reviewed each year for possible loss of value, or impairment.

Intangible assets can be worth an enormous amount for some companies. Consider the value of Coca-Cola's trademark, which over the years has become a familiar and easily recognizable symbol worldwide.

STR/AFP/GETTY IMAGES/Newscom

Liabilities

Liabilities are divided into two categories: current liabilities and long-term liabilities.

Current Liabilities **Current liabilities** are obligations that must be satisfied within one year or within the company's normal operating cycle, whichever is longer. These liabilities are typically paid out of current assets or by incurring new short-term liabilities. Examples include:

- Notes payable
- Accounts payable
- The current portion of long-term debt
- Salaries and wages payable
- Customer advances (unearned revenues)

STUDY NOTE: *The portion of a mortgage due during the next year or the current operating cycle is classified as a current liability. The portion due after the next year or the current operating cycle is classified as a long-term liability.*

Long-Term Liabilities **Long-term liabilities** are debts that fall due more than one year in the future or beyond the normal operating cycle and, thus, will be paid out of noncurrent assets. Examples include:

- Mortgages payable
- Long-term notes
- Bonds payable
- Employee pension obligations
- Long-term lease liabilities

Stockholders' Equity

Although the form of business organization does not usually affect the accounting treatment of assets and liabilities, the equity section of the balance sheet differs depending on whether the business is a sole proprietorship, a partnership, or a corporation.

Sole Proprietorship The terms *owner's equity, proprietorship, owner's capital,* and *net worth* are used to refer to the owner's interest, or equity, in a company. However, the first three terms are preferred to *net worth* because many assets are recorded at their original cost rather than at their current value. The owner's equity section of a sole proprietorship might appear as follows.

Owner's Equity	
J. Bonali, capital	$393,732

STUDY NOTE: *Equity in a sole proprietorship and a partnership differs only in the number of Capital accounts.*

Partnership The equity section of a partnership's balance sheet is called **partners' equity**. It is much like that in a sole proprietorship's balance sheet. It might appear as follows.

Partners' Equity		
R. Hay, capital	$168,750	
J. Bonali, capital	224,982	
Total partners' equity		$393,732

Corporation Corporations are by law separate, legal entities that are owned by their stockholders. The equity section of a balance sheet for a corporation is called **stockholders' equity** (or *shareholders' equity*) and has two parts: contributed capital and retained earnings. The stockholders' equity section of a balance sheet for a corporation would be similar to the one shown for Bonali Company in Exhibit 3:

Stockholders' Equity		
Contributed capital:		
Common stock, $10 par value, 20,000 shares authorized, issued, and outstanding	$200,000	
Additional paid-in capital	40,000	
Total contributed capital	$240,000	
Retained earnings	153,732	
Total stockholders' equity		$393,732

Remember that stockholders' equity and liability accounts show the sources of and claims on assets. These claims are not on any particular asset but on the assets as a whole. It follows, then, that a corporation's contributed and earned capital accounts measure its stockholders' claims on assets and also indicate the sources of the assets. The **Contributed Capital** (or *Paid-in Capital*) accounts reflect the amounts of assets invested by stockholders. Generally, contributed capital is shown on corporate balance sheets by two amounts: (1) the face, or par, value of issued stock and (2) the amounts paid in, or contributed,

Business Perspective

Terminology In Financial Statements Is Not Consistent

Although balance sheets generally resemble the one shown in Exhibit 3 for Bonali Company, no two companies have financial statements that are exactly alike. **CVS**'s balance sheet is a good example of some of the variations. As shown in the Supplement to Chapter 1, it provides data for two years (three years for the income statement) so that users can evaluate changes from one year to the next. Note that its major classifications are similar but not identical to those of Bonali. For instance, Bonali has asset categories for investments, and CVS has an asset category called "other assets," which is a small amount of its total assets. Also, note that CVS has various accounts listed in the liabilities under "Total Current Liabilities." Because these accounts are listed after current liabilities, they represent longer-term liabilities, due more than one year after the balance sheet date.

in excess of the par value per share. In the previous illustration, stockholders invested amounts equal to the par value of the outstanding stock of $200,000 plus $40,000 in additional paid-in capital for a total of $240,000.

The **Retained Earnings** account is sometimes called *Earned Capital* because it represents the stockholders' claim to the assets that are earned from operations and reinvested in corporate operations. Distributions of assets to shareholders, which are called **dividends**, reduce the Retained Earnings account just as withdrawals of assets by the owner of a business reduce the Capital account. Thus, the Retained Earnings balance represents the earnings of the corporation less dividends paid to stockholders over the life of the business.

Overview of the Classified Balance Sheet Accounts

Like accounts on the balance sheet and income statement can be grouped, as shown in Exhibit 4. Such groupings aid in analysis of the statements.

Exhibit 4
Classified Balance Sheet Groups Accounts into Useful Categories

Balance Sheet
December 31, 2014

Assets	**Liabilities**
Current assets	Current liabilities
Investments	Long-term liabilities
Property, plant, and equipment	Total liabilities
Intangible assets	
	Stockholders' Equity
	Contributed capital
	Retained earnings
	Total stockholders' equity
Total Assets =	**Total Liabilities + Stockholders' Equity**

APPLY IT!

Match each account title that follows with the category that appears on a balance sheet or indicate that it does not appear on the balance sheet.

a. Current assets
b. Investments
c. Property, plant, and equipment
d. Intangible assets
e. Current liabilities
f. Long-term liabilities
g. Contributed capital
h. Not on balance sheet

1. Trademark
2. Supplies
3. Land Held for Future Use
4. Property Taxes Payable
5. Note Payable in Five Years
6. Common Stock
7. Land Used in Operations
8. Accumulated Depreciation
9. Accounts Receivable
10. Interest Expense
11. Unearned Revenue
12. Prepaid Rent

SOLUTION

1. d; 2. a; 3. b; 4. e; 5. f; 6. g; 7. c; 8. c; 9. a; 10. h; 11. e; 12. a

TRY IT! SE3, SE4, E3A, E4A, E3B, E4B

SECTION 3 **BUSINESS APPLICATIONS**

BUSINESS APPLICATIONS

- Liquidity
  - Working capital
  - Current ratio
- Profitability
  - Profit margin
  - Asset turnover
  - Return on assets
  - Debt to equity ratio
  - Return on equity

RELEVANT LEARNING OBJECTIVE

LO 3 Use classified financial statements to evaluate liquidity and profitability.

LO3 Using Classified Financial Statements

Owners and creditors base decisions largely on their assessments of a firm's potential liquidity and profitability, often relying on ratios. Ratios use the components of classified financial statements to reflect how well a firm has performed in terms of maintaining liquidity and achieving profitability. Accounts must be classified correctly before the ratios are computed. Otherwise, the ratios will be incorrect.

Evaluation of Liquidity

Liquidity means having enough money on hand to pay bills when they are due and to take care of unexpected needs for cash. Two measures of liquidity are working capital and current ratio.

Working Capital **Working capital**, which uses two elements of the classified balance sheet, is the amount by which current assets exceed current liabilities. It is an important measure of liquidity because current liabilities must be satisfied within one year or one operating cycle, whichever is longer, and current assets are used to pay the current liabilities. Thus, the working capital is what is on hand to continue business operations.

For Bonali Company, working capital is computed as follows.

Current assets	$467,424
Less current liabilities	170,732
Working capital	$296,692

Working capital can be used to buy inventory, obtain credit, and finance expanded sales. Lack of working capital can lead to a company's failure.

Current Ratio The current ratio is closely related to working capital. Many bankers and other creditors believe it is a good indicator of a company's ability to pay its debts on time. The **current ratio** is the ratio of current assets to current liabilities. For Bonali Company, it is computed as follows.

RATIO

Current Ratio: How Did Current Assets Compare to Current Liabilities?

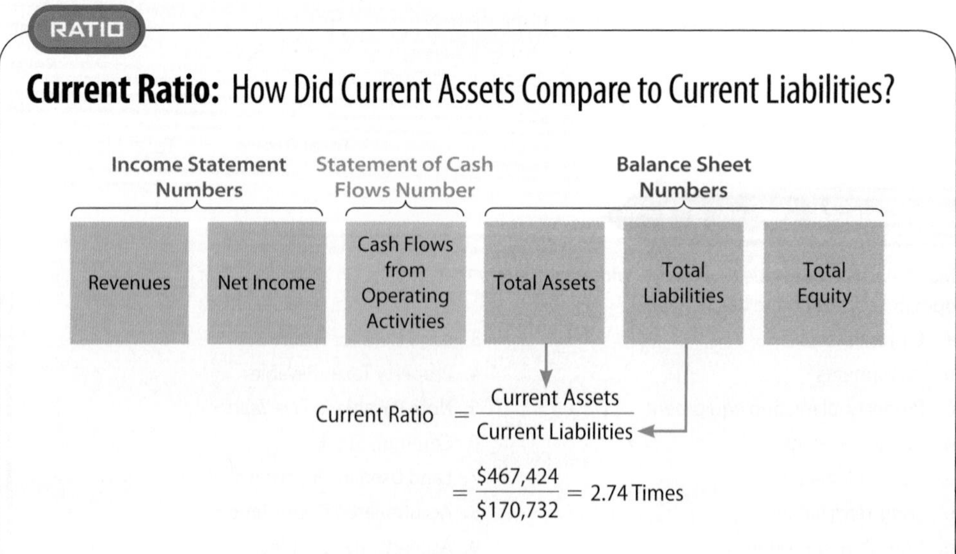

$$\text{Current Ratio} = \frac{\text{Current Assets}}{\text{Current Liabilities}}$$

$$= \frac{\$467,424}{\$170,732} = 2.74 \text{ Times}$$

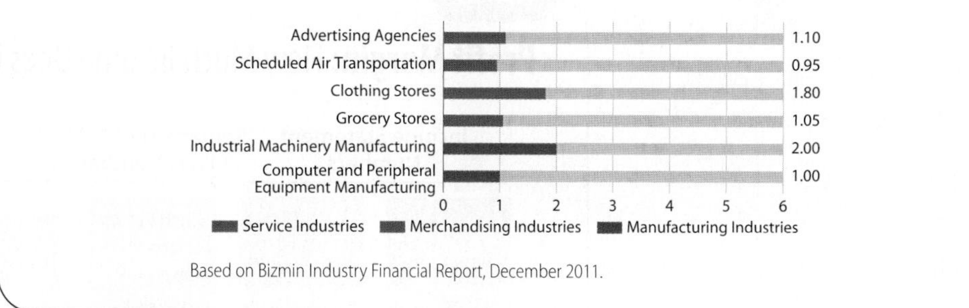

Based on Bizmin Industry Financial Report, December 2011.

Thus, Bonali has $2.74 of current assets for each $1.00 of current liabilities. Is this good or bad? The answer requires a comparison of this year's current ratio with ratios for earlier years and with similar measures for companies in the same industry, which for Bonali is clothing. The average current ratio varies from industry to industry. For the advertising industry, which has large receivables, the current ratio is 1.10. The industrial manufacturing industry, in which companies carry large merchandise inventories, has an average current ratio of 2.00. The current ratio for Bonali, 2.74, exceeds the average for its industry, 1.80.

A very low current ratio can be unfavorable, indicating that a company will not be able to pay its debts on time. But that is not always the case. For example, **McDonald's** and various other successful companies have low current ratios because they carefully plan their cash flows. A very high current ratio may indicate that a company is not using its assets to the best advantage. In other words, it could probably use its excess funds more effectively to increase its overall profit.

Evaluation of Profitability

Just as important as paying bills on time is **profitability**—the ability to earn a satisfactory income. As a goal, profitability competes with liquidity for attention because liquid assets are not the best profit-producing resources. Cash means purchasing power; but a satisfactory profit can be made only if purchasing power is used to buy profit-producing (and less liquid) assets, such as inventory and long-term assets.

To evaluate a company's profitability, you must relate its current performance to its past performance and prospects for the future, as well as to the averages of other companies in the same industry. The following are the ratios commonly used to evaluate a company's ability to earn income:

- Profit margin
- Asset turnover
- Return on assets
- Debt to equity ratio
- Return on equity

Profit Margin The **profit margin** shows the percentage of each sales dollar that results in net income. It is an indication of how well a company is controlling its costs: the lower its costs, the higher its profit margin. The profit margin uses two elements of the income statements: net income and revenues (often called *net sales* or *net revenues*). If Bonali Company had $71,524 of net income and $1,248,624 of revenues, its profit margin would be computed as follows.

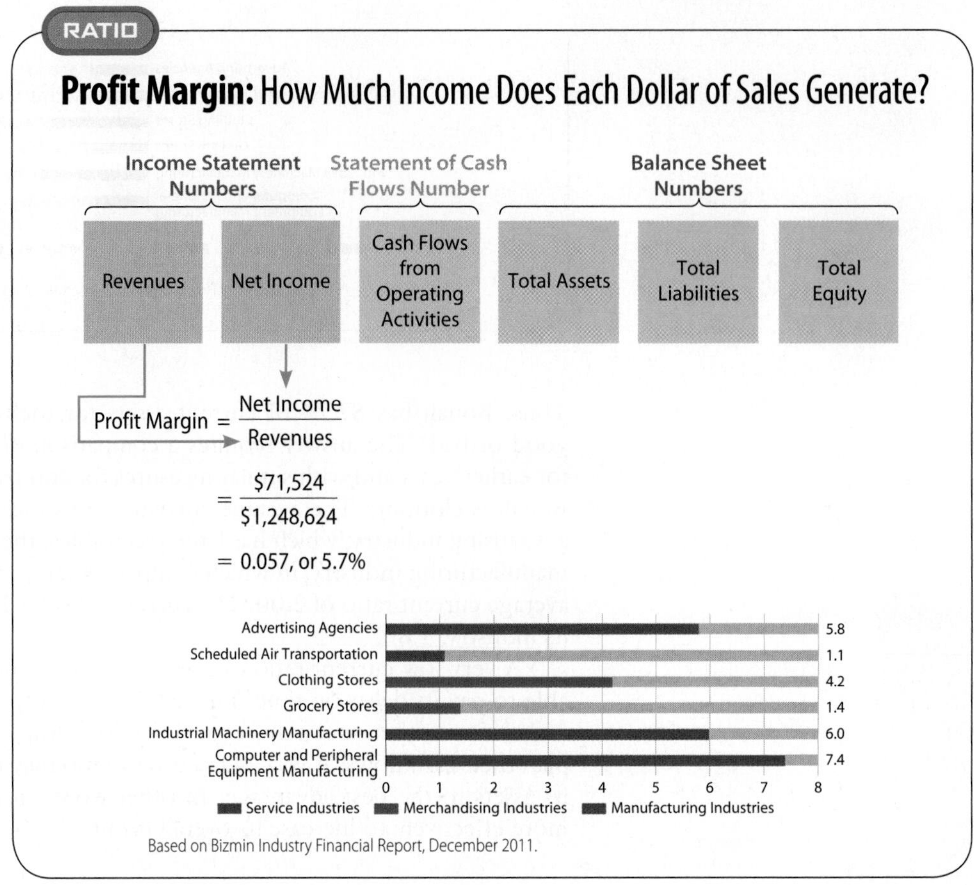

Based on Bizmin Industry Financial Report, December 2011.

Thus, on each dollar of revenue, Bonali makes 5.7 cents. Is this a satisfactory profit? The answer requires a comparison with the profit margin ratios of other companies in the clothing industry, which is 4.2. A difference of 1 or 2 percent in a company's profit margin can be the difference between a fair year and a very profitable one.

Asset Turnover The **asset turnover** ratio measures how efficiently assets are used to produce sales. In other words, how much revenue is generated by each dollar of assets? A company with a high asset turnover uses its assets more productively than one with a low asset turnover.

The asset turnover ratio uses revenues from the income statement and total assets from the balance sheet. It is computed by dividing revenues by average total assets. Since revenues take place over the year, they are compared with average total assets, which is intended to represent the usual level of assets over the year. Average total assets are the sum of assets at the beginning and end of the period divided by 2. If Bonali Company had $1,248,624 of revenues, and $594,480 of assets at the beginning of the year, its asset turnover would be computed as follows.

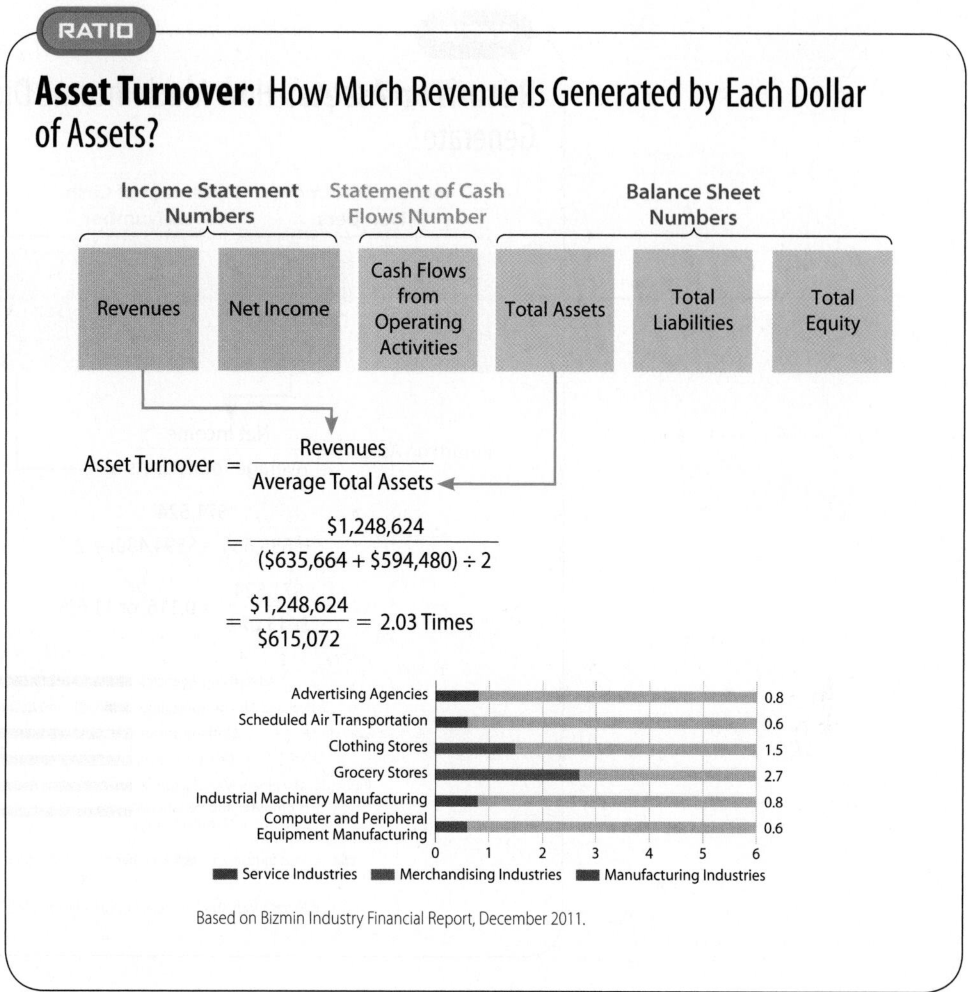

Thus, Bonali produces $2.03 in sales for each dollar invested in assets. Its asset turnover of 2.03 times is greater than the industry average of 1.5 times. In other words, the company is more productive in producing revenue than other companies in the clothing industry.

STUDY NOTE: *Return on assets is a widely used measure of profitability. It is a combination of the profit margin and the asset turnover.*

Return on Assets The profit margin and asset turnover ratios are important measures, but they have limitations. For example, the profit margin ratio does not consider the assets necessary to produce income, and the asset turnover ratio does not take into account the amount of income produced. The **return on assets** ratio overcomes these deficiencies by relating net income to average total assets. If Bonali Company had $71,524 of net income, its return on assets would be computed as follows.

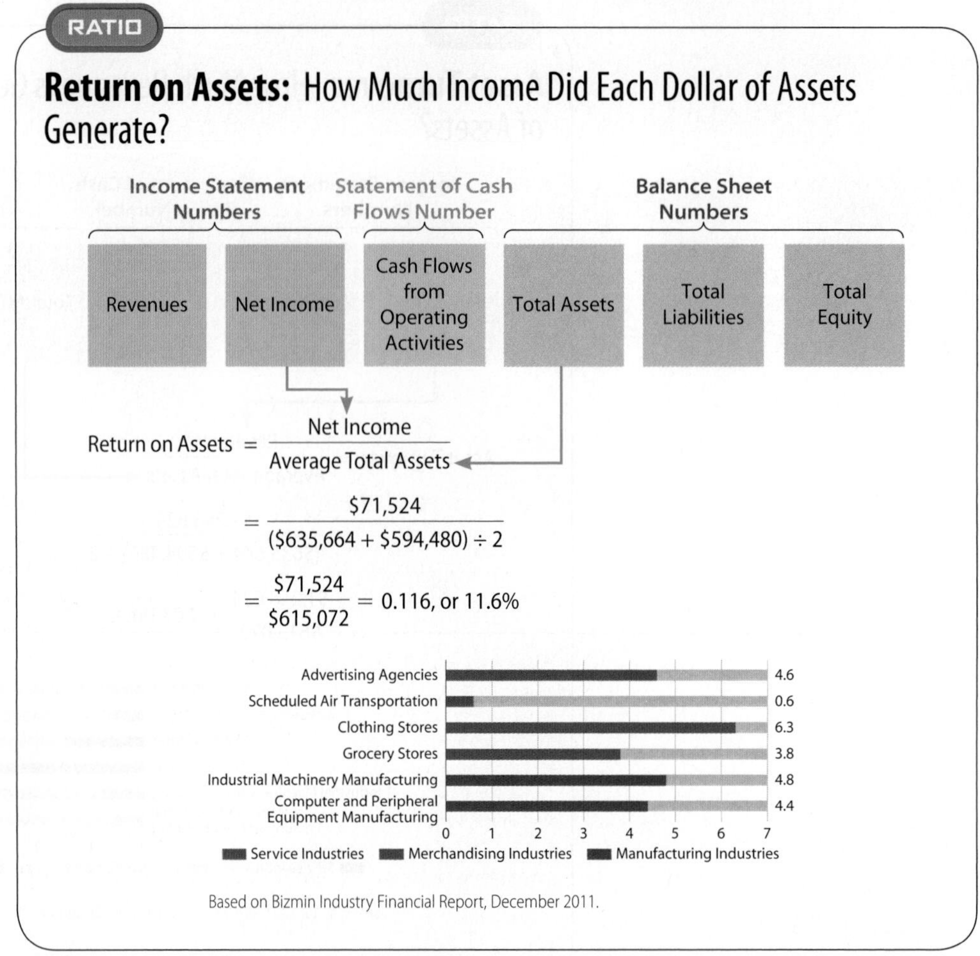

For each dollar of invested assets, Bonali earned 11.6 cents of net income. This ratio combines the firm's income-generating strength (profit margin) and its revenue-generating effectiveness (asset turnover):

$$\frac{\text{Net Income}}{\text{Net Sales}} \times \frac{\text{Net Sales}}{\text{Average Total Assets}} = \frac{\text{Net Income}}{\text{Average Total Assets}}$$

$$\text{Profit Margin} \times \text{Asset Turnover} = \text{Return on Assets}$$

$$5.7\% \times 2.03 \text{ Times} = 11.6\%$$

A company's management can improve overall profitability by increasing the profit margin, the asset turnover, or both. A financial statement user must consider how these two ratios interact to produce return on assets.

Bonali's profit margin of 5.7 percent is above the clothing industry's average of 4.2 percent. Its asset turnover of 2.03 times is the higher than the industry average of 1.5 percent. Bonali is able to achieve a higher profit margin than the industry norm without sacrificing asset turnover. Clearly, its strategy is working because the company's return on assets of 11.6 percent is greater than the industry average of 6.3 percent.

You can see the different ways in which various industries combine profit margin and asset turnover to produce return on assets. For instance, by comparing the return on assets for grocery stores and computer and peripheral equipment manufacturing companies, you can see how they achieve that return in very different ways. The grocery store industry has a profit margin of 1.4 percent, which, when multiplied by an asset turnover of 2.7 times, gives a return on assets of 3.8 percent. The computer and peripheral equipment manufacturing industry has a higher profit margin, 7.4 percent, and a lower asset turnover, 0.6 times, and produces a return on assets of 4.4 percent.

© Alija / iStockphoto.com

Business Perspective

What Performance Measures Do Top Companies Use to Compensate Executives?

The boards of directors of public companies often use financial ratios to judge the performance of their top executives and determine annual bonuses. Public companies must disclose the ratios or performance measures they use in creating these compensation plans. Studies show that the most successful companies use earnings goals combined with sales growth 61 percent of the time compared to 43 percent for less successful companies. Among the most common earnings goals are return on assets and return on equity. Clearly, successful companies set objectives that will provide management with performance incentives.[12]

Debt to Equity Ratio The **debt to equity ratio** reflects a company's strategy for financing its operations. It shows the proportion of a company's assets financed by creditors and the proportion financed by stockholders. It is thus a measure of financial risk; the more debt a company has in relation to its stockholders' equity, the greater its financial risk. Creditors and interest on debt must be paid on time regardless of how well or poorly a company is performing. Stockholders' equity, on the other hand, does not have to be repaid, and dividends can be deferred when a company's performance is poor.

The debt to equity ratio uses two elements of the balance sheet: total liabilities and total equity. Since the balance sheets of most companies do not show total liabilities, a short way of determining them is to deduct the total stockholders' equity from total assets. For Bonali Company, it is computed as follows.

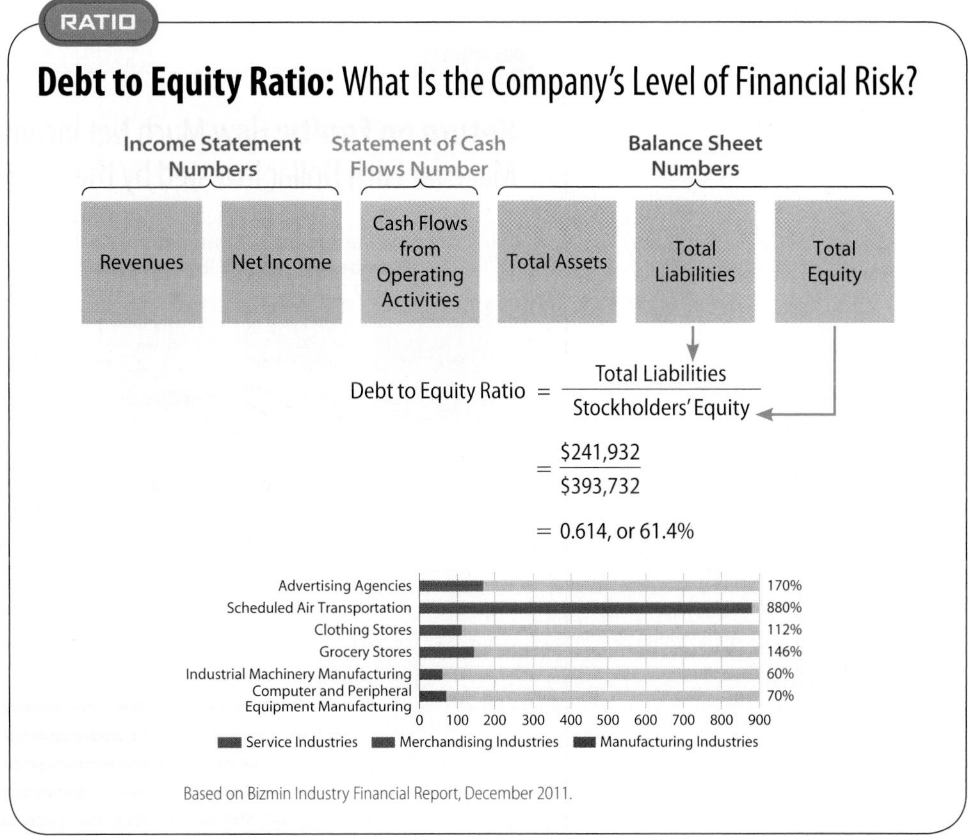

Based on Bizmin Industry Financial Report, December 2011.

A debt to equity ratio of 1.0 means that equal amounts of liabilities and stockholders' equity are used to finance a company's assets. A ratio of 0.5 means that if a company has 50 cents of liabilities for every dollar of equity, one-third of a company's total assets are financed by creditors. Bonali's debt to equity ratio of 61.4 percent means that Bonali relied more on owners than on creditors to finance its assets.

The debt to equity ratio does not fit neatly into either the liquidity or profitability category. It is clearly very important to liquidity analysis because it relates to debt and its repayment. It is also relevant to profitability for two reasons:

- Creditors are interested in the proportion of the business that is debt-financed because the more debt a company has, the more profit it must earn to ensure the payment of interest to creditors.
- Stockholders are interested in the proportion of the business that is debt-financed because the amount of interest paid on debt affects the amount of profit left to provide a return on the stockholders' investment.

The debt to equity ratio also shows how much expansion is possible through borrowing additional long-term funds.

Return on Equity **Return on equity** is the ratio of net income to average stockholders' equity. It indicates whether a company has earned a favorable return for the stockholders. Return on equity will always be greater than return on assets because total equity will always be less than total assets. While greater return on assets is an advantage, the more debt a company has, the greater its financial risk. A company must, therefore, carefully balance the amount of financial risk it assumes with its desire to increase its return to the stockholders.

Using the total stockholders' equity from Bonali Company's balance sheet and assuming that the beginning stockholders' equity was $402,212, and that the company had net income of $71,524, Bonali's return on equity is computed as follows.

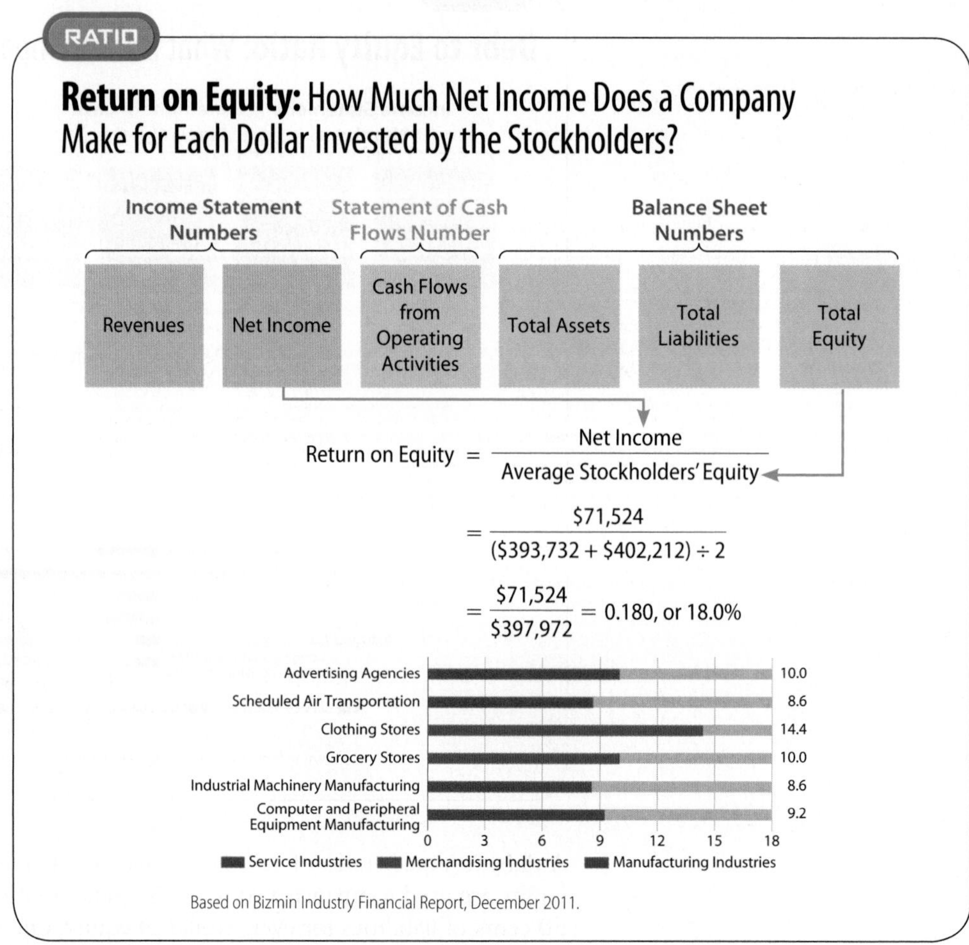

Based on Bizmin Industry Financial Report, December 2011.

International Perspective

IFRS How Has the Goal of Convergence of U.S. GAAP and IFRS Made Financial Analysis More Difficult?

Although the SEC believes that the ideal outcome of an international standard-setting process would be worldwide use of a single set of accounting standards for both domestic and international financial reporting, the reality is that such consistency does not now exist and will be a challenge to implement.[13] For a period of time, financial statement users will have difficulty comparing companies' performance. Profitability measures of foreign firms that file in the United States using IFRS will not be comparable to profitability measures of companies that file using U.S. GAAP. For instance, consider the reporting earnings of the following European companies under both standards in a recent year (earnings in millions of euros):

	IFRS Earnings	GAAP Earnings	% Diff.
Bayer AG	1,695	269	530.1%
Reed Elsevier	625	399	56.6
Benetton Group	125	100	25.0

Given that assets and equity for these companies are also likely to differ as well as the use of fair value in valuing assets and liabilities, all profitability ratios—profit margin, asset turnover, return on assets, debt to equity ratio, and return on equity—will be affected.

Bonali earned 18.0 cents for every dollar invested by stockholders. Is this an acceptable return? Bonali's average return on equity of 18.0 percent is better than the average of 14.4 percent for the clothing industry. Although the air transportation industry's return on equity of 8.6 percent is one of the lowest of the selected industries, it also has the highest debt to equity ratio (880 percent).

APPLY IT!

Roth Company is considering applying for a bank loan. Various data from Roth's classified financial statements follows.

	2014	2013		2014	2013
Current assets	$200,000	$170,000	Stockholders' equity	$ 640,000	$ 610,000
Total assets	880,000	710,000	Sales	1,200,000	1,050,000
Current liabilities	90,000	50,000	Net income	60,000	80,000
Long-term liabilities	150,000	50,000			

Its total assets and stockholders' equity at the beginning of 2013 were $690,000 and $590,000, respectively.

1. Use (a) liquidity analysis and (b) profitability analysis to document Roth's financial position.
2. Discuss Roth's profitability and liquidity. Do you think it will qualify for a bank loan?

SOLUTION

1. (a) Liquidity analysis

	Current Assets	Current Liabilities	Working Capital	Current Ratio
2013	$170,000	$50,000	$120,000	3.40
2014	200,000	90,000	110,000	2.22
Decrease in working capital			$ 10,000	
Decrease in current ratio				1.18

(b) Profitability analysis

	Net Income	Sales	Profit Margin	Average Total Assets	Assets Turnover	Return on Assets	Average Stockholders' Equity	Return on Equity
2013	$80,000	$1,050,000	7.6%	$700,000[a]	1.50	11.4%	$600,000[c]	13.3%
2014	60,000	1,200,000	5.0%	795,000[b]	1.51	7.5%	625,000[d]	9.6%
Increase (decrease)	($20,000)	$ 150,000	(2.6)%	$ 95,000	0.01	(3.9)%	$ 25,000	(3.7)%

[a] ($710,000 + $690,000) ÷ 2
[b] ($880,000 + $710,000) ÷ 2
[c] ($610,000 + $590,000) ÷ 2
[d] ($640,000 + $610,000) ÷ 2

2. Both working capital and the current ratio declined between 2013 and 2014 because the $40,000 increase in current liabilities ($90,000 – $50,000) was greater than the $30,000 increase in current assets.

   Net income decreased by $20,000 despite an increase in sales of $150,000 and an increase in average total assets of $95,000. Thus, the profit margin fell from 7.6 percent to 5.0 percent, and return on assets fell from 11.4 percent to 7.5 percent. Asset turnover showed almost no change and so did not contribute to the decline in profitability. The decrease in return on equity, from 13.3 percent to 9.6 percent, was not as great as the decrease in return on assets because the growth in total assets was financed mainly by debt, as shown in the capital structure analysis below.

	Total Liabilities	Stockholders' Equity	Debt to Equity Ratio
2013	$100,000	$610,000	16.4%
2014	240,000	640,000	37.5%
Increase	$140,000	$ 30,000	21.1%

Total liabilities increased by $140,000, while stockholders' equity increased by $30,000. Thus, the amount of the business financed by debt increased between 2013 and 2014.

Both liquidity and profitability have declined. Roth will probably have to focus on improving current operations before expanding or getting a bank loan.

TRY IT! SE5, SE6, SE7, E5A, E6A, E7A, E8A, E5B, E6B, E7B, E8B

A Look Back At: McDonald's Corporation

Directphoto.org/Alamy

McDonald's Corporation

The beginning of this chapter focused on **McDonald's**. In judging whether any company has achieved its objectives (McDonald's focused on sales and earnings growth, return to stockholders, and cash provided by operations), investors, creditors, and others analyze relationships between key numbers in the company's financial statements. Complete the following requirements in order to answer the questions posed at the beginning of the chapter.

Section 1: Concepts
Why are relevance and faithful representation as well as enhancing qualitative characteristics important to understanding financial statements?

Section 2: Accounting Applications
How should the balance sheet be organized to provide relevant information for statement users?

Section 3: Business Applications
How does McDonald's perform on key profitability measures?

SOLUTION

Section 1: Concepts

Relevance means that the information has a direct bearing on a decision and includes the concepts of *predictive value* and *confirmative value*, and *materiality*, subject to the *cost constraint*. *Faithful representation* means that the financial information is *complete*, *neutral*, and *free from material error*. Enhancing qualitative characteristics include *comparability* to enable users to identify similarities and differences between two sets of financial data, *verifiability* to assure users that information as presented can be substantiated, *timeliness* to enable users to receive information in time to influence their decisions, and *understandability* to enable users to comprehend the meaning of the information. Further, the benefits of information must exceed the costs of providing it. The accounting conventions of *consistency*, *full disclosure*, and *conservatism* help accountants to decide what information to present when uncertainties exist.

Section 2: Accounting Applications

McDonald's uses a classified balance sheet to provide relevant information to those interested in assessing the company's financial performance. McDonald's uses the following classifications:

Assets	**Liabilities**
Current assets	Current liabilities
Other assets	Long-term debt and other long-term liabilities
Property and equipment	**Shareholders' equity**
Total assets	Total liabilities and shareholders' equity

Section 3: Business Applications

Using key elements from the McDonald's Financial Highlights presented at the beginning of the chapter, as well as total assets of $30,225 million and total stockholders' equity of $14.034 million in 2009, the profitability ratios may be computed as follows (numbers in millions; percentages rounded).

Profit Margin:
Net Income ÷ Total Revenues
2011: $5,503 ÷ $27,006 = 20.4%
2010: $7,473 ÷ $24,075 = 31.0%

Asset Turnover:
Revenue ÷ Average Total Assets
2011: $27,006 ÷ [($32,990 + $31,975 ÷ 2] = $27,006 ÷ $32,482.5 = 0.83 Times
2010: $24,075 ÷ [($31,975 + $30,225 ÷ 2] = $24,075 ÷ $31,100 = 0.77 Times

Return on Assets:
Net Income ÷ Average Total Assets
2011: $5,503 ÷ [($32,990 + $31,975 ÷ 2] = $5,503 ÷ $32,482.5 = 16.9%
2010: $7,473 ÷ [($31,975 + $30,225 ÷ 2] = $7,473 ÷ $31,100 = 24.0%

Debt to Equity Ratio:
Total Liabilities ÷ Total Equity
2011: $18,600 ÷ $14,390 = 1.29
2010: $17,341 ÷ $14,634 = 1.18

Return on Equity:
Net Income ÷ Average Stockholders' Equity
$5,503 ÷ [($14,390 + $14,634) ÷ 2] = $5,503 ÷ $14,512 = 37.9%
$7,473 ÷ [($14,634 + $14,034) ÷ 2] = $7,473 ÷ $14,334 = 52.1%

McDonald's is a very profitable company. It obtains a high return on assets by achieving a high profit margin with a relatively low asset turnover. Similarly, its return on equity is very high due to the high return on assets and the debt to equity ratio that exceeds 1.0.

Review Problem

Surf-with-Park Company is a retailer of casual beach wear for college students. The post-closing trial balance for Surf-with-Park follows.

	A	B	C
1	Surf-with-Park Company		
2	Post-Closing Trial Balance		
3	December 31, 2014		
4	Account Name	Debit	Credit
5	Cash	16,000	
6	Short-Term Investments	16,500	
7	Notes Receivable	5,000	
8	Accounts Receivable	138,000	
9	Merchandise Inventory	72,500	
10	Prepaid Rent	800	
11	Prepaid Insurance	2,400	
12	Sales Supplies	640	
13	Office Supplies	220	
14	Deposit for Future Advertising	1,840	
15	Building, Not in Use	24,800	
16	Land	11,700	
17	Delivery Equipment	20,600	
18	Accumulated Depreciation—Delivery Equipment		14,200
19	Trademark	2,000	
20	Accounts Payable		57,300
21	Salaries Payable		2,600
22	Interest Payable		420
23	Long-Term Notes Payable		40,000
24	Common Stock		100,000
25	Retained Earnings		98,480
26		313,000	313,000
27			

REQUIRED

1. Prepare a classified balance sheet for Surf-with-Park Company.
2. What key measures from the balance sheet best capture a company's financial performance?

SOLUTION

	A	B	C	D
1	**Surf-with-Park Company**			
2	**Balance Sheet**			
3	**June 30, 2014**			
4	**Assets**			
5	**Current assets:**			
6	Cash		$ 16,000	
7	Short-term investments		16,500	
8	Notes receivable		5,000	
9	Accounts receivable		138,000	
10	Merchandise inventory		72,500	
11	Prepaid rent		800	
12	Prepaid insurance		2,400	
13	Sales supplies		640	
14	Office supplies		220	
15	Deposit for future advertising		1,840	
16	Total current assets			$253,900
17	**Investments:**			
18	Building, not in use			24,800
19	**Property, plant, and equipment:**			
20	Land		$ 11,700	
21	Delivery equipment	$ 20,600		
22	Less accumulated depreciation	14,200	6,400	
23	Total property, plant, and equipment			18,100
24	**Intangible assets:**			
25	Trademark			2,000
26	**Total assets**			$298,800
27	**Liabilities**			
28	**Current liabilities:**			
29	Accounts payable		$ 57,300	
30	Salaries payable		2,600	
31	Interest payable		420	
32	Total current liabilities			$ 60,320
33	**Long-term liabilities:**			
34	Long-term notes payable			40,000
35	**Total liabilities**			$100,320
36	**Stockholders' Equity**			
37	Common stock		$100,000	
38	Retained earnings		98,480	
39	Total stockholders' equity			198,480
40	Total liabilities and stockholders' equity			$298,800
41				

2. A user of the classified balance sheet would want to know the working capital and current ratio because it is a good indicator of a company's ability to pay its bills and repay outstanding loans. The other measure, the debt to equity ratio, shows the proportion of the company financed by creditors in comparison with that financed by owners. That measure is very important to liquidity analysis, because it is related to debt and its repayment. It is also relevant to profitability analysis, because the amount of debt affects the amount of interest expense and the return on equity.

Chapter Review

Describe the objective of financial reporting, and identify the conceptual framework underlying accounting information. LO 1

The objective of financial reporting is to provide financial information about the reporting entity to present to potential equity investors, lenders, and other creditors in their capacity as capital providers. Financial information must enable the reader to assess cash flow prospects and management's stewardship. Financial information must exhibit the concepts of relevance and faithful representation. To be relevant, it must have predictive value, confirmative value, or both, subject to materiality. To be faithfully represented, it must be complete, neutral, and free from error. Enhancing qualitative characteristics are comparability, verifiability, timeliness, and understandability, all subject to the cost constraint. Because accountants' measurements are not exact, certain conventions are applied to help users interpret financial statements. Consistency requires the use of the same accounting procedures from period to period and enhances the comparability of financial statements. Full disclosure means including all relevant information in the financial statements. Conservatism entails using the procedure that is least likely to overstate assets and income. Since the passage of the Sarbanes-Oxley Act, CEOs and CFOs have been required to certify that their companies' financial statements are accurate and complete.

Identify and define the basic components of financial reporting, and prepare a classified balance sheet. LO 2

The basic components of a classified balance sheet are as follows.

Assets	Liabilities	Stockholders' Equity
Current assets	Current liabilities	Contributed capital
Investments	Long-term liabilities	Retained earnings
Property, plant, and equipment		
Intangible assets		

Current assets are cash and other assets that a firm can reasonably expect to convert to cash or use up during the next year or the normal operating cycle, whichever is longer. Investments are assets, usually long-term, that are not used in the normal operation of a business. Property, plant, and equipment are tangible long-term assets used in day-to-day operations. Intangible assets are long-term assets with no physical substance whose value stems from the rights or privileges they are accruing to their owners.

A current liability is an obligation that must be satisfied within the next year or the normal operating cycle, whichever is longer. Long-term liabilities are debts that fall due more than one year in the future or beyond the normal operating cycle.

The equity section of a corporation's balance sheet differs from the equity section of a partnership's or sole proprietorship's balance sheet in that it has subcategories for contributed capital (the assets invested by stockholders) and retained earnings (stockholders' claim to assets earned from operations and reinvested in operations).

Use classified financial statements to evaluate liquidity and profitability. LO 3

In evaluating a company's performance, investors (owners) and creditors rely on the data provided in financial statements. Two measures of liquidity are working capital and the current ratio. Five measures of profitability are profit margin, asset turnover, return on assets, debt to equity ratio, and return on equity. Data from multiple years and industry averages are useful in interpreting these ratios.

Key Terms and Ratios

accounting conventions 206 (LO1)
classified financial statements 209 (LO2)
comparability 206 (LO1)
complete information 206 (LO1)
confirmative value 205 (LO1)
conservatism 207 (LO1)
consistency 206 (LO1)
Contributed Capital 212 (LO2)
cost constraint (cost-benefit) 206 (LO1)
current assets 209 (LO2)
current liabilities 211 (LO2)
dividends 213 (LO2)
faithful representation 206 (LO1)
free from material error 206 (LO1)
full disclosure 207 (LO1)
goodwill 211 (LO2)
intangible assets 211 (LO2)
investments 211 (LO2)
liquidity 214 (LO3)
long-term liabilities 212 (LO2)
material 205 (LO1)
materiality 205 (LO1)
neutral information 206 (LO1)
normal operating cycle 209 (LO2)
other assets 209 (LO2)
partners' equity 212 (LO2)
predictive value 205 (LO1)
profitability 215 (LO3)
property, plant, and equipment 211 (LO2)
qualitative characteristics 205 (LO1)
relevance 205 (LO1)
Retained Earnings 213 (LO2)
stockholders' equity 212 (LO2)
timeliness 206 (LO1)
understandability 206 (LO1)
verifiability 206 (LO1)

RATIOS

asset turnover 216 (LO3)
current ratio 214 (LO3)
debt to equity ratio 219 (LO3)
profit margin 215 (LO3)
return on assets 217 (LO3)
return on equity 220 (LO3)
working capital 214 (LO3)

Chapter Assignments

DISCUSSION QUESTIONS

LO 1 **DQ1. CONCEPT ▶** How do the four basic financial statements meet the stewardship objective of financial reporting?

LO 1 **DQ2. CONCEPT ▶** What are some areas that require estimates to record transactions under the matching rule?

LO 1 **DQ3. CONCEPT ▶** How can financial information be consistent but not comparable?

LO 1 **DQ4. CONCEPT ▶** When might an amount be material to management but not to the CPA auditing the financial statements?

LO 2 **DQ5.** Why is it that land held for future use and equipment not currently used in the business are classified as investments rather than as property, plant, and equipment?

LO 3 **DQ6. BUSINESS APPLICATION ▶** Why is it important to compare a company's financial performance with industry standards?

LO 3 **DQ7. BUSINESS APPLICATION ▶** Is the statement "Return on assets is a better measure of profitability than profit margin" true or false and why?

SHORT EXERCISES

LO 1 **Objectives and Qualitative Characteristics**

SE1. CONCEPT ▶ Identify each of the following statements as related to either an objective (O) of financial information or as a qualitative (Q) characteristic of accounting information:

a. Information about business resources, claims to those resources, and changes in them should be provided.

(Continued)

b. Decision makers must be able to interpret accounting information.
c. Information that is useful in making investment and credit decisions should be furnished.
d. Accounting information must exhibit relevance and faithful representation.
e. Information useful in assessing cash flow prospects should be provided.

LO 1

Enhancing Qualitative Characteristics and Accounting Conventions

SE2. CONCEPT ▶ State which of these selected enhancing qualitative characteristics and accounting conventions—comparability, verifiability, timeliness, cost constraint, consistency, full disclosure, materiality, or conservatism—is being followed in each case that follows.

1. Management provides detailed information about the company's long-term debt in the notes to the financial statements.
2. A company does not account separately for discounts received for prompt payment of accounts payable because few of these transactions occur and the total amount of the discounts is small.
3. Management eliminates a weekly report on property, plant, and equipment acquisitions and disposals because no one finds it useful.
4. A company follows the policy of recognizing a loss on inventory when the market value of an item falls below its cost but does nothing if the market value rises.
5. When several accounting methods are acceptable, management chooses a single method and follows that method from year to year.
6. The internal audit department comes up with similar estimates to management's determination of fair value of investments.
7. The company makes every effort to complete its financial statements within one week after the end of the accounting period.

LO 2

Classification of Accounts: Balance Sheet

SE3. Tell whether each of the following accounts is a current asset; an investment; property, plant, and equipment; an intangible asset; a current liability; a long-term liability; stockholders' equity; or not on the balance sheet:

1. Delivery Trucks
2. Accounts Payable
3. Note Payable (due in 90 days)
4. Delivery Expense
5. Common Stock
6. Prepaid Insurance
7. Trademark
8. Investment to Be Held Six Months
9. Factory Not Used in Business

LO 2

Classified Balance Sheet

SE4. Using the following accounts, prepare a classified balance sheet at year end, May 31, 2014: Accounts Payable, $1,600; Accounts Receivable, $2,200; Accumulated Depreciation—Equipment, $1,400; Cash, $400; Common Stock, $2,000; Equipment, $6,000; Franchise, $400; Investments (long-term), $1,000; Merchandise Inventory, $1,200; Notes Payable (long-term), $800; Retained Earnings, $?; Wages Payable, $200. Assume that this is the company's first year of operations.

LO 3

Liquidity Ratios

SE5. BUSINESS APPLICATION ▶ Using the following accounts and balances taken from a year-end balance sheet, compute working capital and the current ratio:

Accounts Payable	$3,500	Merchandise Inventory	$ 6,000
Accounts Receivable	5,000	Notes Payable in Three Years	6,500
Cash	2,000	Property, Plant, and Equipment	20,000
Marketable Securities	1,000	Common Stock	24,000

LO 3
Profitability Ratios

SE6. BUSINESS APPLICATION ▶ Using the following information from a balance sheet and an income statement, compute the (1) profit margin, (2) asset turnover, (3) return on assets, (4) debt to equity ratio, and (5) return on equity. (The previous year's total assets were $200,000, and stockholders' equity was $140,000.) (Round to one decimal place.)

Total assets	$240,000	Net sales	$260,000
Total liabilities	60,000	Cost of goods sold	140,000
Total stockholders' equity	180,000	Operating expenses	80,000

LO 3
Profitability Ratios

SE7. BUSINESS APPLICATION ▶ Assume that a company has a profit margin of 12.0 percent, an asset turnover of 6.4 times, and a debt to equity ratio of 50 percent. What are the company's return on assets and return on equity? (Round to one decimal place.)

EXERCISES: SET A

LO 1
Financial Accounting Concepts

E1A. CONCEPT ▶ The lettered items that follow represent a classification scheme for the concepts of financial accounting. Match each numbered term in the list with the letter of the category in which it belongs.

a. Qualitative characteristics
b. Financial statements
c. Objective of accounting information
d. Accounting measurement considerations
e. Accounting processing considerations
f. Decision makers (users of accounting information)
g. Accounting conventions
h. Business activities or entities relevant to accounting measurement

1. Conservatism
2. Verifiability
3. Statement of cash flows
4. Materiality
5. Faithful representation
6. Recognition
7. Cost-benefit
8. Predictive value
9. Business transactions
10. Consistency
11. Full disclosure
12. Furnishing information that is useful to investors and creditors
13. Specific business entities
14. Classification
15. Management
16. Neutrality
17. Internal accounting control
18. Valuation
19. Investors
20. Completeness
21. Relevance
22. Furnishing information that is useful in assessing cash flow prospects

LO 1
Qualitative Characteristics and Accounting Conventions

E2A. CONCEPT ▶ Each of the statements that follow violates one or more accounting concepts. State which of these selected qualitative characteristics and accounting conventions—relevance, faithful representation, comparability, verifiability, timeliness, understandability, cost constraint, consistency, materiality, conservatism, or full disclosure—is (are) violated.

1. A company changes its method of accounting for depreciation.
2. The asset account for a pickup truck still used in the business is written down to what the truck could be sold for, even though the carrying value under conventional depreciation methods is higher.
3. A series of reports that are time-consuming and expensive to prepare are presented to the stockholders each month, even though they are never used.

(*Continued*)

4. The company in **1** does not indicate in the financial statements that the method of depreciation was changed, nor does it specify the effect of the change on net income.
5. A company's new office building, which is built next to the company's existing factory, is debited to the factory account because it represents a fairly small dollar amount in relation to the factory.
6. Information is presented in a way that is not useful to users.
7. A transaction is recorded that does not represent the substance of the economic event.
8. Information is presented in a way that is confusing to users.
9. Similar transactions are recorded using different accounting principles.
10. Information is reported long after the economic events they represent.
11. Various experts come up with widely different estimates of an amount.

LO 2

Classification of Accounts: Balance Sheet

E3A. The lettered items that follow represent a classification scheme for a balance sheet, and the numbered items in the list are account titles. Match each account with the letter of the category in which it belongs.

a. Current liabilities
b. Stockholders' equity
c. Current assets
d. Intangible assets
e. Property, plant, and equipment
f. Investments
g. Long-term liabilities
h. Not on balance sheet

1. Patent
2. Building Held for Sale
3. Prepaid Rent
4. Wages Payable
5. Note Payable in Five Years
6. Building Used in Operations
7. Fund Held to Pay Off Long-Term Debt
8. Inventory
9. Prepaid Insurance
10. Depreciation Expense
11. Accounts Receivable
12. Interest Expense
13. Unearned Revenue
14. Short-Term Investments
15. Accumulated Depreciation
16. Common Stock

LO 2

Classified Balance Sheet Preparation

E4A. The following data pertain to Wagoner, Inc.: Accounts Payable, $20,400; Accounts Receivable, $15,200; Accumulated Depreciation—Building, $5,600; Accumulated Depreciation—Equipment, $6,800; Bonds Payable, $24,000; Building, $28,000; Cash, $12,480; Copyright, $2,480; Equipment, $60,800; Inventory, $16,000; Investment in Corporate Securities (long-term), $8,000; Investment in Six-Month Government Securities, $6,560; Common Stock, $18,000; Income Taxes Payable, $2,600; Land, $3,200; Prepaid Rent, $480; and Revenue Received in Advance, $1,120. Prepare a classified balance sheet at December 31, 2014. Assume that this is Wagoner's first year of operations.

LO 3

Liquidity Ratios

E5A. BUSINESS APPLICATION ▶ The accounts and balances that follow are from Kellman, Inc.'s general ledger. Compute the (1) working capital and (2) current ratio. (Round to one decimal place.)

Accounts Payable	$13,280
Accounts Receivable	8,160
Cash	1,200
Current Portion of Long-Term Debt	8,000
Long-Term Investments	8,320
Marketable Securities	10,080
Merchandise Inventory	20,320

(Continued)

Notes Payable (90 days)	$12,000
Notes Payable (2 years)	16,000
Notes Receivable (90 days)	20,800
Notes Receivable (2 years)	8,000
Prepaid Insurance	320
Property, Plant, and Equipment	48,000
Property Taxes Payable	1,000
Income Taxes Payable	1,580
Common Stock	15,200
Retained Earnings	5,860
Salaries Payable	680
Supplies	280
Unearned Revenue	600

LO 3

Profitability Ratios

E6A. BUSINESS APPLICATION ▶ The following amounts are from Shimura Company's financial statements at the end of the current year: total assets, $426,000; total liabilities, $172,000; stockholders' equity, $254,000; net sales, $782,000; cost of goods sold, $486,000; operating expenses, $178,000; and dividends, $40,000. During the current year, total assets increased by $75,000. Total stockholders' equity was affected only by net income and dividends. Compute the (1) profit margin, (2) asset turnover, (3) return on assets, (4) debt to equity ratio, and (5) return on equity. (Round to one decimal place.)

LO 3

Liquidity and Profitability Ratios

E7A. BUSINESS APPLICATION ▶A company's simplified balance sheet and income statement follow.

Balance Sheet
December 31, 2014

Assets		Liabilities	
Current assets	$ 50,000	Current liabilities	$ 20,000
Investments	10,000	Long-term liabilities	30,000
Property, plant, and equipment	146,500	Total liabilities	$ 50,000
Intangible assets	13,500	**Stockholders' Equity**	
		Stockholders' equity	170,000
Total assets	$220,000	Total liabilities and stockholders' equity	$220,000

Income Statement
For the Year Ended December 31, 2014

Net sales	$410,000
Cost of goods sold	250,000
Gross margin	$160,000
Operating expenses	135,000
Net income	$ 25,000

Total assets and stockholders' equity at the beginning of 2014 were $180,000 and $140,000, respectively.

1. Compute the following liquidity measures: (a) working capital and (b) current ratio. (Round to one decimal place.)
2. Compute the following profitability measures: (a) profit margin, (b) asset turnover, (c) return on assets, (d) debt to equity ratio, and (e) return on equity. (Round to one decimal place.)

LO 3 **Liquidity and Profitability Ratios**

E8A. BUSINESS APPLICATION ▶ Villegas Corporation is considering applying for a bank loan. Various data from Villegas's classified financial statements follow.

	2014	2013
Current assets	$100,000	$ 85,000
Total assets	440,000	355,000
Current liabilities	45,000	25,000
Long-term liabilities	75,000	25,000
Stockholders' equity	320,000	305,000
Sales	600,000	525,000
Net income	30,000	40,000

Its total assets and stockholders' equity at the beginning of 2013 were $345,000 and $295,000, respectively.

1. Use (a) liquidity analysis and (b) profitability analysis to document Villegas's financial position. (Round to two decimal places.)
2. Discuss Villegas's profitability and liquidity. Do you think it will qualify for a bank loan?

EXERCISES: SET B

Visit the textbook companion website at www.cengagebrain.com to access Exercise Set B for this chapter.

PROBLEMS

LO 1 **Qualitative Characteristics and Accounting Conventions**

P1. CONCEPT ▶ In each case that follows, accounting conventions may have been violated.

1. After careful study, Schuss Company, which has offices in 40 states, has determined that its method of depreciating office furniture should be changed. The new method is adopted for the current year, and the change is noted in the financial statements.
2. In the past, Waldemar Company has recorded operating expenses in general accounts (e.g., Salaries Expense and Utilities Expense). Management has determined that despite the additional recordkeeping costs, the company's income statement should break down each operating expense into its components of selling expense and administrative expense.
3. Leon Company's auditor discovered that a company official had authorized the payment of a $1,200 bribe to a local official. Management argued that, because the item was so small in relation to the size of the company ($1,700,000 in sales), the illegal payment should not be disclosed.
4. J&J Bookstore built a small addition to its main building to house a new computer games section. Because no one could be sure that the computer games section would succeed, the accountant took a conservative approach and recorded the addition as an expense.
5. Since it began operations ten years ago, Reed Company has used the same generally accepted inventory method. The company does not disclose in its financial statements what inventory method it uses.
6. Go-Fast Gas has a number of aged service stations around the local community. The company has not included the buildings at these locations on its financial statements because it does not plan on selling them.
7. Social Internet Company is planning to ask the bank for a loan. It asks its accountants to make its financial prospects look as attractive as possible.
8. Acre Company's auditors are having difficulty reproducing estimates in Acre's financial statements due to estimates that cannot be substantiated.

REQUIRED

In each of these cases, identify the qualitative characteristic or accounting convention that applies, state whether or not the treatment is in accord with the accounting concept and generally accepted accounting principles, and briefly explain why.

LO **2, 3**

RATIO

SPREADSHEET

✔ Total assets: $597,600

Classified Balance Sheet

P2. The information that follows is from Jason's Hardware Corporation's June 30, 2014, post-closing trial balance.

Account Name	Debit	Credit
Cash	32,000	
Short-Term Investments	33,000	
Notes Receivable	10,000	
Accounts Receivable	276,000	
Merchandise Inventory	145,000	
Prepaid Rent	1,600	
Prepaid Insurance	4,800	
Sales Supplies	1,280	
Office Supplies	440	
Deposit for Future Advertising	3,680	
Building, Not in Use	49,600	
Land	23,400	
Delivery Equipment	41,200	
Accumulated Depreciation—Delivery Equipment		28,400
Trademark	4,000	
Accounts Payable		114,600
Salaries Payable		5,200
Interest Payable		840
Long-Term Notes Payable		80,000
Income Taxes Payable		910
Common Stock		140,300
Retained Earnings		255,750
Totals	626,000	626,000

REQUIRED

1. Prepare a classified balance sheet for Jason's Hardware Corporation.
2. **BUSINESS APPLICATION** ▶ Compute Jason's Hardware's current ratio and debt to equity ratio. (Round to one decimal place.)
3. **BUSINESS APPLICATION** ▶ As a user of the classified balance sheet, why would you want to know the current ratio or the debt to equity ratio?

LO **3**

RATIO

SPREADSHEET

✔ 2014 current ratio, 2.3;
✔ 2014 return on equity, 15.6%

Liquidity and Profitability Ratios

P3. BUSINESS APPLICATION ▶ Julio Company has had poor operating results for the past two years. As Julio's accountant, you have the following information available to you:

	2014	2013
Current assets	$ 45,000	$ 35,000
Total assets	145,000	110,000
Current liabilities	20,000	10,000
Long-term liabilities	20,000	—
Stockholders' equity	105,000	100,000
Net sales	262,000	200,000
Net income	16,000	11,000

Total assets and stockholders' equity at the beginning of 2013 were $90,000 and $80,000, respectively.

(Continued)

REQUIRED

1. Compute the following measures of liquidity for 2013 and 2014: (a) working capital and (b) current ratio. Comment on the differences between the years. (Round to one decimal place.)
2. Compute the following measures of profitability for 2013 and 2014: (a) profit margin, (b) asset turnover, (c) return on assets, (d) debt to equity ratio, and (e) return on equity. Comment on the change in performance from 2013 to 2014. (Round to one decimal place.)

LO 2, 3

Classified Balance Sheet

P4. The information that follows is from Cullen's Hardware Company's June 30, 2014, post-closing trial balance.

✔ Total assets: $625,800

Account Name	Debit	Credit
Cash	42,800	
Short-Term Investments	34,300	
Sales Supplies	1,280	
Merchandise Inventory	145,000	
Prepaid Rent	2,100	
Income Taxes Payable		3,780
Prepaid Insurance	4,800	
Accounts Receivable	287,000	
Office Supplies	440	
Common Stock		290,000
Notes Receivable	10,000	
Land	31,400	
Delivery Equipment	43,200	
Accumulated Depreciation—Delivery Equipment		28,400
Trademark	4,000	
Accounts Payable		124,600
Salaries Payable		7,700
Deposit for Future Advertising	3,680	
Interest Payable		840
Retained Earnings		118,880
Long-Term Notes Payable		80,000
Building, Not in Use	44,200	
Totals	654,200	654,200

REQUIRED

1. Prepare a classified balance sheet for Cullen's Hardware Company.
2. **BUSINESS APPLICATION** ▶ Compute Cullen's Hardware's current ratio and debt to equity ratio. (Round to one decimal place.)
3. **BUSINESS APPLICATION** ▶ As a user of the classified balance sheet, why would you want to know the current ratio or the debt to equity ratio?

ALTERNATE PROBLEMS

LO 1

Accounting Conventions

P5. CONCEPT ▶ In each case that follows, qualitative characteristics and accounting conventions may have been violated.

1. Elite Manufacturing Company uses the cost method for computing the balance sheet amount of inventory unless the market value of the inventory is less than the cost, in which case the market value is used. At the end of the current year, the market value is $302,000 and the cost is $324,000. The company uses the $302,000 figure to compute the value of inventory because management believes it is the more cautious approach.

2. Livery Service Company has annual sales of $20,000,000. It follows the practice of recording any items costing less than $500 as expenses in the year purchased. During the current year, it purchased several chairs for the executive conference room at $490 each, including freight. Although the chairs were expected to last for at least ten years, they were recorded as an expense in accordance with company policy.
3. Stardust Company closed its books on October 31, 2013, before preparing its annual report. On November 3, 2013, a fire destroyed one of the company's two factories. Although the company had fire insurance and would not suffer a loss on the building, it seemed likely that it would suffer a significant decrease in sales in 2014 because of the fire. It did not report the fire damage in its 2013 financial statements because the fire had not affected its operations during that year.
4. Primal Drug Company spends a substantial portion of its profits on research and development. The company had been reporting its $12,000,000 expenditure for research and development as a lump sum, but management recently decided to begin classifying the expenditures by project, even though its recordkeeping costs will increase.
5. During the current year, Ziegler Company changed from one generally accepted method of accounting for inventories to another method "without disclosing the change" because changing methods is not per se a violation.
6. Due to pressing business issues, Judson Products is consistently behind schedule in preparing its financial statements.
7. Thomas Electronics is a complex global business whose financial statements use many technical terms not known by the typical investor.
8. Siro Company produces financial statements that are not helpful in assessing the company's prospects in the future.

REQUIRED

For each of these cases, identify the accounting concept that applies, state whether or not the treatment is in accord with the concept, and briefly explain why.

LO 2, 3

RATIO

SPREADSHEET

✓ Total assets: $595,600

Classified Balance Sheet

P6. The information that follows is from Matt's Hardware Company's April 30, 2014, post-closing trial balance.

Account Name	Debit	Credit
Cash	31,000	
Short-Term Investments	33,000	
Notes Receivable	10,000	
Accounts Receivable	276,000	
Merchandise Inventory	145,000	
Prepaid Rent	1,600	
Prepaid Insurance	4,800	
Sales Supplies	1,280	
Office Supplies	440	
Deposit for Future Advertising	3,680	
Building, Not in Use	49,600	
Land	22,400	
Delivery Equipment	41,200	
Accumulated Depreciation—Delivery Equipment		28,400
Trademark	4,000	
Accounts Payable		114,600
Salaries Payable		5,200
Interest Payable		840
Income Taxes Payable		4,750
Long-Term Notes Payable		80,000
Common Stock		129,000
Retained Earnings		261,210
Totals	624,000	624,000

(Continued)

REQUIRED

1. Prepare a classified balance sheet for Matt's Hardware.
2. **BUSINESS APPLICATION ▶** Compute Matt's Hardware's current ratio and debt to equity ratio. (Round to one decimal place.)
3. **BUSINESS APPLICATION ▶** As a user of the classified balance sheet, why would you want to know the current ratio or the debt to equity ratio?

LO **3**

SPREADSHEET

✔ 2014 current ratio, 2.0;
✔ 2014 return on equity, 25.2%

Liquidity and Profitability Ratios

P7. BUSINESS APPLICATION ▶ A summary of data from Pinder Construction Supply Company's income statements and balance sheets for 2014 and 2013 follows.

	2014	2013
Current assets	$ 366,000	$ 310,000
Total assets	2,320,000	1,740,000
Current liabilities	180,000	120,000
Long-term liabilities	800,000	580,000
Stockholders' equity	1,340,000	1,040,000
Net sales	4,600,000	3,480,000
Net income	300,000	204,000

Total assets and stockholders' equity at the beginning of 2013 were $1,360,000 and $840,000, respectively.

REQUIRED

1. Compute the following liquidity measures for 2013 and 2014: (a) working capital and (b) current ratio. Comment on the differences between the years. (Round to one decimal place.)
2. Compute the following measures of profitability for 2013 and 2014: (a) profit margin, (b) asset turnover, (c) return on assets, (d) debt to equity ratio, and (e) return on equity. Comment on the change in performance from 2013 to 2014. (Round to one decimal place.)

LO **2, 3**

RATIO

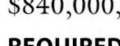

✔ Total assets: $571,470

Classified Balance Sheet

P8. The information that follows is from Rodriguez's Tools Company's April 30, 2014, post-closing trial balance.

Account Name	Debit	Credit
Cash	31,000	
Short-Term Investments	43,500	
Accounts Receivable	239,000	
Merchandise Inventory	113,000	
Notes Receivable	10,000	
Interest Payable		930
Sales Supplies	1,280	
Office Supplies	540	
Deposit for Future Advertising	3,120	
Income Taxes Payable		820
Long-Term Notes Payable		99,000
Land	34,700	
Delivery Equipment	42,230	
Accumulated Depreciation—Delivery Equipment		28,400
Building, Not in Use	72,100	
Accounts Payable		129,600
Salaries Payable		4,600
Prepaid Rent	1,800	
Prepaid Insurance	3,600	
Common Stock		139,900
Retained Earnings		196,620
Trademark	4,000	
Totals	599,870	403,250

REQUIRED

1. Prepare a classified balance sheet for Rodriguez's Tools.
2. **BUSINESS APPLICATION ▶** Compute Rodriguez's Tools' current ratio and debt to equity ratio. (Round to one decimal place.)
3. **BUSINESS APPLICATION ▶** As a user of the classified balance sheet, why would you want to know the current ratio or the debt to equity ratio?

CASES

LO 1

Conceptual Understanding: Consistency, Full Disclosure, and Materiality

C1. CONCEPT ▶ Metro Parking, which operates a seven-story parking building, has a calendar year-end. It serves daily and hourly parkers, as well as monthly parkers who pay a fixed monthly rate in advance. The company traditionally has recorded all cash receipts as revenues when received. Most monthly parkers pay in full during the month prior to that in which they have the right to park. The company's auditors have said that, beginning in 2014, the company should consider recording the cash receipts from monthly parking on an accrual basis, crediting Unearned Revenues. Total cash receipts for 2014 were $1,250,000, and the cash receipts received in 2014 and applicable to January 2015 were $62,500. Discuss the relevance of the accounting concepts of consistency, full disclosure, and materiality to the decision to record the monthly parking revenues on an accrual basis.

LO 1

Conceptual Understanding: Materiality

C1. CONCEPT ▶ Laskowski, Inc., operates a chain of consumer electronics stores. This year, the company achieved annual sales of $75 million, on which it earned a net income of $3 million. At the beginning of the year, management implemented a new inventory system that enabled it to track all purchases and sales. At the end of the year, a physical inventory revealed that the actual inventory was $120,000 below what the new system indicated it should be. The inventory loss, which probably resulted from shoplifting, was reflected in a higher cost of goods sold. The problem concerns management but seems to be less important to the company's auditors. What is materiality? Why might the inventory loss concern management more than it does the auditors? Do you think the amount of inventory loss is material?

LO 3

Interpreting Financial Reports: Comparison of Profitability

C3. BUSINESS APPLICATION ▶ Two of the largest chains of grocery stores in the United States are **The Gap, Inc.**, and **Abercrombie & Fitch Co.** In fiscal 2011, The Gap had net income of $833 million, and Abercrombie & Fitch had net income of $128 million. It is difficult to judge from these figures alone which company is more profitable, because they do not take into account the relative sales, sizes, and investments of the companies. Data (in millions) needed for a complete financial analysis of the two companies follow.[14]

	Gap	Abercrombie & Fitch*
Net sales	$14,549	$4,158
Beginning total assets	7,065	2,941
Ending total assets	7,422	3,048
Beginning total liabilities	2,985	1,051
Ending total liabilities	4,667	1,186
Beginning stockholders' equity	4,080	1,891
Ending stockholders' equity	2,755	1,862

* Abercrombie & Fitch's data is rounded to the nearest dollar.

1. Determine which company was more profitable by computing profit margin, asset turnover, the debt to equity ratio, return on assets, and return on equity for the two companies. Comment on the relative profitability of the two companies. (Round to one decimal place.)
2. What do the ratios tell you about the factors that go into achieving an adequate return on assets in the clothing store industry? For industry data, refer to the graphs in the ratio boxes throughout the chapter.
3. How would you characterize the use of debt financing in the clothing store industry and the use of debt by these two companies?

LO **2, 3**

Annual Report Case: Classified Balance Sheet

C4. BUSINESS APPLICATION ▶ Refer to the **CVS** annual report in the Supplement to Chapter 1 to answer the following questions.

1. Does CVS use a classified balance sheet?
2. Did CVS's debt to equity ratio change from 2010 to 2011?
3. What is the contributed capital for 2011? How does contributed capital compare with retained earnings?

LO **3**

Comparison Case: Financial Performance

C5. BUSINESS APPLICATION ▶ Compare the financial performance of **CVS** and **Southwest Airlines Co.** on the basis of profitability in 2011 and 2010. Use the following ratios: profit margin, asset turnover, return on assets, and return on equity. In 2009, total assets, total stockholders' equity, and cash flows from operating activities for CVS were \$61,141 million, \$35,768 million, and \$4.035 million, respectively. Southwest's total assets were \$14,269 million in 2009, and its total stockholders' equity and cash flow from operating activities were \$5,454 million and \$985 million, respectively. Comment on the relative performance of the two companies. In general, how does Southwest's performance compare to CVS's with respect to profitability? What distinguishes Southwest's profitability performance from that of CVS?

LO **1**

Ethical Dilemma: Ethics and Financial Reporting

C6. Beacon Systems develops computer software and licenses it to financial institutions. The firm records revenues from the software it has developed on a percentage of completion basis. For example, if a project is 50 percent complete, then 50 percent of the contracted revenue is recognized. Preliminary estimates for a \$7 million project now in development are that the project is 75 percent complete. Estimates of completion are a matter of judgment, and management therefore feels justified in asking for a new report showing that the project is 90 percent complete. The change will enable senior managers to meet their financial goals for the year and thus receive substantial year-end bonuses. Do you think management's action is ethical? If you were the company controller and were asked to prepare the new report, would you do it? What action would you take?

Continuing Case: Annual Report Project

C7. BUSINESS APPLICATION ▶ Using the most recent annual report of the company you have chosen to study and that you have accessed online at the company's website, use the classified balance sheet together with the income statement to compute the following ratios for the last two years and indicate whether each has improved. (Round to one decimal place or to the nearest tenth of a percent.)

a. Current ratio
b. Profit margin
c. Asset turnover
d. Return on assets
e. Debt to equity ratio
f. Return on equity

CHAPTER 5

LEARNING OBJECTIVES

LO1 Define *merchandising accounting*, and differentiate perpetual from periodic inventory systems.

LO2 Describe the features of multistep and single-step classified income statements.

LO3 Describe the terms of sale related to merchandising transactions.

LO4 Prepare an income statement, and record merchandising transactions under the perpetual inventory system.

LO5 Prepare an income statement, and record merchandising transactions under the periodic inventory system.

LO6 Explain the role of the operating cycle and foreign business transactions in evaluating the liquidity of a merchandising company.

ACCOUNTING FOR MERCHANDISING OPERATIONS

Business Insight
Walmart Stores, Inc.

Walmart is one of the most successful merchandising companies of all time. Like all merchandisers, it has two key decisions to make: the price at which it will sell goods and the level of service it will provide. A department store may set the price of its merchandise at a relatively high level and provide a great deal of service. A discount store, such as Walmart, may price its merchandise at a low level and provide less service amenities. It purchases merchandise in large quantities from many suppliers, sells the merchandise to customers at the lowest prices it can afford (while still making a profit), and provides limited, but good, service.

As you can see in the company's Financial Highlights,[1] Walmart is having difficulty controlling its cost of sales and operating expenses, which are both growing at a faster rate than net revenues and gross margin, respectively. As a result, operating income has not keep pace with net revenues.

Walmart's Financial Highlights Operating Results (in millions)

Fiscal Year Ended	**2012**	**2011**	**Change**
Net revenues	$446,950	$421,849	6.0%
Cost of sales	335,127	314,946	6.4%
Gross margin	108,727	104,006	4.5%
Operating expenses	85,265	81,361	4.8%
Operating income	26,558	25,542	4.0%

1. **CONCEPT** ▶ How do faithful representation and classification apply to merchandise operations?
2. **ACCOUNTING APPLICATION** ▶ How can merchandising transactions be recorded to reflect the company's performance?
3. **BUSINESS APPLICATION** ▶ How can Walmart manage its operating cycle so that it has adequate cash to maintain liquidity?

SECTION 1 CONCEPTS

CONCEPTS

- Faithful representation
- Classification

RELEVANT LEARNING OBJECTIVE

LO 1 Define *merchandising accounting* and differentiate perpetual from periodic inventory systems.

LO 1 Concepts Underlying Merchandising Accounting

A **merchandising company** earns income by buying and selling goods, which are called **merchandise inventory**. Whether a merchandiser is a wholesaler or a retailer, it uses the same basic accounting methods as a service company. However, the buying and selling of goods adds to the complexity of the accounting process. One complexity is the *classification* of items on the merchandising income statement so that the statement *faithfully represents* the operations of the company. Further, merchandise inventory is an important component on the **operating cycle**, which is the cycle of buying and holding merchandise until it is sold and then collecting payment for the sales.

To *faithfully represent* accounting for merchandising inventories, two basic systems of accounting for merchandise inventory are used: the *perpetual inventory system* and the *periodic inventory system*.

- Under the **perpetual inventory system**, continuous records are kept of the quantity and, usually, the cost of individual items as they are bought and sold. The cost of each item is recorded in the Merchandise Inventory account when it is purchased. As merchandise is sold, its cost is transferred from the Merchandise Inventory account to the Cost of Goods Sold account. Thus, at all times the balance of the Merchandise Inventory account equals the cost of goods on hand, and the balance in Cost of Goods Sold equals the cost of merchandise sold to customers.
- Under the **periodic inventory system**, the inventory not yet sold is counted periodically. This physical count is called **physical inventory**, which is usually taken at the end of the accounting period. No detailed records of the inventory are maintained during the accounting period. The figure for inventory is accurate only on the balance sheet date. (Note that the value of ending inventory on the balance sheet is determined by multiplying the quantity of each inventory item by its unit cost.) As soon as any purchases or sales are made in the new accounting period, the inventory figure becomes a historical amount, and it remains so until the new ending inventory amount is entered at the end of this accounting period.

Note that the perpetual inventory system does not eliminate the need for a physical count of the inventory. One should be taken periodically to ensure that the actual number of goods on hand matches the quantity indicated by the computer records.

Each system has advantages. Managers use the detailed data from the perpetual inventory system to respond to customers' inquiries about product availability, to order inventory more effectively in order to avoid running out of stock, and to control the costs associated with investments in inventory. Managers may choose the periodic inventory system because it reduces the amount of clerical work. If a business is fairly small, management can maintain control over its inventory simply through observation or by use of an offline system of cards or computer records. However, for larger companies, the lack of detailed records may lead to lost sales or high operating costs.

Business Perspective
How Have Bar Codes Influenced the Choice of Inventory Systems?

© Alija / iStockphoto.com

Most grocery stores, which traditionally used the periodic inventory system, now employ bar coding to update the physical inventory as items are sold. At the checkout counter, the cashier scans into the cash register the electronic marking, called a *bar code* or *universal product code* (*UPC*), that appears on each product. The cash register is linked to a computer that records the sale. Bar coding has become common in all types of retail companies, manufacturing firms, and hospitals. It has also become a major factor in the increased use of the perpetual inventory system. Interestingly, some retail businesses now use the perpetual inventory system for keeping track of the physical flow of inventory and the periodic inventory system for preparing their financial statements.

Because of the difficulty and expense of accounting for the purchase and sale of each item, companies that sell items of low value in high volume have traditionally used the periodic inventory system. Examples of such companies include small retailers, drugstores, and grocery stores. In contrast, companies that sell items that have a high unit value, such as appliances, have tended to use the perpetual inventory system. The distinction between high and low unit value for inventory systems has blurred considerably in recent years. Although the periodic inventory system is still widely used, computerization has led to an increase in the use of the perpetual inventory system.

APPLY IT!

Indicate whether each of the statements that follow is more applicable to (a) perpetual inventory system, (b) periodic inventory system, or (c) both systems.

1. Requires a physical count of inventory at end of period.
2. No detailed records of the inventory are maintained during the accounting period.
3. Continuous records are kept of the quantity.
4. Inventory figure is accurate only on the balance sheet date.
5. The balance in Cost of Goods Sold equals the cost of merchandise sold to customers at all times.
6. Helps to manage inventory more effectively and thus avoid running out of stock.
7. Is less costly to maintain but may lead to lost sales.

SOLUTION

1. c; 2. b; 3. a; 4. b; 5. a; 6. a; 7. b

TRY IT! SE1, E1A, E1B

SECTION 2 ACCOUNTING APPLICATIONS

ACCOUNTING APPLICATIONS

- Prepare a multistep income statement
- Prepare a single-step income statement
- Record inventory transactions under the perpetual method
- Record inventory transactions under the periodic method

RELEVANT LEARNING OBJECTIVES

LO2 Describe the features of multistep and single-step classified income statements.

LO3 Describe the terms of sale related to merchandising transactions.

LO4 Prepare an income statement, and record merchandising transactions under the perpetual inventory system.

LO5 Prepare an income statement, and record merchandising transactions under the periodic inventory system.

LO2 Forms of the Income Statement

In the income statements we have presented thus far, expenses have been deducted from revenue in a single step to arrive at net income. Here, we look at a multistep income statement and a more complex single-step format.

Multistep Income Statement

A **multistep income statement** goes through a series of steps, or subtotals, to arrive at net income. In a service company's multistep income statement, the operating expenses are deducted from revenues in a single step to arrive at income from operations. In contrast, because manufacturing and merchandising companies make or buy goods for sale, their income statements include an additional step of calculating gross margin by subtracting the cost of goods from net sales. Exhibit 1 compares the multistep income

Exhibit 1

A Comparison of the Components of Multistep Income Statements for Service and Merchandising or Manufacturing Companies

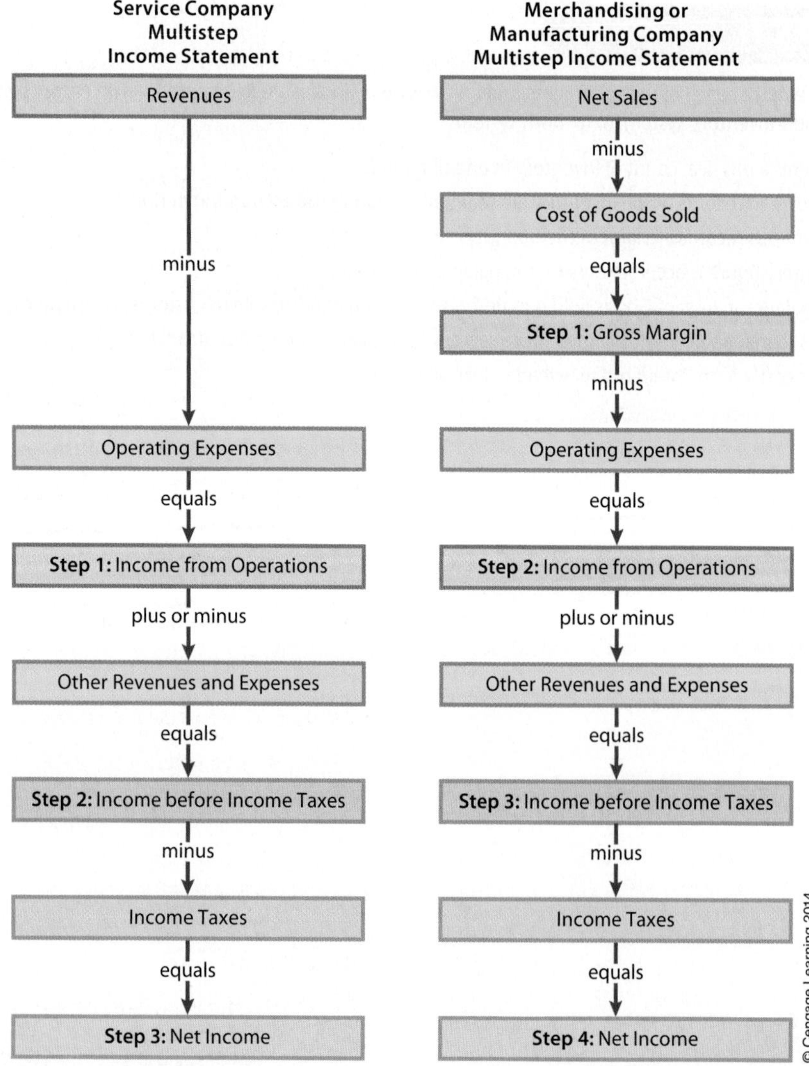

statement of a service company (which provides services as opposed to products) with that of a merchandising company (which buys and sells products) and a **manufacturing company** (which makes and sells products).

We will use Davila Corporation, a merchandising company, to illustrate the multistep income statement. Davila's multistep income statement is presented in Exhibit 2. Like balance sheets, income statements vary among companies. You will rarely, if ever, find an income statement exactly like the one presented for Davila Corporation. Companies use different terms and different structures.

Exhibit 2
Multistep Income Statement for Davila Corporation

Davila Corporation
Income Statement
For the Year Ended December 31, 2014

Step 1	Gross sales	$1,300,924	
	Less sales returns and allowances	52,300	
	Net sales		$1,248,624
	Cost of goods sold		815,040
	Gross margin		$ 433,584
Step 2	Operating expenses:		
	Selling expenses	$ 219,120	
	General and administrative expenses	138,016	
	Total operating expenses		357,136
	Income from operations		$ 76,448
Step 3	Other revenues and expenses:		
	Interest income	$ 5,600	
	Less interest expense	10,524	
	Excess of other expenses over other revenues		4,924
	Income before income taxes		$ 71,524
Step 4	Income tax expense		13,524
	Net income		$ 58,000

Net Sales (or Net Revenue) **Net sales** (or *net revenue*) is computed as follows.

Net Sales = Gross Sales − Sales Returns and Allowances

- **Gross sales** consist of the total revenue from cash and credit sales during a period. Under the revenue recognition concept, even when cash from a credit sale is not received during the current period, it is recorded if title to the merchandise has passed to the buyer.
- **Sales returns and allowances** include cash refunds and credits on account. They also include any discounts from selling prices made to customers who have returned defective products or products that are otherwise unsatisfactory. If other types of discounts are given to customers, they also should be deducted from gross sales.

For Davila, net sales is computed as follows.

$1,300,924 − $52,300 = $1,248,624

Cost of Goods Sold (or Cost of Sales) **Cost of goods sold** (or *cost of sales* or *cost of revenue*) is the amount a merchandiser paid for the merchandise it sold during a period. For a manufacturer, it is the cost of making the products it sold during a period. Davila's cost of goods sold is $815,040.

Gross Margin (or Gross Profit) **Gross margin** (or *gross profit*) is computed as follows.

Gross Margin = Net Sales − Cost of Goods Sold

International Perspective

IFRS Income Statements Under IFRS May Not Show Cost of Goods Sold

Under U.S. GAAP, the Cost of Goods Sold account is needed because the income statement requires listing costs and expense by function, such as cost of goods sold, selling expenses, and general and administrative expenses. IFRS, on the other hand, give companies the option of listing by function, like the U.S. GAAP, or by nature, such as materials costs, labor costs, and so forth. Most European companies choose the latter option, thus not showing any cost of goods sold, gross margin, or operating income on their income statements.

STUDY NOTE: *Gross margin measures profitability. When it is less than operating expenses, the company suffers a net loss from operations.*

A company's gross margin must be sufficient to cover operating expenses and provide an adequate net income. Davila's gross margin is computed as follows (as shown in Step 1 in Exhibit 2).

$1,248,624 − $815,040 = $433,584

Managers and owners are interested in both the amount and **percentage of gross margin**. The percentage is computed as follows.

Percentage of Gross Margin = Gross Margin ÷ Net Sales

For Davila, percentage of gross margin is computed as follows.

$433,584 ÷ $1,248,624 = 34.7%*

*Rounded

Business Application Gross margin information is useful in planning business operations.

- For instance, management may try to increase total sales of a product by reducing the selling price. Although this strategy reduces the percentage of gross margin, it will work if the number of items sold increases enough to raise the absolute amount of gross margin. Discount warehouse stores like **Sam's Club** and **Costco Wholesale Corporation** follow this strategy.
- On the other hand, management may decide to keep a high gross margin from sales and try to increase sales and the amount of gross margin by increasing operating expenses, such as advertising. Upscale specialty stores like **Neiman Marcus** and **Tiffany & Co.** use this strategy.

Other strategies to increase gross margin include using better purchasing methods to reduce the cost of goods sold.

Operating Expenses **Operating expenses** are the expenses, other than the cost of goods sold, that are incurred in running a business. They are often grouped into the categories of selling expenses and general and administrative expenses and computed as follows.

Operating Expenses = Selling Expenses + General and Administrative Expenses

- **Selling expenses** include the costs of storing goods and preparing them for sale; preparing displays, advertising, and otherwise promoting sales; and delivering goods to a buyer if the seller has agreed to pay the cost of delivery.
- **General and administrative expenses** include expenses for accounting, personnel, credit checking, collections, and any other expenses that apply to overall operations. Although occupancy expenses, such as expenses of rent, insurance, and utilities, are often classified as general and administrative expenses, they can also be allocated between selling expenses and general and administrative expenses.

For Davila, operating expenses are computed as follows.

$219,120 + $138,016 = $357,136

Business Application Careful planning and control of operating expenses can improve a company's profitability.

Income from Operations (or Operating Income) **Income from operations** (or *operating income*) is the income from a company's main business and is computed as follows.

Income from Operations = Gross Margin − Operating Expenses

For Davila, income from operations is computed as follows (as shown in Step 2 in Exhibit 2).

$433,584 − $357,136 = $76,448

STUDY NOTE: *Income from operations is a key measure of profitability for financial analysts.*

Business Application Income from operations is often used to compare the profitability of two or more companies or divisions within a company.

Other Revenues and Expenses (or Nonoperating Revenues and Expenses) **Other revenues and expenses** (or *nonoperating revenues and expenses*) are not related to a company's operating activities. Among the items included in this section are revenues from investments (such as dividends and interest on stocks, bonds, and savings accounts) and interest expense and other expenses that result from borrowing money. Davila's other revenues and expenses appear in Step 3 of Exhibit 2.

Income before Income Taxes **Income before income taxes** is the amount on which income taxes will be determined. It is computed as follows.

Income before Income Taxes = Income from Operations +/− Other Revenues and Expenses

For Davila, income before income taxes is computed as follows.

$76,448 − $4,924 = $71,524

Net Income (or Net Earnings) **Net income** (or *net earnings*) is the final figure, or "bottom line," of an income statement and is computed as follows.

Net Income = Income before Income Taxes − Income Tax Expense

For Davila, net income is computed as follows (as shown in Step 4 of Exhibit 2).

$71,524 − $13,524 = $58,000

Net income is an important performance measure because it represents the amount of earnings that accrue to stockholders. It is the amount transferred to retained earnings from all the income that business operations have generated during a period.

STUDY NOTE: *If you encounter income statement components not covered in this chapter, refer to the index at the end of the book to find the topic and read about it.*

Single-Step Income Statement

Exhibit 3 shows a **single-step income statement** for Davila Corporation. In this statement, net income is derived in a single step by putting the major categories of revenues in the first part of the statement and the major categories of costs and expenses in the

Exhibit 3
Single-Step Income Statement for Davila Corporation

Davila Corporation
Income Statement
For the Year Ended December 31, 2014

Revenues:		
Net sales		$1,248,624
Interest income		5,600
Total revenues		$1,254,224
Costs and expenses:		
Cost of goods sold	$815,040	
Selling expenses	219,120	
General and administrative expenses	138,016	
Interest expense	10,524	
Total costs and expenses		1,182,700
Income before income taxes		$ 71,524
Income tax expense		13,524
Net income		$ 58,000

APPLY IT!

A single-step income statement follows. Present the information in a multistep income statement, and indicate what insights can be obtained from the multistep form as opposed to the single-step form.

Diviney Corporation
Income Statement
For the Year Ended December 31, 2014

Revenues:		
Net sales		$500,000
Interest income		50,000
Total revenues		$550,000
Costs and expenses:		
Cost of goods sold	$300,000	
Selling expenses	100,000	
General and administrative expenses	75,000	
Interest expense	25,000	
Total costs and expenses		500,000
Income before income taxes		$ 50,000
Income tax expense		12,000
Net income		$ 38,000

SOLUTION

Diviney Corporation
Income Statement
For the Year Ended December 31, 2014

Net sales		$500,000
Cost of goods sold		300,000
Gross margin		$200,000
Operating expenses:		
Selling expenses	$100,000	
General and administrative expenses	75,000	
Total operating expenses		175,000
Income from operations		$ 25,000
Other revenues and expenses:		
Interest income	$ 50,000	
Less interest expense	25,000	
Excess of other revenues over other expenses		25,000
Income before income taxes		$ 50,000
Income tax expense		12,000
Net income		$ 38,000

TRY IT! SE2, SE3, E1A, E2A, E3A, E4A, E1B, E2B, E3B, E4B

second part. Both the multistep form and the single-step form have advantages: the multistep form shows the components used in deriving net income, and the single-step form has the advantage of simplicity.

LO3 Terms of Sale

When goods are sold on credit, both parties should understand the amount and timing of payment as well as other terms of the purchase. Sellers quote prices in different ways. Many merchants quote the price at which they expect to sell their goods. Others, particularly manufacturers and wholesalers, quote prices as a percentage (usually 30 percent or more) off their list or catalogue prices. Such a reduction is called a **trade discount**.

For example, if an article is listed at $1,000 with a trade discount of 40 percent, or $400, the seller records the sale at $600, and the buyer records the purchase at $600. The seller may raise or lower the trade discount depending on the quantity purchased. The list price and related trade discount are used only to arrive at an agreed-upon price. They do not appear in the accounting records.

Sales and Purchases Discounts

The terms of sale are usually printed on the sales invoice and are part of the sales agreement. Terms differ from industry to industry. In some industries, payment is expected in a short period of time. In these cases, the invoice is marked "n/10" ("net 10") or "n/30" ("net 30"), meaning that the amount of the invoice is due either 10 days or 30 days after the invoice date. If the invoice is due 10 days after the end of the month, it is marked "n/10 eom."

STUDY NOTE: *A trade discount applies to the list or catalogue price. A sales discount applies to the sales price.*

Sales Discount In some industries, it is customary to give a **sales discount** for early payment. An invoice that offers a sales discount might be labeled "2/10, n/30," which means that the buyer either can pay within 10 days of the invoice date and take a 2 percent discount or can wait 30 days and pay the full amount. It is often advantageous for a buyer to take the discount because the saving of 2 percent over a period of 20 days (from the 11th day to the 30th day) represents an effective annual rate of 36.5 percent (365 days ÷ 20 days × 2% = 36.5%). Most companies would be better off borrowing money from a lender so that they can take advantage of the discount from the supplier.

STUDY NOTE: *Early collection also reduces the probability of a customer's defaulting.*

Because it is not possible to know at the time of a sale whether the customer will take advantage of a sales discount, the discounts are recorded by the seller only at the time the customer pays. For example, suppose Kawar Motor Company sells merchandise to a customer on September 20 for $600 on terms of 2/10, n/30. Kawar records the sale on September 20 for the full amount of $600. If the customer pays on or before September 30, Kawar will receive $588 in cash and will reduce its accounts receivable by $600. The difference of $12 ($600 × 0.02) will be debited to an account called *Sales Discounts.* Sales Discounts is a contra-revenue account with a normal debit balance that is deducted from sales on the income statement.

Although sales discounts were intended to increase the seller's liquidity by reducing the amount of money tied up in accounts receivable, the practice of giving sales discounts has been declining. Sales discounts are costly to the seller, and from the buyer's viewpoint, the amount of the discount is usually very small in relation to the price of the purchase.

Purchase Discounts **Purchase discounts** are discounts that a buyer takes for the early payment of merchandise. For example, the buyer that purchased the merchandise from Kawar Motor Company will record the purchase on September 20 at $600. If the buyer pays on or before September 30, it will record cash paid of $588 and reduce its Accounts Payable by $600. The difference of $12 is recorded as a credit to an account called *Purchases Discounts.* The Purchases Discounts account reduces the Cost of Goods Sold account or the Purchases account, depending on the inventory method used. As a result of the decline in the use of sales discounts, the use of purchase discounts is also declining.

Transportation Costs

In some industries, the seller usually pays transportation costs and charges a price that includes those costs. In other industries, it is customary for the purchaser to pay transportation charges. The following special terms designate whether the seller or the purchaser pays the freight charges.

- **FOB shipping point** means that the seller places the merchandise "free on board" at the point of origin and the buyer bears the shipping costs. The title to the merchandise passes to the buyer at that point. For example, when the sales agreement for the purchase of a car says "FOB factory," the buyer must pay the freight from the factory where the car was made to wherever he or she is located, and the buyer owns the car from the time it leaves the factory.
- **FOB destination** means that the seller bears the transportation costs to the delivery point. The seller retains title until the merchandise reaches its destination and usually prepays the shipping costs, in which case the buyer makes no accounting entry for freight.

The effects of these special shipping terms are summarized as follows.

Shipping Term	Where Title Passes	Who Pays the Cost of Transportation
FOB shipping point	At origin	Buyer
FOB destination	At destination	Seller

Shipping terms affect the financial statements. FOB shipping point means the buyer pays the freight charges. When relatively small, these charges are usually included in the cost of goods sold on the buyer's income statement. FOB destination means the seller pays the freight charges. They are included in selling expenses on the seller's income statement.

When the buyer pays the transportation charge, it is called **freight-in**, and it is added to the cost of merchandise purchased. Thus, freight-in increases the buyer's cost of inventory, as well as the cost of goods sold after they are sold. When freight-in is a relatively small amount, most companies include the cost in the cost of goods sold on the income statement rather than allocating part of it to merchandise inventory.

When the seller pays the transportation charge, it is called **delivery expense** (or *freight-out*). Because the seller incurs this cost to facilitate the sale of its product, the cost is included in selling expenses on the income statement.

Terms of Debit and Credit Card Sales

Many retailers allow customers to use debit or credit cards to charge their purchases. Debit cards deduct directly from a person's bank account, whereas a credit card allows for payment later. Three of the most widely used credit cards are **American Express**, **MasterCard**, and **Visa**. The customer establishes credit with the lender (the credit card issuer) and receives a card to use in making purchases. If a seller accepts the card, the customer signs an invoice at the time of the sale. The sale is communicated to the seller's bank, resulting in a cash deposit in the seller's bank account. Thus, the seller does not have to establish the customer's credit, collect from the customer, or tie up money in accounts receivable. The lender takes a discount, which is a selling expense for the merchandiser. For example, if a restaurant makes sales of $1,000 on Visa credit cards and Visa takes a 4 percent discount on the sales, the restaurant would record Cash in the amount of $960 and Credit Card Expense in the amount of $40.

Business Perspective

Are We Becoming a Cashless Society?

Are checks and cash obsolete? Do you "swipe it"? Most Americans do. About 71 percent of Americans (including 41 percent of college students) use credit or debit cards rather than checks. Consumers who have cards like the convenience and have on average 3.5 cards. Retailers, like **McDonald's** and **Starbucks**, like the cards, even though there are fees, because the use of cards usually increases the amount of sales.[2]

APPLY IT!

A local appliance dealer sells refrigerators that it buys from the manufacturer.

1. The manufacturer sets a list or catalogue price of $1,200 for a refrigerator. The manufacturer offers its dealers a 40 percent trade discount.
2. Assume the same terms as **1**, except the manufacturer sells the machine under terms of FOB shipping point. The cost of shipping is $120.
3. Assume the same terms as **2**, except the manufacturer offers a sales discount of 2/10, n/30. Sales discounts do not apply to shipping costs.

What is the net cost of the refrigerator to the dealer, assuming payment is made within 10 days of purchase?

SOLUTION

1. $1,200 − ($1,200 × 0.40) = $720
2. $720 + $120 = $840
3. $840 − ($720 × 0.02) = $825.60

TRY IT! SE4, SE5, E5A, E5B

LO 4 Perpetual Inventory System

We will use Kawar Motor Company to illustrate merchandising transactions under the perpetual inventory system. Kawar's income statement is presented in Exhibit 4. The focal point of the statement is cost of goods sold, which is deducted from net sales to arrive at gross margin. Under the perpetual inventory system, the Merchandise Inventory and Cost of Goods Sold accounts are continually updated during the accounting period as purchases, sales, and other inventory transactions occur.

Exhibit 4
Income Statement Under the Perpetual Inventory System

STUDY NOTE: On the income statement, freight-in is included as part of cost of goods sold, and delivery expense (freight-out) is included as an operating (selling) expense.

Kawar Motor Company
Income Statement
For the Year Ended December 31, 2014

Net sales	$957,300
Cost of goods sold*	525,440
Gross margin	$431,860
Operating expenses	313,936
Income before income taxes	$117,924
Income tax expense	20,000
Net income	$ 97,924

*Freight-in has been included in cost of goods sold.

Purchases of Merchandise

Exhibit 5 shows how transactions involving purchases of merchandise are recorded under the perpetual inventory system. The focus of these journal entries is Accounts Payable. In this section, we present a summary of the entries made for merchandise purchases.[3]

Exhibit 5
Recording Purchase Transactions Under the Perpetual Inventory System

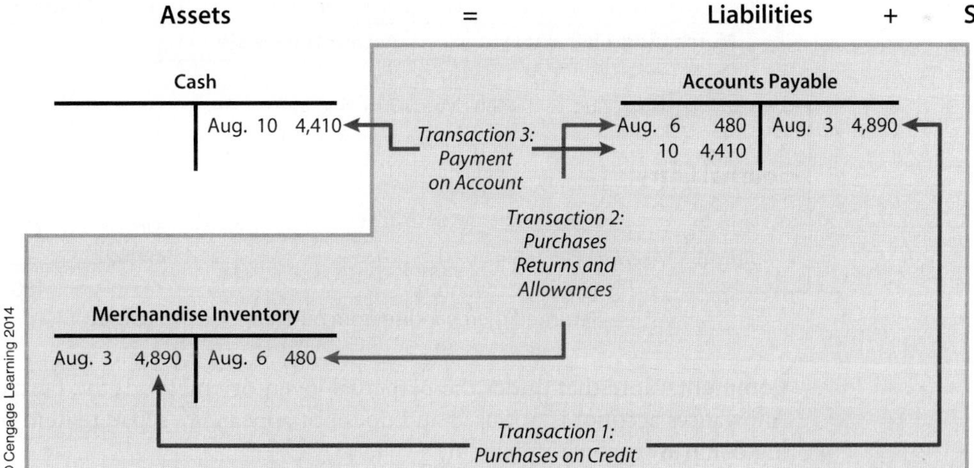

The examples that follow show how Kawar Motor Company would record purchase transactions under the perpetual inventory system.

Purchase on Credit

Transaction 1 On August 3, Kawar received merchandise purchased on credit, invoice dated August 1, terms n/10, $4,890.

Analysis Under the perpetual inventory system, the cost of merchandise is recorded in the Merchandise Inventory account at the time of purchase, which

▲ *increases* the *Merchandise Inventory* account

▲ *increases* the *Accounts Payable* account

Application of Double Entry

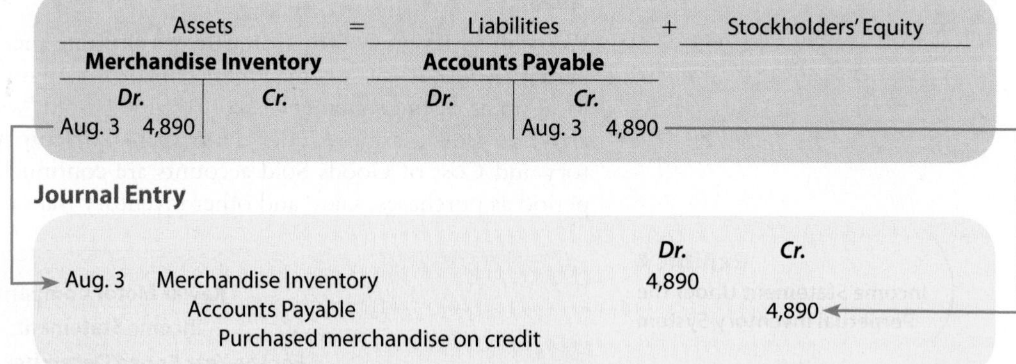

Assets = Liabilities + Stockholders' Equity
Merchandise Inventory
Dr. Cr.
Aug. 3 4,890
Accounts Payable
Dr. Cr.
Aug. 3 4,890
Journal Entry
Dr. Cr.
Aug. 3 Merchandise Inventory 4,890
Accounts Payable 4,890
Purchased merchandise on credit

Comment In this transaction, payment is due ten days from the invoice date. If an invoice includes a charge for shipping or if shipping is billed separately, it should be *recognized* as a debit to Freight-In.

Purchases Returns and Allowances

Transaction 2 On August 6, Kawar returned part of merchandise received on August 3 for credit, $480.

Analysis Under the perpetual inventory system, when a buyer is allowed to return all or part of a purchase or is given an allowance, accounts payable is reduced and merchandise inventory is decreased for the cost of the merchandise returned. This journal entry

- ▼ *decreases* the *Accounts Payable* account
- ▼ *decreases* the *Merchandise Inventory* account

Application of Double Entry

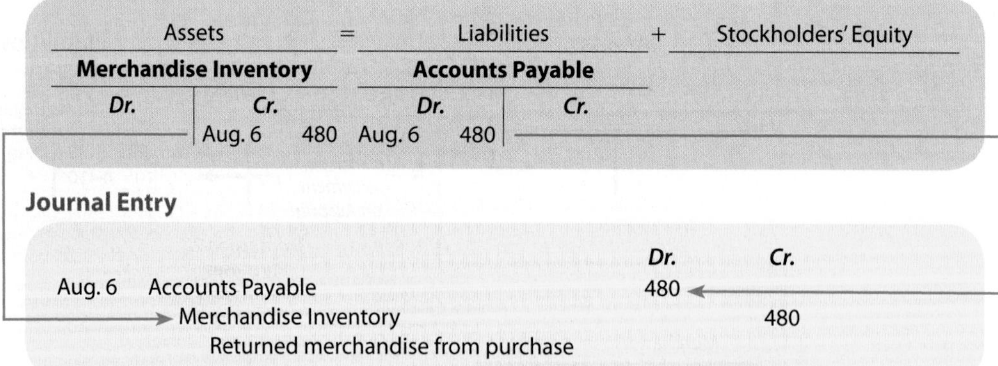

Assets = Liabilities + Stockholders' Equity
Merchandise Inventory
Dr. Cr.
Aug. 6 480
Accounts Payable
Dr. Cr.
Aug. 6 480
Journal Entry
Dr. Cr.
Aug. 6 Accounts Payable 480
Merchandise Inventory 480
Returned merchandise from purchase

Comment Note that under the perpetual inventory method, the Purchase Returns and Allowances account is not used and does not appear as a separate item on a merchandising company income statement.

Payments on Account

Transaction 3 On August 10, Kawar paid amount in full due for the purchase of August 3, part of which was returned on August 6, $4,410.

Analysis The journal entry to record the payment for the net amount due of $4,410 ($4,890 – $480)

- ▼ *decreases* the *Accounts Payable* account
- ▼ *decreases* the *Cash* account

Application of Double Entry

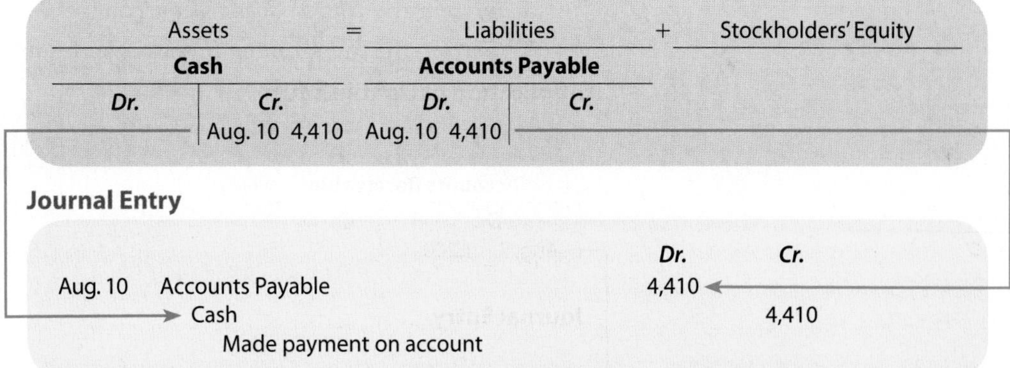

Comment Kawar pays the purchase price less the price of merchandise returned. After the payment, the balance of accounts payable for the purchase recorded on August 3 is zero.

Sales of Merchandise

Exhibit 6 shows how transactions involving sales of merchandise are recorded under the perpetual inventory system. These transactions involve several accounts, including Cash, Accounts Receivable, Merchandise Inventory, Sales Returns and Allowances, and Cost of Goods Sold. The following sections present a summary of the entries made for sales of merchandise.

Exhibit 6
Recording Sales Transactions Under the Perpetual Inventory System

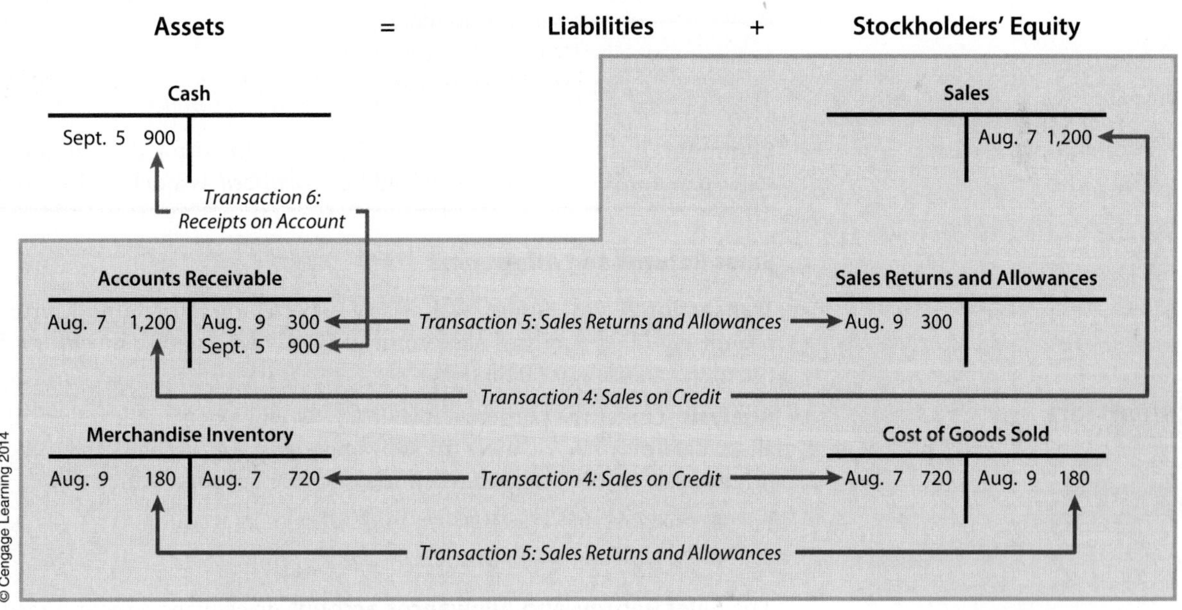

Sales on Credit

Transaction 4 On August 7, Kawar sold merchandise on credit, terms n/30, FOB shipping point, $1,200. The cost of the merchandise was $720.

Analysis Under the perpetual inventory system, sales always require two entries, as shown in Exhibit 6. First, the sale is recorded, which

- ▲ *increases* the *Accounts Receivable* account
- ▲ *increases* the *Sales* account

Second, Cost of Goods Sold is updated by a transfer from Merchandise Inventory, which

▲ *increases* the *Cost of Goods Sold* account

▼ *decreases* the *Merchandise Inventory* account

Application of Double Entry

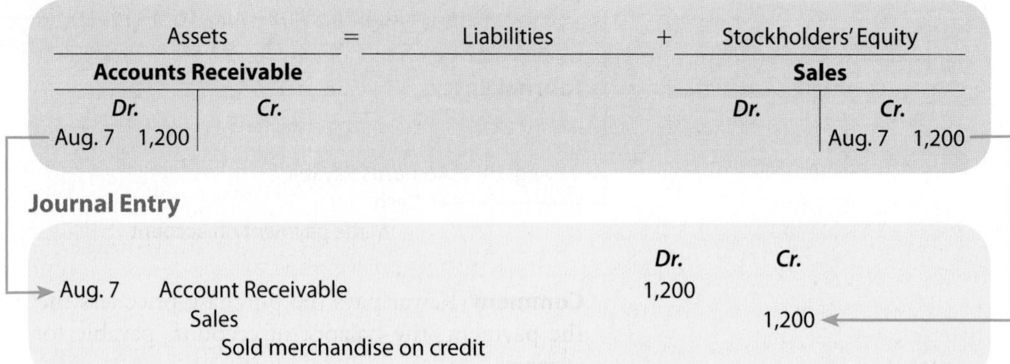

Application of Double Entry

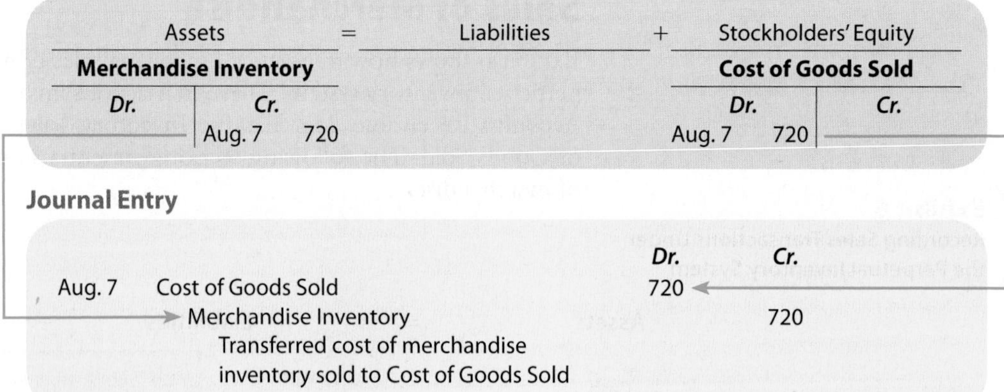

Comment In the case of cash sales, Cash is debited for the amount of the sale. If the seller pays for the shipping, it should be *recognized* as a debit to Delivery Expense.

Sales Returns and Allowances

Transaction 5 On August 9, Kawar accepted, for full credit, a return of part of merchandise sold on August 7, and returned it to merchandise inventory, $300. The cost of the merchandise was $180.

STUDY NOTE: *Because the Sales account is established with a credit, its contra account, Sales Returns and Allowances, is established with a debit.*

Analysis Under the perpetual inventory system, when a seller allows the buyer to return all or part of a sale or gives an allowance, two journal entries are necessary. First, the original sale is reversed using a contra-revenue account, which

▲ *increases* the *Sales Returns and Allowances* account

▼ *decreases* the *Accounts Receivable* account

The **Sales Returns and Allowances account** gives management a readily available measure of unsatisfactory products and dissatisfied customers. This account is a contra-revenue account with a normal debit balance, and it is deducted from sales on the income statement.

Second, the cost of the merchandise must also be transferred from the Cost of Goods Sold account back into the Merchandise Inventory account, which

▲ *increases* the *Merchandise Inventory* account

▼ *decreases* the *Cost of Goods Sold* account

Application of Double Entry

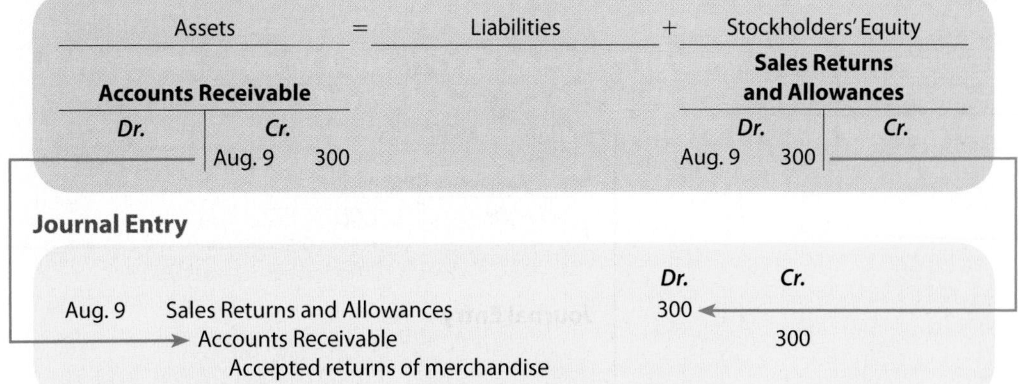

Assets = Liabilities + Stockholders' Equity
Accounts Receivable
Dr. Cr.
Aug. 9 300
Sales Returns and Allowances
Dr. Cr.
Aug. 9 300
Journal Entry
Dr. Cr.
Aug. 9 Sales Returns and Allowances 300
Accounts Receivable 300
Accepted returns of merchandise

Application of Double Entry

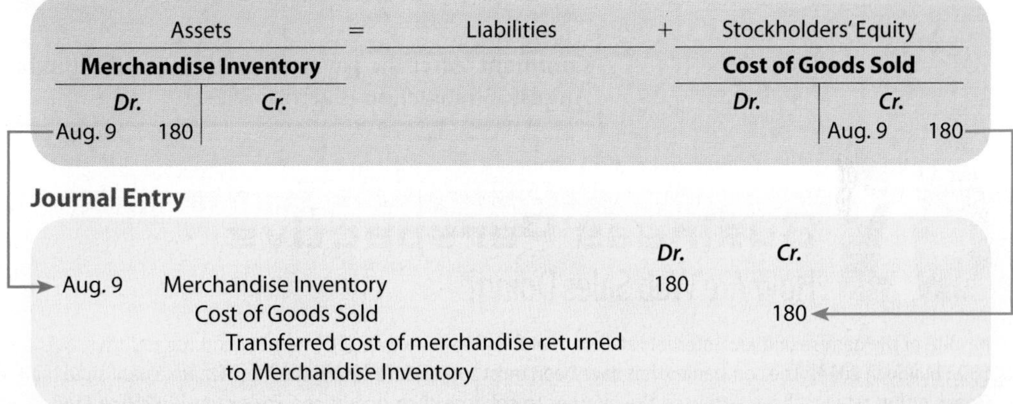

Comment If the company makes an allowance instead of accepting a return, or if the merchandise cannot be returned to inventory and resold, this second entry transferring into Merchandise Inventory and reducing Cost of Goods Sold is not made.

Receipts on Account

Transaction 6 On September 5, Kawar collected in full for sale of merchandise on August 7, less the return on August 9, $900.

Analysis The journal entry to record the collection for the net amount due of $900 ($1,200 − $300)

▲ *increases* the *Cash* account

▼ *decreases* the *Accounts Receivable* account

Application of Double Entry

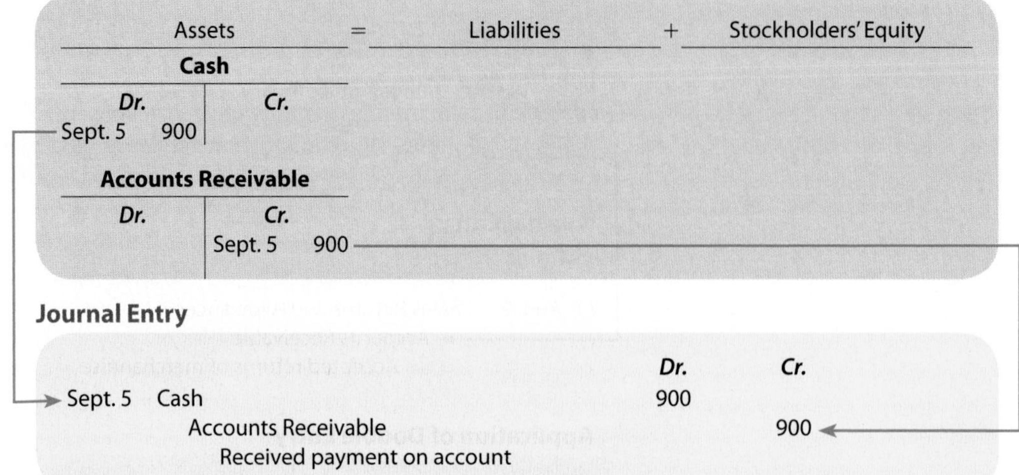

Journal Entry

		Dr.	Cr.
Sept. 5	Cash	900	
	Accounts Receivable		900
	Received payment on account		

Comment After the payment on the account, the balance in accounts receivable for the August 7 transaction is zero.

Business Perspective

How Are Web Sales Doing?

In spite of the demise of many Internet retailers, merchandise sales over the Internet continue to thrive. U.S. Internet sales are expected to reach almost $300 billion in 2014.[4] The companies that have been most successful in using the Internet are established mail-order retailers like **Lands' End** and **L.L. Bean**. Other retailers have also used the Internet to enhance their operations. For example, **Office Depot**, which focuses primarily on business-to-business Internet sales, has set up customized webpages for tens of thousands of corporate clients. These webpages allow customers to make online purchases and check store inventories. Although Internet transactions are recorded in the same way as on-site transactions, the technology adds a level of complexity to the transactions.

APPLY IT!

For each lettered transaction that follows, indicate which numbered accounts are debited or credited by placing the account numbers in the appropriate columns, assuming the use of a perpetual inventory system. (*Note*: Some may require more than one transaction.)

1. Cash
2. Accounts Receivable
3. Merchandise Inventory
4. Accounts Payable
5. Sales
6. Sales Returns and Allowances
7. Cost of Goods Sold

	Account Debited	Account Credited
a. Purchase on credit	___	___
b. Purchase return for credit	___	___
c. Purchase for cash	___	___
d. Sale on credit	___	___
e. Sale for cash	___	___
f. Sales return for credit	___	___
g. Payment on account	___	___
h. Receipt on account	___	___

SOLUTION

	Account Debited	Account Credited
a. Purchase on credit	3	4
b. Purchase return for credit	4	3
c. Purchase for cash	3	1
d. Sale on credit	2, 7	3, 5
e. Sale for cash	1, 7	3, 5
f. Sales return for credit	3, 6	2, 7
g. Payment on account	4	1
h. Receipt on account	1	2

TRY IT! SE6, E6A, E8A, E9A, E10A, E6B, E8B, E9B, E10B

LO 5 Periodic Inventory System

To illustrate merchandising transactions under the periodic inventory system, we will continue with the Kawar Motor Company example. Kawar's income statement appears in Exhibit 7. A major feature of this statement is the computation of cost of goods sold. The cost of goods sold must be computed on the income statement because it is not updated for purchases, sales, and other transactions during the accounting period, as it is under the perpetual inventory system.

Exhibit 7
Income Statement Under the Periodic Inventory System

STUDY NOTE: *Most published financial statements are condensed, eliminating the detail shown here under cost of goods sold.*

Kawar Motor Company
Income Statement
For the Year Ended December 31, 2014

Net sales			$957,300
Cost of goods sold:			
Merchandise inventory, December 31, 2013		$211,200	
Purchases	$505,600		
Less purchases returns and allowances	31,104		
Net purchases	$474,496		
Freight-in	32,944		
Net cost of purchases		507,440	
Cost of goods available for sale		$718,640	
Less merchandise inventory, December 31, 2014		193,200	
Cost of goods sold			525,440
Gross margin			$431,860
Operating expenses			313,936
Income before income taxes			$117,924
Income tax expense			20,000
Net income			$ 97,924

It is important to distinguish between the cost of goods available for sale and the cost of goods sold. The **cost of goods available for sale** is the total cost of merchandise that *could* be sold in the accounting period. The *cost of goods sold* is the cost of merchandise *actually* sold. The difference between the two numbers is the amount *not* sold, or the ending merchandise inventory. The cost of goods available for sale is the sum of the following two factors.

- The amount of merchandise on hand at the beginning of the period.
- The net cost of purchases during the period. (**Net cost of purchases** consist of total purchases plus freight-in less any deductions such as purchases returns and allowances and discounts from suppliers for early payment.)

In Exhibit 7, Kawar has cost of goods available for sale of $718,640 ($211,200 + $507,440). The ending inventory of $193,200 is deducted from this figure to determine the cost of goods sold of $525,440 ($718,640 – $193,200). Exhibit 8 illustrates these relationships.

Exhibit 8
The Components of Cost of Goods Sold

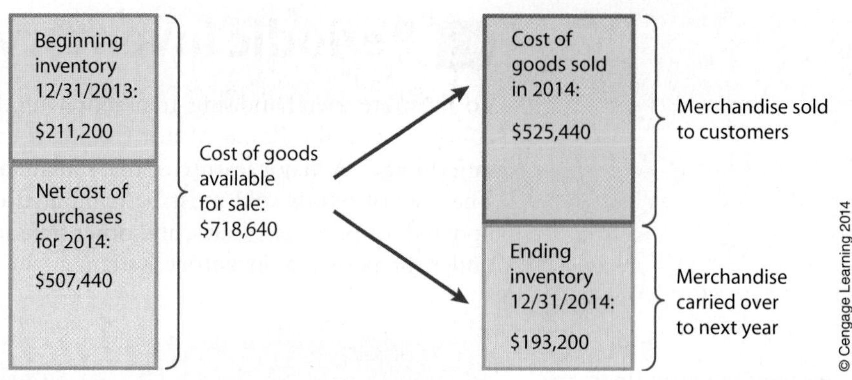

Purchases of Merchandise

STUDY NOTE: *Purchases and Purchases Returns and Allowances accounts are used only in a periodic inventory system.*

Exhibit 9 shows how purchases of merchandise are recorded under the periodic inventory system. In the perpetual inventory system, the Merchandise Inventory account is adjusted each time a purchase, a sale, or another inventory transaction occurs. In the periodic inventory system, the Merchandise Inventory account stays at its beginning balance until the physical inventory is recorded at the end of the period. The periodic system uses a Purchases account to accumulate purchases and a Purchases Returns and Allowances account to accumulate returns of and allowances on purchases.

Exhibit 9
Recording Purchase Transactions Under the Periodic Inventory System

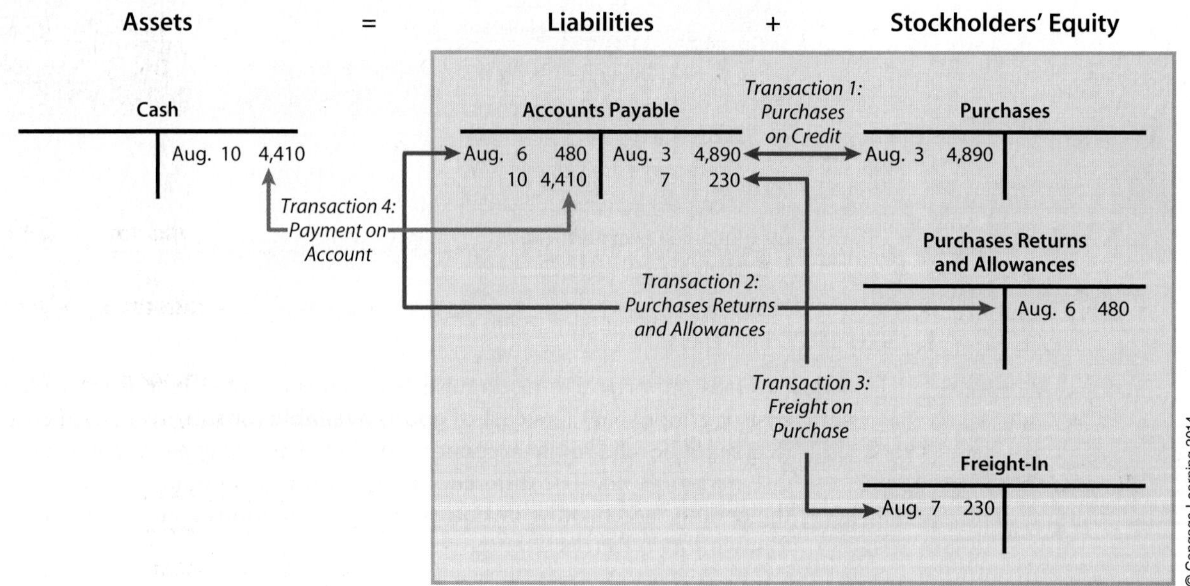

The examples that follow show how Kawar Motor Company would record purchase transactions under the periodic inventory system.

Purchases on Credit

Transaction 1 On August 3, Kawar received merchandise purchased on credit, invoice dated August 1, terms n/10, $4,890.

Analysis Under the periodic inventory system, the cost of merchandise is recorded in the **Purchases account** at the time of purchase. The Purchases account does not indicate whether merchandise has been sold or is still on hand. The journal entry to record purchases made by a company

▲ *increases* the *Purchases* account

▲ *increases* the *Accounts Payable* account

Application of Double Entry

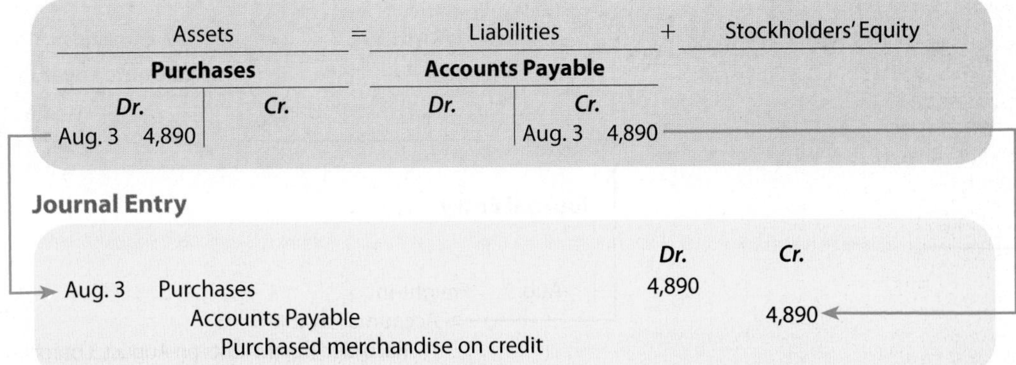

Comment Under the periodic inventory system, purchased merchandise is temporarily *classified* as Purchases. Its sole purpose is to accumulate the total cost of merchandise purchased for resale during a period. (Purchases of other assets, such as equipment, are recorded and *classified* in the appropriate asset account, not in the Purchases account.)

Purchases Returns and Allowances

Transaction 2 On August 6, Kawar returned part of merchandise received on August 3 for credit, $480.

Analysis Purchases Returns and Allowances is a contra-purchases account with a normal credit balance, and it is deducted from purchases on the income statement to arrive at net purchases, which

▼ *decreases* the *Accounts Payable* account

▲ *increases* the *Purchases Returns and Allowances* account

Application of Double Entry

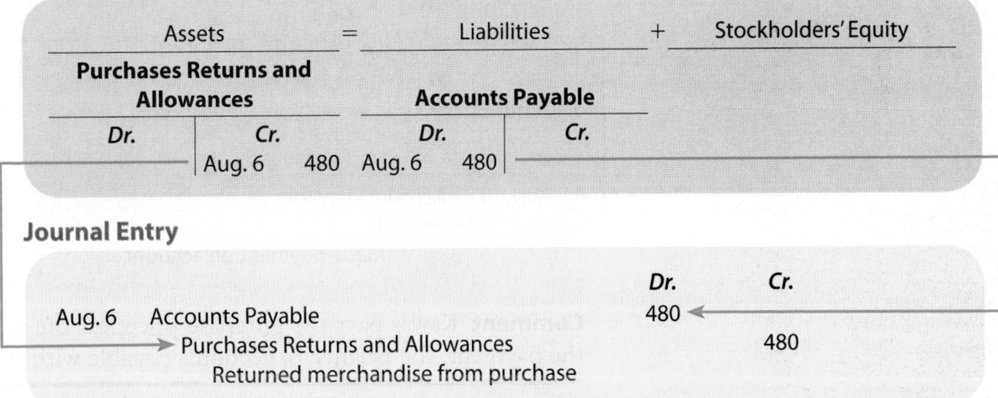

STUDY NOTE: *Because debits establish the Purchases account, credits create its contra account, Purchases Returns and Allowances.*

Comment The **Purchases Returns and Allowances account** is used in a periodic inventory system.

Freight-In

Transaction 3 On August 7, Kawar received a bill for freight costs of the purchases on August 3, $230.

Analysis The journal entry to record freight costs on purchases

▲ *increases* the *Freight-In* account

▲ *increases* the *Accounts Payable* account

Application of Double Entry

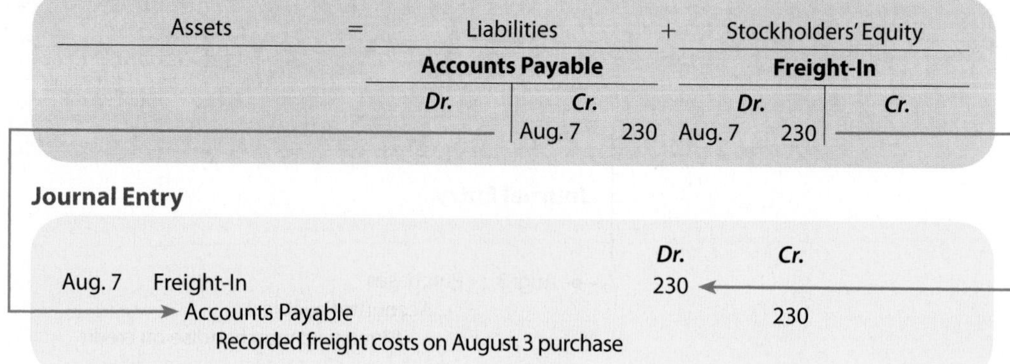

Journal Entry

		Dr.	Cr.
Aug. 7	Freight-In	230	
	Accounts Payable		230
	Recorded freight costs on August 3 purchase		

Comment Freight-In is added on the income statement to net purchases to arrive at the net cost of purchases under the periodic method.

Payments on Account

Transaction 4 On August 10, Kawar paid amount in full due for the purchase of August 3, part of which was returned on August 6, $4,410.

Analysis The journal entry to record payment for the net amount due of $4,410 ($4,890 – $480)

- ▼ *decreases* the *Accounts Payable* account
- ▼ *decreases* the *Cash* account

Application of Double Entry

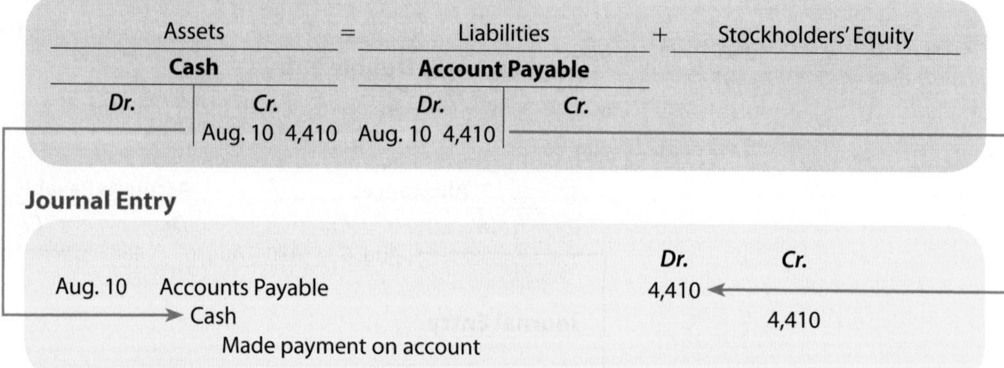

Journal Entry

		Dr.	Cr.
Aug. 10	Accounts Payable	4,410	
	Cash		4,410
	Made payment on account		

Comment Kawar pays the purchase price less the price of merchandise returned. After the payment, the balance of accounts payable with the supplier is zero.

Sales of Merchandise

Exhibit 10 shows how transactions involving sales of merchandise are recorded under the periodic inventory system.

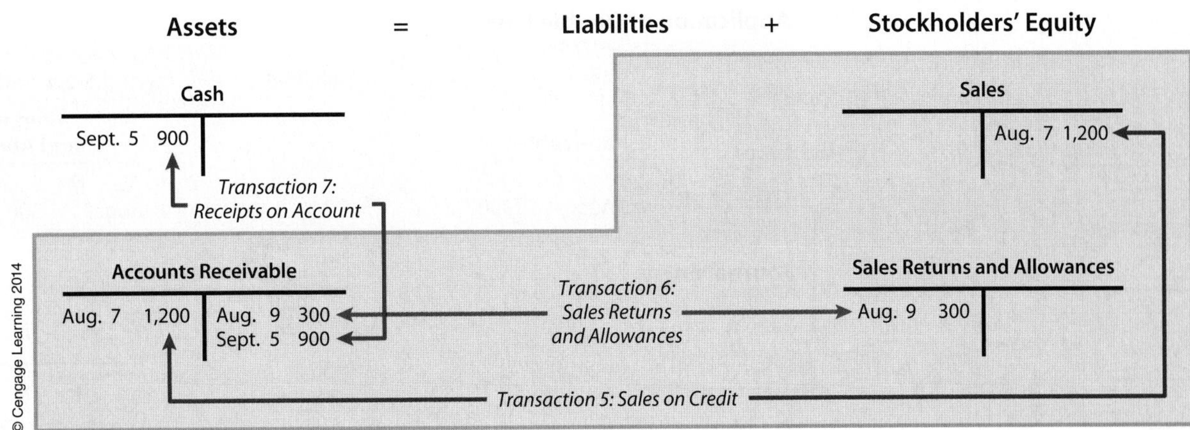

Exhibit 10
Recording Sales Transactions Under the Periodic Inventory System

Sales on Credit

Transaction 5 On August 7, Kawar sold merchandise on credit, terms n/30, FOB destination, $1,200. The cost of the merchandise was $720.

Analysis As shown in Exhibit 10, under the periodic inventory system, credit sales require only one entry, which

▲ *increases* the *Accounts Receivable* account

▲ *increases* the *Sales* account

Application of Double Entry

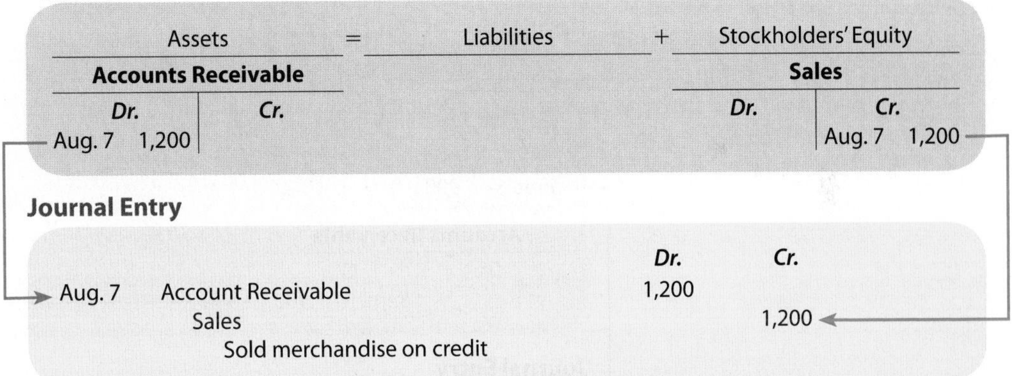

Comment In the case of cash sales, Cash is debited for the amount of the sale. If the seller pays for the shipping, the amount should be debited to Delivery Expense.

Sales Returns and Allowances

Transaction 6 On August 9, Kawar accepted return of part of merchandise sold on August 7 for full credit and returned it to merchandise inventory, $300. The cost of the merchandise was $180.

Analysis Under the periodic inventory system, when a seller allows the buyer to return all or part of a sale or gives an allowance, only one journal entry is needed, which

▲ *increases* the *Sales Returns and Allowances* account

▼ *decreases* the *Accounts Receivable* account

Application of Double Entry

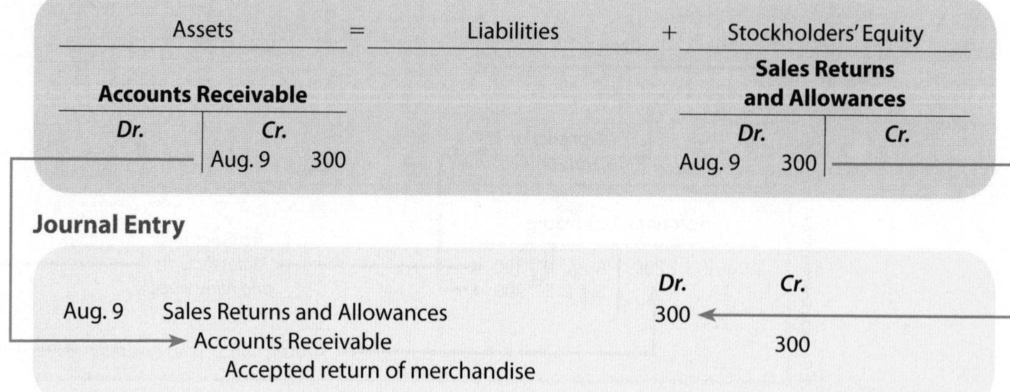

Journal Entry

		Dr.	Cr.
Aug. 9	Sales Returns and Allowances	300	
	Accounts Receivable		300
	Accepted return of merchandise		

Comment The Sales Returns and Allowances account is a contra-revenue account with a normal debit balance and is deducted from sales on the income statement.

Receipts on Account

Transaction 7 On September 5, Kawar collected in full for sale of merchandise on August 7, less the return on August 9, $900.

Analysis The journal entry to record collection for the net amount due of $900 ($1,200 – $300)

▲ *increases* the *Cash* account

▼ *decreases* the *Accounts Receivable* account

Application of Double Entry

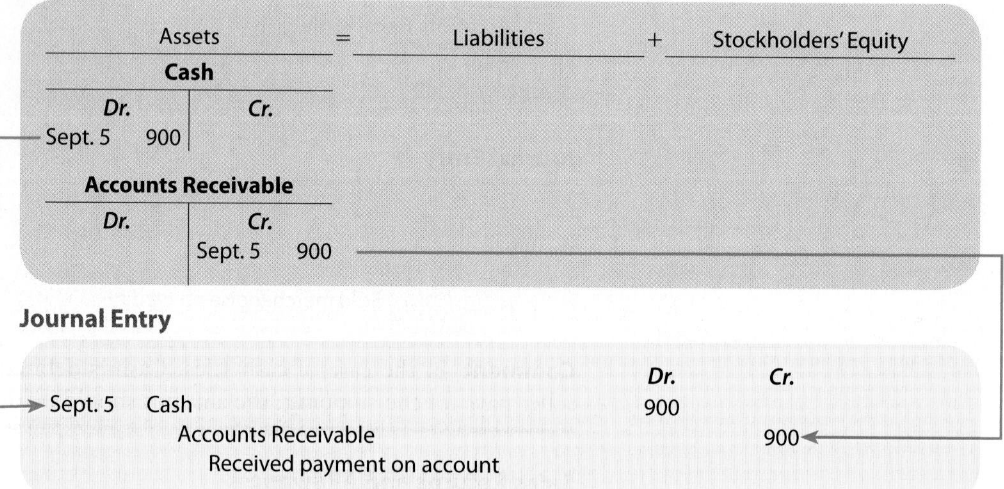

Journal Entry

		Dr.	Cr.
Sept. 5	Cash	900	
	Accounts Receivable		900
	Received payment on account		

Comment After the payment on the account, the balance in accounts receivable for that transaction is zero.

Business Perspective

Are Sales Returns Worth Accounting For?

Some industries routinely have a high percentage of sales returns. More than 6 percent of all nonfood items sold in stores are eventually returned to vendors. This amounts to over $100 billion a year, or more than the gross national product of two-thirds of the world's nations.[5] Book publishers like **Simon & Schuster** often have returns as high as 30 to 50 percent because to gain the attention of potential buyers, they must distribute large numbers of copies to many outlets. Magazine publishers like **AOL Time Warner** expect to sell no more than 35 to 38 percent of the magazines they send to newsstands and other outlets.[6] In all these businesses, it pays management to scrutinize the Sales Returns and Allowances account for ways to reduce returns and increase profitability.

Merchandising Transactions and the Financial Statements

Merchandising transactions can affect all the financial statements, as shown in Exhibit 11.

Exhibit 11
Merchandising Income Statement Groups Accounts in Useful Categories

Income Statement
For the Year Ended December 31, 2014

Net sales
Cost of goods sold
  Gross margin
Operating expenses
  Income from operations
Other revenues and expenses
  Income before income taxes
Income tax expense
  Net income

APPLY IT!

For each lettered transaction that follows, indicate which numbered accounts are debited or credited by placing the account numbers in the appropriate columns, assuming the use of a periodic inventory system.

1. Cash
2. Accounts Receivable
3. Merchandise Inventory
4. Accounts Payable
5. Sales
6. Sales Returns and Allowances
7. Purchases
8. Purchases Returns and Allowances

	Account Debited	Account Credited
a. Purchase on credit	___	___
b. Purchase return for credit	___	___
c. Purchase for cash	___	___
d. Sale on credit	___	___
e. Sale for cash	___	___
f. Sales return for credit	___	___
g. Payment on account	___	___
h. Receipt on account	___	___

SOLUTION

	Account Debited	Account Credited
a. Purchase on credit	7	4
b. Purchase return for credit	4	8
c. Purchase for cash	7	1
d. Sale on credit	2	5
e. Sale for cash	1	5
f. Sales return for credit	6	2
g. Payment on account	4	1
h. Receipt on account	1	2

TRY IT! SE7, SE8, SE9, E7A, E11A, E12A, E13A, E14A, E7B, E11B, E12B, E13B, E14B

SECTION 3 BUSINESS APPLICATIONS

BUSINESS APPLICATIONS
- Calculating operating cycle
- Liquidity

RELEVANT LEARNING OBJECTIVE

LO 6 Explain the role of the operating cycle and the effect of foreign business transactions in evaluating the liquidity of a merchandising company.

LO 6 The Operating Cycle and Foreign Business Transactions

Maintaining adequate liquidity in the operating cycle is important to managing a merchandising company.

CASH FLOW Operating Cycle

Merchandising businesses engage in a series of transactions to buy, sell, and collect for merchandise inventory called the *operating cycle*. Exhibit 12 shows these transactions. Some companies buy merchandise for cash and sell it for cash, but these companies are usually small companies, such as a produce market or a hot dog stand. Most companies buy merchandise on credit and sell it on credit, thereby engaging in the following four transactions:

1. Purchase of merchandise inventory for cash or on credit
2. Sales of merchandise inventory for cash or on credit
3. Collection of cash from credit sales
4. Payment for purchases made on credit

The first three transactions represent the time it takes to purchase inventory, sell it, and collect for it. Merchandisers must be able to do without the cash for this period of time either by relying on cash flows from other sources within the company or by borrowing. If they lack the cash to pay bills when they come due, they can be forced out of business. Thus, managing cash flow is a critical concern.

Exhibit 12
Cash Flows in the Operating Cycle

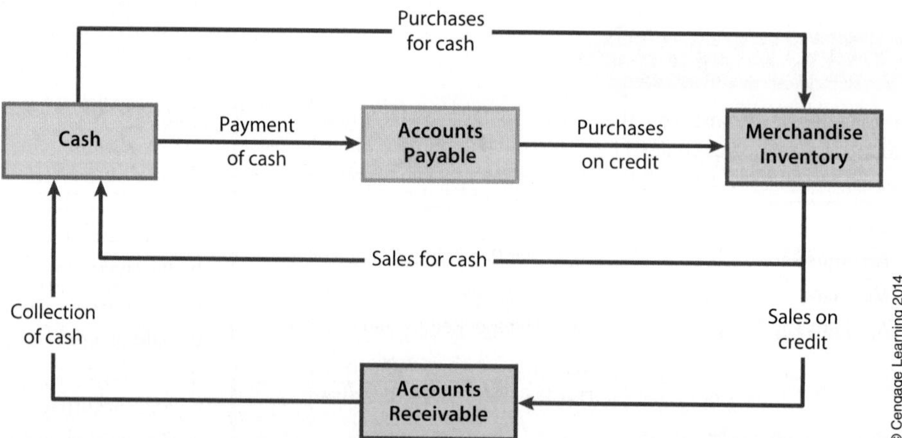

The suppliers that sell the company the merchandise usually also sell on credit, thus helping alleviate the cash flow problem by providing financing for a period of time before they require payment (transaction 4). However, this period is rarely as long as the operating cycle. The period between the time the supplier must be paid and the end of the operating cycle is called the *financing period* (or *cash gap*).

The **financing period**, illustrated in Exhibit 13, is the amount of time from the purchase of inventory until it is sold and payment is collected, less the amount of time

Exhibit 13
The Financing Period

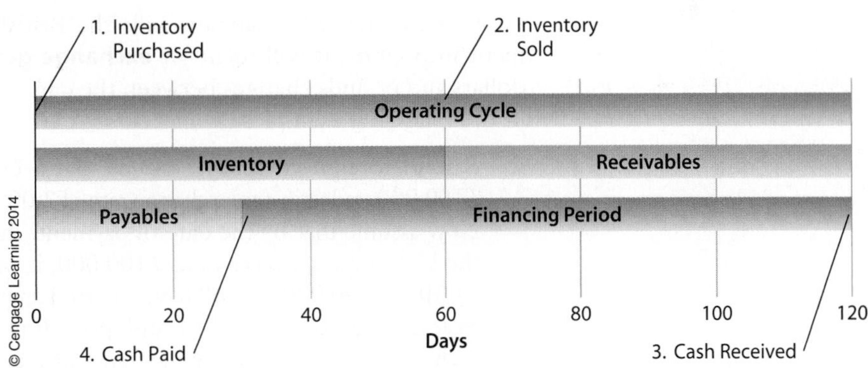

creditors give the company to pay for the inventory. Thus, if it takes 60 days to sell the inventory, 60 days to collect for the sale, and creditors' payment terms are 30 days, the financing period is 90 days [(60 + 60) – 30]. During the financing period, the company will be without cash from this series of transactions and will need either to have funds available internally or to borrow from a bank.

***STUDY NOTE:** A company must provide financing for the average days' inventory plus the average number of days to collect credit sales less the average number of days it is allowed to pay its suppliers.*

The way in which a merchandising company manages its inventories, receivables, and payables will affect its financing period. For example, compare **Costco**'s financing period with that of a traditional discount store chain, **Target Corporation**:

	Target	Costco	Difference
Days' inventory	58 days	29 days	(29) days
Days' receivables	35	4	(31)
Less days' payable	(60)	(31)	29
Financing period	33 days	2 days	(31) days

Costco has an advantage over Target because it sells inventory and collects receivables much faster. Its very short financing period is one of the reasons Costco can charge such low prices.[7]

By reducing its financing period, a company can improve its cash flow. Many merchandisers, including Costco, do this by selling as much as possible for cash. Cash sales include sales made on bank *credit cards,* such as Visa or MasterCard, and on *debit cards,* which draw directly on the purchaser's bank account. They are considered cash sales because funds from them are available to the merchandiser immediately. Small retail stores may have mostly cash sales and very few credit sales, whereas large wholesale concerns may have almost all credit sales.

Foreign Business Transactions

Most large merchandising and manufacturing firms and even many small ones transact some of their business overseas. For example, a U.S. manufacturer may expand by selling its product to foreign customers, or it may lower its product cost by buying a less expensive part from a source in another country. Such sales and purchase transactions may take place in Japanese yen, British pounds, or some other foreign currency.

While all transactions involve money measures, an international transaction is measured in two different currencies, and one currency has to be translated into another by using an *exchange rate.* As noted earlier, the values of other currencies in relation to the dollar rise and fall daily according to supply and demand. Thus, if there is a delay between the date of sale or purchase and the date of payment, the amount of cash involved in an international transaction may differ from the originally agreed-upon amount.

If the billing of an international sale and the payment for it are both in the domestic currency, no accounting problem arises. For example, if a U.S. maker of precision tools sells $160,000 worth of its products to a British company and bills the British company in dollars, the U.S. company will receive $160,000 when it collects payment.

However, if the U.S. company bills the British company in pounds and accepts payment in pounds, it will incur an **exchange gain or loss** if the exchange rate between dollars and pounds changes between the date of sale and the date of payment, as shown in the following examples.

- **Sale in foreign currency**: Assume that a U.S. company billed a sale of \$200,000 at £100,000, reflecting an exchange rate of 2.00 (that is, \$2.00 per pound) on the sale date. Now assume that by the date of payment, the exchange rate has fallen to 1.90. When the U.S. company receives its £100,000, it will be worth only \$190,000 (£100,000 × \$1.90 = \$190,000). It will have incurred an exchange loss of \$10,000 because it agreed to accept a fixed number of British pounds in payment for its products, and the value of each pound dropped before the payment was made. Had the value of the pound in relation to the dollar increased, the company would have made an exchange gain.
- **Purchase in foreign currency**: The same logic applies to purchases as to sales. Assume that a U.S company purchases products from a British company for \$200,000. If the payment is to be made in U.S. dollars, no accounting problem arises. However, if the British company expects to be paid in pounds, the U.S. company will have an exchange gain of \$10,000 because it agreed to pay a fixed £100,000, and between the dates of purchase and payment, the exchange value of the pound decreased from \$2.00 to \$1.90. To make the £100,000 payment, the U.S. company has to expend only \$190,000.

Exchange gains and losses are reported on the income statement. Because of their bearing on financial performance, they are of interest to managers and investors.

APPLY IT!

Rola Company's management made the following decisions. Indicate whether each decision pertains primarily to (a) cash flow management, (b) choice of inventory system, or (c) foreign transactions.

1. Decided to decrease the credit terms offered to customers from 30 days to 20 days to speed up collection of accounts.
2. Decided to purchase goods made by a supplier in India.
3. Decided that sales would increase if salespeople knew how much inventory was on hand at any one time.
4. Decided to try to negotiate a longer time to pay suppliers than had been previously granted.

SOLUTION

1. a; 2. c; 3. b; 4. a

TRY IT! SE10, SE11, E1A, E15A, E1B, E15B

A Look Back At: Walmart

Marc F. Henning/Alamy

Walmart

The beginning of this chapter focused on merchandising results for **Walmart**. Complete the following requirements in order to answer the questions posed at the beginning of the chapter.

Section 1: Concepts
How do faithful representation and classification apply to merchandise operations?

Section 2: Accounting Applications
How can merchandising transactions be recorded and presented to reflect the company's performance?

Section 3: Business Applications
How can Walmart manage its operating cycle so that it has adequate cash to maintain liquidity?

SOLUTION

Section 1: Concepts
Classification of items on the merchandising company financial statements is important because how the amount of goods available for sale is split between ending inventory and cost of goods sold impacts both the income statement and the balance sheet. Thus, a merchandising company needs to classify its accounts properly so that the statements *faithfully represent* the operations of the company. In order to faithfully represent accounting for merchandising inventories, a company can choose between the perpetual inventory system and the periodic inventory system. The perpetual inventory system is a system in which continuous records are kept of the quantity and the cost of individual items as they are bought and sold. The periodic inventory system is a system in which continuous records are not kept but the inventory not yet sold is counted periodically.

Section 2: Accounting Applications
From the Financial Highlights presented at the beginning of the chapter, in 2012, Walmart made only a 4 percent increase in operating income in spite of a 6 percent increase in net revenues. To maintain its policy of selling at low prices and still making a profit, Walmart must have a system of recording sales and purchase transactions that accurately reflects its financial performance. Further, its use of a multistep income statement enables it to see clearly where it needs to make improvements in controlling costs.

Section 3: Business Applications
Walmart engages in all parts of the merchandising cycle. It buys goods on credit, which gives it time to carry the large amount of inventory in its stores until customers buy the items. It sells the goods mostly for cash (with a small amount to businesses on credit), which helps its cash cycle. Accounts payable help the company finance inventory, but when necessary, the company can arrange for short-term financing to ensure that it has enough cash on hand to maintain liquidity.

Review Problem

Mink Company is a fast-growing, discount merchandising company that specializes in selling stylish, low-priced fashions to young people. Mink engaged in the transactions that follow.

July	1	Sold merchandise to Eric Ortega on credit, terms n/30, FOB shipping point, $2,100 (cost, $1,260).
	2	Purchased merchandise on credit from Debra Company, terms n/30, FOB shipping point, $3,800.
	2	Paid Custom Freight $290 for freight charges on merchandise received.
	9	Purchased merchandise on credit from RBT Company, terms n/30, FOB shipping point, $3,600, including $200 freight costs paid by RBT Company.
	11	Accepted from Eric Ortega a return of merchandise, which was returned to inventory, $300 (cost, $180).
	14	Returned for credit $600 of merchandise purchased on July 2.
	16	Sold merchandise for cash, $1,000 (cost, $600).
	22	Paid Debra Company for purchase of July 2 less return on July 14.
	23	Received full payment from Eric Ortega for his July 1 purchase, less return on July 11.

Prepare journal entries to record these transactions, assuming Mink uses (1) the perpetual inventory system and (2) the periodic inventory system.

SOLUTION (1) and (2). (*Note:* Accounts that differ under the two systems are in bold type.)

	A	B	C	D	E	F	G	H	I	J	K	L	M	N
1				**1. Perpetual Inventory System**						**2. Periodic Inventory System**				
2	July	1		Accounts Receivable			2,100			Accounts Receivable			2,100	
3					Sales			2,100			Sales			2,100
4						Sold merchandise on						Sold merchandise on		
5						account to Eric Ortega,						account to Eric Ortega,		
6						terms n/30, FOB shipping						terms n/30, FOB shipping		
7						point						point		
8		1		**Cost of Goods Sold**			1,260							
9					**Merchandise Inventory**			1,260						
10						Transferred cost of								
11						merchandise sold to Cost								
12						of Goods Sold account								
13		2		**Merchandise Inventory**			3,800			**Purchases**			3,800	
14					Accounts Payable			3,800			Accounts Payable			3,800
15						Purchased merchandise						Purchased merchandise		
16						on account from Debra						on account from Debra		
17						Company, terms n/30, FOB						Company, terms n/30, FOB		
18						shipping point						shipping point		
19		2		Freight-In			290			Freight-In			290	
20					Cash			290			Cash			290
21						Paid freight on July 2						Paid freight on July 2		
22						purchase						purchase		
23		9		**Merchandise Inventory**			3,400			**Purchases**			3,400	
24				Freight-In			200			Freight-In			200	
25					Accounts Payable			3,600			Accounts Payable			3,600
26						Purchased merchandise on						Purchased merchandise on		
27						account from RBT Company,						account from RBT Company,		
28						terms n/30, FOB shipping						terms n/30, FOB shipping		
29						point, freight paid by supplier						point, freight paid by supplier		
30		11		Sales Returns and Allowances			300			Sales Returns and Allowances			300	
31					Accounts Receivable			300			Accounts Receivable			300
32						Accepted return of						Accepted return of		
33						merchandise from Eric						merchandise from Eric		
34						Ortega						Ortega		

	A	B	C	D	E	F	G	H	I	J	K	L	M	N
1				**1. Perpetual Inventory System**						**2. Periodic Inventory System**				
2	July	11		**Merchandise Inventory**			180							
3					**Cost of Goods Sold**			180						
4						Transferred cost of								
5						merchandise returned to								
6						Merchandise Inventory								
7						account								
8		14		Accounts Payable			600			Accounts Payable			600	
9					**Merchandise Inventory**			600			**Purchases Returns and Allowances**			600
10						Returned portion of						Returned portion of		
11						merchandise purchased						merchandise purchased		
12						from Debra Company						from Debra Company		
13		16		Cash			1,000			Cash			1,000	
14					Sales			1,000			Sales			1,000
15						Sold merchandise for cash						Sold merchandise for cash		
16		16		**Cost of Goods Sold**			600							
17					**Merchandise Inventory**			600						
18						Transferred cost of								
19						merchandise sold to Cost of								
20						Goods Sold account								
21		22		Accounts Payable			3,200			Accounts Payable			3,200	
22					Cash			3,200			Cash			3,200
23						Made payment on account to						Made payment on account to		
24						Debra Company						Debra Company		
25						$3,800 − $600 = $3,200						$3,800 − $600 = $3,200		
26		23		Cash			1,800			Cash			1,800	
27					Accounts Receivable			1,800			Accounts Receivable			1,800
28						Received payment on						Received payment on		
29						account from Eric Ortega						account from Eric Ortega		
30						$2,100 − $300 = $1,800						$2,100 − $300 = $1,800		

Chapter Review

Define *merchandising accounting*, and differentiate perpetual from periodic inventory systems. LO 1

Merchandising companies differ from service companies in that they earn income by buying and selling goods. The buying and selling of goods adds to the complexity of the business and requires choosing whether to use the perpetual or the periodic inventory system. Using these systems and use of the multistep income statement, properly classified, results in faithful representation of the company's operations.

Describe the features of multistep and single-step classified income statements. LO 2

Classified income statements for external reporting can be in multistep or single-step form. The multistep form arrives at net income through a series of steps, usually with a separate section for other revenues and expenses; the single-step form arrives at net income in a single step.

Describe the terms of sale related to merchandising transactions. LO 3

A trade discount is a reduction from the list or catalogue price of a product. A sales discount is a discount given for early payment of a sale on credit. Terms of 2/10, n/30 mean that the buyer can take a 2 percent discount if the invoice is paid within 10 days of the invoice date. Otherwise, the buyer is obligated to pay the full amount in 30 days. Discounts on sales are recorded in the Sales Discounts account, and discounts on purchases are recorded in the Purchases Discounts account. FOB shipping point means that the buyer bears the cost of transportation and that title to the goods passes to the buyer at the shipping origin. FOB destination means that the seller bears the cost of transportation and that title does not pass to the buyer until the goods reach their destination. Debit and credit card sales are considered cash sales and involve a fee paid by the seller for convenience.

Prepare an income statement, and record merchandising transactions under the perpetual inventory system. LO 4

Under the perpetual inventory system, the Merchandise Inventory account is continuously adjusted by entering purchases, sales, and other inventory transactions as they occur. Purchases increase the Merchandise Inventory account, and purchases returns decrease it. As goods are sold, their cost is transferred from the Merchandise Inventory account to the Cost of Goods Sold account.

Prepare an income statement, and record merchandising transactions under the periodic inventory system. LO 5

When the periodic inventory system is used, the cost of goods sold section of the income statement must include the following elements.

Purchases − Purchases Returns and Allowances + Freight-In = Net Cost of Purchases

Beginning Merchandise Inventory + Net Cost of Purchases = Cost of Goods Available for Sale

Cost of Goods Available for Sale − Ending Merchandise Inventory = Cost of Goods Sold

Under the periodic inventory system, the Merchandise Inventory account stays at the beginning level until the physical inventory is recorded at the end of the period. A Purchases account is used to accumulate purchases of merchandise during the period, and a Purchases Returns and Allowances account is used to accumulate returns of purchases and allowances on purchases.

Explain the role of the operating cycle and foreign business transactions in evaluating the liquidity of a merchandising company. LO 6

The series of transactions (the operating cycle) of a merchandising company requires careful cash flow management. Also, if a company has international transactions, it must deal with changing exchange rates.

Key Terms

cost of goods available for sale 257 (LO5)
cost of goods sold 245 (LO2)
delivery expense 250 (LO3)
exchange gain or loss 266 (LO6)
financing period 264 (LO6)
FOB destination 249 (LO3)
FOB shipping point 249 (LO3)
freight-in 250 (LO3)
general and administrative expenses 246 (LO2)
gross margin 245 (LO2)
gross sales 245 (LO2)
income before income taxes 247 (LO2)
income from operations 246 (LO2)
manufacturing company 245 (LO2)
merchandise inventory 242 (LO1)
merchandising company 242 (LO1)
multistep income statement 244 (LO2)
net cost of purchases 257 (LO5)
net income 247 (LO2)
net sales 245 (LO2)
operating cycle 242 (LO1)
operating expenses 246 (LO2)
other revenues and expenses 247 (LO2)
percentage of gross margin 246 (LO2)
periodic inventory system 242 (LO1)
perpetual inventory system 242 (LO1)
physical inventory 242 (LO1)
purchase discounts 249 (LO3)
Purchases account 258 (LO5)
Purchases Returns and Allowances account 259 (LO5)
sales discount 249 (LO3)
sales returns and allowances 245 (LO2)
Sales Returns and Allowances account 254 (LO4)
selling expenses 246 (LO2)
single-step income statement 247 (LO2)
trade discount 248 (LO3)

Chapter Assignments

DISCUSSION QUESTIONS

LO 1 **DQ1. CONCEPT ▶** In what ways does having merchandise inventory impact faithful representation and classification?

LO 1 **DQ2.** Why is a physical inventory needed under both the periodic and perpetual inventory systems?

LO 2 **DQ3.** Which is the better measure of a company's performance—income from operations or net income?

LO 3 **DQ4.** Assume a large shipment of uninsured merchandise to your company is destroyed when the delivery truck has an accident and burns. Would you want the terms to be FOB shipping point or FOB destination?

LO 4 **DQ5.** Under the perpetual inventory system, the Merchandise Inventory account is constantly updated. What would cause it to have the wrong balance?

LO 6 **DQ6. BUSINESS APPLICATION ▶** Can a company have a "negative" financing period?

LO 6 **DQ7. BUSINESS APPLICATION ▶** Suppose you sold goods to a company in Europe at a time when the exchange rate for the dollar was declining in relation to the euro. Would you want the European company to pay you in dollars or euros?

SHORT EXERCISES

LO 1 **Characteristics of Inventory Systems**

SE1. Indicate whether each of the statements that follow is more applicable to a perpetual inventory system, periodic inventory system, or both.

1. Inventory figure is not accurate until the balance sheet date.
2. Requires a physical count of inventory at end of period.

(Continued)

3. No detailed records of the inventory are maintained during the accounting period.
4. Continuous records are kept of the quantity of inventory on hand.
5. Cost of Goods Sold is calculated only at the end of the accounting period.
6. Effective system for managing inventory and thus avoiding running out of stock.
7. Is more costly to maintain but may lead to increased sales.

LO 2 **Single-Step Income Statement**

SE2. Using the following accounts, prepare a single-step income statement at year end, May 31, 2014: Cost of Goods Sold, $1,680; General Expenses, $900; Interest Expense, $420; Interest Income, $180; Net Sales, $4,800; Selling Expenses, $1,110; Income Tax Expense, $350.

LO 2 **Multistep Income Statement**

SE3. Using the accounts presented in **SE2**, prepare a multistep income statement.

LO 3 **Terms of Sale**

SE4. A dealer buys tooling machines from a manufacturer and resells them to its customers.

a. The manufacturer sets a list or catalogue price of $6,000 for a machine. The manufacturer offers its dealers a 20 percent trade discount.
b. The manufacturer sells the machine under terms of FOB shipping point. The cost of shipping is $350.
c. The manufacturer offers a sales discount of 2/10, n/30. The sales discount does not apply to shipping costs.

What is the net cost of the machine to the dealer, assuming it is paid for within 10 days of purchase?

LO 3 **Sales and Sales Returns**

SE5. On April 15, Sanborn Company sold merchandise to Barr Company for $3,000 on terms of 2/10, n/30. Assume a return of merchandise on April 20 of $600 and collection in full on April 25. What is the amount collected by Sanborn on April 25?

LO 4 **Purchases of Merchandise: Perpetual Inventory System**

SE6. Record each of the following transactions using T accounts, assuming the perpetual inventory system is used:

Aug.	2	Purchased merchandise on credit from Vera Company, invoice dated August 1, terms n/10, FOB shipping point, $1,150.
	3	Received bill from Strauss Shipping Company for transportation costs on August 2 shipment, invoice dated August 1, terms n/30, $105.
	7	Returned damaged merchandise received from Vera on August 2 for credit, $180.
	10	Paid in full the amount due to Vera for the purchase of August 2, part of which was returned on August 7.

LO 5 **Purchases of Merchandise: Periodic Inventory System**

SE7. Record the transactions in **SE6** using T accounts, assuming the periodic inventory system is used.

LO 5 **Cost of Goods Sold: Periodic Inventory System**

SE8. Using the data that follows and assuming cost of goods sold is $273,700, prepare the cost of goods sold section of a merchandising income statement (periodic inventory system). Include the amount of purchases for the month of October.

Freight-in	$13,800
Merchandise inventory, September 30, 2014	37,950
Merchandise inventory, October 31, 2014	50,600
Purchases	?
Purchases returns and allowances	10,350

LO 5 **Sales of Merchandise: Periodic Inventory System**

SE9. Record the following transactions using T accounts, assuming the periodic inventory system is used:

Aug.	4	Sold merchandise on credit to Rock Company, terms n/30, FOB destination, $2,520.
	5	Paid transportation costs for sale of August 4, $231.
	9	Part of the merchandise sold on August 4 was accepted back from Rock for full credit and returned to merchandise inventory, $735.
Sept.	3	Collected in full the amount due from Rock for merchandise sold on August 4, less the return on August 9.

LO 6 **Operating Cycle**

SE10. BUSINESS APPLICATION ▶ On average, Obras Company holds its inventory 40 days before it is sold, waits 25 days for customers' payments, and takes 33 days to pay suppliers. For how many days must it provide financing in its operating cycle?

LO 1, 6 **Identification of Management Issues**

SE11. BUSINESS APPLICATION ▶ Identify each of the following decisions as most directly related to (a) cash flow management, (b) choice of inventory system, or (c) foreign merchandising transactions:

1. Determination of the amount of time from the purchase of inventory until it is sold and the amount due is collected.
2. Determination of the effects of changes in exchange rates.
3. Determination of policies governing sales of merchandise on credit.
4. Determination of whether to use the periodic or the perpetual inventory system.

EXERCISES: SET A

LO 1, 2 **Concept Identification**

E1A. CONCEPT ▶ Sutton Hills Company's management made the decisions that follow. Indicate which of the decisions relates primarily to (a) classification, (b) merchandising inventory, (c) periodic inventory system, or (d) operating cycle.

1. Decided to purchase and sell goods.
2. Decided to use a form of income statement that would show gross margin separately from operating income.
3. Decided to reduce the credit terms offered to customers from 30 days to 20 days to speed up collection of accounts.
4. Decided that the benefits of keeping track of each item of inventory as it is bought and sold would exceed the costs of such a system.

LO 2 **Classification of Accounts: Income Statement**

E2A. Using the classification scheme below for a multistep income statement, match each account with the letter of the category in which it belongs.

a. Other revenues and expenses
b. Cost of sales
c. General and administrative expenses
d. Selling expenses
e. Net sales
f. Not on income statement

1. Sales Discounts
2. Cost of Goods Sold
3. Dividend Income
4. Advertising Expense
5. Office Salaries Expense
6. Freight-Out Expense
7. Prepaid Insurance
8. Utilities Expense
9. Sales Salaries Expense
10. Rent Expense
11. Depreciation Expense—Delivery Equipment
12. Interest Expense
13. Income Taxes Payable

LO 2 **Preparation of Income Statements**

E3A. A company has the following data: net sales, $405,000; cost of goods sold, $220,000; selling expenses, $90,000; general and administrative expenses, $60,000; interest expense, $4,000; interest income, $3,000; and income tax expense, $2,500.

1. Prepare a single-step income statement.
2. Prepare a multistep income statement.

LO 2 **Multistep Income Statement**

E4A. ACCOUNTING CONNECTION ▶ A single-step income statement follows. Present the information in a multistep income statement, and indicate what insights can be obtained from the multistep form as opposed to the single-step form.

Nomar Parra Company
Income Statement
For the Year Ended December 31, 2014

Revenues:		
Net sales		$1,197,132
Interest income		5,720
Total revenues		$1,202,852
Costs and expenses:		
Cost of goods sold	$777,080	
Selling expenses	203,740	
General and administrative expenses	100,688	
Interest expense	13,560	
Total costs and expenses		1,095,068
Income before income taxes		$ 107,784
Income tax expense		11,640
Net income		$ 96,144

LO 3 **Terms of Sale**

E5A. A household appliance dealer buys microwave ovens from a manufacturer and resells them to its customers.

a. The manufacturer sets a list or catalogue price of $1,500 for a microwave. The manufacturer offers its dealers a 30 percent trade discount.
b. The manufacturer sells the machine under terms of FOB destination. The cost of shipping is $150.
c. The manufacturer offers a sales discount of 2/10, n/30. Sales discounts do not apply to shipping costs.

What is the net cost of the microwave to the dealer, assuming it is paid for within 10 days of purchase?

LO 3, 4 **Purchases Involving Discounts: Perpetual Inventory System**

E6A. Linear Company engaged in the following transactions:

July	2	Purchased merchandise on credit from Green Company, terms 2/10, n/30, FOB destination, invoice dated July 1, $2,000.
	6	Returned some merchandise to Green for full credit, $250.
	11	Paid Green for purchase of July 2 less return and discount.
	14	Purchased merchandise on credit from Green, terms 2/10, n/30, FOB destination, invoice dated July 12, $2,250.
	31	Paid amount owed Green for purchase of July 14.

Prepare journal entries and, assuming the perpetual inventory system, determine the total amount paid to Green.

LO 3, 5 **Sales Involving Discounts: Periodic Inventory System**

E7A. Given the following transactions engaged in by Fournier Company, prepare journal entries and, assuming the periodic inventory system, determine the total amount received from Brook Company:

Dec. 1 Sold merchandise on credit to Brook Company, terms 2/10, n/30, FOB shipping point, $500.
3 Accepted a return from Brook for full credit, $200.
10 Collected amount due from Brook for the sale, less the return and discount.
11 Sold merchandise on credit to Brook, terms 2/10, n/30, FOB shipping point, $800.
31 Collected amount due from Brook for the sale of December 11.

LO 4 **Preparation of the Income Statement: Perpetual Inventory System**

E8A. Selected account balances at December 31, 2014, for Infosys Company follow. Prepare a multistep income statement for the year ended December 31, 2014. Show detail of net sales. The company uses the perpetual inventory system, and Freight-In has not been included in Cost of Goods Sold.

Account Name	Debit	Credit
Sales		$475,000
Sales Returns and Allowances	$ 23,500	
Cost of Goods Sold	280,000	
Freight-In	13,500	
Selling Expenses	43,000	
General and Administrative Expenses	87,000	
Income Tax Expense	7,900	

LO 4 **Recording Purchases: Perpetual Inventory System**

E9A. The transactions that follow took place under the perpetual inventory system. Record each transaction using T accounts.

a. Purchased merchandise on credit, terms n/30, FOB shipping point, $5,000.
b. Paid freight on the shipment in transaction **a**, $270.
c. Purchased merchandise on credit, terms n/30, FOB destination, $2,800.
d. Purchased merchandise on credit, terms n/30, FOB shipping point, $5,200, which includes freight paid by the supplier of $400.
e. Returned part of the merchandise purchased in transaction **c**, $1,000.
f. Paid the amount owed on the purchase in transaction **a**.
g. Paid the amount owed on the purchase in transaction **d**.
h. Paid the amount owed on the purchase in transaction **c** less the return in **e**.

LO 4 **Recording Sales: Perpetual Inventory System**

E10A. On November 15, TCS Company sold merchandise for $2,600 on terms of n/30 to Quaker Company. On November 20, Quaker returned some of the merchandise for a credit of $600, and on November 25, Quaker paid the balance owed. Use T accounts to record the sale, return, and receipt of cash under the perpetual inventory system for TCS. The cost of the merchandise sold on November 15 was $1,500, and the cost of the merchandise returned to inventory on November 20 was $350.

LO 5 **Preparation of the Income Statement: Periodic Inventory System**

E11A. Using the selected year-end account balances at December 31, 2014, for Proof General Store that follow, prepare a 2014 multistep income statement. Show detail of net sales. The company uses the periodic inventory system. Beginning merchandise inventory was $26,000; ending merchandise inventory is $22,000.

(Continued)

Account Name	Debit	Credit
Sales		$297,000
Sales Returns and Allowances	$ 15,200	
Purchases	114,800	
Purchases Returns and Allowances		4,000
Freight-In	5,600	
Selling Expenses	48,500	
General and Administrative Expenses	37,200	
Income Tax Expense	6,800	

LO 5

Merchandising Income Statement: Missing Data, Multiple Years

E12A. Determine the missing data for each letter in the following three income statements for Fulco Company (in thousands):

	2014	2013	2012
Sales	$ **q**	$ **i**	$1,144
Sales returns and allowances	96	76	**a**
Net sales	**r**	1,268	**b**
Merchandise inventory, beginning	**s**	**j**	152
Purchases	768	676	**c**
Purchases returns and allowances	124	**k**	68
Freight-in	**t**	116	88
Net cost of purchases	756	**l**	**d**
Cost of goods available for sale	888	848	728
Merchandise inventory, ending	156	**m**	168
Cost of goods sold	**u**	716	**e**
Gross margin	568	**n**	504
Selling expenses	**v**	312	**f**
General and administrative expenses	156	**o**	132
Total operating expenses	520	512	**g**
Income before income taxes	**w**	40	108
Income tax expense	12	**p**	27
Net income	**x**	29	**h**

LO 5

Recording Purchases: Periodic Inventory System

E13A. Using the data in **E9A**, use T accounts to record each of the transactions under the periodic inventory system.

LO 5

Recording Sales: Periodic Inventory System

E14A. Using the relevant data in **E10A**, use T accounts to record each of the transactions under the periodic inventory system.

LO 6

Foreign Merchandising Transactions

E15A. BUSINESS APPLICATION ▶ Winter Treats Company purchased a special-purpose machine from Blanco Company, a French firm, on credit for €50,000. At the date of purchase, the exchange rate was $1.00 per euro. On the date of the payment, which was made in euros, the value of the euro was $1.25. Did Winter Treats incur an exchange gain or loss? How much was it?

EXERCISES: SET B

Visit the textbook companion website at www.cengagebrain.com to access Exercise Set B for this chapter.

PROBLEMS

LO 2

Forms of the Income Statement

✔1: Income from operations 2014: $66,426
✔ 1: Income from operations 2013: $110,628

P1. Matuska Tools Corporation's income statements follow.

Matuska Tools Corporation
Income Statements
For the Years Ended July 31, 2014 and 2013

	2014	2013
Revenues:		
Net sales	$525,932	$475,264
Interest income	800	700
Total revenues	$526,732	$475,964
Costs and expenses:		
Cost of goods sold	$234,948	$171,850
Selling expenses	161,692	150,700
General and administrative expenses	62,866	42,086
Interest expense	3,600	850
Total costs and expenses	$463,106	$365,486
Income before income taxes	$ 63,626	$110,478
Income tax expense	4,900	7,100
Net income	$ 58,726	$103,378

REQUIRED

1. Prepare a multistep income statement for 2013 and 2014 showing percentages of net sales for each component (e.g., cost of goods sold divided by net sales). (Round percentages to one decimal place.)
2. **ACCOUNTING CONNECTION ▶** Did income from operations increase or decrease between 2013 and 2014? Write a short explanation of why this change occurred.

LO 2, 4, 6

Merchandising Income Statement: Perpetual Inventory System

✔ 1: Net income: $12,735

P2. Selected accounts from Murray's Furniture Store's adjusted trial balance as of June 30, 2014, the end of the fiscal year, follow.

Murray's Furniture Store
Partial Adjusted Trial Balance
June 30, 2014

Sales		162,000
Sales Returns and Allowances	2,000	
Cost of Goods Sold	61,400	
Freight-In	2,300	
Store Salaries Expense	32,625	
Office Salaries Expense	12,875	
Advertising Expense	24,300	
Rent Expense	2,400	
Insurance Expense	1,200	
Utilities Expense	1,560	
Store Supplies Expense	2,880	
Office Supplies Expense	1,175	
Depreciation Expense—Store Equipment	1,050	
Depreciation Expense—Office Equipment	800	
Income Tax Expense	2,700	

REQUIRED

1. Prepare a multistep income statement for Murray's. Freight-In should be combined with Cost of Goods Sold. Store Salaries Expense, Advertising Expense, Store Supplies Expense, and Depreciation Expense—Store Equipment are selling expenses. The other expenses are general and administrative expenses. The company uses the perpetual inventory system. Show details of net sales and operating expenses.

(Continued)

2. **BUSINESS APPLICATION ▶** Based on your knowledge at this point in the course, how would you use Murray's income statement to evaluate the company's profitability? What other financial statement should you consider and why?

LO **4**

GENERAL LEDGER

SPREADSHEET

Merchandising Transactions: Perpetual Inventory System

P3. Fulco Company engaged in the following transactions in March 2014:

Mar. 7 Sold merchandise on credit to James William, terms n/30, FOB shipping point, $3,000 (cost, $1,800).
8 Purchased merchandise on credit from Leverage Company, terms n/30, FOB shipping point, $6,000.
9 Paid Leverage Company for shipping charges on merchandise purchased on March 8, $254.
10 Purchased merchandise on credit from Rourke Company, terms n/30, FOB shipping point, $9,600, including $600 freight costs paid by Rourke.
14 Sold merchandise on credit to Deepak Soni, terms n/30, FOB shipping point, $2,400 (cost, $1,440).
14 Returned damaged merchandise received from Leverage Company on March 8 for credit, $600.
17 Received check from James William for his purchase of March 7.
19 Sold merchandise for cash, $1,800 (cost, $1,080).
20 Paid Rourke Company for purchase of March 10.
21 Paid Leverage Company the balance from the transactions of March 8 and March 14.
24 Accepted from Deepak Soni a return of merchandise, which was put back in inventory, $200 (cost, $120).

REQUIRED

1. Prepare journal entries to record the transactions, assuming use of the perpetual inventory system. (*Hint:* Refer to the Review Problem.)
2. **ACCOUNTING CONNECTION ▶** Receiving cash rebates from suppliers based on the past year's purchases is a common practice in some industries. If, at the end of the year, Fulco receives rebates in cash from a supplier, should these cash rebates be reported as revenue? Why or why not?

LO **2, 5, 6**

✓ 1: Net income: $23,431

Merchandising Income Statement: Periodic Inventory System

P4. Selected accounts from Dence's Gourmet Shop's adjusted trial balance as of March 31, 2014, the end of the current fiscal year, follow. The merchandise inventory for Dence's was $81,222 at the beginning of the year and $76,664 at the end of the year.

Dence's Gourmet Shop
Partial Adjusted Trial Balance
March 31, 2014

Account		
Sales		433,912
Sales Returns and Allowances	11,250	
Purchases	221,185	
Purchases Returns and Allowances		30,238
Freight-In	10,078	
Store Salaries Expense	107,550	
Office Salaries Expense	26,500	
Advertising Expense	18,200	
Rent Expense	14,400	
Insurance Expense	2,800	
Utilities Expense	18,760	
Store Supplies Expense	464	
Office Supplies Expense	814	
Depreciation Expense—Store Equipment	1,800	
Depreciation Expense—Office Equipment	1,850	
Income Tax Expense	510	

REQUIRED

1. Prepare a multistep income statement for Dence's. Store Salaries Expense, Advertising Expense, Store Supplies Expense, and Depreciation Expense—Store Equipment are selling expenses. The other expenses are general and administrative expenses. The company uses the periodic inventory system. Show details of net sales and operating expenses.
2. **BUSINESS APPLICATION ▶** Based on your knowledge at this point in the course, how would you use Dence's income statement to evaluate the company's profitability? What other financial statements should you consider, and why?

LO 5

Merchandising Transactions: Periodic Inventory System

P5. Refer to the data in **P3**.

REQUIRED

1. Prepare journal entries to record the transactions, assuming use of the periodic inventory system. (*Hint:* Refer to the Review Problem.)
2. **ACCOUNTING CONNECTION ▶** Most companies call the first line of the income statement *net sales*. Other companies call it *sales*. Do you think these terms are equivalent and comparable? What would be the content of net sales? Why might a company use *sales* instead of *net sales?*

LO 4

GENERAL LEDGER

Merchandising Transactions: Perpetual Inventory System

P6. Teague Company engaged in the following transactions in October 2014:

Oct. 7 Sold merchandise on credit to Mel Forde, terms n/30, FOB shipping point, $12,000 (cost, $7,200).

8 Purchased merchandise on credit from Surf Company, terms n/30, FOB shipping point, $24,000.

9 Paid Surf Company for shipping charges on merchandise purchased on October 8, $1,016.

10 Purchased merchandise on credit from Tata Company, terms n/30, FOB shipping point, $38,400, including $2,400 freight costs paid by Tata.

14 Sold merchandise on credit to David Johnson, terms n/30, FOB shipping point, $9,600 (cost, $5,760).

14 Returned damaged merchandise received from Surf Company on October 8 for credit, $2,400.

17 Received check from Mel Forde for her purchase of October 7.

19 Sold merchandise for cash, $7,200 (cost, $4,320).

20 Paid Tata Company for purchase of October 10.

21 Paid Surf Company the balance from the transactions of October 8 and October 14.

24 Accepted from David Johnson a return of merchandise, which was put back in inventory, $800 (cost, $480).

REQUIRED

1. Prepare journal entries to record the transactions, assuming use of the perpetual inventory system. (*Hint:* Refer to the Review Problem.)
2. **ACCOUNTING CONNECTION ▶** Receiving cash rebates from suppliers based on the past year's purchases is a common practice in some industries. If, at the end of the year, Teague receives rebates in cash from a supplier, should these cash rebates be reported as revenue? Why or why not?

ALTERNATE PROBLEMS

LO 2

Forms of the Income Statement

✔ 1: Income from operations 2014: $132,852
✔ 1: Income from operations 2013: $221,256

P7. Sigma Company's single-step income statements for 2014 and 2013 follow.

Sigma Company
Income Statements
For the Years Ended April 30, 2014 and 2013

	2014	2013
Revenues:		
Net sales	$1,051,864	$950,528
Interest income	3,600	1,700
Total revenues	$1,055,464	$952,228
Costs and expenses:		
Cost of goods sold	$ 469,896	$343,700
Selling expenses	323,384	301,400
General and administrative expenses	125,732	84,172
Interest expense	7,200	3,400
Total costs and expenses	$ 926,212	$732,672
Income before income taxes	$ 129,252	$219,556
Income tax expense	15,400	7,200
Net income	$ 113,852	$212,356

REQUIRED

1. Prepare multistep income statements for 2013 and 2014 showing percentages of net sales for each component (e.g., cost of goods sold divided by net sales). (Round percentages to one decimal place.)
2. **ACCOUNTING CONNECTION ▶** Did income from operations increase or decrease from 2013 to 2014? Write a short explanation of why this change occurred.

LO 2, 4, 6

Merchandising Income Statement: Perpetual Inventory System

✔ 1: Net income: $8,622

P8. Selected accounts from Keystone Furniture's adjusted trial balance as of August 31, 2014, the end of the fiscal year, follow.

Keystone Furniture
Partial Adjusted Trial Balance
August 31, 2014

Sales		867,824
Sales Returns and Allowances	22,500	
Cost of Goods Sold	442,370	
Freight-In	20,156	
Store Salaries Expense	215,100	
Office Salaries Expense	53,000	
Advertising Expense	36,400	
Rent Expense	28,800	
Insurance Expense	5,600	
Utilities Expense	17,520	
Store Supplies Expense	4,928	
Office Supplies Expense	3,628	
Depreciation Expense—Store Equipment	3,600	
Depreciation Expense—Office Equipment	3,700	
Income Tax Expense	1,900	

REQUIRED

1. Prepare a multistep income statement for Keystone. Store Salaries Expense, Advertising Expense, Store Supplies Expense, and Depreciation Expense—Store Equipment are selling expenses. The other expenses are general and administrative expenses. The company uses the perpetual inventory system. Show details of net sales and operating expenses.
2. **BUSINESS APPLICATION ▶** Based on your knowledge at this point in the course, how would you use the income statement for Keystone to evaluate the company's profitability? What other financial statement should be considered, and why?

LO 4

GENERAL LEDGER

SPREADSHEET

Merchandising Transactions: Perpetual Inventory System

P9. Naib Company engaged in the following transactions in July 2014:

July	1	Sold merchandise to Lina Lopez on credit, terms n/30, FOB shipping point, \$4,200 (cost, \$2,520).
	3	Purchased merchandise on credit from Ruff Company, terms n/30, FOB shipping point, \$7,600.
	5	Paid Craft Freight for freight charges on merchandise received, \$580.
	8	Purchased merchandise on credit from Kansas Supply Company, terms n/30, FOB shipping point, \$7,200, which includes \$400 freight costs paid by Kansas Supply.
	12	Returned some of the merchandise purchased on July 3 for credit, \$1,200.
	15	Sold merchandise on credit to Peter Watts, terms n/30, FOB shipping point, \$2,400 (cost, \$1,440).
	17	Sold merchandise for cash, \$2,000 (cost, \$1,200).
	18	Accepted for full credit a return from Lina Lopez and returned merchandise to inventory, \$400 (cost, \$240).
	24	Paid Ruff Company for purchase of July 3 less return of July 12.
	25	Received check from Lina Lopez for July 1 purchase less the return on July 18.

REQUIRED

1. Prepare journal entries to record the transactions, assuming use of the perpetual inventory system. (*Hint:* Refer to the Review Problem.)
2. **ACCOUNTING CONNECTION ▶** Most companies call the first line of the income statement *net sales.* Other companies call it *sales.* Do you think these terms are equivalent and comparable? What would be the content of net sales? Why might a company use *sales* instead of *net sales?*

LO 5

Merchandising Transactions: Periodic Inventory System

P10. Refer to the data in **P9**.

REQUIRED

1. Prepare journal entries to record the transactions, assuming use of the periodic inventory system. (*Hint:* Refer to the Review Problem.)
2. **ACCOUNTING CONNECTION ▶** Receiving cash rebates from suppliers based on the past year's purchases is common in some industries. If at the end of the year, Naib receives rebates in cash from a supplier, should these cash rebates be reported as revenue? Why or why not?

LO 2, 5, 6

✔ 1: Net income: \$2,655

Merchandising Income Statement: Periodic Inventory System

P11. Selected accounts from Will's Sports Equipment's adjusted trial balance on September 30, 2014, the fiscal year end, follow. The company's beginning merchandise inventory was \$38,200 and ending merchandise inventory is \$29,400 for the period.

(Continued)

Will's Sports Equipment
Partial Adjusted Trial Balance
September 30, 2014

Sales		165,000
Sales Returns and Allowances	2,000	
Purchases	70,200	
Purchases Returns and Allowances		2,600
Freight-In	2,300	
Store Salaries Expense	32,625	
Office Salaries Expense	12,875	
Advertising Expense	24,300	
Rent Expense	2,400	
Insurance Expense	1,200	
Utilities Expense	1,560	
Store Supplies Expense	2,880	
Office Supplies Expense	1,175	
Depreciation Expense—Store Equipment	1,050	
Depreciation Expense—Office Equipment	800	
Income Tax Expense	780	

REQUIRED

1. Prepare a multistep income statement for Will's. Store Salaries Expense, Advertising Expense, Store Supplies Expense, and Depreciation Expense—Store Equipment are selling expenses. The other expenses are general and administrative expenses. The company uses the periodic inventory system. Show details of net sales and operating expenses.
2. **BUSINESS APPLICATION ▶** Based on your knowledge at this point in the course, how would you use Will's income statement to evaluate the company's profitability? What other financial statements should you consider and why?

LO 5 **Merchandising Transactions: Periodic Inventory System**

P12. Refer to the data in **P6**.

REQUIRED

Prepare journal entries to record the transactions, assuming use of the periodic inventory system. (*Hint:* Refer to the Review Problem.)

CASES

LO 1 **Conceptual Understanding: Periodic versus Perpetual Inventory Systems**

C1. Books Unlimited is a well-established chain of 20 bookstores in western Ohio. In recent years, the company has grown rapidly, adding five new stores in regional malls. Each store's manager selects stock based on the market in his or her region. Managers select books from a master list of titles that the central office provides. Every six months, a physical inventory is taken, and financial statements are prepared using the periodic inventory system. At that time, books that have not sold well are placed on sale or, whenever possible, returned to the publisher.

Management has found that when selecting books, managers of the new stores are not judging the market as well as the managers of the older, more established stores. Management is therefore thinking of implementing a perpetual inventory system and carefully monitoring sales from the central office. Do you think Books Unlimited should switch to the perpetual inventory system or stay with the periodic inventory system it has used in the past? Discuss the advantages and disadvantages of each system.

LO 6 **Conceptual Understanding: Effects of a Weak Dollar**

C2. BUSINESS APPLICATION ▶ McDonald's reports that its sales in Europe exceed its sales in the United States. This performance, while reflective of the company's phenomenal success in Europe, was also attributed to the weak dollar in relation to the euro. McDonald's reports its sales wherever they take place in U.S. dollars. Explain why a weak dollar relative to the euro would lead to an increase in McDonald's reported European sales. Why is a weak dollar not relevant to a discussion of McDonald's sales in the United States?

LO 6 **Conceptual Understanding: Cash Flow Management**

C3. BUSINESS APPLICATION ▶ Amazing Sound Source, Inc., has been in business for 30 years. It carries a large inventory so that it can offer customers a wide selection of merchandise and deliver purchases quickly. It accepts credit cards and checks but also provides 90 days' credit to reliable customers who have made purchases in the past. It maintains good relations with suppliers by paying invoices quickly.

To pay bills during the past year, the company has had to borrow from its bank. An analysis of the company's financial statements reveals that, on average, inventory is on hand for 70 days before being sold and that receivables are held for 90 days before being paid. Accounts payable are, on average, paid in 20 days.

What are the operating cycle and financing period? How long are Amazing Sound Source's operating cycle and financing period? Describe three ways in which this company can improve its cash flow management.

LO 6 **Annual Report Case: The Operating Cycle and Financing Period**

C4. BUSINESS APPLICATION ▶ Write a brief memorandum to your instructor describing **CVS**'s operating cycle and financing period. To do this, refer to the CVS annual report in the Supplement to Chapter 1 and to Exhibits 5 and 8. Your memorandum should identify the most common transactions in the operating cycle as they apply to CVS. It should also refer to the importance of accounts receivable, accounts payable, and merchandise inventory in CVS's financial statements. Recall that CVS had inventory days on hand of about 44 days, days' receivable of 19 days, and days payable of 21 days. Complete the memorandum by explaining why CVS's operating cycle and financing period are favorable to the company.

LO 2 **Comparison Analysis: Income Statement Analysis**

C5. Refer to the **CVS** annual report in the Supplement to Chapter 1 and to the following data (in millions) for **Walgreens** in 2011: net sales, $72,184; cost of sales, $51,692; total operating expenses, $16,561; and inventories, $8,044. Determine which company—CVS or Walgreens—had more profitable merchandising operations in 2011 by preparing a schedule that compares the companies based on net sales, cost of sales, gross margin, total operating expenses, and income from operations as a percentage of sales. (*Hint:* You should put the income statements in comparable formats.) In addition, for each company, compute inventories as a percentage of the cost of sales. Which company has the highest prices in relation to costs of sales? Which company is more efficient in its operating expenses? Which company manages its inventories better? Overall, on the basis of the income statement, which company is more profitable? Explain your answers.

LO 1, 2, 4, 5 **Decision Analysis: Analysis of a Merchandising Income Statement**

C6. In 2013, Lisa Perry opened Lisa's Jeans Company, a small store that sold designer jeans in a suburban mall. Perry worked 14 hours a day and controlled all aspects of the operation. The company was such a success that in 2014, Perry opened a second store in another mall. Because the new shop needed her attention, she hired a manager for the original store.

During 2014, the new store was successful, but the original store's performance did not match its performance in 2013. Concerned about this, Perry compared the two years' results for the original store. Her analysis showed the following:

(Continued)

	2014	2013
Net sales	$325,000	$350,000
Cost of goods sold	225,000	225,000
Gross margin	$100,000	$125,000
Operating expenses	75,000	50,000
Income before income taxes	$ 25,000	$ 75,000

Perry's analysis also revealed that the cost and the selling price of the jeans were roughly the same in both years, as was the level of operating expenses, except for the new manager's $25,000 salary. The amount of sales returns and allowances was insignificant in both years.

Studying the situation further, Perry discovered the following about the cost of goods sold.

	2014	2013
Purchases	$200,000	$271,000
Total purchases allowances	15,000	20,000
Freight-in	19,000	27,000
Physical inventory, end of year	32,000	53,000

Still not satisfied, Perry went through all the individual sales and purchase records for 2014. She found that they were correct, but given the unit purchases and sales during the year, the 2014 ending inventory should have been $57,000. After puzzling over all this information, Perry has come to you for accounting help.

1. Using Perry's new information, compute the cost of goods sold for 2013 and 2014 and account for the difference in income before income taxes between 2013 and 2014.
2. Suggest at least two reasons for the discrepancy in the 2014 ending inventory. How might Perry improve the management of the original store?

Continuing Case: Annual Report Project

C7. Using the most recent annual report of the company you have chosen to study and that you have accessed online at the company's website, examine the income statement of your company. Answer the following questions.

1. Does your company use a multistep income statement?
2. For the most recent year, what is the company's gross margin, operating income, and net income? Briefly explain why these numbers are different.

CHAPTER 6

LEARNING OBJECTIVES

LO 1 Explain the concepts underlying inventory accounting.

LO 2 Calculate inventory cost under the periodic inventory system using various costing methods.

LO 3 Explain the effects of inventory costing methods on income determination and income taxes.

LO 4 Calculate inventory cost under the perpetual inventory system using various costing methods.

LO 5 Use the retail method and gross profit method to estimate the cost of ending inventory.

LO 6 Evaluate inventory level, and demonstrate the effects of inventory misstatements on income measurement.

Elimantas Buzas/Shutterstock.com

INVENTORIES

Business Insight
Cisco Systems, Inc.

Cisco Systems manufactures and sells networking and communications products. It is the world's leading producer of the switches, hubs, gateways, and firewalls that make the Internet possible. As you can see from Cisco's Financial Highlights,[1] inventory is an important component of the company's total assets.

Cisco's Financial Highlights (in millions)

	2011	2010	Change
Sales of products	$34,526	$32,420	6.5%
Cost of goods sold	13,647	11,620	17.4
Operating income (loss)	7,674	9,164	(16.3)
Inventories*	1,233	1,114	10.7
Total current assets**	20,308	13,859	46.5

* Excludes service-related spares and demonstration systems
**Excludes investments

1. **CONCEPT ▶** Why is the relationship between accrual accounting and valuation important for inventory accounting?
2. **ACCOUNTING APPLICATION ▶** Cisco accounts for inventory using the FIFO method adjusted for lower of cost or market. Would you expect inventory at the end of the year to reflect the most recent or least recent inventory purchased? If inventory is adjusted for lower of cost or market, would the market be less than what the inventory was purchased for or what it could be sold for?
3. **BUSINESS APPLICATION ▶** How do decisions about inventory valuation and inventory levels affect operating results?

SECTION 1 CONCEPTS

CONCEPTS

- Accrual accounting (matching rule)
- Valuation
- Conservatism
- Disclosure

RELEVANT LEARNING OBJECTIVE

LO 1 Explain the concepts underlying inventory accounting.

LO 1 Concepts Underlying Inventory Accounting

For any company that makes or sells merchandise, inventory is an extremely important asset. Managing this asset requires not only protecting goods from theft or loss, but also ensuring that operations are highly efficient. Further, as you will see in this chapter, proper accounting for inventory is essential because misstatements will affect net income in at least two years.

Inventory is considered a current asset because a company normally sells it within a year or within its operating cycle. For a merchandising company like **CVS** or **Walgreens**, inventory consists of all goods owned and held for sale in the regular course of business. Because manufacturing companies like **Cisco Systems** are engaged in making products, they have three kinds of inventory:

- Raw materials (goods used in making products)
- Work in process (partially completed products)
- Finished goods ready for sale

In a note to its financial statements, Cisco showed the following breakdown of its inventories (figures are in millions):[2]

Inventories	**2011**	**2010**
Raw materials (includes supplies)	$ 219	$ 217
Work in process	52	50
Finished goods	962	847
Total inventories	$1,233	$1,114

The work in process and the finished goods inventories have three cost components:

- Cost of the raw materials that go into the product
- Cost of the labor used to convert the raw materials to finished goods
- Overhead costs that support the production process

Overhead costs include the costs of indirect materials (such as packing materials), indirect labor (such as the salaries of supervisors), factory rent, depreciation of plant assets, utilities, and insurance.

Accrual Accounting and Valuation of Inventories

The primary objective of **inventory accounting** is to apply *accrual accounting* to the determination of cost of inventory sold during the accounting period. *Valuation* of inventories is usually at cost. **Inventory cost** includes the following:

- Invoice price less purchases discounts
- Freight-in, including insurance in transit
- Applicable taxes and tariffs

Other costs—for ordering, receiving, and storing—should, in principle, be included in inventory cost. In practice, however, it is so difficult to allocate such costs to specific inventory items that they are usually considered expenses of the period.

Inventory *valuation* depends on the prices of goods, which usually vary during the year. A company may have purchased identical lots of merchandise at different prices. Also, for identical items, it is often impossible to tell which have been sold and which are still in inventory. Thus, it is necessary to make an assumption about the order in which items have been sold. Because the assumed order of sale may or may not be the same as the actual order of sale, the assumption is really about the *flow of costs* rather than the *flow of physical inventory*.

Goods Flows and Cost Flows

STUDY NOTE: *The assumed flow of inventory costs does not have to correspond to the physical flow of goods.*

Goods flow refers to the actual physical movement of goods in the operations of a company. **Cost flow** refers to the association of costs with their *assumed* flow. The assumed cost flow may or may not be the same as the actual goods flow. A difference arises because several choices of assumed cost flow are available under generally accepted accounting principles. In fact, it is sometimes preferable to use an assumed cost flow that bears no relationship to goods flow because it results in a better estimate of income, which is the main goal of inventory accounting.

Merchandise in Transit Because merchandise inventory includes all items that a company owns and holds for sale, the status of any merchandise in transit, whether the company is selling it or buying it, must be evaluated to see if the merchandise should be included in the inventory count. Neither the seller nor the buyer has *physical* possession of merchandise in transit. As Exhibit 1 shows, ownership is determined by the terms of the shipping agreement, which indicate when title passes. Outgoing goods shipped FOB (free on board) destination are included in the seller's merchandise inventory, whereas those shipped FOB shipping point are not. Conversely, incoming goods shipped FOB shipping point are included in the buyer's merchandise inventory, but those shipped FOB destination are not.

Exhibit 1
Merchandise in Transit

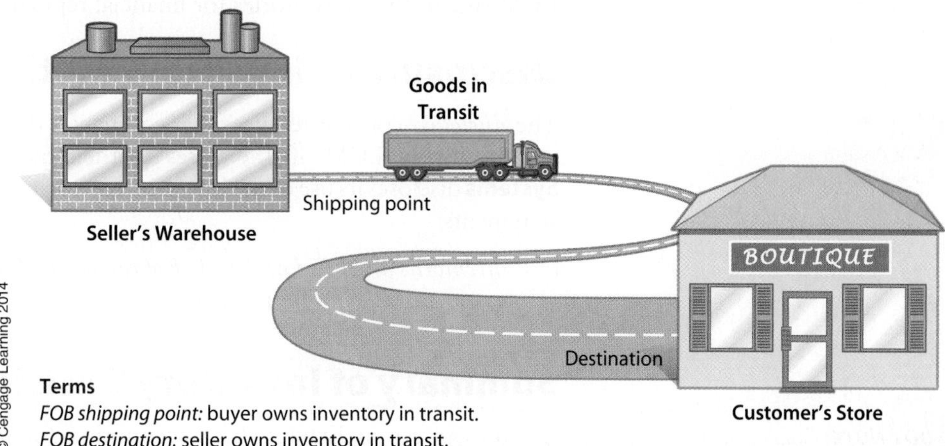

Merchandise Not Included in Inventory At the time a company takes a physical inventory, it may have merchandise to which it does not hold title. For example, it may have sold goods but not yet delivered them to the buyer, but because the sale has been completed, title has passed to the buyer. Thus, the merchandise should be included in the buyer's inventory, not the seller's. Goods held on consignment also fall into this category. A **consignment** is merchandise that its owner (the consignor) places on the premises of another company (the consignee) with the understanding that payment is expected only when the merchandise is sold and that unsold items may be returned to the consignor. Title to consigned goods remains with the consignor until the consignee sells the goods. Consigned goods should not be included in the consignee's physical inventory.

Conservatism and the Lower-of-Cost-or-Market (LCM) Rule

Although cost is usually the most appropriate *valuation* basis, inventory may at times be properly shown in the financial statements at less than its historical, or original, cost. If

International Perspective

IFRS Is "Market" the Same as Fair Value Under IFRS?

When the lower-of-cost-or-market rule is used, what does "market" mean? Under international financial reporting standards (IFRS), market is considered fair value, which is defined as the amount at which an asset can be sold. However, in valuing inventory under U.S. standards, market is normally considered the replacement cost, or the amount at which an identical asset can be purchased. The two "market" values, selling price and purchasing price, can often be quite different for the same asset. This is an issue that will have to be addressed if the U.S. and international standards are to achieve convergence.

STUDY NOTE: *Cost must be determined by one of the inventory costing methods before it can be compared with the market value.*

the market value of inventory falls below its historical cost because of physical deterioration, obsolescence, or decline in price level, a loss has occurred. This loss is recognized by writing the inventory down to **market**—that is, to its current replacement cost. For a merchandising company, market is the amount that it would pay at the present time for the same goods, purchased from the usual suppliers and in the usual quantities.

When the replacement cost of inventory falls below its historical cost (as determined by an inventory costing method), the **lower-of-cost-or-market (LCM) rule** requires that the inventory be written down to the lower value and that a loss be recorded. This rule is an example of the *conservatism* concept because the loss is recognized before an actual transaction takes place. It is also an application of conservatism because, if the replacement cost rises, no gain is recognized and the inventory remains at cost until it is sold. According to an AICPA survey, approximately 80 percent of large companies apply the LCM rule to their inventories for financial reporting.[3]

Disclosure of Inventory Methods

The *disclosure* concept requires that companies disclose their inventory methods, including the use of LCM, in the notes to their financial statements. For example, **Cisco Systems** discloses its use of the lower-of-cost-or-market method in this note to its financial statements:

> *Inventories are stated at the lower of cost or market. Cost is computed using . . . actual cost, on a first-in, first-out basis.*[4]

Summary of Inventory Decisions

STUDY NOTE: *Management considers the behavior of inventory costs over time when selecting inventory costing methods.*

As you can see in Exhibit 2, in accounting for inventory, management must choose among different processing systems, costing methods, and *valuation* methods. These different systems and methods usually result in different amounts of reported net income. Thus, management's choices affect investors' and creditors' evaluations of a company, as well as the internal performance reviews on which bonuses and executive compensation are based.

The *consistency* concept requires that once a company has decided on the accounting systems and methods it will use for inventory, it must use them from one period to the next. When a change is justifiable, the *full disclosure convention* requires that the company clearly describes the change and its effects in the notes to the financial statements.

Because the *valuation* of inventory affects income, it can have a large impact on the income taxes a company pays—and the taxes it pays can impact its cash flows. Federal income tax regulations are specific about the valuation methods a company may use. As a result, management is sometimes faced with the dilemma of how to apply GAAP to income determination and still minimize income taxes.

Exhibit 2
Management Choices in Accounting for Inventories

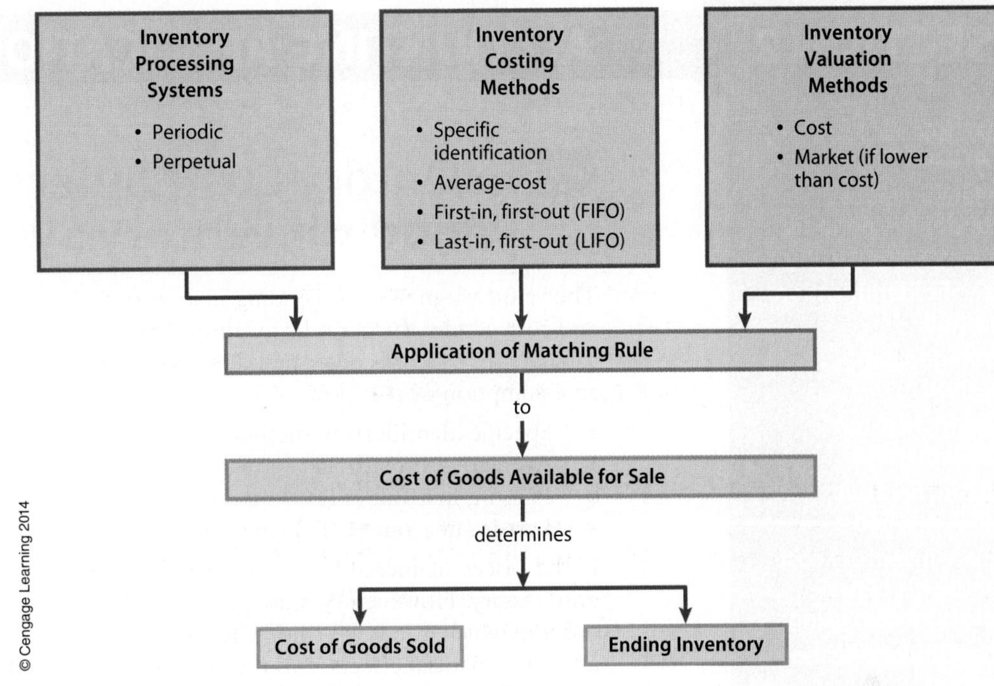

APPLY IT!

Match each lettered item or convention that follows with its related numbered item.

a. An inventory cost
b. An assumption used in the valuation of inventory
c. Full disclosure convention
d. Conservatism convention
e. Consistency convention
f. Not an inventory cost or assumed flow

1. Cost of consigned goods
2. A note to the financial statements explaining inventory policies
3. Application of the LCM rule
4. Goods flow
5. Transportation charge for merchandise shipped FOB shipping point
6. Cost flow
7. Choosing a method and sticking with it
8. Transportation charge for merchandise shipped FOB destination

SOLUTION

1. f; 2. c; 3. d; 4. b; 5. a; 6. b; 7. e; 8. f

TRY IT! SE1, E1A, E1B

SECTION 2 ACCOUNTING APPLICATIONS

ACCOUNTING APPLICATIONS

- Calculate inventory cost under the periodic inventory system using:
  - Specific identification method
  - Average-cost method
  - First-in, first-out (FIFO) method
  - Last-in, first-out (LIFO) method
- Calculate inventory cost under the perpetual inventory system using:
  - Specific identification method
  - Average-cost method
  - First-in, first-out (FIFO) method
  - Last-in, first-out (LIFO) method
- Use the retail method to estimate the cost of ending inventory
- Use the gross profit method to estimate the cost of ending inventory

RELEVANT LEARNING OBJECTIVES

LO2 Calculate inventory cost under the periodic inventory system using various costing methods.

LO3 Explain the effects of inventory costing methods on income determination and income taxes.

LO4 Calculate inventory cost under the perpetual inventory system using various costing methods.

LO5 Use the retail method and gross profit method to estimate the cost of ending inventory.

LO2 Inventory Cost Under the Periodic Inventory System

The value assigned to the ending inventory is the result of two measurements: quantity and cost. Under the periodic inventory system, quantity is determined by taking a physical inventory. Cost is determined by using one of the following methods, each based on an assumption of cost flow:

- Specific identification method
- Average-cost method
- First-in, first-out (FIFO) method
- Last-in, first-out (LIFO) method

If the prices of merchandise purchased never changed, inventory methods would be unnecessary. However, because prices do change, assumptions must be made about the order in which goods are sold. The choice of method depends on the nature of the business, the financial effects, and the cost of implementation.

To illustrate how each method is used under the periodic inventory system, we use Boilen Company. The following data for April, a month in which prices were rising, are available:

April	1	Inventory	160 units @ $10.00	$ 1,600
	6	Purchase	440 units @ $12.50	5,500
	25	Purchase	400 units @ $14.00	5,600
Goods available for sale			1,000 units	$12,700
Sales			560 units	
On hand April 30			440 units	

The problem of inventory costing is to divide the cost of the goods available for sale ($12,700) between the 560 units sold and the 440 units on hand.

Specific Identification Method

The **specific identification method** identifies the cost of each item in the ending inventory. It can be used only when it is possible to identify the units as coming from specific purchases. For instance, if Boilen's April 30 inventory consisted of 100 units from the April 1 inventory, 200 units from the April 6 purchase, and 140 units from the April 25 purchase, the specific identification method would assign the costs as follows.

Periodic Inventory System—Specific Identification Method

100 units @ $10.00	$1,000	Cost of goods available for sale	$12,700
200 units @ $12.50	2,500		
140 units @ $14.00	1,960	Less April 30 inventory	5,460
440 units at a cost of	$5,460	Cost of goods sold	$ 7,240

Although the specific identification method may appear logical, most companies do not use it for the following reasons:

- It is usually impractical, if not impossible, to keep track of the purchase and sale of individual items.
- When a company deals in items that are identical but bought at different prices, deciding which items were sold becomes arbitrary. If the company were to use the

specific identification method, it could raise or lower income by choosing the lower- or higher-priced items.

Average-Cost Method

Under the **average-cost method** (or *weighted average method*), inventory is priced at the average cost of the goods available for sale during the period. Average cost is computed as follows.

$$\text{Average Cost} = \frac{\text{Total Cost of Goods Available for Sale}}{\text{Total Units Available for Sale}}$$

This gives an average unit cost that is applied to the units in the ending inventory. For Boilen, the ending inventory would be $5,588, or $12.70 per unit, determined as follows.

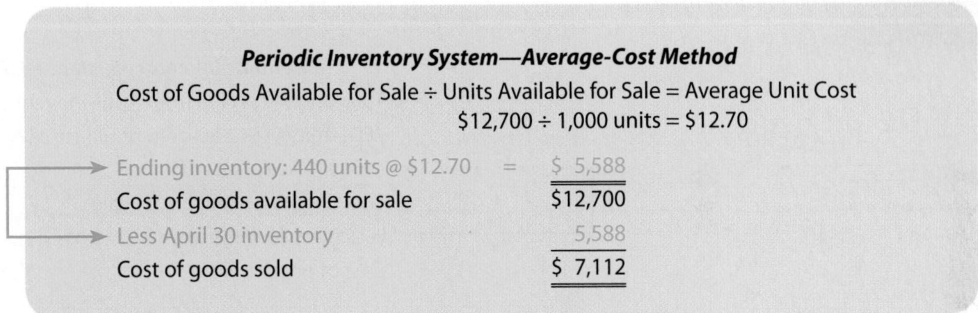

Periodic Inventory System—Average-Cost Method

Cost of Goods Available for Sale ÷ Units Available for Sale = Average Unit Cost
$12,700 ÷ 1,000 units = $12.70

Ending inventory: 440 units @ $12.70 =	$ 5,588
Cost of goods available for sale	$12,700
Less April 30 inventory	5,588
Cost of goods sold	$ 7,112

The average-cost method tends to level out the effects of cost increases and decreases because the cost of the ending inventory is influenced by all the prices paid during the year and by the cost of the beginning inventory. Some analysts, however, believe that recent costs are more relevant for income measurement and decision making.

First-In, First-Out (FIFO) Method

STUDY NOTE: *Because of their perishable nature, some products, such as milk, require a* physical flow *of first-in, first-out. However, the inventory method used to account for them can be based on an assumed* cost flow *that differs from FIFO, such as average-cost or LIFO.*

The **first-in, first-out (FIFO) method** assumes that the costs of the first items acquired should be assigned to the first items sold. The costs of the goods on hand at the end of a period are assumed to be from the most recent purchases, and the costs assigned to goods that have been sold are assumed to be from the earliest purchases. Any business, regardless of its goods flow, can use the FIFO method because the assumption underlying it is based on the flow of costs, not the flow of goods. For Boilen, the FIFO method would result in an ending inventory of $6,100, computed as follows.

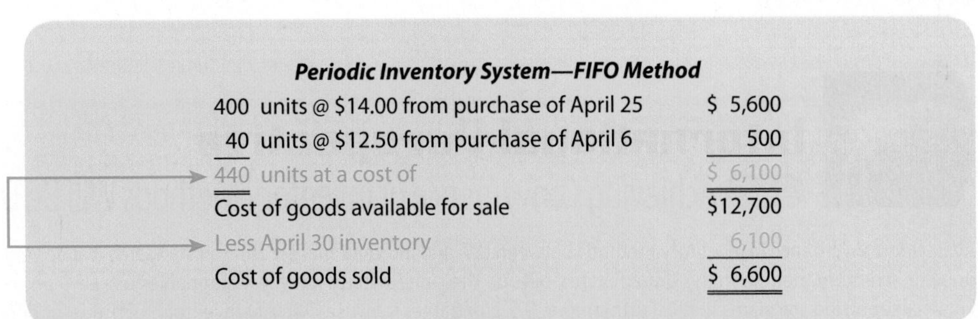

Periodic Inventory System—FIFO Method

400 units @ $14.00 from purchase of April 25	$ 5,600
40 units @ $12.50 from purchase of April 6	500
440 units at a cost of	$ 6,100
Cost of goods available for sale	$12,700
Less April 30 inventory	6,100
Cost of goods sold	$ 6,600

Thus, the FIFO method values the ending inventory at the most recent costs and includes earlier costs in the cost of goods sold.

▲ During periods of rising prices, FIFO yields the highest possible amount of net income because the cost of goods sold shows the earliest costs incurred, which are lower during periods of inflation. Another reason for this is that businesses tend to raise selling prices as costs increase, even when they purchased the goods before the cost increase.

▼ In periods of declining prices, FIFO tends to charge the older and higher prices against revenues, thus reducing income. Consequently, a major criticism of FIFO is that it magnifies the effects of the business cycle on income.

Last-In, First-Out (LIFO) Method

STUDY NOTE: *Physical flow under LIFO can be likened to the changes in a gravel pile as the gravel is sold. As the gravel on top leaves the pile, more is purchased and added to the top. The gravel on the bottom may never be sold.*

The **last-in, first-out (LIFO) method** of costing inventories assumes that the costs of the last items purchased should be assigned to the first items sold and that the cost of the ending inventory should reflect the cost of the goods purchased earliest. Under LIFO, Boilen's April 30 inventory would be $5,100, computed as follows.

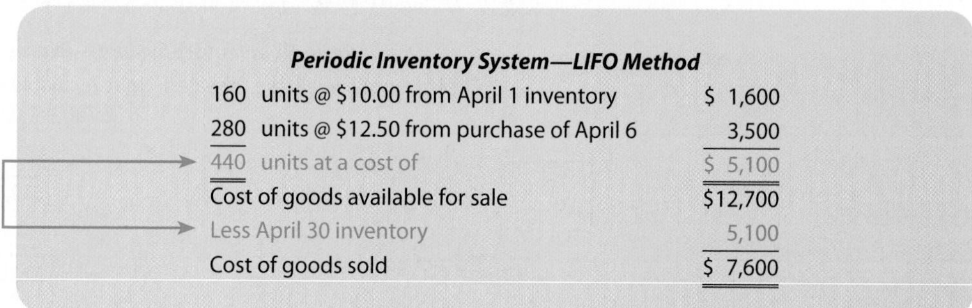

Periodic Inventory System—LIFO Method

160 units @ $10.00 from April 1 inventory	$ 1,600
280 units @ $12.50 from purchase of April 6	3,500
440 units at a cost of	$ 5,100
Cost of goods available for sale	$12,700
Less April 30 inventory	5,100
Cost of goods sold	$ 7,600

The effect of LIFO is to value inventory at the earliest prices and to include the cost of the most recently purchased goods in the cost of goods sold. The logical argument for LIFO is that a certain size of inventory is necessary in a going concern. When inventory is sold, it must be replaced with more goods. The supporters of LIFO reason that the fairest determination of income occurs if the current costs of merchandise are matched against current sales prices, regardless of which physical units of merchandise are sold. When prices are moving either up or down, the cost of goods sold will, under LIFO, show costs closer to the price level at the time the goods are sold. Thus, the LIFO method tends to show a smaller net income during inflationary times and a larger net income during deflationary times than other methods of inventory *valuation*. The peaks and valleys of the business cycle tend to be smoothed out.

STUDY NOTE: *In inventory valuation, the flow of costs—and hence income determination—is more important than the physical movement of goods and balance sheet valuation.*

An argument can also be made against LIFO. Because the inventory *valuation* on the balance sheet reflects earlier prices, it often gives an unrealistic picture of the inventory's current value. Balance sheet measures like working capital and current ratio may be distorted and must be interpreted carefully.

International Perspective

IFRS Achieving Convergence of Inventory Methods Will Be Difficult

Achieving convergence in inventory methods between U.S. and international accounting standards will be very difficult. While, LIFO is the second most popular inventory method in the United States, outside the United States, very few companies use LIFO because it is not allowed under international financial reporting standards (IFRS). Furthermore, U.S. companies may use different inventory methods for different portions of their inventory as long as there is proper *disclosure*; but international standards only allow this practice in very limited cases. Also, as noted earlier in the chapter, U.S. and international standards have different ways of measuring the "market" value of inventories. Because these differences are so significant, the FASB and IASB have decided not to pursue convergence with regard to inventories at this time.[5]

Summary of Inventory Costing Methods

Exhibit 3 summarizes how the four inventory costing methods affect the cost of goods sold and inventory when a company uses the periodic inventory system. In periods of rising prices, FIFO yields the highest inventory *valuation*, the lowest cost of goods sold, and hence a higher net income. LIFO yields the lowest inventory valuation, the highest cost of goods sold, and thus a lower net income.

Exhibit 3
The Impact of Costing Methods on the Income Statement and Balance Sheet Under the Periodic Inventory System

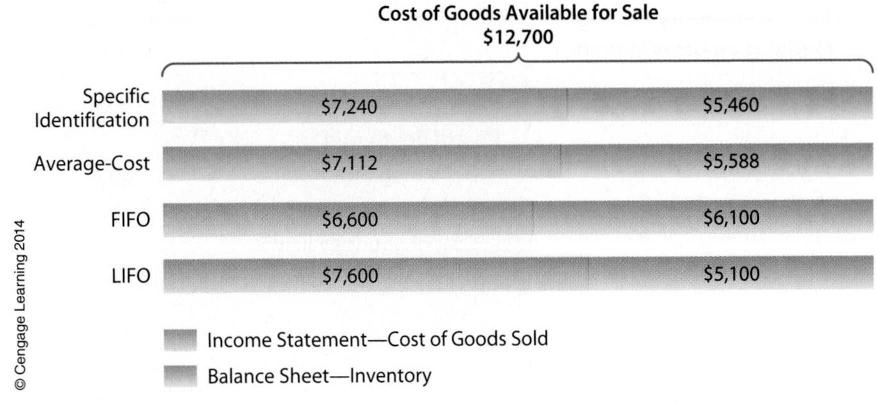

APPLY IT!

Using the data that follows and the periodic inventory system, determine the cost of goods sold associated with the sale on May 6 under the following methods: (a) average-cost, (b) FIFO, and (c) LIFO.

Inventory Data—April 30

May	1	Inventory	100 units @ $4.00
	5	Purchase	200 units @ $5.00
	Sales in May		250 units

SOLUTION

a. Average-cost method:

100 units × $4	$ 400
200 units × $5	1,000
300 units	$1,400
$1,400 ÷ 300 = $4.67* per unit	
Cost of goods sold = 250 units × $4.67* =	$1,168*

*Rounded

b. FIFO method:

100 units × $4	$ 400
150 units × $5	750
Cost of goods sold	$1,150

c. LIFO method:

200 units × $5	$1,000
50 units × $4	200
Cost of goods sold	$1,200

TRY IT! SE2, SE3, SE4, SE5, E2A, E3A, E2B, E3B

LO3 Impact of Inventory Decisions

Continuing with the Boilen Company example and assuming Boilen had April sales of $10,000, Exhibit 4 shows how the specific identification, average-cost, FIFO, and LIFO methods of pricing inventory affect gross margin. Differences in gross margin will affect net income to the same extent.

Exhibit 4
Effects of Inventory Costing Methods on Gross Margin

	Specific Identification Method	Average-Cost Method	FIFO Method	LIFO Method
Sales	$10,000	$10,000	$10,000	$10,000
Cost of goods sold				
Beginning inventory	$ 1,600	$ 1,600	$ 1,600	$ 1,600
Purchases	11,100	11,100	11,100	11,100
Cost of goods available for sale	$12,700	$12,700	$12,700	$12,700
Less ending inventory	5,460	5,588	6,100	5,100
Cost of goods sold	$ 7,240	$ 7,112	$ 6,600	$ 7,600
Gross margin	$ 2,760	$ 2,888	$ 3,400	$ 2,400

Keeping in mind that April was a period of rising prices, Exhibit 4 shows that LIFO, which charges the most recent—and, for Boilen, the highest—prices to the cost of goods sold, resulted in the lowest gross margin. Conversely, FIFO, which charges the earliest—and, in this case, the lowest—prices to the cost of goods sold, produced the highest gross margin. The gross margin under the average-cost method falls between the gross margins produced by LIFO and FIFO. During a period of declining prices, the LIFO method would produce a higher gross margin than the FIFO method because the cost of goods sold would be lower, thus the higher gross margin. Both methods have the greatest impact on gross margin during prolonged periods of price changes, whether up or down.

Effects on the Financial Statements

As Exhibit 5 shows, the FIFO, LIFO, and average-cost methods are widely used. Each method has its advantages and disadvantages. Among the factors managers should consider in choosing an inventory costing method are the trend of prices and the effects of each method on financial statements, income taxes, and cash flows.

Exhibit 5
Inventory Costing Methods Used by 500 Large Companies

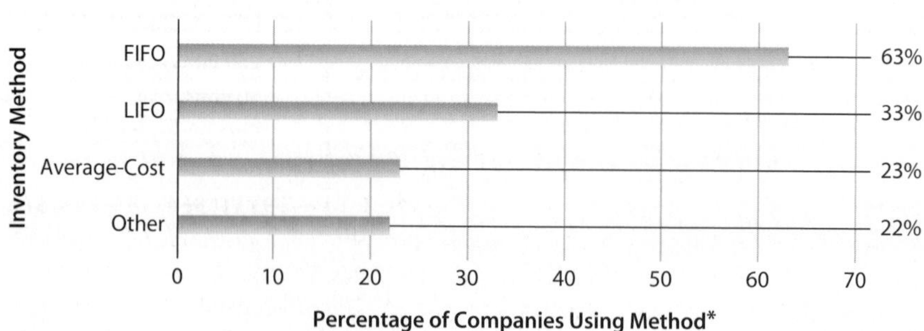

Totals more than 100% due to use of more than one method.

Source: "Industry Costing Methods Used by 500 Large Companies." Copyright © 2011 by AICPA. Reproduced with permission.

As noted, inventory costing methods have different effects on the income statement and balance sheet. The LIFO method is best suited for the income statement because it *matches* revenues and the cost of goods sold. But it is not the best method for *valuing* inventory on the balance sheet, particularly during a prolonged period of price increases or decreases. FIFO, on the other hand, is well suited to the balance sheet because the ending inventory is closest to current values, thus giving a more realistic view of a company's current assets.

Effects on Income Taxes

The Internal Revenue Service governs how inventories must be valued for federal income tax purposes. IRS regulations give companies a wide choice of inventory costing methods, including specific identification, average-cost, FIFO, and LIFO. Except when companies use the LIFO method, they may use the lower-of-cost-or-market rule. However, if a company wants to change the *valuation* method it uses for income tax purposes, it must have advance approval from the IRS.* This requirement conforms to the *consistency convention*. A company should change its inventory method only if there is a good reason to do so. The company must show the nature and effect of the change in its financial statements.

Many accountants believe that using the FIFO and average-cost methods in periods of rising prices causes businesses to overstate their profit, resulting in excess income tax. Profit is overstated because the cost of goods sold is understated relative to current prices. Thus, the company must buy replacement inventory at higher prices, and at the same time pay income taxes. During periods of rapid inflation, billions of dollars reported as profits and paid in income taxes were believed to be the result of the poor matching of current costs and revenues under the FIFO and average-cost methods. Consequently, many companies, believing that prices would continue to rise, switched to the LIFO inventory method. When a company uses the LIFO method for tax purposes, the IRS requires that it use the same method in its accounting records.

STUDY NOTE: *In periods of rising prices, LIFO results in lower net income and lower taxes.*

Over a period of rising prices, a business that uses the LIFO method may find that its inventory is valued at a figure far below what it currently pays for the same items. Management must monitor such a situation carefully. If it lets the inventory quantity at year end fall below the level at the beginning of the year, the company will pay higher income taxes. Higher income before taxes results because the company expenses the historical costs of inventory, which are below current costs.

When sales have reduced inventories below the levels set in prior years, it is called a **LIFO liquidation**—that is, units sold exceed units purchased for the period. Managers can prevent a LIFO liquidation by making enough purchases before the end of the year to restore the desired inventory level. Sometimes, however, a LIFO liquidation cannot be avoided because products are discontinued or supplies are interrupted, as in the case of a strike. In a recent year, 28 out of 500 large companies reported a LIFO liquidation in which their net income increased due to the matching of historical costs with present sales dollars.[6]

Effects on Cash Flows

Generally speaking, a company's choice of average cost, FIFO, or LIFO does not affect cash flows. However, the choice of inventory method will affect the amount of income tax paid. Therefore, choosing a method that results in lower income will result in lower income taxes. In most other cases where there is a choice of accounting method, a company may choose different methods for income tax computations and financial reporting.

*A single exception to this rule is that when companies change to LIFO from another method, they do not need advance approval from IRS.

APPLY IT!

Match the following inventory costing methods with the related statements:
(a) Average cost, (b) FIFO, or (c) LIFO

1. In periods of rising prices, this method results in the highest cost of goods sold.
2. In periods of rising prices, this method results in the highest income.
3. In periods of rising prices, this method results in the lowest ending inventory cost.
4. In periods of rising prices, this method results in the lowest income tax.
5. In periods of decreasing prices, this method results in neither the highest inventory cost nor the lowest income.
6. In periods of decreasing prices, this method results in the lowest income.
7. In periods of decreasing prices, this method results in the highest cost of goods sold.
8. In periods of decreasing prices, this method results in the lowest income tax.

SOLUTION
1. c; 2. b; 3. c; 4. c; 5. a; 6. b; 7. b; 8. b

TRY IT! SE6, E4A, E5A, E4B, E5B

LO4 Inventory Cost Under the Perpetual Inventory System

Under the perpetual inventory system, inventory is updated as purchases and sales take place. The cost of goods sold is accumulated as sales are made and costs are transferred from the Inventory account to the Cost of Goods Sold account. The cost of the ending inventory is the balance of the Inventory account. Goods are valued using one of the following inventory costing methods: specific identification, average-cost, first-in, first-out (FIFO), or last-in, first-out (LIFO). To illustrate costing methods under the perpetual inventory system, we continue with the Boilen Company example. The following data for April, a month in which prices were rising, are available:

Inventory Data—April 30

April 1	Inventory	160 units @ $10.00
6	Purchase	440 units @ $12.50
10	Sale	560 units
25	Purchase	400 units @ $14.00
30	Inventory	440 units

Specific Identification Method

STUDY NOTE: *The specific identification method produces the same inventory cost and cost of goods sold under the perpetual system as under the periodic system because the cost of goods sold and the ending inventory are based on the cost of the identified items sold and on hand.*

The detailed records of purchases and sales maintained under the perpetual system facilitate the use of the specific identification method. For instance, if Boilen's April 30 inventory consisted of 100 units from the April 1 inventory, 200 units from the April 6 purchase, and 140 units from the April 25 purchase, the specific identification method would assign the costs as follows.

Perpetual Inventory System—Specific Identification Method

100 units @ $10.00	$1,000	Cost of goods available for sale	$12,700
200 units @ $12.50	2,500		
140 units @ $14.00	1,960	Less April 30 inventory	5,460
440 units at a cost of	$5,460	Cost of goods sold	$ 7,240

Average-Cost Method

Under the perpetual system, an average is computed after each purchase or series of purchases, as follows.

Perpetual Inventory System—Average-Cost Method

April	1	Inventory	160 units @ $10.00	$ 1,600
	6	Purchase	440 units @ $12.50	5,500
	6	Balance	600 units @ $11.83*	$ 7,100
				(new average computed)
	10	Sale	560 units @ $11.83*	(6,625)
	10	Balance	40 units @ $11.83*	$ 475
	25	Purchase	400 units @ $14.00	5,600
	30	Inventory	440 units @ $13.81*	$ 6,075
				(new average computed)
Cost of goods sold				$ 6,625

*Rounded

STUDY NOTE: *The average-cost method produces different results under the perpetual and periodic systems. Under the periodic system, the average cost is computed for all goods available for sale during the period.*

The costs applied to sales become the cost of goods sold, $6,625. The ending inventory is the balance, $6,075.

FIFO Method

When costing inventory with the FIFO and LIFO methods, it is necessary to keep track of the components of inventory because, as sales are made, the costs must be assigned in the proper order. The FIFO method is applied as follows.

STUDY NOTE: *Under the FIFO perpetual inventory system, Boilen's ending inventory of $6,100 and the cost of goods sold of $6,600 are the same as under the periodic inventory system. This will always occur because the ending inventory under both systems consists of the last items purchased—in this case, the entire purchase of April 25 and 40 units from the purchase of April 6.*

Perpetual Inventory System—FIFO Method

April	1	Inventory	160 units @ $10.00		$ 1,600
	6	Purchase	440 units @ $12.50		5,500
	10	Sale	160 units @ $10.00	$(1,600)	
			400 units @ $12.50	(5,000)	(6,600)
	10	Balance	40 units @ $12.50		$ 500
	25	Purchase	400 units @ $14.00		5,600
	30	Inventory	40 units @ $12.50	$ 500	
			400 units @ $14.00	5,600	$ 6,100
Cost of goods sold					$ 6,600

Business Perspective

More Companies Enjoy LIFO!

The availability of better technology may partially account for the increasing use of LIFO in the United States. Using the LIFO method under the perpetual inventory system has always been a tedious process, especially if done manually. The development of faster and less expensive computer systems has made it easier for companies that use the perpetual inventory system to switch to LIFO and enjoy its economic benefits.

LIFO Method

The LIFO method is applied as follows.

Perpetual Inventory System—LIFO Method

April 1	Inventory	160 units @ $10.00		$ 1,600
6	Purchase	440 units @ $12.50		5,500
10	Sale	440 units @ $12.50	$(5,500)	
		120 units @ $10.00	(1,200)	(6,700)
10	Balance	40 units @ $10.00		$ 400
25	Purchase	400 units @ $14.00		5,600
30	Inventory	40 units @ $10.00	$ 400	
		400 units @ $14.00	5,600	$ 6,000
Cost of goods sold				$ 6,700

STUDY NOTE: The LIFO method produces different results under the perpetual and periodic systems. Under the perpetual method system, the cost of good sold is computed after each sale during the period rather than for all sales.

The ending inventory of $6,000 includes 40 units from the beginning inventory and 400 units from the April 25 purchase.

Summary of Inventory Costing Methods

STUDY NOTE: The rank of the results is the same as under the periodic inventory system, but some amounts have changed.

Exhibit 6 compares the specific identification, average-cost, FIFO, and LIFO methods under the perpetual inventory system for Boilen. In this period of rising prices, FIFO produces the highest inventory value and lowest cost of goods sold, and LIFO produces the lowest inventory cost and highest cost of goods sold. The average-cost method is in between. Specific identification is the same as under the periodic inventory system.

Exhibit 6
The Impact of Costing Methods on the Income Statement and Balance Sheet Under the Perpetual Inventory System

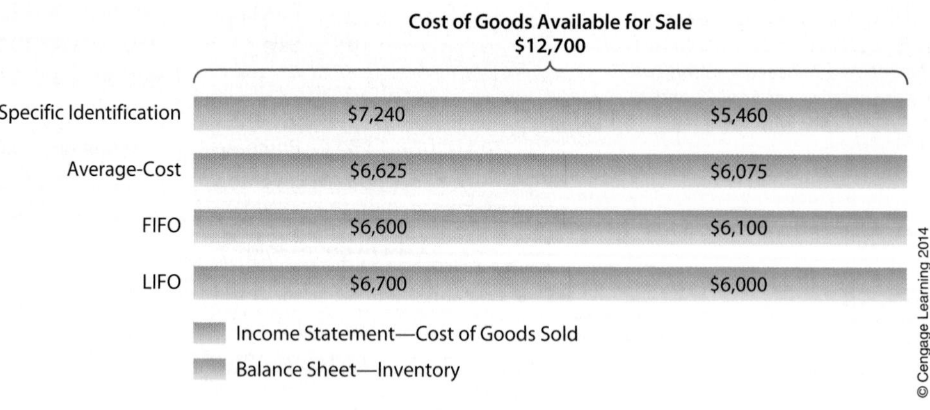

APPLY IT!

Using the data that follows and the perpetual inventory system, determine the cost of goods sold associated with the sale on May 6 under the following methods: (a) average-cost, (b) FIFO, and (c) LIFO.

Inventory Data—April 30

May	1	Inventory	120 units @ $8.00
	5	Purchase	200 units @ $10.00
	6	Sale	220 units

SOLUTION

a. Average-cost method:

120 units × $8	$ 960
200 units × $10	2,000
320 units	$2,960
$2,960 ÷ 320 = $9.25 per unit	
Cost of goods sold = 220 units × $9.25 =	$2,035

b. FIFO method:

120 units × $8	$ 960
100 units × $10	1,000
Cost of goods sold	$1,960

c. LIFO method:

200 units × $10	$2,000
20 units × $8	160
Cost of goods sold	$2,160

TRY IT! SE7, SE8, SE9, E6A, E7A, E6B, E7B

LO5 Valuing Inventory by Estimation

It is sometimes necessary or desirable to estimate the value of the ending inventory. The retail method and gross profit method are most commonly used for this purpose.

Retail Method

The **retail method** estimates the cost of the ending inventory by using the ratio of cost to retail price. Retail merchandising businesses use this method for two main reasons:

STUDY NOTE: *When estimating inventory by the retail method, the inventory need not be counted.*

- To prepare financial statements for each period, the retail method can be used to estimate the cost without taking the time or going to the expense of determining the cost of each item in the inventory.
- Because items in a retail store normally have a price tag or a universal product code, it is common practice to take the physical inventory "at retail" from these price tags or codes and to reduce the total value to cost by using the retail method. *At retail* means the amount of the inventory at the marked selling prices of the items.

When the retail method is used, the records must show the beginning inventory at cost and at retail. They must also show the amount of goods purchased during the period at cost and at retail. The net sales at retail is the balance of the Sales account less returns and allowances. A simple example of the retail method is shown in Exhibit 7.

As shown in Exhibit 7, goods available for sale is determined at cost and at retail by listing the beginning inventory and net purchases for the period at cost and at their expected selling price, adding freight-in to the Cost column, and totaling. The ratio of these two amounts (cost to retail price) provides an estimate of the cost of each dollar of retail sales value. The estimated ending inventory at retail is then determined, as shown in Exhibit 7, by deducting sales for the period from the retail price of the goods that were available for sale during the period. The inventory at retail is then converted to cost on the basis of the ratio of cost to retail.

The cost of the ending inventory can also be estimated by applying the ratio of cost to retail price to the total retail value of the physical count of the ending inventory.

Exhibit 7
Retail Method of Inventory Estimation

	Cost	Retail
Beginning inventory	$ 80,000	$110,000
Net purchases for the period (excluding freight-in)	214,000	290,000
Freight-in	6,000	
Goods available for sale	$300,000	$400,000
Ratio of cost to retail price: $\frac{\$300{,}000}{\$400{,}000} = 75\%$		
Net sales during the period		320,000
Estimated ending inventory at retail		$ 80,000
Ratio of cost to retail	75%	
Estimated cost of ending inventory	$ 60,000	

***STUDY NOTE:** Freight-in does not appear in the Retail column because retailers automatically price their goods high enough to cover freight charges.*

Applying the retail method in practice is often more difficult than this simple example because of such complications as changes in retail price during the period, different markups on different types of merchandise, and varying volumes of sales for different types of merchandise.

Gross Profit Method

The **gross profit method** (or *gross margin method*) assumes that the ratio of gross margin for a business remains relatively stable from year to year. The gross profit method is used in place of the retail method when records of the retail prices of the beginning inventory and purchases are not available. It is a useful way of estimating the amount of inventory lost or destroyed by theft, fire, or other hazards. Insurance companies often use it to verify loss claims. The gross profit method is acceptable for estimating the cost of inventory for interim reports, but it is not acceptable for valuing inventory in the annual financial statements.

As Exhibit 8 shows, the gross profit method involves the following steps:

- **Step 1.** Calculate the cost of goods available for sale in the usual way (add purchases to beginning inventory).
- **Step 2.** Estimate the cost of goods sold by deducting the estimated gross margin of 30 percent from sales.
- **Step 3.** Deduct the estimated cost of goods sold from the goods available for sale to arrive at the estimated cost of the ending inventory.

Exhibit 8
Gross Profit Method of Inventory Estimation

Step 1.	Beginning inventory at cost		$100,000
	Purchases at cost (including freight-in)		580,000
	Cost of goods available for sale		$680,000
Step 2.	Less estimated cost of goods sold		
	Sales at selling price	$800,000	
	Less estimated gross margin		
	($800,000 × 30%)	240,000	
	Estimated cost of goods sold		560,000
Step 3.	Estimated cost of ending inventory		$120,000

Inventory and the Financial Statements

Cost of goods sold is created by the transfer from the balance sheet the cost of the inventories sold to the income statement during the period. The amount of the transfer depends on the *valuation* of inventories using one of the methods illustrated in this chapter. The transfer is depicted in Exhibit 9.

Exhibit 9
Valuation of Inventory on the Balance Sheet Impacts Cost of Goods Sold on the Income Statement

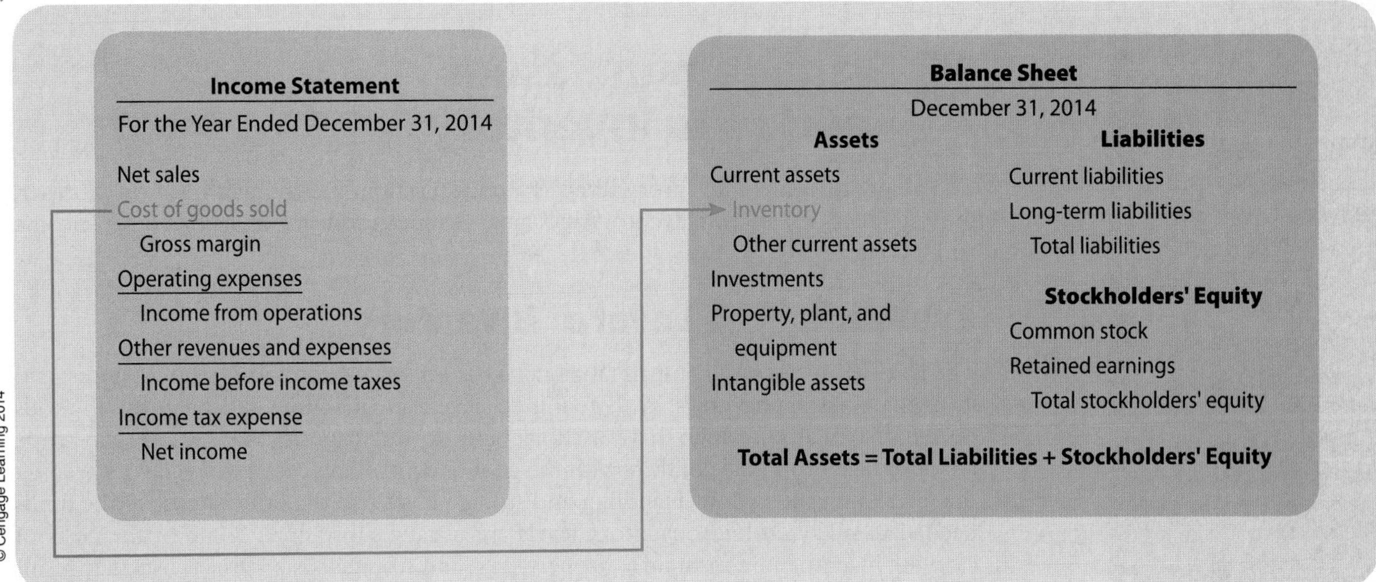

APPLY IT!

Tommy's Vintage Shop had net retail sales of $195,000 during the current year. The following additional information was obtained from the company's accounting records:

	At Cost	At Retail
Beginning inventory	$ 40,000	$ 60,000
Net purchases (excluding freight-in)	130,000	210,000
Freight-in	5,500	

Using the retail method, estimate the company's ending inventory at cost. Assuming that a physical count taken at year-end revealed an inventory of $66,000 at retail value, what is the estimated amount of inventory shrinkage (loss due to theft, damage, etc.) at cost using the retail method?

SOLUTION

	Cost	Retail
Beginning inventory	$ 40,000	$ 60,000
Net purchases for the period (excluding freight-in)	130,000	210,000
Freight-in	5,500	
Goods available for sale	$175,500	$270,000

Ratio of cost to retail price: $\frac{\$175{,}500}{\$270{,}000} = 65\%$

	Cost	Retail
Net sales during the period		195,000
Estimated ending inventory at retail		$ 75,000
Ratio of cost to retail	65%	
Estimated cost of ending inventory	$ 48,750	

Estimated Inventory Loss = Estimated Cost − (Retail Inventory Count × 65%)
= $48,750 − ($66,000 × 65%) = $48,750 − $42,900
= $5,850

TRY IT! SE10, E8A, E9A, E8B, E9B

SECTION 3

BUSINESS APPLICATIONS

BUSINESS APPLICATIONS

- Evaluate the level of inventory
  - Inventory turnover
  - Days' inventory on hand
- Manage the level of inventory
  - Supply-chain management
  - Just-in-time operating environment
- Evaluate the effects of inventory misstatements on income measurement

RELEVANT LEARNING OBJECTIVE

LO 6 Evaluate inventory level, and demonstrate the effects of inventory misstatements on income measurement.

LO 6 Management Issues Related to Inventory

The ability to control inventory levels is a critical skill in managing a business. Further, misstatements in *valuing* inventory will have significant effects on reported net income and income taxes.

Evaluating the Level of Inventory

The level of inventory a company maintains has important economic consequences, and it involves conflicting goals. One goal is to have a great variety and quantity of goods on hand so that customers have a choice and do not have to wait for an item to be restocked. But this goal conflicts with the goal of controlling costs, which favors keeping the level of inventory low. Handling and storage costs and the interest cost of the funds needed to maintain high inventory levels are usually substantial. Some of the costs of carrying inventory are insurance, property tax, and storage costs. Other costs may result from spoilage and theft. However, low inventory levels can result in disgruntled customers and lost sales. Managers control inventory by closely observing two ratios: inventory turnover and days' inventory on hand.

Inventory Turnover **Inventory turnover** is the average number of times a company sells an amount equal to its average level of inventory during a period. For example, using **Cisco Systems**' annual report, we can compute the company's inventory turnover for 2011 as follows (amounts are in millions).

RATIO

Inventory Turnover: How Many Times Did the Company Sell Its Inventory During an Accounting Period?

$$\text{Inventory Turnover} = \frac{\text{Cost of Goods Sold}}{\text{Average Inventory}}$$

$$\text{Cisco Systems Inventory Turnover} = \frac{\$13{,}647}{(\$1{,}233 + \$1{,}114) \div 2}$$

$$= \frac{\$13{,}647}{\$1{,}174^*} = 11.6^* \text{ times}$$

*Rounded

Based on Bizmin Industry Financial Report, December 2011.

Days' Inventory on Hand **Days' inventory on hand** is the average number of days it takes a company to sell an amount equal to its average inventory. It is computed using the inventory turnover. For **Cisco**, it is computed as follows.

STUDY NOTE: Inventory turnover will be systematically higher if year-end levels are low. For example, many merchandisers' year-end is in January when inventories are lower than at any other time of the year.

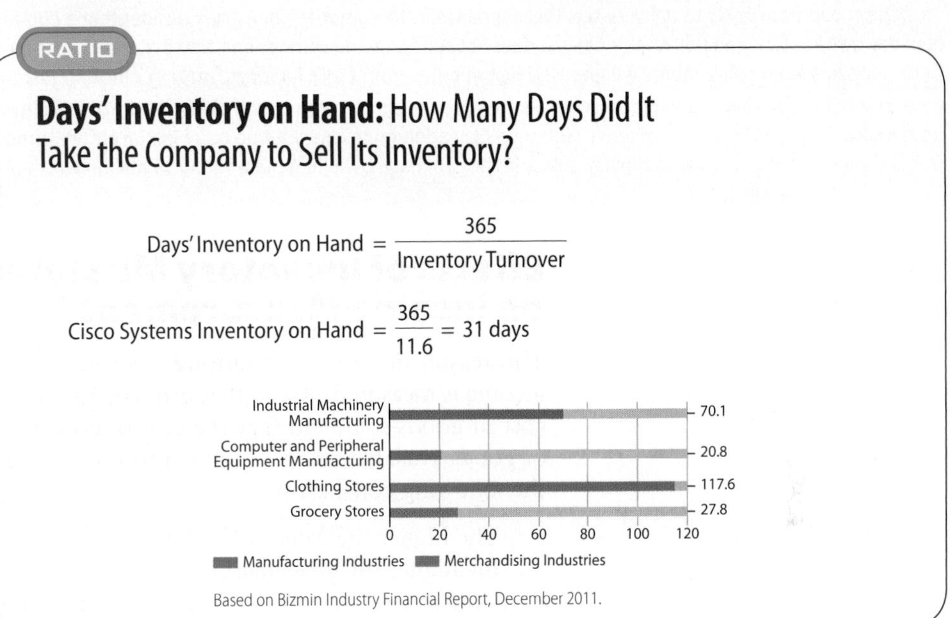

Harley-Davidson uses a just-in-time operating environment when producing its legendary motorcycles—often with only 8 to 10 hours of inventory on hand. A lack of supply can therefore shut down assembly lines, so the company is careful when considering where to source parts because of the longer lead times and customs delays that can occur.

Cisco turned its inventory over 11.6 times in 2011 or, on average, about every 31 days. Thus, on average, products are held in inventory for almost one month before being sold. Until the products are sold, Cisco either has to tie up its own money or obtain outside financing.

Hupeng/Dreamstime

Inventory Management

To reduce their levels of inventory, many merchandisers and manufacturers use supply-chain management in conjunction with a just-in-time operating environment. With **supply-chain management**, a company uses the Internet to order and track goods that it needs immediately. A **just-in-time (JIT) operating environment** is one in which goods arrive just at the time they are needed.

Cisco uses supply-chain management to increase inventory turnover. Given rapidly changing technology and customer requirements, inventory and supply chain management are focus areas as the company balances the need to maintain supply chain flexibility to help ensure competitive lead times with the risk of inventory obsolescence.

© Alija / iStockphoto.com

Business Perspective

A Whirlwind Inventory Turnover—How Does Dell Do It?

Dell Computer Corporation turns its inventory over every 10 days. How can it do this when other computer companies have inventory on hand for 60 days or even longer? Technology and good inventory management are a big part of the answer.

Dell's speed from order to delivery sets the standard for the computer industry. Consider that a computer ordered by 9 A.M. can be delivered the next day by 9 P.M. How can Dell do this when it does not start ordering components and assembling computers until a customer places an order? First, Dell's suppliers keep components warehoused just minutes from Dell's factories, making efficient, just-in-time operations possible. Dell also saves time by sending an e-mail message for some finished products to a shipper, such as **United Parcel Service**, and the shipper picks up the product from a supplier and schedules it to arrive with the PC. In addition to contributing to a high inventory turnover, this practice saves Dell in freight costs. Dell is showing the world how to run a business in the cyber age by selling more than $39 million worth of computers a day on its website.[7]

Effects of Inventory Misstatements on Income Measurement

The reason inventory accounting is so important to income measurement is the way income is measured. Recall that gross margin is the difference between net sales and the cost of goods sold, and that the cost of goods sold depends on the portion of the cost of goods available for sale assigned to the ending inventory. These relationships lead to the following conclusions:

- The higher the value of the ending inventory, the lower the cost of goods sold and the higher the gross margin.
- Conversely, the lower the value of the ending inventory, the higher the cost of goods sold and the lower the gross margin.

Because the amount of gross margin has a direct effect on net income, the value assigned to the ending inventory also affects net income. In effect, the value of the ending inventory determines what portion of the cost of goods available for sale is assigned to the cost of goods sold and what portion is assigned to inventory.

The basic issue in separating goods sold and goods not sold is to assign a value to the goods not sold, the ending inventory. The goods not assigned to the ending inventory are used to determine the cost of goods sold. Because the figures for the ending inventory and the cost of goods sold are related, a misstatement in the inventory figure at the end of a period will cause an equal misstatement in gross margin and income before income taxes. The amount of assets and stockholders' equity will be misstated by the same amount.

Inventory Misstatements and Fraud Inventory is particularly susceptible to fraudulent financial reporting. For example, it is easy to overstate or understate inventory by including end-of-the-year purchase and sales transactions in the wrong fiscal year or by simply misstating inventory by mistake. A misstatement can also occur because of deliberate manipulation of operating results motivated by a desire to enhance the market's perception of the company, obtain bank financing, or achieve compensation incentives.

In one case, **Rite Aid Corporation**, the large drugstore chain, falsified income by manipulating its computerized inventory system to cover losses from shoplifting, employee theft, and spoilage.[8] In another case, bookkeepers at **Rent-Way, Inc.**, which rents furniture to apartment dwellers, boosted income artificially over several years by overstating inventory in small increments.[9]

Inventory Misstatements Illustrated Whatever the causes of an overstatement or understatement of inventory, the three examples that follow illustrate the effects. In each case, the beginning inventory, the net cost of purchases, and the cost of goods available for sale are stated correctly. In Example 1, the ending inventory is correctly stated; in Example 2, it is overstated by $3,000; and in Example 3, it is understated by $3,000.

Example 1. Ending Inventory Correctly Stated at $5,000

Cost of Goods Sold for the Year		*Income Statement for the Year*	
Beginning inventory	$ 6,000	Net sales	$50,000
Net cost of purchases	29,000	Cost of goods sold	30,000
Cost of goods available for sale	$35,000	Gross margin	$20,000
Ending inventory	5,000	Operating expenses	16,000
Cost of goods sold	$30,000	Income before income taxes	$ 4,000

Example 2. Ending Inventory Overstated by $3,000

Cost of Goods Sold for the Year		*Income Statement for the Year*	
Beginning inventory	$ 6,000	Net sales	$50,000
Net cost of purchases	29,000	Cost of goods sold	27,000
Cost of goods available for sale	$35,000	Gross margin	$23,000
Ending inventory	8,000	Operating expenses	16,000
Cost of goods sold	$27,000	Income before income taxes	$ 7,000

Example 3. Ending Inventory Understated by $3,000

Cost of Goods Sold for the Year		*Income Statement for the Year*	
Beginning inventory	$ 6,000	Net sales	$50,000
Net cost of purchases	29,000	Cost of goods sold	33,000
Cost of goods available for sale	$35,000	Gross margin	$17,000
Ending inventory	2,000	Operating expenses	16,000
Cost of goods sold	$33,000	Income before income taxes	$ 1,000

In all three examples, the cost of goods available for sale was $35,000. The difference in income before income taxes resulted from how this $35,000 was divided between the ending inventory and the cost of goods sold.

STUDY NOTE: *A misstatement of inventory has the opposite effect in two successive accounting periods.*

Because the ending inventory in one period becomes the beginning inventory in the following period, a misstatement in inventory *valuation* affects both the current period and the following period. Over two periods, the errors in income before income taxes will offset, or counterbalance, each other. For instance, in Example 2, the overstatement of the ending inventory will cause a $3,000 overstatement of the beginning inventory in the following year, which will result in a $3,000 understatement of income. Because the total income before income taxes for the two periods is the same, it may appear that one need not worry about inventory misstatements. However, the misstatements violate the *accrual accounting*. In addition, management, creditors, and investors base many decisions on the accountant's determination of net income. The accountant has an obligation to make the net income figure for each period as useful as possible.

The effects of inventory misstatements on income before income taxes are as follows.

Year 1	Year 2
Ending inventory overstated	**Beginning inventory overstated**
Cost of goods sold understated	Cost of goods sold overstated
Income before income taxes overstated	Income before income taxes understated
Ending inventory understated	**Beginning inventory understated**
Cost of goods sold overstated	Cost of goods sold understated
Income before income taxes understated	Income before income taxes overstated

APPLY IT!

During 2014, Tom's Sporting Goods had beginning inventory of \$500,000, ending inventory of \$700,000, and cost of goods sold of \$2,100,000. Compute the inventory turnover and days' inventory on hand.

SOLUTION

$$\text{Inventory Turnover} = \frac{\text{Cost of Goods Sold}}{\text{Average Inventory}}$$

$$= \frac{\$2{,}100{,}000}{(\$700{,}000 + \$500{,}000)/2} = \frac{\$2{,}100{,}000}{\$600{,}000}$$

$$= 3.5 \text{ times}$$

$$\text{Day's Inventory on Hand} = \frac{365}{\text{Inventory Turnover}}$$

$$= \frac{365}{3.5} = 104.3^{*} \text{ days}$$

*Rounded

TRY IT! SE11, SE12, E10A, E11A, E12A, E10B, E11B, E12B

A Look Back At: Cisco Systems

Blue Jean Images/Alamy Limited

Cisco Systems 

The beginning of this chapter focused on **Cisco Systems**' operations and inventories. Complete the following requirements in order to answer the questions posed at the beginning of the chapter.

Section 1: Concepts
Why is the relationship between accrual accounting and valuation important for inventory accounting?

Section 2: Accounting Applications
Cisco accounts for inventory using the FIFO method adjusted for lower of cost or market. Would you expect inventory at the end of the year to reflect the most recent or least recent inventory purchased? If inventory is adjusted for lower of cost or market, would the market be less than what the inventory was purchased for or what it could be sold for?

Section 3: Business Applications
How do decisions about inventory valuation and inventory levels affect operating results?

SOLUTION

Section 1: Concepts
Accrual accounting requires that costs associated with goods that are sold be transferred from the balance sheet to cost of goods sold on the income statement. To determine what dollar amount will be transferred, one of various acceptable *valuation* methods must be chosen.

Section 2: Accounting Applications
Using the FIFO method, Cisco's inventory at the end of the year will reflect the most recent purchases. If adjusted to lower of cost or market, the market would be less than the inventory purchase price because market in this context is defined as replacement cost.

Section 3: Business Applications
The decisions that Cisco makes about the valuation of inventory affect a company's net income, the amount of taxes it pays, and its cash flows. Decisions about inventory levels also have important economic consequences: too low a level can result in disgruntled customers and too high a level can result in substantial storage, handling, and interest costs.

SOLUTION • SOLUTION • SOLUTION

Review Problem

Grabs Company is a new store that sells a variety of stylish leather boots and bags. The following data about Grabs' inventory and purchases from May is available.

	A	B	C	D	E	F	G
1				Beginning Inventory and Purchases			
2	Date			Units	Cost	Total	Sales Units
3	May	1	Inventory	2,800	$20	$ 56,000	
4		8	Purchase	1,200	22	26,400	
5		10	Sale				3,200
6		24	Purchase	1,600	24	38,400	
7							
8	Totals			5,600		$120,800	3,200
9							

1. Assuming that Grabs uses the periodic inventory system, compute the cost that should be assigned to the ending inventory and to the cost of goods sold, using (a) the average-cost method, (b) the FIFO method, and (c) the LIFO method.
2. Assuming that Grabs uses the perpetual inventory system, compute the cost that should be assigned to the ending inventory and to the cost of goods sold, using (a) the average-cost method, (b) the FIFO method, and (c) the LIFO method.
3. To better understand the situation, compute Grabs' inventory turnover and days' inventory on hand under each of the inventory cost flow assumptions requirement **1**. What conclusion can you draw from this comparison?

SOLUTION

	Units	Amount
Beginning inventory	2,800	$ 56,000
Purchases	2,800	64,800
Available for sale	5,600	$120,800
Sales	3,200	
Ending inventory	2,400	

1. Periodic inventory system:
   a. Average-cost method

Cost of goods available for sale		$120,800
Less ending inventory consisting of 2,400 units at $21.57*		51,768
Cost of goods sold		$ 69,032

*$120,800 ÷ 5,600 units = $21.57 (rounded)

   b. FIFO method

Cost of goods available for sale		$120,800
Less ending inventory consisting of		
May 24 purchase (1,600 × $24)	$38,400	
May 8 purchase (800 × $22)	17,600	56,000
Cost of goods sold		$ 64,800

c. LIFO method

Cost of goods available for sale	$120,800
Less ending inventory consisting of beginning inventory (2,400 × $20)	48,000
Cost of goods sold	$ 72,800

2. Perpetual inventory system:

a. Average-cost method

Date			Units	Cost	Amount
May	1	Inventory	2,800	$20.00	$56,000
	8	Purchase	1,200	22.00	26,400
	8	Balance	4,000	20.60	$82,400
	10	Sale	(3,200)	20.60	(65,920)
	10	Balance	800	20.60	$16,480
	24	Purchase	1,600	24.00	38,400
	31	Inventory	2,400	22.87*	$54,880
Cost of goods sold					$65,920

*Rounded

b. FIFO method

Date			Units	Cost	Amount
May	1	Inventory	2,800	$20	$56,000
	8	Purchase	1,200	22	26,400
	8	Balance	2,800	20	
			1,200	22	$82,400
	10	Sale	(2,800)	20	
			(400)	22	(64,800)
	10	Balance	800	22	$17,600
	24	Purchase	1,600	24	38,400
	31	Inventory	800	22	
			1,600	24	$56,000
Cost of goods sold					$64,800

c. LIFO method

Date			Units	Cost	Amount
May	1	Inventory	2,800	$20	$56,000
	8	Purchase	1,200	22	26,400
	8	Balance	2,800	20	
			1,200	22	$82,400
	10	Sale	(1,200)	22	
			(2,000)	20	(66,400)
	10	Balance	800	20	$16,000
	24	Purchase	1,600	24	38,400
	31	Inventory	800	20	
			1,600	24	$54,400
Cost of goods sold					$66,400

3. Inventory ratios computed

	Average-Cost	FIFO	LIFO
Cost of Goods Sold / Average Inventory	$69,032 / ($51,768 + $56,000) / 2 =	$64,800 / ($56,000 + $56,000) / 2 =	$72,800 / ($48,000 + $56,000) / 2 =
	$69,032 / $53,884 = 1.3	$64,800 / $56,000 = 1.2	$72,800 / $52,000 = 1.4
Inventory Turnover:	1.3 times	1.2 times	1.4 times
Days' Inventory on Hand:	(365 days / 1.3 times)	(365 days / 1.2 times)	(365 days / 1.4 times)
	280.8 days*	304.2 days*	260.7 days*

*Rounded

In periods of rising prices, the LIFO method will always result in a higher inventory turnover and lower days' inventory on hand than the other costing methods. When comparing inventory ratios for two or more companies, their inventory methods should be considered.

Chapter Review

Explain the concepts underlying inventory accounting. LO 1

Inventory cost includes the invoice price less purchases discounts; freight-in, including insurance in transit; and applicable taxes. Goods flow refers to the actual physical flow of merchandise in a business, whereas cost flow refers to the assumed flow of costs. The lower-of-cost-or-market rule states that if the replacement cost (market cost) of the inventory is lower than the original cost, the lower figure should be used.

The objective of inventory accounting is the proper determination of income through the matching of costs and revenues. Management must choose the type of processing system, costing method, and valuation method the company will use. Because the value of inventory affects a company's net income, management's choices will affect not only external and internal evaluations of the company but also the amount of income taxes the company pays and its cash flows.

Calculate inventory cost under the periodic inventory system using various costing methods. LO 2

The value assigned to the ending inventory is the result of two measurements: quantity and cost. Under the periodic inventory system, quantity is determined by taking a physical inventory. Cost is determined by using one of four inventory methods, each based on a different assumption of cost flow. The specific identification method identifies the actual cost of each item in inventory. The average-cost method assumes that the cost of inventory is the average cost of goods available for sale during the period. The first-in, first-out (FIFO) method assumes that the costs of the first items acquired should be assigned to the first items sold. The last-in, first-out (LIFO) method assumes that the costs of the last items acquired should be assigned to the first items sold.

Explain the effects of inventory costing methods on income determination and income taxes. LO 3

During periods of rising prices, the LIFO method will show the lowest gross margin and thus net income; FIFO, the highest; and average-cost, in between. LIFO and FIFO have the opposite effects in periods of falling prices. The Internal Revenue Service requires a company that uses LIFO for tax purposes to use LIFO in its accounting records. It also does not allow a company that uses LIFO to apply the lower-of-cost-or-market rule.

Calculate inventory cost under the perpetual inventory system using various costing methods. LO 4

Under the perpetual inventory system, the cost of goods sold is accumulated as sales are made and costs are transferred from the Inventory account to the Cost of Goods Sold account. The cost of the ending inventory is the balance of the Inventory account. The specific identification method and the FIFO method produce the same results under both the perpetual and periodic inventory systems. The results differ for the average-cost method because an average is calculated after each sale rather than at the end of the accounting period. Results also differ for the LIFO method because the cost components of inventory change constantly as goods are bought and sold.

Use the retail method and gross profit method to estimate the cost of ending inventory. LO 5

Two methods of estimating the value of inventory are the retail method and the gross profit method. Under the retail method, inventory is determined at retail prices and is then reduced to estimated cost by applying a ratio of cost to retail price. Under the gross profit method, the cost of goods sold is estimated by reducing sales by the estimated gross margin. The estimated cost of goods sold is then deducted from the cost of goods available for sale to estimate the cost of the ending inventory.

Evaluate inventory level, and demonstrate the effects of inventory misstatements on income measurement. LO 6

The level of inventory has important economic consequences. To evaluate inventory levels, managers commonly use inventory turnover and its related measure, days' inventory on hand. Supply-chain management and a just-in-time operating environment are a means of increasing inventory turnover and reducing inventory carrying costs.

If the value of the ending inventory is understated or overstated, a corresponding error—dollar for dollar—will be made in income before income taxes. Furthermore, because the ending inventory of one period is the beginning inventory of the next, the misstatement affects two accounting periods, although the effects are opposite.

Key Terms and Ratios

average-cost method 293 (LO2)
consignment 289 (LO1)
cost flow 289 (LO1)
first-in, first-out (FIFO) method 293 (LO2)
goods flow 289 (LO1)
gross profit method 302 (LO5)
inventory accounting 288 (LO1)
inventory cost 288 (LO1)
just-in-time (JIT) operating environment 305 (LO6)
last-in, first-out (LIFO) method 294 (LO2)
LIFO liquidation 297 (LO3)
lower-of-cost-or-market (LCM) rule 290 (LO1)
market 290 (LO1)
retail method 301 (LO5)
specific identification method 292 (LO2)
supply-chain management 305 (LO6)

RATIOS

days' inventory on hand 305 (LO6)
inventory turnover 304 (LO6)

Chapter Assignments

DISCUSSION QUESTIONS

LO 1 **DQ1. CONCEPT ▶** Which is more important from the standpoint of inventory costing: accrual accounting or valuation?

LO 2, 4 **DQ2.** Which of the following methods do not require a physical inventory: periodic inventory system, perpetual inventory method, retail method, or gross profit method?

LO 1, 6 **DQ3. CONCEPT ▶** Given that the LCM rule is an application of the conservatism convention in the current accounting period, is the effect of this application also conservative in the next period?

LO 2, 3, 4 **DQ4.** Under what condition would all four methods of inventory pricing produce exactly the same results?

LO 4 **DQ5.** Under the perpetual inventory system, why is the cost of goods sold not determined by deducting the ending inventory from goods available for sale, as it is under the periodic method?

LO 6 **DQ6. BUSINESS APPLICATION ▶** Is it good or bad for a retail store to have a large inventory?

LO 6 **DQ7. BUSINESS APPLICATION ▶** Why is misstatement of inventory one of the most common means of financial statement fraud?

SHORT EXERCISES

LO 1 **Inventory Concepts**

SE1. CONCEPT ▶ Match the items that follow with their related statements.

a. Inventory accounting
b. Goods flow
c. Cost flow
d. Lower-of-cost-or-market (LCM) rule
e. Valuation
f. Conservatism

1. Refers to the association of costs with their assumed flow.
2. Has the objective of matching costs of the period against revenues for the period.
3. Requires that the inventory be written down to the lower value and that a loss be recorded.
4. Refers to the actual physical movement of goods in the operations of a company.
5. Related to the lower-of-cost-or-market (LCM) rule.
6. Can vary depending on the assumptions about the flow of costs.

LO 2 **Specific Identification Method**

SE2. Assume the following data with regard to inventory for Vegan Company:

Aug. 1	Inventory	40 units	@ $10 per unit	$ 400
8	Purchase	50 units	@ $11 per unit	550
22	Purchase	35 units	@ $12 per unit	420
Goods available for sale		125 units		$1,370
Aug. 15	Sale	45 units		
28	Sale	25 units		
Inventory, Aug. 31		55 units		

Assuming that the inventory consists of 30 units from the August 8 purchase and 25 units from the purchase of August 22, calculate the cost of ending inventory and cost of goods sold.

LO 2 **Average-Cost Method: Periodic Inventory System**

SE3. Using the data in **SE2**, calculate the cost of ending inventory and cost of goods sold according to the average-cost method under the periodic inventory system. (Round your final answer to the nearest dollar.)

LO 2 **FIFO Method: Periodic Inventory System**

SE4. Using the data in **SE2**, calculate the cost of ending inventory and cost of goods sold according to the FIFO method under the periodic inventory system.

LO 2 **LIFO Method: Periodic Inventory System**

SE5. Using the data in **SE2**, calculate the cost of ending inventory and cost of goods sold according to the LIFO method under the periodic inventory system.

LO 3 **Effects of Inventory Costing Methods and Changing Prices**

SE6. Prepare a table with four columns that shows the ending inventory and cost of goods sold for each of the results from your calculations in **SE2** through **SE5**, including the effects of the different prices at which the merchandise was purchased. Which method(s) would result in the lowest income taxes?

LO 4 **Average-Cost Method: Perpetual Inventory System**

SE7. Using the data in **SE2**, calculate the cost of ending inventory and cost of goods sold according to the average-cost method under the perpetual inventory system. (Round to the nearest dollar.)

LO 4 **FIFO Method: Perpetual Inventory System**

SE8. Using the data in **SE2**, calculate the cost of ending inventory and cost of goods sold according to the FIFO method under the perpetual inventory system.

LO 4 **LIFO Method: Perpetual Inventory System**

SE9. Using the data in **SE2**, calculate the cost of ending inventory and cost of goods sold according to the LIFO method under the perpetual inventory system.

LO 5 **Retail Inventory Method**

SE10. Blue Jeans Shop had net retail sales of $390,000 during the current year. The following additional information was obtained from the company's accounting records:

	At Cost	At Retail
Beginning inventory	$ 80,000	$120,000
Net purchases (excluding freight-in)	260,000	420,000
Freight-in	16,400	

Using the retail method, estimate the company's ending inventory at cost. Assuming that a physical count taken at year-end revealed an inventory of $132,000 at retail value, what is the estimated amount of inventory shrinkage (loss due to theft, damage, etc.) at cost using the retail method?

LO 6 **Management Issues**

SE11. BUSINESS APPLICATION ▶ Indicate whether each of the following items is associated with (a) allocating the cost of inventories in accordance with the accrual accounting, (b) assessing the impact of inventory decisions, (c) evaluating the level of inventory, or (d) engaging in an unethical practice:

1. Calculating days' inventory on hand.
2. Ordering a supply of inventory to satisfy customer needs.
3. Valuing inventory at an amount to achieve a specific profit objective.
4. Calculating the income tax effect of an inventory method.
5. Deciding the cost to place on ending inventory.

LO 6 **Inventory Turnover and Days' Inventory on Hand**

SE12. BUSINESS APPLICATION ▶ During 2014, Victoria's Fashion had beginning inventory of $480,000, ending inventory of $560,000, and cost of goods sold of $2,200,000. Compute the inventory turnover and days' inventory on hand. (Round to one decimal place.)

EXERCISES: SET A

LO 1, 2, 3 **Accounting Conventions and Inventory Valuation**

E1A. CONCEPT ▶ Dynamic Company, a telecommunications equipment company, has used the LIFO method adjusted for lower of cost or market for a number of years. Due to falling prices of its equipment, it has had to adjust (reduce) the cost of inventory to market each year for two years. The company is considering changing its method to FIFO adjusted for lower of cost or market in the future. Explain how the accounting conventions of consistency, full disclosure, and conservatism apply to this decision. If the change were made, why would management expect fewer adjustments to market in the future?

LO 2 **Periodic Inventory System and Inventory Costing Methods**

E2A. Portia's Parts Shop recorded the following purchases and sales during the past year:

Jan. 1	Beginning inventory	125 cases @ $23	$ 2,875
Feb. 25	Purchase	100 cases @ $26	2,600
June 15	Purchase	200 cases @ $28	5,600
Oct. 15	Purchase	150 cases @ $28	4,200
Dec. 15	Purchase	100 cases @ $30	3,000
Goods available for sale		675	$18,275
Total sales		500 cases	
Dec. 31	Ending inventory	175 cases	

Assume that the company sold all of the June 15 purchase and 100 cases each from the January 1 beginning inventory, the October 15 purchase, and the December 15 purchase.

Determine the costs that should be assigned to ending inventory and cost of goods sold according to the periodic inventory method under each of the assumptions that follow. (Round to the nearest dollar and assume the periodic inventory system.)

1. Costs are assigned by the specific identification method.
2. Costs are assigned by the average-cost method.
3. Costs are assigned by the FIFO method.
4. Costs are assigned by the LIFO method.
5. **ACCOUNTING CONNECTION ▶** What conclusions can be drawn about the effect of each method on the income statement and the balance sheet of Portia's Parts Shop?

LO **2**

Periodic Inventory System and Inventory Costing Methods

E3A. During its first year of operation, Lux Company purchased 5,600 units of a product at $42 per unit. During the second year, it purchased 6,000 units of the same product at $48 per unit. During the third year, it purchased 5,000 units at $60 per unit. Lux managed to have an ending inventory each year of 1,000 units. The company uses the periodic inventory system.

Prepare cost of goods sold statements that compare the value of ending inventory and the cost of goods sold for each of the three years using

1. the FIFO inventory costing method.
2. the LIFO method.
3. **ACCOUNTING CONNECTION ▶** From the resulting data, what conclusions can you draw about the relationships between the changes in unit price and the changes in the value of ending inventory?

LO **2, 3**

Periodic Inventory System and Inventory Costing Methods

E4A. In chronological order, the inventory, purchases, and sales of a single product for a recent month are as follows.

		Units	Amount per Unit
June 1	Beginning inventory	150	$30
4	Purchase	400	33
12	Purchase	800	36
16	Sale	1,300	60
24	Purchase	300	39

1. Using the periodic inventory system, compute the cost of ending inventory, cost of goods sold, and gross margin. Use the average-cost, FIFO, and LIFO inventory costing methods. (Round unit costs to cents and totals to dollars.)
2. **ACCOUNTING CONNECTION ▶** Explain the differences in gross margin produced by the three methods.

LO 3

Effects of Inventory Costing Methods on Cash Flows

E5A. ACCOUNTING CONNECTION ▶ Mills, Inc., sold 120,000 cases of glue at $20 per case during 2014. Its beginning inventory consisted of 20,000 cases at a cost of $12 per case. During 2014, it purchased 60,000 cases at $14 per case and, later, 50,000 cases at $15 per case. Operating expenses were $550,000, and the applicable income tax rate was 30 percent.

1. Using the periodic inventory system, compute net income using the FIFO method and the LIFO method for costing inventory. Which alternative produces the larger cash flow?
2. The company is considering a purchase of 10,000 cases at $15 per case just before the year end. What effect on net income and on cash flow will this proposed purchase have under each method? (*Hint:* What are the income tax consequences?)

LO 4

Perpetual Inventory System and Inventory Costing Methods

E6A. Refer to the data provided in **E4A.**

1. Using the perpetual inventory system, compute the cost of ending inventory, cost of goods sold, and gross margin. Use the average-cost, FIFO, and LIFO inventory costing methods. (Round unit costs to the nearest cent.)
2. **ACCOUNTING CONNECTION ▶** Explain the reasons for the differences in gross margin produced by the three methods.

LO 2, 4

Periodic and Perpetual Systems and Inventory Costing Methods

E7A. During July 2014, Micanopy, Inc., sold 500 units of its product Empire for $8,000. The following units were available:

	Units	Cost
Beginning inventory	200	$ 2
Purchase 1	80	4
Purchase 2	120	6
Purchase 3	300	9
Purchase 4	180	12

A sale of 500 units was made after purchase 3. Of the units sold, 200 came from beginning inventory and 300 came from purchase 3.

Determine cost of goods available for sale and ending inventory in units. Then determine the costs that should be assigned to cost of goods sold and ending inventory under each of the following assumptions. (For each alternative, show the gross margin. Round unit costs to cents and totals to dollars.)

1. Costs are assigned under the periodic inventory system using (a) the specific identification method, (b) the average-cost method, (c) the FIFO method, and (d) the LIFO method.
2. Costs are assigned under the perpetual inventory system using (a) the average-cost method, (b) the FIFO method, and (c) the LIFO method.

LO 5

Retail Method

E8A. Warmer's Dress Shop had net retail sales of $250,000 during the current year. The following additional information was obtained from the company's accounting records:

	At Cost	At Retail
Beginning inventory	$ 40,000	$ 60,000
Net purchases (excluding freight-in)	140,000	220,000
Freight-in	10,400	

1. Using the retail method, estimate the company's ending inventory at cost.
2. Assume that a physical inventory taken at year end revealed an inventory on hand of $18,000 at retail value. What is the estimated amount of inventory shrinkage (loss due to theft, damage, etc.) at cost using the retail method?

LO 5

Gross Profit Method

E9A. David Patel was at home when he received a call from the fire department telling him his store had burned. His business was a total loss. The insurance company asked him to prove his inventory loss. For the year, until the date of the fire, Patel's company had sales of $450,000 and purchases of $280,000. Freight-in amounted to $13,700, and beginning inventory was $45,000. Patel always priced his goods to achieve a gross margin of 40 percent. Compute Patel's estimated inventory loss.

LO 6

Management Issues

E10A. BUSINESS APPLICATION ▶ Indicate whether each of the following items is associated with (a) allocating the cost of inventories in accordance with the accrual accounting, (b) assessing the impact of inventory decisions, (c) evaluating the level of inventory, or (d) engaging in an unethical action.

1. Application of the just-in-time operating environment.
2. Determining the effects of inventory methods on income taxes.
3. Computing inventory turnover.
4. Valuing inventory at an amount to meet management's targeted net income.
5. Determining the effects of inventory decisions on cash flows.
6. Apportioning the cost of goods available for sale to ending inventory and cost of goods sold.
7. Determining the assumption about the flow of costs into and out of the company.

LO 6

Inventory Ratios

E11A. BUSINESS APPLICATION ▶ Big Sale Stores is assessing its levels of inventory for 2013 and 2014 and has gathered the following data:

	2014	2013	2012
Ending inventory	$192,000	$162,000	$138,000
Cost of goods sold	960,000	900,000	

Compute the inventory turnover and days' inventory on hand for 2013 and 2014 (round to one decimal place), and comment on the results.

LO 6

Effects of Inventory Errors

E12A. BUSINESS APPLICATION ▶ Necessary Toys Company's condensed income statements for two years follow.

	2014	2013
Sales	$252,000	$210,000
Cost of goods sold	150,000	108,000
Gross margin	$102,000	$102,000
Operating expenses	60,000	60,000
Income before income taxes	$ 42,000	$ 42,000

After the end of 2014, the company discovered that an error had resulted in an $18,000 understatement of the 2013 ending inventory.

Compute the corrected operating income for 2013 and 2014. What effect will the error have on operating income and stockholders' equity for 2015?

EXERCISES: SET B

Visit the textbook companion website at www.cengagebrain.com to access Exercise Set B for this chapter.

PROBLEMS

LO **2, 6**

Periodic Inventory System and Inventory Costing Methods

RATIO

SPREADSHEET

✔ 1: Cost of goods available for sale: $10,560,000
✔ 2c: Income before income taxes using LIFO: $740,000

P1. Midori Company merchandises a single product called Gloss. The following data represent beginning inventory and purchases of Gloss during the past year: January 1 inventory, 68,000 units at $11.00; February purchases, 80,000 units at $12.00; March purchases, 160,000 units at $12.40; May purchases, 120,000 units at $12.60; July purchases, 200,000 units at $12.80; September purchases, 160,000 units at $12.60; and November purchases, 60,000 units at $13.00. Sales of Gloss totaled 786,000 units at $20.00 per unit. Selling and administrative expenses totaled $5,102,000 for the year. Midori uses the periodic inventory system.

REQUIRED

1. Prepare a schedule to compute the cost of goods available for sale.
2. Compute income before income taxes under each of the following inventory cost flow assumptions: (a) the average-cost method, (b) the FIFO method, and (c) the LIFO method. (Round cost to the nearest cent.)
3. **BUSINESS APPLICATION ▶** Compute inventory turnover and days' inventory on hand under each of the inventory cost flow assumptions listed in requirement **2**. (Round to one decimal place.) What conclusion can you draw?

LO **2, 3**

Periodic Inventory System and Inventory Costing Methods

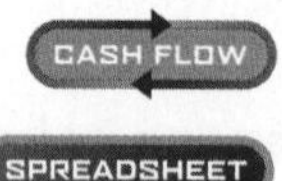

SPREADSHEET

✔ 1: Cost of goods sold for average-cost method: April, $19,320; May, $44,237

P2. The inventory of Wood4Fun and data on purchases and sales for a two-month period follow. The company closes its books at the end of each month. It uses the periodic inventory system.

Apr.	1	Beginning inventory	50 units @ $204
	10	Purchase	100 units @ $220
	17	Sale	90 units
	30	Ending inventory	60 units
May	2	Purchase	100 units @ $216
	14	Purchase	50 units @ $224
	22	Purchase	60 units @ $234
	30	Sale	200 units
	31	Ending inventory	70 units

REQUIRED

1. Compute the cost of ending inventory of Wood4Fun on April 30 and May 31 using the average-cost method. In addition, determine cost of goods sold for April and May. (Round unit costs to the nearest cent.)
2. Compute the cost of the ending inventory on April 30 and May 31 using the FIFO method. In addition, determine cost of goods sold for April and May.
3. Compute the cost of the ending inventory on April 30 and May 31 using the LIFO method. In addition, determine cost of goods sold for April and May.
4. **ACCOUNTING CONNECTION ▶** Do the cash flows from operations for April and May differ depending on which inventory costing method is used—average-cost, FIFO, or LIFO? Explain.

LO 3, 4, 6

RATIO

✔ 3: Cost of goods sold for LIFO method: April, $19,800; May, $44,680

Perpetual Inventory System and Inventory Costing Methods

P3. Use the data provided in **P2**, but assume that the company uses the perpetual inventory system. (*Hint:* In preparing the solutions, it is helpful to determine the balance of inventory after each transaction, as shown in the Review Problem.)

REQUIRED

1. Determine the cost of ending inventory and cost of goods sold for April and May using the average-cost method. (Round unit costs to the nearest cent.)
2. Determine the cost of ending inventory and cost of goods sold for April and May using the FIFO method.
3. Determine the cost of ending inventory and cost of goods sold for April and May using the LIFO method.
4. **BUSINESS APPLICATION ▶** Assume that this company grows for many years in a long period of rising prices. How realistic do you think the balance sheet value for inventory would be and what effect would it have on the inventory turnover ratio?

LO 5

✔ 3: Estimated inventory shortage: at cost, $24,208; at retail, $35,600

Retail Method

P4. Quester Company operates a large discount store and uses the retail method to estimate the cost of ending inventory. Management suspects that in recent weeks there have been unusually heavy losses from shoplifting or employee pilferage. To estimate the amount of the loss, the company has taken a physical inventory and will compare the results with the estimated cost of inventory. Data from Quester's accounting records follow.

	At Cost	At Retail
August 1 beginning inventory	$205,952	$297,200
Purchases	286,932	434,000
Purchases returns and allowances	(8,172)	(12,800)
Freight-in	3,800	
Sales		436,732
Sales returns and allowances		(3,732)
August 31 physical inventory at retail		249,800

REQUIRED

1. Using the retail method, prepare a schedule to estimate the dollar amount of the store's month-end inventory at cost.
2. Use the store's cost to retail ratio to reduce the retail value of the physical inventory to cost.
3. Calculate the estimated amount of inventory shortage at cost and at retail.
4. **ACCOUNTING CONNECTION ▶** Many retail chains use the retail method because it is efficient. Why do you think using this method is an efficient way for these companies to operate?

LO 5

✔ 1: Estimated loss of inventory in fire: $326,513.50

Gross Profit Method

P5. Groh Brothers is a large retail furniture company that operates in two adjacent warehouses. One warehouse is a showroom, and the other is used to store merchandise. On the night of June 22, 2014, a fire broke out in the storage warehouse and destroyed the merchandise stored there. Fortunately, the fire did not reach the showroom, so all the merchandise on display was saved.

Although the company maintained a perpetual inventory system, its records were rather haphazard, and the last reliable physical inventory had been taken on December 31. In addition, there was no control of the flow of goods between the showroom and the warehouse. Thus, it was impossible to tell what goods should have been in either place. As a result, the insurance company required an independent estimate of the amount of loss. The insurance company examiners were satisfied when they received the following information:

(Continued)

Merchandise inventory on December 31, 2013	$363,700.00
Purchases, January 1 to June 22, 2014	603,050.00
Purchases returns, January 1 to June 22, 2014	(2,676.50)
Freight-in, January 1 to June 22, 2014	13,275.00
Sales, January 1 to June 22, 2014	989,762.50
Sales returns, January 1 to June 22, 2014	(7,450.00)
Merchandise inventory in showroom on June 22, 2014	100,740.00
Average gross margin	44%

REQUIRED

1. Prepare a schedule that estimates the amount of the inventory lost in the fire.
2. **ACCOUNTING CONNECTION ▶** What are some other reasons management might need to estimate the amount of inventory?

ALTERNATE PROBLEMS

LO 2, 6

SPREADSHEET

✔ 1: Cost of goods available for sale: $157,980
✔ 2c: Income before income taxes using LIFO: $101,850

Periodic Inventory System and Inventory Costing Methods

P6. Aberdeen Company sold 2,200 cabinets during 2014 at $160 per cabinet. Its beginning inventory on January 1 was 130 cabinets at $56. Purchases made during the year were as follows.

February	225 cabinets @ $62.00
April	350 cabinets @ $65.00
June	700 cabinets @ $70.00
August	300 cabinets @ $66.00
October	400 cabinets @ $68.00
November	250 cabinets @ $72.00

The company's selling and administrative expenses for the year were $101,000. The company uses the periodic inventory system.

REQUIRED

1. Prepare a schedule to compute the cost of goods available for sale.
2. Compute income before income taxes under each of the following inventory cost flow assumptions: (a) the average-cost method, (b) the FIFO method, and (c) the LIFO method. (Round unit cost to the nearest cent, and total costs to the nearest dollar.)
3. **BUSINESS APPLICATION ▶** Compute inventory turnover and days' inventory on hand under each of the inventory cost flow assumptions in requirement **2**. (Round to one decimal place.) What conclusion can you draw from this comparison?

LO 2, 3

SPREADSHEET

✔ 1: Cost of goods sold for average-cost method: March, $4,578; April, $10,660

Periodic Inventory System and Inventory Costing Methods

P7. DiPaolo's inventory, purchases, and sales for March and April follow. The company closes its books at the end of each month. It uses the periodic inventory system.

Mar.	1	Beginning inventory	60 units @ $49
	10	Purchase	100 units @ $52
	19	Sale	90 units
	31	Ending inventory	70 units
Apr.	4	Purchase	120 units @ $53
	15	Purchase	50 units @ $54
	23	Sale	200 units
	25	Purchase	100 units @ $55
	30	Ending inventory	140 units

REQUIRED

1. Compute the cost of the ending inventory on March 31 and April 30 using the average-cost method. In addition, determine cost of goods sold for March and April. (Round unit costs to the nearest cent.)
2. Compute the cost of the ending inventory on March 31 and April 30 using the FIFO method. Also determine cost of goods sold for March and April.
3. Compute the cost of the ending inventory on March 31 and April 30 using the LIFO method. Also determine cost of goods sold for March and April.
4. **ACCOUNTING CONNECTION ▶** Do the cash flows from operations for March and April differ depending on which inventory costing method is used—average-cost, FIFO, or LIFO? Explain.

LO 3, 4, 6

Perpetual Inventory System and Inventory Costing Methods

✔ 3: Cost of goods sold for LIFO method: March, $4,680; April, $10,560

P8. Use the data provided in **P7**, but assume that the company uses the perpetual inventory system. (*Hint*: In preparing the solutions, it is helpful to determine the balance of inventory after each transaction, as shown in the Review Problem.)

REQUIRED

1. Determine the cost of ending inventory and cost of goods sold for March and April using the average-cost method. (Round unit costs to the nearest cent.)
2. Determine the cost of ending inventory and cost of goods sold for March and April using the FIFO method.
3. Determine the cost of ending inventory and cost of goods sold for March and April using the LIFO method.
4. **BUSINESS APPLICATION ▶** Assume that this company grows for many years in a long period of rising prices. How realistic do you think the balance sheet value for inventory would be and what effect would it have on the inventory turnover ratio?

LO 5

Retail Method

✔ 3: Estimated inventory shortage: at cost, $3,456; at retail, $4,800

P9. Alberta Company operates a large discount store and uses the retail method to estimate the cost of ending inventory. Management suspects that in recent weeks there have been unusually heavy losses from shoplifting or employee pilferage. To estimate the amount of the loss, the company has taken a physical inventory and will compare the results with the estimated cost of inventory. Data from Alberta's accounting records follow.

	At Cost	At Retail
October 1 beginning inventory	$184,000	$239,200
Purchases	261,500	383,300
Purchases returns and allowances	(7,360)	(10,500)
Freight-in	2,500	
Sales		514,300
Sales returns and allowances		(2,700)
October 31 physical inventory at retail		95,600

REQUIRED

1. Using the retail method, prepare a schedule to estimate the dollar amount of the store's month-end inventory at cost.
2. Use the store's cost to retail ratio to reduce the retail value of the physical inventory to cost.
3. Calculate the estimated amount of inventory shortage at cost and at retail.
4. **ACCOUNTING CONNECTION ▶** Many retail chains use the retail method because it is efficient. Why do you think using this method is an efficient way for these companies to operate?

LO 5

Gross Profit Method

✓ 1: Estimated loss of inventory in fire: $1,306,054

P10. Zubac Company is a large retail furniture company that operates in two adjacent warehouses. One warehouse is a showroom, and the other is used to store merchandise. On the night of April 22, 2014, a fire broke out in the storage warehouse and destroyed the merchandise stored there. Fortunately, the fire did not reach the showroom, so all the merchandise on display was saved.

Although the company maintained a perpetual inventory system, its records were rather haphazard, and the last reliable physical inventory had been taken on December 31. In addition, there was no control of the flow of goods between the showroom and the warehouse. Thus, it was impossible to tell what goods should have been in either place. As a result, the insurance company required an independent estimate of the amount of loss. The insurance company examiners were satisfied when they received the following information:

Merchandise inventory on December 31, 2013	$1,454,800
Purchases, January 1 to April 22, 2014	2,412,200
Purchases returns, January 1 to April 22, 2014	(10,706)
Freight-in, January 1 to April 22, 2014	53,100
Sales, January 1 to April 22, 2014	3,959,050
Sales returns, January 1 to April 22, 2014	(29,800)
Merchandise inventory in showroom on April 22, 2014	402,960
Average gross margin	44%

REQUIRED

1. Prepare a schedule that estimates the amount of the inventory lost in the fire.
2. **ACCOUNTING CONNECTION ▶** What are some other reasons management might need to estimate the amount of inventory?

CASES

LO 2, 3

Conceptual Understanding: LIFO Inventory Method

C1. Sixty-eight percent of chemical companies use the LIFO inventory method for the costing of inventories, whereas only 13 percent of computer equipment companies use LIFO.[10]

Describe the LIFO inventory method. What effects does it have on reported income, cash flows, and income taxes during periods of price changes? Why do you think so many chemical companies use LIFO and most companies in the computer industry do not?

LO 1

Interpreting Financial Reports: LCM and Conservatism

C2. CONCEPT ▶ ExxonMobil Corporation, the world's second-largest company, uses the LIFO inventory method for most of its inventories. Its inventory costs are heavily dependent on the cost of oil. When the price of oil was down, ExxonMobil, following the lower-of-cost-or-market (LCM) rule, wrote down its inventory by $325 million. In the next year, when the price of oil recovered, the company reported that market price exceeded the LIFO carrying values by $6.8 billion.[11] Explain why the LCM rule resulted in a write-down in the first year. What is the inconsistency between the first- and second-year treatments of the change in the price of oil? How does the accounting convention of conservatism explain the inconsistency? If the price of oil declined substantially in a third year, what would be the likely consequence?

LO 2, 3

Interpreting Financial Reports: FIFO and LIFO

C3. ExxonMobil Corporation had net income of $41.0 billion in 2011. Inventories under the LIFO method used by the company were $11.7 billion in 2011. Inventory would have been $25.6 billion higher if the company had used FIFO.[12] Why do you suppose ExxonMobil's management chooses to use the LIFO inventory method? On what economic conditions, if any, do those reasons depend?

LO 1, 3, 5, 6

Annual Report Case: Inventory Costing Methods and Ratios

C4. BUSINESS APPLICATION ▶ Refer to the note related to inventories in the **CVS** annual report in the Supplement to Chapter 1 to answer the following questions: What inventory method(s) does CVS use? Do you think many of the company's inventories are valued at market? Why or why not? Few companies use the retail method, so why do you think CVS uses it? Compute and compare the inventory turnover and days' inventory on hand for CVS for 2011 and 2010. Ending inventories in 2009 were $10,343 million. (Round to one decimal place.)

LO 6

Comparison Analysis: Inventory Efficiency

C5. BUSINESS APPLICATION ▶ Refer to **CVS**'s annual report in the Supplement to Chapter 1 and to the following data (in millions) for **Walgreens**: cost of goods sold, $51,692 and $48,444 for 2011 and 2010, respectively; inventories, $8,044, $7,378, and $6,789 for 2011, 2010, and 2009, respectively.[13] Ending inventories for 2009 for CVS were $10,343 million.

Calculate inventory turnover and days' inventory on hand for 2010 and 2011. (Round to one decimal place.) If you did **C4**, refer to your answer there for CVS. Has either company improved its performance in these areas over the past two years? If so, what advantage does this give the company? Which company appears to make the most efficient use of inventories? Explain your answers.

LO 6

Evaluation of Inventory Levels

RATIO

C6. BUSINESS APPLICATION ▶ JCPenney, a large retail company with many stores, has an inventory turnover of about 3.8 times. **Dell Computer Corporation**, an Internet mail-order company, has an inventory turnover of about 36.0. Dell achieves its high turnover through supply-chain management in a just-in-time operating environment. Why is inventory turnover important to companies like JCPenney and Dell? Why are comparisons among companies important? Are JCPenney and Dell a good match for comparison? Describe supply-chain management and a just-in-time operating environment. Why are they important to achieving a favorable inventory turnover?

LO 3, 6

Ethical Dilemma: Inventories, Income Determination, and Ethics

C7. Lady, Inc., whose fiscal year ends on December 31, designs and sells fashions for young professional women. Margaret Lutz, president of the company, fears that the forecasted profitability goals for 2014 will not be reached. She is pleased when Lady, Inc., receives a large order on December 30, 2014, from The Executive Woman, a retail chain of upscale stores for businesswomen. Lutz immediately directs the controller to record the sale, which represents 13 percent of Lady's annual sales. At the same time, she directs the inventory control department not to separate the goods for shipment until after January 1, 2015. Separated goods are not included in inventory because they have been sold.

On December 31, 2014, the company's auditors arrive to observe the year-end taking of the physical inventory under the periodic inventory system. How will Lutz's actions affect Lady's profitability in 2014? How will they affect Lady's profitability in 2015? Were Lutz's actions ethical? Why or why not?

Continuing Case: Annual Report Project

C8. Using the most recent annual report of the company you have chosen to study and that you have accessed online at the company's website, examine inventory(ies) on the balance sheet and accompanying note on inventory(ies) of your company. Answer the following questions:

(Continued)

1. What percentage is inventory(ies) to total current assets? Do you think this percentage represents the importance of inventory(ies) to the company's operations?
2. Find the note about inventory(ies) in the notes to the financial statements. Does the company have more than one type of inventory? If so, what are they? What method(s) are used to value inventory(ies)? What other facts, if any, are disclosed about inventory(ies) in the note?
3. **BUSINESS APPLICATION ▶** Calculate inventory turnover and days' inventory on hand for the most recent two years. (Round to one decimal place.) Has the company improved its performance in these areas over the past two years?

CHAPTER 7

LEARNING OBJECTIVES

LO 1 Describe the components of internal control, control activities, and limitations on internal control.

LO 2 Apply internal control activities to common merchandising transactions.

LO 3 Define *cash equivalents*, and explain methods of controlling cash, including bank reconciliations.

LO 4 Demonstrate the use of a simple imprest (petty cash) system.

LO 5 Identify the internal control roles of management and the auditor.

Ulrich Baumgarten/Getty Images

CASH AND INTERNAL CONTROL

Business Insight
Subway

Subway, a popular sandwich restaurant chain with over 37,000 locations in more than 100 countries, is one of the largest privately owned companies in the United States. Each location handles large amounts of food and hundreds of cash transactions per day, which means that the owners must protect against possible theft of inventory and cash and ensure that all transactions are recorded properly. Subway often borrows money to finance its operations and for expansion.

1. **CONCEPT ▶** Why are each of the five components of internal control important to the faithful representation of a company's operations in its financial statements?
2. **ACCOUNTING APPLICATION ▶** How can Subway maintain control over its inventory and cash?
3. **BUSINESS APPLICATION ▶** How can Subway's bank and other users of its financial statements be confident that the restaurant has an adequate system of internal control?

SECTION 1 CONCEPTS

CONCEPT
- Faithful representation

RELEVANT LEARNING OBJECTIVE

LO 1 Describe the components of internal control, control activities, and limitations on internal control.

LO 1 Concepts Underlying Internal Control

It is important that a company's financial statements *faithfully represent* the company's operations. This means, for instance, that the financial statements are *free from material error.* **Internal control** is a process that achieves this goal by establishing the *reliability* of the accounting records and financial statements and ensures that the company's assets are protected.[1]

The Need for Internal Controls

Buying and selling, the principal transactions of merchandising businesses, involve assets—cash, accounts receivable, and merchandise inventory—that are vulnerable to theft and embezzlement. This potential for embezzlement exists because the large number of transactions that are usually involved in a merchandising business (e.g., cash receipts, receipts on account, payments for purchases, and receipts and shipments of inventory) makes monitoring the accounting records difficult. If a merchandising company does not take steps to protect its assets, it can suffer high losses of both cash and inventory. Management's responsibility is to establish an environment, accounting systems, and internal control procedures that will protect the assets.

A company's merchandise inventory includes the following:

- all goods intended for sale regardless of where they are located—on shelves, in storerooms, in warehouses, or in trucks between warehouses and stores
- goods in transit from suppliers if title to the goods has passed to the merchandiser

Ending inventory does not include the following:

- merchandise that a company has sold but not yet delivered to customers
- goods that it cannot sell because they are damaged or obsolete

Taking a **physical inventory** facilitates control over merchandise inventory. This process involves an actual count of all merchandise on hand. A physical inventory must be taken under both the periodic and the perpetual inventory systems. Merchandisers usually take a physical inventory after the close of business on the last day of their fiscal year. To facilitate the process, they often end the fiscal year in a slow season, when inventories are at relatively low levels. For example, many department stores end their fiscal year in January or February. After hours—at night, on a weekend, or when the store closes for taking inventory—employees count all items and record the results on numbered inventory tickets or sheets, following procedures to ensure that no items will be missed. Using bar coding to take inventory electronically has greatly facilitated the process in many companies.

Most companies experience losses of merchandise inventory from spoilage, shoplifting, and theft. Inventory shortages can also result from honest mistakes, such as accidentally tagging inventory with the wrong number. The periodic inventory system provides no means of identifying these losses because the costs are automatically included in the cost of goods sold. For example, suppose a company has lost $1,250 in stolen merchandise during a period. When the physical inventory is taken, the missing items are not in stock, so they cannot be counted. Because the ending inventory does not contain these items, the amount subtracted from the cost of goods available for sale is less than it would be if the goods were in stock. The cost of goods sold, then, is overstated by $1,250.

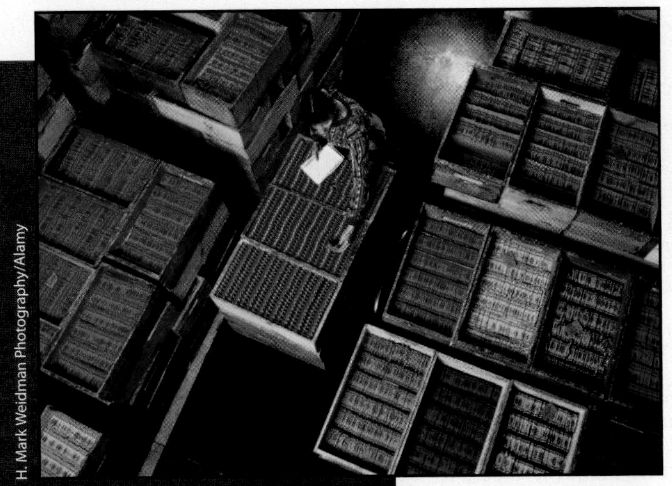
H. Mark Weidman Photography/Alamy

Merchandise inventory includes all goods intended for sale wherever they are located—on store shelves, in warehouses, on car lots, or in transit from suppliers if title to the goods has passed to the merchandiser. To prevent loss of inventory, a merchandiser must have an effective system of internal control.

The perpetual inventory system makes it easier to identify such losses. Because the Merchandise Inventory account is continuously updated for sales, purchases, and returns, the loss will show up as the difference between the inventory records and the physical inventory taken at the end of the accounting period. Once the amount of the loss has been identified, the ending inventory is updated by crediting the Merchandise Inventory account. The offsetting debit is usually an increase in Cost of Goods Sold because the loss is considered a cost that reduces the company's gross margin.

Components of Internal Control

An effective system of internal control has five interrelated components.[2]

Control Environment The **control environment** is created by management's overall attitude, awareness, and actions. It encompasses the following:

- a company's ethics, philosophy and operating style
- organizational structure
- method of assigning authority and responsibility
- personnel policies and practices

Personnel should be qualified to handle responsibilities, which means that they must be trained and informed about what is expected of them. For example, the manager of a retail store should train employees to follow prescribed procedures for handling cash sales, credit card sales, and returns and refunds.

Risk Assessment **Risk assessment** involves identifying areas in which risks of loss of assets or inaccuracies in accounting records are high so that adequate controls can be implemented. Among the greater risks in a retail store are that employees or customers may steal cash or goods.

STUDY NOTE: *An adjustment to the Merchandise Inventory account will be needed if the physical inventory reveals a difference between the actual inventory and the amount in the records.*

Control Activities The policies and procedures management puts in place to see that its directives are carried out are called **control activities**.

Information and Communication **Information and communication** pertains to the way the accounting system gathers and treats information about the company's transactions and to how it communicates individual responsibilities within the system.

Monitoring Management's regular assessment of the quality of internal control, including periodic review of compliance with all policies and procedure, is part of **monitoring**. Large companies often have a staff of internal auditors who review the system of internal control to determine if it is working properly and if procedures are being followed. In smaller businesses, owners and managers conduct these reviews.

Control Activities

The goal of control activities is to safeguard a company's assets and ensure the reliability of its accounting records. Some standard control activities follow.

Authorization **Authorization** is the approval of certain transactions and activities. In a retail store, for example, cashiers customarily authorize cash sales; but other transactions, such as issuing a refund, may require a manager's approval.

Recording Transactions To establish accountability for assets, all transactions should be recorded. For example, if a retail store uses a cash register that records sales, refunds, and other transactions on a paper tape or computer disk, the cashier can be held accountable for the cash received and the merchandise removed during his or her shift.

Business Perspective

Shoplifters: Beware!

With theft from shoplifting approaching $30 billion per year, retailers are increasing their use of physical controls beyond the usual electronic warning if a customer tries to walk out without paying. Companies, such as **Macy's** and **Babies 'R' Us**, have installed more than 6 million video cameras in stores across the country. Advanced surveillance software can compare a shopper's movements between video images and recognize unusual activity. For instance, removing 10 items from a shelf or opening a drawer that normally is closed would trigger the system to alert a security guard.[3]

Documents and Records Well-designed documents help ensure that transactions are properly recorded. For example, using prenumbered invoices and other documents is a way of ensuring that all transactions are recorded.

Physical Controls **Physical controls** limit access to assets. For example, in a retail store, only the person responsible for the cash register should have access to it. Other employees should not be able to open the cash drawer when the cashier is not present. Similarly, only authorized personnel should have access to warehouses and storerooms. Access to accounting records, including those stored in company computers, should also be controlled.

Periodic Independent Verification **Periodic independent verification** means that someone other than the people responsible for the accounting records and assets should periodically check the records against the assets. For example, at the end of each shift or day in a retail store, the owner or manager should count the cash in the cash drawer and compare the amount with the amount recorded on the tape or computer disk in the cash register. Other examples of independent verification are periodic counts of physical inventory and reconciliations of monthly bank statements.

Separation of Duties **Separation of duties** means that no one person should authorize transactions, handle assets, and keep records of assets. For example, in a well-managed electronics store, each employee oversees only a single part of a transaction. A sales employee takes the order and creates an invoice. Another employee receives the customer's cash or credit card payment and issues a receipt. Once the customer has a receipt, and only then, a third employee obtains the item from the warehouse and gives it to the customer. A person in the accounting department subsequently compares all sales recorded in the cash register with the sales invoices and updates the inventory in the accounting records. The separation of duties means that a mistake, careless or not, cannot be made without being seen by at least one other person.

Sound Personnel Practices: Personnel practices that promote internal control include the following:

- adequate supervision
- rotation of key people among different jobs
- insistence that employees take vacations
- bonding of personnel who handle cash or inventory

Bonding is the process of carefully checking an employee's background and insuring the company against theft by that person. Bonding does not guarantee against theft, but it does prevent or reduce loss if theft occurs. Prudent personnel practices help ensure that employees know their jobs, are honest, and will find it difficult to carry out and conceal embezzlement over time.

Internal Control and Achieving Control Objectives

A system of internal control applied effectively to merchandising transactions can achieve important management objectives. As noted, it can prevent losses of cash and inventory due to theft or fraud, and it can ensure that records of transactions and account balances are accurate. It can also help managers achieve the following broader objectives:

- Keep enough inventory on hand to sell to customers without overstocking merchandise.
- Keep sufficient cash on hand to pay for purchases in time to receive discounts.
- Keep credit losses as low as possible by making credit sales only to customers who are likely to pay on time.

Limitations on Internal Control

STUDY NOTE: *While no control procedure can guarantee the prevention of theft, the more that are in place, the less likely it is that theft will occur.*

No system of internal control is without weaknesses. As long as people perform control procedures, an internal control system will be vulnerable to human error. Errors can arise from misunderstandings, mistakes in judgment, carelessness, distraction, or fatigue. Separation of duties can be defeated through collusion by employees who secretly agree to deceive a company. In addition, established procedures may be ineffective against employees' errors or dishonesty, and controls that were initially effective may become ineffective when conditions change.

In some cases, the costs of establishing and maintaining elaborate control systems may exceed the benefits. In a small business, for example, active involvement by the owner can be a practical substitute for the separation of some duties.

Business Perspective
Which Frauds Are Most Common in Retail?

The frauds commonly facing retailers are credit card, check fraud, false invoices and phantom vendors, and expense account abuse. The most common reasons for the occurrences of these frauds are poor internal controls over cashiers, management override of internal controls, and collusion. The most common methods of detecting them are good control procedures over cash receipts at the cash register, internal auditor review, notification by a customer, and accidental discovery. Companies that are successful in preventing fraud have a good system of internal control, a formal code of ethics, and a program to monitor compliance that includes a system for reporting incidents of fraud. These companies routinely communicate the existence of the program to their employees.[4]

APPLY IT!

Match the internal control components with the related statements that follow.

a. Control environment
b. Risk assessment
c. Control activities
d. Information and communication
e. Monitoring

1. Establishes separation of duties.
2. Communicates appropriate information to employees.
3. Has an internal audit department.
4. Periodic independent verification of employees' work.
5. Assesses the possibility of losses.
6. Instructs and trains employees.
7. Has well-designed documents and records.
8. Limits physical access to authorized personnel.

SOLUTION

1. c; 2. d; 3. e; 4. c; 5. b; 6. a; 7. c; 8. c

TRY IT! SE1, SE2, SE3, SE4, E1A, E2A, E3A, E1B, E2B, E3B

SECTION 2 ACCOUNTING APPLICATIONS

ACCOUNTING APPLICATIONS

- Account for merchandising transactions
- Implement control of cash
- Prepare a bank reconciliation
- Use petty cash

RELEVANT LEARNING OBJECTIVES

LO 2 Apply internal control activities to common merchandising transactions.

LO 3 Define *cash equivalents*, and explain methods of controlling cash, including bank reconciliations.

LO 4 Demonstrate the use of a simple imprest (petty cash) system.

LO 2 Internal Control over Merchandising Transactions

It's clear that sound internal control activities are needed when assets are involved. We now turn our attention to how merchandising companies apply internal control activities to business transactions. Maintaining internal control is especially difficult for a merchandiser because management must not only establish controls for cash sales, receipts, purchases, and cash payments, but also protect its inventory. Service and manufacturing businesses use similar procedures.

One control that managers use is the cash budget, which projects future cash receipts and disbursements. By maintaining adequate cash balances, a company is able to take advantage of discounts on purchases, prepared to borrow money when necessary, and able to avoid the damaging effects of being unable to pay bills when they are due. By investing excess cash, the company can earn interest until the cash is needed.

A more specific control is the separation of duties that involve the handling of cash. Such separation makes theft without detection extremely unlikely unless two or more employees conspire. The separation of duties is easier in large businesses than in small ones, where one person may have to carry out several duties. The effectiveness of internal control over cash varies, based on the size and nature of the company. Most firms, however, should use the following procedures:

- Separate the functions of authorization, recordkeeping, and custodianship of cash.
- Limit the number of people who have access to cash, and designate who those people are.
- Bond all employees who have access to cash.
- Keep the amount of cash on hand to a minimum by using banking facilities as much as possible.
- Physically protect cash on hand by using cash registers, cashiers' cages, and safes.
- Record and deposit all cash receipts promptly, and make payments by check rather than by currency.
- Have a person who does not handle or record cash make unannounced audits of the cash on hand.
- Have a person who does not authorize, handle, or record cash transactions reconcile the Cash account each month.

Each of these procedures helps safeguard cash by making it more difficult for any one individual to steal or misuse it without being detected.

Business Perspective

Are Money Market Funds Always a Safe Bet?

When companies have more cash than they need for current operations, they often earn interest on their excess cash by investing it in money market funds. Investments in money market funds have traditionally been considered safe because these funds have usually invested in very safe securities. However, in recent years, in an attempt to earn a slightly higher interest rate, a few money market funds invested in batches of subprime mortgages. This turned out to be a very poor decision. **Bank of America**, for instance, had to shut down its $34 billion money market fund—called Columbia Strategic Cash Portfolio—when investors pulled out $21 billion because the fund was losing a great deal of money due to its investment in subprime loans.[5]

Control of Cash Receipts

Cash payments for sales of goods and services can be received by mail or over the counter in the form of checks, credit or debit cards, or currency. Whatever the source of the cash, it should be recorded immediately in a cash receipts journal. Such a journal establishes a written record that should prevent errors and make theft more difficult.

Control of Cash Received by Mail Cash received by mail is vulnerable to theft by the employees who handle it. For that reason, companies that deal in mail-order sales generally ask customers to pay by credit card, check, or money order instead of with currency.

When cash is received in the mail, two or more employees should handle it. The employee who opens the mail should make a list in triplicate of the money received. The list should contain each customer's name, the purpose for which the money was sent, and the amount. One copy goes with the cash to the cashier, who deposits the money. The second copy goes to the accounting department for recording. The person who opens the mail keeps the third copy. Errors can be easily caught because the amount deposited by the cashier must agree with the amount received and the amount recorded in the cash receipts journal.

STUDY NOTE: *The cashier should not be allowed to remove the cash register tape or to record the day's cash receipts.*

Control of Cash Received Over the Counter Cash registers and prenumbered sales tickets are common tools for controlling cash received over the counter. The amount of a cash sale is rung up on the cash register at the time of the sale. The register should be placed so that the customer can see the amount recorded. Each cash register should have a locked-in tape on which it prints the day's transactions. At the end of the day, the cashier counts the cash in the register and turns it in to the cashier's office. Another employee takes the tape out of the cash register and records the cash receipts for the day in the cash receipts journal. The amount of cash turned in and the amount recorded on the tape should agree; if not, any differences must be explained.

Large retail chains like **Costco** commonly monitor cash receipts by having each cash register tied directly into a computer that records each transaction. Whether the elements are performed manually or with a computer, separating responsibility for cash receipts, cash deposits, and recordkeeping is necessary to ensure good internal control.

In some stores, internal control is further strengthened by the use of prenumbered sales tickets and a central cash register or cashier's office, where all sales are rung up and collected by a person who does not participate in the sale. The salesperson completes a prenumbered sales ticket at the time of the sale, giving one copy to the customer and keeping a copy. At the end of the day, all sales tickets must be accounted for, and the sales total computed from the sales tickets must equal the total sales recorded on the cash register.

Control of Purchases and Cash Disbursements

Cash disbursements are particularly vulnerable to fraud and embezzlement. In one case, the treasurer of one of the nation's largest jewelry retailers was charged with stealing

Business Perspective
How Do Computers Promote Internal Control?

Building good internal controls into accounting programs is a difficult challenge for computer programmers. These programs must include controls that prevent unintentional errors, as well as unauthorized access and tampering. They prevent errors through reasonableness checks (such as not allowing any transactions over a specified amount), mathematical checks that verify the arithmetic of transactions, and sequence checks that require documents and transactions to be in proper order. They typically use passwords and questions about randomly selected personal data to prevent unauthorized access to computer records. They may also use *firewalls*, which are strong electronic barriers to unauthorized access, and *data encryption*, which is a way of coding data so that if they are stolen, they are useless to the thief.

over $500,000 by systematically overpaying the company's federal income taxes and keeping the refund checks.

To avoid this type of theft, cash payments should be made only after they have been specifically authorized and supported by documents that establish the validity and amount of the claims. A company should also separate the duties involved in purchasing goods and services and the duties involved in paying for them. The degree of separation that is possible varies, depending on the size of the business.

Exhibit 1 shows how a large company can maximize the separation of duties. Five internal units (the requesting department, the purchasing department, the accounting department, the receiving department, and the treasurer) and two firms outside the company (the vendor and the bank) play a role in this control plan. Notice that business documents are crucial components of the plan.

Exhibit 1
Internal Controls in a Large Company: Separation of Duties and Documentation

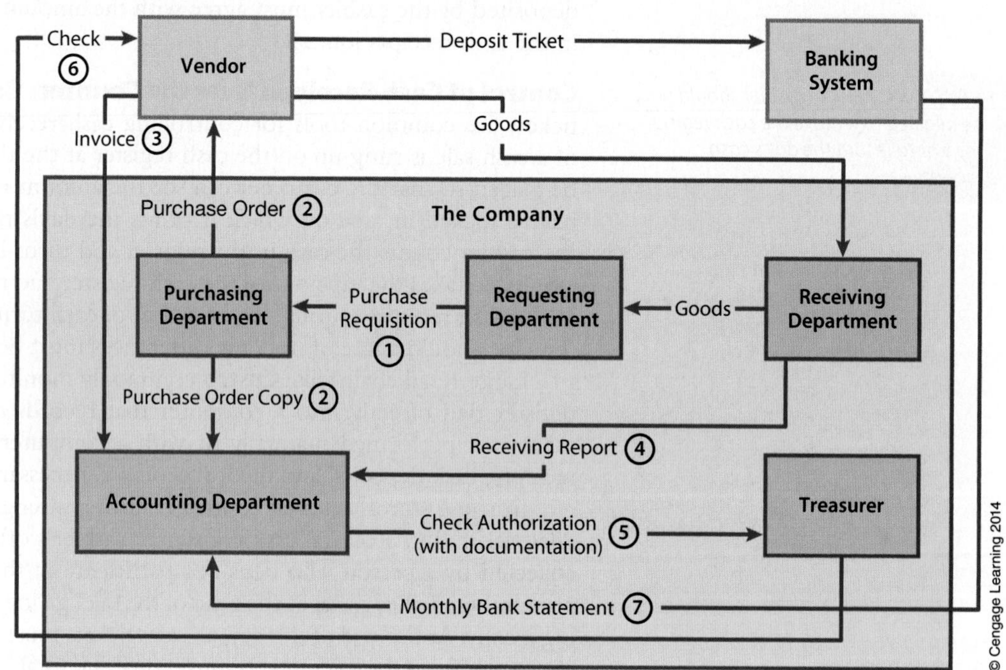

Note: Circled numbers refer to documents in Exhibit 2.

***STUDY NOTE:** Every business document must have a number for purposes of reference.*

Exhibit 2 illustrates the typical sequence in which documents are used in a company's internal control plan for purchases and cash disbursements.

Exhibit 2
Internal Control Plan for Purchases and Cash Disbursements

① PURCHASE REQUISITION No. 7077

Wagon Sportswear Corporation

From: Credit Office Date: July 1, 2014

To: Purchasing Department Suggested Vendor: Henderson Supply Company

Please purchase the following items:

Quantity	Number	Description
20 boxes	X 144	Office supplies

Reason for Request: Six months' supply for office

Approved: J.P.

To be filled in by Purchasing Department

Date ordered 7/2/2014 P.O. No. J 102

② PURCHASE ORDER No. J 102

Wagon Sportswear Corporation
8428 Rocky Island Avenue
Chicago, Illinois 60643

To: Henderson Supply Company
2525 25th Street
Mesa, Illinois 61611

Date: July 2, 2014
FOB: Destination
Ship by: July 5, 2014
Terms: 2/10, n/30

Ship to: Laboda Sportswear Corporation
Above Address

Please ship the following:

Quantity	✓	Number	Description	Price	Per	Amount
20 boxes		X 144	Office Supplies	260.00	box	$5,200.00

Purchase order number must appear on all shipments and invoices.

Ordered by Marsha Owen

③ INVOICE No. 0468

Henderson Supply Company
2525 25th Street
Mesa, Illinois 61611

Date: July 5, 2014
Your Order No.: J 102

Sold to:
Wagon Sportswear Corporation
8428 Rocky Island Avenue
Chicago, Illinois 60643

Ship to: Same

Sales Representative: Joe Jacobs

Quantity		Description	Price	Per	Amount
Ordered	Shipped				
20	20	Office Supplies	260.00	box	$5,200.00

FOB Destination | Terms: 2/10, n/30 | Date Shipped: 7/5/2014 Via: Self

④ RECEIVING REPORT No. JR065

Wagon Sportswear Corporation
8428 Rocky Island Avenue
Chicago, Illinois 60643

Date: July 5, 2014

Quantity	Number	Description	Condition
20 boxes	X 144	Office Supplies	O.K.

Received by B.M.

⑤ CHECK AUTHORIZATION

	NO.	CHECK
Purchase Order	J 102	✓
Receiving Report	JR065	✓
INVOICE	0468	✓
Price		✓
Calculations		✓
Terms		✓

Approved for Payment J. Joseph

⑥

Wagon Sportswear Corporation
8428 Rocky Island Avenue
Chicago, Illinois 60643

NO. 2570
61-153/313

7/14 20 14

PAY TO THE ORDER OF Henderson Supply Company $ 5,096.00

Five thousand ninety-six and 00/100 Dollars

THE LAKE PARK NATIONAL BANK
Chicago, Illinois

Wagon Sportswear Corporation

⑆031301532⑆ ⑈8030 647 4⑈ by Arthur Martin

Remittance Advice

Date	P.O. No.	DESCRIPTION	AMOUNT
7/14/2010	J 102	20 X 144 office supplies Supplier Inv. No. 0468 Less 2% discount Net Wagon Sportswear Corporation	 $5,200.00 104.00 $5,096.00

⑦ Statement of Account with THE LAKE PARK NATIONAL BANK
Chicago, Illinois

Wagon Sportswear Corporation
8428 Rocky Island Avenue
Chicago, Illinois 60643

Checking Acct No 8030-647-4
Period covered June 30-July 31, 2014

CHECKS/DEBITS			DEPOSITS/CREDITS		DAILY BALANCES	
Posting Date	Check No.	Amount	Posting Date	Amount	Date	Amount
7/14	2570	5,096.00				

(Continued)

Business Document	Description	Prepared by	Sent to	Verification and Related Procedures
① Purchase requisition	To begin, the credit office (requesting department) of Wagon Sportswear Corporation fills out a formal request for a purchase, or **purchase requisition**, for office supplies. The head of the requesting department approves it and forwards it to the purchasing department.	Requesting department	Purchasing department	Purchasing verifies authorization.
② Purchase order	The purchasing department prepares a **purchase order**. The purchase order indicates that Wagon Sportswear will not pay any bill that does not include a purchase order number. The purchase order is addressed to the vendor (seller) and contains a description of the quantity and type of items ordered, the expected price, the shipping date and terms, and other instructions.	Purchasing department	Vendor	Vendor sends goods or services in accordance with purchase order.
③ Invoice	After receiving the purchase order, the vendor, Henderson Supply Company, ships the goods and sends an **invoice** to Wagon Sportswear. The invoice shows the quantity of goods delivered, describes what they are, and lists the price and terms of payment. If all the goods cannot be shipped immediately, the invoice indicates the estimated date of shipment for the remaining goods.	Vendor	Accounting department	Accounting receives invoice from vendor.
④ Receiving report	When the goods reach Wagon Sportswear's receiving department, an employee notes the quantity, type of goods, and their condition on a **receiving report**. The receiving department does not receive a copy of the purchase order or the invoice, so its employees don't know what should be received or its value. Thus, they are not tempted to steal any excess that may be delivered.	Receiving department	Accounting department	Accounting compares invoice, purchase order, and receiving report. Accounting verifies prices.
⑤ Check authorization	The receiving report goes to the accounting department, where it is compared to the purchase order and the invoice. If everything is correct, the accounting department completes a **check authorization** and attaches it to the three supporting documents. The check authorization form shown in Exhibit 2 has a space for each item to be checked off as it is examined. Notice that the accounting department has all the documentary evidence for the transaction, but it does not have access to the assets purchased, nor does it write the check for payment. Thus, the accounting department cannot conceal fraud by falsifying documents.	Accounting department	Treasurer	Accounting attaches check authorization to invoice, purchase order, and receiving report.
⑥ Check	The treasurer examines all the documents. If the treasurer approves them, he or she signs or authorizes an electronic **check**, which is an authorization for the bank to pay the vendor in the amount of the invoice less any applicable discount. The check is then sent to the vendor or the vendor's bank, with a remittance advice showing what the check is for. A vendor that is not paid the proper amount will complain, thus providing a form of outside control over the payment.	Treasurer	Vendor	Treasurer verifies all documents before preparing check.
⑦ Bank statement	The vendor deposits the check in its bank, and the canceled check appears in Wagon Sportswear's monthly **bank statement**, which may be in either paper or electronic form. If the treasurer has made the check out for the wrong amount (or altered an amount that was already filled in), the problem will show up in the company's bank reconciliation.	Buyer's bank	Accounting department	Accounting compares amount and payee's name on returned check with check authorization.

Note: Circled numbers refer to documents on the previous page.

APPLY IT!

Items **a–e** below are a company's departments. Items **f** and **g** are firms with which the company has transactions.

a. Requesting department
b. Purchasing department
c. Receiving department
d. Accounting department
e. Treasurer
f. Vendor
g. Bank

Use the letter of the department or firm to indicate which one prepares and sends the business documents that follow.

	Prepared by	Received by
1. Receiving report	____	____
2. Purchase order	____	____
3. Purchase requisition	____	____
4. Check	____	____
5. Invoice	____	____
6. Check authorization	____	____
7. Bank statement	____	____

SOLUTION

	Prepared by	Received by
1. Receiving report	c	d
2. Purchase order	b	f
3. Purchase requisition	a	b
4. Check	d, e	f
5. Invoice	f	d
6. Check authorization	d	e
7. Bank statement	g	d

TRY IT! SE4, SE5, SE6, SE7, E2A, E3A, E4A, E5A, E2B, E3B, E4B, E5B

LO3 Cash Equivalents and Cash Control

Cash Equivalents

STUDY NOTE: *The statement of cash flows explains the change in the balance of cash and cash equivalents from one period to the next.*

At times, a company may have more cash than it needs to pay its debts. Excess cash should not remain idle, especially during periods of high interest rates. Management may decide to invest the excess cash in short-term interest-bearing accounts or certificates of deposit (CDs) at banks and other financial institutions, in government securities (such as U.S. Treasury notes), or in other securities. If these investments have a term of 90 days or less when they are purchased, they are called **cash equivalents** because the funds revert to cash so quickly they are treated as cash on the balance sheet.

Nike describes its treatment of cash and cash equivalents as follows.

> *Cash and equivalents represent cash and short-term, highly liquid investments with maturities of three months or less at date of purchase. The carrying amounts reflected in the consolidated balance sheets for cash and equivalents approximate fair value.*[6]

Like Nike, most companies record cash equivalents at their approximate fair value, that is, their market value.

According to a survey of large U.S. corporations, 2.5 percent use the term *cash* as the balance sheet caption, and 96 percent use either *cash and cash equivalents* or *cash and equivalents*. The rest either combine cash with marketable securities or have no cash.[7]

Cash Control Methods

Earlier in the chapter, we discussed the concept of internal control and how it applies to cash transactions. Here, we address additional ways of controlling cash.

Imprest Systems Most companies need to keep some currency and coins on hand. Currency and coins are needed for cash registers, for paying expenses that are impractical to pay by check, and for situations that require cash advances—for example, when sales representatives need cash for travel expenses. One way to control a cash fund and cash advances is by using an **imprest system**. A common form of imprest system is a *petty cash fund*, which is discussed in more depth later in the chapter.

Banking Services Banks provide safe depositories for cash, negotiable instruments, and other valuable business documents such as stocks and bonds. The checking accounts that they provide improve control by minimizing the amount of currency a company needs to keep on hand and by supplying permanent records of all cash payments. Banks also serve as agents in a variety of transactions, such as the collection and payment of certain kinds of debts and the exchange of foreign currencies.

Electronic funds transfer (EFT) is a method of conducting business transactions that does not involve the actual transfer of cash. With EFT, a company electronically transfers cash from its bank to another company's bank. For the banks, the electronic transfer is simply a bookkeeping entry. Companies today rely heavily on this method of payment. **Wal-Mart**, for example, makes 75 percent of its payments to suppliers through EFT.

Automated teller machines (ATMs) allow bank customers to make deposits, withdraw cash, transfer funds among accounts, and pay bills. Large consumer banks like **Citibank**, **Chase**, and **Bank of America** process hundreds of thousands of ATM transactions each week. Many banks also give customers the option of paying bills online or over the telephone with debit cards. In 2011, debit cards accounted for more than $1.5 trillion in transactions.[8] When a customer makes a retail purchase using a debit card, the amount of the purchase is deducted directly from the buyer's bank account. The bank usually documents debit card transactions for the retailer, but the retailer must develop new internal controls to ensure that the transactions are recorded properly and that unauthorized transfers do not occur.

STUDY NOTE: *Bank reconciliations are an important factor in internal control. If carried out by someone who cannot access the company's bank account, they provide an independent check on people who do have access.*

Bank Reconciliations Rarely does the balance of a company's Cash account exactly equal the cash balance on its bank statement. The bank may not yet have recorded certain transactions that appear in the company's records, and the company may not yet have recorded certain bank transactions. A **bank reconciliation** is the process of accounting for the difference between the balance on a company's bank statement and the balance in its Cash account.

The following transactions commonly appear in a company's records but not on its bank statement:

- **Outstanding checks:** Checks that a company has issued and recorded but that do not yet appear on its bank statement.
- **Deposits in transit:** Deposits a company has sent to its bank but that the bank did not receive in time to enter on the bank statement.

Transactions that may appear on the bank statement but not in the company's records include the following:

- **Service charges (SC):** Banks often charge a fee for the use of a checking account. Many banks base this service charge on a number of factors, such as the average balance of the account during the month or the number of checks drawn.
- **NSF (nonsufficient funds) checks:** An NSF check is a check that a company has deposited but that is not paid when the bank presents it to the issuer's bank. The bank charges the company's account and returns the check so that the company can try to collect the amount due. If the bank has deducted the NSF check on the bank statement but the company has not deducted it from its book balance, an adjustment

STUDY NOTE: A credit memorandum means that an amount was added to the bank balance; a debit memorandum means that an amount was deducted.

must be made in the bank reconciliation. The company usually reclassifies the NSF check from Cash to Accounts Receivable because it must now collect from the person or company that wrote the check.

- **Miscellaneous debits and credits:** Banks also charge for other services, such as stopping payment on checks and printing checks. The bank notifies the depositor of each deduction by including a debit memorandum with the monthly statement. A bank also sometimes serves as an agent in collecting on promissory notes for the depositor. When it does, it includes a credit memorandum in the bank statement, along with a debit memorandum for the service charge.
- **Interest income:** Banks commonly pay interest on a company's average balance. Accounts that pay interest are sometimes called NOW or money market accounts.

STUDY NOTE: The ending balance on a company's bank statement does not represent the amount of cash that should appear on its balance sheet. At the balance sheet date, deposits may be in transit to the bank, and some checks may be outstanding. That is why companies must prepare a bank reconciliation.

An error by either the bank or the depositor will require immediate correction.

To illustrate the preparation of a bank reconciliation, suppose that Kalita Services Company's bank statement for August shows a balance of $1,735.53 on August 31 and that on the same date, the company's records show a cash balance of $1,207.95. Exhibit 3 shows Kalita Services' bank reconciliation for August.

Exhibit 3
Bank Reconciliation

Kalita Services Company
Bank Reconciliation
August 31, 2014

Balance per bank, August 31		$ 1,735.53
① Add deposit of August 31 in transit		138.00
		$ 1,873.53
② Less outstanding checks:		
No. 551, issued on July 14	$ 75.00	
No. 576, issued on Aug. 30	20.34	
No. 578, issued on Aug. 31	250.00	
No. 579, issued on Aug. 31	185.00	
No. 580, issued on Aug. 31	65.25	595.59
Adjusted bank balance, August 31		**$1,277.94**
Balance per books, August 31		$ 1,207.95
Add:		
④ Note receivable collected by bank	$140.00	
④ Interest income on note	10.00	
⑦ Interest income	7.81	157.81
		$ 1,365.76
Less:		
③ Overstatement of deposit of August 6	$ 15.00	
④ Collection fee	2.50	
⑤ NSF check of Austin Chase	64.07	
⑥ Service charge	6.25	87.82
Adjusted book balance, August 31		**$1,277.94**

Note: Circled numbers refer to documents In Exhibit 2.

STUDY NOTE: It is possible to place an item in the wrong section of a bank reconciliation and arrive at equal adjusted balances that are not correct. The correct (and equal) adjusted balances must be obtained.

The circled numbers in the exhibit refer to the following:

1. The bank has not recorded a deposit in the amount of $138.00 that the company mailed to the bank on August 31.
2. The bank has not paid the five checks that the company issued in July and August. Even though the July 14 check was deducted in the July 30 reconciliation, it must be deducted again in each subsequent month in which it remains outstanding.
3. The company incorrectly recorded a $150.00 deposit from cash sales as $165.00. On August 6, the bank received the deposit and correctly recorded the amount.
4. Among the returned checks was a credit memorandum showing that the bank had collected a promissory note from K. Diaz in the amount of $140.00, plus

$10.00 in interest on the note. A debit memorandum was also enclosed for the $2.50 collection fee. The company had not entered these amounts in its records.

5. Also returned with the bank statement was an NSF check for $64.07 that the company had received from a customer named Austin Chase. The NSF check was not reflected in the company's records.
6. A debit memorandum was enclosed for the regular monthly service charge of $6.25. The company had not yet recorded this charge.
7. Interest earned on the company's average balance was $7.81.

In Exhibit 3, starting from their separate balances, both the bank and book amounts are adjusted to the amount of $1,277.94. This adjusted balance is the amount of cash the company owns on August 31 and thus is the amount that should appear on its August 31 balance sheet.

When outstanding checks are presented to the bank for payment and the bank receives and records the deposit in transit, the bank balance will automatically become correct. However, the company must update its book balance by recording all the items reported by the bank. Thus, Kalita Services would record an increase (debit) in Cash with the following items:

▼ *Decrease* (credit) in *Notes Receivable*, $140.00

▲ *Increase* (credit) in *Interest Income*, $10.00 (interest on note)

▲ *Increase* (credit) in *Interest Income*, $7.81 (interest on average bank balance)

The company would record a reduction (credit) in Cash with the following items:

▼ *Decrease* (debit) in *Sales*, $15.00 (error in recording deposit)

▲ *Increase* (debit) in *Accounts Receivable*, $64.07 (return of NSF check)

▲ *Increase* (debit) in *Bank Service Charges*, $8.75 ($6.25 + $2.50)

APPLY IT!

At year end, Binsu Company had currency and coins in cash registers of $1,100, money orders from customers of $2,000, deposits in checking accounts of $12,000, U.S. Treasury bills due in 80 days of $50,000, certificates of deposit at the bank that mature in six months of $200,000, and U.S. Treasury bonds due in one year of $100,000. Calculate the amount of cash and cash equivalents that will be shown on the company's year-end balance sheet.

SOLUTION

Currency and coins	$ 1,100
Money orders	2,000
Checking accounts	12,000
U.S. Treasury bills (due in 80 days)	50,000
Cash and cash equivalents	$65,100

The certificates of deposit and U.S. Treasury Bonds mature in more than 90 days and thus are not cash equivalents.

TRY IT! SE8, SE9, E6A, E7A, E6B, E7B

LO 4 Petty Cash Funds

It is not always practical to use checks. For example, it is sometimes necessary to make small payments of cash for postage stamps, shipping charges due, or minor purchases of pens, paper, and other office supplies. For situations in which it is inconvenient to pay by check, most companies set up a **petty cash fund**. One of the best ways to control a petty cash fund is through an imprest system, in which the fund is established for a fixed amount. A voucher documents each cash payment made from the fund. The fund is periodically reimbursed, based on the vouchers, by the exact amount necessary to restore its original cash balance.

Establishing the Petty Cash Fund

Some companies have a regular cashier or other employee who administers the petty cash fund.

Establishing the Petty Cash Fund

Transaction On October 14, Davis Company establishes the petty cash fund by issuing a check for $100 intended to cover two to four weeks of small expenditures. The check is cashed and the money placed in the petty cash box, drawer, or envelope.

Analysis The journal entry to establish the petty cash fund

▲ *increases* the *Petty Cash* account

▼ *decreases* the *Cash* account

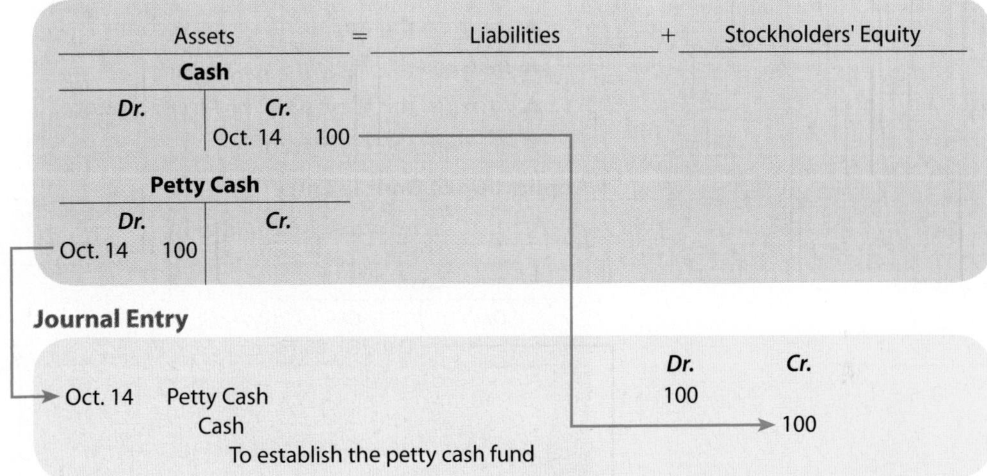

Comment The only entry required when the fund is established is to record the check.

Making Disbursements from the Petty Cash Fund

The custodian of the petty cash fund should prepare a **petty cash voucher**, or written authorization, for each expenditure, as shown in Exhibit 4. On each petty cash voucher, the custodian enters the date, amount, and purpose of the expenditure. The person who receives the payment signs the voucher.

Exhibit 4
Petty Cash Voucher

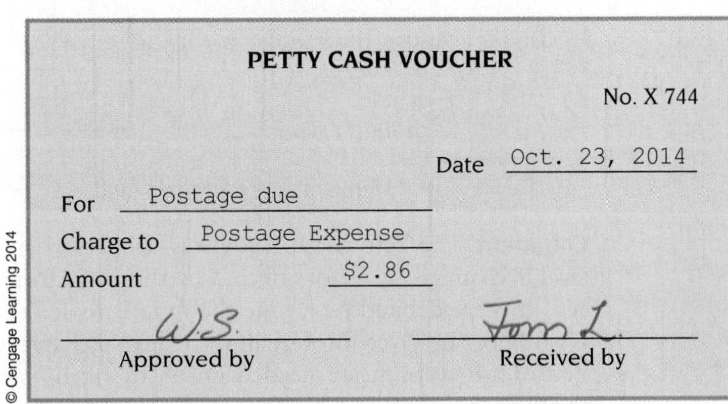
PETTY CASH VOUCHER

No. X 744

Date Oct. 23, 2014

For Postage due

Charge to Postage Expense

Amount $2.86

W.S. — Approved by

Tom L. — Received by

STUDY NOTE: *Even though withdrawals from petty cash are generally small, the cumulative total over time can represent a substantial amount. Accordingly, an effective system of internal control must be established for the fund.*

The custodian should be informed that unannounced audits of the fund will be made occasionally. The cash in the fund plus the sum of the petty cash vouchers should at all times equal the amount shown in the Petty Cash account.

Reimbursing the Petty Cash Fund

At specified intervals, when the fund becomes low, and at the end of a period, the petty cash fund is replenished by a check issued to the custodian for the exact amount of the expenditures. From time to time, there may be minor discrepancies in the amount of cash left in the fund at the time of reimbursement. In those cases, the amount of the discrepancy is recorded in a Cash Short or Over account—as a debit if short or as a credit if over.

Reimbursing the Petty Cash Fund

Transaction On October 28 (after two weeks), Davis Company replenishes its petty cash fund, established earlier, which has a cash balance of $14.27 and petty cash vouchers as follows: postage, $25.00; supplies, $30.55; and freight-in, $30.00.

Analysis The journal entry to replenish the fund

- ▲ *increases* the *Postage Expense* account
- ▲ *increases* the *Supplies Expense* account
- ▲ *increases* the *Freight-In* account
- ▲ *increases* the *Cash Short or Over* account
- ▼ *decreases* the *Cash* account

Application of Double Entry

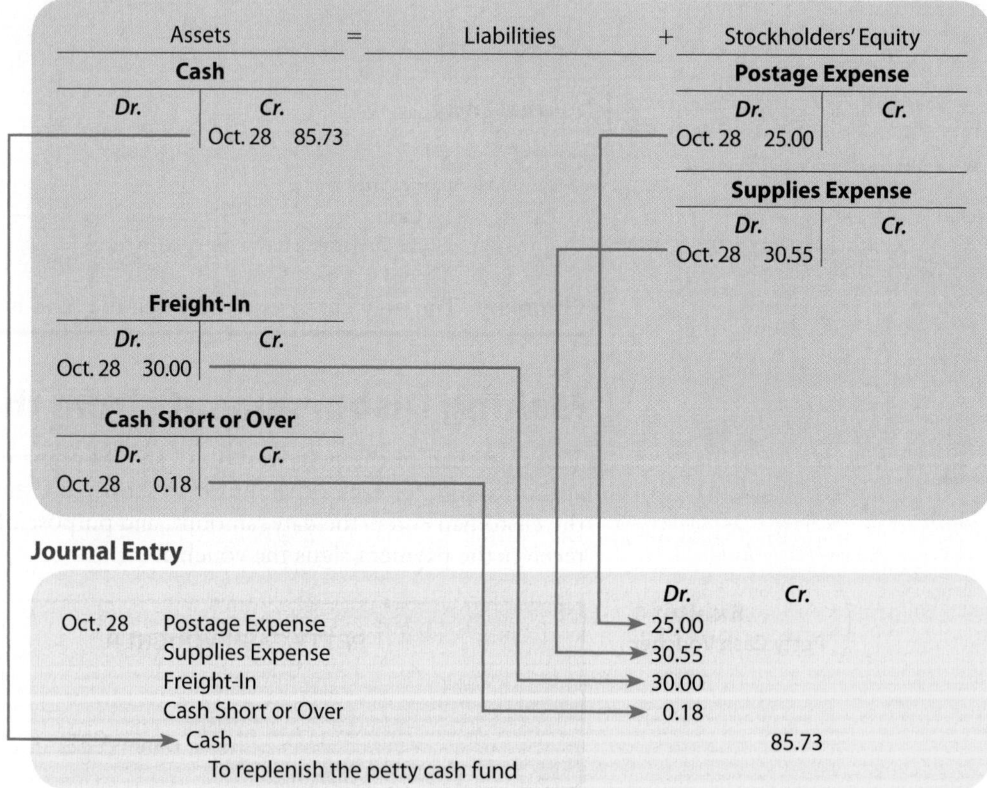

Journal Entry

		Dr.	Cr.
Oct. 28	Postage Expense	25.00	
	Supplies Expense	30.55	
	Freight-In	30.00	
	Cash Short or Over	0.18	
	Cash		85.73
	To replenish the petty cash fund		

Comment The Petty Cash account is debited when the fund is established or the fund level is changed. It is not affected by the entry to replenish the fund. Expense or asset accounts are debited each time the fund is replenished, including in this case $0.18 to Cash Short or Over for a small cash shortage. In most cases, no further entries to the Petty Cash account are needed unless the firm wants to change the fixed amount of the fund.

The petty cash fund should be replenished at the end of a period to bring it up to its fixed amount and ensure that changes in the other accounts involved are reflected in the current period's financial statements. If the petty cash fund is not replenished at the end of the period, expenditures are shown through an adjusting entry debiting the expense accounts and crediting Petty Cash. The result is a reduction in the petty cash fund and the Petty Cash account by the amount of the adjusting entry. In the financial statements, the balance of the Petty Cash account is usually combined with other cash accounts.

Internal Control and the Financial Statements

Internal control applies to all transactions and ensures the fair presentation of the financial statements as shown in Exhibit 5.

Exhibit 5
Internal Control and the Income Statement and Balance Sheet

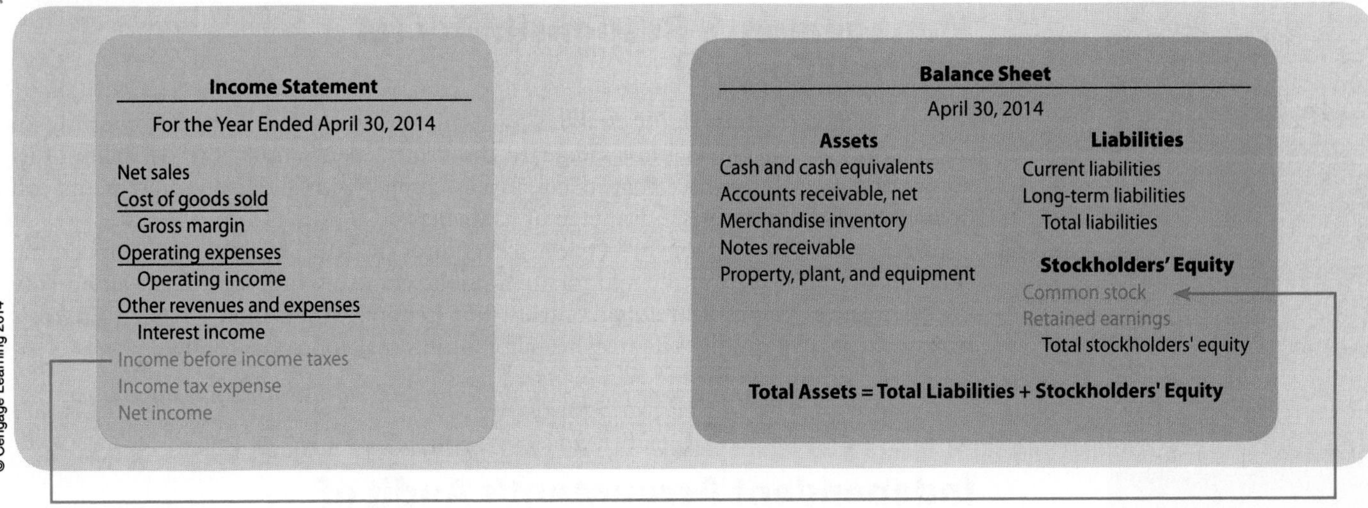

APPLY IT!

A petty cash fund is established at $150 on July 1. At the end of July, the fund has a cash balance of $59 and petty cash vouchers for postage, $37, and office supplies, $52. Prepare the journal entry to establish the fund on July 1 and the entry on July 31 to replenish the fund.

SOLUTION

July 1	Petty Cash	150	
	Cash		150
	To establish petty cash fund		
July 31	Postage Expense	37	
	Office Supplies Expense	52	
	Cash Over or Short	2	
	Cash		91
	To replenish petty cash fund		

TRY IT! SE10, E8A, E9A, E8B, E9B

SECTION 3 BUSINESS APPLICATIONS

BUSINESS APPLICATIONS

- Management's responsibility
- Independent auditor's audit

RELEVANT LEARNING OBJECTIVE

LO5 Identify the internal control roles of management and the auditor.

LO5 Management Issues Related to Internal Control

A company's management and its auditor have important responsibilities for the internal control of a company.

Management's Responsibility for Internal Control

Management is responsible for establishing a satisfactory system of internal controls. In other words, management must safeguard the firm's assets, ensure the reliability of its accounting records, and see that its employees comply with all legal requirements and operate the firm to the best advantage of its owners.

Section 404 of the Sarbanes-Oxley Act requires that the chief executive officer, the chief financial officer, and the auditors of a public company fully document and certify the company's system of internal controls. For example, in its annual report, **Costco**'s management acknowledges its responsibility for internal control as follows.

> *Our management is responsible for establishing and maintaining adequate internal control over financial reporting.*[9]

Independent Accountant's Audit of Internal Control

Although privately owned companies usually are not required to have an independent certified public accountant audit their financial statements, many companies choose to do so. These companies are also not required to have their internal control systems audited. Public companies like **Costco**, on the other hand, are required to not only have an independent audit of their financial statements, they must also have an audit of their internal control. For instance, Costco's auditors state:

> *In our opinion, the Company maintained, in all material respects, effective internal control over financial reporting...*[10]

© Alija / iStockphoto.com

Business Perspective

Will Sarbanes-Oxley Stop Fraud?

Although the Sarbanes-Oxley Act has heightened awareness of internal control and has required increased diligence, it will never stop fraud from occurring. For instance, a recent study of 350 alleged accounting fraud cases investigated by the SEC found that fraud affects companies of all sizes. The average fraud was \$12.1 million, and more than 30 cases involved fraud over \$500 million. Additional guidance with regard to internal controls are expected to be issued.[11]

APPLY IT!

Match the items with the related statements that follow.

a. Internal control
b. A need of internal control
c. Management's responsibility
d. Independent accountant's audit

1. Provides reasonable assurance to outside parties that management maintains internal control over financial reporting.
2. Established by management to ensure the reliability of accounting records and financial statements in accordance with GAAP.
3. Human error can cause errors in the financial statements.
4. To assure the establishment of a system of internal control and assess its effectiveness.

SOLUTION

1. d; 2. a; 3. b; 4. c

TRY IT! SE1, E10A, E10B

A Look Back At: Subway

Subway

Ulrich Baumgarten/Getty Images

The beginning of this chapter focused on **Subway** and how it tries to ensure its assets are protected and its hundreds of daily cash transactions are recorded properly. Complete the following requirements in order to answer the questions posed at the beginning of the chapter.

Section 1: Concepts
Why are each of the five components of internal control important to the faithful representation of a company's operations in its financial statements?

Section 2: Accounting Applications
How can Subway maintain control over its inventory and cash?

Section 3: Business Applications
How can Subway's bank and other users of its financial statements be confident that the restaurant has an adequate system of internal control?

SOLUTION

Section 1: Concepts
An effective system of internal control contributes to the *faithful representation* of a company's operations through five interrelated components: control environment, risk assessment, control activities, information and communication, and monitoring. Since internal control is a process, all of these components need to be present if the company wants to have an effective internal control, for example, management needs to create an environment that encourages compliance with laws, regulations, and standards. Management has to also identify and assess possible risks and implement control activities that will ensure safeguard of its assets and reliability of its accounting records. Information and communication is also crucial because it encompasses the accounting system and how information and data are communicated within the company and to the external parties. Finally, effective system of internal control requires continuous monitoring which means that management reviews compliance with required laws and regulations to make sure everything works as planned and takes necessary actions when problems arise.

Section 2: Accounting Applications
To maintain control over food inventory and cash, Subway must insure that all transactions are recorded in accordance with management's authorization, that proper documents and records are maintained, and that physical controls are used such as store rooms and cash registers. There must also be separation of authorization, from record keeping and custody among employees. Further, an outside representative of management should periodically examine the inventory and count the cash and compare the results to the records. Finally, Subway must make every effort to hire honest and capable employees.

Section 3: Business Applications
The owners of Subway are responsible for establishing an effective system of internal control, which is essential for reliable financial reporting. The best way for any business to assure users of the integrity of its financial statements is to have an independent auditor assess the reliability of its internal control system. Although not a public company, Subway hires independent auditors to audit its financial statements and to audit its system of internal control. The auditor's report is a credible source of information for banks and any other users of Subway's financial statements.

Review Problem

Emma Sung owns a popular neighborhood restaurant. In order to have better control over cash, Emma has established several rules for cashiers. Match each of the internal controls with the control activities that follow. (*Note:* Some may have more than one answer.)

a. Authorization
b. Recording transactions
c. Documents and records
d. Physical controls
e. Periodic independent verification
f. Separation of duties
g. Sound personnel practices

1. Emma Sung hires experienced cashiers who are bonded and checks the references of all new employees.
2. New cashiers are trained in all procedures before being allowed to handle cash.
3. All food bills are prenumbered sequentially.
4. When a customer finishes a meal, the waiter writes up a bill that describes the food items purchased, including the total price.
5. The waiters are not allowed to access the cash register.
6. If the sale is by credit card, the cashier runs the credit card through a scanner that verifies the customer's credit. The scanner prints out a receipt and a slip for the customer to sign. The signed slip is put in the cash register, and the customer is given the receipt and a copy of the sales invoice.
7. All sales, whether cash or credit, are rung up on the cash register.
8. The cash register must be locked when the cashier is not present. The cashier is the only person other than Emma Sung who has a key.
9. Refunds or discounts are made only with Emma Sung's approval.
10. At the end of each day, Emma counts the cash and checks in the cash register and compares the total with the amount recorded on the tape inside the register. She totals all the signed credit card slips and ensures that the total equals the amount recorded by the scanner.

SOLUTION

1. g
2. g
3. c
4. a, c
5. d, f
6. b, c
7. b, d
8. d
9. a, f
10. e

Chapter Review

Describe the components of internal control, control activities, and limitations on internal control. LO 1

Internal control establishes the reliability of the accounting records and financial statements in accordance with generally accepted accounting principles (GAAP) and ensures that the company's assets are protected. Internal control consists of all the policies and procedures a company uses to ensure the reliability of financial reporting, compliance with laws and regulations, and the effectiveness and efficiency of operations. Internal control has five components: the control environment, risk assessment, control activities, information and communication, and monitoring. Control activities include having managers authorize certain transactions, recording all transactions to establish accountability for assets, using well-designed documents to ensure proper recording of transactions, instituting physical controls, periodically checking records and assets, separating duties, and using sound personnel practices. A system of internal control relies on the people who implement it. Human error, collusion, and failure to recognize changed conditions can contribute to a system's failure.

Apply internal control activities to common merchandising transactions. LO 2

To implement internal control over cash sales, receipts, purchases, and disbursements, the functions of authorization, recordkeeping, and custodianship of cash should be kept separate. The people who have access to cash should be specifically designated and their number limited. Employees who have access to cash should be bonded. The control system should also provide for the use of banking services, physical protection of assets, prompt recording and deposit of cash receipts, and payment by check. A person who does not authorize, handle, or record cash transactions should make unannounced audits of the cash on hand, and the Cash account should be reconciled each month.

Define *cash equivalents*, and explain methods of controlling cash, including bank reconciliations. LO 3

Cash equivalents are investments that have a term of 90 days or less. Most companies record cash equivalents at their approximate fair value. Methods of controlling cash include imprest systems; banking services, including electronic funds transfer; and bank reconciliations. A bank reconciliation accounts for the difference between the balance on a company's bank statement and the balance in its Cash account. It involves adjusting for outstanding checks, deposits in transit, service charges, NSF checks, miscellaneous debits and credits, and interest income.

Demonstrate the use of a simple imprest (petty cash) system. LO 4

An imprest system is a method of controlling small cash expenditures by setting up a fund at a fixed amount and periodically reimbursing the fund to restore the original balance. A petty cash fund, one example of an imprest system, is established by a debit to Petty Cash and a credit to Cash. It is replenished by debits to various expense or asset accounts and a credit to Cash. Each expenditure should be supported by a petty cash voucher.

Identify the internal control roles of management and the auditor. LO 5

Management's responsibility is to establish an environment, accounting systems, and internal control procedures that will protect the assets. Public companies must engage an independent CPA to verify that management is indeed meeting these goals.

Key Terms

authorization 329 (LO1)
bank reconciliation 338 (LO3)
bank statement 336 (LO2)
bonding 330 (LO1)
cash equivalents 337 (LO3)
check 336 (LO2)
check authorization 336 (LO2)
control activities 329 (LO1)
control environment 329 (LO1)
deposits in transit 338 (LO3)
electronic funds transfer (EFT) 338 (LO3)
imprest system 338 (LO3)
information and communication 329 (LO1)

internal control 328 (LO1)
invoice 336 (LO2)
monitoring 329 (LO1)
NSF (nonsufficient funds) checks 338 (LO3)
outstanding checks 338 (LO3)
periodic independent verification 330 (LO1)
petty cash fund 340 (LO4)
petty cash voucher 341 (LO4)
physical controls 330 (LO1)
physical inventory 328 (LO1)
purchase order 336 (LO2)
purchase requisition 336 (LO2)
receiving report 336 (LO2)
risk assessment 329 (LO1)
separation of duties 330 (LO1)

Chapter Assignments

DISCUSSION QUESTIONS

LO 1 **DQ1.** Why is a system of internal control not able to overcome collusion by employees?

LO 1 **DQ2. CONCEPT ▶** In what way does internal control contribute to faithful representation in its financial statements?

LO 2 **DQ3.** Which of the following accounts would be assigned a higher level of risk: Building or Merchandising Inventory?

LO 2 **DQ4.** Why is it important to record the amount of cash received through the mail or over the counter?

LO 3 **DQ5.** What role does a bank reconciliation play in internal control over cash?

LO 3 **DQ6.** Name some businesses whose needs for cash fluctuate during the year. Name some whose needs for cash are relatively stable over the year.

LO 5 **DQ7. BUSINESS APPLICATION ▶** Why is it important for public companies to have an audit of management's assessment of internal control?

SHORT EXERCISES

LO 1, 5 **Internal Control**

SE1. Match the items with the related statements that follow.

a. Internal control
b. A need of internal control
c. Management's responsibility
d. Independent accountant's audit

1. Evaluates management's assessment of internal control over financial reporting.
2. A process that establishes reliability of accounting records and financial statements in accordance with GAAP.
3. Many assets such as cash and inventories are at risk of loss.
4. Establishes a system of internal control and assesses its effectiveness

LO 1, 2 **Components of Internal Control**

SE2. Match the items with the related statements that follow.

a. Control environment
b. Risk assessment
c. Control activities
d. Information and communication
e. Monitoring

1. Policies and procedures management puts in place to see that its directives are carried out.
2. Identifying areas where losses may occur.
3. Regular assessment of the quality of internal controls.
4. Management's overall attitude, awareness, and actions.
5. Pertains to the accounting system.

LO 1 **Limitations of Internal Control**

SE3. Internal control is subject to several inherent limitations. Indicate whether each of the following situations is an example of (a) human error, (b) collusion among employees, (c) changed conditions, or (d) cost-benefit considerations:

1. Effective separation of duties in a restaurant is impractical because the business is too small.
2. The cashier and the manager of a retail shoe store work together to avoid the internal controls for the purpose of embezzling funds.
3. The cashier in a pizza shop does not understand the procedures for operating the cash register and thus fails to ring up all the sales and count the cash at the end of the day.
4. At a law firm, computer supplies are mistakenly delivered to the reception area instead of the receiving area because the supplier began using a different system of shipment. As a result, the receipt of supplies is not recorded.

LO 1, 2 **Separation of Duties**

SE4. Match the functions for collecting cash by Sonja Cleaners with the statements that follow.

a. Authorization
b. Custody
c. Recordkeeping

1. The cashier is responsible for funds in the cash register.
2. All sales are recorded on prenumbered invoices and rung up on the cash register.
3. All refunds must be approved by the manager.

LO 2 **Physical Controls**

SE5. Match the assets of a small retail store with the related physical controls that follow.

a. Cash
b. Merchandise inventory
c. Supplies
d. Computers

1. An alarm that signals if unsold items leave the store.
2. Cash register.
3. A locked cabinet in the supplies closet.
4. A cable with a lock.
5. A locked showcase.

LO 1, 2 **Internal Control Activities**

SE6. Match the check-writing policies for a small business to the control activities that follow.

a. Authorization
b. Recording transactions
c. Documents and records
d. Physical controls
e. Periodic independent verification
f. Separation of duties
g. Sound personnel practices

1. The person who writes the checks to pay bills is different from the people who authorize the payments and keep records of the payments.
2. The checks are kept in a locked drawer. The only person who has the key is the person who writes the checks.
3. The person who writes the checks is bonded.
4. Once each month the owner compares and reconciles the amount of money shown in the accounting records with the amount in the bank account.
5. The owner of the business approves each check before it is mailed.
6. Information pertaining to each check is recorded on the check stub.
7. Every day, all checks are recorded in the accounting records, using the information on the check stubs.

LO 2 **Business Documents**

SE7. Arrange the following business documents in the normal order in which they would be prepared:

1. Invoice
2. Purchase order
3. Check
4. Receiving report
5. Bank statement
6. Purchase requisition
7. Check authorization

LO 3 **Cash and Cash Equivalents**

SE8. Compute the amount of cash and cash equivalents on Steen Wash Company's balance sheet if, on the balance sheet date, it has currency and coins on hand of $250, deposits in checking accounts of $1,500, U.S. Treasury bills due in 80 days of $15,000, and U.S. Treasury bonds due in 200 days of $25,000.

LO 3 **Bank Reconciliation**

SE9. Prepare a bank reconciliation from the following information:

a. Balance per bank statement as of June 30, $4,862.77
b. Balance per books as of June 30, $2,479.48
c. Deposits in transit, $654.24
d. Outstanding checks, $3,028.89
e. Interest on average balance, $8.64

LO 4 **Petty Cash Fund**

SE10. A petty cash fund is established at $100. At the end of May, the fund has a cash balance of $36 and petty cash vouchers for postage, $29, and office supplies, $34. Prepare the journal entry on May 31, 2014, to replenish the fund.

EXERCISES: SET A

LO 1 **Components of Internal Control**

E1A. Match the items with the related statements that follow.

a. Control environment
b. Risk assessment
c. Control activities
d. Information and communication
e. Monitoring

1. Management encourages employees to follow the rules.
2. The company has an internal audit department.
3. Management regularly considers what losses the company might face.
4. The company gathers appropriate information and communicates it to employees.
5. Management puts separation of duties in place.
6. Personnel are well trained and instructed in their duties.
7. The company employs good physical controls.
8. The company has a good accounting system.
9. Managers are observant and review how procedures by those who report to them are carried out.

LO 1, 2 **Control Procedures**

E2A. Some conditions for internal control follow.

a. Transactions are executed in accordance with management's general or specific authorization.
b. Transactions are recorded as necessary to permit preparation of financial statements and maintain accountability for assets.
c. Access to assets is permitted only as allowed by management.
d. At reasonable intervals, the records of assets are compared with the existing assets.

Marika Jonssen, who operates a small grocery store, has established the following policies with regard to the checkout cashiers:

1. Cashiers may accept checks for purchases under $100 with proper identification. For checks over $100, they must receive approval from Jonssen.

2. Each cashier has his or her own cash drawer, to which no one else has access.
3. Every sale must be rung up on the cash register and a receipt given to the customer. Each sale is recorded on a tape inside the cash register.
4. At the end of each day, Jonssen counts the cash in the drawer and compares it with the amount on the tape inside the cash register.

Match the conditions for internal control to each of the policies listed.

LO **1, 2**

Internal Control Procedures

E3A. A list of control procedures follows.

a. Authorization
b. Recording transactions
c. Documents and records
d. Physical controls
e. Periodic independent verification
f. Separation of duties
g. Sound personnel practices

Real Video Store maintains the following policies with regard to purchases of new DVDs at each of its branch stores:

1. Once each month a person from the home office visits each branch store to examine the receiving records and to compare the inventory of DVDs with the accounting records.
2. Employees are required to take vacations, and the duties of employees are rotated periodically.
3. Purchases of new DVDs must be authorized by purchase order in the home office and paid for by the treasurer in the home office. Receiving reports are prepared in each branch and sent to the home office.
4. All new personnel receive one hour of training in how to receive and catalogue new DVDs.
5. The company maintains a perpetual inventory system that keeps track of all DVDs purchased, sold, and on hand.

Match the control procedures to each of the policies listed. (*Hint:* Some may have more than one answer.)

LO **2**

Business Documents

E4A. Items **a–e** below are a company's departments. Items **f** and **g** are firms with which the company has transactions.

a. Requesting department
b. Purchasing department
c. Receiving department
d. Accounting department
e. Treasurer
f. Vendor
g. Bank

Use the letter of the department or firm to indicate which one prepares and sends the following business documents:

	Prepared by	Received by
1. Purchase requisition	____	____
2. Bank statement	____	____
3. Purchase order	____	____
4. Check authorization	____	____
5. Invoice	____	____
6. Check	____	____
7. Receiving report	____	____

LO **2**

Use of Accounting Records in Internal Control

E5A. ACCOUNTING CONNECTION ▶ Careful scrutiny of accounting records and financial statements can lead to the discovery of fraud or embezzlement. Each of

(Continued)

the situations that follow may indicate a breakdown in internal control. Indicate the nature of the possible fraud or embezzlement in each of these situations.

1. Wages expense for a branch office was 15 percent higher in 2014 than in 2013, even though the office was authorized to employ only the same four employees and raises were only 2.5 percent in 2014.
2. Sales returns and allowances increased from 2.5 percent to 10 percent of sales in the first two months of 2014, after record sales in 2013 resulted in large bonuses for the sales staff.
3. Gross margin decreased from 20 percent of net sales in 2013 to 10 percent in 2014, even though there was no change in pricing. Ending inventory was 25 percent less at the end of 2014 than it was at the beginning of the year. There is no immediate explanation for the decrease in inventory.
4. A review of daily records of cash register receipts shows that one cashier consistently accepts more discount coupons for purchases than do the other cashiers.

LO 3

Cash and Cash Equivalents

E6A. At year end, Bottle Water Company had currency and coins in cash registers of $5,600, money orders from customers of $10,000, deposits in checking accounts of $64,000, U.S. Treasury bills due in 80 days of $180,000, certificates of deposit at the bank that mature in six months of $200,000, and U.S. Treasury bonds due in one year of $100,000. Calculate the amount of cash and cash equivalents that will be shown on the company's year-end balance sheet.

LO 3

Bank Reconciliation

E7A. Prepare a bank reconciliation from the following information:

a. Balance per bank statement as of May 31, $16,655.44
b. Balance per books as of May 31, $12,091.94
c. Deposits in transit, $2,234.81
d. Outstanding checks, $6,808.16
e. Bank service charge, $9.85

LO 4

Imprest System

E8A. ACCOUNTING CONNECTION ▶ Developing a convenient means of providing sales representatives with cash for their incidental expenses, such as entertaining a client at lunch, is a problem many companies face. Under one company's plan, the sales representatives receive advances in cash from the petty cash fund. Each advance is supported by an authorization from the sales manager. The representative returns the receipt for the expenditure and any unused cash, which is replaced in the petty cash fund. The cashier of the petty cash fund is responsible for seeing that the receipt and the cash returned equal the advance. When the petty cash fund is reimbursed, the amount of the representative's expenditure is debited to Direct Sales Expense.

What is the weak point in this system? What fundamental principle of internal control is being ignored? What improvement in the procedure can you suggest?

LO 4

Petty Cash Transactions

E9A. A small company maintains a petty cash fund for minor expenditures. In February and March 2014, the following transactions took place:

a. The fund was established in the amount of $200.00 on Feb. 1 from the proceeds of check no. 2717.
b. On Feb. 28, the petty cash fund had cash of $30.92 and the following receipts on hand: postage, $80.00; supplies, $49.88; delivery service, $24.80; and rubber stamp, $14.40. Check no. 2748 was drawn to replenish the fund.
c. On March 31, the petty cash fund had cash of $44.12 and these receipts on hand: postage, $68.40; supplies, $65.68; and delivery service, $12.80. The petty cash custodian could not account for the shortage. Check no. 2897 was drawn to replenish the fund.

Prepare the journal entries necessary to record each transaction.

LO 5 **Management and Auditor Responsibility for Internal Control**

E10A. BUSINESS APPLICATION ▶ Match the items with the related statements that follow.

a. Management's responsibility
b. Section 404 of Sarbanes-Oxley Act
c. Independent accountant's responsibility
d. Internal control

1. Provides reasonable assurance to outside parties that management maintains internal control over financial reporting.
2. Established by management to ensure the reliability of accounting records and financial statements in accordance with GAAP.
3. Requires that the chief executive officer, the chief financial officer, and the auditors of a public company fully document and certify the company's system of internal controls.
4. To assure the establishment of a system of internal control and assess its effectiveness.

EXERCISES: SET B

Visit the textbook companion website at www.cengagebrain.com to access Exercise Set B for this chapter.

PROBLEMS

LO 1 **Internal Control Components**

P1. Arcadia Company, a small retail bookstore, has experienced losses of inventory over the past year. Jason Arcadia, the owner, on the advice of his accountant, has adopted a set of internal controls in an effort to stop the losses. Arcadia has taken the following steps:

1. He regularly considers ways in which inventory losses might occur.
2. He had his accountant set up an accounting system over inventory.
3. He requires all new and existing employees to attend a training session in which they are instructed in their duties.
4. He makes sure that different employees perform the duties of authorization, custody, and recordkeeping.
5. He spends time "on the floor" encouraging employees to follow the procedures.
6. He periodically gathers appropriate information about inventory situations and communicates his findings to employees.
7. He had all items in inventory marked with an electronic bar code that signals an alarm if someone tries to take an item out of the store without paying for it.
8. He observes and reviews how internal control procedures are carried out.
9. He hires his accountant to periodically conduct internal audit work.

REQUIRED

1. Show that Arcadia's new system engages all the components of internal control by matching each of the steps with the internal control components that follow. (*Hint:* Some may have more than one answer.)
   a. Control environment
   b. Risk assessment
   c. Control activities
   d. Information and communication
   e. Monitoring
2. **BUSINESS APPLICATION ▶** As the owner of a small company, why is it important that Jason Arcadia take an active part in the management of the internal control system?

LO 1, 2 **Internal Control Procedures**

P2. Transco Printers makes printers for personal computers and maintains a factory outlet showroom through which it sells its products to the public. The company's management has set up a system of internal controls over the inventory of printers to prevent theft and to ensure the accuracy of the accounting records.

(Continued)

All printers in inventory at the factory outlet are kept in a secured warehouse behind the showroom, except for the sample printers on display. Only authorized personnel may enter the warehouse. When a customer buys a printer, a sales invoice is written in triplicate by the cashier and is marked "paid." The sales invoices are sequentially numbered, and all must be accounted for. The cashier sends the pink copy of the completed invoice to the warehouse, gives the blue copy to the customer, and keeps the green copy. The customer drives around to the warehouse entrance. The warehouse attendant takes the blue copy of the invoice from the customer and gives the customer the printer and the pink copy of the invoice.

The company maintains a perpetual inventory system for the printers at the outlet. The warehouse attendant at the outlet signs an inventory transfer sheet for each printer received. An accountant at the factory is assigned responsibility for maintaining the inventory records based on copies of the inventory transfer sheets and the sales invoices. The records are updated daily and may be accessed by computer but not modified by the sales personnel and the warehouse attendant. The accountant also sees that all prenumbered inventory transfer sheets are accounted for and compares copies of them with the ones signed by the warehouse attendant. Once every three months, the company's internal auditor takes a physical count of the printer inventory and compares the results with the perpetual inventory records.

All new employees are required to read a sales and inventory manual and attend a two-hour training session about the internal controls. They must demonstrate that they can perform the functions required of them.

REQUIRED

1. Give an example of how each of the following control activities is applied to internal control over inventory at Transco Printers:
   a. Authorization
   b. Recording transactions
   c. Documents and records
   d. Physical controls
   e. Periodic independent verification
   f. Separation of duties
   g. Sound personnel practices
2. **ACCOUNTING CONNECTION ▶** Can the described system protect against an employee who picks up a printer and carries it off when leaving work?

LO 1, 2

Internal Control Activities

P3. East-West Sports Shop is a small neighborhood sporting goods store. The shop's owner, Sunny Hazel, has set up a system of internal control over sales to prevent theft and to ensure the accuracy of the accounting records.

When a customer buys a product, the cashier writes up a sales invoice that describes the purchase, including the total price. All sales invoices are prenumbered sequentially.

If the sale is by credit card, the cashier runs the credit card through a scanner that verifies the customer's credit. The scanner prints out a receipt and a slip for the customer to sign. The signed slip is put in the cash register, and the customer is given the receipt and a copy of the sales invoice.

If the sale is by cash or check, the cashier rings it up on the cash register and gives change, if appropriate. Checks must be written for the exact amount of the purchase and must be accompanied by identification. The sale is recorded on a tape inside the cash register that cannot be accessed by the cashier. The cash register may be locked with a key. The cashier is the only person other than Hazel who has a key. The cash register must be locked when the cashier is not present. Refunds are made only with Hazel's approval, are recorded on prenumbered credit memorandum forms, and are rung up on the cash register.

At the end of each day, Hazel counts the cash and checks in the cash register and compares the total with the amount recorded on the tape inside the register. Hazel totals all the signed credit card slips and ensures that the total equals the amount recorded by the scanner. Hazel also makes sure that all sales invoices and credit memoranda are accounted for. Hazel prepares a bank deposit ticket for the cash, checks, and signed credit card slips, less $40 in change to be put in the cash register the next day, and removes the record of the day's credit card sales from the scanner. All the records are placed in an envelope that is sealed and sent to the company's accountant for verification and recording in the company records. On the way home, Hazel places the bank deposit in the night deposit box.

The company hires experienced cashiers who are bonded. Hazel spends the first half-day with new cashiers, showing them the procedures and overlooking their work.

REQUIRED

1. Give an example of how each of the following control activities is applied to internal control over sales and cash at East-West Sports Shop: (Do not address controls over inventory.)
   a. Authorization
   b. Recording transactions
   c. Documents and records
   d. Physical controls
   e. Periodic independent verification
   f. Separation of duties
   g. Sound personnel practices
2. **ACCOUNTING CONNECTION ▶** Can the system as described protect against a cashier who accepts cash for a sale but does not ring up the sale and pockets the cash? If so, how does it prevent this action?

LO 3

✔ 1: Adjusted book balance, May 31: $54,485.60

SPREADSHEET

GENERAL LEDGER

Bank Reconciliation

P4. The following information is available for Sedona, Inc., as of May 31, 2014:

a. Cash on the books as of May 31 amounted to $42,754.16. Cash on the bank statement for the same date was $52,351.46.
b. A deposit of $5,220.94, representing cash receipts of May 31, did not appear on the bank statement.
c. Outstanding checks totaled $3,936.80.
d. A check for $1,920.00 returned with the statement was recorded incorrectly in the check register as $1,380.00. The check was for a cash purchase of merchandise.
e. The bank service charge for May amounted to $25.
f. The bank collected $12,360.00 for Sedona, on a note. The face value of the note was $12,000.00.
g. An NSF check for $183.56 from a customer, Eva Mendez, was returned with the statement.
h. The bank mistakenly charged to the company account a check for $850.00 drawn by another company.
i. The bank reported that it had credited the account for $120.00 in interest on the average balance for May.

REQUIRED

1. Prepare a bank reconciliation for Sedona as of May 31, 2014.
2. Prepare the journal entries necessary to adjust the accounts.
3. What amount of cash should appear on Sedona's balance sheet as of May 31?
4. **ACCOUNTING CONNECTION ▶** Why is a bank reconciliation considered an important control over cash?

LO 4

✔ 1: June 30 credit to Cash: $507.24

SPREADSHEET

Imprest (Petty Cash) Transaction

P5. A small company maintains a petty cash fund for minor expenditures. The following transactions occurred in June and July 2014:

a. The fund was established in the amount of $600.00 on June 1 from the proceeds of check no. 30.
b. On June 30, the petty cash fund had cash of $92.76 and the following receipts on hand: postage, $240.00; supplies, $149.64; delivery service, $74.40; and rubber stamp, $43.20. Check no. 1577 was drawn to replenish the fund.
c. On July 31, the petty cash fund had cash of $132.36 and the following receipts on hand: postage, $205.20; supplies, $197.04; and delivery service, $38.40. The petty

(Continued)

cash custodian could not account for the shortage. Check no. 1628 was written to replenish the fund.

REQUIRED

1. Prepare the journal entries necessary to record each of these transactions.
2. **ACCOUNTING CONNECTION ▶** A charity reimburses volunteers for small out-of-pocket expenses such as parking and gasoline when the volunteers are carrying out the business of the charity. How might an imprest (petty cash) fund be helpful in controlling these expenditures?

ALTERNATE PROBLEMS

LO 1

Internal Control Components

P6. Faubert Company, a small electronics distributor, has experienced losses of inventory over the past year. Melissa Faubert, the owner, on the advice of her accountant, has adopted a set of internal controls in an effort to stop the losses. Faubert has taken the following steps:

1. She encourages employees to follow the rules.
2. She regularly considers ways in which inventory losses might occur.
3. She puts separation of duties in place.
4. She gathers appropriate information and communicates it to employees.
5. She sees that new and existing employees are well trained and instructed in their duties.
6. She makes sure inventories are physically protected with locked storage and electronic monitors.
7. She observes and reviews how procedures by those who report to her are carried out.
8. She had her accountant install a better accounting system over inventory.
9. She trains new employees in how to properly carry out control procedures.

REQUIRED

1. Show that Faubert's new system engages all the components of internal control by matching each of the steps with the internal control components that follow. (*Hint:* Some may have more than one answer.)
   a. Control environment
   b. Risk assessment
   c. Information and communication
   d. Control activities
   e. Monitoring
2. **BUSINESS APPLICATION ▶** As the owner of a small company, why is it important that Melissa take an active part in the management of the internal control system?

LO 1, 2

Control Activities

P7. Midori Cabinet Company provides maintenance services to factories in and around Boca-Raton, Florida. The company, which buys a large amount of cleaning supplies, consistently has been over budget in its expenditures for these items. In the past, supplies were left out in the open in the warehouse to be taken each evening as needed by the onsite supervisors. A clerk in the accounting department periodically ordered additional supplies from a long-time supplier. No records were maintained other than to record purchases. Once a year, an inventory of supplies was made for the preparation of the financial statements.

To solve the budgetary problem, management decides to implement a new system for purchasing and controlling supplies. The following actions take place:

1. Management places a supplies clerk in charge of a secured storeroom for cleaning supplies.
2. Supervisors use a purchase requisition to request supplies for the jobs they oversee.
3. Each job receives a predetermined amount of supplies based on a study of each job's needs.

4. In the storeroom, the supplies clerk notes the levels of supplies and completes the purchase requisition when new supplies are needed.
5. The purchase requisition goes to the purchasing clerk, a new position. The purchasing clerk is solely responsible for authorizing purchases and preparing the purchase orders.
6. Supplier prices are monitored constantly by the purchasing clerk to ensure that the lowest price is obtained.
7. When supplies are received, the supplies clerk checks them in and prepares a receiving report. The supplies clerk sends the receiving report to accounting, where each payment to a supplier is documented by the purchase requisition, the purchase order, and the receiving report.
8. The accounting department also maintains a record of supplies inventory, supplies requisitioned by supervisors, and supplies received.
9. Once each month, the warehouse manager takes a physical inventory of cleaning supplies in the storeroom and compares it against the supplies inventory records that the accounting department maintains.

REQUIRED

1. Indicate which of the control activities that follow applies to each of the improvements in the internal control system. (*Hint:* More than one may apply.)
   a. Authorization
   b. Recording transactions
   c. Documents and records
   d. Physical controls
   e. Periodic independent verification
   f. Separation of duties
   g. Sound personnel practices
2. **ACCOUNTING CONNECTION ▶** Explain why each new control activity (a through g) is an improvement over the activities of the old system.

LO **1, 2**

Internal Control Activities

P8. ACCOUNTING CONNECTION ▶ Fuentes is a retail store with several departments. Its internal control procedures for cash sales and purchases are as follows.

Cash sales. The sales clerk in each department rings up every cash sale on the department's cash register. The cash register produces a sales slip, which the clerk gives to the customer along with the merchandise. A continuous tape locked inside the cash register makes a carbon copy of the sales ticket. At the end of each day, the sales clerk presses a "total" key on the register, and it prints the total sales for the day on the continuous tape. The sales clerk then unlocks the tape, reads the total sales figure, and makes the entry in the accounting records for the day's cash sales. Next, she counts the cash in the drawer, places the $200 change fund back in the drawer, and gives the cash received to the cashier. Finally, she files the cash register tape and is ready for the next day's business.

Purchases. At the request of the various department heads, the purchasing agent orders all goods. When the goods arrive, the receiving clerk prepares a receiving report in triplicate. The receiving clerk keeps one copy; the other two copies go to the purchasing agent and the department head. Invoices are forwarded immediately to the accounting department to ensure payment before the discount period elapses. After payment, the invoice is forwarded to the purchasing agent for comparison with the purchase order and the receiving report and is then returned to the accounting office for filing.

REQUIRED

1. Identify the significant internal control weaknesses in each of the above situations.
2. In each case identified in requirement 1, recommend changes that would improve the system.

LO 3

Bank Reconciliation

✔ 1: Adjusted book balance, April 30: $149,473.28

SPREADSHEET

GENERAL LEDGER

P9. The following information is available for Delta Company as of April 30, 2014:

a. Cash on the books as of April 30 amounted to $114,175.28. Cash on the bank statement for the same date was $141,717.08.
b. A deposit of $14,249.84, representing cash receipts of April 30, did not appear on the bank statement.
c. Outstanding checks totaled $7,293.64.
d. A check for $2,420.00 returned with the statement was recorded as $2,024.00. The check was for advertising.
e. The bank service charge for April amounted to $26.00.
f. The bank collected $36,400.00 for Delta Company on a note. The face value of the note was $36,000.00.
g. An NSF check for $1,140.00 from a customer, Hasan Ali, was returned with the statement.
h. The bank mistakenly deducted a check for $800.00 that was drawn by Alpha Corporation.
i. The bank reported a credit of $460.00 for interest on the average balance.

REQUIRED

1. Prepare a bank reconciliation for Delta as of April 30, 2014.
2. Prepare the necessary journal entries from the reconciliation.
3. State the amount of cash that should appear on Delta's balance sheet as of April 30.
4. **ACCOUNTING CONNECTION ▶** Why is a bank reconciliation a necessary internal control?

LO 4

Imprest (Petty Cash) Fund Transactions

✔ 1: July 31 credit to Cash: $737.16

SPREADSHEET

P10. On July 1, 2014, Acting Company established an imprest (petty cash) fund in the amount of $800.00 in cash from a check drawn for the purpose of establishing the fund. On July 31, the petty cash fund has cash of $62.84 and the following receipts on hand: for merchandise received, $408.60; freight-in, $131.48; laundry service, $168.00; and miscellaneous expense, $29.08. A check was drawn to replenish the fund.

On Aug. 31, the petty cash fund has cash of $110.00 and the following receipts on hand: merchandise, $393.68; freight-in, $152.60; laundry service, $168.00; and miscellaneous expense, $15.72. The petty cash custodian is not able to account for the excess cash in the fund. A check is drawn to replenish the fund.

REQUIRED

1. Prepare the journal entries necessary to record each of these transactions. The company uses the periodic inventory system.
2. **ACCOUNTING CONNECTION ▶** What are two examples of why a local semiprofessional baseball team might have need for an imprest (petty cash) system?

CASES

LO 1, 2

Conceptual Understanding: Control Systems

C1. In the spring of each year, Steinbrook College's theater department puts on a contemporary play. Before the performance, the theater manager instructs student volunteers in their duties as cashier, ticket taker, and usher.

The cashier, who is located in a box office at the entrance to the auditorium, receives cash from customers and enters the number of tickets and the amount paid into a computer, which prints out serially numbered tickets. The cashier puts the cash in a locked cash drawer and gives the tickets to the customer.

Customers give their tickets to the ticket taker. The ticket taker tears each ticket in half, gives one half to the customer, and puts the other half in a locked box.

When customers present their ticket stubs to an usher, the usher shows them to their seats.

1. Describe how each of the control activities discussed in this chapter (authorization, recording transactions, documents and records, physical controls, periodic independent verification, separation of duties, and sound personnel practices) apply to the to the control system that includes the cashier, ticket taker, and usher.
2. Could the cashier issue a ticket to a friend without taking in cash? Could the ticket taker allow friends to enter without a ticket? If so, how might they be caught?

LO **1, 2**

Interpreting Financial Reports: Internal Control Lapse

C2. Starbucks Corporation accused an employee and her husband of embezzling $3.7 million by billing the company for services from a fictitious consulting firm. The couple created a phony company called RAD Services, Inc., and charged Starbucks for work they never provided. The employee worked in Starbucks' Information Technology Department.[12] RAD Services charged Starbucks as much as $492,800 for consulting services in a single week. For such a fraud to have taken place, certain control activities were likely not implemented. Identify and describe these activities.

LO **1, 2**

Conceptual Understanding: Internal Controls

C3. Go to a local retail business, such as a bookstore, clothing shop, gift shop, grocery store, hardware store, or car dealership. Ask to speak to someone who is knowledgeable about the store's methods of internal control. After you and other members of the class have completed this step individually, your instructor will divide the class into groups. Group members will compare their findings and develop answers to the questions that follow. A member of each group will then present the group's answers to the class.

1. How does the company protect itself against inventory theft and loss?
2. What control activities, including authorization, recording transactions, documents and records, physical controls, periodic independent verification, separation of duties, and sound personnel practices, does the company use?
3. Can you see these control procedures in use?

LO **1, 5**

Annual Report Case: Internal Control Responsibilities

C4. BUSINESS APPLICATION ▶ To answer the questions that follow, refer to "Management's Report on Internal Control Over Financial Reporting" and the "Report of Independent Registered Public Accounting Firm" in **CVS**'s annual report in the Supplement to Chapter 1.

1. What is management's responsibility with regard to internal control over financial reporting?
2. What is management's conclusion regarding its assessment of internal control over financial reporting?
3. Does CVS's auditor agree with management's assessment?
4. What does the auditor say about the limitations or risks associated with internal control?

LO **1**

Comparison Analysis: Contrasting Internal Control Needs

C5. BUSINESS APPLICATION ▶ In a typical **CVS** store, customers wheel carts down aisles to select items for purchase and take them to a checkout counter where they pay with cash or credit card. The company is concerned that customers might leave the store with merchandise that they have not paid for. Typically, customers of **Southwest Airlines** have already paid for their tickets when they arrive at the gate. The company is concerned that customers who do not have tickets might be allowed on the plane. (Southwest does not have assigned seating.) Compare the risks for each company in the situations just described and the internal control process.

LO 1, 2

Ethical Dilemma: Personal Responsibility for Mistakes

C6. Suppose you have a part-time sales position over the winter break in a small clothing store that is part of a national chain. The store's one full-time employee, with whom you have become friendly, hired you. Explain what you would do in the situations described below, and identify two internal control problems that exist in each situation.

1. You arrive at the store at 6 P.M. to take over the evening shift from the full-time employee who hired you. You notice that this person takes a coat from a rack, puts it on, and leaves by the back door. You are not sure if the coat is one that was for sale or if it belonged to the employee.
2. You are the only person in the store on a busy evening. At closing time, you total the cash register and the receipts and discover that the cash register is $20 short of cash. You consider replacing the $20 out of your pocket because you think you may have made a mistake and are afraid you might lose your job if the company thinks you took the money.

Continuing Case: Annual Report Project

C7. Using the most recent annual report of the company you have chosen to study and that you have accessed online at the company's website, examine the balance sheet and accompanying notes of your company. Answer the following questions:

1. What percentage is cash to total current assets? Do you think this percentage represents the importance of cash to the company's operations?
2. Find the note about cash in the notes to the financial statements. What is included in cash?
3. Given the industry your company is in, what do you think are some of its most important internal control issues?

CHAPTER 8

LEARNING OBJECTIVES

LO 1 Define receivables, and explain the allowance method for valuation of receivables as an application of accrual accounting.

LO 2 Apply the allowance method of accounting for uncollectible accounts.

LO 3 Make common calculations for notes receivable.

LO 4 Show how to evaluate the level of receivables, and identify alternative means of financing receivables.

RECEIVABLES

Business Insight
Hewlett-Packard (HP) Company

Hewlett-Packard Company (HP) is one of the largest and best-known companies in the computer industry. It sells its computers, printers, and related products to individual consumers, small and large businesses, and government, health, and educational organizations. Like any company that sells on credit, HP must give its customers time to pay for their purchases while at the same time retaining enough cash to pay its suppliers. As you can see from HP's Financial Highlights, cash and accounts receivable have made up over 50 percent of the company's current assets in recent years.[1] HP must therefore plan and control its cash flows very carefully.

HP'S FINANCIAL HIGHLIGHTS (in millions)

	2011	2010	2009
Cash	$ 8,043	$ 10,929	$ 13,279
Accounts receivable, net	18,224	18,481	16,537
Total current assets	51,021	54,184	52,539
Net revenue	127,245	126,033	114,552

1. **CONCEPT** ▶ How does HP apply accrual accounting to its receivables, and how does it properly disclose their value?
2. **ACCOUNTING APPLICATION** ▶ How can HP estimate the value of its receivables?
3. **BUSINESS APPLICATION** ▶ How can HP evaluate the effectiveness of its credit policies and the level of its accounts receivable?

SECTION 1 CONCEPTS

CONCEPTS

- Accrual accounting (matching principle)
- Valuation
- Disclosure

RELEVANT LEARNING OBJECTIVE

LO 1 Define receivables, and explain the allowance method for valuation of receivables as an application of accrual accounting.

LO 1 Concepts Underlying Notes and Accounts Receivable

The most common receivables are accounts receivable and notes receivable. The *allowance method* is used to apply *accrual accounting* to the *valuation* of accounts receivable. Proper *disclosure* in the financial statements and the notes to them is important for users of the statements to interpret them.

Accounts Receivable

Accounts receivable are short-term financial assets that arise from sales on credit and are often called **trade credit**. Terms of trade credit usually range from 5 to 60 days, depending on industry practice, and may allow customers to pay in installments. Credit sales or loans not made in the ordinary course of business, such as those made to employees, officers, or owners, should appear separately under asset titles like Receivables from Employees. Exhibit 1 shows the level of accounts receivable in selected industries.

Exhibit 1
Accounts Receivable as a Percentage of Total Assets for Selected Industries

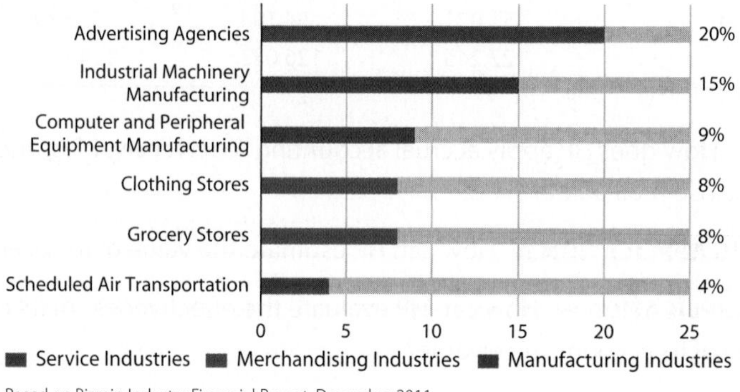

Based on Bizmin Industry Financial Report, December 2011.

Companies that sell on credit do so to be competitive and to increase sales. In setting credit terms, a company must keep in mind the credit terms of its competitors and the needs of its customers. Obviously, any company that sells on credit wants customers who will pay their bills on time. To increase the likelihood of selling only to customers who will pay on time, most companies develop control procedures and maintain a credit department. The credit department's responsibilities include examining each person or company that applies for credit and approving or rejecting a credit sale to that customer. Typically, the credit department asks for information about the customer's financial resources and debts. It may also check personal references and credit bureaus for further information. Based on the information it has gathered, it decides whether to extend credit to the customer.

Companies that are too lenient in granting credit can run into difficulties when customers don't pay. For example, **Sprint**, one of the weaker companies in the competitive cell phone industry, targeted customers with poor credit histories. It attracted so many who failed to pay their bills that its stock dropped by 50 percent, to $2.50, because of the losses that resulted.[2]

Design Pics/Jupiter Images

You may already be familiar with promissory notes if you have taken out student loans or car loans. When you take out these loans, you sign a contract with a lender promising to repay the loan under certain terms.

Companies that extend credit to customers know that some of these customers cannot or will not pay. The accounts of such customers are called **uncollectible accounts** (or *bad debts*), and they are expenses of selling on credit. In accordance with *accrual accounting*, to match these expenses to the revenues they help generate, they should be recognized at the time credit sales are made.

Some companies recognize a loss when they determine that an account is uncollectible by reducing Accounts Receivable and increasing Uncollectible Accounts Expense. Federal regulations require companies to use this method—called the **direct charge-off method**—in computing taxable income. However, because a direct charge-off is usually recorded in a different period from the one in which the sale takes place, this method is not in accord with *accrual accounting*. Generally accepted accounting principles, therefore, require the use of the allowance method of accounting for uncollectible accounts.

Notes Receivable

STUDY NOTE: *Accounts receivable and accounts payable are distinguished from notes receivable and notes payable because the former were not created by a formal promissory note.*

Notes receivable are short-term financial assets supported by written agreements called promissory notes. A **promissory note** is an unconditional promise to pay a definite sum of money on demand or at a future date. The person or company that signs the note and, thereby, promises to pay is the *maker* of the note. The entity to whom payment is to be made is the *payee*. The promissory note shown in Exhibit 2 is an unconditional promise by the maker, Samuel Mason, to pay a definite sum—or principal ($1,000)—to the payee, Cook County Bank & Trust, on August 18, 2014. The note is dated May 20, 2014, and bears an interest rate of 8 percent. This interest accrues by a small amount each day the note is outstanding, increasing the payee's interest receivable and interest income.

Exhibit 2
A Promissory Note

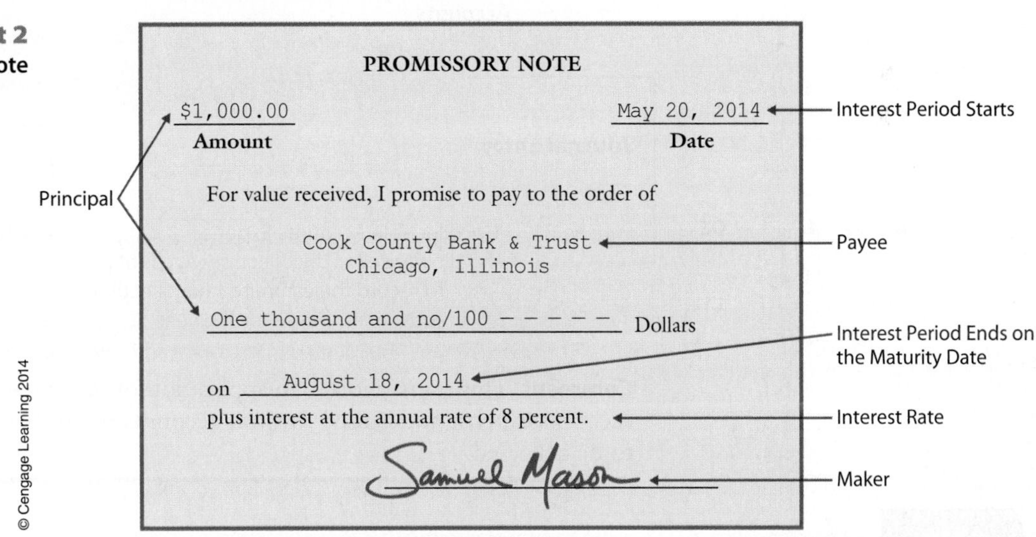
PROMISSORY NOTE

$1,000.00 Amount   May 20, 2014 Date

For value received, I promise to pay to the order of

Cook County Bank & Trust
Chicago, Illinois

One thousand and no/100 - - - - - Dollars

on August 18, 2014

plus interest at the annual rate of 8 percent.

Samuel Mason

The nature of a company's business generally determines how frequently it receives promissory notes from customers. Firms that sell durable goods of high value, such as farm machinery and automobiles, often accept promissory notes. Among the advantages of these notes are that they produce interest income and represent a stronger legal claim against a debtor than accounts receivable do. In addition, selling—or discounting—promissory notes to banks is a common financing method. Almost all companies occasionally accept promissory notes, and many companies obtain them in settlement of past-due accounts receivable.

The Allowance Method: Using Accrual Accounting to Value Receivables

STUDY NOTE: *The allowance method relies on an estimate of uncollectible accounts; but unlike the direct charge-off method, it is in accord with accrual accounting.*

The **allowance method** is an application of *accrual accounting*, which requires estimated losses from bad debts to be matched with the revenues they help to produce. Further, they serve to *value* accounts receivable on the balance sheet. As mentioned earlier, when management extends credit to increase sales, it knows it will incur some losses from uncollectible accounts. Losses from credit sales should be recognized when the sales are made. Of course, at that time, management cannot identify which customers will not pay their debts, nor can it predict the exact amount of money the company will lose. Therefore, to follow accrual accounting (*the matching principle*), losses from uncollectible accounts must be estimated, and the estimate becomes an expense in the period in which the sales are made.

Uncollectible Accounts: The Allowance Method

Transaction Mandy Sales Company made most of its sales on credit during its first year of operation, 2014. At the end of the year, accounts receivable amounted to $200,000. On December 31, 2014, management reviewed the collectible status of the accounts receivable. Approximately $12,000 of the $200,000 of accounts receivable were estimated to be uncollectible.

Analysis The adjusting entry to record estimated uncollectible accounts

▲ *increases* the *Uncollectible Accounts Expense* account

▲ *increases* the *Allowance for Uncollectible Accounts* account

Application of Double Entry

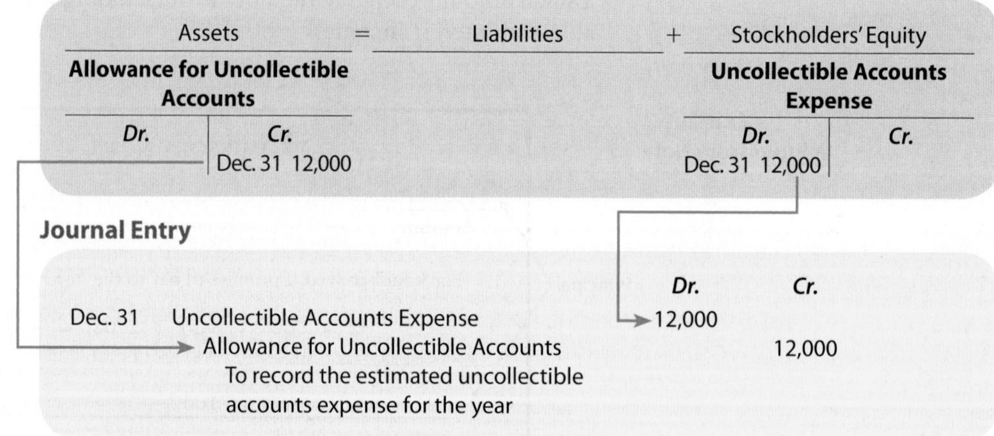

Assets	=	Liabilities	+	Stockholders' Equity	
Allowance for Uncollectible Accounts				**Uncollectible Accounts Expense**	
Dr.	Cr.			Dr.	Cr.
	Dec. 31 12,000			Dec. 31 12,000	

Journal Entry

A	=	L	+	OE
−12,000				−12,000

		Dr.	Cr.
Dec. 31	Uncollectible Accounts Expense	12,000	
	Allowance for Uncollectible Accounts		12,000
	To record the estimated uncollectible accounts expense for the year		

Comment This transaction is an application of *accrual accounting* in that uncollectible accounts expense and is used to *value* accounts receivable at the amount that is expected to be collected.

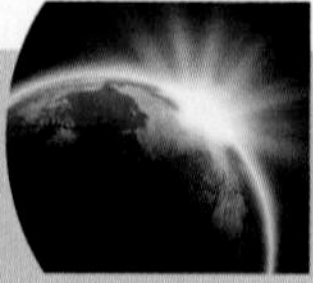

International Perspective

IFRS Can Users Depend on the Allowance for Uncollectible Accounts?

Financial statements contain many estimates, one of which is the allowance for uncollectible accounts. In their effort to converge U.S. GAAP and IFRS, the FASB and the IASB have agreed that estimates must be a faithful representation of what they purport to represent and that they be verifiable. Under their agreement, faithful information is unbiased and contains no errors or omissions. Further, verifiability means that two independent experts could reach agreement as to the estimate.[3] In other words, users can be assured that net accounts receivable (accounts receivable less the allowance) represent the best estimate of the future cash receipts from the receivables.

Disclosure of Receivables

A payee includes all the promissory notes it holds that are due in less than one year as notes receivable in the current assets section of its balance sheet. Any interest accrued on these notes is also included in the current assets section—as **interest receivable**. Because notes are financial instruments, companies may voluntarily *disclose* their fair value. In most cases, fair value approximates the amount in the account records.

STUDY NOTE: *The allowance account often has other titles, such as* Allowance for Doubtful Accounts *and* Allowance for Bad Debts. Bad Debts Expense *is a title often used for* Uncollectible Accounts Expense.

Uncollectible Accounts Expense appears on the income statement as an operating expense. **Allowance for Uncollectible Accounts** appears on the balance sheet as a contra account, deducted from accounts receivable in the current assets section. It reduces the accounts receivable to the amount expected to be collectible (net realizable value), as follows.

Current assets:		
Cash		$ 20,000
Short-term investments		30,000
Notes receivable		15,000
Accounts receivable	$200,000	
Less allowance for uncollectible accounts	12,000	188,000
Interest receivable		1,000
Inventory		112,000
Total current assets		$366,000

A variation of the *disclosure* of accounts receivable on the balance sheet follows.

Accounts receivable (net of allowance for uncollectible accounts of $12,000) $188,000

Accounts receivable may also be shown at "net," with the amount of the allowance for uncollectible accounts identified in a note to the financial statements. For most companies, the "net" amount of accounts receivable approximates fair value. Fair value disclosures are not required for accounts receivable, but 59 percent of large companies made this disclosure voluntarily. Of those, 85 percent indicated that the net accounts receivable approximated fair value.[4]

APPLY IT!

Match the concepts that follow to the related statements.

1. Preparing an adjusting entry to record the estimated uncollectible accounts expense.
2. Subtracting the allowance for uncollectible accounts from accounts receivable.
3. Preparing an adjusting entry to record interest earned on notes receivable.
4. Reporting the net realizable value of receivables on the balance sheet.
5. Separating accounts receivable from receivables from employees.

a. valuation
b. accrual accounting
c. periodicity
d. disclosure

SOLUTION

1. b; 2. a; 3. b; 4. d; 5. d

SECTION 2 ACCOUNTING APPLICATIONS

ACCOUNTING APPLICATIONS

- Estimate uncollectible accounts and uncollectible accounts expense using
  - Percentage of net sales method
  - Accounts receivable aging method
- Write off uncollectible accounts
- Make common calculations for notes receivable

RELEVANT LEARNING OBJECTIVES

LO2 Apply the allowance method of accounting for uncollectible accounts.

LO3 Make common calculations for Notes Receivable.

LO2 Uncollectible Accounts

The allowance account is necessary because the specific uncollectible accounts will not be identified until later. It is not like another contra account, Accumulated Depreciation, whose purpose is to show how much of the plant and equipment cost has been allocated as an expense to previous periods.

If management takes an optimistic view and projects a small loss from uncollectible accounts, the resulting net accounts receivable will be larger than if management takes a pessimistic view. The net income will also be larger under the optimistic view because the estimated expense will be smaller. The company's accountant makes an estimate based on past experience and current economic conditions. For example, losses from uncollectible accounts are normally expected to be greater in a recession than during a period of economic growth. The final decision on the amount of the expense will depend on objective information, such as the accountant's analyses, and on certain qualitative factors, such as how investors, bankers, creditors, and others view the performance of the debtor company. Regardless of the qualitative considerations, the estimated losses from uncollectible accounts should be realistic.

Two common methods of estimating uncollectible accounts expense are the percentage of net sales method and the accounts receivable aging method.

Percentage of Net Sales Method

The basis for the **percentage of net sales method** is the amount of this year's *net sales* that will not be collected. The answer determines the amount of uncollectible accounts expense for the year.

Uncollectible Accounts: The Percentage of Net Sales Method

Transaction The following balances represent Varta Company's ending figures for 2014:

Sales

Dr.		*Cr.*	
		Dec. 31	322,500

Sales Returns and Allowances

Dr.		*Cr.*	
Dec. 31	20,000		

Sales Discounts

Dr.		*Cr.*	
Dec. 31	2,500		

Allowance for Uncollectible Accounts

Dr.		*Cr.*	
		Dec. 31	1,800

Business Perspective
Cash Collections Can Be Hard to Estimate

Companies must not only sell goods and services but also must generate cash flows by collecting on those sales. When there are changes in the economy, some companies make big mistakes in estimating the amount of accounts they will collect. For example, when the dot-com bubble burst in the early 2000s, companies like **Nortel Networks**, **Cisco Systems**, and **Lucent Technologies** increased their estimates of allowances for uncollectible accounts—actions that eliminated previously reported earnings and caused the companies' stock prices to fall.[5] However, it turned out that these companies had overestimated how bad the losses would be. In later years, they reduced their allowances for credit losses, thereby increasing their reported earnings.[6]

The following are Varta's actual losses from uncollectible accounts for the past three years:

Year	Net Sales	Losses from Uncollectible Accounts	Percentage
2011	$260,000	$ 5,100	1.96
2012	297,500	6,950	2.34
2013	292,500	4,950	1.69
Total	$850,000	$17,000	2.00

Varta's management believes that its uncollectible accounts will continue to average about 2 percent of net sales. The uncollectible accounts expense for the year 2014 is therefore estimated as follows.

$$0.02 \times (\$322,500 - \$20,000 - \$2,500) = 0.02 \times \$300,000 = \$6,000$$

Analysis The journal entry to record the estimated uncollectible accounts

▲ *increases* the *Uncollectible Accounts Expense* account

▲ *increases* the *Allowance for Uncollectible Accounts* account

Application of Double Entry

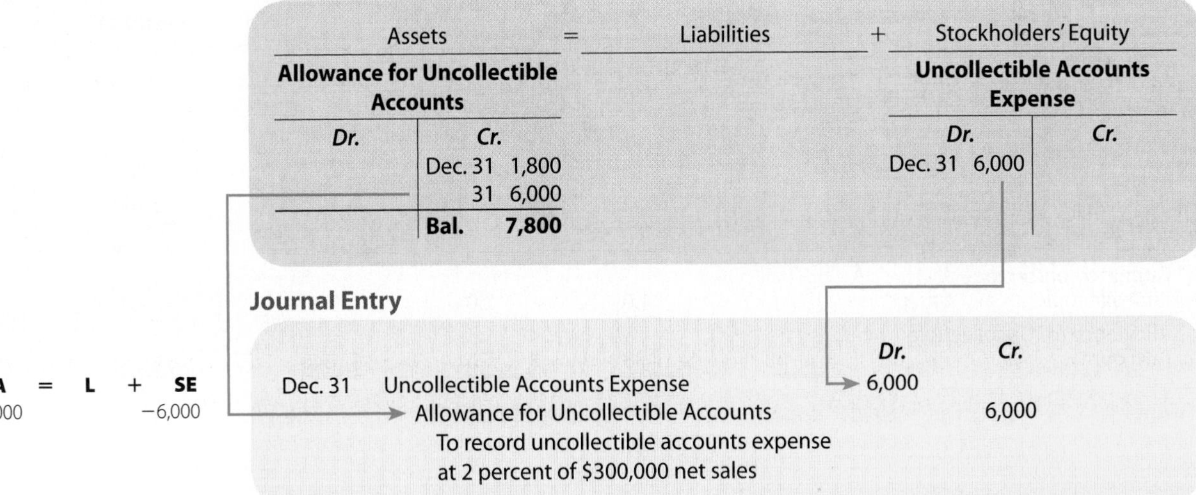

A	=	L	+	SE
−6,000				−6,000

Comment This application of *accrual accounting* leaves the Allowance for Uncollectible Accounts with a balance of $7,800. The balance consists of the $6,000 estimated uncollectible accounts receivable from 2014 sales and the $1,800 estimated uncollectible accounts receivable from previous years.

Accounts Receivable Aging Method

The basis for the **accounts receivable aging method** is the amount of the *ending balance of accounts receivable* that will not be collected. With this method, the ending balance of Allowance for Uncollectible Accounts is determined directly through an analysis of accounts receivable. The difference between the amount determined to be uncollectible and the actual balance of Allowance for Uncollectible Accounts is the expense for the period. In theory, this method should produce the same result as the percentage of net sales method, but in practice it rarely does.

STUDY NOTE: *An aging of accounts receivable is an important tool in cash management because it helps to determine what amounts are likely to be collected in the months ahead.*

The **aging of accounts receivable** is the process of listing each customer's receivable account according to the due date of the account. If the customer's account is past due, there is a possibility that the account will not be paid. And that possibility increases as the account extends further beyond the due date. The aging of accounts receivable helps management evaluate its credit and collection policies and alerts it to possible problems.

To illustrate the accounts receivable aging method, we will use Radko Company. Exhibit 3 illustrates the aging of accounts receivable for Radko. Each account receivable is classified as being not yet due or as being 1–30 days, 31–60 days, 61–90 days, or over 90 days past due. Based on past experience, the estimated percentage for each category is determined and multiplied by the amount in each category to determine the estimated, or target, balance of Allowance for Uncollectible Accounts. In total, it is estimated that $4,918 of the $88,800 in accounts receivable will not be collected.

Exhibit 3
Analysis of Accounts Receivable by Age

Radko Company
Analysis of Accounts Receivable by Age
December 31, 2014

Customer	Total	Not Yet Due	1–30 Days Past Due	31–60 Days Past Due	61–90 Days Past Due	Over 90 Days Past Due
K. Lee	$ 300		$ 300			
F. Moll	800			$ 800		
T. Orr	2,000	$ 1,800	200			
P. Govin	500				$ 500	
Others	85,200	42,000	28,000	7,600	4,400	$3,200
Totals	$88,800	$43,800	$28,500	$8,400	$4,900	$3,200
Estimated percentage uncollectible		1.0	2.0	10.0	30.0	50.0
Allowance for Uncollectible Accounts	$ 4,918	$ 438	$ 570	$ 840	$1,470	$1,600

Once the target balance for Allowance for Uncollectible Accounts has been determined, the amount of the adjustment depends on the current balance of the allowance account. We will assume two cases for the balance of Radko's Allowance for Uncollectible Accounts on December 31: (1) a credit balance of $1,600 and (2) a debit balance of $1,600.

Adjusting the Allowance Account: Credit Balance

Transaction In the first case, an adjustment of $3,318 is needed to bring the balance of the allowance account to a $4,918 credit balance.

Targeted balance for allowance for uncollectible accounts	$4,918
Less current credit balance of allowance for uncollectible accounts	1,600
Uncollectible accounts expense	$3,318

Analysis The journal entry to record the estimated uncollectible accounts

▲ *increases* the *Uncollectible Accounts Expense* account

▲ *increases* the *Allowance for Uncollectible Accounts* account

Application of Double Entry

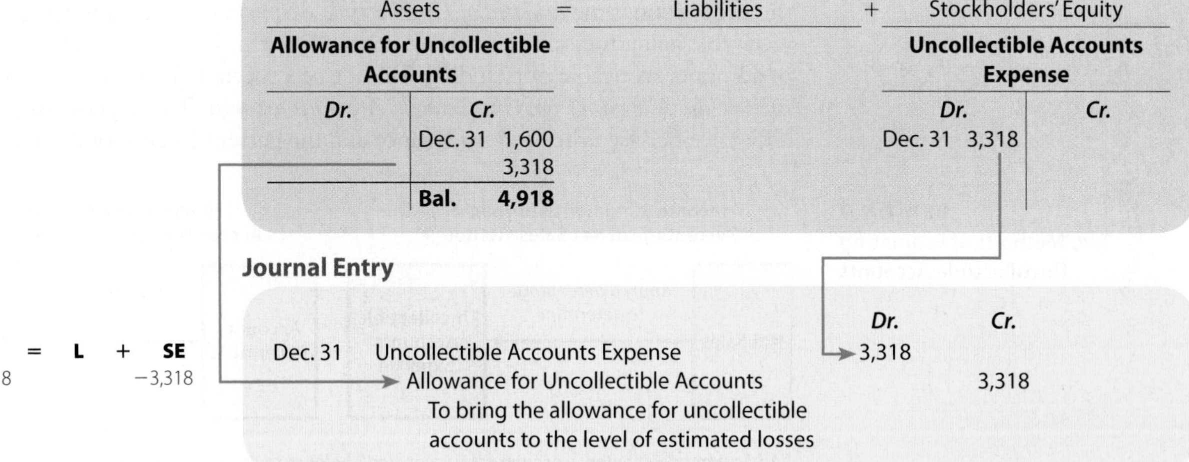

Assets = Liabilities + Stockholders' Equity
Allowance for Uncollectible Accounts
Dr. Cr.
Dec. 31 1,600
3,318
Bal. 4,918
Uncollectible Accounts Expense
Dr. Cr.
Dec. 31 3,318
Journal Entry
A = L + SE
−3,318 −3,318
Dr. Cr.
Dec. 31 Uncollectible Accounts Expense 3,318
Allowance for Uncollectible Accounts 3,318
To bring the allowance for uncollectible accounts to the level of estimated losses

Comment This application of *accrual accounting* results in a balance of Allowance for Uncollectible Accounts of $4,918.

Adjusting the Allowance Account: Debit Balance

STUDY NOTE: *When the write-offs in a period exceed the amount of the allowance, a debit balance in Allowance for Uncollectible Accounts results.*

Transaction In the second case, because Allowance for Uncollectible Accounts has a debit balance of $1,600, the estimated uncollectible accounts expense for the year will have to be $6,518 to reach the targeted balance of $4,918, calculated as follows.

Targeted balance for allowance for uncollectible accounts	$4,918
Plus current debit balance of allowance for uncollectible accounts	1,600
Uncollectible accounts expense	$6,518

Analysis The journal entry to record the estimated uncollectible accounts

- ▲ *increases* the *Uncollectible Accounts Expense* account
- ▲ *increases* the *Allowance for Uncollectible Accounts* account

Application of Double Entry

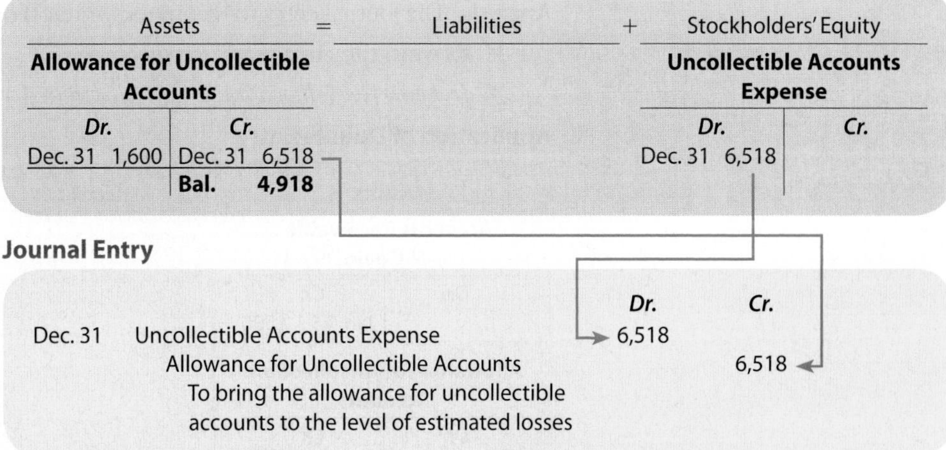

Assets = Liabilities + Stockholders' Equity
Allowance for Uncollectible Accounts
Dr. Cr.
Dec. 31 1,600 Dec. 31 6,518
Bal. 4,918
Uncollectible Accounts Expense
Dr. Cr.
Dec. 31 6,518
Journal Entry
A = L + SE
−6,518 −6,518
Dr. Cr.
Dec. 31 Uncollectible Accounts Expense 6,518
Allowance for Uncollectible Accounts 6,518
To bring the allowance for uncollectible accounts to the level of estimated losses

Comment After this entry applying *accrual accounting*, Allowance for Uncollectible Accounts has a credit balance *valuation* of $4,918, which represents the amount of losses expected in the future.

Comparison of the Two Methods

Both the percentage of net sales method and the accounts receivable aging method estimate the uncollectible accounts expense in accordance with *accrual accounting*, but as shown in

STUDY NOTE: *Describing the aging method as the balance sheet approach emphasizes that the computation is based on ending accounts receivable rather than on net sales for the period.*

Exhibit 4, they do so in different ways. The percentage of net sales method is an income statement approach. It assumes that a certain proportion of sales will not be collected, and this proportion is the *amount of Uncollectible Accounts Expense* for the period. The accounts receivable aging method is a balance sheet approach. It assumes that a certain proportion of accounts receivable outstanding will not be collected. This amount is the *targeted balance of the Allowance for Uncollectible Accounts account.* The expense for the period is the difference between the targeted balance and the current balance of the allowance account.

Exhibit 4
Two Methods of Estimating Uncollectible Accounts

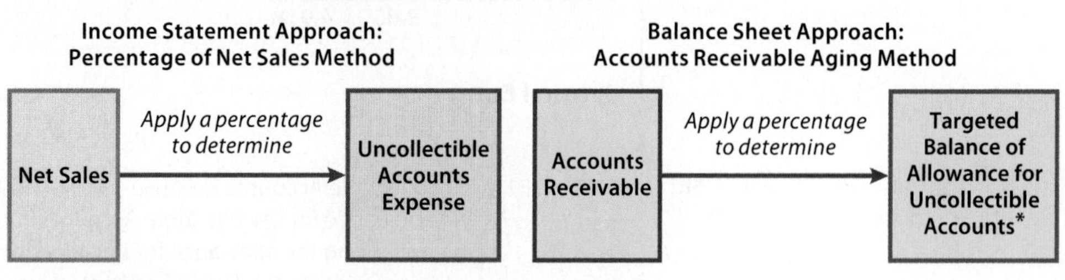

*Add current debit balance or subtract current credit balance to determine uncollectible accounts expense.

Writing Off Uncollectible Accounts

STUDY NOTE: *When writing off an individual account, debit Allowance for Uncollectible Accounts, not Uncollectible Accounts Expense.*

Regardless of the method used to estimate uncollectible accounts, the total of accounts receivable written off in a period will rarely equal the estimated uncollectible amount. The allowance account will show a credit balance when the total written off is less than the estimated uncollectible amount. It will show a debit balance when the total written off is greater than the estimated uncollectible amount.

When it becomes clear that a specific account receivable will not be collected, the amount should be written off to Allowance for Uncollectible Accounts. Remember that the uncollectible amount was already accounted for as an expense when the allowance was established.

Writing Off Uncollectible Accounts

Transaction On January 15, 2015, P. Govin, who owes Radko Company $500, is declared bankrupt by a federal court.

Analysis The journal entry to record the write-off of an account receivable as uncollectible

▼ *decreases* the *Accounts Receivable* account

▼ *decreases* the *Allowance for Uncollectible Accounts* account

Application of Double Entry

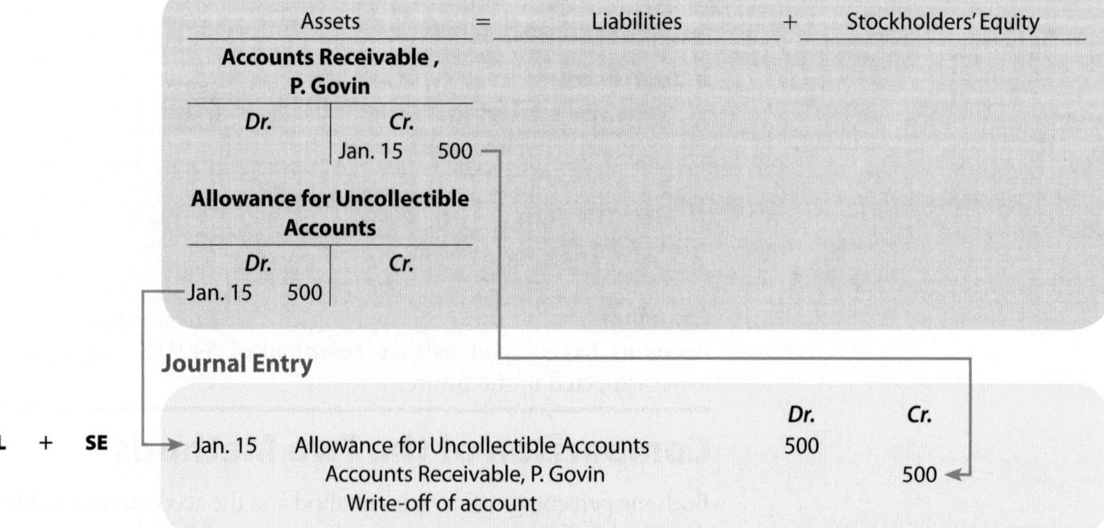

Journal Entry

		Dr.	Cr.
Jan. 15	Allowance for Uncollectible Accounts	500	
	Accounts Receivable, P. Govin		500
	Write-off of account		

A	=	L	+	SE
+500				
−500				

Comment The application of *accrual accounting* recognized the failure to collect this account through the estimate of uncollectible accounts occurred in a prior period. In the earlier period, it was not possible to identify which accounts would not be received.

Although the write-off removes the uncollectible amount from Accounts Receivable, it does not affect the estimated net realizable value of accounts receivable. It simply reduces P. Govin's account to zero and reduces Allowance for Uncollectible Accounts by $500, as shown below.

	Balances Before Write-Off	Balances After Write-Off
Accounts receivable	$88,800	$88,300
Less allowance for uncollectible accounts	4,918	4,418
Estimated net realizable value of accounts receivable	$83,882	$83,882

Occasionally, a customer whose account has been written off as uncollectible will later be able to pay some or all of the amount owed. When that happens, two entries must be made: one to reverse the earlier write-off (which is now incorrect) and another to show the collection of the account.

APPLY IT!

Drums Instruments Co. sells its merchandise on credit. In the company's last fiscal year, which ended July 31, it had net sales of $7,000,000. At the end of the fiscal year, it had Accounts Receivable of $1,800,000 and a credit balance of $11,200 in Allowance for Uncollectible Accounts. In the past, the company has been unable to collect on approximately 1 percent of its net sales. An aging analysis of accounts receivable has indicated that $80,000 of current receivables are estimated to be uncollectible.

1. Calculate the amount of uncollectible accounts expense, and use T accounts to determine the resulting balance of Allowance for Uncollectible Accounts under the percentage of net sales method and the accounts receivable aging method.
2. How would your answers change if Allowance for Uncollectible Accounts had a debit balance of $11,200 instead of a credit balance?

SOLUTION

1. Percentage of net sales method:

Allowance for Uncollectible Accounts

Dr.	*Cr.*	
	July 31	11,200
	31 UA Exp.	70,000*
	July 31 Bal.	**81,200**

*Uncollectible Accounts Expense = $7,000,000 × 0.01

Aging Method:

Allowance for Uncollectible Accounts

Dr.	*Cr.*	
	July 31	11,200
	31 UA Exp.	68,800*
	July 31 Bal.	**80,000**

*Uncollectible Accounts Expense = $80,000 − $11,200

2. Under the percentage of net sales method, the amount of the expense is the same. However, if the allowance account (before adjustment) has a debit balance, its ending balance will be $58,800 ($70,000 − $11,200). Under the accounts receivable aging method, the ending balance in the allowance account is the same. However, if the allowance account (before adjustment) has a debit balance, the amount of the expense will be $91,200 ($80,000 + $11,200).

TRY IT! SE3, SE4, SE5, E2A, E3A, E4A, E5A, E6A, E7A, E2B, E3B, E4B, E5B, E6B, E7B

LO3 Common Calculations for Notes Receivable

As defined previously, notes are promises to pay a definite amount at a definite future date. Such notes typically state a rate of interest that must also be paid at that future date. These features are the basis for several calculations that are common to promissory notes:

- Maturity date
- Duration of a note
- Interest
- Maturity value
- Accrued interest

Maturity Date

The **maturity date** is the date on which a promissory note must be paid. This date must be stated on the note or be determinable from the facts stated on the note. The following are among the most common statements of maturity date:

- A specific date, such as "November 14, 2014"
- A specific number of months after the date of the note, such as "three months after November 14, 2014"
- A specific number of days after the date of the note, such as "60 days after November 14, 2014"

The maturity date is obvious when a specific date is stated. When the maturity date is a number of months from the date of the note, one simply uses the same day in the appropriate future month. For example, a note dated January 20 that is due in two months would be due on March 20.

When the maturity date is a specific number of days from the date of the note, however, the exact maturity date must be determined. In computing this date, it is important to exclude the date of the note. For example, a note dated May 20 and due in 90 days would be due on August 18, determined as follows.

Days remaining in May (31 – 20)	11
Days in June	30
Days in July	31
Days in August	18
Total days	90

Duration of a Note

The **duration of a note** is the time between a promissory note's issue date and its maturity date. Interest is calculated on the basis of the duration of a note. Identifying the duration is easy when the maturity date is a specific number of days from the date of the note. However, when the maturity date is stated as a specific date, the exact number of days must be determined. Assume that a note issued on May 10 matures on August 10. The duration of the note is 92 days.

Days remaining in May (31 – 10)	21
Days in June	30
Days in July	31
Days in August	10
Total days	92

Interest

Interest is the cost of borrowing money or the return on lending money, depending on whether one is the borrower or the lender. The amount of interest is based on three factors:

- Principal (the amount of money borrowed or lent)
- Rate of interest
- Length of the loan

The formula used in computing interest follows.

$$\text{Principal} \times \text{Rate of Interest} \times \text{Time} = \text{Interest}$$

Interest rates are usually stated on an annual basis. For example, the interest on a one-year, 8 percent, $1,000 note would be:

$$\text{Principal} \times \text{Rate of Interest} \times \text{Time} = \text{Interest}$$
$$\$1{,}000 \times 8/100 \times 1 = \$80$$

If the term of the note is three months instead of a year, the interest charge would be calculated as follows.

$$\$1{,}000 \times 8/100 \times 3/12 = \$20$$

When the term of a note is expressed in days, the exact number of days must be used in computing the interest. Thus, if the term of the note described was 45 days, the interest would be $9.86, computed as follows.

$$\$1{,}000 \times 8/100 \times 45/365 = \$9.86^*$$

*Rounded

Maturity Value

The **maturity value** is the total proceeds of a promissory note—face value plus interest—at the maturity date. The maturity value of a 90-day, 8 percent, $1,000 note is computed as follows.

$$\begin{aligned} \text{Maturity Value} &= \text{Principal} + \text{Interest} \\ &= \$1{,}000 + (\$1{,}000 \times 8/100 \times 90/365) \\ &= \$1{,}000 + \$19.73^* \\ &= \$1{,}019.73 \end{aligned}$$

*Rounded

Some notes, called *non-interest-bearing notes*, do not specify an interest rate. The maturity value of these notes is the face value, or principal amount. The principal includes an implied interest cost.

Accrued Interest

Accrued interest must be apportioned to the periods in which it belongs. For example, assume that the $1,000, 90-day, 8 percent note discussed previously was received on August 31 and that the fiscal year ended on September 30. In this case, interest for 30 days, or $6.58, is calculated as follows.

$$\text{Principal} \times \text{Rate of Interest} \times \text{Time} = \text{Interest}$$

$$\$1{,}000 \times 8/100 \times 30/365 = \$6.58^*$$

*Rounded

The $6.58 of interest would be earned in the fiscal year that ends on September 30. The remainder of the interest income, $13.15, would be calculated as follows.

$$\$1{,}000 \times 8/100 \times 60/365 = \$13.15^*$$

*Rounded

This amount would be recorded as income, and the interest receivable ($6.58) would be shown as received when the note is paid. Note that all the cash for the interest is received when the note is paid, but the interest income is apportioned to two fiscal years.

Dishonored Note

A note not paid at maturity is called a **dishonored note**. The holder, or payee, of a dishonored note should transfer the total amount due (including interest income) from Notes Receivable to an individual account receivable for the debtor. This transfer accomplishes two things:

- It leaves only notes that are presumably collectible in the Notes Receivable account.
- It establishes a record showing that the customer has dishonored a note receivable, which may be helpful in deciding whether to extend credit to that customer in the future.

Receivables and the Financial Statements

Exhibit 5 shows that accounts receivable on the balance sheet is closely related to sales on the income statement. The estimation of uncollectible credit sales affects the amount of net accounts receivable and operating expenses. Interest income on notes receivable affects the amount of assets and revenues.

Exhibit 5
Valuation of Accounts Receivable on the Balance Sheet Impacts Net Sales on the Income Statement

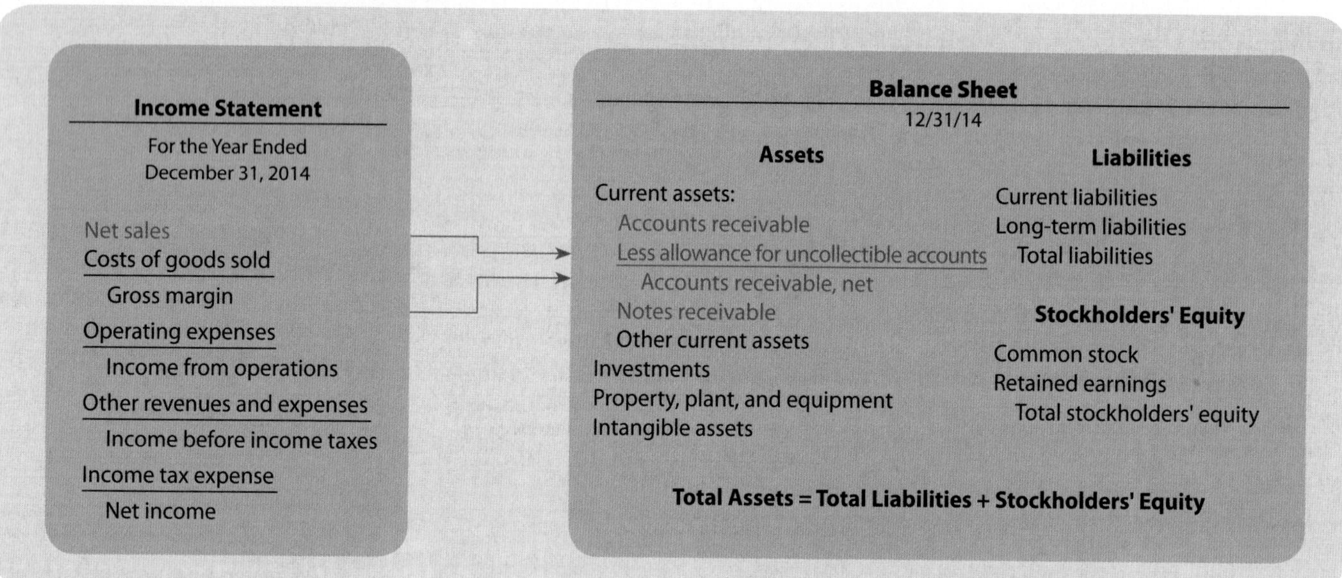

APPLY IT!

Assume that on December 1, 2014, a company receives a 90-day, 8 percent, $5,000 note and that the company prepares financial statements monthly.

1. What is the maturity date of the note?
2. How much interest will be earned on the note if it is paid when due?
3. What is the maturity value of the note?
4. If the company's fiscal year ends on December 31, describe the adjusting entry that would be made, including the amount.
5. How much interest will be earned on this note in 2015?

SOLUTION

1. Maturity date is March 1, 2015, determined as follows.

Days remaining in December (31 − 1)	30
Days in January	31
Days in February	28
Days in March	1
Total days	90

2. Interest: $5,000 × 8/100 × 90/365 = $98.63*
3. Maturity value: $5,000 + $98.63 = $5,098.63
4. An adjusting entry to accrue 30 days of interest income in the amount of $32.88* ($5,000 × 8/100 × 30/365) would be needed.
5. Interest earned in 2015: $65.75 ($98.63 − $32.88)

* Rounded

TRY IT! SE6, SE7, SE8, E8A, E9A, E10A, E11A, E8B, E9B, E10B, E11B

SECTION 3 BUSINESS APPLICATIONS

SINESS APPLICATIONS
- Receivables turnover
- Days' sales uncollected
- Financing receivables
  - Factoring of accounts receivable
  - Securitization of accounts receivable
  - Discounting of accounts receivable
- Ethics

LEVANT ARNING OBJECTIVE

4 Show how to evaluate the level of receivables, d identify alternative means financing receivables.

LO 4 Evaluating the Level of Accounts Receivable and Ethical Ramifications

Receivables are an important asset for any company that sells on credit. For them, it is critical to manage the level of receivables. Two common measures of the effect of a company's credit policies are receivables turnover and days' sales uncollected. Further, many companies manage their receivables by using various means to finance them. Finally, the judgments in estimating uncollectible accounts are a temptation for unethical behavior.

Receivables Turnover

The **receivables turnover** shows how many times, on average, a company turned its receivables into cash during a period. It reflects the relative size of a company's accounts receivable and the success of its credit and collection policies. It may also be affected by external factors, such as seasonal conditions and interest rates.

The receivables turnover is computed by dividing net sales by the average accounts receivable (net of allowances). Theoretically, the numerator should be net credit sales; but since the amount of net credit sales is rarely available in public reports, investors use total net sales. Using data from **HP**'s annual report (presented at the beginning of the chapter), we can compute the company's receivables turnover in 2011 as follows (dollar amounts are in millions).

RATIO

Receivables Turnover: How Many Times Did the Company Collect Its Accounts Receivable During an Accounting Period?

$$\text{Receivables Turnover} = \frac{\text{Net Sales}}{\text{Average Accounts Receivable}}$$

$$\frac{\$127{,}245}{(\$18{,}224 + \$18{,}481)/2} = \frac{\$127{,}245}{\$18{,}352.50} = 6.9 \text{ times*}$$

* Rounded

Based on Bizmin Industry Financial Report, December 2011.

To interpret a company's ratios, you must take into consideration the norms of the industry in which it operates. As shown, the receivables turnover ratio varies substantially from industry to industry. Because grocery stores have few receivables, they have a very high turnover (37.7). The turnover in the computer and peripheral equipment manufacturing industry is much lower (4.5) because that industry tends to have longer credit terms. HP, however, compares very favorably to the industry average with a receivables turnover of 6.9 times.

Days' Sales Uncollected

Days' sales uncollected shows, on average, how long it takes to collect accounts receivable. To determine the days' sales uncollected, the number of days in a year is divided by the receivables turnover. For **HP**, it is computed as follows.

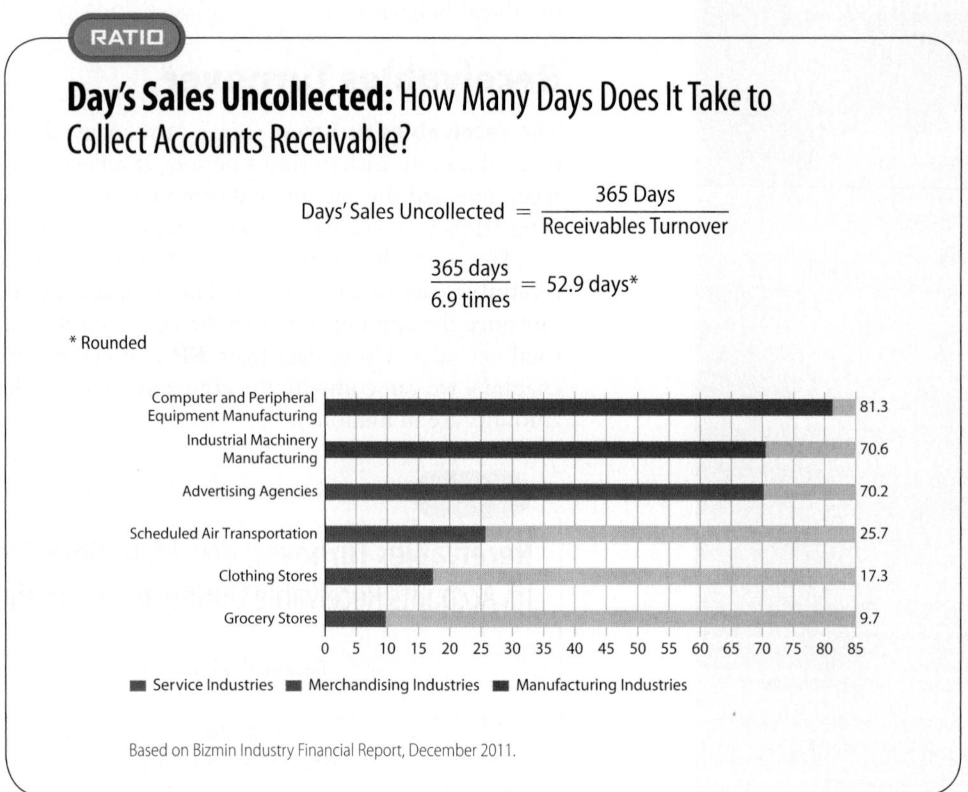

STUDY NOTE: For many businesses with seasonal sales activity, such as ***Nordstrom, Dillard's,*** *and* ***Macy's,*** *receivables are highest at the balance sheet date, resulting in an artificially low receivables turnover and a high days' sales uncollected.*

As you can see, grocery stores have the lowest days' sales uncollected (9.7 days), and they therefore require the least amount of receivables financing. The computer and peripheral equipment manufacturing industry, on the other hand, has more days' sales uncollected (81.3). Again, HP is better than the industry with only 52.9 days. This means that HP must wait fewer days to collect its receivables.

Financing Receivables

Companies that have significant amounts of assets tied up in accounts receivable may be unwilling or unable to wait until they collect cash from their receivables. Many corporations have set up finance companies to help their customers pay for the purchase of their products. For example, **Ford** has set up Ford Motor Credit Company (FMCC) and **Sears** has set up Sears Roebuck Acceptance Corporation (SRAC). Other companies borrow funds by pledging their accounts receivable as collateral. If a company does not pay back its loan, the creditor can take the collateral (in this case, the accounts receivable) and convert it to cash to satisfy the loan.

Companies can also finance their receivables by selling or transferring accounts receivable to another entity. Three methods of financing receivables in this way are factoring, securitization, and discounting.

STUDY NOTE: *A company that factors its receivables will have a better receivables turnover and days' sales uncollected than a company that does not.*

Factoring As illustrated in Exhibit 6, **factoring** is the sale or transfer of accounts receivable to an entity, called a **factor**. Factoring can be done with or without recourse. *With recourse* means that the seller of the receivables is liable to the factor (i.e., the purchaser) if a receivable cannot be collected. *Without recourse* means that the factor bears any losses from unpaid accounts. A company's acceptance of credit cards like **Visa**, **MasterCard**, or **American Express** is an example of factoring without recourse because the issuers of the cards accept the risk of nonpayment.

Exhibit 6
How Factoring Works

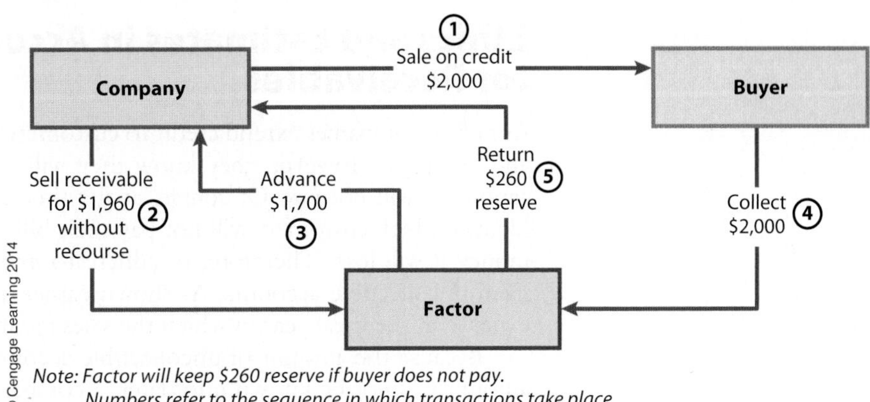

The factor's fee for sales with recourse is usually about 2 percent of the accounts receivable. The fee is higher for sales without recourse because the factor's risk is greater. In accounting terminology, a seller of receivables with recourse is said to be contingently liable. A **contingent liability** is a potential liability that can develop into a real liability if a particular event occurs. In this case, the event would be a customer's nonpayment of a receivable. A contingent liability generally requires *disclosure* in the notes to the financial statements.

Securitization **Securitization** is a process in which a company groups its receivables in batches and sells them at a discount to other companies or investors. When the receivables are paid, the buyers get the full amount. Their profit depends on the amount of the discount. **Circuit City** tried to avoid bankruptcy by selling all its receivables without recourse and, therefore, have no further liability. If Circuit City had sold its receivables with recourse and a customer did not pay, it would have had to make good on the debt.[7] However, by selling without recourse, it had to accept a lower price for its receivables, and it still went bankrupt.

Business Perspective
Why Are Subprime Loans Bad?

Although subprime loans (home loans to individuals with poor credit ratings and low incomes) represent only a small portion of the mortgage loan market, they have caused huge problems in the real estate market. These loans are a form of securitization in that they are batched together and sold in units as safe investments, when in fact they are quite risky. When people were unable to keep up with their mortgage payments, the investments were marked down to their fair value. This loss of value led to the demise of such venerable firms as **Lehman Brothers**, the sale of **Merrill Lynch**, and ultimately a massive government bailout of several well-known financial institutions.[8]

Discounting **Discounting** is a method of financing receivables by selling promissory notes held as notes receivable to a financial lender, usually a bank. The bank derives its profit by deducting the interest from the maturity value of the note. The holder of the note (usually the payee) endorses the note and turns it over to the bank. The bank expects to collect the maturity value of the note (principal plus interest) on the maturity date, but it also has recourse against the note's endorser.

For example, if Company X holds a $20,000 note from Company Z and the note will pay $1,200 in interest, a bank may be willing to buy the note for $19,200. If Company Z pays, the bank will receive $21,200 at maturity and realize a $2,000 profit. If it fails to pay, Company X is liable to the bank for payment. In the meantime, Company X has a contingent liability in the amount of the discounted note plus interest that it must *disclose* in the notes to its financial statements.

Ethics and Estimates in Accounting for Receivables

As noted, companies extend credit to customers because they want to increase their sales and earnings. However, they know they will always have some credit customers who cannot or will not pay. Of course, at the time a company makes credit sales, it cannot identify which customers will not pay their bills, nor can it predict the exact amount of money it will lose. Therefore, to adhere to *accrual accounting*, it must estimate losses from uncollectible accounts. As shown earlier in the chapter, the estimate becomes an expense in the fiscal year in which the sales are made.

Because the amount of uncollectible accounts can only be estimated and the exact amount will not be known until later, a company's earnings can be easily manipulated. Earnings can be overstated by underestimating the amount of losses from uncollectible accounts and understated by overestimating the amount of the losses. Misstatements of earnings can occur simply because of a bad estimate. But, as we have noted elsewhere, they can be deliberately made to meet analysts' estimates of earnings, reduce income taxes, or meet benchmarks for bonuses.

Examples of unethical or questionable practices in dealing with uncollectible accounts include the following cases investigated by the SEC:

- The policy of **Household International**, a large personal finance company, seems to be flexible about when to declare loans delinquent. As a result, the company can vary its estimates of uncollectible accounts from year to year.[9]
- By making large allowances for estimated uncollectible accounts and then gradually reducing them, **Bank One** improved its earnings over several years.[10]
- **HealthSouth** manipulated its income by varying its estimates of the difference between what it charged patients and what it could collect from insurance companies.[11]

Companies with high ethical standards try to be accurate in their estimates of uncollectible accounts, and they *disclose* the basis of their estimates. For example, **HP**'s management describes, in the statement that follows, the basis for its estimates of uncollectible accounts.

> *HP maintains [uncollectible account] reserves based on a variety of factors, including the length of time the receivable is past due, trends in overall weighted-average risk rating of the total portfolio, macroeconomic conditions, significant one-time events, historical experience, [and other factors].*[12]

APPLY IT!

Toni Company has net accounts receivable of $60,000 and net sales of $500,000. Last year's net accounts receivable were $40,000. Compute Toni's receivables turnover and days' sales uncollected.

SOLUTION

$$\text{Receivables Turnover} = \frac{\text{Net Sales}}{\text{Average Accounts Receivable}}$$

$$= \frac{\$500{,}000}{(\$60{,}000 + \$40{,}000) \div 2}$$

$$= \frac{\$500{,}000}{\$50{,}000} = 10.0 \text{ times}$$

$$\text{Days' Sales Uncollected} = \frac{365 \text{ days}}{\text{Receivables Turnover}} = \frac{365 \text{ days}}{10.0 \text{ times}} = 36.5 \text{ days}$$

TRY IT! SE9, SE10, E12A, E13A, E12B, E13B

A Look Back At: Hewlett-Packard Company

Aldo Murillo/iStockphoto.com

Hewlett-Packard Company

The beginning of this chapter focused on **Hewlett-Packard Company**. Complete the following requirements in order to answer the questions posed at the beginning of the chapter.

Section 1: Concepts
How does HP apply accrual accounting to its receivables, and how does it properly disclose their value?

Section 2: Accounting Applications
How can HP estimate the value of its receivables?

Section 3: Business Applications
How can HP evaluate the effectiveness of its credit policies and the level of its accounts receivable?

SOLUTION

Section 1: Concepts
HP makes credit sales now but collects money on those sales in the future. Some of the customers who purchased a product or service on credit will not pay their bills. Due to the uncertainty in regards to the *value* of receivables, HP must estimate how much of their receivables will not be collected. U.S. GAAP requires companies to use the allowance method to estimate the level of uncollectible accounts. The allowance method follows *accrual accounting* and results in the proper *valuation* of accounts receivable because it deducts the amount of estimated uncollectible accounts from accounts receivable on the balance sheet. It also *matches* the expense of uncollectible accounts with the revenues generated by the receivables. Accounts receivable are *disclosed* on the balance sheet at their net of allowance amount and notes to the financial statements disclose pertinent information about accounts receivable and notes receivable.

Section 2: Accounting Applications
In order to estimate the value of its receivables, HP will compute Uncollectible Accounts Expense and determine the ending balance of Allowance for Uncollectible Accounts and Accounts Receivable, Net. It is likely that HP uses a combination of the percentage of net sales method during the year and the accounts receivable aging method periodically during the year.

Section 3: Business Applications
An efficient way for HP to evaluate the effectiveness of its credit policies and the level of its accounts receivable is to compare the current year's receivables turnover and days' sales uncollected with those ratios from previous years.

SOLUTION • SOLUTION • SOLUTION • SOLUTION • SOLUTION

Review Problem

Smart Computer Company sells computer products for cash or on credit. In part because of uncollectible accounts, Smart's management is concerned that, in the coming year, the company may not have enough cash to cover operations before sales begin to increase in late summer. The following data (in thousands) are from Smart's records for year-end 2014, before adjustments:

	2014
Cash	$ 100
Accounts receivable	800
Allowance for doubtful accounts	(42)
Net sales	2,400

1. Compute Uncollectible Accounts Expense for 2014, and determine the ending balance of Allowance for Uncollectible Accounts and Accounts Receivable, Net, under (a) the percentage of net sales method assuming 1.5 percent of net sales to be uncollectible and (b) the accounts receivable aging method, assuming year-end uncollectible accounts to be $76,000.
2. Compute the receivables turnover and days' sales uncollected, using the data above and assuming that the prior year's net accounts receivable were $620,000.
3. Why do the two methods of calculating Uncollectible Accounts Expense produce different results?
4. What are the implications of the receivables turnover and days' sales uncollected results for Smart?

SOLUTION

1.

a. Percentage of net sales method:

Uncollectible Accounts Expense = 1.5 percent × $2,400,000 = $36,000

Allowance for Uncollectible Accounts = $36,000 + $42,000 = $78,000

Accounts Receivable, Net = $800,000 – $78,000 = $722,000

b. Accounts receivable aging method:

Uncollectible Accounts Expense = $76,000 – $42,000 = $34,000

Allowance for Uncollectible Accounts = $76,000

Accounts Receivable, Net = $800,000 – $76,000 = $724,000

2.

$$\text{Receivables Turnover} = \frac{\text{Net Sales}}{\text{Average Accounts Receivable}} = \frac{\$2{,}400{,}000}{(\$724{,}000 + \$620{,}000) \div 2}$$

$$= \frac{\$2{,}400{,}000}{\$672{,}000}$$

$$= \underline{\underline{3.6}}\text{ times*}$$

$$\text{Days' Sales Uncollected} = \frac{365\text{ days}}{\text{Receivable Turnover}} = \frac{365\text{ days}}{3.6\text{ times}} = \underline{\underline{101.4}}\text{ days*}$$

* Rounded

3. Both methods of computing Uncollectible Accounts Expense are estimates and thus are likely to give different results. Ideally, the results would be similar.
4. It takes Smart 101.4 days on average to collect its sales. This is almost four months, which means the company must manage its cash and borrowings carefully or revise its credit terms.

SOLUTION • SOLUTION • SOLUTION • SOLUTION • SOLUTION • SOLUTION

Chapter Review

Define receivables, and explain the allowance method for valuation of receivables as an application of accrual accounting. LO 1

Accounts receivable are short-term financial assets that arise from sales on credit. Notes receivable consists of promissory notes. A promissory note is an unconditional promise to pay a definite sum of money on demand or at a future date. The allowance method matches estimated losses from bad debts with the revenues they help to generate. It also aids in valuing the accounts receivable on the balance sheet. Notes receivable that are due in less than one year may be shown at their fair value in the current assets section of the balance sheet. Accounts receivable are also shown in the current assets section at their net realizable value; i.e., reduced by the allowance for uncollectible accounts. Interest receivable is also included in the current assets section. The uncollectible accounts expense is deducted from revenues on the income statement.

Apply the allowance method of accounting for uncollectible accounts. LO 2

Uncollectible accounts expense is estimated by using either the percentage of net sales method or the accounts receivable aging method. Under the first method, bad debts are judged to be a certain percentage of sales. Under the second method, certain percentages are applied to groups of accounts receivable that have been arranged by due dates.

The estimate of uncollectible accounts is debited to Uncollectible Accounts Expense and credited to the allowance account. When an individual account is determined to be uncollectible, it is removed from Accounts Receivable by debiting the allowance account and crediting Accounts Receivable. If the written-off account is later collected, the earlier entry is reversed and the collection is recorded in the normal way.

Make common calculations for notes receivable. 

In accounting for promissory notes, common calculations include the maturity date, the duration of a note, the interest and interest rate, and the maturity value.

Show how to evaluate the level of receivables, and identify alternative means of financing receivables. LO 4

The management of receivables is critical to maintaining adequate liquidity. Management must (1) consider the need for short-term investing and borrowing as cash fluctuates during seasonal cycles, (2) establish credit policies that balance the need for sales with the ability to collect, (3) evaluate the level of receivables using receivables turnover and days' sales uncollected, (4) assess the need to increase cash flows through alternative means of the financing of receivables, and (5) understand the importance of ethics in estimating credit losses.

Key Terms and Ratios

accounts receivable 364 (LO1)
accounts receivable aging method 369 (LO2)
aging of accounts receivable 369 (LO2)
Allowance for Uncollectible Accounts 367 (LO1)
allowance method 366 (LO1)
contingent liability 379 (LO4)
direct charge-off method 365 (LO1)
discounting 380 (LO4)
dishonored note 375 (LO3)
duration of a note 374 (LO3)
factor 379 (LO4)
factoring 379 (LO4)
interest 374 (LO3)
interest receivable 367 (LO1)
maturity date 374 (LO3)
maturity value 375 (LO3)
notes receivable 365 (LO1)
percentage of net sales method 368 (LO2)
promissory note 365 (LO1)
securitization 379 (LO4)
trade credit 364 (LO1)
uncollectible accounts 365 (LO1)

RATIOS

days' sales uncollected 378 (LO4)
receivables turnover 377 (LO4)

Chapter Assignments

DISCUSSION QUESTIONS

LO 1 **DQ1. CONCEPT ▶** What accounting concepts are violated by the direct charge-off method of recognizing uncollectible accounts? Why?

LO 1, 2 **DQ2.** In what ways is Allowance for Uncollectible Accounts similar to Accumulated Depreciation? In what ways is it different?

LO 3 **DQ3.** Under what circumstances would an accrual of interest income on an interest-bearing note receivable not be required at the end of an accounting period?

LO 4 **DQ4. BUSINESS APPLICATION ▶** Why is it advantageous for a company to finance its receivables?

LO 4 **DQ5. BUSINESS APPLICATION ▶** To increase its sales, a company decides to increase its credit terms from 15 to 30 days. What effect will this change in policy have on receivables turnover and days' sales uncollected?

LO 4 **DQ6. BUSINESS APPLICATION ▶** How might the receivables turnover and days' sales uncollected reveal that management is consistently underestimating the amount of losses from uncollectible accounts? Is this action ethical?

SHORT EXERCISES

LO 1 Accounts Receivable and Notes Receivable

SE1. Indicate which of the following is more closely associated with (a) accounts receivable or (b) notes receivable:

1. Backed by a written promissory note.
2. Appears separate from receivables from employees.
3. Requires an estimate of uncollectible accounts.
4. Banks often have this type of receivable.
5. Often referred to as trade credit.

LO 1 Evaluating the Level of Accounts Receivable

SE2. During its first year of operation in 2014, Browne Sales Corporation made most of its sales on credit. At the end of the year, accounts receivable amounted to $199,000. On December 31, 2014, management reviewed the collectible status of the accounts receivable. Approximately $16,500 of the $199,000 of accounts receivable were estimated to be uncollectible. What adjusting entry would be made December 31, 2014?

LO 2 Percentage of Net Sales Method

SE3. At the end of October, Santa Fe Company's management estimates the uncollectible accounts expense to be 1 percent of net sales of $1,385,000. Prepare the journal entry to record the uncollectible accounts expense, assuming the Allowance for Uncollectible Accounts has a debit balance of $7,000.

LO 2 Accounts Receivable Aging Method

SE4. An aging analysis on June 30 of the accounts receivable of U-Z Door Corporation indicates that uncollectible accounts amount to $86,000. Prepare the journal entry to record uncollectible accounts expense under each of the following independent assumptions:

a. Allowance for Uncollectible Accounts has a credit balance of $18,000 before adjustment.
b. Allowance for Uncollectible Accounts has a debit balance of $14,000 before adjustment.

LO 2 **Write-off of Accounts Receivable**

SE5. Chicago Corporation, which uses the allowance method, has accounts receivable of $25,400 and an allowance for uncollectible accounts of $4,900. An account receivable from Tom Novak of $2,200 is deemed to be uncollectible and is written off. What is the amount of net accounts receivable before and after the write-off?

LO 3 **Interest Computations**

SE6. Determine the interest on the following notes. (Round to the nearest cent.)

a. $58,940 at 6 percent for 60 days.
b. $14,280 at 9 percent for 30 days.
c. $30,600 at 12 percent for 60 days.
d. $21,070 at 10 percent for 90 days.
e. $46,360 at 15 percent for 120 days.

LO 3 **Notes Receivable Calculations**

SE7. Determine the maturity date, interest at maturity, and maturity value for a 120-day, 8 percent, $34,000 note from Archer Corporation dated July 7. (Round to the nearest cent.)

LO 3 **Notes Receivable Calculations**

SE8. On August 25, Intercontinental Company received a 90-day, 9 percent note in settlement of an account receivable in the amount of $20,000. Determine the maturity date, amount of interest on the note, and maturity value. (Round to the nearest cent.)

LO 4 **Management Issues**

SE9. BUSINESS APPLICATION ▶ Indicate whether each of the following actions is related to (a) managing cash needs, (b) setting credit policies, (c) financing receivables, or (d) ethically reporting receivables:

1. Selling accounts receivable to a factor.
2. Borrowing funds for short-term needs during slow periods.
3. Conducting thorough checks of new customers' ability to pay.
4. Making every effort to reflect possible future losses accurately.

LO 4 **Short-Term Liquidity Ratios**

SE10. BUSINESS APPLICATION ▶ Wellman Company has cash of $80,000, net accounts receivable of $180,000, and net sales of $1,440,000. Last year's net accounts receivable were $140,000. Compute the following ratios: (a) receivables turnover and (b) days' sales uncollected. (Round to the nearest whole day.)

EXERCISES: SET A

LO 1 **Evaluating the Level of Accounts Receivable**

E1A. During its first year of operation in 2014, Jameson Sales Corporation made most of its sales on credit. At the end of the year, accounts receivable amounted to $175,000. On December 31, 2014, management reviewed the collectible status of the accounts receivable. Approximately 7.5% of the $175,000 of accounts receivable were estimated to be uncollectible. What adjusting entry would be made December 31, 2014?

LO 2 **Percentage of Net Sales Method**

E2A. At the end of the year, Bertha Enterprises estimates the uncollectible accounts expense to be 0.7 percent of net sales of $15,150,000. The current credit balance of Allowance for Uncollectible Accounts is $25,800. Prepare the entry to record the uncollectible accounts expense. What is the balance of Allowance for Uncollectible Accounts after this adjustment?

LO 2 **Accounts Receivable Aging Method**

E3A. Security Service Company's Accounts Receivable account shows a debit balance of $104,000 at the end of the year. An aging analysis of the individual accounts indicates estimated uncollectible accounts to be $6,700.

Prepare the journal entry to record the uncollectible accounts expense under each of the following independent assumptions: (a) Allowance for Uncollectible Accounts has a credit balance of $800 before adjustment, and (b) Allowance for Uncollectible Accounts has a debit balance of $800 before adjustment. What is the balance of Allowance for Uncollectible Accounts after each of these adjustments?

LO 2 **Aging Method and Net Sales Method Contrasted**

E4A. At the beginning of 2014, the balances for Accounts Receivable and Allowance for Uncollectible Accounts were $215,000 and $15,700 (credit), respectively. During the year, credit sales were $1,600,000 and collections on account were $1,475,000. In addition, $17,500 in uncollectible accounts was written off.

Using T accounts, determine the year-end balances of Accounts Receivable and Allowance for Uncollectible Accounts. Then prepare the year-end adjusting entry to record the uncollectible accounts expense under each of the following conditions. Also show the year-end balance sheet presentation of accounts receivable and allowance for uncollectible accounts.

a. Management estimates the percentage of uncollectible credit sales to be 1.2 percent of total credit sales.
b. Based on an aging of accounts receivable, management estimates the end-of-year uncollectible accounts receivable to be $19,350.

Post the results of each of the entries to the T account for Allowance for Uncollectible Accounts.

LO 2 **Aging Method and Net Sales Method Contrasted**

E5A. ACCOUNTING CONNECTION ▶ During 2014, DeLuca Company had net sales of $5,700,000. Most of the sales were on credit. At the end of 2014, the balance of Accounts Receivable was $700,000 and Allowance for Uncollectible Accounts had a debit balance of $24,000. DeLuca's management uses two methods of estimating uncollectible accounts expense: the percentage of net sales method and the accounts receivable aging method. The percentage of uncollectible sales is 1.5 percent of net sales, and based on an aging of accounts receivable, the end-of-year uncollectible accounts total $70,000.

Prepare the year-end adjusting entry to record the uncollectible accounts expense under each method. What will the balance of Allowance for Uncollectible Accounts be after each adjustment? Why are the results different? Which method is likely to be more reliable? Why?

LO 2 **Aging Method and Net Sales Method Contrasted**

E6A. ACCOUNTING CONNECTION ▶ Dapper Hat Makers Company sells merchandise on credit. During the fiscal year ended July 31, the company had net sales of $2,300,000. At the end of the year, it had Accounts Receivable of $600,000 and a debit balance in Allowance for Uncollectible Accounts of $3,400. In the past, approximately 1.4 percent of net sales have proved to be uncollectible. Also, an aging analysis of accounts receivable reveals that $30,000 of the receivables appears to be uncollectible.

Prepare journal entries to record uncollectible accounts expense using (a) the percentage of net sales method and (b) the accounts receivable aging method. What is the resulting balance of Allowance for Uncollectible Accounts under each method? How would your answers under each method change if Allowance for Uncollectible Accounts had a credit balance of $3,400 instead of a debit balance? Why do the methods result in different balances?

LO 2 **Write-off of Accounts Receivable**

E7A. Norcia Company, which uses the allowance method, began the year with Accounts Receivable of $32,500 and an allowance for uncollectible accounts of $3,200 (credit). The company sold merchandise to Bruce Willis for $3,600 and later received $1,200 from Willis. The rest of the amount due from Willis had to be written off as uncollectible. Using T accounts, show the beginning balances and the effects of the Willis transactions on Accounts Receivable and Allowance for Uncollectible Accounts. What is the amount of net accounts receivable before and after the write-off?

LO 3 **Interest Computations**

E8A. Determine the interest on the following notes. (Round to the nearest cent.)

a. $38,760 at 10 percent for 90 days.
b. $27,200 at 12 percent for 60 days.
c. $30,600 at 9 percent for 30 days.
d. $51,000 at 15 percent for 120 days.
e. $18,360 at 6 percent for 60 days.

LO 3 **Notes Receivable Calculations**

E9A. Determine the maturity date, interest at maturity, and maturity value for a 90-day, 10 percent, $18,000 note from Archer Corporation dated February 15. (Round to the nearest cent.)

LO 3 **Notes Receivable Calculations**

E10A. Determine the maturity date, interest in 2013 and 2014, and maturity value for a 90-day, 12 percent, $15,000 note from a customer dated December 1, 2013, assuming a December 31 year end. (Round to the nearest cent.)

LO 3 **Notes Receivable Calculations**

E11A. Determine the maturity date, interest at maturity, and maturity value for each of the following notes. (Round to the nearest cent.)

a. A 60-day, 10 percent, $2,400 note dated January 5 received from S. William for granting a time extension on a past-due account.
b. A 60-day, 12 percent, $1,500 note dated March 9 received from E. Watson for granting a time extension on a past-due account.

LO 4 **Management Issues**

E12A. BUSINESS APPLICATION ▶ Indicate whether each of the following actions is primarily related to (a) managing cash needs, (b) setting credit policies, (c) financing receivables, or (d) ethically reporting accounts receivable:

1. Selling notes receivable to a financing company.
2. Changing the terms for credit sales in an effort to reduce the days' sales uncollected.
3. Buying a U.S. Treasury bill with cash that is not needed for a few months.
4. Comparing receivable turnovers for two years.
5. Setting a policy that allows customers to buy on credit.
6. Making careful estimates of losses from uncollectible accounts.
7. Establishing a department whose responsibility is to approve customers' credit.
8. Borrowing funds for short-term needs in a period when sales are low.
9. Revising estimated credit losses in a timely manner when conditions change.

LO 4

Short-Term Liquidity Ratios

E13A. BUSINESS APPLICATION ▶ Using the following data from Moontrust Corporation's financial statements, compute the receivables turnover and the days' sales uncollected. (Round to one decimal place or to the nearest whole day.)

Current assets:	
Cash	$ 70,000
Short-term investments	170,000
Notes receivable	240,000
Accounts receivable, net	400,000
Inventory	500,000
Prepaid assets	50,000
Total current assets	$1,430,000
Current liabilities:	
Notes payable	$ 600,000
Accounts payable	150,000
Accrued liabilities	20,000
Total current liabilities	$ 770,000
Net sales	$3,200,000
Last year's accounts receivable, net	$ 360,000

EXERCISES: SET B

Visit the textbook companion website at www.cengagebrain.com to access Exercise Set B for this chapter.

PROBLEMS

LO 2, 4

Methods of Estimating Uncollectible Accounts and Receivables Analysis

SPREADSHEET

GENERAL LEDGER

✔ 2a: Uncollectible accounts expense, percentage of net sales method: $24,965
✔ 2b: Accounts receivable aging method: $27,100

P1. McLennon Company had an Accounts Receivable balance of $320,000 and a credit balance in Allowance for Uncollectible Accounts of $16,700 at January 1, 2014. During the year, the company recorded the following transactions:

a. Sales on account, $1,052,000.
b. Sales returns and allowances by credit customers, $53,400.
c. Collections from customers, $993,000.
d. Worthless accounts written off, $19,800.

The company's past history indicates that 2.5 percent of its net credit sales will not be collected.

REQUIRED

1. Prepare T accounts for Accounts Receivable and Allowance for Uncollectible Accounts. Enter the beginning balances, and show the effects on these accounts of the items listed above, summarizing the year's activity. Determine the ending balance of each account.
2. Compute Uncollectible Accounts Expense, determine the ending balance of Allowance for Uncollectible Accounts and net Accounts Receivable under (a) the percentage of net sales method and (b) the accounts receivable aging method, assuming an aging of the accounts receivable shows that $24,000 may be uncollectible.
3. Compute the receivables turnover and days' sales uncollected, using the data from the accounts receivable aging method in requirement **2**. (Round to one decimal place or to the nearest whole day.)
4. **ACCOUNTING CONNECTION ▶** How do you explain that the two methods used in requirement **2** result in different amounts for Uncollectible Accounts Expense? What rationale underlies each method?

LO 2

✔ 3: Amount of uncollectible accounts expense: $72,714

Accounts Receivable Aging Method

P2. Techno Designs Store uses the accounts receivable aging method to estimate uncollectible accounts. On February 1, 2014, the balance of the Accounts Receivable account was a debit of $442,341, and the balance of Allowance for Uncollectible Accounts was a credit of $43,700. During the year, the store had sales on account of $3,722,000, sales returns and allowances of $60,000, worthless accounts written off of $44,300, and collections from customers of $3,211,000. As part of the end-of-year (January 31, 2015) procedures, an aging analysis of accounts receivable is prepared. The analysis, which is partially complete, follows.

Customer Account	Total	Not Yet Due	1–30 Days Past Due	31–60 Days Past Due	61–90 Days Past Due	Over 90 Days Past Due
Balance Forward	$793,791	$438,933	$149,614	$106,400	$57,442	$41,402

To finish the analysis, the following accounts need to be classified:

Account	Amount	Due Date
J. Curtis	$11,077	Jan. 15
T. Dawson	9,314	Feb. 15 (next fiscal year)
L. Zapata	8,664	Dec. 20
R. Copa	780	Oct. 1
E. Land	14,710	Jan. 4
S. Qadri	6,316	Nov. 15
A. Rosenthal	4,389	Mar. 1 (next fiscal year)
	$55,250	

From past experience, the company has found that the following rates are realistic for estimating uncollectible accounts:

Time	Percentage Considered Uncollectible
Not yet due	2
1–30 days past due	5
31–60 days past due	15
61–90 days past due	25
Over 90 days past due	50

REQUIRED

1. Complete the aging analysis of accounts receivable.
2. Compute the end-of-year balances (before adjustments) of Accounts Receivable and Allowance for Uncollectible Accounts.
3. Prepare an analysis computing the estimated uncollectible accounts. (Round to the nearest whole dollar.)
4. How much is Techno Designs Store's estimated uncollectible accounts expense for the year? (Round the adjustment to the nearest whole dollar.)
5. **ACCOUNTING CONNECTION ▶** What role do estimates play in applying the aging analysis? What factors might affect these estimates?

LO 4

CASH FLOW

SPREADSHEET

✔ 2: Total accrued interest income as of June 30: $3,856.44

Notes Receivable Calculations

P3. West Palm Company engaged in the following transactions involving promissory notes:

May 3 Sold engines to Mittal Company for $120,000 in exchange for a 90-day, 12 percent promissory note.

16 Sold engines to Tata Company for $64,000 in exchange for a 60-day, 13 percent note.

31 Sold engines to Arsenal Company for $60,000 in exchange for a 90-day, 11 percent note.

(Continued)

REQUIRED

1. For each of the notes, determine the (a) maturity date, (b) interest on the note, and (c) maturity value. (Round to the nearest cent.)
2. Assume that the fiscal year for West Palm ends on June 30. How much interest income should be recorded on that date? (Round to the nearest cent.)
3. **ACCOUNTING CONNECTION ▶** What are the effects of the transactions in May on cash flows for the year ended June 30?

LO **3**

Notes Receivable Calculations

✔ 5: Interest in 2015: $425.34

P4. Assume that on December 16, 2014, Harris Company receives a 90-day, 9 percent, $23,000 note, payable in full with interest at maturity, and that the company prepares monthly financial statements.

REQUIRED

1. What is the maturity date of the note?
2. How much interest will be earned on the note if it is paid when due? (Round to the nearest cent.)
3. What is the maturity value of the note?
4. If the company's fiscal year ends on December 31, 2014, calculate the amount of the adjusting entry that would be made for interest.
5. How much interest will be earned on this note in 2015? (Round to the nearest cent.)
6. **ACCOUNTING CONNECTION ▶** How much cash will be received for interest in 2014? Why does the amount of cash received for interest differ from the amount of interest earned?

ALTERNATE PROBLEMS

LO **2, 4**

Methods of Estimating Uncollectible Accounts and Receivables Analysis

RATIO

SPREADSHEET

GENERAL LEDGER

✔ 2a: Uncollectible accounts expense, percentage of net sales method: $17,952

✔ 2b: Accounts receivable aging method: $15,700

P5. On December 31 of last year, Target System Company's balance sheet had Accounts Receivable of $298,000 and a credit balance in Allowance for Uncollectible Accounts of $20,300. During the current year, Target System's records included the following selected activities: (a) sales on account, $1,195,000; (b) sales returns and allowances, $73,000; (c) collections from customers, $1,150,000; and (d) accounts written off as worthless, $16,000. In the past, 1.6 percent of Target System's net sales have been uncollectible.

REQUIRED

1. Prepare T accounts for Accounts Receivable and Allowance for Uncollectible Accounts. Enter the beginning balances, and show the effects on these accounts of the items listed above, summarizing the year's activity. Determine the ending balance of each account.
2. Compute Uncollectible Accounts Expense, determine the ending balance of Allowance for Uncollectible Accounts and net Accounts Receivable under (a) the percentage of net sales method and (b) the accounts receivable aging method. Assume that an aging of the accounts receivable shows that $20,000 may be uncollectible.
3. Compute the receivables turnover and days' sales uncollected, using the data from the accounts receivable aging method in requirement 2. (Round to one decimal place or to the nearest whole day.)
4. **ACCOUNTING CONNECTION ▶** How do you explain that the two methods used in requirement 2 result in different amounts for Uncollectible Accounts Expense? What rationale underlies each method?

LO 2

Accounts Receivable Aging Method

✔ 4: Amount of uncollectible accounts expense: $9,110

P6. Flossmoor Company uses the accounts receivable aging method to estimate uncollectible accounts. At the beginning of the year, the balance of the Accounts Receivable account was a debit of $88,430, and the balance of Allowance for Uncollectible Accounts was a credit of $7,200. During the year, the company had sales on account of $473,000, sales returns and allowances of $4,200, worthless accounts written off of $7,900, and collections from customers of $450,730. At the end of year (December 31, 2014), a junior accountant for Flossmoor was preparing an aging analysis of accounts receivable. At the top of page 6 of the report, the following totals appeared:

Customer Account	Total	Not Yet Due	1–30 Days Past Due	31–60 Days Past Due	61–90 Days Past Due	Over 90 Days Past Due
Balance Forward	$89,640	$49,030	$24,110	$9,210	$3,990	$3,300

To finish the analysis, the following accounts need to be classified:

Account	Amount	Due Date
B. Singh	$ 930	Jan. 14 (next year)
L. Wells	620	Dec. 24
A. Rocky	1,955	Sept. 28
T. Cila	2,100	Aug. 16
M. Mix	375	Dec. 14
S. Prince	2,685	Jan. 23 (next year)
J. Wendt	295	Nov. 5
	$8,960	

From past experience, the company has found that the following rates are realistic for estimating uncollectible accounts:

Time	Percentage Considered Uncollectible
Not yet due	2
1–30 days past due	5
31–60 days past due	15
61–90 days past due	25
Over 90 days past due	50

REQUIRED

1. Complete the aging analysis of accounts receivable.
2. Compute the end-of-year balances (before adjustments) of Accounts Receivable and Allowance for Uncollectible Accounts.
3. Prepare an analysis computing the estimated uncollectible accounts. (Round to the nearest dollar.)
4. Calculate Flossmoor's estimated uncollectible accounts expense for the year. (Round to the nearest whole dollar).
5. **ACCOUNTING CONNECTION ▶** What role do estimates play in applying the aging analysis? What factors might affect these estimates?

LO 3

Notes Receivable Calculations

CASH FLOW

SPREADSHEET

✔ 2: Total accrued interest income as of August 31: $6,025.64

P7. Vision Importing Company engaged in the following transactions involving promissory notes:

July 2 Sold engines to Morgan Company for $180,000 in exchange for a 90-day, 12 percent promissory note.

15 Sold engines to Level Company for $96,000 in exchange for a 60-day, 13 percent note.

30 Sold engines to Level Company for $90,000 in exchange for a 90-day, 11 percent note.

(Continued)

REQUIRED

1. For each of the notes, determine the (a) maturity date, (b) interest on the note, and (c) maturity value. (Round to the nearest cent.)
2. Assume that the fiscal year for Vision Importing ends on August 31. How much interest income should be recorded on that date? (Round to the nearest cent.)
3. **ACCOUNTING CONNECTION ▶** What are the effects of the transactions in July on cash flows for the year ended August 31?

LO **3**

Notes Receivable Calculations

✔ 5: Interest in 2015: $3.92

P8. Assume that on November 3, 2014, Harris Company receives a 60-day, 6.5 percent, $11,000 note, payable in full with interest at maturity, and that the company prepares monthly financial statements.

REQUIRED

1. What is the maturity date of the note?
2. How much interest will be earned on the note if it is paid when due? (Round to the nearest cent.)
3. What is the maturity value of the note?
4. If the company's fiscal year ends on December 31, calculate the amount of the adjusting entry that would be made.
5. How much interest will be earned on this note in 2015? (Round to the nearest cent.)
6. **ACCOUNTING CONNECTION ▶** How much cash will be received for interest in 2014? Why does the amount of cash received for interest differ from the amount of interest earned?

CASES

LO **1**

Conceptual Understanding: Role of Credit Sales

C1. CONCEPT ▶ Mitsubishi Corp., a broadly diversified Japanese company, instituted a credit plan called Three Diamonds for customers who buy its major electronic products, such as large-screen televisions, from specified retail dealers.[13] Under the plan, approved customers who make purchases in July of one year do not have to make any payments until September of the next year. Nor do they have to pay interest during the intervening months. Mitsubishi pays the dealer the full amount less a small fee, sends the customer a Mitsubishi credit card, and collects from the customer at the specified time. What was Mitsubishi's motivation for establishing such generous credit terms? What costs are involved? What are the accounting implications?

LO **1, 2**

Conceptual Understanding: Role of Estimates in Accounting for Receivables

C2. CONCEPT ▶ CompuCredit is a credit card issuer in Atlanta. It prides itself on making credit cards available to almost anyone in a matter of seconds over the Internet. The cost to the consumer is an interest rate of 28 percent, about double that of companies that provide cards only to customers with good credit. Despite its high interest rate, CompuCredit was successful for many years. To calculate its income, the company estimated that 10 percent of its $1.3 billion in accounts receivable would not be paid; the industry average is 7 percent. Some analysts were critical of CompuCredit for being too optimistic in its projections of losses.[14] In fact, during the recent recession, CompuCredit losses from uncollectible accounts increased and exceeded its interest income and the company reported large operating losses.[15] Why are estimates necessary in accounting for receivables? If CompuCredit were to use the same estimate of losses as other companies in its industry, would it have been better or worse off? How would one determine if CompuCredit's estimate of losses is reasonable?

LO 4

Conceptual Understanding: Receivables Financing

C3. Gerard Appliances Inc. is a small manufacturer of washing machines and dryers. It sells its products to large, established discount retailers that market the appliances under their own names. Gerard generally sells the appliances on trade credit terms of n/60, but if a customer wants a longer term, it will accept a note with a term of up to nine months. At present, the company is having cash flow troubles and needs $10 million immediately. Its Cash balance is $400,000, its Accounts Receivable balance is $4.6 million, and its Notes Receivable balance is $7.4 million. How might Gerard Appliances use its accounts receivable and notes receivable to raise the cash it needs? What are its prospects for raising the needed cash?

LO 1, 4

Interpreting Financial Reports: Accounting for Accounts Receivable

C4. BUSINESS APPLICATION ▶ Robinson Products Co., a major consumer goods company, sells more than 3,000 products in 135 countries. Its report to the Securities and Exchange Commission in 2014 presented the following data:

	2014	2013	2012
Net sales	$9,820,000	$9,730,000	$9,888,000
Accounts receivable	1,046,000	1,048,000	1,008,000
Allowance for uncollectible accounts	37,200	42,400	49,000
Uncollectible accounts expense	30,000	33,400	31,600
Uncollectible accounts written off	38,600	40,200	35,400
Recoveries of accounts previously written off	3,400	200	2,000

1. Compute the ratio of uncollectible accounts expense to net sales and to accounts receivable and the ratio of allowance for uncollectible accounts to accounts receivable for 2012, 2013, and 2014. (Round to two decimal places for net sales and one decimal place for accounts receivable.)
2. Compute the receivables turnover and days' sales uncollected for each year assuming that net accounts receivable in 2011 were $930,000. (Round to one decimal place or to the nearest whole day.)
3. What is your interpretation of the ratios? Describe management's attitude toward the collectability of accounts receivable over the three-year period.

LO 1, 2, 4

Annual Report Case: Cash and Receivables

C5. Refer to the **CVS** annual report in the Supplement to Chapter 1 to answer the following questions:

1. Which customers represent the main source of CVS's accounts receivable, and how much is CVS's allowance for uncollectible accounts?
2. What do you think CVS's seasonal needs for cash are? Where in CVS's financial statements is the seasonality of sales discussed?

LO 1, 4

Comparison Analysis: Accounts Receivable Analysis

C6. BUSINESS APPLICATION ▶ Refer to the **CVS** annual report in the Supplement to Chapter 1 and to the following data (in millions) for **Walgreens**: net sales, $72,184 and $67,420 for 2011 and 2010, respectively; accounts receivable, net, $2,497 and $2,450 for 2011 and 2010, respectively.[16]

1. Compute receivables turnover and days' sales uncollected for 2011 and 2010 for CVS and Walgreens. Accounts receivable in 2009 were $5,457 million for CVS and $2,496 million for Walgreens. (Round to one decimal place.)
2. Do you discern any differences in the two companies' credit policies? Explain your answer.

LO 1, 4

Ethical Dilemma: Uncollectible Accounts

C7. BUSINESS APPLICATION ▶ Mullin Interiors, a successful retailer of high-quality furniture, is located in an affluent suburb where a large insurance company has just announced that it will lay off 4,000 employees. Because most of Mullin Interiors' sales are made on credit, accounts receivable is one of its major assets. Although the company's annual losses from uncollectible accounts are not out of line, they represent a sizable amount. The company depends on bank loans for its financing. Sales and net income have declined in the past year, and some customers are falling behind in paying their accounts.

Veronica Mullin, the owner, knows that the bank's loan officer likes to see a steady performance. She has therefore instructed the company's controller to underestimate the uncollectible accounts this year to show a small growth in earnings. Mullin believes this action is justified because earnings in future years will average out the losses. Since the company has a history of success, she believes the adjustments are meaningless accounting measures anyway.

Are Mullin's actions ethical? Would any parties be harmed by her actions? How important is it to try to be accurate in estimating losses from uncollectible accounts?

RATIO

Continuing Case: Annual Report Project

C8. Using the most recent annual report of the company you have chosen to study and that you have accessed online at the company's website, examine the balance sheet and accompanying notes of your company. Answer the following questions:

1. What percentage of total current assets is accounts receivable? Is this figure the total accounts receivable or net accounts receivable? Why or why not?
2. Find the disclosures about accounts receivable in the notes to the financial statements. What is the amount of the allowance account and what percentage of total accounts receivable is it?
3. Does the company have notes receivable on the balance sheet? If so, read the note to the financial statements on notes receivable. What do you learn from it about the business?
4. **BUSINESS APPLICATION ▶** Compute receivables turnover and days' sales uncollected for the most recent year.

CHAPTER 9

LEARNING OBJECTIVES

LO1 Identify the classifications of long-term assets, and describe how they are valued by allocating their costs to the periods that they benefit.

LO2 Account for the acquisition costs of property, plant, and equipment.

LO3 Compute depreciation under the straight-line, production, and declining-balance methods.

LO4 Account for the disposal of depreciable assets.

LO5 Identify the issues related to accounting for natural resources, and compute depletion.

LO6 Identify the issues related to accounting for intangible assets, including research and development costs and goodwill.

LO7 Describe the disclosure of acquiring and financing long-term assets, and calculate free cash flow.

Songquan Deng/Shutterstock.com

LONG-TERM ASSETS

Business Insight
Apple Computer

Long known for its innovative technology and design, **Apple Computer** revolutionized the music industry with its iPod, and it hopes to do the same in the computer industry with its iPad tablet. The company's success stems from its willingness to invest in research and development and long-term assets to create new products. In 2011, it spent almost $2,429 million on research and development and about $4,260 million on new long-term assets. About 61 percent of its assets are long-term. You can get an idea of the extent and importance of Apple's long-term assets by looking at the Financial Highlights from the company's balance sheet.[1]

Apple Computer's Financial Highlights (in millions)

	2011	**2010**
Long-term marketable securities	$55,618	$25,391
Property, Plant, and Equipment:		
Land and buildings	$ 2,059	$ 1,471
Machinery, equipment, and internal-use software	6,926	3,589
Office furniture and equipment	184	144
Leasehold improvements	2,599	2,030
	11,768	7,234
Less accumulated depreciation and amortization	3,991	2,466
Total property, plant, and equipment, net	$ 7,777	$ 4,768
Other Noncurrent Assets:		
Goodwill	$ 896	$ 741
Acquired intangible assets	3,536	342
Other noncurrent assets	3,556	2,263
Total other noncurrent assets	$ 7,988	$ 3,346

Questions

1. **CONCEPT ▶** What is the classification of long-term assets, how are the assets valued, and what is the distinction in recognizing capital and revenue expenditures?
2. **ACCOUNTING APPLICATION ▶** What questions need to be answered in order to properly account for long-term assets?
3. **BUSINESS APPLICATION ▶** How does management decide to acquire, finance, and evaluate long-term assets?

SECTION 1

CONCEPTS

CONCEPTS

- Valuation
- Classification
- Accrual Accounting (matching rule)
- Disclosure
- Recognition

RELEVANT LEARNING OBJECTIVE

LO 1 Identify the classifications of long-term assets, and describe how they are valued by allocating their costs to the periods that they benefit.

LO 1 Concepts Underlying Long-Term Assets

Long-term assets (or *fixed assets*) have the following characteristics:

- **They have a useful life of more than one year.** This distinguishes them from current assets, which a company expects to use up or convert to cash within 1 year or during its operating cycle, whichever is longer. The most common criterion for the useful life of a long-term asset is that it be capable of repeated use for more than a year.
- **They are used in the operation of a business.** For an asset to be *classified* as property, plant, and equipment, it must be "put in use," which means it is available for its intended purpose. An emergency generator is "put in use" when it is available for emergencies, even if it is never used. Assets not used in the normal course of business, such as land held for speculative reasons or buildings no longer used in ordinary operations, should be *classified* as investments.
- **They are not intended for resale to customers.** An asset that a company intends to resell to customers should be *classified* as inventory, no matter how durable it is. For example, a computer that a company uses in an office is a long-term plant asset. An identical computer that a company sells to customers is inventory.

Exhibit 1 shows the relative importance of long-term assets in various industries.

Exhibit 1
Long-Term Assets as a Percentage of Total Assets for Selected Industries

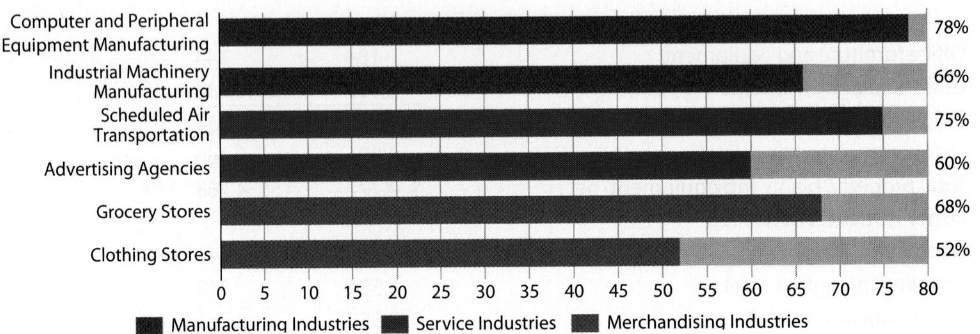

Based on Bizmin Industry Financial Report, December 2011.

Classification, Accrual Accounting, and Disclosure of Long-Term Assets

Long-terms assets are *classified* as property, plant, and equipment; natural resources; and intangible assets. **Property, plant, and equipment** is land and other long-term assets that have physical substance. **Natural resources** are assets purchased for the economic value that can be extracted from them, such as oil and gas. **Intangible assets** are long-term assets that have no physical substance, such as copyrights and patents. Under *accrual accounting* the cost of these assets, with the exception of land and some intangible assets, is allocated to the periods they benefit, as follows.

- The periodic allocation of the costs of plant and equipment over their estimated useful lives is called **depreciation**. Although land is property, it is not depreciated because it has an unlimited life.
- The allocation of the costs of natural resources is called **depletion**.
- The allocation of the costs of most long-term intangible assets, which represent a legal right or advantage, is called **amortization**. Some intangible assets not subject to amortization.

The methods used to determine depreciation, depletion, and amortization are *disclosed* in the notes to the financial statements. Exhibit 2 shows how long-term assets are *classified* and defines the *accrual accounting* methods of allocating their cost of their use to the income statement.

Exhibit 2
Classification of Long-Term Assets and Methods of Accounting for Them

	Balance Sheet Long-Term Assets	Income Statement Expenses
	**Property, Plant, and Equipment:** long-term assets with physical substance used in business operations • Land • Plant Assets – Plant – Buildings – Equipment	Land is not expensed because it has an unlimited life. **Depreciation:** periodic allocation of the cost of a tangible long-lived asset (other than land and natural resources) over its estimated useful life
	**Natural Resources:** long-term assets purchased for the economic value that can be taken from the land and used up, as with ore, lumber, oil, and gas or other resources contained in the land • Mines • Timberland • Oil and Gas Fields	**Depletion:** exhaustion of a natural resource through mining, cutting, pumping, or other extraction and the way in which the cost is allocated
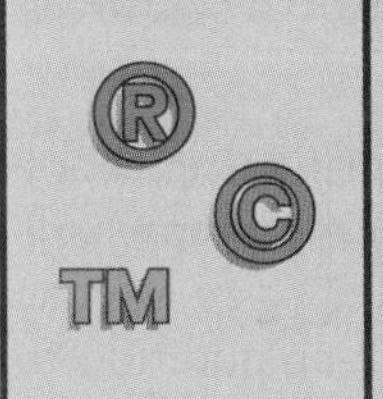	**Intangible Assets:** long-term assets that have no physical substance but have a value based on rights or advantages accruing to the owner *Subject to Amortization and Impairment Test* • Copyrights • Customer lists • Franchises • Licenses • Leaseholds • Noncompete covenants • Patents • Software *Subject Only to Annual Impairment Test* • Brand names • Goodwill • Trademarks	**Amortization:** periodic allocation of the cost of an intangible asset to the periods it benefits **Impairment:** occurs when the fair value of the asset falls below the carrying value; all long-term assets are subject to an annual test for impairment

Valuation and Disclosure of Long-Term Assets

Long-term assets are generally reported and *valued* at carrying value. **Carrying value** (or *book value*) is the unexpired part of an asset's cost, computed as shown in Exhibit 3. If a long-term asset loses some or all of its potential to generate revenue before the end of its useful life, it is *impaired*, and its carrying value is reduced.

Asset impairment occurs when the carrying value of a long-term asset exceeds its fair value.[2] *Fair value* is the amount for which the asset could be bought or sold in a current transaction. For example, if the sum of the expected cash flows from an asset is less than its carrying value, the asset would be impaired, and a loss would be recorded. When the market prices used to establish fair value are not available, the amount of an impairment must be estimated from the best available information.

Exhibit 3
Carrying Value of Long-Term Assets on the Balance Sheet

Building	$200,000
Less Accumulated Depreciation	30,000
Total Plant Assets	$170,000

Mines	$100,000
Less Accumulated Depletion	40,000
Total Natural Resources	$ 60,000

Patents	$20,000
Less Accumulated Amortization	5,000
Total Intangible Assets	$15,000

Business Perspective

Impairments reflect valuations at a point in time. For example, in 2004, **Apple Computer** recognized losses of $5.5 million in asset impairments. With the huge success of the iPhone and iPad in subsequent years, the company had no occasion to recognize impairments in subsequent years. Taking a large write-down in a bad year is often called "taking a big bath" because it "cleans" future years of the bad year's costs and thus can help a company return to a profitable status. In other words, by taking the largest possible loss in a bad year, companies hope to reduce the costs of depreciation or amortization on the asset in subsequent years.[3]

Recognition of the Acquisition Cost of Long-Term Assets

An **expenditure** is a payment or an obligation to make a future payment for an asset or a service. Expenditures are *classified* as capital expenditures or revenue expenditures.

- A **capital expenditure** is for the purchase or expansion of a long-term asset. Capital expenditures are recorded in asset accounts because they benefit more than the current period.
- A **revenue expenditure** is for the ordinary repairs and maintenance needed to keep a long-term asset in good operating condition. For example, trucks, machines, and other equipment require periodic tune-ups and routine repairs. Expenditures of this type are recorded in expense accounts because their benefits are realized in the current period.

Capital expenditures include outlays for plant assets, natural resources, and intangible assets. They also include the following:

- **Additions** are enlargements to the physical layout of a plant asset. For example, if a new wing is added to a building, the benefits from the expenditure will be received over several years, and the amount paid should be debited to an asset account.
- **Betterments** are improvements to a plant asset but not an addition to the plant's physical layout. Installation of an air-conditioning system is an example. Because betterments provide benefits over a period of years, their costs should be debited to an asset account.
- **Extraordinary repairs** are repairs that significantly enhance a plant asset's estimated useful life or residual value. For example, the overhaul of a building's heating and cooling system may extend the system's useful life by five years. Extraordinary repairs are typically recorded by reducing the Accumulated Depreciation account. The effect is to increase the asset's carrying value by the cost of the extraordinary repair. The new carrying value should be depreciated over the asset's new estimated useful life.

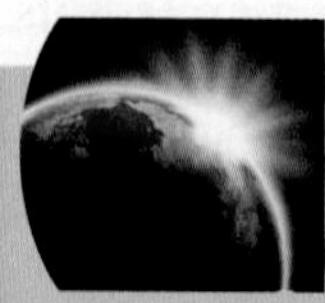

International Perspective

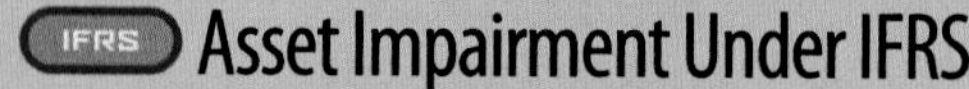

Asset Impairment Under IFRS

The IFRS method of evaluating asset impairment does not consider the sum of the expected cash flows as is done under U. S. GAAP. Instead, it compares the carrying value with the recoverable amount. The recoverable amount is the greater of either the *net selling price* (the market value of the asset less disposal costs) or the *value in use*, which is based on the cash generating ability of the asset adjusted for interest rates. This is called *present value*, which will be explained in a later chapter.

Because the recoverable value is usually less than the sum of the expected cash flows, the IFRS method is much more likely than the GAAP method to result in write-offs due to impairment. The IFRS method also allows reversals of impairment write-offs if the value later increases because of revaluation, whereas the GAAP method prohibits future impairment reversals. One exception under IFRS is that goodwill impairments cannot be reversed.

The distinction between capital and revenue expenditures is important in applying *accrual accounting*, as illustrated in the examples that follow.

	Asset Incorrectly Recorded as Revenue Expenditure	Revenue Expenditure Incorrectly Recorded as Asset
Example	The purchase of a machine that will benefit a company for several years is mistakenly recorded as a revenue expenditure.	A revenue expenditure, such as the routine overhaul of a piece of machinery, is charged to an asset account.
Result	The total cost of the machine becomes an expense on the income statement in the current period. ▼ Current net income will be reported at a lower amount *(understated)*. ▲ In future periods, net income will be reported at a higher amount *(overstated)*.	▼ The expense of the current period will be *understated*. ▲ Current net income will be *overstated* by the same amount. ▼ The net income of future periods will be *understated*.

APPLY IT!

Match each term that follows with the corresponding action.

1. Addition
2. Betterment
3. Extraordinary repair
4. Revenue expenditure
5. Impairment

a. Repainting of an existing building.
b. Installation of a new roof that extends an existing building's useful life.
c. Erection of a new storage facility at the back of an existing building.
d. Decrease in value of intangible asset below carrying value.
e. Installation of a new heating system in an existing building.

SOLUTION

1. c; 2. e; 3. b; 4. a; 5. d

TRY IT! E1A, E1B

SECTION 2 ACCOUNTING APPLICATIONS

ACCOUNTING APPLICATIONS

- Computing acquisition cost
- Computing depreciation
  - Straight-line method
  - Production method
  - Declining-balance method
- Accounting for the disposition of depreciable assets
- Accounting for natural resources
- Accounting for intangible assets

RELEVANT LEARNING OBJECTIVES

LO 2 Account for the acquisition costs of property, plant, and equipment.

LO 3 Compute depreciation under the straight-line, production, and declining-balance methods.

LO 4 Account for the disposal of depreciable assets.

LO 5 Identify the issues related to accounting for natural resources, and compute depletion.

LO 6 Identify the issues related to accounting for intangible assets, including research and development costs and goodwill.

LO 2 Acquisition Cost of Property, Plant, and Equipment

The acquisition cost of property, plant, and equipment includes all expenditures reasonable and necessary to get an asset in place and ready for use. For example, the cost of installing and testing a machine is a legitimate cost of acquiring the machine. However, if the machine is damaged during installation, the cost of repairs is an operating expense.

The cost of an asset is equal to its purchase price plus other costs:

Cost of Asset = Purchase Price + Additional Expenditures (freight, installation, etc.)

Thus, expenditures for freight, insurance while in transit, and installation are included in the cost of the asset because they are necessary for the asset to function. In accordance with *accrual accounting*, these expenditures are allocated over the asset's useful life.

Any interest charges incurred in purchasing an asset are not a cost of the asset. They are a cost of borrowing the money to buy the asset and are, therefore, an operating expense. An exception to this rule is that interest costs incurred during the construction of an asset are properly included as a cost of the asset.[4]

Many companies establish policies that define when an expenditure should be recorded as an expense or as an asset. For example, small expenditures for items that qualify as long-term assets may be treated as expenses because the amounts involved are not *material*. Thus, although a wastebasket may last for years, it would be recorded as an expense rather than as a depreciable asset.

Specific Applications of Determining the Acquisition Cost of Property, Plant, and Equipment

The sections that follow discuss some of the problems of determining the cost of long-term plant assets.

Land The purchase price of land should be debited to the Land account. Other expenditures that should be debited to Land include:

- Commissions to real estate agents
- Lawyers' fees
- Accrued taxes paid by the purchaser
- Costs of preparing the land to build on, such as the costs of tearing down old buildings and grading the land
- Assessments for local improvements, such as putting in streets and sewage systems
- Landscaping

Land is not depreciated because it has an unlimited useful life.

Assume that a company pays $340,000 for land, $16,000 in brokerage and legal fees, $20,000 to have an old building on the site torn down, and $2,000 to have the site graded. It receives $8,000 in salvage from the old building. The cost of the land is $370,000, calculated as follows.

Net purchase price		$340,000
Brokerage and legal fees		16,000
Tearing down old building	$20,000	
Less salvage	8,000	12,000
Grading		2,000
Total cost		$370,000

REUTERS/Str Old

Like other costs involved in preparing land for use, the cost of implosion is debited to Land. Other expenditures debited to Land include the purchase price of the land, brokerage and legal fees involved in the purchase, taxes paid by the purchaser, and landscaping.

Land Improvements Some improvements to real estate, such as driveways, parking lots, and fences, have a limited life and, thus, are subject to depreciation. They should be recorded in an account called Land Improvements.

Buildings When a company buys a building, the cost includes the purchase price and all expenditures required to put the building in usable condition. When a company uses a contractor to construct a building, the cost includes the net contract price plus other expenditures necessary to put the building in usable condition. When a company constructs its own building, the cost includes:

- Costs of materials, labor, overhead and other indirect costs
- Architects' fees and lawyers' fees
- Insurance during construction
- Interest on construction loans during the period of construction
- Building permits

Because buildings have a limited useful life, they are subject to depreciation.

Leasehold Improvements Improvements to leased property on the books of the lessee that become the property of the lessor (the owner of the property) at the end of the lease are called **leasehold improvements**. For example, a tenant's installation of light fixtures, carpets, or walls would be considered a leasehold improvement. These improvements are usually classified in the property, plant, and equipment section of the balance sheet.[5] The cost of a leasehold improvement is depreciated over the remaining term of the lease or the useful life of the improvement, whichever is shorter.

A study of large companies showed that 26 percent report leasehold improvements. The percentage is likely to be much higher for small businesses because they generally operate in leased premises.[6]

STUDY NOTE: *The wiring and plumbing of a dental chair are included in the cost of the asset because they are a necessary cost of preparing the asset for use.*

Equipment The cost of equipment includes all expenditures connected with purchasing the equipment and preparing it for use. These expenditures include:

- Invoice price less cash discounts
- Freight, including insurance
- Excise taxes and tariffs
- Buying expenses
- Installation costs
- Test runs to ready the equipment for operation

Equipment is subject to depreciation.

Group Purchases Companies sometimes purchase land and other assets for a lump sum. The lump-sum purchase price must be apportioned between the land and the other assets. For example, suppose that a company buys a building and land for $170,000. The company can determine what it would have paid for the building and for the land if it had purchased them separately and apply the appropriate percentages to the lump-sum price. If appraisals yield estimates of $20,000 for the land and $180,000 for the building, the lump-sum price would be allocated as follows.

	Appraisal	Percentage	Apportionment
Land	$ 20,000	10% ($ 20,000 ÷ $200,000)	$ 17,000 ($170,000 × 10%)
Building	180,000	90% ($180,000 ÷ $200,000)	153,000 ($170,000 × 90%)
Totals	$200,000	100%	$170,000

APPLY IT!

Match each term that follows with the corresponding action.

1. Land
2. Land improvement
3. Leasehold improvement
4. Buildings
5. Equipment

a. Purchase of a computer.
b. Purchase of a lighting system for a parking lot.
c. Construction of a foundation for a new building.
d. Installation of partitions and shelves in a leased space.
e. Clearing of land in preparation for construction of a new building.

SOLUTION

1. e; 2. b; 3. d; 4. c; 5. a

TRY IT! SE1, SE2, E2A, E3A, E4A, E2B, E3B, E4B

LO3 Depreciation

As noted earlier, depreciation is the periodic allocation of the cost of property, plant, and equipment (other than land) over the asset's estimated useful life. In accounting for depreciation, it is important to keep the following points in mind:

- All plant assets, except land, have a limited useful life, and the costs of these assets must be distributed as expenses over the years they benefit.
- Depreciation refers to the allocation of the cost of a plant asset to the periods it benefits, not to the asset's physical deterioration or its decrease in market value. The term *depreciation* describes the gradual conversion of the cost of the asset into an expense.
- Depreciation is not a process of *valuation*. Accounting records are not indicators of changing price levels. They are kept in accordance with the *cost principle*. Because of an advantageous purchase price and market conditions, the value of a building may increase. Nevertheless, because depreciation is a process of allocation, not valuation, depreciation on the building must continue to be recorded.

STUDY NOTE: *Depreciation is the allocation of the acquisition cost of a plant asset. Any similarity between carrying value and current market value is pure coincidence.*

Physical deterioration and obsolescence are the major factors in limiting a depreciable asset's useful life.

- **Physical deterioration:** The result of use or exposure to the elements, such as wind and sun. Periodic repairs and a sound maintenance policy may keep buildings and equipment in good operating order, but every machine or building must, at some point, be discarded.
- **Obsolescence:** The process of going out of date. Because of fast-changing technology and demands, machinery and even buildings often become obsolete before they wear out.

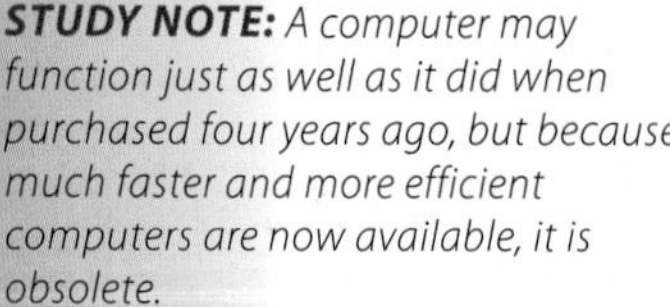

STUDY NOTE: *A computer may function just as well as it did when purchased four years ago, but because much faster and more efficient computers are now available, it is obsolete.*

Accountants do not distinguish between physical deterioration and obsolescence because they are interested in the length of an asset's useful life, not in what limits its useful life.

Business Perspective

How Long Is the Useful Life of an Airplane?

Most airlines depreciate their planes over an estimated useful life of 10 to 20 years. But how long will a properly maintained plane really last? **Western Airlines** paid $3.3 million for a new Boeing 737 in July 1968. More than 78,000 flights and 30 years later, this aircraft was still flying for **Vanguard Airlines**, a no-frills airline. Among the other airlines that have owned this plane are **Piedmont**, **Delta**, and **US Airways**. Virtually every part of the plane has been replaced over the years. **Boeing** believes the plane could theoretically make double the number of flights before it is retired.

The useful lives of many types of assets can be extended indefinitely if the assets are correctly maintained. However, each airline that owned the plane would have depreciated it over a "reasonable" useful life.

Factors in Computing Depreciation

Four factors affect the computation of depreciation:

- **Cost** is the net purchase price of an asset plus all reasonable and necessary expenditures to get it in place and ready for use.
- **Residual value** (or *salvage value*, *disposal value*, and *trade-in value*) is the portion of an asset's acquisition cost that a company expects to recover when it disposes of the asset.
- **Depreciable cost** is an asset's cost less its residual value. For example, a truck that cost $24,000 and that has a residual value of $6,000 would have a depreciable cost of $18,000. Depreciable cost must be allocated over the estimated useful life of the asset.
- **Estimated useful life** is the total number of service units expected from a long-term asset. Service units may be measured in terms of the years an asset is expected to be used, the units it is expected to produce, the miles it is expected to be driven, or similar measures. In computing an asset's estimated useful life, an accountant should consider all relevant information, including past experience with similar assets, the asset's present condition, the company's repair and maintenance policy, and current technological and industry trends.

STUDY NOTE: *Depreciable cost, not acquisition cost, is allocated over a plant asset's useful life.*

At the end of a period, depreciation is recorded with an adjusting entry that takes the following form:

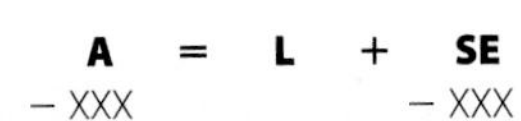

Depreciation Expense—Asset Name	XXX	
Accumulated Depreciation—Asset Name		XXX
To record depreciation for the period		

Methods of Computing Depreciation

Many methods are used to allocate the cost of plant assets to accounting periods. The most common methods are the straight-line method, the production method, and the declining-balance method (an accelerated method).

Straight-Line Method

Method When the **straight-line method** is used, the asset's depreciable cost is spread evenly over the estimated useful life of the asset. The straight-line method is based on the assumption that depreciation depends only on the passage of time.

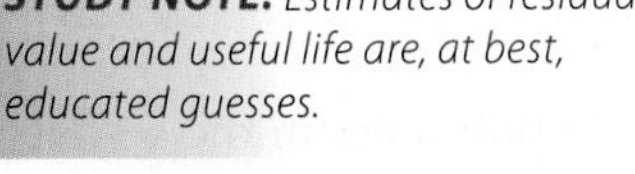

STUDY NOTE: *Estimates of residual value and useful life are, at best, educated guesses.*

Formula The depreciation expense for each period is computed by dividing the depreciable cost (cost less estimated residual value) by the number of accounting periods in the asset's estimated useful life:

Depreciation Expense = (Cost − Residual Value) ÷ Estimated Useful Life

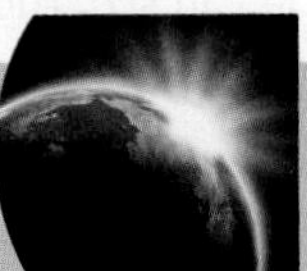

International Perspective

IFRS Depreciation of Buildings Under IFRS

Under GAAP, the costs of a building and its components, such as a heating and air conditioning system, are usually lumped together as one asset and are depreciated over the life of the building. Under IFRS, however, a building and its components are depreciated on an individual basis. In other words, each component of a building—each property, plant. and equipment asset—is considered to have its own useful life and fair value and is depreciated on that basis. Because many of a building's assets often have shorter useful lives than the building itself, IFRS tend to increase depreciation expense. These standards also require more precise record keeping.

Example A delivery truck cost $20,000 and has an estimated residual value of $2,000 at the end of its estimated useful life of five years. Under the straight-line method, the annual depreciation would be $3,600, calculated as follows.

$$\text{Depreciation Expense} = \frac{\text{Cost} - \text{Residual Value}}{\text{Estimated Useful Life}} = \frac{\$20{,}000 - \$2{,}000}{5 \text{ Years}} = \$3{,}600 \text{ per Year}$$

Exhibit 4 shows the depreciation schedule for the five years. Note that in addition to annual depreciation being the same each year, the accumulated depreciation increases uniformly and the carrying value decreases uniformly until it reaches the estimated residual value.

Exhibit 4
Depreciation Schedule, Straight-Line Method

	Cost	Annual Depreciation	Accumulated Depreciation	Carrying Value
Date of purchase	$20,000	—	—	$20,000
End of first year	20,000	$3,600	$ 3,600	16,400
End of second year	20,000	3,600	7,200	12,800
End of third year	20,000	3,600	10,800	9,200
End of fourth year	20,000	3,600	14,400	5,600
End of fifth year	20,000	3,600	18,000	2,000

Production Method

Method The **production method** (or *units of production method*) is based on the assumption that depreciation is solely the result of use and that the passage of time plays no role in the process. The production method is appropriate when a company has widely fluctuating rates of production. For example, carpet mills often close during the first two weeks in July but may run double shifts in September. With the production method, depreciation would be in direct relation to a mill's units of output.

Formula Under the production method, depreciation is calculated as follows.

$$\text{Depreciation Expense} = \frac{\text{Cost} - \text{Residual Value}}{\text{Estimated Units of Useful Life}}$$

Example Assume that the delivery truck in the previous example has an estimated useful life of 90,000 miles. The depreciation cost per mile would be determined as follows.

$$\text{Depreciation Expense} = \frac{\text{Cost} - \text{Residual Value}}{\text{Estimated Units of Useful Life}} = \frac{\$20{,}000 - \$2{,}000}{90{,}000} = \$0.20 \text{ per Mile}$$

If the truck were driven 20,000 miles in the first year, 30,000 miles in the second, 10,000 miles in the third, 20,000 miles in the fourth, and 10,000 miles in the fifth, the depreciation schedule for the truck would be as shown in Exhibit 5. As you can see, the amount of depreciation each year is directly related to the units of use. The carrying value decreases each year until it reaches the estimated residual value.

Exhibit 5
Depreciation Schedule, Production Method

	Cost	Miles	Annual Depreciation	Accumulated Depreciation	Carrying Value
Date of purchase	$20,000	—	—	—	$20,000
End of first year	20,000	20,000	$4,000	$ 4,000	16,000
End of second year	20,000	30,000	6,000	10,000	10,000
End of third year	20,000	10,000	2,000	12,000	8,000
End of fourth year	20,000	20,000	4,000	16,000	4,000
End of fifth year	20,000	10,000	2,000	18,000	2,000

In considering whether to use the production method, it is important to keep the following points in mind:

- It must be possible to estimate with reasonable accuracy the output of an asset over its useful life.
- The unit used to measure the estimated useful life of an asset must be appropriate for the asset.

Declining-Balance Method An **accelerated method** of depreciation results in relatively large amounts of depreciation in the early years of an asset's life and smaller amounts in later years. This type of method is based on the assumption that many plant assets are most efficient when new and so provide the greatest benefits in their first years.

Under an accelerated method, depreciation charges will be highest in years when revenue generation from the asset is highest. Fast-changing technologies often cause equipment to become obsolete and lose service value rapidly. In addition, repair expense is likely to increase as an asset ages. In such cases, using an accelerated method is appropriate. Thus, the total of repair plus depreciation expense will remain fairly constant over the years.

Declining-Balance Method

Method The **declining-balance method** is the most common accelerated method of depreciation. With this method, depreciation is computed by applying a fixed rate to the declining carrying value of a long-term asset. It therefore results in higher depreciation charges in the early years of the asset's life. Though any fixed rate can be used, the most common rate is a percentage equal to twice the straight-line depreciation percentage. When this rate is used, the method is usually called the **double-declining-balance method**.

Example In our example of the straight-line method, the delivery truck had an estimated useful life of five years, and the annual depreciation rate for the truck was therefore 20 percent:

$$\text{Annual Depreciation Rate} = \frac{\text{Percent of Useful Life}}{\text{Estimated Useful Life}}$$

$$= \frac{100\%}{5 \text{ Years}}$$

$$= 20\%$$

STUDY NOTE: The double-declining-balance method is the only method presented here in which the residual value is not deducted before calculating depreciation.

$$\text{Declining-Balance Depreciation Rate} = 2 \times 20\% = 40\%$$

Under the double-declining-balance method, the fixed rate would be 40 percent, or "double" the straight-line rate.

This rate is applied to the carrying value at the end of the previous year. With this method, the depreciation schedule would be as shown in Exhibit 6.

Exhibit 6
Depreciation Schedule, Double-Declining-Balance Method

	Cost	Annual Depreciation	Accumulated Depreciation	Carrying Value
Date of purchase	$20,000	—	—	$20,000
End of first year	20,000	(40% × $20,000) = $8,000	$ 8,000	12,000
End of second year	20,000	(40% × $12,000) = 4,800	12,800	7,200
End of third year	20,000	(40% × $ 7,200) = 2,880	15,680	4,320
End of fourth year	20,000	(40% × $ 4,320) = 1,728	17,408	2,592
End of fifth year	20,000	592*	18,000	2,000

*Depreciation is limited to the amount necessary to reduce carrying value to residual value: $2,592 (previous carrying value) − $2,000 (residual value) = $592.

Comparison of the Three Methods Exhibit 7 compares yearly depreciation and carrying value under the three methods. The graph on the left shows yearly depreciation.

- Straight-line depreciation is uniform at $3,600 per year over the 5-year period.
- The double-declining-balance method begins at $8,000 and decreases each year to amounts that are less than straight-line (ultimately, $592).
- The production method does not generate a regular pattern because of the random fluctuation of the depreciation from year to year.

The graph on the right side of Exhibit 7 shows the carrying value under the three methods. Each method starts in the same place (cost of $20,000) and ends at the same place (residual value of $2,000). However, the patterns of carrying value during the asset's useful life differ. For instance, the carrying value under the straight-line method is always greater than under the double-declining-balance method, except at the beginning and end of the asset's useful life.

Exhibit 7
Graphic Comparison of Three Methods of Determining Depreciation

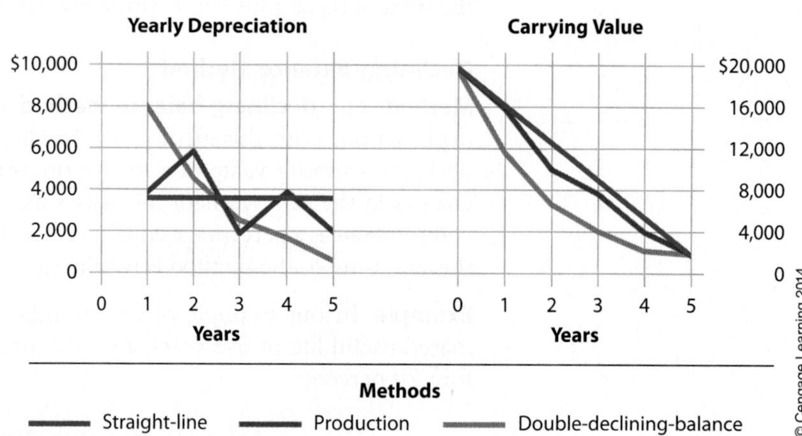

Business Perspective
Accelerated Methods Save Money!

As shown in the graph below, an AICPA study of 500 large companies found that the overwhelming majority used the straight-line method of depreciation for financial reporting. Only about 5 percent used some type of accelerated method, and 3 percent used the production method. However, these figures tend to be misleading about the importance of accelerated depreciation methods. Federal income tax laws allow either the straight-line method or an accelerated method, and, for tax purposes, about 75 percent of the 500 companies studied preferred an accelerated method. The straight-line method can be advantageous for financial reporting because it can produce the highest net income, and an accelerated method can be beneficial for tax purposes because it can result in lower income taxes.

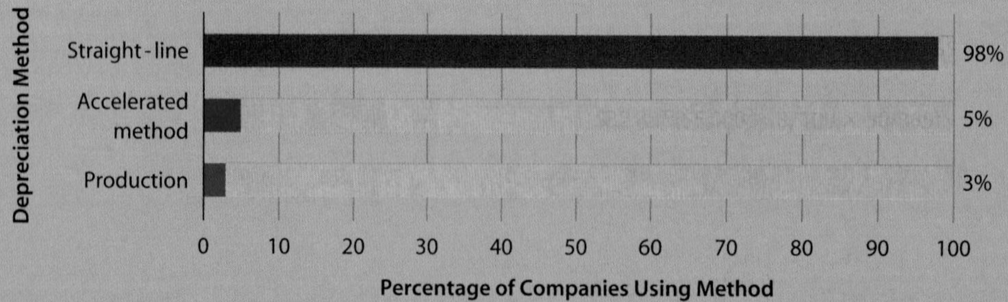

Note: Calculation more than 100% due to companies using more than one method.

Source: "Depreciation Methods Used by 600 Large Companies for Financial Reporting." Copyright © 2011 by AICPA. Reproduced with permission.

Special Issues in Determining Depreciation

Other issues in depreciating assets include group depreciation, depreciation for partial years, revision of depreciation rates, and accelerated cost recovery for tax purposes.

Group Depreciation The estimated useful life of an asset is the average length of time assets of the same type are expected to last. For example, the average useful life of a particular type of machine may be six years. However, some machines in this category may last only two or three years, while others may last eight or nine years or longer. For this reason, and for convenience, large companies group similar assets, such as machines, to calculate depreciation. A survey of large businesses indicated that 67 percent used this method, called **group depreciation**, for all or part of their plant assets.[7]

Depreciation for Partial Years To simplify our examples of depreciation, we have assumed that plant assets were purchased at the beginning or end of a period. However, the time of year is normally not a factor in the decision to buy or sell assets. Thus, it is often necessary to calculate depreciation for partial years. Some companies compute depreciation to the nearest month. Others use the half-year convention, in which one-half year of depreciation is taken in the year the asset is purchased and one-half year is taken in the last year of the asset's life.

Revision of Depreciation Rates The periodic depreciation charge is seldom precise. Sometimes, the estimate of useful life is revised, so that the periodic depreciation expense increases or decreases over the asset's remaining useful life. For example, suppose a delivery truck cost $14,000 and has a residual value of $2,000. The truck was expected to last six years, and it was depreciated on the straight-line basis. However, after two years of intensive use, it is determined that the truck will last only two more years, but its residual value at the end of the two years will still be $2,000. At the end of the second year, the asset account and its related accumulated depreciation account would be as follows.

Delivery Truck

	Dr.	*Cr.*
Cost	14,000	

Accumulated Depreciation—Delivery Truck

Dr.	*Cr.*	
	Depreciation, Year 1	2,000
	Depreciation, Year 2	2,000

The remaining depreciable cost is computed as follows.

Cost − Depreciation Already Taken − Residual Value = Depreciable Cost
$14,000 − $4,000 − $2,000 = $8,000

The new annual periodic depreciation charge is computed by dividing the remaining depreciable cost of $8,000 by the remaining useful life of two years. Therefore, the new periodic depreciation charge is $4,000.[8]

Special Rules for Tax Purposes Over the years, Congress has revised the federal income tax law to encourage businesses to invest in new plant and equipment. For instance, the tax law allows rapid write-offs of plant assets, which differs considerably from the depreciation methods most companies use for financial reporting. Tax methods of depreciation are usually not acceptable for financial reporting because the periods over which deductions may be taken are often shorter than the assets' estimated useful lives. A change in the federal income tax law—the result of the **Economic Stimulus Act of 2008**—allows a small company to expense the first $250,000 of equipment expenditures rather than record them as assets and depreciate them over their useful lives. Also, for assets that are subject to depreciation, there is a bonus first-year deduction.

APPLY IT!

On January 13, 2014, Miko Company purchased a company car for $47,500. Miko expects the car to last five years or 120,000 miles, with an estimated residual value of $7,500. During 2015, the car is driven 27,000 miles. Miko's year-end is December 31. Compute the depreciation for 2015 under each of the following methods: (1) straight-line, (2) production, and (3) double-declining-balance. Using the amount computed in (3), prepare the journal entry to record depreciation expense for the second year and compute carrying value of the company car as it would appear on the balance sheet.

SOLUTION

Depreciation computed:

1. Straight-line method: ($47,500 − $7,500) ÷ 5 years = $8,000
2. Production method: ($47,500 – $7,500) ÷ 120,000 miles = $0.3333 per mile
   27,000 miles × $0.3333 = $9,000*
3. Double-declining-balance method: (1 ÷ 5) × 2 = 0.40
   2014: $47,500 × 0.40 = $19,000
   2015: ($47,500 − $19,000) × 0.40 = $11,400

* Rounded

Journal entry:

Depreciation Expense	11,400	
Accumulated Depreciation		11,400
To record depreciation of car: ($47,500 − $19,000) × 0.40		

Balance sheet carrying value:

Company car	$47,500	
Less accumulated depreciation	30,400	$17,100

TRY IT! SE3, SE4, SE5, E4A, E5A, E6A, E7A, E4B, E5B, E6B, E7B

LO4 Disposal of Depreciable Assets

When plant assets, like buildings and equipment, are no longer useful because they have physically deteriorated or become obsolete, a company can:

- Discard them
- Sell them
- Trade them in on the purchase of a new asset

STUDY NOTE: *When a company disposes of an asset, it must bring the depreciation up to date and remove all evidence of ownership of the asset, including the contra account Accumulated Depreciation.*

Regardless of how a company disposes of a plant asset, it must record depreciation expense for the partial year up to the date of disposal. This step is required because the company used the asset until that date and, under accrual accounting, the accounting period should receive the proper allocation of depreciation expense.

To illustrate how a company records each type of disposal, we will use BTL Company.

Discarded Plant Assets

If an asset remains in use beyond the end of its estimated life, its cost and accumulated depreciation remain in the ledger accounts. Thus, proper records will be available for maintaining control over plant assets. If the residual value is zero, the carrying value of a fully depreciated asset is zero. When the asset is discarded, no gain or loss results. For assets with a carrying value, however, a loss equal to the carrying value should be recorded.

Discarding Assets with a Carrying Value

Transaction BTL purchases a machine on January 2, 2014, for $13,000 and plans to depreciate it on a straight-line basis over an estimated useful life of eight years. The machine's residual value at the end of eight years is estimated to be $600. On December 31, 2019, the balances of the relevant accounts are as shown below. On January 2, 2020, management disposes of the asset.

Machinery		Accumulated Depreciation—Machinery	
Dr.	Cr.	Dr.	Cr.
13,000			9,300

The discarded equipment has a carrying value of $3,700 at the time of its disposal ($13,000 less accumulated depreciation of $9,300).

Analysis A loss equal to the carrying value should be recorded. This journal entry

▼ *decreases* the asset *Machinery* with a credit

▼ *decreases* Machinery's related *Accumulated Depreciation* with a debit

▲ *increases* the *Loss on Disposal of Machinery* account with a debit

Application of Accrual Accounting

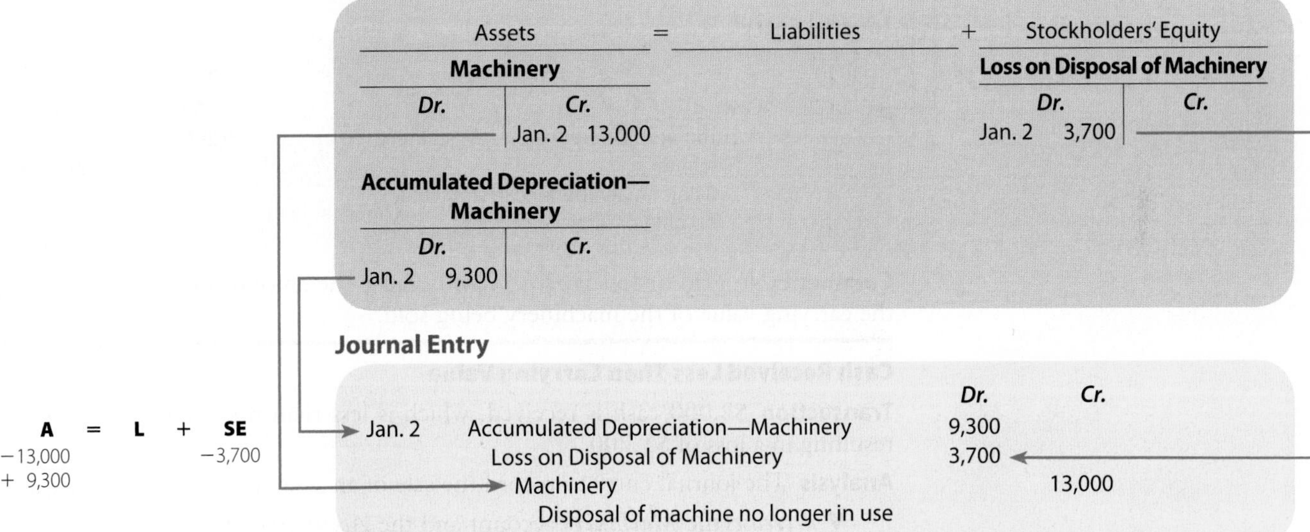

Comment *Recognized* gains and losses on disposals of plant assets are *classified* as other revenues and expenses on the income statement.

Plant Assets Sold for Cash

STUDY NOTE: *When an asset is discarded or sold for cash, the gain or loss equals cash received minus the carrying value.*

The entry to record a plant asset sold for cash is similar to the one just illustrated, except that the receipt of cash should also be recorded. The following entries show how to record the sale of a machine at three different selling prices.

Cash Received Equal to Carrying Value

Transaction $3,700 cash is received and is exactly equal to the $3,700 carrying value of the machine.

Analysis The journal entry to record the sale of an asset at carrying value

▼ *decreases* the *Machinery* account and the *Accumulated Depreciation* account

▲ *increases* the *Cash* account

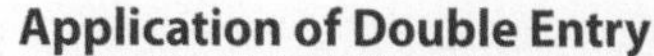

Application of Double Entry

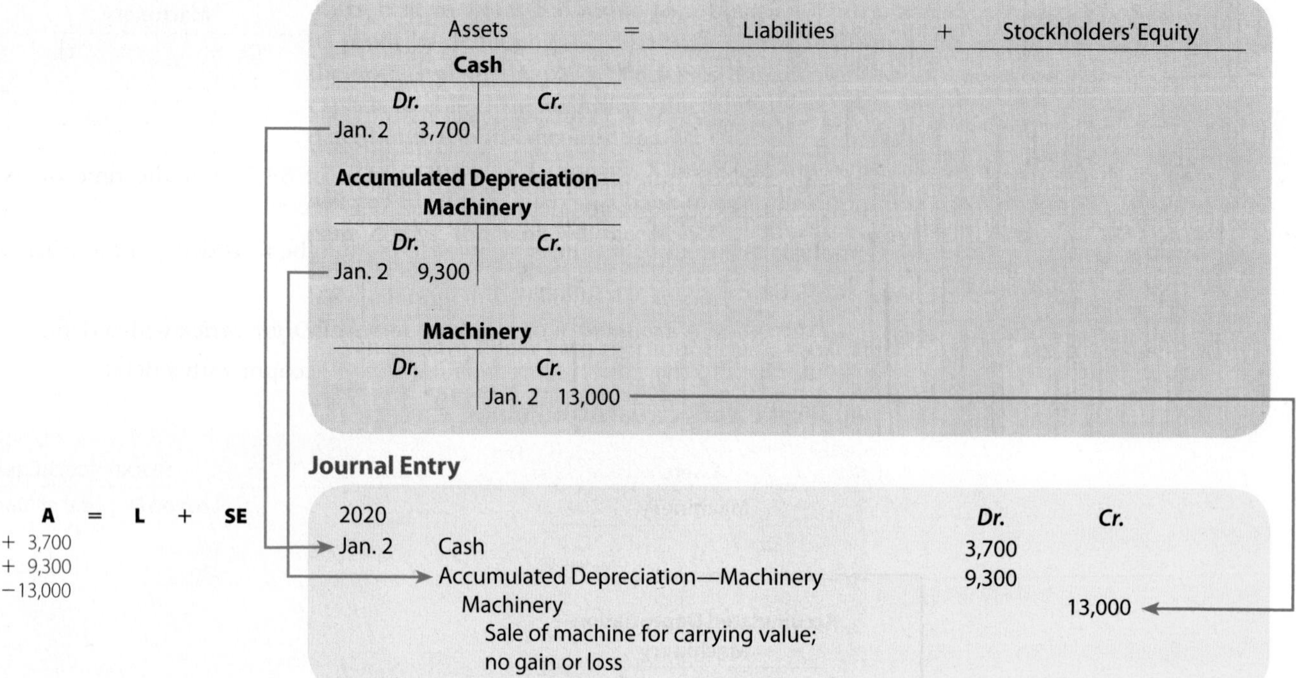

Comment No gain or loss is *recognized* because the amount of cash is exactly equal to the carrying value of the machinery being sold.

Cash Received Less Than Carrying Value

Transaction $2,000 cash is received, which is less than the carrying value of $3,700, resulting in a loss of $1,700.

Analysis The journal entry to record the sale of an asset at less than carrying amount

- ▼ *decreases* the *Machinery* account and the *Accumulated Depreciation* account
- ▲ *increases* the *Cash* account
- ▲ *increases* the *Loss on Sale of Machinery* account for the difference

Application of Double Entry

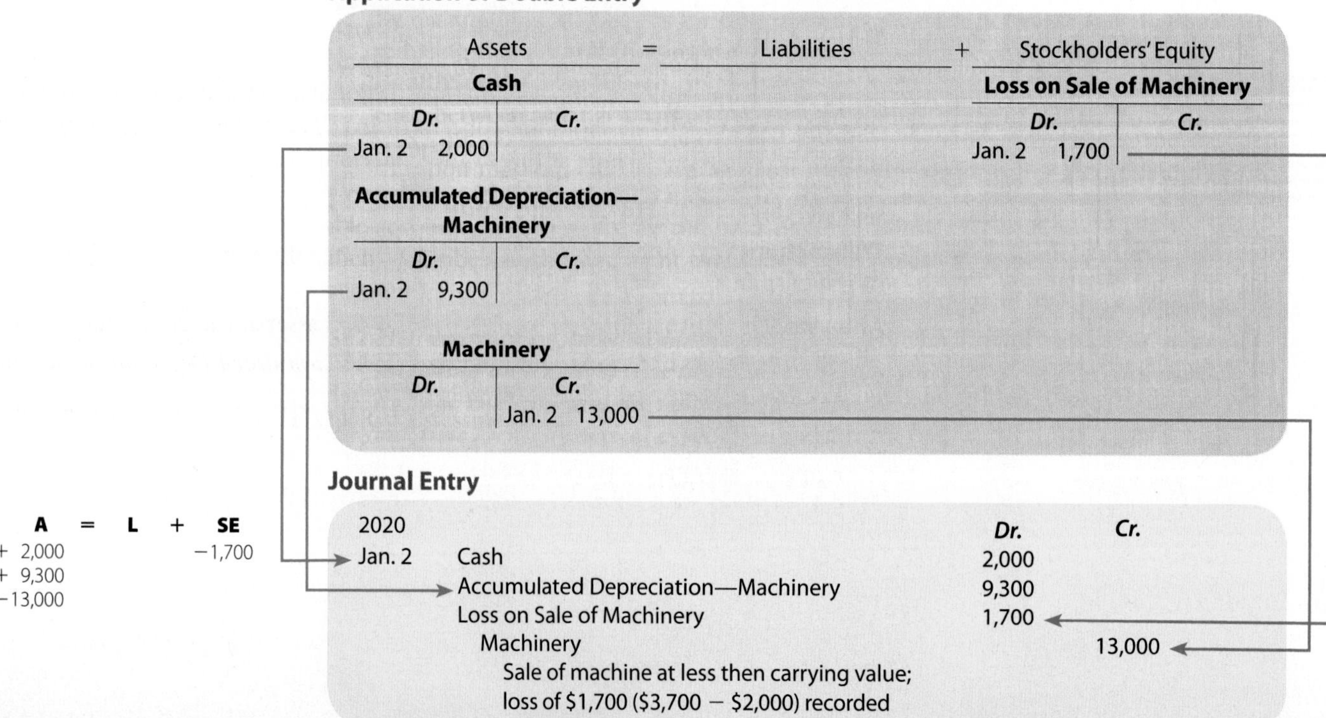

Comment A loss is *recognized* because the amount of cash is less than the carrying value of the machinery being sold.

Cash Received More Than Carrying Value

Transaction $4,000 cash is received, which exceeds the carrying value of $3,700, resulting in a gain of $300.

Analysis The journal entry to record the sale of an asset at less than carrying amount

- ▼ *decreases* the *Machinery* account and the *Accumulated Depreciation* account
- ▲ *increases* the *Cash* account
- ▲ *increases* the *Gain on Sale of Machinery* account for the difference

Application of Double Entry

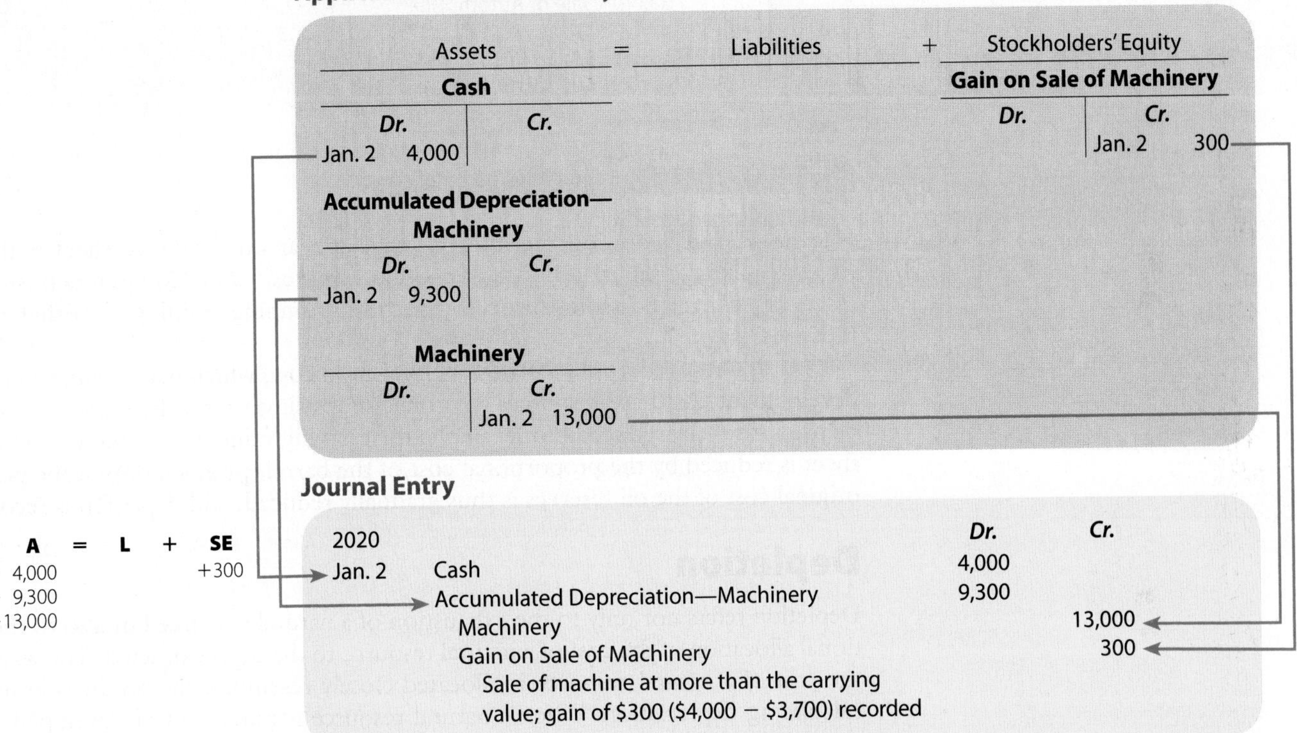

Journal Entry

2020		Dr.	Cr.
Jan. 2	Cash	4,000	
	Accumulated Depreciation—Machinery	9,300	
	Machinery		13,000
	Gain on Sale of Machinery		300
	Sale of machine at more than the carrying value; gain of $300 ($4,000 − $3,700) recorded		

Comment A gain is *recognized* because the amount of cash is more than the carrying value of the machinery being sold.

Exchanges of Plant Assets

Exchanges may involve similar assets, such as an old machine traded in on a newer model, or dissimilar assets, such as a cement mixer traded in on a truck. In either case, the purchase price is reduced by the amount of the trade-in allowance.

Basically, accounting for exchanges of plant assets is similar to accounting for sales of plant assets.

- ▲ If the trade-in allowance is greater than the asset's carrying value, the company realizes a gain.
- ▼ If the allowance is less, it suffers a loss.[9]

APPLY IT!

On January 2, the first day of business of the current year, Kamila Company sold a car that cost $47,500 and on which $30,400 of accumulated depreciation had been recorded. For each of the following assumptions, prepare the journal entry (without explanation) for the disposal: (1) The car was sold for $17,100 cash. (2) The car was sold for $15,000 cash. (3) The car was sold for $20,000 cash.

SOLUTION

	Dr.	Cr.
1. Cash	17,100	
Accumulated Depreciation—Automobile	30,400	
Automobile		47,500
2. Cash	15,000	
Accumulated Depreciation—Automobile	30,400	
Loss on Sale of Automobile	2,100	
Automobile		47,500
3. Cash	20,000	
Accumulated Depreciation—Automobile	30,400	
Automobile		47,500
Gain on Sale of Automobile		2,900

TRY IT! SE6, E8A, E9A, E8B, E9B

LO5 Natural Resources

Natural resources are long-term assets that appear on a balance sheet with descriptive titles like "Timberlands," "Oil and gas reserves," and "Mineral deposits." These assets are converted to inventory by cutting, pumping, mining, or other extraction methods.

Natural resources are recorded at acquisition cost, which may include some costs of development. As these resources are converted to inventory, their asset accounts must be proportionally reduced. For example, the carrying value of oil reserves on the balance sheet is reduced by the proportional cost of the barrels pumped during the period. The original cost of the oil reserves is thus gradually reduced, and depletion is recognized.

Depletion

Depletion refers not only to the exhaustion of a natural resource but also to the proportional allocation of the cost of a natural resource to the units extracted. The way in which the cost of a natural resource is allocated closely resembles the production method of calculating depreciation. When a natural resource is purchased or developed, the total units that will be available, such as tons of coal, must be estimated. The depletion cost per unit is computed as follows.

$$\text{Depletion Cost per Unit} = \frac{\text{Cost} - \text{Residual Value}}{\text{Estimated Number of Units}}$$

Depletion of a Natural Resource

Transaction A mine was purchased for $3,600,000. It has an estimated residual value of $600,000, and it contains an estimated 3,000,000 tons of coal. The depletion charge per ton of coal is $1, calculated as follows.

$$\text{Depletion Cost per Unit} = \frac{\text{Cost} - \text{Residual Value}}{\text{Estimated Number of Units}}$$

$$\frac{\$3{,}600{,}000 - \$600{,}000}{3{,}000{,}000 \text{ Tons}} = \$1 \text{ per Ton}$$

The amount of the depletion cost for each accounting period is then computed by multiplying the depletion cost per unit by the number of units extracted and sold. Thus, if 230,000 tons of coal are mined and sold during the first year, the depletion charge for the year is $230,000.

Analysis The journal entry to record the depletion of a natural resource

▲ *increases* the *Depletion Expense* account

▲ *increases* the *Accumulated Depletion* account

Application of Double Entry

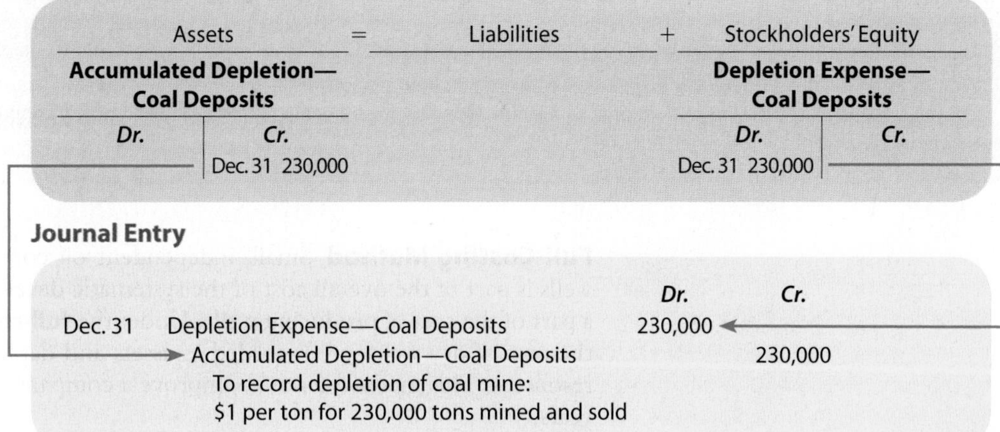

Assets = Liabilities + Stockholders' Equity
Accumulated Depletion—Coal Deposits
Dr. Cr.
Dec. 31 230,000
Depletion Expense—Coal Deposits
Dr. Cr.
Dec. 31 230,000

Journal Entry

A = L + SE
−230,000 −230,000

		Dr.	Cr.
Dec. 31	Depletion Expense—Coal Deposits	230,000	
	Accumulated Depletion—Coal Deposits		230,000
	To record depletion of coal mine: $1 per ton for 230,000 tons mined and sold		

On the balance sheet, data for the mine would be presented as follows.

Coal deposits	$3,600,000	
Less accumulated depletion	230,000	$3,370,000

Comment If a natural resource is not sold in the year it is extracted, it is reported as inventory. It would be *recorded* as a depletion *expense* in the year it is *sold*.

Depreciation of Plant Assets Related to Natural Resources

STUDY NOTE: *A company may abandon equipment that is still in good working condition because of the expense involved in dismantling the equipment and moving it to another site.*

The extraction of natural resources generally requires special on-site buildings and equipment (e.g., conveyors, drills, and pumps). The useful life of these plant assets may be longer than the estimated time it will take to deplete the resources. However, a company may plan to abandon these assets after all the resources have been extracted because they no longer serve a useful purpose. In this case, they should be depreciated on the same basis as the depletion.

For example, suppose machinery with a useful life of ten years is installed on an oil field that is expected to be depleted in eight years. The machinery should be depreciated over the eight-year period, using the production method. That way, each year's depreciation will be proportional to the year's depletion.[10]

Development and Exploration Costs in the Oil and Gas Industry

The costs of exploring and developing oil and gas resources can be accounted for under one of two methods: successful efforts or full costing. The Financial Accounting Standards Board permits the use of either method.[11]

Successful Efforts Accounting Under **successful efforts accounting**, the cost of successful exploration—for example, an exploration that produces an oil well—is a cost of the resource. It should be recorded as an asset and depleted over the resource's estimated life. The cost of an unsuccessful exploration—such as one that produces a dry well—is written off immediately as a loss. Because of these immediate write-offs, successful efforts accounting is considered the more conservative method and is used by most large oil companies.

Business Perspective
How Do You Measure What's Underground? With a Good Guess.

Accounting standards require publicly traded energy companies to *disclose* in their annual reports their production activities, estimates of their proven oil and gas reserves, and estimates of the future cash flows those reserves are expected to generate. Since the reserves are often miles underground or beneath deep water, these figures are considered "supplementary" and not reliable enough to be audited independently. As a result, some companies have overestimated their reserves and, thus, overestimated their future prospects. Apparently, some managers at **Royal Dutch/Shell Group** were receiving bonuses based on the amount of new reserves added to the annual report. When the company announced that it was reducing its reported reserves by 20 percent, the price of its stock dropped.[12]

Full-Costing Method Small, independent oil companies argue that the cost of dry wells is part of the overall cost of the systematic development of an oil field and is, thus, a part of the cost of producing wells. Under the **full-costing method**, all costs, including the cost of dry wells, are recorded as assets and depleted over the estimated life of the resources. This method tends to improve a company's earnings performance in its early years.

APPLY IT!

Sharp Mining Company paid $8,800,000 for land containing an estimated 40 million tons of ore. The land without the ore is estimated to be worth $2,000,000. The company spent $1,380,000 to erect buildings on the site and $2,400,000 on equipment installed on site. The buildings have an estimated useful life of 30 years, and the equipment has an estimated useful life of 10 years. Neither the buildings nor the equipment has a residual value. The company expects to mine all the usable ore in 10 years. During its first year of operation, it mined and sold 2,800,000 tons of ore.

1. Compute the depletion charge per ton.
2. Compute the depletion expense that Sharp Mining should record for its first year of operation.
3. Determine the depreciation expense for the year for the buildings, making it proportional to the depletion.
4. Determine the depreciation expense for the year for the equipment, using two alternatives:

   (a) making the expense proportional to the depletion, and

   (b) using the straight-line method.

SOLUTION

1. $\frac{\$8{,}800{,}000 - \$2{,}000{,}000}{40{,}000{,}000 \text{ tons}} = \$0.17 \text{ per ton}$
2. 2,800,000 tons × $0.17 per ton = $476,000
3. $\frac{2{,}800{,}000 \text{ tons}}{40{,}000{,}000 \text{ tons}} \times \$1{,}380{,}000 = \$96{,}600$
4. a. $\frac{2{,}800{,}000 \text{ tons}}{40{,}000{,}000 \text{ tons}} \times \$2{,}400{,}000 = \$168{,}000$

   b. $\frac{\$2{,}400{,}000}{10 \text{ years}} \times 1 \text{ year} = \$240{,}000$

TRY IT! SE7, E10A, E10B

LO6 Intangible Assets

An intangible asset is both long-term and nonphysical. Its value comes from the long-term rights it affords its owner. Exhibit 8 describes the following most common types of intangible assets and their accounting treatment. Like intangible assets, some current assets—for example, accounts receivable and certain prepaid expenses—have no physical substance; but because they are short-term, they are not classified as intangible assets.

Exhibit 8
Accounting for Intangible Assets

Type	Description	Usual Accounting Treatment
	Subject to Amortization and Annual Impairment Test	
Copyright	An exclusive right granted by the federal government to reproduce and sell literary, musical, and other artistic materials and computer programs for a period of the author's life plus 70 years.	Record at acquisition cost, and amortize over the asset's useful life, which is often much shorter than its legal life. For example, the cost of paperback rights to a popular novel would typically be amortized over a useful life of 2 to 4 years.
Patent	An exclusive right granted by the federal government for a period of 20 years to make a particular product or use a specific process. A design may be granted a patent for 14 years.	The cost of successfully defending a patent in a patent infringement suit is added to the acquisition cost of the patent. Amortize over the asset's useful life, which may be less than its legal life.
Leasehold	A right to occupy land or buildings under a long-term rental contract. For example, if Company A sells or subleases its right to use a retail location to Company B for 10 years in return for one or more rental payments, Company B has purchased a leasehold.	The lessor (Company A) debits Leasehold for the amount of the rental payment and amortizes it over the remaining life of the lease. The lessee (Company B) debits payments to Lease Expense.
Software	Capitalized costs of computer programs developed for sale, lease, or internal use.	Record the amount of capitalizable production costs, and amortize over the estimated economic life of the product.
Noncompete covenant	A contract limiting the rights of others to compete in a specific industry or line of business for a specified period.	Record at acquisition cost, and amortize over the contract period.
Franchise, License	A right to an exclusive territory or market or the right to use a formula, technique, process, or design.	Debit Franchise or License for the acquisition cost, and amortize it over a reasonable life.
Customer list	A list of customers or subscribers.	Debit Customer List for amount paid, and amortize over the asset's expected life.
	Subject to Annual Impairment Test Only	
Goodwill	The excess of the amount paid for a business over the fair market value of the business's net assets.	Debit Goodwill for the acquisition cost, and review impairment annually.
Trademark, Brand name	A registered symbol or name that can be used only by its owner to identify a product or service.	Debit Trademark or Brand Name for the acquisition cost, and review impairment annually.

Exhibit 9 shows the percentage of companies (out of those surveyed) that report various intangible assets. For some companies, intangible assets make up a substantial portion of total assets. For example, **Apple**'s goodwill and other acquired intangible assets amounted to $4.4 billion in 2011. How these assets are accounted for has a major effect on Apple's performance. For example, acquired intangible assets are amortized over six years, and amortization expenses for these costs amounted to $192 million in 2011.

Exhibit 9
Assets Reported by Large Companies

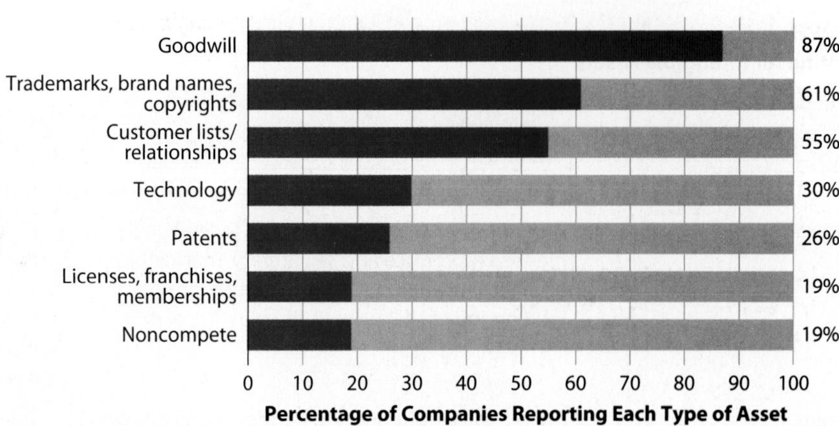

Source: Data from American Institute of Certified Public Accountants, *Accounting Trends & Techniques* (New York: AICPA, 2011).

The purchase of an intangible asset is a special kind of capital expenditure. Such assets are accounted for at the amount that a company paid for them. Some intangible assets, such as goodwill and trademarks, may be acquired at little or no cost. Even though these assets may have great value and may be needed for profitable operations, a company should include them on its balance sheet only if it purchased them from another party at a price established in the marketplace. When a company develops its own intangible assets, it should record the costs of development as expenses. An exception is the cost of internally developed computer software after a working prototype of the software has been developed.

Purchased intangible assets are recorded at cost or at fair value when purchased as part of a group of assets. The useful life of an intangible asset is the period over which the asset is expected to contribute to the company's future cash flows. The useful life may be definite or indefinite.[13]

- **Definite useful life:** A definite useful life is subject to a legal limit or can be reasonably estimated. Examples include patents, copyrights, and leaseholds. The estimated useful lives of these assets are often less than their legal limits. The cost of an intangible asset with a definite useful life should be allocated to expense through periodic amortization.
- **Indefinite useful life:** An indefinite useful life is not limited by legal, regulatory, contractual, competitive, economic, or other factors. This definition does not imply that these assets last forever. Examples can include trademarks and brands, which can last for as short or as long as the company is successful in using them. The costs of intangible assets with an indefinite life are not amortized as long as circumstances continue to support an indefinite life.

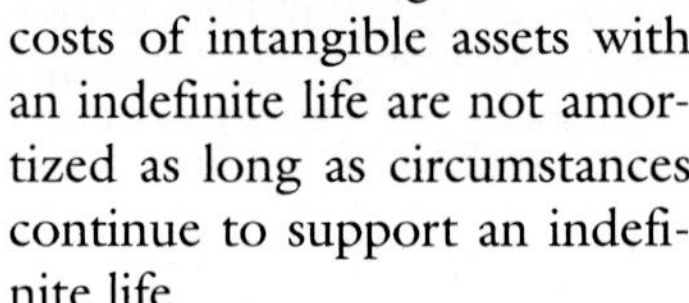

Business Perspective
Who's Number One in Brands?

Brands are intangible assets that often do not appear on a company's balance sheet because, rather than purchasing them, the company has developed them over time. According to one report, the 10 most valuable brands were: [14]

Apple	**Coca-Cola**
Google	**AT&T**
IBM	**Marlboro**
McDonald's	**China Mobile**
Microsoft	**GE**

Apple's brand was valued at almost $153 billion, whereas GE's brand was valued at $50 billion.

All intangible assets, whether definite or indefinite, are subject to an annual impairment test to determine if the assets justify their value on the balance sheet. If they have lost some or all of their value in producing future cash flows, they should be written down to their fair value or to zero if they have no fair value. The amount of the write-down is shown on the income statement as an impairment charge (deduction) in determining income from operations.

To illustrate accounting for intangible assets with limited useful lives, suppose Soda Bottling Company purchases a patent on a unique bottle cap for $36,000. The purchase would be recorded with an entry of $36,000 in the asset Patents.[15] Although the patent for the bottle cap will last for 20 years, Soda determines that it will sell the product that uses the cap for only six years. Thus, the annual amortization expense is $6,000 ($36,000 ÷ 6 years). When the expense is recorded, the Patents account is reduced directly by the amount of the amortization expense (in contrast to the treatment of other long-term assets, for which depreciation or depletion is accumulated in separate contra accounts). The journal entry would be as follows.

A	=	L	+	SE
−6,000				−6,000

Dec. 31	Amortization Expense—Patents	6,000	
	Patents		6,000
	To record amortization of patient		

Research and Development Costs

Most successful companies carry out research and development (R&D) activities, often within a separate department. Among these activities are development of new products, testing of existing and proposed products, and pure research. The costs of these activities are substantial for many companies. In a recent year, **General Motors** spent $8.1 billion, or about 5.4 percent of its revenues, on R&D.[16] R&D costs can be even greater in high-tech fields like pharmaceuticals. For example, **Abbott Laboratories** recently spent $4.1 billion, or 10.6 percent of its revenues, on R&D.[17]

The Financial Accounting Standards Board requires that all R&D costs be charged to expense in the period in which they are incurred.[18] The reasoning is that it is too hard to trace specific costs to specific profitable developments. Also, the costs of research and development are continuous and necessary for the success of a business and so should be treated as current expenses.

Computer Software Costs

The costs that companies incur in developing computer software for sale or lease or for their own internal use are considered research and development costs until the product has proved feasible. Thus, costs incurred before that point should be charged to expense as they are incurred. A product is deemed feasible when a detailed working program has been designed. Once that occurs, all software production costs are recorded as assets and are amortized over the software's estimated economic life, using the straight-line method. If at any time a company cannot expect to realize the amount of the unamortized software costs, the asset should be written down to the amount expected to be realized.[19]

International Perspective

IFRS R&D Costs Under IFRS

In contrast to GAAP, under which all research and development costs are expensed, IFRS require that research costs be expensed and that development costs be capitalized and amortized. This requires a judgment about what constitutes research and what constitutes development. These differences in accounting treatments—immediate expensing versus amortization over time—can have considerable impact on reported income over many years.

Goodwill

Goodwill generally refers to a company's good reputation. From an accounting standpoint, goodwill exists when a purchaser pays more for a business than the fair market value of the business's net assets. In other words, the purchaser would pay less if it bought the assets separately. Most businesses are worth more as going concerns than as collections of assets.

Goodwill reflects all the factors that allow a company to earn a higher-than-market rate of return on its assets, including:

- Customer satisfaction
- Good management
- Manufacturing efficiency
- The advantages of having a monopoly
- Good locations
- Good employee relations

The FASB requires that purchased goodwill be reported as a separate line item on the balance sheet and that it be reviewed annually for impairment. If the fair value of goodwill is less than its carrying value, it is considered impaired. In that case, it is reduced to its fair value, and the impairment charge is reported on the income statement.[20]

A company should record goodwill only when it acquires a controlling interest in another business. The amount to be recorded as goodwill can be determined by writing the identifiable net assets up to their fair market values at the time of purchase and subtracting the total from the purchase price. For example, suppose a company pays \$11,400,000 to purchase another business.

- If the net assets of the business (total assets − total liabilities) are *fairly valued* at \$10,000,000, the amount of the goodwill is \$1,400,000 (\$11,400,000 − \$10,000,000).
- If the fair market value of the net assets is more or less than \$10,000,000, an entry is made in the accounting records to adjust the assets to the fair market value. The goodwill would then represent the difference between the adjusted net assets and the purchase price of \$11,400,000.

Long-Term Assets and the Financial Statements

Exhibit 10 shows that purchase, use, and disposal of long-term assets affect all financial statements. As you can see, the acquisition cost of long-term assets increases by the amount of capital expenditures and accumulated depreciation increases by the amount of depreciation expense.

Business Perspective
Wake up! Goodwill Is Growing!

© Alija / iStockphoto.com

Eighty-nine percent of 500 large companies separately report goodwill as an asset.[21] Because much of the growth of these companies has come through purchasing other companies, goodwill as a percentage of total assets has also grown. As shown right, the amount of goodwill can be material.[22]

	Goodwill (in billions)	Percentage of Total Assets
General Mills	\$ 8,205	38%
Heinz	\$ 3,298	32%
Cisco Systems	\$16,823	19%

Exhibit 10
Relationship of Long-Term Assets to the Financial Statements

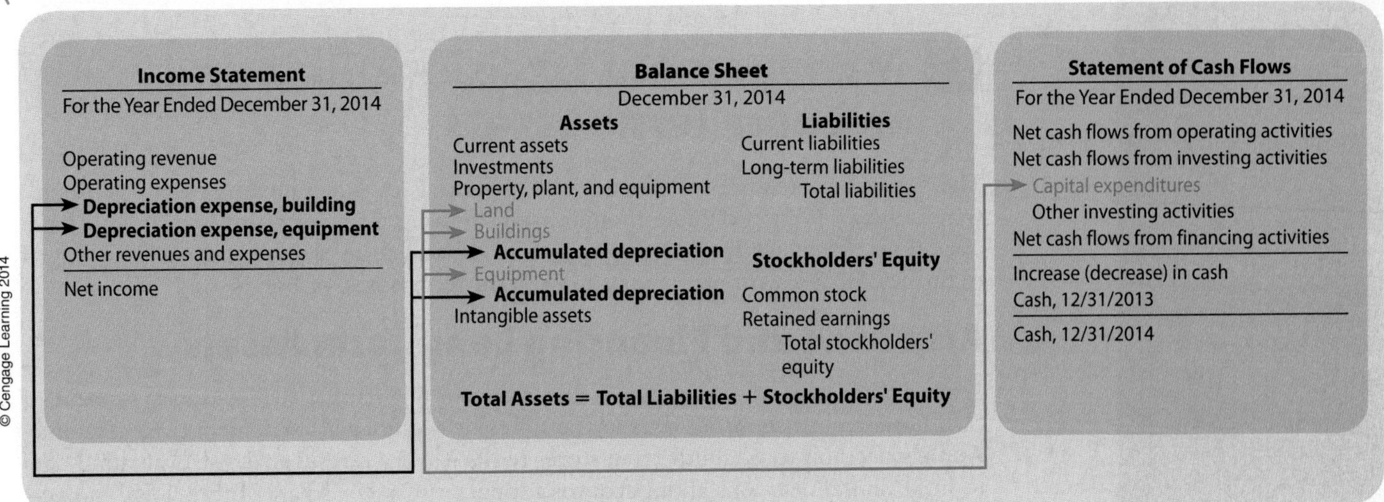

Income Statement
For the Year Ended December 31, 2014
Operating revenue
Operating expenses
Depreciation expense, building
Depreciation expense, equipment
Other revenues and expenses
Net income
Balance Sheet
December 31, 2014
Assets
Current assets
Investments
Property, plant, and equipment
Land
Buildings
Accumulated depreciation
Equipment
Accumulated depreciation
Intangible assets
Liabilities
Current liabilities
Long-term liabilities
Total liabilities
Stockholders' Equity
Common stock
Retained earnings
Total stockholders' equity
Total Assets = Total Liabilities + Stockholders' Equity
Statement of Cash Flows
For the Year Ended December 31, 2014
Net cash flows from operating activities
Net cash flows from investing activities
Capital expenditures
Other investing activities
Net cash flows from financing activities
Increase (decrease) in cash
Cash, 12/31/2013
Cash, 12/31/2014

APPLY IT!

For each of the following intangible assets, indicate (a) if the asset is to be amortized over its useful life or (b) if the asset is not amortized but only subject to annual impairment test:

1. Goodwill
2. Copyright
3. Brand name
4. Patent
5. Trademark

SOLUTION

1. b; 2. a; 3. b; 4. a; 5. b

TRY IT! SE8, E11A, E12A, E11B, E12B

SECTION 3 **BUSINESS APPLICATIONS**

BUSINESS APPLICATIONS
- Acquiring and Financing Long-Term Assets
- Free Cash Flow
- Ethics

RELEVANT LEARNING OBJECTIVE

LO 7 Describe the disclosure of acquiring and financing long-term assets, and calculate free cash flow.

LO 7 Management Decisions Relating to Long-Term Assets

The decision to acquire and finance a long-term asset is a complex process. Although some companies are profitable enough to pay for long-term assets out of cash flows from operations, for major long-term acquisitions of long-term assets, a company may need to finance them it with the issue of stock, long-term notes, or bonds.

Acquiring and Financing Long-Term Assets

A good place to study a company's investing and financing activities is its statement of cash flows and in the *disclosures* in the notes to the financial statements. For example, **Apple**'s decision to establish retail stores required very careful analysis. Evaluating data to make sound decisions about acquiring long-term assets is part of the capital budgeting process, a topic covered in detail in managerial accounting texts. However, information about acquisitions of long-term assets appears in the investing activities section of the statement of cash flows. The investing section of Apple's statement of cash flows in its 2011 annual report shows acquisition of property, plant, and equipment to be $4.3 billion in 2011. Apple's management reveals the portion of this amount spent on retail stores in 2011 and its plans for 2012 in the notes, as follows.

> *The Company's actual cash payments for capital expenditures during 2011 were $4.3 billion, of which $612 million relates to retail store facilities. . . . The Company anticipates utilizing approximately $8.0 billion for capital expenditures during 2012, including approximately $900 million for retail store facilities and approximately $7.1 billion for product tooling and manufacturing process equipment, and corporate facilities and infrastructure, including information systems hardware, software and enhancements.*

The financing section of Apple's statement of cash flows reveals that the company raised $831 million through the issuance of common stock in 2011. Since this is much less than the $4.3 billion in acquisitions, the company must have used funds it already had from its operations. A measure of the company's success in funding these acquisitions is free cash flow, discussed in the next section.

Free Cash Flow Although not a financial ratio, **free cash flow** is an important measure of a company's ability to finance long-term assets. It is the amount of cash that remains after deducting the funds a company must commit to continue operating at its planned level. These commitments include:

- Current or continuing operations
- Interest
- Income taxes
- Dividends
- Net capital expenditures (purchases of plant assets minus sales of plant assets)

If a company fails to pay for current or continuing operations, interest, and income taxes, its creditors or the government can take legal action. Although the payment of dividends is not required, dividends represent a commitment to stockholders. If they are reduced or eliminated, stockholders may be unhappy, which will cause the price of the company's stock to fall.

A positive free cash flow means that a company has met all its cash commitments and has cash available to reduce debt or to expand operations. A negative free cash flow means that it will have to sell investments, borrow money, or issue stock to continue at its planned level. If its free cash flow remains negative for several years, a company may not be able to raise cash by issuing stock or bonds.

Using data from **Apple**'s statement of cash flows in its 2011 annual report, we can compute the company's free cash flow as follows (in millions).

$$\begin{aligned}\text{Free Cash Flow} &= \text{Net Cash Flows from Operating Activities} - \text{Dividends}\\ &\quad - \text{Purchases of Plant Assets} + \text{Sales of Plant Assets}\\ &= \$37{,}529 - \$0 - \$4{,}260 + \$0\\ &= \$33{,}269\end{aligned}$$

This analysis confirms Apple's strong financial position. Its cash flow from operating activities far exceeded its net capital expenditures of $4,260 million. A factor in its positive free cash flow of $33,269 million is that the company pays no dividends. In addition, the financing activities section of Apple's statement of cash flows indicates that the company, rather than incurring debt for expansion, actually made net investments of $32,464 million.

Ethics in Acquiring and Financing Long-Term Assets

When a company records a long-term asset, it defers some of the asset's cost to later periods. Thus, the current period's profitability looks better than it would have if the asset's total cost had been expensed immediately. Management has considerable latitude in making the judgments and estimates necessary to account for long-term assets, and this latitude has sometimes been used unethically. For example, in the **WorldCom** accounting fraud, management ordered that expenditures that should have been recorded as operating expenses be recorded as long-term assets and written off over several years. The result was an overstatement of income by about $10 billion, which ultimately led to one of the largest bankruptcies in the history of U.S. business.

To avoid fraudulent reporting of long-term assets, a company's management must apply accrual accounting in resolving properly two important issues:

- The amount of the total cost of a long-term asset to allocate to expense in the current period.
- The amount to retain on the balance sheet as an asset.

To resolve these issues, management must answer four important questions about the acquisition, use, and disposal of each long-term asset. These questions are illustrated in Exhibit 11.

Exhibit 11
Issues in Accounting for Long-Term Assets

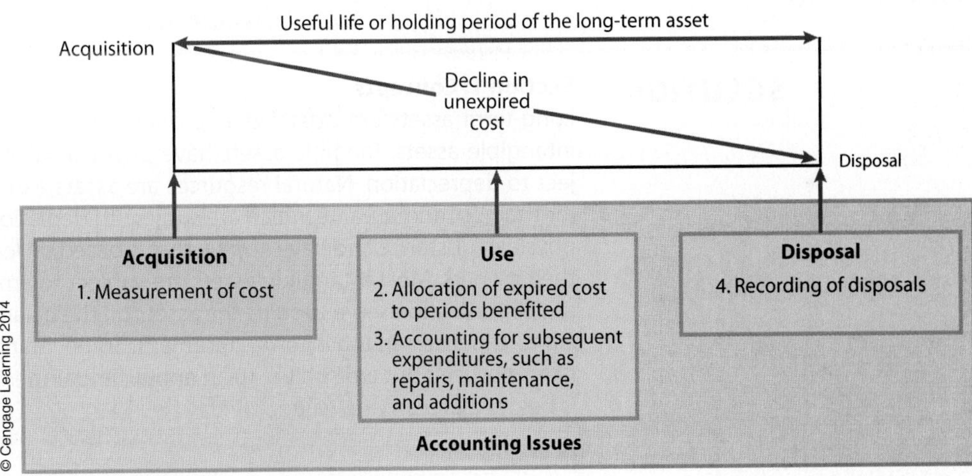

1. How is the cost of the long-term asset determined?
2. How should the expired portion of the cost of the long-term asset be allocated against revenues over time?
3. How should subsequent expenditures, such as repairs and additions, be treated?
4. How should disposal of the long-term asset be recorded?

Management's answers to these questions can be found in the company's annual report under management's discussion and analysis and in the notes to the financial statements.

APPLY IT!

In the past year, Bivak Company had net cash flows of $133,000 from operating activities. It expended $61,000 for property, plant, and equipment; sold property, plant, and equipment for $14,000; and paid dividends of $20,000. Calculate the company's free cash flow. What does the result tell you about the company?

SOLUTION

Net cash flows from operating activities	$133,000
Purchases of property, plant, and equipment	(61,000)
Sales of property, plant, and equipment	14,000
Dividends	(20,000)
Free cash flow	$ 66,000

Bivak's operations provide sufficient cash flows to fund its current expansion and its payment of dividends without raising additional capital.

TRY IT! SE9, SE10, E13A, E14A, E13B, E14B

A Look Back At: Apple Computer

Songquan Deng/Shutterstock.com

Apple Computer

We began the chapter by emphasizing that **Apple**'s success as an innovator and marketer is a result of its wise and steady investments in research and development and long-term assets. Complete the following requirements in order to answer the questions posed at the beginning of the chapter.

Section 1: Concepts
What is the classification of long-term assets, how are the assets valued, and what is the distinction in recognizing capital and revenue expenditures?

Section 2: Accounting Applications
What questions need to be answered in order to properly account for long-term assets?

Section 3: Business Applications
How does management decide to acquire, finance, and evaluate long-term assets?

SOLUTION

Section 1: Concepts
Long-term assets are *classified* as property, plant, and equipment, natural resources, or intangible assets. Tangible assets have physical substance and, except for land, are subject to depreciation. Natural resources are assets extracted from the land and purchased for their economic value which are subject to depletion. Finally, intangible assets have no physical substance and have a value that is based on legal rights or advantages accruing to their owners. Most intangible assets are subject to amortization. Depreciation, depletion, and amortization serve to *value* the assets on the balance sheet and apply *accrual accounting* to expenses on the income statement. Some intangible assets, including goodwill, are not amortized but are subject to an annual impairment test to determine if their fair value is below their carrying value.

OLUTION • SOLUTION • SOLUTION

Expenditures related to long-term assets are *recognized* either as capital expenditures or revenue expenditures. A capital expenditure is for the purchase or expansion of a long-term asset and is recorded in asset accounts because it benefits several future accounting periods. On the other hand, a revenue expenditure is for the ordinary repairs and maintenance needed to keep a long-term asset in good operating condition.

Section 2: Accounting Applications
When acquiring and recording long-term assets, such as a computer, the company needs to apply accrual accounting in deciding how to allocate the total cost of the asset to expense in the current period and over time (whether the purchase is a capital or revenue expenditure and choosing a deprecation method), how to treat subsequent expenditures (repair and maintenance, betterments, etc.), and how to record the disposal of the asset. These decisions will impact the long-term asset's value presented on the balance sheet as well as the net income amount in current and future periods.

Section 3: Business Applications
The decision to acquire a long-term asset involves determining if the company has sufficient funds to make the purchase and, if not, to obtain appropriate financing. A company can finance a long-term asset purchase with cash or by issuing stocks, long-term notes, or bonds. Management needs to analyze the company's statement of cash flows and calculate free cash flow as follows.

Free Cash Flow = Net Cash Flows from Operating Activities − Dividends −
Purchases of Plant Assets + Sales of Plant Assets

Review Problem

Hubert Building Company purchased a cement mixer on January 2, 2014, for $29,000. The mixer was expected to have a useful life of five years and a residual value of $2,000. The company's engineers estimated that the mixer would have a useful life of 15,000 hours. It was used for 3,000 hours in 2014; 5,250 hours in 2015; 4,500 hours in 2016; 1,500 hours in 2017; and 750 hours in 2018. The company's fiscal year ends on December 31. Using this information, complete the requirements that follow.

1. Compute the depreciation expense and carrying value of the cement mixer for 2014 to 2018 using the following methods: (a) straight-line, (b) production, and (c) double-declining-balance.
2. Assuming the straight-line method is used and that the cement mixer is sold for $5,000 on December 31, 2018, show the entry to record the sale.
3. What conclusions can you draw from the patterns of yearly depreciation?

SOLUTION

1.

	A	B	C	D	E	F	G	H
1		Depreciation						Carrying
2		Method	Year	Computation			Depreciation	Value
3	a.	Straight-line	2014	$27,000	÷	5	$5,400	$23,600
4			2015	27,000	÷	5	5,400	18,200
5			2016	27,000	÷	5	5,400	12,800
6			2017	27,000	÷	5	5,400	7,400
7			2018	27,000	÷	5	5,400	2,000
8								
9	b.	Production	2014	$27,000	×	3,000	$5,400	$23,600
10						15,000		
11								
12			2015	27,000	×	5,250	9,450	14,150
13						15,000		
14								
15			2016	27,000	×	4,500	8,100	6,050
16						15,000		
17								
18			2017	27,000	×	1,500	2,700	3,350
19						15,000		
20								
21			2018	27,000	×	750	1,350	2,000
22						15,000		
23								
24	c.	Double-	2014	$29,000	×	0.40	$11,600	$17,400
25		declining-	2015	17,400	×	0.40	6,960	10,440
26		balance	2016	10,440	×	0.40	4,176	6,264
27			2017	6,264	×	0.40	2,506*	3,758
28			2018	3,758	–	$2,000	1,758**	2,000
29	*	Rounded						
30	**	Remaining depreciation to reduce carrying value to residual value						
31		($3,758 – $2,000)						
32								

2.

		Debit	Credit
Dec. 31	Cash	5,000	
	Accumulated Depreciation—Cement Mixer	27,000	
	Cement Mixer		29,000
	Gain on Sale of Cement Mixer		3,000
	To record the sale of cement mixer		

3. In the earlier years, the amount of depreciation under the double-declining-balance method is significantly greater than the amount under the straight-line method. In the later years, the opposite is true. The carrying value under the straight-line method is greater than under the double-declining-balance method at the end of all years except the fifth year. Depreciation under the production method differs from depreciation under the other methods in that it follows no regular pattern. It varies with the amount of use. Consequently, depreciation is greatest in 2015 and 2016, which are the years of greatest use.

Chapter Review

LO 1 Identify the classifications of long-term assets, and describe how they are valued by allocating their costs to the periods that they benefit.

Long-term assets have a useful life of more than one year, are used in the operation of a business, and are not intended for resale. They are classified as property, plant, and equipment; natural resources; or intangible assets. In the latter category are patents, trademarks, franchises, and other rights, as well as goodwill. Accrual accounting and valuation of long-term asset are applied through depreciation, depletion, amortization, or impairment tests, depending on the classification of the asset.

Capital expenditures are classifed as assets, whereas revenue expenditures are classified as expenses of the current period. Capital expenditures include not only outlays for plant assets, natural resources, and intangible assets, but also expenditures for additions, betterments, and extraordinary repairs that increase an asset's residual value or extend its useful life. Revenue expenditures are made for ordinary repairs and maintenance. The error of classifying a capital expenditure as a revenue expenditure, or vice versa, has an important effect on net income.

LO 2 Account for the acquisition costs of property, plant, and equipment.

The acquisition cost of property, plant, and equipment includes all expenditures reasonable and necessary to get the asset in place and ready for use. Among these expenditures are the purchase price, installation cost, freight charges, and insurance during transit. The acquisition cost of a plant asset is allocated over the asset's useful life.

LO 3 Compute depreciation under the straight-line, production, and declining-balance methods.

Depreciation—the periodic allocation of the cost of a plant asset over its estimated useful life—is commonly computed by using the straight-line method, the production method, or an accelerated method. The straight-line method is related directly to the passage of time, whereas the production method is related directly to use or output. An accelerated method, which results in relatively large amounts of depreciation in earlier years and reduced amounts in later years, is based on the assumption that plant assets provide greater economic benefits in their earlier years than in later ones. The most common accelerated method is the declining-balance method.

LO 4 Account for the disposal of depreciable assets.

A company can dispose of a long-term plant asset by discarding or selling it or exchanging it for another asset. An asset being disposed of must have depreciation recorded up to the date of disposal. To record the disposal, the carrying value must be removed from the asset account and the depreciation to date must be removed from the accumulated depreciation account. When a company sells a depreciable long-term asset at a price that differs from its carrying value, it should report the gain or loss on its income statement. In recording exchanges of similar plant assets, a gain or loss may arise.

LO 5 Identify the issues related to accounting for natural resources, and compute depletion.

Natural resources are depletable assets that are converted to inventory by cutting, pumping, mining, or other forms of extraction. They are recorded at cost as long-term assets. As natural resources are sold, their costs are allocated as expenses through depletion charges. The depletion charge is based on the ratio of the resource extracted to the total estimated resource. A major issue related to this subject is accounting for oil and gas reserves.

LO 6 Identify the issues related to accounting for intangible assets, including research and development costs and goodwill.

The purchase of an intangible asset should be treated as a capital expenditure and recorded at acquisition cost. All intangible assets are subject to annual tests for impairment of value. Intangible assets with a definite life are also amortized annually. The FASB requires that research and development costs be expensed. Software costs are treated as research and development costs and expensed until a feasible working program is developed, after which time the costs may be capitalized and amortized over a reasonable estimated life. Goodwill is the excess of the amount paid for a business over the fair market value of the net assets and is usually related to the business's superior earning potential. It should be recorded only when a company purchases an entire business, and it should be reviewed annually for possible impairment.

LO 7 Describe the disclosure of acquiring and financing long-term assets and calculate free cash flow.

Information about the acquisition and financing of long-term assets is found in the statement of cash flows and in the disclosures in the notes to the financial statements. Free cash flow is the amount of cash that remains after deducting the funds a company must commit to continue operating at its planned level.

Key Terms

Chapter Assignments

DISCUSSION QUESTIONS

LO 1 **DQ1. CONCEPT ▶** Is carrying value ever the same as market value?

LO 2 **DQ2.** What incentive does a company have to allocate more of a group purchase price to land than to building?

LO 3 **DQ3.** Which depreciation method would best reflect the risk of obsolescence from rapid technological changes?

LO 4 **DQ4.** When would the disposal of a long-term asset result in no gain or loss?

LO 5 **DQ5.** When would annual depletion not equal depletion expense?

LO 6 **DQ6.** Why would a firm amortize a patent over fewer years than the patent's life?

LO 6 **DQ7.** Why would a company spend millions of dollars on goodwill?

LO 7 **DQ8. BUSINESS APPLICATION ▶** What major advantage does a company that has positive free cash flow have over a company that has negative free cash flow?

SHORT EXERCISES

LO 2 **Classifying Cost of Long-Term Assets**

SE1. CONCEPT ▶ Gallon Auto purchased a neighboring lot for a new building and parking lot. Indicate whether each of the following expenditures is properly charged to (a) Land, (b) Land Improvements, or (c) Buildings:

1. Paving costs
2. Architects' fee for building design
3. Cost of clearing the property
4. Cost of the property
5. Building construction costs
6. Lights around the property
7. Building permit
8. Interest on the construction loan

LO 2 **Group Purchase**

SE2. Pattia Company purchased property with a warehouse and parking lot for $1,500,000. An appraiser valued the components of the property if purchased separately as follows.

Land	$ 400,000
Land improvements	200,000
Building	1,000,000
Total	$1,600,000

Determine the cost to be assigned to each component.

LO 3 **Straight-Line Method**

SE3. Sunburn Fitness Center purchased a new step machine for $8,250. The apparatus is expected to last four years and have a residual value of $750. What will the depreciation expense be for each year under the straight-line method?

LO 3 **Production Method**

SE4. Assume that the step machine in **SE3** has an estimated useful life of 8,000 hours and was used for 2,400 hours in year 1; 2,000 hours in year 2; 2,200 hours in year 3; and 1,400 hours in year 4. How much would depreciation expense be in each year? (Round to the nearest dollar.)

LO 3 **Double-Declining-Balance Method**

SE5. Assume that the step machine in **SE3** is depreciated using the double-declining-balance method. How much would depreciation expense be in each year?

LO 4 **Disposal of Plant Assets: No Trade-In**

SE6. Times Printing owned a piece of equipment that cost $32,400 and on which it had recorded $18,000 of accumulated depreciation. The company disposed of the equipment on January 2, the first day of business of the current year.

1. Calculate the carrying value of the equipment.
2. Calculate the gain or loss on the disposal under each of the following assumptions:
   a. The equipment was discarded as having no value.
   b. The equipment was sold for $6,000 cash.
   c. The equipment was sold for $16,000 cash.

LO 5 **Natural Resources**

SE7. Walden Green Company purchased land containing an estimated 4,000,000 tons of ore for $16,000,000. The land will be worth $2,400,000 without the ore after 8 years of active mining. Although the equipment needed for the mining will have a useful life of 20 years, it is not expected to be usable and will have no value after the mining on this site is complete. Compute the depletion charge per ton and the amount of depletion expense for the first year of operation, assuming that 600,000 tons of ore are mined and sold. Also, compute the first-year depreciation on the mining equipment using the production method, assuming a cost of $19,200,000 with no residual value.

LO 6 **Intangible Assets: Computer Software**

SE8. Satyam Company has created a new software application for PCs. Its costs during research and development were $500,000. Its costs after the working program was developed were $350,000. Although the company's copyright may be amortized over 40 years, management believes that the product will be viable for only 5 years. How should the costs be accounted for? At what value will the software appear on the balance sheet after 1 year?

LO 7

Management Issues

SE9. BUSINESS APPLICATION ▶ Indicate whether each of the following actions is primarily related to (a) acquisition of long-term assets, (b) evaluating the adequacy of financing of long-term assets, or (c) applying accrual accounting to long-term assets:

1. Deciding between common stock and long-term notes for the raising of funds.
2. Relating the acquisition cost of a long-term asset to the cash flows generated by the asset.
3. Determining how long an asset will benefit the company.
4. Deciding to use cash flows from operations to purchase long-term assets.
5. Determining how much an asset will sell for when it is no longer useful to the company.
6. Calculating free cash flow.

LO 7

Free Cash Flow

SE10. BUSINESS APPLICATION ▶ Maki Corporation had cash flows from operating activities during the past year of $194,000. During the year, the company expended $25,000 for dividends; expended $158,000 for property, plant, and equipment; and sold property, plant, and equipment for $12,000. Calculate the company's free cash flow. What does the result tell you about the company?

EXERCISES: SET A

LO 1

Recognition and Classification of Capital Expenditures

E1A. CONCEPT ▶ Tell whether each of the following transactions related to an office building is a revenue expenditure (RE) or a capital expenditure (CE). In addition, indicate whether each transaction is an ordinary repair (OR), an extraordinary repair (ER), an addition (A), a betterment (B), or none of these (N).

1. The hallways and ceilings in the building are repainted at a cost of $4,150.
2. The hallways, which have tile floors, are carpeted at a cost of $14,000.
3. A new wing is added to the building at a cost of $87,500.
4. Furniture is purchased for the entrance to the building at a cost of $8,250.
5. The air-conditioning system is overhauled at a cost of $14,250. The overhaul extends the useful life of the air-conditioning system by 10 years.
6. A cleaning firm is paid $100 per week to clean the newly installed carpets.

LO 2

Recognizing and Classifying the Cost of Long-Term Assets

E2A. CONCEPT ▶ Fraser Manufacturing purchased land next to its factory to be used as a parking lot. The following expenditures were incurred by the company: purchase price, $300,000; broker's fees, $24,000; title search and other fees, $2,200; demolition of a cottage on the property, $8,000; general grading of property, $4,200; paving parking lots, $40,000; lighting for parking lots, $32,000; and signs for parking lots, $6,400. Determine the amounts that should be debited to the Land account and the Land Improvements account.

LO 2

Group Purchase

E3A. Sea Scout purchased a car wash for $240,000. If purchased separately, the land would have cost $60,000, the building $135,000, and the equipment $105,000. Determine the amount that should be recorded in the new business's records for land, building, and equipment.

LO 2, 3

Cost of Long-Term Asset and Depreciation

E4A. Melissa Mertz purchased a used tractor for $17,500. Before the tractor could be used, it required new tires, which cost $1,100, and an overhaul, which cost $1,400. Its first tank of fuel cost $75. The tractor is expected to last six years and have a residual value of $2,000. Determine the cost and depreciable cost of the tractor and calculate the first year's depreciation under the straight-line method.

LO 3 **Depreciation Methods**

E5A. On January 13, 2013, Precision Oil Company purchased a drilling truck for $90,000. Precision expects the truck to last five years or 200,000 miles, with an estimated residual value of $15,000 at the end of that time. During 2014, the truck is driven 48,000 miles. Precision's year end is December 31. Compute the depreciation for 2014 under each of the following methods: (1) straight-line, (2) production, and (3) double-declining-balance. Using the amount computed in (3), prepare the journal entry to record depreciation expense for the second year, and show how the Drilling Truck account would appear on the balance sheet.

LO 3 **Double-Declining-Balance Method**

E6A. Crescendo Company purchased a computer for $1,120. It has an estimated useful life of four years and an estimated residual value of $120. Compute the depreciation charge for each of the four years using the double-declining-balance method.

LO 3 **Revision of Depreciation Rates**

E7A. NewLife Hospital purchased a special X-ray machine. The machine, which cost $623,120, was expected to last ten years, with an estimated residual value of $63,120. After two years of operation (and depreciation charges using the straight-line method), it became evident that the X-ray machine would last a total of only seven years. The estimated residual value, however, would remain the same. Given this information, determine the new depreciation charge for the third year on the basis of the revised estimated useful life.

LO 4 **Disposal of Plant Assets**

E8A. A piece of equipment that cost $64,800 and on which $36,000 of accumulated depreciation had been recorded was disposed of on January 2, the first day of business of the current year. For each of the following assumptions, compute the gain or loss on the disposal:

1. The equipment was discarded as having no value.
2. The equipment was sold for $12,000 cash.
3. The equipment was sold for $36,000 cash.

LO 4 **Disposal of Plant Assets**

E9A. Star Company purchased a computer on January 2, 2012, at a cost of $2,500. The computer is expected to have a useful life of five years and a residual value of $250. Assume that the computer is disposed of on July 1, 2015. Using the straight-line method, record the depreciation expense for half a year and the disposal under each of the following assumptions:

1. The computer is discarded.
2. The computer is sold for $400.
3. The computer is sold for $1,100.

LO 5 **Natural Resource Depletion and Depreciation of Related Plant Assets**

E10A. Mertz Company purchased land containing an estimated 5 million tons of ore for a cost of $8,800,000. The land without the ore is estimated to be worth $500,000. During its first year of operation, the company mined and sold 750,000 tons of ore. Compute the depletion charge per ton. Compute the depletion expense that Mertz should record for the year.

LO 6 **Amortization of Copyrights and Trademarks**

E11A. Complete the following requirements regarding amortizing copyrights and trademarks:

1. Argyle Publishing Company purchased the copyright to a basic computer textbook for $40,000. The usual life of a textbook is about four years. However, the copyright will remain in effect for another 50 years. Calculate the annual amortization of the copyright.
2. **ACCOUNTING CONNECTION ▶** Scion Company purchased a trademark from a well-known supermarket for $320,000. The company's management argued that the trademark's useful life was indefinite. Explain how the cost should be accounted for.

LO 6

Accounting for a Patent

E12A. At the beginning of the fiscal year, David Company purchased for $1,030,000 a patent that applies to the manufacture of a unique tamper-proof lid for medicine bottles. David incurred legal costs of $450,000 in successfully defending use of the lid by a competitor. David estimated that the patent would be valuable for at least ten years.

During the first two years of operations, David successfully marketed the lid. At the beginning of the third year, a study appeared in a consumer magazine showing that children could in fact remove the lid. As a result, all orders for the lids were canceled, and the patent was rendered worthless.

Prepare journal entries to record the following: (a) purchase of the patent, (b) successful defense of the patent, (c) amortization expense for the first year, and (d) write-off of the patent as worthless.

LO 7

Management Issues

E13A. BUSINESS APPLICATION ▶ Indicate whether each of the following actions is primarily related to (a) acquisition of long-term assets, (b) evaluating the financing of long-term assets, or (c) applying accrual accounting to long-term assets:

1. Deciding whether to rent or buy a piece of equipment.
2. Allocating costs on a group purchase.
3. Deciding to use the production method of depreciation.
4. Determining the total units a machine will produce.
5. Deciding to borrow funds to purchase equipment.
6. Estimating the savings a new machine will produce and comparing that amount to cost.
7. Examining the trend of free cash flow over several years.

LO 7

Free Cash Flow

E14A. BUSINESS APPLICATION ▶ Zee Corporation had net cash flows from operating activities during the past year of $432,000. During the year, the company expended $924,000 for property, plant, and equipment; sold property, plant, and equipment for $108,000; and paid dividends of $100,000. Calculate the company's free cash flow. What does the result tell you about the company?

EXERCISES: SET B

Visit the textbook companion website at www.cengagebrain.com to access Exercise Set B for this chapter.

PROBLEMS

LO 1

Identification of Long-Term Assets Terminology

P1. Common terms associated with long-term assets follow.

a. Tangible assets
b. Natural resources
c. Intangible assets
d. Additions
e. Betterments
f. Extraordinary repair
g. Depreciation
h. Depletion
i. Amortization
j. Revenue expenditure

REQUIRED

1. For each of the statements that follow, identify the term with which it is associated. (If two terms apply, choose the one that is most closely associated.)
   1. Periodic cost associated with intangible assets.
   2. Cost of constructing a new wing on a building.
   3. A group of assets encompassing property, plant, and equipment.
   4. Cost associated with enhancing a building but not expanding it.

5. Periodic cost associated with tangible assets.
6. A group of assets that gain their value from contracts or rights.
7. Cost of normal repairs to a building.
8. Assets whose value derives from what can be extracted from them.
9. Periodic cost associated with natural resources.
10. Cost of a repair that extends the useful life of a building.

2. **ACCOUNTING CONNECTION ▶** Assuming the company uses cash for all its expenditures, which of the terms listed above would you expect to see on the income statement? Which ones would not result in an outlay of cash?

LO 2

✔ 1: Land: $723,900
✔ 1: Land Improvements: $142,000
✔ 1: Buildings: $1,383,600
✔ 1: Equipment: $210,800

Determining Cost of Assets

P2. Cergo Computers constructed a new training center in 2014, which you have been hired to manage. A review of the accounting records shows the following expenditures debited to an asset account called Training Center:

Attorney's fee, land acquisition	$ 34,900
Cost of land	598,000
Architect's fee, building design	102,000
Building	1,020,000
Parking lot and sidewalk	135,600
Electrical wiring, building	164,000
Landscaping	55,000
Cost of surveying land	9,200
Training equipment, tables, and chairs	136,400
Installation of training equipment	68,000
Cost of grading the land	14,000
Cost of changes in building to soundproof rooms	59,200
Total account balance	$2,396,300

During the center's construction, an employee of Cergo worked full-time overseeing the project. He spent two months on the purchase and preparation of the site, six months on the construction, one month on land improvements, and one month on equipment installation and training-room furniture purchase and setup. His salary of $64,000 during this ten-month period was charged to Administrative Expense. The training center was placed in operation on November 1.

REQUIRED

1. Prepare a schedule with the following four column (account) headings: Land, Land Improvements, Building, and Equipment. Place each of the above expenditures in the appropriate column. Total the columns.
2. **CONCEPT ▶** What impact does the classification of the items among several accounts have on evaluating the profitability performance of the company?

LO 3, 4

CASH FLOW

✔ 1a: Depreciation, year 3: $165,000
✔ 1b: Depreciation, year 3: $132,000
✔ 1c: Depreciation, year 3: $90,000

Comparison of Depreciation Methods

P3. Zeigler Manufacturing Company purchased a robot for $720,000 at the beginning of year 1. The robot has an estimated useful life of four years and an estimated residual value of $60,000. The robot, which should last 20,000 hours, was operated 6,000 hours in year 1; 8,000 hours in year 2; 4,000 hours in year 3; and 2,000 hours in year 4.

REQUIRED

1. Compute the annual depreciation and carrying value for the robot for each year assuming the following depreciation methods: (a) straight-line, (b) production, and (c) double-declining-balance.
2. If the robot is sold for $750,000 after year 2, what would be the amount of gain or loss under each method?
3. **ACCOUNTING CONNECTION ▶** What conclusions can you draw from the patterns of yearly depreciation and carrying value in requirement 1? Do the three methods differ in their effect on the company's profitability? Do they differ in their effect on the company's operating cash flows? Explain.

LO 3, 4

Comparison of Depreciation Methods

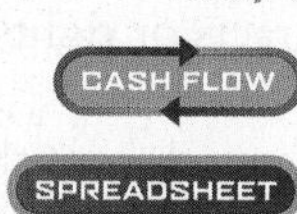

✔ 1a: Depreciation, year 3: $54,250
✔ 1b: Depreciation, year 3: $81,375
✔ 1c: Depreciation, year 3: $53,407

P4. Italian Construction Company purchased a new crane for $360,500 at the beginning of year 1. The crane has an estimated residual value of $35,000 and an estimated useful life of six years. The crane is expected to last 10,000 hours. It was used 1,800 hours in year 1; 2,000 hours in year 2; 2,500 hours in year 3; 1,500 hours in year 4; 1,200 hours in year 5; and 1,000 hours in year 6.

REQUIRED

1. Compute the annual depreciation and carrying value for the new crane for each of the six years under each of the following methods: (a) straight-line, (b) production, and (c) double-declining-balance (round percentage to two decimal places.)
2. If the crane is sold for $250,000 after year 3, what would be the amount of gain or loss under each method?
3. **ACCOUNTING CONNECTION ▶** Do the three methods differ in their effect on the company's profitability? Do they differ in their effect on the company's operating cash flows? Explain.

LO 5

Natural Resource Depletion and Depreciation of Related Plant Assets

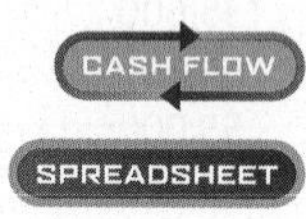

✔ 2: Depletion expense: $121,500

P5. Bychowski Company purchased land containing an estimated 10 million tons of ore for a cost of $3,300,000. The land without the ore is estimated to be worth $600,000. The company expects that all the usable ore can be mined in 10 years. Buildings costing $300,000 with an estimated useful life of 20 years were erected on the site. Equipment costing $360,000 with an estimated useful life of 10 years was installed. Because of the remote location, neither the buildings nor the equipment has an estimated residual value. During its first year of operation, the company mined and sold 450,000 tons of ore.

REQUIRED

1. Compute the depletion charge per ton.
2. Compute the depletion expense that Bychowski should record for the year.
3. Determine the depreciation expense for the year for the buildings, making it proportional to the depletion.
4. Determine the depreciation expense for the year for the equipment under two alternatives: (a) making the expense proportional to the depletion and (b) using the straight-line method.
5. **ACCOUNTING CONNECTION ▶** Suppose the company mined and sold 250,000 tons of ore (instead of 450,000) during the first year. Would the change in the results in requirements 2 or 3 affect earnings or cash flows? Explain.

ALTERNATE PROBLEMS

LO 2

Determining Cost of Assets

✔ 1: Land: $426,212
✔ 1: Land Improvements: $166,560
✔ 1: Buildings: $833,940
✔ 1: Machinery: $1,262,640
✔ 1: Expense: $18,120

P6. Krall Company was formed on January 1, 2014, and began constructing a new plant. At the end of 2014, its auditor discovered that all expenditures involving long-term assets had been debited to an account called Fixed Assets. An analysis of the Fixed Assets account, which had a year-end balance of $2,644,972, disclosed that it contained the following items:

Cost of land	$ 316,600
Surveying costs	4,100
Transfer of title and other fees required by the county	920
Broker's fees for land	21,144
Attorney's fees associated with land acquisition	7,048
Cost of removing timber from land	50,400
Cost of grading land	4,200
Cost of digging building foundation	34,600
Architect's fee for building and land improvements (80 percent building)	64,800
Cost of building construction	710,000
Cost of sidewalks	11,400
Cost of parking lots	54,400
Cost of lighting for grounds	80,300
Cost of landscaping	11,800
Cost of machinery	989,000
Shipping cost on machinery	55,300
Cost of installing machinery	176,200
Cost of testing machinery	22,100
Cost of changes in building to comply with safety regulations pertaining to machinery	12,540
Cost of repairing building that was damaged in the installation of machinery	8,900
Cost of medical bill for injury received by employee while installing machinery	2,400
Cost of water damage to building during heavy rains prior to opening the plant for operation	6,820
Account balance	$2,644,972

Krall sold the timber it cleared from the land to a firewood dealer for $5,000. This amount was credited to Miscellaneous Income. During the construction period, two of Krall's supervisors devoted full time to the construction project. Their annual salaries were $48,000 and $42,000, respectively. They spent two months on the purchase and preparation of the land, six months on the construction of the building (approximately one-sixth of which was devoted to improvements on the grounds), and one month on machinery installation. When the plant began operation on October 1, the supervisors returned to their regular duties. Their salaries were debited to Factory Salaries Expense.

REQUIRED

1. Prepare a schedule with the following column headings: Land, Land Improvements, Buildings, Machinery, and Expense. Place each of the above expenditures in the appropriate column. Negative amounts should be shown in parentheses. Total the columns.
2. **CONCEPT ▶** What impact does the classification of the items among several accounts have on evaluating the profitability performance of the company?

LO **3, 4**

✔ 1a: Depreciation, year 3: $5,000
✔ 1b: Depreciation, year 3: $8,000
✔ 1c: Depreciation, year 3: $2,813

Comparison of Depreciation Methods

P7. Bao Wao Designs, Inc., purchased a computerized blueprint printer that will assist in the design and display of plans for factory layouts. The cost of the printer was $22,500, and its expected useful life is four years. The company can probably sell the printer for $2,500 at the end of four years. The printer is expected to last 6,000 hours. It was used 1,200 hours in year 1; 1,800 hours in year 2; 2,400 hours in year 3; and 600 hours in year 4.

REQUIRED

1. Compute the annual depreciation and carrying value for the new blueprint printer for each of the four years (round to the nearest dollar where necessary) under each of the following methods: (a) straight-line, (b) production, and (c) double-declining-balance.

(Continued)

2. If the printer is sold for $12,000 after year 2, what would be the gain or loss under each method?
3. **ACCOUNTING CONNECTION ▶** What conclusions can you draw from the patterns of yearly depreciation and carrying value in requirement **1**? Do the three methods differ in their impact on profitability? Do they differ in their effect on the company's operating cash flows? Explain.

LO **3, 4**

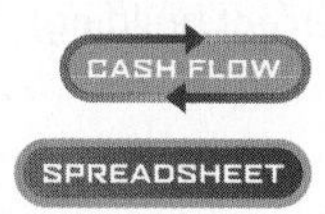

✔ 1a: Depreciation, year 3: $51,667
✔ 1b: Depreciation, year 3: $77,500
✔ 1c: Depreciation, year 3: $51,852

Comparison of Depreciation Methods

P8. Niles Construction Company purchased a new crane for $350,000 at the beginning of year 1. The crane has an estimated residual value of $40,000 and an estimated useful life of six years. The crane is expected to last 10,000 hours. It was used 1,800 hours in year 1; 2,000 hours in year 2; 2,500 hours in year 3; 1,500 hours in year 4; 1,200 hours in year 5; and 1,000 hours in year 6.

REQUIRED

1. Compute the annual depreciation and carrying value for the new crane for each of the six years (round to the nearest dollar where necessary) under each of the following methods: (a) straight-line, (b) production, and (c) double-declining-balance (round percentage to two decimal places).
2. If the crane is sold for $500,000 after year 3, what would be the amount of gain or loss under each method?
3. **ACCOUNTING CONNECTION ▶** Do the three methods differ in their effect on the company's profitability? Do they differ in their effect on the company's operating cash flows? Explain.

LO **5**

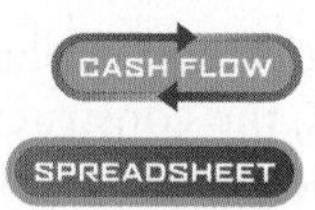

✔ 2: Depletion expense: $288,000

Natural Resource Depletion and Depreciation of Related Plant Assets

P9. Crystler Mining Company purchased land containing an estimated 10 million tons of ore for a cost of $4,400,000. The land without the ore is estimated to be worth $800,000. The company expects that all the usable ore can be mined in 10 years. Buildings costing $400,000 with an estimated useful life of 30 years were erected on the site. Equipment costing $480,000 with an estimated useful life of 10 years was installed. Because of the remote location, neither the buildings nor the equipment has an estimated residual value. During its first year of operation, the company mined and sold 800,000 tons of ore.

REQUIRED

1. Compute the depletion charge per ton.
2. Compute the depletion expense that Crystler Mining should record for the year.
3. Determine the depreciation expense for the year for the buildings, making it proportional to the depletion.
4. Determine the depreciation expense for the year for the equipment under two alternatives: (a) making the expense proportional to the depletion and (b) using the straight-line method.
5. **ACCOUNTING CONNECTION ▶** Suppose the company mined and sold 1,000,000 tons of ore (instead of 800,000) during the first year. Would the change in the results in requirements **2** or **3** affect earnings or cash flows? Explain.

CASES

LO **7**

Conceptual Understanding: Effect of Change in Estimates

C1. The airline industry was hit particularly hard after the 9/11 attacks on the World Trade Center in 2001. In 2002, **Southwest Airlines**, one of the healthier airline companies, decided to lengthen the useful lives of its aircraft from 22 to 27 years. Shortly thereafter, following Southwest's lead, other airlines made the same move.[23] What advantage, if any, did the airlines gain by making this change in estimate? Would it have changed earnings or cash flows, and if it did, would the change have been favorable or negative?

Some people argue that the useful lives and depreciation of airplanes are irrelevant. They claim that because of the extensive maintenance and testing that airline companies are required by law to perform, the planes theoretically can be in service for an indefinite future period. What is wrong with this argument?

LO **1**

Conceptual Understanding: Impairment Test

C2. BUSINESS APPLICATION ▶ An annual report of **Costco Wholesale Corporation**, the large discount company, contained the following statement:

> *The Company periodically evaluates long-lived assets for impairment when ... circumstances occur that may indicate the carrying amount of the asset group ... may not be fully recoverable.*[24]

What does the concept of impairment mean in accounting? What effect does impairment have on profitability and cash flows? Why would the concept of impairment be referred to as a conservative accounting approach?

LO **3**

Conceptual Understanding: Accounting Estimates

C3. IBM, the large computer equipment and services company, stated in one of its annual reports that "Property, plant and equipment are carried at cost and depreciated over their estimated useful lives using the straight-line method."[25] What estimates are necessary to carry out this policy? What factors should be considered in making each of the estimates?

LO **6**

Interpreting Financial Reports: Brands

C4. CONCEPT ▶ Starwood Hotels & Resorts Worldwide, Inc., and **Marriott International** provide hospitality services. Starwood Hotels' well-known brands include St. Regis, The Luxury Collection, W Hotels, Westin Hotels & Resorts, Le Meridien, Sheraton Hotels & Resorts, Four Points by Sheraton, Aloft by W Hotels, and Element by Westin. Marriott also owns or manages properties with recognizable brand names, such as Marriott Hotels & Resorts, Ritz-Carlton Hotel Company and Destination Club, Bulgari Hotels & Resorts, Marriott ExecuStay, Marriott Executive Apartments, Marriott Vacation Club, Grand Residences by Marriott, Spring Hill Suites by Marriott, Renaissance Hotels & Resorts, AC Hotels by Marriott, JW Marriott Hotels & Resorts, EDITION Hotels, Autograph Collection, Courtyard by Marriott, Residence Inn by Marriott, Fairfield Inn & Suites by Marriott, TownePlace Suites by Marriott, and Marriott Conference Centers.

On its balance sheet, Starwood Hotels & Resorts includes brands of $313 million (see note 7), or 3.3 percent of total assets. Marriott International, however, does not list brands among its intangible assets.[26] What principles of accounting for intangibles require Starwood to record brands as an asset while Marriott does not? How do these differences in accounting for brands generally affect the net income and return on assets of these two competitors?

LO **1, 2, 3**

Annual Report Case: Long-Term Assets

C5. To answer the following questions, refer to the **CVS** annual report in the Supplement to Chapter 1. Examine the balance sheets, as well as the summary of significant accounting policies on property and equipment in the notes to the financial statements.

1. What percentage of total assets in 2011 was property and equipment, net? Identify the major categories of CVS's property and equipment. Which types of property and equipment are most significant? What are leasehold improvements? How significant are these items, and what are their effects on CVS's earnings?
2. What method of depreciation does CVS use? How long does management estimate its buildings will last as compared with furniture and equipment? What does this say about the company's need to remodel its stores?
3. How does the company determine if it has impaired assets?

LO 7

Comparison Analysis: Long-Term Assets and Free Cash Flows

C6. To complete the assignments listed below, refer to the **CVS** annual report and the financial statements of **Southwest Airlines Co.** in the Supplement to Chapter 1.

1. Prepare a table that shows the net amount each company spent on property and equipment (from the statement of cash flows), the net amount of its property and equipment (from the balance sheet), and the percentage of net amount spent to the net amount of property and equipment for each of the past two years. (Round percentages to one decimal place.) In which company did the amount of property and equipment grow more rapidly?
2. **BUSINESS APPLICATION ▶** Calculate free cash flow for both companies for the past two years. What conclusions can you draw about each company's need to raise funds from debt and equity and its ability to grow?

LO 2

Ethical Dilemma: Ethics and Allocation of Acquisition Costs

C7. BUSINESS APPLICATION ▶ Hamlin Company has purchased land and a warehouse for \$18,000,000. The warehouse is expected to last 20 years and to have a residual value equal to 10 percent of its cost. The chief financial officer (CFO) and the controller are discussing the allocation of the purchase price. The CFO believes that the largest amount possible should be assigned to the land because that would improve reported net income in the future. Depreciation expense would be lower because land is not depreciated. He suggests allocating one-third, or \$6,000,000, of the cost to the land. This would result in depreciation expense each year of \$540,000 [(\$12,000,000 − \$1,200,000) ÷ 20 years].

The controller disagrees. She argues that the smallest amount possible, say one-fifth of the purchase price, should be allocated to the land because the depreciation of the warehouse, which is tax-deductible, would be greater and thus reduce income taxes. Under this plan, annual depreciation would be \$648,000 [(\$14,400,000 − \$1,440,000) ÷ 20 years]. The annual tax savings at a 30 percent tax rate is \$32,400 [(\$648,000 − \$540,000) × 0.30].

How would each decision affect the company's cash flows? Ethically, how should the purchase cost be allocated? Who would be affected by the decision?

Continuing Case: Annual Report Project

C8. Using the most recent annual report of the company you have chosen to study and that you have accessed online at the company's website, examine the balance sheet and the statement of cash flows and accompanying notes of your company. Answer the following questions:

1. **CONCEPT ▶** What percentage of total assets is property, plant, and equipment? What items are classified in this category?
2. **CONCEPT ▶** What percentage of total assets are intangible assets? What items are classified in this category?
3. How much did the company invest in property, plant, and equipment during the year?
4. **BUSINESS APPLICATION ▶** Compute free cash flow for the most recent year.
5. Find the disclosures about property, plant, and equipment in the notes to the financial statements. What depreciation methods does the company use?
6. Find the disclosures about intangible assets in the notes to the financial statements. What intangible assets are amortized and which are not? Has the company recognized any impairments of intangible assets?

CHAPTER 10

LEARNING OBJECTIVES

LO 1 **Define *current liabilities*, and identify the concepts underlying them.**

LO 2 **Identify, compute, and record definitely determinable and estimated current liabilities.**

LO 3 **Distinguish contingent liabilities from commitments.**

LO 4 **Identify the valuation approaches to fair value accounting, define *time value of money* and *interest*, and apply them to present values.**

LO 5 **Apply the present value concept to simple valuation situations.**

LO 6 **Use ratio analysis to manage the impact of current liabilities' impact on liquidity.**

Hilz, Peter/Hollandse Hoogte/Redux

CURRENT LIABILITIES AND FAIR VALUE ACCOUNTING

Business Insight
Microsoft

Microsoft is the world's leading computer software company. It earns revenue by developing, manufacturing, licensing, and supporting a wide range of software products, such as Windows 7®, its latest operating system, and Xbox360®, its most recent game console. As you can see from Microsoft's Financial Highlights, the company's total current liabilities in 2011 were almost $29.0 billion, which is about 50 percent of its stockholders' equity of $57,083 billion.[1]

Managing liabilities is important to achieving profitability and liquidity. If a company has too few liabilities, it may not be earning up to its full potential. If it has too many liabilities, it may be incurring excessive risks. A company that does not manage its debt carefully is vulnerable to failure.

MICROSOFT'S FINANCIAL HIGHLIGHTS (in millions)

Current Liabilities	**2011**	**2010**
Accounts payable	$ 4,197	$ 4,025
Short-term debt	—	1,000
Accrued compensation	3,575	3,283
Income taxes payable	580	1,074
Short-term unearned revenue	15,722	13,652
Securities lending payable and other	4,700	3,113
Total current liabilities	$28,774	$26,147
Long-term debt	11,921	4,939
Long-term unearned revenue and other long-term liabilities	10,926	8,852
Total liabilities	$51,621	$39,938

1. **CONCEPT ▶** How do the concepts of recognition, valuation, classification, and disclosure apply to current liabilities?
2. **ACCOUNTING APPLICATION ▶** How does a company identify and account for all its current liabilities?
3. **BUSINESS APPLICATION ▶** Why is it important for Microsoft to identify and account for all the company's current liabilities?

SECTION 1 CONCEPTS

CONCEPTS
- Recognition
- Valuation
- Classification
- Disclosure

RELEVANT LEARNING OBJECTIVE

LO 1 Define *current liabilities*, and identify the concepts underlying them.

LO1 Concepts Underlying Current Liabilities

Current liabilities are debts and obligations that a company expects to satisfy within one year or within its normal operating cycle, whichever is longer. They require not only careful management of liquidity and cash flows but also close monitoring. Managers must understand how current liabilities should be *recognized*, *valued*, *classified*, and *disclosed*.

Recognition

Timing is important in the *recognition* of liabilities. Failure to record a liability often goes along with failure to record an expense. The two errors lead to an understatement of expense and an overstatement of income.

Generally accepted accounting principles require that a liability be recorded when an obligation occurs, as when goods are bought on credit. However, some current liabilities are not the result of direct transactions. One reason for making adjusting entries is to *recognize* unrecorded liabilities that accrue during the period. Accrued liabilities include salaries payable and interest payable. Other liabilities that can only be estimated, such as taxes payable, must also be recognized through adjusting entries.

Agreements for future transactions do not have to be *recognized*. For instance, **Microsoft** might agree to pay an executive $250,000 a year for a period of three years, or it might agree to buy an unspecified amount of advertising at a certain price over the next five years. Such contracts, though they are definite commitments, are not considered liabilities because they are for future—not past—transactions. Because there is no current obligation, no liability is recognized. However, if the amounts involved are material, these commitments would be mentioned in the notes to the financial statements.

Valuation

On the balance sheet, a liability is generally *valued* at the amount of money needed to pay the debt or reported at the fair market value of the goods or services to be delivered. For most liabilities, at least one of these amounts is definitely known. For example, **Amazon.com** sells a large number of gift certificates that are redeemable in the future. The amount of the liability (unearned revenue) is known, but the exact timing is not known.

Some companies, however, must estimate future liabilities. For example, if an automobile dealer sells a car with a one-year warranty on parts and service, the obligation is definite because the sale has occurred; but the amount of the obligation can only be estimated.

Classification

As discussed earlier, current liabilities are due in the next year or within the normal operating cycle, whichever is longer, and are normally paid out of current assets or with cash generated by operations. They contrast with **long-term liabilities**, which are liabilities due beyond one year or beyond the normal operating cycle. For example, a company may incur long-term liabilities to finance its expansion to a larger location. The distinction between current and long-term liabilities affects the evaluation of a company's liquidity.

Disclosure

STUDY NOTE: *Disclosure of the fair value and the bases for estimating the fair value of short-term notes payable, loans payable, and other short-term debt are required unless it is not practical to estimate the value.*

In addition to reporting current liabilities in the balance sheet, a company may need to include additional explanation in the notes to its financial statements. For example, if a company's Notes Payable account is large, it should *disclose* the balances, maturity dates, interest rates, and other features of the debts in an explanatory note. Any special credit arrangements should also be disclosed. For example, in this note to its 2011 financial statements, **Hershey Foods Corporation** discloses the nature of its credit arrangements:

Short-Term Debt

> *As a source of short-term financing, . . . we entered into a new five-year agreement establishing an unsecured revolving [letter of credit] to borrow up to $1.1 billion, with an option to increase borrowings by an additional $400 million with the consent of the lenders.*[2]

A **line of credit** with a bank allows a company to borrow funds when they are needed to finance current operations. Unused lines of credit allow a company to borrow on short notice up to the credit limit, with little or no negotiation. Thus, the type of *disclosure* in Hershey's note is helpful in assessing whether a company has additional borrowing power.

APPLY IT!

Indicate whether each of the following actions relates to (a) recognition of liabilities, (b) valuation of liabilities, (c) classification of liabilities, or (d) disclosure of liabilities:

1. Determining whether a liability is current or long-term.
2. Determining the dollar amount of a liability.
3. Determining what information should be reported about a liability.
4. Determining that a liability exists.

SOLUTION

1. c; 2. b; 3. d; 4. a

TRY IT! SE1, E1A, E1B

SECTION 2

ACCOUNTING APPLICATIONS

ACCOUNTING APPLICATIONS

- Record definitely determinable current liabilities
- Record estimated current liabilities
- Account for contingent liabilities
- Compute present value

RELEVANT LEARNING OBJECTIVES

LO2 Identify, compute, and record definitely determinable and estimated current liabilities.

LO3 Distinguish contingent liabilities from commitments.

LO4 Identify the valuation approaches to fair value accounting, define *time value of money* and *interest*, and apply them to present values.

LO5 Apply the present value concept to simple valuation situations.

LO2 Common Types of Current Liabilities

As noted earlier, a company incurs current liabilities to meet its needs for cash during the operating cycle. These liabilities fall into two major groups: definitely determinable liabilities and estimated liabilities.

Definitely Determinable Liabilities

Current liabilities that are set by contract or statute and that can be measured exactly are called **definitely determinable liabilities**. The objectives in accounting for these liabilities are to:

- determine their existence and amount
- record them properly

The most common definitely determinable liabilities are described in the sections that follow.

Accounts Payable **Accounts payable** (or *trade accounts payable*) are short-term obligations to suppliers for goods and services. The amount in the Accounts Payable control account is supported by an accounts payable subsidiary ledger. This separate ledger contains an individual account for each person or company to whom money is owed.

Notes Payable **Short-term notes payable** are represented by **promissory notes**, which are written agreements to pay according to certain terms. A company may sign promissory notes to obtain bank loans, pay suppliers for goods and services, or secure credit from other sources. The interest rate is usually stated separately on the face of the note, as shown in Exhibit 1.

Exhibit 1
Promissory Note

Chicago, Illinois January 1, 2013

Sixty days after date I promise to pay First Federal Bank the sum of $16,000 with interest at the rate of 3% per annum.

Teresa Madej
Teresa's Fitness Center

Issuance of Note Payable

Transaction Borrowed $16,000 from bank and signed 60-day, 3% promissory note.

Analysis The journal entry to record the issuance of the note payable

▲ *increases* the *Cash* account

▲ *increases* the *Notes Payable* account

Application of Double Entry

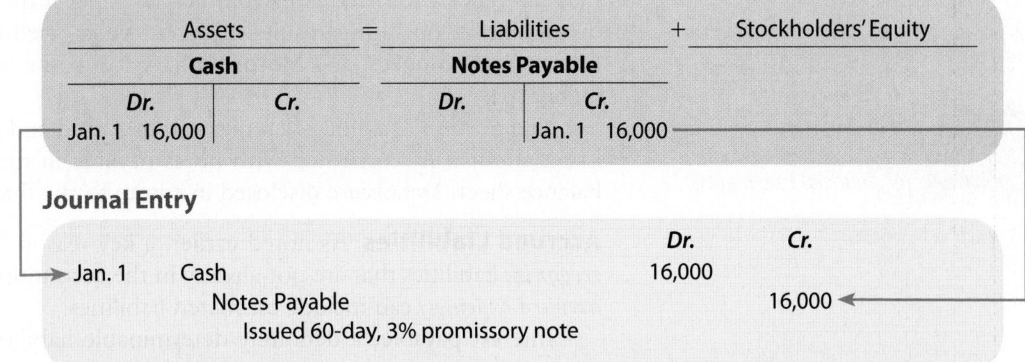

Journal Entry

A	=	L	+	SE
+16,000		+16,000		

		Dr.	Cr.
Jan. 1	Cash	16,000	
	Notes Payable		16,000
	Issued 60-day, 3% promissory note		

Comment The transaction is *recognized* by an increase in assets and liabilities.

Payment of Note with Interest

Transaction On March 1, Teresa repays the $16,000 plus interest.

Analysis The journal entry to record the payment of the note with interest after 60 days

▲ *increases* the *Interest Expense* account
▼ *decreases* the *Notes Payable* account
▼ *decreases* the *Cash* account

Application of Double Entry

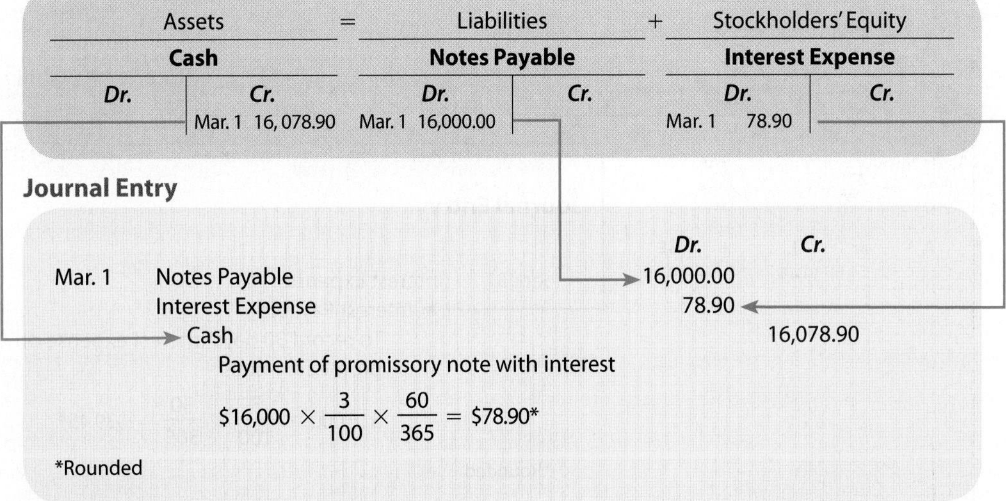

Comment The transaction is *recognized* by a decrease in assets and liabilities and an increase in interest expense.

Bank Loans and Commercial Paper Although a company signs a promissory note for the full amount of a line of credit, it has great flexibility in using the available funds. It can increase its borrowing up to the limit when it needs cash and reduce the amount borrowed when it generates enough cash of its own. Both the amount borrowed and the interest rate charged by the bank may change daily. The bank may require the company to meet certain financial goals (such as maintaining specific profit margins, current ratios, or debt to equity ratios) to retain its line of credit.

Companies with excellent credit ratings can borrow short-term funds by issuing commercial paper. **Commercial paper** refers to unsecured loans (i.e., loans not backed up by any specific assets) that are sold to the public, usually investment firms. Companies can quickly lose access to commercial paper if their credit rating drops. Because of disappointing operating results in recent years, well-known companies like **Chrysler**, **Lucent Technologies**, and **Motorola** have lost some or all of their ability to issue commercial paper.

STUDY NOTE: *Only the used portion of a line of credit is recognized as a liability in the financial statements.*

The portion of a line of credit currently used and the amount of commercial paper issued are usually combined with notes payable in the current liabilities section of the balance sheet. Details are disclosed in a note to the financial statements.

Accrued Liabilities As noted earlier, a key reason for making adjusting entries is to *recognize* liabilities that are not already in the accounting records. **Accrued liabilities** (or *accrued expenses)* can include estimated liabilities.

Interest payable, a definitely determinable liability, is an accrued liability. Interest accrues daily on interest-bearing notes. An adjusting entry is made at the end of each period to record the interest obligation up to that point.

Recognizing Accrual Interest Expense

Transaction The accounting period of Teresa's note in Exhibit 1 ends on January 31, or 30 days after the issuance of the 60-day note.

Analysis The adjusting entry to record the payment of the note with interest after 30 days

▲ *increases* the *Interest Expense* account

▲ *increases* the *Interest Payable* account

Application of Double Entry

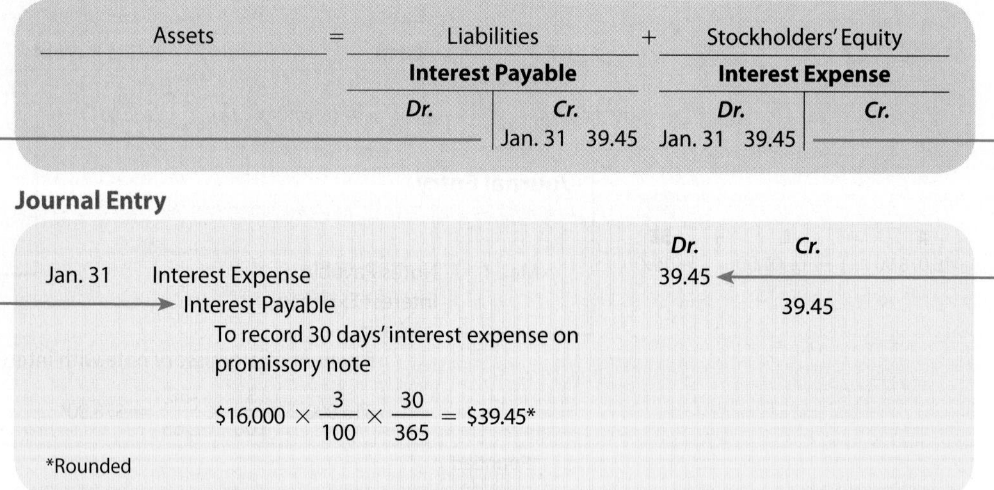

Assets	=	Liabilities		+	Stockholders' Equity	
		Interest Payable			**Interest Expense**	
		Dr.	*Cr.*		*Dr.*	*Cr.*
			Jan. 31 39.45		Jan. 31 39.45	

Journal Entry

A	=	L	+	SE
		+39.45		−39.45

		Dr.	*Cr.*
Jan. 31	Interest Expense	39.45	
	Interest Payable		39.45
	To record 30 days' interest expense on promissory note		

$$\$16{,}000 \times \frac{3}{100} \times \frac{30}{365} = \$39.45^*$$

*Rounded

Comment The accrued interest is *recognized* by an increase in expense and liabilities.

Dividends Payable **Cash dividends** are a distribution of earnings to a corporation's stockholders, and a corporation's board of directors has the sole authority to declare them. The corporation has no liability for dividends until the date of declaration. During the brief time between that date and the date of payment, the dividends declared are considered current liabilities of the corporation.

Sales and Excise Taxes Payable Most states and many cities levy a sales tax on retail transactions, and the federal government imposes an excise tax on some products, such as gasoline. A merchant that sells goods subject to these taxes must collect the taxes and forward them periodically to the appropriate government agency. Until the merchant remits the amount it has collected to the government, that amount represents a current liability.

Recording Sales and Excise Taxes

Transaction On June 1, Teresa's Fitness Center makes a $200 sale of nutritional supplements that is subject to a 5 percent sales tax and a 10 percent excise tax.

Analysis The journal entry to record the sale

- ▲ *increases* the *Cash* account
- ▲ *increases* the *Sales* account
- ▲ *increases* the *Sales Tax Payable* account
- ▲ *increases* the *Excise Tax Payable* account

Application of Double Entry

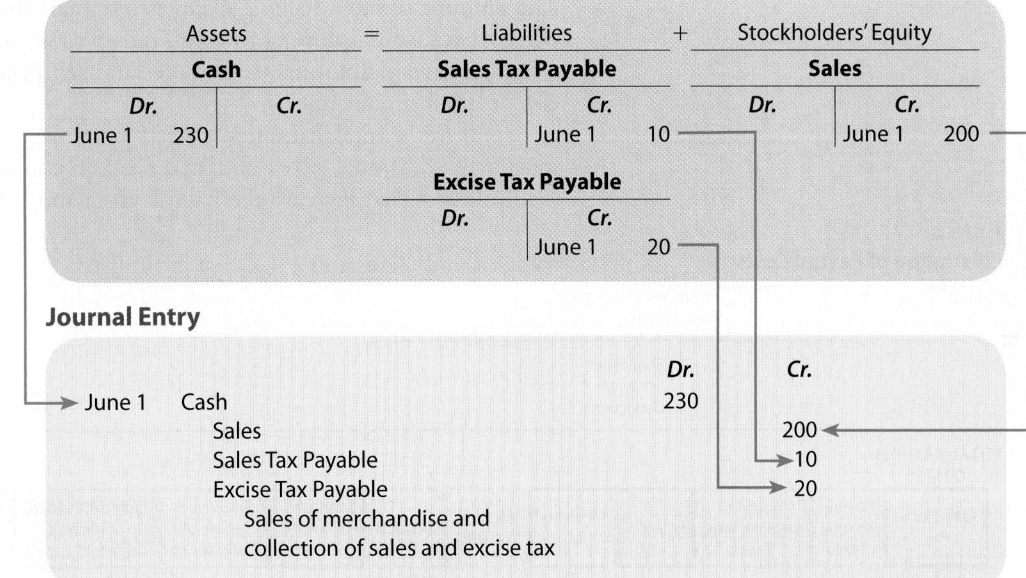

Journal Entry

A	=	L	+	SE
+230		+10		+200
		+20		

		Dr.	Cr.
June 1	Cash	230	
	Sales		200
	Sales Tax Payable		10
	Excise Tax Payable		20
	Sales of merchandise and collection of sales and excise tax		

Comment The sale is properly *recognized* at $200, and the taxes collected, which are not revenues, are *classified* as liabilities to be remitted to the appropriate government agencies.

Companies that have a physical presence in many cities and states require a complex accounting system for sales taxes because the rates vary from state to state and city to city. For Internet companies, the sales tax situation is simpler. For example, **Amazon.com** is an Internet company without a physical presence in most states. Thus, it does not always have to collect sales tax from its customers. This situation may change in the future, but so far Congress has exempted most Internet sales from sales tax.

Current Portion of Long-Term Debt The portion of long-term debt that is due within the next year and is to be paid from current assets is *classified* as a current liability. No journal entry is necessary when this is the case. The total debt is simply reclassified as short-term and long-term when the company prepares its balance sheet and other financial statements.

Payroll Liabilities In the banking and airlines industries, payroll costs represent more than half of all operating costs. Payroll accounting is important because complex laws and significant liabilities are involved. The employer is liable to employees for wages and salaries and to various agencies for amounts withheld from wages and salaries and for related taxes. **Wages** are compensation of employees at an hourly rate; **salaries** are compensation of employees at a monthly or yearly rate.

Because payroll accounting applies only to an organization's employees, it is important to distinguish between employees and independent contractors, as follows.

- An **employee** is paid a wage or salary by the organization and is under its direct supervision and control.
- An **independent contractor** offers services for a fee but is not under the organization's direct control or supervision. Certified public accountants, advertising agencies, and lawyers, for example, often act as independent contractors.

Exhibit 2 shows how payroll liabilities relate to employee earnings and employer taxes and other costs. When accounting for payroll liabilities, it is important to keep the following in mind:

- The amount payable to employees is less than the amount of their earnings. This occurs because employers are required by law or are requested by employees to withhold certain amounts from wages and send them directly to government agencies or other organizations.
- An employer's total liabilities exceed employees' earnings because the employer must pay additional taxes and make other contributions (e.g., for pensions and medical care) that increase the payroll costs and liabilities.

Exhibit 2
Illustration of Payroll Costs

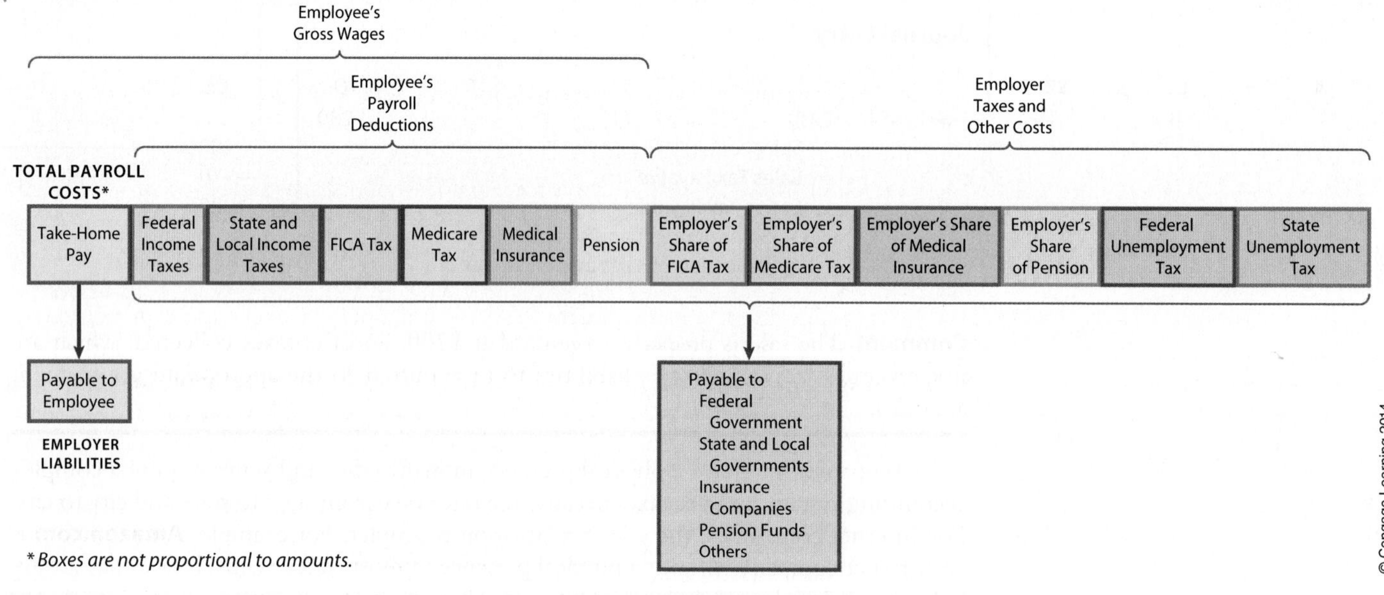

Boxes are not proportional to amounts.

STUDY NOTE: *Vacation pay, sick pay, personal days, health insurance, life insurance, and pensions are additional costs that may be negotiated between employers and employees.*

The most common withholdings, taxes, and other payroll costs are described below.

- **Federal income taxes:** Employers are required to withhold federal income taxes from employees' paychecks and pay them to the U.S. Treasury. These taxes are collected each time an employee is paid.
- **State and local income taxes:** Most states and some local governments levy income taxes. In most cases, the procedures for withholding are similar to those for federal income taxes.
- **Social security (FICA) tax:** The social security program (the Federal Insurance Contribution Act) provides retirement and disability benefits and survivor's benefits. The 2012 Social Security tax rate of 6.2 percent was paid by both employee and employer on the first $110,100 earned by an employee during the calendar year.* Both the rate and the base to which it applies are subject to change in future years.

*A temporary reduction in the employee social security contribution to 4.2 percent was enacted in 2011 and continued in 2012; but since it is not possible to predict if it will continue, the full 6.2 percent rate is used in the examples in this text.

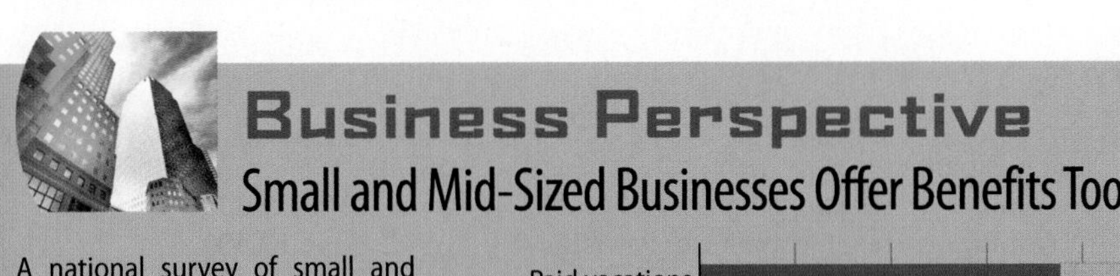

Business Perspective
Small and Mid-Sized Businesses Offer Benefits Too

A national survey of small and mid-sized businesses focused on the employee benefits that these companies offer. The graph at the right presents the results. As you can see, 75 percent of respondents provided paid vacation and 61 percent provided health/medical benefits.[3]

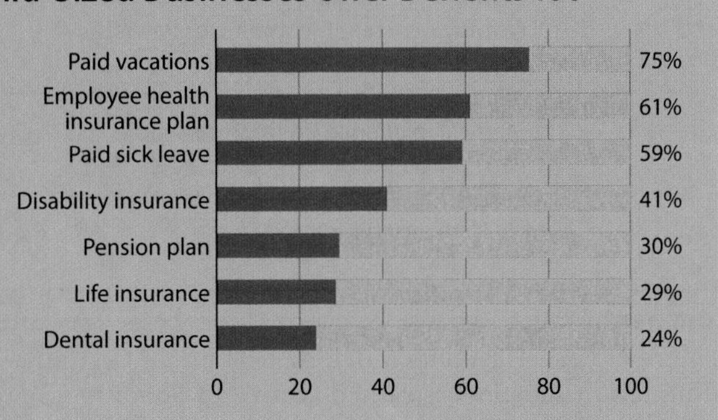

© Alija / iStockphoto.com

- **Medicare tax:** A major extension of the social security program is Medicare, which provides hospitalization and medical insurance for persons over age 65. In 2012, the Medicare tax rate was 1.45 percent of gross income, with no limit, paid by *both* employee and employer.
- **Medical insurance:** Many organizations provide medical benefits to employees. Often, the employee contributes a portion of the cost through withholdings from income and the employer pays the rest—usually a greater amount—to the insurance company.
- **Pension contributions:** Many organizations also provide pension benefits to employees. A portion of the pension contribution is withheld from the employee's income, and the organization pays the rest of the amount into the pension fund.
- **Federal unemployment insurance (FUTA) tax:** This tax pays for programs for unemployed workers. It is paid *only* by employers and recently was 6.2 percent of the first $7,000 earned by each employee. (This rate may vary from state to state.) The employer is allowed a credit for unemployment taxes it pays to the state. The maximum credit is 5.4 percent of the first $7,000 earned by each employee. Most states set their rate at this maximum. Thus, the FUTA tax most often paid is 0.8 percent (6.2 percent – 5.4 percent) of the taxable wages.
- **State unemployment insurance tax:** State unemployment programs provide compensation to eligible unemployed workers. The compensation is paid out of the fund provided by the 5.4 percent of the first $7,000 (or the amount the state sets) earned by each employee. In some states, employers with favorable employment records may be entitled to pay less than 5.4 percent.

STUDY NOTE: *The employee pays all federal, state, and local taxes on income. The employer and employee share FICA and Medicare taxes. The employer bears FUTA and state unemployment taxes.*

Recording Payroll and Related Withholdings

Transaction On February 15, Teresa's Fitness Center's wages for employees total $65,000, and withholdings for employees are as follows.

- $10,800 for federal income taxes
- $2,400 for state income taxes
- $4,030 for social security tax
- $942 for Medicare tax
- $1,800 for medical insurance
- $2,600 for pension contributions

Analysis The journal entry to record payroll and related withholdings

▲ *increases* the *Wages Expense* account

▲ *increases* a *Payable* account for each type of withholding

▲ *increases* the *Wages Payable* account

Journal Entry

A	=	L	+	SE
		+10,800		−65,000
		+2,400		
		+4,030		
		+942		
		+1,800		
		+2,600		
		+42,428		

		Debit	Credit
Feb. 15	Wages Expense	65,000	
	Employees' Federal Income Taxes Payable		10,800
	Employees' State Income Taxes Payable		2,400
	Social Security Tax Payable		4,030
	Medicare Tax Payable		942
	Medical Insurance Premiums Payable		1,800
	Pension Contributions Payable		2,600
	Wages Payable		42,428
	To record the payroll		

Comment Wages Expense is recorded for the gross wages, but the various withholding are *recognized* as liabilities before net amount payable to employees is determined. Although the employees earned at total of $65,000, their take-home pay total was only $42,428.

Recording Employer Payroll Taxes and Health Insurance Cost and Pension Benefits

Transaction On February 15, Teresa records the fitness center's share of payroll taxes (50 percent), the health insurance premiums (80 percent) and the pension contributions (50 percent).

Analysis The journal entry to record employer payroll taxes, health insurance costs, and pension benefits

- ▲ *increases* the *Payroll Taxes and Benefits Expense* account
- ▲ *increases* each *Tax Payable* account
- ▲ *increases* the *Medical Insurance Premiums Payable* account
- ▲ *increases* the *Pension Contributions Payable* account

Journal Entry

A	=	L	+	SE
		+4,030		−18,802
		+942		
		+7,200		
		+2,600		
		+520		
		+3,510		

		Debit	Credit
Feb. 15	Payroll Taxes and Benefits Expense	18,802	
	Social Security Tax Payable		4,030
	Medicare Tax Payable		942
	Medical Insurance Premiums Payable		7,200*
	Pension Contributions Payable		2,600
	Federal Unemployment Tax Payable		520
	State Unemployment Tax Payable		3,510
	To record payroll taxes and other costs		

*The employees' share of premiums is 20%. Thus, the employer's share is: ($1,800 ÷ 0.20) − $1,800 = $7,200

Comment Note that the payroll taxes and benefits expense increases the total cost of the payroll to $83,802 ($18,802 + $65,000), which exceeds the amount earned by the employees by almost 29 percent.

Unearned Revenues **Unearned revenues** are advance payments for goods or services that a company must provide in a future period. The company *recognizes* the revenue over that period.

Recording Unearned Revenues

Transaction On June 1, Teresa's Fitness Center receives cash from a customer in advance for a one-year membership in the fitness center in the amount of $360.

Analysis The journal entry to record unearned revenues

▲ *increases* the *Cash* account

▲ *increases* the *Unearned Revenue* account

Application of Double Entry

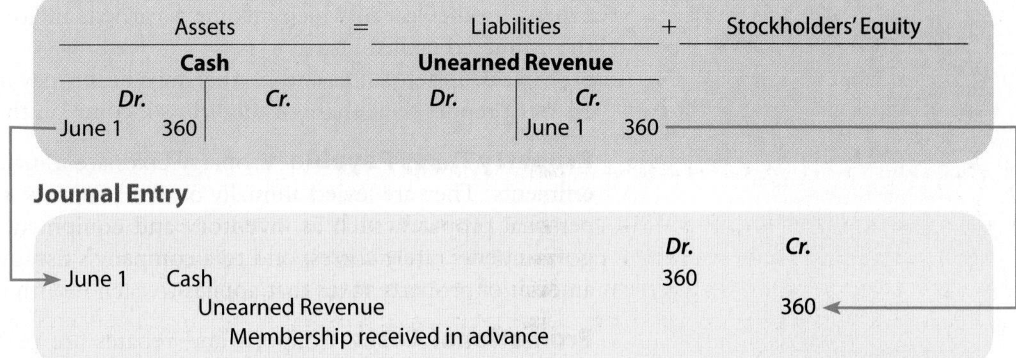

A	=	L	+	SE
+360		+360		

Comment Teresa's Fitness Center has a liability of $360 that will slowly be reduced over the year as it provides the service.

Recognizing Unearned Revenues That Are Now Earned

Transaction On June 30, Teresa needs to record the amount of revenues earned at the end of the first month.

Analysis The journal entry to record unearned revenues that have been earned

▲ *increases* the *Revenue* account

▼ *decreases* the *Unearned Revenue* account

Application of Double Entry

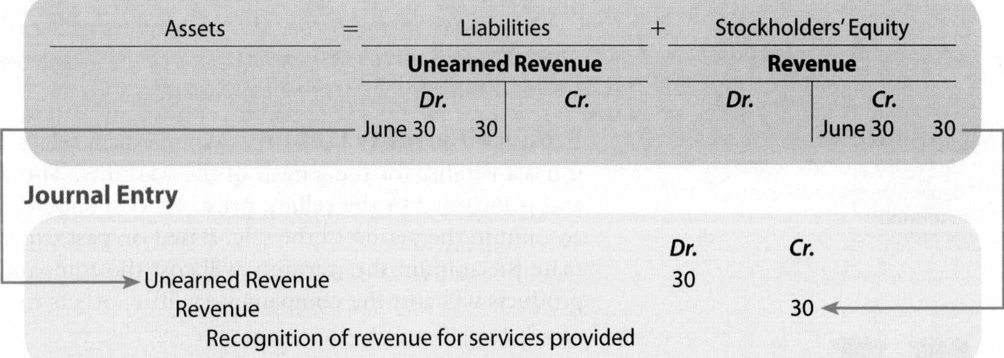

A	=	L	+	SE
		−30		+30

Comment Many businesses, including special-order firms, repair companies, and construction companies, ask for a deposit. Until they deliver the goods or services, these deposits are *classified* as current liabilities.

Estimated Liabilities

STUDY NOTE: *Estimated liabilities are recorded and presented on the financial statements in the same way as definitely determinable liabilities. The only difference is that the computation of estimated liabilities involves some uncertainty.*

Estimated liabilities are definite debts or obligations whose exact dollar amount cannot be known until a later date. The primary accounting problem is to estimate and record the amount of the liability. The following are examples of estimated liabilities.

Income Taxes Payable The federal government, most state governments, and some cities and towns levy a tax on a corporation's income. The amount of the liability depends on the results of a corporation's operations, which are often not known until after the end of the corporation's fiscal year. However, because income taxes are an expense in the year in which income is earned, an adjusting entry is necessary to record the estimated tax liability.

Sole proprietorships and partnerships do *not* pay income taxes. However, their owners must report their share of the firm's income on their individual tax returns.

Property Taxes Payable Property taxes are a main source of revenue for local governments. They are levied annually on real property, such as land and buildings, and on personal property, such as inventory and equipment. Because the fiscal years of local governments rarely correspond to a company's fiscal year, it is necessary to estimate the amount of property taxes that applies to each month of the year.

Promotional Costs Coupons and rebates are part of many companies' marketing programs. Because of frequent flyer programs, for example, U.S. airline companies today have more than 10 trillion "free miles" outstanding. What are the accounting implications of these promotional programs? Companies usually record the costs as a reduction in sales (a contra-sales account) rather than as an expense with a corresponding current liability.

Hershey Foods Corporation accrues almost $1 billion in promotional costs each year. In its annual report, Hershey acknowledged the difficulty of estimating the accrued liability for promotional programs:

> *Accrued liabilities requiring the most difficult or subjective judgments include liabilities associated with marketing promotion programs. . . . We determine the amount of the accrued liability by analysis of programs offered, historical trends, expectations regarding customer and consumer participation, sales and payment trends; and experience with payment patterns associated with similar, previously offered programs. The estimated costs of these programs are reasonably likely to change in the future due to changes in trends with regard to customer and consumer participation, particularly for new programs and for programs related to the introduction of new products.*[4]

STUDY NOTE: *Recording a product warranty expense in the period of the sale is an application of* accrual accounting.

Product Warranty Liability When a firm sells a product or service with a warranty, it has a liability for the length of the warranty. The warranty is a feature of the product and is included in the selling price. Its cost should therefore be debited to an expense account in the period of the sale. Based on past experience, it should be possible to estimate the amount the warranty will cost the company in the future. Warranties on some products will cost the company very little; others may cost a lot.

Business Perspective
What Is the Cost of Frequent Flyer Miles?

In the early 1980s, **American Airlines** developed a frequent flyer program that awards free trips and other bonuses to customers based on the number of miles they fly on the airline. It is estimated that 180 million people now participate in similar programs. Estimated liabilities for these tickets have become an important consideration in evaluating an airline's financial position. Complicating the estimate is that almost half the miles have been earned through purchases from hotels, car rental and telephone companies, Internet service providers like **AOL**, and bank credit cards.[5]

Recording Product Liability

Transaction A muffler company like **Midas** guarantees that it will replace free of charge any muffler it sells that fails during the time the buyer owns the car. The company charges a small service fee for replacing the muffler. In the past, 6 percent of the mufflers sold have been returned for replacement under the warranty. The average cost of a muffler is $50. On July 31, Midas must record the accrued liability and related expense. The company sold 700 mufflers during the month.

Analysis The journal entry to record the accrued liability and related expense

▲ *increases* the *Product Warranty Expense* account

▲ *increases* the *Estimated Product Warranty Liability* account

Application of Double Entry

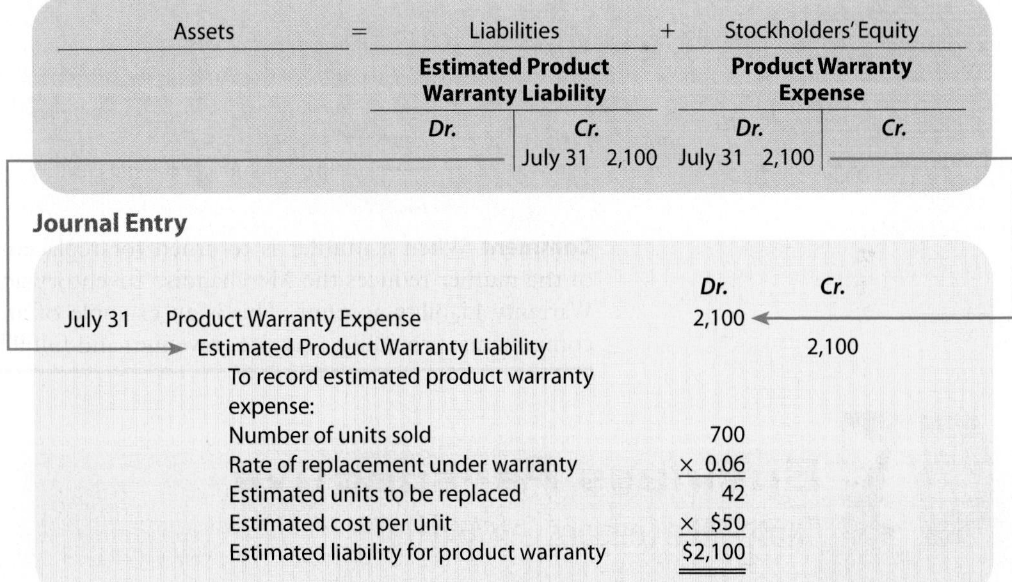

Assets	=	Liabilities		+	Stockholders' Equity	
		Estimated Product Warranty Liability			**Product Warranty Expense**	
		Dr.	*Cr.*		*Dr.*	*Cr.*
			July 31 2,100		July 31 2,100	

Journal Entry

A	=	L	+	SE
		+2,100		−2,100

		Dr.	*Cr.*
July 31	Product Warranty Expense	2,100	
	Estimated Product Warranty Liability		2,100
	To record estimated product warranty expense:		
	Number of units sold	700	
	Rate of replacement under warranty	× 0.06	
	Estimated units to be replaced	42	
	Estimated cost per unit	× $50	
	Estimated liability for product warranty	$2,100	

Comment The expense and liability for the estimated warranty are *recognized* at the time of sale of the product.

Recording Product Liability and Service

Transaction On December 5, a customer returns with a defective muffler, which cost $60, and pays a $30 service fee to have it replaced.

Analysis The journal entry to record this liability and service

▲ *increases* the *Cash* account

▲ *increases* the *Service Revenue* account

▼ *decreases* the *Merchandise Inventory* account

▼ *decreases* the *Estimated Product Warranty Liability* account

Application of Double Entry

Assets			=	Liabilities			+	Stockholders' Equity		
Cash				**Estimated Product Warranty Liability**				**Service Revenue**		
Dr.		Cr.		Dr.		Cr.		Dr.	Cr.	
Dec. 5	30			Dec. 5	60				Dec. 5	30
Merchandise Inventory										
Dr.	Cr.									
	Dec. 5	60								

Journal Entry

A	=	L	+	SE
+30		−60		+30
−60				

		Dr.	Cr.
Dec. 5	Cash	30	
	Estimated Product Warranty Liability	60	
	Service Revenue		30
	Merchandise Inventory		60
	Replacement of muffler under warranty		

Comment When a muffler is returned for replacement under the warranty, the cost of the muffler reduces the Merchandise Inventory account and the Estimated Product Warranty Liability account. This is an example of an entry for a transaction with two components: providing a service (revenue) and fulfilling an obligation (liability).

Business Perspective

Those Little Coupons Can Add Up

© Alija / iStockphoto.com

Many companies promote their products by issuing coupons that offer "cents off" or other enticements. Because four out of five shoppers use coupons, companies are forced by competition to distribute them. The total value of unredeemed coupons, each of which represents a potential liability for the issuing company, is staggering. In 2011, marketers distributed approximately 305 billion coupons, of which less than 1% of all coupons were digital coupons. In total, the coupons were worth about \$470 billion, but consumers redeemed only \$4.6 billion in savings.[6] Thus, a big advertiser can issue millions of coupons and expect less than 1 percent to be redeemed.

Vacation Pay Liability In most companies, employees accrue paid vacation as they work during the year. For example, an employee may earn 52 weeks' salary for 50 weeks' work. The cost of the two weeks' vacation should be allocated as an expense over the year so that month-to-month costs will not be distorted. The vacation pay represents 4 percent (two weeks' vacation divided by 50 weeks) of an employee's pay.

Recording Vacation Pay Expense

Transaction Diviney Company has a vacation policy of two weeks of paid vacation for each 50 weeks of work, has a payroll of \$42,000, and paid \$2,000 of that amount to employees on vacation for the week ended April 20. Because of past experience with employee turnover, the company assumes that only 75 percent of the employees will ultimately collect vacation pay. The computation of vacation pay expense based on the payroll of employees not on vacation (\$42,000 − \$2,000) is as follows.

\$40,000 × 4 percent × 75 percent = \$1,200

Diviney must record vacation pay expense for the week ended April 20.

Analysis The journal entry to record vacation pay expense

▲ *increases* the *Vacation Pay Expense* account

▲ *increases* the *Estimated Liability for Vacation Pay* account

Application of Double Entry

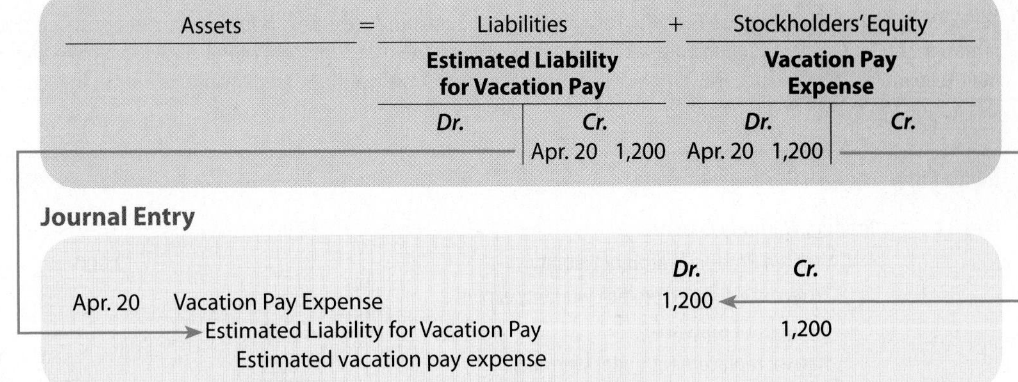

Journal Entry

A	=	L	+	SE
		+1,200		−1,200

		Dr.	Cr.
Apr. 20	Vacation Pay Expense	1,200	
	Estimated Liability for Vacation Pay		1,200
	Estimated vacation pay expense		

Comment Vacation Pay Expense and corresponding liability are ***recognized*** on this date because the employee earned the vacation pay in the week working rather than when the vacation is taken.

Just as employees earn paid vacation days and holidays when working, employers incur expenses and liabilities for those paid days off.

YanLev/Shutterstock.com

Recording Payment When Vacation is Taken

Transaction On August 31, Diviney Company needs to record the $2,000 paid to employees on vacation during August.

Analysis The journal entry for a company to record payment for employees on vacation

▼ *decreases* the *Estimated Liability for Vacation Pay* account

▼ *decreases* the *Cash* account

Application of Double Entry

Assets		=	Liabilities		+	Stockholders' Equity
Cash			**Estimated Liability for Vacation Pay**			
Dr.	Cr.		Dr.	Cr.		
	Aug. 31 2,000		Aug. 31 2,000			

Journal Entry

A*	=	L	+	SE
−2,000		−2,000		

*Assumes Cash paid.

		Dr.	Cr.
Aug. 31	Estimated Liability for Vacation Pay	2,000	
	Cash		2,000
	Wages of employees on vacation		

Comment The treatment of vacation pay presented here can also be applied to other payroll costs, such as bonus plans and contributions to pension plans.

APPLY IT!

Tellex Corp. manufactures and sells clocks. Each clock costs $30 to produce and sells for $60. In addition, each clock carries a warranty that provides for free replacement if it fails during the two years following the sale. In the past, 2 percent of the clocks sold have had to be replaced under the warranty. During May, Tellex sold 20,000 clocks, and 350 clocks were replaced under the warranty. Prepare journal entries to record the estimated liability for product warranties during the month and the clocks replaced under warranty during the month (use May 31).

SOLUTION

May 31	Product Warranty Expense	12,000	
	Estimated Product Warranty Liability		12,000
	To record estimated product warranty expense:		
	Number of units sold	20,000	
	Rate of replacement under warranty	× 0.02	
	Estimated units to be replaced	400	
	Estimated cost per unit	× $30	
	Estimated liability for product warranty	$12,000	
May 31	Estimated Product Warranty Liability	10,500	
	Merchandise Inventory		10,500
	Replacement of clocks under warranty		
	350 clocks × $30 = $10,500		

TRY IT! SE2, SE3, SE4, E2A, E3A, E4A, E5A, E6A, E2B, E3B, E4B, E5B, E6B

LO3 Contingent Liabilities and Commitments

The FASB requires companies to *disclose* in a note to their financial statements any contingent liabilities and commitments. A **contingent liability** is a *potential* liability because it depends on a future event arising out of a past transaction. Contingent liabilities often involve the following:

- Lawsuits
- Income tax disputes
- Discounted notes receivable
- Guarantees of debt
- Failure to follow government regulations

For instance, a construction company that signed a contract with a state to build a bridge may be sued by the state for using poor materials. The past transaction is the contract for building the bridge. The future event is the outcome of the lawsuit, which is not yet known.

STUDY NOTE: *Contingencies are recorded when they are probable and can be reasonably estimated.*

The FASB has established two conditions for determining when a contingency should be entered in the accounting records:

- The liability must be probable.
- The liability can be reasonably estimated.[7]

Estimated liabilities like those for income taxes, warranties, and vacation pay that we described earlier meet those conditions. They are, therefore, accrued in the accounting records.

International Perspective

IFRS Balance Sheet Liabilities Are Often Greater Under IFRS

U.S. GAAP do not record commitments, such as purchase agreements, as liabilities even though they are a *legal* obligation, since they do not meet the technical definition of a liability. *Disclosure* in a note to the financial statements is required. Under IFRS, however, these agreements are *recognized* when an entity has a demonstrable commitment.

In a survey of large companies, lawsuits involving many different issues and environmental concerns, including toxic waste cleanup, were among the most common types of contingencies reported.[8] In a note to its 2011 financial statements, **Microsoft** described its contingent liabilities as lawsuits involving infringement of European competition law, antitrust and overcharge actions, and patent and intellectual property claims, among other matters. Microsoft's management stated:

> *We also are subject to a variety of other claims and suits. . . . While we intend to vigorously defend these matters, there exists the possibility of adverse outcomes that we estimate could reach approximately $800 million in aggregate beyond recorded amounts. Were unfavorable final outcomes to occur, there exists the possibility of a material adverse impact on our financial statements for the period in which the effects become reasonably estimable.*[9]

A **commitment** is a legal obligation that does not meet the technical requirements for *recognition* as a liability and so is not recorded. Common examples are purchase agreements, construction or acquisition of long-term assets, and leases.[10] For example, **Microsoft** also reported in its notes to its financial statements that it had construction commitments of $263 million and purchase commitments of $5.6 billion.[11] Knowledge of these amounts is very important for planning cash flows in the coming years.

APPLY IT!

Indicate whether each of the following is (a) a contingent liability or (b) a commitment:

1. A tax dispute with the IRS
2. A long-term lease agreement
3. An agreement to purchase goods in the future
4. A potential lawsuit over a defective product

SOLUTION

1. a; 2. b; 3. b; 4. a

TRY IT! SE5, E7A, E7B

LO4 Valuation Approaches to Fair Value Accounting

Recall that *fair value* is the price for which an asset or liability could be sold, or exit the company, as opposed to the price for which the company could buy the asset or liability. As pointed out previously, the concept of fair value applies to some financial assets, such as cash equivalents and investments, and to some liabilities, such as notes payable. Fair value is also applicable to determining whether tangible assets such as inventories and long-term assets have sustained a permanent decline in value below their cost. The FASB identifies three approaches to measurement of fair value:[12]

- **Market approach:** External market transactions are ideal for *valuing* investments and liabilities for which there is an active market and quoted prices are available

International Perspective

IFRS Do the FASB and IASB Agree on Fair Value Measurement?

As part of their effort to converge U.S. GAAP with IFRS, the FASB and the IASB agreed in 2011, after almost ten years of effort, to issue a converged fair value measurement standard ASU 2011-04 (Topic 820) by the FASB and IFRS 13 by the IASB. In this standard, they agree on a common definition of fair value, including concepts and assumptions as well as *disclosures*. This is a major step forward in the effort to bring U.S. GAAP closer to global accounting standards.[13]

for the specific asset or liability. However, an active market or a quoted price is not always available. For example, there may not be a market for special-purpose equipment. In these cases, it may be possible to observe quoted prices for comparable types of equipment.

- **Income (or cash flow) approach:** The income approach, as defined by the FASB, converts future cash flows to a single present value. This approach is used when the market approach cannot be used because there are no identical or comparable quoted prices available. It is based on management's best determination of the future cash amounts generated by an asset or payments that will be made for a liability. It is based on internally generated information, which should be reasonable for the circumstances. For instance, management may estimate the cash flows or cost savings expected to be generated by the special-purpose equipment.
- **Cost approach:** The cost approach is based on the amount that currently would be required to replace an asset with the same or a comparable asset. For example, inventory is usually *valued* at lower of cost or market, where market is the replacement cost. For plant assets like special-purpose equipment, the replacement cost of a new asset must be adjusted to take into account the asset's age, condition, depreciation, and obsolescence.

The following sections, which focus on the income or cash flow approach, require knowledge of interest and the time value of money and present value techniques.

Interest, the Time Value of Money, and Future Value

The concept of the **time value of money** refers to the costs or benefits of holding or not holding money over time. **Interest** is the cost of using money for a specific period. For example, if you have $100 and hold that amount for one year without putting it in a savings account, you have forgone the interest that the money would have earned. However, if you put the $100 in an interest-bearing checking account, you will have the $100 plus the interest at the end of the year.

The amount of principal plus interest after one or more periods is known as **future value**. Future value may be computed using either simple interest or compound interest.

- **Simple interest** is the interest cost for one or more periods when the principal sum—the amount on which interest is computed—stays the same from period to period.
- **Compound interest** is the interest cost for two or more periods when, after each period, the interest earned in that period is added to the amount on which interest is computed in future periods. In other words, the principal sum is increased at the end of each period by the interest earned in that period.

STUDY NOTE: *Compound interest is useful in business because it helps decision makers choose among alternative courses of action.*

The examples that follow illustrate these concepts.

Future Value Using Simple Interest

Measure *Simple interest* is the interest cost for one or more periods when the principal sum stays the same from period to period.

Example Willy Wang accepts an 8 percent, $15,000 note due in 90 days. How much will he receive at that time? The interest is calculated as follows.

$$\begin{aligned}\text{Interest} &= \text{Principal} \times \text{Rate} \times \text{Time}\\ &= \$15{,}000.00 \times 8/100 \times 90/365\\ &= \$295.89\end{aligned}$$

Therefore, the future value that Wang will receive is $15,295.89, calculated as follows.

$$\begin{aligned}\text{Total} &= \text{Principal} + \text{Interest}\\ &= \$15{,}000.00 + \$295.89\\ &= \$15{,}295.89\end{aligned}$$

Future Value Using Compound Interest

Measure *Compound interest* is the interest cost for two or more periods when, after each period, the interest earned in that period is added to the amount on which interest is computed in future periods.

Example Terry Soma deposits $10,000 in an account that pays 6 percent interest. She expects to leave the principal and accumulated interest in the account for three years. If the interest is paid at the end of each year and is then added to the principal and this amount in turn earns interest, how much will Soma's account total at the end of three years? The amount is computed as follows.

Year	Principal Amount at Beginning of Year	Annual Amount of Interest (Principal at Beginning of Year x 6%)	Accumulated Amount at End of Year (Principal at Beginning of Year + Annual Amount of Interest)
1	$10,000.00	$600.00	$10,600.00
2	10,600.00	636.00	11,236.00
3	11,236.00	674.16	11,910.16

Soma will have $11,910.16 in her account at the end of three years. Note that the amount of interest increases each year by the interest rate times the interest of the previous year. For example, between year 1 and year 2, the interest increased by $36, which equals 6 percent times $600.

Present Value

STUDY NOTE: *Present value is a method of determining* today *the value of future cash flows. Financial analysts commonly compute present value to determine the* value *of potential investments.*

Suppose you had the choice of receiving $100 today or one year from today. No doubt you would choose to receive it today. Why? If you have the money today, you can put it in a savings account to earn interest so you will have more than $100 a year from today. In other words, because the amount today (present value) does not include any interest, it is less than the amount in the future (future value). **Present value** is the amount that must be invested today at a given rate of interest to produce a given future value. Thus, present value and future value are closely related.

Present Value

Measure *Present value* is the amount that must be invested today at a given rate of interest to produce a given future value.

Example Lucia Fontaine needs $10,000 one year from now. How much does she have to invest today to achieve that goal if the interest rate is 5 percent? From earlier examples, we can establish the following equation:

Present Value × (1.0 + Interest Rate)	= Future Value
Present Value × 1.05	= $10,000.00
Present Value	= $10,000.00 ÷ 1.05
Present Value	= $9,523.81*

*Rounded

To achieve a future value of $10,000, Fontaine must invest a present value of $9,523.81. Interest of 5 percent on $9,523.81 for one year equals $476.19, and these two amounts added together equal $10,000.

Present Value of a Single Sum Due in the Future

Measure The present value of a single amount of cash is the amount to be received at a specified date in the future.

Example Ron Moore wants to be sure of having $8,000 at the end of three years. How much must he invest today in a 5 percent savings account to achieve this goal?

Manual Computation We can compute the present value of $8,000 at compound interest of 5 percent for three years by adapting the above equation:

Year	Amount at End of Year		Divide by		Present Value at Beginning of Year
3	$8,000.00	÷	1.05	=	$7,619.05*
2	7,619.05	÷	1.05	=	7,256.24*
1	7,256.24	÷	1.05	=	6,910.70*

*Rounded

Moore must invest $6,910.70 today to achieve a value of $8,000 in three years.

Table Computation We can simplify the calculation by using a table of present values. Refer to Table 1 in Appendix C. The point at which the 5 percent column and the row for period 3 intersect shows a factor of 0.864, as shown in Exhibit 3. This factor, when multiplied by $1, gives the present value of $1 to be received three years from now at 5 percent interest. Thus, we solve the problem as follows.

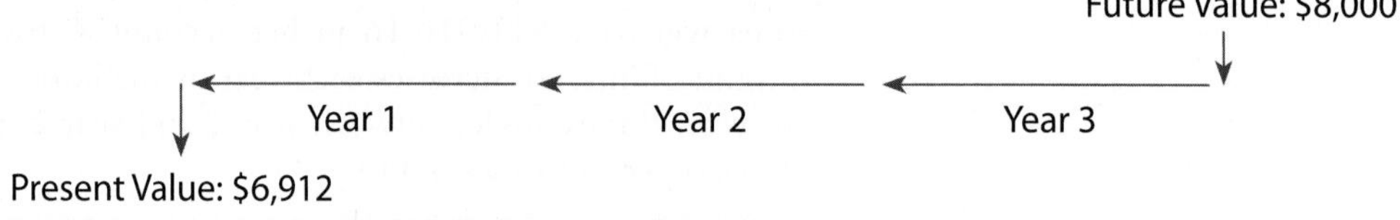

Future Value	×	Factor	=	Present Value
$8,000	×	0.864	=	$6,912

Except for a rounding difference of $1.30, this result is the same as our earlier one.

Exhibit 3
Present Value of $1 to Be Received at the End of a Given Number of Periods

Period	1%	2%	3%	4%	5%	6%	7%	8%	9%	10%
1	0.990	0.980	0.971	0.962	0.952	0.943	0.935	0.926	0.917	0.909
2	0.980	0.961	0.943	0.925	0.907	0.890	0.873	0.857	0.842	0.826
3	0.971	0.942	0.915	0.889	**0.864**	0.840	0.816	0.794	0.772	0.751

Present Value of an Ordinary Annuity

It is often necessary to compute the present value of a series of receipts or payments equally spaced over time, with compound interest—in other words, the present value of an **ordinary annuity**.

Present Value of an Ordinary Annuity

Measure An *ordinary annuity* is a series of equal payments or receipts that will begin one time period from the current date.

Example Vickie Long has sold a piece of property and is to receive $18,000 in three equal annual payments of $6,000 beginning one year from today. What is the present value of this sale if the current interest rate is 5 percent?

Manual Computation Using Table 1 in Appendix C, we can compute the present value by calculating a separate value for each of the three payments and summing the results, as follows.

Future Receipts (Annuity) Year 1	Year 2	Year 3		Present Value Factor at 5 Percent (from Exhibit 3)		Present Value
$6,000			×	0.952	=	$ 5,712
	$6,000		×	0.907	=	5,442
		$6,000	×	0.864	=	5,184
Total Present Value						$16,338

The present value of the sale is $16,338. Thus, there is an implied interest cost (given the 5 percent rate) of $1,662 ($18,000 − $16,338) associated with the payment plan.

Table Computation We can make this calculation more easily by using Table 2 in Appendix C. The point at which the 5 percent column intersects the row for period 3 shows a factor of 2.723 (as shown in Exhibit 4), which is the sum of the three present value factors in the table above (0.952 + 0.907 + 0.864 = 2.723). When multiplied by $1, this factor gives the present value of a series of three $1 payments (spaced one year apart) at compound interest of 5 percent. Thus, we solve the problem as follows.

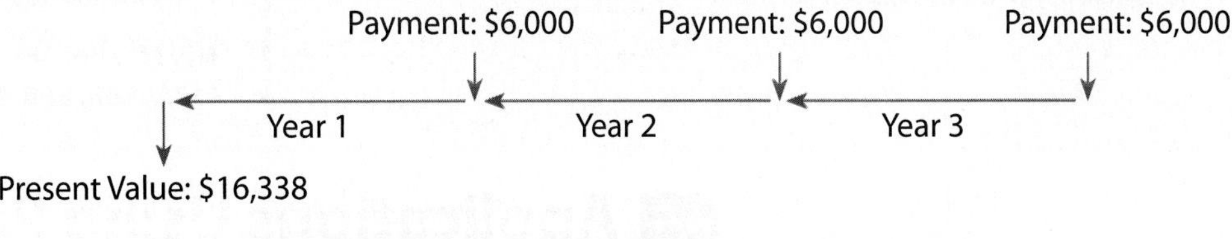

Periodic Payment	×	Factor	=	Present Value
$6,000	×	2.723	=	$16,338

This result is the same as the one we computed earlier.

Exhibit 4
Present Value of an Ordinary $1 Annuity Received in Each Period for a Given Number of Periods

Period	1%	2%	3%	4%	5%	6%	7%	8%	9%	10%
1	0.990	0.980	0.971	0.962	0.952	0.943	0.935	0.926	0.917	0.909
2	1.970	1.942	1.913	1.886	1.859	1.833	1.808	1.783	1.759	1.736
3	2.941	2.884	2.829	2.775	**2.723**	2.673	2.624	2.577	2.531	2.487

Time Periods As in all our examples, the compounding period is in most cases one year, and the interest rate is stated on an annual basis. However, in Tables 1 and 2 in Appendix C, the far left columns refer not to years but to periods. This wording

STUDY NOTE: The interest rate used when compounding interest for less than one year is the annual rate divided by the number of periods in a year.

accommodates compounding periods of less than one year. Savings accounts that record interest quarterly and bonds that pay interest semiannually are cases in which the compounding period is less than one year. To use the tables in these cases, you must divide the annual interest rate by the number of periods in the year and multiply the number of periods in one year by the number of years.

Present Value When Compounding Period Is Less than One Year

Measure The present value is the amount of interest calculated or compounded more than once per year.

Example Compute the present value of a $6,000 payment that is to be made in two years. The annual interest rate of 8 percent, and the compounding period is semiannual.

Manual Computation Before using present value tables in this computation, we must compute the interest rate that applies to each compounding period and the total number of compounding periods.

- The interest rate to use is 4 percent (8% annual rate ÷ 2 periods per year).
- The total number of compounding periods is 4 (2 periods per year × 2 years).

Table Computation We can then use Table 1 in Appendix C to compute the present value of the payment, $5,130, as follows.

Principal	×	Factor	=	Present Value
$6,000	×	0.855	=	$5,130

This procedure is used whenever the corresponding period is less than one year. For example, a monthly compounding requires dividing the annual interest rate by 12 and multiplying the number of years by 12 to use the tables. This method can be used with the present value tables in Appendix C.

APPLY IT!

Use Tables 1 and 2 in Appendix C to determine the present value of the following:

1. A single payment of $10,000 at 5 percent for 10 years
2. 10 annual payments of $1,000 at 5 percent
3. A single payment of $10,000 at 7 percent for 5 years
4. 10 annual payments of $1,000 at 9 percent

SOLUTION

1. From Table 1: $10,000 × 0.614 = $6,140
2. From Table 2: $1,000 × 7.722 = $7,722
3. From Table 1: $10,000 × 0.713 = $7,130
4. From Table 2: $1,000 × 6.418 = $6,418

TRY IT! SE6, SE7, SE8, E8A, E9A, E10A, E11A, E12A, E13A, E8B, E9B, E10B, E11B, E12B, E13B

LO5 Applications Using Present Value

The concept of present value is widely used in business decision making and financial reporting. For example, the *value* of a long-term note receivable or payable can be determined by calculating the present value of the future interest payments. As mentioned earlier, the FASB has made present value an important component of its approach in determining the fair value of assets and liabilities when a market price is not available.

The SEC has issued guidance on how to apply fair value accounting.[14] For instance, it states that management's internal assumptions about expected cash flows may be used to measure fair value and that market quotes may be used when they are from an orderly, active market. Thus, **Microsoft** may determine the expected present value of the future cash flows of an investment by using its internal cash flow projections and a market rate of interest. By comparing the result to the current value of the investment, Microsoft can determine if an adjustment needs to be made to record a gain or loss.

In the sections that follow, we illustrate two useful applications of present value. These applications will be helpful in understanding the uses of present value that we discuss in later chapters.

Valuing an Asset at Present Value

As already discussed, an asset is something that will provide future benefits to the company that owns it. Usually, the purchase price of an asset represents the present value of those future benefits. It is possible to evaluate a proposed purchase price by comparing it with the present value of the asset to the company.

The Present Value of an Asset

Measure The present value of an asset is based on the saving it will generate over its useful life.

Example Mike Yeboah is thinking of buying a new machine that will reduce his annual labor cost by $1,400 per year. The machine will last eight years. The interest rate that Yeboah assumes for making equipment purchases is 10 percent. What is the maximum amount (present value) that Yeboah should pay for the machine?

Table Computation The present value of the machine is equal to the present value of an ordinary annuity of $1,400 per year for eight years at compound interest of 10 percent. Using the present value factor from Appendix C, we compute the present value as follows.

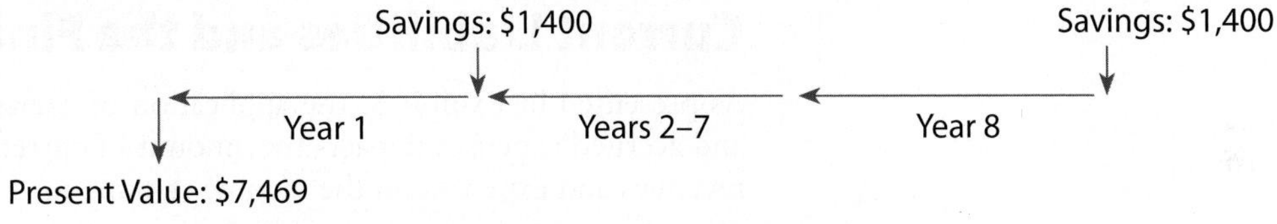

Periodic Savings	×	Factor	=	Present Value
$1,400	×	5.335	=	$7,469

Yeboah should not pay more than $7,469 for the machine because this amount equals the present value of the benefits he would receive from owning it.

Present Value of a Deferred Payment

To encourage buyers to make a purchase, sellers sometimes agree to defer payment for a sale. This practice is common among companies that sell agricultural equipment to farmers who need new equipment in the spring but cannot pay for it until they sell their crops in the fall.

Present Value of a Deferred Payment

Measure The present value is the amount of a payment to be received later.

Example Field Helpers Corporation sells a tractor to Sasha Ptak for $100,000 on February 1 and agrees to take payment ten months later, on December 1. With such an agreement, the future payment includes not only the selling price but also an implied (imputed) interest cost.

Table Computation If the prevailing annual interest rate for such transactions is 12 percent compounded monthly, the actual price of the tractor would be the present value of the future payment, computed using the factor from Appendix C [10 periods, 1 percent (12 percent ÷ 12 months)], as follows.

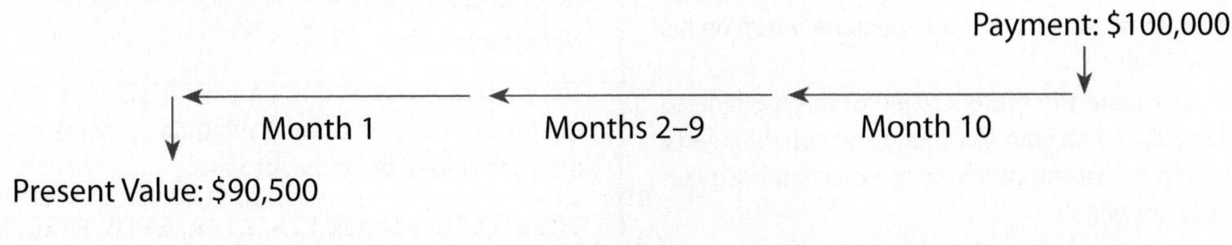

Future Payment	×	Factor	=	Present Value
$100,000	×	0.905	=	$90,500

Ptak records the present value, $90,500, in his purchase records, and Field Helpers Corporation records it in its sales records. The balance consists of interest expense or interest income.

Other Applications

Other applications of present value in accounting include the following:

- Computing imputed interest on non-interest-bearing notes
- Accounting for installment notes
- Valuing a bond
- Recording lease obligations
- Pension obligations
- Valuing debt
- Depreciating property, plant, and equipment
- Making capital expenditure decisions
- Accounting for any item in which time is a factor

Current Liabilities and the Financial Statements

As presented in Exhibit 5, the application of *accrual accounting* to unearned revenues and accrued expenses impacts the amount of current liabilities on the balance sheet and revenues and expenses on the income statement.

Exhibit 5
Accrued Expenses and Related Accrued Liabilities

Income Statement

For the Year Ended December 31, 2014

Net sales
Operating expenses
Accrued expenses
Other revenues and expenses
Income before income tax expense
Income taxes
Net income

Balance Sheet

December 31, 2014

Assets	**Liabilities**
Current assets	Current liabilities
Investments	Accrued liabilities
Property, plant, and equipment	Other current liabilities
Intangible assets	Long-term liabilities
	Total liabilities
	Stockholders' Equity
	Common stock
	Retained earnings
	Total stockholders' equity

Total Assets = Total Liabilities + Stockholders' Equity

APPLY IT!

Jerry owns a restaurant and has the opportunity to buy a high-quality espresso coffee machine for $5,000. After carefully studying expected costs and revenues, Jerry estimates that the machine will produce a net cash inflow of $1,600 annually and will last for five years. He determines that an interest rate of 10 percent is an adequate return on his investment.

Calculate the present value of the machine to Jerry. Based on your calculation, do you think Jerry would be wise to purchase the machine? Explain your answer.

SOLUTION

Calculation of the present value:

Annual cash inflow	$ 1,600.00
Factor from Table 2, Appendix C (5 years at 10%)	× 3.791
Present value of net cash flows	$ 6,065.60
Less purchase price	−5,000.00
Net present value	$ 1,065.60

The present value of the net cash flows from the machine exceeds the purchase price. Thus, the investment will return more than 10 percent to Jerry's business. A decision to purchase the machine would, therefore, be wise.

TRY IT! SE8, E11A, E12A, E13A, E11B, E12B, E13B

SECTION 3 **BUSINESS APPLICATIONS**

BUSINESS APPLICATIONS
- Liquidity
- Cash flows

RELEVANT LEARNING OBJECTIVE

LO 6 Use ratio analysis to manage the impact of current liabilities' impact on liquidity.

LO 6 Business Issues Related to Current Liabilities

The primary reason a company incurs current liabilities is to meet its needs for cash during the operating cycle. Failure to manage the cash flows related to current liabilities can have serious consequences for a business. For instance, if suppliers are not paid on time, they may withhold vital shipments. Continued failure to pay current liabilities can lead to bankruptcy.

RATIO

Working Capital and the Current Ratio

As explained in Chapter 5, the *operating cycle* is the length of time it takes to purchase inventory, sell the inventory, and collect the resulting receivable. Most current liabilities arise from purchases of inventory, accrued expenses arise from operating costs, and unearned revenues arise from customers' advance payments. Companies incur short-term debt to raise cash during periods of inventory buildup or while waiting for the collection of receivables. They use the cash to pay the portion of long-term debt that is currently due and to pay liabilities arising from operations.

To evaluate a company's ability to pay its current liabilities, analysts often use two measures of liquidity, both of which we defined in an earlier chapter:

- Working Capital = Current Assets − Current Liabilities
- Current Ratio = Current Assets ÷ Current Liabilities

As shown below (in millions), **Nike**'s short-term liquidity as measured by working capital and the current ratio was positive in 2010 but decreased in 2011.

	Current Assets	−	Current Liabilities	=	Working Capital	Current Ratio*
2010	$10,959	−	$3,364	=	$7,595	3.26**
2011	$11,297	−	$3,958	=	$7,339	2.85**

*Current Assets ÷ Current Liabilities
**Rounded

The decrease in Nike's working capital and current ratio was caused primarily by a large decrease in cash and equivalents and an increase in all current liabilities. Overall, Nike is in a strong current situation.

Evaluating Accounts Payable

Another consideration in managing liquidity and cash flows is the time suppliers give a company to pay for purchases. Measurements commonly used to assess a company's ability to pay within a certain time frame are payables turnover and days' payable.

Payables Turnover **Payables turnover** is the number of times, on average, that a company pays its accounts payable in an accounting period. This measure reflects the relative size of accounts payable, the credit terms offered by suppliers, and a company's diligence in paying its suppliers.

To measure payables turnover for **Nike**, we must first calculate purchases by adjusting the cost of goods sold for the change in inventory.

▲ An *increase* in inventory means purchases were more than the cost of goods sold.

▼ A *decrease* means purchases were less than the cost of goods sold.

Nike's cost of goods sold in 2011 was \$20,862 million, and its inventory increased by \$674 million. Using these data, we can compute Nike's payables turnover as follows (in millions).

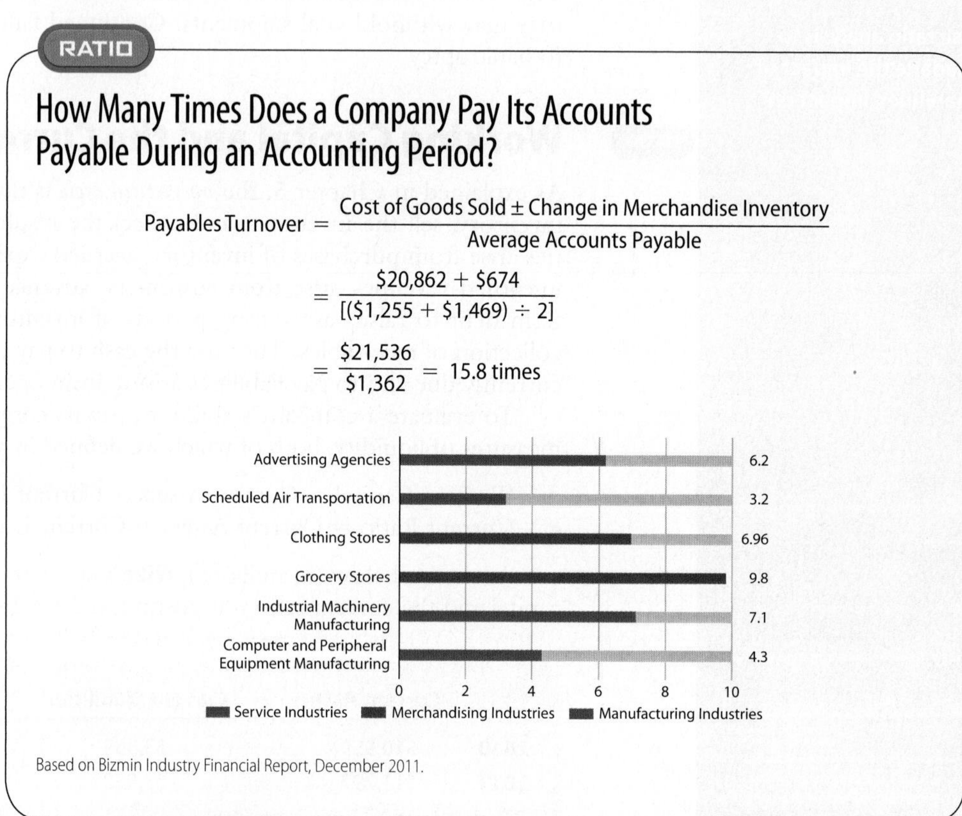

RATIO
How Many Times Does a Company Pay Its Accounts Payable During an Accounting Period?
Payables Turnover = (Cost of Goods Sold ± Change in Merchandise Inventory) / Average Accounts Payable
= (\$20,862 + \$674) / [(\$1,255 + \$1,469) ÷ 2]
= \$21,536 / \$1,362 = 15.8 times
Advertising Agencies 6.2
Scheduled Air Transportation 3.2
Clothing Stores 6.96
Grocery Stores 9.8
Industrial Machinery Manufacturing 7.1
Computer and Peripheral Equipment Manufacturing 4.3
0 2 4 6 8 10
Service Industries
Merchandising Industries
Manufacturing Industries

Based on Bizmin Industry Financial Report, December 2011.

As you can see, Nike's payables turnover is greater than the industries illustrated. This indicates that Nike pays its suppliers very quickly.

Days' Payable **Days' payable** shows how long, on average, a company takes to pay its accounts payable. For **Nike**, it is computed as follows.

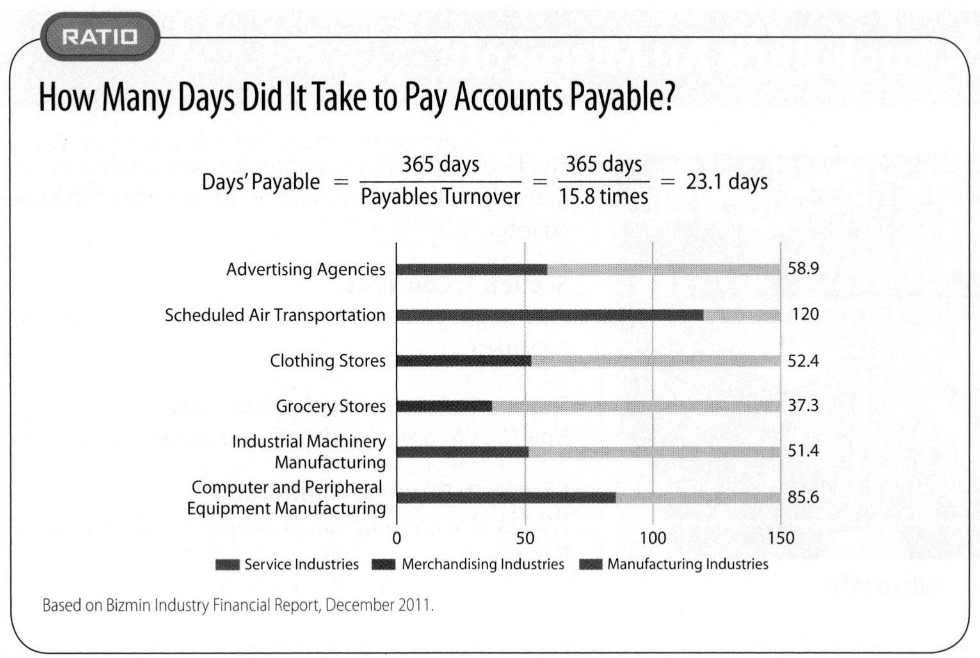

As shown, Nike's days' payable of 23.1 days, like its payables turnover of 15.8 times, indicates that Nike is prompt in paying its suppliers.

APPLY IT!

Jackie's Cookie Company has current assets of \$30,000 and current liabilities of \$20,000, of which accounts payable are \$15,000. Jackie's cost of goods sold is \$125,000, its merchandise inventory increased by \$5,000, and accounts payable were \$11,000 the prior year. Calculate Jackie's working capital, payables turnover, and days' payable.

SOLUTION

Working Capital = Current Assets − Current Liabilities
= \$30,000 − \$20,000
= \$10,000

$$\text{Payables Turnover} = \frac{\text{Cost of Goods Sold} \pm \text{Change in Inventory}}{\text{Average Accounts Payable}}$$

$$= \frac{\$125{,}000 + \$5{,}000}{(\$15{,}000 + \$11{,}000) \div 2} = \frac{\$130{,}000}{\$13{,}000}$$

= 10 Times

Days' Payable = 365 days ÷ Payables Turnover

$$= \frac{365 \text{ days}}{10 \text{ times}} = 36.5 \text{ days}$$

TRY IT! SE9, E15A, E15B

A Look Back At: Microsoft

Hilz, Peter/Hollandse Hoogte/Redux

Microsoft

The beginning of this chapter focused on the extent of **Microsoft**'s current liabilities. Complete the following requirements to answer the questions posed at the beginning of the chapter.

Section 1: Concepts
How do the concepts of recognition, valuation, classification, and disclosure apply to current liabilities?

Section 2: Accounting Applications
How does a company identify and account for all its current liabilities?

Section 3: Business Applications
Why is it important for Microsoft to identify and account for all her company's current liabilities?

SOLUTION

Section 1: Concepts
First of all, generally accepted accounting principles require that a liability be recorded when an obligation occurs, which refers to the *recognition* of liabilities. In addition, liabilities must be properly *valued*, which refers to knowing or properly estimating the amount of money needed to pay the debt. Furthermore, because of the impact that *classification* can have on a company's reported liquidity, it is very important to distinguish between current and long-term liabilities. Finally, to allow financial statement users to more clearly understand how a company uses some liability accounts, any special arrangements or additional explanation should be *disclosed* in the notes to the financial statements.

Section 2: Accounting Applications
Microsoft has all types of current liabilities. It has definitely determinable current liabilities, such as account payable, short-term debt, and securities lending payable. The rest of the current liabilities must be estimated. The estimated liabilities consist of accruals such as accrued compensation and income taxes payable and deferrals, such as short-term unearned revenue.

Section 3: Business Applications
It is important for Microsoft to identify and account for all its current liabilities because these amounts are taken into consideration when evaluating the company's liquidity. Working capital shows a company's ability to pay its current liabilities. Payables turnover shows the relative size of accounts payable, the credit terms offered by suppliers, and a company's diligence in paying its suppliers, and days' payable shows how long, on average, a company takes to pay its accounts payables.

Review Problem

In January 2014, Teresa Madej started a business called Teresa's Fitness Center. Teresa has not yet filed any tax reports for her business and, therefore, owes taxes. Because she has limited experience in running a business, she has brought you all her business records—a checkbook, canceled checks, deposit slips, suppliers' invoices, a notice of annual property taxes of $3,600 due to the city, and a promissory note to her bank for $16,000.

You analyzed all her records and determined the following as of December 31, 2014:

Unpaid invoices for nutritional supplements	$12,000
Sales of nutritional supplements (excluding sales tax)	57,000
Cost of supplements sold	33,600
Exercise instructors' salaries	22,800
Exercise revenues	81,400
Current assets	40,000
Supplements inventory, December 31, 2014	27,000
Supplements inventory, December 31, 2013	21,000

You learned that the company sold gift certificates in the amount of $700 that have not been redeemed and that it deducted $1,374 from its two employees' salaries for federal income taxes owed to the government. The current social security tax is 6.2 percent on maximum earnings of $110,100 for each employee, and the current Medicare tax is 1.45 percent (no maximum earnings). The FUTA tax is 5.4 percent to the state and 0.8 percent to the federal government on the first $7,000 earned by each employee; both employees earned more than $7,000. Teresa's Fitness Center has not filed a sales tax report to the state (6 percent of supplements sales).

Determine Teresa's Fitness center's current liabilities and their total amount.

SOLUTION

	A	B	C	D	E	F	G
1	Accounts payable						$12,000.00
2	Notes payable						16,000.00
3	Property taxes payable						3,600.00
4	Sales tax payable	(	$57,000	×	0.06	)	3,420.00
5	Social security tax payable	(	$22,800	×	0.062	) × 2	2,827.20
6	Medicare tax payable	(	$22,800	×	0.0145	) × 2	661.20
7	State unemployment tax payable	(	$ 7,000	×	0.054	) × 2	756.00
8	Federal unemployment tax payable	(	$ 7,000	×	0.008	) × 2	112.00
9	Employees' federal income taxes payable						1,374.00
10	Unearned revenues						700.00
11	Total current liabilities						$41,450.40
12							

Note: The company may have current liabilities for which you have not seen any documentary evidence. For instance, invoices for accounts payable could be missing. In addition, the company may have accrued liabilities, such as vacation pay for its two employees, which would require establishing an estimated liability. If the promissory note to Madej's bank is interest-bearing, it also would require an adjustment to accrue interest payable, and the company could have other loans outstanding for which you have not seen documentary evidence. Moreover, the company may have to pay penalties and interest to the federal and state governments because of its failure to remit tax payments on a timely basis. City and state income tax withholdings for the employees could be other overlooked liabilities.

Chapter Review

Define *current liabilities*, and identify the concepts underlying them. LO1

Liabilities result from past transactions and should be recognized at the time a transaction obligates a company to make future payments. They are valued at the amount of money necessary to satisfy the obligation or at the fair value of the goods or services to be delivered. Liabilities are classified as current or long-term. Companies are required to provide supplemental disclosure when the nature or details of the obligations would help in understanding the liability.

Identify, compute, and record definitely determinable and estimated current liabilities. LO2

The two major categories of current liabilities are definitely determinable liabilities and estimated liabilities. Definitely determinable liabilities include accounts payable, bank loans and commercial paper, notes payable, accrued liabilities, dividends payable, sales and excise taxes payable, the current portion of long-term debt, payroll liabilities, and unearned revenues. Estimated liabilities definitely exist, but their amounts are uncertain and must be estimated. They include liabilities for income taxes, property taxes, promotional costs, product warranties, and vacation pay.

Distinguish contingent liabilities from commitments. LO3

A contingent liability is a potential liability that arises from a past transaction and is dependent on a future event. Contingent liabilities often involve lawsuits, income tax disputes, discounted notes receivable, guarantees of debt, and failure to follow government regulations. A commitment is a legal obligation, such as a purchase agreement, that is not recorded as a liability.

Identify the valuation approaches to fair value accounting, define *time value of money* and *interest*, and apply them to present values. LO4

The FASB identifies three approaches to measuring fair value. The market approach is useful when there is an active market in which quoted prices are available for the specific asset or liability. The income (or cash flow) approach converts future cash flows to a single present value. The cost approach is based on the amount that currently would be required to replace an asset with a comparable one.

The time value of money refers to the costs or benefits derived from holding or not holding money over time. Interest is the cost of using money for a specific period. The amount on which simple interest is computed stays the same from period to period. In the computation of compound interest, the interest for a period is added to the principal amount before the interest for the next period is computed.

Future value is the amount an investment will be worth at a future date if invested at compound interest. Present value is the amount that must be invested today at a given rate of interest to produce a given future value. An ordinary annuity is a series of equal payments made at the end of equal intervals of time, with compound interest on the payments. The present value of an ordinary annuity is the present value of a series of payments. Calculations of present values are simplified by using the appropriate tables, which appear in an appendix to this book.

Apply the present value concept to simple valuation situations. LO5

Present value is commonly used in determining fair value and may be used in determining the value of an asset, in computing the present value of deferred payments, and in establishing a fund for loan repayment. Present value can also be applied to numerous other accounting situations in which time is a factor.

Use ratio analysis to manage the impact of current liabilities' impact on liquidity. LO6

Current liabilities are an important consideration in managing a company's liquidity and cash flows. Key measures of liquidity are working capital, payables turnover, and days' payable.

Key Terms and Ratios

accounts payable 444 (LO2)
accrued liabilities 446 (LO2)
cash dividends 446 (LO2)
commercial paper 445 (LO2)
commitment 457 (LO3)
compound interest 458 (LO4)
contingent liability 456 (LO3)
current liabilities 442 (LO1)
definitely determinable liabilities 444 (LO2)
employee 448 (LO2)
estimated liabilities 452 (LO2)
future value 458 (LO4)
independent contractor 448 (LO2)
interest 458 (LO4)
line of credit 443 (LO1)
long-term liabilities 442 (LO1)
ordinary annuity 461 (LO4)
present value 459 (LO4)
promissory notes 444 (LO2)
salaries 447 (LO2)
short-term notes payable 444 (LO2)
simple interest 458 (LO4)
time value of money 458 (LO4)
unearned revenues 450 (LO2)
wages 447 (LO2)

RATIOS
days' payable 466 (LO6)
payables turnover 465 (LO6)

Chapter Assignments

DISCUSSION QUESTIONS

LO 1, 2 **DQ1. CONCEPT ▶** James Williams, a star college basketball player, received a contract from the Midwest Blazers to play professional basketball. The contract calls for a salary of $420,000 a year for four years, dependent on his making the team in each of those years. Should this contract be considered a liability and recorded on the books of the basketball team? Why or why not?

LO 1, 3 **DQ2. CONCEPT ▶** When would a commitment be recognized in the accounting records?

LO 2 **DQ3.** Do adjusting entries involving estimated liabilities and accruals ever affect cash flows?

LO 4 **DQ4.** Is a friend who borrows money from you for three years and agrees to pay you interest after each year paying you simple or compound interest?

LO 4 **DQ5.** Ordinary annuities assume that the first payment is made at the end of each year. In a transaction, who is better off in this arrangement, the payer or the receiver? Why?

LO 4, 5 **DQ6.** Why is present value one of the most useful concepts in making business decisions?

LO 6 **DQ7. BUSINESS APPLICATION ▶** Is increasing payables turnover good or bad for a company? Why or why not?

SHORT EXERCISES

LO 1, 6 **Issues in Accounting for Liabilities**

SE1. CONCEPT ▶ Indicate whether each of the following actions relates to (a) managing liquidity and cash flow, (b) recognition of liabilities, (c) valuation of liabilities, (d) classification of liabilities, or (e) disclosure of liabilities:

1. Determining that a liability will be paid in less than one year.
2. Estimating the amount of a liability.
3. Providing information about when liabilities are due and their interest rates.
4. Determining when a liability arises.
5. Assessing working capital and payables turnover.

LO 2 **Interest Expense on Note Payable**

SE2. On the last day of August, Broadway Company borrowed $120,000 on a bank note for 60 days at 10 percent interest. Assume that interest is stated separately. Prepare the following journal entries: (1) August 31, recording of note; and (2) October 30, payment of note plus interest. (Round to the nearest cent.)

LO 2 **Payroll Expenses**

SE3. The following payroll totals for the month of April are from the payroll register of Myth Corporation: salaries, $446,000; federal income taxes withheld, $62,880; Social Security tax withheld, $27,652; Medicare tax withheld, $6,467; medical insurance deductions, $13,160; and salaries subject to unemployment taxes, $313,200.

Determine the total and components of (1) the monthly payroll and (2) employer payroll expenses, assuming Social Security and Medicare taxes equal to the amounts for employees, a federal unemployment insurance tax of 0.8 percent, a state unemployment tax of 5.4 percent, and medical insurance premiums for which the employer pays 80 percent of the cost.

LO 2 **Product Warranty Liability**

SE4. Maiden Corp. manufactures and sells travel clocks. Each clock costs $12.50 to produce and sells for $25. In addition, each clock carries a warranty that provides for free replacement if it fails during the two years following the sale. In the past, 5 percent of the clocks sold have had to be replaced under the warranty. During October, Maiden sold 52,000 clocks, and 2,800 clocks were replaced under the warranty. Prepare journal entries to record the estimated liability for product warranties during the month and the clocks replaced under warranty during the month.

LO 2, 3 **Types of Liabilities**

SE5. Indicate whether each of the following is (a) a definitely determinable liability, (b) an estimated liability, (c) a commitment, or (d) a contingent liability:

1. Dividends payable
2. Pending litigation
3. Income taxes payable
4. Current portion of long-term debt
5. Vacation pay liability
6. Guaranteed loans of another company
7. Purchase agreement

LO 4 **Simple and Compound Interest**

SE6. Maruti Motors, Inc., receives a one-year note that carries a 12 percent annual interest rate on $3,000 for the sale of a used car. Compute the maturity value under each of the following assumptions: (1) Simple interest is charged. (2) The interest is compounded semiannually. (3) The interest is compounded quarterly. (Round to the nearest cent.)

LO 4 **Present Value Calculations**

SE7. Find the present value of (1) a single payment of $24,000 at 6 percent for 12 years, (2) 12 annual payments of $2,000 at 6 percent, (3) a single payment of $5,000 at 9 percent for five years, and (4) five annual payments of $5,000 at 9 percent. (*Hint:* Use Tables 1 and 2 in Appendix C.)

LO 4, 5

Valuing an Asset for the Purpose of Making a Purchasing Decision

SE8. ACCOUNTING CONNECTION ▶ Luke Ricci owns a machine shop and has the opportunity to purchase a new machine for $60,000. After carefully studying projected costs and revenues, Ricci estimates that the new machine will produce a net cash flow of $14,400 annually and will last for eight years. Ricci believes that an interest rate of 10 percent is adequate for his business.

Calculate the present value of the machine to Ricci. Does the purchase appear to be a smart business decision? Why? (*Hint:* Use Table 2 in Appendix C.)

LO 6

Measuring Short-Term Liquidity

SE9. BUSINESS APPLICATION ▶ Luster Company has current assets of $130,000 and current liabilities of $80,000, of which accounts payable are $70,000. Luster's cost of goods sold is $460,000, its merchandise inventory increased by $20,000, and accounts payable were $50,000 the prior year. Calculate Luster's working capital, payables turnover, and days' payable. (Round to one decimal place.)

EXERCISES: SET A

LO 1, 6

Issues in Accounting for Liabilities

E1A. CONCEPT ▶ Indicate whether each of the following actions relates to (a) managing liquidity and cash flows, (b) recognition of liabilities, (c) valuation of liabilities, (d) classification of liabilities, or (e) disclosure of liabilities:

1. Providing information about financial instruments on the balance sheet.
2. Measuring working capital.
3. Setting a liability at the fair market value of goods to be delivered.
4. Relating the payment date of a liability to the length of the operating cycle.
5. Recording a liability in accordance with the accrual accounting.
6. Estimating the amount of "cents-off" coupons that will be redeemed.
7. Categorizing a liability as long-term debt.
8. Comparing days' payable with last year.

LO 2

Interest Expense on Note Payable

E2A. On the last day of October, Lake Company borrows $60,000 on a bank note for 60 days at 12 percent interest. Interest is not included in the face amount. Prepare the following journal entries: (1) October 31, recording of note; (2) November 30, accrual of interest expense (round to the nearest cent); and (3) December 30, payment of note plus interest.

LO 2

Sales and Excise Taxes

E3A. Lindstrom Design Services billed its customers a total of $245,100 for the month of August, including 9 percent federal excise tax and 5 percent sales tax.

1. Determine the proper amount of service revenue to report for the month.
2. Prepare a journal entry to record the revenue and related liabilities for the month.

LO 2

Payroll Expenses

E4A. At the end of October, the payroll register for Noir Tool Corporation contained the following totals: wages, $371,000; federal income taxes withheld, $94,884; state income taxes withheld, $15,636; Social Security tax withheld, $23,002; Medicare tax withheld, $5,379.50; medical insurance deductions, $12,870; and wages subject to unemployment taxes, $57,240.

(Continued)

Determine the total and components of the (1) monthly payroll and (2) employer payroll expenses, assuming Social Security and Medicare taxes equal to the amount for employees, a federal unemployment insurance tax of 0.8 percent, a state unemployment tax of 5.4 percent, and medical insurance premiums for which the employer pays 80 percent of the cost.

LO 2

Product Warranty Liability

E5A. Boulware Company manufactures and sells electronic games. Each game costs $25 to produce, sells for $45, and carries a warranty that provides for free replacement if it fails during the two years following the sale. In the past, 7 percent of the games sold had to be replaced under the warranty. During July, Boulware sold 13,000 games, and 1,400 games were replaced under the warranty.

1. Prepare a journal entry to record the estimated liability for product warranties during the month.
2. Prepare a journal entry to record the games replaced under warranty during the month.

LO 2

Vacation Pay Liability

E6A. Funz Corporation gives three weeks' paid vacation to each employee who has worked at the company for one year. Based on studies of employee turnover and previous experience, management estimates that 65 percent of the employees will qualify for vacation pay this year.

1. Assume that Funz's July payroll is $300,000, of which $20,000 is paid to employees on vacation. Figure the estimated employee vacation benefit for the month. (Round to the nearest thousandth.)
2. Prepare a journal entry to record the employee benefit for July.
3. Prepare a journal entry to record the pay to employees on vacation.

LO 3

Contingencies and Commitments

E7A. Indicate whether each of the following related to an airline company relates to (a) contingency or (b) commitment:

1. The company has agreed to purchase 10 new airplanes over the next three years.
2. The company has a lawsuit pending against it.

LO 4

Determining an Advance Payment

E8A. Katie Davis is contemplating paying five years' rent in advance. Her annual rent is $12,600. Calculate the single sum that would have to be paid now for the advance rent. Assume compound interest of 8 percent. (*Hint:* Use Table 2 in Appendix C.)

LO 4

Present Value Calculations

E9A. Find the present value of (1) a single payment of $12,000 at 6 percent for 12 years, (2) 12 annual payments of $1,000 at 6 percent, (3) a single payment of $2,500 at 9 percent for five years, and (4) 5 annual payments of $2,500 at 9 percent. (*Hint:* Use Tables 1 and 2 in Appendix C.)

LO 4

Present Value of a Lump-Sum Contract

E10A. A contract calls for a lump-sum payment of $30,000. Find the present value of the contract, assuming that (1) the payment is due in five years and the current interest rate is 9 percent; (2) the payment is due in ten years and the current interest rate is 9 percent; (3) the payment is due in five years and the current interest rate is 5 percent; and (4) the payment is due in ten years and the current interest rate is 5 percent. (*Hint:* Use Table 1 in Appendix C.)

LO 4, 5

Present Value of an Annuity Contract

E11A. A contract calls for annual payments of $2,400. Find the present value of the contract, assuming that (1) the number of payments is 7 and the current interest rate is 6 percent; (2) the number of payments is 14 and the current interest rate is 6 percent; (3) the number of payments is 7 and the current interest rate is 8 percent; and (4) the number of payments is 14 and the current interest rate is 8 percent. (*Hint:* Use Table 2 in Appendix C.)

LO 4, 5

Valuing an Asset for the Purpose of Making a Purchasing Decision

E12A. ACCOUNTING CONNECTION ▶ Sid Patel owns a service station and has the opportunity to purchase a car-wash machine for $15,000. After carefully studying projected costs and revenues, Patel estimates that the car-wash machine will produce a net cash flow of $2,600 annually and will last for eight years. He determines that an interest rate of 14 percent is adequate for his business. Calculate the present value of the machine to Patel. (*Hint:* Use Table 2 in Appendix C.) Does the purchase appear to be a smart business decision? Why?

LO 4, 5

Deferred Payment

E13A. Alligood Equipment Corporation sold a precision tool machine with computer controls to Kaui Corporation for $400,000 on January 2 and agreed to take payment nine months later on October 2. Assuming that the prevailing annual interest rate for such a transaction is 16 percent compounded quarterly, what is the actual sale (purchase) price of the machine tool? (*Hint:* Use Table 1 in Appendix C.)

LO 4, 5

Negotiating the Sale of a Business

E14A. Knight Enterprises, Inc., is attempting to sell the business to Bosh Corporation. The company has assets of $1,800,000, liabilities of $1,600,000, and stockholders' equity of $200,000. Both parties agree that the proper rate of return to expect is 12 percent; however, they differ on other assumptions. Knight believes that the business will generate at least $200,000 per year of cash flows for 20 years. Bosh thinks that $160,000 in cash flows per year is more reasonable and that only 10 years in the future should be considered. Determine the range for negotiation by computing the present value of Knight's offer to sell and of Bosh's offer to buy. (*Hint:* Use Table 2 in Appendix C.)

LO 6

Measuring Short-Term Liquidity

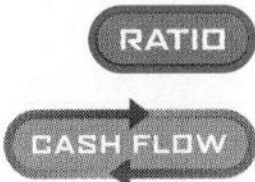

E15A. BUSINESS APPLICATION ▶ In 2013, Copia Company had current assets of $155,000 and current liabilities of $100,000, of which accounts payable were $65,000. Cost of goods sold was $425,000, merchandise inventory increased by $40,000, and accounts payable were $55,000 in the prior year. In 2014, Copia had current assets of $210,000 and current liabilities of $160,000, of which accounts payable were $75,000. Cost of goods sold was $475,000, and merchandise inventory decreased by $15,000. Calculate Copia's working capital, payables turnover, and days' payable for 2013 and 2014. Assess Copia's liquidity and cash flows in relation to the change in payables turnover from 2013 to 2014. (Round to one decimal place.)

EXERCISES: SET B

Visit the textbook companion website at www.cengagebrain.com to access Exercise Set B for this chapter.

PROBLEMS

LO 1, 2, 3

Identification of Current Liabilities, Contingencies, and Commitments

P1. Common types of current liabilities, contingencies, and commitments follow.

a. Accounts payable
b. Bank loans and commercial paper
c. Notes payable
d. Dividends payable
e. Sales and excise taxes payable
f. Current portion of long-term debt
g. Payroll liabilities
h. Unearned revenues
i. Income taxes payable
j. Property taxes payable
k. Promotional costs
l. Product warranty liability
m. Vacation pay liability
n. Contingent liability
o. Commitment

REQUIRED

1. For each of the following statements, identify the type of current liability, contingency, or commitment to which it gives rise or with which it is most closely associated:
    1. A company agrees to replace parts of a product if they fail.
    2. An employee earns one day off for each month worked.
    3. A company signs a contract to lease a building for five years.
    4. A company puts discount coupons in the newspaper.
    5. A company agrees to pay insurance costs for employees.
    6. A portion of a mortgage on a building is due this year.
    7. The board of directors declares a dividend.
    8. A company has trade payables.
    9. A company has a pending lawsuit against it.
    10. A company arranges for a line of credit.
    11. A company signs a note due in 60 days.
    12. A company operates in a state that has a sales tax.
    13. A company earns a profit that is taxable.
    14. A company owns buildings that are subject to property taxes.
2. **ACCOUNTING CONNECTION ▶** Of the items listed from **a** to **o**, which ones would you not expect to see listed on the balance sheet with a dollar amount? Of those items that would be listed on the balance sheet with a dollar amount, which ones would you consider to involve the most judgment or discretion on the part of management?

LO 2

Notes Payable and Wages Payable

✔ 1: Part A: December 31 Interest Expense: $426.08
✔ 2: Part B: October 31 Payroll Taxes and Benefits Expense: $23,444.88

P2. Part A: Blue Blaze Company, whose fiscal year ends December 31, completed the following transactions involving notes payable:

2013		
Nov.	25	Purchased a new loading cart by issuing a 60-day 10 percent note for $43,200.
Dec.	31	Made the end-of-year adjusting entry to accrue interest expense. (Round to the nearest cent.)
2014		
Jan.	24	Paid off the loading cart note. (Round to the nearest cent.)

REQUIRED

1. Prepare journal entries for Blue Blaze's notes payable transactions.
2. **ACCOUNTING CONNECTION ▶** When notes payable appears on the balance sheet, what other current liability would you look for to be associated with the notes? What would it mean if this other current liability did not appear?

Part B: At the end of October, the payroll register for Blue Blaze Company contained the following totals: wages, $92,750; federal income taxes withheld, $23,721; state income taxes withheld, $3,909; Social Security tax withheld, $5,751; Medicare tax withheld, $1,345; medical insurance deductions, $3,200; and wages subject to unemployment taxes, $57,240.

REQUIRED

Prepare journal entries to record the (1) monthly payroll and (2) employer payroll expenses, assuming Social Security and Medicare taxes equal to the amount for employees, a federal unemployment insurance tax of 0.8 percent, a state unemployment tax of 5.4 percent, and medical insurance premiums for which the employer pays 80 percent of the cost.

LO **2**

✔ 2: End of month estimated product warranty liability: $168,160

Product Warranty Liability

P3. Reliance Company manufactures and sells wireless video cell phones, which it guarantees for five years. If a cell phone fails, it is replaced free, but the customer is charged a service fee for handling. In the past, management has found that only 3 percent of the cell phones sold required replacement under the warranty. The average cell phone costs the company $240. At the beginning of September, the account for estimated liability for product warranties had a credit balance of $208,000. During September, 250 cell phones were returned under the warranty. The company collected $9,860 of service fees for handling. During the month, the company sold 2,800 cell phones.

REQUIRED

1. Prepare journal entries to record (a) the cost of cell phones replaced under warranty and (b) the estimated liability for product warranties for cell phones sold during the month.
2. Compute the balance of the Estimated Product Warranty Liability account at the end of the month.
3. **ACCOUNTING CONNECTION** ▶ If the company's product warranty liability is underestimated, what are the effects on current and future years' income?

LO **2, 6**

✔ 1: Total current liabilities: $20,152.10

Identification and Evaluation of Current Liabilities

P4. Stan Styka opened a small dryer repair shop, Styka Repair Shop, on January 2, 2014. The shop also sells a limited number of dryer parts. In January 2015, Styka realized he had never filed any tax reports for his business and therefore probably owes a considerable amount of taxes. Since he has limited experience in running a business, he has brought you all his business records, including a checkbook, canceled checks, deposit slips, suppliers' invoices, a notice of annual property taxes of $2,310 due to the city, and a promissory note to his father-in-law for $2,500. He wants you to determine what his business owes the government and other parties (but not employees).

You analyze all his records and determine the following as of December 31, 2014:

Unpaid invoices for dryer parts	$ 9,000
Parts sales (excluding sales tax)	44,270
Cost of parts sold	31,125
Workers' salaries	18,200
Repair revenues	60,300
Current assets	16,300
Dryer parts inventory	11,750

You learn that the company has deducted $476 from the two employees' salaries for federal income taxes owed to the government. The current Social Security tax is 6.2 percent on maximum earnings of $110,100 for each employee, and the current Medicare tax is 1.45 percent (no maximum earnings). The FUTA tax is 5.4 percent to the state and .8 percent to the federal government on the first $7,000 earned by each employee, and each employee earned more than $7,000. Styka has not filed a sales tax report to the state (5 percent of sales).

(Continued)

REQUIRED

1. Determine Styka Repair Shop's current liabilities as of December 31, 2014.
2. **ACCOUNTING CONNECTION ▶** What additional information would you want from Styka to satisfy yourself that all current liabilities have been identified?
3. **BUSINESS APPLICATION ▶** Evaluate Styka's liquidity by calculating working capital, payables turnover, and days' payable. (Round to one decimal place.) Comment on the results. (Assume average accounts payable were the same as year-end accounts payable.)

LO **4, 5**

Applications of Present Value

SPREADSHEET

✔ 1a: Present value of liability: $187,750
✔ 1b: Cost of buyout: $79,250

P5. Austin Corporation's management took the following actions, which went into effect on January 2, 2014. Each action involved an application of present value.

a. Austin Corporation enters into a purchase agreement that calls for a payment of $250,000 three years from now.
b. Bought out the contract of a member of top management for a payment of $25,000 per year for four years beginning January 2, 2015.

REQUIRED

1. Assuming an annual interest rate of 10 percent and using Tables 1 and 2 in Appendix C, answer the following questions:
   a. In action **a**, what is the present value of the liability for the purchase agreement?
   b. In action **b**, what is the cost (present value) of the buyout?
2. **ACCOUNTING CONNECTION ▶** Many businesses analyze present value extensively when making decisions about investing in long-term assets. Why is this type of analysis particularly appropriate for such decisions?

ALTERNATE PROBLEMS

LO **1, 2, 3**

Identification of Current Liabilities, Contingencies, and Commitments

P6. Common types of current liabilities, contingencies, and commitments follow.

a. Accounts payable
b. Bank loans and commercial paper
c. Notes payable
d. Dividends payable
e. Sales and excise taxes payable
f. Current portion of long-term debt
g. Payroll liabilities
h. Unearned revenues
i. Income taxes payable
j. Property taxes payable
k. Promotional costs
l. Product warranty liability
m. Vacation pay liability
n. Contingent liability
o. Commitment

REQUIRED

1. For each of the following statements, identify the type of current liability, contingency, or commitment to which it gives rise or with which it is most closely associated:
   1. The board of directors declares a dividend.
   2. A company signs a note due in 60 days.
   3. A company has a pending lawsuit against it.
   4. A company signs a contract to lease a building for five years.
   5. A company arranges for a line of credit.
   6. A company agrees to pay insurance costs for employees.
   7. A portion of a mortgage on a building is due this year.
   8. A company agrees to replace parts of a product if they fail.
   9. A company has trade payables.
   10. A company operates in a state that has a sales tax.
   11. A company puts discount coupons in the newspaper.
   12. A company earns a profit that is taxable.

13. A company owns buildings that are subject to property taxes.
14. An employee earns one day off for each month worked.

2. **ACCOUNTING CONNECTION ▶** Of the items listed from **a** to **o**, which ones would you not expect to see listed on the balance sheet with a dollar amount? Of those items that would be listed on the balance sheet with a dollar amount, which ones would you consider to involve the most judgment or discretion on the part of management?

LO 2

SPREADSHEET

GENERAL LEDGER

✔ 1: Part A: June 30 Interest Expense: $552.33
✔ 2: Part B: July 31 Payroll Taxes and Benefits Expense: $70,334.64

Notes Payable and Wages Payable

P7. Part A: Candlelight Corporation, whose fiscal year ended June 30, 2014, completed the following transactions involving notes payable:

May 21	Obtained a 60-day extension on an $36,000 trade account payable owed to a supplier by signing a 60-day $36,000 note. Interest is in addition to the face value, at the rate of 14 percent.
June 30	Made the end-of-year adjusting entry to accrue interest expense. (Round to the nearest cent.)
July 20	Paid off the note plus interest due the supplier. (Round to the nearest cent.)

REQUIRED

1. Prepare journal entries for the notes payable transactions.
2. **ACCOUNTING CONNECTION ▶** When notes payable appears on the balance sheet, what other current liability would you look for to be associated with the notes? What would it mean if this other current liability did not appear?

Part B: The payroll register for Candlelight Corporation contained the following totals at the end of July: wages, $278,250; federal income taxes withheld, $71,163; state income taxes withheld, $11,727; Social Security tax withheld, $17,253; Medicare tax withheld, $4,035; medical insurance deductions, $9,600; and wages subject to unemployment taxes, $171,720.

REQUIRED

Prepare journal entries to record the (1) monthly payroll and (2) employer payroll expenses, assuming Social Security and Medicare taxes equal to the amount for employees, a federal unemployment insurance tax of 0.8 percent, a state unemployment tax of 5.4 percent, and medical insurance premiums for which the employer pays 80 percent of the cost.

LO 2

GENERAL LEDGER

✔ 2: End of the month estimated product warranty liability: $21,870

Product Warranty Liability

P8. Treetech Company is engaged in the retail sale of high-definition televisions (HDTVs). Each HDTV has a 24-month warranty on parts. If a repair under warranty is required, a charge for the labor is made. Management has found that 20 percent of the HDTVs sold require some work before the warranty expires. Furthermore, the average cost of replacement parts has been $120 per repair. At the beginning of January, the account for the estimated liability for product warranties had a credit balance of $28,600. During January, 112 HDTVs were returned under the warranty. The cost of the parts used in repairing the HDTVs was $17,530, and $18,884 was collected as service revenue for the labor involved. During January, the month before the Super Bowl, Treetech sold 450 new HDTVs.

REQUIRED

1. Prepare journal entries to record each of the following: (a) the warranty work completed during the month, including related revenue; (b) the estimated liability for product warranties for HDTVs sold during the month.
2. Compute the balance of the Estimated Product Warranty Liability account at the end of the month.
3. **ACCOUNTING CONNECTION ▶** If the company's product warranty liability is overestimated, what are the effects on current and future years' income?

LO 1

Identification and Evaluation of Current Liabilities

✔ 1: Total current liabilities: $36,988.20

P9. Daisy Luna opened a small motorcycle repair shop, Luna Cycle Repair, on January 2, 2014. The shop also sells a limited number of motorcycle parts. In January 2015, Luna realized she had never filed any tax reports for her business and therefore probably owes a considerable amount of taxes. Since she has limited experience in running a business, she has brought you all her business records, including a checkbook, canceled checks, deposit slips, suppliers' invoices, a notice of annual property taxes of $4,620 due to the city, and a promissory note to her father-in-law for $5,000. She wants you to determine what her business owes the government and other parties (but not employees).

You analyze all her records and determine the following as of December 31, 2014:

Unpaid invoices for motorcycle parts	$ 18,000
Parts sales (excluding sales tax)	88,540
Cost of parts sold	62,250
Workers' salaries	20,400
Repair revenues	120,600
Current assets	32,600
Motorcycle parts inventory	23,500

You learn that the company has deducted $952 from the two employees' salaries for federal income taxes owed to the government. The current Social Security tax is 6.2 percent on maximum earnings of $110,100 for each employee, and the current Medicare tax is 1.45 percent (no maximum earnings). The FUTA tax is 5.4 percent to the state and 0.8 percent to the federal government on the first $7,000 earned by each employee, and each employee earned more than $7,000. Luna has not filed a sales tax report to the state (5 percent of sales).

REQUIRED

1. Determine Luna Cycle Repair's current liabilities as of December 31, 2014.
2. **ACCOUNTING CONNECTION ▶** What additional information would you want from Luna to satisfy yourself that all current liabilities have been identified?
3. **BUSINESS APPLICATION ▶** Evaluate Luna's liquidity by calculating working capital, payables turnover, and days' payable. (Round to one decimal place.) Comment on the results. (Assume average accounts payable were the same as year-end accounts payable.)

LO **4, 5**

Applications of Present Value

SPREADSHEET

✔ 1a: Present value of initial deposit: $110,250
✔ 1b: Purchase price: $393,300

P10. Lisette, Inc.'s management took the following actions that went into effect on January 2, 2014. Each action involved an application of present value.

a. Asked for another fund to be established by a single payment to accumulate to $150,000 in four years.
b. Approved the purchase of a parcel of land for future plant expansion. Payments are to start January 2, 2014, at $100,000 per year for five years.

REQUIRED

1. Assuming an annual interest rate of 8 percent and using Tables 1 and 2 in Appendix C, answer the following questions:
   a. In action **a**, how much will need to be deposited initially to accumulate the desired amount?
   b. In action **b**, what is the purchase price (present value) of the land?
2. **ACCOUNTING CONNECTION ▶** What is the fundamental reason present value analysis is a useful tool in making business decisions?

CASES

LO 2

Conceptual Understanding: Frequent Flyer Plan

C1. CONCEPT ▶ JetFly Airways instituted a frequent flyer program in which passengers accumulate points toward a free flight based on the number of miles they fly on the airline. One point was awarded for each mile flown, and a minimum of 750 miles was awarded for any one flight. Because of competition in 2014, the company began a bonus plan in which passengers receive triple the normal mileage points. In the past, about 1.5 percent of passenger miles were flown by passengers who had converted points to free flights; with the triple mileage program, JetFly expects that the rate will increase to 2.5 percent.

During 2014, the company had passenger revenues of $966.3 million and passenger transportation operating expenses of $802.8 million before depreciation and amortization. Operating income was $86.1 million. What is the appropriate rate to use to estimate free miles? What effect would the estimated liability for free travel by frequent flyers have on 2014 net income? Describe several ways to estimate the amount of this liability. Be prepared to discuss the arguments for and against recognizing this liability.

LO 3

Conceptual Understanding: Lawsuits and Contingent Liabilities

C2. CONCEPT ▶ When faced with lawsuits, many companies recognize a loss and therefore credit a liability or reserve account for any future losses that may result. For instance, in the famous **WorldCom** case, **Citibank**, one of the world's largest financial services firms, announced it was setting up reserves or liabilities of $5.6 billion because of pending lawsuits due to its relationship with WorldCom.[15] Were these pending lawsuits contingent liabilities? According to the FASB, what conditions must exist before a liability related to a pending lawsuit can be entered in the accounting records?

LO 4, 5

Conceptual Understanding: Present Value

C3. In its "Year-End Countdown Sale," a local car dealer advertised "0% interest for 60 months!"[16] What role does the time value of money play in this promotion? Assuming that the car dealer is able to borrow funds at 8 percent interest, what is the cost to the dealer of every customer who takes advantage of this offer? If you could borrow money to buy a car from this dealer, which rate would be more relevant in determining how much you might offer for the car: the rate at which you borrow money, or the rate at which the dealer borrows money?

LO 6

Interpreting Financial Reports: Comparison of Two Companies' Ratios with Industry Ratios

C4. BUSINESS APPLICATION ▶ Both **Oracle Corporation** and **Cisco Systems** are in the computer industry. The data that follows (in millions) are from the end of their fiscal years 2011.[17]

	Oracle	Cisco
Accounts payable	$ 701	$ 876
Cost of goods sold	8,398	16,682
Increase (decrease) in inventory	(28)	(147)

Compare the payables turnover and days' payable for both companies. How are cash flows affected by days' payable? How do Oracle's and Cisco Systems' ratios compare with the computer industry ratios shown in the chapter? (Use year-end amounts for ratios and round to one decimal place.)

LO 1, 3

Annual Report Case: Commitments and Contingencies

C5. CONCEPT ▶ Read **CVS**'s note on commitments and contingencies in the Supplement to Chapter 1. What commitments and contingencies does the company have? Why is it important to consider this information when analyzing accounts payable? What two conditions have to be met to record commitments and contingencies as liabilities on the balance sheet?

LO 6

Comparison Case: Payables Analysis

C6. BUSINESS APPLICATION ▶ Refer to **CVS**'s financial statements in the Supplement to Chapter 1 and to the following data for **Walgreens** (amounts in millions):

	2011	2010	2009
Cost of goods sold	$51,692	$48,444	$45,722
Accounts payable	4,810	4,585	4,308
Increase (decrease) in merchandise inventory	(592)	(307)	533

Compute the payables turnover and days' payable for CVS and Walgreens in 2010 and 2011. (Round to one decimal place.) In 2009, CVS had accounts payable of $3,560 million, and in 2010, its merchandise inventory decreased by $352. Which company do you think made the most use of financing from creditors during the operating cycle? Did the trend change?

LO 2

Ethical Dilemma: Known Legal Violations

C7. Surf and Turf is a large restaurant in the suburbs of Chicago. Ronald Swift, an accounting student at a nearby college, recently secured a full-time accounting job there. He felt fortunate to have a good job that accommodated his class schedule. After a few weeks on the job, Swift realized that his boss, the owner of the business, was paying the kitchen workers in cash and not withholding federal and state income taxes or social security and Medicare taxes. Swift knows that federal and state laws require these taxes to be withheld and paid to the appropriate agency in a timely manner. He also realizes that if he raises this issue, he could lose his job. What alternatives are available to Swift? What action would you take if you were in his position? Why did you make this choice?

LO 4, 5

Business Communication: Baseball Contract

C8. Devon Turner, who has been playing shortstop for the St. Louis Titans for five years, made the All-Star team in 2014. He has three years left on a contract that pays him $2.4 million a year. He wants to renegotiate his contract because other players with records similar to his are receiving as much as $10.5 million per year for five years.

Titans' management has a policy of never renegotiating a current contract but is willing to consider extending Turner's contract to additional years. In fact, the Titans have offered Turner an additional three years at $6.0 million, $9.0 million, and $12.0 million, respectively. They have also added an option year at $15.0 million. Management points out that this package is worth $42.0 million, or $10.5 million per year on average. Turner is considering this offer and is also thinking of asking for a bonus if and when he signs the contract.

Write a memorandum to Turner that comments on management's position and evaluates the offer, assuming a current interest rate of 10 percent. (*Hint*: Use present values.) Propose a range for the signing bonus. Finally, include other considerations that may affect the value of the offer.

Continuing Case: Annual Report Project

C9. BUSINESS APPLICATION ▶ Using the most recent annual report of the company you have chosen to study and that you have accessed online at the company's website, identify on the balance sheet the current liabilities that are definitely determinable and those that are probably estimates. Also, calculate the following for the most recent two years:

1. Working capital
2. Payables turnover
3. Days' payable

CHAPTER 11

LEARNING OBJECTIVES

LO 1 Explain the concepts underlying long-term liabilities, and identify the types of long-term liabilities.

LO 2 Describe the features of a bond issue and the major characteristics of bonds.

LO 3 Record bonds issued at face value and at a discount or premium.

LO 4 Use present values to determine the value of bonds.

LO 5 Amortize bond discounts and bond premiums using the straight-line and effective interest methods.

LO 6 Account for the retirement of bonds and the conversion of bonds into stock.

LO 7 Record bonds issued between interest dates, and record year-end adjustments.

LO 8 Explain and demonstrate the accounting issues related to leases and pensions.

LO 9 Evaluate the decision to issue long-term debt, including analyzing long-term debt.

Kim Karpeles/Alamy

LONG-TERM LIABILITIES

Business Insight
McDonald's

McDonald's, the world's largest restaurant chain, passed a milestone in 2004 when it earned more revenues in Europe than in the United States. To finance its continued global expansion, the company raises funds by issuing both debt and capital stock. As you can see in its Financial Highlights, McDonald's relies heavily on debt financing. In 2011, its total long-term liabilities were 105 percent of total stockholders' equity, and its total current and long-term liabilities amounted to over 129 percent of stockholders' equity. The company's long-term debt includes bonds and notes payable. Among its other long-term obligations are numerous leases on real estate and employee pension and health plans.[1]

MCDONALD'S FINANCIAL HIGHLIGHTS (in millions)

	2011	**2010**
Total current liabilities	$ 3,509.2	$ 2,924.7
Long-term debt	$12,133.8	$11,497.0
Other long-term liabilities	1,612.6	1,586.9
Deferred income taxes	1,344.1	1,332.4
Total long-term liabilities	$15,090.5	$14,416.3
Total stockholders' equity	$14,390.2	$14,634.2
Total liabilities and stockholders' equity	$32,989.9	$31,975.2

1. **CONCEPT** ▶ *How do the concepts of recognition, valuation, classification, and disclosure apply to long-term liabilities?*

2. **ACCOUNTING APPLICATION** ▶ *How are long-term bonds accounted for in the company's records?*

3. **BUSINESS APPLICATION** ▶ *What should McDonald's consider in deciding whether to issue long-term debt?*

SECTION 1 CONCEPTS

CONCEPTS
- Recognition
- Valuation
- Classification
- Disclosure

RELEVANT LEARNING OBJECTIVE

LO 1 Explain the concepts underlying long-term liabilities, and identify the types of long-term liabilities.

LO 1 Concepts Underlying Long-Term Liabilities

Profitable operations and short-term credit seldom provide sufficient funds for a growing business. Growth usually requires investments in long-term assets, research and development, and other activities to expand the business. To finance these assets and activities, the company needs funds that will be available for longer periods. Capital contributed by stockholders is one source of long-term funds. Long-term liabilities are another source. **Long-term liabilities** are debts and obligations that a company expects to satisfy in more than one year or beyond its normal operating cycle, whichever is longer. Managers must understand how long-term liabilities should be *recognized*, *valued*, *classified*, and *disclosed*.

Recognition

Generally accepted accounting principles require that long-term liabilities be *recognized* and recorded when an obligation occurs even though the obligation may not be due for many years. Some long-term liabilities, such as a note payable due in five years, are easy to identify, but others, such as promises to pay employees pensions after they retire, are more difficult. Nevertheless, recognition of long-term liabilities is important because managers and stockholders need to know how much a company is obligated to pay in the future.

Valuation

On the balance sheet, long-term liabilities are generally *valued* at the amount of money needed to pay the debt or at the fair market value of the goods or services to be delivered. The amount of most liabilities is definitely known (as with notes payable). Other long-term liabilities require judgment and estimates about conditions in the future (as with pension obligations).

Classification

In contrast to current liabilities, a liability is *classified* as long-term when it is due beyond one year or beyond the normal operating cycle. The distinction between current and long-term liabilities affects the evaluation of a company's liquidity. For example, when a portion of a long-term liability becomes due in the next year and will be paid out of current assets, it should be classified as a current liability. The investor or creditor can then see what current obligations will need to be paid soon.

Disclosure

Because of the complex nature of many long-term liabilities, extensive *disclosures* in the notes to the financial statements are often required. For example, the disclosures for long-term notes should include the balances, maturity dates, interest rates, and other features of the debts. Any special credit arrangements should also be disclosed. When estimates and judgments are involved, as with pension liabilities, these should also be disclosed.

Types of Long-Term Debt

To structure long-term financing to the best advantage of their companies, managers must know the characteristics of the various types of long-term debt. Long-term debt includes bonds payable, notes payable, mortgages, and other more complex obligations.

Bonds Payable Long-term **bonds payable** are the most common type of long-term debt. They can have many different characteristics, including the amount of interest, whether the company can elect to repay them before their maturity date, and whether they can be converted to common stock. We cover bonds in detail in later sections of this chapter.

Notes Payable Long-term **notes payable**, those that come due in more than one year, are also very common. They differ from bonds mainly in the way the contract with the creditor is structured. A long-term note is a promissory note that represents a loan from a bank or other creditor, whereas a bond is a more complex financial instrument that usually involves debt to many creditors. Analysts often do not distinguish between long-term notes and bonds because they have similar effects on the financial statements.

Mortgages Payable A **mortgage** is a long-term debt secured by real property. It is usually paid in equal monthly installments. Each monthly payment includes interest on the debt and a reduction in the debt. Exhibit 1 shows the first three monthly payments on a $100,000, 9 percent mortgage.

Exhibit 1
Monthly Payment Schedule on a $100,000, 9 Percent Mortgage

	A	B	C	D	E
Payment Date	Unpaid Balance at Beginning of Period	Monthly Payment	Interest for 1 Month at ¾% on Unpaid Balance* (¾% × A)	Reduction in Debt (B – C)	Unpaid Balance at End of Period (A – D)
June 1					$100,000
July 1	$100,000	$1,200	$750	$450	99,550
August 1	99,550	1,200	747	453	99,097
September 1	99,097	1,200	743	457	98,640

*Rounded

Mortgages Payable

Transaction The mortgage was obtained on June 1, and the monthly payments are $1,200.

Analysis The journal entry to record the July 1 mortgage payment

▼ *decreases* the *Mortgage Payable* account with a debit of $450

▲ *increases* the *Mortgage Interest Expense* account with a debit of $750

▼ *decreases* the *Cash* account with a credit of $1,200

Application of Double Entry

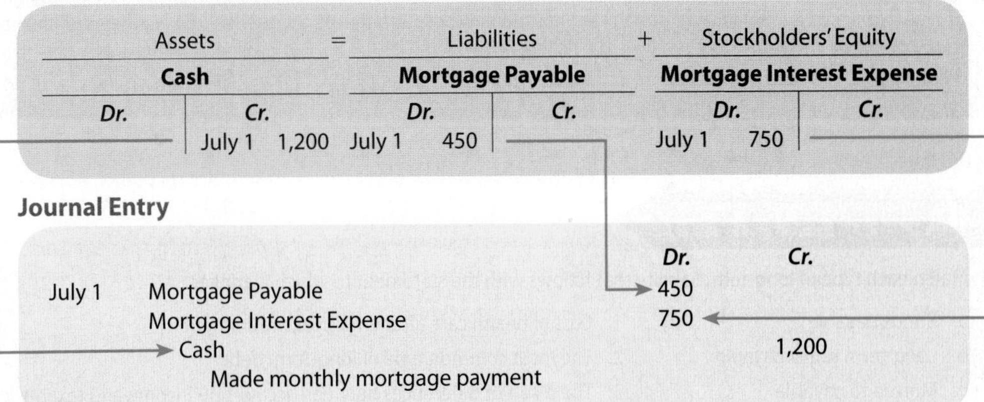

A	=	L	+	SE
−1,200		−450		−750

Comment Notice from the entry and from Exhibit 1 that the July 1 payment represents the following:

- Interest expense: $\$100,000 \times 0.09 \times 1/12 = \$750$
- Reduction in debt: $\$1,200 - \$750 = \$450$

Therefore, the July payment reduces the unpaid balance to $99,550. August's interest expense is slightly less than July's because of the decrease in the debt.

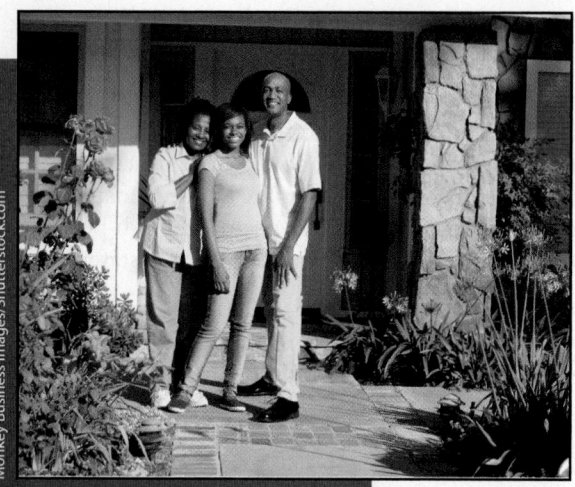

A mortgage is a type of long-term debt that is secured by real property. Most mortgages are paid in equal monthly installments.

Other Long-Term Obligations Other common long-term obligations consist of the following:

- **Long-term leases:** When a long-term lease has a term that corresponds closely to the life of the asset and, thus, is more like a purchase of an asset than a shorter-term lease, it is called a **capital lease**. In this case, a long-term asset with a corresponding long-term liability is *recognized* on the balance sheet. Long-term leases are covered in more detail later in the chapter.
- **Pension liabilities:** A liability arises from a contract that requires a company to make payments to its employees after they retire. Pension obligations are covered in more detail later in the chapter.
- **Other post-retirement benefits:** A liability arises from a contract that requires a company to provide medical and other benefits to its employees after they retire. *Recognition* and *valuation* of the liability requires estimates and assumptions about retirement age, mortality, and, most significantly, future trends in health care benefits.
- **Deferred income taxes:** A common long-term liability on the balance sheets of many companies, **deferred income taxes** are the result of using different accounting methods to calculate income taxes on the income statement and income tax liability on the income tax return. For instance, companies often use straight-line depreciation for financial reporting and an accelerated method to calculate income tax liability. Because straight-line depreciation is less than accelerated depreciation in the early years of an asset's life, the assumption is that the income taxes will eventually have to be paid. Thus, the difference is listed as deferred income taxes. Because companies try to manage their affairs to minimize income taxes paid, deferred income taxes can become quite large. For example, **Southwest Airlines** has deferred income taxes of about $2.6 billion or almost 23 percent of its total liabilities.[2]

Business Perspective

Post-Retirement Liabilities Affect Everyone

The rule requiring *recognition* of unfunded pension plans as liabilities impacts even government entities. Most government entities have defined benefit pension plans and provide post-retirement medical benefits. As a result, states, school districts, and municipalities are all encountering previously ignored pension and health care liabilities. For example, the state of New Jersey actually stopped setting aside funds to pay for health care in order to give a tax cut. No one added up the cost until the new accounting rule required it. The estimated cost to provide the health care promised to New Jersey's current and future retirees was $58 billion, or twice the state's annual budget.[3] These cases, while extreme, are not unusual, especially in light of the decrease in government tax collections during the recent recession. Citizens across the country will face tax increases to pay for these liabilities.

APPLY IT!

Match each type of long-term liability that follows with the statement to which it applies.

a. Bonds payable	1. Cost of health care after employees' retirement
b. Long-term notes payable	2. The most common type of long-term debt
c. Mortgage payable	3. The result of differences between accounting income and taxable income
d. Long-term lease	4. Debt that is secured by real estate
e. Pension liabilities	5. Promissory note that is due in more than one year
f. Other post-retirement benefits	6. Company requirement to make payments to its employees after they retire
g. Deferred income taxes	7. Often similar in form to purchasing a long-term asset

SOLUTION

1. f, 2. a, 3. g, 4. c, 5. b, 6. e, 7. d

TRY IT! SE1, SE2, E1A, E1B

SECTION 2

ACCOUNTING APPLICATIONS

OUNTING
LICATIONS

ecord bonds issued at
ace value, at a discount,
nd at a premium
alue bonds
mortize bond discounts
nd bond premiums
ecord the retirement of
onds
ecord the conversion of
onds into stock
ecord bonds issued
etween interest dates
ecord year-end
djustments
ccount for leases
ccount for pensions

LEVANT
ARNING OBJECTIVES

2 Describe the features of a bond issue and the jor characteristics of bonds.

3 Record bonds issued at face value and at a count or premium.

4 Use present values to determine the value of nds.

5 Amortize bond discounts and bond emiums using the straight-e and effective interest ethods.

6 Account for the retirement of bonds and e conversion of bonds into ck.

7 Record bonds issued between interest dates, d record year-end iustments.

8 Explain and demonstrate the counting issues related to ses and pensions.

LO2 The Nature of Bonds

A **bond** is a security, usually long term, representing money that a corporation borrows from the investing public. (The federal, state, and local governments also issue bonds to raise money, as do foreign countries.) A bond entails a promise to repay the amount borrowed, called the *principal,* on a specified date and to pay interest at a specified rate at specified times—usually semiannually. In contrast to stockholders, who are the owners of a corporation, bondholders are a corporation's creditors.

When a public corporation decides to issue bonds, it must submit the appropriate legal documents to the Securities and Exchange Commission (SEC) for permission to borrow the funds. The SEC reviews the corporation's financial health and the specific terms of the **bond indenture**, which is a contract that defines the rights, privileges, and limitations of the bondholders. The bond indenture generally describes such things as:

- the maturity date of the bonds
- interest payment dates
- the interest rate

It may also cover repayment plans and restrictions.

Once the bond issue is approved, the corporation has a limited time in which to issue the authorized bonds. As evidence of its debt to the bondholders, the corporation provides each of them with a **bond certificate**.

Bond Issue: Prices and Interest Rates

A **bond issue** is the total value of bonds issued at one time. For example, a $1,000,000 bond issue could consist of one thousand $1,000 bonds. The prices of bonds are stated in terms of a percentage of the face value, or principal, of the bonds. A bond issue quoted at 103½ means that a $1,000 bond costs $1,035 ($1,000 × 1.035). When a bond sells at exactly 100, it is said to sell at **face value** (or *par value*). When it sells below 100, it is said to sell at a *discount*; above 100, at a *premium*. For instance, a $1,000 bond quoted at 87.62 would be selling at a discount and would cost the buyer $876.20.

Face Interest Rate and Market Interest Rate Two interest rates relevant to bond prices are the face interest rate and the market interest rate.

- The **face interest rate** is the fixed rate of interest paid to bondholders based on the face value of the bonds. To allow time to file with the SEC, publicize the bond issue, and print the bond certificates, a company must decide in advance what the face interest rate will be. Most companies try to set the face interest rate as close as possible to the market interest rate.
- The **market interest rate** (or *effective interest rate*) is the rate of interest paid in the market on bonds of similar risk.* The market interest rate fluctuates daily. Because a company has no control over it, the market interest rate often differs from the face interest rate on the issue date.

Discounts and Premiums If the market interest rate fluctuates from the face interest rate before the issue date, the issue price will not equal the bonds' face value.

* At the time this chapter was written, the market interest rates on corporate bonds were volatile. Therefore, we use a variety of interest rates in our examples.

STUDY NOTE: *A bond sells at face value when the face interest rate of the bond is identical to the market interest rate for similar bonds on the date of issue. When the face interest and the market interest rates are different, a discount or premium arises.*

This fluctuation in market interest rate causes the bonds to sell at either a discount or a premium.

- A **discount** equals the excess of the face value over the issue price. The issue price will be less than the face value when the market interest rate is higher than the face interest rate.
- A **premium** equals the excess of the issue price over the face value. The issue price will be more than the face value when the market interest rate is lower than the face interest rate.

Discounts or premiums are contra-accounts that are subtracted from or added to bonds payable on the balance sheet.

Characteristics of Bonds

A bond indenture can be written to fit an organization's financing needs. As a result, the bonds issued in today's financial markets have many different features. We describe several of the more important features in the following paragraphs.

Unsecured and Secured Bonds Bonds can be either unsecured or secured.

STUDY NOTE: *Do not confuse the terms* indenture *and* debenture. *An indenture is a bond contract, whereas a debenture is an unsecured bond. A debenture bond of a stable company actually might be a less risky investment than a secured bond of an unstable company.*

- **Unsecured bonds** (or *debenture bonds*) are issued on the basis of a corporation's general credit.
- **Secured bonds** carry a pledge of certain corporate assets as a guarantee of repayment. A pledged asset may be a specific asset, such as a truck, or a general category of asset, such as property, plant, and equipment.

Term and Serial Bonds When all the bonds of an issue mature at the same time, they are called **term bonds**. For instance, a company may decide to issue $1,000,000 worth of bonds, all due 20 years from the date of issue.

STUDY NOTE: *An advantage of issuing serial bonds is that the organization retires the bonds over a period of years, rather than all at once.*

When the bonds of an issue mature on different dates, they are called **serial bonds**. For example, suppose that a $1,000,000 bond issue calls for paying $200,000 of the principal every five years. This arrangement means that after the issuing company makes the first $200,000 payment, $800,000 of the bonds would remain outstanding for the next five years, $600,000 for the next five years, and so on. A company may issue serial bonds to ease the task of paying off what it owes on the bonds.

Callable and Convertible Bonds When bonds are callable and convertible, a company may be able to retire them before their maturity dates. When a company does retire a bond issue before its maturity date, it is called **early extinguishment of debt**. Doing so can be to a company's advantage.

Callable bonds give the issuer the right to buy back and retire the bonds before maturity at a specified **call price**, which is usually above face value. Callable bonds give a company flexibility in financing its operations. For example, if bond interest rates drop, the company can call the bonds and reissue debt at a lower interest rate. A company might also call its bonds if it has earned enough to pay off the debt, if the reason for having the debt no longer exists, or if it wants to restructure its debt to equity ratio. The bond indenture states the time period and the prices at which the bonds can be redeemed.

Convertible bonds allow the bondholder to exchange a bond for a specified number of shares of common stock. The face value of a convertible bond when issued is greater than the market value of the shares to which it can be converted. However, if the market price of the common stock rises above a certain level, the value of the bond rises in relation to the value of the common stock. Even if the stock price does not rise, the investor still holds the bond and receives both the periodic interest payments and the face value at the maturity date.

One advantage of issuing convertible bonds is that the interest rate is usually lower because investors are willing to give up some current interest in the hope that the value of the stock will increase and the value of the bonds will, therefore, also increase. In addition, if the bonds are both callable and convertible and the market value of the stock rises to a level at which the bond is worth more than face value, management can avoid repaying the bonds by calling them for redemption, thereby forcing the bondholders to convert their bonds into common stock. The bondholders will agree to convert because no gain or loss results from the transaction.

Registered and Coupon Bonds **Registered bonds** are issued in the names of the bondholders. The issuing organization keeps a record of the bondholders' names and addresses and pays them interest by check. Most bonds today are registered.

Coupon bonds are not registered with the organization. Instead, they bear coupons stating the amount of interest due and the payment date. The bondholder removes the coupons from the bonds on the interest payment dates and presents them at a bank for collection.

APPLY IT!

Match each term that follows with the term that could be an alternate (or sometimes opposite) term.

a. Face interest rate	1. Secured
b. Discount	2. Coupon
c. Unsecured	3. Convertible
d. Term	4. Premium
e. Registered	5. Market interest rate
f. Callable	6. Serial

SOLUTION

1. c, 2. e, 3. f, 4. b, 5. a, 6. d

TRY IT! SE3, E2A, E2B

LO 3 Accounting for the Issuance of Bonds

When the board of directors decides to issue bonds, it is not necessary to make an entry to record the SEC's authorization of the bond issue. However, most companies *disclose* the authorization in the notes to their financial statements. The note lists the number and *value* of bonds authorized, the interest rate, the interest payment dates, and the life of the bonds.

If the face interest rate on the bonds issued equals the market interest rate, the bonds will sell at their face value. If the face rate is less than the market rate, the bonds will sell at a discount. If the face rate is greater than the market rate, the bonds will sell at a premium.

Bonds Issued at Face Value

Transaction Carrot Corporation issues $200,000 of 7 percent, five-year bonds on January 1, 2014, and sells them on the same date for their face value. The bond indenture states that interest is to be paid on January 1 and July 1 of each year.

Analysis The journal entry to record the issuance of the bonds at face value

▲ *increases* the *Cash* account with a debit

▲ *increases* the *Bonds Payable* account with a credit

Application of Double Entry

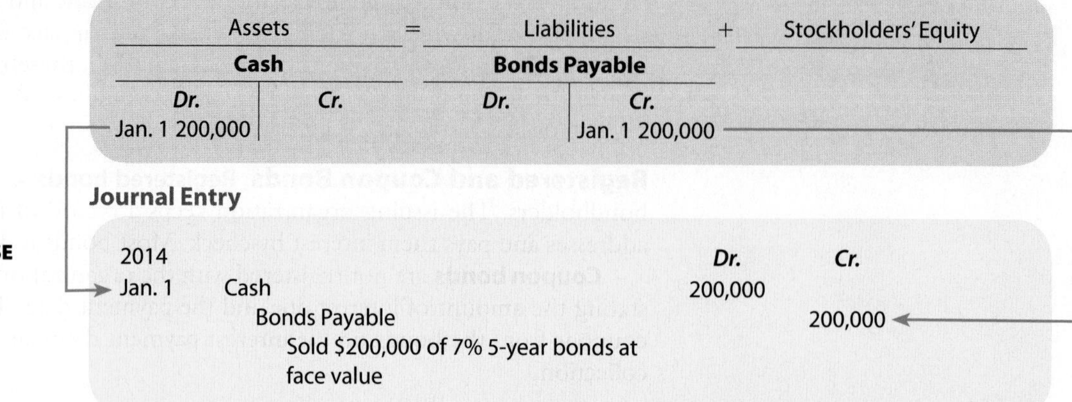

Journal Entry

A	=	L	+	SE
+200,000		+200,000		

2014		Dr.	Cr.
Jan. 1	Cash	200,000	
	Bonds Payable		200,000
	Sold $200,000 of 7% 5-year bonds at face value		

STUDY NOTE: *When calculating semiannual interest, multiply the annual rate by one-half year.*

Interest Expense Carrot pays interest on January 1 and July 1 of each year. Thus, Carrot would owe the bondholders $7,000 interest on July 1, 2014:

$$\text{Interest} = \text{Principal} \times \text{Rate} \times \text{Time}$$
$$= \$200{,}000 \times \frac{7}{100} \times 6/12 \text{ year}$$
$$= \$7{,}000$$

Analysis The journal entry to record the interest paid to the bondholders on each semiannual interest payment date (January 1 or July 1)

▲ *increases* the *Bond Interest Expense* account with a debit

▼ ▲ *decreases* the *Cash* account with a credit (or *increases* the *Interest Payable* account with a credit)

Application of Double Entry

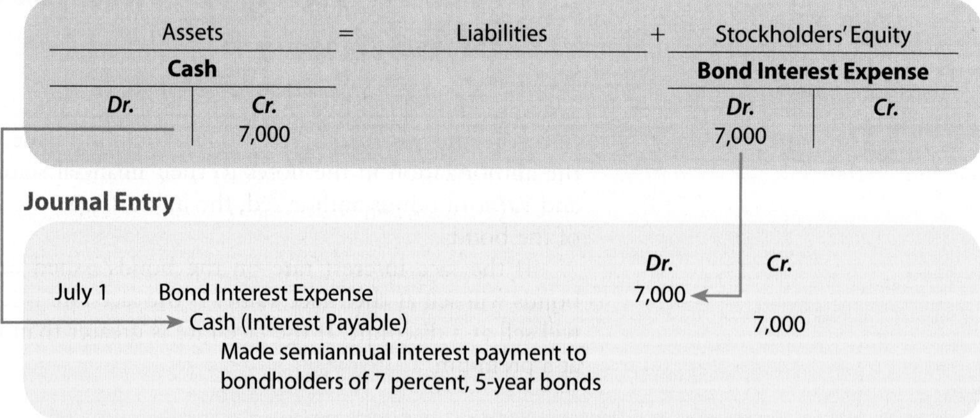

Journal Entry

A*	=	L	+	SE
−7,000				−7,000

*Assumes cash paid.

		Dr.	Cr.
July 1	Bond Interest Expense	7,000	
	Cash (Interest Payable)		7,000
	Made semiannual interest payment to bondholders of 7 percent, 5-year bonds		

Comment It is common for bond interest to be paid twice per year.

Bonds Issued at a Discount

Transaction Carrot issues $200,000 of 7 percent, five-year bonds at 95.9445 on January 1, 2014, when the market interest rate is 8 percent. In this case, the bonds are being issued at a discount because the market interest rate exceeds the face interest rate.

Analysis The entry to record the issuance of the bonds at a discount

- ▲ *increases* the *Cash* account with a debit for the amount of the bond issue less the discount
- ▲ *increases* the *Unamortized Bond Discount* account with a debit for the amount of discount
- ▲ *increases* the *Bonds Payable* account with a credit for the amount of the bond issued

Application of Double Entry

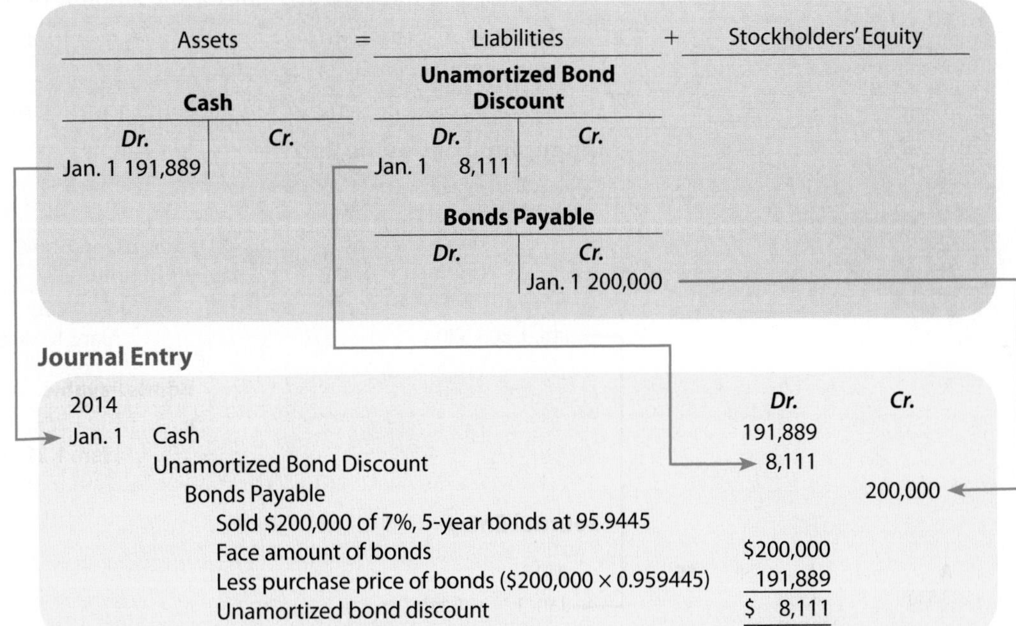

Journal Entry

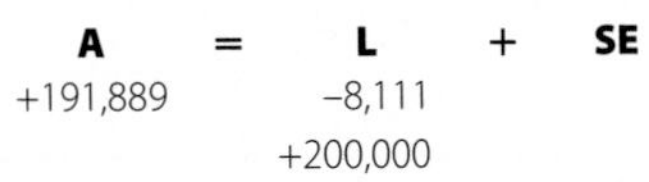

2014		Dr.	Cr.
Jan. 1	Cash	191,889	
	Unamortized Bond Discount	8,111	
	Bonds Payable		200,000
	Sold $200,000 of 7%, 5-year bonds at 95.9445		
	Face amount of bonds	$200,000	
	Less purchase price of bonds ($200,000 × 0.959445)	191,889	
	Unamortized bond discount	$ 8,111	

Comment If a balance sheet is prepared immediately after the bonds are issued at a discount, the liability for bonds payable is reported as follows.

Long-term liabilities		
7% bonds payable, due 1/1/2019	$200,000	
Less unamortized bond discount	8,111	$191,889

Unamortized Bond Discount is a contra-liability account. Its balance is deducted from the face amount of the bonds to arrive at the carrying value, or present value, of the bonds. The bond discount is described as unamortized because it will be amortized (written off) over the life of the bonds.

Business Perspective

100-Year Bonds Are Not for Everyone

With interest rates on long-term debt at historically low levels, some companies attempt to lock in those low costs for long periods. In 1993, in a classic example, **The Walt Disney Company** aggressively issued $150 million of 100-year bonds at a yield of only 7.5 percent. Among the others that followed Walt Disney's lead by issuing 100-year bonds were the **Coca-Cola Company, Columbia HCA Healthcare, Bell South, IBM**, and even the People's Republic of China. Some analysts wondered if even Mickey Mouse could survive 100 years. In fact, in 2012, interest rates had dropped so far that Disney is now paying more than the market rate of only 5.7 percent. Investors who purchased the bonds have had a gain because the bonds are now selling at a premium at $132.[4]

Bonds Issued at a Premium

Transaction Carrot issues $200,000 of 7 percent, five-year bonds for $208,530 on January 1, 2014, when the market interest rate is 6 percent. This means that investors will purchase the bonds at 104.265 percent of their face value. In this case, the bonds are being issued at a premium because the face interest rate exceeds the market rate for similar investments.

Analysis The journal entry to record the bond issuance at a premium

- ▲ *increases* the *Cash* account for the amount of the bond issue plus the premium
- ▲ *increases* the *Unamortized Bond Premium* account for the amount of the premium
- ▲ *increases* the *Bonds Payable* account for the amount of the bond issue

Application of Double Entry

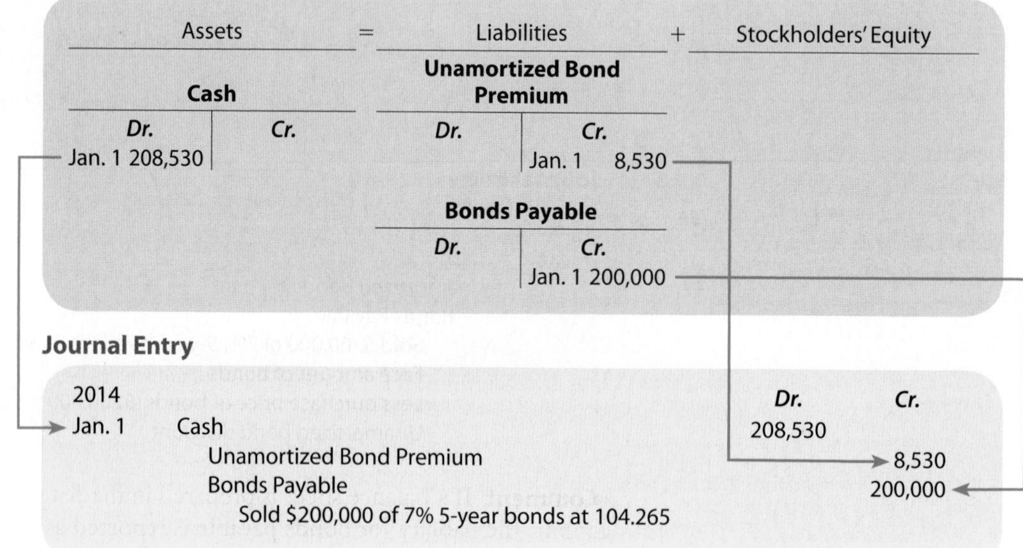

Journal Entry

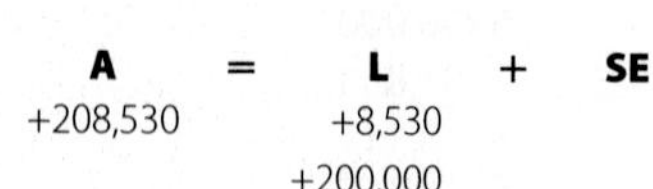

2014		Dr.	Cr.
Jan. 1	Cash	208,530	
	Unamortized Bond Premium		8,530
	Bonds Payable		200,000
	Sold $200,000 of 7% 5-year bonds at 104.265		

Comment Immediately after this entry is made, bonds payable would be presented on the balance sheet as follows.

Long-term liabilities		
7% bonds payable, due 1/1/2019	$200,000	
Plus unamortized bond premium	8,530	$208,530

STUDY NOTE: The carrying amount is always the face value of the bonds less the unamortized discount or plus the unamortized premium.

Here, the carrying value of the bonds payable is $208,530, which equals the face value of the bonds plus the unamortized bond premium. This means that the purchasers were willing to pay a premium of $8,530 to buy these bonds because their face interest rate was higher than the market interest rate.

Bond Issue Costs

The costs of issuing bonds can amount to as much as 5 percent of a bond issue. These costs often include the fees of underwriters, whom corporations hire to take care of the details of marketing a bond issue. Because the issue costs benefit the whole life of a bond issue, they are spread over that period. It is generally accepted practice to establish a separate account for these costs and to amortize them over the life of the bonds.

Because issue costs decrease the amount of money a company receives from a bond issue, they have the effect of raising the discount or lowering the premium on the issue. Thus, bond issue costs can be spread over the life of the bonds through the amortization of a discount or premium. This method simplifies recordkeeping. In the rest of our discussion, we assume that all bond issue costs increase the discounts or decrease the premiums on bond issues.

APPLY IT!

Nico Foods is planning to issue $1,000,000 in long-term bonds. Depending on market conditions, Nico's CPA advises that the bonds could be issued at (a) 99, (b) 100, or (b) 101. Calculate the amount that Nico would receive under each alternative. Indicate whether it is at face value, a discount or a premium, and the amount of discount or premium of each.

SOLUTION

(a) $1,000,000 × 0.99 = $990,000; a discount of $10,000

(b) $1,000,000 × 1.00 = $1,000,000; at face value; no discount or premium

(c) $1,000,000 × 1.01 = $1,010,000; a premium of $10,000

TRY IT! SE5, E6A, E6B

LO4 Using Present Value to Value a Bond

A bond's value is determined by summing the following two present value amounts, based on concepts presented previously in Chapter 11:

- a series of fixed interest payments
- a single payment at maturity

As noted, the amount of interest a bond pays is fixed over its life. The market interest rate, on the other hand, varies from day to day and is the rate used to determine the bond's present value. Thus, the amount investors are willing to pay for a bond varies because the bond's present value changes as the market interest rate changes. In the next sections, we show how to calculate the present value of a bond when the market rate is above the face value and when it is below the face value. Exhibit 2 illustrates both examples.

Exhibit 2
Using Present Value to Value a $20,000, 9 Percent, Five-Year Bond

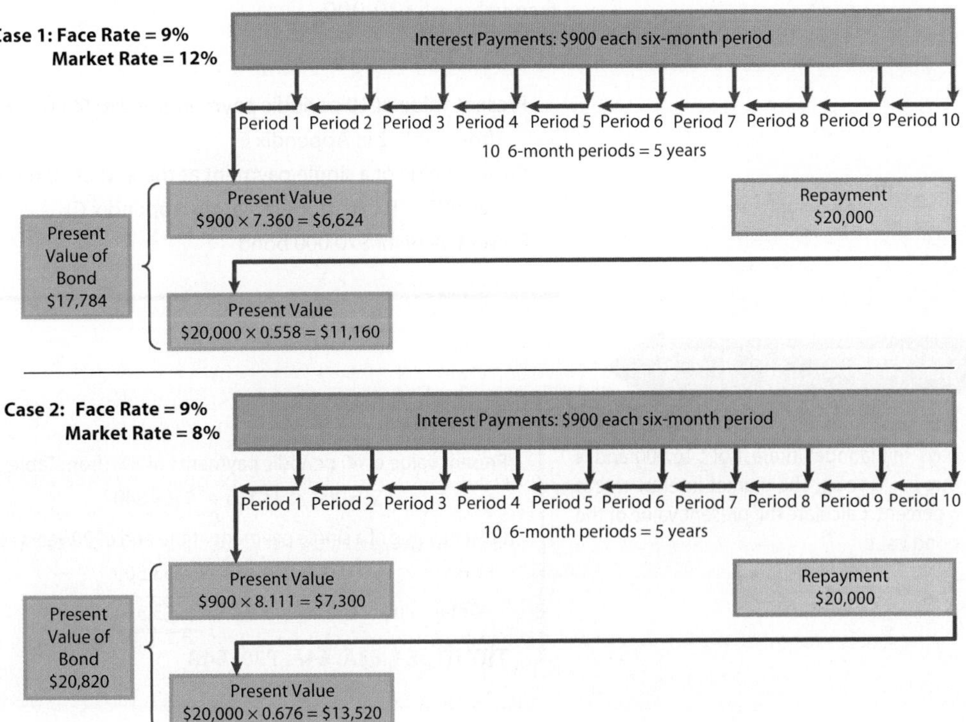

Market Rate Above Face Rate

Measure Calculate the present value of a bond when the market rate is above the face value.

Example A bond has a face value of $20,000 and pays fixed interest of $900 every six months (a 9 percent annual rate). The bond is due in five years. If the market interest rate today is 12 percent, what is the present value of the bond?

Table Computation Use Table 2 in Appendix C to calculate the present value of the periodic interest payments of $900, and use Table 1 in the same appendix to calculate the present value of the single payment of $20,000 at maturity. Because interest payments are made every six months, the compounding period is half a year. Thus, we have to convert the annual rate to a semiannual rate of 6 percent (12% ÷ 2 six-month periods per year) and use ten periods (5 years × 2 six-month periods per year). The present value of the bond is therefore computed as follows.

Present value of 10 periodic payments at 6%: $900 × 7.360 (from Table 2 Appendix C)	$ 6,624
Present value of a single payment at the end of 10 periods at 6%: $20,000 × 0.558 (from Table 1 in Appendix C)	11,160
Present value of $20,000 bond	$17,784

The market interest rate has increased so much since the bond was issued—from 9 percent to 12 percent—that the value of the bond today is only $17,784. That amount is all investors would be willing to pay at this time for a bond that provides income of $900 every six months and a return of the $20,000 principal in five years.

Market Rate Below Face Rate

Measure Calculate the present value of a bond when the market rate is below the face value.

Example Suppose the market interest rate on the bond described above falls to 8 percent (4 percent semiannually). The present value of the bond will be greater than the face value of $20,000.

Table Computation

Present value of 10 periodic payments at 4%: $900 × 8.111 (from Table 2 in Appendix C)	$ 7,300
Present value of a single payment at the end of 10 periods at 4%: $20,000 × 0.676 (from Table 2 in Appendix C)	13,520
Present value of $20,000 bond	$20,820

APPLY IT!

Romero Company's $500,000 bond issue pays semiannual interest of $16,000 and is due in 20 years. The market interest rate is 6 percent. Calculate the present value of the bond issue.

SOLUTION

Present value of 40 periodic payments of 3% (from Table 2 in Appendix C):

$16,000 × 23.115 = $369,840

Present value of a single payment at the end of 20 years (40 periods) at 3% (from Table 1 in Appendix C):

$500,000 × 0.307 = 153,500

Total value of the bond issue = $523,340

TRY IT! SE4, E3A, E4A, E3B, E4B

LO 5 Amortization of Bond Discounts and Premiums

To record interest expense properly and ensure that the carrying value of bonds payable at maturity equals face value, it is necessary to systematically reduce the bond discount or premium—that is, to *amortize* them—over the life of the bonds. This can be accomplished by using either the straight-line method or the effective interest method.

Amortizing a Bond Discount

In one of our earlier examples, Carrot Corporation issued $200,000 of five-year bonds at a time when the market interest rate of 8 percent exceeded the face interest rate of 7 percent. The bonds sold for $191,889, resulting in an unamortized bond discount of $8,111.

STUDY NOTE: *The carrying amount always approaches the face value over the life of the bond.*

Because it affects interest expense each year, the bond discount should be amortized over the life of the bond issue. In this way, the unamortized bond discount will decrease gradually over time, and the carrying value of the bond issue (face value less unamortized discount) will increase gradually. By the maturity date, the carrying value of the bond issue will equal its face value, and the unamortized bond discount will be zero.

STUDY NOTE: *A bond discount is a component of interest cost because it represents the amount in excess of the issue price that a corporation must pay on the maturity date.*

Calculating Total Interest Expense When a corporation issues bonds at a discount, the market (or effective) interest rate that it pays is greater than the face interest rate on the bonds. The reason is that the interest expense is the stated interest payments *plus* the amount of the bond discount. That is, although the company does not receive the full face value of the bonds on issue, it still must pay back the full face value at maturity. The difference between the issue price and the face value must be added to the total interest payments to arrive at the actual interest expense.

Interest Expense for Bond Issued at a Discount

To have each year's interest expense reflect the market interest rate, the discount must be allocated over the remaining life of the bonds as an increase in the interest expense each period. Thus, interest expense for each period will exceed the actual payment of interest by the amount of the bond discount amortized over the period. This process of allocation is called *amortization of the bond discount.*

The total expense to Carrot of issuing its $200,000 bonds at a discount is as follows.

Cash to be paid to bondholders	
Face value at maturity	$200,000
Interest payments ($200,000 × 0.07 × 5 years)	70,000
Total cash paid to bondholders	$270,000
Less cash received from bondholders	191,889
Total interest cost	$ 78,111

Or, alternatively:

Interest payments ($200,000 × 0.07 × 5 years)	$ 70,000
Bond discount	8,111
Total interest cost	$ 78,111

The total interest cost of $78,111 is made up of $70,000 in interest payments and the $8,111 bond discount. Thus, the bond discount *increases* the interest paid on the bonds from the face interest rate to the market interest rate. The market (or effective) interest rate is the real interest cost of the bond over its life.

STUDY NOTE: *The discount on a zero coupon bond represents the interest that will be paid (in its entirety) on the maturity date.*

Some bonds do not require periodic interest payments. These bonds, called **zero coupon bonds**, are simply a promise to pay a fixed amount at the maturity date. They are issued at a large discount because the only interest that the buyer earns or the issuer pays is the discount. For example, a five-year, $200,000 zero coupon bond issued when the market rate is 10 percent, compounded semiannually, would sell for only $122,800. That amount is the present value of a single payment of $200,000 at the end of five years. The discount of $77,200 ($200,000 − $122,800) is the total interest expense, which is amortized over the life of the bond.

Straight-Line Method The **straight-line method** equalizes amortization of a bond discount for each interest period in the life of the bonds.

Amortizing a Bond Discount Using the Straight-Line Method

Transaction Using the Carrot Corporation example, the interest payment dates of the bond issue are January 1 and July 1 of each year, and the bonds mature in five years.

Bond Discount Amortized and Interest Expense With the straight-line method, the amount of the bond discount amortized and the interest expense for each semiannual period are calculated in four steps.

Step 1: Determine the total number of interest payments.

$$\text{Total Interest Payments} = \text{Interest Payments per Year} \times \text{Life of Bonds}$$
$$= 2 \times 5 = 10$$

Step 2: Determine the amount of bond discount amortization per period.

$$\text{Amortization of Bond Discount per Interest Period} = \frac{\text{Bond Discount}}{\text{Total Interest Payments}}$$
$$= \frac{\$8{,}111}{10}$$
$$= \$811^*$$

* Rounded

Step 3: Determine the cash interest payment.

$$\text{Cash Interest Payment} = \text{Face Value} \times \text{Face Interest Rate} \times \text{Time}$$
$$= \$200{,}000 \times 0.07 \times 6/12 = \$7{,}000$$

Step 4: Determine the interest expense per period.

$$\text{Interest Expense per Interest Period} = \text{Interest Payment} + \text{Amortization of Bond Discount}$$
$$= \$7{,}000 + \$811 = \$7{,}811$$

Analysis The journal entry to record the bond discount amortized and interest expense

▲ *increases* the *Bond Interest Expense* account with a debit for the amount calculated in Step 4,

▼ *decreases* the *Unamortized Bond Discount* account with a credit for the amount calculated in Step 2, and

▼▲ *decreases* the *Cash* account (or *increases* the *Interest Payable* account with a credit) for the amount in Step 3.

Application of Double Entry

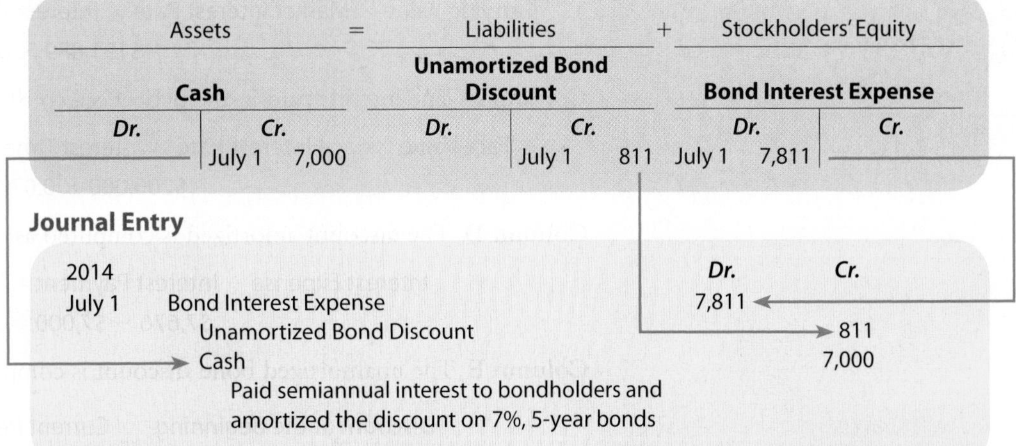

Journal Entry

A*	=	L	+	SE
−7,000		+811		−7,811

*Assumes cash paid.

		Dr.	Cr.
2014			
July 1	Bond Interest Expense	7,811	
	Unamortized Bond Discount		811
	Cash		7,000
	Paid semiannual interest to bondholders and amortized the discount on 7%, 5-year bonds		

Comment Notice that the bond interest expense is $7,811, but the amount paid to the bondholders is the $7,000 face interest payment. The difference of $811 is the credit to Unamortized Bond Discount. This lowers the debit balance of Unamortized Bond Discount and raises the carrying value of the bonds payable by $811 each interest period. If no changes occur in the bond issue, this entry will be made every six months during the life of the bonds. When the bond issue matures, the Unamortized Bond Discount account will have a zero balance, and the carrying value of the bonds will be $200,000—exactly equal to the amount due the bondholders.

Although the straight-line method has long been used, it has a certain weakness. When it is used to amortize a discount, the carrying value goes up each period, but the bond interest expense stays the same; thus, the rate of interest falls over time. Conversely, when this method is used to amortize a premium, the rate of interest rises over time. The Accounting Principles Board, therefore, holds that the straight-line method should be used only when it does not lead to a material difference from the effective interest method.[5] A *material difference* is one that affects the evaluation of a company.

Effective Interest Method When the **effective interest method** is used to compute the interest and amortization of a bond discount, a constant interest rate is applied to the carrying value of the bonds at the beginning of each interest period. This constant rate is the market rate (i.e., the effective rate) at the time the bonds were issued. The amount amortized each period is the difference between the interest computed by using the market rate and the actual interest paid to bondholders.

Amortizing a Bond Discount Using the Effective Interest Method

Transaction Use the same facts for Carrot that we used earlier—a $200,000 bond issue at 7 percent, with a five-year maturity and interest to be paid twice a year. The market rate at the time the bonds were issued was 8 percent, so the bonds sold for $191,889, a discount of $8,111. Exhibit 3 shows the interest and amortization of the bond discount.

Carrying Value, Interest Expense, Discount Amortized, and Discount Unamortized The amounts in Exhibit 3 for period 1 were computed as follows. (Amounts are rounded to the nearest dollar.)

Column A The carrying value of the bonds is computed as:

Face Value − Unamortized Discount = Carrying Value

$200,000 − $8,111 = $191,889

Column B The interest expense to be recorded is the effective interest, computed as:

$$\text{Carrying Value} \times \text{Market Interest Rate} \times \text{Interest Time Period} = \text{Interest Expense}$$
$$\$191{,}889 \times 0.08 \times 6/12 = \$7{,}676$$

Column C The interest paid in the period is a constant amount, computed as:

$$\text{Face Value} \times \text{Face Interest Rate} \times \text{Interest Time Period} = \text{Interest Payments}$$
$$\$200{,}000 \times 0.07 \times 6/12 = \$7{,}000$$

Column D The discount amortized is computed as:

$$\text{Interest Expense} - \text{Interest Payment} = \text{Amortized Discount}$$
$$\$7{,}676 - \$7{,}000 = \$676$$

Column E The unamortized bond discount is computed as:

$$\text{Discount at the Beginning of the Period} - \text{Current Period Amortization} = \text{Unamortized Discount}$$
$$\$8{,}111 - \$676 = \$7{,}435$$

The unamortized discount decreases in each interest payment period because it is amortized as a portion of interest expense.

Column F The carrying value of the bonds at the end of the period is computed as:

$$\text{Carrying Value at Beginning of Period} + \text{Amortization During Period} = \text{Carrying Value at End of Period}$$
$$\$191{,}889 + \$676 = \$192{,}565$$

***STUDY NOTE:** Whether a bond is sold at a discount or a premium, its carrying value will equal its face value on the maturity date.*

Notice that the sum of the carrying value and the unamortized discount (column F + column E) always equals the face value of the bonds (for example, $192,565 + $7,435 = $200,000).

Analysis The journal entry to record the bond discount amortized and interest expense is exactly like the one when the straight-line method is used. However, the amounts debited and credited to the various accounts are different. This journal entry

▲ *increases* the *Bond Interest Expense* account with a debit for the amount calculated in column B

▼ *decreases* the *Unamortized Bond Discount* account with a credit for the amount calculated in column D

▼▲ *decreases* the *Cash* account (or *increases* the *Interest Payable* account) with a credit for the amount in column C

Application of Double Entry

Assets	=	Liabilities	+	Stockholders' Equity
Cash		**Unamortized Bond Discount**		**Bond Interest Expense**
Dr. / Cr.		Dr. / Cr.		Dr. / Cr.
Cr.: July 1 7,000		Cr.: July 1 676		Dr.: July 1 7,676

Journal Entry

A*	=	L	+	SE
−7,000		+676		−7,676

*Assumes cash paid.

2014		Dr.	Cr.
July 1	Bond Interest Expense	7,676	
	Unamortized Bond Discount		676
	Cash		7,000
	Paid semiannual interest to bondholders and amortized the discount on 7%, 5-year bonds		

Comment Although an interest and amortization table is useful because it can be prepared in advance for all periods, it is not necessary to have one to determine the amortization of a discount for any one interest payment period. It is necessary only to multiply the carrying value by the effective interest rate and subtract the interest payment from the result. For example, the amount of discount to be amortized in the seventh interest payment period is $855, calculated as:

(Carrying Value × Interest Rate) − Interest Payment = Amortized Discount

($196,370 × 0.04) − $7,000 = $855

Exhibit 3
Interest and Amortization Table of a Bond Discount: Effective Interest Method

Semiannual Interest Period	A Carrying Value at Beginning of Period	B Semiannual Interest Expense at 8% to Be Recorded* (4% × A)	C Semiannual Interest Payment to Bondholders (3½% × $200,000)	D Amortization of Bond Discount (B − C)	E Unamortized Bond Discount at End of Period (E − D)	F Carrying Value at End of Period (A + D)
0					$8,111	$191,889
1	$191,889	$7,676	$7,000	$676	7,435	192,565
2	192,565	7,703	7,000	703	6,732	193,268
3	193,268	7,731	7,000	731	6,001	193,999
4	193,999	7,760	7,000	760	5,241	194,759
5	194,759	7,790	7,000	790	4,451	195,549
6	195,549	7,822	7,000	822	3,629	196,371
7	196,371	7,855	7,000	855	2,774	197,226
8	197,226	7,889	7,000	889	1,885	198,115
9	198,115	7,925	7,000	925	960	199,040
10	199,040	7,960**	7,000	960	—	200,000

* Rounded

** Last period's interest expense equals $7,960 ($7,000 + $960). It does not equal $7,962 ($199,040 × 0.04) because of the cumulative effect of rounding.

STUDY NOTE: *The bond interest increases each period because the carrying value of the bonds (the principal on which the interest is calculated) increases each period.*

Exhibit 4, which is based on the data in Exhibit 3, shows how the effective interest method affects the amortization of a bond discount. Notice that the carrying value at the beginning of Period 1 (the issue price) is initially less than the face value but that it gradually increases toward the face value over the life of the bond issue. Notice also that interest expense exceeds interest payments by the amount of the bond discount amortized. Interest expense increases gradually over the life of the bond because it is based on the gradually increasing carrying value (multiplied by the market interest rate).

Exhibit 4
Carrying Value and Interest Expense—Bonds Issued at a Discount

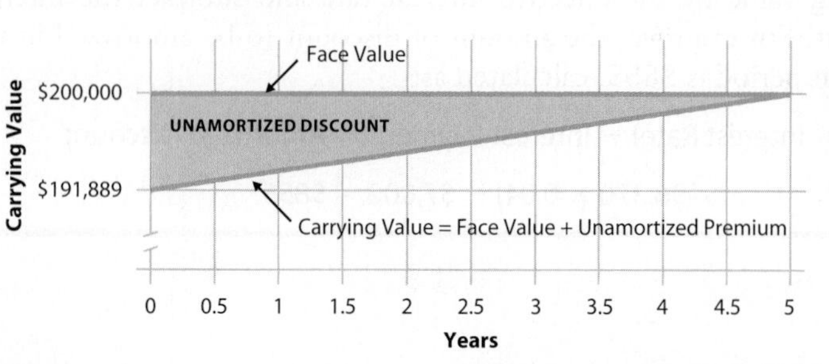

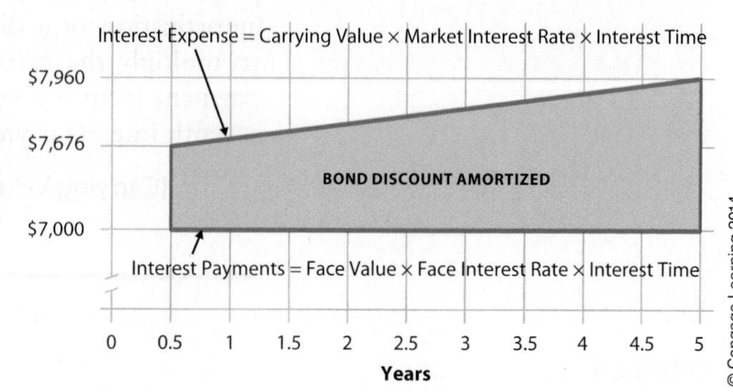

Amortizing a Bond Premium

STUDY NOTE: *The bond interest expense recorded is less than the amount of the interest paid because of the amortization of the bond premium. Accrual accounting dictates that the premium be amortized over the life of the bond.*

Like a discount, a bond premium must be amortized over the life of the bonds so that it can be matched to its effects on interest expense during that period. In the following sections, we calculate Carrot's total interest expense and amortize its bond premium using the straight-line and effective interest methods.

Calculation of Total Interest Expense When bondholders pay more than face value for the bonds, the premium represents an amount that they will not receive at maturity. The premium is in effect a reduction, in advance, of the total interest paid on the bonds over the life of the bond issue. The total interest expense over the issue's life needs to be determined.

STUDY NOTE: *A bond premium is deducted from interest payments in calculating total interest expense because a bond premium represents an amount over the face value of a bond that the corporation never has to return to bondholders. In effect, it reduces the higher-than-market interest the corporation is paying on the bond.*

Interest Expense for a Bond Issued at a Premium

In our earlier example of bonds issued at a premium, Carrot issued $200,000 of five-year bonds when the market interest rate was 6 percent and the face interest rate was 7 percent. The bonds sold for $208,530, which resulted in an unamortized bond premium of $8,530 ($208,530 − $200,000).

The total interest expense over the bond issue's life is computed as follows.

Cash to be paid to bondholders	
Face value at maturity	$200,000
Interest payments ($200,000 × 0.07 × 5 years)	70,000
Total cash paid to bondholders	$270,000
Less cash received from bondholders	208,530
Total interest expense	$ 61,470

Alternatively, the total interest expense can be computed as follows:

Interest payments ($200,000 × 0.07 × 5 years)	$ 70,000
Less bond premium	8,530
Total interest expense	$ 61,470

Notice that the total interest payments of $70,000 exceed the total interest expense of $61,470 by $8,530, the amount of the bond premium.

Straight-Line Method Under the straight-line method, the bond premium is spread evenly over the life of the bond issue.

Amortizing a Bond Premium Using the Straight-Line Method

Transaction When bonds are issued at a premium, interest expense will be less than the interest rate on the bonds due to the amortization of the premium.

Bond Premium Amortized and Interest Expense As with bond discounts, the amount of the bond premium amortized and the interest expense for each semiannual period are computed in four steps.

Step 1: Determine the number of interest payments.

$$\text{Total Interest Payments} = \text{Interest Payments per Year} \times \text{Life of Bonds}$$
$$= 2 \times 5 = 10$$

Step 2: Determine the amount of bond premium amortization per period.

$$\text{Amortization of Bond Premium per Interest Period} = \frac{\text{Bond Premium}}{\text{Total Interest Payments}}$$
$$= \frac{\$8,530}{10}$$
$$= \$853$$

Step 3: Determine the cash interest payment.

$$\text{Cash Interest Payment} = \text{Face Value} \times \text{Face Interest Rate} \times \text{Time}$$
$$= \$200,000 \times 0.07 \times 6/12 = \$7,000$$

Step 4: Determine the interest expense per period.

$$\text{Interest Expense per Interest Period} = \text{Interest Payment} - \text{Amortization of Bond Premium}$$
$$= \$7,000 - \$853 = \$6,147$$

Analysis The journal entry to record the bond premium amortized and interest expense

- ▲ *increases* the *Bond Interest Expense* account with a debit for the amount calculated in Step 4
- ▼ *decreases* the *Unamortized Bond Premium* account with a debit for the amount calculated in Step 2
- ▼▲ *decreases* the *Cash* account (or *increases* the *Interest Payable* account) with a credit for the amount in Step 3

Application of Double Entry

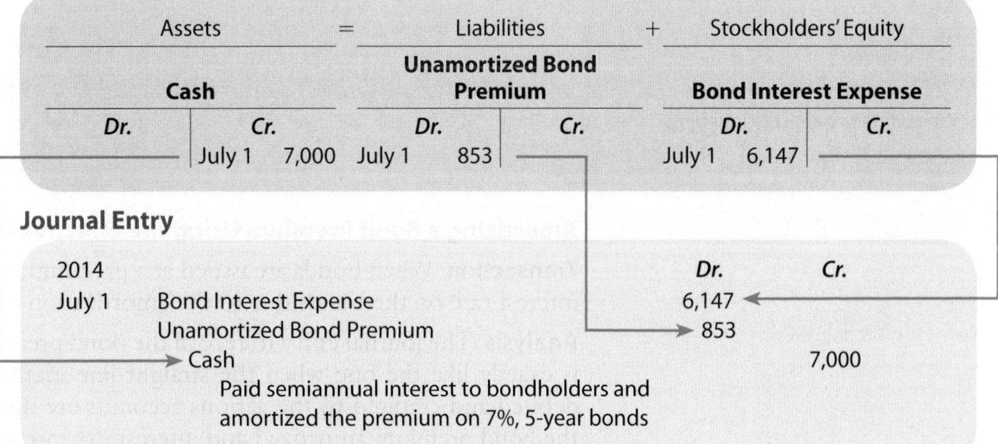

Assets	=	Liabilities	+	Stockholders' Equity
Cash		**Unamortized Bond Premium**		**Bond Interest Expense**
Dr. / Cr.		Dr. / Cr.		Dr. / Cr.
Cr.: July 1 7,000		Dr.: July 1 853		Dr.: July 1 6,147

Journal Entry

2014		Dr.	Cr.
July 1	Bond Interest Expense	6,147	
	Unamortized Bond Premium	853	
	Cash		7,000
	Paid semiannual interest to bondholders and amortized the premium on 7%, 5-year bonds		

A	=	L	+	SE
−7,000		−853		−6,147

STUDY NOTE: *The bond interest expense recorded exceeds the amount of interest paid because of the amortization of the bond discount. Accrual accounting dictates that the discount be amortized over the life of the bond.*

Comment Note that the bond interest expense is $6,147, but the amount that bondholders receive is the $7,000 face interest payment. The difference of $853 is the debit to Unamortized Bond Premium. This lowers the credit balance of the Unamortized Bond Premium account and the carrying value of the bonds payable by $853 each interest period. If the bond issue remains unchanged, the same entry will be made on every semiannual interest date over the life of the bond issue. When the bond issue matures, the balance in the Unamortized Bond Premium account will be zero, and the carrying value of the bonds payable will be $200,000—exactly equal to the amount due the bondholders.

Effective Interest Method Under the straight-line method, the effective interest rate changes constantly, because it is determined by comparing the fixed interest expense with a carrying value that changes as a result of amortizing the discount or premium. To apply a fixed interest rate over the life of the bonds based on the actual market rate at the time of the bond issue, one must use the effective interest method. With this method, the interest expense decreases slightly each period (see Exhibit 5, column B) because the amount of the bond premium amortized increases slightly (column D). This occurs because a fixed rate is applied each period to the gradually decreasing carrying value (column A).

Exhibit 5

Interest and Amortization Table of a Bond Premium: Effective Interest Method

	A	B	C	D	E	F
Semiannual Interest Period	Carrying Value at Beginning of Period	Semiannual Interest Expense at 6% to Be Recorded* (3% × A)	Semiannual Interest Payment to Bondholders (3½% × $200,000)	Amortization of Bond Premium (C – B)	Unamortized Bond Premium at End of Period (E – D)	Carrying Value at End of Period (A – D)
0					$8,530	$208,530
1	$208,530	$6,256	$7,000	$744	7,786	207,786
2	207,786	6,234	7,000	766	7,020	207,020
3	207,020	6,211	7,000	789	6,231	206,231
4	206,231	6,187	7,000	813	5,418	205,418
5	205,418	6,163	7,000	837	4,581	204,581
6	204,581	6,137	7,000	863	3,718	203,718
7	203,718	6,112	7,000	888	2,830	202,830
8	202,830	6,085	7,000	915	1,915	201,915
9	201,915	6,057	7,000	943	972	200,972
10	200,972	6,028**	7,000	972	—	200,000

* Rounded

** Last period's interest expense equals $6,028 ($7,000 – $972); it is actually equal to $6,029 ($200,972 × 0.03) but the difference is because of the cumulative effect of rounding.

Amortizing a Bond Premium Using the Effective Interest Method

Transaction When bonds are issued at a premium, interest expense will be less than the interest rate on the bonds due to the amortization of the premium.

Analysis The journal entry to record the bond premium amortized and interest expense is exactly like the one when the straight-line method is used. However, the amounts debited and credited to the various accounts are different. The journal entry to record the bond premium amortized and interest expense using the effective interest method

- ▲ *increases* the *Bond Interest Expense* account with a debit for the amount calculated in column B
- ▼ *decreases* the *Unamortized Bond Premium* account with a debit for the amount calculated in column D
- ▼▲ *decreases* the *Cash* account (or *increases* the *Interest Payable* account) with a credit for the amount in column C

Application of Double Entry

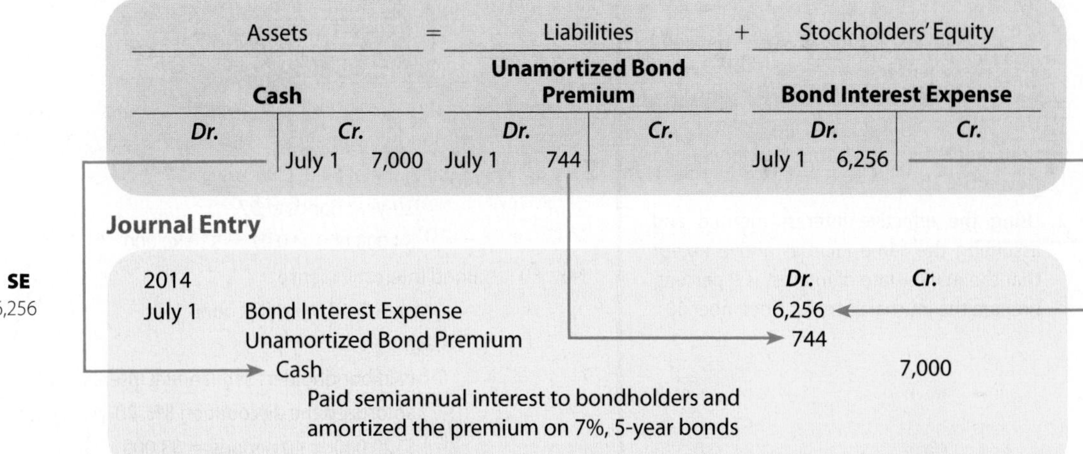

A	=	L	+	SE
–7,000		–744		–6,256

Comment Note that the unamortized bond premium (column E) decreases gradually to zero as the carrying value decreases to the face value (column F). To find the amount of premium amortized in any one interest payment period, subtract the effective interest expense (the carrying value times the effective interest rate, column B) from the interest payment (column C). In semiannual interest period 5, for example, the amortization of premium is $837, which is calculated as follows.

$$\text{Interest Payment} - (\text{Carrying Value} \times \text{Interest Rate}) = \text{Amortized Premium}$$

$$\$7{,}000 - (\$205{,}418 \times 0.03) = \$837$$

Exhibit 6, which is based on the data in Exhibit 5, shows how the effective interest method affects the amortization of a bond premium. Note that the carrying value at the beginning of Period 1 (issue price) is initially greater than the face value, but that it gradually decreases toward the face value over the bond issue's life. Also, the interest payments exceed interest expense by the amount of the premium amortized. Interest expense decreases gradually over the life of the bond because it is based on the gradually decreasing carrying value (multiplied by the market interest rate).

Exhibit 6
Carrying Value and Interest Expense—Bonds Issued at a Premium

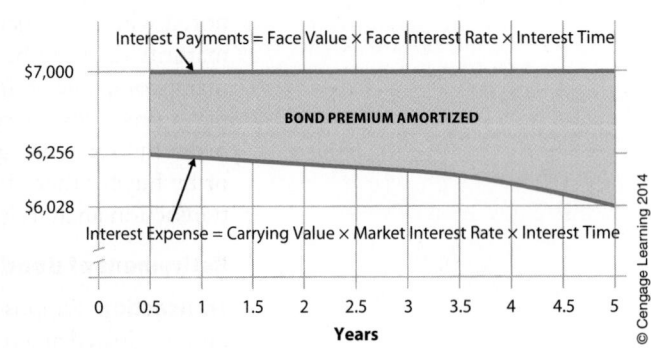

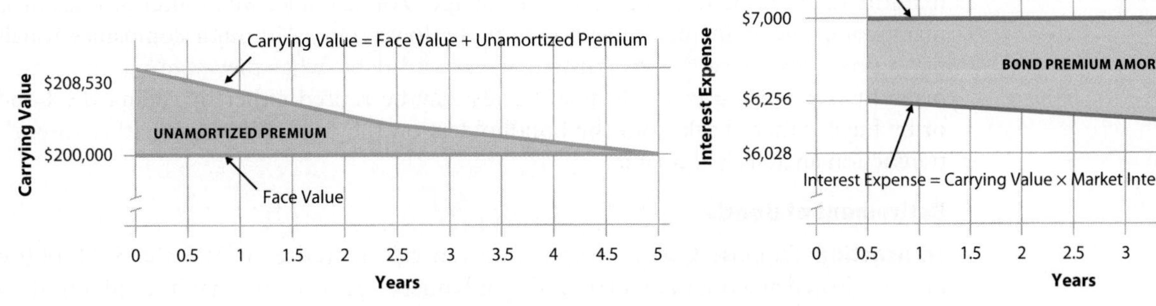

APPLY IT!

On June 1, Scott Corporation issues $4,000,000 of 8 percent, 20-year bonds at 97. Interest is payable semiannually, on May 31 and November 30. Scott's fiscal year ends on November 30.

1. Using the straight-line method of amortization, prepare journal entries for June 1 and November 30.
2. Using the effective interest method and assuming the same facts as above except that the market rate of interest is 9 percent, prepare the journal entry for November 30.

SOLUTION

1.

		Dr.	Cr.
June 1	Cash	3,880,000	
	Unamortized Bond Discount	120,000	
	Bonds Payable		4,000,000
	Issue of $4,000,000 of 8%, 20-year bonds at 97		
	$4,000,000 × 0.97 = $3,880,000		
Nov. 30	Bond Interest Expense	163,000	
	Unamortized Bond Discount		3,000
	Cash		160,000
	Paid bondholders semiannual interest and amortized the discount on 8%, 20-year bonds		
	$120,000 ÷ 40 periods = $3,000		
	$4,000,000 × 0.04 = $160,000		

2.

		Dr.	Cr.
Nov. 30	Bond Interest Expense	174,600	
	Unamortized Bond Discount		14,600
	Cash		160,000
	Paid bondholders semiannual interest and amortized the discount on 8%, 20-year bonds		
	$3,880,000 × 0.045 = $174,600		
	$4,000,000 × 0.04 = $160,000		

TRY IT! SE5, SE6, SE7, E6A, E7A, E8A, E9A, E12A, E16A, E6B, E7B, E8B, E9B, E12B, E16B

LO6 Retirement and Conversion of Bonds

Two ways in which a company can reduce its bond debt are by:

- retiring the bonds or
- converting the bonds into common stock.

Retirement of Bonds

Usually, companies repay bonds when they are due—on the maturity date. However, as noted when discussing callable and convertible bonds, retiring a bond issue before its maturity date can be to a company's advantage. For example, when interest rates drop, many companies refinance their bonds at the lower rate. Although companies usually pay a premium for early extinguishment of bond debt, what they save on interest can make the refinancing cost-effective. Bonds may be retired either by calling the bonds or by buying them back from the bondholders on the open market. In either case, the transaction analysis is the same.

Retirement of Bonds

Transaction Suppose Carrot Corporation can call, or retire, at 105 the $200,000 of bonds it issued at a premium (104.265) on January 1, 2014, and that it decides to do so on July 1, 2017. The retirement thus takes place on the seventh interest payment date. Assume that the entry for the required interest payment and the amortization of the premium has been made.

Analysis The journal entry to record the retirement of the bonds

▼ *decreases* the *Bonds Payable* account with a debit for the face amount to remove the bonds from the balance sheet

▼ *decreases* the *Unamortized Bond Premium* account with a debit (or the Unamortized Bond Discount account with a credit) to remove the related premium (or discount) from the records

▼ *decreases* the *Cash* account for the amount required to call the bonds

▲ *increases* the *Loss on Retirement of Bonds* account with a debit (or *increases* the *Gain on Retirement of Bonds* account with a credit) for the net amount

Application of Double Entry

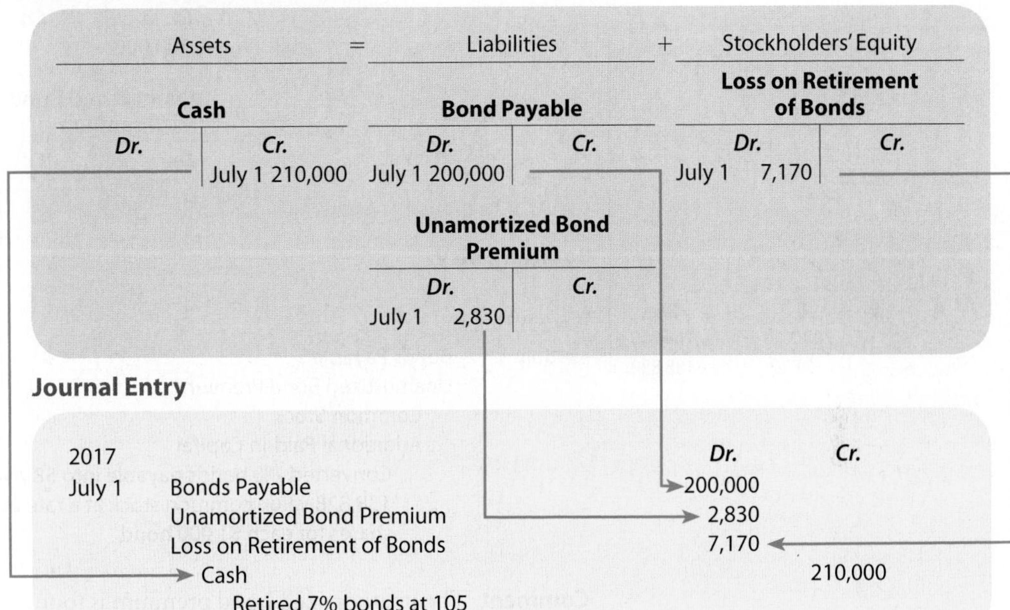

Journal Entry

A	=	L	+	SE
−210,000		−200,000		−7,170
		−2,830		

		Dr.	Cr.
2017			
July 1	Bonds Payable	200,000	
	Unamortized Bond Premium	2,830	
	Loss on Retirement of Bonds	7,170	
	Cash		210,000
	Retired 7% bonds at 105		

Comment In this entry, the cash paid is the face value times the call price ($200,000 × 1.05 = $210,000). The unamortized bond premium can be found in column E of Exhibit 5 on the seventh period line. The loss on retirement of bonds occurs because the call price of the bonds is greater than the carrying value ($210,000 − $202,830 = $7,170). Sometimes, a rise in the market interest rate can cause the market value of bonds to fall considerably below their face value. If it has the cash to do so, the company may find it advantageous to purchase the bonds on the open market and retire them. For example, if Carrot were able to purchase the above bonds on the open market at 85, a gain would be *recognized* for the difference between the purchase price of the bonds and the carrying value of the retired bonds.

Conversion of Bonds

When a bondholder converts bonds to common stock, the company records the common stock at the carrying value of the bonds. The bond liability and the unamortized discount or premium are written off the books. For this reason, no gain or loss on the transaction is recorded.

Conversion of Bonds to Common Stock

Transaction Suppose that Carrot Corporation does not call its bonds on July 1, 2017. Instead, the corporation's bondholders decide to convert all their bonds to $8 par value common stock under a convertible provision of 40 shares of common stock for each $1,000 bond.

Analysis The journal entry to record the conversion of bonds to common stock

▼ *decreases* the *Bonds Payable* account with a debit for the face amount to remove the bonds from the balance sheet

▼ *decreases* the *Unamortized Bond Premium* account with a debit (or the *Unamortized Bond Discount* account with a credit) to remove the related premium (or discount) from the records

- ▲ *increases* the *Common Stock* account for the par value of the shares
- ▲ *increases* the *Additional Paid-in Capital* account for the amount required to balance the entry

Application of Double Entry

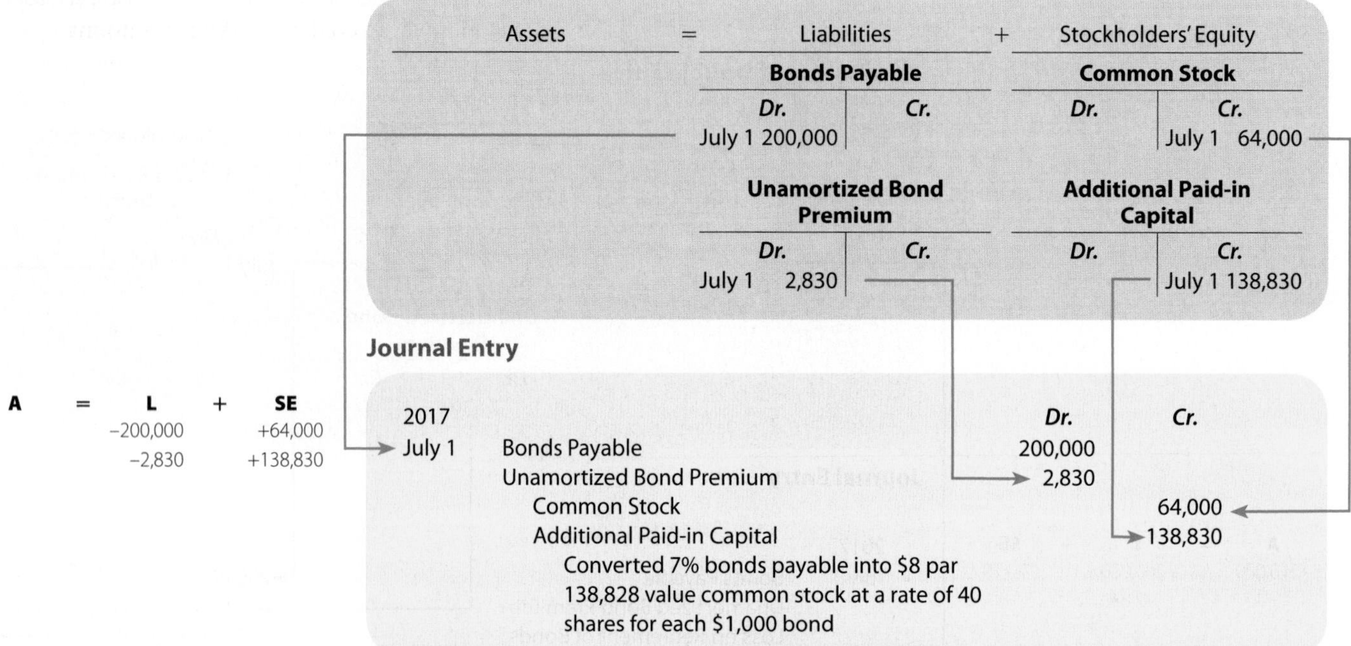

Comment The unamortized bond premium is found in column E of Exhibit 5 on the seventh period line. At a rate of 40 shares for each $1,000 bond, 8,000 shares will be issued, with a total par value of $64,000 (8,000 × $8). The Common Stock account is credited for the amount of the par value of the stock issued. In addition, Additional Paid-in Capital is credited for the difference between the carrying value of the bonds and the par value of the stock issued ($202,830 − $64,000 = $138,830). No gain or loss is recorded.

APPLY IT!

Assume that in the Carrot example of retirement in this section the company is able to buy the $200,000 in bonds on the open market at 95 and retire them. The Unamortized Bond Premium remains at $2,830. Prepare the journal entry to record the purchase and retirement on July 1, 2017.

SOLUTION

2017			
July 1	Bonds Payable	200,000	
	Unamortized Bond Premium	2,830	
	Gain on Retirement of Bonds		12,830
	Cash		190,000
	Retired 7% bonds at 95		

TRY IT! SE8, SE9, E10A, E11A, E13A, E10B, E11B, E13B

LO7 Other Bonds Payable Issues

Among the other issues involved in accounting for bonds payable are the sale of bonds between interest payment dates and the year-end accrual of bond interest expense.

Sale of Bonds Between Interest Dates

Although corporations may issue bonds on an interest payment date, as in the previous examples, they often issue them between interest payment dates. When that is the case, they generally collect from the investors the interest that would have accrued for the partial period preceding the issue date. At the end of the first interest period, they pay the interest for the entire period. In other words, the interest collected when bonds are sold is returned to investors on the next interest payment date.

There are two reasons for following this procedure:

- From a practical standpoint, if a company issued bonds on several different days and did not collect the accrued interest, records would have to be maintained for each bondholder and date of purchase. The interest due each bondholder would, therefore, have to be computed for a different time period. Clearly, this procedure would involve large bookkeeping costs. On the other hand, if accrued interest is collected when the bonds are sold, the corporation can pay the interest due for the entire period on the interest payment date, thereby eliminating the extra computations and costs.
- When accrued interest is collected in advance, the amount is subtracted from the full interest paid on the interest payment date. Thus, the resulting interest expense represents the amount for the time the money was borrowed.

Bonds Issued Between Interest Payment Dates

Transaction Suppose Carrot Corporation sold $200,000 of 7 percent, five-year bonds for face value on May 1, 2014, rather than on January 1, 2014. Carrot pays interest on January 1 and July 1 of each year.

Analysis The journal entry to record bonds sold between interest dates

▲ *increases* the *Cash* account for the amount the bond issue plus the accrued interest

▼ *decreases* the *Bond Interest Expense* account for the amount of the accrued interest

▲ *increases* the *Bonds Payable* account for the amount of the bond issue

Application of Double Entry

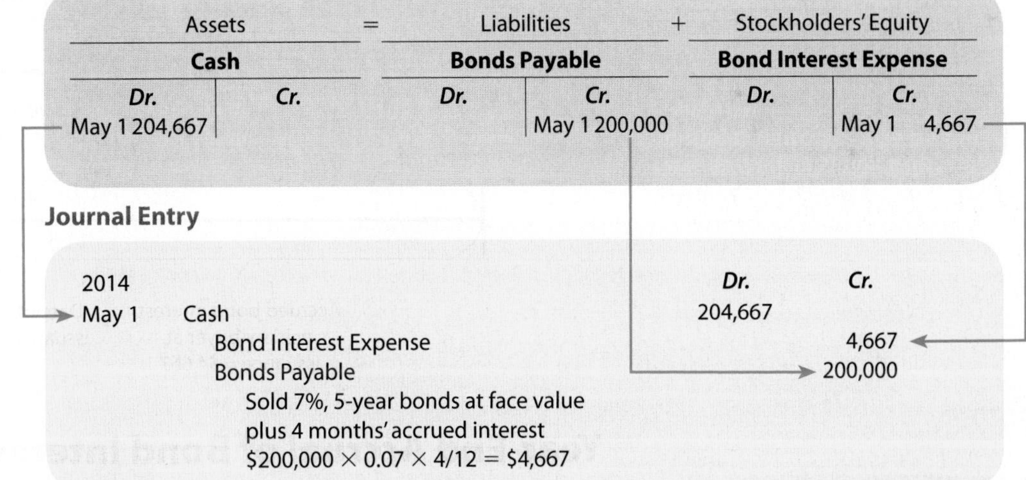

A	=	L	+	SE
+204,667		+200,000		+4,667

Comment Cash is debited for the amount received, $204,667 (the face value of $200,000 plus four months' accrued interest of $4,667). Bond Interest Expense is credited for the $4,667 of accrued interest, and Bonds Payable is credited for the face value of $200,000.

Interest Payment for Bonds Issued Between Interest Payment Dates

Transaction On July 1, the first semiannual interest payment is made.

Analysis The journal entry to record the first semiannual interest payment

▲ *increases* the *Bond Interest Expense* account for the amount of interest paid

▼ *decreases* the *Cash* account for the amount of cash paid

Application of Double Entry

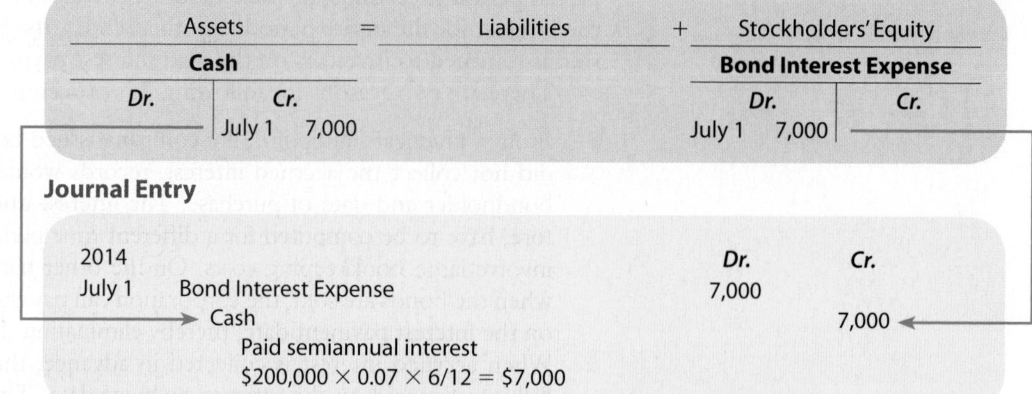

Journal Entry

A	=	L	+	SE
−7,000				−7,000

		Dr.	Cr.
2014			
July 1	Bond Interest Expense	7,000	
	Cash		7,000
	Paid semiannual interest		
	$200,000 × 0.07 × 6/12 = $7,000		

Comment Notice that the entire half-year interest is debited to Bond Interest Expense and credited to Cash because Carrot pays bond interest every six months, in full six-month amounts. Exhibit 7 illustrates this process. The actual interest expense for the two months that the bonds were outstanding is $2,333. This amount is the net balance of the $7,000 debit to Bond Interest Expense on July 1 less the $4,667 credit to Bond Interest Expense on May 1. The following T account clearly shows these steps:

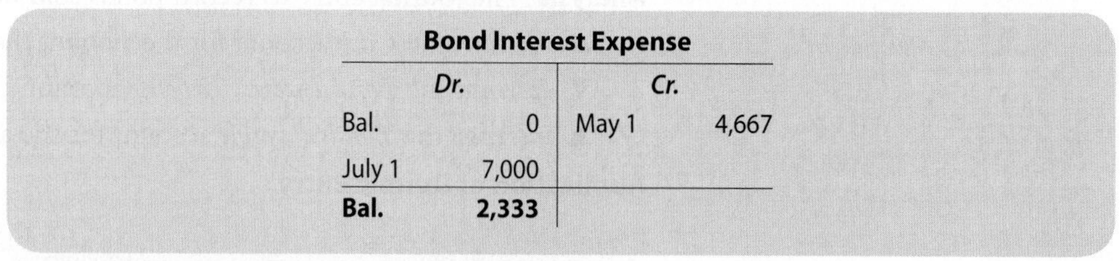

Bond Interest Expense

	Dr.		Cr.
Bal.	0	May 1	4,667
July 1	7,000		
Bal.	**2,333**		

Exhibit 7
Interest Expense When Bonds Are Issued Between Interest Dates

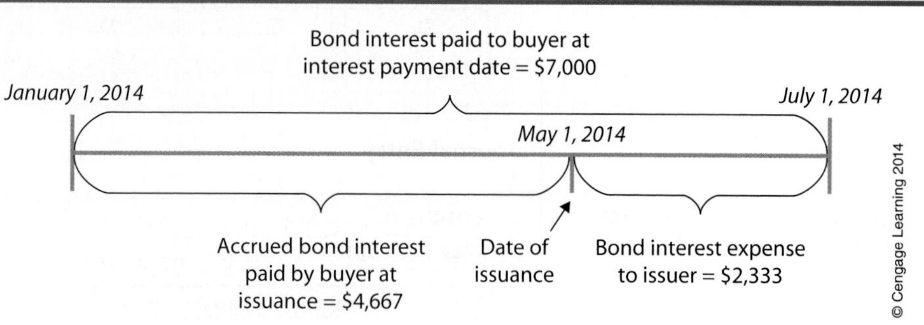

Year-End Accrual of Bond Interest Expense

***STUDY NOTE:** Accrual accounting dictates that both the accrued interest and the amortization of a premium or discount be recorded at year-end.*

Bond interest payment dates rarely correspond with a company's fiscal year. Therefore, an adjustment must be made to accrue the interest expense on the bonds from the last interest payment date to the end of the fiscal year. In addition, any discount or premium on the bonds must be amortized for the partial period.

Year-End Accrual of Bond Interest Expense When Year-End Falls Between Bond Interest Dates

Transaction In the example of bonds issued at a premium, Carrot Corporation issued $200,000 of bonds on January 1, 2014, at 104.265 percent of face value. Suppose Carrot's fiscal year ends on September 30, 2014. In the period since the interest payment and amortization of the premium on July 1, three months' worth of interest has accrued.

Analysis Under the effective interest method, the adjusting entry

▲ *increases* the *Bond Interest Expense* account

▼ *decreases* the *Unamortized Bond Premium* account

▲ *increases* the *Bond Interest Payable* account

Application of Double Entry

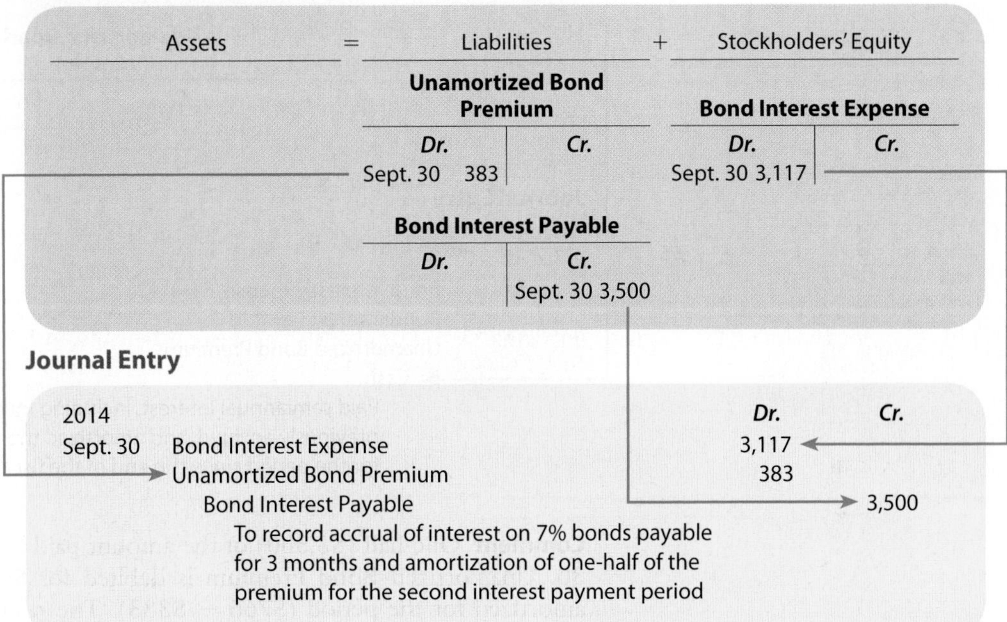

Assets = Liabilities + Stockholders' Equity
Unamortized Bond Premium
Dr. Cr.
Sept. 30 383
Bond Interest Expense
Dr. Cr.
Sept. 30 3,117
Bond Interest Payable
Dr. Cr.
Sept. 30 3,500

Journal Entry

2014		Dr.	Cr.
Sept. 30	Bond Interest Expense	3,117	
	Unamortized Bond Premium	383	
	Bond Interest Payable		3,500
	To record accrual of interest on 7% bonds payable for 3 months and amortization of one-half of the premium for the second interest payment period		

Comment This entry covers one-half of the second interest period. Unamortized Bond Premium is debited for \$383, which is one-half of \$766, the amortization of the premium for the second period from Exhibit 5. Bond Interest Payable is credited for \$3,500, which is three months' interest on the face value of the bonds (\$200,000 × 0.07 × 3/12). Bond Interest Expense is debited for \$3,117 (\$3,500 − \$383), which is the bond interest expense for the three-month period (or one-half of \$6,234).

Payment of Interest When the Interest Payment Date Falls After Year-End Accrual

Transaction On the interest payment date of January 1, 2015, Carrot Corporation makes the entry to pay the bondholders and amortize the premium.

Analysis The journal entry to pay the bondholders and amortize the premium

▲ *increases* the *Bond Interest Expense* account

▼ *decreases* the *Bond Interest Payable* account

▼ *decreases* the *Unamortized Bond Premium* account

▼ *decreases* the *Cash* account

Application of Double Entry

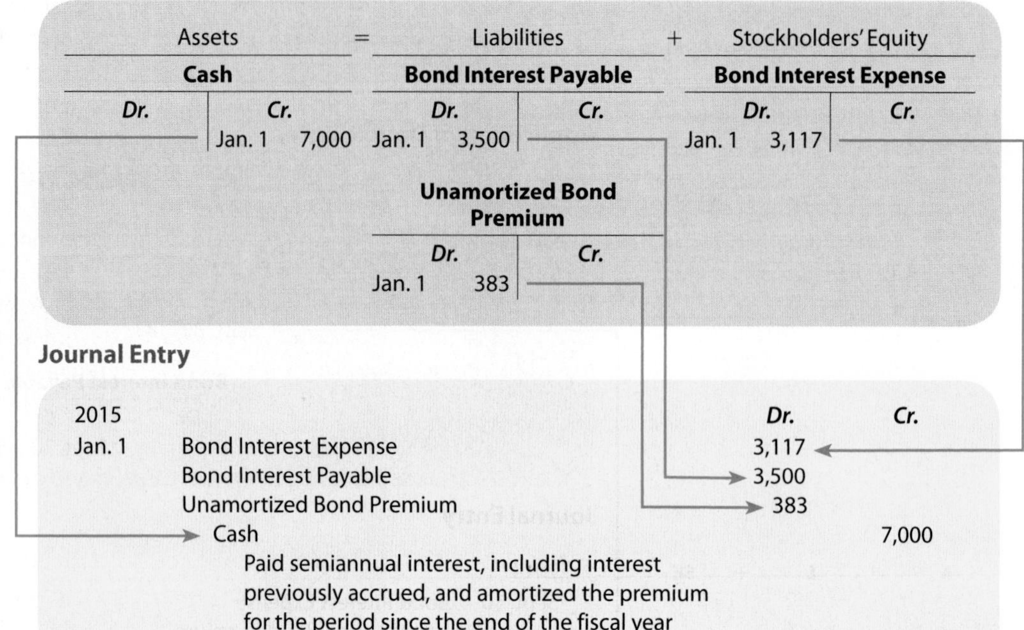

Assets = Liabilities + Stockholders' Equity
Cash
Dr. Cr.
Jan. 1 7,000
Bond Interest Payable
Dr. Cr.
Jan. 1 3,500
Bond Interest Expense
Dr. Cr.
Jan. 1 3,117
Unamortized Bond Premium
Dr. Cr.
Jan. 1 383

Journal Entry

2015		Dr.	Cr.
Jan. 1	Bond Interest Expense	3,117	
	Bond Interest Payable	3,500	
	Unamortized Bond Premium	383	
	Cash		7,000
	Paid semiannual interest, including interest previously accrued, and amortized the premium for the period since the end of the fiscal year		

Comment One-half ($3,500) of the amount paid ($7,000) was accrued on September 30. Unamortized Bond Premium is debited for $383, the remaining amount to be amortized for the period ($766 − $383). The resulting bond interest expense is the amount that applies to the three-month period from October 1 to December 31.

Bond discounts are recorded at year-end in the same way as bond premiums. The difference is that the amortization of a bond discount increases interest expense instead of decreasing it.

APPLY IT!

Flis Associates sold $1,000,000 in bonds on April 1. The bonds carry a face interest rate of 8 percent, which is to be paid on January 1 and July 1. Prepare journal entries for (a) the issue of the bonds on April 1 at 100 and (b) the interest payment on July 1. (c) How much was the total interest expense for the first six months of the year?

SOLUTION

(a) Apr. 1	Cash	1,020,000	
	Bonds Payable		1,000,000
	Bond Interest Expense		20,000
	Issuance of 8 percent bonds		
(b) July 1	Bond Interest Expense	40,000	
	Cash		40,000
	Interest payment		

(c) Total interest expense: $40,000 − $20,000 = $20,000

TRY IT! SE7, SE10, E12A, E14A, E15A, E16A, E12B, E14B, E15B, E16B

LO 8 Long-Term Leases

A company can obtain an operating asset in the following ways:

- **By borrowing money and buying the asset:** When a company uses this method, it records the asset and liability at the amount paid, and the asset is subject to periodic depreciation.
- **By renting the asset on a short-term lease:** When a company uses this method, the risks of ownership of the asset remain with the lessor (the owner), and the lease

is shorter than the asset's useful life. This type of agreement is called an **operating lease**. Payments on operating leases are properly treated as rent expense.

- **By obtaining the asset on a long-term lease:** This is one of the fastest-growing ways of financing plant assets in the United States today. A long-term lease on a plant asset has several advantages. It requires no immediate cash payment, the rental payment is deducted in full for tax purposes, and it costs less than a short-term lease. Acquiring the use of plant assets under long-term leases does create several accounting challenges, however.

Capital Leases Long-term leases may be carefully structured, as they are by companies like **CVS**, so that they can be accounted for as operating leases. However, accounting standards require that a long-term lease be treated as a capital lease when it meets *all* of the following conditions:

- It cannot be canceled.
- Its duration is about the same as the useful life of the asset.
- It stipulates that the lessee has the option to buy the asset at a nominal price at the end of the lease.

STUDY NOTE: *A capital lease is, in substance, an installment purchase, and the leased asset and related liability must be recognized at their present value.*

A capital lease is, thus, more like a purchase or sale on installment than a rental. The lessee in a capital lease should record an asset, depreciation on the asset, and a long-term liability equal to the present value of the total lease payments during the lease term.[6] Much like a mortgage payment, each lease payment consists partly of interest expense and partly of repayment of debt.

To illustrate capital leases, we will use Urban Manufacturing Company, which enters into a long-term lease for a machine. The lease terms call for an annual payment of $8,000 for six years, which approximates the useful life of the machine. At the end of the lease period, the title to the machine passes to Urban. This lease is clearly a capital lease and should be recorded as an asset and a liability. Present value techniques can be used to place a value on the asset and on the corresponding liability in a capital lease. An example of a payment schedule for a capital lease is presented in Exhibit 8.

Exhibit 8
Payment Schedule on an 8 Percent Capital Lease

	A	B	C	D
Year	Lease Payment	Interest (8%) on Unpaid Obligation* (D × 8%)	Reduction of Lease Obligation (A – B)	Balance of Lease Obligation (D – C)
Beginning				$36,984
1	$ 8,000	$ 2,959	$ 5,041	31,943
2	8,000	2,555	5,445	26,498
3	8,000	2,120	5,880	20,618
4	8,000	1,649	6,351	14,267
5	8,000	1,141	6,859	7,408
6	8,000	592**	7,408	—
	$48,000	$11,016	$36,984	

* Rounded

** The last year's interest equals $592 ($8,000 − $7,408). It does not exactly equal $593 ($7,408 × $\frac{8}{100}$ × 1) because of the cumulative effect of rounding.

Capital Lease Recognition

Transaction Urban's interest cost on the unpaid part of its obligation is 8 percent. Using the factor for 8 percent and six periods in Table 2 in Appendix C, the present value of the lease payments can be computed as follows.

Periodic Payment × Factor = Present Value
$8,000 × 4.623 = $36,984

Analysis The journal entry to record the lease

▲ *increases* the *Capital Lease Equipment* account with a debit

▲ *increases* the *Capital Lease Obligations* account with a credit

Application of Double Entry

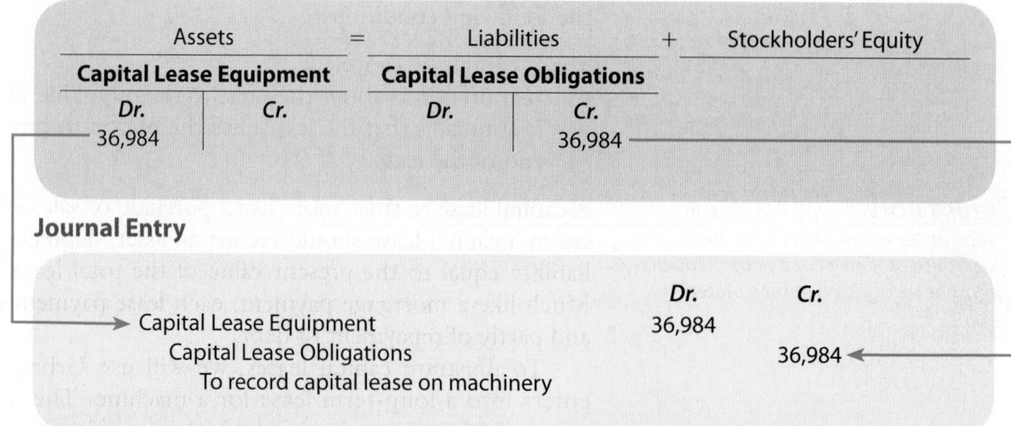

Journal Entry

A	=	L	+	SE
+36,984		+36,984		

	Dr.	Cr.
Capital Lease Equipment	36,984	
Capital Lease Obligations		36,984
To record capital lease on machinery		

Comment Capital Lease Equipment is *classified* as a long-term asset. Capital Lease Obligations is *classified* as a long-term liability.

Depreciation Recorded

Transaction Each year, Urban must record depreciation on the leased asset. Assume straight-line depreciation, a six-year life, and no residual value.

Analysis The journal entry to record depreciation

▲ *increases* the *Depreciation Expense—Capital Lease Equipment* account with a debit

▲ *increases* the contra-asset account *Accumulated Depreciation—Capital Lease Equipment* with a credit

Application of Double Entry

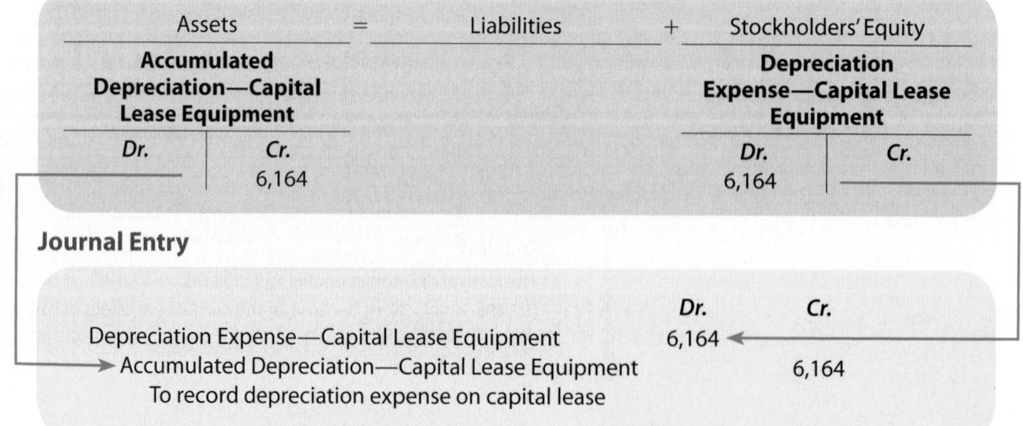

Journal Entry

A	=	L	+	SE
−6,164				−6,164

	Dr.	Cr.
Depreciation Expense—Capital Lease Equipment	6,164	
Accumulated Depreciation—Capital Lease Equipment		6,164
To record depreciation expense on capital lease		

Comment The depreciation expense is computed by dividing the present value of the capital lease by the term of the lease ($36,984 ÷ 6 = $6,164).

Lease Payment

Transaction Refer to the data in Exhibit 8. Urban makes the first payment on its capital lease.

Analysis The journal entry to record the first lease payment

▲ *increases* the *Interest Expense* account with a debit

▼ *decreases* the *Capital Lease Obligations* account with credit

▼ *decreases* the *Cash* account with a credit

Application of Double Entry

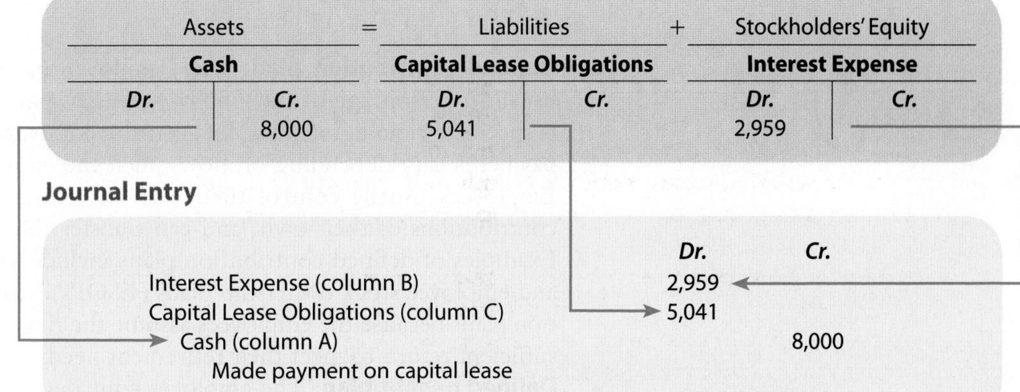

Assets		=	Liabilities		+	Stockholders' Equity	
Cash			**Capital Lease Obligations**			**Interest Expense**	
Dr.	*Cr.*		*Dr.*	*Cr.*		*Dr.*	*Cr.*
	8,000		5,041			2,959	

Journal Entry

A	=	L	+	SE
−8,000		−5,041		−2,959

	Dr.	*Cr.*
Interest Expense (column B)	2,959	
Capital Lease Obligations (column C)	5,041	
Cash (column A)		8,000
Made payment on capital lease		

Comment The interest expense for each year is computed by multiplying the interest rate (8 percent) by the amount of the remaining lease obligation. Exhibit 8 shows these calculations. This example suggests why companies are motivated to engage in off-balance-sheet financing for leases. By structuring long-term leases so that they can be accounted for as operating leases, companies avoid recording them on the balance sheet as long-term assets and liabilities. This practice, which is legal, not only improves the debt to equity ratio by showing less debt on the balance sheet, but also improves the return on assets by reducing the total assets.

International Perspective

IFRS Recording Liabilities and Assets Will Not Look the Same Under IFRS

Under U.S. GAAP, most leases are accounted for as operating expenses. Current lease payments are generally recorded as operating expenses, and future lease obligations appear as described in the footnotes to the financial statements. Under International Financial Reporting Standards (IFRS), lease obligations are recorded at fair value as a liability, and the related debt is recorded as an asset. Fair value is usually measured at the discounted present value of the future lease payments. The result is that more assets and liabilities will appear to be greater under IFRS than under GAAP.

Pension Liabilities

Most employees of medium-sized and large companies are covered by a **pension plan**, a contract that requires a company to pay benefits to its employees after they retire. Some companies pay the full cost of the pension plan; but in many companies, employees share the cost by contributing part of their salaries or wages. The contributions from employer and employees are usually paid into a **pension fund**, which is invested on behalf of the employees. Pension benefits typically consist of monthly payments to retired employees and other payments upon disability or death.

Employers whose pension plans do not have sufficient assets to cover the present value of their pension obligations must record the amount of the shortfall as a liability. If a pension plan has sufficient assets to cover its obligations, no balance sheet reporting is required or permitted.

There are two kinds of pension plans:

- **Defined contribution plan:** The employer makes a fixed annual contribution, usually a percentage of the employee's gross pay. The amount of the contribution is specified in an agreement between the company and the employees. Retirement payments vary depending on how much the employee's retirement account earns. Employees usually control their own investment accounts, can make additional contributions of their own, and can transfer the funds if they leave the company. Examples of defined contribution plans include 401(k) plans, profit-sharing plans, and employee stock ownership plans (ESOPs). Companies prefer defined contribution plans because the employees assume the risk that their pension assets will earn a sufficient return to meet their retirement needs.
- **Defined benefit plan:** The employer contributes an amount annually to fund estimated future pension liability. The exact amount of the liability will not be known until the retirement or death of the current employees. Although the amount of future benefits is fixed, the annual contributions vary depending on assumptions about how much the pension fund will earn.

Annual pension expense under a defined contribution plan is simple and predictable. Pension expense equals the fixed amount of the annual contribution. In contrast, annual expense under a defined benefit plan is one of the most complex topics in accounting. The intricacies are reserved for advanced courses, but in concept, the procedure is simple. Computation of the annual expense takes into account the estimation of such factors as the average remaining service life of active employees, the long-run return on pension plan assets, and future salary increases. An accounting standard requires companies and other entities with defined benefit plans not backed by a fund sufficient to pay them to record the unfunded portion as a liability.[7] For many companies this can amount to millions or even billions of dollars.

Because pension expense under a defined benefit plan is not predictable and can vary from year to year, many companies are adopting the more predictable defined contribution plans.

Long-Term Liabilities and the Financial Statements

As presented in Exhibit 9, long-term liabilities arise from a variety of financing and obligations. Long-term liabilities are amounts to be paid more than one year after the balance sheet date.

Exhibit 9
Long-Term Liabilities on the Balance Sheet

Balance Sheet
December 31, 2014

Assets	**Liabilities**
Current assets	Current liabilities
Investments	Long-term liabilities:
Property, plant, and equipment	Bonds payable
Intangible assets	Notes payable
	Mortgage payable
	Capital lease obligation
	Pension and post-retirement liabilities
	Deferred income taxes
	Total long-term liabilities
	Total liabilities
	Stockholders' Equity
	Contributed capital
	Retained earnings
	Total stockholders' equity

Total Assets = Total Liabilities + Stockholders' Equity

APPLY IT!

Eureka Corporation has leased a machine that has a useful life of 10 years. The terms of the lease are payments of $60,000 per year for 10 years. Eureka currently is able to borrow money at a long-term interest rate of 12 percent. Calculate (a) the present value of the lease and (b) prepare the journal entry to record the lease agreement.

SOLUTION

(a) Present value of the lease is equal to periodic payment × factor (Table 2 in Appendix C: 12%, 10 periods)

$60,000 × 5.650 = $339,000

(b) The journal entry to record the lease is:

Capital Lease Machine	339,000	
Capital Lease Obligations		339,000
To record the lease contract		

TRY IT! SE11, E17A, E17B

SECTION 3 **BUSINESS APPLICATIONS**

BUSINESS APPLICATIONS

- Evaluate a company's level of debt
  - Debt to equity ratio
  - Interest coverage ratio

RELEVANT LEARNING OBJECTIVE

LO 9 Evaluate the decision to issue long-term debt, including analyzing long-term debt.

LO 9 Management Issues Related to Long-Term Debt Financing

A key decision for management is whether to rely solely on stockholders' equity for long-term funds or to rely partially on long-term debt. Some companies, such as **Microsoft** and **Apple**, do not issue long-term debt; but like **CVS** and **Southwest Airlines**, most companies find it useful to do so. To make a decision, it is important to know the advantages and disadvantages of issuing long-term debt and to analyze the risks of the issue of the company's finances. Further, it is also important to understand the long-term effects of more complex obligations such as leases and pensions.

Evaluating the Decision to Issue Long-Term Debt

Because long-term debt must be paid at maturity and usually requires periodic payments of interest, issuing common stock has two advantages over issuing long-term debt:

- **Permanent financing:** Common stock does not have to be paid back.
- **Dividend payment optional:** Dividends on common stock are normally paid only if the company earns sufficient income.

Issuing long-term debt, however, has the following advantages over issuing common stock:

- **Stockholder control:** When a corporation issues long-term debt, common stockholders do not relinquish any of their control over the company because bondholders and other creditors do not have voting rights. In contrast, when a corporation issues additional shares of common stock, the votes of the new stockholders may force current stockholders and management to give up some control.
- **Tax advantage:** The interest on debt is tax-deductible, whereas dividends on common stock are not. For example, if a corporation pays $100,000 in interest and its income tax rate is 30 percent, its net cost will be $70,000 because it will save $30,000 on income taxes. To pay $100,000 in dividends on common stock, the corporation would have to earn $142,857 before income taxes [$100,000 ÷ (1 − 0.30)].
- **Financial leverage:** If a corporation earns more from the funds it raises by incurring long-term debt than it pays in interest on the debt, the excess will increase its earnings for the stockholders. This concept is called **financial leverage** (or *trading on equity*). For example, if a company earns 10 percent on a $1,000,000 investment financed by long-term 8 percent notes, it will earn $20,000 before income taxes ($100,000 – $80,000). The debt to equity ratio, which we will discuss later in this chapter, is considered an overall measure of a company's financial leverage.

Despite these advantages, debt financing is not always in a company's best interest. It may entail the following:

- **Financial risk:** A high level of debt exposes a company to financial risk. A company whose plans for earnings do not pan out, whose operations are subject to the ups and downs of the economy, or whose cash flow is weak may be unable to pay the principal amount of its debt at the maturity date or even to make periodic interest payments. Creditors can then force the company into bankruptcy. **TWA**, **Continental Airlines**, and **United Airlines** filed for bankruptcy protection because they could not make payments on their long-term debt and other liabilities. (While in bankruptcy, they restructured their debt and interest payments: TWA sold off its assets; Continental and United subsequently came out of bankruptcy. The latter two airlines have since merged.)

Business Perspective

How Does Debt Affect a Company's Ability to Borrow?

Credit ratings by agencies like **Standard & Poor's (S&P)** reflect the fact that the greater a company's debt, the greater its financial risk. S&P rates companies from AAA (best) to CCC (worst) based on various factors, including a company's debt to equity ratio, as shown below.

Rating	AAA	AA	A	BBB	BB	B	CCC
Debt to Equity Ratio*	4.5	34.1	42.9	47.9	59.8	76.0	75.7

*Averages of companies with similar ratings. Ratings also take into effect other factors, such as the companies' profitability, interest coverage, and stability.

These ratings affect not only how much a company can borrow but also what the interest will cost. The lower its rating, the more a company must pay in interest, and vice versa.

For a company in a heavily debt-laden industry such as the auto industry, a change in credit rating can mean millions of dollars. For instance, when S&P lowered **General Motors**' credit ratings to "junk status" (i.e., BB), it meant that GM had to pay 1 or more percentage points in additional interest. On GM's $291 billion debt, this amounted to about $2–$3 billion.[8] S&P proved to be correct in its downgrade, as GM subsequently went bankrupt and had to be bailed out by the federal government.

- **Negative financial leverage:** Financial leverage can work against a company if the earnings from its investments do not exceed its interest payments. For example, many small retail companies failed in recent years because they relied too heavily on debt financing before developing sufficient resources to ensure their survival.

Evaluating Long-Term Debt

Financial leverage is advantageous as long as a company is able to make timely interest payments and repay the debt at maturity. Because failure to do so can force a company into bankruptcy, a company must assess the financial risk involved. Financial risk is measured by the debt to equity ratio and the interest coverage ratio.

Debt to Equity Ratio To assess how much debt to carry, managers compute the **debt to equity ratio**, which shows the amount of debt a company carries in relation to its stockholders' equity. The higher this ratio, the greater the company's financial risk. Using data for **McDonald's** (presented at the beginning of the chapter), we can compute its debt to equity ratio in 2011 as follows (in millions).

RATIO

Debt to Equity Ratio: How Much Debt Does a Company Have in Relation to Its Stockholders' Equity?

$$\text{Debt to Equity Ratio} = \frac{\text{Total Liabilities}}{\text{Total Stockholders' Equity}}$$

$$= \frac{\$18{,}599.7}{\$14{,}390.2} = 1.29 \text{ Times (or 129\%)*}$$

* Rounded

As illustrated, a debt to equity ratio of 1.29 times (or 129%) is relatively high, but it does not tell the whole story. As noted in the chapter opener, McDonald's also has long-term leases on various properties, which require annual payments of $1,200 million. McDonald's structures these leases in such a way that they do not appear as liabilities on the balance sheet. This practice is called **off-balance-sheet financing** and, as used by McDonald's, is entirely legal. The leases are, however, long-term commitments of cash payments and so have the effect of long-term liabilities.

Interest Coverage Ratio

The **interest coverage ratio** measures the degree of protection a company has from default on interest payments. The lower this ratio, the greater the financial risk.

Most analysts want to see an interest coverage ratio of at least 3 or 4 times. Lower interest coverage would mean the company is at risk from a downturn in the economy. The 2011 **McDonald's** income statement shows that the company had income before income taxes of $8,012.2 million and interest expense of $2,509.1 million. Using these figures, we can compute the company's interest coverage ratio as follows.

RATIO

Interest Coverage Ratio: How Many Times Does the Company's Income Exceed Its Interest Expense?

$$\text{Interest Coverage Ratio} = \frac{\text{Income Before Income Taxes} + \text{Interest Expense}}{\text{Interest Expense}}$$

$$= \frac{\$8{,}012.2 + \$2{,}509.1}{\$2{,}509.1}$$

$$= \frac{\$10{,}521.3}{\$2{,}509.1}$$

$$= 4.2 \text{ Times}$$

In comparison, its strong interest coverage ratio of 4.2 times shows that McDonald's is in no danger of being unable to make interest payments. However, in computing this ratio, management will add the company's off-balance-sheet rent expense of $1,200 million to its interest expense. This procedure decreases the interest coverage ratio to about 3.1 times. Although still adequate to cover interest payments, the adjusted coverage ratio is less robust, which demonstrates the significant effect that off-balance-sheet financing for leases can have on a company's financial situation.

Cash Flow Information

The best source of information concerning cash flows about short-term and long-term debt is the financing activities section of the statement of cash flows. For instance, **McDonald's** cash flows are clearly revealed in this excerpt from its 2011 statement of cash flows (in millions):[9]

Financing Activities	2011	2010	2009
Net short-term borrowings	$ 260.6	$ 3.1	$ (285.4)
Long-term financing issuances	1,367.3	1,931.8	1,169.3
Long-term financing repayments	(624.0)	(1,147.5)	(664.6)

Note that McDonald's has little short-term borrowing and that the company's cash inflows for long-term borrowing for the three years exceeded cash outflows for long-term borrowing by $2,032.3 million.

APPLY IT!

Compute the interest coverage ratios for 2013 and 2014 from Travis Corporation's partial income statements that follow.

	2014	2013
Income from operations	$27,500	$34,000
Interest expense	5,000	4,000
Income before income taxes	$22,500	$30,000
Income taxes	8,250	10,200
Net income	$14,250	$19,800

SOLUTION

2013

$$\frac{\$30{,}000 + \$4{,}000}{\$4{,}000} = \frac{\$34{,}000}{\$4{,}000} = 8.5 \text{ Times}$$

2014

$$\frac{\$22{,}500 + \$5{,}000}{\$5{,}000} = \frac{\$27{,}500}{\$5{,}000} = 5.5 \text{ Times}$$

TRY IT! SE12, E18A, E18B

A Look Back At: McDonald's

Kim Karpeles/Alamy

McDonald's

The beginning of this chapter focused on the extent of long-term liabilities at **McDonald's**. Complete the following requirements to answer the questions posed at the beginning of the chapter.

Section 1: Concepts
How do the concepts of recognition, valuation, classification, and disclosure apply to long-term liabilities?

Section 2: Accounting Applications
How are long-term bonds accounted for in the company's records?

Section 3: Business Applications 
What should McDonald's consider in deciding to issue long-term debt?

To answer this question, compute the debt to equity and interest coverage ratios for McDonald's for 2010 and 2011.

SOLUTION

Section 1: Concepts
Generally accepted accounting principles require that long-term liabilities be *recognized* and recorded when an obligation occurs even though the obligation may not be due for many years. On the balance sheet, long-term liabilities are generally *valued* at the amount of money needed to pay the debt or at the fair market value of the goods or services to be delivered. A liability is *classified* as a long-term liability when it is due beyond one year or beyond the normal operating cycle. Because of the complex nature of many long-term liabilities, extensive *disclosures* in the notes to the financial statements are often required.

Section 2: Accounting Applications
McDonald's has all types of current liabilities. It has definitely determinable current liabilities such as accounts payable, short-term debt, and securities lending payable. The rest of the current liabilities must be estimated. The estimated liabilities consist of accruals such as accrued compensation and income taxes payable and deferrals such as short-term unearned revenue.

Section 3: Business Applications

In addition to bonds, notes payable, and mortgages, it is important to consider the company's numerous leases on properties in evaluating its long-term debt. McDonald's also has deferred income taxes and pension and health plans. Its purpose in taking on long-term debt is to foster growth and increase earnings. By using financial leverage in this way, McDonald's, like any other company, assumes financial risk. For McDonald's, the risk is partially offset because much of its long-term debt relates to leases on real estate, an area in which the company has great experience and expertise. Management commits the company to long-term leases not only because it believes the company will stay in the leased locations for a long time, but also because it is a way of financing expansion.

The company's 2011 annual report includes a detailed description of management's approach to debt financing. It points out that Standard & Poor's gives McDonald's an "A" credit rating and that management carefully monitors critical credit ratios that "incorporate capitalized operating leases to estimate total adjusted debt."

Review Problem

Swan Manufacturing Company is considering issuing long-term bonds in order to finance an expansion of its metal window division. Swan's bond indenture states that the company would issue $2,500,000 of 8 percent, five-year bonds on January 1, 2015, and would pay interest semiannually on June 30 and December 31 in each of the five years. It also stated that the bonds would be callable at 104 and that each $1,000 bond would be convertible to 30 shares of $10 par value common stock.

Swan sold the bonds on January 1, 2015, at 96 because the market rate of interest for similar investments was 9 percent. It decided to amortize the bond discount by using the effective interest method. On July 1, 2017, management called and retired half the bonds, and investors converted the other half to common stock.

1. Prepare an interest and amortization schedule for the first five interest periods.
2. Prepare journal entries to record the sale of the bonds, the first two interest payments, the bond retirement, and the bond conversion.

SOLUTION

Section 1: Accounting Applications

1.

	A	B	C	D	E	F	G
1	Interest and Amortization of Bond Discount						
2	Semiannual Interest Payment Date	Carrying Value at Beginning of Period	Semiannual Interest Expense* (9% × 1/2)	Semiannual Interest Expense (8% × 1/2)	Amortization of Discount	Unamortized Bond Discount at End of Period	Carrying Value at End of Period
3	Jan. 1, 2015					$100,000	$2,400,000
4	June 30, 2015	$2,400,000	$108,000	$100,000	$8,000	92,000	2,408,000
5	Dec. 31, 2015	2,408,000	108,360	100,000	8,360	83,640	2,416,360
6	June 30, 2016	2,416,360	108,736	100,000	8,736	74,904	2,425,096
7	Dec. 31, 2016	2,425,096	109,129	100,000	9,129	65,775	2,434,225
8	June 30, 2017	2,434,225	109,540	100,000	9,540	56,235	2,443,765
9							
10	*Rounded						

2.

	A	B	C	D	E
1	2015				
2	Jan.	1	Cash	2,400,000	
3			Unamortized Bond Discount	100,000	
4			Bonds Payable		2,500,000
5			Sold $2,500,000 of 8%, 5-year bonds at 96		
6	June	30	Bond Interest Expense	108,000	
7			Unamortized Bond Discount		8,000
8			Cash		100,000
9			Paid semiannual interest and amortized		
10			the discount on 8%, 5-year bonds		
11	Dec.	31	Bond Interest Expense	108,360	
12			Unamortized Bond Discount		8,360
13			Cash		100,000
14			Paid semiannual interest and amortized		
15			the discount on 8%, 5-year bonds		
16	2017				
17	July	1	Bonds Payable	1,250,000	
18			Loss on Retirement of Bonds	78,118	
19			Unamortized Bond Discount		28,118
20			Cash		1,300,000
21			Called $1,250,000 of 8% bonds and retired		
22			them at 104 ($56,235 × 1/2 = $28,118*)		
23			Bonds Payable	1,250,000	
24			Unamortized Bond Discount		28,117
25			Common Stock		375,000
26			Additional Paid-in Capital		846,883
27			Converted $1,250,000 of 8% bonds into		
28			common stock		
29			1,250 × 30 shares = 37,500 shares		
30			37,500 shares × $10 = $375,000		
31			$56,235 – $28,118 = $28,117		
32			$1,250,000 – ($28,117 + $375,000) = $846,883		
33					

SOLUTION • SOLUTION • SOLUTION • SOLUTION • SOLUTION • SOLUTION • SOLUTION • SOLUTION • SOLUTION • SOLUTION • SOLUTION

Chapter Review

Explain the concepts underlying long-term liabilities, and identify the types of long-term liabilities. LO 1

Long-term debt is used to finance assets and business activities, such as research and development, that will produce income in future years. The management issues related to long-term debt are whether to take on long-term debt, how much debt to carry, and what types of debt to incur. Common types of long-term debt are bonds, notes, mortgages, long-term leases, pension liabilities, other post-retirement benefits, and deferred income taxes.

Describe the features of a bond issue and the major characteristics of bonds. LO 2

A bond is a security that represents money borrowed from the investing public. When a corporation issues bonds, it enters into a contract, called a bond indenture, with the bondholders. The bond indenture defines the terms of the bond issue. A bond issue is the total value of bonds issued at one time. The prices of bonds are stated in terms of a percentage of the face value, or principal, of the bonds. The face interest rate is the fixed rate of interest paid to bondholders based on the face value. The market interest rate is the rate of interest paid in the market on bonds of similar risk. If the market rate fluctuates from the face interest rate before the bond issue date, the bonds will sell at either a discount or a premium.

A corporation can issue several types of bonds, each having different characteristics. For example, a bond issue may or may not require security (secured versus unsecured bonds). It may be payable at a single time (term bonds) or at several times (serial bonds). And the holder may receive interest automatically (registered bonds) or may have to return coupons to receive interest payable (coupon bonds). Bonds may also be callable and convertible.

Record bonds issued at face value and at a discount or premium. LO 3

Bondholders pay face value for bonds when the interest rate on the bonds approximates the market rate for similar investments. The issuing corporation records the bond issue at face value as a long-term liability in the Bonds Payable account. Bonds are issued at a discount when their face interest rate is lower than the market rate for similar investments. The difference between the face value and the issue price is debited to Unamortized Bond Discount. Bonds are issued at a premium when their face interest rate is greater than the market interest rate on similar investments. The difference between the issue price and the face value is credited to Unamortized Bond Premium.

Use present values to determine the value of bonds. LO 4

The value of a bond is determined by summing the present values of (1) the series of fixed interest payments of the bond issue and (2) the single payment of the face value at maturity. Tables 1 and 2 in the appendix on present value tables should be used in making these computations.

Amortize bond discounts and bond premiums using the straight-line and effective interest methods. LO 5

The straight-line method allocates a fixed portion of a bond discount or premium each interest period to adjust the interest payment to interest expense. The effective interest method, which is used when the effects of amortization are material, applies a constant rate of interest to the carrying value of the bonds. To find interest and the amortization of discounts or premiums, the effective interest rate is applied to the carrying value of the bonds (face value minus the discount or plus the premium) at the beginning of the interest period. The amount of the discount or premium to be amortized is the difference between the interest figured by using the effective rate and that obtained by using the face rate. The results of using the effective interest method on bonds issued at a discount or a premium are summarized below and compared with issuance at face value:

	Bonds Issued at		
	Face Value	**Discount**	**Premium**
Trend in carrying value over bond term	Constant	Increasing	Decreasing
Trend in interest expense over bond term	Constant	Increasing	Decreasing
Interest expense versus interest payments	Interest expense = interest payments	Interest expense > interest payments	Interest expense < interest payments
Classification of bond discount or premium	Not applicable	Contra-liability (deducted from Bonds Payable)	Adjunct-liability (added to Bonds Payable)

LO 6 Account for the retirement of bonds and the conversion of bonds into stock.

Callable bonds can be retired before maturity at the option of the issuing corporation. The call price is usually an amount greater than the face value of the bonds, in which case the corporation recognizes a loss on the retirement of the bonds. Sometimes, a rise in the market interest rate causes the market value of the bonds to fall below face value. If a company purchases its bonds on the open market at a price below carrying value, it recognizes a gain on the transaction.

Convertible bonds allow the bondholder to convert bonds to the issuing corporation's common stock. When bondholders exercise this option, the common stock issued is recorded at the carrying value of the bonds being converted. No gain or loss is recognized.

LO 7 Record bonds issued between interest dates, and record year-end adjustments.

When bonds are sold between the interest payment dates, the issuing corporation collects from investors the interest that has accrued since the last interest payment date. When the next interest payment date arrives, the corporation pays the bondholders interest for the entire interest period.

When the end of a corporation's fiscal year does not fall on an interest payment date, the corporation must accrue bond interest expense from the last interest payment date to the end of its fiscal year. This accrual results in the inclusion of the interest expense in the year it is incurred.

LO 8 Explain and demonstrate the accounting issues related to leases and pensions.

An operating lease is a contract under which a company rents an asset. Payments on operating leases are properly treated as rent expense. On the other hand, a capital lease is a lease that cannot be canceled, has duration about the same as the useful life of the asset, or stipulates that the lessee has the option to buy the asset at a nominal price at the end of the lease. A capital lease is like a purchase or sale on installment. The lessee in a capital lease records an asset, depreciation on the asset, and a long-term liability equal to the present value of the total lease payments during the lease term.

A pension plan is a contract that requires a company to pay benefits to its employees after they retire. The two types of pension plans are defined contribution plans and defined benefit plans.

LO 9 Evaluate the decision to issue long-term debt, including analyzing long-term debt.

Management needs to decide between issuing long-term debt and issuing common stock or a combination of these two options. The advantages of issuing long-term debt are that common stockholders do not relinquish any control, interest on debt is tax-deductible, and financial leverage can increase earnings. The disadvantages are that interest and principal must be paid on time and financial leverage can work against a company if an investment is not successful. The level of debt can be evaluated using the debt to equity ratio and the interest coverage ratio.

Key Terms and Ratios

bond 489 (LO2)
bond certificate 489 (LO2)
bond indenture 489 (LO2)
bond issue 489 (LO2)
bonds payable 486 (LO1)
call price 490 (LO2)
callable bonds 490 (LO2)
capital lease 488 (LO1)
convertible bonds 490 (LO2)
coupon bonds 491 (LO2)
deferred income taxes 488 (LO1)
defined benefit plan 516 (LO8)
defined contribution plan 516 (LO8)
discount 490 (LO2)
early extinguishment of debt 490 (LO2)
effective interest method 499 (LO5)
face interest rate 489 (LO2)
face value 489 (LO2)
financial leverage 518 (LO9)
long-term liabilities 486 (LO1)
market interest rate 489 (LO2)
mortgage 487 (LO1)
notes payable 487 (LO1)
off-balance-sheet financing 519 (LO9)
operating lease 513 (LO8)
pension fund 516 (LO8)
pension plan 516 (LO8)
premium 490 (LO2)
registered bonds 491 (LO2)
secured bonds 490 (LO2)
serial bonds 490 (LO2)
straight-line method 498 (LO5)
term bonds 490 (LO2)
unsecured bonds 490 (LO2)
zero coupon bonds 498 (LO5)

RATIOS

debt to equity ratio 519 (LO9)
interest coverage ratio 519 (LO9)

Chapter Assignments

DISCUSSION QUESTIONS

LO 2, 9 RATIO **DQ1. BUSINESS APPLICATION ▶** If a company with a high debt to equity ratio wants to increase its debt when the economy is weak, what kind of bond might it issue?

LO 3 **DQ2.** What determines whether bonds are issued at a discount, premium, or face value?

LO 4 **DQ3.** Why does the market price of a bond vary over time?

LO 5 **DQ4.** When is it acceptable to use the straight-line method to amortize a bond discount or premium?

LO 6 **DQ5.** Why are callable and convertible bonds considered to add to management's future flexibility in financing a business?

LO 7 **DQ6. CONCEPT ▶** Why must the accrual of bond interest be recorded at the end of an accounting period?

LO 9 **DQ7. BUSINESS APPLICATION ▶** How does a lender assess the risk that a borrower may default—that is, not pay interest and principal when due?

LO 8 **DQ8. BUSINESS APPLICATION ▶** Why might a company lease a long-term asset rather than buy it and issue long-term bonds?

SHORT EXERCISES

LO 1 **Types of Long-Term Liabilities**

SE1. Match the liabilities that follow with the statement to which it applies.

1. Bonds payable	a. May result in a capital lease
2. Long-term notes payable	b. Differences in income taxes on accounting income and taxable income
3. Mortgage payable	c. The most popular form of long-term financing
4. Long-term lease	d. Often used to purchase land and buildings
5. Pension liabilities	e. Often used interchangeably with bonds payable
6. Other post-retirement benefits	f. Future health care costs are a major component
7. Deferred income taxes	g. May include 401(k), ESOPs, or profit-sharing

LO 1 **Mortgage Payable**

SE2. Hagler Corporation purchased a building by signing a $150,000 long-term mortgage with monthly payments of $1,200. The mortgage carries an interest rate of 8 percent per year. Prepare a monthly payment schedule showing the monthly payment, the interest for the month, the reduction in debt, and the unpaid balance for the first three months. (Round to the nearest dollar.)

LO 2 **Bond Characteristics**

SE3. Match each term that follows with the related term.

1. Discount	a. Convertible
2. Callable	b. Secured
3. Face interest rate	c. Coupon
4. Unsecured	d. Market interest rate
5. Registered	e. Serial
6. Term	f. Premium

LO 4 **Valuing Bonds Using Present Value**

SE4. Sanchez, Inc., is considering the sale of two bond issues. Choice A is a $1,200,000 bond issue that pays semiannual interest of $64,000 and is due in 20 years. Choice B is a $1,200,000 bond issue that pays semiannual interest of $60,000 and is due in 15 years. Assume that the market interest rate for each bond is 12 percent. Calculate the amount that Sanchez will receive if both bond issues occur. (*Hint:* Calculate the present value of each bond issue and sum.)

LO 3, 5 **Straight-Line Method**

SE5. On April 1, 2014, Angel Corporation issued $8,000,000 in 8.5 percent, five-year bonds at 98. The semiannual interest payment dates are April 1 and October 1. Prepare journal entries to record the issue of the bonds by Angel on April 1, 2014, and the first two interest payments on October 1, 2014, and April 1, 2015. Use the straight-line method and ignore year-end accruals.

LO 3, 5 **Effective Interest Method**

SE6. On March 1, 2014, Smart Way Freight Company sold $200,000 of its 9.5 percent, 20-year bonds at 106. The semiannual interest payment dates are March 1 and September 1. The market interest rate is 8.9 percent. The firm's fiscal year ends August 31. Prepare journal entries to record the sale of the bonds on March 1, the accrual of interest and amortization of premium on August 31, and the first interest payment on September 1. Use the effective interest method to amortize the premium.

LO 3, 5, 7 **Year-End Accrual of Bond Interest**

SE7. On October 1, 2014, Tender Corporation issued $250,000 of 9 percent bonds at 96. The bonds are dated October 1 and pay interest semiannually. The market rate of

(Continued)

interest is 10 percent, and the company's year-end is December 31. Prepare the journal entries to record the issuance of the bonds, the accrual of the interest on December 31, 2014, and the payment of the first semiannual interest on April 1, 2015. Assume the company uses the effective interest method to amortize the bond discount.

LO 6 **Bond Retirement**

SE8. Noble Corporation has outstanding $400,000 of 8 percent bonds callable at 104. On December 1, immediately after the payment of the semiannual interest and the amortization of the bond discount were recorded, the unamortized bond discount equaled $10,500. On that date, $240,000 of the bonds were called and retired. Prepare the journal entry to record the retirement of the bonds on December 1.

LO 6 **Bond Conversion**

SE9. Evergreen Corporation has $2,000,000 of 6 percent bonds outstanding. There is $40,000 of unamortized discount remaining on the bonds after the March 1, 2014, semiannual interest payment. The bonds are convertible at the rate of 20 shares of $10 par value common stock for each $1,000 bond. On March 1, 2014, bondholders presented $1,200,000 of the bonds for conversion. Prepare the journal entry to record the conversion of the bonds.

LO 7 **Bond Issue Between Interest Dates**

SE10. Dawn Corporation sold $400,000 of 9 percent, 10-year bonds for face value on September 1, 2014. The issue date of the bonds was May 1, 2014. The company's fiscal year ends on December 31, and this is its only bond issue. Prepare the journal entry to record the sale of the bonds on September 1 and the first semiannual interest payment on November 1, 2014. What is the bond interest expense for the year ended December 31, 2014?

LO 8 **Leases and Pensions Definitions**

SE11. Match each term that follows with the appropriate definition.

1. Defined benefit plan
2. Capital lease
3. Pension plan
4. Operating lease
5. Defined contribution plan

a. A contract that requires a company to pay benefits to its employees after they retire.
b. A short-term lease used for renting assets where ownership of the asset remain with the lessor, and the lease is shorter than the asset's useful life.
c. A plan in which the employer makes a fixed specified annual contribution, usually a percentage of the employee's gross pay.
d. A long-term lease that cannot be canceled, has duration about the same as the useful life of the asset, and stipulates that the lessee has the option to buy the asset at a nominal price at the end of the lease.
e. A plan in which the employer contributes an amount annually to fund estimated future pension liability.

LO 9 **Bond Versus Common Stock Financing**

SE12. BUSINESS APPLICATION ▶ Indicate whether each of the following is an advantage or a disadvantage of using long-term bond financing rather than issuing common stock:

1. Interest paid on bonds is tax-deductible.
2. Investments are sometimes not as successful as planned.
3. Financial leverage can have a negative effect when investments do not earn as much as the interest payments on the related debt.
4. Bondholders do not have voting rights in a corporation.
5. Positive financial leverage may be achieved.

EXERCISES: SET A

LO 1 Mortgage Payable

E1A. Pittman Corporation purchased a building by signing a $75,000 long-term mortgage with monthly payments of $1,000. The mortgage carries an interest rate of 12 percent.

1. Prepare a monthly payment schedule showing the monthly payment, the interest for the month, the reduction in debt, and the unpaid balance for the first three months. (Round to the nearest dollar.)
2. Prepare the journal entries to record the purchase and the first two monthly payments.

LO 2 Bond Issue Features and Bond Characteristics

E2A. Match each term that follows with the appropriate definition.

1. Face interest rate
2. Bond indenture
3. Secured bonds
4. Bond issue
5. Coupon bonds
6. Callable bonds
7. Market interest rate
8. Convertible bonds
9. Registered bonds

a. A contract that defines the rights, privileges, and limitations of the bondholders.
b. Bonds that allow the bondholder to exchange a bond for a specified number of shares of common stock.
c. The fixed rate of interest paid to bondholders based on the face value of the bonds.
d. Bonds that give the issuer the right to buy back and retire the bonds before maturity at a specified price, which is usually above face value.
e. The rate of interest paid in the market on bonds of similar risk.
f. The total value of bonds issued at one time.
g. Bonds issued in the names of the bondholders.
h. Bonds that carry a pledge of certain corporate assets as a guarantee of repayment.
i. Bonds not registered with the organization but bearing coupons stating the amount of interest due and the payment date.

LO 4 Valuing Bonds Using Present Value

E3A. Tsang, Inc., is considering the sale of two bond issues. Choice A is a $1,600,000 bond issue that pays semiannual interest of $128,000 and is due in 20 years. Choice B is a $1,600,000 bond issue that pays semiannual interest of $120,000 and is due in 15 years. Assume that the market interest rate for each bond is 12 percent. Calculate the amount that Tsang will receive if both bond issues are made. (*Hint:* Calculate the present value of each bond issue and sum.)

LO 4 Valuing Bonds Using Present Value

E4A. Use the present value tables in Appendix C to calculate the issue price of a $600,000 bond issue in each of the following independent cases. Assume interest is paid semiannually.

a. A 10-year, 8 percent bond issue; the market interest rate is 10 percent.
b. A 10-year, 8 percent bond issue; the market interest rate is 6 percent.
c. A 10-year, 10 percent bond issue; the market interest rate is 8 percent.
d. A 20-year, 10 percent bond issue; the market interest rate is 12 percent.
e. A 20-year, 10 percent bond issue; the market interest rate is 6 percent.

LO 4 Zero Coupon Bonds

E5A. The state of Idaho needs to raise $50,000,000 for highway repairs. Officials are considering issuing zero coupon bonds, which do not require periodic interest payments. The current market interest rate for the bonds is 10 percent. What face value of

(Continued)

bonds must be issued to raise the needed funds, assuming the bonds will be due in 30 years and compounded annually? How would your answer change if the bonds were due in 50 years? How would both answers change if the market interest rate were 8 percent instead of 10 percent?

LO **3, 5** **Straight-Line Method**

E6A. Norris Corporation issued $2,000,000 in 10.5 percent, 10-year bonds on February 1, 2014, at 104. Semiannual interest payment dates are January 31 and July 31. Use the straight-line method and ignore year-end accruals.

1. With regard to the bond issue on February 1, 2014:
   a. How much cash is received?
   b. How much is Bonds Payable?
   c. What is the difference between **a** and **b** called and how much is it?
2. With regard to the bond interest payment on July 31, 2014:
   a. How much cash is paid in interest?
   b. How much is the amortization?
   c. How much is interest expense?
3. With regard to the bond interest payment on January 31, 2015:
   a. How much cash is paid in interest?
   b. How much is the amortization?
   c. How much is interest expense?

LO **3, 5** **Straight-Line Method**

E7A. Waterbury Corporation issued $16,000,000 in 8.5 percent, five-year bonds on March 1, 2014, at 96. The semiannual interest payment dates are September 1 and March 1. Prepare the journal entries to record the issue of the bonds by Waterbury on March 1, 2014, and the first two interest payments on September 1, 2014, and March 1, 2015. Use the straight-line method and ignore year-end accruals.

LO **3, 5** **Effective Interest Method**

E8A. Linz Company sold $250,000 of 9.5 percent, 20-year bonds on April 1, 2014, at 106. The semiannual interest payment dates are March 31 and September 30. The market interest rate is 8.9 percent. The company's fiscal year ends September 30. Use the effective interest method to calculate the amortization. (Round to the nearest cent.)

1. With regard to the bond issue on April 1, 2014:
   a. How much cash is received?
   b. How much is Bonds Payable?
   c. What is the difference between **a** and **b** called and how much is it?
2. With regard to the bond interest payment on September 30, 2014:
   a. How much cash is paid in interest?
   b. How much is the amortization?
   c. How much is interest expense?
3. With regard to the bond interest payment on March 31, 2015:
   a. How much cash is paid in interest?
   b. How much is the amortization?
   c. How much is interest expense?

LO **3, 5** **Effective Interest Method**

E9A. On March 1, 2014, Minnow Corporation issued $600,000 of 10 percent, five-year bonds. The semiannual interest payment dates are February 28 and August 31. Because the market rate for similar investments was 11 percent, the bonds had to be issued at a discount. The discount on the issuance of the bonds was $24,335. The company's fiscal year ends February 28. Prepare the journal entries to record the bond issue on March 1, 2014, the payment of interest, and the amortization of the discount on August 31, 2014 and on February 28, 2015. Use the effective interest method. (Round to the nearest dollar.)

LO 6

Bond Retirement

E10A. Freed Corporation has outstanding $800,000 of 8 percent bonds callable at 104. On September 1, immediately after recording the payment of the semiannual interest and the amortization of the discount, the unamortized bond discount equaled $21,000. On that date, $480,000 of the bonds was called and retired.

1. How much cash must be paid to retire the bonds?
2. Is there a gain or loss on retirement, and if so, how much is it?

LO 6

Bond Conversion

E11A. Marisol Corporation has $800,000 of 6 percent bonds outstanding. There is $40,000 of unamortized discount remaining on these bonds after the July 1, 2014, semiannual interest payment. The bonds are convertible at the rate of 40 shares of $5 par value common stock for each $1,000 bond. On July 1, 2014, bondholders presented $600,000 of the bonds for conversion.

1. Is there a gain or loss on conversion, and if so, how much is it?
2. How many shares of common stock are issued in exchange for the bonds?
3. In dollar amounts, how does this transaction affect the total liabilities and the total stockholders' equity of the company? In your answer, show the effects on four accounts.

LO 5, 7

Effective Interest Method and Interest Accrual

E12A. The long-term debt section of Karidis Corporation's balance sheet at the end of its fiscal year, December 31, 2013, follows.

Long-term liabilities		
Bonds payable—8%, interest payable		
1/1 and 7/1, due 12/31/16	$500,000	
Less unamortized bond discount	40,000	$460,000

Using the effective interest method, prepare the journal entries relevant to the interest payments on July 1, 2014, December 31, 2014, and January 1, 2015. Assume a market interest rate of 10 percent.

LO 4, 6

Time Value of Money and Early Extinguishment of Debt

E13A. Flanders, Inc., has a $700,000, 8 percent bond issue that was issued a number of years ago at face value. There are now 10 years left on the bond issue, and the market interest rate is 16 percent. Interest is paid semiannually. The company purchases the bonds on the open market at the calculated current market value and retires the bonds.

1. Using present value tables, calculate the current market value of the bond issue.
2. Is there a gain or loss on retirement of the bonds, and if so, how much is it?

LO 3, 7

Bond Issue on and Between Interest Dates

E14A. O'Brien, Inc., is authorized to issue $3,600,000 in bonds on June 1. The bonds carry a face interest rate of 9 percent, which is to be paid on June 1 and December 1. Prepare journal entries to record the issue of the bonds by O'Brien under the assumptions that (a) the bonds are issued on September 1 at 100 and (b) the bonds are issued on June 1 at 105.

LO 7 **Bond Issue Between Interest Dates**

E15A. Fleetwood Corporation sold $800,000 of 12 percent, 10-year bonds at face value on September 1, 2014. The issue date of the bonds was May 1, 2014.

1. Prepare the journal entries to record the sale of the bonds on September 1 and the first semiannual interest payment on November 1, 2014.
2. The company's fiscal year ends on December 31, and this is its only bond issue. What is the bond interest expense for the year ended December 31, 2014?

LO 3, 5, 7 **Year-End Accrual of Bond Interest**

E16A. Rapid Tech Corporation issued $2,000,000 of 9 percent bonds on October 1, 2014, at 96. The bonds are dated October 1 and pay interest semiannually. The market interest rate is 10 percent, and Rapid Tech's fiscal year ends on December 31. Prepare the journal entries to record the issuance of the bonds, the accrual of the interest on December 31, 2014, and the first semiannual interest payment on April 1, 2015. Assume the company uses the effective interest method to amortize the bond discount.

LO 8 **Recording Lease Obligations**

E17A. BUSINESS APPLICATION ▶ Rigby Corporation has leased a piece of equipment that has a useful life of 12 years. This capital lease requires payments of $86,000 per year for 12 years. Rigby currently is able to borrow money at a long-term interest rate of 15 percent. (Round to the nearest dollar.)

1. Calculate the present value of the lease.
2. Prepare the journal entry to record the lease agreement.
3. Prepare the journal entry to record depreciation of the equipment for the first year using the straight-line method.
4. Prepare the journal entries to record the lease payments for the first two years.

LO 9 **Interest Coverage Ratio**

E18A. BUSINESS APPLICATION ▶ Compute the interest coverage ratios for 2013 and 2014 from Dasbol Corporation's partial income statements that follow. (Round to one decimal place.) State whether the ratio improved or worsened over time.

	2014	2013
Income from operations	$47,780	$36,920
Interest expense	11,600	6,600
Income before income taxes	$36,180	$30,320
Income taxes	10,800	9,000
Net income	$25,380	$21,320

EXERCISES: SET B

Visit the textbook companion website at www.cengagebrain.com to access Exercise Set B for this chapter.

PROBLEMS

LO 1, 2 **Bond Terminology**

P1. Some common terms associated with bonds follow.

a. Bond certificate
b. Bond issue
c. Bond indenture
d. Unsecured bonds
e. Debenture bonds
f. Secured bonds
g. Term bonds
h. Serial bonds
i. Registered bonds
j. Coupon bonds
k. Callable bonds
l. Convertible bonds
m. Face interest rate
n. Market interest rate
o. Effective interest rate
p. Bond premium
q. Bond discount

REQUIRED

1. For each of the statements that follow, identify the category above with which it is associated. (If two statements apply, choose the category with which it is most closely associated.)
   1. Occurs when bonds are sold at more than face value
   2. Rate of interest that will vary depending on economic conditions
   3. Bonds that may be exchanged for common stock
   4. Bonds that are not registered
   5. A bond issue in which all bonds are due on the same date
   6. Occurs when bonds are sold at less than face value
   7. Rate of interest that will be paid regardless of market conditions
   8. Bonds that may be retired at management's option
   9. A document that is evidence of a company's debt
   10. Same as market rate of interest
   11. Bonds for which the company knows who owns them
   12. A bond issue for which bonds are due at different dates
   13. The total value of bonds issued at one time
   14. Bonds whose payment involves a pledge of certain assets
   15. Same as debenture bonds
   16. Contains the terms of the bond issue
   17. Bonds issued on the general credit of the company
2. **ACCOUNTING CONNECTION ▶** What effect will a decrease in interest rates below the face interest rate and before a bond is issued have on the cash received from the bond issue? What effect will the decrease have on interest expense? What effect will the decrease have on the amount of cash paid for interest?

LO **3, 5, 6, 9**

Bond Basics—Straight-Line Method, Retirement, and Conversion

SPREADSHEET

✔ 1d(3): Interest expense: $374,400
✔ 2d(3): Interest expense: $385,600

P2. Sasina Corporation has $8,000,000 of 9.5 percent, 25-year bonds dated May 1, 2014, with interest payable on April 30 and October 31. The company's fiscal year ends on December 31, and it uses the straight-line method to amortize bond premiums or discounts. The bonds are callable after 10 years at 103, or each $1,000 bond is convertible into 40 shares of $10 par value common stock.

REQUIRED

1. Assume the bonds are issued at 103.5 on May 1, 2014.
   a. How much cash is received?
   b. How much is Bonds Payable?
   c. What is the difference between **a** and **b** called, and how much is it?
   d. With regard to the bond interest payment on October 31, 2014:
      (1) How much cash is paid in interest?
      (2) How much is the amortization?
      (3) How much is interest expense?
2. Assume the bonds are issued at 96.5 on May 1, 2014.
   a. How much cash is received?
   b. How much is Bonds Payable?
   c. What is the difference between **a** and **b** called, and how much is it?
   d. With regard to the bond interest payment on October 31, 2014:
      (1) How much cash is paid in interest?
      (2) How much is the amortization?
      (3) How much is interest expense?
3. Assume the issue price in requirement **1** and that the bonds are called and retired 10 years later.
   a. How much cash will have to be paid to retire the bonds?
   b. Is there a gain or loss on the retirement, and if so, how much is it?

(Continued)

4. Assume the issue price in requirement **2** and that the bonds are converted to common stock 10 years later.
   a. Is there a gain or loss on conversion, and if so, how much is it?
   b. How many shares of common stock are issued in exchange for the bonds?
   c. In dollar amounts, how does this transaction affect the total liabilities and the total stockholders' equity of the company? In your answer, show the effects on four accounts.
5. **BUSINESS APPLICATION** ▶ Assume that after 10 years market interest rates have dropped significantly and that the price of the company's common stock has risen significantly. Also assume that management wants to improve its credit rating by reducing its debt to equity ratio and that it needs what cash it currently has for expansion. Would management prefer the approach and result in requirement **3** or **4**? Explain your answer. What would be a disadvantage of the approach you chose?

LO **3, 5**

GENERAL LEDGER

✔ 1: Bond Interest Expense, May 31: $439,184
✔ 2: Bond Interest Expense, May 31: $457,350

Bond Transactions—Effective Interest Method

P3. Zapala Corporation has $10,000,000 of 9 percent, 20-year bonds dated June 1, 2014, with interest payment dates of May 31 and November 30. The company's fiscal year ends November 30. It uses the effective interest method to amortize bond premiums or discounts.

REQUIRED

1. Assume the bonds are issued at 109.9 on June 1 to yield an effective interest rate of 8 percent. Prepare the journal entries for June 1, 2014, November 30, 2014, and May 31, 2015. (Round to the nearest dollar.)
2. Assume the bonds are issued at 91.4 on June 1 to yield an effective interest rate of 10 percent. Prepare the journal entries for June 1, 2014, November 30, 2014, and May 31, 2015. (Round to the nearest dollar.)
3. **ACCOUNTING CONNECTION** ▶ Explain the role that market interest rates play in causing a premium in requirement **1** and a discount in requirement **2**.

LO **3, 5, 7**

SPREADSHEET

✔ 2a: Total interest expense in 2014: $474,200
✔ 2b: Total cash paid for interest in 2014: $380,000

Bonds Issued at a Discount and a Premium—Effective Interest Method

P4. Yacuma Corporation issued bonds twice during 2014. The transactions follow.

2014

Jan. 1	Issued $2,000,000 of 9.2 percent, 10-year bonds dated January 1, 2014, with interest payable on June 30 and December 31. The bonds were sold at 98.1, resulting in an effective interest rate of 9.5 percent.
Apr. 1	Issued $4,000,000 of 9.8 percent, 10-year bonds dated April 1, 2014, with interest payable on March 31 and September 30. The bonds were sold at 101, resulting in an effective interest rate of 9.5 percent.
June 30	Paid semiannual interest on the January 1 issue and amortized the discount, using the effective interest method.
Sept. 30	Paid semiannual interest on the April 1 issue and amortized the premium, using the effective interest method.
Dec. 31	Paid semiannual interest on the January 1 issue and amortized the discount, using the effective interest method.
31	Made an end-of-year adjusting entry to accrue interest on the April 1 issue and to amortize half the premium applicable to the second interest period.

2015

Mar. 31	Paid semiannual interest on the April 1 issue and amortized the premium applicable to the second half of the second interest period.

REQUIRED

1. Prepare the journal entries to record the bond transactions. (Round to the nearest dollar.)

2. **ACCOUNTING CONNECTION ▶** Describe the effect of the above transactions on profitability and liquidity by answering the following questions:
   a. What is the total interest expense in 2014 for each of the bond issues?
   b. What is the total cash paid in 2014 for each of the bond issues?
   c. What differences, if any, do you observe, and how do you explain them?

LO **8**

Lease Versus Purchase

✔ 1a: Present value of lease: $171,864
✔ 2a: Unpaid balance at the end of third month: $157,582

P5. Wooster Corporation can either lease or buy a small garage next to its business that will provide parking for its customers. The company can lease the building for a period of 12 years, which approximates the useful life of the facility and thus qualifies as a capital lease. The terms of the lease are payments of $24,000 per year for 12 years. Wooster currently is able to borrow money at a long-term interest rate of 9 percent. The company can purchase the building by signing an $160,000 long-term mortgage with monthly payments of $2,000. The mortgage also carries an interest rate of 9 percent.

REQUIRED

1. With regard to the lease option:
   a. Calculate the present value of the lease. (Round to the nearest dollar.)
   b. Prepare the journal entry to record the lease agreement.
   c. Prepare the journal entry to record depreciation of the building for the first year using the straight-line method.
   d. Prepare the journal entries to record the lease payments for the first two years.
2. With regard to the purchase option:
   a. Prepare a monthly payment schedule showing the monthly payment, the interest for the month, the reduction in debt, and the unpaid balance for the first three months. (Round to the nearest dollar.)
   b. Prepare the journal entries to record the purchase and the first two monthly payments.
3. **BUSINESS APPLICATION ▶** Based on your calculations, which option seems to be best? Aside from cost, name an advantage and a disadvantage of each option.

ALTERNATE PROBLEMS

LO **3, 5, 6, 9**

Bond Basics—Straight-Line Method, Retirement, and Conversion

✔ 1d(3): Interest Expense: $517,500
✔ 2d(3): Interest expense: $532,500

P6. Cozumel Corporation has $10,000,000 of 10.5 percent, 20-year bonds dated June 1, 2014, with interest payment dates of May 31 and November 30. After 10 years, the bonds are callable at 104, and each $1,000 bond is convertible into 25 shares of $20 par value common stock. The company's fiscal year ends on December 31. It uses the straight-line method to amortize bond premiums or discounts.

REQUIRED

1. Assume the bonds are issued at 103 on June 1, 2014.
   a. How much cash is received?
   b. How much is Bonds Payable?
   c. What is the difference between **a** and **b** called, and how much is it?
   d. With regard to the bond interest payment on November 30, 2014:
      (1) How much cash is paid in interest?
      (2) How much is the amortization?
      (3) How much is interest expense?
2. Assume the bonds are issued at 97 on June 1, 2014.
   a. How much cash is received?
   b. How much is Bonds Payable?

(Continued)

   c. What is the difference between **a** and **b** called, and how much is it?
   d. With regard to the bond interest payment on November 30, 2014:
      (1) How much cash is paid in interest?
      (2) How much is the amortization?
      (3) How much is interest expense?
3. Assume the issue price in requirement **1** and that the bonds are called and retired 10 years later.
   a. How much cash will have to be paid to retire the bonds?
   b. Is there a gain or loss on the retirement, and if so, how much is it?
4. Assume the issue price in requirement **2** and that the bonds are converted to common stock 10 years later.
   a. Is there a gain or loss on the conversion, and if so, how much is it?
   b. How many shares of common stock are issued in exchange for the bonds?
   c. In dollar amounts, how does this transaction affect the total liabilities and the total stockholders' equity of the company? In your answer, show the effects on four accounts.
5. **BUSINESS APPLICATION** ▶ Assume that after 10 years, market interest rates have dropped significantly and that the price on the company's common stock has risen significantly. Also assume that management wants to improve its credit rating by reducing its debt to equity ratio and that it needs what cash it has for expansion. Which approach would management prefer—the approach and result in requirement **3** or **4**? Explain your answer. What would be a disadvantage of the approach you chose?

LO **3, 5**

Bond Transactions—Effective Interest Method

GENERAL LEDGER

✓ 1: Bond Interest Expense, Feb. 28: $377,071
✓ 2: Bond Interest Expense, Feb. 28: $382,308

P7. Krabna Corporation has $8,000,000 of 9.5 percent, 25-year bonds dated March 1, 2014, with interest payable on February 28 and August 31. The company's fiscal year end is February 28. It uses the effective interest method to amortize bond premiums or discounts. (Round to the nearest dollar.)

REQUIRED

1. Assume the bonds are issued at 102.5 on March 1, 2014, to yield an effective interest rate of 9.2 percent. Prepare the journal entries for March 1, 2014, August 31, 2014, and February 28, 2015.
2. Assume the bonds are issued at 97.5 on March 1, 2014, to yield an effective interest rate of 9.8 percent. Prepare the journal entries for March 1, 2014, August 31, 2014, and February 28, 2015.
3. **ACCOUNTING CONNECTION** ▶ Explain the role that market interest rates play in causing a premium in requirement **1** and a discount in requirement **2**.

LO **3, 5, 7**

Bonds Issued at a Discount and a Premium—Effective Interest Method

SPREADSHEET

✓ 2a: Total interest expense in 2014: $889,352
✓ 2b: Total cash paid for interest in 2014: $778,000

P8. Hart Corporation issued bonds twice during 2014. A summary of the transactions involving the bonds follows.

2014

Jan. 1	Issued $6,000,000 of 9.9 percent, 10-year bonds dated January 1, 2014, with interest payable on June 30 and December 31. The bonds were sold at 102.6, resulting in an effective interest rate of 9.4 percent.
Mar. 1	Issued $4,000,000 of 9.2 percent, 10-year bonds dated March 1, 2014, with interest payable March 1 and September 1. The bonds were sold at 98.2, resulting in an effective interest rate of 9.5 percent.
June 30	Paid semiannual interest on the January 1 issue and amortized the premium, using the effective interest method.
Sept. 1	Paid semiannual interest on the March 1 issue and amortized the discount, using the effective interest method.

Dec. 31 Paid semiannual interest on the January 1 issue and amortized the premium, using the effective interest method.

31 Made an end-of-year adjusting entry to accrue interest on the March 1 issue and to amortize two-thirds of the discount applicable to the second interest period.

2015

Mar. 1 Paid semiannual interest on the March 1 issue and amortized the remainder of the discount applicable to the second interest period.

REQUIRED

1. Prepare journal entries to record the bond transactions. (Round to the nearest dollar.)
2. **ACCOUNTING CONNECTION ▶** Describe the effect on profitability and liquidity by answering the following questions:
   a. What is the total interest expense in 2014 for each of the bond issues?
   b. What is the total cash paid in 2014 for each of the bond issues?
   c. What differences, if any, do you observe and how do you explain them?

LO **8**

Lease Versus Purchase

✔ 1a: Present value of lease: $343,728
✔ 2a: Unpaid balance at the end of third month: $315,164

P9. Martha Corporation can either lease or buy a small garage next to its business that will provide parking for its customers. The company can lease the building for a period of 12 years, which approximates the useful life of the facility and thus qualifies as a capital lease. The terms of the lease are payments of $48,000 per year for 12 years. Martha currently is able to borrow money at a long-term interest rate of 9 percent. The company can purchase the building by signing a $320,000 long-term mortgage with monthly payments of $4,000. The mortgage also carries an interest rate of 9 percent.

REQUIRED

1. With regard to the lease option:
   a. Calculate the present value of the lease. (Round to the nearest dollar.)
   b. Prepare the journal entry to record the lease agreement.
   c. Prepare the journal entry to record depreciation of the building for the first year using the straight-line method.
   d. Prepare the journal entries to record the lease payments for the first two years.
2. With regard to the purchase option:
   a. Prepare a monthly payment schedule showing the monthly payment, the interest for the month, the reduction in debt, and the unpaid balance for the first three months. (Round to the nearest dollar.)
   b. Prepare the journal entries to record the purchase and the first two monthly payments.
3. **BUSINESS APPLICATION ▶** Based on your calculations, which option seems to be best? Aside from cost, name an advantage and a disadvantage of each option.

CASES

LO **1, 2, 6**

Conceptual Understanding: Bond Issue

C1. Eastman Kodak, the more than 100-year-old photography company, recently declared bankruptcy after struggling for many years. One of its efforts to survive was a $1 billion bond issue several years ago. Even though the company's credit rating was low at the time, the bond issue was well received by the investment community because the company offered attractive terms. The offering comprised $500 million of 10-year unsecured notes and $500 million of 30-year convertible bonds. The convertibles were callable after seven years and would be convertible into common stock about 40 to 45 percent higher than the current price.[10]

(Continued)

What are unsecured notes? Why would they carry a relatively high interest rate? What are convertible securities? Why are they good for the investor and for the company? Why would they carry a relatively low interest rate? What does *callable* mean? What advantage does this feature give the company?

LO 2, 3

Conceptual Understanding: Bond Interest Rates and Market Prices

C2. Dow Chemical is one of the largest chemical companies in the world. Among its long-term liabilities was a bond due in 2011 that carried a face interest rate of 6.125 percent.[11] This bond sold on the New York Stock Exchange at 104 5/8. Did this bond sell at a discount or a premium? Assuming the bond was originally issued at face value, did interest rates rise or decline after the date of issue? Would you have expected the market rate of interest on this bond to be more or less than 6.125 percent? Did the current market price affect either the amount that the company paid in semiannual interest or the amount of interest expense for the same period? Explain your answers.

LO 6, 9

Conceptual Understanding: Characteristics of Convertible Debt

C3. Intel Corporation designs and manufactures advanced integrated digital technology platforms. The company has never earned a profit. In 2009, Intel issued $2,000,000,000 of junior subordinated convertible notes at 3.25 percent due in 2039 at face value. The notes are convertible into common stock at a price of $22.45 per share, which at the time of issue was above the market price. The market value of Intel's common stock ranged from $19.16 to $25.66 in 2011.[12] What reasons can you suggest for Intel's management choosing notes that are convertible into common stock rather than simply issuing nonconvertible notes or issuing common stock directly? Are there any disadvantages to this approach? If the price of the company's common stock goes to $17 per share, what would be the total theoretical value of the notes? If the holders of the notes were to elect to convert the notes into common stock, what would be the effect on the company's debt to equity ratio, and what would be the effect on the percentage ownership of the company by other stockholders?

LO 8, 9

Conceptual Understanding: Effect of Long-Term Leases

C4. BUSINESS APPLICATION ▶ Many companies use long-term leases to finance long-term assets. Although these leases are similar to mortgage payments, they are structured in such a way that they qualify as operating leases. As a result, the lease commitments do not appear on the companies' balance sheets.

In a recent year, **Continental Airlines** had almost $15 billion in total operating lease commitments, of which $1.5 billion was due in the current year. Further, the airline had total assets of $12.686 billion and total liabilities of $12.581 billion. Because of heavy losses in previous years, its stockholders' equity was only $0.105 billion.

What effect do these types of leases have on the balance sheet? Why would the use of these long-term leases make a company's debt to equity ratio, interest coverage ratio, and free cash flow look better than they really are? What is a capital lease? How does the application of capital lease accounting provide insight into a company's financial health?

LO 1, 8

Interpreting Financial Reports: Long-Term Debt, Leases, and Pensions

C5. BUSINESS APPLICATION ▶ To answer the following questions, refer to the financial statements and the notes to the financial statements in **CVS Corporation**'s annual report in the Supplement to Chapter 1:

1. Is it the practice of CVS to own or lease most of its buildings?
2. Does CVS lease property predominantly under capital leases or under operating leases? How much was rental expense for operating leases in 2011?
3. Does CVS have a defined benefit pension plan? Does it offer post-retirement benefits?

LO 1, 9

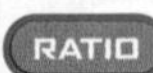

Interpreting Financial Reports: Use of Debt Financing

C6. BUSINESS APPLICATION ▶ Refer to the annual report of **CVS Corporation** and the financial statements of **Southwest Airlines Co.** in the Supplement to Chapter 1. Calculate the debt to equity ratio and the interest coverage ratio for both companies' two most recent years. (Round to one decimal place.) Find the note to the financial statements that contains information on leases and lease commitments by CVS. Southwest's lease expenses were $847 million and $631 million in 2011 and 2010, respectively, and total lease commitments for future years were $5,583 million. What effect do the total lease commitments and lease expense have on your assessment of the ratios you calculated? Evaluate and comment on the relative performance of the two companies with regard to debt financing. Which company has more risk of not being able to meet its interest obligations? How does leasing affect the analysis? Explain.

Continuing Case: Annual Report Project

C7. Using the most recent annual report of the company you have chosen to study and that you have accessed online at the company's website, examine the balance sheet and accompanying notes of your company. Answer the following questions:

1. What percentage of total liabilities and stockholders' equity is long-term liabilities? Does the company have long-term notes or bonds and deferred income taxes? How do these liabilities differ from each other?
2. Find the disclosures about these leases in the notes to the financial statements. What are the total lease obligations of the company?
3. Find the disclosures about pensions in the notes to the financial statements. What kind of pension plan does the company have? Does it offer post-retirement benefits?

CHAPTER 12

LEARNING OBJECTIVES

LO 1 Define the *corporate* form of business and its characteristics.

LO 2 Identify the components of stockholders' equity and their characteristics.

LO 3 Account for the issuance of stock for cash and other assets.

LO 4 Account for treasury stock.

LO 5 Account for cash dividends.

LO 6 Account for stock dividends and stock splits.

LO 7 Describe the statement of stockholders' equity, and compute book value per share.

LO 8 Calculate dividend yield and return on equity, and define stock options.

Alex Segre/Alamy

STOCKHOLDERS' EQUITY

Business Insight

Google, Inc.

When a company issues stock to the public for the first time, it is called an **initial public offering (IPO)**. There are many initial public offerings in any given year, but when **Google**, the popular Internet search engine company, went to market with its IPO in August 2004, it created a national sensation for two reasons. First, it was one of the most successful IPOs in history. Second, Google provides a very well-known and widely used search service. Those who bought shares at $85 each saw the price per share soar to $135 in a few days. Although volatile in subsequent years, ranging to as high at $700 per share, it remains almost $600 per share in early 2012. Google's Financial Highlights show the components of its stockholders' equity.[1]

Google's Financial Highlights (in millions)

	Dec. 31, 2011	Dec. 31, 2010
Stockholders' equity		
Preferred stock	$ —	$ —
Common stock ($0.001 par value)	321	325
Additional paid-in capital	19,943	17,910
Retained earnings	37,605	27,868
Accumulated other comprehensive income	276	138
Total stockholders' equity	$ 58,145	$ 46,241
Total assets	$40,496,778	$31,767,575

1. **CONCEPT** ▶ How does the separate entity concept apply to the stockholders in a corporation like Google?
2. **ACCOUNTING APPLICATION** ▶ How would Google account for its initial public offering?
3. **BUSINESS APPLICATION** ▶ What measures should stockholders use to evaluate the return on their investments?

SECTION 1 CONCEPTS

CONCEPT

- Separate entity

RELEVANT LEARNING OBJECTIVE

LO1 Define the *corporate* form of business and its characteristics.

LO1 Concepts Underlying the Corporate Form of Business

The corporate form of business is well suited to today's trends toward large organizations, international trade, and professional management. Although fewer in number than sole proprietorships and partnerships, corporations dominate the U.S. economy, in part because of their ability to raise large amounts of capital. In 2007, the peak market year, the amount of new capital that corporations raised was $2.7 trillion. Even though the following years were not the best for markets, the amount of new capital raised by corporations was $1.4 trillion.[2]

In Chapter 1, we defined a *corporation* as a *separate entity* chartered by the state and *legally separate* from its owners—that is, its stockholders. **Contributed capital**, which refers to stockholders' investments in a corporation, is a major means of financing a corporation. Managing contributed capital requires an understanding of the advantages and disadvantages of the corporate form of business and of the issues involved in equity financing. It also requires familiarity with dividend policies, with how to use return on equity to evaluate performance, and with stock option plans.

Advantages of Incorporation

Some of the advantages of the corporate form of business follow.

- **Separate legal entity:** As a *separate legal entity*, a corporation can buy and sell property, sue other parties, enter into contracts, hire and fire employees, and be taxed.
- **Limited liability:** Because a corporation is a *legal entity, separate* from its owners, its creditors can satisfy their claims only against the assets of the corporation, not against the personal property of the corporation's owners. Because the owners are not responsible for the corporation's debts, their liability is limited to the amount of their investment. In contrast, the personal property of sole proprietors and partners generally is available to creditors.
- **Ease of capital generation:** It is fairly easy for a corporation to raise capital because shares of ownership in the business are available to a great number of potential investors for a small amount of money. As a result, a single corporation can have many owners.
- **Ease of transfer of ownership:** A stockholder can normally buy and sell shares of stock without affecting the corporation's activities or needing the approval of other owners.
- **Lack of mutual agency:** If a stockholder tries to enter into a contract for a corporation, the corporation is not bound by the contract. In a partnership, because of what is called *mutual agency*, all the partners can be bound by one partner's actions.
- **Continuous existence:** Because a corporation is a *separate legal entity*, an owner's death, incapacity, or withdrawal does not affect the life of the corporation. A corporation's life is set by its charter and regulated by state laws.
- **Centralized authority and responsibility:** The board of directors represents the stockholders and delegates the responsibility and authority for day-to-day operation to a single person, usually the president. Operating power is centralized rather than divided among the multiple owners of the business. The president may delegate authority over certain segments of the business to others, but he or she is held accountable to the board of directors. If the board is dissatisfied with the performance of the president, it can replace that person.
- **Professional management:** Large corporations have many owners, most of whom are not able to make timely decisions about business operations. Thus, management and ownership are usually separate. This allows management to hire the best talent available to run the business.

Disadvantages of Incorporation

Some of the disadvantages of corporations follow.

- **Government regulation:** As "creatures of the state," corporations are subject to greater control and regulation than are other forms of business. They must file many reports with the state in which they are chartered. Publicly held corporations must also file reports with the Securities and Exchange Commission and with the stock exchanges on which they are listed. They must also maintain internal controls and have audits conducted in compliance with regulations set by the Public Company Accounting Oversight Board (PCAOB). Meeting these requirements is very costly.
- **Double taxation:** A major disadvantage of the corporate form of business is **double taxation**. Because a corporation is a *separate legal entity*, its earnings are subject to federal and state income taxes, which may be as much as 35 percent of corporate earnings. If any of a corporation's after-tax earnings are paid out as dividends, the earnings are taxed again as income to the stockholders. In contrast, the earnings of sole proprietorships and partnerships are taxed only once, as income to the owners.
- **Limited liability:** Limited liability restricts the ability of a small corporation to borrow money. Because creditors can lay claim only to the assets of a corporation, they may limit their loans to the level secured by those assets or require stockholders to guarantee the loans personally.
- **Separation of ownership and control:** Just as limited liability can be a drawback of incorporation, so can the separation of ownership and control. Management sometimes makes decisions that are not good for the corporation. Poor communication can also make it hard for stockholders to exercise control over the corporation or even to recognize that management's decisions are harmful.

STUDY NOTE: *Lenders to a small corporation may require the corporation's officers to sign a promissory note, which makes them personally liable for the debt.*

Equity Financing

Equity financing is accomplished by issuing stock to investors in exchange for assets, usually cash. Once the stock has been issued to them, the stockholders can transfer their ownership at will. Large corporations can have millions of shares of stock, thousands of which change ownership every day. They, therefore, often appoint independent **registrars** and **transfer agents** (usually banks and trust companies) to help perform the transfer duties. The outside agents are responsible for transferring the corporation's stock, maintaining stockholders' records, preparing a list of stockholders for stockholders' meetings, and paying dividends.

Two important terms in equity financing are par value and legal capital:

- **Par value** is an arbitrary amount assigned to each share of stock. It must be recorded in the capital stock accounts. Par value usually bears little, if any, relationship to the market value of the shares. For example, although **Google**'s stock initially sold for $85 per share and the market value is now much higher, its par value per share is only $0.001.
- **Legal capital** is the number of shares issued multiplied by the par value. It is the minimum amount that a corporation can report as contributed capital. For example, even though the total market value of **Google**'s shares now exceeds $200 billion, Google's legal capital is only about $325,140 (325.14 million shares × $0.001).

To help with its initial public offering (IPO), a corporation often uses an **underwriter**—an intermediary between the corporation and the investing public. For a fee—usually less than 1 percent of the selling price—the underwriter guarantees the sale of the stock. The corporation records the amount of the net proceeds of the offering in its Capital Stock and Additional Paid-in Capital accounts. The net proceeds are what the public paid less the underwriter's fees, legal expenses, and any other direct costs of the offering. Because of the size of its IPO, **Google** used a group of investment banks headed by two well-known investment bankers, **Morgan Stanley** and **Credit Suisse First Boston**.

The costs of forming a corporation are called **start-up and organization costs**. These costs include:

- State incorporation fees
- Attorneys' fees for drawing up the articles of incorporation
- The cost of printing stock certificates
- Accountants' fees for registering the firm's initial stock
- Other expenditures necessary for the formation of the corporation

STUDY NOTE: *Start-up and organization costs are expensed as they are incurred.*

Theoretically, start-up and organization costs benefit the entire life of a corporation. For that reason, a case can be made for recording them as intangible assets and amortizing them over the life of the corporation. However, a corporation's life normally is not known, so accountants expense start-up and organization costs as they are incurred.

Advantages of Equity Financing Financing a business by issuing common stock has several advantages.

- **Decreased financial risk:** Issuing common stock is less risky than financing with long-term debt because a company does not pay dividends on common stock unless the board of directors decides to pay them. In contrast, if a company does not pay interest on long-term debt, it can be forced into bankruptcy.
- **Increased cash for operations:** When a company does not pay a cash dividend, it can shift the cash generated by profitable operations back into the company's operations. **Google**, for instance, does not currently pay any dividends, and its issuance of common stock provides it with funds for expansion.
- **Better debt to equity ratio:** A company can use the proceeds of a common stock issue to maintain or improve its debt to equity ratio.

Disadvantages of Equity Financing Issuing common stock also has certain disadvantages.

- **Increased tax liability:** Whereas the interest on debt is tax-deductible, the dividends paid on stock are not tax-deductible.
- **Decreased stockholder control:** When a corporation issues more stock, it dilutes its ownership. Thus, the current stockholders must yield some control to the new stockholders.

APPLY IT!

Match each item that follows with the topic to which it pertains.

a. Advantage of the corporate form of business
b. Disadvantage of the corporate form of business
c. Dividend policies

1. U.S. tax policies
2. Separate legal entity
3. Ease of ownership transfer
4. Distributing cash to stockholders
5. Need to deal with government regulation

SOLUTION

1. b; 2. a; 3. a; 4. c; 5. b

TRY IT! SE1, SE2, E1A, E1B

SECTION 2 **ACCOUNTING APPLICATIONS**

COUNTING PLICATIONS
- Prepare the statement of stockholders' equity
- Record the issuance of stock for cash and other assets
- Record the purchase, sale, and retirement of treasury stock
- Account for cash dividends
- Account for stock dividends and stock splits

LEVANT ARNING OBJECTIVES

2 Identify the components of ckholders' equity and their racteristics.

3 Account for the issuance of stock for h and other assets.

4 Account for treasury stock.

5 Account for cash dividends.

6 Account for stock dividends and ck splits.

7 Describe the statement of stockholders' equity, d compute book value share.

LO2 Components of Stockholders' Equity

As shown in Exhibit 1, the stockholders' equity section of a corporate balance sheet usually has at least three components.

- **Contributed capital:** The stockholders' investments in the corporation.
- **Retained earnings:** The earnings of the corporation since its inception, less any losses, dividends, or transfers to contributed capital. Retained earnings are reinvested in the business. They are not a pool of funds to be distributed to the stockholders; instead, they represent the stockholders' claim to assets resulting from profitable operations.
- **Treasury stock:** Shares of the corporation's own stock that it has bought back on the open market are called **treasury stock**. The cost of these shares is treated as a reduction in stockholders' equity. By buying back the shares, the corporation reduces the ownership of the business.

Exhibit 1
Stockholders' Equity Section of a Balance Sheet

Stockholders' Equity		
Contributed capital:		
Preferred stock, $50 par value, 2,000 shares authorized, issued, and outstanding		$100,000
Common stock, $5 par value, 60,000 shares authorized, 40,000 shares issued, 36,000 shares outstanding	$200,000	
Additional paid-in capital	100,000	300,000
Total contributed capital		$400,000
Retained earnings		120,000
Total contributed capital and retained earnings		$520,000
Less: Treasury stock, common (4,000 shares at cost)		40,000
Total stockholders' equity		$480,000

In keeping with the convention of *full disclosure*, the stockholders' equity section of a balance sheet gives a great deal of information about the corporation's stock. Under contributed capital, it lists the kinds of stock, their par values, and the number of shares authorized, issued, and outstanding. Corporations may disclose more detail in a **statement of stockholders' equity** (or *statement of changes in stockholders' equity*). This statement summarizes changes in the components of the stockholders' equity section of the balance sheet.

International Perspective

IFRS How Does a Stock Become a Debt Under IFRS?

A significant difference between International Financial Reporting Standards (IFRS) and U.S. GAAP is the issue of what constitutes stockholders' equity. This issue is important because it affects financial ratios such as return on assets, requirements under loan agreements, and the capital requirements of banks. Under U.S. GAAP, most preferred stocks are *classified* as stockholders' equity. In contrast, under IFRS, most preferred stocks are *classified* as liabilities because they resemble debt in that they have fixed dividends rates and are often cumulative.

The FASB is considering a proposal that would require these special preferred stocks to be classified as a liability on the balance sheet, which would be more in line with IFRS.[3]

A corporation can issue two types of stock:

- **Common stock** is the basic form of stock. If a corporation issues only one type of stock, it is common stock. Because shares of common stock carry voting rights, they generally provide their owners with the means of controlling the corporation. Common stock is also called *residual equity*, which means that if the corporation is liquidated, the claims of all creditors and usually those of preferred stockholders rank ahead of the claims of common stockholders.
- **Preferred stock** is stock that a corporation may issue to attract investors whose goals differ from those of common stockholders. Preferred stock gives its owners preference over common stockholders, usually in terms of receiving dividends and in terms of claims to assets if the corporation is liquidated.

In addition to identifying the kind of stock and its par value, the description of contributed capital in Exhibit 1 specifies the number of shares authorized, issued, and outstanding.

- **Authorized shares** are the maximum number of shares that a corporation's state charter allows it to issue. Most corporations are authorized to issue more shares than they need to issue at the time they are formed. Thus, they are able to raise more capital in the future by issuing additional shares. When a corporation issues all of its authorized shares, it cannot issue more without a change in its state charter.
- **Issued shares** are those that a corporation sells or otherwise transfers to stockholders. The owners of a corporation's issued shares own 100 percent of the business. Unissued shares have no rights or privileges until they are issued.
- **Outstanding shares** are shares that a corporation has issued and that are still in circulation. Treasury stock is not outstanding because it consists of shares that a corporation has issued but has bought back and thereby put out of circulation. Thus, a corporation can have more shares issued than are currently outstanding.

Exhibit 2 shows the relationship of authorized shares to issued, unissued, outstanding, and treasury shares. For example, **Google** has 9 billion authorized shares of stock and only about 325 million shares issued. With its excess of authorized shares, Google has plenty of flexibility for future stock transactions.

Business Perspective

Are You a First-Class or Second-Class Stockholder?

When companies go public, the founders of the company or top management often get first-class shares with extra votes, while outsiders get second-class shares with fewer votes. The class A and class B shares of **Adolph Coors Company**, the large brewing firm, are an extreme example. The company's class B shares, owned by the public, have no votes except in the case of a merger. Its class A shares, held by the Coors family trust, have all the votes on all other issues.

Google also has two classes of identical common shares, except that each class B share is entitled to ten votes and each class A share is entitled to only one vote. Class A shares are the ones that Google offered to the public in its IPO. As a result, Class B holders control 70 percent of the company.[4]

Shareholder advocates maintain that this practice gives a privileged few shareholders all or most of the control of a company and that it denies other shareholders voting power consistent with the risk they are taking. Defenders of the practice argue that it shields top executives from the market's obsession with short-term results and allows them to make better long-term decisions. They also point out that many investors don't care about voting rights as long as the stock performs well.

Exhibit 2
Relationship of Authorized Shares to Unissued, Issued, Outstanding, and Treasury Shares

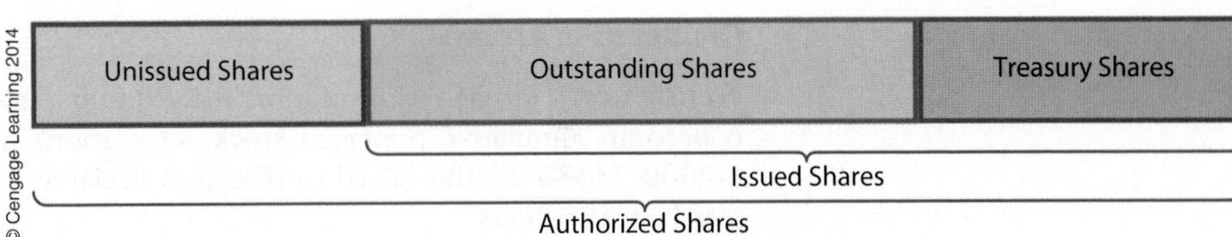

Characteristics of Preferred Stock

STUDY NOTE: Preferred stock has many different characteristics. They are rarely exactly the same from company to company.

Most preferred stock has one or more of the following characteristics: preference as to dividends, preference as to assets if a corporation is liquidated, convertibility, and a callable option. A corporation may offer several different classes of preferred stock, each with distinctive characteristics to attract different investors.

Preference as to Dividends Preferred stockholders ordinarily must receive a certain amount of dividends before common stockholders receive anything. The amount that preferred stockholders must be paid before common stockholders can be paid is usually stated in dollars per share or as a percentage of the par value of the preferred shares. For example, a company might pay an annual dividend of $4 per share on preferred stock, or it might issue preferred stock at $50 par value and pay an annual dividend of 8 percent of par value, which would also be $4 per share.

Preferred stockholders have no guarantee of receiving dividends. A company's board of directors must declare dividends on preferred stock before any liability arises. The consequences of not granting an annual dividend on preferred stock vary according to whether the stock is noncumulative or cumulative.

- If the stock is **noncumulative preferred stock** and the board of directors fails to declare a dividend on it in any given year, the company is under no obligation to make up the missed dividend in future years.
- If the stock is **cumulative preferred stock**, the dividend amount per share accumulates from year to year, and the company must pay the whole amount before it pays any dividends on common stock.

Dividends not paid in the year they are due are called **dividends in arrears**. If a corporation has dividends in arrears, it should report the amount either in the body of its financial statements or in a note to its financial statements. The following note is typical of one that might appear in a corporation's annual report:

> *On December 31, 2014, the company was in arrears by $37,851,000 ($1.25 per share) on dividends to its preferred stockholders. The company must pay all dividends in arrears to preferred stockholders before paying any dividends to common stockholders.*

Business Perspective
How Does a Stock Become a Debt?

Some companies have used the flexibility of preferred stocks to create a type of stock that is similar to debt. Usually, stocks do not have maturity dates, and companies do not buy them back except at the option of management. However, **CMS Energy**, **Time Warner**, **Xerox**, and other companies have issued preferred stock that is "mandatorily redeemable." This means that the issuing companies are required to buy back the stock at fixed future dates or under predetermined conditions. Thus, these special preferred stocks are similar to long-term debt in that they have a fixed maturity date. In addition, in much the same way as long-term debt requires periodic interest payments at a fixed rate, these stocks require an annual dividend payment, also at a fixed rate. Even though companies list these stocks in the stockholders' equity section of their balance sheets, the astute analyst will treat them as debt when calculating a company's debt to equity ratio.[5]

Dividends in Arrears

Transaction Harbach Corporation has 20,000 outstanding shares of $10 par value, 6 percent cumulative preferred stock. Operations in 2015 produced income of only $8,000. However, the board of directors declared a $6,000 cash dividend to the preferred stockholders.

Computation Dividends in arrears are calculated as follows.

2015 dividends due preferred stockholders (20,000 × $10 × 0.06)	$12,000
Less 2015 dividends declared to preferred stockholders	6,000
2015 preferred stock dividends in arrears	$ 6,000

Comment Before the corporation can pay a dividend in 2016 to common stockholders, it must pay the preferred stockholders the $6,000 in arrears from 2015, plus $12,000 for 2016 for a total of $18,000.

Dividend Distribution

Transaction In 2016, Harbach Corporation earns income of $60,000 and wants to pay dividends to both preferred and common stockholders. The board of directors declares a $24,000 dividend.

Computation The dividend would be distributed as follows.

2016 declaration of dividends	$24,000
Less 2015 preferred stock dividends in arrears	6,000
Amount available for 2016 dividends	$18,000
Less 2016 dividends due preferred stockholders (20,000 × $10 × 0.06)	12,000
Remainder available to common stockholders	$ 6,000

Preference as to Assets Preferred stockholders often have preference in terms of their claims to a corporation's assets if the corporation goes out of business. If a corporation is liquidated, these preferred stockholders have a right to receive the par value of their stock or a larger stated liquidation value per share before the common stockholders receive any share of the assets. This preference can also extend to any dividends in arrears owed to the preferred stockholders.

STUDY NOTE: *When preferred stockholders convert their shares to common stock, they gain voting rights but lose the dividend and liquidation preference. Conversion back to preferred stock is not an option.*

Convertible Preferred Stock Owners of **convertible preferred stock** can exchange their shares of preferred stock for shares of common stock at a ratio stated in the preferred stock contract. If the market value of the common stock increases, the conversion feature allows these stockholders to share in the increase by converting their stock to common stock. For example, if you look back at **Google**'s Financial Highlights at the beginning of the chapter, you will see that Google has preferred stock, but none of it is outstanding. The reason for this is that early investors who bought the company's convertible preferred stock took advantage of the steep increase in the price of common stock by converting their shares to common stock. The preferred stock is still authorized, and Google may decide to issue it again in the future.

As another example, suppose that a company issues 1,000 shares of 8 percent, $100 par value convertible preferred stock for $100 per share. Each share of stock can be converted to five shares of the company's common stock at any time. The market value of the common stock when the company issues the convertible preferred stock is $15 per share. The owner of one share of preferred stock purchased for $100, therefore, has an investment if converted into common stock with a market value of about $75. The investor would not convert at this point, preferring to receive the 8 percent dividend.

Now suppose that in the next few years, the market value of a share of the common stock increases from $15 to $30. By converting each of their shares to five common shares, preferred stockholders can realize $150 (5 shares × $30 per share) or a gain of $50 above the $100 they paid per share of preferred stock.

Callable Preferred Stock Most preferred stock is **callable preferred stock**—that is, the issuing corporation can redeem it at a price stated in the preferred stock contract. An owner of callable preferred stock that is not convertible must surrender it to the issuing corporation when asked to do so. If the preferred stock is convertible, the stockholder can either surrender the stock to the corporation or convert it to common stock when the corporation calls the stock. The *call price*, or *redemption price*, is usually higher than the stock's par value. For example, preferred stock that has a $100 par value might be callable at $103 per share.

When preferred stock is called and surrendered, the stockholder is entitled to the following:

- The par value of the stock
- The call premium
- Any dividends in arrears
- The current period's dividend prorated by the proportion of the year to the call date

A corporation may decide to call its preferred stock for any of the following reasons:

- It may want to force conversion of the preferred stock to common stock because the dividend that it pays on preferred shares is higher than the dividend that it pays on the equivalent number of common shares.
- It may be able to replace the outstanding preferred stock with a preferred stock at a lower dividend rate or with long-term debt, which can have a lower after-tax cost.
- It may simply be profitable enough to retire the preferred stock.

APPLY IT!

Romeo Corporation has 2,000 shares of $100 par value, 7 percent cumulative preferred stock outstanding and 200,000 shares of $1 par value common stock outstanding. In the corporation's first three years of operation, its board of directors declared cash dividends as follows:

2014: None
2015: $20,000
2016: $30,000

Determine the total cash dividends paid to the preferred and common stockholders during each of the three years.

SOLUTION

2014:	None	
2015:	Preferred dividends in arrears (2,000 shares × $100 × 0.07)	$14,000
	Current year remainder to preferred ($20,000 – $14,000)	6,000
	Total to preferred stockholders	$20,000
2016:	Preferred dividends in arrears ($14,000 – $6,000)	$ 8,000
	Current year to preferred (2,000 shares × $100 × 0.07)	14,000
	Total to preferred stockholders	$22,000
	Total to common stockholders ($30,000 – $22,000)	8,000
	Total dividends in 2016	$30,000

TRY IT! SE4, SE5, E2A, E3A, E4A, E5A, E2B, E3B, E4B, E5B

LO3 Issuance of Common Stock

A share of capital stock may be either par or no-par. The value of par stock is stated in the corporate charter and on each stock certificate. It can be $0.01, $1, $5, $100, or any other amount established by the organizers of the corporation. The par values of common stocks tend to be lower than those of preferred stocks.

A corporation cannot declare a dividend that would cause stockholders' equity to fall below the legal capital. Par value is thus a minimum cushion of capital that protects a corporation's creditors.

No-par stock does not have a par value. A corporation may issue stock without a par value for several reasons. For one thing, rather than recognizing par value as an arbitrary figure, investors may confuse it with the stock's market value. For another, most states do not allow a stock issue below par value, and this limits a corporation's flexibility in obtaining capital.

To illustrate accounting for the issuance of stock, we will use Rexio Corporation.

Accounting for Par Value Stock

When a corporation issues par value stock, the appropriate Capital Stock account (usually Common Stock or Preferred Stock) is credited for the par value regardless of whether the proceeds are more or less than the par value. When a corporation issues stock at a price greater than par value, as is usually the case, the proceeds in excess of par are credited to an account called Additional Paid-in Capital.

Issuing Stock Above Par Value

Transaction Rexio Corporation is authorized to issue 10,000 shares of $10 par value common stock. On January 1, 2014, it issues 5,000 shares at $12 each.

Analysis The journal entry to record the issuance of the stock above par value

- ▲ *increases Cash* with a debit for the proceeds of $60,000 (5,000 shares × $12)
- ▲ *increases Common Stock* with a credit for the total par value of $50,000 (5,000 shares × $10)
- ▲ *increases Additional Paid-in Capital* with a credit for the difference of $10,000 (5,000 shares × $2)

Application of Double Entry

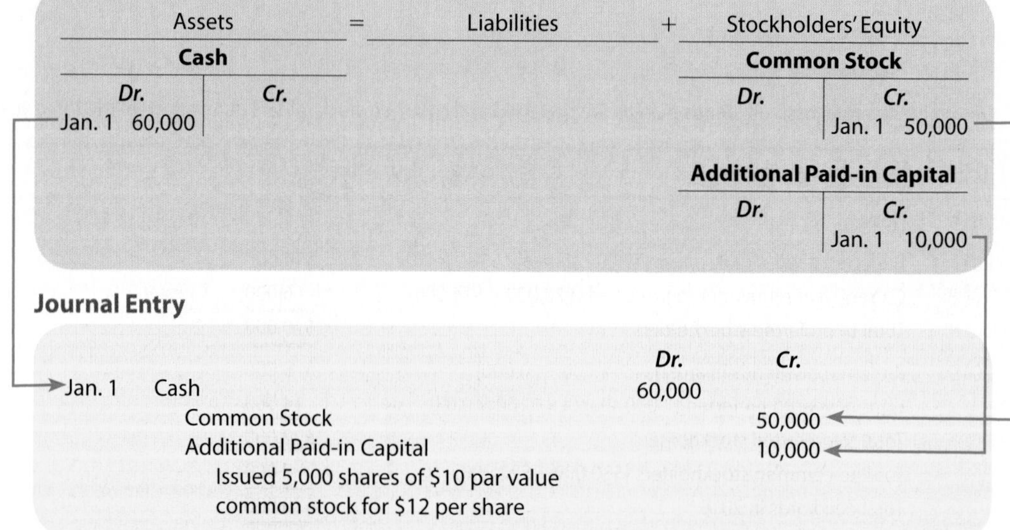

A	=	L	+	SE
+60,000				+50,000
				+10,000

STUDY NOTE: *If a corporation issues stock for less than par value, an account called Discount on Capital Stock is debited for the difference. The issuance of stock at a discount rarely occurs. It is illegal in many states.*

Comment The amount in excess of par value is part of Rexio's contributed capital and will be included in the stockholders' equity section of its balance sheet. Immediately after the stock issue, this section of Rexio's balance sheet would appear as follows.

Contributed capital:	
Common stock, $10 par value, 10,000 shares authorized, 5,000 shares issued and outstanding	$50,000
Additional paid-in capital	10,000
Total contributed capital	$60,000
Retained earnings	—
Total stockholders' equity	$60,000

No-Par Stock

STUDY NOTE: When no-par stock has a stated value, the stated value serves the same purpose as par value in that it represents the minimum legal capital.

Most states require that all or part of the proceeds from a corporation's issuance of no-par stock be designated as legal capital, which cannot be used unless the corporation is liquidated. The purpose of this requirement is to protect the corporation's assets for creditors.

State laws often require corporations to place a **stated value** on each share of stock that they issue, but even when this is not required, a corporation's board of directors may do so as a matter of convenience. The stated value can be any value set by the board unless the state specifies a minimum amount, which is sometimes the case. The stated value can be set before or after the shares are issued if the state law is not specific.

Issuing No-Par Stock with No Stated Value

Transaction On January 1, 2014, Rexio issues 5,000 shares of no-par common stock at $15 per share.

Analysis The journal entry to record this no-par stock with no stated value

▲ *increases Cash* with a debit of $75,000 (5,000 shares × $15)

▲ *increases Common Stock* with a credit of $75,000

Application of Double Entry

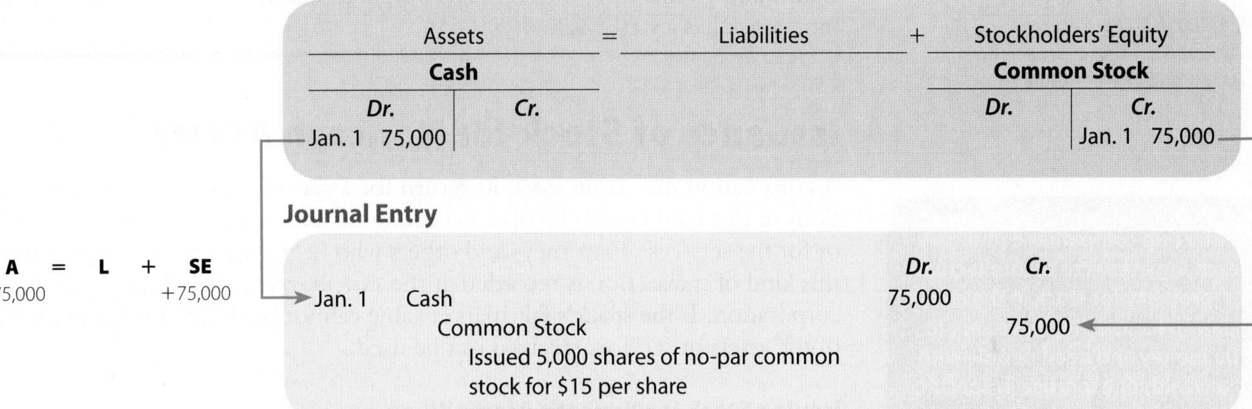

Comment Because the stock does not have a stated or par value, all proceeds ($75,000) of the issue are *credited* to Common Stock and are part of the company's legal capital.

Issuing No-Par Stock with a Stated Value

Event Assume the same facts as were provided previously, except that Rexio puts a $10 stated value on each share of its no-par stock.

Analysis The journal entry to record this no-par stock with a stated value

▲ *increases Cash* with a debit of $75,000 (5,000 shares × $15)

▲ *increases Common Stock* with a credit of $50,000 (the stated value decided by Rexio's board of directors)

▲ *increases Additional Paid-in Capital* with a credit of $25,000, which is the difference between the proceeds ($75,000) and the total stated value ($50,000)

Application of Double Entry

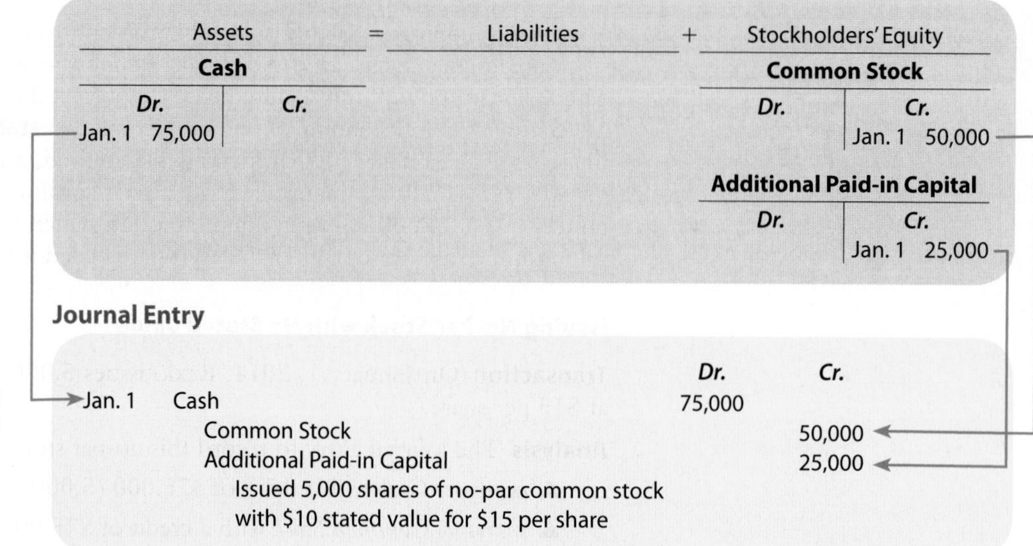

Journal Entry

A	=	L	+	SE
+75,000				+50,000
				+25,000

	Dr.	Cr.
Jan. 1 Cash	75,000	
Common Stock		50,000
Additional Paid-in Capital		25,000
Issued 5,000 shares of no-par common stock with $10 stated value for $15 per share		

Comment In this case, the company's legal capital is $50,000 because the no-par common stock has a stated value.

STUDY NOTE: *In establishing the fair market value of property that a corporation exchanges for stock, a board of directors cannot be arbitrary. It must use all the information at its disposal.*

Issuance of Stock for Noncash Assets

A corporation may issue stock in return for assets or services other than cash. Transactions of this kind usually involve a corporation's exchange of stock for land or buildings or for the services of attorneys and others who help organize the corporation. Generally, this kind of transaction is recorded at the *fair market value* of the stock given up by the corporation. If the stock's fair market value cannot be determined, the fair market value of the assets or services received can be used.

Start-up companies commonly exchange services or intellectual property for stock in the company because they have very little money and need people with a wealth of expertise in specific areas. For example, Mark Zuckerberg and Adam D'Angelo, the founders of Facebook, essentially traded the intellectual property involved in creating programming language and their time investment for stock in the company.

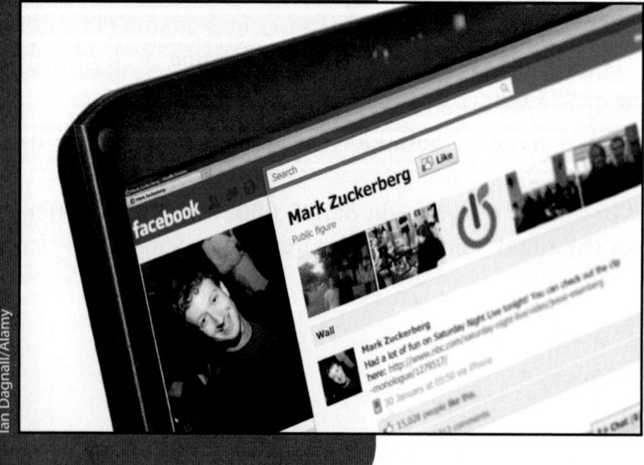

Ian Dagnall/Alamy

Issuing Stock for Noncash Assets When No Market Value for the Stock Exists

Transaction When Rexio was formed on January 1, 2014, its attorney agreed to accept 200 shares of its $10 par value common stock for services rendered. At that time, the market value of the stock could not be determined. However, for similar services, the attorney would have charged Rexio $3,000.

Analysis The journal entry to record stock exchanged for noncash assets when no market value for the stock exists

- ▲ *increases Legal Expenses* with a debit of $3,000 (estimated cost for attorney services)
- ▲ *increases Common Stock* with a credit for the total par value of $2,000 (200 shares × $10)
- ▲ *increases Additional Paid-in Capital* with a credit for the difference of the proceeds ($3,000) and the total stated value ($2,000)

Application of Double Entry

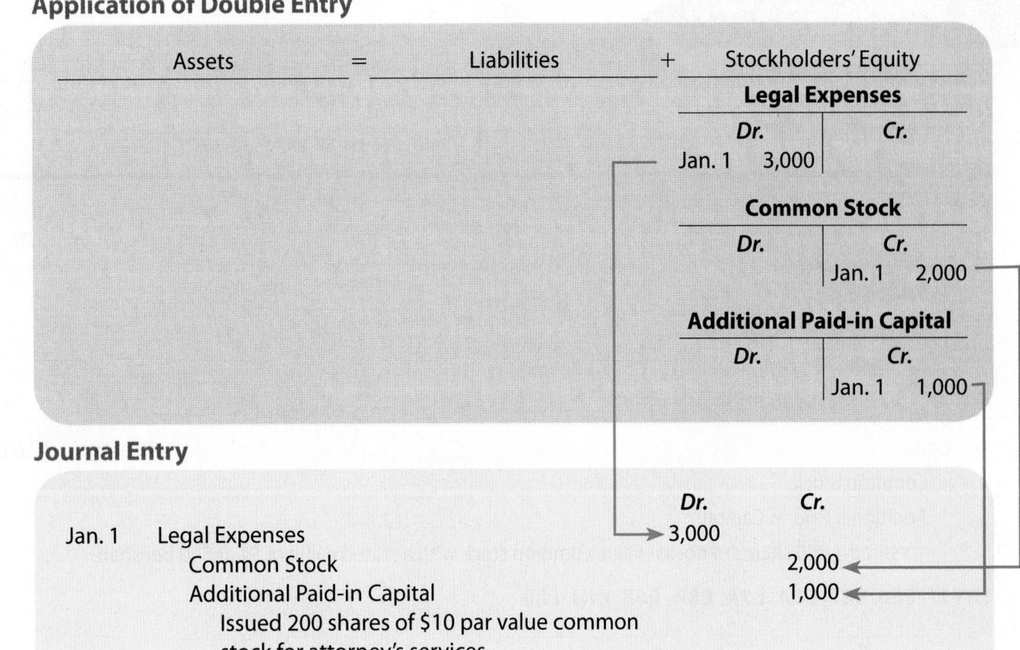

Journal Entry

A	=	L	+	SE
				−3,000
				+2,000
				+1,000

		Dr.	Cr.
Jan. 1	Legal Expenses	3,000	
	Common Stock		2,000
	Additional Paid-in Capital		1,000
	Issued 200 shares of $10 par value common stock for attorney's services		

Comment As a stockholder, the attorney becomes a part-owner of the business. Even though the corporation is a *separate entity* from its owners for accounting purposes, the owners have the right vote on corporate board members and, at times, other important issues.

Issuance of Stock for Noncash Assets When Market Value for the Stock Exists

Transaction Two years later, Rexio exchanged 500 shares of its $10 par value common stock for a piece of land. At the time of the exchange, Rexio's stock was selling on the market for $16 per share.

Analysis In this case, the market value of the land is irrelevant because the value of the stock is known. The journal entry to record stock exchanged for noncash assets when a market value for the stock exists

- ▲ *increases Land* with a debit of $8,000 (500 shares × $16)
- ▲ *increases Common Stock* with a credit of $5,000 (500 shares × $10)
- ▲ *increases Additional Paid-in Capital* with a credit for $3,000 ($8,000 − $5,000)

Application of Double Entry

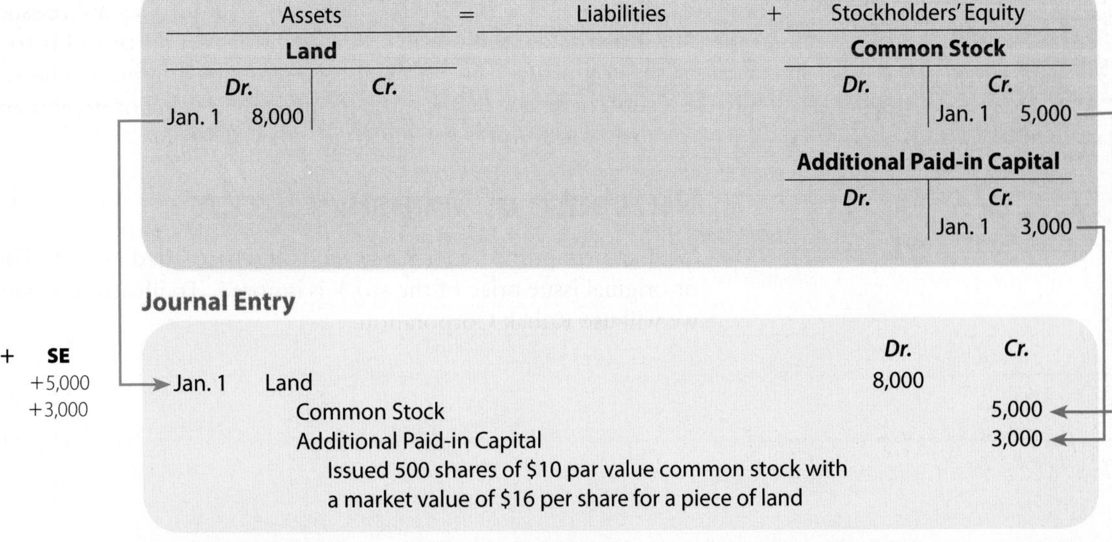

Journal Entry

A	=	L	+	SE
+8,000				+5,000
				+3,000

		Dr.	Cr.
Jan. 1	Land	8,000	
	Common Stock		5,000
	Additional Paid-in Capital		3,000
	Issued 500 shares of $10 par value common stock with a market value of $16 per share for a piece of land		

APPLY IT!

Norma Company is authorized to issue 10,000 shares of common stock. The company sold 1,000 shares at $10 per share. Prepare the journal entries to record the sale of stock for cash under each of the following independent alternatives: (1) The stock has a par value of $2, and (2) the stock has no par value but a stated value of $1 per share.

SOLUTION

1.	***Dr.***	***Cr.***
Cash	10,000	
Common Stock		2,000
Additional Paid-in Capital		8,000
Issued 1,000 shares of $2 par value common stock at $10 per share		
2.		
Cash	10,000	
Common Stock		1,000
Additional Paid-in Capital		9,000
Issued 1,000 shares of no-par value common stock with a stated value of $1 at $10 per share		

TRY IT! SE6, SE7, E6A, E7A, E8A, E6B, E7B, E8B

LO4 Accounting for Treasury Stock

As noted earlier, treasury stock is stock that the issuing company has reacquired, usually by purchasing shares on the open market. Although repurchasing its own stock can be a drain on a corporation's cash, it is common practice. In a recent year, 323, or 65 percent, of 500 large companies held treasury stock.[6]

A company may want to buy back its own stock for any of the following reasons:

- To distribute to employees through stock option plans.
- To maintain a favorable market for its stock.
- To increase its earnings per share or stock price per share.
- To have additional shares of stock available for purchasing other companies.
- To prevent a hostile takeover.

STUDY NOTE: *Treasury stock is not the same as unissued stock. Treasury stock represents shares that have been issued but are no longer outstanding. Unissued shares, on the other hand, have never been in circulation.*

Treasury stock is not considered a purchase of assets but is a reduction in stockholders' equity. A company can hold treasury shares for an indefinite period or reissue or retire them. Treasury shares have no rights until they are reissued. Like unissued shares, they do not have voting rights, rights to dividends, or rights to assets during liquidation of the company. However, there is one major difference between unissued shares and treasury shares. A share of stock issued at par value or greater and that was reacquired as treasury stock can be reissued at less than par value.

Purchase of Treasury Stock

When a firm purchases treasury stock, it is recorded at cost. The par value, stated value, or original issue price of the stock is ignored. To illustrate accounting for treasury stock, we will use Kobak Corporation.

Purchase of Treasury Stock

Transaction On September 15, Kobak Corporation purchases 2,000 shares of its common stock on the market at a price of $50 per share.

Analysis The entry to record this purchase of treasury stock

▲ *increases Treasury Stock, Common* with a debit of $100,000 (2,000 shares × $50)

▼ *decreases Cash* with a credit of $100,000 (2,000 shares × $50)

Application of Double Entry

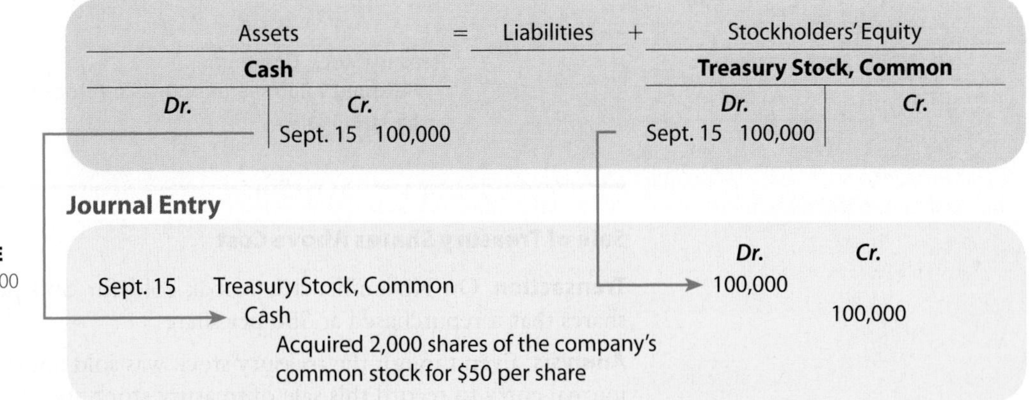

A	=	L	+	SE
−100,000				−100,000

Comment In the stockholders' equity section of Kobak's balance sheet, $100,000 would be deducted from total contributed capital and retained earnings, as shown below.

Contributed capital:	
Common stock, $5 par value, 200,000 shares authorized, 60,000 shares issued, 58,000 shares outstanding	$ 300,000
Additional paid-in capital	60,000
Total contributed capital	$ 360,000
Retained earnings	1,800,000
Total contributed capital and retained earnings	$2,160,000
Less: Treasury stock, common (2,000 shares at cost)	100,000
Total stockholders' equity	$2,060,000

Note that the number of shares issued, and therefore the legal capital, has not changed. However, the number of shares outstanding has *decreased* as a result of the transaction.

Sale of Treasury Stock

Treasury shares can be sold at cost, above cost, or below cost.

Sale of Treasury Shares at Cost

Transaction On November 15, Kobak sold 2,000 shares of its $5 par value common stock on the market at a price of $50 per share.

Analysis When treasury shares are sold at cost, the entry is the reverse of the previous transaction for the purchase of the shares. The journal entry to record this sale of treasury stock at cost

▲ *increases Cash* with a debit for the sales amount

▼ *decreases Treasury Stock, Common* with a credit for the same amount

Application of Double Entry

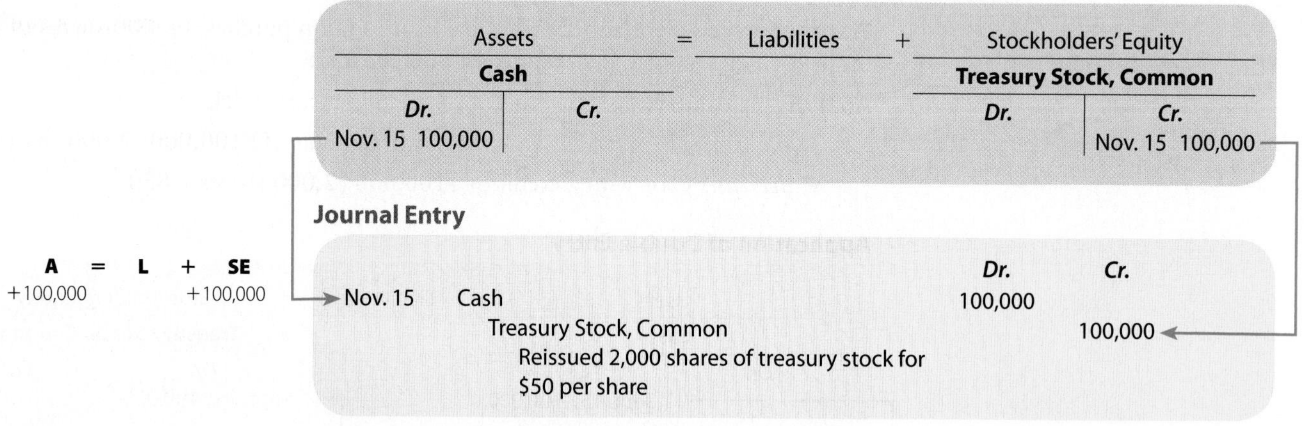

A = L + SE
+100,000 +100,000

Sale of Treasury Shares Above Cost

Transaction On November 15, Kobak sold for $60 per share 1,000 of the treasury shares that it repurchased at $50 per share.

Analysis Even though the treasury stock was sold above cost, no gain is recorded. The journal entry to record this sale of treasury stock above cost

- ▲ *increases Cash* with a debit of $60,000 (1,000 shares × $60)
- ▼ *decreases Treasury Stock, Common* with a credit of $50,000 (1,000 shares × $50)
- ▲ *increases Paid-in Capital, Treasury Stock* with a credit of $10,000 ($60,000 − $50,000)

Application of Double Entry

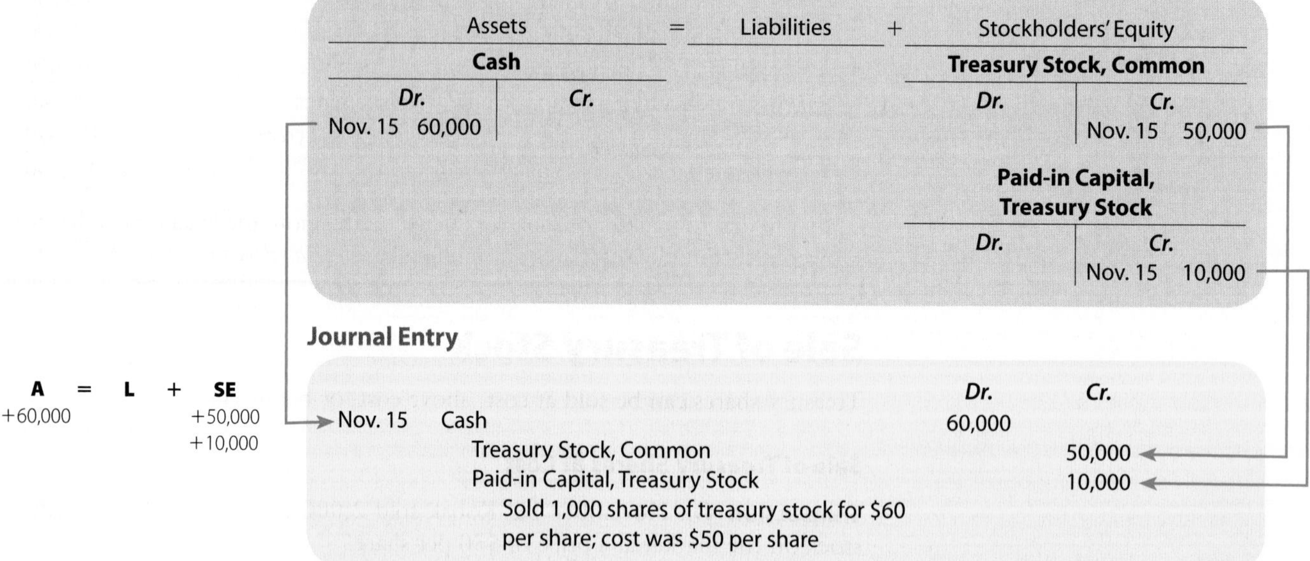

A = L + SE
+60,000 +50,000
+10,000

Comment When treasury shares are sold for an amount greater than their cost, the excess of the sales price over the cost is not considered a gain but is credited to Paid-in Capital, Treasury Stock.

Sale of Treasury Shares Below Cost

Transaction On December 15, Kobak sells its remaining 1,000 treasury shares for $38 per share.

Analysis When treasury shares are sold below their cost, the difference is deducted from Paid-in Capital, Treasury Stock. If this account does not exist or if its balance is insufficient to cover the excess of cost over the reissue price, Retained Earnings absorbs the excess. The journal entry to record the sale of treasury stock below cost

- ▲ *increases Cash* with a debit of $38,000 (1,000 shares × $38)
- ▼ *decreases Paid-in Capital, Treasury Stock* with a debit of $10,000
- ▼ *decreases Retained Earnings* with a debit for the remaining $2,000 by which the shares were sold below their cost ($50,000 – $38,000 – $10,000)
- ▼ *decreases Treasury Stock, Common* with a credit of $50,000 ($38,000 + $10,000 + $2,000)

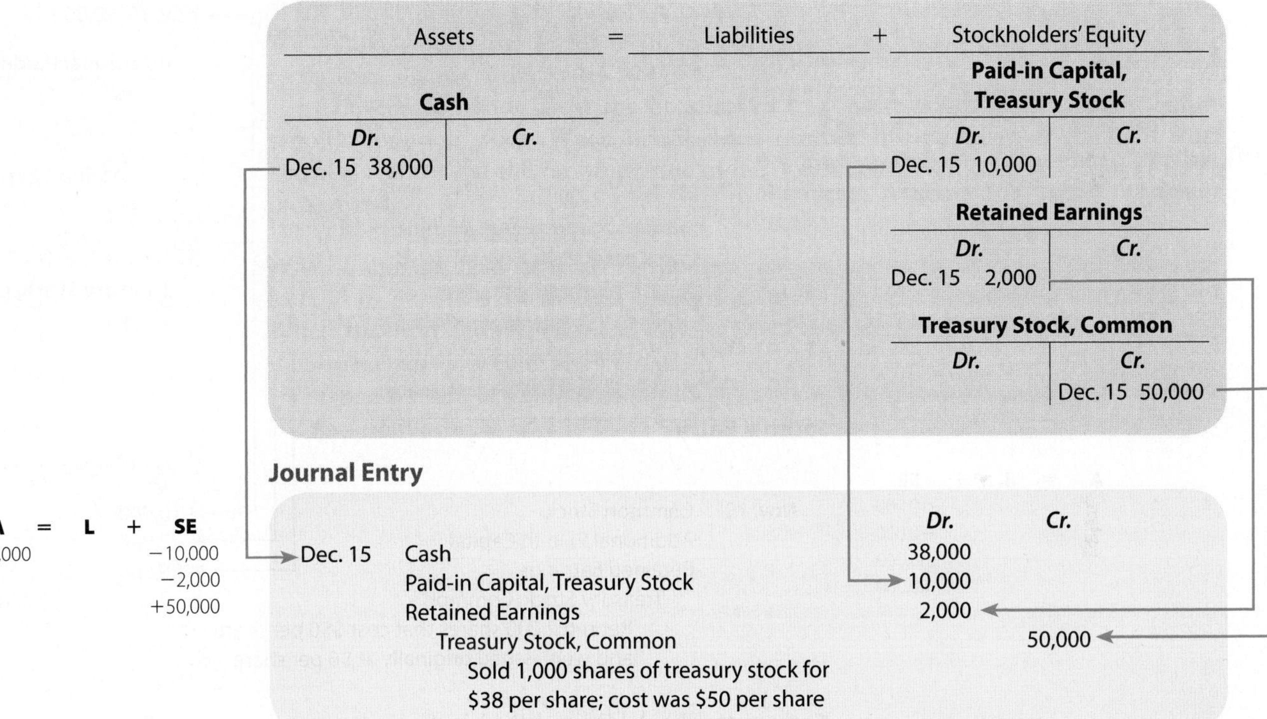

		Dr.	Cr.
Dec. 15	Cash	38,000	
	Paid-in Capital, Treasury Stock	10,000	
	Retained Earnings	2,000	
	Treasury Stock, Common		50,000
	Sold 1,000 shares of treasury stock for $38 per share; cost was $50 per share		

Comment Note that the *decrease* in Treasury Stock, Common *increases* stockholders' equity. Also, note that no loss is recorded. Further, Retained Earnings is debited only when the Paid-in Capital, Treasury Stock account does not exist or has been depleted. For Kobak, the Paid-in Capital, Treasury Stock had a balance of $10,000 so the remaining $2,000 had to come from Retained Earnings.

Retirement of Treasury Stock

If a company decides not to reissue treasury stock, it can retire the stock. All items related to those shares are then removed from the associated capital accounts. If the cost of buying back the treasury stock is less than the company received when it issued the stock, the difference is recorded in Paid-in Capital, Retirement of Stock. If the cost is more than was received when the stock was first issued, the difference is a reduction in stockholders' equity and is debited to Retained Earnings.

Retiring Treasury Stock

Transaction On November 15, Kobak decides to retire the 2,000 shares of stock that it bought back for $100,000.

Analysis If the $5 par value common stock was originally issued at $6 per share, the journal entry to record this retirement of treasury stock

- ▼ *decreases Common Stock* with a debit of $10,000 (2,000 shares × $5)
- ▼ *decreases Additional Paid-in Capital* with a debit of $2,000 [2,000 shares × ($6 − $5)]
- ▼ *decreases Retained Earnings* with a debit of $88,000 ($100,000 − $10,000 − $2,000)
- ▼ *decreases Treasury Stock, Common* with a credit of $100,000 (2,000 shares × $50)

Application of Double Entry

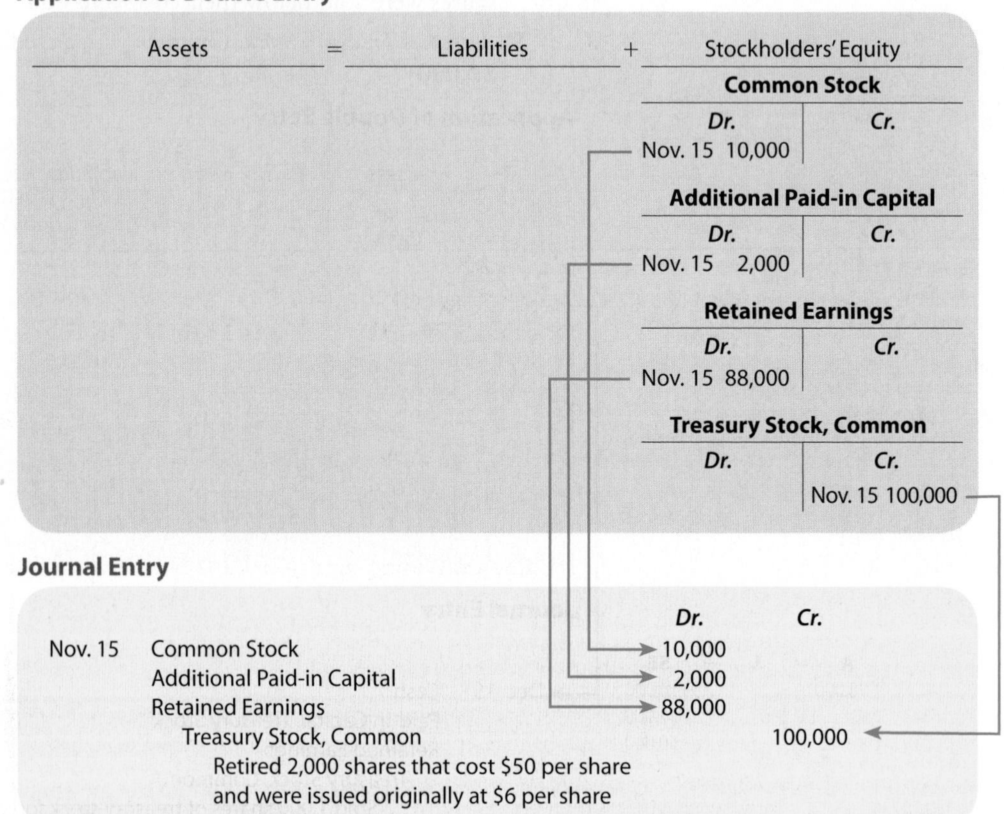

Assets = Liabilities + Stockholders' Equity
Common Stock
Dr. Cr.
Nov. 15 10,000
Additional Paid-in Capital
Dr. Cr.
Nov. 15 2,000
Retained Earnings
Dr. Cr.
Nov. 15 88,000
Treasury Stock, Common
Dr. Cr.
Nov. 15 100,000

Journal Entry

A	=	L	+	SE
				−10,000
				−2,000
				−88,000
				+100,000

		Dr.	Cr.
Nov. 15	Common Stock	10,000	
	Additional Paid-in Capital	2,000	
	Retained Earnings	88,000	
	Treasury Stock, Common		100,000
	Retired 2,000 shares that cost $50 per share and were issued originally at $6 per share		

Comment The Additional Paid-in Capital was reduced by $2,000 because this is how much was in that account since the stock had a $5 par value and was sold at $6 share [2,000 shares × ($6 − $5)]. Note that this transaction does not change the total stockholders' equity because all accounts are in stockholders' equity.

APPLY IT!

Prepare journal entries to record the following stock transactions for Junior Company during 2015:

May 1 Purchased 5,000 shares of its own $1 par value common stock for $10 per share, the current market price.
17 Sold 1,000 shares of treasury stock purchased on May 1 for $11 per share.

SOLUTION

	Dr.	Cr.
May 1		
Treasury Stock, Common	50,000	
Cash		50,000
Purchased 5,000 shares of Junior Company's common stock at $10 per share		
May 17		
Cash	11,000	
Treasury Stock, Common		10,000
Paid-in Capital, Treasury Stock		1,000
Sold 1,000 shares of treasury stock for $11 per share		

TRY IT! SE8, SE9, E9A, E10A, E9B, E10B

LO5 Accounting for Cash Dividends

A **dividend** is a distribution of the assets that a corporation's earnings have generated. Stockholders receive these assets, usually cash, in proportion to the number of shares they own. A corporation's board of directors has sole authority to declare dividends; but senior managers, who usually serve as members of the board, influence dividend policies. Receiving dividends is one of two ways in which stockholders can earn a return on their investment in a corporation. The other way is to sell their shares for more than they paid for them.

Although a corporation may have sufficient cash and retained earnings to pay a dividend, its board of directors may not declare dividends for several reasons:

- The corporation may need the cash for expansion.
- It may want to improve its overall financial position by liquidating debt.
- It may be facing major uncertainties, such as a pending lawsuit, strike, or a projected decline in the economy.

A corporation pays dividends quarterly, semiannually, annually, or at other times. Most states do not allow a corporation to declare a dividend that exceeds its retained earnings. When a corporation does declare a dividend that exceeds retained earnings, it is, in essence, returning to the stockholders part of their contributed capital. This is called a **liquidating dividend**. A corporation usually pays a liquidating dividend only when it is going out of business or reducing its operations.

Having sufficient retained earnings in itself does not justify the declaration of a dividend. If a corporation does not have cash or other assets readily available for distribution, it might have to borrow money to pay the dividend—an action most boards of directors want to avoid.

Companies usually pay dividends only when they have had profitable operations. For example, **Apple** began paying dividends in 1987, but it stopped those payments in 1996 to conserve cash after it suffered large operating losses in 1995. Factors other than earnings also affect the decision to pay dividends. Among them are the following:

- **Industry policies:** A company may change its dividend policy to bring it into line with the prevailing policy in its industry. For example, despite positive earnings, **AT&T Corporation** slashed its dividends by 83 percent in 2002. This action put AT&T's policy more in line with the policies of its peers in the telecommunications industry, most of which do not pay dividends.
- **Volatility of earnings:** If a company has years of good earnings followed by years of poor earnings, it may want to keep dividends low to avoid giving a false impression of sustained high earnings. For example, for many years, **General Motors** paid a fairly low but stable dividend but declared a bonus dividend in especially good years.

- **Effect on cash flows:** A company may not pay dividends because its operations do not generate enough cash to do so or because it wants to invest cash in future operations. **Abbott Laboratories** increases its dividends per share each year to reward its stockholders but also keeps back a portion of its earnings to spend for other purposes, such as researching and developing new drugs. In a recent year, for example, the company with earnings per share of $3.03 paid a $1.92 per share dividend.[7]

In recent years, because of a 15 percent reduction in the tax rate on dividends, attitudes toward dividends have changed. Many firms have either increased their dividends or started to pay dividends for the first time.

Dividend Dates Three important dates are associated with dividends: the declaration date, the record date, and the payment date.

- The **declaration date** is the date on which the board of directors formally declares that the corporation is going to pay a dividend. Because the legal obligation to pay the dividend arises at this time, a liability for Dividends Payable is recorded and the Dividends account is debited. In the accounting process, Retained Earnings will be reduced by the total dividends declared.
- The **record date** is the date on which ownership of stock, and therefore the right to receive a dividend, is determined. Persons who own the stock on the record date will receive the dividend. No entry is made on this date. Between the record date and the date of payment, the stock is said to be **ex-dividend**. If the owner on the date of record sells the shares of stock before the date of payment, the right to the dividend remains with that person; it does not transfer with the shares to the second owner.
- The **payment date** is the date on which the dividend is paid to the stockholders of record. On this date, the Dividends Payable account is eliminated, and the Cash account is reduced.

Dividend Transactions Assume a board of directors declares a cash dividend of $28,000 on December 21. The record date is December 31, which is also the end of the company's accounting period. The dividend payment date is January 11.

Declaration Date

Transaction On December 21, the company declared a cash dividend of $28,000.

Analysis The journal entry to record the dividend on the declaration date (December 21)

▲ *increases* the equity account *Dividends* with a debit on the declaration date

▲ *increases* the liability account *Dividends Payable* with a credit in the amount of the total dividends declared

Journal Entry

A	=	L	+	SE
		+28,000		−28,000

		Dr.	*Cr.*
Dec. 21	Dividends	28,000	
	Dividends Payable		28,000
	Declaration of dividends		

Comment The Dividends account reduces equity by appearing as a deduction from retained earnings on the statement of stockholders' equity, and Dividends Payable appears as a liability on the balance sheet.

Record Date

Event December 31, the record date for the dividends declared on December 21.

Analysis As noted, no journal entry is made on the record date (December 31).

Comment Journal entries for dividends are made only on the declaration date and the payment date.

Payment Date

Transaction On January 11, the company made the dividend payment.

Analysis The journal entry to record the dividend on the payment date (January 11)

- ▼ *decreases* the liability account *Dividends Payable* with a debit in the amount of the total dividends declared
- ▼ *decreases* the asset account *Cash* with a credit

Journal Entry

A	=	L	+	SE
−28,000		−28,000		

		Dr.	Cr.
Jan. 11	Dividends Payable	28,000	
	Cash		28,000
	Payment of dividends		

Comment When the date of declaration and the payment date occur in the same period, the amount of dividends shown on the statement of stockholders' equity and on the statement of cash flows will be equal. In this example, however, the accounting period ended between the dates of declaration and payment. Thus, dividends declared during the period ending December 31 exceed the amount paid for dividends. As a result,

- The statement of stockholders' equity for the accounting period will show a *decrease* of $28,000 in the amount of the dividends declared.
- The statement of cash flows will not show the dividends because the cash has not yet been paid out.

APPLY IT!

Jask Corporation has authorized 100,000 shares of $1 par value common stock, of which 80,000 are issued and 70,000 are outstanding. On March 15, the board of directors declared a cash dividend of $0.10 per share, payable on April 15 to stockholders of record on May 1. Prepare the journal entries, as necessary, for each of the three dates.

SOLUTION

Journal Entry:

Mar. 15	Dividends	7,000	
	Dividends Payable		7,000
	Declaration of dividends		

April 15: no entry

Journal Entry:

May 1	Dividends Payable	7,000	
	Cash		7,000
	Payment of dividends		

TRY IT! SE10, E11A, E12A, E11B, E12B

LO 6 Stock Dividends and Stock Splits

Two transactions that commonly modify the content of stockholders' equity are stock dividends and stock splits.

Stock Dividends

A **stock dividend** is a proportional distribution of shares among a corporation's stockholders. Unlike a cash dividend, a stock dividend involves no distribution of assets, and so it has no effect on assets or liabilities. A board of directors may declare a stock dividend for the following reasons:

- To give stockholders some evidence of the company's success without affecting working capital (which would be the case if it paid a cash dividend).
- To reduce the stock's market price by increasing the number of shares outstanding (a goal, however, more often met by a stock split).
- To make a nontaxable distribution to stockholders (because stock dividends that meet certain conditions are not considered income and are thus not taxed).
- To increase the company's permanent capital by transferring an amount from retained earnings to contributed capital.

STUDY NOTE: The declaration of a stock dividend results in a reshuffling of stockholders' equity—that is, a portion of retained earnings is converted to contributed capital (by closing the Stock Dividends account). Total stockholders' equity is not affected.

A stock dividend does not affect total stockholders' equity. Basically, it transfers a dollar amount from retained earnings to contributed capital. The amount transferred is the fair market value (usually, the market price) of the additional shares. When stock distributions are small—less than 20 to 25 percent of a company's outstanding common stock—generally accepted accounting principles require that the market price be used to account for the stock dividends.[8]

Stock Dividend Transactions To illustrate accounting for stock dividends, we will use Wing Corporation. Stockholders' equity in Wing is as follows.

Contributed capital:	
Common stock, $5 par value, 50,000 shares authorized, 15,000 shares issued and outstanding	$ 75,000
Additional paid-in capital	15,000
Total contributed capital	$ 90,000
Retained earnings	450,000
Total stockholders' equity	$540,000

Declaration Date

Transaction On February 24, when the market price of Wing's $5 par value common stock is $20 per share, the board of directors declares a 10 percent stock dividend to be distributed on March 31 to stockholders of record on March 15.

STUDY NOTE: For a small stock dividend, the portion of retained earnings transferred is determined by multiplying the number of shares to be distributed by the stock's market price on the declaration date.

Analysis The journal entry to record this stock dividend on the declaration date (February 24)

- ▲ *increases* the *Stock Dividends* account with a debit of $30,000 (0.10 × 15,000 shares × $20), the total market value of the stock dividend
- ▲ *increases Common Stock Distributable* (a temporary account until the 1,500 shares are distributed on March 31) with a credit at total par value of $7,500 (1,500 shares × $5)
- ▲ *increases Additional Paid-in Capital* with a credit of $22,500 ($30,000 − $7,500), the amount by which the total market value of the stock to be issued exceeds its total par value

Journal Entry

A	=	L	+	SE
				−30,000
				+7,500
				+22,500

		Dr.	Cr.
Feb. 24	Stock Dividends	30,000	
	Common Stock Distributable		7,500
	Additional Paid-in Capital		22,500
	Declared a 10 percent stock dividend on common stock, distributable on March 31 to stockholders of record on March 15:		
	15,000 shares × 0.10 = 1,500 shares		
	1,500 shares × \$20 per share = \$30,000		
	1,500 shares × \$5 per share = \$7,500		

Comment Because Common Stock Distributable represents an obligation to distribute additional shares of capital stock, it is a stockholders' equity account, not a liability account, as Cash Dividends Payable is. Also, the Stock Dividends account appears as a deduction from retained earnings on the statement of stockholders' equity.

Record Date

Analysis No entry is needed on the date of record (March 15).

Payment Date

Analysis The journal entry to record the stock dividend on the distribution, or payment, date (March 31)

▼ *decreases Common Stock Distributable* to zero with debit of \$7,500 (1,500 shares × \$5)

▲ *increases Common Stock* with a credit of \$7,500 (1,500 shares × \$5)

Journal Entry

A	=	L	+	SE
				−7,500
				+7,500

		Dr.	Cr.
Mar. 31	Common Stock Distributable	7,500	
	Common Stock		7,500
	Distributed a stock dividend of 1,500 shares of common stock		

Effect of a Stock Dividend on Stockholders' Equity If financial statements are prepared between the declaration date and the date of distribution, Common Stock Distributable should be reported as part of contributed capital.

Contributed capital:	
Common stock, \$5 par value, 50,000 shares authorized, 15,000 shares issued and outstanding	\$ 75,000
Common stock distributable, 1,500 shares	7,500
Additional paid-in capital	37,500
Total contributed capital	\$120,000
Retained earnings	420,000
Total stockholders' equity	\$540,000

Note that after the stock dividend has been distributed:

- Total stockholders' equity is the same before and after the stock dividend.
- The assets of the corporation are not reduced, as they would be by a cash dividend.
- The proportionate ownership in the corporation of any individual stockholder is the same before and after the stock dividend.

Large Stock Dividends All stock dividends have some effect on the market price of a company's stock, but some are so large that they have a material effect. For example, a 50 percent stock dividend would cause the market price of a stock to drop about 33 percent because the increase would be one-third of the shares outstanding. The AICPA has ruled that large stock dividends—those greater than 20 to 25 percent—should be accounted for by transferring the par or stated value of the stock on the declaration date from retained earnings to contributed capital.[9]

Stock Splits

STUDY NOTE: Stock dividends and stock splits reduce earnings per share because they increase the number of shares issued and outstanding. Cash dividends have no effect on earnings per share.

A **stock split** occurs when a corporation increases the number of shares of stock issued and outstanding and reduces the par or stated value proportionally. A company may plan a stock split for the following reasons:

- To lower its stock's market price per share and, thereby, increase the demand and volume of trading for its stock at this lower price.
- To signal to the market its success in achieving its operating goals.

Business Application Nike achieved these strategic objectives in 2007 by increasing its cash dividend and declaring a 2-for-1 stock split.[10] After the stock split, the number of the company's outstanding shares doubled, thereby cutting the share price from about $80 per share to $40 per share. The stock split left each stockholder's total wealth unchanged but increased the income stockholders received from dividends. Although there is no fundamental reason why a stock should go up because of a stock split, the stock split was a sign that Nike has continued to do well. In fact, Nike's stock continued to rise during the difficult years for the economy that followed to over $100 per share in 2012.[11]

Stock Split

Transaction Wing has 15,000 shares of $5 par value stock outstanding and the market value is $70 per share. The corporation plans a 2-for-1 split.

Analysis The journal entry to record this split

▼ *decreases* the par value to $2.50 per share ($5.00 ÷ 2)

▲ *increases* the number of shares outstanding to 30,000 (15,000 shares × 2)

After the split, a stockholder who previously owned 200 shares of the $5 par value stock will own:

- 400 shares of the $2.50 par value stock in outstanding shares of stock
- the same proportionate share of the company as before the split
- approximately the same total market value of stock because the 2-for-1 stock split will cause the price of the stock to drop by approximately 50 percent, to about $35

Journal Entry A stock split does not increase the number of shares authorized, nor does it change the balances in the stockholders' equity section of the balance sheet. It simply changes the par value and the number of shares issued for both shares outstanding and treasury stock. Thus, a journal entry is unnecessary. However, it is appropriate to document the change with a memorandum entry in the general journal.

Business Perspective

Do Stock Splits Help Increase a Company's Market Price?

When **General Mills**, the cereal company, completed a 2-for-1 split in May 2010, its stock dropped from about $70 per share to about $35 per share. Since then, the price has trended upward.[12]

July 15 The 15,000 shares of $5 par value common stock issued and outstanding were split 2 for 1, resulting in 30,000 shares of $2.50 par value common stock issued and outstanding.

The stockholders' equity before and after the stock split follows.

Before Stock Split

Contributed capital:	
Common stock, $5 par value, 50,000 shares authorized; 15,000 shares issued and outstanding	$ 75,000
Additional paid-in capital	15,000
Total contributed capital	$ 90,000
Retained earnings	450,000
Total stockholders' equity	$540,000

After Stock Split

Contributed capital:	
Common stock, $2.50 par value, 50,000 shares authorized, 30,000 shares issued and outstanding	$ 75,000
Additional paid-in capital	15,000
Total contributed capital	$ 90,000
Retained earnings	450,000
Total stockholders' equity	$540,000

Comment The balances of all accounts remain the same. Only the par value and number of shares issued and outstanding change. If the number of split shares exceeds the number of authorized shares, the corporation's board of directors must secure state and stockholders' approval before it can issue the additional shares.

APPLY IT!

Kelly Corporation's board of directors declared a 2 percent stock dividend applicable to the outstanding shares of its $10 par value common stock, of which 1,000,000 shares are authorized, 300,000 are issued, and 100,000 are held in the treasury. Then, the board declared a 2-for-1 stock split on issued shares. How many authorized, issued, and treasury shares existed after each of these transactions? What is the par value per share?

SOLUTION

Stock dividend applies to outstanding shares:
(300,000 shares − 100,000 shares) × 0.02 = 4,000 shares

Stock split applies to all issued shares:
304,000 shares × 2 = 608,000 shares

Authorized shares are unchanged (1,000,000, but par value is now $5 per share); issued shares are 608,000; and outstanding shares are 408,000 (608,000 − 200,000 treasury shares).

TRY IT! SE11, SE12, SE13, E13A, E14A, E15A, E13B, E14B, E15B

LO 7 The Statement of Stockholders' Equity and Book Value per Share

The following sections describe the statement of stockholders' equity and show how to calculate book value per share.

Statement of Stockholders' Equity

STUDY NOTE: *The statement of stockholders' equity is a labeled calculation of the change in each stockholder's equity account over an accounting period.*

Most companies use the statement of stockholders' equity in place of the statement of retained earnings because it reveals much more about the stockholders' equity transactions that took place during the period. For example, in the statement of stockholders' equity in Exhibit 3, the first line shows the beginning balance of each account in the stockholders' equity section of Snow Corporation's balance sheet. Each subsequent line *discloses* the effects of transactions on those accounts.

Exhibit 3
Statement of Stockholders' Equity

Snow Corporation
Statement of Stockholders' Equity
For the Year Ended December 31, 2015

	Preferred Stock $100 Par Value 8% Convertible	Common Stock $10 Par Value	Additional Paid-in Capital	Retained Earnings	Treasury Stock	Total
Balance, December 31, 2014	$ 800,000	$600,000	$ 600,000	$1,200,000		$3,200,000
Net income				540,000		540,000
Issuance of 10,000 shares of common stock		100,000	400,000			500,000
Conversion of 2,000 shares of preferred stock to 6,000 shares of common stock	(200,000)	60,000	140,000			—
10 percent stock dividend on common stock, 7,600 shares		76,000	304,000	(380,000)		—
Purchase of 1,000 shares of treasury stock					$(48,000)	(48,000)
Cash dividends:						
Preferred stock				(48,000)		(48,000)
Common stock				(95,200)		(95,200)
Balance, December 31, 2015	$ 600,000	$836,000	$1,444,000	$1,216,800	$(48,000)	$4,048,800

As shown in Exhibit 3, Snow had the following:

- Net income of $540,000
- 10,000 shares of common stock issued for $500,000
- Conversion of $200,000 of preferred stock to common stock
- A 10 percent stock dividend on common stock
- Treasury stock purchases of $48,000
- Cash dividends on both preferred and common stock

***STUDY NOTE:** The ending balances on the statement of stockholders' equity appear in the stockholders' equity section of the balance sheet.*

The ending balances of the accounts appear at the bottom of the statement. Those accounts and balances make up the stockholders' equity section of Snow's balance sheet on December 31, 2015, as shown in Exhibit 4.

Exhibit 4
Stockholders' Equity Section of a Balance Sheet

Snow Corporation
Balance Sheet
December 31, 2015

Stockholders' Equity

Contributed capital:		
Preferred stock, $100 par value, 8 percent convertible, 20,000 shares authorized. 6,000 shares issued and outstanding		$ 600,000
Common stock, $10 par value, 200,000 shares authorized, 83,600 shares issued. 82,600 shares outstanding	$ 836,000	
Additional paid-in capital	1,444,000	2,280,000
Total contributed capital		$2,880,000
Retained earnings		1,216,800
Total contributed capital and retained earnings		$4,096,800
Less: Treasury stock, common (1,000 shares, at cost)		48,000
Total stockholders' equity		$4,048,800

Book Value per Share

The word *value* is associated with shares of stock in several ways. Par value or stated value is set when the stock is authorized, and it establishes a company's legal capital. Neither par value nor stated value has any relationship to a stock's book value or market value. The **book value** of stock represents a company's total assets less its liabilities. It is simply the stockholders' equity in a company or, to put it another way, it represents a company's net assets. The **book value per share** is, therefore, the equity of the owner of one share of stock in the net assets of a company. That value generally does not equal the amount a stockholder receives if the company is sold or liquidated because, in most cases, assets are recorded at historical cost, not at their current market value.

Book Value per Share of Common Stock If a company has only common stock outstanding, book value per share is calculated as follows.

Stockholders' Equity ÷ Common Shares Outstanding = Book Value per Share

Common stock distributable is included in the number of shares outstanding, but treasury stock is not. For example, if a firm has total stockholders' equity of $2,060,000 and 58,000 shares outstanding, the book value per share of its common stock would be $35.52 ($2,060,000 ÷ 58,000 shares, rounded).

Book Value for Common and Preferred Stock If a company has both preferred and common stock, determining the book value per share is not so simple. Generally, the preferred stock's call value (or par value, if a call value is not specified) and any dividends in arrears are subtracted from stockholders' equity to determine the equity pertaining to common stock. Refer to the stockholders' equity section of Snow's balance sheet in Exhibit 4. If Snow has no dividends in arrears and its preferred stock is callable at $105, the equity pertaining to its common stock would be calculated as follows.

Total stockholders' equity	$4,048,800
Less equity allocated to preferred stockholders (6,000 shares × $105)	630,000
Equity pertaining to common stockholders	$3,418,800

As indicated in Exhibit 4, Snow has 82,600 shares of common stock outstanding (83,600 shares issued less 1,000 shares of treasury stock). Its book values per share are computed as follows.

Preferred stock: $630,000 ÷ 6,000 shares = $105 per share
Common stock: $3,418,800 ÷ 82,600 shares = $41.39 per share (rounded)

Book Value for Dividends in Arrears Assume the same facts except that Snow's preferred stock is 8 percent cumulative and that one year of dividends is in arrears. The stockholders' equity would be allocated as follows.

Total stockholders' equity		$4,048,800
Less call value of outstanding preferred shares	$630,000	
Dividends in arrears ($600,000 × 0.08)	48,000	
Equity allocated to preferred stockholders		678,000
Equity pertaining to common stockholders		$3,370,800

The book values per share would then be as follows.

Preferred stock: $678,000 ÷ 6,000 shares = $113 per share
Common stock: $3,370,800 ÷ 82,600 shares = $40.81 per share (rounded)

Stockholders' Equity and the Financial Statements

The stockholders' equity of a corporation, as shown on the balance sheet in Exhibit 5, is separated into contributed capital, retained earnings, and treasury stock.

Exhibit 5
Stockholders' Equity on the Balance Sheet

Balance Sheet
December 31, 2014

Assets	**Liabilities**
Current assets	Current liabilities
Investments	Long-term liabilities
Property, plant, and equipment	Total liabilities
Intangible assets	**Stockholders' Equity**
	Preferred stock, par value
	Common stock, par value
	Paid in capital in excess of par value, common
	Paid in capital in excess of par value, treasury
	Total contributed capital
	Retained earnings
	Less treasury stock
	Total stockholders' equity

Total Assets = Total Liabilities + Stockholders' Equity

APPLY IT!

Using the data from the stockholders' equity section of Puskin Corporation's balance sheet that follows, compute the book value per share for both the preferred and common stock.

Contributed capital:	
Preferred stock, $100 par value, 6 percent cumulative, 20,000 shares authorized, 2,000 shares issued and outstanding*	$ 200,000
Common stock, $5 par value, 200,000 shares authorized. 100,000 shares issued and outstanding	500,000
Additional paid-in capital	300,000
Total contributed capital	$1,000,000
Retained earnings	500,000
Total stockholders' equity	$1,500,000

*The preferred stock is callable at $104 per share, and one year's dividends are in arrears.

SOLUTION

Total stockholders' equity		$1,500,000
Less call value of outstanding preferred shares	$208,000	
Dividends in arrears ($200,000 × 0.06)	12,000	
Equity allocated to preferred stockholders		220,000
Equity pertaining to common stockholders		$1,280,000

Preferred stock book value per share: $220,000 ÷ 2,000 shares = $110, or $104 + $6 = $110 per share
Common stock book value per share: ($1,500,000 − $220,000) ÷ 100,000 common shares = $12.80 per share

TRY IT! SE14, SE15, E16A, E17A, E16B, E17B

SECTION 3 BUSINESS APPLICATIONS

SINESS APPLICATIONS
- Evaluate dividend policies
  - Dividend yield
- Evaluate profitability
  - Return on equity
- Evaluate investors' confidence in a company's future
  - Price/earnings ratio
- Evaluate stock options

EVANT RNING OBJECTIVE

3 Calculate dividend yield and return equity, and define k options.

LO 8 Evaluating Dividend Policies, Company Performance, and Stock Options

Investors use the dividend yield ratio to evaluate the amount of dividends they receive. In addition to evaluating dividends, investors will also want to evaluate a firm's past and future performance, using return on equity, the price-earnings ratio, and cash flow information. Both employees and investors evaluate stock options to determine their effects on compensation (employees) and the financial performance of the company (investors).

Dividend Yield

Dividend yield is computed by dividing the dividends per share by the market price per share. Companies that pay no dividends, such as **Google**, have a dividend yield of zero. To illustrate, **Microsoft** built up a large cash balance through its years of profitable operations, with no dividends paid. In 2005, it paid a large dividend of $3.40 per share and began paying regular dividends thereafter ($0.35 per share in 2006). By 2011, Microsoft's annual dividend increased to $5.4 billion ($0.64 per share).[13] Microsoft's dividend yield is computed as follows.

RATIO

Dividend Yield: What Is the Return from Dividends on Each Share of Stock?

$$\text{Dividend Yield} = \frac{\text{Dividends per Share}}{\text{Market Price per Share}} = \frac{\$0.64}{\$26} = 2.5\%^*$$

*Rounded

Because the yield is relatively low, Microsoft shareholders must expect some of their return to come from increases in the price of the shares. This expectation is even greater for stockholders of companies that pay no dividends, such as Google.

Return on Equity

Return on equity is the most important ratio associated with stockholders' equity. It is also a common measure of management's performance. For instance, when *Business Week* and *Forbes* rate companies on their success, return on equity is the major basis of their evaluations. In addition, the compensation of top executives is often tied to return on equity benchmarks. Return on equity is the ratio of net income to average total stockholders' equity. **Google**'s return on equity in 2011 is computed as follows.

RATIO

Return on Equity: How Much Does the Company Earn on the Stockholders' Investment in the Company?

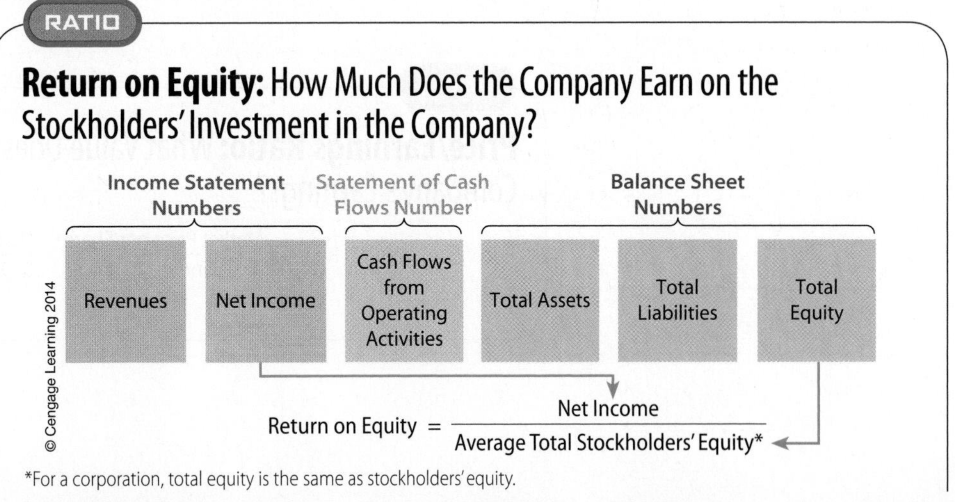

*For a corporation, total equity is the same as stockholders' equity.

$$= \frac{\$9{,}737}{(\$58{,}145 + \$46{,}241) \div 2}$$

$$= \frac{\$9{,}737}{\$52{,}193}$$

$$= 18.7\%^{**}$$

**Rounded

Google's 18.7 percent return on equity depends, of course, on the amount of net income the company earns. However, it also depends on the level of stockholders' equity, which in turn depends on management decisions about the amount of stock the company sells to the public. As a company sells more shares,

▲ stockholders' equity *increases*

▼ return on equity *decreases*

Management can keep stockholders' equity at a minimum, thereby increasing return on equity, by financing the business with cash flows from operations and by issuing long-term debt instead of stock. However, issuing long-term debt increases a company's financial risk because the interest and principal of the debt must be paid in a timely manner.

Management can also reduce stockholders' equity, thereby increasing return on equity, by buying back the company's shares on the open market. The cost of treasury stock has the following effect:

▼ Stockholders' equity *decreases*

▲ Return on equity *increases*

Many companies buy back their own stock instead of paying or increasing dividends. Their reason for doing so is that it puts money into the hands of stockholders in the form of market price appreciation without creating a commitment to higher dividends in the future. For instance, in 2011, **Microsoft** purchased $11.6 billion of its common stock on the open market.[14] Microsoft's stock repurchases will improve the company's return on equity, increase its earnings per share, and lower its price/earnings ratio.

Price-Earnings Ratio

The **price/earnings (P/E) ratio** is a measure of investors' confidence in a company's future. It is calculated by dividing the market price per share by the earnings per share. The price/earnings ratio will vary as market price per share fluctuates daily and the amount of earnings per share changes. Using the annual earnings per share from **Google**'s 2011 income statement, its P/E ratio can be calculated as follows.

RATIO

Price/Earnings Ratio: What Value Does the Market Place on the Company's Earnings?

$$\text{Price/Earnings (P/E) Ratio} = \frac{\text{Market Price per Share}}{\text{Earnings per Share}} = \frac{\$564}{\$29.76} = 19.0 \text{ times}^{*}$$

*Rounded

Because the market price is 19.0 times earnings, investors are paying a moderately high price in relation to earnings. They do so expecting that Google will continue to be successful.

Cash Flow Information

The best source of information concerning cash flows related to stock transactions and dividends is the financing activities section of the statement of cash flows. For instance, **Microsoft**'s cash flows from these activities are clearly revealed in this partial section of the company's statement of cash flows (in millions):

	2011	**2010**
Financing Activities		
Common stock issued	$ 2,422	$ 2,311
Common stock repurchased	(11,555)	(11,269)
Common stock cash dividend	**(5,180)**	**(4,578)**

Note the increasing amounts of common stock repurchased (treasury stock) and the small amount of new common stock issued in 2011. Both actions are a reflection of the company's success.

Stock Options as Compensation

More than 98 percent of public companies encourage employees to invest in their common stock through **stock option plans**.[15] Most such plans give employees the right to purchase stock in the future at a fixed price. Investors evaluate these plans to determine their effect on current and future financial statements and the value of their investment.

Some companies offer stock option plans only to management personnel, but others, including **Google**, make them available to all employees. Because the market value of a company's stock is tied to a company's performance, these plans are a means of both motivating and compensating employees. As the market value of the stock goes up, the difference between the option price and the market price grows, which increases the amount of compensation. Another key benefit of stock option plans is that compensation expense is tax-deductible.

In one example of how firms value stock options, **Google** recognized $1.97 billion of stock-based compensation expense in 2011. This amount represented about 7.6 percent of the company's total expenses and 20.3 percent of the net income.[16]

Business Perspective
Politics and Accounting Don't Mix

The FASB has long held that stock options should be treated as an expense, because they are a form of compensation. However, technology industry leaders have maintained that expensing stock options would hurt their companies' profits and growth. The U.S. Congress pressured the FASB to back down, using the companies' reasoning that stock options essentially have no value and, thus, are not an expense on the income statement, although they should be mentioned in a note to the financial statements. Many stock options were being granted, and the companies granting them were very loose in how they accounted for them. Many of the stock transactions were back-dated so that the exercise price would be most advantageous to the executives who were benefiting. By 2010, the SEC had settled more than 60 criminal investigations related to stock options, usually resulting in settlements and significant fines.[17]

APPLY IT!

In 2014, Chalet Corporation earned $2.20 per share and paid a dividend of $0.88 per share. At year-end, the price of its stock was $44 per share. Calculate the dividend yield and the price/earnings ratio.

SOLUTION

$$\text{Dividend Yield} = \frac{\text{Dividends per Share}}{\text{Market Price per Share}}$$

$$= \frac{\$0.88}{\$44.00} = 2.0\%$$

$$\text{Price/Earnings (P/E) Ratio} = \frac{\text{Market Price per Share}}{\text{Earnings per Share}}$$

$$= \frac{\$44.00}{\$2.20} = 20.0 \text{ times}$$

TRY IT! SE3, SE16, E18A, E18B

A Look Back At: Google, Inc.

Google

Alex Segre/Alamy

The beginning of this chapter focused on the extent of **Google, Inc.**'s stockholders' equity. Complete the following requirements to answer the questions posed at the beginning of the chapter.

Section 1: Concepts
How does the separate entity concept apply to the stockholders in a corporation like Google?

Section 2: Accounting Applications
How would Google account for its initial public offering?

Section 3: Business Applications 
What measures should stockholders use to evaluate the return on their investments?

SOLUTION

Section 1: Concepts
Google, Inc., is an *entity*, chartered by the state, that is separate from its owners both legally and from an accounting standpoint. Google's founders chose the corporate form of business rather than a partnership because it is relatively easy for a corporation to raise capital by issuing stock. Moreover, this approach to financing does not burden a company with debt and interest payments. Among the several other advantages that corporations have over proprietorships and partnerships are limited liability, ease of transfer of ownership, and continuous existence.

Section 2: Accounting Applications
Google stock has a low par value of only $.001 per share, even thought the shares were issued for $85 per share in cash. Thus, for each share of stock sold, Google credited common stock for $0.001 and additional paid in capital for $84.999. Legally, corporations must keep separate accounts for the amount of par or stated value and the additional amount received.

Section 3: Business Applications*
An efficient way for Google to evaluate the effectiveness of its credit policies and the level of its accounts receivable is to compare the current year's receivables turnover and days' sales uncollected with those ratios from previous years.

Return on equity is a critical measure of management's performance. Google's return on equity for 2011 should be compared to prior years' return on equity.

The price/earnings ratio is a measure of investors' confidence in Google's future. Google's price earnings ratio is very high. Evidently, despite Google not paying dividends, investors are rewarding the company's high return on equity and considering the company's future very bright.

* *Note:* These ratios were computed in the chapter.

Review Problem

In 2014, a group of investors in Wisconsin formed a corporation called Vietecha, Inc. The corporation's state charter authorized it to issue 2 million shares of $1 par value common stock and 50,000 shares of 4 percent, $20 par value cumulative and convertible preferred stock. Vietecha engaged in a number of transactions involving stock and dividends during 2014. These transactions were as follows.

Feb.	1	Issued 200,000 shares of common stock for $250,000.
	15	Issued 6,000 shares of common stock for accounting and legal services. The bills for these services totaled $7,200.
Mar.	15	Issued 240,000 shares of common stock to Jesus Miko in exchange for a building and land appraised at $200,000 and $50,000, respectively.
Apr.	2	Purchased 40,000 shares of its own common stock at $1.25 per share from a person who changed her mind about investing in the company.
July	1	Issued 50,000 shares of preferred stock for $1,000,000.
Sept.	30	Sold 20,000 of the shares in the treasury for $1.50 per share.
Dec.	31	Vietecha's board of directors declared dividends of $49,820, payable on January 15, 2015, to stockholders of record on January 7. Dividends included preferred stock dividends of $20,000 for one-half year.

For the period ended December 31, 2014, Vietecha reported net income of $80,000 and earnings per common share of $0.14. At December 31, the market price per common share was $1.60.

1. Record Vietecha's stock transactions using T accounts.
2. Prepare the stockholders' equity section of Vietecha's balance sheet as of December 31, 2014. (*Hint:* Use net income and dividends to calculate retained earnings.)

SOLUTION

1.

	A	B	C	D	E	F	G	H	I	J	K	L	M	N	O	P	Q	R	S	T
1			Assets				=			Liabilities				+			Stockholders' Equity			
2																				
3			Cash							Dividends Payable							Preferred Stock			
4	Feb.	1	250,000	Apr.	2	50,000					Dec.	31	49,820					July	1	1,000,000
5	July	1	1,000,000																	
6	Sept.	30	30,000														Common Stock			
7	Bal.		1,230,000															Feb.	1	200,000
8			Building																15	6,000
9	Mar.	15	200,000															Mar.	15	240,000
10																		Bal.		446,000
11			Land																	
12	Mar.	15	50,000														Additional Paid-in Capital			
13																		Feb.	1	50,000
14																			15	1,200
15																		Mar.	15	10,000
16																		Bal.		61,200
17																				
18																	Paid-in Capital, Treasury Stock			
19																		Sept.	30	5,000
20																				
21			Assets				=			Liabilities				+			Stockholders' Equity			
22																				
23																	Dividends			
24															Dec.	31	49,820			
25																				
26																	Treasury Stock			
27															Apr.	2	50,000	Sept.	30	25,000
28															Bal.		25,000			
29																				
30																	Start-up and Organization Costs			
31															Feb.	15	7,200			
32																				

2.

	A	B	C	
1	Vietecha, Inc.			
2	Balance Sheet			
3	December 31, 2014			
4				
5	Stockholders' Equity			
6				
7	Contributed capital:			
8	Preferred stock, 4 percent cumulative convertible, $20 par value, 50,000 shares authorized, issued, and outstanding			$1,000,000
9	Common stock $1 par value, 2,000,000 shares authorized, 446,000 shares issued, and 426,000 shares outstanding			446,000
10	Additional paid-in capital		$61,200	
11	Paid-in capital, treasury stock		5,000	66,200
12	Total contributed capital			$1,512,200
13	Retained earnings			30,180*
14	Total contributed capital and retained earnings			$1,542,380
15	Less treasury stock (20,000 shares, at cost)			25,000
16	Total stockholders' equity			$1,517,380
17				
18	*Retained Earnings = Net Income – Cash Dividends Declared Retained Earnings = $80,000 – $49,820 = $30,180			

Chapter Review

Define the *corporate* form of business and its characteristics. LO 1

The corporate form of business has definite advantages over sole proprietorships and partnerships, such as limited liability and the ability to raise large amounts of capital, but choosing a corporate form of business requires a careful weighing of the advantages and disadvantages as well as the issues involved in using equity financing.

Most states require corporations to issue stock at a minimum value called legal capital. Legal capital is represented by the stock's par or stated value.

Identify the components of stockholders' equity and their characteristics. LO 2

The stockholders' equity section of a corporate balance sheet usually has at least three components: contributed capital, retained earnings, and treasury stock. Contributed capital consists of money raised through stock issues. A corporation can issue two types of stock: common stock and preferred stock. Common stockholders have voting rights; they also share in the earnings of the corporation. Preferred stockholders usually have preference over common stockholders in one or more areas. Retained earnings are reinvested in the corporation. They represent stockholders' claims to assets resulting from profitable operations. Treasury stock is stock that the issuing corporation has reacquired. It is treated as a deduction from stockholders' equity.

Preferred stock generally gives its owners first right to dividend payments. Only after these stockholders have been paid can common stockholders receive any portion of a dividend. If the preferred stock is cumulative and dividends are in arrears, a corporation must pay the amount in arrears to preferred stockholders before it pays any dividends to common stockholders. Preferred stockholders also usually have preference over common stockholders in terms of their claims to assets if the corporation is liquidated. In addition, preferred stock may be convertible to common stock, and it is often callable at the option of the corporation.

Account for the issuance of stock for cash and other assets. LO 3

Corporations normally issue their stock in exchange for cash or other assets. When stock is issued for cash at par or stated value, Cash is debited and Common Stock or Preferred Stock is credited. When stock is sold at an amount greater than par or stated value, the excess is recorded in Additional Paid-in Capital.

When stock is issued for noncash assets, the general rule is to record the stock at its market value. If this value cannot be determined, the fair market value of the asset received is used to record the transaction.

Account for treasury stock. LO 4

Treasury stock is stock that the issuing company has reacquired. A company may buy back its own stock for several reasons, including a desire to create stock option plans, maintain a favorable market for the stock, increase earnings per share, or purchase other companies. The purchase of treasury stock is recorded at cost and is deducted from stockholders' equity. Treasury stock can be reissued or retired. It is similar to unissued stock in that it does not have rights until it is reissued.

Account for cash dividends. LO 5

The liability for payment of dividends arises on the date the board of directors declares a dividend. The declaration is recorded with a debit to Dividends and a credit to Dividends Payable. The record date—the date on which ownership of the stock, and thus of the right to receive a dividend, is determined—requires no entry. On the payment date, the Dividends Payable account is eliminated, and the Cash account is reduced.

Account for stock dividends and stock splits. LO 6

A stock dividend is a proportional distribution of shares among a corporation's stockholders. The following is a summary of the key dates and accounting treatments of stock dividends:

Key Date	Stock Dividend
Declaration date	Debit Stock Dividends for the market value of the stock to be distributed (if the stock dividend is small) and credit Common Stock Distributable for the stock's par value and Additional Paid-in Capital for the excess of the market value over the stock's par value.
Record date	No entry is needed.
Date of distribution	Debit Common Stock Distributable and credit Common Stock for the par value of the stock

A company usually declares a stock split to reduce the market value of its stock and thereby increase the demand for the stock. Because the par value of the stock normally decreases in proportion to the number of additional shares issued, a stock split has no effect on the dollar amount in stockholders' equity. A stock split does not require a journal entry, but a memorandum entry in the general journal is appropriate.

Describe the statement of stockholders' equity, and compute book value per share. LO 7

The statement of stockholders' equity summarizes changes during a period in each component of the stockholders' equity section of the balance sheet.

Book value per share is calculated by dividing stockholders' equity by the number of common shares outstanding. If a company has both preferred and common stock, the call or par value of the preferred stock and any dividends in arrears are deducted from stockholders' equity before dividing by the common shares outstanding.

Calculate dividend yield and return on equity, and define stock options. LO 8

Investors evaluate dividend policies and company performance by determining the dividend yield, return on equity, and the price/earnings ratio. Another issue involved in managing contributed capital is using stock options as compensation.

Key Terms and Ratios

authorized shares 546 (LO2)
book value 567 (LO7)
book value per share 567 (LO7)
callable preferred stock 549 (LO2)
common stock 546 (LO2)
contributed capital 542 (LO1)
convertible preferred stock 548 (LO2)
cumulative preferred stock 547 (LO2)
declaration date 560 (LO5)
dividend 559 (LO5)
dividends in arrears 547 (LO2)
double taxation 543 (LO1)
ex-dividend 560 (LO5)
initial public offering (IPO) 541
issued shares 546 (LO2)
legal capital 543 (LO1)
liquidating dividend 559 (LO5)
noncumulative preferred stock 547 (LO2)
no-par stock 550 (LO3)
outstanding shares 546 (LO2)
par value 543 (LO1)
payment date 560 (LO5)
preferred stock 546 (LO2)
record date 560 (LO5)
registrars 543 (LO1)
start-up and organization costs 544 (LO1)
stated value 551 (LO3)
statement of stockholders' equity 545 (LO2)
stock dividend 562 (LO6)
stock option plans 571 (LO8)
stock split 564 (LO6)
transfer agents 543 (LO1)
treasury stock 545 (LO2)
underwriter 543 (LO1)

RATIOS

dividend yield 569 (LO8)
price/earnings (P/E) ratio 570 (LO8)
return on equity 569 (LO8)

Chapter Assignments

DISCUSSION QUESTIONS

LO 1 **DQ1.** Why are most large companies established as corporations rather than as partnerships?

LO 2 **DQ2.** Why does a company usually not want to issue all its authorized shares?

LO 2 **DQ3.** Why would a company want to issue callable preferred stock?

LO 2 **DQ4.** What arguments can you give for treating preferred stock as debt rather than equity when carrying out financial analysis?

LO 4 **DQ5.** Why is treasury stock not considered an investment or an asset?

LO 5 **DQ6.** If an investor sells shares after the declaration date but before the date of record, does the seller still receive the dividend?

LO 6 **DQ7.** Upon receiving shares of stock from a stock dividend, why should the stockholder not consider the value of the stock as income?

LO 6, 7 **DQ8.** What is the effect of a stock dividend or a stock split on book value per share?

LO 8 **DQ9. BUSINESS APPLICATION ▶** Why do many companies like to give stock options as compensation?

LO 8 **DQ10. BUSINESS APPLICATION ▶** What relevance does par value or stated value have to a financial ratio, such as return on equity or debt to equity?

SHORT EXERCISES

LO 1 Advantages and Disadvantages of a Corporation

SE1. CONCEPT ▶ Identify whether each of the following characteristics is an advantage or a disadvantage of the corporate form of business:

1. Ease of transfer of ownership
2. Taxation
3. Separate legal entity
4. Lack of mutual agency
5. Government regulation
6. Continuous existence

LO 1 Effect of Start-up and Organization Costs

SE2. At the beginning of 2014, Salinas Company incurred the following start-up and organization costs: (1) attorneys' fees with a market value of $10,000, paid with 6,000 shares of $1 par value common stock, and (2) incorporation fees of $6,000 cash. Calculate total start-up and organization costs. What will be the effect of these costs on the income statement and balance sheet?

LO 1, 5, 8 Management Issues

SE3. BUSINESS APPLICATION ▶ Indicate whether each of the following actions is related to (a) managing under the corporate form of business, (b) using equity financing, (c) determining dividend policies, (d) evaluating performance using return on equity, or (e) issuing stock options:

1. Considering whether to make a distribution to stockholders.
2. Controlling day-to-day operations.
3. Determining whether to issue preferred or common stock.
4. Compensating management based on the company's meeting or exceeding the targeted return on equity.
5. Compensating employees by giving them the right to purchase shares at a given price.
6. Transferring shares without the approval of other owners.

LO 2 Stockholders' Equity

SE4. Prepare the stockholders' equity section of Waldemar Corporation's balance sheet from the following accounts and balances on December 31, 2014:

Common Stock, $10 par value, 30,000 shares authorized, 20,000 shares issued, and 19,500 shares outstanding	$200,000
Additional Paid-in Capital	100,000
Retained Earnings	15,000
Treasury Stock, Common (500 shares, at cost)	7,500

LO 2 **Preferred Stock Dividends with Dividends in Arrears**

SE5. Mazurka Corporation has 2,000 shares of $100, 8 percent cumulative preferred stock outstanding and 40,000 shares of $1 par value common stock outstanding. In the company's first three years of operation, its board of directors paid the following cash dividends: 2013, none; 2014, $40,000; and 2015, $80,000. Determine the total cash dividends and dividends per share paid to the preferred and common stockholders during each of the three years.

LO 3 **Issuance of Stock**

SE6. Sigma Company is authorized to issue 100,000 shares of common stock. The company sold 5,000 shares at $12 per share. Prepare journal entries to record the sale of stock for cash under each of the following independent alternatives: (1) The stock has a par value of $5, and (2) the stock has no par value but a stated value of $1 per share.

LO 3 **Issuance of Stock for Noncash Assets**

SE7. Tulip Corporation issued 16,000 shares of its $1 par value common stock in exchange for land that had a fair market value of $100,000. Prepare the journal entries necessary to record the issuance of the stock for the land under each of these conditions: (1) The stock was selling for $7 per share on the day of the transaction; (2) management attempted to place a value on the common stock but could not do so.

LO 4 **Treasury Stock Transactions**

SE8. Prepare the journal entries necessary to record Dao Company's following stock transactions during 2014:

Oct.	1	Purchased 2,000 shares of its own $2 par value common stock for $20 per share, the current market price.
	17	Sold 500 shares of treasury stock purchased on October 1 for $25 per share.
	21	Sold 800 shares of treasury stock purchased on October 1 for $18 per share.

LO 4 **Retirement of Treasury Stock**

SE9. Refer to the information for Dao Company in **SE8**. On October 28, 2014, Dao retired the remaining 700 shares of treasury stock. The shares were originally issued at $5 per share. Prepare the necessary journal entry.

LO 5 **Cash Dividends**

SE10. Leon Corporation has authorized 400,000 shares of $1 par value common stock, of which 320,000 are issued and 280,000 are outstanding. On May 15, the board of directors declared a cash dividend of $0.20 per share, payable on June 15 to stockholders of record on June 1. Prepare the entries using T accounts, as necessary, for each of the three dates.

LO 6 **Stock Dividends**

SE11. On February 15, Mite Corporation's board of directors declared a 2 percent stock dividend applicable to the outstanding shares of its $10 par value common stock, of which 400,000 shares are authorized, 260,000 are issued, and 40,000 are held in the treasury. The stock dividend was distributed on March 15 to stockholders of record on March 1. On February 15, the market value of the common stock was $15 per share. On March 30, the board of directors declared a $0.50 per share cash dividend. No other stock transactions have occurred. Prepare journal entries to record, as necessary, the transactions of February 15, March 1, March 15, and March 30.

LO 6 **Stock Split**

SE12. On August 10, 2014, Geller, Inc.'s board of directors declared a 3-for-1 stock split of its $9 par value common stock, of which 400,000 shares were authorized and 125,000 were issued and outstanding. The market value on that date was $60 per share. On the same date, the balance of additional paid-in capital was $3,000,000, and the balance of retained earnings was $3,250,000. Prepare the stockholders' equity section of the company's balance sheet after the stock split. What entry, if any, is needed to record the stock split?

LO 6, 7 **Effects of Stockholders' Equity Actions**

SE13. Tell whether each of the following actions will increase, decrease, or have no effect on total assets, total liabilities, and total stockholders' equity:

1. Declaration of a stock dividend
2. Declaration of a cash dividend
3. Stock split
4. Purchase of treasury stock

LO 7 **Statement of Stockholders' Equity**

SE14. Refer to Snow Corporation's statement of stockholders' equity in Exhibit 3 to answer the following questions: (1) At what price per share were the 10,000 shares of common stock sold? (2) What was the conversion price per share of the common stock? (Round to the nearest cent.) (3) At what price was the common stock selling on the date of the stock dividend? (4) At what price per share was the treasury stock purchased?

LO 7 **Book Value for Preferred and Common Stock**

SE15. Using data from the stockholders' equity section of Tramot Corporation's balance sheet that follows, and assuming one year's dividend in arrears, compute the book value per share for both the preferred and the common stock. (Round to the nearest cent.)

Contributed capital:	
Preferred stock, $100 par value, 8 percent cumulative, 20,000 shares authorized, 1,000 shares issued and outstanding	$ 100,000
Common stock, $10 par value, 200,000 shares authorized, 80,000 shares issued and outstanding	800,000
Additional paid-in capital	1,032,000
Total contributed capital	$1,932,000
Retained earnings	550,000
Total stockholders' equity	$2,482,000

LO 8 **Dividend Yield and Price/Earnings Ratio**

SE16. BUSINESS APPLICATION ▶ In 2014, Konstan Corporation earned $3.30 per share and paid a dividend of $1.65 per share. At year-end, the price of its stock was $33 per share. Calculate the dividend yield and the price/earnings ratio.

EXERCISES: SET A

LO 1 **Advantages and Disadvantages of a Corporation**

E1A. CONCEPT ▶ Identify whether each of the following characteristics is an advantage (A) or a disadvantage (D) of the corporate form of business:

1. Continuous existence
2. Government regulation
3. Separate legal entity
4. Double taxation
5. Professional management

LO 2 **Stockholders' Equity**

E2A. The accounts and balances that follow are from Hastings Corporation's records on December 31, 2014.

Preferred Stock, $100 par value, 9 percent cumulative, 10,000 shares authorized, 6,000 shares issued and outstanding	$600,000
Common Stock, $12 par value, 45,000 shares authorized, 30,000 shares issued, and 28,500 shares outstanding	360,000
Additional Paid-in Capital	194,000
Retained Earnings	23,000
Treasury Stock, Common (1,500 shares, at cost)	30,000

Prepare the stockholders' equity section of Hastings' balance sheet as of December 31, 2014.

LO 2 **Characteristics of Common and Preferred Stock**

E3A. Indicate whether each of the following characteristics is more closely associated with common stock (C) or preferred stock (P):

1. Can be callable
2. Generally receives dividends before other classes of stock
3. Often receives dividends at a set rate
4. Is considered the residual equity of a company
5. Can be convertible
6. More likely to have dividends that vary in amount from year to year
7. Can be entitled to receive dividends not paid in past years
8. Likely to have full voting rights
9. Receives assets first in liquidation

LO 2 **Cash Dividends with Dividends in Arrears**

E4A. Rutherford Corporation has 20,000 shares of its $100 par value, 7 percent cumulative preferred stock outstanding and 100,000 shares of its $1 par value common stock outstanding. In Rutherford's first four years of operation, its board of directors paid the following cash dividends: 2011, none; 2012, $240,000; 2013, $280,000; 2014, $280,000. Determine the dividends per share and total cash dividends paid to the preferred and common stockholders during each of the four years.

LO 2 **Cash Dividends on Preferred and Common Stock**

E5A. Ex-Act Corporation pays dividends at the end of each year. The dividends that it paid for 2012, 2013, and 2014 were $160,000, $120,000, and $360,000, respectively. Calculate the total amount of dividends Ex-Act paid in each of these years to its common and preferred stockholders under both of the following capital structures: (1) 40,000 shares of $100 par, 6 percent noncumulative preferred stock and 120,000 shares of $10 par common stock; (2) 20,000 shares of $100 par, 7 percent cumulative preferred stock and 120,000 shares of $10 par common stock. Ex-Act had no dividends in arrears at the beginning of 2012.

LO 2, 3 **Stock Entries Using T Accounts; Stockholders' Equity**

E6A. Gormanus Corporation was organized in 2014. It was authorized to issue 400,000 shares of no-par common stock with a stated value of $5 per share, and 80,000 shares of $100 par value, 6 percent noncumulative preferred stock. On March 1, the company issued 120,000 shares of its common stock for $15 per share and 16,000 shares of its preferred stock for $100 per share.

1. Record the issuance of the stock using T accounts.
2. Prepare the stockholders' equity section of Gormanus' balance sheet as it would appear immediately after the company issued the common and preferred stock.

LO 3 **Issuance of Stock**

E7A. Sussex Company is authorized to issue 100,000 shares of common stock. On August 1, the company issued 5,000 shares at $25 per share. Prepare journal entries to record the issuance of stock for cash under each of the following alternatives: (1) the stock has a par value of $25; (2) the stock has a par value of $10; (3) the stock has no par value; and (4) the stock has a stated value of $1 per share.

LO 3 **Issuance of Stock for Noncash Assets**

E8A. On July 1, 2014, Jones Corporation, a new corporation, issued 40,000 shares of its common stock to finance a corporate headquarters building. The building has a fair market value of $1,200,000 and a book value of $800,000. Because Jones is a new corporation, it is not possible to establish a market value for its common stock. Prepare journal entries to record the issuance of stock for the building, assuming the following conditions: (1) the par value of the stock is $10 per share; (2) the stock is no-par stock; and (3) the stock has a stated value of $4 per share.

LO 4 **Treasury Stock Transactions**

E9A. Record DeMeo Corporation's following stock transactions, which represent all the company's treasury stock transactions during 2014, using T accounts:

May	5	Purchased 800 shares of its own $2 par value common stock for $20 per share, the current market price.
	17	Sold 300 shares of treasury stock purchased on May 5 for $22 per share.
	21	Sold 200 shares of treasury stock purchased on May 5 for $20 per share.
	28	Sold the remaining 300 shares of treasury stock purchased on May 5 for $19 per share.

LO 4 **Treasury Stock Transactions Including Retirement**

E10A. Record Carmel Corporation's following stock transactions, which represent all its treasury stock transactions for the year, using T accounts:

June	1	Purchased 1,000 shares of its own $30 par value common stock for $70 per share, the current market price.
	10	Sold 250 shares of treasury stock purchased on June 1 for $80 per share.
	20	Sold 350 shares of treasury stock purchased on June 1 for $58 per share.
	30	Retired the remaining shares purchased on June 1. The original issue price was $42 per share.

LO 5 **Cash Dividends**

E11A. Nogel Corporation secured authorization from the state for 200,000 shares of $10 par value common stock. It has 80,000 shares issued and 70,000 shares outstanding. On June 5, the board of directors declared a $0.25 per share cash dividend to be paid on June 25 to stockholders of record on June 15. Record these events using T accounts.

LO 5 **Cash Dividends**

E12A. Bennett Corporation has 500,000 authorized shares of $1 par value common stock, of which 200,000 are issued, including 20,000 shares of treasury stock. On October 15, the corporation's board of directors declared a cash dividend of $0.50 per share payable on November 15 to stockholders of record on November 1. Record these events using T accounts.

LO 6 **Journal Entries: Stock Dividends**

E13A. Panza Corporation has 60,000 shares of its $1 par value common stock outstanding. Prepare journal entries to record the following transactions as they relate to the company's common stock:

July	17	Declared a 10 percent stock dividend on common stock to be distributed on August 10 to stockholders of record on July 31. Market value of the stock was $5 per share on this date.
	31	Date of record.
Aug.	10	Distributed the stock dividend declared on July 17.
Sept.	1	Declared a $0.50 per share cash dividend on common stock to be paid on September 16 to stockholders of record on September 10.

LO 6 **Stock Split**

E14A. Charles Corporation currently has 250,000 shares of $1 par value common stock authorized with 100,000 shares outstanding. The board of directors declared a 2-for-1 split on May 15, 2014, when the market value of the common stock was $2.50 per share. The retained earnings balance on May 15 was $350,000. Additional paid-in capital on this date was $10,000. Prepare the stockholders' equity section of the company's balance sheet before and after the stock split. What entry, if any, would be necessary to record the stock split?

LO 6 **Stock Split**

E15A. On January 15, 2014, Agard International's board of directors declared a 3-for-1 stock split of its $12 per value common stock, of which 1,600,000 shares were authorized and 400,000 were issued and outstanding. The market value on that date was $45 per share. On the same date, the balance of additional paid-in capital was $8,000,000, and the balance of retained earnings was $16,000,000. Prepare the stockholders' equity section of Agard's balance sheet before and after the stock split. What entry, if any, is needed to record the stock split?

LO 7 **Statement of Stockholders' Equity**

E16A. The stockholders' equity section of Manco Corporation's balance sheet on December 31, 2014, follows.

Contributed capital:	
Common stock, $2 par value, 250,000 shares authorized, 200,000 shares issued and outstanding	$ 400,000
Additional paid-in capital	600,000
Total contributed capital	$1,000,000
Retained earnings	2,100,000
Total stockholders' equity	$3,100,000

Prepare a statement of stockholders' equity for the year ended December 31, 2015, assuming these transactions occurred in sequence in 2015:

a. Issued 5,000 shares of $100 par value, 9 percent cumulative preferred stock at par after obtaining authorization from the state.
b. Issued 20,000 shares of common stock in connection with the conversion of bonds having a carrying value of $300,000.
c. Declared and issued a 2 percent common stock dividend. The market value on the date of declaration was $14 per share.
d. Purchased 5,000 shares of common stock for the treasury at a cost of $16 per share.
e. Earned net income of $230,000.
f. Declared and paid the full-year's dividend on preferred stock and a dividend of $0.40 per share on common stock outstanding at the end of the year.

LO 7

Book Value for Preferred and Common Stock

E17A. The stockholders' equity section of Plaka Corporation's balance sheet follows. Assuming one year's dividend in arrears, determine the book value per share for both the preferred and the common stock. (Round to the nearest cent.)

Contributed capital:	
Preferred stock, $100 par value, callable at $105 per share, 6 percent cumulative, 5,000 shares authorized, 100 shares issued and outstanding	$10,000
Common stock, $5 par value, 50,000 shares authorized, 5,000 shares issued, 4,500 shares outstanding	25,000
Additional paid-in capital	14,000
Total contributed capital	$49,000
Retained earnings	47,500
Total contributed capital and retained earnings	$96,500
Less treasury stock, common (500 shares at cost)	7,500
Total stockholders' equity	$89,000

LO 8

Dividend Yield and Price/Earnings Ratio

E18A. BUSINESS APPLICATION ▶ In 2014, Konstan Corporation earned $4.40 per share and paid a dividend of $2.00 per share. At year-end, the price of its stock was $66 per share. Calculate the dividend yield and the price/earnings ratio. (Round the dividend yield to the nearest tenth of a percent.)

EXERCISES: SET B

Visit the textbook companion website at www.cengagebrain.com to access Exercise Set B for this chapter.

PROBLEMS

LO 1, 2, 3, 4, 5

✔ 2: Total stockholders' equity: $302,400

Common Stock Transactions and Stockholders' Equity

P1. On March 1, 2014, Kissell Corporation began operations with a charter from the state that authorized 100,000 shares of $4 par value common stock. Over the next quarter, the company engaged in the transactions that follow.

Mar.	1	Issued 30,000 shares of common stock, $200,000.
	2	Paid fees associated with obtaining the charter and starting up and organizing the corporation, $24,000.
Apr.	10	Issued 13,000 shares of common stock, $130,000.
	15	Purchased 5,000 shares of common stock, $50,000.
May	31	The board of directors declared a $0.20 per share cash dividend to be paid on June 15 to shareholders of record on June 10.

REQUIRED

1. Record the above transactions using T accounts.
2. Prepare the stockholders' equity section of Kissell's balance sheet on May 31, 2014. Net income earned during the first quarter was $30,000.
3. **ACCOUNTING CONNECTION ▶** What effect, if any, will the cash dividend declaration on May 31 have on Kissell's net income, retained earnings, and cash flows?

LO 2, 8

✔ 1: Total dividends in 2014: preferred, $40,000; common, $90,000

Preferred and Common Stock Dividends and Dividend Yield

P2. Avaya Corporation had the following stock outstanding from 2011 through 2014:

Preferred stock: $100 par value, 8 percent cumulative, 5,000 shares authorized, issued, and outstanding

Common stock: $10 par value, 100,000 shares authorized, issued, and outstanding

(Continued)

The company paid $30,000, $30,000, $94,000, and $130,000 in dividends during 2011, 2012, 2013, and 2014, respectively. The market price per common share was $7.25 and $8.00 per share at the end of years 2013 and 2014, respectively.

REQUIRED

1. Determine the dividends per share and the total dividends paid to common stockholders and preferred stockholders in 2011, 2012, 2013, and 2014.
2. Perform the same computations, with the assumption that the preferred stock was noncumulative.
3. **BUSINESS APPLICATION ▶** Calculate the 2013 and 2014 dividend yield for common stock, using the dividends per share computed in requirement **2**. (Round to the nearest tenth of a percent.)
4. **ACCOUNTING CONNECTION ▶** How are cumulative preferred stock and noncumulative preferred stock similar to long-term bonds? How do they differ from long-term bonds?

LO **1, 2, 3, 4, 5**

Comprehensive Stockholders' Equity Transactions

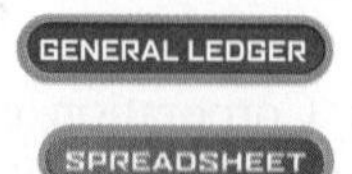

P3. In January 2014, Vanowski Corporation was organized and authorized to issue 2,000,000 shares of no-par common stock and 50,000 shares of 5 percent, $50 par value, noncumulative preferred stock. The stock-related transactions for the first year's operations follow.

			Account			
			Debited		Credited	
			Account Number	Dollar Amount	Account Number	Dollar Amount
Jan.	19	Sold 15,000 shares of common stock for $31,500. State law requires a minimum of $1 stated value per share.	110	$31,500	310 312	$15,000 $16,500
	21	Issued 5,000 shares of common stock to attorneys and accountants for services valued at $11,000 and provided during the organization of the corporation.	___	___	___	___
Feb.	7	Issued 30,000 shares of common stock for a building that had an appraised value of $78,000.	___	___	___	___
Mar.	22	Purchased 10,000 shares of its common stock at $3 per share.	___	___	___	___
July	15	Issued 5,000 shares of common stock to employees under a stock option plan that allows any employee to buy shares at the current market price, which is now $3 per share.	___	___	___	___
Aug.	1	Sold 2,500 shares of treasury stock for $4 per share.	___	___	___	___
Sept.	1	Declared a cash dividend of $0.15 per common share to be paid on September 25 to stockholders of record on September 15.	___	___	___	___

Sept.	15	Date of record for cash dividends.	___	___	___	___
	25	Paid cash dividends to stockholders of record on September 15.	___	___	___	___
Oct.	30	Issued 4,000 shares of common stock for a piece of land. The stock was selling for $3 per share, and the land had a fair market value of $12,000.	___	___	___	___
Dec.	15	Issued 2,200 shares of preferred stock for $50 per share.	___	___	___	___

REQUIRED

1. For each of these transactions, indicate the account numbers and dollar amounts (as shown in the example) for the account(s) debited and credited, using the account numbers that follow.

110 Cash	312 Additional Paid-in Capital
120 Land	313 Paid-in Capital, Treasury Stock
121 Building	340 Retained Earnings
220 Dividends Payable	341 Dividends
305 Preferred Stock	350 Treasury Stock, Common
310 Common Stock	510 Start-up and Organization Costs

2. **BUSINESS APPLICATION ▶** Why is the stockholders' equity section of the balance sheet an important consideration in analyzing the performance of a company?

LO **2, 3, 4, 5, 8**

RATIO

GENERAL LEDGER

✔ 2: Total stockholders' equity: $236,520

Comprehensive Stockholders' Equity Transactions and Stockholders' Equity

P4. Kraft Unlimited, Inc., was organized and authorized to issue 5,000 shares of $100 par value, 9 percent preferred stock and 50,000 shares of no par, $5 stated value common stock on July 1, 2014. Stock-related transactions for Kraft Unlimited follow.

July	1	Issued 10,000 shares of common stock at $11 per share.
	1	Issued 500 shares of common stock at $11 per share for services rendered in connection with the organization of the company.
	2	Issued 1,000 shares of preferred stock at par value for cash.
	10	Issued 2,500 shares of common stock for land on which the asking price was $35,000. Market value of the stock was $12. Management wishes to record the land at the market value of the stock.
Aug.	2	Purchased 1,500 shares of its common stock at $13 per share.
	10	Declared a cash dividend for one month on the outstanding preferred stock and $0.02 per share on common stock outstanding, payable on August 22 to stockholders of record on August 12.
	12	Date of record for cash dividends.
	22	Paid cash dividends.

REQUIRED

1. Prepare journal entries to record these transactions.
2. Prepare the stockholders' equity section of Kraft's balance sheet as it would appear on August 31, 2014. Net income for July was zero and August was $11,500.
3. **BUSINESS APPLICATION ▶** Calculate dividend yield, price/earnings ratio, and return on equity. Assume earnings per common share are $1.00 and market price per common share is $20. For beginning stockholders' equity, use the balance after the July transactions. (Round to the nearest tenth of a percent.)

(*Continued*)

4. **BUSINESS APPLICATION** ▶ Discuss the results in requirement 3, including the effect on investors' returns and the company's profitability as it relates to stockholders' equity.

LO 4

Treasury Stock

GENERAL LEDGER

SPREADSHEET

✔ 1: Balance in Retained Earnings: $17,200 debit

P5. Rolex Company was involved in the following treasury stock transactions during 2014:

a. Purchased 80,000 shares of its $1 par value common stock on the market for $2.50 per share.
b. Purchased 16,000 shares of its $1 par value common stock on the market for $2.80 per share.
c. Sold 44,000 shares purchased in (a) for $131,000.
d. Sold the other 36,000 shares purchased in (a) for $72,000.
e. Sold 6,000 of the remaining shares of treasury stock for $1.60 per share.
f. Retired all the remaining shares of treasury stock. All shares originally were issued at $1.50 per share.

REQUIRED

1. Record the treasury stock transactions using T accounts.
2. **ACCOUNTING CONNECTION** ▶ What is the reasoning behind treating the purchase of treasury stock as a reduction in stockholders' equity as opposed to treating it as an investment asset?

LO 6, 7

Dividends, Stock Splits, and Stockholders' Equity

GENERAL LEDGER

SPREADSHEET

✔ 2: Total retained earnings: $423,200
✔ 2: Total stockholders' equity: $1,049,000

P6. The stockholders' equity section of Minh, Inc.'s balance sheet as of December 31, 2013, follows.

Contributed capital:	
Common stock, $3 par value, 1,000,000 shares authorized, 80,000 shares issued and outstanding	$240,000
Additional paid-in capital	75,000
Total contributed capital	$315,000
Retained earnings	240,000
Total stockholders' equity	$555,000

A review of Minh's stockholders' equity records disclosed the following transactions during 2014:

Mar. 25	The board of directors declared a 5 percent stock dividend to stockholders of record on April 20 to be distributed on May 1. The market value of the common stock was $21 per share.
Apr. 20	Date of record for stock dividend.
May 1	Issued stock dividend.
Sept. 10	Declared a 3-for-1 stock split.
Dec. 15	Declared a 10 percent stock dividend to stockholders of record on January 15 to be distributed on February 15. The market price on this date is $9 per share.

REQUIRED

1. Record the stockholders' equity components of these transactions using T accounts.
2. Prepare the stockholders' equity section of Minh's balance sheet as of December 31, 2014. Assume net income for 2014 is $494,000.
3. **ACCOUNTING CONNECTION** ▶ If you owned 2,000 shares of Minh stock on March 1, 2014, how many shares would you own on February 15, 2015? Would your proportionate share of the ownership of the company be different on the latter date from what it was on the former date? Explain your answer.

LO 3, 4, 5, 6, 7

GENERAL LEDGER

✔ 2: Total stockholders' equity: $5,605,600

Comprehensive Stockholders' Equity Transactions

P7. On December 31, 2014, the stockholders' equity section of Delux Corporation's balance sheet appeared as follows:

Contributed capital:	
Common stock, $8 par value, 400,000 shares authorized, 120,000 shares issued and outstanding	$ 960,000
Additional paid-in capital	2,560,000
Total contributed capital	$3,520,000
Retained earnings	1,648,000
Total stockholders' equity	$5,168,000

Selected transactions involving stockholders' equity in 2015 follow.

Jan.	4	The board of directors obtained authorization for 40,000 shares of $40 par value noncumulative preferred stock that carried an indicated dividend rate of $4 per share and was callable at $42 per share.
	14	The company sold 24,000 shares of the preferred stock at $40 per share and issued another 4,000 in exchange for a building valued at $160,000.
Mar.	8	The board of directors declared a 2-for-1 stock split on the common stock.
Apr.	20	After the stock split, the company purchased 6,000 shares of common stock for the treasury at a price of $12 per share.
May	4	The company sold 2,000 of the shares purchased on April 20, at an average price of $16 per share.
July	15	The board of directors declared a cash dividend of $4 per share on the preferred stock and $0.40 per share on the common stock.
	25	Date of record.
Aug.	15	Paid the cash dividend.
Nov.	28	The board of directors declared a 15 percent stock dividend when the common stock was selling for $20 per share to be distributed on January 5 to stockholders of record on December 15.
Dec.	15	Date of record for the stock dividend.

REQUIRED

1. Prepare journal entries to record these transactions.
2. Prepare the stockholders' equity section of Delux's balance sheet as of December 31, 2015. Net loss for 2015 was $436,000. (*Hint:* Use T accounts to keep track of transactions.)
3. **ACCOUNTING CONNECTION ▶** Compute the book value per share for preferred and common stock (including common stock distributable) on December 31, 2014 and 2015, using end-of-year shares outstanding. (Round to the nearest cent.) What effect would you expect the change in book value to have on the market price per share of the company's stock?

ALTERNATE PROBLEMS

LO 1, 2, 3, 4, 5

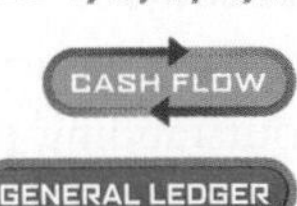

✔ 2: Total retained earnings: $32,000
✔ 2: Total stockholders' equity: $1,342,000

Common Stock Transactions and Stockholders' Equity

P8. Canterbury Corporation began operations on September 1, 2014. The corporation's charter authorized 300,000 shares of $8 par value common stock. Canterbury engaged in the transactions that follow during its first quarter.

Sept.	1	Issued 50,000 shares of common stock, $500,000.
	1	Paid an attorney $32,000 to help start up and organize the corporation and obtain a corporate charter from the state.

(*Continued*)

Oct. 2 Issued 80,000 shares of common stock, $960,000.
15 Purchased 10,000 shares of common stock for $150,000.
Nov. 30 Declared a cash dividend of $0.40 per share to be paid on December 15 to stockholders of record on December 10.

REQUIRED

1. Prepare entries using T accounts to record the above transactions.
2. Prepare the stockholders' equity section of Canterbury's balance sheet on November 30, 2014. Net income for the quarter was $80,000.
3. **ACCOUNTING CONNECTION ▶** What effect, if any, will the cash dividend declaration on November 30 have on net income, retained earnings, and cash flows?

LO 2, 8

RATIO

✔ 1: Total dividends in 2014: preferred, $280,000; common, $820,000

Preferred and Common Stock Dividends and Dividend Yield

P9. Rhinehart Corporation had both common stock and preferred stock outstanding from 2012 through 2014. Information about each stock for the three years follows.

Type	Par Value	Shares Outstanding	Other
Preferred	$100	40,000	7% cumulative
Common	20	600,000	

The company paid $140,000, $800,000, and $1,100,000 in dividends for 2012 through 2014, respectively. The market price per common share was $15 and $17 per share at the end of years 2013 and 2014, respectively.

REQUIRED

1. Determine the dividends per share and total dividends paid to the common and preferred stockholders each year. (Round to the nearest cent.)
2. Assuming that the preferred stock was noncumulative, repeat the computations performed in requirement **1**. (Round to the nearest cent.)
3. **BUSINESS APPLICATION ▶** Calculate the 2013 and 2014 dividend yield for common stock using dividends per share computed in requirement **2**. (Round to the nearest tenth of a percent.)
4. **ACCOUNTING CONNECTION ▶** How are cumulative preferred stock and noncumulative preferred stock similar to long-term bonds? How do they differ from long-term bonds?

LO 2, 3, 4, 5, 8

RATIO

GENERAL LEDGER

✔ 2: Total stockholders' equity: $1,765,900

Comprehensive Stockholders' Equity Transactions and Financial Ratios

P10. Gorlin Corporation was chartered in the Commonwealth of Massachusetts. The company was authorized to issue 20,000 shares of $100 par value, 6 percent preferred stock and 100,000 shares of no-par common stock. The common stock has a $2 stated value. The stock-related transactions for the quarter ended October 31, 2014, follow.

Aug. 3 Issued 20,000 shares of common stock at $22 per share.
15 Issued 16,000 shares of common stock for land. Asking price for the land was $200,000. Common stock's market value was $12 per share. Management wishes to record the land at the market value of the stock.
22 Issued 10,000 shares of preferred stock for $1,000,000.
Oct. 4 Issued 10,000 shares of common stock for $120,000.
10 Purchased 5,000 shares of common stock for the treasury for $13,000.
15 Declared a quarterly cash dividend on the outstanding preferred stock and $0.10 per share on common stock outstanding, payable on October 31 to stockholders of record on October 25.
25 Date of record for cash dividends.
31 Paid the cash dividends declared on October 15.

REQUIRED

1. Record transactions for the quarter ended October 31, 2014, using T accounts.
2. Prepare the stockholders' equity section of Gorlin's balance sheet as of October 31, 2014. Net income for the quarter was $46,000.
3. **BUSINESS APPLICATION ▶** Calculate dividend yield, price/earnings ratio, and return on equity. (Round the dividend yield and return on equity to the nearest tenth of a percent. Round the price/earnings ratio to the nearest tenth.) Assume earnings per common share are $1.97 and market price per common share is $25. For beginning stockholders' equity, use the balance after the August transactions.
4. **BUSINESS APPLICATION ▶** Discuss the results in requirement **3**, including the effect on investors' returns and the firm's profitability as it relates to stockholders' equity.

LO 1, 2, 3, 4, 5

Comprehensive Stockholders' Equity Transactions

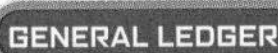

P11. In January 2014, Imperial Corporation was organized and authorized to issue 4,000,000 shares of no-par common stock and 100,000 shares of 5 percent, $50 par value, noncumulative preferred stock. The stock-related transactions for the first year's operations follow.

			Account Debited		Account Credited	
			Account Number	Dollar Amount	Account Number	Dollar Amount
Jan.	19	Sold 30,000 shares of common stock for $63,000. State law requires a minimum of $1 stated value per share.	110	$63,000	310 312	$30,000 $33,000
	21	Issued 10,000 shares of common stock to attorneys and accountants for services valued at $22,000 and provided during the organization of the corporation.	—	—	—	—
Feb.	7	Issued 60,000 shares of common stock for a building that had an appraised value of $156,000.	—	—	—	—
Mar.	22	Purchased 20,000 shares of its common stock at $3 per share.	—	—	—	—
July	15	Issued 10,000 shares of common stock to employees under a stock option plan that allows any employee to buy shares at the current market price, which is now $3 per share.	—	—	—	—
Aug.	1	Sold 5,000 shares of treasury stock for $4 per share.	—	—	—	—
Sept.	1	Declared a cash dividend of $0.15 per common share to be paid on September 25 to stockholders of record on September 15.	—	—	—	—
	15	Date of record for cash dividends.	—	—	—	—

(*Continued*)

Sept. 25	Paid cash dividends to stockholders of record on September 15.	___	___	___	___
Oct. 30	Issued 8,000 shares of common stock for a piece of land. The stock was selling for $3 per share, and the land had a fair market value of $24,000.	___	___	___	___
Dec. 15	Issued 4,400 shares of preferred stock for $50 per share.	___	___	___	___

REQUIRED

1. For each of these transactions, provided the account numbers and dollar amounts (as shown in the example) for the account(s) debited and credited using the account numbers that follow.

110 Cash	312 Additional Paid-in Capital
120 Land	313 Paid-in Capital, Treasury Stock
121 Building	340 Retained Earnings
220 Dividends Payable	341 Dividends
305 Preferred Stock	350 Treasury Stock, Common
310 Common Stock	510 Start-up and Organization Costs

2. **BUSINESS APPLICATION** ▶ Why is the stockholders' equity section of the balance sheet an important consideration in analyzing the performance of a company?

LO **4**

✔ 1: Balance in Retained Earnings: $34,400 debit

Treasury Stock

P12. Khandi Company was involved in the following treasury stock transactions during 2014:

a. Purchased 160,000 shares of its $1 par value common stock on the market for $2.50 per share.
b. Purchased 32,000 shares of its $1 par value common stock on the market for $2.80 per share.
c. Sold 88,000 shares purchased in (a) for $262,000.
d. Sold the other 72,000 shares purchased in (a) for $144,000.
e. Sold 12,000 of the remaining shares of treasury stock for $1.60 per share.
f. Retired all the remaining shares of treasury stock. All shares originally were issued at $1.50 per share.

REQUIRED

1. Record the treasury stock transactions using T accounts.
2. **ACCOUNTING CONNECTION** ▶ What is the reasoning behind treating the purchase of treasury stock as a reduction in stockholders' equity as opposed to treating it as an investment asset?

LO **6, 7**

GENERAL LEDGER

✔ 2: Total retained earnings: $798,100
✔ 2: Total stockholders' equity: $2,964,000

Dividends, Stock Splits, and Stockholders' Equity

P13. The stockholders' equity section of Villa Corporation's balance sheet as of December 31, 2013, follows.

Contributed capital:	
Common stock, $4 par value, 500,000 shares authorized, 200,000 shares issued and outstanding	$ 800,000
Additional paid-in capital	1,000,000
Total contributed capital	$1,800,000
Retained earnings	1,200,000
Total stockholders' equity	$3,000,000

Villa had the following transactions in 2014:

Feb.	28	The board of directors declared a 10 percent stock dividend to stockholders of record on March 25 to be distributed on April 5. The market value on this date is $16.
Mar.	25	Date of record for stock dividend.
Apr.	5	Issued stock dividend.
Aug.	3	Declared a 2-for-1 stock split.
Nov.	20	Purchased 18,000 shares of the company's common stock at $8 per share for the treasury.
Dec.	31	Declared a 5 percent stock dividend to stockholders of record on January 25 to be distributed on February 5. The market value per share was $9.

REQUIRED

1. Record the stockholders' equity components of these transactions using T accounts.
2. Prepare the stockholders' equity section of Villa's balance sheet as of December 31, 2014. Assume net income for 2014 is $108,000.
3. **ACCOUNTING CONNECTION ▶** If you owned 1,000 shares of Villa stock on February 1, 2014, how many shares would you own on February 5, 2015? Would your proportionate share of the ownership of the company be different on the latter date from what it was on the former date? Explain your answer.

LO **3, 4, 5, 6, 7**

Comprehensive Stockholders' Equity Transactions

RATIO

GENERAL LEDGER

✔ 2: Total stockholders' equity: $11,211,200

P14. On December 31, 2014, the stockholders' equity section of Torez Corporation's balance sheet appeared as follows.

Contributed capital:	
Common stock, $8 par value, 800,000 shares authorized, 240,000 shares issued and outstanding	$ 1,920,000
Additional paid-in capital	5,120,000
Total contributed capital	$ 7,040,000
Retained earnings	3,296,000
Total stockholders' equity	$10,336,000

The following are selected transactions involving stockholders' equity in 2015. On January 4, the board of directors obtained authorization for 80,000 shares of $40 par value noncumulative preferred stock that carried an indicated dividend rate of $4 per share and was callable at $42 per share. On January 14, the company sold 48,000 shares of the preferred stock at $40 per share and issued another 8,000 in exchange for a building valued at $320,000. On March 8, the board of directors declared a 2-for-1 stock split on the common stock. On April 20, after the stock split, the company purchased 12,000 shares of common stock for the treasury at a price of $12 per share; 4,000 of these shares subsequently were sold on May 4 at an average price of $16 per share. On July 15, the board of directors declared a cash dividend of $4 per share on the preferred stock and $0.40 per share on the common stock. The date of record was July 25. The dividends were paid on August 15. The board of directors declared a 15 percent stock dividend on November 28, when the common stock was selling for $20. The date of record for the stock dividend was December 15, and the dividend was to be distributed on January 5.

REQUIRED

1. Prepare journal entries to record these transactions.
2. Prepare the stockholders' equity section of Torez's balance sheet as of December 31, 2015. Net loss for 2015 was $872,000. (*Hint:* Use T accounts to keep track of transactions.)

(*Continued*)

3. **BUSINESS APPLICATION ▶** Compute the book value per share for preferred and common stock (including common stock distributable) on December 31, 2014 and 2015, using end-of-year shares outstanding. (Round to the nearest cent.) What effect would you expect the change in book value to have on the market price per share of the company's stock?

CASES

LO 1

Conceptual Understanding: Reasons for Issuing Common Stock

C1. DreamWorks Animation, led by billionaire **Microsoft** founder Paul Allen, went public in a recent year with its class A common stock at $28 per share, raising $650 million. By the end of the first day, it was up 27 percent to $38 per share, giving the company a value of almost $1 billion. This initial enthusiasm did not last. By the end of 2007, the price was only around $25 per share.[18] As a growing company that has produced such animated hits as Shrek, DreamWorks could have borrowed significant funds by issuing long-term debt. What are some advantages of issuing common stock as opposed to long-term debt? What are some disadvantages?

LO 4

Conceptual Understanding: Purposes of Treasury Stock

C2. BUSINESS APPLICATION ▶ Many companies in recent years have bought back their common stock. For example, **IBM**, with large cash holdings, spent almost $350 billion over three years repurchasing its stock.[19] What are the reasons companies buy back their own shares? What is the effect of common stock buybacks on earnings per share, return on equity, return on assets, debt to equity, and the current ratio?

LO 2, 3

Interpreting Financial Reports: Effect of Stock Issue

C3. When **Google, Inc.**, went public with an IPO, it used an auction system that allowed everyone to participate rather than allocating shares of stock to a few insiders. The company's IPO drew widespread attention. Announcements of the IPO would have been similar to the following:

22,500,000 Shares
GOOGLE, INC.
$0.001 Par Value Common Stock
Price $85 a share

The gross proceeds of the IPO before issue costs were $1.9 billion.

A portion of the stockholders' equity section of the balance sheet adapted from Google's annual report, which was issued prior to this stock offering, follows.

Stockholders' Equity
(Dollar amounts in thousands)

Common stock, $0.001 par value, 700,000,000 shares authorized; 161,000,000 shares issued and outstanding	$ 161
Additional paid-in capital	725,219
Retained earnings	191,352

1. Assume that the net proceeds to Google after issue costs were $1.8 billion. Prepare the journal entry to record the stock issuance on Google's accounting.
2. Prepare the stockholders' equity section portion of Google's balance sheet shown above after the issue of the common stock, based on the information given. (Round all answers to the nearest thousand.)
3. Based on your answer in **2**, did Google have to increase its authorized shares to undertake this stock issue?
4. What amount per share did Google receive and how much did Google's underwriters receive to help in issuing the stock? What do underwriters do to earn their fee?

LO 6

Conceptual Understanding: Stock Split

C4. When **Crocs**, the shoe company, reported in early 2007 that its first-quarter earnings had increased from the previous year, its stock price jumped to over $80 per share. At the same time, the company announced a 2-for-1 stock split.[20] What is a stock split and what effect does it have on the company's stockholders' equity? What effect will it likely have on the market value of the company's stock? In light of your answers, do you think the stock split is positive for the company and for its stockholders?

LO 2, 8

Interpreting Financial Reports: Stockholders' Equity

C5. Refer to the **CVS Corporation** annual report in the Supplement to Chapter 1 to answer the following questions:

1. What type of capital stock does CVS have? What is the par value? How many shares were authorized, issued, and outstanding at the end of fiscal 2011?
2. **BUSINESS APPLICATION ▶** What is the dividend yield (use average price of stock in last quarter) for CVS and its relationship to the investors' total return? (Round the average price to the nearest cent; round the dividend yield to the nearest tenth of a percent.) Does the company rely mostly on stock or on earnings for its stockholders' equity? (CVS's fourth quarter of 2011 high and low market prices were $41.35 and $32.28, respectively.)
3. **BUSINESS APPLICATION ▶** Does the company have a stock option plan? To whom do the stock options apply? Do employees have significant stock options? Given the market price of the stock shown in the report, do these options represent significant value to the employees?

LO 3, 4, 5, 8

Interpreting Financial Reports: Return on Equity, Treasury Stock, and Dividends Policy

C6. Refer to the annual report of **CVS Corporation** and the financial statements of **Southwest Airlines Co.** in the Supplement to Chapter 1.

1. **BUSINESS APPLICATION ▶** Compute the return on equity for both companies for fiscal 2011 and 2010. Total stockholders' equity for CVS and Southwest in 2009 was $35,768 million and $5,454 million, respectively.
2. **BUSINESS APPLICATION ▶** Did either company purchase treasury stock during these years? How will the purchase of treasury stock affect return on equity and earnings per share?
3. Did either company issue stock during these years? What are the details?
4. Compare the dividend policy of the two companies.

Continuing Case: Annual Report Project

C7. Using the most recent annual report of the company you have chosen to study and that you have accessed online at the company's website, examine the balance sheet and accompanying notes of your company. Answer the following questions:

1. What percentage of total liabilities and stockholders' equity is stockholders' equity? What kinds of stock does the company have?
2. Is retained earnings a significant component of stockholders' equity?
3. Does the company have treasury stock? What effect does it have on total stockholders' equity?
4. **BUSINESS APPLICATION ▶** Compute return on equity for your company.

CHAPTER 13

LEARNING OBJECTIVES

LO 1 Describe the principal purposes and concepts underlying the statement of cash flows, and identify its components and format.

LO 2 Use the indirect method to determine cash flows from operating activities.

LO 3 Determine cash flows from investing activities.

LO 4 Determine cash flows from financing activities.

LO 5 Analyze the statement of cash flows.

Annette Shaff/Shutterstock.com

THE STATEMENT OF CASH FLOWS

Business Insight

Amazon.com, Inc.

Founded in 1995, **Amazon.com, Inc.**, is now the largest online merchandising company in the world and one of the 500 largest companies in the United States. The company's financial focus is on "long-term sustainable growth" in cash flows.

Strong cash flows are critical to achieving and maintaining liquidity. If cash flows exceed the amount a company needs for operations and expansion, it will not have to borrow additional funds. It can use its excess cash to reduce debt, thereby lowering its debt to equity ratio and improving its financial position. That, in turn, can increase the market value of its stock.

Amazon.com's Financial Highlights summarize key components of the company's statement of cash flows.[1]

AMAZON.COM'S FINANCIAL HIGHLIGHTS:
Consolidated Statement of Cash Flows (In millions)

	2011	2010	2009
Net cash provided by operating activities	$ 3,903	$ 3,495	$ 3,293
Net cash provided by (used in) investing activities	(1,930)	(3,360)	(2,337)
Net cash provided by (used in) financing activities	(482)	181	(280)
Foreign currency effects	1	17	(1)
Increase (decrease) in cash and equivalents	$ 1,492	$ 333	$ 675

1. **CONCEPT ▶** How do relevance and classification apply to the statement of cash flows?

2. **ACCOUNTING APPLICATION ▶** How is the statement of cash flows prepared using the indirect method?

3. **BUSINESS APPLICATION ▶** Are Amazon.com's operations generating sufficient operating cash flows?

SECTION 1 CONCEPTS

CONCEPTS
- Relevance
- Classification
- Disclosure

RELEVANT LEARNING OBJECTIVE

LO1 Describe the principal purposes and concepts underlying the statement of cash flows, and identify its components and format.

LO1 Concepts Underlying the Statement of Cash Flows

CASH FLOW

Cash flows enable a company to pay expenses, debts, employees' wages, and taxes and to invest in the assets it needs for its operations. Without sufficient cash flows, a company cannot grow and prosper. Because of the importance of cash flows, one must be alert to the possibility that items may be incorrectly *classified* in a statement of cash flows and that the statement may not fully *disclose* all pertinent information. This chapter identifies the classifications used in a statement of cash flows and explains how to analyze the statement.

The **statement of cash flows** shows how a company's operating, investing, and financing activities have affected cash during a period. It explains the net increase (or decrease) in cash during the period. For purposes of this statement, **cash** is defined as including both cash and cash equivalents. **Cash equivalents** are investments that can be quickly converted to cash. They have a maturity of 90 days or less when they are purchased, and they include the following:

- Money market accounts
- Commercial paper (short-term corporate notes)
- U.S. Treasury bills

A company invests in cash equivalents to earn interest on cash that would otherwise be temporarily idle. Suppose, for example, that a company has $1,000,000 that it will not need for 30 days. To earn a return on this amount, the company could place the cash in an account that earns interest (such as a money market account), lend the cash to another corporation by purchasing that corporation's short-term notes (commercial paper), or purchase a short-term obligation of the U.S. government (a Treasury bill).

Cash equivalents should not be confused with short-term investments, also called **marketable securities**. Marketable securities have a maturity of more than 90 days but are intended to be held only until cash is needed for current operations. Purchases of marketable securities are treated as cash outflows, and sales of marketable securities are treated as cash inflows. Conversely, transfers between the Cash account and cash equivalents are not treated as cash inflows or cash outflows.

Relevance of the Statement of Cash Flows

The statement of cash flows provides information about a company's cash receipts and cash payments during a period, as well as about a company's operating, investing, and financing activities. Some information about those activities may be inferred from other financial statements, but the statement of cash flows summarizes *all* transactions that affect cash.

International Perspective

IFRS **How Universal Is the Statement of Cash Flows?**

Despite the importance of the statement of cash flows in assessing the liquidity of companies in the United States, there has been considerable variation in its use and format in other countries. For example, in many countries, the statement shows the change in working capital rather than the change in cash and cash equivalents. Although the European Union's principal directives for financial reporting do not address the statement of cash flows, international accounting standards require it, and international financial markets expect it to be presented. As a result, most multinational companies include the statement in their financial reports. Most European countries adopted the statement of cash flows when the European Union adopted international accounting standards.

The information provided by the statement of cash flows is relevant to management in operating the business, as well as to investors and creditors in making investment and lending decisions. Management uses the statement of cash flows to:

- assess liquidity (e.g., to determine whether short-term financing is needed to pay current liabilities).
- determine dividend policy.
- evaluate the effects of major policy decisions involving investments and financing needs.

Investors and creditors use the statement of cash flows to assess a company's ability to:

- manage cash flows.
- generate positive future cash flows.
- pay its liabilities.
- pay dividends and interest.
- anticipate the need for additional financing.

Classification of Cash Flows

Amazon.com is the largest online retailer in the world and one of the 500 largest companies in the United States. Exhibit 1 shows the company's consolidated statements of cash flows for 2011, 2010, and 2009. As you can see, this statement has three major classifications: operating, investing, and financing activities.

The *classifications* of operating, investing, and financing activities are illustrated in Exhibit 2 and summarized next.

Operating Activities The first section of the statement of cash flows is cash flow from operating activities. **Operating activities** involve the cash inflows and outflows from activities that enter into the determination of net income. Cash inflows in this category include cash receipts from the sale of goods and services and from the sale of trading securities. **Trading securities** are a type of marketable security that a company buys and sells for making a profit in the near term as opposed to holding them indefinitely for investment purposes. Cash inflows from operating activities also include interest received on loans and dividends received on investments. Cash outflows from operating activities include cash payments for wages, inventory, expenses, interest, taxes, and the purchase of trading securities.

Investing Activities The second section of the statement of cash flows is cash flows from investing activities. **Investing activities** involve the acquisition and sale of property, plant, and equipment and other long-term assets, including long-term investments. They also involve the acquisition and sale of short-term marketable securities, other than trading securities, and the making and collecting of loans. Cash flows provided by investing activities include the cash received from selling marketable securities and long-term assets and from collecting on loans. Cash flows used by investing activities include the cash expended on purchasing these securities and assets and the cash lent to borrowers. Cash outflows for property, plant, and equipment, or capital expenditures, are usually shown separately from cash inflows from sales of these assets, as they are in **Amazon.com**'s statement in Exhibit 1. However, when the inflows are not material, some companies combine these two lines to show the net amount of outflow.

STUDY NOTE: *Operating activities involve the day-to-day sale of goods and services, investing activities involve long-term assets and investments, and financing activities deal with stockholders' equity accounts and debt (borrowing).*

Financing Activities The third section of the statement of cash flows is cash flows from financing activities. **Financing activities** involve obtaining resources from stockholders and creditors. Cash inflows include the proceeds from stock issues and from short- and long-term borrowing. Cash outflows include the repayments of loans (excluding interest) and payments to stockholders, including cash dividends. Treasury stock transactions are also considered financing activities. Repayments of accounts payable or accrued liabilities are not considered repayments of loans. They are classified as cash outflows under operating activities.

Cash Balances A reconciliation of the beginning and ending balances of cash appears at the bottom of the statement. These cash balances will tie into the cash balances on the balance sheet.

Exhibit 1
Consolidated Statement of Cash Flows

Amazon.com, Inc.
Consolidated Statements of Cash Flows

	For the Years Ended		
(In millions)	**2011**	**2010**	**2009**
Operating Activities:			
Net income	$ 631	$ 1,152	$ 902
Adjustments to reconcile net income to net cash from operating activities:			
Depreciation and amortization	1,083	568	378
Stock-based compensation	557	424	341
Other operating expense (income), net	154	106	103
Losses (gains) on sales of marketable securities, net	(4)	(2)	(4)
Other expense (income), net	(56)	(79)	(15)
Deferred income taxes	136	4	81
Excess tax benefits from stock-based compensation	(62)	(259)	(105)
Changes in operating assets and liabilities:			
Inventories	(1,777)	(1,019)	(531)
Accounts receivable, net and other	(866)	(295)	(481)
Accounts payable	2,997	2,373	1,859
Accrued expenses and other	1,067	740	300
Additions to unearned revenue	1,064	687	1,054
Amortization of previously unearned revenue	(1,021)	(905)	(589)
Net cash provided by operating activities	$ 3,903	$ 3,495	$ 3,293
Investing Activities:			
Purchases of fixed assets, including internal-use software and website development	(1,811)	(979)	(373)
Acquisitions, net of cash received and other	(705)	(352)	(40)
Sales and maturities of marketable securities and other investments	6,843	4,250	1,966
Purchases of marketable securities and other investments	(6,257)	(6,279)	(3,890)
Net cash provided by (used in) investing activities	$ (1,930)	$(3,360)	$(2,337)
Financing Activities:			
Excess tax benefits from exercises of stock options	62	259	105
Common stock repurchased (treasury stock)	(277)	—	—
Proceeds from long-term debt and other	177	143	87
Repayments of long-term debt and capital lease obligations	(444)	(221)	(472)
Net cash provided by (used in) financing activities	$ (482)	$ 181	$ (280)
Foreign-currency effect on cash and cash equivalents	1	17	(1)
Net (decrease) increase in cash and cash equivalents	$ 1,492	$ 333	$ 675
Cash and cash equivalents, beginning of year	3,777	3,444	2,769
Cash and cash equivalents, end of year	$ 5,269	$ 3,777	$ 3,444

Source: Amazon.com, Inc., *Annual Report*, 2011 (adapted).

Exhibit 2
Classification of Cash Inflows and Cash Outflows

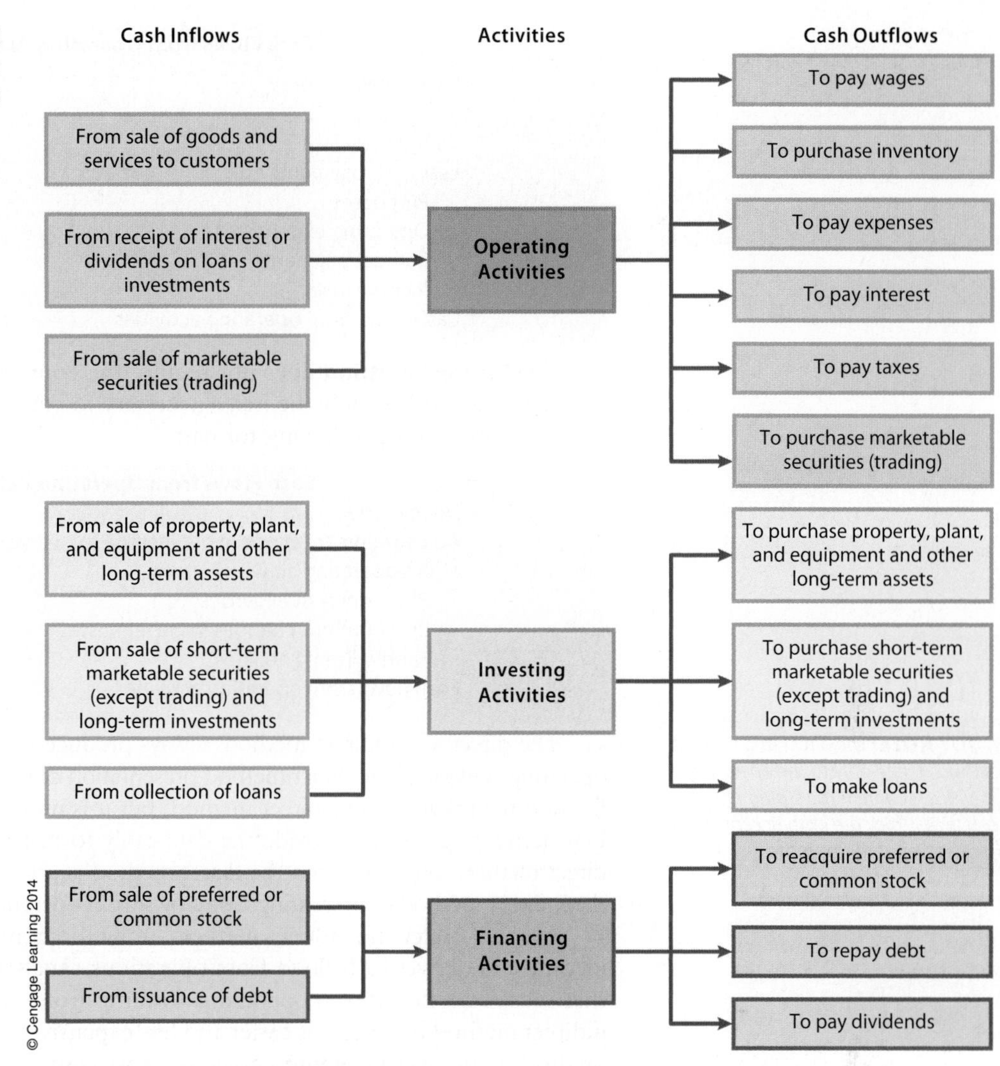

Required Disclosure of Noncash Investing and Financing Transactions

Companies occasionally engage in significant **noncash investing and financing transactions**. These transactions involve *only* long-term assets, long-term liabilities, or stockholders' equity. For instance, a company might exchange a long-term asset for a long-term liability, settle a debt by issuing capital stock, or take out a long-term mortgage to purchase real estate. Although noncash transactions represent significant investing and financing activities, they are not reflected in the body of the statement of cash flows because they do not affect current cash inflows or outflows. They will, however, affect future cash flows. For this reason, they must be *disclosed* in a separate schedule, usually following the statement of cash flows.

Alternate Presentations of Operating Activities

There are two ways of presenting operating activities on the statement of cash flows.

- The **direct method** converts each item on the income statement from the accrual basis to the cash basis. The operating activities section of the statement of cash flows under the direct method follows in simplified format.

Cash Flows from Operating Activities		
Cash receipts from:		
Sales	XXX	
Interest	XXX	XXX
Less cash payments for:		
Purchases	XXX	
Operating expenses	XXX	
Interest payments	XXX	
Income taxes	XXX	XXX
Cash flows from operating activities		XXX

- The **indirect method** does not require the conversion of each item on the income statement. It lists only the items necessary to convert net income to cash flows from operations in the following format:

Cash Flows from Operating Activities		
Net income		XXX
Adjustments to reconcile net income to net cash flows from operating activities:		
Plus non-cash expenses	XXX	
Plus or minus changes in current assets and current liabilities	XXX	
Cash flows from operating activities		XXX

STUDY NOTE: *The direct and indirect methods relate only to the operating activities section of the statement of cash flows. They are both acceptable for financial reporting purposes.*

The direct and indirect methods always produce the same amount of cash flows from operating activities. The direct method presentation of operating cash flows is more straightforward than that of the indirect method, but it is more difficult to implement in practice. Few accounting systems provide the data easily to make the calculations necessary for the direct method. Further, when the direct method is presented, preparation and *disclosure* of the indirect method of presenting cash flows from operating activities is also required.

Analysts prefer the indirect method to the direct method because it begins with net income and derives cash flows from operations. Analysts can readily identify the factors that cause cash flows from operations to differ from net income. Companies prefer the indirect method because it is easier and less expensive to prepare. As a result, the indirect method is the overwhelming choice of most companies and accountants. A survey of large companies shows that 98 percent use this method.[2]

International Perspective

IFRS The Direct Method May Become More Important Under IFRS

In the interest of converging U.S. GAAP with international financial reporting standards (IFRS), the IASB is promoting the use of the direct method, even though it is more costly for companies to prepare. IFRS will continue to require a reconciliation of net income and net cash flows from operating activities similar to what is now done in the indirect method. **CVS**'s statement of cash flows, as shown in the Supplement to Chapter 1, is one of the few U.S. companies to use the direct method with a reconciliation. Thus, its approach is very similar to what all companies may do if the U.S. adopts IFRS.

APPLY IT!

Mango Corporation engaged in the transactions that follow. Identify each transaction as (a) an operating activity, (b) an investing activity, (c) a financing activity, (d) a noncash transaction, or (e) not on the statement of cash flows.

1. Purchased office equipment, a long-term investment.
2. Decreased accounts receivable.
3. Sold land at cost.
4. Issued long-term bonds for plant assets.
5. Increased inventory.
6. Issued common stock.
7. Repurchased common stock.
8. Issued notes payable.
9. Increased income taxes payable.
10. Purchased a 60-day Treasury bill.
11. Purchased a long-term investment.
12. Declared and paid a cash dividend.

SOLUTION

1. b; 2. a; 3. b; 4. d; 5. a; 6. c; 7. c; 8. c; 9. a; 10. e (cash equivalent); 11. b; 12. c

TRY IT! SE1, SE6, E1A, E1B

SECTION 2 **ACCOUNTING APPLICATIONS**

ACCOUNTING APPLICATIONS

- Determining cash flows from operating activities using the indirect method
- Determining cash flows from investing activities
- Determining cash flows from financing activities

RELEVANT LEARNING OBJECTIVES

LO 2 Use the indirect method to determine cash flows from operating activities.

LO 3 Determine cash flows from investing activities.

LO 4 Determine cash flows from financing activities.

LO 2 CASH FLOW Step 1: Determining Cash Flows from Operating Activities

As shown in Exhibit 3, preparing a statement of cash flows involves four steps:

- **Step 1:** Determine cash flows from operating activities.
- **Step 2:** Determine cash flows from investing activities.
- **Step 3:** Determine cash flows from financing activities.
- **Step 4:** Prepare the statement of cash flows.

In this section, we begin with determining cash flows from operating activities.

Exhibit 3
Preparation of the Statement of Cash Flows

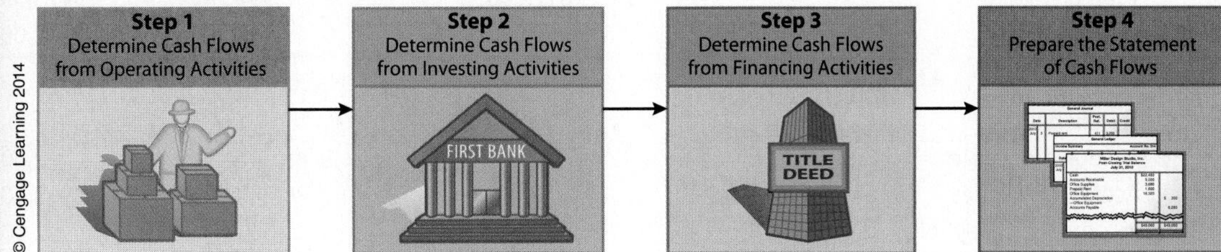

To demonstrate the preparation of the statement of cash flows, we will use data for Eureka Corporation. Eureka's income statement for 2014 is presented in Exhibit 4, and its balance sheets for December 31, 2014 and 2013 appear in Exhibit 5. Exhibit 5 also shows the balance sheet accounts that we use for analysis and whether the change in each account is an increase or a decrease.

Exhibit 4
Income Statement

Eureka Corporation
Income Statement
For the Year Ended December 31, 2014

Sales		$698,000
Cost of goods sold		520,000
Gross margin		$178,000
Operating expenses (including depreciation expense of $37,000)		147,000
Operating income		$ 31,000
Other income (expenses):		
Interest expense	$(23,000)	
Interest income	6,000	
Gain on sale of investments	12,000	
Loss on sale of plant assets	(3,000)	(8,000)
Income before income taxes		$ 23,000
Income taxes expense		7,000
Net income		$ 16,000

Exhibit 5
Comparative Balance Sheets Showing Changes in Accounts

Eureka Corporation
Comparative Balance Sheets
December 31, 2014 and 2013

	2014	**2013**	**Change**	**Increase or Decrease**
Assets				
Current assets:				
Cash	$ 47,000	$ 15,000	$ 32,000	Increase
Accounts receivable (net)	47,000	55,000	(8,000)	Decrease
Inventory	144,000	110,000	34,000	Increase
Prepaid expenses	1,000	5,000	(4,000)	Decrease
Total current assets	$ 239,000	$185,000	$ 54,000	
Investments	$ 115,000	$127,000	$ (12,000)	Decrease
Plant assets	$ 715,000	$505,000	$210,000	Increase
Less accumulated depreciation	(103,000)	(68,000)	(35,000)	Increase
Total plant assets	$ 612,000	$437,000	$175,000	
Total assets	$ 966,000	$749,000	$217,000	
Liabilities				
Current liabilities:				
Accounts payable	$ 50,000	$ 43,000	$ 7,000	Increase
Accrued liabilities	12,000	9,000	3,000	Increase
Income taxes payable	3,000	5,000	(2,000)	Decrease
Total current liabilities	$ 65,000	$ 57,000	$ 8,000	
Long-term liabilities:				
Bonds payable	295,000	245,000	50,000	Increase
Total liabilities	$ 360,000	$302,000	$ 58,000	
Stockholders' Equity				
Common stock, $5 par value	$ 276,000	$200,000	$ 76,000	Increase
Additional paid-in capital	214,000	115,000	99,000	Increase
Retained earnings	141,000	132,000	9,000	Increase
Treasury stock	(25,000)	0	(25,000)	Increase
Total stockholders' equity	$ 606,000	$447,000	$159,000	
Total liabilities and stockholders' equity	$ 966,000	$749,000	$217,000	

The income statement indicates how successful a company has been in earning an income from its operating activities. However, because that statement is prepared on an accrual basis, it does not reflect the inflow and outflow of cash related to operating activities. Revenues are recorded even though the company may not yet have received the cash, and expenses are recorded even though the company may not yet have expended the cash. Thus, to ascertain cash flows from operations in step 1 in preparing the statement of cash flows, the figures on the income statement must be converted from an accrual basis to a cash basis.

As Exhibit 6 shows, the indirect method focuses on adjusting items on the income statement to reconcile net income to net cash flows from operating activities. These items include the following:

- Depreciation, amortization, and depletion
- Gains and losses
- Changes in the balances of current asset and current liability accounts.

Exhibit 6
Indirect Method of Determining Net Cash Flows from Operating Activities

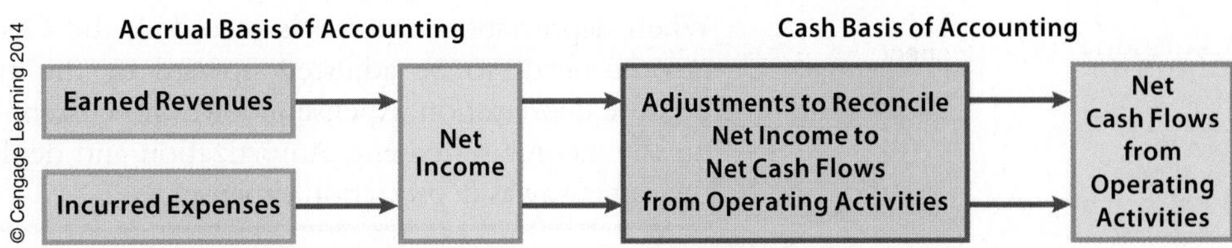

These adjusting items can be seen in the schedule in Exhibit 7, which shows the reconciliation of Eureka's net income to net cash flows from operating activities. Each adjusting item requires a different type of analysis as illustrated in the sections that follow.

Exhibit 7
Schedule of Cash Flows from Operating Activities: Indirect Method

Eureka Corporation
Schedule of Cash Flows from Operating Activities
For the Year Ended December 31, 2014

Cash flows from operating activities:		
Net income		$16,000
Adjustments to reconcile net income to net cash flows from operating activities:		
Depreciation	$ 37,000	
Gain on sale of investments	(12,000)	
Loss on sale of plant assets	3,000	
Changes in current assets and current liabilities:		
Decrease in accounts receivable	8,000	
Increase in inventory	(34,000)	
Decrease in prepaid expenses	4,000	
Increase in accounts payable	7,000	
Increase in accrued liabilities	3,000	
Decrease in income taxes payable	(2,000)	14,000
Net cash flows from operating activities		$30,000

Depreciation, Amortization, and Depletion

STUDY NOTE: *Operating expenses on the income statement include depreciation expense, which does not require a cash outlay.*

Although the cash payments made for plant assets, intangible assets, and natural resources appear in the investing activities section of the statement of cash flows, the depreciation expense, amortization expense, and depletion expense associated with these assets appear in the operating activities section. The amount of these expenses can usually be found in the income statement or in a note to the financial statements.

Depreciation

Financial Statement Information Eureka's income statement (Exhibit 4) shows $37,000 of depreciation expense.

Journal Entry

A	=	L	+	SE
−37,000				−37,000

	Dr.	Cr.
Depreciation Expense	37,000	
Accumulated Depreciation		37,000
To record annual depreciation on plant assets		

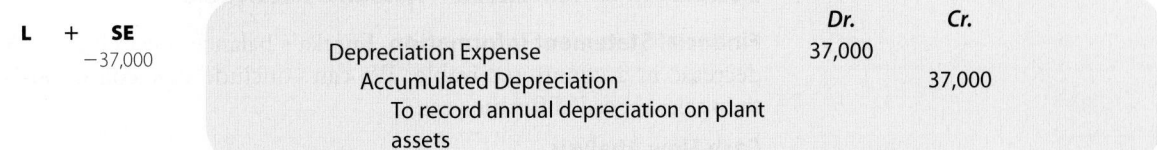

Cash Flow Analysis

Depreciation	$37,000

When depreciation expense is recorded, the Cash account is not affected. Thus, net income needs to be adjusted upward by the amount of depreciation, or $37,000, because depreciation expense involves no current outlay of cash even though it appears on the income statement. Amortization and depletion expenses are handled in exactly the same way as depreciation expense.

Gains and Losses

STUDY NOTE: Gains and losses by themselves do not represent cash flows; they are merely bookkeeping adjustments. For example, when a long-term asset is sold, the proceeds (cash received), not the gain or loss, constitute cash flow.

Like depreciation expense, gains and losses that appear on the income statement do not affect cash flows from operating activities and need to be subtracted from or added to net income. The actual cash flows from these transactions are reflected in the investing and financing activities sections of the statement of cash flows.

Gain—Sale of Investments

Financial Statement Information Eureka's income statement (Exhibit 4) shows a $12,000 gain on the sale of investments.

Cash Flow Analysis

Gain on sale of investments	($12,000)

This amount is subtracted from net income to reconcile net income to net cash flows from operating activities. The reason for doing this is that the $12,000 is included in the investing activities section of the statement of cash flows as part of the cash from the sale of the investment. Because the gain has already been included in the calculation of net income, the $12,000 gain must be subtracted to prevent double counting.

Loss—Sale of Plant Assets

Financial Statement Information Eureka's income statement shows a $3,000 loss on the sale of plant assets.

Cash Flow Analysis

Loss on sale of plant assets	$3,000

As was the case with depreciation expense, a loss on the sale of assets is added to net income to reconcile net income to net cash flows from operating activities. The cash received associated with the transaction that resulted in this loss is reflected in the investing activities section of the statement of cash flows.

Changes in Current Assets

As explained in this section and the next, changes in current assets and current liabilities require a different approach to reconcile net income to cash flows from operating activities.

Decreases in current assets other than cash have positive effects on cash flows, and increases in current assets have negative effects on cash flows:

- ▼ A *decrease* in a current asset frees up invested cash, thereby increasing cash flow.
- ▲ An *increase* in a current asset consumes cash, thereby decreasing cash flow.

Decrease in Current Assets—Accounts Receivable

Financial Statement Information Eureka's balance sheet (Exhibit 5) shows an $8,000 decrease in accounts receivable. We can conclude that collections were $8,000 more than sales recorded for the year.

Cash Flow Analysis

Decrease in account receivable	$8,000

Because net sales in 2014 were $698,000, the total cash received from sales can be calculated as follows.

Net Sales + Additional Cash Collections = Total Cash Collections Received
$698,000 + $8,000 = $706,000

The effect on Accounts Receivable can be illustrated as follows.

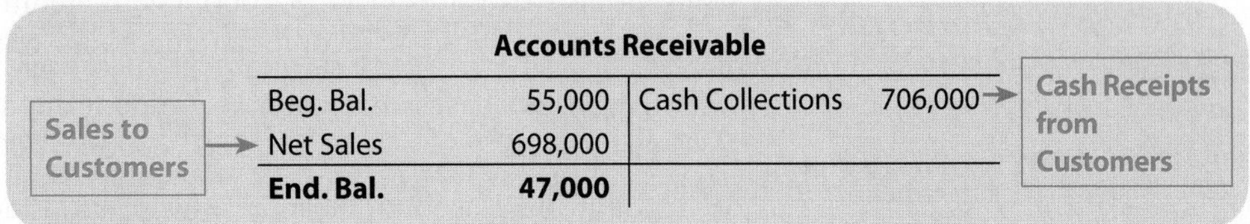

Accounts Receivable
Sales to Customers
Beg. Bal. 55,000
Net Sales 698,000
End. Bal. 47,000
Cash Collections 706,000
Cash Receipts from Customers

To reconcile net income to net cash flows from operating activities, the $8,000 decrease in accounts receivable is added to net income.

Increase in Current Assets—Inventory

Financial Statement Information Eureka's balance sheet (Exhibit 5) shows a $34,000 increase in inventory.

Cash Flow Analysis

Increase in inventory	($34,000)

Because the cost of goods sold in 2014 was $520,000, the total cash paid for inventory can be calculated as follows, as was done with accounts receivable.

Cost of Goods Sold + Additional Purchases = Total Purchases
$520,000 + $34,000 = $554,000

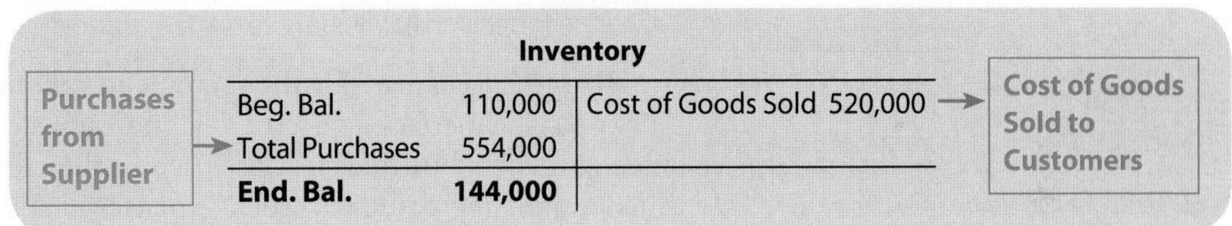

Inventory
Purchases from Supplier
Beg. Bal. 110,000
Total Purchases 554,000
End. Bal. 144,000
Cost of Goods Sold 520,000
Cost of Goods Sold to Customers

Thus, Eureka expended $34,000 more in cash for purchases than it included in the cost of goods sold on its income statement. Because of this expenditure, net income is higher than net cash flows from operating activities, so $34,000 must be deducted from net income.

Decrease in Current Assets—Prepaid Expenses

Financial Statement Information Continuing with current assets, Eureka's balance sheet (Exhibit 5) shows a $4,000 decrease in prepaid expenses.

Cash Flow Analysis

Decrease in prepaid expenses	$4,000

Using the same logic, the decrease shown on the balance sheet is added to net income because Eureka expended less cash on prepaid expenses than was included on the income statement.

Changes in Current Liabilities

The effect that changes in current liabilities have on cash flows is the opposite of the effect of changes in current assets:

- ▲ An *increase* in a current liability represents a postponement of a cash payment, which frees up cash and increases cash flow in the current period; thus, it is added to net income.
- ▼ A *decrease* in a current liability consumes cash, which decreases cash flow; thus, it is deducted from net income.

Increase in Current Liabilities—Accounts Payable

Financial Statement Information Eureka's balance sheet (Exhibit 5) shows a $7,000 increase in accounts payable.

Cash Flow Analysis

Increase in accounts payable	$7,000

This means that Eureka paid $7,000 less to creditors than the amount indicated in the cost of goods sold on its income statement, illustrated as follows.

Purchases on Account* – Amount Unpaid = Total Cash Payments
$554,000 – $7,000 = $547,000

The following T account illustrates this relationship:

	Accounts Payable				
Cash Payments to Suppliers →	Payments on Account 547,000	Beg. Bal.	43,000	
		Purchases on Account	554,000*	← Purchases
		End. Bal.	**50,000**	

*Purchases = Cost of Goods Sold ($520,000) + Increase in Inventory ($34,000)

Thus, $7,000 must be added to net income to reconcile net income to net cash flows from operating activities.

Increase in Current Liabilities—Accrued Liabilities

Financial Statement Information Eureka's balance sheet (Exhibit 5) shows a $3,000 increase in accrued liabilities.

Cash Flow Analysis

Increase in accrued liabilities	$3,000

Using the same logic as with the increase in accounts payable, this amount is added to net income. The increase in accrued liabilities was created by an adjusting entry that also increases expenses but does not use cash in the current period. Since expenses decrease net income, the increase in accrued expenses needs to be added to net income.

Decrease in Current Liabilities—Income Taxes Payable

Financial Statement Information Eureka's balance sheet (Exhibit 5) shows a $2,000 decrease in income taxes payable.

Cash Flow Analysis

Decrease in income taxes payable	($2,000)

This amount is deducted from net income because the decrease in income taxes payable means the company paid this year's taxes plus an amount from the prior year, as follows.

Income Taxes Expense + Additional Payment = Total Income Taxes Payments
$7,000 + $2,000 = $9,000

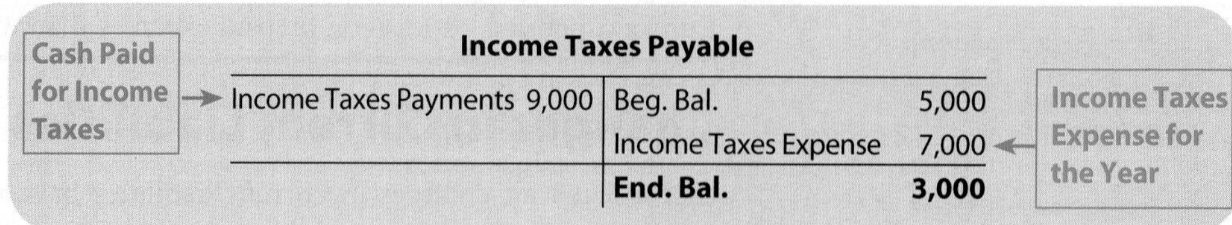

	Income Taxes Payable				
Cash Paid for Income Taxes →	Income Taxes Payments 9,000	Beg. Bal.	5,000	
		Income Taxes Expense	7,000	← Income Taxes Expense for the Year
		End. Bal.	**3,000**	

Schedule of Cash Flows from Operating Activities

In summary, Exhibit 7 shows that by using the indirect method, net income of $16,000 has been adjusted by reconciling items totaling $14,000 to arrive at net cash flows from operating activities of $30,000:

Net Income +/– Reconciling Items = Cash Flows from Operating Activities
$16,000 + $14,000 = $30,000

Although Eureka's net income was $16,000, the company actually had net cash flows of $30,000 from operating activities to use for purchasing assets, reducing debts, and paying dividends. The rules for reconciling items from the income statement that do not affect cash flows can be summarized as follows.

	Add to or Deduct from Net Income
Depreciation expense	+ Add
Amortization expense	+ Add
Depletion expense	+ Add
Losses	+ Add
Gains	– Deduct

The following summarizes the adjustments from the balance sheet for increases and decreases in current assets and current liabilities:

	Add to Net Income +	*Deduct from Net Income* –
Current assets:		
Accounts receivable (net)	▼ Decrease	▲ Increase
Inventory	▼ Decrease	▲ Increase
Prepaid expenses	▼ Decrease	▲ Increase
Current liabilities:		
Accounts payable	▲ Increase	▼ Decrease
Accrued liabilities	▲ Increase	▼ Decrease
Income taxes payable	▲ Increase	▼ Decrease

Business Perspective

What Is EBITDA, and Is It Any Good?

Some companies and analysts like to use EBITDA (an acronym for Earnings Before Interest, Taxes, Depreciation, and Amortization) as a shortcut measure of cash flows from operations. But experiences of the past decade have caused many analysts to reconsider this measure of performance. For instance, when **WorldCom** transferred $3.8 billion from expenses to capital expenditures in one year, it touted its EBITDA. At the time, the firm was, in fact, nearly bankrupt. The demise of **Vivendi**, the big French company that imploded when it did not have enough cash to pay its debts and that also touted its EBITDA, is another reason that analysts have had second thoughts about relying on this measure of performance.

Some analysts are now saying that EBITDA is "to a great extent misleading" and that it "is a confusing metric. . . . Some take it for a proxy for profits and some take it for a proxy for cash flow, and it's neither."[3] Cash flows from operations and free cash flow, both of which take into account interest, taxes, and depreciation, are better and more comprehensive measures of a company's ability to generate sufficient cash flows.

APPLY IT!

For the year ended June 30, 2015, RAK Corporation's net income was $7,400. Its depreciation expense was $2,000. During the year, its accounts receivable increased by $4,400, inventories increased by $7,000, prepaid rent decreased by $1,400, accounts payable increased by $14,000, salaries payable increased by $1,000, and income taxes payable decreased by $600. The company also had an $1,800 gain on the sale of investments. Use the indirect method to prepare a schedule of cash flows from operating activities.

SOLUTION

RAK Corporation
Schedule of Cash Flows from Operating Activities
For the Year Ended June 30, 2015

Cash flows from operating activities:		
Net income		$ 7,400
Adjustments to reconcile net income to net cash flows from operating activities:		
Depreciation	$ 2,000	
Gain on sale of investments	(1,800)	
Changes in current assets and current liabilities:		
Increase in accounts receivable	(4,400)	
Increase in inventories	(7,000)	
Decrease in prepaid rent	1,400	
Increase in accounts payable	14,000	
Increase in salaries payable	1,000	
Decrease in income taxes payable	(600)	4,600
Net cash flows from operating activities		$12,000

TRY IT! SE2, SE3, SE6, E2A, E3A, E4A, E8A, E2B, E3B, E4B, E8B

LO3 Step 2: Determining Cash Flows from Investing Activities

CASH FLOW

STUDY NOTE: *Investing activities involve long-term assets and short- and long-term investments. Inflows and outflows of cash are shown in the investing activities section of the statement of cash flows.*

Determining cash flows from investing activities is step 2 in preparing the statement of cash flows. In this step, accounts involving cash receipts and cash payments from investing activities are examined individually. The objective is to explain the change in each account balance from one period to the next.

Although investing activities relate mainly to the long-term assets shown on the balance sheet, they also include any short-term investments shown under current assets on the balance sheet and any investment gains and losses on the income statement. The balance sheets in Exhibit 5 show that Eureka had no short-term investments and that its long-term assets consisted of investments and plant assets. The income statement in Exhibit 4 shows that Eureka had a gain on the sale of investments and a loss on the sale of plant assets.

The following transactions pertain to Eureka's investing activities in 2014:

1. Purchased investments in the amount of $78,000.
2. Sold for $102,000 investments that cost $90,000.
3. Purchased plant assets in the amount of $120,000.
4. Sold for $5,000 plant assets that cost $10,000 and that had accumulated depreciation of $2,000.
5. Issued $100,000 of bonds at face value in a noncash exchange for plant assets.

In the sections that follow, we explain the effects of these transactions on Eureka's cash flows by analyzing their impact on the accounts related to investing activities.

Investments

Financial Statement Information Eureka's balance sheet (Exhibit 5) shows a $12,000 decrease in investments. To explain this decrease and its effects on the statement of cash flows, we will analyze the increases and decreases in Eureka's Investments account.

Purchase of Investments

Transaction 1 Purchased investments in the amount of $78,000.

Journal Entry

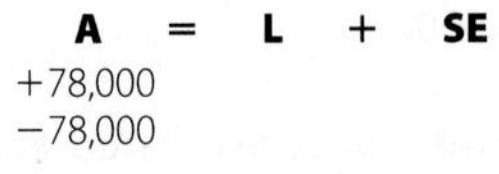

	Dr.	Cr.
Investments	78,000	
Cash		78,000
Purchase of investments		

Cash Flow Analysis

Purchase of investments	($78,000)

Sale of Investments

Transaction 2 Sold for $102,000 investments that cost $90,000.

Journal Entry

A	=	L	+	SE
+102,000				+12,000
−90,000				

	Dr.	Cr.
Cash	102,000	
Investments		90,000
Gain on Sale of Investments		12,000
Sale of Investments for a gain		

Cash Flow Analysis

Sale of investments	$102,000

STUDY NOTE: The $102,000 price obtained, not the $12,000 gained, constitutes the cash flow.

Note that the gain on the sale is included in the $102,000. This is the reason we excluded it in computing cash flows from operations. If it had not been excluded in that section, it would have been counted twice.

Reconciliation We have now explained the $12,000 decrease in the Investments account during 2014, as illustrated in the following T account:

Investments

Dr.		Cr.	
Beg. Bal.	127,000	Sales	90,000
Purchases	78,000		
End. Bal.	**115,000**		

Purchases and sales are listed separately as cash outflows and inflows to give analysts a complete view of investing activities. However, some companies prefer to list them as a single net amount. If Eureka Corporation had short-term investments or marketable securities, the analysis of cash flows would be the same.

Plant Assets

Financial Statement Information Eureka's balance sheet shows the following:

- $210,000 increase in plant assets
- $35,000 increase in accumulated depreciation

Purchase of Plant Assets

Transaction 3 Purchased plant assets in the amount of $120,000.

Journal Entry

A	=	L	+	SE
+120,000				
−120,000				

	Dr.	Cr.
Plant Assets	120,000	
Cash		120,000

Cash Flow Analysis

Purchase of plant assets	($120,000)

Comment Cash outflows and cash inflows related to plant assets are listed separately, but companies sometimes combine them into a single net amount, called *capital expenditures*, when the cash inflows from sales are immaterial.

Sale of Plant Assets

Transaction 4 Sold for $5,000 plant assets that cost $10,000 and that had accumulated depreciation of $2,000.

Journal Entry

A	=	L	+	SE
+5,000				+3,000
+2,000				
−10,000				

	Dr.	Cr.
Cash	5,000	
Accumulated Depreciation	2,000	
Loss on Sale of Plant Assets	3,000	
Plant Assets		10,000
Sale of plant assets at a loss		

Cash Flow Analysis

Sale of plant assets	$5,000

STUDY NOTE: The amount of a loss or gain on the sale of an asset is determined by the amount of cash received and does not represent a cash outflow or inflow.

Note that this transaction results in a positive cash flow of $5,000, even though the plant assets were sold at a loss of $3,000. As noted in our analysis of operating activities, the loss on the sale of plant assets is added back to net income. This action avoids counting the loss in two sections of the statement of cash flows.

Issued Bonds in Exchange for Plant Assets

Transaction 5 Issued $100,000 of bonds at face value in a noncash exchange for plant assets.

Journal Entry

A	=	L	+	SE
+100,000		+100,000		

	Dr.	Cr.
Plant Assets	100,000	
Bonds Payable		100,000
Issued bonds at face value for plant assets		

Cash Flow Analysis

Schedule of Noncash Investing and Financing Transactions	
Issue of bonds payable for plant assets	$100,000

Although this transaction does not involve an inflow or outflow of cash, it is a significant transaction involving both an investing activity (the purchase of plant assets) and a financing activity (the issue of bonds payable). Because one purpose of the statement of cash flows is to show important investing and financing activities, the transaction is *disclosed* at the bottom of the statement of cash flows or in a separate schedule.

Reconciliation We have now explained all the changes related to Eureka's Plant Assets account. The following T accounts summarize these changes:

Plant Assets

Dr.		Cr.	
Beg. Bal.	505,000	Sales	10,000
Cash Purchase	120,000		
Noncash Purchase	100,000		
End. Bal.	**715,000**		

Accumulated Depreciation

Dr.		Cr.	
Sale	2,000	Beg. Bal.	68,000
		Depreciation Expense	37,000
		End. Bal.	**103,000**

Had the balance sheet included specific plant asset accounts (e.g., Equipment and the related accumulated depreciation account) or other long-term asset accounts (e.g., Intangibles), the analysis would have been the same.

APPLY IT!

The following T accounts show Andre Company's plant assets and accumulated depreciation at the end of 2015:

Plant Assets

Dr.		Cr.	
Beg. Bal.	65,000	Disposals	23,000
Purchases	33,600		
End. Bal.	**75,600**		

Accumulated Depreciation

Dr.		Cr.	
Disposals	14,700	Beg. Bal.	34,500
		Depreciation	10,200
		End. Bal.	**30,000**

Andre's income statement shows a $4,400 gain on the sale of plant assets. Compute the amounts that should be shown as cash flows from investing activities and show how they should appear on Andre's 2015 statement of cash flows.

SOLUTION

Cash flows from investing activities:

Purchase of plant assets	$(33,600)
Sale of plant assets	12,700

The T accounts show total purchases of plant assets of $33,600, which is an outflow of cash, and the disposal of plant assets that cost $23,000 and that had accumulated depreciation of $14,700. The cash inflow from the disposal was as follows.

Plant assets	$23,000
Less accumulated depreciation	14,700
Book value	$ 8,300
Add gain on sale	4,400
Cash inflow from sale of plant assets	$12,700

Because the gain on the sale is included in the $12,700 in the investing activities section of the statement of cash flows, it should be deducted from net income in the operating activities section.

TRY IT! SE4, SE6, E5A, E6A, E8A, E5B, E6B, E8B

LO4 CASH FLOW Step 3: Determining Cash Flows from Financing Activities

Determining cash flows from financing activities is step 3 in preparing the statement of cash flows. It is very similar to determining cash flows from investing activities, but the accounts analyzed relate to short-term borrowings, long-term liabilities, and stockholders' equity. Because Eureka Corporation does not have short-term borrowings, we deal only with long-term liabilities and stockholders' equity accounts.

The following transactions pertain to Eureka's financing activities in 2014:

1. Issued $100,000 of bonds at face value in a noncash exchange for plant assets.
2. Repaid $50,000 of bonds at face value at maturity.
3. Issued 15,200 shares of $5 par value common stock for $175,000.
4. Paid cash dividends in the amount of $7,000.
5. Purchased treasury stock for $25,000.

Bonds Payable

Financial Statement Information Eureka's balance sheet (Exhibit 5) shows a $50,000 increase in Bonds Payable.

Issued Bonds

Transaction 1 Issued $100,000 of bonds at face value in a noncash exchange for plant assets. We have already analyzed Transaction 1 in connection with plant assets, but we also need to account for the change in the Bonds Payable account. As noted, this transaction is reported on the schedule of noncash investing and financing transactions.

Redeemed Bonds

Transaction 2 Repaid $50,000 of bonds at face value at maturity.

Journal Entry

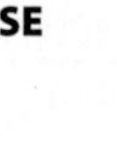

A	=	L	+	SE
−50,000		−50,000		

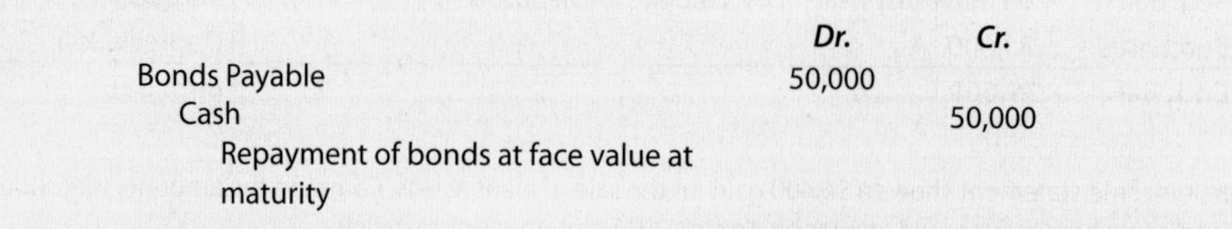

	Dr.	Cr.
Bonds Payable	50,000	
Cash		50,000
Repayment of bonds at face value at maturity		

Cash Flow Analysis

Repayment of bonds	($50,000)

Reconciliation The following T account explains the change in Bonds Payable:

Bonds Payable			
Dr.		**Cr.**	
Repayment	50,000	Beg. Bal.	245,000
		Noncash Issue	100,000
		End. Bal.	**295,000**

If Eureka Corporation had any notes payable, the analysis would be the same.

Common Stock

Increase in Common Stock and Additional Paid-in Capital

Financial Statement Information Eureka's balance sheet (Exhibit 5) shows a $76,000 increase in common stock and a $99,000 increase in additional paid-in capital.

Transaction 3 Issued 15,200 shares of $5 par value common stock for $175,000.

Journal Entry

A	=	L	+	SE
+175,000				+76,000
				+99,000

	Dr.	Cr.
Cash	175,000	
Common Stock		76,000
Additional Paid-in Capital		99,000
Issued 15,200 shares of $5 par value common stock		

Cash Flow Analysis

Issuance of common stock	$175,000

Reconciliation The following analysis of this transaction is all that is needed to explain the changes in the two accounts during 2014:

Common Stock Dr.	Common Stock Cr.		Additional Paid-in Capital Dr.	Additional Paid-in Capital Cr.	
	Beg. Bal.	200,000		Beg. Bal.	115,000
	Issue	76,000		Issue	99,000
	End. Bal.	**276,000**		**End. Bal.**	**214,000**

STUDY NOTE: *Dividends paid, not dividends declared, appear on the statement of cash flows.*

Retained Earnings

Increase in Retained Earnings

Financial Statement Information Eureka's balance sheet (Exhibit 5) shows a $9,000 increase in retained earnings.

Transaction 4 Paid cash dividends in the amount of $7,000.

Journal Entry

A	=	L	+	SE
				−7,000
				+7,000

	Dr.	Cr.
Retained Earnings	7,000	
Cash Dividends		7,000
To close the Cash Dividends account		

Cash Flow Analysis

Payment of dividends	($7,000)

Reconciliation Recall that dividends will reduce Retained Earnings and that net income appears in the operating activities section of the statement of cash flows. Thus, we have now explained all the changes related to Eureka's Retained Earnings account. This T account shows the change in the Retained Earnings account:

Retained Earnings Dr.		Retained Earnings Cr.	
Cash Dividends	7,000	Beg. Bal.	132,000
		Net Income	16,000
		End. Bal.	**141,000**

High-tech companies with large amounts of intangible assets can lose up to 80 percent of their value in times of financial stress. As a hedge against economic downturns, these companies need to build cash reserves and may therefore choose to hoard cash rather than pay dividends.

Patryk Kosmider/Shutterstock.com

Treasury Stock

Increase in Treasury Stock

Financial Statement Information Eureka's balance sheet (Exhibit 5) shows a $25,000 increase in treasury stock.

Transaction 5 Purchased treasury stock for $25,000.

Journal Entry

A	=	L	+	SE
−25,000				−25,000

	Dr.	Cr.
Treasury Stock	25,000	
Cash		25,000
Purchased treasury stock		

STUDY NOTE: *The purchase of treasury stock qualifies as a financing activity, but it is also a cash outflow.*

Cash Flow Analysis

Purchase of treasury stock	($25,000)

Reconciliation The following T account explains the change in Treasury Stock:

Treasury Stock

Dr.		Cr.	
Purchase	25,000		

Step 4: Preparing the Statement of Cash Flows

We have now analyzed all of Eureka Corporation's income statement items, explained all balance sheet changes, and taken all additional information into account. Exhibit 8 shows how these data are assembled in Eureka's statement of cash flows.

Exhibit 8
Statement of Cash Flows: Indirect Method

Eureka Corporation
Statement of Cash Flows
For the Year Ended December 31, 2014

Cash flows from operating activities:		
Net income		$ 16,000
Adjustments to reconcile net income to net cash flows from operating activities:		
Depreciation	$ 37,000	
Gain on sale of investments	(12,000)	
Loss on sale of plant assets	3,000	
Changes in current assets and current liabilities:		
Decrease in accounts receivable	8,000	
Increase in inventory	(34,000)	
Decrease in prepaid expenses	4,000	
Increase in accounts payable	7,000	
Increase in accrued liabilities	3,000	
Decrease in income taxes payable	(2,000)	14,000
Net cash flows from operating activities		$ 30,000
Cash flows from investing activities:		
Purchase of investments	$ (78,000)	
Sale of investments	102,000	
Purchase of plant assets	(120,000)	
Sale of plant assets	5,000	
Net cash flows from investing activities		(91,000)
Cash flows from financing activities:		
Repayment of bonds	$ (50,000)	
Issuance of common stock	175,000	
Payment of dividends	(7,000)	
Purchase of treasury stock	(25,000)	
Net cash flows from financing activities		93,000
Net increase in cash		$ 32,000
Cash at beginning of year		15,000
Cash at end of year		$ 47,000
Schedule of Noncash Investing and Financing Transactions		
Issue of bonds payable for plant assets		$100,000

Cash Flows and the Financial Statements

As shown in Exhibit 9, the statement of cash flows explains the changes in cash on the balance sheet and reconciles the change in Cash (reported on the Balance Sheet) from one period to the next.

Exhibit 9
Relationship of the Statement of Cash Flows to the Balance Sheet

Balance Sheet
December 31, 2014

Assets	**Liabilities**
Current assets	Current liabilities
Cash	Long-term liabilities
Other current assets	Total liabilities
Total current assets	**Stockholders' Equity**
Investments	Contributed capital
Property, plant, and equipment	Retained earnings
Intangible assets	Total stockholders' equity

Total Assets = Total Liabilities + Stockholders' Equity

Statement of Cash Flows
For the Year Ended December 31, 2014

Net cash flows from (used by) operating activities
Net cash flows from (used by) investing activities
Net cash flows from (used by) financing activities
Increase (decrease) in cash
Cash, 12/31/13
Cash, 12/31/14

APPLY IT!

During 2015, Brown Company issued $1,000,000 in long-term bonds at par, repaid $200,000 of notes payable at face value, issued notes payable of $40,000 for equipment, paid interest of $40,000, paid dividends of $25,000, and repurchased common stock in the amount of $50,000. Prepare the cash flows from financing activities section of the statement of cash flows.

SOLUTION

Cash flows from financing activities:	
Issuance of long-term bonds	$1,000,000
Repayment of notes payable	(200,000)
Payment of dividends	(25,000)
Purchase of treasury stock	(50,000)
Net cash flows from financing activities	$ 725,000

Note: Interest is an operating activity. The exchange of the notes payable for equipment is a noncash investing and financing transaction.

TRY IT! SE5, SE6, E7A, E8A, E7B, E8B

SECTION 3 BUSINESS APPLICATIONS

BUSINESS APPLICATIONS

- Evaluate a company's cash-generating efficiency
  - Cash flow yield
  - Cash flows to sales
  - Cash flows to assets
  - Free cash flow
- Ethics

RELEVANT LEARNING OBJECTIVE

LO5 Analyze the statement of cash flows.

LO5 Analyzing Cash Flows

An analysis of the statement of cash flows can reveal significant relationships. One area on which analysts focus is the cash inflows and outflows from operating activities, the first section on the statement of cash flows. Analysts use the information in this section to compute cash flow yield, cash flows to sales, cash flows to assets, and free cash flow.

Cash Flow Ratios

Cash flows from operating activities represent the cash generated from current or continuing operations. They are a measure of the ability to pay bills on time and to meet unexpected needs for cash, as well as how management spends the company's cash.

While the level of cash at the bottom of the statement of cash flows is certainly an important consideration, such information can be obtained from the balance sheet. The focal point of cash flow analysis is on cash inflows and outflows from operating activities. These cash flows are used in ratios that measure **cash-generating efficiency**, which is a company's ability to generate cash from its current or continuing operations. The ratios that analysts use to compute cash-generating efficiency are cash flow yield, cash flows to sales, and cash flows to assets.

In this section, we compute these ratios for **Amazon.com** in 2011 using data for net income and net cash flows from Exhibit 1 and the following information from Amazon.com's 2011 annual report (all dollar amounts are in millions):

	2011	2010
Net sales	$48,077	$34,204
Total assets	25,278	18,797

Cash Flow Yield **Cash flow yield** is the ratio of net cash flows from operating activities to net income. For **Amazon.com**, it is calculated as follows.

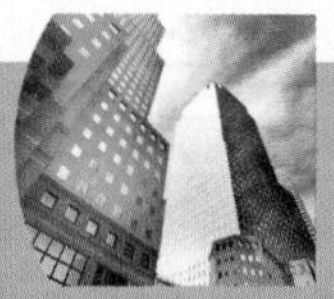

© Alija / iStockphoto.com

Business Perspective

Can a Company Have Too Much Cash?

Having a surplus of cash on hand can be a benefit or a risk. Many companies put their excess cash to good use by investing in productive assets, conducting research and development, paying off debt, buying back stock, or paying dividends. Of course, companies must also keep enough cash on hand for emergencies; but when companies like **ExxonMobil**, **Microsoft**, and **Cisco Systems** accumulated large amounts of cash before the market crash in 2008, some commentators argued that this was poor management. They pointed out that shareholders suffer when executives are too conservative and keep the money in low-paying money market accounts or make unwise acquisitions.[4] However, these companies and others, like **Ford** and **Google**, that had cash reserves not only survived the down years, but also were prospering by 2010.[5] For financial statement users, it is important to look closely at the components of the statement of cash flows.

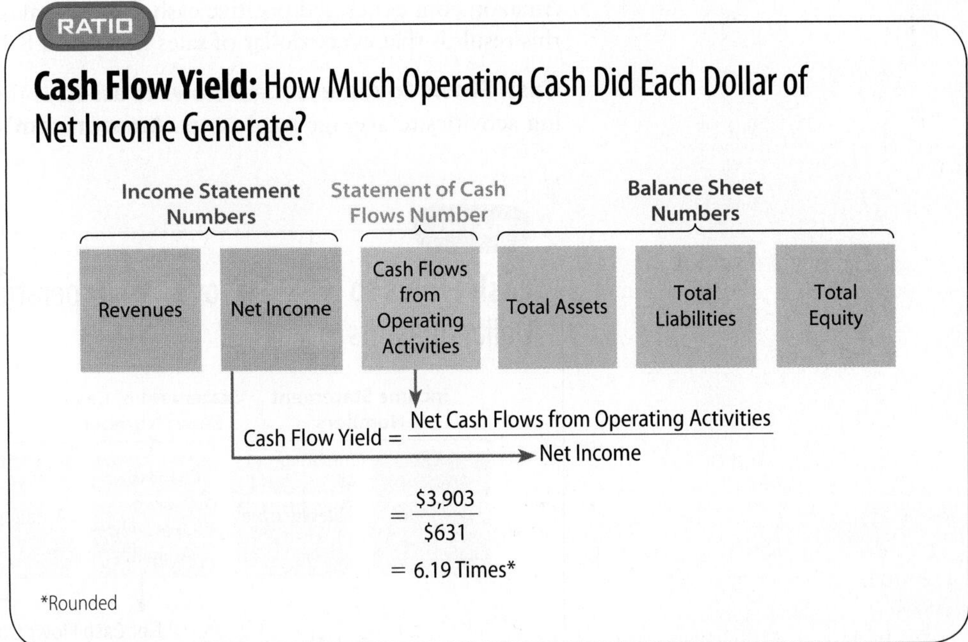

RATIO
Cash Flow Yield: How Much Operating Cash Did Each Dollar of Net Income Generate?
Income Statement Numbers
Statement of Cash Flows Number
Balance Sheet Numbers
Revenues
Net Income
Cash Flows from Operating Activities
Total Assets
Total Liabilities
Total Equity
Cash Flow Yield = Net Cash Flows from Operating Activities / Net Income
= $3,903 / $631
= 6.19 Times*
*Rounded

Cash flow yield is an important financial ratio because it shows whether a company is generating sufficient cash flow in relation to its net income or profitability. For most companies, the cash flow yield should exceed 1.0. Amazon.com's cash flow yield in 2011 was much better than that. With a cash flow yield of 6.19 times, Amazon.com was generating about $6.19 of cash for every dollar of net income.

The cash flow yield needs to be examined carefully. For instance, a firm with significant depreciable assets should have a cash flow yield greater than 1.0 because depreciation expense is added back to net income to arrive at cash flows from operating activities. If special items, such as discontinued operations, appear on the income statement and are material, income from continuing operations (from the income statement) should be used as the denominator. Also, an artificially high cash flow yield may result because a firm has very low net income, which is the denominator in the ratio.

Cash Flows to Sales **Cash flows to sales** is the ratio of net cash flows from operating activities to net sales. For **Amazon.com**, it is calculated as follows.

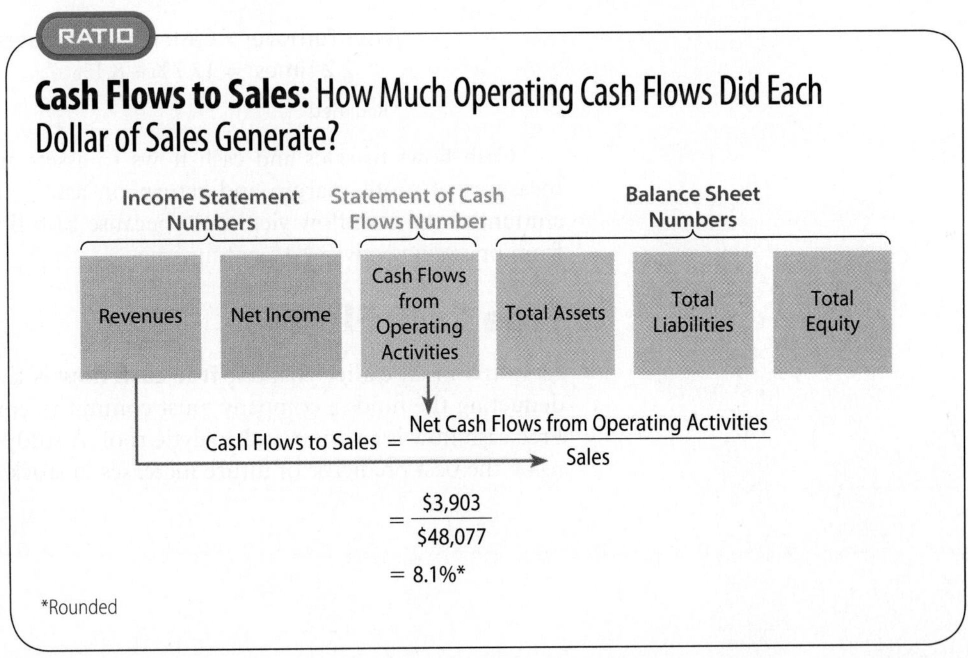

Amazon.com generated positive cash flows to sales of 8.1 percent. Another way to state this result is that every dollar of sales generated 8.1 cents in cash.

Cash Flows to Assets **Cash flows to assets** is the ratio of net cash flows from operating activities to average total assets. **Amazon.com**'s ratio is calculated as follows.

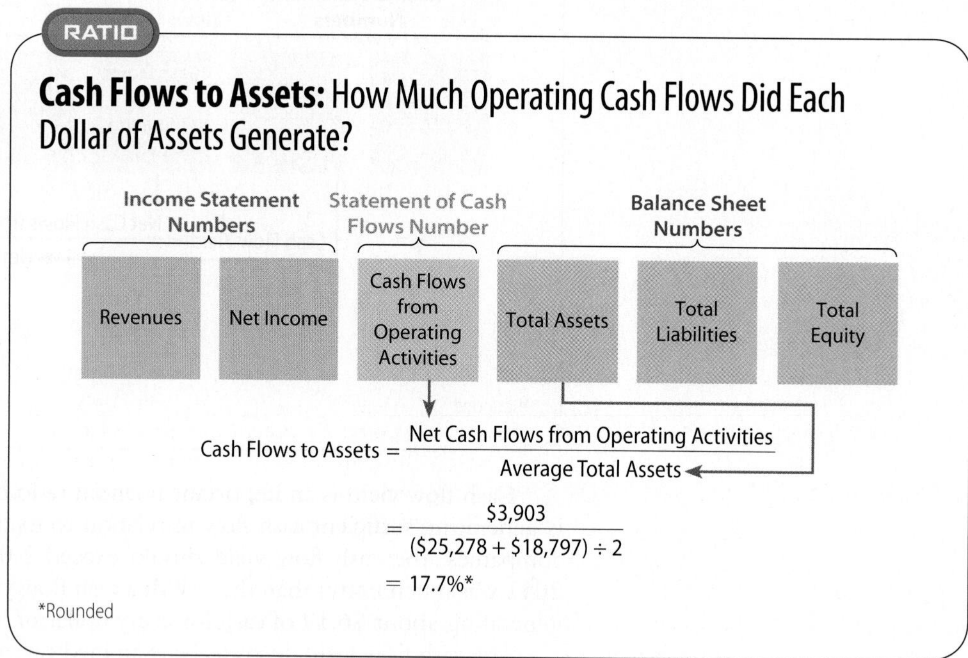

At 17.7 percent, Amazon.com's cash flows to assets ratio indicates that for every dollar of assets, the company generated almost 18 cents. This excellent result is higher than its cash flows to sales ratio because of its good asset turnover ratio:

Asset Turnover = Sales ÷ Average Total Assets
2.2 Times* = $48,077 ÷ $22,038
or
Asset Turnover = Cash Flows to Assets ÷ Cash Flows to Sales
2.2 Times* = 17.7% ÷ 8.1%

* Rounded

Cash flows to sales and cash flows to assets are closely related to the profitability measures of profit margin and return on assets. They exceed those measures by the amount of the cash flow yield ratio because cash flow yield is the ratio of net cash flows from operating activities to net income.

Free Cash Flow

As noted in an earlier chapter, **free cash flow** is the amount of cash that remains after deducting the funds a company must commit to continue operating at its planned level. Free cash flow is a very useful analytic tool. A study of 100 different measures showed it to be the best predictor of future increases in stock price.[6]

Free cash flow can be positive or negative:

- *Positive free cash flow* means that the company has met all of its planned cash commitments and has cash available to reduce debt or to expand.
- *Negative free cash flow* means that the company will have to sell investments, borrow money, or issue stock in the short term to continue at its planned level. If a company's free cash flow remains negative for several years, it may not be able to raise cash by issuing stocks or bonds. On the statement of cash flows, cash commitments for current and continuing operations, interest, and income taxes are incorporated in cash flows from current operations.

Amazon.com has a stated primary financial objective of "long-term sustainable growth in free cash flow."[7] The company definitely achieved this objective in 2011, as shown in the computation (in millions) that follows.

STUDY NOTE: *The computation for free cash flow sometimes uses net capital expenditures in place of purchases plus sales of plant assets.*

$$\text{Free Cash Flow} = \text{Net Cash Flows from Operating Activities} - \text{Dividends} - \text{Purchases of Plant Assets} + \text{Sales of Plant Assets}$$

$$= \$3{,}903 - \$0 - \$1{,}811 + \$0$$

$$= \$2{,}092$$

Purchases of plant assets (capital expenditures) and sales (dispositions) of plant assets, if any, appear in the investing activities section of the statement of cash flows. Dividends, if any, appear in the financing activities section. Amazon.com is a growing company and does not have material sales of plant assets and does not pay dividends. The company's positive free cash flow of $2,092 million was due primarily to its strong operating cash flow of $3,903 million. Consequently, the company does not have to borrow money to expand.

Asking the Right Questions About the Statement of Cash Flows

Most readers of financial statements are accustomed to looking at the "bottom line" to get an overview of a company's financial status. They look at total assets on the balance sheet and net income on the income statement. However, the statement of cash flows requires a different approach because changes in the components of the statement during the year are far more revealing.

In interpreting a statement of cash flows, it pays to know the right questions to ask. To illustrate, we will use **Amazon.com** as an example.

Cash Flows and Net Income *What are the primary reasons that Amazon.com's cash flows from operating activities differed from net income in 2011?*

For Amazon.com, the largest positive items in 2011 were accounts payable and depreciation. They are added to net income for different reasons. Accounts payable represents

Business Perspective
What Do You Mean, "Free Cash Flow"?

Because the statement of cash flows has been around for less than 25 years, no generally accepted analyses have yet been developed. For example, the term *free cash flow* is commonly used in the business press, but there is no agreement on its definition. An article in *Forbes* defines *free cash flow* as "cash available after paying out capital expenditures and dividends, but *before taxes and interest*" [emphasis added].[8] An article in *The Wall Street Journal* defines it as "operating income less maintenance-level capital expenditures."[9] The definition with which we are most in agreement is the one used in *BusinessWeek:* free cash flow is net cash flows from operating activities less net capital expenditures and dividends. This "measures truly discretionary funds—company money that an owner could pocket without harming the business."[10]

an increase in the amount owed to creditors, whereas depreciation represents a noncash expense that is deducted in arriving at net income. Amazon.com's two largest negative items were increases in inventories and amortization of unearned revenue. As a growing company, Amazon.com was managing its operating cycle by generating cash from creditors to pay for increases in inventories.

Investing Activities *What were Amazon.com's most important investing activities other than capital expenditures?*

Amazon.com was actively buying and selling investments. However, sales of marketable securities and other investments were not sufficient to offset the purchase of marketable securities and other investments and the purchase of various assets.

Financing Activities *How did Amazon.com manage its financing activities during 2011?*

Excess tax benefits from stock-based compensation and proceeds from long-term debt provided some funds to buy back treasury stock and pay off some long-term debt, but the inflows were less than the outflows. Because of its good cash flow from operations, Amazon.com did not need long-term financing.

Cash Flow Trends *What has been the trend of cash flows for Amazon.com?*

Because cash flows can vary from year to year, analysts should look at trends in cash flow measures over several years. For example, Amazon.com's management states:

> *Because of our model we are able to turn our inventory quickly and have a cash-generating operating cycle. On average our high inventory velocity means we generally collect from consumers before our payments to suppliers come due. Inventory turnover was 10, 11, and 12 for 2011, 2010, and 2009. We expect variability in inventory turnover over time since it is affected by several factors, including our product mix, the mix of sales by us and by other sellers, our continuing focus on in-stock inventory availability, our investment in new geographies and product lines, and the extent to which we choose to utilize outsource fulfillment providers. Accounts payable days were 74, 72, and 68 for 2011, 2010, and 2009. We expect some variability in accounts payable days over time since they are affected by several factors, including the mix of product sales, the mix of sales by other sellers, the mix of suppliers, seasonality, and changes in payment terms over time, including the effect of balancing pricing and timing of payment terms with suppliers.*[11]

Ethical Considerations in Analyzing the Statement of Cash Flows

Although cash inflows and outflows are not as subject to manipulation as earnings are, managers are acutely aware of users' emphasis on cash flows from operations as an important measure of performance. Thus, an incentive exists to overstate these cash flows.

In earlier chapters, we cited an egregious example of earnings management. As you may recall, by treating operating expenses of about $10 billion over several years as purchases of equipment, **WorldCom** reduced reported expenses and improved reported earnings. In addition, by classifying payments of operating expenses as investments on the statement of cash flows, it was able to show an improvement in cash flows from operations. The inclusion of the expenditures in the investing activities section did not draw special attention because the company normally had large capital expenditures.

Another way a company can show an apparent improvement in its performance is through lack of transparency, or lack of full disclosure, in its financial statements. For instance, securitization—the sale of batches of accounts receivable—is clearly a means of financing, and the proceeds from it should be shown in the financing activities section of the statement of cash flows. However, because the accounting standards are somewhat vague about where these proceeds should go, some companies net the proceeds against the accounts receivable in the operating activities section of the statement and bury the explanation in the notes to the financial statements. By doing so, they make collections of receivables look better than they actually were. It is not illegal to do this; but from an ethical standpoint, it obscures the company's true performance.

APPLY IT!

In 2015, Benson Corporation had year-end assets of \$2,400,000, sales of \$2,000,000, net income of \$400,000, net cash flows from operating activities of \$360,000, dividends of \$100,000, purchases of plant assets of \$200,000, and sales of plant assets of \$40,000. In 2014, year-end assets were \$2,200,000. Calculate cash flow yield, cash flows to sales, cash flows to assets, and free cash flow.

SOLUTION

$$\text{Cash Flow Yield} = \frac{\$360{,}000}{\$400{,}000} = 0.9 \text{ Times}$$

$$\text{Cash Flows to Sales} = \frac{\$360{,}000}{\$2{,}000{,}000} = 0.18, \text{ or } 18\%$$

$$\text{Cash Flows to Assets} = \frac{\$360{,}000}{(\$2{,}400{,}000 + \$2{,}200{,}000) \div 2} = 0.16, \text{ or } 16\% \text{ (rounded)}$$

$$\text{Free Cash Flow} = \$360{,}000 - \$100{,}000 - \$200{,}000 + \$40{,}000 = \$100{,}000$$

TRY IT! SE7, SE8, E9A, E9B

A Look Back At: Amazon.com, Inc.

Annette Shaff/Shutterstock.com

Amazon.com

The beginning of this chapter focused on the extent of **Amazon.com**'s cash flow. Complete the following requirements to answer the questions posed at the beginning of the chapter.

Section 1: Concepts
How do relevance and classification apply to the statement of cash flows?

Section 2: Accounting Applications
How is the statement of cash flows prepared using the indirect method?

Section 3: Business Applications
Are Amazon.com's operations generating sufficient operating cash flows?

SOLUTION

Section 1: Concepts

The statement of cash flows is *relevant* to management, investors, and creditors for assessing the current and future liquidity of a company, its dividend policy, and its financing needs. Operating activities *classify* inflows and outflows from operating activities and include among other things cash inflows from the sales of goods and services, sale of trading securities, as well as interest and dividends on loans and investments while cash outflows include cash spent for wages, inventory, expenses, interest, taxes, and purchase of trading securities. Investing activities *classify* the acquisition and sale of short-term marketable securities, long-term investments, and property, plant, and equipment and the making and collecting of loans. Financing activities *classify* obtaining resources from stockholders and creditors and show proceeds from stock issues and from short- and long-term borrowings and deductions for repayment of loans, payment of dividends, and purchase of treasury stock. Finally, noncash investment and financing activities are *disclosed* in a separate schedule.

SOLUTION • SOLUTION

Section 2: Accounting Applications

The indirect method of preparing the statement of cash flows begins with net income and derives cash flows from operations by adjusting for items that reconcile net income to cash flows from operations. These include expense items like depreciation that do not use cash in the current year, gains and losses, and changes in current assets and current liabilities.

Section 3: Business Applications

Amazon.com's operations are generating sufficient cash flows, as evidenced by its cash flow yield of 6.19 times in 2011. This cash flow yield is more than twice that of 2010 (3.03 times = $3,495 / $1,152).

Both years easily exceeded the 1.0 level normally considered the minimum acceptable cash flow yield. Although net income decreased from 2010 to 2011, net cash flows from operating activities grew by $408 million.

Free cash flow measures the sufficiency of cash flows in a different way, and as mentioned earlier in the chapter, it is a key financial objective of Amazon.com's management. The free cash flow in 2011 was $2,092, compared to $2,516 ($3,495 − $0 − $979 + $) in 2010. Although Amazon.com's free cash flow decreased by $424 million it still has sufficient free cash flow.

An examination of Amazon.com's statement of cash flows in Exhibit 1 shows how the company is investing its free cash flow. In addition to investing in long-term assets ($1,811 million in 2011 and $979 million in 2010), the company increased its investment in marketable securities because purchases exceeded sales each year. Thus, the company did not have to rely on borrowing money (because repayments exceeded proceeds from debt) or issuing stock to finance its growth. Although it did not pay a cash dividend, Amazon.com did repurchase common stock in the amount of $277 million in 2011. Finally, cash and cash equivalents increased from $3,444 million in 2010 to $3,777 million in 2011. One must conclude that Amazon.com is a very successful and growing company. It will be interesting to see if it can maintain its success.

Review Problem

Deliga Corporation is a distributor of accessories for cell phones, iPods, iPhones, and other small electronic devices. Its income statement for 2015 and comparative balance sheets for 2015 and 2014 follow.

	A	B	C	D	E
1			**Deliga Corporation**		
2			**Income Statement**		
3			**For the Year Ended December 31, 2015**		
4	Net sales				$825,000
5	Cost of goods sold				460,000
6	Gross margin				$365,000
7	Operating expenses (including depreciation expense of $6,000				
8	on buildings and $11,550 on equipment and amortization				
9	expense of $2,400)				235,000
10	Operating income				$130,000
11	Other income:				
12		Interest expense		$(27,500)	
13		Dividend income		1,700	
14		Gain on sale of investments		6,250	
15		Loss on disposal of equipment		(1,150)	(20,700)
16	Income before income taxes				$109,300
17	Income taxes expense				26,100
18	Net income				$ 83,200

	A	B	C	D	E	F
1		**Deliga Corporation**				
2		**Comparative Balance Sheets**				
3		**December 31, 2015 and 2014**				
4						**Increase or**
5			**2015**	**2014**	**Change**	**Decrease**
6		**Assets**				
7		Cash	$ 52,925	$ 60,925	$ (8,000)	Decrease
8		Accounts receivable (net)	148,000	157,250	(9,250)	Decrease
9		Inventory	161,000	150,500	10,500	Increase
10		Prepaid expenses	3,900	2,900	1,000	Increase
11		Long-term investments	18,000	43,000	(25,000)	Decrease
12		Land	75,000	62,500	12,500	Increase
13		Buildings	231,000	231,000	—	—
14		Accumulated depreciation—buildings	(45,500)	(39,500)	(6,000)	Increase
15		Equipment	79,865	83,615	(3,750)	Decrease
16		Accumulated depreciation—equipment	(21,700)	(22,800)	1,100	Decrease
17		Intangible assets	9,600	12,000	(2,400)	Decrease
18		Total assets	$712,090	$741,390	$(29,300)	
19						
20		**Liabilities and Stockholders' Equity**				
21		Accounts payable	$ 66,875	$116,875	$(50,000)	Decrease
22		Notes payable (current)	37,850	72,850	(35,000)	Decrease
23		Accrued liabilities	2,500	—	2,500	Increase
24		Income taxes payable	10,000	—	10,000	Increase
25		Bonds payable	105,000	155,000	(50,000)	Decrease
26		Mortgage payable	165,000	175,000	(10,000)	Decrease
27		Common stock, $10 par value	200,000	170,000	30,000	Increase
28		Additional paid-in capital	45,000	25,000	20,000	Increase
29		Retained earnings	104,865	46,665	58,200	Increase
30		Treasury stock	(25,000)	(20,000)	(5,000)	Increase
31		Total liabilities and stockholders' equity	$712,090	$741,390	$(29,300)	

The company's records for 2015 provide this additional information:

a. Sold long-term investments that cost $35,000 for a gain of $6,250; made other long-term investments in the amount of $10,000.
b. Purchased five acres of land to build a parking lot for $12,500.
c. Sold equipment that cost $18,750 and that had accumulated depreciation of $12,650 at a loss of $1,150; purchased new equipment for $15,000.
d. Repaid notes payable in the amount of $50,000; borrowed $15,000 by signing new notes payable.
e. Converted $50,000 of bonds payable into 3,000 shares of common stock.
f. Reduced the Mortgage Payable account by $10,000.
g. Declared and paid cash dividends of $25,000.
h. Purchased treasury stock for $5,000.

1. Prepare Deluga's statement of cash flows for 2015.
2. Compute the company's cash flow yield, cash flows to sales, cash flows to assets, and free cash flow for 2015. (Round ratios to one decimal place.)

SOLUTION • SOLUTION • SOLUTION • SOLUTION • SOLUTION • SOLUTION • SOLUTION • SOLUTION

SOLUTION

1.

	A	B	C	D	E
1			**Deliga Corporation**		
2			**Statement of Cash Flows**		
3			**For the Year Ended December 31, 2015**		
4	Cash flows from operating activities:				
5	Net income				$83,200
6	Adjustments to reconcile net income to net cash flows				
7	from operating activities:				
8		Depreciation expense—buildings		$ 6,000	
9		Depreciation expense—equipment		11,550	
10		Amortization expense—intangible assets		2,400	
11		Gain on sale of investments		(6,250)	
12		Loss on disposal of equipment		1,150	
13		Changes in current assets and current liabilities:			
14			Decrease in accounts receivable	9,250	
15			Increase in inventory	(10,500)	
16			Increase in prepaid expenses	(1,000)	
17			Decrease in accounts payable	(50,000)	
18			Increase in accrued liabilities	2,500	
19			Increase in income taxes payable	10,000	(24,900)
20	Net cash flows from operating activities				$58,300
21	Cash flows from investing activities:				
22	Sale of long-term investments			$ 41,250[a]	
23	Purchase of long-term investments			(10,000)	
24	Purchase of land			(12,500)	
25	Sale of equipment			4,950[b]	
26	Purchase of equipment			(15,000)	
27	Net cash flows from investing activities				8,700
28	Cash flows from financing activities:				
29	Repayment of notes payable			$(50,000)	
30	Issuance of notes payable			15,000	
31	Reduction in mortgage			(10,000)	
32	Dividends paid			(25,000)	
33	Purchase of treasury stock			(5,000)	
34	Net cash flows from financing activities				(75,000)
35	Net (decrease) in cash				$ (8,000)
36	Cash at beginning of year				60,925
37	Cash at end of year				$52,925
38					
39			**Schedule of Noncash Investing and Financing Transactions**		
40	Conversion of bonds payable into common stock				$50,000
41					
42	[a]$35,000 + $6,250 (gain) = $41,250				
43	[b]$18,750 – $12,650 = $6,100 (book value) – $1,150 (loss) = $4,950				

2.

$$\text{Cash Flow Yield} = \frac{\$58{,}300}{\$83{,}200} = 0.7 \text{ Time*}$$

$$\text{Cash Flows to Sales} = \frac{\$58{,}300}{\$825{,}000} = 7.1\%*$$

$$\text{Cash Flows to Assets} = \frac{\$58{,}300}{(\$712{,}090 + \$741{,}390) \div 2} = 8.0\%*$$

$$\text{Free Cash Flow} = \$58{,}300 - \$25{,}000 - \$12{,}500 - \$15{,}000 + \$4{,}950 = \$10{,}750$$

*Rounded

Chapter Review

LO 1 Describe the principal purposes and concepts underlying the statement of cash flows, and identify its components and format.

The statement of cash flows is relevant to investors and creditors by providing information about a company's cash receipts and cash payments during a period in order to assess the company's cash-generating ability. It is relevant to management to assess liquidity, determine dividend policy, and plan investing and financing activities. Investors and creditors use it to assess the company's cash-generating ability.

The statement of cash flows has three major classifications: (1) operating activities, which involve the cash effects of transactions and other events that enter into the determination of net income; (2) investing activities, which involve the acquisition and sale of marketable securities and long-term assets and the making and collecting of loans; and (3) financing activities, which involve obtaining resources from stockholders and creditors. Noncash investing and financing transactions are also important because they affect future cash flows.

LO 2 Use the indirect method to determine cash flows from operating activities.

The indirect method adjusts net income for all items in the income statement that do not have cash flow effects (such as depreciation, amortization, and gains and losses on sales of assets) and for changes in assets and liabilities that affect operating cash flows. Generally, increases in current assets have a negative effect on cash flows, and decreases have a positive effect. Conversely, increases in current liabilities have a positive effect on cash flows, and decreases have a negative effect.

LO 3 Determine cash flows from investing activities.

Investing activities involve the acquisition and sale of property, plant, and equipment and other long-term assets, including long-term investments. They also involve the acquisition and sale of short-term marketable securities, other than trading securities, and the making and collecting of loans. Cash flows from investing activities are determined by analyzing the cash flow effects of changes in each account related to investing activities. The effects of gains and losses reported on the income statement must also be considered.

LO 4 Determine cash flows from financing activities.

Determining cash flows from financing activities is almost identical to determining cash flows from investing activities. The difference is that the accounts analyzed relate to short-term borrowings, long-term liabilities, and stockholders' equity. After the changes in the balance sheet accounts from one accounting period to the next have been explained, all the cash flow effects should have been identified, and the statement of cash flows can be prepared.

LO 5 Analyze the statement of cash flows.

Analysts tend to focus on a firm's degree of liquidity, which is determined by cash inflows and outflows. The ratios used to measure a firm's ability to generate sufficient cash are cash flow yield, cash flows to sales, and cash flows to assets. Free cash flow—the cash that remains after deducting the funds a firm must commit to continue operating at its planned level—is another important measure of the adequacy of cash flow.

Key Terms and Ratios

cash 596 (LO1)
cash equivalents 596 (LO1)
direct method 599 (LO1)
financing activities 597 (LO1)
indirect method 600 (LO1)
investing activities 597 (LO1)
marketable securities 596 (LO1)
noncash investing and financing transactions 599 (LO1)
operating activities 597 (LO1)
statement of cash flows 596 (LO1)
trading securities 597 (LO1)

RATIOS
cash flow yield 616 (LO5)
cash flows to assets 618 (LO5)
cash flows to sales 617 (LO5)
cash-generating efficiency 616 (LO5)
free cash flow 618 (LO5)

Chapter Assignments

DISCUSSION QUESTIONS

LO 1 **DQ1.** Which statement is more useful—the income statement or the statement of cash flows?

LO 2 **DQ2.** If a company has positive earnings, can cash flows from operating activities ever be negative?

LO 2, 3 **DQ3.** Which adjustments to net income in the operating activities section of the statement of cash flows are directly related to cash flows in other sections?

LO 5 **DQ4.** How would you respond to someone who says that the most important item on the statement of cash flows is the change in the cash balance for the year?

LO 5 **DQ5. BUSINESS APPLICATION ▶** If a company's cash flow yield is less than 1.0, would its cash flows to sales and cash flows to assets be greater or less than profit margin and return on assets, respectively?

LO 5 **DQ6. BUSINESS APPLICATION ▶** In computing free cash flow, what is an argument for treating the purchases of treasury stock like dividend payments?

SHORT EXERCISES

LO 1 **Classification of Cash Flow Transactions**

SE1. CONCEPT ▶ The list that follows itemizes Alpha Pro Corporation's transactions. Identify each as (a) an operating activity, (b) an investing activity, (c) a financing activity, (d) a noncash transaction, or (e) none of the above.

1. Sold land.
2. Declared and paid a cash dividend.
3. Paid interest.
4. Issued common stock for plant assets.
5. Issued preferred stock.
6. Borrowed cash on a bank loan.

LO 2 **Computing Cash Flows from Operating Activities: Indirect Method**

SE2. Stewart Construction Corporation had a net income of $16,500 during 2014. In that year, the company had depreciation expense of $7,000. Accounts Receivable increased by $5,500, and Accounts Payable increased by $2,500. Those were the company's only current assets and current liabilities. Use the indirect method to determine net cash flows from operating activities.

LO 2 **Computing Cash Flows from Operating Activities: Indirect Method**

SE3. During 2014, Cupello Corporation had a net income of $144,000. Included on its income statement were depreciation expense of $16,000 and amortization expense of $1,800. During the year, Accounts Receivable decreased by $8,200, Inventories increased by $5,400, Prepaid Expenses decreased by $1,000, Accounts Payable decreased by $14,000, and Accrued Liabilities decreased by $1,700. Use the indirect method to determine net cash flows from operating activities.

LO 3 **Cash Flows from Investing Activities and Noncash Transactions**

SE4. During 2014, Fargo Company purchased land for $375,000. It paid $125,000 in cash and signed a $250,000 mortgage for the rest. The company also sold for $95,000 cash a building that originally cost $90,000, on which it had $70,000 of accumulated depreciation, making a gain of $75,000. Prepare the cash flows from investing activities section and the schedule of noncash investing and financing transactions of the statement of cash flows.

LO 4 **Cash Flows from Financing Activities**

SE5. During 2014, North Dakota Company issued $1,000,000 in long-term bonds at 96, repaid $150,000 of bonds at face value, paid interest of $80,000, and paid dividends of $50,000. Prepare the cash flows from the financing activities section of the statement of cash flows.

LO 1, 2, 3, 4 **Identifying Components of the Statement of Cash Flows**

SE6. CONCEPT ▶ Assuming the indirect method is used to prepare the statement of cash flows, tell whether each of the following items would be reported (a) in cash flows from operating activities, (b) in cash flows from investing activities, (c) in cash flows from financing activities, (d) in the schedule of noncash investing and financing transactions, or (e) not on the statement of cash flows at all:

1. Dividends paid
2. Cash receipts from sales
3. Decrease in accounts receivable
4. Sale of plant assets
5. Gain on sale of investments
6. Issue of stock for plant assets
7. Issue of common stock
8. Net income

LO 5 **Cash-Generating Efficiency Ratios and Free Cash Flow**

SE7. BUSINESS APPLICATION ▶ In 2014, Melvin Corporation had year-end assets of $1,100,000, sales of $1,580,000, net income of $180,000, net cash flows from operating activities of $360,000, purchases of plant assets of $240,000, and sales of plant assets of $40,000, and it paid dividends of $80,000. In 2013, year-end assets were $1,000,000. Calculate the cash-generating efficiency ratios of cash flow yield, cash flows to sales, and cash flows to assets. Also calculate free cash flow. (Round to the nearest tenth of a percent.)

LO 5 **Cash-Generating Efficiency Ratios and Free Cash Flow**

SE8. BUSINESS APPLICATION ▶ Examine the cash flow measures in requirement 2 of the Review Problem at the end of this chapter. Discuss the meaning of these ratios.

EXERCISES: SET A

LO 1

Classification of Cash Flow Transactions

E1A. CONCEPT ▶ VIP Corporation engaged in the transactions that follow. Identify each transaction as (a) an operating activity, (b) an investing activity, (c) a financing activity, (d) a noncash transaction, or (e) not on the statement of cash flows. Assume the indirect method is used. (*Hint:* More than one answer may apply.)

1. Paid interest.
2. Increased dividends receivable.
3. Declared and paid a cash dividend.
4. Purchased a long-term investment.
5. Increased accounts receivable.
6. Sold equipment at a loss.
7. Issued long-term bonds for plant assets.
8. Issued common stock.
9. Declared and issued a stock dividend.
10. Decreased wages payable.
11. Purchased a 60-day Treasury bill.
12. Repaid notes payable.
13. Purchased land.

LO 2

Cash Flows from Operating Activities: Indirect Method

E2A. The condensed single-step income statement for the year ended December 31, 2014, of Conti Chemical Company, a distributor of farm fertilizers and herbicides, follows.

Sales		$26,000,000
Less: Cost of goods sold	$15,200,000	
Operating expenses (including depreciation of $1,640,000)	7,600,000	
Income taxes expense	800,000	23,600,000
Net income		$ 2,400,000

Selected accounts from Conti Chemical's balance sheets for 2014 and 2013 follow.

	2014	2013
Accounts receivable	$4,800,000	$3,400,000
Inventory	1,680,000	2,040,000
Prepaid expenses	520,000	360,000
Accounts payable	1,920,000	1,440,000
Accrued liabilities	120,000	200,000
Income taxes payable	280,000	240,000

Prepare a schedule of cash flows from operating activities using the indirect method.

LO 2

Computing Cash Flows from Operating Activities: Indirect Method

E3A. During 2014, Ortega Corporation had net income of $82,000. Included on its income statement were depreciation expense of $4,600 and amortization expense of $600. During the year, Accounts Receivable increased by $6,800, Inventories decreased by $3,800, Prepaid Expenses decreased by $400, Accounts Payable increased by $10,000, and Accrued Liabilities decreased by $900. Determine net cash flows from operating activities using the indirect method.

LO 2

Preparing a Schedule of Cash Flows from Operating Activities: Indirect Method

E4A. For the year ended June 30, 2014, net income for Flake Corporation was $14,800. Depreciation expense was $4,000. During the year, Accounts Receivable increased by

$8,800, Inventories increased by $14,000, Prepaid Rent decreased by $2,800, Accounts Payable increased by $28,000, Salaries Payable increased by $2,000, and Income Taxes Payable decreased by $1,200. Use the indirect method to prepare a schedule of cash flows from operating activities.

LO 3

Computing Cash Flows from Investing Activities: Investments

E5A. Wilma Company's T account for long-term available-for-sale investments at the end of 2014 follows.

Investments

Dr.		*Cr.*	
Beg. Bal.	76,000	Sales of Investments	78,000
Purchases of Investments	116,000		
End. Bal.	**114,000**		

In addition, Wilma's income statement shows a loss on the sale of investments of $13,000. Compute the amounts to be shown as cash flows from investing activities, and show how they appear in the statement of cash flows.

LO 3

Computing Cash Flows from Investing Activities: Plant Assets

E6A. The T accounts for plant assets and accumulated depreciation for Street Company at the end of 2014 follow.

Plant Assets

Dr.		*Cr.*	
Beg. Bal.	130,000	Disposals	46,000
Purchases	67,200		
End. Bal.	**151,200**		

Accumulated Depreciation

Dr.		*Cr.*	
Disposals	29,400	Beg. Bal.	69,000
		Depreciation	20,400
		End. Bal.	**60,000**

In addition, Street's income statement shows a gain on sale of plant assets of $8,800. Compute the amounts to be shown as cash flows from investing activities, and show how they appear on the statement of cash flows.

LO 4

Determining Cash Flows from Financing Activities: Notes Payable

E7A. All transactions involving Notes Payable and related accounts of Sally Company during 2014 follow.

	Dr.	*Cr.*
Cash	36,000	
Notes Payable		36,000
Bank loan		

	Dr.	*Cr.*
Patent	60,000	
Notes Payable		60,000
Purchase of patent by issuing note payable		

	Dr.	*Cr.*
Notes Payable	10,000	
Interest Expense	1,000	
Cash		11,000
Repayment of note payable at maturity		

Determine the amounts of the transactions affecting financing activities and show how they appear on the statement of cash flows for 2014.

LO 2, 3, 4

Preparing the Statement of Cash Flows: Indirect Method

E8A. Keeper Corporation's income statement for the year ended June 30, 2014, and its comparative balance sheets for June 30, 2014 and 2013 follow.

Keeper Corporation
Income Statement
For the Year Ended June 30, 2014

Sales	$234,000
Cost of goods sold	156,000
Gross margin	$ 78,000
Operating expenses	45,000
Operating income	$ 33,000
Interest expense	2,800
Income before income taxes	$ 30,200
Income taxes expense	12,300
Net income	$ 17,900

Keeper Corporation
Comparative Balance Sheets
June 30, 2014 and 2013

	2014	2013
Assets		
Cash	$ 69,900	$ 12,500
Accounts receivable (net)	21,000	26,000
Inventory	43,400	48,400
Prepaid expenses	3,200	2,600
Furniture	55,000	60,000
Accumulated depreciation—furniture	(9,000)	(5,000)
Total assets	$183,500	$144,500
Liabilities and Stockholders' Equity		
Accounts payable	$ 13,000	$ 14,000
Income taxes payable	1,200	1,800
Notes payable (long-term)	37,000	35,000
Common stock, $10 par value	115,000	90,000
Retained earnings	17,300	3,700
Total liabilities and stockholders' equity	$183,500	$144,500

Keeper issued a $22,000 note payable for purchase of furniture; sold at carrying value furniture that cost $27,000 with accumulated depreciation of $15,300; recorded depreciation on the furniture for the year, $19,300; repaid a note in the amount of $20,000; issued $25,000 of common stock at par value; and paid dividends of $4,300. Prepare Keeper's statement of cash flows for the year 2014 using the indirect method.

LO 5

Cash-Generating Efficiency Ratios and Free Cash Flow

E9A. BUSINESS APPLICATION ▶ In 2014, Andy's Corporation had year-end assets of $2,400,000, sales of $3,300,000, net income of $280,000, net cash flows from operating activities of $390,000, dividends of $120,000, purchases of plant assets of $500,000, and sales of plant assets of $90,000. In 2013, year-end assets were $2,100,000. Calculate free cash flow and the cash-generating efficiency ratios of cash flow yield, cash flows to sales, and cash flows to assets. (Round to one decimal point or the nearest tenth of a percent.)

EXERCISES: SET B

Visit the textbook companion website at www.cengagebrain.com to access Exercise Set B for this chapter.

PROBLEMS

LO 1

Classification of Cash Flow Transactions

P1. CONCEPT ▶ Analyze each transaction listed in the table that follows and place X's in the appropriate columns to indicate the transaction's classification and its effect on cash flows using the indirect method.

Transaction	Cash Flow Classification: Operating Activity	Investing Activity	Financing Activity	Noncash Transaction	Effect on Cash Flows: Increase	Decrease	No Effect
1. Paid a cash dividend.							
2. Decreased accounts receivable.							
3. Increased inventory.							
4. Incurred a net loss.							
5. Declared and issued a stock dividend.							
6. Retired long-term debt with cash.							
7. Sold available-for-sale securities at a loss.							
8. Issued stock for equipment.							
9. Decreased prepaid insurance.							
10. Purchased treasury stock with cash.							
11. Retired a fully depreciated truck (no gain or loss).							
12. Increased interest payable.							
13. Decreased dividends receivable on investment.							
14. Sold treasury stock.							
15. Increased income taxes payable.							
16. Transferred cash to money market account.							
17. Purchased land and building with a mortgage.							

LO 1, 5

✓ 2: Free cash flow, 2013: ($183,114)
✓ 2: Free cash flow, 2014: $290,316

Interpreting and Analyzing the Statement of Cash Flows

P2. The comparative statements of cash flows for Wung Corporation, a manufacturer of high-quality suits for men, follow. To expand its markets and familiarity with its brand, the company attempted a new strategic diversification in 2013 by acquiring a chain of retail men's stores in outlet malls. Its plan was to expand in malls around the country, but department stores viewed the action as infringing on their territory.

Wung Corporation
Statement of Cash Flows
For the Years Ended December 31, 2014 and 2013

(In thousands)	2014	2013
Cash flows from operating activities:		
Net income (loss)	$ (43,090)	$ 76,030
Adjustments to reconcile net income to net cash flows from operating activities:		
Depreciation	$ 70,438	$ 50,036
Loss on closure of retail outlets	70,000	
Changes in current assets and current liabilities:		
Decrease (increase) in accounts receivable	100,000	(89,606)
Decrease (increase) in inventory	120,814	(102,290)
Decrease (increase) in prepaid expenses	2,734	4,492
Increase (decrease) in accounts payable	61,158	2,532
Increase (decrease) in accrued liabilities	3,000	(5,576)
Increase (decrease) in income taxes payable	(16,600)	(12,562)
	$ 411,544	$(152,974)

(Continued)

Net cash flows from operating activities	$ 368,454	$ (76,944)
Cash flows from investing activities:		
Capital expenditures, net	$ (32,290)	$ (66,224)
Purchase of Retail Division, cash portion	—	(402,000)
Net cash flows from investing activities	$ (32,290)	$(468,224)
Cash flows from financing activities:		
Increase (decrease) in notes payable to banks	$ (247,000)	$ 456,800
Reduction in long-term debt	(18,476)	(21,622)
Payment of dividends	(45,848)	(39,946)
Purchase of treasury stock	—	(25,000)
Net cash flows from financing activities	$ (311,324)	$ 370,232
Net increase (decrease) in cash	$ 24,840	$(174,936)
Cash at beginning of year	32,064	207,000
Cash at end of year	$ 56,904	$ 32,064

Schedule of Noncash Investing and Financing Transactions

Issue of bonds payable for retail acquisition	$ 100,000

REQUIRED

Evaluate the success of the company's strategy by answering the questions that follow.

1. **ACCOUNTING CONNECTION ▶** What are the primary reasons cash flows from operating activities differ from net income in 2013 and in 2014? What is the effect of the acquisition in 2013? What conclusions can you draw from the changes in 2014?
2. **BUSINESS APPLICATION ▶** Compute free cash flow for both years. What was the total cost of the acquisition? Was the company able to finance expansion in 2013 by generating internal cash flow? What was the situation in 2013?
3. **ACCOUNTING CONNECTION ▶** What are the most significant financing activities in 2013? How did the company finance the acquisition? Do you think this is a good strategy? What other issues might you question in financing activities?
4. **ACCOUNTING CONNECTION ▶** Based on results in 2014, what actions was the company forced to take and what is your overall assessment of the company's diversification strategy?

LO **2, 3, 4, 5**

Statement of Cash Flows: Indirect Method

RATIO

SPREADSHEET

✔ 1: Net cash flows from operating activities: $23,400
✔ 1: Net cash flows from investing activities: ($7,200)
✔ 1: Net cash flows from financing activities: $51,000

P3. Chaplin Arts, Inc.'s comparative balance sheets for December 31, 2014 and 2013, follow.

Chaplin Arts, Inc.
Comparative Balance Sheets
December 31, 2014 and 2013

	2014	2013
Assets		
Cash	$ 94,560	$ 27,360
Accounts receivable (net)	102,430	75,430
Inventory	112,890	137,890
Prepaid expenses	—	20,000
Land	25,000	—
Building	137,000	—
Accumulated depreciation—building	(15,000)	—
Equipment	33,000	34,000
Accumulated depreciation—equipment	(14,500)	(24,000)
Patents	4,000	6,000
Total assets	$479,380	$276,680

Liabilities and Stockholders' Equity		
Accounts payable	$ 10,750	$ 36,750
Notes payable (current)	10,000	—
Accrued liabilities	—	12,300
Mortgage payable	162,000	—
Common stock, $10 par value	180,000	150,000
Additional paid-in capital	57,200	37,200
Retained earnings	59,430	40,430
Total liabilities and stockholders' equity	$479,380	$276,680

The following additional information about Chaplin Arts's operations during 2013 is available: (a) net income, $28,000; (b) building and equipment depreciation expense amounts, $15,000 and $3,000, respectively; (c) equipment that cost $13,500 with accumulated depreciation of $12,500 sold at a gain of $5,300; (d) equipment purchases, $12,500; (e) patent amortization, $3,000; purchase of patent, $1,000; (f) funds borrowed by issuing notes payable, $25,000; notes payable repaid, $15,000; (g) land and building purchased for $162,000 by signing a mortgage for the total cost; (h) 1,500 shares of $20 par value common stock issued for a total of $50,000; and (i) paid cash dividends, $9,000.

REQUIRED

1. Using the indirect method, prepare a statement of cash flows for Chaplin Arts.
2. **ACCOUNTING CONNECTION ▶** Why did Chaplin Arts have an increase in cash of $67,200 when it recorded net income of only $28,000? Discuss and interpret.
3. **BUSINESS APPLICATION ▶** Compute and assess cash flow yield and free cash flow for 2014. (Round to one decimal place.) What is your assessment of Chaplin Arts' cash-generating ability?

LO **2, 3, 4, 5**

Statement of Cash Flows: Indirect Method

RATIO

✔ 1: Net cash flows from operating activities: ($106,000)
✔ 1: Net cash flows from investing activities: $34,000
✔ 1: Net cash flows from financing activities: $24,000

P4. Ben Tools, Inc.'s comparative balance sheets for December 31, 2014 and 2013, follow.

Ben Tools, Inc.
Comparative Balance Sheets
December 31, 2014 and 2013

	2014	**2013**
Assets		
Cash	$ 257,600	$ 305,600
Accounts receivable (net)	738,800	758,800
Inventory	960,000	800,000
Prepaid expenses	14,800	26,800
Long-term investments	440,000	440,000
Land	361,200	321,200
Building	1,200,000	920,000
Accumulated depreciation—building	(240,000)	(160,000)
Equipment	480,000	480,000
Accumulated depreciation—equipment	(116,000)	(56,000)
Intangible assets	20,000	40,000
Total assets	$4,116,400	$3,876,400
Liabilities and Stockholders' Equity		
Accounts payable	$ 470,800	$ 660,800
Notes payable (current)	40,000	160,000
Accrued liabilities	10,800	20,800
Mortgage payable	1,080,000	800,000
Bonds payable	1,000,000	760,000
Common stock	1,300,000	1,300,000
Additional paid-in capital	80,000	80,000
Retained earnings	254,800	194,800
Treasury stock	(120,000)	(100,000)
Total liabilities and stockholders' equity	$4,116,400	$3,876,400

(Continued)

During 2014, the company had net income of $96,000 and building and equipment depreciation expenses of $80,000 and $60,000, respectively. It amortized intangible assets in the amount of $20,000; purchased investments for $116,000; sold investments for $150,000, on which it recorded a gain of $34,000; issued $240,000 of long-term bonds at face value; purchased land and a warehouse through a $320,000 mortgage; paid $40,000 to reduce the mortgage; borrowed $60,000 by issuing notes payable; repaid notes payable in the amount of $180,000; declared and paid cash dividends in the amount of $36,000; and purchased treasury stock in the amount of $20,000.

REQUIRED

1. Using the indirect method, prepare a statement of cash flows for Ben Tools.
2. **ACCOUNTING CONNECTION ▶** Why did Ben Tools experience a decrease in cash in a year in which it had a net income of $96,000? Discuss and interpret.
3. **BUSINESS APPLICATION ▶** Compute and assess cash flow yield and free cash flow for 2014. Why is each of these measures important in assessing cash-generating ability?

LO **2, 3, 4, 5**

RATIO

✔ 1: Net cash flows from operating activities: $126,600
✔ 1: Net cash flows from investing activities: ($25,800)
✔ 1: Net cash flows from financing activities: $14,000

Statement of Cash Flows: Indirect Method

P5. Yong Company's income statement for the year ended December 31, 2014, and its comparative balance sheets as of December 31, 2014 and 2013, follow.

Yong Company
Income Statement
For the Year Ended December 31, 2014

Sales		$1,609,000
Cost of goods sold		1,127,800
Gross margin		$ 481,200
Operating expenses (including depreciation expense of $46,800)		449,400
Income from operations		$ 31,800
Other income (expenses):		
Gain on sale of furniture and fixtures	$ 7,000	
Interest expense	(23,200)	(16,200)
Income before income taxes		$ 15,600
Income taxes expense		4,600
Net income		$ 11,000

Yong Company
Comparative Balance Sheets
December 31, 2014 and 2013

	2014	2013
Assets		
Cash	$164,800	$ 50,000
Accounts receivable (net)	165,200	200,000
Merchandise inventory	350,000	450,000
Prepaid rent	2,000	3,000
Furniture and fixtures	148,000	144,000
Accumulated depreciation—furniture and fixtures	(42,000)	(24,000)
Total assets	$788,000	$823,000
Liabilities and Stockholders' Equity		
Accounts payable	$143,400	$200,400
Income taxes payable	1,400	4,400
Notes payable (long-term)	40,000	20,000
Bonds payable	100,000	200,000
Common stock, $20 par value	240,000	200,000
Additional paid-in capital	181,440	121,440
Retained earnings	81,760	76,760
Total liabilities and stockholders' equity	$788,000	$823,000

During 2014, the company engaged in these transactions:

a. Sold at a gain of $7,000 furniture and fixtures that cost $35,600, on which it had accumulated depreciation of $28,800.
b. Purchased furniture and fixtures in the amount of $39,600.
c. Paid a $20,000 note payable and borrowed $40,000 on a new note.
d. Converted bonds payable in the amount of $100,000 into 4,000 shares of common stock.
e. Declared and paid $6,000 in cash dividends.

REQUIRED

1. Using the indirect method, prepare a statement of cash flows for Yong. Include a supporting schedule of noncash investing transactions and financing transactions.
2. **ACCOUNTING CONNECTION** ▶ What are the primary reasons for Yong's large increase in cash from 2013 to 2014, despite its low net income?
3. **BUSINESS APPLICATION** ▶ Compute and assess cash flow yield and free cash flow for 2014. (Round to one decimal place.) Compare and contrast what these two performance measures tell you about Yong's cash-generating ability.

ALTERNATE PROBLEMS

Classification of Cash Flow Transactions

LO 1

P6. CONCEPT ▶ Analyze each transaction listed in the table that follows and place X's in the appropriate columns to indicate the transaction's classification and its effect on cash flows using the indirect method.

	Cash Flow Classification				Effect on Cash Flows		
Transaction	**Operating Activity**	**Investing Activity**	**Financing Activity**	**Noncash Transaction**	**Increase**	**Decrease**	**No Effect**
1. Increased accounts payable.							
2. Decreased inventory.							
3. Increased prepaid insurance.							
4. Earned a net income.							
5. Declared and paid a cash dividend.							
6. Issued stock for cash.							
7. Retired long-term debt by issuing stock.							
8. Purchased a long-term investment with cash.							
9. Sold trading securities at a gain.							
10. Sold a machine at a loss.							
11. Retired fully depreciated equipment.							
12. Decreased interest payable.							
13. Purchased available-for-sale securities (long-term).							
14. Decreased dividends receivable.							
15. Decreased accounts receivable.							
16. Converted bonds to common stock.							
17. Purchased 90-day Treasury bill.							

LO **2, 3, 4, 5**

Statement of Cash Flows: Indirect Method

SPREADSHEET

✔ 1: Net cash flows from operating activities: $548,000
✔ 1: Net cash flows from investing activities: $6,000
✔ 1: Net cash flows from financing activities: ($260,000)

P7. Reed Corporation's income statement for the year ended June 30, 2014, and its comparative balance sheets as of June 30, 2014 and 2013, follow.

Reed Corporation
Income Statement
For the Year Ended June 30, 2014

Sales		$8,081,800
Cost of goods sold		7,312,600
Gross margin		$ 769,200
Operating expenses (including depreciation expense of $120,000)		378,400
Income from operations		$ 390,800
Other income (expenses)		
Loss on sale of equipment	$ (8,000)	
Interest expense	(75,200)	(83,200)
Income before income taxes		$ 307,600
Income taxes expense		68,400
Net income		$ 239,200

Reed Corporation
Comparative Balance Sheets
June 30, 2014 and 2013

	2014	2013
Assets		
Cash	$ 334,000	$ 40,000
Accounts receivable (net)	200,000	240,000
Inventory	360,000	440,000
Prepaid expenses	1,200	2,000
Property, plant, and equipment	1,256,000	1,104,000
Accumulated depreciation—property, plant, and equipment	(366,000)	(280,000)
Total assets	$1,785,200	$1,546,000
Liabilities and Stockholders' Equity		
Accounts payable	$ 128,000	$ 84,000
Notes payable (due in 90 days)	60,000	160,000
Income taxes payable	52,000	36,000
Mortgage payable	720,000	560,000
Common stock, $5 par value	400,000	400,000
Retained earnings	425,200	306,000
Total liabilities and stockholders' equity	$1,785,200	$1,546,000

During 2014, the corporation sold at a loss of $8,000 equipment that cost $48,000, on which it had accumulated depreciation of $34,000. It also purchased land and a building for $200,000 through an increase of $200,000 in Mortgage Payable; made a $40,000 payment on the mortgage; repaid $160,000 in notes but borrowed an additional $60,000 through the issuance of a new note payable; and declared and paid a $120,000 cash dividend.

REQUIRED

1. Using the indirect method, prepare a statement of cash flows. Include a supporting schedule of noncash investing and financing transactions.
2. **ACCOUNTING CONNECTION** ▶ What are the primary reasons for Reed's large increase in cash from 2013 to 2014?
3. **BUSINESS APPLICATION** ▶ Compute and assess cash flow yield and free cash flow for 2014. (Round to one decimal place.) How would you assess the corporation's cash-generating ability?

LO 2, 3, 4, 5

✔ 1: Net cash flows from operating activities: $93,600
✔ 1: Net cash flows from investing activities: ($28,800)
✔ 1: Net cash flows from financing activities: $204,000

Statement of Cash Flows: Indirect Method

P8. Shah Fabrics, Inc.'s comparative balance sheets for December 31, 2014 and 2013, follow.

Shah Fabrics, Inc.
Comparative Balance Sheets
December 31, 2014 and 2013

	2014	2013
Assets		
Cash	$ 378,240	$ 109,440
Accounts receivable (net)	409,720	301,720
Inventory	451,560	551,560
Prepaid expenses	—	80,000
Land	100,000	—
Building	548,000	—
Accumulated depreciation—building	(60,000)	—
Equipment	132,000	136,000
Accumulated depreciation—equipment	(58,000)	(96,000)
Patents	16,000	24,000
Total assets	$1,917,520	$1,106,720
Liabilities and Stockholders' Equity		
Accounts payable	$ 43,000	$ 147,000
Notes payable (current)	40,000	—
Accrued liabilities	—	49,200
Mortgage payable	648,000	—
Common stock, $10 par value	720,000	600,000
Additional paid-in capital	228,800	148,800
Retained earnings	237,720	161,720
Total liabilities and stockholders' equity	$1,917,520	$1,106,720

Additional information about Shah Fabrics' operations during 2014 is as follows: (a) net income, $112,000; (b) building and equipment depreciation expense amounts, $60,000 and $12,000, respectively; (c) equipment that cost $54,000 with accumulated depreciation of $50,000 sold at a gain of $21,200; (d) equipment purchases, $50,000; (e) patent amortization, $12,000; purchase of patent, $4,000; (f) funds borrowed by issuing notes payable, $100,000; notes payable repaid, $60,000; (g) land and building purchased for $648,000 by signing a mortgage for the total cost; (h) 6,000 shares of $40 par value common stock issued for a total of $200,000; and (i) paid cash dividend, $36,000.

REQUIRED

1. Using the indirect method, prepare a statement of cash flows for Shah Fabrics.
2. **ACCOUNTING CONNECTION ▶** Why did Shah Fabrics have an increase in cash of $268,800 when it recorded net income of only $112,000? Discuss and interpret.
3. **BUSINESS APPLICATION ▶** Compute and assess cash flow yield and free cash flow for 2014. (Round to one decimal place.) What is your assessment of Shah Fabrics' cash-generating ability?

LO **2, 3, 4, 5**

✔ 1: Net cash flows from operating activities: ($212,000)
✔ 1: Net cash flows from investing activities: $68,000
✔ 1: Net cash flows from financing activities: $48,000

Statement of Cash Flows: Indirect Method

P9. Kohl Ceramics, Inc.'s comparative balance sheets, for December 31, 2014 and 2013, follow.

Kohl Ceramics, Inc.
Comparative Balance Sheets
December 31, 2014 and 2013

	2014	2013
Assets		
Cash	$ 515,200	$ 611,200
Accounts receivable (net)	1,477,600	1,517,600
Inventory	1,920,000	1,600,000
Prepaid expenses	29,600	53,600
Long-term investments	880,000	880,000
Land	722,400	642,400
Building	2,400,000	1,840,000
Accumulated depreciation—building	(480,000)	(320,000)
Equipment	960,000	960,000
Accumulated depreciation—equipment	(232,000)	(112,000)
Intangible assets	40,000	80,000
Total assets	$8,232,800	$7,752,800
Liabilities and Stockholders' Equity		
Accounts payable	$ 941,600	$1,321,600
Notes payable (current)	80,000	320,000
Accrued liabilities	21,600	41,600
Mortgage payable	2,160,000	1,600,000
Bonds payable	2,000,000	1,520,000
Common stock	2,600,000	2,600,000
Additional paid-in capital	160,000	160,000
Retained earnings	509,600	389,600
Treasury stock	(240,000)	(200,000)
Total liabilities and stockholders' equity	$8,232,800	$7,752,800

During 2014, the company had net income of $192,000 and building and equipment depreciation expenses of $160,000 and $120,000, respectively. It amortized intangible assets in the amount of $40,000; purchased investments for $232,000; sold investments for $300,000, on which it recorded a gain of $68,000; issued $480,000 of long-term bonds at face value; purchased land and a warehouse through a $640,000 mortgage; paid $80,000 to reduce the mortgage; borrowed $120,000 by issuing notes payable; repaid notes payable in the amount of $360,000; declared and paid cash dividends in the amount of $72,000; and purchased treasury stock in the amount of $40,000.

REQUIRED

1. Using the indirect method, prepare a statement of cash flows for Kohl Ceramics.
2. **ACCOUNTING CONNECTION** ▶ Why did Kohl Ceramics experience a decrease in cash in a year in which it had a net income of $192,000? Discuss and interpret.
3. **BUSINESS APPLICATION** ▶ Compute and assess cash flow yield and free cash flow for 2014. Why is each of these measures important in assessing cash-generating ability?

LO **2, 3, 4, 5**

✔ 1: Net cash flows from operating activities: $126,600
✔ 1: Net cash flows from investing activities: ($25,800)
✔ 1: Net cash flows from financing activities: $14,000
✔ 3: Free cash flow, 2014: $94,800

Statement of Cash Flows: Indirect Method

P10. William Corporation's income statement for the year ended December 31, 2014, and its comparative balance sheets as of December 31, 2014 and 2013, follow.

William Corporation
Income Statement
For the Year Ended December 31, 2014

Sales		$1,609,000
Cost of goods sold		1,127,800
Gross margin		$ 481,200
Operating expenses (including depreciation expense of $46,800)		449,400
Income from operations		$ 31,800
Other income (expenses)		
Gain on sale of furniture and fixtures	$ 7,000	
Interest expense	(23,200)	(16,200)
Income before income taxes		$ 15,600
Income taxes expense		4,600
Net income		$ 11,000

William Corporation
Comparative Balance Sheets
December 31, 2014 and 2013

	2014	2013
Assets		
Cash	$164,800	$ 50,000
Accounts receivable (net)	165,200	200,000
Merchandise inventory	350,000	450,000
Prepaid rent	2,000	3,000
Furniture and fixtures	148,000	144,000
Accumulated depreciation—furniture and fixtures	(42,000)	(24,000)
Total assets	$788,000	$823,000
Liabilities and Stockholders' Equity		
Accounts payable	$143,400	$200,400
Income taxes payable	1,400	4,400
Notes payable (long-term)	40,000	20,000
Bonds payable	100,000	200,000
Common stock, $20 par value	240,000	200,000
Additional paid-in capital	181,440	121,440
Retained earnings	81,760	76,760
Total liabilities and stockholders' equity	$788,000	$823,000

During 2014, William engaged in these transactions:

a. Sold at a gain of $7,000 furniture and fixtures that cost $35,600, on which it had accumulated depreciation of $28,800.
b. Purchased furniture and fixtures in the amount of $39,600.
c. Paid a $20,000 note payable and borrowed $40,000 on a new note.
d. Converted bonds payable in the amount of $100,000 into 4,000 shares of common stock.
e. Declared and paid $6,000 in cash dividends.

REQUIRED

1. Using the indirect method, prepare a statement of cash flows for William. Include a supporting schedule of noncash investing transactions and financing transactions.
2. **ACCOUNTING CONNECTION ▶** What are the primary reasons for William's large increase in cash from 2013 to 2014, despite its low net income?
3. **BUSINESS APPLICATION ▶** Compute and assess cash flow yield and free cash flow for 2014. (Round to one decimal place.) Compare and contrast what these two performance measures tell you about William's cash-generating ability.

CASES

LO 1, 2

Conceptual Understanding: EBITDA and the Statement of Cash Flows

C1. When **Fleetwood Enterprises, Inc.**, a large producer of recreational vehicles and manufactured housing, warned that it might not be able to generate enough cash to satisfy debt requirements and could be in default of a loan agreement, its cash flow, defined in the financial press as "EBITDA" (earnings before interest, taxes, depreciation, and amortization), was a negative \$2.7 million. The company would have had to generate \$17.7 million in the next accounting period to comply with the loan terms.[12] To what section of the statement of cash flows does EBITDA most closely relate? Is EBITDA a good approximation for this section of the statement of cash flows? Explain your answer, which should include an identification of the major differences between EBITDA and the section of the statement of cash flows you chose.

LO 5

Interpreting Financial Reports: Classic Case—Anatomy of a Disaster

C2. On October 16, 2001, Kenneth Lay, chairman and CEO of **Enron Corporation**, announced the company's earnings for the first nine months of 2001 as follows:

> *Our 26 percent increase in recurring earnings per diluted share shows the very strong results of our core wholesale and retail energy businesses and our natural gas pipelines. The continued excellent prospects in these businesses and Enron's leading market position make us very confident in our strong earnings outlook.*[13]

Less than six months later, the company filed for the biggest bankruptcy in U.S. history. Its stock dropped to less than \$1 per share, and a major financial scandal was underway. Enron's statement of cash flows for the first nine months of 2001 and 2000 (restated to correct the previous accounting errors) follow. Assume you report to an investment analyst, who has asked you to analyze this statement for clues as to why the company went under.

Enron Corporation
Statement of Cash Flows
For the Nine Months Ended September 30, 2001 and 2000

(In millions)	**2001**	**2000**
Cash Flows from Operating Activities:		
Reconciliation of net income to net cash provided by operating activities:		
Net income	\$ 225	\$ 797
Cumulative effect of accounting changes, net of tax	(19)	—
Depreciation, depletion and amortization	746	617
Deferred income taxes	(134)	8
Gains on sales of non-trading assets	(49)	(135)
Investment losses	768	0
Changes in components of working capital:		
Receivables	987	(3,363)
Inventories	1	339
Payables	(1,764)	2,899
Other	464	(455)
Trading investments		
Net margin deposit activity	(2,349)	541
Other trading activities	173	(555)
Other, net	198	(566)
Net Cash Provided by (Used in) Operating Activities	\$ (753)	\$ 127

Cash Flows from Investing Activities:		
Capital expenditures	$(1,584)	$(1,539)
Equity investments	(1,172)	(858)
Proceeds from sales of non-trading investments	1,711	222
Acquisition of subsidiary stock	0	(485)
Business acquisitions, net of cash acquired	(82)	(773)
Other investing activities	(239)	(147)
Net Cash Used in Investing Activities	$(1,366)	$(3,580)
Cash Flows from Financing Activities:		
Issuance of long-term debt	$ 4,060	$ 2,725
Repayment of long-term debt	(3,903)	(579)
Net increase in short-term borrowings	2,365	1,694
Issuance of common stock	199	182
Net redemption of company-obligated preferred securities of subsidiaries	0	(95)
Dividends paid	(394)	(396)
Net (acquisition) disposition of treasury stock	(398)	354
Other financing activities	(49)	(12)
Net Cash Provided by Financing Activities	$ 1,880	$ 3,873
Increase (Decrease) in Cash and Cash Equivalents	$ (239)	$ 420
Cash and Cash Equivalents, Beginning of Period	1,240	333
Cash and Cash Equivalents, End of Period	$ 1,001	$ 753

1. **BUSINESS APPLICATION ▶** For the two time periods shown, compute the cash-generating efficiency ratios of cash flow yield, cash flows to sales (Enron's revenues were $133,762 million in 2001 and $55,494 million in 2000), and cash flows to assets (use total assets of $61,783 million for 2001 and $64,926 million for 2000). Also compute free cash flows for the two years. (Round to one decimal place or the nearest tenth of a percent.)
2. Prepare a memorandum to the investment analyst that assesses Enron's cash generating efficiency in light of the chairman's remarks and that evaluates its available free cash flow, taking into account its financing activities. Identify significant changes in Enron's operating items and any special operating items that should be considered. Include your computations as an attachment.

LO 5

Ethical Dilemma: Ethics and Cash Flow Classifications

C3. BUSINESS APPLICATION ▶ Precise Metals, Inc., a fast-growing company that makes metals for equipment manufacturers, has an $800,000 line of credit at its bank. One section in the credit agreement says that the ratio of cash flows from operations to interest expense must exceed 3.0. If this ratio falls below 3.0, the company must reduce the balance outstanding on its line of credit to one-half the total line if the funds borrowed against the line of credit exceed one-half of the total line.

After the end of the fiscal year, the company's controller informs the president: "We will not meet the ratio requirements on our line of credit in 2010 because interest expense was $1.2 million and cash flows from operations were $3.2 million. Also, we have borrowed 100 percent of our line of credit. We do not have the cash to reduce the credit line by $400,000."

The president says, "This is a serious situation. To pay our ongoing bills, we need our bank to increase our line of credit, not decrease it. What can we do?" "Do you recall the $500,000 two-year note payable for equipment?" replied the controller. "It is now classified as 'Proceeds from Notes Payable' in cash flows provided from financing activities in the statement of cash flows. If we move it to cash flows from operations and call it 'Increase in Payables,' it would increase cash flows from operations to $3.7 million and put us over the limit." "Well, do it," ordered the president. "It surely doesn't make any

(Continued)

difference where it is on the statement. It is an increase in both places. It would be much worse for our company in the long term if we failed to meet this ratio requirement."

What is your opinion of the controller and president's reasoning? Is the president's order ethical? Who benefits and who is harmed if the controller follows the president's order? What are management's alternatives? What would you do?

LO **1, 5**

Conceptual Understanding: Alternative Uses of Cash

C4. Perhaps because of hard times in their start-up years, companies in the high tech sector of American industry seem more prone than those in other sectors to building up cash reserves. For example, companies like **Cisco Systems**, **Intel**, **Dell**, and **Oracle** have amassed large cash balances.

Assume you work for a company in the high-tech industry that has built up a substantial amount of cash. The company is still growing through development of new products, has some debt, and has never paid a dividend or bought treasury stock. The company is doing better than most companies in the current financial crisis but the company's stock price is lagging. Outline at least four strategies for using the company's cash to improve the company's financial outlook.

LO **1**

Interpreting Financial Reports: Analysis of the Statement of Cash Flows

C5. Refer to the statement of cash flows in the **CVS Corporation** annual report in the Supplement to Chapter 1 to answer the following questions:

1. Does CVS use the indirect method of reporting cash flows from operating activities? Other than net earnings, what are the most important factors affecting the company's cash flows from operating activities? Explain the trend of each of these factors.
2. Based on the cash flows from investing activities, in 2010 and 2011, would you say that CVS is a contracting or an expanding company? Explain.
3. Has CVS used external financing during 2010 and 2011? If so, where did it come from?

LO **1, 5**

Interpreting Financial Reports: Cash Flows Analysis

SPREADSHEET

C6. BUSINESS APPLICATION ▶ Refer to the annual report of **CVS Corporation** and the financial statements of **Southwest Airlines** in the Supplement to Chapter 1. Calculate for 2011 and 2010 each company's cash flow yield, cash flows to sales, cash flows to assets, and free cash flow. (Round to one decimal place or to the nearest tenth of a percent.) At the end of 2009, Southwest's total assets were $14,269 million and CVS's total assets were $61,641 million.

Discuss and compare the trends of the cash-generating ability of CVS and Southwest. Comment on each company's change in cash and cash equivalents over the two-year period.

Continuing Case: Annual Report Project

C7. Using the most recent annual report of the company you have chosen to study and that you have accessed online at the company's website, examine the statement of cash flows and accompanying notes of your company. Answer the following questions:

1. Does the company use the direct or indirect method for computing cash flows from operating activities? What effect does depreciation have on cash flows? Have receivables, inventories, and payables had positive or negative effects on cash flows from operating activities?
2. What are the most important investing activities for the company in the most recent year?
3. What are the most important financing activities for the company in the most recent year?
4. **BUSINESS APPLICATION ▶** Calculate cash flow yield, cash flows to sales, cash flows to assets, and free cash flow for the most recent year.

SUPPLEMENT TO CHAPTER 13

The Direct Method of Preparing the Statement of Cash Flows

To this point, the indirect method of preparing the statement of cash flows has been used. In this section, the direct method is presented.

Determining Cash Flows from Operating Activities

The principal difference between the indirect and the direct methods appears in the cash flows from operating activities section of the statement of cash flows.

- The indirect method starts with net income from the income statement and converts it to net cash flows from operating activities by adding or subtracting items that do not affect net cash flows.
- The direct method converts each item on the income statement to its cash equivalent, as illustrated in Exhibit 1. For instance, sales are converted to cash receipts from sales and purchases are converted to cash payments for purchases.

Exhibit 1
Direct Method of Determining Net Cash Flows from Operating Activities

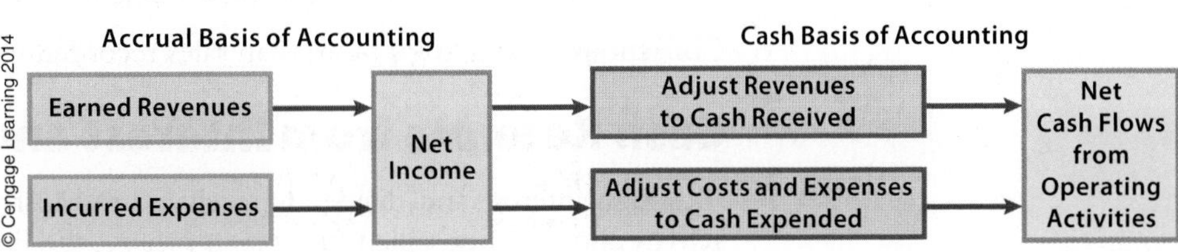

To illustrate how to determine cash flows from operating activities under the direct method, we will use Eureka Corporation. Eureka's schedule of cash flows from operating activities is presented in Exhibit 2.

Exhibit 2
Schedule of Cash Flows from Operating Activities: Direct Method

Eureka Corporation
Schedule of Cash Flows from Operating Activities
For the Year Ended December 31, 2014

Cash receipts from:		
Sales	$706,000	
Interest received	6,000	$712,000
Cash payments for:		
Purchases	$547,000	
Operating expenses	103,000	
Interest	23,000	
Income taxes	9,000	682,000
Net cash flows from operating activities		$ 30,000

Cash Receipts from Sales

Sales result in a positive cash flow for a company. Cash sales are direct cash inflows. Credit sales are not direct cash inflows because some receivables may be uncollectible. For example, you cannot assume that credit sales are automatically inflows of cash, because the collections of accounts receivable in any one accounting period are not likely to equal credit sales. Some receivables may be uncollectible, sales from a prior period may be collected in the current period, or sales from the current period may be collected in the next period.

- ▲ If accounts receivables *increase* from one accounting period to the next, cash receipts from sales will not be as great as sales.
- ▼ If accounts receivable *decrease* from one accounting period to the next, cash receipts from sales will exceed sales.

The relationships among sales, changes in the accounts receivable, and cash receipts from sales are reflected in the formula that follows.

$$\text{Sales} \begin{cases} + \text{Decrease in Accounts Receivable} \\ \text{or} \\ - \text{Increase in Accounts Receivable} \end{cases} = \text{Cash Receipts from Sales}$$

Refer to the balance sheets and the income statement for Eureka Corporation in Exhibits 4 and 5 in Chapter 13. Note that sales were $698,000 in 2014 and that accounts receivable decreased by $8,000. Thus, cash received from sales is $706,000:

$$\$698{,}000 + \$8{,}000 = \$706{,}000$$

Collections were $8,000 more than sales recorded for the year.

Cash Receipts from Interest and Dividends

Although interest and dividends received are most closely associated with investment activity and are often called *investment income*, the FASB *classifies* the cash received from these items as operating activities. To simplify the examples in this text, it is assumed that interest income equals interest received and that dividend income equals dividends received. Thus, based on Exhibit 4 in Chapter 13, interest received by Eureka Corporation is assumed to equal $6,000, which is the amount of interest income.

Cash Payments for Purchases

The cost of goods sold (from the income statement) must be adjusted for changes in two balance sheet accounts to arrive at cash payments for purchases. First, the cost of goods sold must be adjusted for changes in inventory to arrive at net purchases. Then, net purchases must be adjusted for the change in accounts payable to arrive at cash payments for purchases.

- ▲ If inventory has *increased* from one accounting period to another, net purchases will be greater than the cost of goods sold because net purchases during the period have exceeded the dollar amount of the items sold during the period.
- ▼ If inventory has *decreased*, net purchases will be less than the cost of goods sold.
- ▲ If accounts payable have *increased*, cash payments for purchases will be less than net purchases.
- ▼ If accounts payable have *decreased*, cash payments for purchases will be greater than net purchases.

These relationships may be stated in equation form as follows.

$$\text{Cost of Goods Sold} \begin{cases} + \text{Increase in Inventory} \\ \text{or} \\ - \text{Decrease in Inventory} \end{cases} \begin{cases} + \text{Decrease in Accounts Payable} \\ \text{or} \\ - \text{Increase in Accounts Payable} \end{cases} = \text{Cash Payments for Purchases}$$

From Exhibits 4 and 5 in Chapter 13, cost of goods sold is \$520,000, inventory increased by \$34,000, and accounts payable increased by \$7,000. Thus, cash payments for purchases for Eureka are computed as follows.

$$\$520{,}000 + \$34{,}000 - \$7{,}000 = \$547{,}000$$

Eureka purchased \$34,000 more inventory than it sold and paid out \$7,000 less in cash than it made in purchases. The net result is that cash payments for purchases exceeded the cost of goods sold by \$27,000 (\$547,000 – \$520,000).

Cash Payments for Operating Expenses

Just as the cost of goods sold does not represent the amount of cash paid for purchases during an accounting period, operating expenses do not match the amount of cash paid to employees, suppliers, and others for goods and services. Three adjustments must be made to operating expenses to arrive at the cash outflows. The first adjustment is for changes in prepaid expenses, such as prepaid insurance or prepaid rent.

- ▲ If prepaid assets *increase* during the accounting period, more cash will have been paid out than appears on the income statement as expenses.
- ▼ If prepaid assets *decrease*, the expenses shown on the income statement will exceed the cash spent.

The second adjustment is for changes in liabilities resulting from accrued expenses, such as wages payable and payroll taxes payable.

- ▲ If accrued liabilities *increase* during the accounting period, operating expenses on the income statement will exceed the cash spent.
- ▼ If accrued liabilities *decrease*, operating expenses will fall short of cash spent.

The third adjustment is made because certain expenses do not require a current outlay of cash; those expenses must be subtracted from operating expense to arrive at cash payments for operating expenses. The most common expenses in this category are depreciation expense, amortization expense, and depletion expense. For example, in 2014, Eureka recorded depreciation expense of \$37,000. No cash payment was made in this transaction. Therefore, to the extent that operating expenses include depreciation and similar items, an adjustment is needed to reduce operating expenses to the amount of cash expended.

The three adjustments to operating expenses are summarized in the equations that follow.

$$\text{Operating Expenses} \begin{cases} + \text{Increase in Prepaid Expenses} \\ \text{or} \\ - \text{Decrease in Prepaid Expenses} \end{cases} \begin{cases} + \text{Decrease in Accrued Liabilities} \\ \text{or} \\ - \text{Increase in Accrued Liabilities} \end{cases} \begin{cases} - \text{Depreciation and Other Noncash Expenses} \end{cases} = \text{Cash Payments for Operating Expenses}$$

According to Exhibits 4 and 5 in Chapter 13, Eureka's operating expenses (including depreciation of $37,000) were $147,000, prepaid expenses decreased by $4,000, and accrued liabilities increased by $3,000. As a result, Eureka's cash payments for operating expenses are computed as follows.

$$\$147{,}000 - \$4{,}000 - \$3{,}000 - \$37{,}000 = \$103{,}000$$

If there are prepaid expenses and accrued liabilities that are *not* related to specific operating expenses, they are not included in these computations. One example is income taxes payable, which is the accrued liability related to income taxes expense. The cash payment for income taxes will be discussed shortly.

Cash Payments for Interest

The FASB classifies cash payments for interest as operating activities. For the sake of simplicity, all examples in this text assume that interest payments are equal to interest expense on the income statement. Thus, based on Exhibit 4 in Chapter 13, Eureka's interest payments are assumed to be $23,000 in 2014.

Cash Payments for Income Taxes

The amount of income taxes expense that appears on the income statement rarely equals the amount of income taxes actually paid during the year. To determine cash payments for income taxes, income taxes are adjusted by the change in Income Taxes Payable.

- ▲ If Income Taxes Payable *increased* during the accounting period, cash payments for taxes will be less than the expense shown on the income statement.
- ▼ If Income Taxes Payable *decreased*, cash payments for taxes will exceed income taxes on the income statement.

In other words, the following equation is applicable:

$$\text{Income Taxes} \begin{cases} + \text{ Decrease in Income Taxes Payable} \\ \text{or} \\ - \text{ Increase in Income Taxes Payable} \end{cases} = \text{Cash Payments for Income Taxes}$$

In 2014, Eureka reported income taxes of $7,000 on its income statement and a decrease of $2,000 in Income Taxes Payable on its balance sheets (see Exhibits 4 and 5 in Chapter 13). As a result, cash payments for income taxes for Eureka during 2014 are calculated as follows.

$$\$7{,}000 + \$2{,}000 = \$9{,}000$$

Compiling the Statement of Cash Flows

Eureka's statement of cash flows under the direct method is presented in Exhibit 3. The only differences between that statement of cash flows and the one based on the indirect method shown in Exhibit 8 in Chapter 13 occur in the first and last sections. The middle sections, which present cash flows from investing activities and financing activities, net increases or decreases in cash, and the schedule of non-cash investing and financing activities, are the same under both methods.

The first section of the statement in Exhibit 3 shows the net cash flows from operating activities on a direct basis, as presented in Exhibit 2. The last section is the same as the cash flows from operating activities section of the statement of cash flows under the indirect method (see Exhibit 8 in Chapter 13). The FASB believes that when the direct method is used, a schedule must be provided that reconciles net income to net cash flows from operating activities. Thus, the statement of cash flows under the direct method includes a section that accommodates the main difference between it and the indirect method.

Exhibit 3
Statement of Cash Flows: Direct Method

Eureka Corporation
Statement of Cash Flows
For the Year Ended December 31, 2014

Cash flows from operating activities:		
Cash receipts from:		
Sales	$ 706,000	
Interest received	6,000	$712,000
Cash payments for:		
Purchases	$ 547,000	
Operating expenses	103,000	
Interest	23,000	
Income taxes	9,000	682,000
Net cash flows from operating activities		$ 30,000
Cash flows from investing activities:		
Purchase of investments	$ (78,000)	
Sale of investments	102,000	
Purchase of plant assets	(120,000)	
Sale of plant assets	5,000	
Net cash flows from investing activities		(91,000)
Cash flows from financing activities:		
Repayment of bonds	$ (50,000)	
Issue of common stock	150,000	
Dividends paid	(7,000)	
Net cash flows from financing activities		93,000
Net increase in cash		$ 32,000
Cash at beginning of year		15,000
Cash at end of year		$ 47,000

Schedule of Noncash Investing and Financing Transactions

Issue of bonds payable for plant assets		$100,000

Reconciliation of Net Income to Net Cash Flows from Operating Activities

Net income		$ 16,000
Adjustments to reconcile net income to net cash flows from operating activities:		
Depreciation	$ 37,000	
Gain on sale of investments	(12,000)	
Loss on sale of plant assets	3,000	
Changes in current assets and current liabilities:		
Decrease in accounts receivable	8,000	
Increase in inventory	(34,000)	
Decrease in prepaid expenses	4,000	
Increase in accounts payable	7,000	
Increase in accrued liabilities	3,000	
Decrease in income taxes payable	(2,000)	14,000
Net cash flows from operating activities		$ 30,000
Cash flows from investing activities:		
Purchase of investments	$ (78,000)	
Sale of investments	102,000	
Purchase of plant assets	(120,000)	
Sale of plant assets	5,000	
Net cash flows from investing activities		(91,000)
Cash flows from financing activities:		
Repayment of bonds	$ (50,000)	
Issuance of common stock	175,000	
Payment of dividends	(7,000)	
Purchase of treasury stock	(25,000)	
Net cash flows from financing activities		93,000
Net increase in cash		$ 32,000
Cash at beginning of year		15,000
Cash at end of year		$ 47,000

Assignments

SHORT EXERCISES

SE1. Cash Receipts from Sales and Cash Payments for Purchases: Direct Method

During 2014, Nebraska Wheat Company, a maker of whole-grain products, had sales of \$426,500. The ending balance of accounts receivable was \$127,400 in 2013 and \$96,200 in 2014. Also, during 2014, Nebraska Wheat had cost of goods sold of \$294,200. The ending balance of inventory was \$36,400 in 2013 and \$44,800 in 2014. The ending balance of accounts payable was \$28,100 in 2013 and \$25,900 in 2014. Using the direct method, calculate cash receipts from sales and cash payments for purchases in 2014.

SE2. Cash Payments for Operating Expenses and Income Taxes: Direct Method

During 2014, Nebraska Wheat Company had operating expenses of \$79,000 and income tax expense of \$12,500. Depreciation expense of \$20,000 for 2014 was included in operating expenses. The ending balance of prepaid expenses was \$3,600 in 2013 and \$2,300 in 2014. The ending balance of accrued liabilities (excluding income taxes payable) was \$3,000 in 2013 and \$2,000 in 2014. The ending balance of income taxes payable was \$4,100 in 2013 and \$3,500 in 2014. Calculate cash payments for operating expenses and income taxes in 2014 using the direct method.

EXERCISES

E1. Computing Cash Flows from Operating Activities: Direct Method

Vlieg Corporation engaged in the transactions that follow in 2014. Using the direct method, compute the various cash flows from operating activities as required.

a. During 2014, Vlieg had cash sales of \$41,300 and sales on credit of \$123,000. During the same year, accounts receivable decreased by \$18,000. Determine the cash receipts from sales during 2014.
b. During 2014, Vlieg's cost of goods sold was \$119,000. During the same year, merchandise inventory increased by \$12,500 and accounts payable decreased by \$4,300. Determine the cash payments for purchases during 2014.
c. During 2014, Vlieg had operating expenses of \$45,000, including depreciation of \$15,600. Also during 2014, related prepaid expenses decreased by \$3,100 and relevant accrued liabilities increased by \$1,200. Determine the cash payments for operating expenses to suppliers of goods and services during 2014.
d. Vlieg's income tax expense for 2014 was \$4,300. Income taxes payable decreased by \$230 that year. Determine the cash payments for income taxes during 2014.

E2. Preparing a Schedule of Cash Flows from Operating Activities: Direct Method

Vasquez Corporation's income statement follows.

Vasquez Corporation
Income Statement
For the Year Ended June 30, 2014

Sales		\$122,000
Cost of goods sold		60,000
Gross margin		\$ 62,000
Operating expenses:		
Salaries expense	\$32,000	
Rent expense	16,800	
Depreciation expense	2,000	50,800
Income before income taxes		\$ 11,200
Income taxes		2,400
Net income		\$ 8,800

Additional information: (a) Accounts receivable increased by $4,400 during the year; (b) inventories increased by $7,000, and accounts payable increased by $14,000 during the year; (c) prepaid rent decreased by $1,400, while salaries payable increased by $1,000; and (d) income taxes payable decreased by $600 during the year.

Using the direct method, prepare a schedule of cash flows from operating activities.

PROBLEMS

P1. Cash Flows from Operating Activities: Direct Method

✔ Total operating activities: $47,600 inflows

Tanucci Clothing Store's income statement follows.

Tanucci Clothing Store
Income Statement
For the Year Ended June 30, 2014

Net sales		$4,900,000
Cost of goods sold:		
Beginning inventory	$1,240,000	
Net cost of purchases	3,040,000	
Goods available for sale	$4,280,000	
Ending inventory	1,400,000	
Cost of goods sold		2,880,000
Gross margin		$2,020,000
Operating expenses:		
Sales and administrative salaries expense	$1,112,000	
Other sales and administrative expenses	624,000	
Total operating expenses		1,736,000
Income before income taxes		$ 284,000
Income taxes		78,000
Net income		$ 206,000

Additional information: (a) other sales and administrative expenses include depreciation expense of $104,000 and amortization expense of $36,000; (b) accrued liabilities for salaries were $24,000 less than the previous year, and prepaid expenses were $40,000 more than the previous year; and (c) during the year accounts receivable (net) increased by $288,000, accounts payable increased by $228,000, and income taxes payable decreased by $14,400.

REQUIRED

Using the direct method, prepare a schedule of cash flows from operating activities.

P2. Statement of Cash Flows: Direct Method

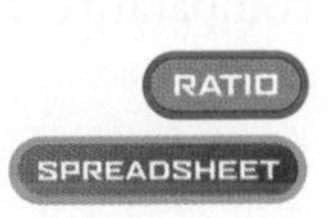

✔ 1: Total operating activities: $548,000 inflows
✔ 1: Total financing activities: $260,000 outflows

Flanders Corporation's 2014 income statement and comparative balance sheet as of June 30, 2014 and 2013 follow.

Flanders Corporation
Income Statement
For the Year Ended June 30, 2014

Sales		$2,081,800
Cost of goods sold		1,312,600
Gross margin		$ 769,200
Operating expenses (including depreciation expense of $120,000)		378,400
Income from operations		$ 390,800
Other income (expenses):		
Loss on disposal of equipment	$ 8,000	
Interest expense	75,200	83,200
Income before income taxes		$ 307,600
Income taxes		68,400
Net income		$ 239,200

(Continued)

Flanders Corporation
Comparative Balance Sheets
For Years Ended June 30, 2014 and 2013

	2014	2013
Assets		
Cash	$ 334,000	$ 40,000
Accounts receivable (net)	200,000	240,000
Inventory	360,000	440,000
Prepaid expenses	1,200	2,000
Property, plant, and equipment	1,256,000	1,104,000
Accumulated depreciation—property, plant, and equipment	(366,000)	(280,000)
Total assets	$1,785,200	$1,546,000
Liabilities and Stockholders' Equity		
Accounts payable	$ 128,000	$ 84,000
Notes payable (due in 90 days)	60,000	160,000
Income taxes payable	52,000	36,000
Mortgage payable	720,000	560,000
Common stock, $5 par value	400,000	400,000
Retained earnings	425,200	306,000
Total liabilities and stockholders' equity	$ 1,785,200	$1,546,000

The following is additional information about 2014: (a) equipment that cost $48,000 with accumulated depreciation of $34,000 was sold at a loss of $8,000; (b) land and building were purchased in the amount of $200,000 through an increase of $200,000 in the mortgage payable; (c) a $40,000 payment was made on the mortgage; (d) the notes were repaid, but the company borrowed an additional $60,000 through the issuance of a new note payable; and (e) a $120,000 cash dividend was declared and paid.

REQUIRED

1. Use the direct method to prepare a statement of cash flows. Include a supporting schedule of noncash investing and financing transactions. Do not include a reconciliation of net income to net cash flows from operating activities.
2. What are the primary reasons for Flanders' large increase in cash from 2013 to 2014?
3. Compute and assess cash flow yield and free cash flow for 2014. (Round to one decimal place.)

P3. Statement of Cash Flows: Direct Method

RATIO
SPREADSHEET

Saudade Corporation's 2014 income statement and comparative balance sheet as of June 30, 2014 and 2013 follow.

✔ 1: Total operating activities: $638,400 inflows
✔ 1: Total financing activities: $303,000 outflows

Saudade Corporation
Income Statement
For the Year Ended June 30, 2014

Sales		$2,252,700
Cost of goods sold		1,451,200
Gross margin		$ 801,500
Operating expenses (including depreciation expense of $140,000)		397,300
Income from operations		$ 404,200
Other income (expenses):		
Loss on disposal of equipment	$ 7,500	
Interest expense	74,800	82,300
Income before income taxes		$ 321,900
Income taxes		69,200
Net income		$ 252,700

Saudade Corporation
Comparative Balance Sheets
For Years Ended June 30, 2014 and 2013

	2014	2013
Assets		
Cash	$ 393,900	$ 50,000
Accounts receivable (net)	180,000	250,000
Inventory	330,000	420,000
Prepaid expenses	1,400	2,300
Property, plant, and equipment	1,365,000	1,213,000
Accumulated depreciation—property, plant, and equipment	(404,000)	(297,000)
Total assets	$1,866,300	$1,638,300
Liabilities and Stockholders' Equity		
Accounts payable	$ 148,000	$ 85,000
Notes payable (due in 90 days)	75,000	150,000
Income taxes payable	53,300	39,000
Mortgage payable	740,000	587,000
Common stock, $5 par value	415,000	415,000
Retained earnings	435,000	362,300
Total liabilities and stockholders' equity	$1,866,300	$1,638,300

The following is additional information about 2014: (a) equipment that cost $49,000 with accumulated depreciation of $33,000 was sold at a loss of $7,500; (b) land and building were purchased in the amount of $201,000 through an increase of $201,000 in the mortgage payable; (c) a $48,000 payment was made on the mortgage; (d) the notes were repaid, but the company borrowed an additional $75,000 through the issuance of a new note payable; and (e) a $180,000 cash dividend was declared and paid.

REQUIRED

1. Use the direct method to prepare a statement of cash flows. Include a supporting schedule of noncash investing and financing transactions. Do not include a reconciliation of net income to net cash flows from operating activities.
2. What are the primary reasons for Saudade's large increase in cash from 2013 to 2014?
3. Compute and assess cash flow yield and free cash flow for 2014. (Round to one decimal place.)

CHAPTER 14

LEARNING OBJECTIVES

LO 1 Describe the concepts, standards of comparison, and sources of information used in measuring financial performance.

LO 2 Apply horizontal analysis, trend analysis, vertical analysis, and ratio analysis to financial statements.

LO 3 Apply financial ratio analysis in a comprehensive evaluation of a company's financial performance.

LO 4 Define *quality of earnings*, and identify the factors that affect quality of earnings and related management compensation issues.

AP Photo/Ted S. Warren

FINANCIAL STATEMENT ANALYSIS

Business Insight
Starbucks Corporation

Formed in 1985, **Starbucks** is today a well-known specialty retailer. The company purchases, roasts, and sells whole coffee beans, along with a variety of freshly brewed coffees and other beverages and food items. It also produces and sells bottled coffee drinks and a line of premium ice creams.

Like many other companies, Starbucks uses financial performance measures, primarily earnings per share, in determining compensation for top management. Earnings per share and the six financial measures used in computing the most critical financial ratios appear in the company's Financial Highlights.[1] By linking compensation to financial performance, Starbucks provides its executives with incentive to improve the company's performance. Compensation and financial performance are thus linked to increasing shareholders' value.

STARBUCKS' FINANCIAL HIGHLIGHTS
(in millions, except earnings per share)

	2011	2010	2009
Net revenues	$11,700.4	$10,383.0	$9,774.6
Net earnings	1,245.7	948.3	390.8
Total assets	7,360.4	6,385.9	5,576.8
Total liabilities	2,973.1	2,703.6	2,531.1
Total equity	4,387.3	3,674.7	3,045.7
Cash flows from operating activities	1,612.4	1,704.9	1,389.0
Earnings per share—basic	$ 1.66	$ 1.27	$ 0.53

***1.* CONCEPT** ▶ *What concepts underlie the standards that Starbucks can use to evaluate performance?*

***2.* ACCOUNTING APPLICATION** ▶ *What analytical tools can Starbucks use to measure financial performance?*

***3.* BUSINESS APPLICATION** ▶ *In what ways would having access to prior years' information aid this analysis? Why is earnings management important in your assessment?*

SECTION 1 CONCEPTS

CONCEPTS
- Relevance
- Predictive value
- Comparability
- Timeliness

RELEVANT LEARNING OBJECTIVE

LO1 Describe the concepts, standards of comparison, and sources of information used in measuring financial performance.

LO1 Concepts Underlying Financial Performance Measurement

Financial statement analysis (or *financial performance measurement*) is used to show how items in a company's financial statements relate to the company's financial performance objectives. Users of accounting information interested in measuring a company's financial performance fall into two groups:

- A company's top managers, who set and strive to achieve financial performance objectives; middle-level managers of business processes; and lower-level employees who own stock in the company
- Creditors and investors, as well as customers who have cooperative agreements with the company

Both these groups of users want measures of financial performance that meet these underlying concepts:

- **Relevance:** The measures need to make a difference in the analysis of a company's performance.
- **Predictive value:** The users want measures that will help them make decisions about future actions.
- **Comparability:** The users want measures that make useful comparison of one period of the company's performance with another and of the company's performance to other companies.
- **Timeliness:** The users want measures that enable them to make decisions made in time to have the desired effects.

In the analysis of accounting information, managers, creditors, and investors want measures that relate to the following objectives:

- **Profitability:** To continue operating, a company must earn a satisfactory net income. Management is responsible for monitoring and measuring net income, determining the causes of any deviations from financial performance plans, and correcting the deviations. Creditors and investors look at a company's past and present net income to identify trends and to judge potential earnings ability.
- **Total Asset Management:** A company uses its assets to generate revenues. These assets are part of the cost of operating a business. To maximize net income, management must use all of the company's assets in a way that maximizes revenues while minimizing the investment in these assets.
- **Liquidity:** A company must be able to pay its bills when they come due and meet unexpected needs for cash. Management must use cash, like other assets, to fund operations that generate maximum revenues. Creditors focus on liquidity because they expect to be paid what they are owed at the appropriate time.
- **Financial Risk:** Management must use debt and stockholders' investments effectively without jeopardizing the company's future. Creditors and stockholders judge the risk involved in making a loan or an investment by looking at a company's past performance and current position. The more difficult it is to predict future profitability and liquidity, the greater the risk.
- **Operating Asset Management:** Managing operating assets is much like managing total assets. Managers must use current assets and current liabilities in a way that supports revenue growth and minimizes investment.

Standards of Comparison

When analyzing financial statements, decision makers must judge whether the relationships they find in the statements are favorable or unfavorable. Three standards of comparison that they commonly use are rule-of-thumb measures, a company's past performance, and industry norms.

Rule-of-Thumb Measures Many financial analysts, investors, and lenders apply general standards, or *rule-of-thumb measures*, to key financial ratios. For example, the credit-rating firm of **Dun & Bradstreet** offers the following rules of thumb:

- **Current Ratio:** The higher the ratio, the more likely the company will be able to meet its liabilities. A ratio of 2 to 1 (2.0) or higher is desirable.
- **Current Liabilities to Net Worth Ratio (%):** Normally a business starts to have trouble when this relationship exceeds 80%.[2]

Past Performance Comparing financial measures or ratios of the same company over time is an improvement over using rule-of-thumb measures. Such a comparison gives the analyst some basis for judging whether the measure or ratio is getting better or worse. Thus, it may be helpful in showing future trends. However, such projections must be made with care. Trends reverse over time, and a company's needs may change. For example, even if a company improves its return on investment from 3 percent in one year to 4 percent the next year, the 4 percent return may not be adequate for the company's current needs. In addition, using a company's past performance as a standard of comparison is not helpful in judging its performance relative to that of other companies.

Industry Norms Using industry norms as a standard of comparison overcomes some of the limitations of comparing a company's measures over time. Industry norms show how a company compares with other companies in the same industry. For example, if companies in a particular industry have an average rate of return on investment of 8 percent, a 3 or 4 percent rate of return is probably not adequate. Using industry norms as standards has the following limitations:

- **Comparability:** Companies in the same industry may not be strictly comparable. For example, one company in the oil industry purchases oil products and markets them through service stations. The other, an international company, discovers, produces, refines, and markets its own oil products. Because of the disparity in their operations, these two companies cannot be directly compared.
- **Accounting differences:** Companies in the same industry with similar operations may not use the same accounting procedures. For example, they may use different methods of valuing inventories and of depreciating assets.
- **Diversity: Diversified companies** (or *conglomerates*) are large companies that have multiple segments and operate in more than one industry. They may not be comparable to any other company.

International Perspective

IFRS **The Use and Evaluation of Performance Measures Must Change When Using IFRS**

Financial statement users must carefully consider evaluations and comparisons of historical performance under IFRS for a variety of reasons. When a company switches from U.S. GAAP to IFRS, prior years' performance measures will not likely be comparable. In fact, 80 percent of companies surveyed in a research study of European companies reported higher net income for the same operations under IFRS than under U.S. GAAP. When this occurs, an IFRS profit margin will likely provide a more optimistic evaluation when compared with pre-IFRS results or with a U.S. GAAP- based competitor. Further, the definitions of assets, liabilities, and equity differ under IFRS. The combined effect is that debt to equity, return on equity, and return on assets ratios may not exhibit historical trends. Contracts and management compensation based on these IFRS measures also require a closer look.

STUDY NOTE: Each segment of a diversified company represents an investment that the home office or parent company evaluates and reviews frequently.

The FASB provides a partial solution to the limitation posed by diversified companies. It requires a diversified company to report profit or loss, certain revenue and expense items, and assets for each of its segments. Segment information may be reported for operations in different industries or different geographical areas or for major customers.[3] Exhibit 1 shows how **Goodyear Tire & Rubber Company** reports data on sales, income, and assets for its tire products segments. These data allow the analyst to compute measures of profitability, such as profit margin, asset turnover, and return on assets, for each segment and to compare them with industry norms.

Exhibit 1
Selected Segment Information for Goodyear Tire & Rubber Company

(In millions)	2011	2010	2009
Sales:			
North American Tire	$ 9,859	$ 8,205	$ 6,977
Europe, Middle East and Africa Tire	8,040	6,407	5,801
Latin American Tire	2,472	2,158	1,814
Asia Pacific Tire	2,396	2,062	1,709
Net Sales	**$22,767**	**$18,832**	**$16,301**
Segment Operating Income:			
North American Tire	$ 276	$ 18	$ (305)
Europe, Middle East and Africa Tire	627	319	166
Latin American Tire	231	330	301
Asia Pacific Tire	234	250	210
Total Segment Operating Income	**$ 1,368**	**$ 917**	**$ 372**
Assets:			
North American Tire	$ 5,744	$ 5,243	$ 4,836
Europe, Middle East and Africa Tire	5,915	5,266	5,144
Latin American Tire	2,141	1,809	1,672
Asia Pacific Tire	2,482	2,150	1,548
Total Segment Assets	**$16,282**	**$14,468**	**$13,200**
Corporate	1,347	1,162	1,210
Total Assets	**$17,629**	**$15,630**	**$14,410**

Source: Goodyear Tire & Rubber Company, Form 10-K, For the Fiscal Year Ended December 31, 2011 (adapted).

Despite these limitations, if little information about a company's past performance is available, industry norms probably offer the best available standards for judging current performance—as long as they are used with care.

Sources of Information

The major sources of information about public corporations follow.

- **Reports published by a corporation**: A public corporation's annual report is an important source of financial information. Most public corporations also publish **interim financial statements** each quarter and sometimes each month. These reports, which present limited information in the form of condensed financial statements, are not subject to a full audit by an independent auditor. The financial community watches interim statements closely for early signs of change in a company's earnings trend.
- **Reports filed with the Securities and Exchange Commission (SEC):** Public corporations in the United States must file annual reports (**Form 10-K**), quarterly reports (**Form 10-Q**), and current reports (**Form 8-K**) with the SEC. If they have more than $10 million in assets and more than 500 shareholders, they must file these reports electronically at http://www.sec.gov/edgar/searchedgar/webusers.htm, where anyone can access them free of charge.

STUDY NOTE: *Publishers often redefine the content of the ratios that companies provide. While the general content is similar, variations occur. Be sure to ascertain and evaluate the information that a published source uses to calculate ratios.*

- **Business periodicals and credit and investment advisory services:** Financial analysts must keep up with current events in the financial world. One leading source of financial news is *The Wall Street Journal.* It is the most complete financial newspaper in the United States and is published every business day. Credit and investment advisory services such as **Moody's Investors Service**, **Standard & Poor's**, and **Dun and Bradstreet** provide useful information, including details about a company's financial history, industry data, and credit ratings.

APPLY IT!

Identify each of the following as (a) an underlying concept, (b) an objective of financial statement analysis, (c) a standard for financial statement analysis, or (d) a source of information for financial statement analysis:

1. A company's past performance
2. Investment advisory services
3. Assessment of a company's future potential
4. Relevance
5. Industry norms
6. Annual report
7. Form 10-K
8. Timeliness

SOLUTION

1. c; 2. d; 3. b; 4. a; 5. c; 6. d; 7. d; 8. a

TRY IT! SE1, SE2, E1A, E1B

SECTION 2 ACCOUNTING APPLICATIONS

ACCOUNTING APPLICATIONS

- Analyzing financial statements
  - Horizontal analysis
  - Trend analysis
  - Vertical analysis
  - Ratio analysis
- Evaluating profitability and total asset management
  - Profit margin
  - Asset turnover
  - Return on assets
- Evaluating liquidity
  - Cash flow yield
  - Cash flows to sales
  - Cash flows to assets
  - Free cash flow
- Evaluating financial risk
  - Debt to equity ratio
  - Return on equity
  - Interest coverage ratio
- Evaluating operating asset management
  - Inventory turnover
  - Days' inventory on hand
  - Receivable turnover
  - Days' sales uncollected
  - Payables turnover
  - Days' payable
  - Financing period
  - Current ratio
  - Quick ratio
- Evaluating market strength
  - Price/earnings (P/E)
  - Dividend yield

RELEVANT LEARNING OBJECTIVES

LO 2 Apply horizontal analysis, trend analysis, vertical analysis, and ratio analysis to financial statements.

LO 3 Apply financial ratio analysis in a comprehensive evaluation of a company's financial performance.

LO 2 Tools and Techniques of Financial Analysis

To gain insight into a company's financial performance, one must look beyond the individual numbers to the relationship between the numbers and their change from one period to another. The tools of financial analysis—horizontal analysis, trend analysis, vertical analysis, and ratio analysis—are intended to show these relationships and changes.

Horizontal Analysis

Comparative financial statements provide financial information for the current year and the previous year. To gain insight into year-to-year changes, analysts use **horizontal analysis**, in which changes from the previous year to the current year are computed in both dollar amounts and percentages. The percentage change relates the size of the change to the size of the dollar amounts involved. Note that it is important to ascertain the base amount used when a percentage describes an item. For example, inventory may be 50 percent of total current assets but only 10 percent of total assets.

Exhibits 2 and 3 present **Starbucks Corporation**'s comparative balance sheets and income statements and show both the dollar and percentage changes.

The percentage change is computed as follows.

$$\text{Percentage Change} = 100 \times \frac{\text{Comparative Year Amount} - \text{Base Year Amount}}{\text{Base Year Amount}}$$

The **base year** is the first year considered in any set of data. For example, when comparing data for 2010 and 2011, 2010 is the base year. As the balance sheets in Exhibit 2 show, between 2010 and 2011, Starbucks' total current assets increased by \$1,038.5 million, from \$2,756.4 million to \$3,794.9 million, or by 37.7 percent, computed as follows.

$$\text{Percentage Change} = 100 \times \frac{\$1{,}038.5 \text{ million}}{\$2{,}756.4 \text{ million}} = 37.7\%$$

When examining such changes, it is important to consider the dollar amount of the change as well as the percentage change in each component. For example, the difference between the percentage increase in accounts receivable, net (27.7 percent) and total current assets (37.7 percent) is 10 percent. However, the dollar increase in total current assets is more than twelve times the dollar increase in accounts receivable (\$1,038.5 million versus \$83.8 million). Thus, even though the percentage changes differ by 10 percent, current assets require much more cash than accounts receivable.

Starbucks' balance sheets for 2010 and 2011 also show the following:

▲ Total assets *increased* by \$974.5 million, or 15.3 percent.

▲ Shareholders' equity *increased* by \$710.2 million, or 19.3 percent.

Starbucks' income statements in Exhibit 3 show the following:

▲ Net revenues *increased* by \$993.0 million, or 9.3 percent.

▲ Gross margin *increased* by \$502.3 million, or 8.0 percent.

This indicates that the cost of sales grew faster than net revenues. In fact, the cost of sales increased 11.0 percent compared with the 9.3 percent increase in net revenues.

In addition,

▲ Total operating expenses *increased* by $249 million, or 5.0 percent, which is lower than the 9.3 percent increase in net revenues.

▲ Operating income *increased* by $309.1 million, or 21.8 percent.

▲ Net income *increased* by $299.7 million, or 31.6 percent.

Exhibit 2
Comparative Balance Sheets with Horizontal Analysis

Starbucks Corporation
Consolidated Balance Sheets
For the Years Ended October 2, 2011 and October 3, 2010

			Increase (Decrease)	
(Dollar amounts in millions)	**2011**	**2010**	**Amount***	**Percentage***
	Assets			
Current assets:				
Cash and cash equivalents	$1,148.1	$1,164.0	$(15.9)	(1.4)
Short-term investments—available-for-sale securities	855.0	236.5	618.5	261.5
Short-term investments—trading securities	47.6	49.2	(1.6)	(3.3)
Accounts receivable, net	386.5	302.7	83.8	27.7
Inventories	965.8	543.3	422.5	77.8
Prepaid and other current assets	161.5	156.5	5.0	3.2
Deferred income taxes, net	230.4	304.2	(73.8)	(24.3)
Total current assets	$3,794.9	$2,756.4	$1,038.5	37.7
Long-term investments - available-for-sale securities	107.0	191.8	(84.8)	(44.2)
Equity and cost investments	372.3	341.5	30.8	9.0
Property, plant, and equipment, net	2,355.0	2,416.5	(61.5)	(2.5)
Other assets	297.7	346.5	(48.8)	(14.1)
Other intangible assets	111.9	70.8	41.1	58.1
Goodwill	321.6	262.4	59.2	22.6
Total assets	$7,360.4	$6,385.9	$ 974.5	15.3
	Liabilities and Shareholders' Equity			
Current liabilities:				
Accounts payable	540.0	282.6	257.4	91.1
Accrued compensation and related costs	364.4	400.0	(35.6)	(8.9)
Accrued occupancy costs	148.3	173.2	(24.9)	(14.4)
Accrued taxes	109.2	100.2	9.0	9.0
Insurance reserves	145.6	146.2	(0.6)	(0.4)
Other accrued liabilities	319.0	262.8	56.2	21.4
Deferred revenue	449.3	414.1	35.2	8.5
Total current liabilities	$2,075.8	$1,779.1	$ 296.7	16.7
Long-term debt	549.5	549.4	0.1	0.0
Other long-term liabilities	347.8	375.1	(27.3)	(7.3)
Total liabilities	2,973.1	2,703.6	269.5	10.0
Total shareholders' equity	4,384.9	3,674.7	710.2	19.3
Noncontrolling interests	2.4	7.6	(5.2)	(68.4)
Total equity	4,387.3	3,682.3	705.0	19.1
Total liabilities and shareholders' equity	$7,360.4	$6,385.9	$ 974.5	15.3

*Rounded
Source: Data from Starbucks Corporation, Form 10-K, For the Fiscal Year Ended October 2, 2011.

Exhibit 3
Comparative Income Statements with Horizontal Analysis

Starbucks Corporation
Consolidated Income Statements
For the Years Ended October 2, 2011 and October 3, 2010

(Dollar amounts in millions except per share amounts)	2011	2010	Increase (Decrease) Amount*	Increase (Decrease) Percentage*
Net revenues	$11,700.4	$10,707.4	$993.0	9.3
Cost of sales, including occupancy costs	4,949.3	4,458.6	490.7	11.0
Gross margin	$ 6,751.1	$ 6,248.8	$502.3	8.0
Operating expenses				
Store operating expenses	$ 3,665.1	$ 3,551.4	$113.7	3.2
Other operating expenses	402.0	293.2	108.8	37.1
Depreciation and amortization expenses	523.3	510.4	12.9	2.5
General and administrative expenses	636.1	569.5	66.6	11.7
Restructuring charges	—	53.0	(53.0)	(100.0)
Total operating expenses	$ 5,226.5	$ 4,977.5	$249.0	5.0
Gain on sale of properties	30.2	—	30.2	—
Income from equity investees	173.7	148.1	25.6	17.3
Operating income	$ 1,728.5	$ 1,419.4	$309.1	21.8
Interest income and other, net	115.9	50.3	65.6	130.4
Interest expense	(33.3)	(32.7)	(0.6)	1.8
Income before taxes	$ 1,811.1	$ 1,437.0	$374.1	26.0
Income taxes	563.1	488.7	74.4	15.2
Net income	$ 1,248.0	$ 948.3	$299.7	31.6

*Rounded
Source: Data from Starbucks Corporation, Form 10-K, For the Fiscal Year Ended October 2, 2011.

The primary reason for the increases in operating income and net income is that operating expenses increased at a slower rate (5.0 percent) than net revenues (9.3 percent).

Trend Analysis

STUDY NOTE: *To reflect the general five-year economic cycle of the U.S. economy, trend analysis usually covers a five-year period.*

Trend analysis is a variation of horizontal analysis. With this tool, the analyst calculates percentage changes for several successive years instead of for just two years. Because of its long-term view, trend analysis can highlight basic changes in the nature of a business.

Exhibit 4 shows a trend analysis of **Starbucks'** five-year summary of net revenues and operating income.

Trend analysis uses an **index number** to show changes in related items over time. For an index number, the base year is set at 100 percent. Other years are measured in relation to that amount. For example, the 2011 index for Starbucks' net revenues is figured as follows (dollar amounts are in millions).

Exhibit 4
Trend Analysis

Starbucks Corporation
Net Revenues and Operating Income
Trend Analysis

	2011	2010	2009	2008	2007
Dollar values (In millions)					
Net revenues	$11,700.4	$10,707.4	$9,774.6	$10,383.0	$9,411.5
Operating income	1,728.5	1,419.4	562.0	390.3	945.9
Trend analysis (In percentages)					
Net revenues	124.3	113.8	103.9	110.3	100.0
Operating income	182.7	150.1	59.4	41.3	100.0

Source: Data from Starbucks Corporation, Form 10-K, For the Fiscal Year Ended October 2, 2011.

$$\text{Index} = 100 \times \frac{\$11{,}700.4}{\$9{,}411.5} = 124.3\%$$

The trend analysis in Exhibit 4 shows the following:

▲ Net revenues *increased* over the five-year period.

▲ Overall, revenue *increased* 24.3 percent.

Net revenues grew faster than operating income in 2008 and 2009; however, operating income grew faster than net revenues in 2010 and 2011. Exhibit 5 illustrates these trends.

Exhibit 5
Graph of Trend Analysis Shown in Exhibit 4

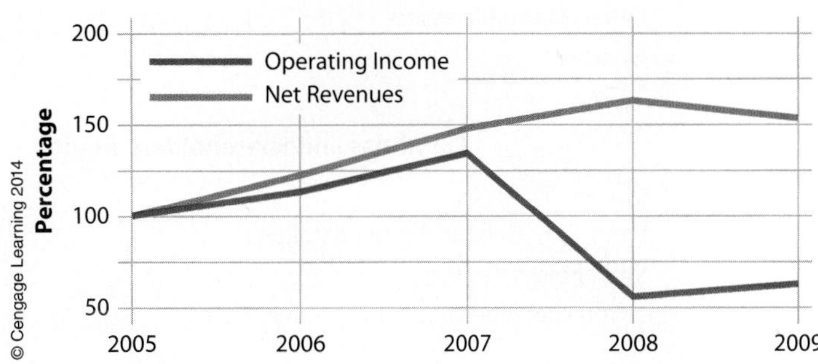

Vertical Analysis

Vertical analysis shows how the different components of a financial statement relate to a total figure in the statement. On the balance sheet, the figure would be total assets or total liabilities and stockholders' equity, and on the income statement, it would be net revenues or net sales. The analyst sets the total figure at 100 percent and computes each component's percentage of that total. The resulting financial statement, which is expressed entirely in percentages, is called a **common-size statement**. Common-size balance sheets and common-size income statements for **Starbucks** are shown in pie-chart form in Exhibits 6 and 8 and in financial statement form in Exhibits 7 and 9.

Exhibit 6
Common-Size Balance Sheets Presented Graphically

2011* **2010**

Assets = 100% **Liabilities and Shareholders' Equity = 100%**

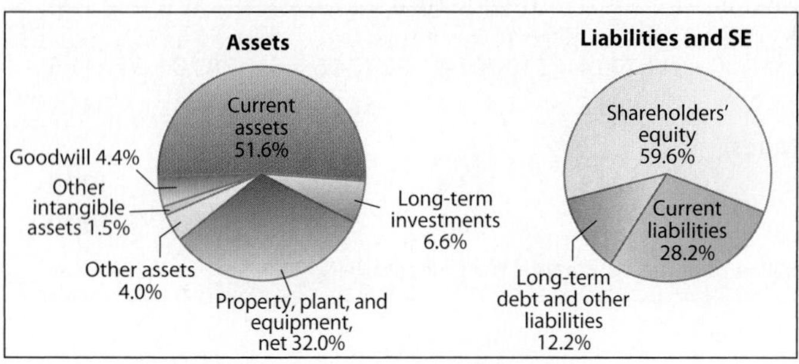

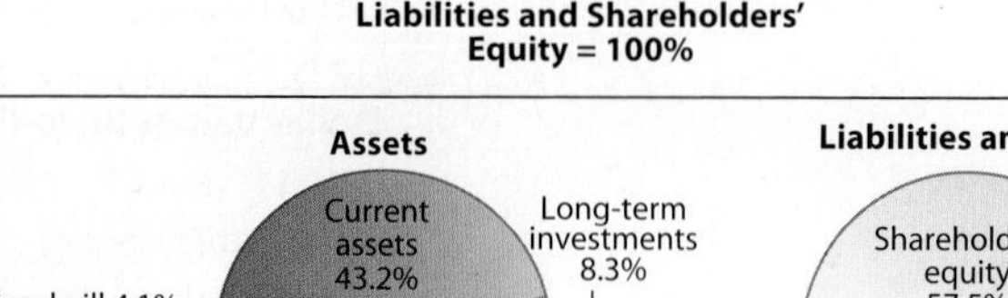

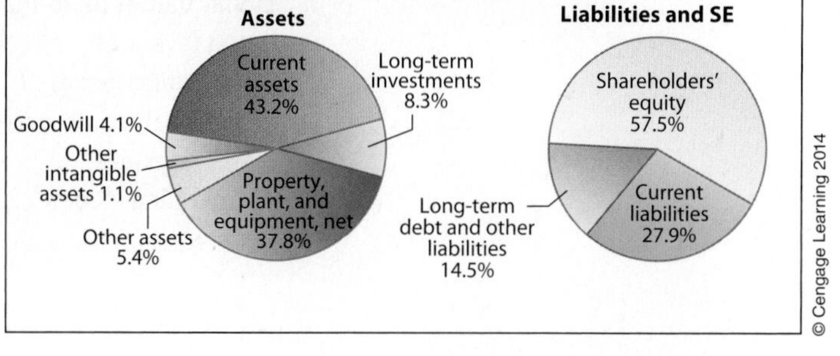

**Rounding causes some additions not to total precisely.*

Exhibit 7
Common-Size Balance Sheets

Starbucks Corporation
Common-Size Balance Sheets
October 2, 2011, and October 3, 2010

	2011	2010
Assets		
Current assets	51.6%	43.2%
Long-term investments	6.6	8.3
Property, plant, and equipment, net	32.0	37.8
Other assets	4.0	5.4
Other intangible assets	1.5	1.1
Goodwill	4.4	4.1
Total assets	100.0%	100.0%
Liabilities and Shareholders' Equity		
Current liabilities	28.2%	27.9%
Long-term debt and other liabilities	12.2	14.5
Shareholders' equity	59.6	57.5
Total liabilities and shareholders' equity	100.0%	100.0%

Note: Amounts do not precisely total 100 percent in all cases due to rounding.
Source: Data from Starbucks Corporation, Form 10-K, For the Fiscal Year Ended October 2, 2011.

Vertical analysis and common-size statements are useful in comparing the importance of specific components in the operation of a business and in identifying important changes in the components from one year to the next. The main conclusions to be drawn from our analysis of Starbucks are the following:

- Starbucks' assets consist largely of current assets and property, plant, and equipment.
- Starbucks finances assets primarily through equity and current liabilities.
- Starbucks has few long-term liabilities.

Looking at the pie charts in Exhibit 6 and the common-size balance sheets in Exhibit 7, you can see the following:

- The composition of Starbucks' assets shifted from property, plant, and equipment (declined from 37.8% to 32.0%), long-term investments (from 8.3% to 6.6%), and other assets (from 5.4% to 4.0%) to current assets (from 43.2% to 51.6%).

- The proportion of long-term debt and other liabilities decreased (from 14.5% to 12.2%) while current liabilities increased (from 27.9% to 28.2%) and shareholders' equity increased (from 57.5% to 59.6%).

The common-size income statements in Exhibit 9, illustrated as pie charts in Exhibit 8, show that Starbucks decreased its operating expenses from 2010 to 2011 by 1.9 percent of revenues (46.5% vs. 44.6%). In other words, revenues grew faster than operating expenses.

Exhibit 8
Common-Size Income Statements Presented Graphically

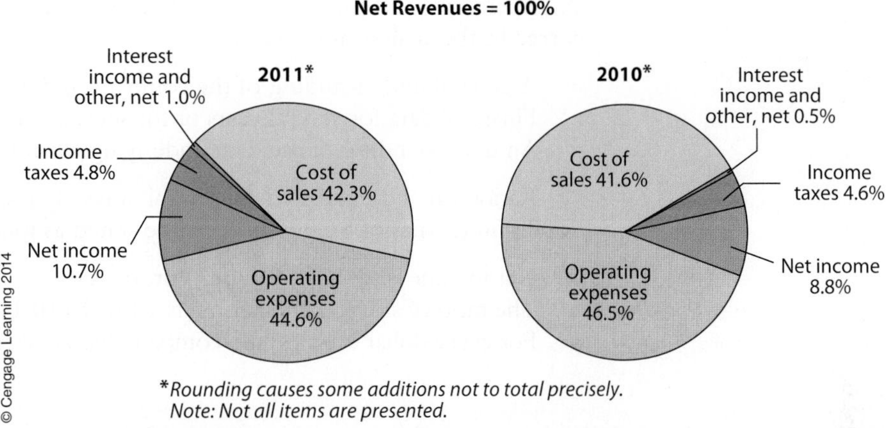

*Rounding causes some additions not to total precisely.
Note: Not all items are presented.

Exhibit 9
Common-Size Income Statements

Starbucks Corporation
Common-Size Income Statements
For the Years Ended October 2, 2011, and October 3, 2010

	2011	2010
Net revenues	100.0%	100.0%
Cost of sales, including occupancy costs	42.3	41.6
Gross margin	57.7%	58.4%
Operating expenses:		
Store operating expenses	31.3%	33.2%
Other operating expenses	3.4	2.7
Depreciation and amortization expenses	4.5	4.8
General and administrative expenses	5.4	5.3
Restructuring charges	—	0.5
Total operating expenses	44.6%	46.5%
Gain on sales of properties	0.3%	—%
Income from equity investees	1.5	1.4
Operating income	14.9%	13.3%
Interest income and other, net	1.0	0.5
Interest expense	(0.3)	(0.3)
Income before taxes	15.5%	13.4%
Income taxes	4.8	4.6
Net income	10.7%	8.9%

Note: Amounts do not precisely total 100 percent in all cases due to rounding.
Source: Data from Starbucks Corporation, Form 10-K, For the Fiscal Year Ended October 2, 2011.

Common-size statements are often used to make comparisons between companies. They allow an analyst to compare the operating and financing characteristics of two companies of different size in the same industry. For example, the analyst might want to compare Starbucks with other specialty retailers in terms of percentage of total assets financed by debt or in terms of operating expenses as a percentage of net revenues. Common-size statements would show those and other relationships. These statements can also be used to compare the characteristics of companies that report in different currencies.

Financial Ratio Analysis

Financial ratio analysis identifies key relationships between the components of the financial statements. Ratios are useful tools for evaluating a company's financial position and operations and may reveal areas that need further investigation. To interpret ratios correctly, the analyst must have:

- A general understanding of the company and its environment
- Financial data for several years or for several companies
- An understanding of the data underlying the numerator and denominator

Ratios can be expressed in several ways. For example, a ratio of net income of $100,000 to sales of $1,000,000 can be stated as follows.

- Net income is 1/10, or 10 percent, of sales.
- The ratio of sales to net income is 10 to 1 (10:1), or sales are 10 times net income.
- For every dollar of sales, the company has an average net income of 10 cents.

APPLY IT!

Using 2012 as the base year, prepare a trend analysis for the data that follow, and tell whether the results suggest a favorable or unfavorable trend. (Round to one decimal place.)

	2014	2013	2012
Net sales	$216,000	$152,000	$100,000
Accounts receivable (net)	40,000	29,000	20,000

SOLUTION

	2014	2013	2012
Net sales	216.0%	152.0%	100.0%
Accounts receivable (net)	200.0%	145.0%	100.0%

These results show favorable trends because the company is increasing sales at a faster pace than the amount of resources tied up in accounts receivable.

TRY IT! SE3, SE4, SE5, E2A, E3A, E4A, E2B, E3B, E4B

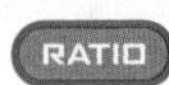

LO 3 Comprehensive Illustration of Financial Ratio Analysis

In this section, we perform a comprehensive financial ratio analysis of **Starbucks'** performance in 2010 and 2011. The following excerpt from the Management's Discussion and Analysis of Financial Condition section of Starbucks' 2011 annual report provides the context for our evaluation:

> *Starbucks results for fiscal 2011 reflect the strength and resiliency of our business model, the global power of our brand and the talent and dedication of our employees. Our business has performed well this year despite significant headwinds from commodity costs and a continuingly challenging consumer environment. Strong global comparable stores sales growth of 8% for the full year (US*

8% and International 5%) drove increased sales leverage and resulted in higher operating margins and net earnings. This helped mitigate the impact of higher commodity costs, which negatively impacted EPS by approximately $0.20 per share for the year, equivalent to approximately 220 basis points of operating margin. Most of the commodity pressure was related to coffee, with dairy, cocoa, sugar and fuel accounting for the rest. . . .

We are aggressively pursuing the profitable expansion opportunities that exist outside the US, including disciplined growth and scale in our more mature markets, and faster expansion in key emerging markets like China.

We will use the ratios introduced earlier in the text, as well as some commonly used supplemental financial ratios, to evaluate Starbucks' performance in relation to the five concepts: profitability, total asset management, liquidity, financial risk, and operating asset management. We will also evaluate Starbucks' market strength. The data that we use in computing all ratios are from Starbucks' Form 10-K, 2011, and Form 10-K, 2010. All dollar amounts shown in the computations are in millions.

Evaluating Profitability and Total Asset Management

Investors and creditors use profit margin to evaluate a company's ability to earn a satisfactory income (*profitability*). They use asset turnover to determine whether the company uses assets in a way that maximizes revenue (*total asset management*). These two ratios require only three numbers: revenue (or net revenue),* net income, and average total assets. Their combined effect is overall earning power—that is, return on assets.

Profit Margin **Profit margin** measures the net income produced by each dollar of sales. **Starbucks**' profit margins in 2011 and 2010 are computed as follows.

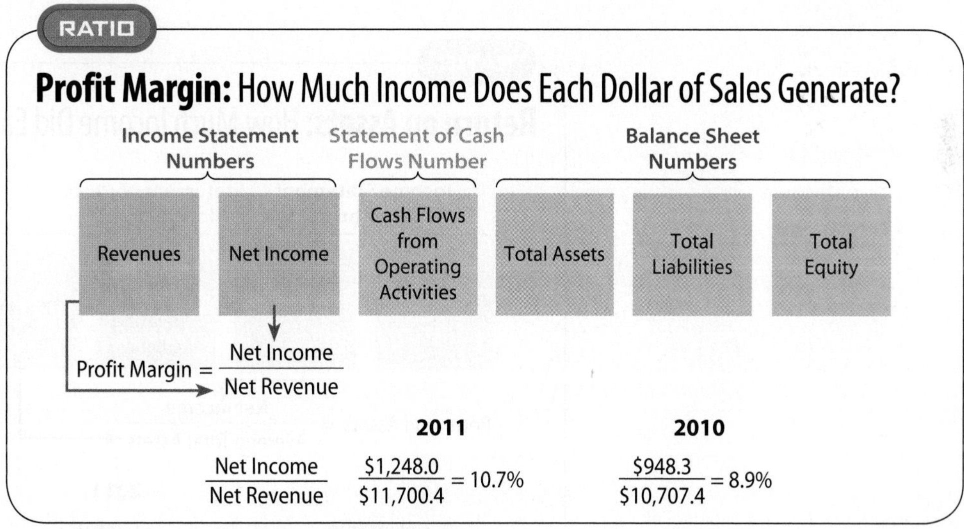

Starbucks' profit margin increased from 8.9 to 10.7 percent between 2011 and 2010 because as a percentage of revenue, operating expenses decreased, as shown in Exhibit 9.

Asset Turnover **Asset turnover** measures how efficiently assets are used to produce sales. **Starbucks**' asset turnover ratios in 2011 and 2010 are computed as follows.

* Starbucks refers to revenue as *net revenue*, and we use that term throughout our examples.

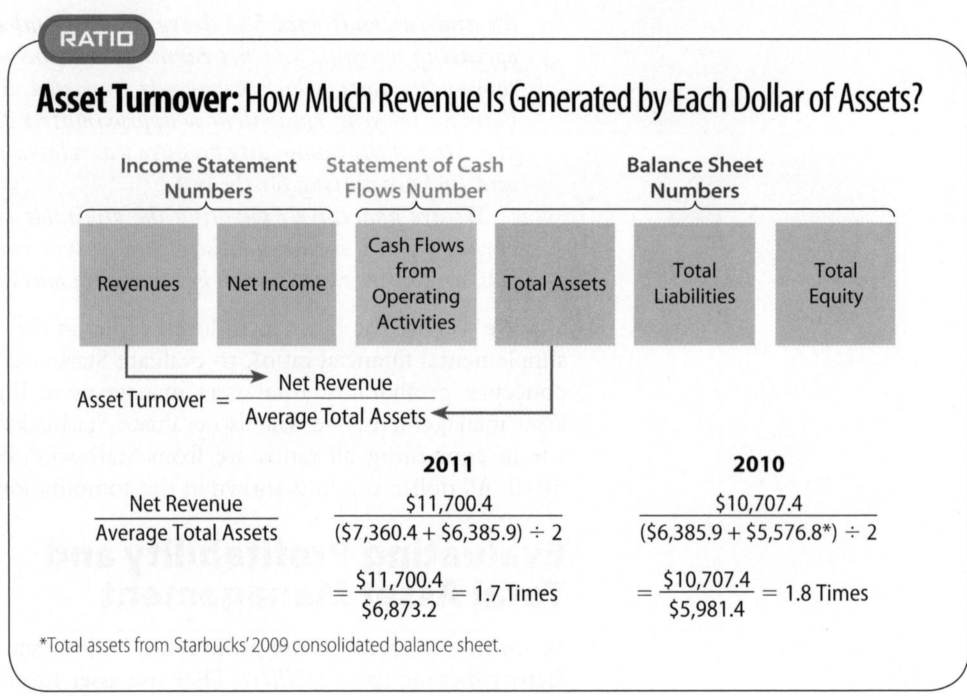

Starbucks' asset turnover decreased slightly to 1.7 times from 1.8 times because net sales increased slightly less in relation to average total assets.

Return on Assets **Return on assets** measures a company's overall earning power, or profitability. **Starbucks**' return on assets ratios in 2011 and 2010 are computed as follows.

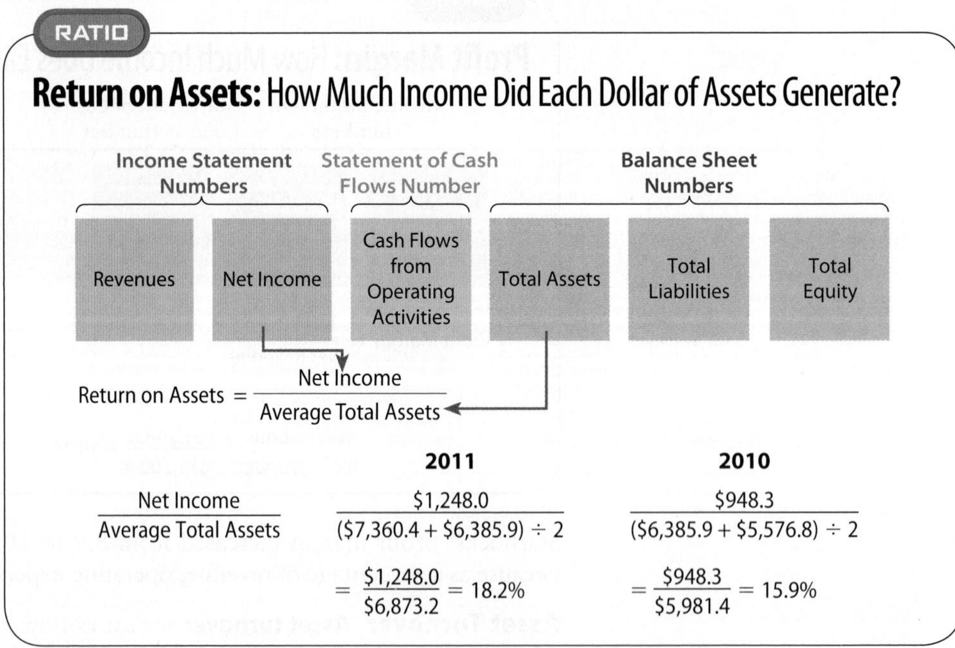

Starbucks' return on assets increased from 15.9 percent in 2010 to 18.2 percent in 2011 because net income increased more in relation to average total assets.

Profitability Ratio Relationships The relationships of the three financial ratios for profitability are as follows.

	Profit Margin		*Asset Turnover*		*Return on Assets*
	$\frac{\text{Net Income}}{\text{Net Sales}}$	×	$\frac{\text{Net Sales}}{\text{Average Total Assets}}$	=	$\frac{\text{Net Income}}{\text{Average Total Assets}}$
2010	8.9%	×	1.8	=	16.0%
2011	10.7%	×	1.7	=	18.2%

Starbucks' return on assets increased in 2011 because of an increase in profit margin. Although Starbucks' profitability and total asset management ratios were relatively low, Starbucks is very good at generating cash from these returns on assets.

STUDY NOTE: *The analysis of both asset turnover and return on assets is improved if only productive assets are used in the calculations. For example, when investments in unfinished new plant construction or in nonoperating plants are removed from the asset base, the result is a better picture of the productivity of assets.*

It is important to note that net income is sometimes not as useful in computing profitability ratios as it is for Starbucks. If a company has one-time items on its income statement, such as gains, or losses on the sale or disposal of discontinued operations, income from continuing operations may be a better measure of sustainable earnings than net income. Some analysts like to use earnings before interest and taxes (EBIT) for the earnings measure because it excludes the effects of the company's borrowings and the tax rates from the analysis. Whatever figure one uses for earnings, it is important to try to determine the effects of various components on future operations.

Evaluating Liquidity

As mentioned, ***liquidity*** is a company's ability to pay bills when they are due and to meet unexpected needs for cash. Analysts compute cash flow yield, cash flows to sales, cash flows to assets, and free cash flow to evaluate a company's liquidity.

Cash Flow Yield **Cash flow yield** is the most important liquidity ratio because it measures a company's ability to generate operating cash flows in relation to net income. **Starbucks**' cash flow yields in 2011 and 2010 are computed as follows.

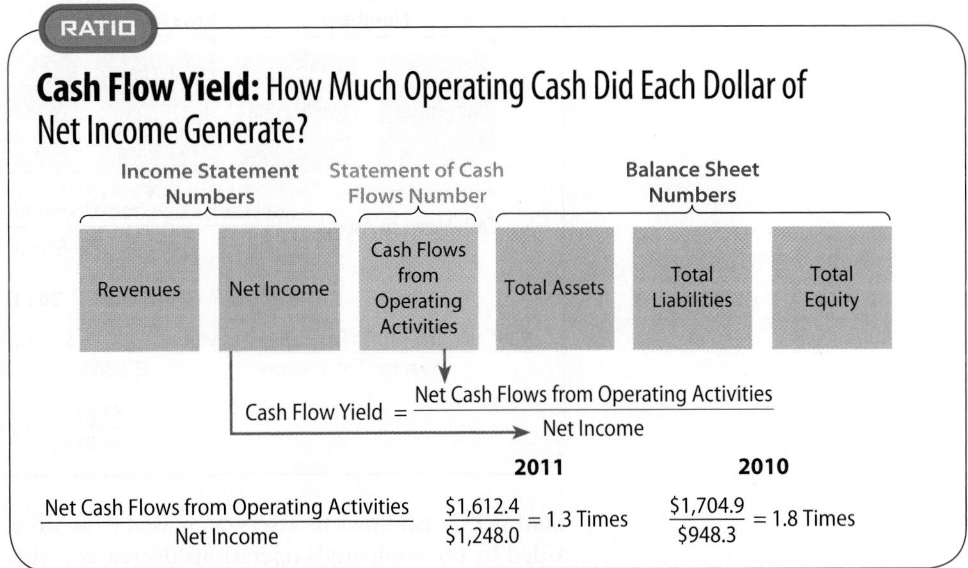

Starbucks' cash flow yield decreased from 1.8 times in 2010 to 1.3 times in 2011 because net cash flows from operating activities decreased while net income increased.

Cash Flows to Sales **Cash flows to sales** refers to the ability of sales to generate operating cash flows. **Starbucks**' cash flows to sales ratios in 2011 and 2010 are computed as follows.

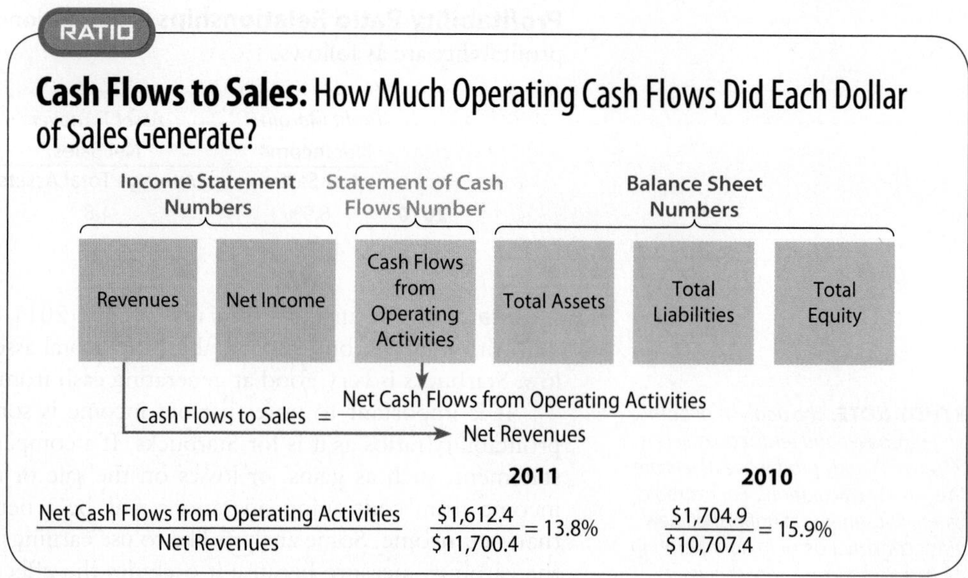

Starbucks' cash flows to sales decreased from 15.9 to 13.8 percent because the company's cash flows provided by its operations decreased while net revenues increased.

Cash Flows to Assets **Cash flows to assets** measures the ability of assets to generate operating cash flows. **Starbucks**' cash flows to assets ratios in 2011 and 2010 are computed as follows.

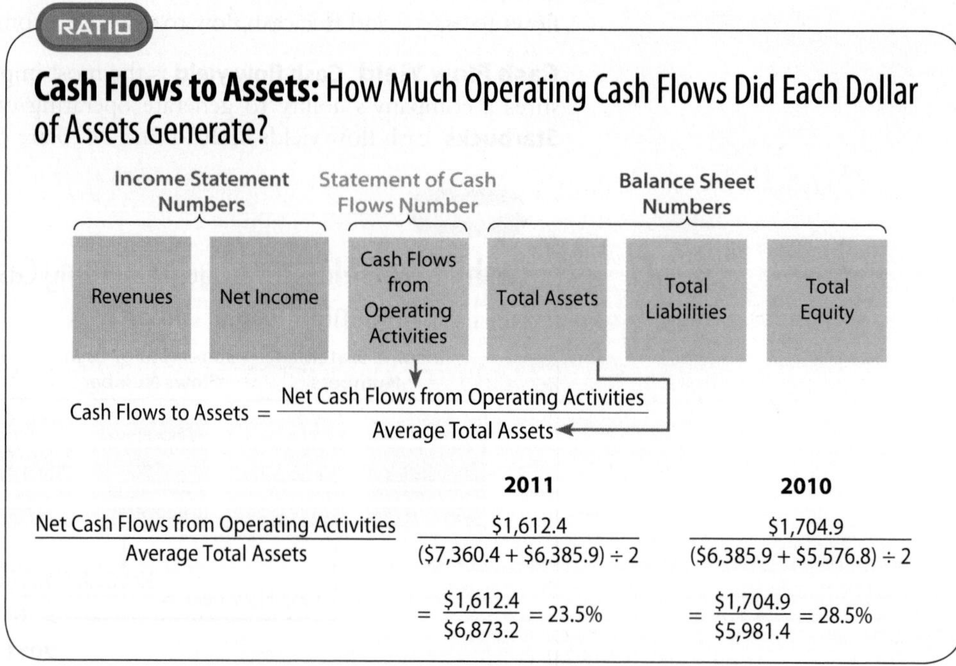

Starbucks' cash flows to assets decreased from 28.5 to 23.5 percent. The cash flows provided by the company's operations decreased, while the average total assets increased.

Free Cash Flow **Free cash flow** is a measure of the cash remaining after providing for commitments. **Starbucks**' free cash flows in 2010 and 2011 are computed as follows.

	2011	2010
Net Cash Flows from Operating Activities − Dividends − Net Capital Expenditures*	$1,612.4 − $389.5 − $531.9 = $691.0	$1,704.9 − $171.0 − $440.7 = $1,093.2

*From the consolidated statements of cash flows.

Starbucks' free cash flow decreased. While the company's net capital expenditures (the difference between purchases and sales of plant assets) increased by $91.2 million ($531.9 − $440.7), the net cash provided by operating activities decreased by $92.5 million ($1,612.4 − $1,704.9). Another unfavorable factor in Starbucks' free cash flow is that the company paid dividends in the past two years. In sum, Starbucks is very proficient in turning its income into cash. It has very good cash flow returns and strong free cash flow.

Evaluating Financial Risk

Financial risk refers to a company's ability to survive in good times and bad. The aim of evaluating financial risk is to detect early signs that a company is headed for financial difficulty through its use of debt, or *financial leverage*, to finance part of the company. Many companies use financial leverage positively. They take advantage of the fact that interest paid on debt is tax-deductible, whereas dividends on stock are not. Because debt usually carries a fixed interest charge and the cost of financing can be limited, leverage can be used to advantage. If a company can earn a return on assets greater than the cost of interest, it increases the return to its stockholders. However, increasing amounts of debt in a company's capital structure can mean that the company is becoming more heavily leveraged. When this occurs, the company runs the risk of not earning a return on assets equal to the cost of financing the assets, thereby incurring a loss. This condition has a negative effect because it represents increasing legal obligations to pay interest periodically and the principal at maturity. Failure to make those payments can result in bankruptcy.

STUDY NOTE: *Because of innovative financing plans and other means of acquiring assets, lease payments and similar types of fixed obligations should be considered when evaluating financial risk.*

Declining profitability and liquidity ratios together with increased leverage are key indicators of possible failure. Ratios related to financial risk include debt to equity, return on equity, and interest coverage.

Debt to Equity Ratio The **debt to equity ratio** measures financial risk by showing the amount of assets provided by creditors in relation to the amount provided by stockholders. A higher ratio indicates more financial risk because it indicates the company is reling more heavily on debt financing. **Starbucks**' debt to equity ratios in 2010 and 2011 are computed as follows.

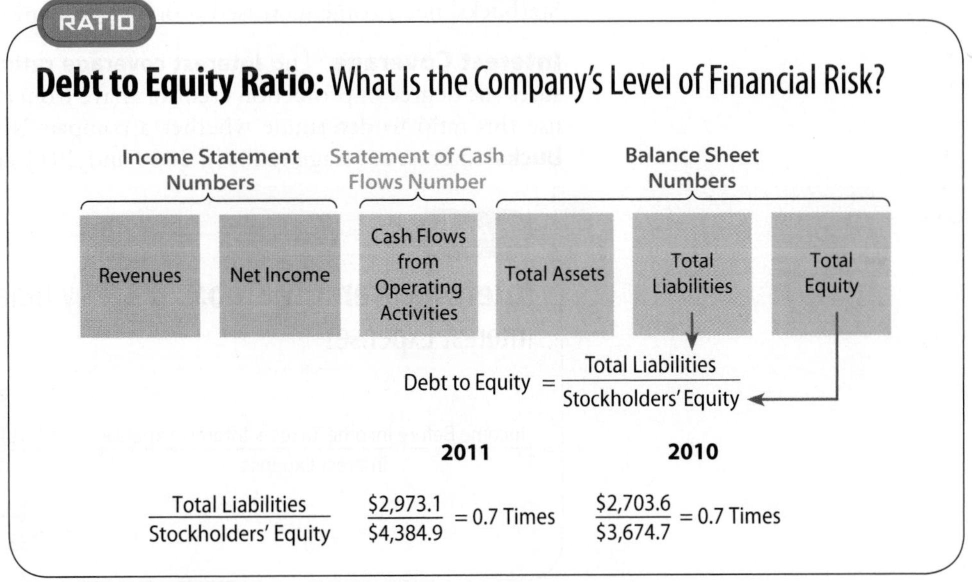

Starbucks' debt to equity ratio was stable at 0.7 times in both 2010 and 2011. Recall from Exhibit 2 that the company increased both its liabilities and its stockholders' equity from 2010 to 2011.

Return on Equity **Return on equity** measures the return to stockholders, or the profitability of stockholders' investments. **Starbucks**' return on equity ratios in 2010 and 2011 are computed as follows.

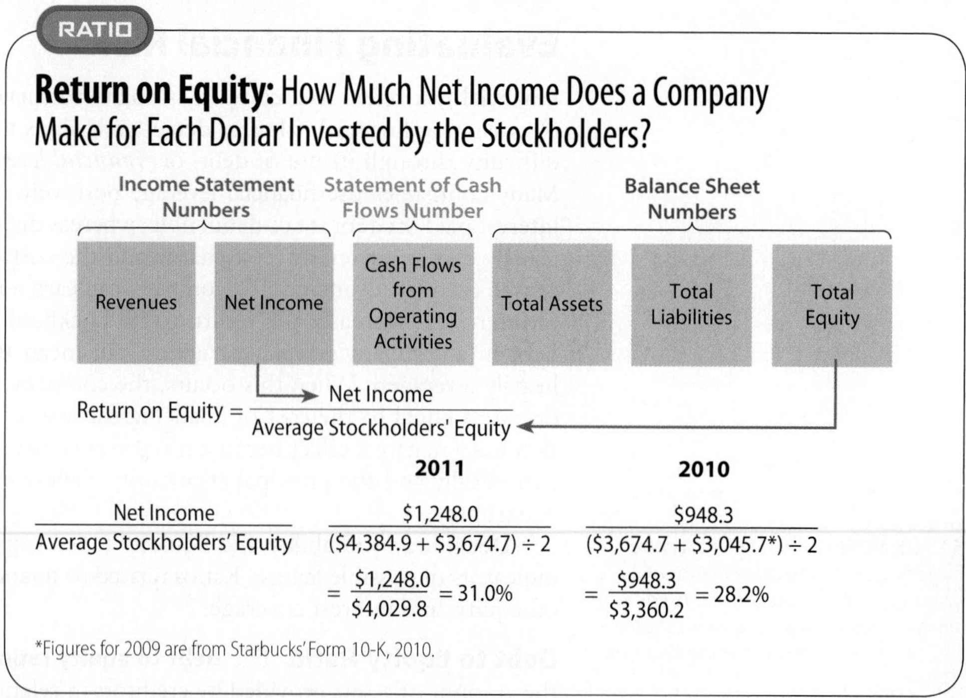

RATIO
Return on Equity: How Much Net Income Does a Company Make for Each Dollar Invested by the Stockholders?
Income Statement Numbers
Statement of Cash Flows Number
Balance Sheet Numbers
Revenues
Net Income
Cash Flows from Operating Activities
Total Assets
Total Liabilities
Total Equity
Return on Equity = Net Income / Average Stockholders' Equity
2011
2010
Net Income / Average Stockholders' Equity
$1,248.0 / ($4,384.9 + $3,674.7) ÷ 2
$948.3 / ($3,674.7 + $3,045.7*) ÷ 2
= $1,248.0 / $4,029.8 = 31.0%
= $948.3 / $3,360.2 = 28.2%
*Figures for 2009 are from Starbucks' Form 10-K, 2010.

Starbucks' return on equity increased from 28.2 percent in 2010 to 31.0 percent in 2011. These are excellent returns compared to return on assets of 15.8 percent in 2010 and 18.1 percent in 2011. Note that both the overall profitability (return on assets) and the return to stockholders (return on equity) increased. The reason for this is that Starbucks' net income increased proportionally more than average stockholders' equity.

Interest Coverage The **interest coverage ratio** is a supplementary ratio that measures the degree of protection creditors have from default on interest payments. Analysts use this ratio to determine whether a company's interest payments are in peril. **Starbucks**' interest coverage ratios in 2010 and 2011 are computed as follows.

RATIO

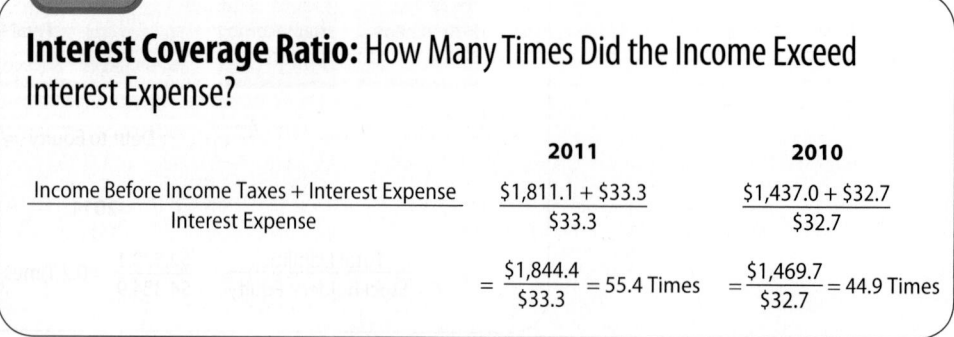

Interest Coverage Ratio: How Many Times Did the Income Exceed Interest Expense?

	2011	2010
Income Before Income Taxes + Interest Expense / Interest Expense	($1,811.1 + $33.3) / $33.3	($1,437.0 + $32.7) / $32.7
	= $1,844.4 / $33.3 = 55.4 Times	= $1,469.7 / $32.7 = 44.9 Times

Starbucks' interest coverage increased from 44.9 times to 55.4 times, due to an increase in income before income taxes. Therefore, the interest coverage is at a very safe level.

Evaluating Operating Asset Management

Research has shown that successful companies carefully manage the operating assets and payables in the **operating cycle**.[4] As discussed in an earlier chapter, the operating cycle involves inventories, accounts receivable, and accounts payable. It spans the time it takes to purchase inventory, sell it, and collect for it. The **financing period**—the period between the time a supplier must be paid and the end of the operating cycle—defines how much additional financing the company must have to support its operations. Because additional debt increases a company's financial risk, it is important to keep the financing period at a manageable level.

The financial ratios that measure operating asset management include inventory turnover, days' inventory on hand, receivables turnover, days' sales uncollected, payables turnover, and days' payable. To determine the days in each component of the cash cycle, the turnover must first be computed by relating the average for each balance sheet account—inventory, accounts receivable, and accounts payable—to the respective income statement account for the period—cost of goods sold and net sales or revenues. The average number of days of each component is then determined by dividing the turnover into 365 days.

Inventory Turnover **Inventory turnover** measures the relative size of inventories. **Starbucks**' inventory turnover ratios in 2010 and 2011 are computed as follows.

RATIO

Inventory Turnover: How Many Times Did the Company Sell Its Inventory During an Accounting Period?

	2011	2010
$\frac{\text{Cost of Goods Sold*}}{\text{Average Inventory}}$	$\frac{\$4,949.3}{(\$965.8 + \$543.3) \div 2}$	$\frac{\$4,458.6}{(\$543.3 + \$664.9^{**}) \div 2}$
	$= \frac{\$4,949.3}{\$754.6} = 6.6 \text{ Times}$	$= \frac{\$4,458.6}{\$604.1} = 7.4 \text{ Times}$

*Starbucks refers to Cost of Goods Sold as Cost of Sales.
**Inventory from Starbucks' 2009 consolidated balance sheet.

Starbucks' inventory turnover decreased from 7.4 times in 2010 to 6.6 times in 2011 because the average inventory increased more in relation to the cost of goods sold.

Days' Inventory on Hand **Days' inventory on hand** measures the average number of days that it takes to sell inventory. **Starbucks**' days' inventory on hand ratios in 2010 and 2011 are computed as follows.

RATIO

Days' Inventory on Hand: How Many Days Did It Take the Company to Sell Its Inventory?

	2011	2010
$\frac{\text{Days in Accounting Period}}{\text{Inventory Turnover}}$	$\frac{365 \text{ Days}}{6.6 \text{ Times}} = 55.3 \text{ Days}$	$\frac{365 \text{ Days}}{7.4 \text{ Times}} = 49.3 \text{ Days}$

Starbucks' days' inventory on hand increased from 49.3 days in 2010 to 55.3 days in 2011 due to the decrease in the inventory turnover.

Receivables Turnover **Receivables turnover** measures the relative size of accounts receivable and the effectiveness of credit policies. **Starbucks**' receivables turnover ratios in 2010 and 2011 are computed as follows.

RATIO

Receivables Turnover: How Many Times Did the Company Collect Its Accounts Receivable During an Accounting Period?

	2011	2010
$\frac{\text{Net Sales}}{\text{Average Accounts Receivable}}$	$\frac{\$11,700.4}{(\$386.5 + \$302.7) \div 2}$	$\frac{\$10,707.4}{(\$302.7 + \$271.0^*) \div 2}$
	$= \frac{\$11,700.4}{\$344.6} = 34.0$ Times	$= \frac{\$10,707.4}{\$286.9} = 37.3$ Times

*Accounts receivable from Starbucks' 2009 consolidated balance sheet.

Because most of Starbucks' sales are for cash or credit card, receivables are not a significant asset for Starbucks. Thus, its receivables turnover is very high. However, it declined slightly, from 37.3 times in 2010 to 34.0 times in 2011.

Days' Sales Uncollected **Days' sales uncollected** measures the average number of days it takes to collect receivables. **Starbucks**' days' sales uncollected ratios in 2010 and 2011 are computed as follows.

RATIO

Days' Sales Uncollected: How Many Days Does It Take to Collect Accounts Receivables?

	2011	2010
$\frac{\text{Days in Accounting Period}}{\text{Receivables Turnover}}$	$\frac{365 \text{ Days}}{34.0 \text{ Times}} = 10.7$ Days	$\frac{365 \text{ Days}}{37.3 \text{ Times}} = 9.8$ Days

Starbucks' high receivables turnover ratios resulted in an increase in days' sales uncollected from 9.8 days in 2010 to 10.7 days in 2011.

Payables Turnover **Payables turnover** measures the relative size of accounts payable and the credit terms extended to a company. **Starbucks**' payables turnover ratios in 2010 and 2011 are computed as follows.

RATIO

Payables Turnover: How Many Times Does a Company Pay Its Accounts Payable During an Accounting Period?

	2011	2010
$\frac{\text{Costs of Goods Sold +/– Change in Inventory}}{\text{Average Accounts Payable}}$	$\frac{\$4,949.3 + \$422.5}{(\$540.0 + \$282.6) \div 2}$	$\frac{\$4,458.6 - \$121.6}{(\$282.6 + \$267.1^*) \div 2}$
	$= \frac{\$5,371.8}{\$411.3} = 13.1$ Times	$= \frac{\$4,337.0}{\$274.9} = 15.8$ Times

*Accounts Payable from Starbucks' 2009 consolidated balance sheet.

Starbucks' payables turnover decreased from 15.8 times in 2010 to 13.1 times in 2011.

Days' Payable **Days' payable** measures the average number of days it takes to pay accounts payable. Starbucks' days' payable ratios in 2010 and 2011 are computed as follows.

RATIO

Days' Payable: How Many Days Did It Take to Pay Accounts Payable?

	2011	2010
$\frac{\text{Days in Accounting Period}}{\text{Payables Turnover}}$	$\frac{\text{365 Days}}{\text{13.1 Times}}$ = 27.9 Days	$\frac{\text{365 Days}}{\text{15.8 Times}}$ = 23.1 Days

Strabucks' decrease in payables turnover resulted in an increase in days' payable from 23.1 days in 2010 to 27.9 days in 2011.

Financing Period We can now assess **Starbucks**' overall operating asset management by computing the financing period—the number of days of financing that must be provided. The financing period is computed by deducting the days' payable from the operating cycle (days' inventory on hand + days' sales uncollected). Starbucks' financing periods in 2010 and 2011 are computed as follows.

2011: 55.3 Days + 10.7 Days – 27.9 Days = 38.1 Days
2010: 49.3 Days + 9.8 Days – 23.1 Days = 36.0 Days

Since both days' inventory on hand and days' sales uncollected increased and days' payable increased, Starbucks had to provide 2.1 (38.1 – 36.0) more days of financing for its operating assets in 2011 than in 2010.

Supplemental Financial Ratios for Assessing Operating Asset Management and Liquidity

In evaluating operating asset management and liquidity, many analysts also consider two supplemental financial ratios: the current ratio and the quick ratio.

Current Ratio

The **current ratio** measures short-term debt-paying ability by comparing current assets with current liabilities. **Starbucks**' current ratios in 2010 and 2011 are computed as follows.

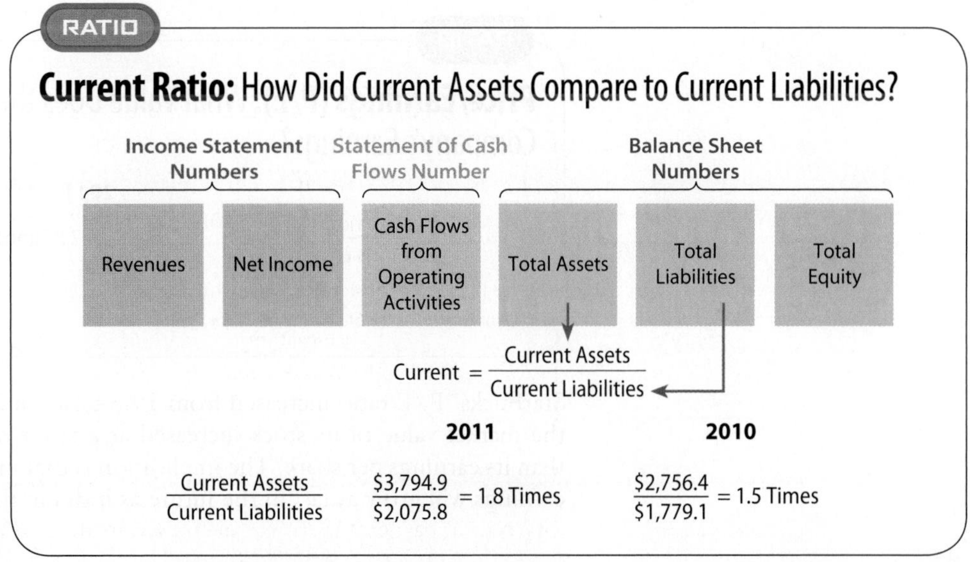

Starbucks' current ratio was increased from 1.5 times in 2010 to 1.8 times in 2011. From 2010 to 2011, its current assets grew faster than its current liabilities.

Quick Ratio The **quick ratio**, another measure of short-term debt-paying ability, differs from the current ratio in that the numerator of the quick ratio excludes inventories and prepaid expenses. Inventories and prepaid expenses take longer to convert to cash than the current assets included in the numerator of the quick ratio. **Starbucks**' quick ratios in 2010 and 2011 are computed as follows.

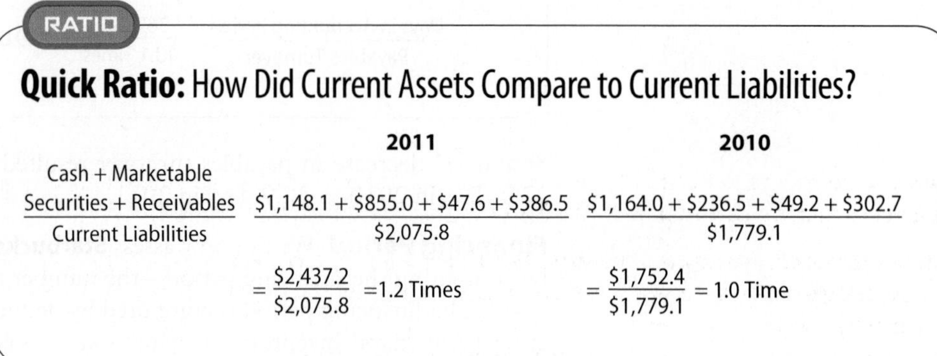

RATIO

Quick Ratio: How Did Current Assets Compare to Current Liabilities?

	2011	2010
(Cash + Marketable Securities + Receivables) / Current Liabilities	($1,148.1 + $855.0 + $47.6 + $386.5) / $2,075.8	($1,164.0 + $236.5 + $49.2 + $302.7) / $1,779.1
	= $2,437.2 / $2,075.8 = 1.2 Times	= $1,752.4 / $1,779.1 = 1.0 Time

Starbucks' quick ratio increased from 1.0 time in 2010 to 1.2 times in 2011.

Evaluating Market Strength with Financial Ratios

Market price is the price at which a company's stock is bought and sold. It indicates how investors view the potential return and risk connected with owning the stock. Market price by itself is not very informative, however, because companies have different numbers of shares outstanding, different earnings, and different dividend policies. Thus, market price must be related to earnings by considering the price/earnings (P/E) ratio and the dividend yield.

Price/Earnings (P/E) **Price/earnings (P/E)**, which measures investors' confidence in a company, is the ratio of the market price per share to earnings per share. The P/E ratio is useful in comparing the earnings of different companies and the value of a company's shares in relation to values in the overall market. With a higher P/E ratio, the investor obtains less earnings per dollar invested. **Starbucks**' P/E ratios in 2010 and 2011 are computed as follows.

RATIO

Price/Earnings (P/E): What Value Does the Market Place on the Company's Earnings?

	2011	2010
Market Price per Share / Earnings per Share**	$37.86* / $1.66 = 22.8 Times	$24.79* / $1.27 = 19.5 Times

*Market price is the average for the fourth quarter reported in Starbucks' 2010 and 2011 annual reports.

**Earnings per share is Starbucks' basic EPS.

Starbucks' P/E ratio increased from 19.5 times in 2010 to 22.8 times in 2011 because the market value of its stock increased at a faster rate (from about $25 to about $38) than its earnings per share. The implication is that investors are confident that Starbucks' earnings will grow as fast in the future as it did in the past.

Dividend Yield **Dividend yield** measures a stock's current return to an investor in the form of dividends. **Starbucks**' dividend yields in 2010 and 2011 are computed as follows.

RATIO

Dividend Yield: What Is the Return from Dividends on Each Share of Stock?

	2011	2010
$\frac{\text{Dividends per Share}}{\text{Market Price per Share}}$	$\frac{\$0.56}{\$37.86} = 1.5\%$	$\frac{\$0.36}{\$24.79} = 1.5\%$

Starbucks's dividend yield was steady and rather low at 1.5 percent for both years 2010 and 2011. Because the dividend yield was rather low, we can conclude that those who invest in the company expect their return to come from increases in the stock's market value.

Financial Statement Analysis and Performance Assessment

The relationships of key financial ratios help the users of financial statements assess financial performance. These relationships are shown in Exhibit 10.

Exhibit 10
Relationships of Financial Ratios

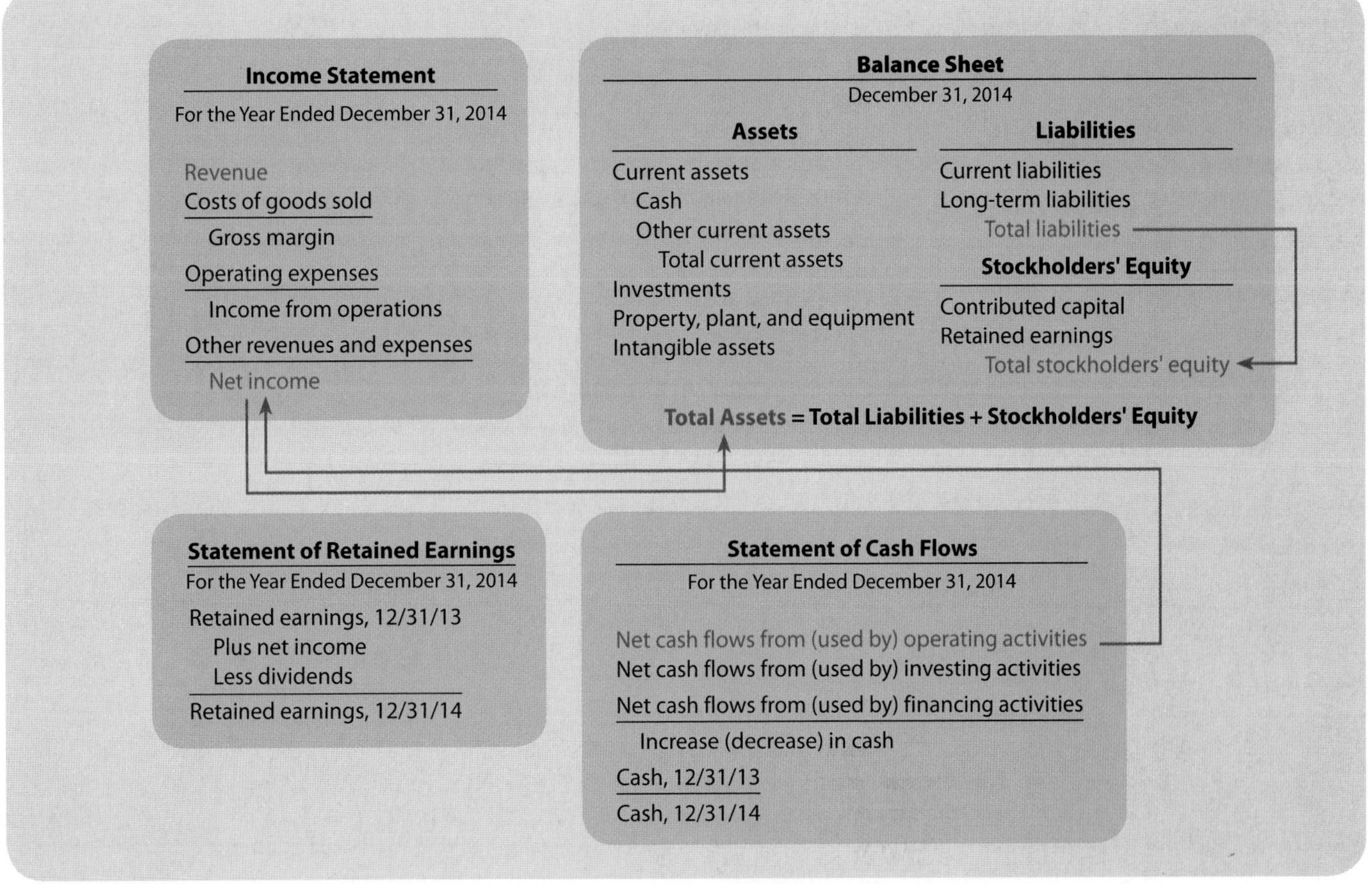

APPLY IT!

Kora's, a retail company, engaged in the transactions that follow. Opposite each transaction is a ratio and space to mark the effect of each transaction on the ratio. Show that you understand the effect of business activities on performance measures by placing an X in the appropriate column to show whether the transaction increased, decreased, or had no effect on the ratio.

Transaction	Ratio	Effect		
		Increase	Decrease	None
a. Accrued salaries.	Current ratio			
b. Purchased inventory.	Quick ratio			
c. Increased allowance for uncollectible accounts.	Receivables turnover			
d. Purchased inventory on credit.	Payables turnover			
e. Sold treasury stock.	Profit margin			
f. Borrowed cash by issuing bond payable.	Asset turnover			
g. Paid wages expense.	Return on assets			
h. Repaid bond payable.	Debt to equity ratio			
i. Accrued interest expense.	Interest coverage ratio			
j. Sold merchandise on account.	Return on equity			
k. Recorded depreciation expense.	Cash flow yield			
l. Sold equipment.	Free cash flow			

SOLUTION

Transaction	Ratio	Effect		
		Increase	Decrease	None
a. Accrued salaries.	Current ratio		X	
b. Purchased inventory.	Quick ratio		X	
c. Increased allowance for uncollectible accounts.	Receivables turnover	X		
d. Purchased inventory on credit.	Payables turnover		X	
e. Sold treasury stock.	Profit margin			X
f. Borrowed cash by issuing bond payable.	Asset turnover		X	
g. Paid wages expense.	Return on assets		X	
h. Repaid bond payable.	Debt to equity ratio	X		
i. Accrued interest expense.	Interest coverage ratio		X	
j. Sold merchandise on account.	Return on equity	X		
k. Recorded depreciation expense.	Cash flow yield	X		
l. Sold equipment.	Free cash flow	X		

TRY IT! SE6, SE7, SE8, SE9, SE10, E5A, E6A, E7A, E8A, E9A, E5B, E6B, E7B, E8B, E9B

SECTION 3 BUSINESS APPLICATIONS

USINESS
PPLICATIONS
- Evaluating quality of earnings
  - Accounting methods
  - Accounting estimates
  - One-time items
- Determining management compensation

ELEVANT
EARNING OBJECTIVE

4 Define *quality of earnings*, and identify he factors that affect quality f earnings and related anagement compensation sues.

LO 4 Evaluating Quality of Earnings

Net income (net earnings) is the measure most commonly used to evaluate a company's profitability. In fact, one survey indicated that the two important measures in evaluating common stocks were expected changes in earnings per share and return on assets.[5] Net income is a key component of both measures.

Because of the importance of net income, or the "bottom line," in measuring a company's prospects, there is significant interest in evaluating the quality of the net income. The **quality of earnings** refers to the substance of earnings and their sustainability into future periods. Quality of earnings is affected by the following:

- Accounting methods
- Accounting estimates
- One-time items

Accounting Methods

The accounting methods a firm uses affect its operating income. Generally accepted accounting methods include:

- Uncollectible receivables methods (percentage of net sales and aging of accounts receivable)
- Inventory methods (LIFO, FIFO, and average cost)
- Depreciation methods (accelerated, production, and straight-line)
- Revenue recognition methods

All these methods are designed to *match* revenues and expenses. However, the expenses are estimates, and the period or periods benefited cannot be demonstrated conclusively. In practice, it is hard to justify one method of estimation over another.

Different accounting methods have different effects on net income. Some methods are more conservative than others because they tend to produce a lower net income in the current period. For example, suppose that Rudy Company and Kanya Company have similar operations, but Rudy uses FIFO for inventory costing and the straight-line (SL) method for computing depreciation. Kanya uses LIFO for inventory costing and the double-declining-balance (DDB) method for computing depreciation. The income statements of the two companies might appear as shown in Exhibit 11.

Exhibit 11
Effects of Different Accounting Methods

	Rudy Company (FIFO and SL)	*Kanya Company (LIFO and DDB)*
Net sales	$462,500	$462,500
Cost of goods available for sale	$200,000	$200,000
Less ending inventory	30,000	25,000
Cost of goods sold	$170,000	$175,000
Gross margin	$292,500	$287,500
Less depreciation expense	$ 20,000	$ 40,000
Less other expenses	85,000	85,000
Total operating expenses	$105,000	$125,000
Income from continuing operations before income taxes	$187,500	$162,500

STUDY NOTE: *To assess the quality of a company's reported earnings, you must know the estimates and methods it uses to compute income.*

Impact of Different Accounting Methods on Income The income from continuing operations before income taxes for the firm that uses LIFO and DDB is lower because in periods of rising prices, the LIFO method produces a higher cost of goods sold. Also, in the early years of an asset's useful life, accelerated depreciation yields a higher depreciation expense. The result is lower operating income. However, future operating income should be higher.

Impact of Different Accounting Methods on Cash Flows Although the choice of accounting method does not affect cash flows except for possible differences in income taxes, the $25,000 difference in operating income stems solely from the choice of accounting methods. Estimates of the useful lives and residual values of plant assets could lead to an even greater difference. In practice, of course, differences in net income occur for many reasons; but the user of financial statements must be aware of the discrepancies that can occur as a result of the accounting methods used. In general, an accounting method or estimate that results in lower current earnings produces a better quality of operating income.

Impact of Different Accounting Methods on Financial Statements The latitude that companies have in their choice of accounting methods could cause problems in the interpretation of financial statements were it not for the conventions of *full disclosure* and *consistency*. As noted in an earlier chapter, **full disclosure** requires management to explain, in a note to the financial statements, the significant accounting policies used. For instance, in a note to its financial statements, **Starbucks** discloses that it uses the straight-line method for depreciation of property, plant, and equipment.[6] **Consistency** requires that the same accounting procedures be used from year to year. If a company changes its accounting procedure, it must explain the nature of the change and its monetary effect in a note to its statements.

Accounting Estimates

Users of financial statements also need to be aware of the impact that accounting estimates have on reported income. To comply with *accrual accounting* (the *matching rule*), accountants must assign revenues and expenses to the periods in which they occur. If they cannot establish a direct relationship between revenues and expenses, they systematically allocate the expenses among the periods that benefit from them. In doing so, they must make estimates and exercise judgment, based on realistic assumptions. However, there is latitude in making the estimate, and the final judgment will affect net income.

For example, when a company acquires an asset, the accountant must estimate the asset's useful life. Technological obsolescence could shorten the asset's expected useful life, and regular maintenance and repairs could lengthen it. Although the actual useful life cannot be known with certainty until some future date, the accountant's estimate of it affects both current and future operating income. Other areas that require accounting estimates include:

- Residual value of assets
- Uncollectible accounts receivable
- Sales returns
- Total units of production
- Total recoverable units of natural resources
- Amortization periods
- Warranty claims
- Environmental cleanup costs

The importance of accounting estimates depends on the industry in which a firm operates. For example, estimated uncollectible receivables for a credit card firm, such as **American Express**, or for a financial services firm, such as **Bank of America**, can have a material impact on earnings; but estimated useful life may be less important because depreciable assets represent a small percentage of the firm's total assets. **Starbucks** has few receivables, but it has major investments in depreciable assets. Thus, estimates of useful life and residual value are more important to Starbucks than an estimate of uncollectible accounts receivable. The company depreciates its equipment over 2 to 15 years and its buildings over 30 to 40 years.[7]

One-Time Items

If earnings increase because of one-time items, that portion of earnings will not be sustained in the future. In contrast, one-time decreases in earnings may not indicate that earnings will be poor in the future. Examples of one-time items include:

- Gains and losses
- Write-downs and restructurings
- Nonoperating items

Because management has choices in the content and positioning of these income statement components, there is a potential for managing earnings to achieve specific income targets. It is, therefore, critical for users of income statements to understand these factors and take them into consideration when evaluating a company's performance.

Exhibit 12 shows the components of a typical income statement. Net income or loss (the "bottom line" of the income statement) includes all revenues, expenses, gains, and losses over the period. When a company has both continuing and discontinued operations, the operating income section is called *income from continuing operations.* Income

Exhibit 12
Corporate Income Statement

Dingo Corporation
Income Statement
For the Year Ended December 31, 2014

Operating items before income taxes →	Revenues		$ 1,850,000
	Costs and expenses		(1,100,000)
	Gain on sale of assets		300,000
	Write-downs of assets		(50,000)
	Restructurings		(150,000)
	Income from continuing operations before income taxes		$ 850,000
Income taxes →	Income taxes expense		289,000
	Income from continuing operations		$ 561,000
Nonoperating items →	Discontinued operations:		
	Income from operations of discontinued segment (net of taxes, $70,000)	$ 180,000	
	Loss on disposal of segment (net of taxes, $84,000)	(146,000)	34,000
	Net income		$ 595,000
Earnings per share information →	Earnings per common share:		
	Income from continuing operations		$2.81
	Discontinued operations (net of taxes)		0.17
	Net income		$2.98

Business Perspective

Beware of the "Bottom Line!"

In the second quarter of 2007, **McDonald's** posted its second-ever loss: $711.7 million. Should this have been cause for concern? The answer is no because the loss resulted from a one-time noncash impairment (decline in value) of $1.6 billion related to investments in Latin America; the company was actually in a period of rapidly growing revenues and profits. In another example, **Campbell Soup** showed unrealistically positive results. Its income jumped by 31 percent due to a tax settlement and an accounting restatement. Without these items, its revenue and income would have been up less than 1 percent; soup sales—its main product—actually dropped by 6 percent. The lesson to be learned is to look beyond the "bottom line" to the components of the income statement when evaluating a company's performance.[8]

from continuing operations before income taxes may include gains or losses on the sale of assets, write-downs, and restructurings.

As you can see in Exhibit 12, the section of the income statement that follows income taxes may contain such nonoperating items as **discontinued operations**—segments that are no longer part of a company's operations—and gains (or losses) on the sale or disposal of these segments. Another item that may appear in this section is the write-off of goodwill when its value has been impaired. Earnings per share information appears at the bottom of the statement

Gains and Losses When a company sells or otherwise disposes of operating assets or marketable securities, a gain or loss generally results. Although these gains or losses appear in the operating section of the income statement, they usually represent one-time events. However, management often has some choice as to their timing. Thus, from an analyst's point of view, they should be ignored when considering operating income.

Write-Downs and Restructurings When management decides that an asset is no longer of value to the company, a write-down or restructuring occurs.

- A **write-down** (or *write-off*) is a reduction in the value of an asset below its carrying value on the balance sheet.
- A **restructuring** is the estimated cost of a change in a company's operations. It usually involves the closing of facilities and the laying off of personnel.

Both write-downs and restructurings reduce current operating income and boost future income by shifting future costs to the current period. They are often an indication of poor management decisions in the past, such as paying too much for the assets of another company or making operational changes that do not work out. Companies sometimes take all possible losses in the current year so that future years will be "clean" of these costs. Such "big baths," as they are called, commonly occur when a company is having a bad year. They also often occur in years when there is a change in management. The new management takes a "big bath" in the current year so it can show improved results in future years.

In a recent year, 34 percent of 500 large companies had write-downs of tangible assets, and 41 percent had restructurings. Another 19 percent had write-downs or charges related to intangible assets, often involving goodwill. In 2011, **Starbucks** did not have any restructuring costs, but in 2009 its restructuring costs were $332.4 million (compared with net income of only $390.8 million) in connection with the closing of a number of its stores.[9]

Nonoperating Items The nonoperating items that appear on the income statement include discontinued operations and gains or losses on the sale or disposal of these segments. These items can significantly affect net income. For example, in Exhibit 12, earnings per common share for income from continuing operations are $2.81; but when all the nonoperating items are taken into consideration, net income per share is $2.98.To

Business Perspective
Look Carefully at the Numbers

In recent years, companies have increasingly used pro forma statements—statements as they would appear without certain items—as a way of presenting a better picture of their operations than would be the case in reports prepared under GAAP. For example, in the first quarter of 2012, **GEO Group, Inc.**, reported pro forma net income of $18.8 million, even though its actual net income was $15.1 million. The higher pro forma figure came about by not deducting certain expenses which are required under GAAP. In addition, a common practice used by such companies as **Google**, **eBay**, and **Starbucks** is to provide in the notes to the financial statements income as it would be without the expense related to compensation for stock options.[10] Pro forma statements, which are unaudited, have come to mean whatever a company's management wants them to mean. As a result, the SEC issued rules that prohibit companies from giving more prominence to non-GAAP measures and from using terms that are similar to GAAP measures.[11] Nevertheless, companies still report pro forma results. Analysts should rely exclusively on financial statements that are prepared using GAAP and that are audited by an independent CPA.

make it easier to evaluate a company's ongoing operations, generally accepted accounting principles require that gains and losses from discontinued operations be reported separately on the income statement.

In Exhibit 12, the *disclosure* of discontinued operations has two parts:

- One part shows that after the decision to discontinue, the income from operations of the disposed segment was $180,000 (net of $70,000 taxes).
- The other part shows that the loss from the disposal of the segment was $146,000 (net of $84,000 tax savings). (The computation of the gains or losses involved in discontinued operations is covered in more advanced accounting courses.)

Management Compensation

Knowledge of performance measurement not only is important for evaluating a company, but also leads to an understanding of the criteria by which a board of directors evaluates and compensates management. Members of management are often paid based on the earnings of the company. As noted earlier, one intent of the Sarbanes-Oxley Act of 2002 was to strengthen the corporate governance of public corporations. Under this act, a public corporation's board of directors must establish a **compensation committee** made up of independent directors to determine how the company's top executives will be compensated. The company must file documents with the SEC, *disclosing* the components of compensation and the criteria used to remunerate top executives.

The components of **Starbucks**' compensation of executive officers are typical of those used by many companies. They include the following:

- Annual base salary
- Annual incentive bonuses
- Long-term incentive compensation (stock option awards)[12]

Incentive bonuses are based on financial performance measures that the compensation committee identifies as important to the company's long-term success, especially in terms of increasing the value of shareholders' investments in the company. Many companies tie incentive bonuses to measures such as growth in revenues and return on assets or return on equity. Starbucks bases 50 percent of its incentive bonus on an "adjusted consolidated operating income or adjusted business unit operating income," 30 percent on "adjusted earnings per share target approved by the compensation committee," and 20 percent on the executive's "specific individual performance goals."[13]

Stock option awards are usually based on how well the company is achieving its long-term strategic goals. In 2011, Starbucks' CEO received a base salary of $1,382,692 and a non-equity incentive plan compensation of $2,982,000. He also received a stock option awards of $11,479,494.[14]

From one vantage point, earnings per share is a "bottom-line" number that encompasses all the other performance measures. However, using a single performance measure as the basis for determining compensation has the potential of leading to practices that are not in the best interests of a company or its stockholders. For instance, management could boost earnings per share by reducing the number of shares outstanding (the denominator in the earnings per share equation) while not improving earnings. It could accomplish this by using cash to repurchase shares of the company's stock (treasury stock), rather than investing the cash in more profitable operations.

APPLY IT!

The following data apply to Kawa, Inc.: net sales, $180,000; cost of goods sold, $87,500; loss from discontinued operations (net of income tax benefit of $17,500), $50,000; loss on disposal of discontinued operations (net of income tax benefit of $4,000), $12,500; operating expenses, $32,500; income taxes expense on continuing operations, $18,000. Prepare the company's income statement for the year ended December 31, 2014. (*Note:* Ignore earnings per share information.)

SOLUTION

Kawa, Inc.
Income Statement
For the Year Ended December 31, 2014

Net sales		$180,000
Cost of goods sold		87,500
Gross margin		$ 92,500
Operating expenses		32,500
Income from continuing operations before income taxes		$ 60,000
Income taxes expense		18,000
Income from continuing operations		$ 42,000
Discontinued operations		
Loss from discontinued operations (net of income tax benefit of $17,500)	$(50,000)	
Loss on disposal of discontinued operations (net of income tax benefit of $4,000)	(12,500)	(62,500)
Net loss		$ (20,500)

TRY IT! SE11, SE12, E10A, E11A, E12A, E10B, E11B, E12B

A Look Back At: Starbucks Corporation

AP Photo/Ted S. Warren

Starbucks Corporation

The beginning of this chapter focused on **Starbucks Corporation**. Complete the following requirements in order to answer the questions posed at the beginning of the chapter.

Section 1: Concepts
What concepts underlie the standards that Starbucks can use to evaluate performance?

Section 2: Accounting Applications
What analytical tools can Starbucks use to measure financial performance?

Section 3: Business Applications
In what ways would having access to prior years' information aid this analysis? Why is earnings management important in your assessment?

SOLUTION

Section 1: Concepts

Rule-of-thumb measures, a company's past performance, and industry norms are standards companies can use to assess financial performance. Rule-of-thumb measures are weak because they often lack *relevance*. A company's past performance is more reliable and it can be used for measuring the improvement (or lack thereof) in a particular ratio, but can be lacking in *predictive value* and *timeliness* because past performance is not a guarantee of future performance and a company's past performance is not helpful in judging its performance relative to the performance of other companies. Finally, Starbucks can use industry norms to *compare* financial performance, though it's important to note that firms even in the same industry are not always *comparable* because of having different accounting procedures and diversity issues.

Section 2: Accounting Applications

Ratio analysis may be used to measure profitability, total asset management, liquidity, financial risk, and operating asset management. Users of Starbucks' financial statements may employ such techniques as horizontal or trend analysis, vertical analysis, and ratio analysis.

Section 3: Business Applications

Prior years' information would be helpful in two ways. First, turnover, return, and cash flows to assets ratios could be based on average amounts. Second, a trend analysis could be performed for each company. Earnings management is important because it can be used to make a company look as if it is performing better than it is in reality

Review Problem

Comparative Analysis of Two Companies

Debra Wright is considering investing in a fast-food restaurant chain. She has narrowed her choice to Slim Burger or Tasty Steak. The 2014 income statements and balance sheets of the two companies follow.

	A B C	D	E
1	**Income Statements**		
2	**For the Year Ended December 31, 2014**		
3	(in thousands, except per share amounts)		
4		**Fast Burger**	**Tasty Steak**
5	Net sales	$53,000	$86,000
6	Costs and expenses:		
7	Cost of goods sold	$37,000	$61,000
8	Selling expenses	7,000	10,000
9	Administrative expenses	4,000	5,000
10	Total costs and expenses	$48,000	$76,000
11	Income from operations	$ 5,000	$10,000
12	Interest expense	1,400	3,200
13	Income before income taxes	$ 3,600	$ 6,800
14	Income taxes expense	1,800	3,400
15	Net income	$ 1,800	$ 3,400
16	Earnings per share	$ 1.80	$ 1.13
17			

	A	B	C	D	E
1			Balance Sheets		
2			December 31, 2014		
3			(in thousands)		
4				Fast Burger	Tasty Steak
5			Assets		
6	Cash			$ 2,000	$ 4,500
7	Accounts receivable (net)			2,000	6,500
8	Inventory			2,000	5,000
9	Property, plant, and equipment (net)			20,000	35,000
10	Other assets			4,000	5,000
11		Total assets		$30,000	$56,000
12					
13			Liabilities and Stockholders' Equity		
14	Accounts payable			$ 2,500	$ 3,000
15	Notes payable			1,500	4,000
16	Bonds payable			10,000	30,000
17	Common stock, $1 par value			1,000	3,000
18	Additional paid-in capital			9,000	9,000
19	Retained earnings			6,000	7,000
20		Total liabilities and stockholders' equity		$30,000	$56,000
21					

The following information pertaining to 2014 is also available to Debra:

- Fast Burger's statement of cash flows shows that it had net cash flows from operations of $2,200,000. Tasty Steak's statement of cash flows shows that its net cash flows from operations were $3,000,000.
- Net capital expenditures were $2,100,000 for Fast Burger and $1,800,000 for Tasty Steak.
- Fast Burger paid dividends of $500,000, and Tasty Steak paid dividends of $600,000.
- The market prices of the stocks of Fast Burger and Tasty Steak were $30 and $20, respectively.
- Debra does not have financial information pertaining to prior years. Thus, she used year-end amounts, rather than average amounts.

Perform a comprehensive ratio analysis of both Fast Burger and Tasty Steak using the steps that follow. Assume that all notes payable of the two companies are current liabilities and that all their bonds payable are long-term liabilities. Show dollar amounts in thousands, use end-of-year balances for averages, assume no change in inventory, and round all ratios and percentages to one decimal place.

1. Prepare an analysis of profitability and total asset management.
2. Prepare an analysis of liquidity.
3. Prepare an analysis of financial risk.
4. Prepare an analysis of operating asset management.
5. Prepare an analysis of market strength.
6. In each analysis, indicate which company apparently had the more favorable ratio. (Consider differences of 0.1 or less to be neutral.)

SOLUTION

1.

Ratio Name	Fast Burger	Tasty Steak	6. Company with More Favorable Ratio
Profit margin	$\frac{\$1,800}{\$53,000} = 3.4\%$	$\frac{\$3,400}{\$86,000} = 4.0\%$	Tasty Steak
Asset turnover	$\frac{\$53,000}{\$30,000} = 1.8$ Times	$\frac{\$86,000}{\$56,000} = 1.5$ Times	Fast Burger
Return on assets	$\frac{\$1,800}{\$30,000} = 6.0\%$	$\frac{\$3,400}{\$56,000} = 6.1\%$	Tasty Steak

2.

Ratio Name	Fast Burger	Tasty Steak	6. Company with More Favorable Ratio
Cash flow yield	$\frac{\$2,200}{\$1,800} = 1.2$ Times	$\frac{\$3,000}{\$3,400} = 0.9$ Time	Fast Burger
Cash flows to sales	$\frac{\$2,200}{\$53,000} = 4.2\%$	$\frac{\$3,000}{\$86,000} = 3.5\%$	Fast Burger
Cash flows to assets	$\frac{\$2,200}{\$30,000} = 7.3\%$	$\frac{\$3,000}{\$56,000} = 5.4\%$	Fast Burger
Free cash flow	$2,200 − $500 − $2,100 = ($400)	$3,000 − $600 − $1,800 = $600	Tasty Steak

3.

Ratio Name	Fast Burger	Tasty Steak	6. Company with More Favorable Ratio
Debt to equity ratio	$\frac{\$2,500 + \$1,500 + \$10,000}{\$1,000 + \$9,000 + \$6,000}$ $\frac{\$14,000}{\$16,000} = 0.9$ Time	$\frac{\$3,000 + \$4,000 + \$30,000}{\$3,000 + \$9,000 + \$7,000}$ $\frac{\$37,000}{\$19,000} = 1.9$ Times	Fast Burger
Return on equity	$\frac{\$1,800}{\$1,000 + \$9,000 + \$6,000}$ $\frac{\$1,800}{\$16,000} = 11.3\%$	$\frac{\$3,400}{\$3,000 + \$9,000 + \$7,000}$ $\frac{\$3,400}{\$19,000} = 17.9\%$	Tasty Steak
Interest coverage ratio	$\frac{\$3,600 + \$1,400}{\$1,400}$ $\frac{\$5,000}{\$1,400} = 3.6$ Times	$\frac{\$6,800 + \$3,200}{\$3,200}$ $\frac{\$10,000}{\$3,200} = 3.1$ Times	Fast Burger

4.

Ratio Name	Fast Burger	Tasty Steak	6. Company with More Favorable Ratio
Inventory turnover	$\frac{\$37,000}{\$2,000} = 18.5$ Times	$\frac{\$61,000}{\$5,000} = 12.2$ Times	Fast Burger
Days' inventory on hand	$\frac{365 \text{ Days}}{18.5 \text{ Times}} = 19.7$ Days	$\frac{365 \text{ Days}}{12.2 \text{ Times}} = 29.9$ Days	Fast Burger
Receivable turnover	$\frac{\$53,000}{\$2,000} = 26.5$ Times	$\frac{\$86,000}{\$6,500} = 13.2$ Times	Fast Burger
Day's sales uncollected	$\frac{365 \text{ Days}}{26.5 \text{ Times}} = 13.8$ Days	$\frac{365 \text{ Days}}{13.2 \text{ Times}} = 27.7$ Days	Fast Burger
Payables turnover	$\frac{\$37,000}{\$2,500} = 14.8$ Times	$\frac{\$61,000}{\$3,000} = 20.3$ Times	Tasty Steak
Days' payable	$\frac{365 \text{ Days}}{14.8 \text{ Times}} = 24.7$ Days	$\frac{365 \text{ Days}}{20.3 \text{ Times}} = 18.0$ Days	Fast Burger

Financing period

Fast Burger: 19.7 Days + 13.8 Days – 24.7 Days = 8.8 Days
Tasty Steak: 29.9 Days + 27.7 Days – 18.0 Days = 39.6 Days

Fast Burger's financing period of only 8.8 days is more favorable.

Current ratio	$\frac{\$2,000 + \$2,000 + \$2,000}{\$2,500 + \$1,500}$ $\frac{\$6,000}{\$4,000} = 1.5$ Times	$\frac{\$4,500 + \$6,500 + \$5,000}{\$3,000 + \$4,000}$ $\frac{\$16,000}{\$7,000} = 2.3$ Times	Tasty Steak
Quick ratio	$\frac{\$2,000 + \$2,000}{\$2,500 + \$1,500}$ $\frac{\$4,000}{\$4,000} = 1.0$ Time	$\frac{\$4,500 + \$6,500}{\$3,000 + \$4,000}$ $\frac{\$11,000}{\$7,000} = 1.6$ Times	Tasty Steak

Note: This analysis indicates the company with the apparently more favorable ratio.

5.

Ratio Name	Fast Burger	Tasty Steak	6. Company with More Favorable Ratio
Price/earnings ratio	$\frac{\$30}{\$1.80} = 16.7$ Times	$\frac{\$20}{\$1.13} = 17.7$ Times	Tasty Steak
Dividend yield	$\frac{\$500,000 \div 1,000,000}{\$30}$ $= \frac{\$0.50}{\$30} = 1.7\%$	$\frac{\$600,000 \div 3,000,000}{\$20}$ $= \frac{\$0.20}{\$20} = 1.0\%$	Fast Burger

Chapter Review

Describe the concepts, standards of comparison, and sources of information used in measuring financial performance. LO 1

Important to measuring financial performance are the concepts of relevance, predictive value, comparability, and timeliness, which underlie the objectives of profitability, total asset management, liquidity, financial risk, and operating asset management. Creditors and investors use financial performance measurement to judge a company's past performance and current position, as well as its future potential and the risk associated with it. Creditors use the information from their analyses to make reliable loans that will be repaid with interest. Investors use the information to make investments that will provide a return that is worth the risk.

Three standards of comparison commonly used in evaluating financial performance are rule-of-thumb measures, a company's past performance, and industry norms. Rule-of-thumb measures are weak because of a lack of evidence that they can be widely applied and that they have predictive value. A company's past performance can offer a guideline for measuring improvement, but it is not helpful in judging performance relative to the performance of other companies. Although the use of industry norms overcomes this last problem, firms are not always comparable, even in the same industry.

The main sources of information about public corporations are annual reports and interim financial statements, reports filed with the SEC, business periodicals, and credit and investment advisory services.

Apply horizontal analysis, trend analysis, vertical analysis, and ratio analysis to financial statements. LO 2

Horizontal analysis involves the computation of changes in both dollar amounts and percentages from year to year.

Trend analysis calculates percentage changes for several years. The analyst computes the changes by setting a base year equal to 100 and calculating the results for subsequent years as percentages of the base year.

Vertical analysis uses percentages to show the relationship of the component parts of a financial statement to a total figure in the statement. The resulting financial statements, which are expressed entirely in percentages, are called common-size statements.

Financial ratio analysis identifies key relationships between the components of the financial statements. To interpret ratios correctly, the analyst must have a general understanding of the company and its environment, financial data for several years or for several companies, and an understanding of the data underlying the numerators and denominators.

Apply financial ratio analysis in a comprehensive evaluation of a company's financial performance. LO 3

A comprehensive ratio analysis includes the evaluation of a company's profitability, total asset management, liquidity, financial risk, operating asset management, and market strength.

Define *quality of earnings*, and identify the factors that affect quality of earnings and related management compensation issues. LO 4

The quality of earnings refers to the substance of earnings and their sustainability into future accounting periods. The quality of a company's earnings may be affected by the accounting methods and estimates it uses and by one-time items that it reports on its income statement. One-time items include gains and losses, write-downs and restructurings, and nonoperating items.

When a company has both continuing and discontinued operations, the operating income section of its income statement is called income from continuing operations. Income from continuing operations before income taxes is affected by choices of accounting methods and estimates and may contain gains and losses on the sale of assets, write-downs, and restructurings. The lower part of the income statement may contain such nonoperating items as discontinued operations. Earnings per share information appears at the bottom of the statement.

In public corporations, a committee made up of independent directors appointed by the board of directors determines the compensation of top executives. Although earnings per share can be regarded as a "bottom-line" number that encompasses all the other performance measures, using it as the sole basis for determining executive compensation may lead to management practices that are not in the best interests of the company or its stockholders.

Key Terms and Ratios

base year 658 (LO2)
common-size statement 661 (LO2)
compensation committee 681 (LO4)
consistency 678 (LO4)
discontinued operations 680 (LO4)
diversified companies 655 (LO1)
financial ratio analysis 664 (LO2)
financial statement analysis 654 (LO1)
financing period 671 (LO3)
Form 8-K 656 (LO1)
Form 10-K 656 (LO1)
Form 10-Q 656 (LO1)
full disclosure 678 (LO4)
horizontal analysis 658 (LO2)
index number 660 (LO2)
interim financial statements 656 (LO1)
operating cycle 671 (LO3)
quality of earnings 677 (LO4)
restructuring 680 (LO4)
trend analysis 660 (LO2)
vertical analysis 661 (LO2)
write-down 680 (LO4)

RATIOS

asset turnover 665 (LO3)
cash flow yield 667 (LO3)
cash flows to assets 668 (LO3)
cash flows to sales 667 (LO3)
current ratio 673 (LO3)
days' inventory on hand 671 (LO3)
days' payable 673 (LO3)
days' sales uncollected 672 (LO3)
debt to equity ratio 669 (LO3)
dividend yield 675 (LO3)
free cash flow 668 (LO3)
interest coverage ratio 670 (LO3)
inventory turnover 671 (LO3)
payables turnover 672 (LO3)
price/earnings (P/E) 674 (LO3)
profit margin 665 (LO3)
quick ratio 674 (LO3)
receivables turnover 672 (LO3)
return on assets 666 (LO3)
return on equity 670 (LO3)

Chapter Assignments

DISCUSSION QUESTIONS

LO 1 **DQ1.** How are past performance and industry norms useful in evaluating a company's performance? What are their limitations?

LO 2 **DQ2.** In a five-year trend analysis, why do the dollar values remain the same for their respective years while the percentages usually change when a new five-year period is chosen?

LO 3 RATIO **DQ3.** Why does a decrease in receivables turnover create the need for cash from operating activities?

LO 3 RATIO **DQ4.** Why would ratios that include one balance sheet account and one income statement account, such as receivables turnover or return on assets, be questionable if they came from quarterly or other interim financial reports?

LO 3 **DQ5.** What is a limitation of free cash flow in comparing one company to another?

LO 4 **DQ6. BUSINESS APPLICATION ▶** In what way is selling an investment for a gain potentially a negative in evaluating quality of earnings?

LO 4 **DQ7. BUSINESS APPLICATION ▶** Is it unethical for new management to take an extra large write-off (a "big bath") in order to reduce future costs? Why or why not?

LO 4 **DQ8. BUSINESS APPLICATION ▶** Why is it useful to disclose discontinued operations separately on the income statement?

LO 4 **DQ9. BUSINESS APPLICATION ▶** Why is it essential that management compensation, including bonuses, be linked to financial goals and strategies that achieve shareholder value?

LO 4 **DQ10. BUSINESS APPLICATION ▶** What is one way a company can improve its earnings per share without improving its earnings or net income?

SHORT EXERCISES

LO 1 Objectives and Standards of Financial Performance Evaluation

SE1. CONCEPT ▶ Indicate whether each of the following items is (a) an underlying concept, (b) an objective or (c) a standard of comparison of financial statement analysis:

1. Industry norms
2. Assessment of a company's past performance
3. Comparability
4. The company's past performance
5. Assessment of future potential and related risk
6. Predictive value

LO 1 Sources of Information

SE2. For each piece of information in the list that follows, indicate whether the best source would be (a) reports published by the company, (b) SEC reports, (c) business periodicals, or (d) credit and investment advisory services.

1. Current market value of a company's stock
2. Management's analysis of the past year's operations
3. Objective assessment of a company's financial performance
4. Most complete body of financial disclosures
5. Current events affecting the company

LO 2 Trend Analysis

SE3. ACCOUNTING CONNECTION ▶ Using 2012 as the base year, prepare a trend analysis for the data that follow, and tell whether the results suggest a favorable or unfavorable trend. (Round to one decimal place.)

	2014	2013	2012
Net sales	$316,000	$272,000	$224,000
Accounts receivable (net)	86,000	64,000	42,000

LO 2 Horizontal Analysis

SE4. ACCOUNTING CONNECTION ▶ Vision, Inc.'s comparative income statements follow. Compute the amount and percentage changes for the income statements, and comment on the changes from 2013 to 2014. (Round the percentage changes to one decimal place.)

(Continued)

Vision, Inc.
Comparative Income Statements
For the Years Ended December 31, 2014 and 2013

	2014	2013
Net sales	$360,000	$290,000
Cost of goods sold	224,000	176,000
Gross margin	$136,000	$114,000
Operating expenses	80,000	60,000
Operating income	$ 56,000	$ 54,000
Interest expense	14,000	10,000
Income before income taxes	$ 42,000	$ 44,000
Income taxes expense	14,000	16,000
Net income	$ 28,000	$ 28,000
Earnings per share	$ 2.80	$ 2.80

LO 2 **Vertical Analysis**

SE5. ACCOUNTING CONNECTION ▶ Vision, Inc.'s comparative balance sheets follow. Prepare common-size statements, and comment on the changes from 2013 to 2014. (Round to one decimal place.)

Vision, Inc.
Comparative Balance Sheets
December 31, 2014 and 2013

	2014	2013
Assets		
Current assets	$ 48,000	$ 40,000
Property, plant, and equipment (net)	260,000	200,000
Total assets	$308,000	$240,000
Liabilities and Stockholders' Equity		
Current liabilities	$ 36,000	$ 44,000
Long-term liabilities	180,000	120,000
Stockholders' equity	92,000	76,000
Total liabilities and stockholders' equity	$308,000	$240,000

LO 3 **Operating Asset Management Analysis**

SE6. ACCOUNTING CONNECTION ▶ Using the information for Vision, Inc., in **SE4** and **SE5**, compute the current ratio, quick ratio, receivables turnover, days' sales uncollected, inventory turnover, days' inventory on hand, payables turnover, days' payable, and financing period for 2013 and 2014. Inventories were $8,000 in 2012, $10,000 in 2013, and $14,000 in 2014. Accounts receivable were $12,000 in 2012, $16,000 in 2013, and $20,000 in 2014. Accounts payable were $18,000 in 2012, $20,000 in 2013, and $24,000 in 2014. The company had no marketable securities or prepaid assets. Comment on the results. (Round to one decimal place.)

LO 3 **Profitability and Total Asset Management Analysis**

SE7. ACCOUNTING CONNECTION ▶ Using the information for Vision, Inc., in **SE4** and **SE5**, compute the profit margin, asset turnover, and return on assets for 2013 and 2014. In 2012, total assets were $200,000. Comment on the results. (Round to one decimal place.)

LO 3 **Financial Risk Analysis**

SE8. ACCOUNTING CONNECTION ▶ Using the information for Vision, Inc., in **SE4** and **SE5**, compute the debt to equity ratio, return on equity, and the interest coverage ratio for 2013 and 2014. In 2012 total stockholders' equity was $60,000. Comment on the results. (Round to one decimal place.)

LO 3 **Liquidity Analysis**

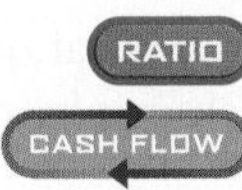

SE9. ACCOUNTING CONNECTION ▶ Using the information for Vision, Inc., in **SE4**, **SE5**, and **SE7**, compute the cash flow yield, cash flows to sales, cash flows to assets, and free cash flow for 2013 and 2014. Net cash flows from operating activities were $42,000 in 2013 and $32,000 in 2014. Net capital expenditures were $60,000 in 2013 and $80,000 in 2014. Cash dividends were $12,000 in both years. Comment on the results. (Round to one decimal place.)

LO 3 **Market Strength Analysis**

SE10. ACCOUNTING CONNECTION ▶ Using the information for Vision, Inc., in **SE4**, **SE5**, and **SE9**, compute the price/earnings (P/E) ratio and dividend yield for 2013 and 2014. The company had 10,000 shares of common stock outstanding in both years. The price of Vision's common stock was $60 in 2013 and $40 in 2014. Comment on the results. (Round to one decimal place.)

LO 4 **Quality of Earnings**

SE11. BUSINESS APPLICATION ▶ Each of the items that follow is a quality of earnings issue. Indicate whether the item is (a) an accounting method, (b) an accounting estimate, or (c) a nonoperating item. For any item for which the answer is (a) or (b), indicate which alternative is usually the more conservative choice.

1. LIFO versus FIFO
2. Extraordinary loss
3. 10-year useful life versus 15-year useful life
4. Straight-line versus accelerated method
5. Discontinued operations
6. Immediate write-off versus amortization
7. Increase versus decrease in percentage of uncollectible accounts

LO 4 **Corporate Income Statement**

SE12. BUSINESS APPLICATION ▶ Assume that Karib Corporation's chief financial officer gave you the following information: net sales, $720,000; cost of goods sold, $350,000; loss from discontinued operations (net of income tax benefit of $70,000), $200,000; loss on disposal of discontinued operations (net of income tax benefit of $16,000), $50,000; operating expenses, $130,000; income taxes expense on continuing operations, $100,000. Prepare the company's income statement for the year ended June 30, 2014. (Ignore earnings per share information.)

EXERCISES: SET A

LO 1 **Issues in Financial Performance Evaluation: Objectives, Standards, Sources of Information, and Executive Compensation**

E1A. CONCEPT ▶ Identify each of the following as (a) an underlying concept, (b) an objective of financial statement analysis, (c) a standard for financial statement analysis, (d) a source of information for financial statement analysis, or (e) an executive compensation issue:

1. Past ratios of the company
2. Linking performance to shareholder value
3. Average ratios of other companies in the same industry
4. Assessment of the future potential of an investment
5. Timeliness
6. Interim financial statements
7. SEC Form 10-K
8. Assessment of risk
9. Comparability
10. A company's annual report

LO 2

Trend Analysis

E2A. ACCOUNTING CONNECTION ▶ Using 2010 as the base year, prepare a trend analysis of the data that follow, and tell whether the situation shown by the trends is favorable or unfavorable. (Round to one decimal place.)

	2014	2013	2012	2011	2010
Net sales	$51,040	$47,960	$48,400	$45,760	$44,000
Cost of goods sold	34,440	30,800	31,080	29,400	28,000
General and administrative expenses	10,560	10,368	10,176	9,792	9,600
Operating income	6,040	6,792	7,144	6,568	6,400

LO 2

Horizontal Analysis

E3A. ACCOUNTING CONNECTION ▶ Compute the amount and percentage changes for Rivera Company's comparative balance sheets, and comment on the changes from 2013 to 2014. (Round the percentage changes to one decimal place.)

Rivera Company
Comparative Balance Sheets
December 31, 2014 and 2013

	2014	2013
Assets		
Current assets	$ 37,200	$ 25,600
Property, plant, and equipment (net)	218,928	194,400
Total assets	$256,128	$220,000
Liabilities and Stockholders' Equity		
Current liabilities	$ 22,400	$ 6,400
Long-term liabilities	70,000	80,000
Stockholders' equity	163,728	133,600
Total liabilities and stockholders' equity	$256,128	$220,000

LO 2

Vertical Analysis

E4A. ACCOUNTING CONNECTION ▶ Express Rivera Company's partial comparative income statements as common-size statements, and comment on the changes from 2013 to 2014.

Rivera Company
Partial Comparative Income Statements
For the Years Ended December 31, 2014 and 2013

	2014	2013
Net sales	$424,000	$368,000
Cost of goods sold	254,400	239,200
Gross margin	$169,600	$128,800
Selling expenses	$106,000	$ 73,600
General expenses	50,880	36,800
Total operating expenses	$156,880	$110,400
Operating income	$ 12,720	$ 18,400

LO 3

RATIO

Operating Asset Management Analysis

E5A. ACCOUNTING CONNECTION ▶ Partial comparative balance sheet and income statement information for Posad Company follows.

	2014	2013
Cash	$ 13,600	$ 10,400
Marketable securities	7,200	17,200
Accounts receivable (net)	44,800	35,600
Inventory	54,400	49,600
Total current assets	$120,000	$112,800
Accounts payable	$ 40,000	$ 28,200
Net sales	$322,560	$220,720
Cost of goods sold	217,600	203,360
Gross margin	$104,960	$ 17,360

In 2012, the year-end balances for Accounts Receivable and Inventory were $32,400 and $51,200, respectively. Accounts Payable was $30,600 in 2012 and is the only current liability. Compute the current ratio, quick ratio, receivables turnover, days' sales uncollected, inventory turnover, days' inventory on hand, payables turnover, days' payable for each year, and financing period. (Round to one decimal place.) Comment on the change in the company's liquidity position, including its operating cycle and required days of financing from 2013 to 2014.

LO 3

Turnover Analysis

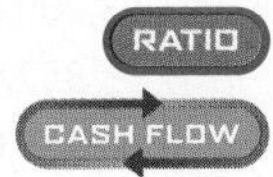

E6A. ACCOUNTING CONNECTION ▶ Designer Suits Rental has been in business for four years. Because the company has recently had a cash flow problem, management wonders whether there is a problem with receivables or inventories. Selected figures from the company's financial statements (in thousands) follow.

	2014	2013	2012	2011
Net sales	$144.0	$112.0	$96.0	$80.0
Cost of goods sold	90.0	72.0	60.0	48.0
Accounts receivable (net)	24.0	20.0	16.0	12.0
Merchandise inventory	28.0	22.0	16.0	10.0
Accounts payable	13.0	10.0	8.0	5.0

Compute the receivables turnover, inventory turnover, and payables turnover for each of the four years, and comment on the results relative to the cash flow problem that the firm has been experiencing. Merchandise inventory was $11,000, accounts receivable were $11,000, and accounts payable were $4,000 in 2010. (Round to one decimal place.)

LO 3

Profitability and Total Asset Management Analysis

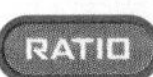

E7A. ACCOUNTING CONNECTION ▶ Elm Company had total assets of $640,000 in 2012, $680,000 in 2013, and $760,000 in 2014. In 2013, Elm had net income of $77,112 on revenues of $1,224,000. In 2014, it had net income of $98,952 on revenues of $1,596,000. Compute the profit margin, asset turnover, and return on assets for 2013 and 2014. Comment on the apparent cause of the increase or decrease in profitability. (Round to one decimal place.)

LO 3

Financial Risk and Market Strength Ratios

E8A. ACCOUNTING CONNECTION ▶ An investor is considering investing in the long-term bonds and common stock of Companies A and B. Both firms operate in the same industry. Both also pay a dividend per share of $8 and have a yield of 10 percent on their long-term bonds. Other data for the two firms follow.

(Continued)

	Company A	Company B
Total assets	$4,800,000	$2,160,000
Total liabilities	2,160,000	1,188,000
Prior year stockholders' equity	2,120,000	750,000
Income before income taxes	576,000	259,200
Interest expense	194,400	106,920
Net income	136,800	74,800
Earnings per share	6.40	10.00
Market price of common stock	80.00	95.00

Compute the debt to equity ratio, return on equity ratio, interest coverage ratio, and price/earnings (P/E) ratio, as well as the dividend yield, and comment on the results. (Round to one decimal place.)

LO 3 **Liquidity Analysis**

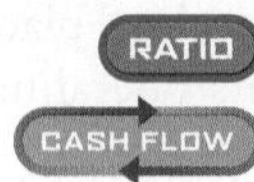

E9A. Using the data from the financial statements of Stanford, Inc., that follow, compute the company's cash flow yield, cash flows to sales, cash flows to assets, and free cash flow. (Round to one decimal place.)

Net sales	$3,200,000
Net income	352,000
Net cash flows from operating activities	456,000
Total assets, beginning of year	2,890,000
Total assets, end of year	3,120,000
Cash dividends	120,000
Net capital expenditures	298,000

LO 4 **Effect of Alternative Accounting Methods**

E10A. BUSINESS APPLICATION ▶ At the end of its first year of operations, a company calculated its ending merchandise inventory according to three different accounting methods, as follows: FIFO, $47,500; average-cost, $45,000; LIFO, $43,000. If the company used the average-cost method, its net income for the year would be $17,000.

1. Determine net income if the company used the FIFO method.
2. Determine net income if the company used the LIFO method.
3. Which method is more conservative?
4. **CONCEPT ▶** Will the consistency convention be violated if the company chooses to use the LIFO method? Why or why not?
5. **CONCEPT ▶** Does the full-disclosure convention require disclosure of the inventory method used in the financial statements?

LO 4 **Corporate Income Statement**

E11A. BUSINESS APPLICATION ▶ Assume that Stream Toy Corporation's chief financial officer gave you the following information: net sales, $3,800,000; cost of goods sold, $2,100,000; extraordinary gain (net of income taxes of $7,000), $25,000; loss from discontinued operations (net of income tax benefit of $60,000), $100,000; loss on disposal of discontinued operations (net of income tax benefit of $26,000), $70,000; selling expenses, $100,000; administrative expenses, $80,000; income taxes expense on continuing operations, $600,000. Prepare the company's income statement for the year ended June 30, 2014. (Ignore earnings per share information.)

LO 4

Corporate Income Statement

E12A. BUSINESS APPLICATION ▶ Components of Van Corporation's income statement for the year ended December 31, 2014 follow. Recast the income statement in multistep form, including allocating income taxes to appropriate items (assume a 30 percent income tax rate) and showing earnings per share figures (200,000 shares outstanding). (Round earnings per share figures to the nearest cent.)

Sales	$1,110,000
Cost of goods sold	(550,000)
Operating expenses	(225,000)
Restructuring	(110,000)
Total income taxes expense for period	(179,100)
Income from discontinued operations	160,000
Gain on disposal of discontinued operations	140,000
Extraordinary gain	72,000
Net income	$ 417,900
Earnings per share	$ 2.09

EXERCISES: SET B

Visit the textbook companion website at www.cengagebrain.com to access Exercise Set B for this chapter.

PROBLEMS

LO 2

Horizontal and Vertical Analysis

SPREADSHEET

✔ 1: Net income: 34.9% increase
✔ 1: Total assets: 3.6% increase
✔ 2: 2014 Net income: 4.2%

P1. Obras Corporation's condensed comparative income statements and comparative balance sheets for 2014 and 2013 follow.

Obras Corporation
Comparative Income Statements
For the Years Ended December 31, 2014 and 2013

	2014	2013
Net sales	$3,276,800	$3,146,400
Cost of goods sold	2,088,800	2,008,400
Gross margin	$1,188,000	$1,138,000
Operating expenses:		
Selling expenses	$ 476,800	$ 518,000
Administrative expenses	447,200	423,200
Total operating expenses	$ 924,000	$ 941,200
Income from operations	$ 264,000	$ 196,800
Interest expense	65,600	39,200
Income before income taxes	$ 198,400	$ 157,600
Income taxes expense	62,400	56,800
Net income	$ 136,000	$ 100,800
Earnings per share	$ 3.40	$ 2.52

(Continued)

Obras Corporation
Comparative Balance Sheets
December 31, 2014 and 2013

	2014	2013
Assets		
Cash	$ 81,200	$ 40,800
Accounts receivable (net)	235,600	229,200
Inventory	574,800	594,800
Property, plant, and equipment (net)	750,000	720,000
Total assets	$1,641,600	$1,584,800
Liabilities and Stockholders' Equity		
Accounts payable	$ 267,600	$ 477,200
Notes payable (short-term)	200,000	400,000
Bonds payable	400,000	—
Common stock, $10 par value	400,000	400,000
Retained earnings	374,000	307,600
Total liabilities and stockholders' equity	$1,641,600	$1,584,800

REQUIRED

1. Prepare schedules showing the amount and percentage changes from 2013 to 2014 for the comparative income statements and the balance sheets. (Round to one decimal place.)
2. Prepare common-size income statements and balance sheets for 2013 and 2014. (Round to one decimal place.)
3. **ACCOUNTING CONNECTION ▶** Comment on the results in requirements **1** and **2** by identifying favorable and unfavorable changes in the components and composition of the statements.

LO 3

Effects of Transactions on Ratios

P2. Davis Corporation, a clothing retailer, engaged in the transactions that follow. Opposite each transaction is a ratio and space to mark the effect of each transaction on the ratio.

		Effect		
Transaction	**Ratio**	**Increase**	**Decrease**	**None**
a. Issued common stock for cash.	Asset turnover	___	___	___
b. Declared cash dividend.	Current ratio	___	___	___
c. Sold treasury stock.	Return on equity	___	___	___
d. Borrowed cash by issuing note payable.	Debt to equity ratio	___	___	___
e. Paid salaries expense.	Inventory turnover	___	___	___
f. Purchased merchandise for cash.	Current ratio	___	___	___
g. Sold equipment for cash.	Receivables turnover	___	___	___
h. Sold merchandise on account.	Quick ratio	___	___	___
i. Paid current portion of long-term debt.	Return on assets	___	___	___
j. Gave sales discount.	Profit margin	___	___	___
k. Purchased marketable securities for cash.	Quick ratio	___	___	___
l. Declared 5% stock dividend.	Current ratio	___	___	___
m. Purchased a building.	Free cash flow	___	___	___

REQUIRED

ACCOUNTING CONNECTION ▶ Show that you understand the effect of business activities on performance measures by placing an *X* in the appropriate column to show whether the transaction increased, decreased, or had no effect on the indicated ratio.

LO 3

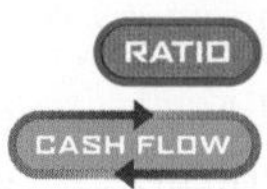

Comprehensive Ratio Analysis

✔ 1a: 2014 Current ratio: 1.5 times
✔ 1e: 2014 Inventory turnover: 3.9 times
✔ 2c: 2014 Return on assets: 5.0%
✔ 3b: 2014 Return on equity: 8.2%
✔ 4a: 2014 Cash flow yield: 1.7 times
✔ 5b: 2014 Dividend yield: 1.3%

P3. Tuxedo Corporation's condensed comparative income statements and balance sheets follow. All figures are given in thousands of dollars, except earnings per share.

Tuxedo Corporation
Comparative Income Statements
For the Years Ended December 31, 2014 and 2013

	2014	2013
Net sales	$800,400	$742,600
Cost of goods sold	454,100	396,200
Gross margin	$346,300	$346,400
Operating expenses:		
Selling expenses	$130,100	$104,600
Administrative expenses	140,300	115,500
Total operating expenses	$270,400	$220,100
Income from operations	$ 75,900	$126,300
Interest expense	25,000	20,000
Income before income taxes	$ 50,900	$106,300
Income taxes expense	14,000	35,000
Net income	$ 36,900	$ 71,300
Earnings per share	$ 2.46	$ 4.76

Tuxedo Corporation
Comparative Balance Sheets
December 31, 2014 and 2013

	2014	2013
Assets		
Cash	$ 31,100	$ 27,200
Accounts receivable (net)	72,500	42,700
Inventory	122,600	107,800
Property, plant, and equipment (net)	577,700	507,500
Total assets	$803,900	$685,200
Liabilities and Stockholders' Equity		
Accounts payable	$104,700	$ 72,300
Notes payable (short-term)	50,000	50,000
Bonds payable	200,000	110,000
Common stock, $10 par value	300,000	300,000
Retained earnings	149,200	152,900
Total liabilities and stockholders' equity	$803,900	$685,200

Additional data for Tuxedo in 2014 and 2013 follow.

	2014	2013
Net cash flows from operating activities	$64,000	$99,000
Net capital expenditures	$119,000	$38,000
Dividends paid	$31,400	$35,000
Number of common shares	30,000	30,000
Market price per share	$80	$120

Balances of selected accounts at the end of 2012 were accounts receivable (net), $52,700; inventory, $99,400; accounts payable, $64,800; total assets, $647,800; and stockholders' equity, $376,600. All of the bonds payable were long-term liabilities.

(Continued)

REQUIRED

Perform the following analyses. (Round to one decimal place.)

1. Prepare an operating asset management analysis by calculating for each year the (a) current ratio, (b) quick ratio, (c) receivables turnover, (d) days' sales uncollected, (e) inventory turnover, (f) days' inventory on hand, (g) payables turnover, (h) days' payable, and (i) financing period.
2. Prepare a profitability and total asset management analysis by calculating for each year the (a) profit margin, (b) asset turnover, and (c) return on assets.
3. Prepare a financial risk analysis by calculating for each year the (a) debt to equity ratio, (b) return on equity, and (c) interest coverage ratio.
4. Prepare a liquidity analysis by calculating for each year the (a) cash flow yield, (b) cash flows to sales, (c) cash flows to assets, and (d) free cash flow.
5. Prepare an analysis of market strength by calculating for each year the (a) price/earnings (P/E) ratio and (b) dividend yield.
6. **ACCOUNTING CONNECTION ▶** After making the calculations, indicate whether each ratio improved or deteriorated from 2013 to 2014 (use *F* for favorable and *U* for unfavorable and consider changes of 0.1 or less to be neutral).

LO 3

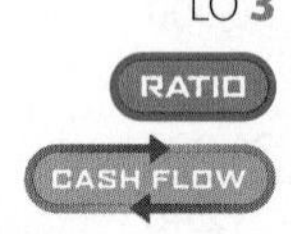

Comprehensive Ratio Analysis of Two Companies

✔ 1b: Single quick ratio: 1.5 times
✔ 1g: Single payables turnover: 17.9 times
✔ 2b: Single asset turnover: 2.5 times
✔ 3a: Single debt to equity ratio: 1.0 time
✔ 4b: Single cash flow to sales: 2.2%
✔ 5a: Single price/earnings ratio: 13.9 times

P4. Mel Filbert is considering an investment in the common stock of a chain of retail department stores. She has narrowed her choice to two retail companies, Single Corporation and Design Corporation, whose income statements and balance sheets follow.

Income Statements

	Single	Design
Net sales	$12,560,000	$25,210,000
Costs and expenses:		
Cost of goods sold	$ 6,142,000	$14,834,000
Selling expenses	4,822,600	7,108,200
Administrative expenses	986,000	2,434,000
Total costs and expenses	$11,950,600	$24,376,200
Income from operations	$ 609,400	$ 833,800
Interest expense	194,000	228,000
Income before income taxes	$ 415,400	$ 605,800
Income taxes expense	200,000	300,000
Net income	$ 215,400	$ 305,800
Earnings per share	$ 4.31	$ 10.19

Balance Sheets

	Single	Design
Assets		
Cash	$ 80,000	$ 192,400
Marketable securities (at cost)	203,400	84,600
Accounts receivable (net)	552,800	985,400
Inventory	629,800	1,253,400
Prepaid expenses	54,400	114,000
Property, plant, and equipment (net)	2,913,600	6,552,000
Intangibles and other assets	553,200	144,800
Total assets	$4,987,200	$9,326,600

(Continued)

Liabilities and Stockholders' Equity		
Accounts payable	$ 344,000	$ 572,600
Notes payable	150,000	400,000
Income taxes payable	50,200	73,400
Bonds payable	2,000,000	2,000,000
Common stock, $20 par value	1,000,000	600,000
Additional paid-in capital	609,800	3,568,600
Retained earnings	833,200	2,112,000
Total liabilities and stockholders' equity	$4,987,200	$9,326,600

During the year, Single paid a total of $50,000 in dividends. The market price per share of its stock is currently $60. In comparison, Design paid a total of $114,000 in dividends, and the current market price of its stock is $76 per share. Single had net cash flows from operations of $271,500 and net capital expenditures of $625,000. Design had net cash flows from operations of $492,500 and net capital expenditures of $1,050,000. Information for prior years is not readily available. Assume that all notes payable are current liabilities and all bonds payable are long-term liabilities and that there is no change in inventory.

REQUIRED

Conduct a comprehensive ratio analysis for each company, using the available information. Compare the results. (Round to one decimal place, and consider changes of 0.1 or less to be indeterminate.)

1. Prepare an operating asset management analysis by calculating for each company the (a) current ratio, (b) quick ratio, (c) receivables turnover, (d) days' sales uncollected, (e) inventory turnover, (f) days' inventory on hand, (g) payables turnover, (h) days' payable, and (i) financing period.
2. Prepare a profitability and total asset management analysis by calculating for each company the (a) profit margin, (b) asset turnover, and (c) return on assets.
3. Prepare a financial risk analysis by calculating for each company the (a) debt to equity ratio, (b) return on equity, and (c) interest coverage ratio.
4. Prepare a liquidity analysis by calculating for each company the (a) cash flow yield, (b) cash flows to sales, (c) cash flows to assets, and (d) free cash flow.
5. Prepare an analysis of market strength by calculating for each company the (a) price/earnings (P/E) ratio and (b) dividend yield.
6. **ACCOUNTING CONNECTION ▶** Compare the two companies by inserting the ratio calculations from 1 through 5 in a table with the following column headings: Ratio Name, Single, Design, and Company with More Favorable Ratio. Indicate in the last column which company had the more favorable ratio in each case.
7. **BUSINESS APPLICATION ▶** How could the analysis be improved if information about these companies' prior years were available?

LO 4

RATIO

SPREADSHEET

✔ 1: Net income using FIFO and straight line: $190,800
✔ 1: Net income using LIFO and double-declining-balance: $93,200

Effect of Alternative Accounting Methods

P5. BUSINESS APPLICATION ▶ Furlong Corporation began operations in 2014. At the beginning of the year, the company purchased plant assets of $900,000, with an estimated useful life of 10 years and no residual value. During the year, the company had net sales of $1,300,000, salaries expense of $200,000, and other expenses of $80,000, excluding depreciation. In addition, Furlong purchased inventory as follows.

Jan. 15	400 units at $400	$160,000
Mar. 20	200 units at $408	81,600
June 15	800 units at $416	332,800
Sept. 18	600 units at $412	247,200
Dec. 9	300 units at $420	126,000
Total	2,300 units	$947,600

At the end of the year, a physical inventory disclosed 500 units still on hand. Furlong's managers know they have a choice of accounting methods, but they are unsure how those

(Continued)

methods will affect net income. They have heard of the FIFO and LIFO inventory methods and the straight-line and double-declining-balance depreciation methods.

REQUIRED

1. Prepare two income statements for Furlong, one using the FIFO and straight-line methods and the other using the LIFO and double-declining-balance methods. Ignore income taxes.
2. Prepare a schedule accounting for the difference in the two net income figures obtained in requirement **1**.
3. What effect does the choice of accounting method have on Furlong's inventory turnover? What conclusions can you draw? Use the year-end balance to compute the ratio. (Round to one decimal place.)
4. How does the choice of accounting methods affect Furlong's return on assets? Assume the company's only assets are cash of $80,000, inventory, and plant assets. Use year-end balances to compute the ratios. Is your evaluation of Furlong's profitability affected by the choice of accounting methods?

LO **4**

Corporate Income Statement

✔ 1: Net income: $145,000

P6. BUSINESS APPLICATION ▶ Information concerning Krall Corporation's operations during 2014 follows.

a. Administrative expenses, $90,000
b. Cost of goods sold, $420,000
c. Extraordinary loss from an earthquake (net of taxes, $36,000), $60,000
d. Sales (net), $900,000
e. Selling expenses, $80,000
f. Income taxes expense applicable to continuing operations, $105,000

REQUIRED

1. Prepare the corporation's income statement for the year ended December 31, 2014 (ignore earnings per share data).
2. Which item in Krall's income statement affects the company's quality of earnings? Why does it have an effect on quality of earnings?

ALTERNATE PROBLEMS

LO **2**

Horizontal and Vertical Analysis

SPREADSHEET

✔ 1: Net income, 34.9% increase
✔ 1: Total assets, 3.6% increase
✔ 2: 2014 Net income: 4.2%

P7. Rylander Corporation's condensed comparative income statements and balance sheets for 2014 and 2013 follow.

Rylander Corporation
Comparative Income Statements
For the Years Ended December 31, 2014 and 2013

	2014	2013
Net sales	$6,553,600	$6,292,800
Cost of goods sold	4,177,600	4,016,800
Gross margin	$2,376,000	$2,276,000
Operating expenses:		
Selling expenses	$ 953,600	$1,036,000
Administrative expenses	894,400	846,400
Total operating expenses	$1,848,000	$1,882,400
Income from operations	$ 528,000	$ 393,600
Interest expense	131,200	78,400
Income before income taxes	$ 396,800	$ 315,200
Income taxes expense	124,800	113,600
Net income	$ 272,000	$ 201,600
Earnings per share	$ 3.40	$ 2.52

Rylander Corporation
Comparative Balance Sheets
December 31, 2014 and 2013

	2014	2013
Assets		
Cash	$ 162,400	$ 81,600
Accounts receivable (net)	471,200	458,400
Inventory	1,149,600	1,189,600
Property, plant, and equipment (net)	1,500,000	1,440,000
Total assets	$3,283,200	$3,169,600
Liabilities and Stockholders' Equity		
Accounts payable	$ 535,200	$ 954,400
Notes payable (short-term)	400,000	800,000
Bonds payable	800,000	—
Common stock, $10 par value	800,000	800,000
Retained earnings	748,000	615,200
Total liabilities and stockholders' equity	$3,283,200	$3,169,600

REQUIRED

1. Prepare schedules showing the amount and percentage changes from 2013 to 2014 for the comparative income statements and the balance sheets. (Round to one decimal place.)
2. Prepare common-size income statements and balance sheets for 2013 and 2014. (Round to one decimal place.)
3. **ACCOUNTING CONNECTION ▶** Comment on the results in requirements **1** and **2** by identifying favorable and unfavorable changes in the components and composition of the statements.

LO **3**

Effects of Transactions on Ratios

P8. Koz Corporation engaged in the transactions that follow. Opposite each transaction is a ratio and space to indicate the effect of each transaction on the ratio.

		Effect		
Transaction	**Ratio**	**Increase**	**Decrease**	**None**
a. Sold merchandise on account.	Current ratio	___	___	___
b. Sold merchandise on account.	Inventory turnover	___	___	___
c. Collected on accounts receivable.	Quick ratio	___	___	___
d. Wrote off an uncollectible account.	Receivables turnover	___	___	___
e. Paid on accounts payable.	Current ratio	___	___	___
f. Declared cash dividend.	Return on equity	___	___	___
g. Incurred advertising expense.	Profit margin	___	___	___
h. Issued stock dividend.	Debt to equity ratio	___	___	___
i. Issued bonds payable.	Asset turnover	___	___	___
j. Accrued interest expense.	Current ratio	___	___	___
k. Paid previously declared cash dividend.	Dividend yield	___	___	___
l. Purchased treasury stock.	Return on assets	___	___	___
m. Recorded depreciation expense.	Cash flow yield	___	___	___

REQUIRED

ACCOUNTING CONNECTION ▶ Show that you understand the effect of business activities on performance measures by placing an *X* in the appropriate column to show whether the transaction increased, decreased, or had no effect on the indicated ratio.

LO 3

RATIO

CASH FLOW

✔ 1a: 2014 Current ratio: 1.9 times
✔ 1e: 2014 Inventory turnover: 3.6 times
✔ 2c: 2014 Return on assets: 8.40%
✔ 3b: 2014 Return on equity: 18.4%
✔ 4d: 2014 Free cash flows: ($280,000)
✔ 5b: 2014 Dividend yield: 3.1%

Comprehensive Ratio Analysis

P9. Data for Obras Corporation in 2014 and 2013 follow. These data should be used in conjunction with the data in **P1**.

	2014	2013
Net cash flows from operating activities	$(196,000)	$144,000
Net capital expenditures	$40,000	$65,000
Dividends paid	$44,000	$34,400
Number of common shares	40,000	40,000
Market price per share	$36	$60

Selected balances at the end of 2012 were accounts receivable (net), $206,800; inventory, $547,200; total assets, $1,465,600; accounts payable, $386,600; and stockholders' equity, $641,200. All of Obras's notes payable were current liabilities; all its bonds payable were long-term liabilities.

REQUIRED

Perform a comprehensive ratio analysis following the steps outlined below. (Round to one decimal place.)

1. Prepare a operating asset management analysis by calculating for each year the (a) current ratio, (b) quick ratio, (c) receivables turnover, (d) days' sales uncollected, (e) inventory turnover, (f) days' inventory on hand, (g) payables turnover, (h) days' payable, and (i) financing period.
2. Prepare a profitability and total asset management analysis by calculating for each year the (a) profit margin, (b) asset turnover, and (c) return on assets.
3. Prepare a financial risk analysis by calculating for each year the (a) debt to equity ratio, (b) return on equity, and (c) interest coverage ratio.
4. Prepare a liquidity analysis by calculating for each year the (a) cash flow yield, (b) cash flows to sales, (c) cash flows to assets, and (d) free cash flow.
5. Prepare a market strength analysis by calculating for each year the (a) price/earnings (P/E) ratio and (b) dividend yield.
6. **ACCOUNTING CONNECTION ▶** After making the calculations, indicate whether each ratio improved or deteriorated from 2013 to 2014 (use *F* for favorable and *U* for unfavorable and consider changes of 0.1 or less to be neutral).

LO 3

RATIO

CASH FLOW

✔ 1b: Lucent quick ratio: 1.5 times
✔ 1g: Lucent payables turnover: 17.9 times
✔ 2b: Lucent asset turnover: 2.5 times
✔ 3a: Lucent debt to equity ratio: 1.0 time
✔ 4b: Lucent cash flow to sales: 2.2%
✔ 5a: Lucent price/earnings ratio: 13.9 times

Comprehensive Ratio Analysis of Two Companies

P10. Lucy Lee is considering an investment in the common stock of a chain of retail department stores. She has narrowed her choice to two retail companies, Lucent Corporation and Ranbaxy Corporation, whose income statements and balance sheets follow.

Income Statements

	Lucent	Ranbaxy
Net sales	$50,240,000	$100,840,000
Costs and expenses:		
Cost of goods sold	$24,568,000	$ 59,336,000
Selling expenses	19,290,400	28,432,800
Administrative expenses	3,944,000	9,736,000
Total costs and expenses	$47,802,400	$ 97,504,800
Income from operations	$ 2,437,600	$ 3,335,200
Interest expense	776,000	912,000
Income before income taxes	$ 1,661,600	$ 2,423,200
Income taxes expense	800,000	1,200,000
Net income	$ 861,600	$ 1,223,200
Earnings per share	$ 8.62	$ 20.38

Balance Sheets

	Lucent	Ranbaxy
Assets		
Cash	$ 320,000	$ 769,600
Marketable securities (at cost)	813,600	338,400
Accounts receivable (net)	2,211,200	3,941,600
Inventory	2,519,200	5,013,600
Prepaid expenses	217,600	456,000
Property, plant, and equipment (net)	11,654,400	26,208,000
Intangibles and other assets	2,212,800	579,200
Total assets	$19,948,800	$37,306,400
Liabilities and Stockholders' Equity		
Accounts payable	$ 1,376,000	$ 2,290,400
Notes payable	600,000	1,600,000
Income taxes payable	200,800	293,600
Bonds payable	8,000,000	8,000,000
Common stock, $20 par value	4,000,000	2,400,000
Additional paid-in capital	2,439,200	14,274,400
Retained earnings	3,332,800	8,448,000
Total liabilities and stockholders' equity	$19,948,800	$37,306,400

During the year, Lucent paid a total of $200,000 in dividends. The market price per share of its stock is currently $120. In comparison, Ranbaxy paid a total of $456,000 in dividends, and the current market price of its stock is $152 per share. Lucent had net cash flows from operations of $1,086,000 and net capital expenditures of $2,500,000. Ranbaxy had net cash flows from operations of $1,970,000 and net capital expenditures of $4,200,000. Information for prior years is not readily available. Assume that all notes payable are current liabilities and all bonds payable are long-term liabilities and that there is no change in inventory.

REQUIRED

Conduct a comprehensive ratio analysis for each company, following the steps below. Compare the results. (Round to one decimal place, and consider changes of 0.1 or less to be indeterminate.)

1. Prepare an operating asset management analysis by calculating for each company the (a) current ratio, (b) quick ratio, (c) receivables turnover, (d) days' sales uncollected, (e) inventory turnover, (f) days' inventory on hand, (g) payables turnover, (h) days' payable, and (i) financing period.
2. Prepare a profitability and total asset management analysis by calculating for each company the (a) profit margin, (b) asset turnover, and (c) return on assets.
3. Prepare a financial risk analysis by calculating for each company the (a) debt to equity ratio, (b) return on equity, and (c) interest coverage ratio.
4. Prepare a liquidity analysis by calculating for each company the (a) cash flow yield, (b) cash flows to sales, (c) cash flows to assets, and (d) free cash flow.
5. Prepare an analysis of market strength by calculating for each company the (a) price/earnings (P/E) ratio and (b) dividend yield.
6. **ACCOUNTING CONNECTION ▶** Compare the two companies by inserting the ratio calculations from 1 through 5 in a table with the following column headings: Ratio Name, Lucent, Ranbaxy, and Company with More Favorable Ratio. Indicate in the last column which company had the more favorable ratio in each case.
7. **BUSINESS APPLICATION ▶** How could the analysis be improved if information about these companies' prior years were available?

LO 4

Effect of Alternative Accounting Methods

RATIO

SPREADSHEET

✔ 1: Net income using FIFO and straight line: $381,600
✔ 1: Net income using LIFO and double-declining-balance: $186,400

P11. BUSINESS APPLICATION ▶ Minnows Corporation began operations in 2014. At the beginning of the year, the company purchased plant assets of $1,800,000, with an estimated useful life of 10 years and no residual value. During the year, the company had net sales of $2,600,000, salaries expense of $400,000, and other expenses of $160,000, excluding depreciation. In addition, Minnows purchased inventory as follows.

Jan. 15	800 units at $400	$ 320,000
Mar. 20	400 units at $408	163,200
June 15	1,600 units at $416	665,600
Sept. 18	1,200 units at $412	494,400
Dec. 9	600 units at $420	252,000
Total	4,600 units	$1,895,200

At the end of the year, a physical inventory disclosed 1,000 units still on hand. Minnows's managers know they have a choice of accounting methods, but they are unsure how those methods will affect net income. They have heard of the FIFO and LIFO inventory methods and the straight-line and double-declining-balance depreciation methods.

REQUIRED

1. Prepare two income statements for Minnows, one using the FIFO and straight-line methods and the other using the LIFO and double-declining-balance methods. Ignore income taxes.
2. Prepare a schedule accounting for the difference in the two net income figures obtained in requirement **1**.
3. What effect does the choice of accounting method have on Minnows's inventory turnover? What conclusions can you draw? Use the year-end balance to compute the ratio. (Round to one decimal place.)
4. How does the choice of accounting methods affect Minnows's return on assets? Assume the company's only assets are cash of $160,000, inventory, and plant assets. Use year-end balances to compute the ratios. Is your evaluation of Minnows's profitability affected by the choice of accounting methods? (Round to one decimal place.)

LO 4

Corporate Income Statement

✔ 1: Net income: $176,000

P12. BUSINESS APPLICATION ▶ Income statement information for Linz Corporation in 2014 follows.

a. Administrative expenses, $220,000
b. Cost of goods sold, $880,000
c. Extraordinary loss from a storm (net of taxes, $20,000), $40,000
d. Income taxes expense, continuing operations, $84,000
e. Net sales, $1,780,000
f. Selling expenses, $380,000

REQUIRED

1. Prepare Linz's income statement for 2014 (ignore earnings per share data).
2. Which item in Linz's income statement affects the company's quality of earnings? Why does it have this effect?

CASES

LO 1, 3

Conceptual Understanding: Standards for Financial Performance Evaluation

C1. In 2005, in a dramatic move, **Standard & Poor's Ratings Group**, the large financial company that evaluates the riskiness of companies' debt, downgraded its rating of **General Motors** and **Ford Motor Co.** debt to "junk" bond status because of concerns about the companies' profitability and cash flows. Despite aggressive cost cutting, both companies still face substantial future liabilities for health care and pension obligations. They are losing money or barely breaking even on auto operations that concentrate on slow-selling SUVs. High gas prices and competition force them to sell the cars at a discount. What standards do you think Standard & Poor's would use to evaluate General Motors' progress? What performance measures would Standard & Poor's most likely use in making its evaluation? Was Standard & Poor's right in light of future events?

LO 1

RATIO

Interpreting Financial Reports: Using Segment Information

C2. Refer to Exhibit 1, which shows the segment information of **Goodyear Tire & Rubber Company**. In what business segments does Goodyear operate? What is the relative size of its business segments in terms of sales and income in the most recent year shown? Which segment is most profitable in terms of return on assets? Which segment is largest, and which segment is most profitable in terms of return on assets? (Round to one decimal place.)

LO 2, 3

RATIO

Interpreting Financial Reports: Effect of a One-Time Item on a Loan Decision

C3. Apple a Day, Inc., and Unforgettable Edibles, Inc., are food catering businesses that operate in the same metropolitan area. Their customers include *Fortune* 500 companies, regional firms, and individuals. The two firms reported similar profit margins for the current year, and both base bonuses for managers on the achievement of a target profit margin and return on equity. Each firm has submitted a loan request to you, a loan officer for City National Bank. They have provided you with the following information:

	Apple a Day	Unforgettable Edibles
Net sales	$625,348	$717,900
Cost of goods sold	225,125	287,080
Gross margin	$400,223	$430,820
Operating expenses	281,300	371,565
Operating income	$118,923	$ 59,255
Gain on sale of real estate	—	81,923
Interest expense	(9,333)	(15,338)
Income before income taxes	$109,590	$125,840
Income taxes expense	25,990	29,525
Net income	$ 83,600	$ 96,315
Average stockholders' equity	$312,700	$390,560

1. Perform a vertical analysis and prepare a common-size income statement for each firm. Compute profit margin and return on equity. (Round to one decimal place.)
2. Discuss these results, the bonus plan for management, and loan considerations. Identify the company that is the better loan risk.

LO 3

RATIO

Interpreting Financial Reports: Comprehensive Ratio Analysis

C4. Using data from **CVS Corporation**'s annual report in the Supplement to Chapter 1, conduct a comprehensive ratio analysis that compares the company's performance in 2011 and 2010. If you have computed ratios for CVS in previous chapters, you may

(Continued)

prepare a table that summarizes the ratios and show calculations only for the ratios not previously calculated. If this is the first ratio analysis you have done for CVS, show all your computations. In either case, after each group of ratios, comment on the performance of CVS. (Round to one decimal place.) Prepare and comment on the following categories of ratios:

- Operating asset management analysis: current ratio, quick ratio, receivables turnover, days' sales uncollected, inventory turnover, days' inventory on hand, payables turnover, days' payable, and financing period (Accounts Receivable, Inventories, and Accounts Payable were [in millions] $5,457, $10,343, and $3,560, respectively, in 2009.)
- Profitability and total asset management analysis: profit margin, asset turnover, and return on assets (Total assets were [in millions] $61,641 in 2009.)
- Financial risk analysis: debt to equity ratio, return on equity, and interest coverage ratio (Total total shareholders' equity was [in millions] $35,768 in 2009.)
- Liquidity analysis: cash flow yield, cash flows to sales, cash flows to assets, and free cash flow
- Market strength analysis: price/earnings (P/E) ratio and dividend yield

LO 3

Interpreting Financial Reports: Comparison of Key Financial Performance Measures

RATIO

C5. Refer to **CVS Corporation**'s annual report and **Southwest Airlines Co.**'s financial statements in the Supplement to Chapter 1. Prepare a table for the following key financial performance measures for the two most recent years for both companies. (Round to one decimal place.) Use your computations in **C4** or perform those analyses if you have not done so. Total assets for Southwest in 2009 were $14,269 million.

- Profitability and total asset management: profit margin, asset turnover, return on assets
- Financial risk: debt to equity ratio
- Liquidity: cash flow yield, free cash flow

Evaluate and comment on the relative performance of the two companies with respect to each of the above categories.

LO 4

Conceptual Understanding: Classic Quality of Earnings Case

C6. BUSINESS APPLICATION ▶ On January 19, 1988, **IBM** reported greatly increased earnings for the fourth quarter of 1987. Despite this reported gain in earnings, the price of IBM's stock on the New York Stock Exchange declined by $6 per share to $111.75. In sympathy with this move, most other technology stocks also declined.[15] IBM's fourth-quarter net earnings rose from $1.39 billion, or $2.28 a share, to $2.08 billion, or $3.47 a share, an increase of 49.6 percent and 52.2 percent over the same period a year earlier. Management declared that these results demonstrated the effectiveness of IBM's efforts to become more competitive and that, despite the economic uncertainties of 1988, the company was planning for growth. The apparent cause of the stock price decline was that the huge increase in income could be traced to nonrecurring gains. Investment analysts pointed out that IBM's high earnings stemmed primarily from such factors as a lower tax rate. Despite most analysts' expectations of a tax rate between 40 and 42 percent, IBM's was a low 36.4 percent, down from the previous year's 45.3 percent. Analysts were also disappointed in IBM's revenue growth. Revenues within the United States were down, and much of the company's growth in revenues came through favorable currency translations, increases that might not be repeated. In fact, some estimates of IBM's fourth-quarter earnings attributed $0.50 per share to currency translations and another $0.25 to tax-rate changes. Other factors contributing to IBM's rise in earnings were one-time transactions, such as the sale of **Intel Corporation** stock and bond redemptions, along with a corporate stock buyback program that reduced the amount of stock outstanding in the fourth quarter by 7.4 million shares. The analysts were concerned about the quality of IBM's earnings. Identify four quality of earnings issues reported in the case and the analysts' concern about each. In percentage terms, what is the impact of the currency changes on fourth quarter earnings? (Round to one decimal place.)

(*Optional*) Comment on management's assessment of IBM's performance.

Continuing Case: Annual Report Project

C7. Using the most recent annual report of the company you have chosen to study and that you have accessed online at the company's website, examine the financial statements and accompanying notes of your company. Conduct a comprehensive financial analysis for the past two years, as follows. (Round to one decimal place.)

- Operating asset management analysis: current ratio, quick ratio, receivables turnover, days' sales uncollected, inventory turnover, days' inventory on hand, payables turnover, days' payable, and financing period
- Profitability and total asset management analysis: profit margin, asset turnover, and return on assets
- Financial risk analysis: debt to equity ratio, return on equity, and interest coverage ratio
- Liquidity analysis: cash flow yield, cash flows to sales, cash flows to assets, and free cash flow
- Market strength analysis: price/earnings (P/E) ratio and dividend yield

CHAPTER 15
Managerial Accounting and Cost Concepts

BUSINESS INSIGHT
The Hershey Company

With net sales in the billions, **The Hershey Company** does indeed fulfill its mission statement of "bringing sweet moments of Hershey happiness to the world every day." To continue achieving business results, Hershey's managers must know a lot about the costs of producing and selling its Reese's, KitKat, Twizzlers, Kisses, Jolly Rancher, Ice Breakers, and other products and be familiar with the managerial accounting concepts discussed in this chapter. Go to Hershey's website (www.hersheys.com) to have a tour of the world's largest chocolate factory and to view how various candy bar brands are made.

***1.* CONCEPT ▶** *How does managerial accounting recognize and define costs?*

***2.* ACCOUNTING APPLICATION ▶** *How do companies like Hershey determine the cost of a candy bar?*

***3.* BUSINESS APPLICATION ▶** *How does managerial accounting facilitate the management process as managers plan, organize, and control costs?*

LEARNING OBJECTIVES

LO1 **Distinguish managerial accounting from financial accounting.**

LO2 **Explain how managers recognize costs and how they define product or service unit cost.**

LO3 **Describe the flow of costs through a manufacturer's inventory accounts.**

LO4 **Compare how service, retail, and manufacturing organizations report costs on their financial statements and how they account for inventories.**

LO5 **Compute the unit cost of a product or service.**

LO6 **Explain how managerial accounting supports the management process to produce business results.**

LO7 **Identify the standards of ethical conduct for management accountants.**

Yurchyks/Shutterstock

SECTION 1

CONCEPTS
- Measurement
- Recognition
- Classification

RELEVANT LEARNING OBJECTIVES

LO1 Distinguish managerial accounting from financial accounting.

LO2 Explain how managers recognize costs and how they define product or service unit cost.

CONCEPTS

LO1 The Role of Managerial Accounting

Both financial and managerial accounting reports adhere to the fundamental concepts of *cost measurement* and *recognition* when providing past, present, and future information about an organization's performance. Financial accounting reports follow strict guidelines defined by generally accepted accounting principles when reporting on past operations to external users. In contrast, to plan, control, and measure an organization's current and future operations and to make decisions about products or services, managers and other internal users rely on the information managerial accounting provides. The role of managerial accounting is to enable managers and people throughout an organization to:

- make informed decisions
- be more effective at their jobs
- improve the organization's performance

The Institute of Management Accountants (IMA) defines **managerial accounting** (or *management accounting*) as follows:

> *Management accounting is a profession that involves partnering in management decision making, devising planning and performance management systems, and providing expertise in financial reporting and control to assist management in the formulation and implementation of an organization's strategy.*[1]

This definition recognizes that regulation, globalization, and technology changes have redefined the management accountant's role to be a strategic partner within an organization. Today, managerial accounting information includes nonfinancial data as well as financial data in performance management, planning and budgeting, corporate governance, risk management, and internal controls.

Managerial Accounting and Financial Accounting: A Comparison

Both managerial accounting and financial accounting assist decision makers by identifying, measuring, processing, and communicating relevant information. Both provide managers with key measures of a company's performance and with cost information for valuing inventories on the balance sheet. However, managerial accounting and financial accounting differ in a number of ways, as summarized in Exhibit 1. Note that managerial accounting is not a subordinate activity to financial accounting. Rather, it is a process that includes financial accounting, tax accounting, information analysis, and other accounting activities.

The primary users of managerial accounting information are people inside the organization, whereas financial accounting prepares financial statements for parties outside the organization (owners or stockholders, lenders, customers, and governmental agencies). Although these reports are prepared primarily for external use, managers also rely on them in evaluating an organization's performance.

Because managerial accounting reports are for internal use, their format is driven by the user's needs. They may report either historical or future-oriented information without any formal guidelines or restrictions. That means that managerial accounting can use innovative analyses and presentation techniques to enhance the usefulness of information to people within the company. In contrast, financial accounting reports, which focus on past performance, must follow generally accepted accounting principles as specified by the Securities and Exchange Commission (SEC).

The information in managerial accounting reports may be objective and verifiable, expressed in monetary terms or in physical measures of time or objects; or they may be more subjective and based on estimates. In contrast, the statements that financial

Exhibit 1
Comparison of Managerial Accounting and Financial Accounting

Areas of Comparison	Managerial Accounting	Financial Accounting
Primary users	Managers, employees, supply-chain partners	Owners or stockholders, lenders, customers, governmental agencies
Report format	Flexible, driven by user's needs	Based on generally accepted accounting principles
Purpose of reports	Provide information for planning, control, performance measurement, and decision making	Provide information on past performance
Nature of information	Objective and verifiable for decision making; more subjective for planning (relies on estimates); confidential and private	Objective and verifiable; publicly available
Units of measure	Monetary at historical or current market or projected values; physical measures of time or number of objects	Monetary at historical or current market values
Frequency of reports	Prepared as needed; may or may not be on a periodic basis	Prepared on a periodic basis

accounting provides must be based on objective and verifiable information, which is generally historical and measured in monetary terms. Managerial accounting reports are prepared annually, quarterly, monthly, or even daily. Financial statements, on the other hand, are usually prepared and distributed on a quarterly and annual basis.

APPLY IT!

Indicate whether each of the characteristics that follows relates to managerial accounting (MA) or financial accounting (FA). (*Hint*: More than one answer may apply.)

a. Focuses on various segments of the business entity
b. Demands objectivity
c. Relies on the criterion of usefulness rather than formal guidelines in reporting information
d. Measures units in historical dollars
e. Reports information on a regular basis
f. Uses only monetary measures for reports
g. Adheres to generally accepted accounting principles
h. Prepares reports whenever needed

SOLUTION

a. MA; b. FA; c. MA; d. FA and MA; e. FA; f. FA; g. FA; h. MA

TRY IT! SE1

LO2 Concepts Underlying Costs

A key question for managers is "How much does it cost?" We begin by looking at how managers in different organizations *recognize* and *classify* information about costs.

Cost Recognition

In addition to *recognizing* costs for financial reporting, a single cost can be *classified* and used in several ways, depending on the purpose of the analysis. Exhibit 2 provides an overview of commonly used cost recognition classifications. These classifications enable managers to do the following:

- Control costs by determining which are traceable to a particular cost object, such as a service or product.
- Calculate the number of units that must be sold to achieve a certain level of profit (cost behavior).

Exhibit 2
Overview of Cost Recognition Classifications

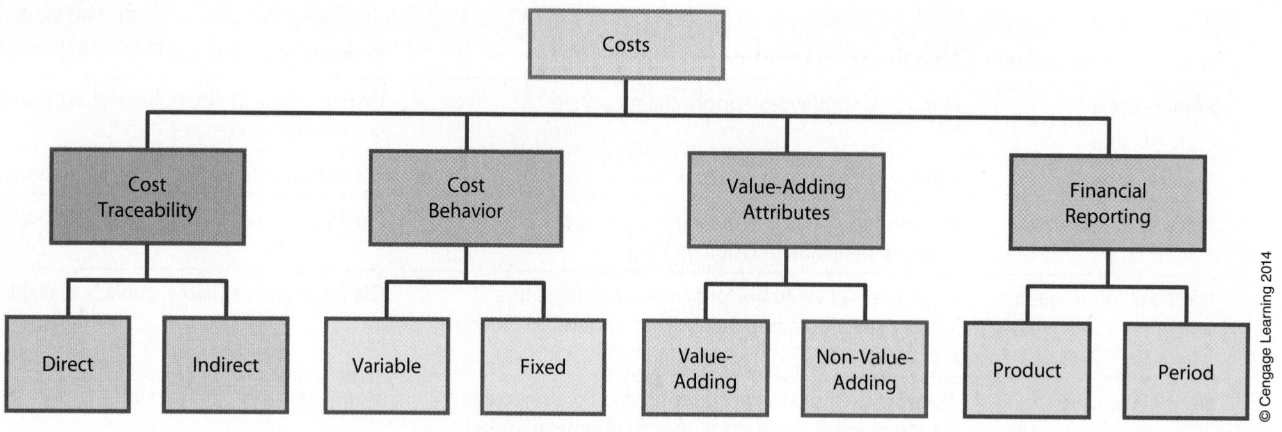

- Identify the costs of activities that do and do not add value to a product or service.
- Recognize and measure costs for the preparation of financial statements.

Managers in manufacturing, retail, and service organizations use cost information to prepare budgets, make pricing and other decisions, calculate variances between estimated and actual costs, and communicate results.

Cost Measurement

Managers *measure* costs by tracing them to cost objects, such as products or services, sales territories, departments, or operating activities.

- **Direct costs** are costs that can be measured conveniently and economically by tracing them to a cost object. For example, the wages of workers who make candy bars can be conveniently traced to a particular batch because of time cards and payroll records. Similarly, the cost of chocolate's main ingredients—chocolate liquor, cocoa butter, sugar, and milk—can be easily traced.
- **Indirect costs** are costs that cannot be measured conveniently and economically by tracing them to a cost object. Some examples include the nails used in furniture, the salt used in candy, and the rivets used in airplanes. For the sake of accuracy, however, these indirect costs must be included in the cost of a product or service. Because they are difficult to trace or an insignificant amount, management uses a formula to assign them to cost objects.

Cost classification involves identifying costs and sorting them into direct or indirect, variable or fixed, value-adding or non-value-adding, or product or period, depending on the purpose of the analysis.

The examples that follow illustrate cost objects and their direct and indirect costs in service, retail, and manufacturing organizations.

- **Service organization:** In organizations such as an accounting firm, costs can be traced to a specific service, such as preparation of tax returns. Direct costs for such a service include the costs of computer usage and the accountant's labor. Indirect costs include the costs of supplies, office rental, utilities, secretarial labor, telephone usage, and depreciation of office furniture.
- **Retail organization:** Costs for retailers can be traced to a department. For example, the direct costs of a grocery store's produce department include the costs of fruits and vegetables and the wages of employees in that department. Indirect costs include the costs of utilities to cool the produce displays and the storage and handling of the produce.

- **Manufacturing organization:** Costs for organizations such as **The Hershey Company** can be traced to the product. Direct costs include the costs of the materials and labor needed to make the candy. Indirect costs include the costs of utilities, depreciation of plant and equipment, insurance, property taxes, inspection, supervision, maintenance of machinery, storage, and handling.

Financial Reporting

In order for managers to make good decisions, they need managerial accounting information about the costs involved in making a product or providing a service. Managers *recognize* and *measure* costs as period costs or product costs.

***STUDY NOTE:** Period costs and product costs can be explained by using the matching rule (accrual accounting). Period costs are charged against the revenue of the current period, and product costs must be charged to the period in which the product generates revenue.*

- **Period costs** (or *noninventoriable costs*) are costs of resources that are not assigned to products. They are *recognized* as operating expenses on the income statement. Selling, administrative, and general expenses are examples of period costs.
- **Product costs** (or *inventoriable costs*) include direct materials, direct labor, and overhead (indirect costs). Product costs are *recognized* on the income statement as cost of goods sold and on the balance sheet as inventory. Product costs can be further *classified* as being either direct costs or indirect costs.

Product unit cost is the cost of manufacturing a single unit of a product. It is made up of the costs of direct materials, direct labor, and overhead. These three cost elements are accumulated as a batch of products is produced. When the batch is completed, the total costs are divided by the units produced to determine product unit cost. **Service unit cost** is the cost to perform one service. The direct materials element does not apply, so only direct labor and overhead would be totaled and divided by the number of services performed. The three elements of product or service cost are defined as follows.

- **Direct materials costs:** The costs of materials that can be conveniently and economically measured when making specific units of the product. Some examples of direct materials are the meat and bun in hamburgers, the oil and additives in a gallon of gasoline, and the sugar used in making candy. Direct materials may also include parts that a company purchases from another manufacturer, e.g., a battery and windshield for an automobile.
- **Direct labor costs:** The costs of the hands-on labor needed to make a product or service that can be measured when making specific units. For example, the wages of production-line workers are direct labor costs.
- **Overhead costs** (or *service overhead, factory overhead, factory burden, manufacturing overhead,* or *indirect production costs*): The costs that cannot be practically or conveniently measured directly to an end product or service. They include **indirect materials costs**, such as the costs of nails, rivets, lubricants, and small tools, and **indirect labor costs**, such as the costs of labor for maintenance, inspection, engineering design, supervision, and materials handling. Other indirect manufacturing costs include the costs of building maintenance, property taxes, property insurance, depreciation on plant and equipment, rent, and utilities.*

To illustrate product costs and the manufacturing process, we'll refer to Choice Candy Company, which has identified the following elements of the product cost of one candy bar:

- **Direct materials costs:** costs of sugar, chocolate, and wrapper
- **Direct labor costs:** costs of labor used in making the candy bar
- **Overhead costs:** indirect materials costs, including the costs of salt and flavorings; indirect labor costs, including the costs of labor to move materials to the production area and to inspect the candy bars during production; and other indirect overhead costs, including depreciation on the building and equipment, utilities, property taxes, and insurance

*Overhead costs are allocated to a product's cost using either traditional or activity-based costing methods, which we discuss in the next chapter.

Business Perspective

Has Technology Shifted the Elements of Product Costs?

New technology and manufacturing processes have created new patterns of product costs. The three elements of product costs are still direct materials, direct labor, and overhead, but the percentage that each contributes to the total cost of a product has changed. From the 1950s through the 1970s, direct material and labor costs accounted for 75 percent of total product cost. Improved production technology caused a dramatic shift in the three product cost elements. Machines replaced people, significantly reducing direct labor costs. Today, only 50 percent of the cost of a product is directly traceable to the product. The other 50 percent is overhead, an indirect cost.

Prime Costs and Conversion Costs The three elements of product cost can be also grouped into prime costs and conversion costs.

- **Prime costs:** The primary costs of production. They are the sum of the direct materials costs and direct labor costs.
- **Conversion costs:** The costs of converting or processing direct materials into a finished product. They are the sum of direct labor costs and overhead costs.

These *classifications* are important for understanding the costing methods discussed in later chapters. Exhibit 3 summarizes the relationships among the product cost recognition classifications presented so far.

Exhibit 3
Relationships Among Product Cost Recognition Classifications

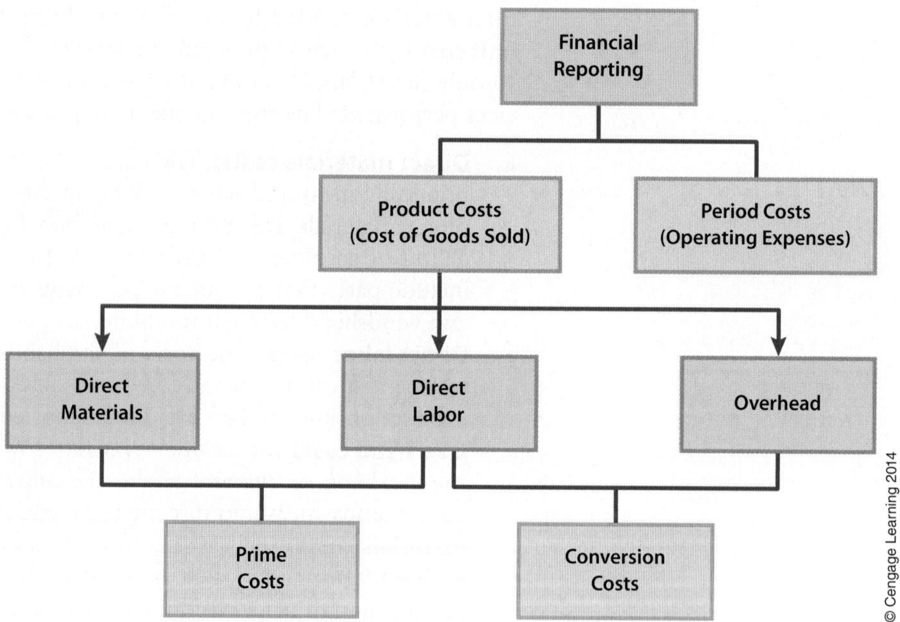

Cost Behavior

Managers are also interested in the way costs respond to changes in volume or activity. By analyzing those variable and fixed patterns of behavior, they gain information to make better management decisions.

- A **variable cost** is a cost that changes in direct proportion to a change in productive output (or some other measure of volume).
- A **fixed cost** is a cost that remains constant within a defined range of activity or time period.

All types of organizations have variable and fixed costs.

- **Service organization:** Because the number of passengers drives the consumption of food and beverages on a flight, the cost of peanuts and beverages is a variable cost for **Southwest Airlines**. Fixed costs include the depreciation on the plane and the salaries and benefits of the flight and ground crews.

- **Retail organization:** The variable costs of a grocery store like **Kroger** or **Trader Joe's** include the cost of groceries sold and any sales commissions. Fixed costs include the costs of building and lot rental, depreciation on store equipment, and the manager's salary.
- **Manufacturing organization:** The variable costs of a manufacturer like **The Hershey Company** or Choice Candy include the costs of direct materials (e.g., sugar, cocoa), direct labor, indirect materials (e.g., salt), and indirect labor (e.g., inspection and maintenance labor). Fixed costs include the costs of supervisors' salaries and depreciation on buildings.

STUDY NOTE: *As more products or services are produced and sold, the variable costs increase proportionately. Fixed costs, however, remain the same for a specified period.*

Value-Adding versus Non-Value-Adding Costs

Costs can also be *classified* as value-adding or non-value-adding.

- A **value-adding cost** is the cost of an activity that increases the market value of a product or service.
- A **non-value-adding cost** is the cost of an activity that adds cost to a product or service but does not increase its market value.

Managers examine the value-adding attributes of their company's operating activities and, wherever possible, reduce or eliminate activities that do not directly add value to the company's products or services. For example, the costs of administrative activities, such as accounting and human resource management, are non-value-adding costs. Because they are necessary for the operation of the business, they are monitored closely but cannot be eliminated.

Exhibit 4 shows how some costs of a manufacturer like Choice Candy can be *recognized* in terms of traceability, behavior, value attribute, and financial reporting.

Exhibit 4
Examples of Cost Recognition Classifications for a Candy Manufacturer

Cost Examples	Traceability to Product	Cost Behavior	Value Attribute	Financial Reporting
Sugar for candy	Direct	Variable	Value-adding	Product (direct materials)
Labor for mixing	Direct	Variable	Value-adding	Product (direct labor)
Labor for supervision	Indirect	Fixed	Non-value-adding	Product (overhead)
Depreciation on mixing machine	Indirect	Fixed	Value-adding	Product (overhead)
Sales commission	—*	Variable	Value-adding**	Period
Accountant's salary	—*	Fixed	Non-value-adding	Period

*Sales commissions and accountants' salaries cannot be directly or indirectly traced to a cost object; they are not product costs.

**Sales commissions can be value-adding because customers' perceptions of the salesperson and the selling experience can strongly affect their perceptions of the product's market value.

APPLY IT!

Indicate whether each of the following costs for a gourmet chocolate candy maker is recognized as a product or a period cost, a variable or a fixed cost, a value-adding or a non-value-adding cost, and, if it is a product cost, a direct or an indirect candy cost:

a. Chocolate
b. Office rent
c. Candy chef wages
d. Dishwasher wages
e. Pinch of salt
f. Utilities to run mixer

SOLUTION

	Cost Recognition Classification			
	Product or Period	**Variable or Fixed**	**Value-Adding or Non-Value-Adding**	**Direct or Indirect**
a. Chocolate	Product	Variable	Value-adding	Direct
b. Office rent	Period	Fixed	Non-value-adding	—
c. Candy chef	Product	Variable	Value-adding	Direct
d. Dishwasher	Product	Variable	Value-adding	Indirect
e. Pinch of salt	Product	Variable	Value-adding	Indirect
f. Utilities to run mixer	Product	Variable	Value-adding	Indirect

TRY IT! SE2, SE3, E1A, E2A, E3A, E1B, E2B, E3B

SECTION 2

ACCOUNTING APPLICATIONS

ACCOUNTING APPLICATIONS

- Describe the materials inventory
- Describe the work in process inventory
- Describe the finished goods inventory
- Prepare the income statement
- Determine the cost of goods sold
- Prepare the statement of cost of goods manufactured
- Determine the product unit cost

RELEVANT LEARNING OBJECTIVES

LO 3 Describe the flow of costs through a manufacturer's inventory accounts.

LO 4 Compare how service, retail, and manufacturing organizations report costs on their financial statements and how they account for inventories.

LO 5 Compute the unit cost of a product or service.

LO 3 Inventory Accounts in Manufacturing Organizations

Transforming materials into finished products requires a number of production and production-related activities. A manufacturing organization's accounting system tracks these activities as product costs flowing through the Materials Inventory, Work in Process Inventory, and Finished Goods Inventory accounts.

Document Flows and Cost Flows Through the Inventory Accounts

Managers accumulate and report manufacturing costs based on documents pertaining to production and production-related activities. Exhibit 5 summarizes the typical relationships among the production activities, the documents for each of the three cost elements, and the inventory accounts affected by the activities. Looking at these relationships provides insight into how costs flow through the three inventory accounts and when an activity must be recorded in the accounting records. To illustrate document flow and changes in inventory balances for production activities in Exhibit 5, we continue with our example of Choice Candy Company, a typical manufacturing business.

Purchase of Materials

- **Step 1. Acquiring the materials.** The purchasing process starts with a *purchase request* submitted for specific quantities of materials needed. A qualified manager approves the request. Based on the information in the purchase request, the Purchasing Department prepares a *purchase order* and sends it to a supplier.
- **Step 2. Receiving the materials.** When the materials arrive, an employee on the receiving dock examines the materials and enters the information into the company database as a *receiving report*. The system matches the information on the receiving report with the descriptions and quantities listed on the purchase order. A materials handler moves the newly arrived materials from the receiving area to the materials storeroom.
- **Step 3. Paying for the materials.** Choice Candy's accounting department receives a *vendor's invoice* from the supplier requesting payment for the materials. The cost of those materials increases the balance of the Materials Inventory account and an account payable is recognized. If all documents match, payment is authorized.

Production of Goods

- **Step 4. Preparing the materials for production.** When candy bars are scheduled for production, the storeroom clerk receives a *materials request form*. In addition to showing authorization, it describes the types and quantities of materials that the storeroom clerk is to send to the production area, and it authorizes the release of those materials from the materials inventory into production.
- **Step 5. Sending the materials into production.** If all is in order, the storeroom clerk has the materials handler move the materials to the production floor.
- **Step 6. Producing goods.** Each of the production employees who make the candy bars prepares a *time card* to record the number of hours he or she has worked on this and other orders each day. A *job order cost card* can be used to record all direct materials, direct labor, and overhead costs incurred as the products move through production.

Exhibit 5
Activities, Documents, and Cost Flows Through the Inventory Accounts of a Manufacturing Organization

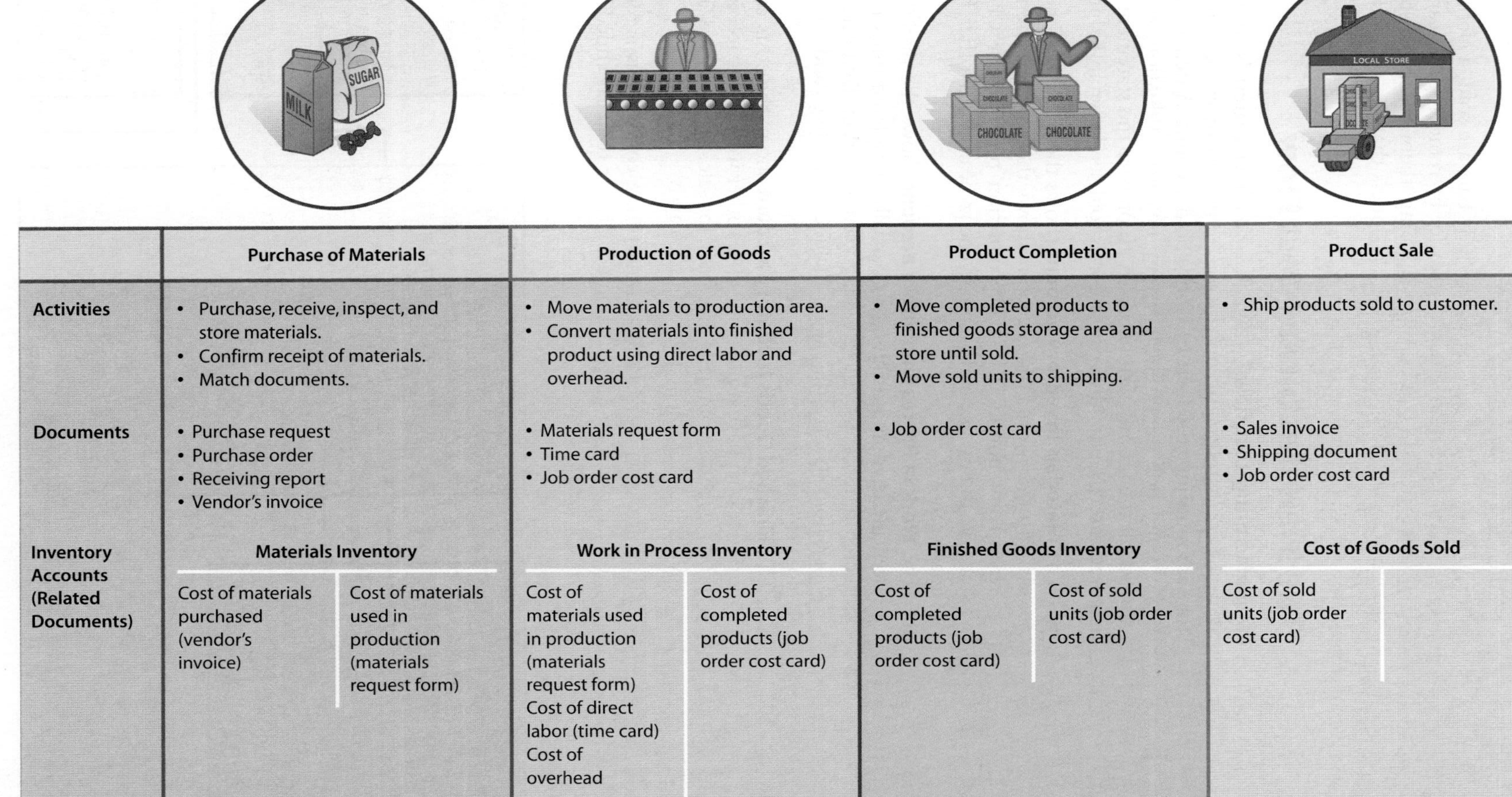

	Purchase of Materials	Production of Goods	Product Completion	Product Sale
Activities	• Purchase, receive, inspect, and store materials. • Confirm receipt of materials. • Match documents.	• Move materials to production area. • Convert materials into finished product using direct labor and overhead.	• Move completed products to finished goods storage area and store until sold. • Move sold units to shipping.	• Ship products sold to customer.
Documents	• Purchase request • Purchase order • Receiving report • Vendor's invoice	• Materials request form • Time card • Job order cost card	• Job order cost card	• Sales invoice • Shipping document • Job order cost card
Inventory Accounts (Related Documents)	**Materials Inventory** Debit: Cost of materials purchased (vendor's invoice) Credit: Cost of materials used in production (materials request form)	**Work in Process Inventory** Debit: Cost of materials used in production (materials request form); Cost of direct labor (time card); Cost of overhead Credit: Cost of completed products (job order cost card)	**Finished Goods Inventory** Debit: Cost of completed products (job order cost card) Credit: Cost of sold units (job order cost card)	**Cost of Goods Sold** Debit: Cost of sold units (job order cost card)

Product Completion and Sale

- **Step 7. Completing goods.** Employees place completed candy bars in cartons and then move the cartons to the finished goods storeroom, where they are kept until they are shipped to customers.
- **Step 8. Selling goods.** When candy bars are sold, a clerk prepares a *sales invoice,* and another employee fills the order by removing the candy bars from the storeroom, packaging them, and shipping them to the customer. A *shipping document* shows the quantity of the products that are shipped and gives a description of them.

The Manufacturing Cost Flow

Manufacturing cost flow is the flow of direct materials, direct labor, and overhead through the Materials Inventory, Work in Process Inventory, and Finished Goods Inventory accounts into the Cost of Goods Sold account. A defined manufacturing cost flow is the foundation for product costing, inventory valuation, and financial reporting. It supplies all the information necessary to prepare the statement of cost of goods manufactured and compute the cost of goods sold, as shown in Exhibit 8.

- The **Materials Inventory account** shows the balance of the cost of unused materials. In other words, this account shows the cost of materials that have been purchased but not used in the production process. For Choice Candy, this might include things like milk, sugar, cocoa beans, and other ingredients necessary to make candy.
- The **Work in Process Inventory account** shows the manufacturing costs that have been incurred and assigned to partially completed units of product. This account therefore represents the costs involved with manufacturing the unfinished product. For Choice Candy, this might include things like candy that is ready to eat but has not yet been packaged for sale.
- The **Finished Goods Inventory account** shows the costs assigned to all completed products that have not been sold. In other words, this account shows the cost of the product that is complete and ready for sale. For Choice Candy, this would include things like the wrapped packages of candy.

Exhibit 6 summarizes the manufacturing cost flow as it relates to Choice Candy's inventory accounts and production activity for the year ended December 31. To show

Exhibit 6
Manufacturing Cost Flow: Choice Candy Company

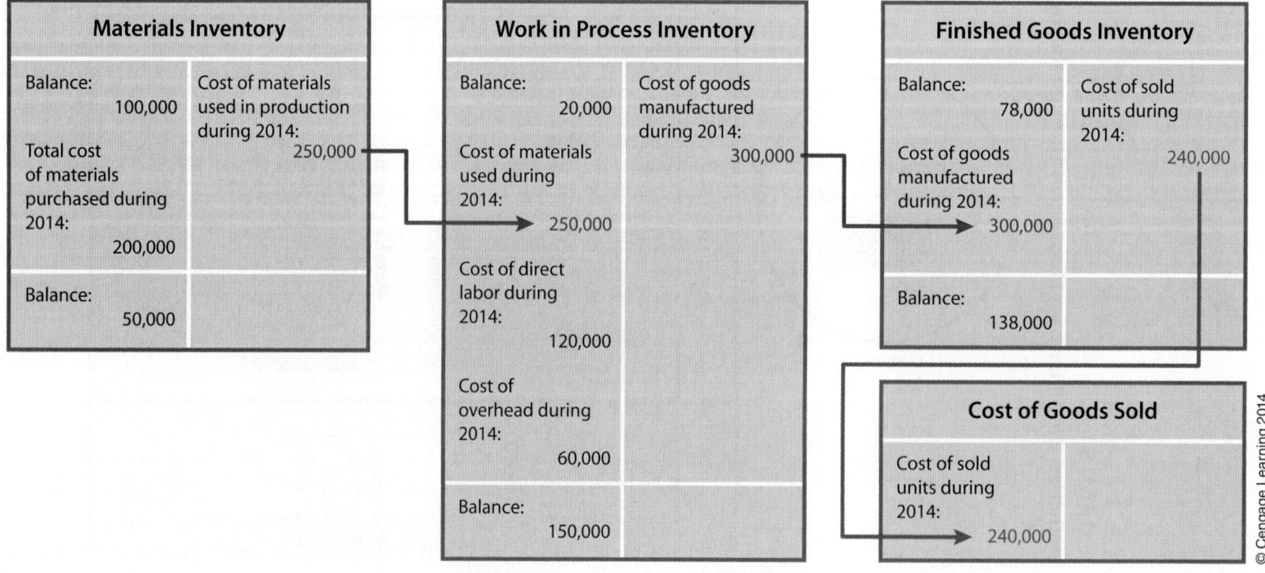

the basic flows in this example, we assume that all materials are direct materials to the candy bars produced.

Materials Inventory The Materials Inventory account holds the balance of the cost of materials that have been purchased, but have not yet been used in the production process.

The Materials Inventory Account

Transactions Choice Candy began the period with $100,000 in Beginning Materials Inventory. During the period, Choice Candy purchased $200,000 of direct materials and used $250,000 of direct materials.

Analysis Because there are no indirect materials in this case, the Materials Inventory account shows the balance of unused direct materials.

- ▲ The cost of direct materials purchased *increases* the balance of the *Materials Inventory* account.
- ▼ The cost of direct materials used by the Production Department *decreases* the *Materials Inventory* account as it flows into the Work in Process Inventory account.

Application of Double Entry

Materials Inventory			
Balance	100,000	Cost of materials used in production during 2014	250,000
Total cost of materials purchased during 2014	200,000		
Balance	50,000		

Comment If indirect materials had been used, the cost of the indirect materials transferred would

- ▲ *increase* the balance of the *Overhead* account
- ▼ *decrease* the balance of the *Materials Inventory* account

We discuss overhead in more detail in the next chapter.

STUDY NOTE: *When costs are transferred from one inventory account to another in a manufacturing company, they remain assets. They are on the balance sheet and are not expensed on the income statement until the finished goods are sold.*

Work in Process Inventory The Work in Process Inventory account records the balance of partially completed units of the product. As direct materials and direct labor enter the production process, their costs are added to the Work in Process Inventory account. The cost of overhead for the current period is also added. The total costs of direct materials, direct labor, and overhead incurred and transferred to the Work in Process Inventory account during a period are called **total manufacturing costs** (or *current manufacturing costs*).

Exhibit 6 recaps the inflows of direct materials, direct labor, and overhead into the Work in Process Inventory T account and the resulting outflow of completed product costs.

The Work in Process Inventory Account

Transactions Choice Candy began the period with $20,000 in beginning Work in Process Inventory. Choice Candy used $250,000 of direct materials, $120,000 of direct labor, and $60,000 of overhead during the period to manufacture $300,000 of goods.

Analysis

- ▲ The costs of the direct materials used to manufacture the candy bars *increase* the balance of the *Work in Process Inventory* account as the costs flow out of the Material Inventory account and into Work in Process Inventory (see previous transaction).

▲ The costs of the direct labor used to manufacture the candy bars *increase* the balance of the *Work in Process Inventory* account.

▲ The costs of overhead used to support the manufacture of the candy bars *increase* the balance of the *Work in Process Inventory* account.

Application of Double Entry

Work in Process Inventory			
Balance	20,000	Cost of goods manufactured during 2014	300,000
Cost of materials used during 2014	250,000		
Cost of direct labor during 2014	120,000		
Cost of overhead during 2014	60,000		
Balance	150,000		

Comment The cost of all units completed and moved to Finished Goods Inventory during a period is the **cost of goods manufactured**.

▼ The cost of goods manufactured *decreases* the balance of the *Work in Process Inventory* account as these costs flow into the Finished Goods Inventory account.

STUDY NOTE: *Materials Inventory and Work in Process Inventory support the production process, while Finished Goods Inventory supports the sales and distribution functions.*

Finished Goods Inventory The Finished Goods Inventory account holds the balance of costs assigned to all completed products that a manufacturing company has not yet sold.

The Finished Goods Inventory Account

Transactions Choice Candy began the period with $78,000 in beginning Finished Goods Inventory. During the period, Choice Candy manufactured $300,000 of goods and sold $240,000 units.

Analysis

▲ The cost of goods manufactured *increases* the balance in the *Finished Goods Inventory* account when the goods are completed and flow out of the Work in Process Inventory account and into the Finished Goods account.

▼ The cost of goods sold *decreases* the balance in the *Finished Goods* account.

Application of Double Entry

Finished Goods Inventory			
Balance	78,000	Cost of sold units during 2014	240,000
Cost of goods manufactured during 2014	300,000		
Balance	138,000		

Cost of Goods Sold			
Cost of sold units during 2014	240,000		

Comment The cost of all units sold during a period that move out of Finished Goods Inventory is called the **cost of goods sold**.

APPLY IT!

Given the following information, use T accounts to compute the ending balances of the Materials Inventory, Work in Process Inventory, and Finished Goods Inventory accounts:

Materials Inventory, beginning balance	$ 230
Work in Process Inventory, beginning balance	250
Finished Goods Inventory, beginning balance	380
Direct materials purchased	850
Direct materials (DM) used	740
Direct labor (DL) costs	970
Overhead (OH) costs	350
Cost of goods manufactured (COGM)	1,230
Cost of goods sold (COGS)	935

SOLUTION

Materials Inventory

Beg. bal.	230	Used	740
Purchased	850		
End. bal.	340		

Work in Process Inventory

Beg. bal.	250	COGM	1,230
DM	740		
DL	970		
OH	350		
End. bal.	1,080		

Finished Goods Inventory

Beg. bal.	380	COGS	935
COGM	1,230		
End. bal.	675		

TRY IT! SE4, SE5

LO 4 Financial Statements and the Reporting of Costs

Managers prepare financial statements at least once a year to communicate the results of their activities. The key to preparing an income statement or a balance sheet in any kind of organization is *recognizing* and *measuring* its cost of goods or services sold and the value of its inventories, if any.

Income Statement and Accounting for Inventories

All organizations—service, retail, and manufacturing—use the following income statement format:

$$\text{Sales} - \begin{matrix}\text{Cost of Sales or}\\ \text{Cost of Goods Sold}\end{matrix} = \text{Gross Margin} - \begin{matrix}\text{Operating}\\ \text{Expenses}\end{matrix} = \begin{matrix}\text{Operating}\\ \text{Income}\end{matrix}$$

How the cost of sales or cost of goods sold is computed, however, varies depending on the organization.

Service organizations like **Southwest Airlines** and **United Parcel Service (UPS)** sell services and not products. They maintain no inventories and they have no inventory accounts. Instead, service organizations use cost of sales. For example, suppose that UPS delivers packages of chocolate to Choice Candy. The cost of sales for UPS would include the wages and salaries of personnel plus the expense of the trucks, planes, supplies, and anything else used to deliver packages for Choice Candy.

In contrast, retail organizations, such as **Wal-Mart** and **The Gap**, which purchase products ready for resale, maintain just one inventory account on the balance sheet. This

Merchandise Inventory account reflects the costs of goods held for resale. Suppose a retailer had a balance of $3,000 in its Merchandise Inventory account at the beginning of the year. During the year, its purchases of products totaled $23,000 (adjusted for purchase discounts, returns and allowances, and freight-in). At year-end, its Merchandise Inventory balance was $4,500. As illustrated in Exhibit 7, the cost of goods sold was thus $21,500 ($3,000 + $23,000 = $26,000 − $4,500 = $21,500).

On the other hand, manufacturing organizations like **The Hershey Company**, **Godiva Chocolatier, Inc.**, or Choice Candy, which make products for sale, maintain three inventory accounts on the balance sheet: Materials Inventory, Work in Process Inventory, and Finished Goods Inventory. Suppose that Choice Candy had a balance of $52,000 in its Finished Goods Inventory account at the beginning of the year. During the year, the cost of the products that the company manufactured totaled $144,000. At year end, its Finished Goods Inventory balance was $78,000. As illustrated in Exhibit 7, the cost of goods sold would be $118,000 ($52,000 + $144,000 = $196,000 − $78,000 = $118,000).

Exhibit 7 compares the financial statements of service, retail, and manufacturing organizations. Note the differences in inventory accounts and cost of goods sold.

Exhibit 7
Financial Statements of Service, Retail, and Manufacturing Organizations

	Service Company	Retail Company	Manufacturing Company
Income Statement	Sales – Cost of sales = Gross margin – Operating expenses = Operating income	Sales – Cost of goods sold* = Gross margin – Operating expenses = Operating income *Cost of goods sold: Beginning merchandise inventory + Net cost of purchases = Cost of goods available for sale – Ending merchandise inventory = Cost of goods sold	Sales – Cost of goods sold† = Gross margin – Operating expenses = Operating income †Cost of goods sold: Beginning finished goods inventory + Cost of goods manufactured = Cost of goods available for sale – Ending finished goods inventory = Cost of goods sold
Balance Sheet (Current Assets Section)	No inventory accounts	One inventory account: Merchandise Inventory (finished product ready for sale)	Three inventory accounts: Materials Inventory (unused materials) Work in Process Inventory (unfinished product) Finished Goods Inventory (finished product ready for sale)
Example With Numbers		Income Statement: Beg. merchandise inventory $ 3,000 + Net cost of purchases 23,000 = Cost of goods available for sale $26,000 – End. merchandise inventory 4,500 = Cost of goods sold $21,500 Balance Sheet: Merchandise inventory, ending $ 4,500	Income Statement: Beg. finished goods inventory $ 52,000 + Cost of goods manufactured 144,000 = Cost of goods available for sale $196,000 – End. finished goods inventory 78,000 = Cost of goods sold $118,000 Balance Sheet:* Finished goods inventory, ending $ 78,000 *The balance sheet would also disclose the following: Materials inventory, ending Work in process inventory, ending

Statement of Cost of Goods Manufactured

STUDY NOTE: It is important not to confuse the cost of goods manufactured *with the* cost of goods sold. *These amounts may differ because not all units produced may be sold in the same period.*

As illustrated in Exhibit 7, for manufacturing companies, the cost of goods manufactured needs to be determined before cost of goods sold can be computed. The cost of goods manufactured is calculated in the **statement of cost of goods manufactured**, which summarizes the flow of all manufacturing costs incurred during the period. Exhibit 8 shows Choice Candy's statement of cost of goods manufactured for the year.

Exhibit 8
Statement of Cost of Goods Manufactured and Partial Income Statement for a Manufacturing Organization

Choice Candy Company
Statement of Cost of Goods Manufactured
For the Year

Direct materials used:		
Beginning materials inventory	$100,000	
Direct materials purchased	200,000	
Cost of direct materials available for use	$300,000	
Less ending materials inventory	50,000	
Step 1: Cost of direct materials used		$250,000
Direct labor		120,000
Overhead		60,000
Step 2: Total manufacturing costs		$430,000
Add beginning work in process inventory		20,000
Total cost of work in process during the year		$450,000
Less ending work in process inventory		150,000
Step 3: Cost of goods manufactured		$300,000

Choice Candy Company
Income Statement
For the Year

Sales		$500,000
Cost of goods sold:		
Beginning finished goods inventory	$ 78,000	
Cost of goods manufactured	300,000	
Cost of goods available for sale	$378,000	
Less ending finished goods inventory	138,000	
Cost of goods sold		240,000
Gross margin		$260,000
Selling and administrative expenses		160,000
Operating income		$100,000

The statement of cost of goods manufactured is developed in three steps.

- **Step 1. Compute the cost of direct materials used during the accounting period.** As shown in Exhibit 8, for Choice Candy, this would be computed as follows.

Beginning Materials Inventory	+	Direct Materials Purchased	=	Direct Materials Available for Use
$100,000	+	$200,000	=	$300,000

Direct Materials Available for Use	−	Ending Materials Inventory	=	Direct Materials Used
$300,000	−	$50,000	=	$250,000

- **Step 2. Calculate total manufacturing costs for the period.** As shown in Exhibit 8, for Choice Candy this would be computed as follows.

Direct Materials	+	Direct Labor	+	Overhead	=	Total Manufacturing Costs
$250,000	+	$120,000	+	$60,000	=	$430,000

- **Step 3. Determine total cost of goods manufactured for the period.** As shown in Exhibit 8, for Choice Candy this would be computed as follows.

Beginning Work in Process Inventory	+	Total Manufacturing Costs	−	Ending Work in Process Inventory	=	Cost of Goods Manufactured
$20,000	+	$430,000	−	$150,000	=	$300,000

Cost of Goods Sold and a Manufacturer's Income Statement

Exhibit 8 shows the relationship between Choice Candy's income statement and its statement of cost of goods manufactured. The total amount of the cost of goods manufactured is carried over to the income statement, where it is used to compute the cost of goods sold. The cost of goods sold is considered an expense in the period in which the goods are sold.

Beginning Finished Goods Inventory	+	Cost of Goods Manufactured	=	Cost of Goods Available for Sale
$78,000	+	$300,000	=	$378,000

Cost of Goods Available for Sale (what was available for sale)	−	Ending Finished Goods Inventory (what was not sold)	=	Cost of Goods Sold
$378,000	−	$138,000	=	$240,000

APPLY IT!

Given the following information, compute the ending balances of the Materials Inventory, Work in Process Inventory, and Finished Goods Inventory accounts:

Materials inventory, beginning balance	$ 230
Work in process inventory, beginning balance	250
Finished goods inventory, beginning balance	380
Direct materials purchased	850
Direct materials used	740
Direct labor costs	970
Overhead costs	350
Cost of goods completed	1,230
Cost of goods sold	935

SOLUTION

Materials Inventory, ending balance:	
Materials Inventory, beginning balance	$ 230
Direct materials purchased	850
Direct materials used	(740)
Materials Inventory, ending balance	$ 340
Work in Process Inventory, ending balance:	
Work in Process Inventory, beginning balance	$ 250
Direct materials used	740
Direct labor costs	970
Overhead costs	350
Cost of goods completed	(1,230)
Work in Process Inventory, ending balance	$ 1,080
Finished Goods Inventory, ending balance:	
Finished Goods Inventory, beginning balance	$ 380
Cost of goods completed	1,230
Cost of goods sold	(935)
Finished Goods Inventory, ending balance	$ 675

TRY IT! SE6, E4A, E5A, E6A, E7A, E4B, E5B, E6B, E7B

LO 5 Measurement of Product Costs

Making or delivering products, selling insurance policies, or preparing a client's income taxes are all examples of a product or service that can be produced and sold, but how much does a single unit cost?

Computing Product Unit Cost

Product unit cost is the cost of manufacturing a single unit of a product. It is made up of the cost of goods manufactured costs of direct materials, direct labor, and overhead. These three cost elements are accumulated as a batch of products is being produced. When the batch has been completed, the product unit cost is computed.

$$\text{Product Unit Cost} = \frac{\text{Direct Materials Cost} + \text{Direct Labor Cost} + \text{Overhead Cost}}{\text{Number of Units Produced}}$$

or

$$\text{Product Unit Cost} = \text{Direct Materials Cost per Unit} + \text{Direct Labor Cost per Unit} + \text{Overhead Cost per Unit}$$

Product Cost Measurement Methods

How products flow physically and how costs are incurred does not always match. For example, Choice Candy physically produces candy bars 24 hours a day, 7 days a week, but the accounting department only does accounting 8 hours a day, 5 days a week. Because product cost data must be available 24/7, managers may use estimates or predetermined standards to compute product costs during the period. At the end of the period, these estimates are reconciled with the actual product costs so actual product costs appear in the financial statements. The three methods managers and accountants can use to calculate product unit cost include:

- Actual costing
- Normal costing
- Standard costing

Exhibit 9 summarizes how these three methods use actual and estimated costs.

Exhibit 9
Three Product Cost-Measurement Methods: Actual and Estimated Costs

Product Cost Elements	Actual Costing	Normal Costing	Standard Costing
Direct materials	Actual costs	Actual costs	Estimated costs
Direct labor	Actual costs	Actual costs	Estimated costs
Overhead	Actual costs	Estimated costs	Estimated costs

Actual Costing Method The **actual costing method** uses the actual costs of direct materials, direct labor, and overhead to calculate the product unit cost. These costs, however, may not be known until the end of the period. In the following example, assume the product unit cost is computed after the job is completed and all cost information is known.

Choice Candy produced 3,000 candy bars for a customer. The company accountant calculated the actual costs for the order as follows: direct materials, $540; direct labor, $420; and overhead, $240. The actual product unit cost for the order was $0.40, calculated as follows.

Actual direct materials ($540 ÷ 3,000 candy bars)	$0.18
Actual direct labor ($420 ÷ 3,000 candy bars)	0.14
Actual overhead ($240 ÷ 3,000 candy bars)	0.08
Actual product cost per candy bar ($1,200 ÷ 3,000 candy bars)	$0.40

STUDY NOTE: The use of normal costing is widespread, since many overhead bills, such as utility bills, are not received until after products or services are produced and sold.

Normal Costing Method The **normal costing method** combines the easy-to-track actual direct costs of materials and labor with estimated overhead costs to determine a product unit cost. The normal costing method is simple and allows a smooth assignment of overhead costs to production during a period. At the end of the period, any difference between the estimated and actual costs must be identified and removed so that the financial statements show only the actual product costs.

For Choice Candy, assume the company accountant used normal costing to price the order for 3,000 candy bars and that overhead was applied to the product's cost using an estimated rate of 50 percent of direct labor costs. In this case, the costs for the order would include the actual direct materials cost of $540, the actual direct labor cost of $420, and an estimated overhead cost of $210 ($420 × 50%). The product unit cost would be $0.39:

Actual direct materials ($540 ÷ 3,000 candy bars)	$0.18
Actual direct labor ($420 ÷ 3,000 candy bars)	0.14
Estimated overhead ($210 ÷ 3,000 candy bars)	0.07
Normal product cost per candy bar ($1,170 ÷ 3,000 candy bars)	$0.39

Standard Costing Method Managers sometimes need product cost information before the accounting period begins so that they can control the cost of operating activities or price a proposed product for a customer. In such situations, product unit costs must be estimated, and the standard costing method can be helpful. The **standard costing method** uses estimated or standard costs of direct materials, direct labor, and overhead to calculate the product unit cost. Standard costing is very useful in performance management and evaluation because a manager can compare actual and standard costs to compute the variances.*

Assume that Choice Candy is placing a bid to manufacture 2,000 candy bars for a new customer. From standard cost information developed at the beginning of the period, the company accountant estimates the following costs: $0.20 per unit for direct materials, $0.15 per unit for direct labor, and $0.09 per unit for overhead (assuming a standard overhead rate of 60 percent of direct labor cost). The standard cost per unit would be $0.44:

Standard direct materials	$0.20
Standard direct labor	0.15
Standard overhead ($0.15 × 60%)	0.09
Standard product cost per candy bar	$0.44

Computing Service Unit Cost

STUDY NOTE: Any material costs in a service organization would be for supplies used in providing services. Because these are indirect materials costs, they are included in overhead.

Delivering products, representing people in courts of law, selling insurance policies, and computing people's income taxes are typical of the services performed in service organizations. Like other services, these are labor-intensive processes supported by indirect materials or supplies, indirect labor, and other overhead costs. The most important cost in a service organization is the direct cost of labor that can be traceable to the service rendered. The indirect costs incurred in performing a service are similar to those incurred in manufacturing a product. They are *classified* as overhead. These service costs appear on service organizations' income statements as cost of sales.

APPLY IT!

Fickle Picking Services provides inexpensive, high-quality labor for farmers growing vegetable and fruit crops. In September, Fickle Picking paid laborers $4,000 to harvest 500 acres of apples. The company incurred overhead costs of $2,400 for apple-picking services in September. This amount included the costs of transporting the laborers to the orchards; of providing facilities, food, and beverages for the laborers; and of scheduling, billing, and collecting from the farmers. Of this amount, 50 percent was related to picking apples. Compute the cost per acre to pick apples.

SOLUTION

Total cost to pick apples:	$4,000 + (0.50 × $2,400) = $5,200
Cost per acre to pick apples:	$5,200 ÷ 500 acres = $10.40 per acre

TRY IT! SE7, E8A, E9A, E8B, E9B

*This is covered in more detail in the chapter on standard costing and variance analysis.

SECTION 3 BUSINESS APPLICATIONS

SINESS APPLICATIONS
- Planning
- Performing
- Evaluating
- Communicating
- Ethics

LEVANT ARNING OBJECTIVES

6 Explain how managerial accounting supports management process to duce business results.

7 Identify the standards of ethical conduct for nagement accountants.

LO 6 Managerial Accounting and the Management Process

The fundamentals of managing an organization include planning and forecasting operations, organizing and coordinating resources and data, and commanding and controlling resources. Managers use managerial accounting principles to guide their actions and decisions in the management process. Although management actions differ from organization to organization, they generally follow a four-stage management process:

- planning
- performing
- evaluating
- communicating

Managerial accounting is essential in each stage of the process.

Planning Exhibit 10 shows the overall framework in which planning takes place. The overriding **goal/vision** of a business is to increase the value of the stakeholders' interest in the business. The fundamental way in which the company will achieve this goal/

Exhibit 10
Overview of the Planning Framework

Goal/Vision: To increase the value of stakeholders' interest in the business
Mission Statement: Fundamental way in which the company will achieve the goal of increasing stakeholders' value
Strategic Objectives: Broad, long-term goals that determine the fundamental nature and direction of the business and that serve as a guide for decision making
Tactical Objectives: Mid-term goals for positioning the business to achieve its long-term strategies
Operating Objectives: Short-term goals that outline expectations for performance of day-to-day operations
Business Plan: A comprehensive statement of how the company will achieve its objectives
Budgets: Expressions of the business plan in financial terms
© Cengage Learning 2014

Business Perspective
What's Going on in the Grocery Business?

Sales at large supermarket chains, such as **Kroger**, **Safeway**, and **Albertson's**, have been flat and profits weak because both ends of their customer market are being squeezed. Large-scale retailers like **Wal-Mart** and **Costco** are attracting cost-conscious grocery shoppers, and upscale grocery customers are being lured by quality to specialty grocers like **Trader Joe's** and **Whole Foods Market**. Other grocery chains are reconsidering their company's mission and strategic options by adding new products and services, such as walk-in medical clinics, closing stores and downsizing, or entering new geographic markets.[2]

vision is described in its **mission statement.** This statement also expresses the company's identity and unique character. For example, **Wal-Mart**'s mission statement says that the company wants "to give ordinary folk the chance to buy the same things as rich people." **The Hershey Company**'s mission is "bringing sweet moments of Hershey happiness to the world every day."

The mission statement is essential to the planning process, which must consider how to add value through strategic, tactical, and operating objectives.

- **Strategic objectives**: Broad, long-term goals that determine the fundamental nature and direction of a business and that serve as a guide for decision making. Strategic objectives involve such basic issues as what a company's main products or services will be, who its primary customers will be, and where it will operate. They stake out a company's strategic position—whether it will be a cost leader, quality leader, or niche satisfier.
- **Tactical objectives**: Mid-term goals that position an organization to achieve its long-term strategies. These objectives, which usually cover a three- to five-year period, lay the groundwork for attaining the company's strategic objectives.
- **Operating objectives**: Short-term goals that outline expectations for the performance of day-to-day operations. Operating objectives link to performance targets and specify how success will be measured.

A **business plan** is a comprehensive statement of how a company will achieve its strategic, tactical, and operating objectives. It is usually expressed in financial terms in the form of budgets, and it often includes performance goals for individuals, teams, products, or services. A business plan provides a full description of the business, including a complete operating budget for the first two years of operations. The **budget** must include a forecasted income statement, a forecasted statement of cash flows, and a forecasted balance sheet.

Performing Planning alone does not guarantee satisfactory operating results. Management must implement the business plan in ways that make optimal use of available resources in an ethical manner.

Critical to managing any retail business is a thorough understanding of the supply chain. As Exhibit 11 shows, the **supply chain** (or *supply network*) is the path that leads from the suppliers to the final consumer. In the supply chain for a company that produces and sells candy, materials and resources flow from growers and suppliers to the company (manufacturer) and then on to candy distributors to retailers to consumers. Managers' knowledge of their supply chain allows them to coordinate deliveries from local growers and international suppliers so that they can meet the demands of customers without having too much or too little inventory on hand.

Exhibit 11
The Supply Chain

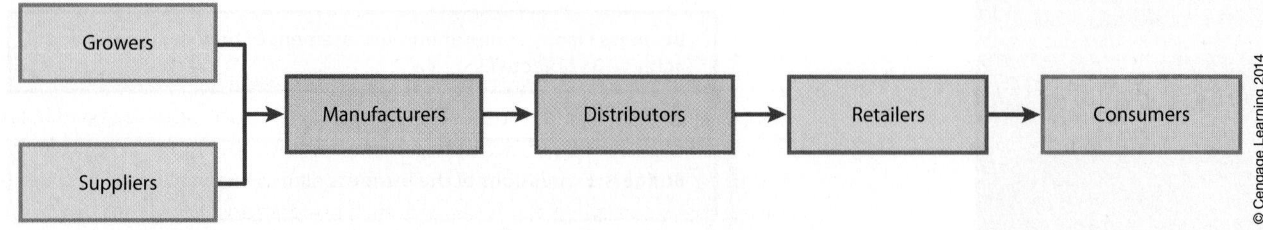

Business Perspective
What Do You Do to Cure a Bottleneck Headache?

A single seat belt can have as many as 50 parts, and getting the parts from suppliers was once a big problem for **Autoliv, Inc.**, a Swedish maker of auto safety devices. Autoliv's plant in Indianapolis was encountering constant bottlenecks in dealing with 125 different suppliers. To keep the production lines going required high-priced, rush shipments on a daily basis. To solve the problem, the company began using supply-chain management, keeping in touch with suppliers through the Internet rather than through faxes and phone calls. This system allowed suppliers to monitor the inventory at Autoliv and thus to anticipate problems. It also provided information on quantity and time of recent shipments, as well as continuously updated forecasts of parts that would be needed in the next 12 weeks. With supply-chain management, Autoliv reduced inventory by 75 percent and rush freight costs by 95 percent.[3]

Evaluating

Managers evaluate operating results by comparing the organization's actual performance with the performance levels established in the planning stage. They earmark any significant variations for further analysis so that they can correct the problems. If the problems are the result of a change in the organization's operating environment, the managers may revise their original estimates and/or objectives.

Communicating

Whether accounting reports are prepared for internal or external use, they must provide accurate information and clearly communicate this information. Inaccurate or confusing internal reports can have a negative effect on a company's operations. Full disclosure and transparency in financial statements issued to external parties is a basic concept of generally accepted accounting principles, and violation of this principle can result in stiff penalties. After several scandals, Congress passed legislation that requires the top management of companies to certify that financial statements filed with the SEC are accurate. The penalty for issuing false public reports can be loss of compensation, fines, and jail time.

The key to producing accurate and useful internal and external reports is to apply the four *w's*:

- **Why?** Know the purpose of the report. Focus on it as you write.
- **Who?** Identify the audience for your report. Communicate at a level that matches your readers' understanding of the issue and their familiarity with accounting information. A detailed, informal report may be appropriate for your manager, but a more concise summary may be necessary for other audiences, such as the president or board of directors of your organization.
- **What?** What information is needed, and what method of presentation is best? Select relevant information from reliable sources. You may draw information from pertinent documents or from interviews with knowledgeable managers and employees. The information should be not only relevant but also easy to read and understand. You may need to include visual aids, such as bar charts or graphs, to present the information clearly.
- **When?** Know the due date for the report. Strive to prepare an accurate report on a timely basis. If the report is urgently needed, you may have to sacrifice some accuracy in the interest of timeliness.

In summary, managerial accounting can provide a constant stream of relevant information to the management process. Managers start with a business plan, implement the plan, and evaluate and report the results. Accounting information helps managers develop their business plan, communicate that plan to their employees or their bank, evaluate their operating performance, and report the results of operations. As you can see in Exhibit 12, accounting plays a critical role in managing the operations of any organization.

Exhibit 12
Producing Results with the Management Process

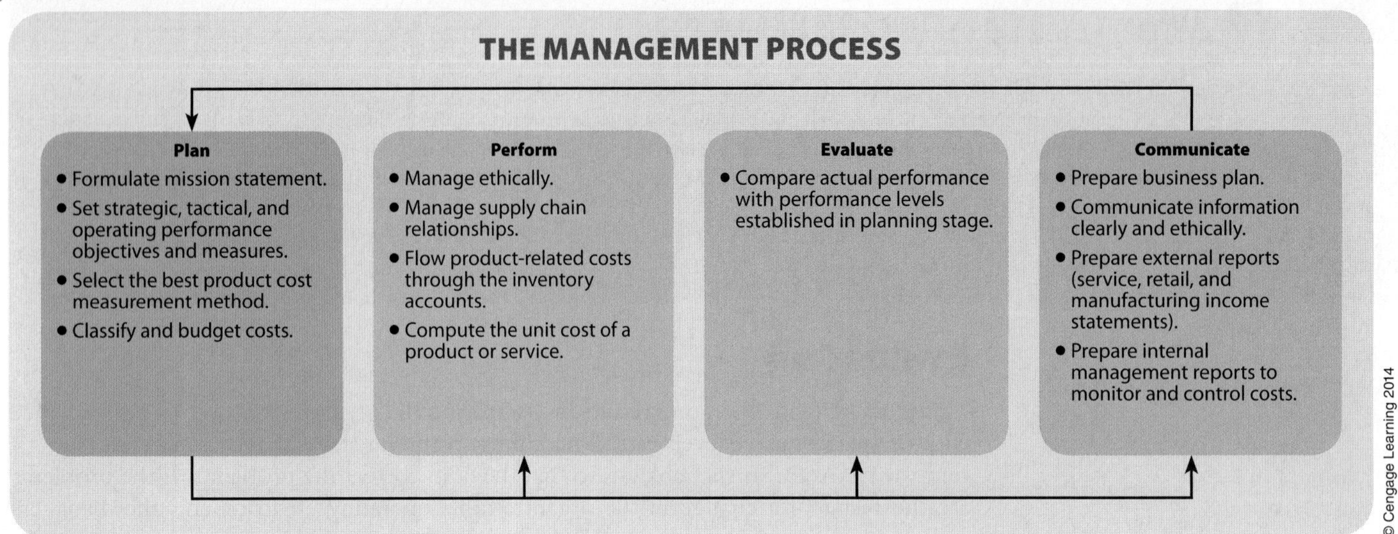

APPLY IT!

Indicate whether each of the following activities takes place during the planning (PL), performing (PE), evaluating (E), or communicating (C) stage of the management process.

a. Changing regular price to clearance price
b. Reporting results to appropriate personnel
c. Preparing budgets of operating costs
d. Comparing estimated and actual costs to determine variances

SOLUTION

a. PE, b. C, c. PL, d. E

TRY IT! SE8, SE9, E10A, E11A, E10B, E11B

LO7 Standards of Ethical Conduct

Managers consider the interests of external parties (e.g., customers, owners, suppliers, governmental agencies, and the local community) when they make decisions about the proper use of organizational resources and the financial reporting of their actions. When ethical conflicts arise, management accountants have a responsibility to help managers balance those interests.

To be viewed credibly by the various parties who rely on the information they provide, management accountants must adhere to the highest standards of performance. To provide guidance, the Institute of Management Accountants has issued standards of ethical conduct for practitioners of managerial accounting and financial management. Those standards, presented in Exhibit 13, emphasize that management accountants have responsibilities in the following areas:

- competence
- confidentiality
- integrity
- credibility

Exhibit 13
Statement of Ethical Professional Practice

Members of IMA shall behave ethically. A commitment to ethical professional practice includes: overarching principles that express our values, and standards that guide our conduct.

PRINCIPLES

IMA's overarching ethical principles include: Honesty, Fairness, Objectivity, and Responsibility. Members shall act in accordance with these principles and shall encourage others within their organizations to adhere to them.

STANDARDS

A member's failure to comply with the following standards may result in disciplinary action.

I. COMPETENCE

Each member has a responsibility to:

1. Maintain an appropriate level of professional expertise by continually developing knowledge and skills.
2. Perform professional duties in accordance with relevant laws, regulations, and technical standards.
3. Provide decision support information and recommendations that are accurate, clear, concise, and timely.
4. Recognize and communicate professional limitations or other constraints that would preclude responsible judgment or successful performance of an activity.

II. CONFIDENTIALITY

Each member has a responsibility to:

1. Keep information confidential except when disclosure is authorized or legally required.
2. Inform all relevant parties regarding appropriate use of confidential information. Monitor subordinates' activities to ensure compliance.
3. Refrain from using confidential information for unethical or illegal advantage.

III. INTEGRITY

Each member has a responsibility to:

1. Mitigate actual conflicts of interest. Regularly communicate with business associates to avoid apparent conflicts of interest. Advise all parties of any potential conflicts.
2. Refrain from engaging in any conduct that would prejudice carrying out duties ethically.
3. Abstain from engaging in or supporting any activity that might discredit the profession.

IV. CREDIBILITY

Each member has a responsibility to:

1. Communicate information fairly and objectively.
2. Disclose all relevant information that could reasonably be expected to influence an intended user's understanding of the reports, analyses, or recommendations.
3. Disclose delays or deficiencies in information, timeliness, processing, or internal controls in conformance with organization policy and/or applicable law.

RESOLUTION OF ETHICAL CONFLICT

In applying the Standards of Ethical Professional Practice, you may encounter problems identifying unethical behavior or resolving an ethical conflict. When faced with ethical issues, you should follow your organization's established policies on the resolution of such conflict. If these policies do not resolve the ethical conflict, you should consider the following courses of action:

Discuss the issue with your immediate supervisor except when it appears that the supervisor is involved. In that case, present the issue to the next level. If you cannot achieve a satisfactory resolution, submit the issue to the next management level. If your immediate superior is the chief executive officer or equivalent, the acceptable reviewing authority may be a group such as the audit committee, executive committee, board of directors, board of trustees, or owners. Contact with levels above the immediate superior should be initiated only with your superior's knowledge, assuming he or she is not involved. Communication of such problems to authorities or individuals not employed or engaged by the organization is not considered appropriate, unless you believe there is a clear violation of the law.

Clarify relevant ethical issues by initiating a confidential discussion with an IMA Ethics Counselor or other impartial advisor to obtain a better understanding of possible courses of action.

Consult your own attorney as to legal obligations and rights concerning the ethical conflict.

Source: *IMA Statement of Ethical Professional Practice*, Institute of Management Accountants, www.imanet.org. Reprinted by permission.

Business Perspective
How to Blow the Whistle on Fraud

According to **PricewaterhouseCoopers**'s fourth biennial survey of more than 5,400 companies in 40 countries, eradicating fraud is extremely difficult. Despite increased attention to fraud detection systems and stronger internal controls, half of the companies interviewed had fallen victim to some type of fraud in the previous two years. The average cost of the fraud was about $3.2 million per company. Fraud appeared most likely to happen in Africa, North America, and Central-Eastern Europe.

The Sarbanes-Oxley Act of 2002 requires that all publicly traded companies have an anonymous incident reporting system. Such a system can help prevent fraud, as can hotlines that provide guidance on ethical dilemmas involved in reporting fraud. An example of such an ethics hotline is the one that the Institute of Management Accountants instituted in 2002. However, PricewaterhouseCoopers's study found that the best fraud deterrents were a company-wide risk management system with a continuous proactive fraud-monitoring component and a strong ethical culture to which all employees subscribe.[4]

© Alija / iStockphoto.com

APPLY IT!

Rank in order of importance the management accountant's four areas of responsibility: competence, confidentiality, integrity, and credibility. Explain the reasons for your ranking.

SOLUTION

Rankings will vary depending on the reasoning used concerning the four areas of responsibility. Ranking differences among individuals also reinforces the fact that we approach ethical behavior in a variety of ways and why a code of ethics is necessary.

TRY IT! SE10, E12A, E13A, E12B, E13B

TriLevel Problem

Yurchyks/Shutterstock

The Hershey Company

The beginning of this chapter focused on **The Hershey Company**, a well-known company that manufactures and sells quality chocolate bars and other candies. Complete the following requirements in order to answer the questions posed at the beginning of the chapter.

Section 1: Concepts

How does managerial accounting recognize and define costs?

In this chapter, we learned that how managers recognize and define costs depends on how the cost information is used for decision making. Based on what you learned, match this chapter's cost classifications and uses.

Cost Classifications	Use of Cost Analysis
a. Direct costs; indirect costs	1. Classify costs for the preparation of financial statements.
b. Product costs; period costs	2. Calculate the number of units that must be sold to achieve a certain level of profit (cost behavior).
c. Variable costs; fixed costs	3. Identify the costs of activities that do and do not add value to a product or service.
d. Value-adding costs; non-value-adding costs	4. Control costs by tracking them to a particular cost object, such as a service or product.

1. Discuss the three elements of product or service cost.
2. Define product or service unit cost.

Section 2: Accounting Applications

How do companies like Hershey determine the cost of a candy bar?

Assume that one of Hershey's factories produces 50-pound blocks of dark chocolate and that it needs to prepare a year-end balance sheet and income statement, as well as a statement of cost of goods manufactured, and compute its product's actual unit cost. During the year, the factory purchased $361,920 of direct materials. The factory's direct labor costs for the year were $99,085 (10,430 hours at $9.50 per hour); its indirect labor costs totaled $126,750 (20,280 hours at $6.25 per hour). Account balances for the year were as follows.

Account	Balance
Plant Supervision	$ 42,500
Factory Insurance	8,100
Utilities, Factory	29,220
Depreciation, Factory Building	46,200
Depreciation, Factory Equipment	62,800
Factory Security	9,460
Factory Repair and Maintenance	14,980
Selling and Administrative Expenses	76,480
Materials Inventory, beginning	26,490
Work in Process Inventory, beginning	101,640
Finished Goods Inventory, beginning	148,290
Materials Inventory, ending	24,910
Work in Process Inventory, ending	100,400
Finished Goods Inventory, ending	141,100

1. Compute the cost of materials used during the year.
2. From the cost of materials used, compute the total manufacturing costs for the year.
3. From the total manufacturing costs for the year, compute the cost of goods manufactured during the year.
4. If 13,397 units (1 unit = 50-pound block of dark chocolate) were manufactured during the year, what was the actual product unit cost? (Round to two decimal places.)

Section 3: Business Applications

How does managerial accounting facilitate the management process as managers plan, organize, and control costs?

To answer this question, match this chapter's management responsibilities with when they occur within the management process.

a. Plan
b. Perform
c. Evaluate
d. Communicate

1. Track the flow of product costs
2. Compare actual and planned results
3. Prepare financial statements
4. Manage ethically
5. Classify costs
6. Prepare internal management reports
7. Communicate clearly and ethically
8. Select the best product cost measurement method
9. Formulate mission statement
10. Set strategic, tactical, and operating performance objectives and measures
11. Prepare business plan
12. Compute the unit cost of a product or service

SOLUTION

Concepts

1. 1. b; 2. c; 3. d; 4. a
2. Managers must analyze the elements of a product or service unit cost, which may include the traceable costs of direct materials and direct labor, and the indirect costs known as overhead.
3. Product unit cost is defined as the cost of manufacturing a single unit of product. Service unit cost is defined as the cost of performing a single service.

Accounting Applications

1. Cost of materials used:

Materials inventory, beginning		$ 26,490
Direct materials purchased		361,920
Cost of materials available for use		$388,410
Less materials inventory, ending		24,910
Cost of materials used		$363,500

2. Total manufacturing costs:

Cost of materials used		$363,500
Direct labor costs		99,085
Overhead costs:		
Indirect labor	$126,750	
Plant supervision	42,500	
Factory insurance	8,100	
Utilities, factory	29,220	
Depreciation, factory building	46,200	
Depreciation, factory equipment	62,800	
Factory security	9,460	
Factory repair and maintenance	14,980	
Total overhead costs		340,010
Total manufacturing costs		$802,595

3. Cost of goods manufactured:

Total manufacturing costs	$802,595
Add work in process inventory, beginning	101,640
Total cost of work in process during the year	$904,235
Less work in process inventory, ending	100,400
Cost of goods manufactured	$803,835

4. Actual product unit cost:

$$\frac{\text{Cost of Goods Manufactured}}{\text{Number of Units Manufactured}} = \frac{\$803{,}835}{13{,}397 \text{ units}} = \$60.00^{*}$$

*Rounded

Section 3: Business Applications

1. b
2. c
3. d
4. b
5. a
6. d
7. d
8. a
9. a
10. a
11. d
12. b

Chapter Review

Distinguish managerial accounting from financial accounting. **LO 1**

Managerial accounting involves partnering with management in decision making, devising planning and performance management systems to assist management in the formulation and implementation of an organization's strategy. Managerial accounting reports provide information for planning, control, performance measurement, and decision making to managers and employees. These reports have a flexible format; they can present either historical or future-oriented information expressed in dollar amounts or physical measures. In contrast, financial accounting reports provide information about an organization's past performance to owners, lenders, customers, and governmental agencies on a periodic basis. Financial accounting reports follow strict guidelines defined by generally accepted accounting principles.

Explain how managers recognize costs and how they define product or service unit cost. **LO 2**

A single cost can be recognized as a direct or an indirect cost, a variable or a fixed cost, a value-adding or a non-value-adding cost, and a product or a period cost. The three measured elements of product costs are direct materials, direct labor, and overhead. Direct materials costs are the costs of materials measured when making a product that can be traced to specific product units. Direct labor costs include all labor costs that can be traced to specific product units. All other production-related costs are measured and recognized as overhead costs. Such costs cannot be easily traced to end products or services, so a cost allocation method is used to assign them to products or services. When a batch of products has been completed, the product unit cost is computed by dividing the total cost of direct materials, direct labor, and overhead by the total number of units produced.

These cost classifications enable managers to control costs by tracing them to cost objects, to calculate the number of units that must be sold to obtain a certain level of profit, to identify the costs of activities that do and do not add value to a product or service, and to prepare financial statements for parties outside the organization. Managers in manufacturing, retail, and service organizations use information about operating costs and product or service unit costs to prepare budgets, make pricing and other decisions, calculate variances between estimated and actual costs, and communicate results.

Describe the flow of costs through a manufacturer's inventory accounts. **LO 3**

The flow of costs through the inventory accounts begins when costs for direct materials, direct labor, and overhead are incurred. Materials costs flow first into the Materials Inventory account, which is used to record the costs of materials when they are received and again when they are issued for use in a production process. All manufacturing-related costs—direct materials, direct labor, and overhead—are recorded in the Work in Process Inventory account. When products are completed, their costs are transferred from the Work in Process Inventory account to the Finished Goods Inventory account. When the products are sold, these costs are transferred to the Cost of Goods Sold account.

Compare how service, retail, and manufacturing organizations report costs on their financial statements and how they account for inventories. **LO 4**

Because the operations of service, retail, and manufacturing organizations differ, their financial statements differ as well. A service organization maintains no inventory accounts on its balance sheet. The cost of sales on its income statement reflects the net cost of the services sold. A retail organization, which purchases products ready for resale, maintains only a Merchandise Inventory account. The cost of goods sold is simply the difference between the cost of goods available for sale and the ending merchandise inventory. A manufacturing organization maintains three inventory accounts: Materials Inventory, Work in Process Inventory, and Finished Goods Inventory. Manufacturing costs flow through all three inventory accounts. During the accounting period, the cost of completed products is transferred to the Finished Goods Inventory account, and the cost of units that have been manufactured and sold is transferred to the Cost of Goods Sold account.

Compute the unit cost of a product or service. 

The product unit cost is computed by dividing the cost of goods manufactured by the total number of units produced. The product unit cost can be calculated using the actual, normal, or standard costing method. Under actual costing, the actual costs are used to compute the product unit cost. Under normal costing, the actual costs of direct materials and direct labor are combined with the estimated cost of overhead to determine the product unit cost. Under standard costing, the estimated costs are used to calculate the product unit cost. The components of product cost may be classified as prime costs or conversion costs. Prime costs are the primary costs of production--the sum of direct materials costs and direct labor costs. Conversion costs are the costs of converting direct materials into finished product—the sum of direct labor costs and overhead costs.

Service organizations have no materials costs; but they do have both direct labor costs and overhead costs. To determine the cost of performing a service, professional labor and service-related overhead costs are included in the analysis.

Explain how managerial accounting supports the management process to produce business results. LO 6

Managerial accounting supports each stage of the management process. When managers plan, they work with managerial accounting to establish strategic, tactical, and operating objectives that reflect their company's mission and to formulate a business plan for achieving those objectives. The plan is usually expressed in the form of budgets. When managers implement the plan, they use the information provided in the budgets to manage the business in the context of its supply chain. In evaluating performance, managers compare actual performance with planned performance and take steps to correct any problems. Reports reflect the results of planning, executing, and evaluating operations and may be prepared for external or internal use.

Identify the standards of ethical conduct for management accountants. LO 7

The Statement of Ethical Professional Practice emphasizes the Institute of Management Accounting members' responsibilities in the areas of competence, confidentiality, integrity, and credibility. These standards of conduct help management accountants recognize and avoid situations that could compromise their ability to supply management with accurate and relevant information.

Key Terms

actual costing method 725 (LO5)
budget 728 (LO6)
business plan 728 (LO6)
conversion costs 714 (LO2)
cost of goods manufactured 720 (LO3)
cost of goods sold 720 (LO3)
direct costs 712 (LO2)
direct labor costs 713 (LO2)
direct materials costs 713 (LO2)
Finished Goods Inventory account 718 (LO3)
fixed cost 714 (LO2)
goal/vision 727 (LO6)
indirect costs 712 (LO2)
indirect labor costs 713 (LO2)
indirect materials costs 713 (LO2)
managerial accounting 710 (LO1)
manufacturing cost flow 718 (LO3)
Materials Inventory account 718 (LO3)
mission statement 728 (LO6)
non-value-adding cost 715 (LO2)
normal costing method 726 (LO5)
operating objectives 728 (LO6)
overhead costs 713 (LO2)
period costs 713 (LO2)
prime costs 714 (LO2)
product costs 713 (LO2)
product unit cost 713 (LO2)
service unit cost 713 (LO2)
standard costing method 726 (LO5)
statement of cost of goods manufactured 723 (LO4)
strategic objectives 728 (LO6)
supply chain 728 (LO6)
tactical objectives 728 (LO6)
total manufacturing costs 719 (LO3)
value-adding cost 715 (LO2)
variable cost 714 (LO2)
Work in Process Inventory account 718 (LO3)

Chapter Assignments

DISCUSSION QUESTIONS

LO 1 **DQ1. CONCEPT ▶ BUSINESS APPLICATION ▶** How do the concepts of cost measurement and cost recognition underlie management accountants partnering with managers?

LO 1 **DQ2. CONCEPT ▶** Explain how this statement: "Managerial accounting and financial accounting work is interrelated and the accountants must work together closely" relates to accounting concepts.

LO 1 **DQ3.** In 1982, the IMA defined management accounting as follows.

> *The process of identification, measurement, accumulation, analysis, preparation, interpretation, and communication of financial information used by management to plan, evaluate, and control within the organization and to assure appropriate use of and accountability for its resources.*[5]

Compare this definition with the updated one that appears in LO1. Has the role of a management accountant changed?

LO 5 **DQ4. CONCEPT ▶** Describe the three cost measurement methods that can be used to compute the unit cost of a product or service.

LO 6 **DQ5. CONCEPT ▶ BUSINESS APPLICATION ▶** How do managers in various organizations use cost information in the management process to measure and recognize costs during a period?

SHORT EXERCISES

LO 1 **Managerial Accounting versus Financial Accounting**

SE1. Indicate whether each of the following characteristics relates to managerial accounting (MA) or financial accounting (FA):

a. Forward looking
b. Publicly reported
c. Complies with accounting standards
d. Usually confidential
e. Reports past performance
f. Uses physical measures as well as monetary ones for reports
g. Driven by user needs
h. Focuses on business decision making

LO 2 **Elements of Manufacturing Costs**

SE2. CONCEPT ▶ Stoney Saure, accountant for Votives, Inc., must group the costs of manufacturing tealights. Indicate whether each of the following items should be classified as direct materials (DM), direct labor (DL), overhead (O), or none of these (N). Also indicate whether each is a prime cost (PC), a conversion cost (CC), or neither (N). (*Hint:* More than one answer per category may apply.)

a. Cost of wax
b. Depreciation of the cost of vats to hold melted wax
c. Cost of Gigi's time to dip the wicks into the wax
d. Rent on the factory where candles are made
e. Cost of coloring for candles
f. Steve's commission to sell candles to Brightlights, Inc.
g. Cost of Ramos's time to design candles for Halloween

LO 2

Cost Recognition

SE3. CONCEPT ▶ Indicate whether each of the following is a direct cost (D), an indirect cost (ID), or neither (N) and whether it is a variable (V) or a fixed (F) cost. Also indicate whether each adds value (VA) or does not add value (NVA) to the product and whether each is a product cost (PD) or a period cost (PER).

a. Production foreman's salary
b. Straight-line depreciation on office equipment
c. Wages of a production-line worker

LO 3

Cost Flow in a Manufacturing Organization

SE4. Given the following information, compute the ending balances of the Materials Inventory, Work in Process Inventory, and Finished Goods Inventory accounts:

Materials Inventory, beginning balance	$ 25,000
Work in Process Inventory, beginning balance	5,750
Finished Goods Inventory, beginning balance	38,000
Direct materials purchased	85,000
Direct materials used	74,000
Direct labor costs	70,000
Overhead costs	35,000
Cost of goods manufactured	133,000
Cost of goods sold	103,375

LO 3

Document Flows in a Manufacturing Organization

SE5. Identify the document needed to support each of the following activities in a manufacturing organization:

a. Recording direct labor time at the beginning and end of each work shift
b. Placing an order for direct materials with a supplier
c. Receiving direct materials at the shipping dock
d. Recording the costs of a specific job's direct materials, direct labor, and overhead
e. Issuing direct materials into production
f. Fulfilling a Production Department request for the purchase of direct materials
g. Billing the customer for a completed order

LO 4

Income Statement for a Manufacturing Organization

SE6. Using the following information from Nathan Company, prepare an income statement through operating income for the year:

Sales	$900,000
Finished goods inventory, beginning	45,000
Cost of goods manufactured	575,000
Finished goods inventory, ending	80,000
Operating expenses	300,000

LO 5

Computation of Product Unit Cost

SE7. What is the product unit cost for Job SZ, which consists of 600 units and has total manufacturing costs of direct materials, $4,800; direct labor, $7,200; and overhead, $3,600? What are the prime costs and conversion costs per unit?

LO 6 **The Management Process**

SE8. BUSINESS APPLICATION ▶ Indicate whether each of the following management activities in a department store is part of planning (PL), performing (PE), evaluating (E), or communicating (C):

a. Completing a balance sheet and income statement at the end of the year
b. Meeting with sales managers to develop performance measures for sales personnel
c. Training a clerk to complete a cash sale
d. Renting a local warehouse to store excess inventory of clothing
e. Preparing an annual sales budget for each department and the entire store
f. Evaluating the performance of the shoe department by examining the significant differences between its actual and planned expenses for the month

LO 6 **Strategic Positioning**

SE9. BUSINESS APPLICATION ▶ Organizations stake out different strategic positions to add value and achieve success. Some strive to be low-cost leaders like **Wal-Mart**, while others become the high-end quality leaders like **Whole Foods Market**. Identify which of the following organizations are low-cost leaders (C) and which are quality leaders (Q):

a. Tiffany & Co.
b. Yale University
c. Local community college
d. Lexus
e. All-you-can-eat restaurant
f. Rent-a-Wreck
g. Apple Computers
h. Coca-Cola
i. Store-brand soda

LO 7 **Ethical Conduct**

SE10. BUSINESS APPLICATION ▶ ABC Cosmetics Company's managerial accountant has lunch every day with his friend who is a managerial accountant for XYZ Cosmetics, Inc., a competitor of ABC. Last week, ABC's accountant couldn't decide how to treat some information in a report he was preparing, so he discussed it with his friend. Is ABC's accountant adhering to the ethical standards of management accountants? Defend your answer.

EXERCISES: SET A

LO 2 **Cost Recognition**

E1A. CONCEPT ▶ Indicate whether each of the following costs for a moped manufacturer is a product or a period cost, a variable or a fixed cost, a value-adding or a non-value-adding cost, and, if it is a product cost, a direct or an indirect cost of the moped:

	Cost Recognition Classifications			
Item	**Product or Period**	**Variable or Fixed**	**Value-Adding or Non-Value-Adding**	**Direct or Indirect**
Example: Motor	Product	Variable	Value-adding	Direct

a. Office rent
b. Labor to assemble moped
c. Labor to inspect moped
d. Accountant's salary
e. Lubricant for brakes

LO 4

Comparison of Income Statement Formats

E2A. Indicate whether each of these equations applies to a service organization (SER), a retail organization (RET), or a manufacturing organization (MANF):

a. Cost of Sales = Net Cost of Services Sold
b. Cost of Goods Sold = Beginning Merchandise Inventory + Net Cost of Purchases − Ending Merchandise Inventory
c. Cost of Goods Sold = Beginning Finished Goods Inventory + Cost of Goods Manufactured − Ending Finished Goods Inventory

LO 4

Characteristics of Organizations

E3A. Indicate whether each of the following is typical of a service organization (SER), a retail organization (RET), or a manufacturing organization (MANF):

a. Purchases products ready for resale
b. Maintains no balance sheet inventory accounts
c. Maintains only one balance sheet inventory account
d. Maintains three balance sheet inventory accounts
e. Designs and makes products for sale
f. Sells services
g. Includes the net cost of purchases in calculating cost of goods sold
h. Determines the net cost of services sold
i. Includes the cost of goods manufactured in calculating cost of goods sold

LO 4

Statement of Cost of Goods Manufactured

E4A. During June, Agron, Inc., purchases of direct materials totaled $119,000; direct labor for the month was 3,400 hours at $10.00 per hour. Agron also incurred the following overhead costs: utilities, $5,870; supervision, $17,300; indirect materials, $6,750; depreciation, $6,200; insurance, $1,830; and miscellaneous, $1,100.

Beginning inventory accounts were as follows: Materials Inventory, $48,600; Work in Process Inventory, $55,250; and Finished Goods Inventory, $38,500. Ending inventory accounts were as follows: Materials Inventory, $55,100; Work in Process Inventory, $48,400; and Finished Goods Inventory, $37,450.

Prepare a statement of cost of goods manufactured.

LO 4

Statement of Cost of Goods Manufactured and Cost of Goods Sold

E5A. FruTee Corp. makes irrigation sprinkler systems for fruit tree nurseries. FruTee's new controller can find only the following partial information for the past year:

	Lime Division	Lemon Division	Orange Division	Fig Division
Direct materials used	$ 4	$ 7	$ (g)	$ 8
Total manufacturing costs	11	(d)	(h)	17
Overhead	5	3	3	(j)
Direct labor	(a)	9	4	4
Ending work in process inventory	(b)	3	2	5
Cost of goods manufactured	12	23	15	(l)
Beginning work in process inventory	2	(e)	5	(k)
Ending finished goods inventory	2	6	(i)	9
Beginning finished goods inventory	3	(f)	5	7
Cost of goods sold	(c)	21	16	12

Compute the unknown values. List the accounts in the proper order, and show subtotals and totals as appropriate.

LO 4 **Missing Amounts—Manufacturing**

E6A. Incomplete inventory and income statement data for Gator Corporation follow. Determine the missing amounts.

	Cost of Goods Sold	Cost of Goods Manufactured	Beginning Finished Goods Inventory	Ending Finished Goods Inventory
a.	$ 15,000	$20,000	$ 1,000	?
b.	$140,000	?	$55,000	$60,000
c.	?	$99,000	$23,000	$29,000

LO 4 **Inventories, Cost of Goods Sold, and Net Income**

E7A. The data that follow are for a retail organization and a manufacturing organization.

1. Fill in the missing data for the retail organization:

	First Quarter	Second Quarter	Third Quarter	Fourth Quarter
Sales	$10	$(e)	$15	$(k)
Gross margin	(a)	4	5	(l)
Ending merchandise inventory	5	(f)	5	(m)
Beginning merchandise inventory	4	(g)	(h)	5
Net cost of purchases	(b)	7	11	(n)
Operating income	3	2	(i)	2
Operating expenses	(c)	2	1	4
Cost of goods sold	5	8	(j)	12
Cost of goods available for sale	(d)	12	15	15

2. Fill in the missing data for the manufacturing organization:

	First Quarter	Second Quarter	Third Quarter	Fourth Quarter
Ending finished goods inventory	$(a)	$3	$(h)	$ 6
Cost of goods sold	6	3	5	(l)
Operating income	2	3	2	(m)
Cost of goods available for sale	8	(d)	10	13
Cost of goods manufactured	5	(e)	(i)	8
Gross margin	4	(f)	(j)	7
Operating expenses	2	(g)	4	5
Beginning finished goods inventory	(b)	2	3	(n)
Sales	(c)	10	(k)	14

LO 5 **Unit Cost Determination**

E8A. Anderson Winery produces a red wine called Old Vines. Recently, management has become concerned about the increasing cost of making Old Vines and needs to determine if the current selling price of $10 per bottle is adequate. The winery wants to achieve a 25 percent gross profit on the sale of each bottle. The following information is given to you for analysis:

Batch size	6,264 bottles
Costs:	
Total direct materials costs	$25,056
Total direct labor costs	12,528
Total overhead costs	21,924
Total production costs	$59,508

(Continued)

1. Compute the unit cost per bottle for materials, labor, and overhead.
2. **ACCOUNTING CONNECTION ▶** How would you advise management regarding the price per bottle of wine? (Round to the nearest cent.)
3. Compute the prime costs per unit and the conversion costs per unit.

LO 5

Unit Costs in a Service Business

E9A. Roll in the Hay, Inc., provides harvesting services. In June, the business earned $3,600 by cutting, turning, and baling 6,000 bales. During the month, the following costs were incurred: gas, $900; tractor maintenance, $360; and labor, $1,200. Annual tractor depreciation is $3,000. What was the company's cost per bale? (Round to the nearest cent.) What was its revenue per bale? Should the price per bale be increased?

LO 6

The Management Process

E10A. BUSINESS APPLICATION ▶ Indicate whether each of the following management activities of a chain of retail stores is part of planning (PL), performing (PE), evaluating (E), or communicating (C):

a. Leasing five delivery trucks for the current year
b. Comparing the actual number with the planned number of customers for the year
c. Developing a strategic plan for a new store
d. Preparing a report showing the past performance of a retail store
e. Developing standards, or expectations, for performance of sales staff for next year
f. Preparing the chain's balance sheet and income statement and distributing them to the board of directors
g. Maintaining an inventory of a variety of merchandise
h. Formulating a corporate policy for the treatment and disposition of recyclables
i. Preparing a report on the types and amounts of recyclables removed from each store in the last three months
j. Recording the time taken to deliver online orders to customers

LO 6

The Planning Framework

E11A. BUSINESS APPLICATION ▶ Yuan Xi has just opened a company that imports fine ceramic gifts from China and sells them over the Internet. In planning his business, Xi did the following:

1. Listed his expected expenses and revenues for the first year of operations
2. Determined that he would keep his expenses low and generate enough revenues during the first four months of operations so that he would have a positive cash flow by the fifth month
3. Decided that he wanted the company to provide him with income for a good lifestyle and funds for retirement
4. Developed a complete list of goals, objectives, procedures, and policies relating to how he would find, buy, store, sell, and ship goods and collect payment
5. Decided to focus his business on providing customers with the finest Chinese ceramics at a favorable price
6. Decided to expand his website to include ceramics from other Far Eastern countries over the next five years
7. Decided to solely rely on the Internet to market the products

Match each of Xi's actions to the components of the planning framework: goal, mission, strategic objectives, tactical objectives, operating objectives, business plan, and budget.

LO 7

Ethical Conduct

E12A. BUSINESS APPLICATION ▶ Dula Gibbon was recently promoted to accounting manager and now has a new boss, Tim Paine, the corporate controller. Last week, they went to a two-day workshop on accounting security. During the first hour of the first day's program, Paine disappeared. The same thing happened on the second day. During the trip home, Gibbon asked Paine about the conference. Paine replied, "I haven't sat in on one of those workshops in years. This is my R&R time. Those sessions are for the new people. My experience is enough to keep me current. Plus, I have excellent people, like you, to help me."

Does Dula Gibbon have an ethical dilemma? If so, what is it? What are her options? How would you solve her problem? Be prepared to defend your answer.

LO 7 **Corporate Ethics**

E13A. BUSINESS APPLICATION ▶ To answer the following questions, conduct a search of several companies' websites: (1) Does the company have an ethics statement? (2) Does it express a commitment to environmental or social issues? (3) In your opinion, is the company ethically responsible? Select one of the companies you researched and write a brief description of your findings.

EXERCISES: SET B

Visit the textbook companion website at www.cengagebrain.com to access Exercise Set B for this chapter.

PROBLEMS

LO 4 **A Manufacturing Organization's Balance Sheet**

✔ 2d: Cost of goods manufactured: $312,100

P1. The information that follows is from Manufacturing Company's trial balance.

	Debits	Credits
Cash	34,000	
Accounts Receivable	27,000	
Materials Inventory, ending	31,000	
Work in Process Inventory, ending	47,900	
Finished Goods Inventory, ending	54,800	
Factory Supplies	5,700	
Small Tools	9,330	
Land	160,000	
Factory Building	575,000	
Accumulated Depreciation—Factory Building		199,000
Factory Equipment	310,000	
Accumulated Depreciation—Factory Equipment		137,000
Patents	33,500	
Accounts Payable		26,900
Insurance Premiums Payable		6,700
Income Taxes Payable		41,500
Mortgage Payable		343,000
Common Stock		200,000
Retained Earnings		334,130
	1,288,230	1,288,230

REQUIRED

1. Manufacturing organizations use asset accounts that are not needed by retail organizations.
   a. List the titles of the asset accounts that are specifically related to manufacturing organizations.
   b. List the titles of the asset, liability, and equity accounts that you would see on the balance sheets of both manufacturing and retail organizations.
2. Assuming that the following information reflects the results of operations for the year, calculate the (a) gross margin, (b) cost of goods sold, (c) cost of goods available for sale, and (d) cost of goods manufactured:

Operating income	$138,130
Operating expenses	53,670
Sales	500,000
Finished goods inventory, beginning	50,900
Finished goods inventory, ending	54,800

LO 4

Statement of Cost of Goods Manufactured

SPREADSHEET

✔ Cost of goods manufactured: $3,645,800

P2. Jackplum Vineyards, whose fiscal year begins on November 1, has just completed a record-breaking year producing and selling wine. Its inventory account balances on October 31 of this year were Materials Inventory, $83,800; Work in Process Inventory, $2,700,500; and Finished Goods Inventory, $1,800,200. At the beginning of the year, the inventory account balances were Materials Inventory, $56,200; Work in Process Inventory, $3,300,000; and Finished Goods Inventory, $1,596,400.

During the fiscal year, the company's purchases of direct materials totaled $750,000. Direct labor hours totaled 140,000, and the average labor rate was $11.00 per hour. The following overhead costs were incurred during the year: depreciation—plant and equipment, $85,600; indirect labor, $207,300; property tax—plant and equipment, $96,000; plant maintenance, $80,000; small tools, $42,400; utilities, $96,500; and employee benefits, $176,100.

REQUIRED

Prepare a statement of cost of goods manufactured for the year ended October 31.

LO 5

Computation of Unit Cost

SPREADSHEET

✔ 2: Total unit cost: $5.20
✔ 4: Dept. 70 prime costs: $3.80
✔ 4: Dept. 70 conversion costs: $1.30

P3. Keep Cool Industries, Inc., manufactures fans for personal use. Department 70 is responsible for assembling the fan. Department 71 packages them for shipment. Keep Cool recently produced 10,000 fans for a national retailer. In fulfilling this order, the departments incurred the following costs:

	Department	
	70	**71**
Direct materials used	$30,000	$4,000
Direct labor	8,000	2,000
Overhead	5,000	3,000

1. Compute the unit cost for each department.
2. Compute the total unit cost for the national retailer order.
3. **ACCOUNTING CONNECTION ▶** The selling price for this order was $10 per unit. Was the selling price adequate? List the assumptions and/or computations upon which you based your answer. What suggestions would you make to Keep Cool's management about the pricing of future orders?
4. Compute the prime costs and conversion costs per unit for each department.

LO 5

Unit Costs in a Service Business

✔ 1: Total cost per patient day: $2,000
✔ 3: Total cost per patient day using industry average: $2,899

P4. Sunny Day Nursing Home relies heavily on cost data to keep its pricing structures in line with those of its competitors. The facility provides a wide range of services, including assisted living and skilled nursing. The facilities' controller is concerned about the profits generated by the 30-bed memory unit, so she is reviewing current billing procedures for that unit. The focus of her analysis is the unit's billing per patient day. This billing equals the per diem cost of the memory unit plus a 40 percent markup to cover other operating costs and generate a profit. Memory unit patient costs include the following:

Memory aids	$30 per patient day (average)
Doctors' care	1 hour per day @ $200 per hour (actual)
Memory therapy care	3 hours per day @ $90 per hour (actual)
Regular nursing care	24 hours per day @ $30 per hour (average)
Medications	$250 per day (average)
Daily living supplies	$80 per day (average)
Room rental	$400 per day (average)
Food services	$50 per day (average)

The nursing home director has asked the controller to compare the current billing procedure with one that uses industry averages to determine the billing per patient day.

REQUIRED

1. Compute the cost per patient per day.
2. Compute the billing per patient day using the memory unit's existing markup rate.
3. Compute the billing per patient day using the following industry averages for markup rates:

Memory aids	30%	Medications	50%
Doctors' care	50	Daily living supplies	50
Memory therapy care	50	Room rental	30
Regular nursing care	50	Food services	20

4. **ACCOUNTING CONNECTION ▶** Based on your findings in requirements 2 and 3, which billing procedure would you recommend? Why?

LO 7

Professional Ethics

P5. BUSINESS APPLICATION ▶ Ted Thalia is Tops Corporation's controller. He has been with the company for 20 years and is being considered for the job of chief financial officer. His boss, who is the current chief financial officer and former company controller, will be Tops's new president. Thalia has just discussed the year-end closing with his boss, who made the following statement during their conversation: "Ted, why are you being so inflexible? I'm only asking you to postpone the $5,000,000 write-off of obsolete inventory for 10 days so that it won't appear on this year's financial statements. Ten days! Do it. Your promotion is coming up, you know. Make sure you keep all the possible outcomes in mind as you complete your year-end work. Oh, and keep this conversation confidential—just between you and me. Okay?"

REQUIRED

1. Identify the ethical issue or issues involved.
2. What do you believe is the appropriate solution to the problem? Be prepared to defend your answer.

ALTERNATE PROBLEMS

LO 4

A Manufacturing Organization's Balance Sheet

✓ 2d: Cost of goods manufactured: $352,000

P6. The information that follows is from Miles Production Company's trial balance.

	Debits	Credits
Cash	40,000	
Accounts Receivable	30,000	
Materials Inventory, ending	41,000	
Work in Process Inventory, ending	37,000	
Finished Goods Inventory, ending	70,000	
Production Supplies	5,000	
Small Tools	3,000	
Land	200,000	
Factory Building	600,000	
Accumulated Depreciation—Factory Building		300,000
Production Equipment	210,000	
Accumulated Depreciation—Production Equipment		100,000
Patents	20,000	
Accounts Payable		40,000
Insurance Premiums Payable		6,000
Income Taxes Payable		40,000
Mortgage Payable		400,000
Common Stock		300,000
Retained Earnings		70,000
	1,256,000	1,256,000

(Continued)

REQUIRED

1. Manufacturing organizations use asset accounts that are not needed by retail organizations.
   a. List the titles of the asset accounts that are specifically related to manufacturing organizations.
   b. List the titles of the asset, liability, and equity accounts that you would see on the balance sheets of both manufacturing and retail organizations.
2. Assuming that the following information reflects the results of operations for the year, calculate the (a) gross margin, (b) cost of goods sold, (c) cost of goods available for sale, and (d) cost of goods manufactured:

Operating income	$ 68,000
Operating expenses	40,000
Sales	450,000
Finished goods inventory, beginning	60,000

LO **4**

SPREADSHEET

✔ Cost of goods manufactured: $10,163,200

Statement of Cost of Goods Manufactured

P7. Reggi Vineyards produces a full line of varietal wines. The company, whose fiscal year begins on November 1, has just completed a record-breaking year. Its inventory account balances on October 31 of this year were Materials Inventory, $1,803,800; Work in Process Inventory, $2,764,500; and Finished Goods Inventory, $1,883,200. At the beginning of the year, the inventory account balances were Materials Inventory, $2,156,200; Work in Process Inventory, $3,371,000; and Finished Goods Inventory, $1,596,400.

During the fiscal year, the company's purchases of direct materials totaled $6,750,000. Direct labor hours totaled 142,500, and the average labor rate was $8.20 per hour. The following overhead costs were incurred during the year: depreciation—plant and equipment, $685,600; indirect labor, $207,300; property tax—plant and equipment, $94,200; plant maintenance, $83,700; small tools, $42,400; utilities, $96,500; and employee benefits, $76,100.

REQUIRED

Prepare a statement of cost of goods manufactured for the fiscal year ended October 31.

LO **5**

SPREADSHEET

✔ 2: Total unit cost: $13.72
✔ 4: Dept. 60 prime costs: $9.06
✔ 4: Dept. 60 conversion costs: $3.54

Computation of Unit Cost

P8. Disco Industries, Inc., manufactures discs for several of the leading recording studios in the United States and Europe. Department 60 is responsible for pressing each disc. Department 61 then packages them for shipment. Disco recently produced 4,000 discs for Vintage Records Company. In fulfilling this order, the departments incurred the following costs:

	Department	
	60	**61**
Direct materials used	$29,440	$3,920
Direct labor	6,800	2,560
Overhead	7,360	4,800

1. Compute the unit cost for each department.
2. Compute the total unit cost for the Vintage Records Company order.
3. **ACCOUNTING CONNECTION ▶** The selling price for this order was $14 per unit. Was the selling price adequate? List the assumptions and/or computations upon which you based your answer. What suggestions would you make to Disco's management about the pricing of future orders?
4. Compute the prime costs and conversion costs per unit for each department.

LO **5**

✔ 1: Total cost per patient day: $2,792
✔ 3: Total cost per patient day using industry average: $4,013

Unit Costs in a Service Business

P9. Everymans Hospital relies heavily on cost data to keep its pricing structures in line with those of its competitors. The hospital provides a wide range of services, including intensive care, intermediate care, and a neonatal nursery. The hospital's controller is concerned about the profits generated by the 30-bed intensive care unit (ICU), so she is reviewing current billing procedures for that unit. The focus of her analysis is the hospital's billing per ICU patient day. This billing equals the per diem cost of intensive care plus a 40 percent markup to cover other operating costs and generate a profit. ICU patient costs include the following:

Equipment usage	\$180 per day (average)
Doctors' care	2 hours per day @ \$360 per hour (actual)
Special nursing care	4 hours per day @ \$85 per hour (actual)
Regular nursing care	24 hours per day @ \$28 per hour (average)
Medications	\$240 per day (average)
Medical supplies	\$150 per day (average)
Room rental	\$350 per day (average)
Food and services	\$140 per day (average)

The hospital director has asked the controller to compare the current billing procedure with one that uses industry averages to determine the billing per patient day.

REQUIRED

1. Compute the cost per patient per day.
2. Compute the billing per patient day using the hospital's existing markup rate. (Round to the nearest dollar.)
3. Compute the billing per patient day using the following industry averages for markup rates:

Equipment	30%	Medications	50%
Doctors' care	50	Medical supplies	50
Special nursing care	40	Room rental	30
Regular nursing care	50	Food and services	25

4. **ACCOUNTING CONNECTION** ▶ Based on your findings in requirements 2 and 3, which billing procedure would you recommend? Why?

LO 7

Professional Ethics

P10. BUSINESS APPLICATION ▶ For almost a year, OK Company has been changing its manufacturing processes. Management has asked for employees' assistance in the transition and has offered bonuses for suggestions that cut time from the production operation. Jim Han and Jerome Smith each identified a time-saving opportunity and turned in their suggestions to their boss.

The boss sent the suggestions to the committee charged with reviewing employees' suggestions, which inadvertently identified them as being the boss's own. The committee decided that the two suggestions were worthy of reward and voted a large bonus for the boss. When notified of this, the boss could not bring himself to identify the true authors of the suggestions.

When Han and Smith heard about their boss's bonus, they confronted him and expressed their grievances. He told them that he needed the recognition to be eligible for an upcoming promotion and promised that if they kept quiet about the matter, he would make sure that they both received significant raises.

REQUIRED

1. Should Han and Smith keep quiet? What other options are open to them?
2. How should their boss have dealt with Han's and Smith's complaints?

CASES

LO 2

Conceptual Understanding: Cost Recognition

C1. CONCEPT ▶ Visit a local fast-food restaurant. Observe all aspects of the operation and take notes on the entire process. Describe the procedures used to take, process, and fill an order and deliver the food to the customer. Based on your observations, make a list of the costs incurred by the restaurant. Then create a table similar to Exhibit 4 in the

(Continued)

text, in which you recognize the costs you have identified by their traceability (direct or indirect), cost behavior (variable or fixed), value attribute (value-adding or non-value-adding), and implications for financial reporting (product or period costs). Bring your notes and your table to class and be prepared to discuss your findings.

LO 2, 6

Business Communication: Management Decision about a Supporting Service Function

C2. As the manager of grounds maintenance for a large insurance company in Missouri, you are responsible for maintaining the grounds surrounding the company's three buildings, the six entrances to the property, and the recreational facilities, which include a golf course, a soccer field, jogging and bike paths, and tennis, basketball, and volleyball courts. Maintenance includes gardening (watering, planting, mowing, trimming, removing debris, and so on) and land improvements (e.g., repairing or replacing damaged or worn concrete and gravel areas).

Early in January, you receive a memo from the company president requesting information about the cost of operating your department for the last 12 months. She has received a bid from Outsource Landscapes, Inc., to perform the gardening activities you now perform. You are to prepare a cost report that will help her decide whether to keep gardening activities within the company or to outsource the work.

1. **BUSINESS APPLICATION ▶** Before preparing your report, answer the following questions:
   a. What kinds of information do you need about your department?
   b. Why is this information relevant?
   c. Where would you go to obtain this information (sources)?
   d. When would you want to obtain this information?
2. Draft a report showing only headings and line items that best communicate the costs of your department. How would you change your report if the president asked you to reduce the costs of operating your department?
3. **CONCEPT ▶** One of your department's cost accounts is the Maintenance Expense—Garden Equipment account.
   a. Is this a direct or an indirect cost?
   b. Is it a product or a period cost?
   c. Is it a variable or a fixed cost?
   d. Does the activity add value to the company business of insurance services?
   e. Is it a budgeted or an actual cost in your report?

LO 4, 6

Conceptual Understanding: Management Information Needs

C3. H&Y Drug Corporation manufactures most of its three pharmaceutical products in India. Inventory balances for March and April follow.

	March 31	April 30
Materials Inventory	$258,400	$228,100
Work in Process Inventory	138,800	127,200
Finished Goods Inventory	111,700	114,100

During April, purchases of direct materials, which include natural materials, basic organic compounds, catalysts, and suspension agents, totaled $612,600. Direct labor costs were $160,000, and actual overhead costs were $303,500. Sales of the company's three products for April totaled $2,188,400. General and administrative expenses were $362,000.

1. Prepare a statement of cost of goods manufactured and an income statement through operating income for the month ended April 30.
2. Why is it that the total manufacturing costs do not equal the cost of goods manufactured?
3. What additional information would you need to determine the profitability of each of the three product lines?
4. **CONCEPT ▶** Indicate whether each of the following is a product cost or a period cost:
   a. Import duties for indirect materials
   b. Shipping expenses to deliver manufactured products to the United States

c. Rent for manufacturing facilities in India
d. Salary of the American manager working at the Indian manufacturing facilities
e. Training costs for an Indian accountant

LO 6

Interpreting Managerial Reports: Financial Performance Measures

C4. Shape It Manufacturing Company makes sheet metal products. For the past several years, the company's income has been declining. Its statements of cost of goods manufactured and income statements for the last two years are shown here. Review and comment on why the ratios for Shape It's profitability have deteriorated.

Shape It Manufacturing Company
Statements of Cost of Goods Manufactured
For the Years Ended December 31

	This Year		Last Year	
Direct materials used:				
Materials inventory, beginning	$ 91,240		$ 93,560	
Direct materials purchased (net)	987,640		959,940	
Cost of direct materials available for use	$1,078,880		$1,053,500	
Less materials inventory, ending	95,020		91,240	
Cost of direct materials used		$ 983,860		$ 962,260
Direct labor		571,410		579,720
Total overhead		482,880		452,110
Total manufacturing costs		$2,038,150		$1,994,090
Add work in process inventory, beginning		148,875		152,275
Total cost of work in process during the period		$2,187,025		$2,146,365
Less work in process inventory, ending		146,750		148,875
Cost of goods manufactured		$2,040,275		$1,997,490

Shape It Manufacturing Company
Income Statements
For the Years Ended December 31

	This Year		Last Year	
Sales		$2,942,960		$3,096,220
Cost of goods sold	$ 142,640		$ 184,820	
Cost of goods manufactured	2,040,275		1,997,490	
Cost of goods available for sale	$2,182,915		$2,182,310	
Less finished goods inventory, ending	186,630		142,640	
Total		1,996,285		2,039,670
Gross margin		$ 946,675		$1,056,550
Selling and administrative expenses:				
Sales salaries and commissions	$ 394,840		$ 329,480	
Advertising expense	116,110		194,290	
Other selling expenses	82,680		72,930	
Administrative expenses	242,600		195,530	
Total selling and administrative expenses		836,230		792,230
Income from operations		$ 110,445		$ 264,320
Other revenues and expenses:				
Interest expense		54,160		56,815
Income before income taxes		$ 56,285		$ 207,505
Income tax expense		19,137		87,586
Net income		$ 37,148		$ 119,919

(Continued)

1. In preparing your comments, compute the following ratios for each year:
   a. Ratios of cost of direct materials used to total manufacturing costs, direct labor to total manufacturing costs, and total overhead to total manufacturing costs. (Round to one decimal place.)
   b. Ratios of sales salaries and commission expense, advertising expense, other selling expenses, administrative expenses, and total selling and administrative expenses to sales. (Round to one decimal place.)
   c. Ratios of gross margin to sales and net income to sales. (Round to one decimal place.)
2. From your evaluation of the ratios computed in **1**, state the probable causes of the decline in net income.
3. What other factors or ratios do you believe should be considered in determining the cause of the company's decreased income?

LO **6, 7**

Ethical Dilemma: Preventing Pollution and the Costs of Waste Disposal

C5. BUSINESS APPLICATION ▶ Lake Waburg Power Plant provides power to a metropolitan area of 4 million people. The plant's controller, Sunny Hope, has just returned from a conference on the Environmental Protection Agency's regulations concerning pollution prevention. She is meeting with the company's president, Guy Poe, to discuss the impact of the EPA's regulations on the plant.

"Guy, I'm really concerned. We haven't been monitoring the disposal of the radioactive material we send to the Willis Disposal Plant. If Willis is disposing of our waste material improperly, we could be sued," said Sunny. "We also haven't been recording the costs of the waste as part of our product cost. Ignoring those costs will have a negative impact on our decision about the next rate hike."

"Sunny, don't worry. I don't think we need to concern ourselves with the waste we send to Willis. We pay the company to dispose of it. The company takes it off our hands, and it's their responsibility to manage its disposal. As for the cost of waste disposal, I think we would have a hard time justifying a rate increase based on a requirement to record the full cost of waste as a cost of producing power. Let's just forget about waste and its disposal as a component of our power cost. We can get our rate increase without mentioning waste disposal," replied Guy.

What responsibility for monitoring the waste disposal practices at the Willis Disposal Plant does Lake Waburg Power Plant have? Should Sunny take Guy's advice to ignore waste disposal costs in calculating the cost of power? Be prepared to discuss your response.

Continuing Case: Cookie Company

C6. BUSINESS APPLICATION ▶ Each of the rest of the chapters in this text includes a "cookie company" case that allows you to explore operating your own cookie business. For this chapter, you will form a company team and assign roles to team members. As a team, you will prepare a mission statement; set strategic, tactical, and operating objectives; decide on a company name; set cookie specifications, decide on a cookie recipe, and answer some questions about product costs.

REQUIRED

1. Join with 4 or 5 other students in the class to form a company team. (Your instructor may assign groups or allow students to organize their own teams.)
2. In researching how to start and run a cookie business, your team found the following three examples of cookie company mission statements:
   - To provide cheap cookies that taste great with fast and courteous service!
   - To make the best chocolate chip cookies that anyone has ever tasted!
   - To handmake the best in custom cookie creations!

   a. Consider which of the mission statements most closely expresses what you want your company's identity and unique character to be. Why?
   b. Will your business focus on cost, quality, or satisfying a specific need?
   c. Write your company's mission statement.

3. Based on your mission statement, describe your company's broad long-term strategic objectives:
   a. What will be your main products?
   b. Who will be your primary customers?
   c. Where will you operate your business?
4. Your team made the following decisions about your business:
   - To list expected expenses and revenues for the first six months of operations
   - To keep expenses low and generate enough revenues during the first two months of operations to have a positive cash flow by the third month
   - To develop a complete list of goals, objectives, procedures, and policies relating to how to find, buy, store, sell, and ship goods and collect payment
   - To rely solely on the Internet to market products
   - To expand the e-commerce website to include 20 varieties of cookies over the next five years

   Match each of the above to the following components of the planning framework: strategic objectives, tactical objectives, operating objectives, business plan, and budget.
5. As a team:
   - Determine the name of your cookie company.
   - Determine team members' tasks, and make team assignments (e.g., mixer, baker, quality controller, materials purchaser, accountant, marketing manager).
   - Assign each task an hourly pay rate or monthly salary based on your team's perception of the job market for the task involved.
   - Give the plan compiled thus far to your instructor and all team members in writing.
6. As a team, determine cookie specifications: quality, size, appearance, and special features (such as types of chips or nuts), as well as quantity and packaging.
7. As a team, select a cookie recipe that best fits the company's mission.
8. As a team, answer the following questions and submit the answers to your instructor:
   - Will your company use actual or normal costing when computing the cost per cookie? Explain your answer.
   - List the types of costs that your company will recognize as overhead.

CHAPTER 16
Costing Systems: Job Order Costing

BUSINESS INSIGHT
Club Car, LLC

Club Car is the world's largest manufacturer of electric vehicles. Its product portfolio includes golf carts, commercial utility vehicles, multi-passenger shuttle vehicles, and rough-terrain and off-road utility vehicles. When Club Car builds made-to-order golf carts, its customers can choose the type of wheels and windshield the golf cart should have, the cart's interior and exterior trim, the upholstery fabric, and a dashboard with or without oversized cup holders. They can also specify whether they want the cart to have a music system, a global positioning system, and a propane heater. They can even specify the sound of the golf cart's horn. In this chapter, we focus on the job order costing system—the type of system that makers of special-order products, such as a customized golf cart, use to account for costs and to make informed product decisions.

1. **CONCEPT** ▶ *Why is a job order costing system appropriate for Club Car to measure and recognize costs?*

2. **ACCOUNTING APPLICATION** ▶ *How does a product costing system account for costs when made-to-order products or services are produced?*

3. **BUSINESS APPLICATION** ▶ *How does a job order costing system help managers organize and control costs and facilitate management decisions?*

LEARNING OBJECTIVES

LO 1 **Distinguish between the two basic types of product costing systems, and identify the information that each provides.**

LO 2 **Explain the cost flow in a manufacturer's job order costing system.**

LO 3 **Prepare a job order cost card, and compute a job order's product or service unit cost.**

LO 4 **Explain cost allocation, and describe how allocating overhead costs figures into calculating product or service unit cost.**

LO 5 **Explain why unit cost measurement is important to the management process in producing business results.**

SECTION 1 CONCEPTS

CONCEPTS
- Cost measurement
- Cost recognition
- Matching rule (accrual accounting)

RELEVANT LEARNING OBJECTIVE

LO1 Distinguish between the two basic types of product costing systems, and identify the information that each provides.

LO1 Concepts Underlying Product Costing Systems

A **product costing system** is used to account for an organization's product costs and to provide timely and accurate unit cost information for pricing, cost planning and control, inventory valuation, and financial statement preparation.

- The product costing system enables managers to measure and recognize costs throughout the management process.
- It provides a measurement and recognition structure for *matching* the recording of the revenues earned from product or service sales to their related cost flows.

Job Order and Process Costing Systems

Two basic types of product costing systems have been developed: job order costing systems and process costing systems.

A **job order costing system** is used by companies that make unique or special-order products, such as custom-tailored suits. A job order costing system *measures* and *recognizes* the costs of direct materials, direct labor, and overhead to a specific batch of products or a specific **job order** (i.e., a customer order for a specific number of specially designed, made-to-order products) by using job order cost cards. A **job order cost card** is usually an electronic or paper document on which all costs incurred in the production of a particular job order—a completed unit—are recorded and *matched* with the job's revenues. In other words, in a job order costing system, the specific job or batch of a product (not a department or work cell) is the focus of *cost measurement* and *recognition*.

A **process costing system** is used by companies that produce large amounts of similar products or liquid products or that have long, continuous production runs of identical products. Makers of soft drinks, candy, bricks, and paper would use such a system. It first traces the costs of direct materials, direct labor, and overhead to processes, departments, or work cells and then assigns the costs to the products manufactured by those processes, departments, or work cells during a specific period using a process cost report. A **process cost report** is usually an electronic or paper document prepared every period for each process, department, or work cell and is explained fully in the next chapter.

The typical product costing system combines parts of job order costing and process costing to create a hybrid system known as an **operations costing system**.

Exhibit 1 summarizes the characteristics of both costing systems.

Exhibit 1
Characteristics of Job Order Costing and Process Costing Systems

Job Order Costing System	Process Costing System
Traces production costs to a specific job order	Traces production costs to processes, departments, or work cells and then assigns the costs to products manufactured
Measures the cost of each completed unit	Measures costs in terms of units completed during a specific period
Uses a single Work in Process Inventory account	Uses several Work in Process Inventory accounts
Measures the cost of all job orders using one inventory account	Measures costs of each process, department, or work cell, using an inventory account for each
Typically used by companies that make unique or special-order products, such as customized publications, built-in cabinets, or made-to-order draperies	Typically used by companies that make large amounts of similar products or liquid products or that have long, continuous production runs of identical products, such as paint, soft drinks, candy, bricks, and paper

APPLY IT!

State whether a job order costing system or a process costing system would typically be used to account for the costs of the following:

a. Manufacturing golf tees
b. Manufacturing custom-designed fencing for a specific golf course
c. Providing pet grooming
d. Manufacturing golf balls
e. Manufacturing dog food
f. Providing private golf lessons

SOLUTION

a. process; b. job order;
c. job order; d. process;
e. process; f. job order

TRY IT! SE1, E1A, E2A, E3A, E1B, E2B, E3B

SECTION 2

ACCOUNTING APPLICATIONS

ACCOUNTING APPLICATIONS

- Prepare a job order cost card
- Compute a job order's product or service unit cost

RELEVANT LEARNING OBJECTIVES

LO2 Explain the cost flow in a manufacturer's job order costing system.

LO3 Prepare a job order cost card, and compute a job order's product or service unit cost.

LO4 Explain cost allocation, and describe how allocating overhead costs figures into calculating product or service unit cost.

LO2 Job Order Costing in a Manufacturing Company

The basic parts of a job order costing system are the cost measurement and recognition procedures, electronic documents, and accounts that a company uses when it incurs costs for direct materials, direct labor, and overhead. Job order cost cards and cost flows through the inventory accounts form the core of a job order costing system.

Let's take a hypothetical company, Custom Golf Carts, which builds both customized and general-purpose golf carts. To study these cost flows, let's look at how Custom operates.

- Direct materials costs include the costs of a cart frame, wheels, upholstered seats, a windshield, a motor, and a rechargeable battery.
- Direct labor costs include the wages of the two production workers who assemble the golf carts.
- Overhead costs include indirect materials costs for upholstery zippers; cloth straps to hold equipment in place; wheel lubricants, screws and fasteners; silicon to attach the windshield; indirect labor costs for moving materials to the production area and inspecting a golf cart during its construction; depreciation on the manufacturing plant and equipment used to make the golf carts; and utilities, insurance, and property taxes related to the manufacturing plant.

Exhibit 2 shows the flow of each of these costs. The beginning balance in the Materials Inventory account means that there are already direct and indirect materials in the materials storeroom. The beginning balance in Work in Process Inventory means that Job CC is in production (with specifics given in the job order cost card). The zero beginning balance in Finished Goods Inventory means that all previously completed golf carts have been shipped.

Materials

The purchasing process begins with a request for specific quantities of direct and indirect materials that are needed for a sales order but are not currently available in the materials storeroom. When the new materials arrive, the Accounting Department records the materials purchased. It is helpful to understand the process of tracking production costs as they flow through the three inventory accounts and the entries that are triggered by the organization's source documents. The entries that track product cost flows are provided as background.

Purchase of Materials

Transactions 1 and 2 During the month, Custom made two purchases on credit. In transaction **1**, the company purchased cart frames costing $572 and wheels costing $340 for a total of $912. In transaction **2**, the company purchased indirect materials costing $82.

Analysis The journal entry to record these purchases

▲ *increases* the *Materials Inventory* account with a debit

▲ *increases* the *Accounts Payable* account with a credit

Journal Entries

	Dr.	*Cr.*
Materials Inventory	912	
Accounts Payable		912
Materials Inventory	82	
Accounts Payable		82

Comment Cost of direct and indirect materials are *recognized* when purchased.

Exhibit 2
The Job Order Costing System—Custom Golf Carts, Inc.

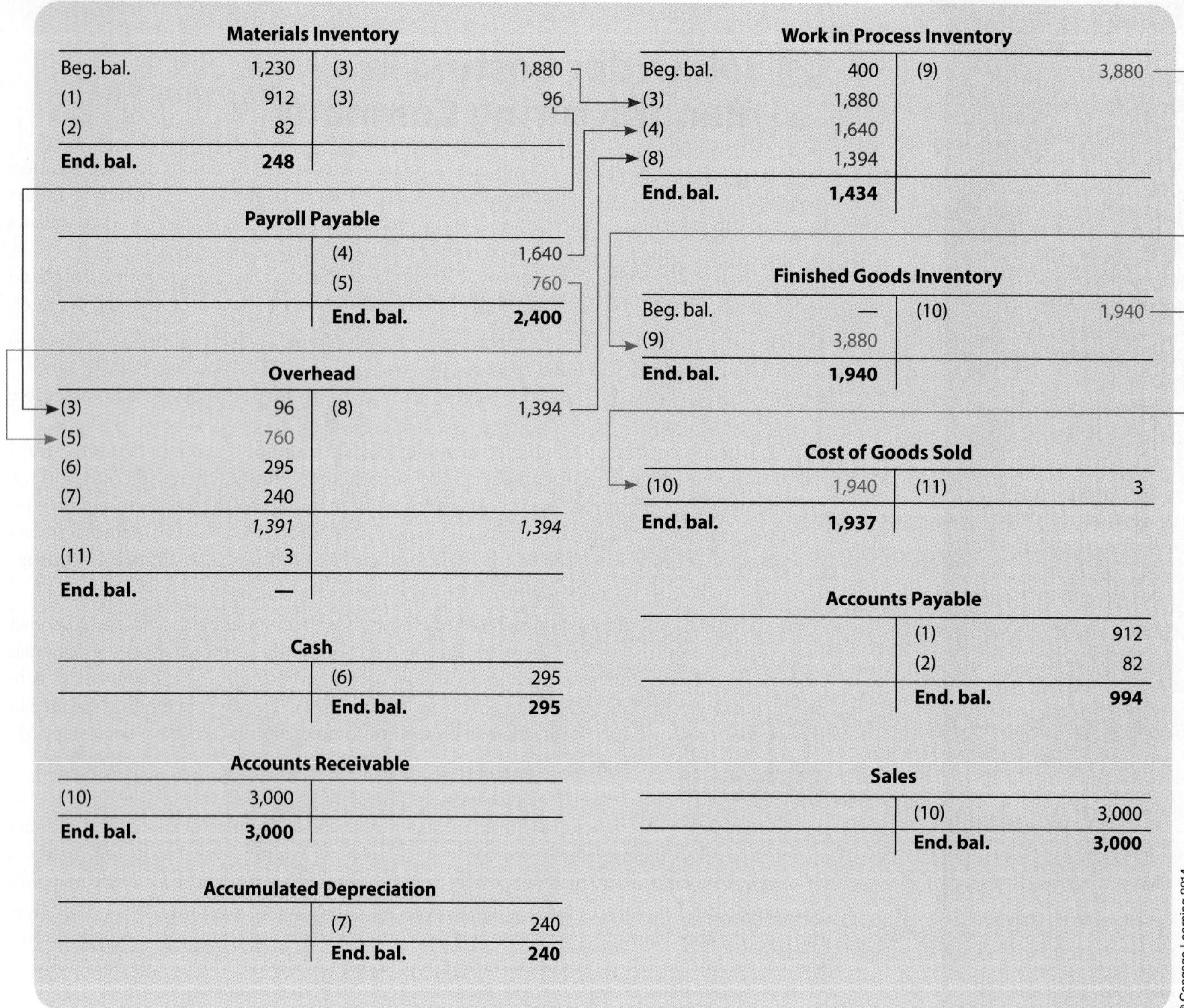

Materials Inventory

Beg. bal.	1,230	(3)	1,880
(1)	912	(3)	96
(2)	82		
End. bal.	**248**		

Work in Process Inventory

Beg. bal.	400	(9)	3,880
(3)	1,880		
(4)	1,640		
(8)	1,394		
End. bal.	**1,434**		

Payroll Payable

		(4)	1,640
		(5)	760
		End. bal.	**2,400**

Finished Goods Inventory

Beg. bal.	—	(10)	1,940
(9)	3,880		
End. bal.	**1,940**		

Overhead

(3)	96	(8)	1,394
(5)	760		
(6)	295		
(7)	240		
	1,391		*1,394*
(11)	3		
End. bal.	—		

Cost of Goods Sold

(10)	1,940	(11)	3
End. bal.	**1,937**		

Accounts Payable

		(1)	912
		(2)	82
		End. bal.	**994**

Cash

		(6)	295
		End. bal.	**295**

Accounts Receivable

(10)	3,000		
End. bal.	**3,000**		

Sales

		(10)	3,000
		End. bal.	**3,000**

Accumulated Depreciation

		(7)	240
		End. bal.	**240**

Transfer of Direct Materials to Production

Transaction 3—Direct Materials When golf carts are scheduled for production, requested materials are sent to the production area. Custom requested $1,880 of direct materials for the production of two jobs. These costs are also recorded on the corresponding job order cost cards. Job CC, a batch run of two general-purpose golf carts already in production, required $1,038 of the additional direct materials. Job JB, a customized golf cart made to the specifications of an individual customer, Alex Special, required $842 of the direct materials.

Analysis The journal entry to record the transfer of direct materials to production

- ▲ *increases* the *Work in Process Inventory* account with a debit (and also *increases* the charges to the corresponding job order cost cards)
- ▼ *decreases* the *Materials Inventory* account with a credit

Journal Entry

	Dr.	Cr.
Work in Process Inventory—Job CC	1,038	
Work in Process Inventory—Job JB	842	
Materials Inventory		1,880

Comment Custom processes requests for direct materials through journal entries to track cost flows and *measure* the cost of each job order.

Transfer of Indirect Materials to Production

Transaction 3—Indirect Materials Custom also requests indirect materials. When indirect materials are requested and sent to production, the indirect materials cost flows from the Materials Inventory account into the Overhead account.

Analysis The journal entry to record the transfer of indirect materials to production

▲ *increases* the *Overhead* account with a debit

▼ *decreases* the *Materials Inventory* account with a credit

Journal Entry

	Dr.	Cr.
Overhead	96	
Materials Inventory		96

Comment Custom processes requests for indirect materials through journal entries to track cost flows and *measure* the actual cost of overhead.

Labor

In general, the payroll costs include salaries and wages for direct and indirect production labor as well as for nonproduction-related employees. Custom's two production employees assemble the golf carts. Several other employees support production by moving materials and inspecting the products.

Payroll Costs Incurred for Production Labor

Transactions 4 and 5 Transactions **4** and **5** show the total production-related wages earned by employees during the period. Custom incurred $1,640 of direct labor costs—$1,320 for Job CC and $320 for Job JB—(transaction **4**) and $760 indirect labor costs (transaction **5**).

Analysis The journal entry to record the direct labor costs

▲ *increases* the *Work in Process Inventory* account with a debit

▲ *increases* the *Payroll Payable* account with a credit

The journal entry to record the indirect labor costs

▲ *increases* the *Overhead* account with a debit

▲ *increases* the *Payroll Payable* account with a credit

Journal Entry

	Dr.	Cr.
Work in Process Inventory—Job CC	1,320	
Work in Process Inventory—Job JB	320	
Payroll Payable		1,640
Overhead (indirect labor costs)	760	
Payroll Payable		760

Comment Custom *recognizes* labor costs through journal entries to *measure* the direct labor cost of each job order and to measure the actual cost of indirect labor and other nonproduction-related labor cost flows into overhead.

Overhead

Thus far, indirect materials and indirect labor have been the only costs debited to the Overhead account. Other actual indirect production costs, such as utilities, property taxes, insurance, and depreciation, are also charged to the Overhead account as they are incurred during the period.

Other Overhead Costs Incurred for Production

Transactions 6 and 7 Transaction **6** shows that other indirect costs amounting to $295 were paid. Transaction 7 records the $240 of production-related depreciation.

Analysis The journal entry to record incurring actual overhead costs

▲ *increases* the *Overhead* account with a debit

▼ *decreases* the *Cash* and *Accumulated Depreciation* accounts with a credit

Journal Entry

	Dr.	*Cr.*
Overhead	295	
Cash		295
Overhead	240	
Accumulated Depreciation		240

Comment Custom *recognizes* actual overhead costs on the debit side of the Overhead account so it can *measure* them against the overhead costs estimated for job orders.

During the period, to *recognize* all product-related costs for a job, an overhead cost estimate is applied to a job using a predetermined rate since the business uses a normal costing method to *measure* product costs. Based on its budget and past experience, Custom currently uses a predetermined overhead rate of 85 percent of direct labor costs.

Estimate of Overhead Costs

Transaction 8 In transaction **8**, Custom estimates the overhead incurred by each job to date by charging each job order in process with a percentage of its labor cost incurred. Total overhead of $1,394 is applied to the job orders, with $1,122 going to Job CC (85 percent of $1,320) and $272 going to Job JB (85 percent of $320).

Analysis The journal entry to record applying overhead using a predetermined rate

▲ *increases* the *Work in Process Inventory* account with a debit for $1,394 (85 percent of $1,640; see transaction **4**)

▼ *decreases* the *Overhead* account with a credit for the applied overhead of $1,394

Journal Entry

	Dr.	*Cr.*
Work in Process Inventory—Job CC	1,122	
Work in Process Inventory—Job JB	272	
Overhead		1,394

Comment Custom compares the actual (debit side of the Overhead account) and applied (credit side of the Overhead account) overhead amounts at the end of the period to determine the accuracy of job order overhead *cost recognition*.

Completed Units

When a custom job or a batch of general-purpose golf carts is completed and ready for sale, the products are moved from the manufacturing area to the finished goods storeroom.

Transfer of Completed Production to Finished Goods

Transaction 9 In transaction **9**, a job order is completed and transferred to the Finished Goods Inventory account since it is ready for sale. Custom's Job CC is completed and its cost of $3,880 is transferred from the Work in Process Inventory account to the Finished Goods Inventory account. The $3,880 includes the beginning balance of $400, materials of $1,038, labor of $1,320, and overhead of $1,122. Thus, the cost to produce one golf cart is $1,940 ($3,880 ÷ 2).

Analysis The journal entry to record completing a job order

▲ *increases* the *Finished Goods Inventory* account with a debit

▼ *decreases* the *Work in Process Inventory* account with a credit

Journal Entry

	Dr.	*Cr.*
Finished Goods Inventory	3,880	
Work in Process Inventory—Job CC		3,880

Comment When a job order is complete, its job order cost card has *measured* and *recognized* all the costs associated with its production. The job's cost of goods manufactured and product unit cost can be computed. The card is also transferred to the finished goods file.

Sold Units

STUDY NOTE: In this example, the company uses a perpetual inventory system. In a periodic inventory system, the cost of goods sold is calculated at the end of the period.

When a company uses a perpetual inventory system, as Custom does, two accounting entries are made when products are sold. One is prompted by the sales invoice and records the quantity and selling price of the products sold. The other entry, prompted by the delivery of products to a customer, records the quantity and cost of the products shipped.

Sales and the Transfer of Production Costs to Cost of Goods Sold

Transaction 10 In transaction **10**, a golf cart is sold to a customer and its cost of the goods sold is recognized. The $3,000 sales price of the one general-purpose golf cart sold on account by Custom is recorded. As was explained in Transaction **9**, the sold golf cart's related cost is $1,940. This cost is now transferred from the Finished Goods Inventory account to the Cost of Goods Sold account.

Analysis The journal entry to record a product's sales price and associated costs

▲ *increases* the *Accounts Receivable* account

▲ *increases* the *Sales* account

▲ *increases* the *Cost of Goods Sold* account

▼ *decreases* the *Finished Goods Inventory* account

Journal Entries

	Dr.	*Cr.*
Accounts Receivable (sales price of 1 unit sold)	3,000	
Sales (sales price of 1 unit sold)		3,000
Cost of Goods Sold (unit cost)	1,940	
Finished Goods Inventory (unit cost)		1,940

Comment When a job or product is sold, its revenues are *matched* with its costs. Since the job or product's revenue and costs have been *measured* and *recognized*, profitability can be analyzed. Notice the Finished Goods Inventory account has an ending balance of $1,940 for the one remaining unsold car from Job CC.

APPLY IT!

Partial operating data for Sample Company follows. Sample's management has set the predetermined overhead rate for the current year at 60 percent of direct labor costs.

Account/Transaction	October
Beginning Materials Inventory	$ 4,000
Beginning Work in Process Inventory	6,000
Beginning Finished Goods Inventory	2,000
Direct materials used	16,000
Direct materials purchased	(a)
Direct labor costs	24,000
Overhead applied	(b)
Cost of units completed	(c)
Cost of Goods Sold	50,000
Ending Materials Inventory	3,000
Ending Work in Process Inventory	10,000
Ending Finished Goods Inventory	(d)

Using T accounts, compute the unknown values. Show all your computations.

SOLUTION

Materials Inventory

Beg. bal.	4,000	Used	16,000
(a) Purchases	15,000		
End. bal.	**3,000**		

Work in Process Inventory

Beg. bal.	6,000	(c) Completed during period	50,400
Direct materials used	16,000		
Direct labor	24,000		
(b) Overhead applied	14,400*		
End. bal.	**10,000**		

Finished Goods Inventory

Beg. bal.	2,000	Cost of goods sold	50,000
(c) Completed during period	50,400		
(d) **End. bal.**	**2,400**		

*$24,000 × 60% = $14,400

TRY IT! SE2, SE3, SE4, E4A, E5A, E6A, E7A, E8A, E4B, E5B, E6B, E7B, E8B

LO3 A Job Order Cost Card and the Computation of Unit Cost

STUDY NOTE: *Traditionally, job order cost cards were paper, but today, most cards reside electronically in a computer system.*

In a job order costing system, each job in production has a job order cost card. As costs are incurred, they are classified by job and recorded on the appropriate card.

A Manufacturer's Job Order Cost Card

A manufacturer's job order cost card typically has space for direct materials, direct labor, and overhead costs, as shown in Exhibit 3. It also includes the job order number, product specifications, customer name, date of the order, projected completion date, and a cost summary. As a job incurs direct materials and direct labor costs, its job order cost card is updated. Overhead is also posted to the job order cost card at the predetermined rate.

Job order cost cards for incomplete jobs make up the subsidiary ledger for the Work in Process Inventory account. To ensure correctness, the ending balance in the Work in Process Inventory account is compared with the total of the costs shown on the job order cost cards.

Computation of Unit Cost

A job order costing system simplifies the calculation of product unit costs. When a job is finished, the costs of direct materials, direct labor, and overhead that have been recorded on its job order cost card are totaled. The product unit cost is then computed and entered on the job order cost card. It will be used to value items in inventory. The job

Exhibit 3
Job Order Cost Card for a Manufacturing Company

Job Order: CC

JOB ORDER COST CARD *
Custom Golf Carts, Inc.
Spring Hill, Florida

Customer: Stock **Batch:** X **Custom:**
Specifications: Two general-purpose golf carts
Date of Order: 2/26/14
Date of Completion: 3/6/14

Costs Charged to Job	Previous Months	Current Month	Total Cost
Direct materials	$165	$1,038	$1,203
Direct labor	127	1,320	1,447
Overhead (85% of direct labor cost)	108*	1,122	1,230*
Totals	$400	$3,480	$3,880
Units completed			÷ 2
Product unit cost			$1,940

*Rounded to nearest dollar

order cost card in Exhibit 3 shows the costs for completed Job CC. The product unit cost is computed as follows.

Product Unit Cost = Total Costs for Job ÷ Number of Good (Salable) Units Produced
= $3,880 ÷ 2
= $1,940

Job Order Costing in a Service Organization

Many service organizations use a job order costing system to compute the cost of rendering services. The most important cost for a service organization is labor, which is accounted for through the use of time cards. The cost flow of services is similar to the cost flow of manufactured products. Job order cost cards are used to keep track of the labor, materials and supplies, and service overhead incurred for each job.

To cover these costs and earn a profit, many service organizations base jobs on **cost-plus contracts**. Such contracts require the customer to pay all costs incurred in performing the job plus a predetermined amount of profit, which is based on the amount of costs incurred. When the job is complete, the costs on the completed job order cost card become the cost of services.

STUDY NOTE: *Job order cost cards for service businesses record costs by activities done for the job. The activity costs may include supplies, labor, and overhead.*

To illustrate how a service organization uses a job order costing system, assume that Dream Golf Retreats earns its revenue by designing and selling golf retreat packages to corporate clients. Exhibit 4 shows Dream Golf Retreats' job order cost card for Work Corporation. Costs have been categorized into three separate activities: planning, golf activities, and nongolf activities.

Exhibit 4
Job Order Cost Card for a Service Organization

Job Order: 2011-A7

JOB ORDER COST CARD
Dream Golf Retreats

Customer: Work Corporation **Batch:** ______ **Custom:** X
Specifications: Golf retreat for 45 executives
Date of Order: 3/24/14 **Date of Completion:** 4/8/14

Costs Charged to Job	Previous Months	Current Month	Total Cost
Planning:			
Supplies	$ 100	$ —	$ 100
Labor	850	—	850
Overhead (40% of planning labor costs)	340	—	340
Totals	$1,290	$ 0	$1,290
Golf activities:			
Supplies	$ 970	$1,200	$2,170
Labor	400	620	1,020
Overhead (50% of on-site labor costs)	200	310	510
Totals	$1,570	$2,130	$3,700
Nongolf activities:			
Cost of outsourcing	$ 90	$ 320	$ 410
Totals	$ 90	$ 320	$ 410

Cost Summary to Date	Total Cost
Planning	$1,290
Golf activities	3,700
Nongolf activities	410
Total	$5,400
Profit margin (15% of total cost)	810
Job revenue	$6,210

As Exhibit 4 illustrates, the service overhead cost for planning is 40 percent of planning labor cost ($850 × 0.40 = $340) and the service overhead cost for golf activities is 50 percent of on-site labor cost ($1,020 × 0.50 = $510). Total costs incurred for this job were $5,400. Dream Golf Retreats' cost-plus contract with Work Corporation has a 15 percent profit guarantee. Therefore, $810 of profit margin ($5,400 × 0.15 = $810) is added to the total cost to arrive at the total contract revenue ($5,400 + $810 = $6,210), which is billed to Work Corporation.

Complete the following job order cost card for six handcrafted sets of golf clubs:

Job Order 16

JOB ORDER COST CARD
Craftsman Golf Clubs
World of Golf, FL

Customer:	Kalpesh Patel	Batch: ___	Custom: X
Specifications:	6 sets of clubs		
Date of Order:	5/4/14		Date of Completion: 6/8/14

Costs Charged to Job	**Previous Months**	**Current Month**	**Total Cost**
Direct materials	$3,500	$2,800	$?
Direct labor	2,300	1,600	?
Overhead applied	1,150	800	?
Totals	$?	$?	$?
Units completed			÷ ?
Product unit cost			$?

SOLUTION

Job Order 16

JOB ORDER COST CARD
Craftsman Golf Clubs
World of Golf, FL

Customer:	Kalpesh Patel	Batch: ___	Custom: X
Specifications:	6 sets of clubs		
Date of Order:	5/4/14		Date of Completion: 6/8/14

Costs Charged to Job	**Previous Months**	**Current Month**	**Total Cost**
Direct materials	$3,500	$2,800	$ 6,300
Direct labor	2,300	1,600	3,900
Overhead applied	1,150	800	1,950
Totals	$6,950	$5,200	$12,150
Units completed			÷ 6
Product unit cost			$ 2,025

TRY IT! SE5, SE6, SE7, E6A, E7A, E8A, E9A, E10A, E11A, E12A, E13A, E6B, E7B, E8B, E9B, E10B, E11B, E12B, E13B

LO4 Cost Allocation

The costs of direct materials and direct labor can be easily traced to a product or service, but overhead costs are indirect costs that must be collected and allocated in some manner since their physical flow and how these costs are incurred do not always match. For example, utilities are used daily, but the utility bill comes once a month.

- **Cost allocation** is the process of assigning a collection of indirect costs, such as overhead, to a specific **cost object**, such as a product or service, a department, or an operating activity, using an allocation base known as a cost driver.
- A **cost driver** might be direct labor hours, direct labor costs, units produced, or another activity base that has a cause-and-effect relationship with the cost.
- As the cost driver increases in volume, it causes the **cost pool**—the collection of indirect costs assigned to a cost object—to increase in amount.

Cost allocation is the process of assigning costs to a specific cost object using a cost driver. This ties the cost to an identifiable and measurable activity base.

Allocating the Costs of Overhead

Allocating overhead costs to products or services is a four-step process.

Step 1. Planning the Overhead Rate Before a period begins, managers determine cost pools and cost drivers and calculate a **predetermined overhead rate** as follows.

$$\text{Predetermined Overhead Rate} = \frac{\text{Estimated Overhead Costs}}{\text{Estimated Cost Driver Activity}}$$

For example, earlier in this chapter, Custom Golf Carts used a predetermined overhead rate of 85 percent of direct labor costs.

Step 2. Applying the Overhead Rate As units of the product or service are produced during the period, the estimated overhead costs are assigned to the product or service using the predetermined overhead rate as follows.

$$\text{Overhead Applied} = \text{Predetermined Overhead Rate} \times \text{Actual Cost Driver Activity}$$

The purpose of this calculation is to assign a consistent overhead cost to each unit produced during the period.

Custom used a predetermined overhead rate of 85 percent of direct labor costs to apply overhead of $1,394, with $1,122 going to Job CC (85% of $1,320 direct labor costs) and $272 going to Job JB (85% of $320 direct labor costs) as shown in Transaction **8** in Exhibit 2.

Step 3. Recording Actual Overhead Costs The actual overhead costs are recorded as they are incurred during the period. These costs include the actual costs of indirect materials, indirect labor, depreciation, property taxes, and other production costs. The entry for the actual overhead costs debits the Overhead account and credits the asset, contra-asset, or liability account(s) affected.

For example, Custom incurred actual overhead costs for indirect materials, indirect labor, other indirect costs, and production-related depreciation by debiting Overhead and crediting the appropriate accounts, as shown in Transactions **3**, **5**, **6**, and **7** in Exhibit 2.

STUDY NOTE: Why do financial statements require the reconciliation of overhead costs? Financial statements report actual cost information; therefore, estimated overhead costs applied during the accounting period must be adjusted to reflect actual overhead costs.

Step 4. Reconciling the Applied and Actual Overhead Amounts At the end of the period, the difference between the applied and actual overhead costs is calculated and reconciled.

For example, Custom incurred actual overhead costs of $1,391 and applied overhead of $1,394, as shown in the Overhead account in Exhibit 2.

Overhead			
(3)	96	(8)	1,394
(5)	760		
(6)	295		
(7)	240		
		Bal. (overapplied)	3

Overapplied Overhead If the overhead costs applied to production during the period are greater than the actual overhead costs, the difference in the amounts represents **overapplied overhead costs**. If this difference is immaterial, the Overhead account is debited or increased and the Cost of Goods Sold or Cost of Sales account is credited or decreased by the difference. If the difference is material for the products produced, adjustments are made to the accounts affected—that is, the Work in Process Inventory, Finished Goods Inventory, and Cost of Goods Sold accounts.

For example, Custom determined that actual overhead cost for the period ($1,391) is less than the overhead applied during the period ($1,394), resulting in the $3 credit balance. This $3 overapplied balance must be closed to the Cost of Goods Sold account, as shown in Transaction **11** in Exhibit 2.

Closing the Overhead Account

Transaction 11 In transaction **11**, Custom closes the Overhead account balance to Cost of Goods Sold at the end of a period so the Cost of Goods Sold account will contain the actual costs of direct materials, direct labor, and overhead. Overhead has a $3 credit balance so Custom has overapplied overhead costs to the jobs produced.

Analysis The journal entry to close immaterial overapplied overhead

▲ *increases* the *Overhead* account with a debit

▼ *decreases* the *Cost of Goods Sold* account with a credit

Journal Entry

	Dr.	Cr.
Overhead	3	
Cost of Goods Sold		3

Comment Custom compares the actual (debit side of the Overhead account) and applied (Credit side of the Overhead account) overhead amounts at the end of the period and closes the difference to improve the accuracy of *cost measurement* of products produced and sold.

Underapplied Overhead If the overhead costs applied to production during the period are less than the actual overhead costs, the difference represents **underapplied overhead costs**. If the difference is immaterial, the Cost of Goods Sold or Cost of Sales account is debited or increased and the Overhead account is credited or decreased by this difference. If the difference is material for the products produced, adjustments are made to the accounts affected—that is, the Work in Process Inventory, Finished Goods Inventory, and Cost of Goods Sold accounts.

If the actual overhead debit balance exceeds the applied overhead credit balance, then the Overhead account is said to be underapplied and the debit balance must be closed to the Cost of Goods Sold account. The journal entry would be as follows.

	Dr.	Cr.
Cost of Goods Sold	XX	
Overhead		XX

Actual Cost of Goods Sold or Cost of Sales

The adjustment for overapplied or underapplied overhead costs is necessary to reflect the actual overhead costs on the income statement. For example, Custom Golf Carts determined Cost of Goods Sold ending balance was actually $1,937 after the overapplied amount of $3 reduced Cost of Goods Sold, as shown in Exhibit 2.

Exhibit 5 summarizes the four steps involved in allocating overhead costs to products or services in terms of their timing, the procedures involved, and the entries required. It also shows how the cost flows in the various steps affect the accounting records.

Exhibit 5
Allocating Overhead Cost: A Four-Step Process

Year 1 — January 1 — Year 2 — December 31

	Step 1: Planning the Overhead Rate	Step 2: Applying the Overhead Rate	Step 3: Recording Actual Overhead Costs	Step 4: Reconciling Applied and Actual Overhead Costs
Timing and Procedure	Before the accounting period begins, determine cost pools and cost drivers. Calculate the overhead rate by dividing the cost pool of total estimated overhead costs by the total estimated cost driver level.	During the accounting period, as units are produced, apply overhead costs to products by multiplying the predetermined overhead rate for each cost pool by the actual cost driver level for that pool. Record costs.	Record actual overhead costs as they are incurred during the accounting period.	At the end of the accounting period, calculate and reconcile the difference between applied and actual overhead costs.
Entry	None	Increase Work in Process Inventory account and decrease Overhead account: Dr. Work in Process Inventory XX Cr. Overhead XX	Increase Overhead account and decrease asset accounts or increase contra-asset or liability accounts: Dr. Overhead XX Cr. Various Accounts XX	Entry will vary depending on how costs have been applied. If overapplied, increase Overhead and decrease Cost of Goods Sold. If underapplied, increase Cost of Goods Sold and decrease Overhead.
Cost Flow Through the Accounts		Overhead (right side) **Overhead applied using predetermined rate** Work in Process Inventory (left side) **Overhead applied using predetermined rate**	Overhead (left side) **Actual overhead costs recorded** Various Asset and Liability Accounts (right side) **Actual overhead costs recorded**	**Overapplied:** Overhead (left side) Actual overhead costs recorded; **Overapplied**; Bal. $0 (right side) Overhead applied using predetermined rate Cost of Goods Sold (left side) Bal.; Actual Bal. (right side) **Overapplied** **Underapplied:** Overhead (left side) Actual overhead costs recorded; Bal. $0 (right side) Overhead applied using predetermined rate; **Underapplied** Cost of Goods Sold (left side) Bal.; **Underapplied**; Actual Bal.

Allocating Overhead: The Traditional Approach

The traditional approach to applying overhead costs to a product or service is to use a single plantwide overhead rate. This approach is especially useful when companies manufacture only one product or a few very similar products that require the same production processes and production-related activities, such as setup, inspection, and materials handling. The total overhead costs constitute one cost pool, and a traditional activity base—such as direct labor hours, direct labor costs, machine hours, or units of production—is the cost driver.

Allocating Overhead: The ABC Approach

Activity-based costing (ABC) is a more accurate method of assigning overhead costs to products or services. It categorizes all indirect costs by activity, traces the indirect costs to those activities, and assigns activity costs to products or services using a cost driver related to the cause of the cost. A company that uses ABC identifies production-related activities or tasks and the events that cause, or drive, those activities, such as number of inspections or maintenance hours. As a result, many smaller activity pools are created from the single overhead cost pool used in the traditional method. This means that managers will calculate many rates. There will be an activity cost rate for each activity pool, which must be applied to products or services produced. Managers must select an appropriate number of activity pools instead of the traditional plantwide rate for overhead.

More careful cost allocation means that managers will have better information for decision making. The ABC approach to allocating overhead will be covered in a later chapter.

APPLY IT!

1. Compute the predetermined overhead rate for Sample Service Company if its estimated overhead costs for the coming year will be $15,000 and 5,000 direct labor hours will be worked.
2. Calculate the amount of overhead costs applied by Sample Company to one of its jobs if the job required 10 direct labor hours to complete.
3. Compute the total cost of the job if prime (direct material and direct labor) costs incurred by Sample Company to complete it were $60. If the job contained 5 units of service, what is the unit cost?
4. Using the traditional overhead rate computed in Step 1, determine the total amount of overhead applied to operations during the year if Sample Company compiles a total of 4,900 labor hours worked.
5. If Sample Company's actual overhead costs for the year are $14,800, compute the amount of under- or overapplied overhead for the year. Will the Cost of Goods Sold account be increased or decreased to correct the under- or overapplication of overhead?

SOLUTION

1. $$\text{Predetermined Overhead Rate} = \frac{\text{Estimated Overhead Costs}}{\text{Estimated Direct Labor Hours (DLH)}} = \frac{\$15{,}000}{5{,}000\ \text{DLH}} = \$3\ \text{per DLH}$$

2. Overhead Costs Applied = Predetermined Overhead Rate × Actual Hours Worked
   = $3 per DLH × 10 Actual Direct Labor Hours Worked
   = $30

3. Total Cost = Prime Costs + Applied Overhead Cost
   = $60 + $30
   = $90

   $$\text{Unit Cost} = \frac{\text{Total Cost of Job}}{\text{Units Produced}} = \frac{\$90}{5\ \text{units}} = \$18\ \text{per unit}$$

4. Overhead Costs Applied = Predetermined Overhead Rate × Actual Hours Worked
   = $3 per DLH × 4,900 Actual Hours Worked
   = $14,700

5. Overhead Costs Applied = $14,700
   Actual Overhead Costs = 14,800
   Underapplied Overhead = $ 100, which will increase the Cost of Goods Sold account

TRY IT! SE8, SE9, SE10, E9A, E10A, E11A, E12A, E13A, E14A, E15A, E9B, E10B, E11B, E12B, E13B, E14B, E15B

SECTION 3 BUSINESS APPLICATIONS

BUSINESS APPLICATIONS
- Planning
- Performing
- Evaluating
- Communicating

RELEVANT LEARNING OBJECTIVE

LO 5 Explain why unit cost measurement is important to the management process in producing business results.

LO 5 Product Unit Cost Information and the Management Process

Managers depend on relevant and reliable information about costs to manage their organizations. Although they vary in their approaches, managers share the same basic concerns as they move through the management process.

Planning

Managers' unit cost knowledge helps them set reasonable selling prices and estimate the cost of their products or services.

- In manufacturing companies, such as **Club Car, LLC**, **Toyota**, and **Levi Strauss & Co.**, managers use unit cost information to develop budgets, establish product prices, and plan production volumes.
- In service organizations, such as **Google**, **H&R Block**, and **UPS**, managers use cost information to develop budgets, establish prices, set sales goals, and determine human resource needs.

Performing

Managers make decisions every day about controlling costs, managing the company's activity volume, ensuring quality, and negotiating prices. They use timely cost and volume information and actual unit costs to support their decisions.

- In manufacturing companies, managers use cost information to decide whether to drop a product line, add a production shift, outsource the manufacture of a subassembly to another company, bid on a special order, or negotiate a selling price.
- In service organizations, managers use cost information to make decisions about bidding on jobs, dropping a current service, outsourcing a task to an independent contractor, adding staff, or negotiating a price.

Evaluating

When managers evaluate results, they watch for changes in cost and quality. They compare actual and targeted total and unit costs, assess relevant price and volume information, and then adjust their planning and decision-making strategies. For example, if a service business's unit cost has risen, managers may break the unit cost down into its many components to analyze where costs can be cut or how the service can be performed more efficiently.

Communicating

Internal and external users analyze the data in the performance evaluation reports to determine whether the business is achieving cost goals. When managers report to stakeholders, they prepare financial statements.

- In manufacturing companies, managers use product unit costs to determine inventory balances and the cost of goods sold.
- In service organizations, managers use unit costs of services to determine the cost of sales.

When managers prepare internal performance evaluation reports, they compare actual unit costs with targeted costs, as well as actual and targeted nonfinancial measures of performance.

Supporting the Management Process

Exhibit 6 shows how managers use unit cost information throughout the management process to fulfill the management concepts of planning and forecasting operations, organizing and coordinating resources and data, and commanding and controlling the organization's resources.

Exhibit 6
Job Order Costing and the Management Process

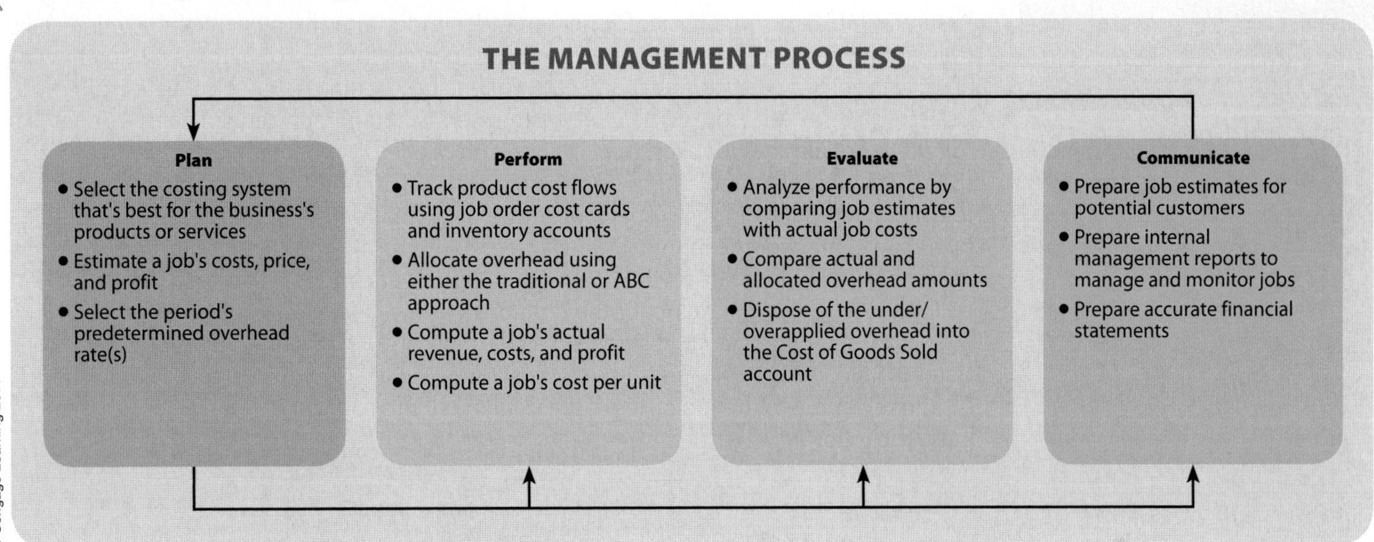

THE MANAGEMENT PROCESS
Plan
• Select the costing system that's best for the business's products or services
• Estimate a job's costs, price, and profit
• Select the period's predetermined overhead rate(s)
Perform
• Track product cost flows using job order cost cards and inventory accounts
• Allocate overhead using either the traditional or ABC approach
• Compute a job's actual revenue, costs, and profit
• Compute a job's cost per unit
Evaluate
• Analyze performance by comparing job estimates with actual job costs
• Compare actual and allocated overhead amounts
• Dispose of the under/overapplied overhead into the Cost of Goods Sold account
Communicate
• Prepare job estimates for potential customers
• Prepare internal management reports to manage and monitor jobs
• Prepare accurate financial statements

APPLY IT!

Shelley's Kennel provides pet boarding. Shelley, the owner, must make several business decisions soon. Write *yes* or *no* to indicate whether knowing the cost to board one animal for one day (i.e., the service unit cost) can help Shelley answer these questions.

a. Is the daily boarding fee high enough to cover the kennel's costs?
b. How much profit will the kennel make if it boards an average of 10 dogs per day for 50 weeks?
c. What costs can be reduced to make the kennel's boarding fee competitive with other kennels?

SOLUTION

a. yes; b. yes; c. yes

TRY IT! SE11

TriLevel Problem

Digital Vision/Jupiter Images

Club Car

The beginning of this chapter focused on **Club Car**, a company that makes both general-purpose and customized golf carts. Complete the following requirements in order to answer the questions posed at the beginning of the chapter.

Section 1: Concepts

Why is a job order costing system appropriate for Club Car to measure and recognize costs?

Section 2: Accounting Applications

How does a product costing system account for costs when made-to-order products or services are produced?

Assume Club Car owners have formed an independent loyalty owners club. Periodically, golf cart owners gather at the company headquarters for reunion parties complete with an owner golf cart parade and a golf cart–shaped cake. Suppose Club Car uses a job order costing system to keep track of the customized costs of each reunion party. Job costs (direct materials and supplies, direct labor, and service overhead) are categorized under three activities: planning and design, reunion, and cleanup. The service overhead charge for planning and design is 30 percent of the party planner's labor costs, and the service overhead charge for the reunion is 50 percent of the cost of the cake created for the party. Assume a cost-plus contract with a 20 percent profit guarantee for each party is used when billing the loyalty owners club for the reunions.

Suppose one manager has tracked all of the costs of the reunion party that was contracted on May 28, 2014, and scheduled for June 5, 2014. Now that the work is finished, it is time to complete the job order cost card and bill the sponsor. The costs for the reunion party job follow.

Costs during May	
Planning and design:	
Supplies	$100
Party planner labor	250
Costs during June	
Reunion:	
Cake creation	500
Direct labor	160
Cleanup:	
Janitorial service cost	400

1. Create the job order cost card for the reunion party job.
2. What amount will the manager bill for the job?
3. Using the format of the Work in Process Inventory account in Exhibit 2, reconstruct the beginning balance and costs for the current month. What is the ending balance for the account?

Section 3: Business Applications

How does a job order costing system help managers organize and control costs and facilitate management decisions? To answer this question, match this chapter's manager responsibilities with when they occur within the management process.

a. Plan
b. Perform
c. Evaluate
d. Communicate

1. Compute a job's cost per unit
2. Select the best product costing system
3. Compare actual and allocated overhead amounts
4. Compute a job's actual costs, price, and profit
5. Estimate a job's costs, price, and profit
6. Prepare accurate financial statements
7. Compare actual job costs with job estimates
8. Compute the predetermined overhead rate(s)
9. Track the flow of product costs
10. Prepare job estimates for potential customers
11. Prepare internal management reports
12. Dispose of under/overapplied overhead to Cost of Goods Sold
13. Allocate overhead using either the traditional or ABC approach

SOLUTION

Concepts

Whether a product costing system is appropriate to *measure* and *recognize* costs depends on the nature of the production process. Because the production of custom-made items and the production of mass-produced items involve different processes, they require different costing systems to measure and recognize product costs. When a product is made to order like the customized golf cart, it is possible to use a job order costing system, which recognizes and collects the costs of each order and *matches* them against the revenue generated by the order. When a product is mass produced, like the general-purpose golf cart, the costs of a specific unit cannot be recognized because there is a continuous flow of similar products. For this reason, a process costing system is used to collect and match a period's costs and revenues for the products sold.

Accounting Applications

1.

JOB ORDER COST CARD

Customer: Loyalty Owners Club Batch: ___ Custom: X

Specifications: Reunion party

Date of Order: 5/28/2014 Date of Completion: 6/5/2014

Cost Charged to Job	Previous Month	Current Month	Total Costs
Planning and design:			
Supplies	$100	$ —	$ 100
Party planner labor	250	—	250
Overhead (30% of planning labor costs)	75	—	75
Totals	$425	$ —	$ 425
Reunion:			
Cake creation	$ —	$ 500	$ 500
Direct labor	—	160	160
Overhead (50% of cake creation cost)	—	250	250
Totals	$ —	$ 910	$ 910
Cleanup:			
Janitorial service costs		$ 400	$ 400
Total		$ 400	$ 400
Cost Summary to Date			
Planning			$ 425
Reunion			910
Cleanup			400
Total			$1,735
Profit margin (20% of total cost)			347
Job revenue			$2,082

2. The manager will bill $2,082.00 for this job.

3.

Work in Process Inventory

Beg. bal.	0	Completed and transferred to Cost of Sales	1,735
Planning and design:			
Supplies	100		
Party planner labor	250		
Overhead	75		
Party:			
Cake creation	500		
Direct labor	160		
Overhead	250		
Cleanup:			
Janitorial service costs	400		
End. bal.	—		

Section 3: Business Applications

1. b
2. a
3. c
4. b
5. a
6. d
7. c
8. a
9. d
10. d
11. d
12. c
13. b

Chapter Review

Distinguish between the two basic types of product costing systems, and identify the information that each provides. LO 1

A job order costing system is a product costing system used by companies that make unique, custom, or special-order products. Such a system traces the costs of direct materials, direct labor, and overhead to a specific batch of products or to a specific job order. A job order costing system measures the cost of each complete unit and summarizes the cost of all jobs in a single Work in Process Inventory account that is supported by job order cost cards.

A process costing system is a product costing system used by companies that produce large amounts of similar products or liquid products or that have long, continuous production runs of identical products. Such a system first traces the costs of direct materials, direct labor, and overhead to processes, departments, or work cells and then assigns the costs to the products manufactured by those processes, departments, or work cells. A process costing system uses several Work in Process Inventory accounts, one for each department, process, or work cell.

Explain the cost flow in a manufacturer's job order costing system. LO 2

In a manufacturer's job order costing system, the costs of materials are first charged to the Materials Inventory account. The actual overhead costs are debited to the Overhead account. As products are manufactured, the costs of direct materials and direct labor are debited to the Work in Process Inventory account and are recorded on each job's job order cost card. Overhead costs are applied and debited to the Work in Process Inventory account and credited to the Overhead account using a predetermined overhead rate. They too are recorded on the job order cost card. When products and jobs are completed, their costs are transferred to the Finished Goods Inventory account. Then, when the products are sold and shipped, their costs are transferred to the Cost of Goods Sold account.

Prepare a job order cost card, and compute a job order's product or service unit cost. LO 3

All costs of direct materials, direct labor, and overhead for a particular job are accumulated on a job order cost card. When the job has been completed, those costs are totaled. The total is then divided by the number of good units produced to find the product unit cost. The product unit cost is entered on the job order cost card and will be used to value items in inventory.

Many service organizations use a job order costing system to track the costs of labor, materials and supplies, and service overhead to specific customer jobs. Labor is an important cost for service organizations. To cover their costs and earn a profit, service organizations often base jobs on cost-plus contracts, which require the customer to pay all costs incurred plus a predetermined amount of profit.

LO4 Explain cost allocation, and describe how allocating overhead costs figures into calculating product or service unit cost.

Cost allocation is the process of assigning indirect costs to a specific cost object using an allocation base known as a cost driver. The allocation of overhead costs requires the pooling of overhead costs that are affected by a common activity and the selection of a cost driver whose activity level causes a change in the cost pool. A cost pool is the collection of overhead costs assigned to a cost object. A cost driver is an activity base that causes the cost pool to increase in amount as the volume of activity increases.

Allocating overhead is a four-step process that involves planning a rate at which overhead costs will be assigned to products or services, assigning overhead costs at this predetermined rate to products or services during production, recording actual overhead costs as they are incurred, and reconciling the difference between the actual and applied overhead costs. The Cost of Goods Sold or Cost of Sales account is corrected for an amount of over- or underapplied overhead costs assigned to the products or services. In manufacturing companies, if the difference is material, adjustments are made to the Work in Process Inventory, Finished Goods Inventory, and Cost of Goods Sold accounts.

The traditional method applies overhead costs by estimating one predetermined overhead rate and multiplying that rate by the actual cost driver level. When the ABC method is used, overhead costs are grouped into a number of cost pools related to specific activities. For each activity pool, cost drivers are identified, and cost driver levels are estimated. Overhead is applied to the product or service by multiplying the various activity rates by their actual cost driver level. The product or service unit cost is computed either by dividing the total product or service cost by the total number of units produced or by determining the cost per unit for each element of the cost and summing those per-unit costs.

LO5 Explain why unit cost measurement is important to the management process in producing business results.

When managers plan, information about costs helps them develop budgets, establish prices, set sales goals, plan production volumes, estimate product or service unit costs, and determine human resource needs. Daily, managers use cost information to make decisions about controlling costs, managing the company's volume of activity, ensuring quality, and negotiating prices. When managers evaluate results, they analyze actual and targeted information to evaluate performance and make any necessary adjustments to their planning and decision-making strategies. When managers communicate with stakeholders, they use unit costs to determine inventory balances and the cost of goods or services sold for the financial statements. They also use internal reports that compare the organization's measures of actual and targeted unit costs to determine whether the cost goals for products or services are being achieved. Reports may also contain nonfinancial measures of performance.

Key Terms

activity-based costing (ABC) 767 (LO4)
cost allocation 763 (LO4)
cost driver 763 (LO4)
cost object 763 (LO4)
cost-plus contracts 761 (LO3)
cost pool 763 (LO4)
job order 754 (LO1)
job order cost card 754 (LO1)
job order costing system 754 (LO1)
operations costing system 754 (LO1)
overapplied overhead costs 764 (LO4)
predetermined overhead rate 764 (LO4)
process cost report 754 (LO1)
process costing system 754 (LO1)
product costing system 754 (LO1)
underapplied overhead costs 765 (LO4)

Chapter Assignments

DISCUSSION QUESTIONS

LO 1 **DQ1. CONCEPT ▶** Describe the accounting concepts that focus on determining the amount of cost, when costs should be recorded, and to what costs should be compared.

LO 1 **DQ2. CONCEPT ▶** What are some of the cost measurement and cost recognition differences between the two basic types of product costing systems?

LO 2 **DQ3. CONCEPT ▶** Why does the concept of matching underlie the cost flows in a job order costing system?

LO 4 **DQ4. CONCEPT ▶** Why do the concepts of cost recognition and cost measurement underlie the four steps necessary to allocate overhead costs?

LO 5 **DQ5. BUSINESS APPLICATION ▶** Why is the determination of unit cost information using job order costing important in the management process?

SHORT EXERCISES

LO 1 Job Order Versus Process Costing Systems

SE1. State whether a job order costing system or a process costing system would typically be used to account for the costs of the following:

a. Manufacturing bottles
b. Manufacturing custom-designed swimming pools
c. Manufacturing one-size-fits-all robes
d. Providing babysitting
e. Manufacturing canned food
f. Providing accounting services

LO 2 Transactions in a Manufacturer's Job Order Costing System

SE2. For each of the following transactions, state which account(s) would be debited and credited in a job order costing system:

a. Purchased materials on account, $12,000.
b. Charged direct labor to production, $3,000.
c. Requested direct materials for production, $6,000.
d. Applied overhead to jobs in process, $4,000.

LO 2 Transactions in a Manufacturer's Job Order Costing System

SE3. Enter the following transactions into T accounts:

a. Incurred $34,000 of direct labor and $18,000 of indirect labor.
b. Applied overhead based on 12,680 labor hours @ $6 per labor hour.

LO 2 Accounts for Job Order Costing

SE4. Identify the accounts in which each of the following transactions for Oak Leaf Furniture, a custom manufacturer of oak tables and chairs, would be debited and credited:

1. Issued oak materials into production for Job ABC.
2. Recorded direct labor time for the first week in February for Job ABC.
3. Purchased indirect materials from a vendor on account.
4. Received a production-related electricity bill.
5. Applied overhead to Job ABC.
6. Completed but did not yet sell Job ABC.

LO 3 **Job Order Cost Card**

SE5. Complete the following job order cost card for five custom-built computer systems:

Job Order 16

JOB ORDER COST CARD
Custom Computers
Kowloon, Hong Kong

Customer: L. Kim Batch: ___ Custom: X
Specifications: 5 Computer Systems
Date of Order: 4/4/2014 Date of Completion: 6/8/2014

Costs Charged to Job	Previous Months	Current Month	Total Cost
Direct materials	$540	$820	$?
Direct labor	340	620	?
Overhead applied	880	550	?
Totals	$?	$?	$?
Units completed			÷ ?
Product unit cost			$?

LO 3 **Job Order Costing in a Service Organization**

SE6. A desert landscaping business is doing custom landscape work for J. Abbott. For each of the following transactions, state which account(s) would be debited and credited by the landscape business:

a. Sent J. Abbott a bill for landscape design.
b. Purchased gravel on credit, which was delivered to J. Abbott's yard.
c. Paid three employees to prepare soil for gravel.
d. Paid for cactus plants and planted them in J. Abbott's yard.

LO 3 **Job Order Costing with Cost-Plus Contracts**

SE7. Complete the following job order cost card for an individual tax return:

Job Order A7

JOB ORDER COST CARD
Doremus Tax Service
Puyallup, Washington

Customer: Arthur Farnsworth Batch: ___ Custom: X
Specifications: Annual Individual Tax Return
Date of Order: 3/24/2014 Date of Completion: 4/8/2014

Costs Charged to Job	Previous Months	Current Month	Total Cost
Client interview:			
Supplies	$ 10	$ —	$?
Labor	50	60	?
Overhead (40% of interview labor costs)	20	24	?
Totals	$?	$?	$?
Preparation of return:			
Supplies	$ —	$ 16	$?
Computer time	—	12	?
Labor	—	240	?
Overhead (50% of preparation labor costs)	—	120	?
Totals	$ —	$?	$?
Delivery:			
Postage	$ —	$ 8	$?
Total	$ —	$?	$?

Cost Summary to Date	Total Cost
Client interview	$?
Preparation of return	?
Delivery	?
Total	$?
Profit margin (20% of total cost)	?
Job revenue	$?

LO 4 **Calculation of Underapplied or Overapplied Overhead**

SE8. At year end, records show that actual overhead costs incurred were $25,870 and the amount of overhead costs applied to production was $27,000. Identify the amount of under- or overapplied overhead, and indicate whether the Cost of Goods Sold account should be increased or decreased to reflect actual overhead costs.

LO 4 **Computation of Overhead Rate**

SE9. Compute the overhead rate per service request for the Maintenance Department if estimated overhead costs are $18,290 and the number of estimated service requests is 3,100.

LO 4 **Allocation of Overhead to Production**

SE10. Calculate the amount of overhead costs applied to production if the predetermined overhead rate is $4 per direct labor hour and 1,200 direct labor hours were worked.

LO 5 **Uses of Unit Cost Information**

SE11. ACCOUNTING CONNECTION ▶ Doug, the owner of a miniature golf course with 36 holes of miniature golf, must make several business decisions soon. Write *yes* or *no* to indicate whether knowing the cost to provide one golf game (i.e., the service unit cost) can help Doug answer these questions:

a. Is the fee for playing a golf game high enough to cover the related cost?
b. How much profit will Miniature Golf make if it sells an average of 100 games per day for 50 weeks?
c. What costs can be reduced to make the fee more competitive?

EXERCISES: SET A

LO 1 **Product Costing**

E1A. Custom Publishers Company specializes in print-on-demand books. The company needs information to budget next year's activities. Write *yes* or *no* to indicate whether each of the following costs is likely to be available in the company's product costing system:

a. cost of paper
b. advertising costs
c. printing machine setup costs
d. depreciation of printing machinery
e. repair costs for printing machinery
f. costs to deliver books to customers
g. office supplies costs
h. sales commissions
i. costs to design a book cover
j. cost of ink

LO 1 **Costing Systems: Industry Linkage**

E2A. Which of the following products would typically be accounted for using a job order costing system? Which would typically be accounted for using a process costing system?

a. glue
b. toothpicks
c. restaurant meal
d. clothing repair by a tailor
e. birthday cake
f. liquid soap
g. propane gas canisters used to barbeque
h. standard compressed-gas cylinders used by scuba divers

LO 1

Costing Systems: Industry Linkage

E3A. Which of the following products would typically be accounted for using a job order costing system? Which would typically be accounted for using a process costing system?

a. standard shirt buttons
b. printed graduation announcements
c. everyday glassware
d. a limited edition sculpture
e. flea collars for cats
f. oatmeal cereal
g. personal weight loss program
h. an original painting

LO 2

Job Order Cost Flow

E4A. ACCOUNTING CONNECTION ▶ The three product cost elements—direct materials, direct labor, and overhead—flow through a job order costing system in a structured, orderly fashion. Specific accounts and subsidiary ledgers are used to verify and record cost information. Write a paragraph describing the cost flow in a job order costing system.

LO 2

Work in Process Inventory: T Account Analysis

E5A. On July 1, Tin Hau Company's Work in Process Inventory account showed a beginning balance of $9,000. The Materials Inventory account showed a beginning balance of $40,000. Production activity for July was as follows: (a) Direct materials costing $28,800 were requested for production; (b) total production-related payroll was $10,600, of which $2,600 was used to pay for indirect labor; (c) indirect materials costing $8,400 were purchased and used; and (d) overhead was applied at a rate of 120 percent of direct labor costs.

1. Record Tin Hau's materials, labor, and overhead costs for July in T accounts.
2. Compute the ending balance in the Work in Process Inventory account. Assume a transfer of $45,000 to the Finished Goods Inventory account during the period.

LO 2, 3

T Account Analysis with Unknowns

E6A. Partial operating data for Census Company follow. Management has set the predetermined overhead rate for the current year at 125 percent of direct labor costs.

Account/Transaction	June	July
Beginning Materials Inventory	$ (a)	$ (e)
Beginning Work in Process Inventory	8,605	(f)
Beginning Finished Goods Inventory	7,764	6,660
Direct materials requested	5,025	(g)
Materials purchased	5,100	6,216
Direct labor costs	4,760	5,540
Overhead applied	(b)	(h)
Cost of units completed	(c)	21,861
Cost of Goods Sold	16,805	(i)
Ending Materials Inventory	3,014	2,628
Ending Work in Process Inventory	(d)	(j)
Ending Finished Goods Inventory	6,660	3,515

Using T accounts, compute the unknown values. Show all your computations.

LO 2, 3

T Account Analysis with Unknowns

E7A. Partial operating data for Brent Cross Company follow. Management has set the predetermined overhead rate for the current year at 90 percent of direct labor costs.

Account/Transaction	December
Beginning Materials Inventory	$142,000
Beginning Work in Process Inventory	66,000
Beginning Finished Goods Inventory	129,000
Direct materials used	256,000
Direct materials purchased	(a)
Direct labor costs	390,000
Overhead applied	(b)
Cost of units completed	(c)
Cost of Goods Sold	953,400
Ending Materials Inventory	50,000
Ending Work in Process Inventory	138,600
Ending Finished Goods Inventory	(d)

Using T accounts and the data provided, compute the unknown values. Show all your computations.

LO 2, 3

Job Order Costing: T Account Analysis

E8A. Custom Floral, Inc., produces special-order artificial flower arrangements, so it uses a job order costing system. Overhead is applied at the rate of 80 percent of direct labor cost. The following is a list of transactions for June:

June 1 Purchased direct materials on account, $300.
2 Purchased indirect materials on account, $50.
4 Requested direct materials costing $250 ($200 used on Job AX and $50 used on Job BY) and indirect materials costing $40 for production.
10 Paid the following overhead costs: utilities, $40; manufacturing rent, $300; and maintenance charges, $10.
15 Recorded the following gross wages and salaries for employees: direct labor, $1,000 ($700 for Job AX and $300 for Job BY); indirect labor, $300.
15 Applied overhead to production.
16 Completed and transferred Job AX and Job BY to finished goods inventory; total cost of both jobs was $2,050.
20 Delivered Job AX to the customer; total production cost was $1,460 and billed customer for the sales price $2,000.
30 Recorded these overhead costs (adjusting entries): prepaid insurance expired, $30; and depreciation—machinery, $150.

REQUIRED

1. Record the entries for all transactions in June using T accounts for the following: Materials Inventory, Work in Process Inventory, Finished Goods Inventory, Overhead, Cash, Accounts Receivable, Prepaid Insurance, Accumulated Depreciation—Machinery, Accounts Payable, Payroll Payable, Sales, and Cost of Goods Sold. Determine the partial account balances. Assume no beginning inventory balances. Also assume that when the payroll was recorded, entries were made to the Payroll Payable account.
2. Compute the amount of underapplied or overapplied overhead as of June 30 and transfer it to the Cost of Goods Sold account.

LO 3, 4

Job Order Cost Card and Computation of Product Unit Cost

E9A. In February 2014, Storage Company worked on five job orders for specialty cedar storage cabinets. It began Job Z-6 for Cedar Safe, Inc., on February 10 and completed it on February 24. Partial data for Job Z-6 are as follows.

(Continued)

	Costs	Machine Hours Used
Direct materials:		
Cedar	$8,000	
Pine	6,000	
Hardware	2,000	
Assembly supplies	1,000	
Direct labor:		
Sawing	3,000	120
Shaping	2,000	210
Finishing	2,500	150
Assembly	3,000	50

Storage Company produced a total of 50 cabinets for Job Z-6. Its current predetermined overhead rate is $20 per machine hour. From the information given, prepare a job order cost card and compute the job order's product unit cost.

LO 3, 4

Computation of Product Unit Cost

E10A. MS Company uses job order costing to determine the product unit cost of one of its products based on the following costs incurred during March: liability insurance, manufacturing, $3,500; rent, sales office, $3,000; depreciation, manufacturing equipment, $5,000; direct materials, $34,000; indirect labor, manufacturing, $3,600; indirect materials, $2,000; heat, light, and power, manufacturing, $2,500; fire insurance, manufacturing, $2,400; depreciation, sales equipment, $5,000; rent, manufacturing, $4,000; direct labor, $20,000; manager's salary, manufacturing, $4,800; president's salary, $6,000; sales commissions, $8,000; and advertising expenses, $3,000. The Inspection Department reported that 40,900 good units were produced during March. Determine the unit product cost.

LO 3, 4

Computation of Product Unit Cost

E11A. China Trade, Inc., manufactures custom-made stuffed animals. Last month the company produced 500 stuffed pandas for the local zoo to sell at a fund-raising event. Using job order costing, determine the product unit cost of a stuffed panda based on the following costs incurred during the month: manufacturing utilities, $200; depreciation on manufacturing equipment, $250; indirect materials, $150; direct materials, $1,000; indirect labor, $400; direct labor, $1,200; sales commissions, $3,000; president's salary, $4,000; insurance on manufacturing plant, $300; advertising expense, $500; rent on manufacturing plant, $2,500; rent on sales office, $4,000; and legal expense, $250.

LO 3, 4

Computation of Product Unit Cost

E12A. Dude Corporation manufactures specialty lines of men's apparel. During February, the company worked on three special orders: B-2, B-3, and B-4. Cost and production data for each order are as follows.

	Job B-2	Job B-3	Job B-4
Direct materials:			
Fabric Q	$1,000	$1,800	$17,600
Fabric Z	2,000	2,200	13,400
Fabric YB	5,000	6,000	2,000
Direct labor:			
Garment maker	4,500	8,000	10,200
Layout	2,500	7,000	9,800
Packaging	3,000	5,000	5,000
Overhead:			
(150% of direct labor costs)	?	?	?
Number of units produced	500	1,200	500

1. Compute the total cost associated with each job. Show the subtotals for each cost category.
2. Compute the product unit cost for each job.

LO **3, 4**

Job Order Costing in a Service Organization

E13A. A job order cost card for Cloud Storage Services follows. Complete the missing information. The profit factor in the organization's cost-plus contract is 60 percent of total cost.

JOB ORDER COST CARD
Cloud Storage Services

Customer:	Jayson Holiday
Job Order No.:	XXYQ
Contract Type:	Cost-Plus
Type of Service:	Annual Internet Storage
Date of Completion:	November 6, 2014

Costs Charged to Job	**Total Cost**
Software installation services:	
Installation labor	$30
Service overhead (?% of installation labor costs)	?
Total	$60
Internet services:	
Internet storage	$10
Service overhead (200% of Internet storage costs)	20
Total	$?

Cost Summary to Date	**Total Cost**
Software installation services	$?
Internet services	?
Total	$?
Profit margin (60% of total cost)	?
Contract revenue	$?

LO **4**

Computation of Overhead Rate

E14A. The overhead costs that Sife Industries, Inc., used to compute its overhead rate for the past year are as follows.

Indirect materials and supplies, repair and maintenance, outside service contracts, indirect labor, factory supervision, factory insurance, heat, light, and power costs	$222,000
Property taxes and miscellaneous overhead costs	13,000
Depreciation, machinery	85,000
Total overhead costs	$320,000

The allocation base for the past year was 40,000 total machine hours. For the next year, all overhead costs except depreciation, property taxes, and miscellaneous overhead are expected to increase by 10 percent. Depreciation should increase by 12 percent, and property taxes and miscellaneous overhead are expected to increase by 20 percent. Plant capacity in terms of machine hours used will increase by 10,000 hours.

1. Compute the past year's overhead rate.
2. Compute the overhead rate for next year.

LO 4

Computation and Application of Overhead Rate

E15A. For Road Patch Company, labor is the highest single expense, totaling $693,000 for 75,000 hours of work last year. Overhead costs for last year were $900,000 and were applied to specific jobs on the basis of labor hours worked. This year, the company anticipates a 25 percent increase in overhead costs. Labor costs will increase by $130,000, and the number of hours worked is expected to increase by 20 percent.

1. Determine the total amount of overhead anticipated this year.
2. Compute the overhead rate for this year.
3. At the end of this year, Road Patch had compiled a total of 89,920 labor hours worked. The actual overhead incurred was $1,143,400.
   a. Using the overhead rate computed in 2, determine the total amount of overhead applied to operations during the year.
   b. Compute the amount of under/overapplied overhead for the year.
   c. **ACCOUNTING CONNECTION ▶** Will the Cost of Goods Sold account be increased or decreased to correct the under/overapplication of overhead?

EXERCISES: SET B

Visit the textbook companion web site at www.cengagebrain.com to access Exercise Set B for this chapter.

PROBLEMS

LO 2

T Account Analysis with Unknowns

✔ d: May ending work in process inventory: $45,770
✔ i: June overhead applied: $57,800

P1. Patriotic Enterprises makes flags. The company's new controller can find only the following partial information for the past two months:

Account/Transaction	May	June
Beginning Materials Inventory	$ 36,240	$ (e)
Beginning Work in Process Inventory	56,480	(f)
Beginning Finished Goods Inventory	44,260	(g)
Materials purchased	(a)	96,120
Direct materials requested	82,320	(h)
Direct labor costs	(b)	72,250
Overhead applied	53,200	(i)
Cost of units completed	(c)	221,400
Cost of Goods Sold	209,050	(j)
Ending Materials Inventory	38,910	41,950
Ending Work in Process Inventory	(d)	(k)
Ending Finished Goods Inventory	47,940	51,180

The current year's predetermined overhead rate is 80 percent of direct labor cost.

REQUIRED

Using T accounts, compute the unknown values.

LO 2, 3, 4

Job Order Costing: T Account Analysis

✔ 2: $260 underapplied overhead

P2. Eagle Carts, Inc., produces special-order golf carts, so Eagle Carts uses a job order costing system. Overhead is applied at the rate of 90 percent of direct labor cost. A list of transactions for January follows.

Jan. 1 Purchased direct materials on account, $215,400.
2 Purchased indirect materials on account, $49,500.
4 Requested direct materials costing $193,200 (all used on Job X) and indirect materials costing $38,100 for production.
10 Paid the following overhead costs: utilities, $4,400; manufacturing rent, $3,800; and maintenance charges, $3,900.

Jan.	15	Recorded the following gross wages and salaries for employees: direct labor, $120,000 (all for Job X); indirect labor, $60,620.
	15	Applied overhead to production.
	19	Purchased indirect materials costing $27,550 and direct materials costing $190,450 on account.
	21	Requested direct materials costing $214,750 (Job X, $178,170; Job Y, $18,170; and Job Z, $18,410) and indirect materials costing $31,400 for production.
	31	Recorded the following gross wages and salaries for employees: direct labor, $132,000 (Job X, $118,500; Job Y, $7,000; Job Z, $6,500); indirect labor, $62,240.
	31	Applied overhead to production.
	31	Completed and transferred Job X (375 carts) and Job Y (10 carts) to finished goods inventory; total cost was $855,990.
	31	Shipped Job X to the customer; total production cost was $824,520 and sales price was $996,800.
	31	Recorded these overhead costs (adjusting entries): prepaid insurance expired, $3,700; property taxes (payable at year end), $3,400; and depreciation—machinery, $15,500.

REQUIRED

1. Record the entries for all transactions in January using T accounts for the following: Materials Inventory, Work in Process Inventory, Finished Goods Inventory, Overhead, Cash, Accounts Receivable, Prepaid Insurance, Accumulated Depreciation—Machinery, Accounts Payable, Payroll Payable, Property Taxes Payable, Sales, and Cost of Goods Sold. Prepare job order cost cards for Job X, Job Y, and Job Z. (Round product unit cost to two decimal places.) Determine the partial account balances. Assume no beginning inventory balances. Also assume that when the payroll was recorded, entries were made to the Payroll Payable account.
2. Compute the amount of underapplied or overapplied overhead as of January 31 and transfer it to the Cost of Goods Sold account.
3. **ACCOUNTING CONNECTION ▶** Why should the Overhead account's underapplied or overapplied overhead be transferred to the Cost of Goods Sold account?

LO 2, 3, 4

Job Order Cost Flow

SPREADSHEET

✔ 2: Cost of units completed during the month: $185,073

P3. On May 31, the inventory balances of Tog Designs, a manufacturer of high-quality children's clothing, were as follows: Materials Inventory, $21,360; Work in Process Inventory, $15,112; and Finished Goods Inventory, $17,120. Job order cost cards for jobs in process as of June 30 had the following totals:

Job No.	Direct Materials	Direct Labor	Overhead
24-A	$1,593	$1,290	$1,677
24-B	1,492	1,380	1,794
24-C	1,987	1,760	2,288
24-D	1,608	1,540	2,002

The predetermined overhead rate is 130 percent of direct labor costs. Materials purchased and received in June were as follows.

June 4	$33,120
June 16	28,600
June 22	31,920

Direct labor costs for June were as follows.

June 15 payroll	$23,680
June 29 payroll	25,960

(Continued)

Direct materials requested by production during June were as follows.

June 6	$37,240
June 23	38,960

On June 30, Tog Designs sold on account finished goods with a cost of $183,000 for $320,000.

REQUIRED

1. Using T accounts for Materials Inventory, Work in Process Inventory, Finished Goods Inventory, Overhead, Accounts Receivable, Payroll Payable, Sales, and Cost of Goods Sold, reconstruct the transactions in June, including applying overhead to production.
2. Compute the cost of units completed during the month.
3. Determine the ending inventory balances.
4. Jobs 24-A and 24-C were completed during the first week of July. No additional materials costs were incurred, but Job 24-A required $960 more of direct labor, and Job 24-C needed an additional $1,610 of direct labor. Job 24-A was composed of 1,800 pairs of trousers; Job 24-C, of 900 shirts. Compute the product unit cost for each job.

LO **4**

Allocation of Overhead

✔ 1: Predetermined overhead rate for this year: $2.40 per machine hour
✔ 3: Overapplied overhead: $475

P4. Nature Cosmetics Company applies overhead costs on the basis of machine hours. The overhead rate is computed by analyzing data from the previous year to determine the percentage change in costs. Thus, this year's overhead rate will be based on the percentage change multiplied by last year's costs.

	Last Year
Machine hours	55,360
Overhead costs:	
Indirect labor	$ 23,500
Employee benefits	28,600
Manufacturing supervision	18,500
Utilities	15,000
Factory insurance	7,800
Janitorial services	12,100
Depreciation, factory and machinery	21,300
Miscellaneous overhead	6,000
Total overhead	$132,800

This year the cost of utilities is expected to increase by 40 percent over the previous year; the cost of indirect labor, employee benefits, and miscellaneous overhead is expected to increase by 30 percent over the previous year; the cost of insurance and depreciation is expected to increase by 20 percent over the previous year; and the cost of supervision and janitorial services is expected to increase by 10 percent over the previous year. Machine hours are expected to total 68,786.

REQUIRED

1. Compute the projected costs, and use those costs to calculate the overhead rate for this year. (Round the rate to two decimal places.)
2. Jobs completed during this year and the machine hours used were as follows.

Job No.	**Machine Hours**
2214	12,300
2215	14,200
2216	9,800
2217	13,600
2218	11,300
2219	8,100

Determine the amount of overhead to be applied to each job and to total production during this year.

3. Actual overhead costs for this year were $165,845. Was overhead underapplied or overapplied? By how much? Should the Cost of Goods Sold account be increased or decreased to reflect actual overhead costs?
4. **ACCOUNTING CONNECTION ▶** At what point during this year was the overhead rate computed? When was it applied? Finally, when was underapplied or overapplied overhead determined and the Cost of Goods Sold account adjusted to reflect actual costs?

LO 4

Allocation of Overhead

✔ Total costs assigned to order: $71,074

P5. Byte Computer Company, a manufacturing organization, has just completed an order that Grater, Ltd., placed for 80 computers. Direct materials, purchased parts, and direct labor costs for the Grater order are as follows.

Cost of direct materials	$36,750
Cost of purchased parts	$21,300
Direct labor hours	220
Average direct labor pay rate	$16

Overhead costs were applied at a single, plantwide overhead rate of 270 percent of direct labor dollars.

REQUIRED

Compute the total cost of the Grater order.

ALTERNATE PROBLEMS

LO 2

T Account Analysis with Unknowns

✔ d: July ending work in process inventory: $38,564
✔ i: August overhead applied: $48,400

P6. Core Enterprises makes peripheral equipment for computers. The company's new controller only has the following partial information for the past two months:

Account/Transaction	July	August
Beginning Materials Inventory	$52,000	$ (e)
Beginning Work in Process Inventory	24,000	(f)
Beginning Finished Goods Inventory	36,000	(g)
Materials purchased	(a)	31,000
Direct materials requested	77,000	(h)
Direct labor costs	(b)	44,000
Overhead applied	53,200	(i)
Cost of units completed	(c)	167,000
Cost of Goods Sold	188,000	(j)
Ending Materials Inventory	27,000	8,000
Ending Work in Process Inventory	(d)	(k)
Ending Finished Goods Inventory	12,000	19,000

The current year's predetermined overhead rate is 110 percent of direct labor cost.

REQUIRED

Using T accounts, compute the unknown values. (Round to the nearest dollar.)

LO 2, 3, 4

Job Order Costing: T Account Analysis

✔ 2: $4,581 underapplied overhead

P7. Rhile Industries, Inc., produces colorful and stylish uniforms to order. During September 2014, Rhile completed the following transactions:

Sept. 1 Purchased direct materials on account, $59,400.
3 Requested direct materials costing $26,850 for production (all for Job A).
4 Purchased indirect materials for cash, $22,830.
8 Issued checks for the following overhead costs: utilities, $4,310; manufacturing insurance, $1,925; and repairs, $4,640.

(Continued)

Sept. 10 Requested direct materials costing $29,510 (all used on Job A) and indirect materials costing $6,480 for production.
15 Recorded the following gross wages and salaries for employees: direct labor, $62,900 (all for Job A); indirect labor, $31,610; manufacturing supervision, $26,900; and sales commissions, $32,980.
15 Applied overhead to production at a rate of 120 percent of direct labor cost.
22 Paid the following overhead costs: utilities, $4,270; maintenance, $3,380; and rent, $3,250.
23 Recorded the purchase on account and receipt of $31,940 of direct materials and $9,260 of indirect materials.
27 Requested $28,870 of direct materials (Job A, $2,660; Job B, $8,400; Job C, $17,810) and $7,640 of indirect materials for production.
30 Recorded the following gross wages and salaries for employees: direct labor, $64,220 (Job A, $44,000; Job B, $9,000; Job C, $11,220); indirect labor, $30,290; manufacturing supervision, $28,520; and sales commissions, $36,200.
30 Applied overhead to production at a rate of 120 percent of direct labor cost.
30 Completed and transferred Job A (58,840 units) and Job B (3,525 units) to finished goods inventory; total cost was $322,400.
30 Shipped Job A to the customer; total production cost was $294,200, and sales price was $418,240.
30 Recorded the following adjusting entries: $2,680 for depreciation—manufacturing equipment; and $1,230 for property taxes, manufacturing, payable at month end.

REQUIRED

1. Record the entries for all Rhile's transactions in September using T accounts for the following: Materials Inventory, Work in Process Inventory, Finished Goods Inventory, Overhead, Cash, Accounts Receivable, Accumulated Depreciation—Manufacturing Equipment, Accounts Payable, Payroll Payable, Property Taxes Payable, Sales, Cost of Goods Sold, and Selling and Administrative Expenses. Prepare job order cost cards for Job A, Job B, and Job C. Determine the partial account balances. Assume no beginning inventory balances. Assume also that when payroll was recorded, entries were made to the Payroll Payable account.
2. Compute the amount of underapplied or overapplied overhead for September and transfer it to the Cost of Goods Sold account.
3. **ACCOUNTING CONNECTION ▶** Why should the Overhead account's underapplied or overapplied overhead be transferred to the Cost of Goods Sold account?

LO 2, 3, 4

Job Order Cost Flow

SPREADSHEET

✔ 2: Cost of units completed during the month: $76,470

P8. Tottham Industries is a company that makes special-order sound systems. The chief financial officer has records for February that reveal the following information:

Beginning inventory balances:	
Materials Inventory	$27,450
Work in Process Inventory	22,900
Finished Goods Inventory	19,200
Direct materials purchased and received:	
February 6	$ 7,200
February 12	8,110
February 24	5,890
Direct labor costs:	
February 14	$13,750
February 28	13,230

Direct materials requested for production:	
February 4	$9,080
February 13	5,940
February 25	7,600

Job order cost cards for jobs in process on February 28 had the following totals:

Job No.	Direct Materials	Direct Labor	Overhead
AJ-10	$3,220	$1,810	$2,534
AJ-14	3,880	2,110	2,954
AJ-15	2,980	1,640	2,296
AJ-16	4,690	2,370	3,318

The predetermined overhead rate for the month was 140 percent of direct labor costs. Sales for February totaled $152,400, the cost of production for the goods sold was $89,000.

REQUIRED

1. Using T accounts for Materials Inventory, Work in Process Inventory, Finished Goods Inventory, Overhead, Accounts Receivable, Payroll Payable, Sales, and Cost of Goods Sold, reconstruct the transactions in February, including applying overhead to production.
2. Compute the cost of units completed during the month.
3. Determine the ending balances in the inventory accounts.
4. During the first week of March, Jobs AJ-10 and AJ-14 were completed. No additional direct materials costs were incurred, but Job AJ-10 needed $720 more of direct labor, and Job AJ-14 needed an additional $1,140 of direct labor. Job AJ-10 was 40 units; Job AJ-14, 50 units. Compute the product unit cost for each completed job.

LO 4

Allocation of Overhead

SPREADSHEET

✔ 1: Predetermined overhead rate for this year: $5.00 per machine hour
✔ 3: Underapplied overhead: $750

P9. Gyllstrom Products, Inc., uses a predetermined overhead rate in its production, assembly, and testing departments. One rate is used for the entire company; it is based on machine hours. The rate is determined by analyzing data from the previous year to determine the percentage change in costs. Thus this year's overhead rate will be based on the percentage change multiplied by last year's costs. The following data are available:

	Last Year's Costs
Machine hours	38,000
Overhead costs	
Indirect materials	$ 58,000
Indirect labor	25,000
Supervision	41,000
Utilities	11,200
Labor-related costs	9,000
Depreciation, factory	10,500
Depreciation, machinery	27,000
Property taxes	3,000
Insurance	2,000
Miscellaneous overhead	5,000
Total overhead	$191,700

This year the cost of indirect materials is expected to increase by 30 percent over the previous year. The cost of indirect labor, utilities, machinery depreciation, property taxes, and insurance is expected to increase by 20 percent over the previous year. All other expenses are expected to increase by 10 percent over the previous year. Machine hours for this year are estimated at 45,858.

(Continued)

REQUIRED

1. Compute the projected costs, and use those costs to calculate the overhead rate for this year.
2. During this year, the company completed the following jobs using the machine hours shown:

Job No.	Machine Hours	Job No.	Machine Hours
H–142	7,840	H–201	10,680
H–164	5,260	H–218	12,310
H–175	8,100	H–304	2,460

   Determine the amount of overhead applied to each job. What was the total overhead applied during this year?
3. Actual overhead costs for this year were $234,000. Was overhead underapplied or overapplied this year? By how much? Should the Cost of Goods Sold account be increased or decreased to reflect actual overhead costs?
4. **ACCOUNTING CONNECTION ▶** At what point during this year was the overhead rate computed? When was it applied? Finally, when was underapplied or overapplied overhead determined and the Cost of Goods Sold account adjusted to reflect actual costs?

LO 4

Allocation of Overhead

P10. Fraser Products, Inc., which produces copy machines, has just completed packaging an order from Kent Company for 150 machines. Direct materials, purchased parts, and direct labor costs for the Kent order are as follows.

Cost of direct materials	$17,450
Cost of purchased parts	$14,800
Direct labor hours	140
Average direct labor pay rate	$16.50

Overhead costs were applied at a single, plantwide overhead rate of 240 percent of direct labor dollars.

REQUIRED

Compute the total cost of the Kent order.

CASES

LO 1, 5

Business Communication: Product Costing Systems

C1. BUSINESS APPLICATION ▶ Hawk Manufacturing manufactures engine parts for motorcycles. Jordan Smith, Hawk Manufacturing's president, wants to improve the quality of the company's operations and products. She believes waste exists in the design and manufacture of standard engine parts. To begin the improvement process, she has asked you to (1) identify the sources of such waste, (2) develop performance measures to account for the waste, and (3) estimate the current costs associated with the waste. She has asked you to submit a memo of your findings within two weeks so that she can begin strategic planning to revise the price at which Hawk sells engine parts to motorcycle manufacturers.

You have identified two sources of costly waste. The Production Department is redoing work that was not done correctly the first time, and the Engineering Design Department is redesigning products that were not initially designed to customer specifications. Having improper designs has caused the company to buy parts that are not used in production. You have also obtained the following information from the product costing system:

Direct labor costs	$673,402
Engineering design costs	124,709
Indirect labor costs	67,200
Depreciation on production equipment	84,300
Supervisors' salaries	98,340
Direct materials costs	432,223
Indirect materials costs	44,332

1. In preparation for writing your memo, answer the following questions:
   a. For whom are you preparing the memo? What is the appropriate length of the memo?
   b. Why are you preparing the memo?
   c. What information is needed for the memo? Where can you get this information? What performance measure would you suggest for each activity? Is the accounting information sufficient for your memo?
   d. When is the memo due? What can be done to provide accurate and timely information?
2. Prepare an outline of the sections you would want to include in your memo.

LO **2, 5**

Group Activity: Job Order Costing

C2. Many businesses accumulate costs for each job performed. Examples of businesses that use a job order costing system include print shops, car repair shops, health clinics, and kennels.

Visit a local business that uses job order costing, and interview the owner, manager, or accountant about the job order process and the documents the business uses to accumulate product costs. Write a paper that summarizes the information you obtained. Include the following in your summary:

1. The name of the business and the type of operations performed
2. The name and position of the individual you interviewed
3. A description of the process of starting and completing a job
4. A description of the accounting process and the documents used to track a job
5. Your responses to these questions:
   a. Did the person you interviewed know the actual amount of direct materials, direct labor, and overhead charged to a particular job? If the job includes some estimated costs, how are the estimates calculated? Do the costs affect the determination of the selling price of the product or service?
   b. Compare the documents discussed in this chapter with the documents used by the company you visited. How are they similar, and how are they different?
   c. In your opinion, does the business record and accumulate its product costs effectively? Explain.

LO **3, 5**

Ethical Dilemma: Costing Procedures and Ethics

C3. Roger Parker, the production manager of Products Company, entered the office of controller Harris Johnson and asked, "Harris, what gives here? I was charged for 330 direct labor hours on Job AD22, and my records show that we spent only 290 hours on that job. That 40-hour difference caused the total cost of direct labor and overhead for the job to increase by over $5,500. Are my records wrong, or was there an error in the direct labor assigned to the job?"

Harris replied, "Don't worry about it, Roger. This job won't be used in your quarterly performance evaluation. Job AD22 was a federal government job, a cost-plus contract, so the more costs we assign to it, the more profit we make. We decided to add a few hours to the job in case there is some follow-up work to do. You know how fussy the feds are." What should Roger Parker do? Discuss Harris Johnson's costing procedure.

LO 3, 5

Conceptual Understanding: Role of Cost Information in Software Development

C4. Software development companies frequently have a problem: When is "good enough" good enough? How many hours should be devoted to developing a new product? The industry's rule of thumb is that developing and shipping new software takes six to nine months. To be the first to market, a company must develop and ship products much more quickly than the industry norm. One performance measure that is used to answer the "good enough" question is a calculation based on the economic value (not cost) of what a company's developers create. The computation takes the estimated current market valuation of a firm and divides it by the number of product developers in the firm, to arrive at the market value created per developer. Some companies refine this calculation further to determine the value that each developer creates per workday. One company has estimated this value to be $10,000. Thus, for one software development company, "good enough" focuses on whether a new product's potential justifies an investment of time by someone who is worth $10,000 per day.

The salary cost of the company's developers is not used in the "good enough" calculation. Why is that cost not relevant?

LO 5

Interpreting Management Reports: Nonfinancial Data

C5. BUSINESS APPLICATION ▶ Hawk Manufacturing supplies engine parts to Cherokee Cycle Company, a major U.S. manufacturer of motorcycles. Like all of Cherokee's suppliers, Hawk has always added a healthy profit margin to its cost when quoting selling prices to Cherokee. Recently, however, several companies have offered to supply engine parts to Cherokee for lower prices than Hawk has been charging.

Because Hawk wants to keep Cherokee's business, a team of Hawk's managers analyzed their company's product costs and decided to make minor changes in the company's manufacturing process. No new equipment was purchased, and no additional labor was required. Instead, the machines were rearranged, and some of the work was reassigned.

To monitor the effectiveness of the changes, Hawk introduced three new performance measures to its information system: inventory levels, lead time (total time required for a part to move through the production process), and productivity (number of parts manufactured per person per day). Hawk's goal was to reduce the quantities of the first two performance measures and to increase the quantity of the third.

A section of a recent management report, shown below, summarizes the quantities for each performance measure before and after the changes in the manufacturing process were made.

Measure	Before	After	Improvement
Inventory in dollars	$21,444	$10,772	50%
Lead time in minutes	17	11	35%
Productivity (parts per person per day)	515	1,152	124%

1. Do you believe that Hawk improved the quality of its manufacturing process and the quality of its engine parts? Explain your answer.
2. Can Hawk lower its selling price to Cherokee? Explain your answer.
3. Did the introduction of the new measures affect the design of the product costing system? Explain your answer.
4. Do you believe that the new measures caused a change in Hawk's cost per engine part? If so, how did they cause the change?

Continuing Case: Cookie Company

C6. In the Cookie Company case in the last chapter, your team selected a cookie recipe for your company. In this chapter, your team will use that recipe to bake a batch of cookies, collect cost and time performance data related to the baking, create a marketing display for your company, and vote for the class's favorite cookie during an in-class cookie taste test. The goal of the taste test is to have your team's product voted the "best in class." One rule of the contest is that you may not vote for your own team's product.

1. Design a job measurement document that includes at least the following measures: cost per cookie; number of cookies produced (= number meeting specs + number rejected + number sampled for quality control + unexplained differences); size of cookies before baking; size of cookies after baking; and total throughput time (= mix time + [bake time for one cookie sheet × number of cookie sheets processed] + packaging time + downtime + cleanup time).
2. Design a job order cost card for your company that resembles one of those displayed in this chapter.
3. Using the recipe your team selected and assigning duties as described in the last chapter, bake a batch of cookies, and complete the job measurement document and job order cost card.
   - Assume an overhead rate of $2 for every $1 of direct material cost.
   - Assign direct labor cost for each production task based on the hourly rate or a monthly salary previously determined by your team.
4. Create a marketing display for your cookie product and bring it to class on the day of the taste test. The marketing display should include 20 cookies on a plate or napkin and a poster that displays your company's name and mission statement, cookie recipe, job measurement document, and job order cost card.
5. During class, each student should look at all of the marketing displays, taste 2 or 3 cookies and, on a ballot provided by your instructor, rank taste test results by giving 1 to the best cookie tasted, 2 to the next best, and so on. Students must sign their ballots before they turn them in to the instructor. (Remember, you cannot cast a vote for your own team's entry.) Your instructor will tabulate the ballots and announce the winning team.
6. Finally, write a review of your team members' efforts and give it to your instructor.

CHAPTER 17
Costing Systems: Process Costing

BUSINESS INSIGHT
Dean Foods

Dean Foods is the largest milk producer and distributor of milk and other dairy products in the United States. Its products are made in over 100 plants under such popular brands as Meadow Gold, Land O'Lakes, Pet, Garelick Farms, Silk, and Horizon Organic. In this chapter, we explain why a company like Dean Foods should use a process costing system and how this system provides the information that managers need to make sound product decisions.

1. **CONCEPT** ▶ *Why is a process costing system appropriate for Dean Foods to measure and recognize costs?*

2. **ACCOUNTING APPLICATION** ▶ *How does a product costing system account for costs when identical products or services are produced?*

3. **BUSINESS APPLICATION** ▶ *How does a process costing system help managers organize and control costs and facilitate management decisions?*

LEARNING OBJECTIVES

LO 1 **Describe a process costing system.**

LO 2 **Relate the patterns of product flows to the cost flow methods in a process costing environment, and explain the role of the Work in Process Inventory accounts.**

LO 3 **Describe equivalent production, and compute equivalent units.**

LO 4 **Prepare a process cost report using the FIFO costing method.**

LO 5 **Prepare a process cost report using the average costing method.**

LO 6 **Explain how managers use a process costing system to produce business results.**

Lasse Kristensen/Shutterstock.com

SECTION 1 CONCEPTS

CONCEPTS
- Cost measurement
- Cost recognition
- Matching principle

RELEVANT LEARNING OBJECTIVE

LO 1 Describe a process costing system.

LO1 Concepts Underlying the Process Costing System

Since it is impossible to identify an individual unit of some products until they have been completed (such as a container of milk, a package of jelly beans, or a gallon of ice cream), process costing is used to track and control costs while products are being made. A **process costing system** first *measures* the costs of direct materials, direct labor, and overhead for each process, department, or work cell and then assigns those costs to the products produced during a particular period. Reports prepared at the end of each period *recognize* the costs assigned to products completed and transferred out or to the products remaining in the process, department, or work cell. It provides the cost information for product revenues to be *matched* with the expenses required to generate them. A product costing system, like process costing, provides managers with unit cost information, cost data for management decisions, and ending values for the Materials Inventory, Work in Process Inventory, and Finished Goods Inventory accounts.

Such a system is used for *cost measurement* by companies that make large amounts of similar products or liquid products or that have continuous production runs of identical products. For example, companies that produce paint or chemicals (like **Dow Chemicals**), beverages (like **Coors** and **Coca-Cola**), foods (like **Kellogg Company**), computer chips (like **Apple Computer**), and gallon containers of ice cream are typical users of a process costing system.

In the previous chapter, we focused on job order costing. It's important to note that the difference between job order costing and process costing is that, in process costing, costs are *measured* and *recognized* by production *processes*, such as the Work in Process Inventory account of the Mixing Department, whereas in job order costing, costs are measured and recognized by *jobs* through the job order cost card.

APPLY IT!

Indicate whether the manufacturer of each of the following products should use a job order costing system or a process costing system to accumulate product costs.

a. baby bottles
b. chocolate milk
c. nuclear submarines
d. generic drugs

SOLUTION

a. Process
b. Process
c. Job order
d. Process

TRY IT! SE1, SE2, E1A, E1B

SECTION 2 ACCOUNTING APPLICATIONS

COUNTING PLICATIONS
Compute equivalent units
Prepare a process cost report using the FIFO costing method
Prepare a process cost report using the average costing method

LEVANT ARNING OBJECTIVES

2 Relate the patterns of product flows to the t flow methods in a cess costing environment, d explain the role of the rk in Process Inventory ounts.

3 Describe equivalent production, and npute equivalent units.

4 Prepare a process cost report using the FIFO ting method.

5 Prepare a process cost report using the erage costing method.

LO2 Patterns of Product Flows and Cost Flow Methods

In a process costing environment, products flow in a first-in, first-out (FIFO) fashion through several processes, departments, or work cells and may undergo many different operations. Exhibit 1 illustrates the simple linear production flow of how milk is produced in a series of three processing steps, or departments. Each department has its own Work in Process Inventory account to accumulate the direct materials, direct labor, and overhead costs associated with it.

- **Homogenization Department:** Raw milk from the cow must be mixed to evenly distribute the butterfat. The homogenized milk and its associated cost then become the direct materials for the next department.
- **Pasteurization Department:** The homogenized milk is heated to 145 degrees to kill the bacteria found in raw milk. The homogenized, pasteurized milk and all associated costs are then transferred on to the next department.
- **Packaging Department:** The milk is put into bottles and transferred to Finished Goods Inventory since it is ready for sale.

The product unit cost of a bottle of milk is the sum of the cost elements in all three departments divided by the number of bottles of milk produced.

Exhibit 1
Product Flows in a Process Costing Environment

Homogenization Department
Resources used:
• Direct materials (raw milk)
• Direct labor
• Overhead

Pasteurization Department
Resources used:
• Milk transferred in
• Direct labor
• Overhead

Packing Department
Resources used:
• Milk transferred in
• Direct materials (bottles)
• Direct labor
• Overhead

Finished Goods Inventory

Even in simple process costing environments, production generally involves a number of separate manufacturing processes, departments, or work cells. For example, the separate processes involved in manufacturing cookies include mixing, baking, and packaging.

To *measure* and *recognize* product costs using process costing requires the preparation of a **process cost report** for each process, department, or work cell as product-related costs flow through the production process. Managers assign these costs to the units that have transferred out of the process and to the units that are still a part of the work in process. They use a cost allocation method, such as the FIFO costing method or the average costing method.

- In the **first-in, first-out (FIFO) costing method**, the cost flow follows the logical physical flow of production—that is, the costs assigned to the first materials processed are the first costs transferred out when those materials flow to the next process, department, or work cell. Thus, in Exhibit 1, the costs assigned to the homogenized milk would be the first costs transferred to the Pasteurization Department.

- In contrast, the **average costing method** assigns an average cost to all products made during a period. This method thus uses total cost averages and does not try to match cost flow with the physical flow of production.

Cost Flows Through the Work in Process Inventory Accounts

As discussed in the previous chapter, a job order costing system uses a single Work in Process Inventory account, whereas a process costing system has a separate Work in Process Inventory account for each process, department, or work cell. As shown in Exhibit 1, these accounts are the focal point of process costing. As products move from one process, department, or work cell to the next, the costs of the direct materials, direct labor, and overhead associated with them flow to the next Work in Process Inventory account. The journal entry to record the transfer of costs from one process, department, or work cell to another is:

	Dr.	*Cr.*
Work in Process Inventory (next department)	XX	
Work in Process Inventory (this department)		XX

Once the products are completed, packaged, and ready for sale, their costs are transferred to the Finished Goods Inventory account. The journal entry to record this transfer out of Work in Process Inventory into Finished Goods Inventory is:

	Dr.	*Cr.*
Finished Goods Inventory	XX	
Work in Process Inventory (last department)		XX

As you will learn later in this chapter, the costs associated with these entries are calculated in a process cost report for the process, department, or work cell.

APPLY IT!

Milk Smoothies, Inc., uses an automated mixing machine in its Mixing Department to combine three raw materials into a product called Strawberry Smoothie Mix. Total costs charged to the Mixing Department's Work in Process Inventory account during the month were $210,000. There were no units in beginning or ending work in process inventory. Prepare the journal entry to transfer the units completed to Finished Goods Inventory.

SOLUTION

Finished Goods Inventory	210,000	
Work in Process Inventory		210,000

TRY IT! SE3, E2A, E3A, E2B, E3B

LO3 Computing Equivalent Production

A process costing system does not associate costs with particular job orders. Instead, it assigns the costs incurred in a process, department, or work cell to the units in production during a period by computing an average cost per unit of effort. Unit cost for the period is computed as follows.

(Direct Materials + Direct Labor + Overhead) ÷ Number of Units = Unit Cost

The number of units in production during the period is a critical question. Do we count only units started and completed during the period? Or should we include partially

While direct materials are usually added to production at the beginning of the process, they can be added at other stages. For example, chocolate chips are added at the end of the mixing process for cookie dough.

completed units in the beginning work in process inventory? And what about incomplete products in the ending work in process inventory?

These questions relate to the concept of equivalent production. **Equivalent production** (or *equivalent units*) applies a percentage-of-completion factor to partially completed units to calculate the equivalent number of whole units produced during a period for each type of input (i.e., direct materials, direct labor, and overhead). The number of equivalent units produced is (1) the sum of total units started and completed during the period and (2) an amount representing the work done on partially completed products in both the beginning and the ending work in process inventories. Equivalent production must be computed separately for each type of input because of differences in the ways in which costs are incurred.

- Direct materials are usually added to production at the beginning of the process.
- The costs of direct labor and overhead are often incurred uniformly throughout the production process. Thus, it is convenient to combine direct labor and overhead when calculating equivalent units. These combined costs are called **conversion costs** (or *processing costs*).

For example, Milk Products Company makes a pint-sized, bottled milk drink. As shown in Exhibit 2, the company started Week 2 with one half-completed unit in process. During Week 2, it started and completed three units, and at the end of Week 2, it had one unit that was three-quarters completed.

Exhibit 2
Computation of Equivalent Production

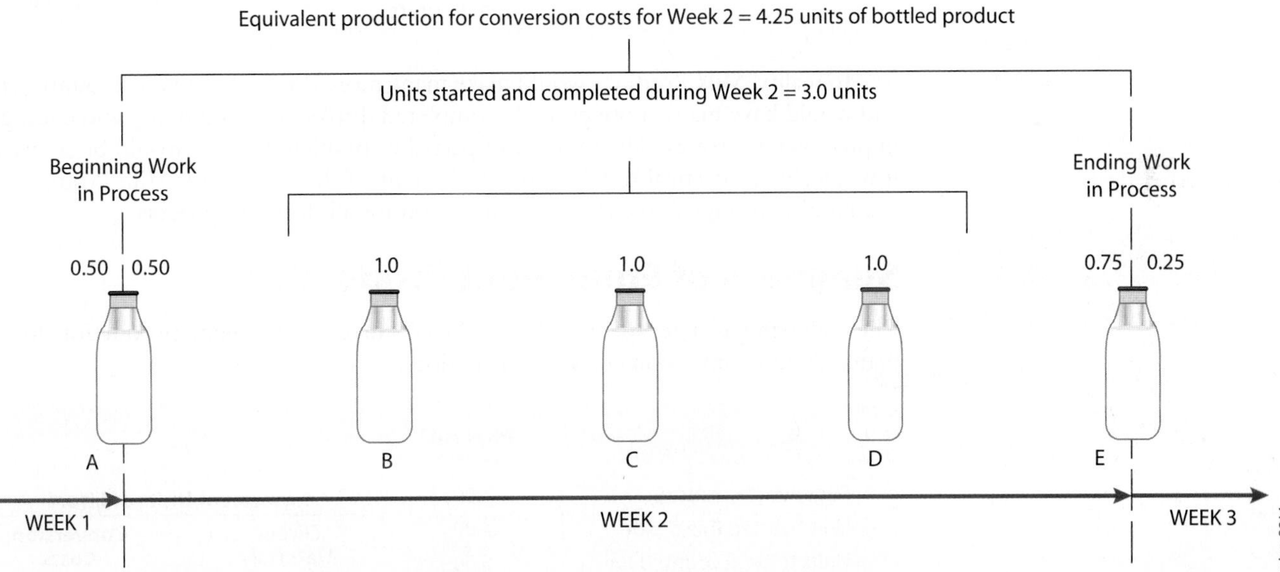

Note: Conversion costs (the cost of direct labor and overhead) are incurred uniformly as each physical unit of drink moves through production. Equivalent production for Week 2 is 4.25 units for conversion costs. But direct materials costs are all added to production at the beginning of the process. Because four physical units of drinks entered production in Week 2, equivalent production for the week is 4.0 units of effort for direct materials costs.

Equivalent Production for Direct Materials

At Milk Products, all direct materials, including liquids and bottles, are added at the beginning of production. Thus, the unit that was half-completed at the beginning of Week 2 had had all its direct materials added during the previous week. No direct materials costs for this unit are included in the computation of Week 2's equivalent units for the beginning inventory units.

STUDY NOTE: The number of units started and completed is not the same as the total number of units completed during the period. Total units completed include both units in beginning work in process inventory that were completed and units started and completed.

During Week 2, work began on four new units—the three units that were completed and the unit that was three-quarters completed at week's end. Because all direct materials are added at the beginning of the production process, all four units were 100 percent complete with regard to direct materials at the end of Week 2. Thus, for Week 2, the equivalent production for direct materials was 4.0 units. This figure includes direct materials for both the 3.0 units that were started and completed and the 1.0 unit that was three-quarters completed.

Equivalent Production for Conversion Costs

Because conversion costs at Milk Products are incurred uniformly throughout the production process, the equivalent production for conversion costs during Week 2 consists of the following three components:

- the cost to finish the half-completed unit in beginning work in process inventory (0.50)
- the cost to begin and finish three completed units (3.0)
- the cost to begin work on the three-quarters-completed unit in ending work in process inventory (0.75)

STUDY NOTE: Work in the current period is assigned to three distinct product groups: units in beginning work in process inventory, which must be completed; goods started and completed during the period; and goods started but not completed by the end of the accounting period.

Thus, For Week 2, the total equivalent production for conversion costs in units is computed as follows:

$$\text{Total Equivalent Units for Conversion Costs} = \text{Beginning Inventory} + \text{Started and Completed} + \text{Ending Inventory}$$

$$= 0.50 \text{ unit} + 3.0 \text{ units} + 0.75 \text{ unit}$$

$$= 4.25 \text{ units}$$

In reality, Milk Products would make many more drinks during an accounting period and would have many more partially completed drinks in its beginning and ending work in process inventories. The number of partially completed drinks would be so great that it would be impractical to take a physical count of them. Instead, Milk Products would estimate an average percentage of completion for all drinks in process.

Summary of Equivalent Production

The following is a recap of Milk Products' current equivalent production for direct materials and conversion costs for the period:

	Physical Units	Equivalent Units of Effort			
		Direct Materials		Conversion Costs	
Beginning inventory	1.00				
Units started this period	4.00				
Units to be accounted for	5.00				
Beginning inventory	1.00	—	0%	0.50	50%
Units started and completed	3.00	3.00	100%	3.00	100%
Ending inventory	1.00	1.00	100%	0.75	75%
Units accounted for	5.00	4.00		4.25	

APPLY IT!

Milk Smoothies, Inc., adds direct materials when it starts its drink mix production process and adds conversion costs uniformly throughout this process. Given the following information from July, compute the current period's equivalent units of production:

- Units in beginning inventory: 2,000
- Units started during the period: 13,000
- Units partially completed: 500
- Percentage of completion of beginning inventory: 100% for direct materials; 40% for conversion costs in previous period
- Percentage of completion of ending work in process inventory: 100% for direct materials; 70% for conversion costs

SOLUTION

Milk Smoothies, Inc.
For the Month Ended July 31

	Physical Units	Equivalent Units of Effort			
		Direct Materials		Conversion Costs	
Beginning inventory	2,000				
Units started this period	13,000				
Units to be accounted for	15,000				
Beginning inventory	2,000	—	0%	1,200	60%
Units started and completed	12,500	12,500	100%	12,500	100%
Ending inventory	500	500	100%	350	70%
Units accounted for	15,000	13,000		14,050	

TRY IT! SE4, E4A, E5A, E6A, E4B, E5B, E6B

LO4 Preparing a Process Cost Report Using the FIFO Costing Method

STUDY NOTE: *The FIFO method focuses on the work done in the current period only.*

As mentioned earlier, a *process cost report* is a report that managers use to track and analyze costs for a process, department, or work cell in a process costing system. In a process cost report that uses the FIFO costing method, the cost flow follows the logical physical flow of production—that is, the costs assigned to the first products processed are the first costs transferred out when those products flow to the next process, department, or work cell.

To continue with the Milk Products example, assume the following for February:

- The beginning work in process inventory consists of 6,200 partially completed units (60% processed in the previous period). Beginning inventory cost of $41,540 consisted of materials cost of $20,150 and conversion cost of $21,390.
- During the period, the 6,200 units in beginning inventory were completed, and 57,500 units were started into production. Current period cost of $510,238 consisted of material cost of $189,750 and conversion cost of $320,488.
- Of the 57,500 units started during the period, 52,500 units were completed. The other 5,000 units remain in ending work in process inventory and are 45% complete.

Exhibit 3 presents a process cost report for Milk Products.

Exhibit 3
Process Cost Report: FIFO Costing Method

		Physical Units					
Step 1: *Account for physical units.*	Beginning inventory (units started last period)	6,200					
	Units started this period	57,500					
	Units to be accounted for	63,700					
			Current Equivalent Units of Effort				
			Direct Materials	**% Incurred During Period**		**Conversion Costs**	**% Incurred During Period**
Step 2: *Account for equivalent units.*	Beginning inventory (units completed this period)	6,200	0	0%		2,480	40%
	Units started and completed this period	52,500	52,500	100%		52,500	100%
	Ending inventory (units started but not completed this period)	5,000	5,000	100%		2,250	45%
	Units accounted for	63,700	57,500			57,230	
		Total Costs					
Step 3: *Account for costs.*	Beginning inventory	$ 41,540 =	$ 20,150	+		$ 21,390	
	Current costs	510,238 =	189,750	+		320,488	
	Total costs	$551,778					
Step 4: *Compute cost per equivalent unit.*	Current Costs / Equivalent Units		$189,750 / 57,500			$320,488 / 57,230	
	Cost per equivalent unit	$8.90 =	$3.30	+		$5.60	
Step 5: *Assign costs to cost of goods manufactured and ending inventory.*	Cost of goods manufactured and transferred out:						
	From beginning inventory	$ 41,540					
	Current costs to complete	13,888 =	$0	+		(2,480 × $5.60)	
	Units started and completed this period	467,250 =	(52,500 × $3.30) +			(52,500 × $5.60)	
	Cost of goods manufactured	$522,678	*(No rounding necessary)*				
	Ending inventory	29,100 =	(5,000 × $3.30) +			(2,250 × $5.60)	
	Total costs	$551,778					

Work in Process Inventory Account: Cost Recap

Beg. bal.	41,540	Cost of goods manufactured and transferred out	522,678
Direct materials	189,750		
Conversion costs	320,488		
End. bal.	**29,100**		

Work in Process Inventory Account: Unit Recap

Beg. bal.	6,200	FIFO units transferred out (from the 6,200 in beginning inventory plus the 52,500 started and completed)	58,700
Units started	57,500		
End. bal.	**5,000**		

As shown in Exhibit 3, the preparation of a process cost report involves five steps. The first two steps account for the units of product being processed. The next two steps account for the costs of the direct materials, direct labor, and overhead being incurred. The final step assigns costs to products being transferred out of the area and to those remaining behind in ending work in process inventory.

Accounting for Units

Managers must account for the physical flow of products through their areas (Step 1) before they can compute equivalent production for the accounting period (Step 2). To continue with the Milk Products example, assume the following for February:

- The beginning work in process inventory consists of 6,200 partially completed units (60 percent processed in the previous period).
- During the period, the 6,200 units in beginning inventory were completed, and 57,500 units were started into production.
- Of the 57,500 units started during the period, 52,500 units were completed. The other 5,000 units remain in ending work in process inventory and are 45 percent complete.

Step 1: Account for Physical Units In Step 1 in Exhibit 3, Milk Products' department manager computes the total units to be accounted for by adding the 6,200 units in beginning inventory to the 57,500 units started into production during this period. These 63,700 units are the actual physical units that the manager is responsible for during the period.

Step 1 continues accounting for physical units. As shown in Exhibit 3, the 6,200 units in beginning inventory that were completed during the period, the 52,500 units that were started and finished in the period, and the 5,000 units remaining in the department at the end of the period are summed, and the total is listed as "units accounted for." (Note that the "units accounted for" must equal the "units to be accounted for" in Step 1.)

Step 2: Account for Equivalent Units The units accounted for in Step 1 are used to compute equivalent production for the department's direct materials and conversion costs for the month in Step 2.

STUDY NOTE: *Units in beginning work in process inventory represent work accomplished in the previous period that has already been assigned a certain portion of its total cost. Those units must be completed in the current period, incurring additional costs. Under FIFO, the amount of effort required to complete beginning work in process inventory is the relevant percentage.*

Beginning Inventory. Because all direct materials are added at the beginning of the production process, the 6,200 partially completed units that began February as work in process were already 100 percent complete in regard to direct materials. They were 60 percent complete in regard to conversion costs on February 1. The remaining 40 percent of their conversion costs were incurred as they were completed during the month. Thus, as shown in the "Conversion Costs" column of Exhibit 3, the current equivalent production for their conversion costs is computed as follows.

$$6{,}200 \text{ units} \times 40\% = 2{,}480 \text{ units}$$

Units Started and Completed During the Period. All the costs of the 52,500 units started and completed during February were incurred during this period. Thus, the full amount of 52,500 is entered as the equivalent units for both direct materials costs and conversion costs since 100% of the work was completed during the current period.

Ending Inventory. Because the materials for the 5,000 drinks still in process at the end of February were added when the drinks went into production during the month, the full amount of 5,000 is entered as the equivalent units for direct materials costs. However, these drinks are only 45 percent complete in terms of conversion costs. Thus, as shown in the Conversion Costs column of Exhibit 3, the equivalent production for their conversion costs is computed as follows.

$$5{,}000 \text{ units} \times 45\% = 2{,}250 \text{ units}$$

Totals. Step 2 is completed by summing all the physical units to be accounted for, all equivalent units for direct materials costs, and all equivalent units for conversion costs. Exhibit 3 shows that for February, Milk Products accounted for 63,700 units. Equivalent units for direct materials costs totaled 57,500, and equivalent units for conversion costs totaled 57,230. Once Milk Products knows February's equivalent unit amounts, it can complete the remaining three steps in the preparation of a process cost report.

Accounting for Costs

Thus far, we have focused on accounting for units of productive output—in our example, bottled milk drinks. We now turn our focus to the cost information portion of preparing a process cost report.

- In Step 3, all costs charged to the Work in Process Inventory account of each production process, department, or work cell are accumulated and analyzed.
- In Step 4, the cost per equivalent unit for direct materials costs and conversion costs is computed.

To continue with the Milk Products example, assume the following for February:

Work in Process Inventory		
Costs from beginning inventory:		
Direct materials costs	20,150	
Conversion costs	21,390	
Current period costs:		
Direct materials costs	189,750	
Conversion costs	320,488	

***STUDY NOTE:** The cost per equivalent unit using the FIFO method measures the current cost divided by current effort. Notice in Exhibit 3 that the cost of beginning work in process inventory is omitted.*

Step 3: Account for Costs As shown in Exhibit 3, all costs for the period are accumulated in the Total Costs column.

Beginning Material Inventory Cost + Conversion Cost = Total Beginning Inventory Cost

$20,150 + $21,390 = $41,540

Current Period Material Cost + Conversion Cost = Total Current Period Cost

$189,750 + $320,488 = $510,238

Beginning Inventory Cost + Current Period Cost = Total Cost

$41,540 + $510,238 = $551,778

Notice that only the Total Costs column is totaled. Because only the current period costs for direct materials and conversion are used in Step 4, there is no need to find the total costs of the direct materials and conversion costs columns in Step 3.

Step 4: Compute Cost per Equivalent Unit Exhibit 3 shows the computation of the current cost per current equivalent unit for direct materials and for conversion costs.

$$\text{Total Cost per Equivalent Unit} = \left(\text{Direct Materials Cost} \div \text{Units of Equivalent Production}\right) + \left(\text{Conversion Costs} \div \text{Units of Equivalent Production}\right)$$

$$= (\$189{,}750 \div 57{,}500) + (\$320{,}488 \div 57{,}230)$$

$$= \$3.30 + \$5.60$$

$$= \underline{\underline{\$8.90}}$$

Note that the equivalent units are taken from Step 2 of Exhibit 3. Prior period costs attached to units in beginning inventory are not included in these computations because the FIFO costing method uses a separate costing analysis for each accounting period. (The FIFO method treats the costs of beginning inventory separately, in Step 5.)

Assigning Costs

We have focused on accounting for units of productive output, analyzed the costs accumulated in the production process, department, or work cell, and computed the cost per equivalent unit for direct material costs and conversion costs. We now turn to the final step, which is to recognize the costs that are transferred out either to the next production process, department, or work cell or to the Finished Goods Inventory account (i.e., the cost of goods manufactured), as well as the costs that remain in the Work in Process Inventory account.

STUDY NOTE: The process cost report is developed for the purpose of assigning a value to one transaction: the transfer of goods from one department to another or to finished goods inventory. The ending balance in the Work in Process Inventory account represents the costs that remain after this transfer.

Step 5: Assign Costs to Cost of Goods Manufactured and Ending Inventory Step 5 in the preparation of a process costing report uses information from Steps 2 and 4 to assign costs, as shown in Exhibit 3. This final step determines the costs that are transferred out or remain in the Work in Process Inventory account. The total costs assigned to units completed and transferred out and to ending inventory must equal the total costs in Step 3.

Cost of Goods Manufactured and Transferred Out. Step 5 in Exhibit 3 shows that the costs transferred to the Finished Goods Inventory account include the $41,540 in direct materials and conversion costs for completing the 6,200 units in beginning inventory. Step 2 shows that 2,480 equivalent units of conversion costs were required to complete these 6,200 units. Because the equivalent unit conversion cost for February is $5.60, the cost to complete the units carried over from January is computed as follows.

$$2{,}480 \text{ units} \times \$5.60 = \$13{,}888$$

Each of the 52,500 units started and completed in February cost $8.90 to produce.

$$52{,}500 \text{ units} \times \$8.90 = \$467{,}250$$

To recap the cost assigned to the work completed during the period and transferred to Finished Goods:

$$\$41{,}540 + \$13{,}888 + \$467{,}250 = \$522{,}678$$

The entry resulting from doing the process cost report for February is:

	Dr.	Cr.
Finished Goods Inventory	522,678	
Work in Process Inventory		522,678

STUDY NOTE: All costs must be accounted for, including both costs from beginning inventory and costs incurred during the current period. All costs must be assigned to either ending inventory or the goods transferred out.

Ending Inventory. All costs remaining in Milk Products' Work in Process Inventory account after the cost of goods manufactured has been transferred out represent the costs of the drinks still in production at the end of February. As shown in Step 5 of Exhibit 3, the balance in the ending Work in Process Inventory is computed as follows.

$$(5{,}000 \text{ units} \times \$3.30 \text{ per unit}) + (2{,}250 \times \$5.60 \text{ per unit}) = \$29{,}100$$

Rounding Differences. As you perform Step 5 in any process cost report, remember that the total costs in Steps 3 and 5 must always be the same number. In Exhibit 3, for example, they are both $551,778.

- If the total costs in Steps 3 and 5 are not the same, first check for omission of any costs and for calculation errors.
- If that does not solve the problem, check whether any rounding was necessary in computing the costs per equivalent unit in Step 4. If rounding was done in Step 4, rounding differences will occur when assigning costs in Step 5. In that case, adjust the total costs transferred out for any rounding difference so that the total costs in Step 5 equal the total costs in Step 3.

STUDY NOTE: Rounding product unit costs to even dollars may lead to a significant difference in total costs, giving the impression that costs have been miscalculated. Round product unit costs to two decimal places where appropriate.

Recap of Work in Process Inventory Account When the process cost report is complete, an account recap will show the effects of the report on the Work in Process Inventory account for the period. Two recaps of Milk Products' Work in Process Inventory account for February—one for costs and one for units—appear at the end of Exhibit 3.

Process Costing for Two or More Production Departments

In this example, Milk Products has only one production department for making milk drinks, so it needs only one Work in Process Inventory account. However, a company that has more than one production process or department must have a Work in Process Inventory account for each process or department.

For instance, a milk producer like Milk Products has a production department for homogenization, another for pasteurization, and another for packaging needs—three Work in Process Inventory accounts.

- When products flow from the Homogenization Department to the Pasteurization Department, their costs flow from the Homogenization Department's Work in Process Inventory account to the Pasteurization Department's Work in Process Inventory account.
- The costs transferred into the Pasteurization Department's Work in Process Inventory account are treated in the same way as the cost of direct materials added at the beginning of the production process.
- When production flows to the Packaging Department, the accumulated costs (incurred in the two previous departments) are transferred to that department's Work in Process Inventory account.
- At the end of the period, a separate process cost report is prepared for each department.

APPLY IT!

Pop Chewing Gum Company produces bubble gum. Direct materials are blended at the beginning of the manufacturing process. No materials are lost in the process, so one kilogram of materials input produces one kilogram of bubble gum. Direct labor and overhead costs are incurred uniformly throughout the blending process.

- On June 30, 16,000 units were in process. All direct materials had been added, but the units were only 70 percent complete in regard to conversion costs in the prior period. Direct materials costs of $8,100 and conversion costs of $11,800 were attached to the beginning inventory.
- During July, 405,000 kilograms of materials were used at a cost of $202,500. Direct labor charges were $299,200, and overhead costs applied during July were $284,000.
- The ending work in process inventory was 21,600 kilograms. All direct materials have been added to those units, and 25 percent of the conversion costs have been assigned. Output from the Blending Department is transferred to the Packaging Department.

Required

1. Prepare a process cost report using the FIFO costing method for the Blending Department for July.
2. Identify the amount that should be transferred out of the Work in Process Inventory account, state where those dollars should be transferred, and prepare the appropriate journal entry.

SOLUTION

1.

Pop Chewing Gum Company
Blending Department
Process Cost Report: FIFO Method
For the Month Ended July 31

		Physical Units
Step 1: *Account for physical units.*	Beginning inventory (units started last period)	16,000
	Units started this period	405,000
	Units to be accounted for	421,000

			Current Equivalent Units of Effort			
			Direct Materials	% Incurred During Period	Conversion Costs	% Incurred During Period
Step 2: *Account for equivalent units.*	Beginning inventory (units completed this period)	16,000	0	0%	4,800	30%
	Units started and completed this period	383,400	383,400	100%	383,400	100%
	Ending inventory (units started but not completed this period)	21,600	21,600	100%	5,400	25%
	Units accounted for	421,000	405,000		393,600	

		Total Costs				
Step 3: *Account for costs.*	Beginning inventory	$ 19,900	=	$ 8,100	+	$ 11,800
	Current costs	785,700	=	202,500	+	583,200
	Total costs	$805,600				
Step 4: *Compute cost per equivalent unit.*	Current Costs			$202,500		$583,200
	Equivalent Units			405,000		393,600
	Cost per equivalent unit	$1.98	=	$0.50	+	$1.48*
						**Rounded to nearest cent*
Step 5: *Assign costs to cost of goods manufactured and ending inventory.*	Cost of goods manufactured and transferred out:					
	From beginning inventory	$ 19,900				
	Current costs to complete	7,104	=	$0	+	(4,800 × $1.48)
	Units started and completed this period	759,132	=	(383,400 × $0.50)	+	(383,400 × $1.48)
	Cost of goods manufactured	$786,808	*[Cost of goods manufactured must be $786,808 (add rounding of $672) since Total costs = Ending inventory + Cost of goods manufactured]*			
	Ending inventory	18,792	=	(21,600 × $0.50)	+	(5,400 × $1.48)
	Total costs	$805,600				

Work in Process Inventory Account: Cost Recap

Beg. bal.	19,900	Cost of goods manufactured and transferred out	786,808
Direct materials	202,500		
Conversion costs	583,200		
End. bal.	**18,792**		

Work in Process Inventory Account: Unit Recap

Beg. bal.	16,000	FIFO units transferred out (from the 16,000 in beginning inventory plus the 383,400 started and completed)	399,400
Units started	405,000		
End. bal.	**21,600**		

(Continued)

2. The amount of $786,808 should be transferred to the Work in Process Inventory account of the Packaging Department.

Work in Process Inventory (Packaging Department)	786,808	
Work in Process Inventory (Blending Department)		786,808

TRY IT! SE5, SE6, E7A, E8A, E9A, E10A, E7B, E8B, E9B, E10B

LO 5 Preparing a Process Cost Report Using the Average Costing Method

When a process cost report uses the average costing method, like the one shown in Exhibit 4, cost flows do not follow the logical physical flow of production as they do when the FIFO method is used. Instead, the costs in beginning inventory are combined with current period costs to compute an average product unit cost. Preparing a process cost report using the average costing method involves the same five steps as using the FIFO method, but the procedures for completing the steps differ. Assume that Milk Products uses the average costing method of process costing.

Accounting for Units

The process cost report accounts for the physical units in a production process, department, or work cell during a period. Managers must account for the physical flow of products through their areas (Step 1) before they can compute equivalent production for the accounting period (Step 2). Units to be accounted for equals the physical units in beginning inventory plus the physical units started during the period.

STUDY NOTE: *Step 1 (accounting for physical units) is identical for the average costing and FIFO costing methods.*

Step 1: Account for Physical Units Step 1 of a process cost report accounts for the physical units in a production process, department, or work cell during a period. Units to be accounted for equals the physical units in beginning inventory plus the physical units started during the period. In Step 1 of Exhibit 4, Milk Product's department manager computes the total units to be accounted for as follows.

6,200 units + 57,500 units = 63,700

STUDY NOTE: *In contrast, as shown in Exhibit 3, the FIFO costing method disregards the previous period costs of units started in the last period and calculates only the equivalent units required in the current period to complete the units in beginning inventory.*

Step 2: Account for Equivalent Units Step 2 also accounts for production during the period in terms of units. After the number of units completed and transferred to finished goods inventory and the number of units in ending inventory have been added to arrive at "units accounted for," the equivalent units in terms of direct materials costs and conversion costs are computed.

Units Completed and Transferred Out. In Exhibit 4, the average costing method treats both the direct materials costs and the conversion costs of the 58,700 units completed in February (6,200 units from beginning inventory + 52,500 started this period) as if they were incurred in the current period. Thus, the full amount of 58,700 is entered as the equivalent units for these costs.

STUDY NOTE: *The average costing method treats ending inventory in exactly the same way as the FIFO costing method.*

Ending Inventory. Because all direct materials are added at the beginning of the production process, the full amount of 5,000 is entered as the equivalent units for direct materials cost. Because the 5,000 units in ending inventory are only 45 percent complete in terms of conversion costs, the amount of equivalent units is computed as follows.

5,000 units × 45% = 2,250 units

Totals. When the average costing method is used, Step 2 in a process cost report is completed by summing all the physical units to be accounted for, all equivalent units for direct

Exhibit 4
Process Cost Report: Average Costing Method

		Physical Units		Direct Materials	% Incurred During Period		Conversion Costs	% Incurred During Period
Step 1: *Account for physical units.*	Beginning inventory (units started last period)	6,200						
	Units started this period	57,500						
	Units to be accounted for	63,700		**Total Equivalent Units of Effort**				
Step 2: *Account for equivalent units.*	Units completed and transferred out	58,700		58,700	100%		58,700	100%
	Ending inventory (units started but not completed this period)	5,000		5,000	100%		2,250	45%
	Units accounted for	63,700		63,700			60,950	
		Total Costs						
Step 3: *Account for costs.*	Beginning inventory	$ 41,540	=	$ 20,150		+	$ 21,390	
	Current costs	510,238	=	189,750		+	320,488	
	Total costs	$551,778		$209,900			$341,878	
Step 4: *Compute cost per equivalent unit.*	Total Costs / Equivalent Units			$209,900 / 63,700			$341,878 / 60,950	
	Cost per equivalent unit	$8.91	=	$3.30*		+	$5.61*	
				*Rounded to nearest cent				
Step 5: *Assign costs to cost of goods manufactured and ending inventory.*	Cost of goods manufactured and transferred out	$522,655	=	(58,700 × $3.30)		+	(58,700 × $5.61)	
				(Cost of goods manufactured must be $522,655 (less rounding of $362) since Total costs = Ending inventory + Cost of goods manufactured)				
	Ending inventory	29,123*	=	(5,000 × $3.30)		+	(2,250 × $5.61)	
		*Rounded to nearest whole dollar						
	Total costs	$551,778						

Work in Process Inventory Account: Cost Recap

Beg. bal.	41,540	Cost of goods manufactured and transferred out	522,655
Direct materials	189,750		
Conversion costs	320,488		
End. bal.	**29,123**		

Work in Process Inventory Account: Unit Cost Recap

Beg. bal.	6,200	Units transferred out	58,700
Units started	57,500		
End. bal.	**5,000**		

materials costs, and all equivalent units for conversion costs. Exhibit 4 shows that for February, Milk Products accounted for 63,700 physical units. Equivalent units for direct materials costs totaled 63,700, and equivalent units for conversion costs totaled 60,950.

Accounting for Costs

Step 3 of the report accumulates and analyzes all costs in the Work in Process Inventory account, and Step 4 computes the cost per equivalent unit for direct materials costs and conversion costs. The costs of Milk Products' beginning inventory were $20,150 for direct materials and $21,390 for conversion. Current period costs were $189,750 for direct materials and $320,488 for conversion.

STUDY NOTE: Comparing Exhibit 4 with Exhibit 3, you will see that the average costing and FIFO costing methods deal with Step 3 in the same manner.

Step 3: Account for Costs All direct materials costs and conversion costs for beginning inventory and the current period are accumulated in the Total Costs column. The total of $551,778 consists of $209,900 in direct materials costs and $341,878 in conversion costs.

Step 4: Compute Cost per Equivalent Unit Step 4 computes the cost per equivalent unit as follows.

$$\text{Total Cost per Equivalent Unit} = \left(\begin{array}{c}\text{Direct}\\ \text{Materials}\\ \text{Cost}\end{array} \div \begin{array}{c}\text{Units of}\\ \text{Equivalent}\\ \text{Production}\end{array}\right) + \left(\begin{array}{c}\text{Conversion}\\ \text{Costs}\end{array} \div \begin{array}{c}\text{Units of}\\ \text{Equivalent}\\ \text{Production}\end{array}\right)$$

$$= (\$209{,}900 \div 63{,}700) + (\$341{,}878 \div 60{,}950)$$

$$= \$3.30 + \$5.61$$

$$= \underline{\underline{\$8.91}}$$

- Notice that the cost per equivalent unit for both direct materials and conversion costs has been rounded to the nearest cent. In this text, any rounding differences are assigned to the units transferred out in Step 5.
- Notice also that the average costing and FIFO costing methods use different numerators and denominators in Step 4. Average costing divides *total* cost by *total* equivalent units, whereas FIFO divides *current* costs by *current* equivalent units.

Assigning Costs

We have focused on accounting for units of productive output, analyzed the costs accumulated in the production process, department, or work cell, and computed the cost per equivalent unit for direct material costs and conversion costs. We now turn to the final step, which is to recognize the costs that are transferred out either to the next production process, department, or work cell or to the Finished Goods Inventory account (i.e., the cost of goods manufactured), as well as the costs that remain in the Work in Process Inventory account.

Step 5: Assign Costs to Cost of Goods Manufactured and Ending Inventory Using information from Steps 2 and 4, Step 5 of a process cost report assigns direct materials and conversion costs to the units transferred out and to the units still in process at the end of the period. As noted, any rounding issues that arise in completing Step 5 are included in units completed and transferred out. Milk Products completes Step 5 as described next.

Cost of Goods Manufactured and Transferred Out. As shown in Exhibit 4, the costs of the units completed and transferred out are assigned by multiplying the equivalent units for direct materials and conversion costs (accounted for in Step 2) by their respective cost per equivalent unit (computed in Step 4) and then totaling these assigned values.

$$\text{Cost of Goods Transferred Out} = (58{,}700 \times \$3.30) + (58{,}700 \times \$5.61) - \$362$$

$$= \$193{,}710 + \$329{,}307 - \$362$$

$$= \underline{\underline{\$522{,}655}}$$

In this case, because the costs per equivalent unit were rounded in Step 4, a rounding difference of $362 has been deducted from the total cost. The $522,655 of transferred costs will go to the Finished Goods Inventory account, since the goods are ready for sale. The entry resulting from doing the process cost report for February is:

	Dr.	Cr.
Finished Goods Inventory	522,655	
Work in Process Inventory		522,655

Ending Inventory. The costs of the units in ending work in process inventory are assigned in the same way as the costs of cost of goods manufactured and transferred out. In Exhibit 4, the total of costs assigned to ending inventory is computed as follows.

$$(5{,}000 \times \$3.30) + (2{,}250 \times \$5.61) = \$29{,}123$$

The $29,123 (rounded) will appear as the ending balance in the Work in Process Inventory account.

Recap of Work in Process Inventory Account As noted earlier, when a process cost report is complete, an account recap shows the effects of the report on the Work in Process Inventory account for the period. Exhibit 4 includes a cost recap and a unit recap of Milk Products' Work in Process Inventory account for February.

APPLY IT!

Pop Chewing Gum Company produces several flavors of bubble gum. Direct materials are blended at the beginning of the manufacturing process. No materials are lost in the process, so one kilogram of materials input produces one kilogram of bubble gum. Direct labor and overhead costs are incurred uniformly throughout the blending process.

- On June 30, 16,000 units (kilograms) were in process. All direct materials had been added, but the units were only 70 percent complete in regard to conversion costs in the prior period. Direct materials costs of $8,100 and conversion costs of $11,800 were attached to the beginning inventory.
- During July, 405,000 kilograms of materials were used at a cost of $202,500. Direct labor charges were $299,200, and overhead costs applied during July were $284,000.
- The ending work in process inventory was 21,600 kilograms. All direct materials have been added to those units, and 25 percent of the conversion costs have been assigned. Output from the Blending Department is transferred to the Packaging Department.

Required

1. Prepare a process cost report using the average costing method for the Blending Department for July.
2. Identify the amount that should be transferred out of the Work in Process Inventory account, state where those dollars should be transferred, and prepare the appropriate journal entry.

(Continued)

SOLUTION

1.

Pop Chewing Gum Company
Blending Department
Process Cost Report: Average Costing Method
For the Month Ended July 31

		Physical Units		Direct Materials Costs	% Incurred During Period		Conversion Costs	% Incurred During Period
Step 1: *Account for physical units.*	Beginning inventory (units started last period)	16,000						
	Units started this period	405,000						
	Units to be accounted for	421,000						
				Total Equivalent Units of Effort				
Step 2: *Account for equivalent units.*	Units completed and transferred out	399,400		399,400	100%		399,400	100%
	Ending inventory (units started but not completed this period)	21,600		21,600	100%		5,400	25%
	Units accounted for	421,000		421,000			404,800	
Step 3: *Account for costs.*		**Total Costs**						
	Beginning inventory	$ 19,900	=	$ 8,100		+	$ 11,800	
	Current costs	785,700	=	202,500		+	583,200	
	Total costs	$805,600		$210,600			$595,000	
Step 4: *Compute cost per equivalent unit.*	Total Costs / Equivalent Units			$210,600 / 421,000			$595,000 / 404,800	
	Cost per equivalent unit	$1.97	=	$0.50*		+	$1.47*	
				*Rounded to nearest cent				
Step 5: *Assign costs to cost of goods manufactured and ending inventory.*	Cost of goods manufactured and transferred out *(Add rounding of $44)*	$786,862	=	(399,400 × $0.50) +			(399,400 × $1.47)	
	Ending inventory	18,738	=	(21,600 × $0.50) +			(5,400 × $1.47)	
	Total costs	$805,600						

Work in Process Inventory Account: Cost Recap

Beg. bal.	19,900	Cost of goods manufactured and transferred out	786,862
Direct materials	202,500		
Conversion costs	583,200		
End. bal.	**18,738**		

Work in Process Inventory Account: Unit Recap

Beg. bal.	16,000	Units transferred out	399,400
Units started	405,000		
End. bal.	**21,600**		

2. The amount of $786,862 should be transferred to the Work in Process Inventory account of the Packaging Department.

Work in Process Inventory (Packaging Department)	786,862	
Work in Process Inventory (Blending Department)		786,862

TRY IT! SE7, SE8, SE9, SE10, E11A, E12A, E13A, E14A, E15A, E11B, E12B, E13B, E14B, E15B

SECTION 3

BUSINESS APPLICATIONS

.NESS
.ICATIONS
anning
erforming
valuating
ommunicating

EVANT
RNING OBJECTIVE

Explain how managers use a process costing m to produce business ts.

LO 6 The Management Process and the Process Costing System

As noted in the previous chapter, a product costing system provides managers with unit cost information, cost data for management decisions, and ending values for the Materials Inventory, Work in Process Inventory, and Finished Goods Inventory accounts. In this chapter, we focused on a process costing system, the product costing system used by managers at companies that make large amounts of similar products or liquid products. To use process costing, managers must understand product and cost flow patterns, equivalent production, and the preparation of process cost reports. Managers use process costing information in every stage of the management process.

- **Planning:** Managers use information about past and projected product costing and customer preferences to decide what a product should cost. After they have determined a target number of units to be sold, all product-related costs for that targeted number of units can be computed and used in the budget.
- **Performing:** During the period, managers control costs by tracking product and cost flows through their departments or processes and prepare process cost reports to assign production costs to the products manufactured.
- **Evaluating:** Managers evaluate performance by comparing targeted costs with actual costs. If costs have exceeded expectations, managers analyze why this has occurred and adjust their planning and decision-making strategies.
- **Communicating:** Managers use actual units and costs to value inventory on the balance sheet and cost of goods sold on the income statement. Managers are also interested in whether goals for product costs are being achieved.

Notice how managers use process costing throughout the management process to fulfill the management process of planning and forecasting operations, organizing and coordinating resources and data, and commanding and controlling the organization's resources, as illustrated in Exhibit 5.

Exhibit 5
The Management Process and the Process Costing System

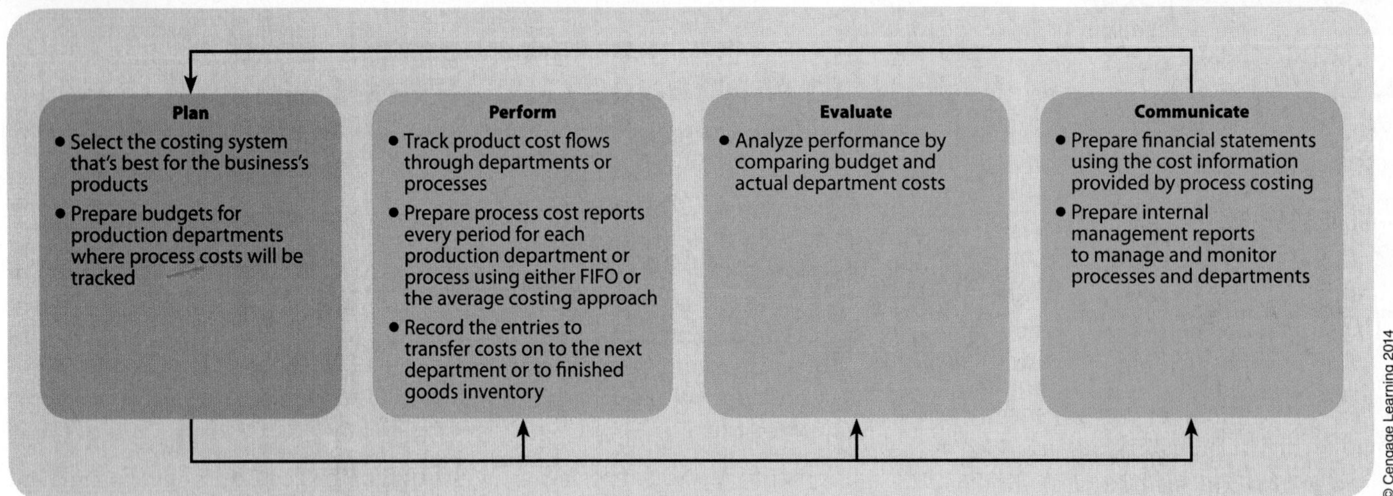

Plan
• Select the costing system that's best for the business's products
• Prepare budgets for production departments where process costs will be tracked
Perform
• Track product cost flows through departments or processes
• Prepare process cost reports every period for each production department or process using either FIFO or the average costing approach
• Record the entries to transfer costs on to the next department or to finished goods inventory
Evaluate
• Analyze performance by comparing budget and actual department costs
Communicate
• Prepare financial statements using the cost information provided by process costing
• Prepare internal management reports to manage and monitor processes and departments
© Cengage Learning 2014

APPLY IT!

Match the activities that follow with one of the stages in the management process.

a. Planning
b. Performing
c. Evaluating
d. Reporting

1. Track the flow of product costs
2 Prepare process cost reports
3. Record entries to transfer costs on to the next department or finished goods inventory
4. Select either the FIFO or weighted average method for process costing

SOLUTION

1. b
2. b
3. b
4. a

TriLevel Problem

Dean Foods

The beginning of this chapter focused on **Dean Foods**, a company known as a leader in the field of milk products. Complete the following requirements in order to answer the questions posed at the beginning of the chapter.

Section 1: Concepts

Why is a process costing system appropriate for Dean Foods to measure and recognize costs?

Section 2: Accounting Applications

How does a product costing system account for costs when identical products or services are produced?

A company like Dean Foods produces several flavors of milk, including chocolate milk. Assume that one of its plants produces chocolate milk. Two basic direct materials, milk and chocolate syrup, are combined by the Mixing Department to make gallons of chocolate milk. No materials are lost in the process, so one gallon of material input produces one gallon of chocolate milk. Direct labor and overhead costs are incurred uniformly throughout the mixing process. How does a product costing system account for costs when identical products like chocolate milk are produced?

Assume that 15,000 units of chocolate milk were in process at the beginning of the month. All direct materials had been added, but the units were only two-thirds complete in regard to conversion costs. Direct materials costs of $19,200 and conversion costs of $14,400 were attached to the beginning inventory.

During the month, 435,000 gallons of materials were used at a cost of $426,300. Direct labor charges were $100,000, and overhead costs applied during the month were $312,000. The ending work in process inventory was 50,000 gallons. All direct materials have now been added to those units, and 20 percent of the conversion costs have been assigned. Output from the Mixing Department has been transferred to the Packaging Department.

1. Using the FIFO costing method, prepare a process cost report for the Mixing Department for the month.
2. What amount should be transferred out of the Work in Process Inventory account, and to where should those dollars be transferred? Prepare the appropriate journal entry.
3. Using the average costing method, repeat requirement **1**.
4. Answer the questions in requirement **2** as they apply to the process cost report that you prepared in requirement **3**.

Section 3: Business Applications

How does a process costing system help managers organize and control costs and facilitate management decisions? To answer this question, match this chapter's manager responsibilities with when they occur within the management process.

a. Plan
b. Perform
c. Evaluate
d. Communicate

1. Track the flow of product costs
2. Compare actual and budgeted departmental costs
3. Prepare financial statements
4. Prepare process cost reports
5. Prepare budgets
6. Prepare internal management reports
7. Record entries to transfer costs on to the next department or finished goods inventory
8. Select the best product costing system

SOLUTION

Section 1: Concepts

Because the processing of milk and the production of dairy products involve a continuous flow of similar products, the process costing system is the most appropriate for a company like Dean Foods. Such a system *measures* costs by process, department, or work cell and assigns them to products as they pass through. Companies like Dean Foods can use either the FIFO method or the average costing method of process costing. The process cost report prepared at the end of each period *recognizes* the costs assigned to products completed and transferred out and to the products remaining in the process, department, or work cell. It provides the cost information for product revenues to be *matched* with the expenses required to generate them. A product costing system, like process costing, provides managers with unit cost information, cost data for management decisions, and ending values for the Materials Inventory, Work in Process, and Finished Goods Inventory accounts.

Section 2: Accounting Applications

1.

Mixing Department
Process Cost Report—FIFO Costing Method
For the Month

	Physical Units
Beginning inventory	15,000
Units started this period	435,000
Units to be accounted for	450,000

		Current Equivalent Units of Effort			
		Direct Materials Costs	**% Incurred During Period**	**Conversion Costs**	**% Incurred During Period**
Beginning inventory	15,000	—	0%	5,000	33%
Units started and completed	385,000	385,000	100%	385,000	100%
Ending inventory	50,000	50,000	100%	10,000	20%
Units accounted for	450,000	435,000		400,000	

	Total Costs				
Beginning inventory	$ 33,600	=	$ 19,200	+	$ 14,400
Current costs	838,300	=	426,300	+	412,000
Total costs	$871,900				
Current Costs / Equivalent Units			$426,300 / 435,000		$412,000 / 400,000
Cost per equivalent unit	$2.01	=	$0.98	+	$1.03
Cost of goods manufactured and transferred out:					
From beginning inventory	$ 33,600				
Current costs to complete	5,150	=	$0		(5,000 × $1.03)
Units started and completed	773,850	=	(385,000 × $0.98)	+	(385,000 × $1.03)
Cost of goods manufactured	$812,600				
Ending inventory	59,300	=	(50,000 × $0.98)	+	(10,000 × $1.03)
Total costs	$871,900				

2. The amount of $812,600 should be transferred to the Work in Process Inventory account of the Packaging Department.

Work in Process (Packaging Inventory Department)	812,600	
Work in Process (Mixing Inventory Department)		812,600

3.

Mixing Department
Process Cost Report—Average Costing Method
For the Month

	Physical Units					
Beginning inventory	15,000					
Units started this period	435,000					
Units to be accounted for	450,000					
		Total Equivalent Units of Effort				
		Direct Materials Costs	**% Incurred During Period**		**Conversion Costs**	**% Incurred During Period**
Units completed and transferred out	400,000	400,000	100%		400,000	100%
Ending inventory	50,000	50,000	100%		10,000	20%
Units accounted for	450,000	450,000			410,000	
	Total Costs					
Beginning inventory	$ 33,600	= $ 19,200		+	$ 14,400	
Current costs	838,300	= 426,300		+	412,000	
Total costs	$871,900	$445,500			$426,400	
Total Costs / Equivalent Units		$445,500 / 450,000			$426,400 / 410,000	
Cost per equivalent unit	$2.03	= $0.99		+	$1.04	
Cost of goods manufactured and transferred out	$812,000	= (400,000 × $0.99)		+	(400,000 × $1.04)	
Ending inventory	59,900	= (50,000 × $0.99)		+	(10,000 × $1.04)	
Total costs	$871,900					

4. The amount of $812,000 should be transferred to the Work in Process Inventory account of the Packaging Department.

Work in Process (Packaging Inventory Department)	812,000	
Work in Process (Mixing Inventory Department)		812,000

Section 3: Business Applications

1. b
2. c
3. d
4. b
5. a
6. d
7. b
8. a

Chapter Review

Describe a process costing system. 

A process costing system is used by companies that produce large amounts of similar products or liquid products or that have long, continuous production runs of identical products. Because these companies have a continuous production flow, it would be impractical for them to use a job order costing system, which tracks costs to a specific batch of products or a specific job order. A process costing system accumulates the costs of direct materials, direct labor, and overhead for each process, department, or work cell and assigns those costs to the products as they are produced during a particular period.

Relate the patterns of product flows to the cost flow methods in a process costing environment, and explain the role of the Work in Process Inventory accounts. LO 2

During production in a process costing environment, products flow in a first-in, first-out (FIFO) fashion through several processes, departments, or work cells. The process costing system accumulates their costs and passes them on to the next process, department, or work cell. A process cost report may assign costs by using the FIFO costing method, in which the costs assigned to the first products processed are the first costs transferred out, or the average costing method, which assigns an average cost to all products made during a period.

The Work in Process Inventory accounts are the focal point of a process costing system. Each production process, department, or work cell has its own Work in Process Inventory account to which costs are charged. A process cost report assigns the costs that have accumulated during the period to the units that have flowed out of the process, department, or work cell (the cost of goods transferred out) and to the units that are still in process (the cost of ending inventory).

Describe equivalent production, and compute equivalent units. LO 3

Equivalent production measures the equivalent number of whole units produced in an accounting period for each type of input. Equivalent units are computed from (1) units in the beginning work in process inventory and their percentage of completion, (2) units started and completed during the period, and (3) units in the ending work in process inventory and their percentage of completion. The computation of equivalent units differs depending on whether the FIFO method or the average costing method is used.

Prepare a process cost report using the FIFO costing method. LO 4

In a process cost report that uses the FIFO costing method, the costs assigned to the first products processed are the first costs transferred out. Preparing a process cost report involves five steps. Steps 1 and 2 account for the physical flow of products and compute the equivalent units of production. In Step 3, all direct materials costs and conversion costs for the current period are added to arrive at total costs. In Step 4, the cost per equivalent unit for both direct materials costs and conversion costs is found by dividing those costs by their respective equivalent units. In Step 5, costs are assigned to the units completed and transferred out during the period, as well as to the ending work in process inventory. These costs include the costs incurred in the preceding period and the conversion costs that were needed to complete those units during the current period. That amount is added to the total cost of producing all units started and completed during the period. The result is the total cost transferred out for the units completed during the period. Step 5 also assigns costs to units still in process at the end of the period by multiplying their direct materials costs and conversion costs by their respective equivalent units. The total equals the balance in the Work in Process Inventory account at the end of the period.

Prepare a process cost report using the average costing method. LO 5

The average costing method is an alternative method of accounting for production costs. A process costing report that uses the average costing method does not differentiate when work was done on inventory. The costs in the beginning inventory are averaged with the current period costs to compute the product unit costs. These unit costs are used to value the ending balance in Work in Process Inventory and the goods completed and transferred out of the process.

Explain how managers use a process costing system to produce business results. LO 6

The product costs provided by a process costing system play a key role in the management process. Managers use past and projected information about product costs to set selling prices and prepare budgets. Each day, managers use cost information to make decisions about controlling costs, the company's volume of activity, ensuring quality, and negotiating prices. They evaluate performance results by comparing targeted costs with actual costs. They use actual units produced and costs incurred to value inventory and the cost of goods sold. They also analyze internal reports that compare the organization's measures of actual and targeted performance to determine whether cost goals for products or services are being achieved.

Key Terms

average costing method 796 (LO2)
conversion costs 797 (LO3)
equivalent production 797 (LO3)
first-in, first-out (FIFO) costing method 795 (LO2)
process cost report 795 (LO2)
process costing system 794 (LO1)

Chapter Assignments

DISCUSSION QUESTIONS

LO 2, 3 **DQ1. CONCEPT ▶** Explain why equivalent units are a measure of production effort instead of a physical unit measure of performance.

LO 2, 4, 5 **DQ2. CONCEPT ▶** Does the concept of cost recognition underlie why a process cost report is prepared every period for each production department?

LO 4, 5 **DQ3. CONCEPT ▶** Why does the concept of cost measurement underlie the five steps in preparing a process cost report?

LO 4, 5 **DQ4. CONCEPT ▶** What is the primary cost measurement and cost recognition differences between the FIFO and average costing methods of preparing a process cost report?

LO 6 **DQ5. CONCEPT ▶ BUSINESS APPLICATION ▶** Why does process costing in the management process reinforce the concepts of cost recognition and cost measurement to produce business results?

SHORT EXERCISES

LO 1 **Accounting Concepts**

SE1. CONCEPT ▶Match the following statements about process costing with its associated accounting concept:

a. Cost measurement
b. Cost recognition
c. Matching concept

1. Because the processing of a continuous flow of similar products makes it difficult to track costs to individual units, the process costing system provides the cost information for product revenues to be measured against the expenses required to generate them. It provides managers with unit cost information, cost data for management decisions, and ending values for the Materials Inventory, Work in Process, and Finished Goods Inventory accounts.
2. Costs are tracked and accumulated by process, department, or work cell.
3. The report prepared at the end of each period assigns costs to products completed and transferred out and to the products remaining in the process, department, or work cell.

LO 1 **Process Costing Versus Job Order Costing**

SE2. Indicate whether each of the following is a characteristic of job order costing or process costing:

1. Several Work in Process Inventory accounts are used, one for each department or work cell in the process.
2. Costs are measured for each completed job.
3. Costs are grouped by process or department.
4. Costs are measured in terms of units completed in specific time periods.
5. Only one Work in Process Inventory account is used.
6. Costs are assigned to specific jobs or batches of product.

LO 2 **Process Costing and a Work in Process Inventory Account**

SE3. Pro Chemicals uses an automated mixing machine in its Mixing Department to combine three raw materials into a product called Trio. On average, each unit of Trio contains $3 of Material X, $6 of Material Y, $9 of Material Z, $2 of direct labor, and $10 of overhead. Total costs charged to the Mixing Department's Work in Process Inventory account during the month were $210,000. There were no units in beginning or ending work in process inventory. How many units were completed and transferred to finished goods inventory during the month?

LO 3 **Equivalent Production: FIFO Costing Method**

SE4. Pearl Glaze adds direct materials at the beginning of its production process and adds conversion costs uniformly throughout the process. Given the following information from Pearl's records for July and using Steps 1 and 2 of the FIFO costing method, compute the equivalent units of production:

Units in beginning inventory	3,000
Units started during the period	17,000
Units partially completed in prior period	2,500
Percentage of completion of ending work in process inventory	100% for direct materials; 70% for conversion costs
Percentage of completion of beginning inventory in prior period	100% for direct materials; 40% for conversion costs

LO 4 **Determining Unit Cost: FIFO Costing Method**

SE5. Using the information from **SE4** and the data that follow, compute the total cost per equivalent unit.

	Beginning Work in Process	Costs for the Period
Direct materials	$7,600	$20,400
Conversion costs	2,545	32,490

LO 4 **Assigning Costs: FIFO Costing Method**

SE6. Using the data in **SE4** and **SE5,** assign costs to the units transferred out and to the units in ending inventory for July.

LO 5 **Equivalent Production: Average Costing Method**

SE7. Using the same data as in **SE4** but Steps 1 and 2 of the average costing method, compute the equivalent units of production for the month.

LO 5 **Determining Unit Cost: Average Costing Method**

SE8. Using the average costing method and the information from **SE4, SE5,** and **SE7,** compute the total cost per equivalent unit.

LO 5 **Assigning Costs: Average Costing Method**

SE9. Using the data in **SE4, SE5, SE7,** and **SE8** and assuming that Pearl Glaze uses the average costing method, assign costs to the units completed and transferred out and to the units in ending inventory for July.

LO 5 **Equivalent Production: Average Costing Method**

SE10. Real Company adds direct materials at the beginning of its production process and adds conversion costs uniformly throughout the process. Given the following information from Real's records for July, compute the current period's equivalent units of production for direct materials and conversion costs using the average costing method.

Units in beginning inventory	2,000
Units started during the period	13,000
Units partially completed in prior period	500
Percentage of completion of beginning inventory	100% for direct materials; 40% for conversion costs
Percentage of completion of ending work in process inventory	100% for direct materials; 70% for conversion costs

EXERCISES: SET A

LO 1 **Process Costing Versus Job Order Costing**

E1A. Indicate whether the manufacturer of each of the following products should use a job order costing system or a process costing system to accumulate product costs:

1. paint
2. tailor-made tuxedo
3. soft drinks
4. soy milk
5. cups printed with your school insignia
6. water slide for a theme park
7. plastic
8. posters for a concert

LO 2 **Use of Process Costing Information**

E2A. ACCOUNTING CONNECTION ▶ Mom's Bakery makes a variety of baked goods for distribution to grocery stores in the area. The company uses a standard manufacturing process for all items except special-order birthday cakes. It currently uses a process costing system. The owner of the company has the following questions:

1. Did the cost of making special-order birthday cakes exceed the cost budgeted for this month?
2. How much does it cost to make one cheesecake?
3. What is the value of the cupcake inventory at the end of May?
4. What were the costs of the cookies sold during May?
5. At what price should Mom's Bakery sell its famous sweet rolls to the grocery store chains?
6. Were the planned production costs of $3,000 for making pies in May exceeded?

Which of these questions can be answered using information from a process costing system? Which can be best answered using information from a job order costing system? Explain your answers.

LO 2 **Work in Process Inventory Accounts in Process Costing Systems**

E3A. Chemical, Inc., which uses a process costing system, makes a chemical used as a preservative. The manufacturing process involves Departments A and B. The company had the following total costs and unit costs for completed production last month, when it manufactured 10,000 pounds of the chemical. Neither Department A nor Department B had any beginning or ending work in process inventories:

(Continued)

	Total Cost	Unit Cost
Department A:		
Direct materials	$ 9,000	$0.90
Direct labor	2,600	0.26
Overhead	1.300	0.13
Total costs	$12,900	$1.29
Department B:		
Direct materials	$ 3,000	$0.30
Direct labor	700	0.07
Overhead	1,000	0.10
Total costs	$ 4,700	$0.47
Totals	$17,600	$1.76

1. How many Work in Process Inventory accounts would Chemical, Inc., use?
2. What dollar amount of the chemical's production cost was transferred from Department A to Department B last month?
3. What dollar amount was transferred from Department B to the Finished Goods Inventory account?
4. What dollar amount is useful in determining a selling price for 1 pound of the chemical?

LO 3

Equivalent Production: FIFO Costing Method

E4A. Brick Company produces bricks. During its first 12 months, it put 600,000 bricks into production and completed and transferred 580,000 bricks to finished goods inventory. The remaining bricks were still in process at the end of the year and were 60 percent complete.

The company's process costing system adds all direct materials costs at the beginning of the production process; conversion costs are incurred uniformly throughout the process. Using the FIFO costing method, compute the equivalent units of production for direct materials and conversion costs for the company's first year, which ended December 31.

LO 3

Equivalent Production: FIFO Costing Method

E5A. Suds Enterprises makes Perfecto Shampoo for professional hair stylists. On July 31, it had 5,000 liters of shampoo in process that were 80 percent complete in regard to conversion costs and 100 percent complete in regard to direct materials costs. During August, it put 210,000 liters of direct materials into production. Data for Work in Process Inventory on August 31 were as follows: shampoo, 10,000 liters; stage of completion, 60 percent for conversion costs and 100 percent for direct materials. Using the FIFO costing method, compute the equivalent units of production for direct materials and conversion costs for the month.

LO 3

Equivalent Production: FIFO Costing Method

E6A. Eco Savers Corporation produces wood pulp that is used in making paper. The data that follow pertain to the company's production of pulp during September.

		Percentage Complete	
	Tons	Direct Materials	Conversion Costs
Work in process, Aug. 31	50,000	100%	60%
Placed into production	250,000	—	—
Work in process, Sept. 30	80,000	100%	40%

Compute the equivalent units of production for direct materials and conversion costs for September using the FIFO costing method.

LO 4 **Work in Process Inventory Accounts: Total Unit Cost**

E7A. Scientists at Amazing Laboratories, Inc., have just perfected Sparkle, a liquid substance that dissolves silver tarnish. The substance, which is generated by a complex process involving five departments, is very expensive. Cost and equivalent unit data for the latest week follow (units are in ounces).

	Direct Materials		Conversion Costs	
Dept.	Cost	Equivalent Units	Cost	Equivalent Units
A	$12,000	2,000	$33,825	4,100
B	21,835	1,985	14,070	1,005
C	24,102	1,030	20,972	2,140
D	—	—	22,000	2,000
E	—	—	15,560	1,945

Compute the unit cost for each department and the total unit cost of producing 1 ounce of Sparkle.

LO 4 **Determining Unit Cost: FIFO Costing Method**

E8A. Cookware, Inc., manufactures sets of heavy-duty pans. It has just completed production for August. At the beginning of August, its Work in Process Inventory account showed direct materials costs of $31,000 and conversion costs of $29,000. The cost of direct materials used in August was $280,000; conversion costs were $120,000. During the month, the company started and completed 10,000 sets. For August, a total of 14,000 equivalent sets for direct materials and 12,000 equivalent sets for conversion costs have been computed. Using the FIFO costing method, determine the cost per equivalent set for August.

LO 4 **Assigning Costs: FIFO Costing Method**

E9A. The Bakery produces cupcakes. It uses a process costing system. In March, its beginning inventory was 450 units, which were 100 percent complete for direct materials costs and 10 percent complete for conversion costs. The cost of beginning inventory was $655. Units started and completed during the month totaled 14,200. Ending inventory was 410 units, which were 100 percent complete for direct materials costs and 70 percent complete for conversion costs. Costs per equivalent unit for March were $1.40 for direct materials costs and $1.00 for conversion costs. Using the FIFO costing method, compute the cost of goods transferred to the Finished Goods Inventory account, the cost remaining in the Work in Process Inventory account, and the total costs to be accounted for.

LO 4 **Process Cost Report: FIFO Costing Method**

E10A. Toy Truck Corporation produces children's toy trucks using a continuous production process. All direct materials are added at the beginning of the process. In November, the beginning work in process inventory was 420 units, which were 50 percent complete; the ending balance was 400 units, which were 70 percent complete.

During November, 15,000 units were started into production. The Work in Process Inventory account had a beginning balance of $937 for direct materials costs and $370 for conversion costs. In the course of the month, $35,300 of direct materials were added to the process, and $31,689 of conversion costs were assigned. Using the FIFO costing method, prepare a process cost report that computes the equivalent units for November, the product unit cost for the toys, and the ending balance in the Work in Process Inventory account. (Round cost per equivalent unit to the nearest cent.)

LO 5

Equivalent Production: Average Costing Method

E11A. Using the data given for Brick Company in **E4A** and assuming that the company uses the average costing method, compute the equivalent units of production for direct materials and conversion costs for the company's first year ended December 31.

LO 5

Equivalent Production: Average Costing Method

E12A. Using the data given for Suds Enterprises in **E5A** and assuming that the company uses the average costing method, compute the equivalent units of production for direct materials and conversion costs for August.

LO 5

Equivalent Production: Average Costing Method

E13A. Using the data given for Eco Savers Corporation in **E6A** and assuming that the company uses the average costing method, compute the equivalent units of production for direct materials and conversion costs for September.

LO 5

Determining Unit Cost: Average Costing Method

E14A. Using the data given for Cookware, Inc., in **E8A** and assuming that the company uses the average costing method, determine the cost per equivalent set for August. Assume equivalent sets are 15,550 for direct materials costs and 14,900 for conversion costs.

LO 5

Process Cost Report: Average Costing Method

E15A. Using the data given for Toy Truck Corporation in **E10A** and assuming that the company uses the average costing method, prepare a process cost report that computes the equivalent units for November, the product unit cost for the toys, and the ending balance in the Work in Process Inventory account. (Round cost per equivalent unit to the nearest cent.)

EXERCISES: SET B

Visit the textbook companion website at www.cengagebrain.com to access Exercise Set B for this chapter.

PROBLEMS

LO 4

Process Costing: FIFO Costing Method

✔ 1: Total cost of goods manufactured and transferred: $125,013

P1. Juice Extracts Company produces a line of fruit extracts for home use in making wine, jams and jellies, pies, and meat sauces. Fruits enter the production process in pounds, and the product emerges in quarts (1 pound of input equals 1 quart of output). On May 31, 4,250 units were in process. All direct materials had been added, and the units were 70 percent complete for conversion costs. Direct materials costs of $4,607 and conversion costs of $3,535 were attached to the units in beginning work in process inventory. During June, 61,300 pounds of fruit were added at a cost of $71,108. Direct labor for the month totaled $19,760, and overhead costs applied were $31,375. On June 30, 3,400 units remained in process. All direct materials for these units had been added, and 50 percent of conversion costs had been incurred.

REQUIRED

1. Using the FIFO costing method, prepare a process cost report for June.
2. From the information in the process cost report, identify the amount that should be transferred out of the Work in Process Inventory account, and state where those dollars should be transferred.

LO 4

✔ 3: August total cost of goods manufactured and transferred: $120,737

Process Costing: One Process and Two Time Periods—FIFO Costing Method

P2. Clean Laboratories produces biodegradable liquid detergents that leave no soap film. The production process has been automated, so the product can now be produced in one operation instead of in a series of heating, mixing, and cooling operations. All direct materials are added at the beginning of the process, and conversion costs are incurred uniformly throughout the process. Operating data for July and August follow.

	July	August
Beginning work in process inventory:		
Units (pounds)	2,300	3,050
Direct materials	$4,699	?*
Conversion costs	$1,219	?*
Production during the period:		
Units started (pounds)	31,500	32,800
Direct materials	$65,520	$66,912
Conversion costs	$54,213	$54,774
Ending work in process inventory:		
Units (pounds)	3,050	3,600

*From calculations at end of July.

The beginning work in process inventory was 30 percent complete for conversion costs. The ending work in process inventory for July was 60 percent complete; for August, it was 50 percent complete. Assume that the loss from spoilage and evaporation was negligible.

REQUIRED

1. Using the FIFO costing method, prepare a process cost report for July.
2. From the information in the process cost report, identify the amount that should be transferred out of the Work in Process Inventory account, and state where those dollars should be transferred.
3. Repeat requirements 1 and 2 for August.

LO 5

SPREADSHEET

✔ 1: May total cost of goods manufactured and transferred: $120,100
✔ 1: June total cost of goods manufactured and transferred: $185,280

Process Costing: Average Costing Method and Two Time Periods

P3. Top Corporation produces a line of beverage lids. The production process has been automated, so the product can now be produced in one operation rather than in the three operations that were needed before the company purchased the automated machinery. All direct materials are added at the beginning of the process, and conversion costs are incurred uniformly throughout the process. Operating data for May and June follow.

	May	June
Beginning work in process inventory:		
Units (May: 40% complete)	220,000	?
Direct materials	$3,440	$400
Conversion costs	$6,480	$420
Production during the month:		
Units started	24,000,000	31,000,000
Direct materials	$45,000	$93,200
Conversion costs	$66,000	$92,796
Ending work in process inventory:		
Units (May: 70% complete; June: 60% complete)	200,000	320,000

1. Using the average costing method, prepare process cost reports for May and June. (Round unit costs to three decimal places.)

(Continued)

2. From the information in the process cost report for May, identify the amount that should be transferred out of the Work in Process Inventory account, and state where those dollars should be transferred.
3. **ACCOUNTING CONNECTION ▶** Compare the product costing results for June with the results for May. What is the most significant change? What are some of the possible causes of this change?

LO 5

Process Costing: Average Costing Method

✔ 1: Total cost of goods manufactured and transferred: $552,720

P4. Energy Products, Inc., makes high-vitamin, calorie-packed wafers that are popular among professional athletes because they supply quick energy. The company produces the wafers in a continuous flow, and it uses a process costing system based on the average costing method. It recently purchased several automated machines so that the wafers can be produced in a single department. All direct materials are added at the beginning of the process. The costs for the machine operators' labor and production-related overhead are incurred uniformly throughout the process.

In February, the company put a total of 231,200 liters of direct materials into production at a cost of $294,780. Two liters of direct materials were used to produce one unit of output (one unit = 144 wafers). Direct labor costs for February were $60,530, and overhead was $181,590. The beginning work in process inventory for February was 14,000 units, which were 100 percent complete for direct materials and 20 percent complete for conversion costs. The total cost of those units was $55,000, $48,660 of which was assigned to the cost of direct materials. The ending work in process inventory of 12,000 units was fully complete for direct materials but only 30 percent complete for conversion costs.

REQUIRED

1. Using the average costing method and assuming no loss due to spoilage, prepare a process cost report for February.
2. From the information in the process cost report, identify the amount that should be transferred out of the Work in Process Inventory account, and state where those dollars should be transferred.

LO 4, 5

Process Costing: FIFO Costing and Average Costing Methods

✔ 1: Total cost of goods manufactured and transferred: $82,280

P5. Goofy Industries specializes in making Go, a high-moisture, low-alkaline wax used to protect and preserve snowboards. The company began producing a new, improved brand of Go on January 1. Materials are introduced at the beginning of the production process. During January, 15,300 pounds were used at a cost of $46,665. Direct labor of $17,136 and overhead costs of $25,704 were incurred uniformly throughout the month. By January 31, 13,600 pounds of Go had been completed and transferred to the finished goods inventory (1 pound of input equals 1 pound of output). Since no spoilage occurred, the leftover materials remained in production and were 40 percent complete on average.

REQUIRED

1. Using the FIFO costing method, prepare a process cost report for January.
2. From the information in the process cost report, identify the amount that should be transferred out of the Work in Process Inventory account, and state where those dollars should be transferred.
3. Repeat requirements **1** and **2** using the average costing method.

ALTERNATE PROBLEMS

LO 4

Process Costing: FIFO Costing Method

✔ 1: Total cost of goods manufactured: $627,790

P6. Canned fruits and vegetables are the main products made by Yummy Foods, Inc. All direct materials are added at the beginning of the Mixing Department's process. When the ingredients have been mixed, they go to the Cooking Department. There the mixture is heated to 100° Celsius and simmered for 20 minutes. When cooled, the mixture goes to the Canning Department for final processing. Throughout the operations, direct labor and overhead costs are incurred uniformly. No direct materials are added in the Cooking Department. Cost data and other information for the Mixing Department for January are as follows.

Production Cost Data	Direct Materials	Conversion Costs
Mixing Department:		
Beginning inventory	$ 28,560	$ 5,230
Current period costs	450,000	181,200
Work in process inventory:		
Beginning inventory (40% complete in prior period)	5,000 liters	
Ending inventory (60% complete)	6,000 liters	
Unit production data:		
Units started during January	90,000 liters	
Units transferred out during January	89,000 liters	

Assume that no spoilage or evaporation loss took place during January.

REQUIRED

1. Using the FIFO costing method, prepare a process cost report for the Mixing Department for January.
2. **ACCOUNTING CONNECTION ▶** Explain how the analysis for the Cooking Department will differ from the analysis for the Mixing Department.

LO 4

SPREADSHEET

✔ 1: April total cost of goods manufactured and transferred: $353,368
✔ 3: May total cost of goods manufactured and transferred: $390,668

Process Costing: One Process and Two Time Periods—FIFO Costing Method

P7. Doover Company produces organic honey, which it sells to health food stores and restaurants. The company owns thousands of beehives. No direct materials other than honey are used. The production operation is a simple one. Impure honey is added at the beginning of the process and flows through a series of filters, leading to a pure finished product. Costs of labor and overhead are incurred uniformly throughout the filtering process. Production data for April and May follow.

	April	May
Beginning work in process inventory:		
Units (liters)	7,100	12,400
Direct materials	$2,480	?*
Conversion costs	$5,110	?*
Production during the period:		
Units started (liters)	288,000	310,000
Direct materials	$100,800	$117,800
Conversion costs	$251,550	$277,281
Ending work in process inventory:		
Units (liters)	12,400	16,900

*From calculations at end of April.

The beginning work in process inventory for April was 80 percent complete for conversion costs, and ending work in process inventory was 20 percent complete. The ending work in process inventory for May was 30 percent complete for conversion costs. Assume no loss from spoilage or evaporation.

REQUIRED

1. Using the FIFO method, prepare a process cost report for April.
2. From the information in the process cost report, identify the amount that should be transferred out of the Work in Process Inventory account, and state where those dollars should be transferred.
3. Repeat requirements **1** and **2** for May.

LO 5

✔ 1: July total cost of goods manufactured and transferred: $168,000
✔ 1: August total cost of goods manufactured and transferred: $162,750

Process Costing: Average Costing Method and Two Time Periods

P8. Box Corporation produces a line of beverage boxes. The production process has been automated, so the product can now be produced in one operation rather than in the three operations that were needed before the company purchased the automated machinery. All direct materials are added at the beginning of the process, and conversion costs are incurred uniformly throughout the process. Operating data for July and August follow.

	July	August
Beginning work in process inventory:		
Units (July: 20% complete)	20,000	?
Direct materials	$20,000	$6,000
Conversion costs	$30,000	$6,000
Production during the month:		
Units started	70,000	90,000
Direct materials	$34,000	$59,000
Conversion costs	$96,000	$130,800
Ending work in process inventory:		
Units (July: 40% complete; August: 60% complete)	10,000	25,000

1. Using the average costing method, prepare process cost reports for July and August.
2. From the information in the process cost report for July, identify the amount that should be transferred out of the Work in Process Inventory account, and state where those dollars should be transferred.
3. **ACCOUNTING CONNECTION ▶** Compare the product costing results for August with the results for July. What is the most significant change? What are some of the possible causes of this change?

LO 5

✔ 1: Total cost of goods manufactured and transferred: $5,463,040

Process Costing: Average Costing Method

P9. Many of the products made by Plastics Company are standard telephone replacement parts that require long production runs and are produced continuously. A unit for Plastics is a box of parts. During April, direct materials for 25,250 units were put into production. The total cost of direct materials used during April was $2,273,000. Direct labor costs totaled $1,135,000, and overhead was $2,043,000. The beginning work in process inventory contained 1,600 units, which were 100 percent complete for direct materials costs and 60 percent complete for conversion costs. Costs attached to the units in beginning inventory totaled $232,515, which included $143,500 of direct materials costs. At the end of the month, 1,250 units were in ending inventory; all direct materials had been added, and the units were 70 percent complete for conversion costs.

REQUIRED

1. Using the average costing method and assuming no loss due to spoilage, prepare a process cost report for April.
2. From the information in the process cost report, identify the amount that should be transferred out of the Work in Process Inventory account, and state where those dollars should be transferred.

LO 4, 5

SPREADSHEET

✔ 1: FIFO total cost of goods manufactured and transferred: $140,892
✔ 3: Average costing total cost of goods manufactured and transferred: $140,892

Process Costing: FIFO Costing and Average Costing Methods

P10. Sunny Company manufactures and sells several different kinds of soft drinks. Direct materials (sugar syrup and artificial flavor) are added at the beginning of production in the Mixing Department. Direct labor and overhead costs are applied to products throughout the process. For August, beginning inventory for the citrus flavor was 2,400 gallons, 80 percent complete. Ending inventory was 3,600 gallons, 50 percent complete. Production data show 240,000 gallons started during August. A total of 238,800 gallons was completed and transferred to the Bottling Department. Beginning inventory costs were \$576 for direct materials and \$672 for conversion costs. Current period costs were \$57,600 for direct materials and \$83,538 for conversion costs.

REQUIRED

1. Using the FIFO costing method, prepare a process cost report for the Mixing Department for August.
2. From the information in the process cost report, identify the amount that should be transferred out of the Work in Process Inventory account, and state where those dollars should be transferred.
3. Repeat requirements **1** and **2** using the average costing method.

CASES

LO **1, 6**

Conceptual Understanding: Process Costing Systems

C1. For more than 60 years, **Dow Chemical Company** has made and sold a tasteless, odorless, and calorie-free substance called Methocel. When heated, this liquid plastic (methyl cellulose) has the unusual characteristic (for plastics) of becoming a gel that resembles cooked egg whites. It is used in over 400 food products, including gravies, soups, and puddings. It was also used as wampa drool in *The Empire Strikes Back* and dinosaur sneeze in *Jurassic Park*. What kind of costing system is most appropriate for the manufacture of Methocel? Why is this system most appropriate? Describe the system, and include in the description a general explanation of how costs are determined.

LO **1, 2, 6**

Ethical Dilemma: Continuing Professional Education

C2. BUSINESS APPLICATION ▶ Paula Woodward is the head of the Information Systems Department at Mo Manufacturing Company. Roland Randolph, the company's controller, is meeting with her to discuss changes in data gathering that relate to the company's new flexible manufacturing system. Woodward opens the conversation by saying, "Roland, the old job order costing methods just will not work with the new flexible manufacturing system. The new system is based on continuous product flow, not batch processing. We need to change to a process costing system for both data gathering and product costing. Otherwise, our product costs will be way off, and it will affect our pricing decisions. I found out about this at a professional seminar I attended last month. You should have been there."

Randolph responds, "Job order costing has provided accurate information for this product line for more than 15 years. Why should we change just because we've purchased a new machine? We've purchased several machines for this line over the years. And as for your seminar, I don't need to learn about costing methods. I was exposed to them all when I studied management accounting in the 1970s."

Is Randolph's behavior ethical? If not, what has he done wrong? What can Woodward do if Randolph continues to refuse to update the product costing system?

LO **3, 4, 6**

SPREADSHEET

Interpreting Managerial Reports: Analysis of Product Cost

C3. BUSINESS APPLICATION ▶ Road Tire Corporation makes several lines of automobile and truck tires. The company operates in a competitive marketplace, so it relies heavily on cost data from its FIFO-based process costing system. It uses that information to set prices for its most competitive tires. The company's radial line has lost some of its market share during each of the past four years. Management believes that price breaks allowed by the company's three biggest competitors are the main reason for the decline in sales.

The company controller has been asked to review the product costing information that supports pricing decisions on the radial line. In preparing her report, she collected the following data for last year, the most recent full year of operations:

(Continued)

	Units	Dollars
Equivalent units:		
Direct materials	84,200	
Conversion costs	82,800	
Manufacturing costs:		
Direct materials		$1,978,700
Direct labor		800,400
Overhead		1,600,800
Unit cost data:		
Direct materials		23.50
Conversion costs		29.00
Work in process inventory:		
Beginning (70% complete)	4,200	
Ending (30% complete)	3,800	

Units started and completed last year totaled 80,400. Attached to the beginning Work in Process Inventory account were direct materials costs of $123,660 and conversion costs of $57,010. A review of the conversion costs revealed, however, an error in the production account. The correct conversion cost being charged to the production account should have been $2,129,616 instead of $2,401,200. This resulted in overly high overhead costs being charged to the production account.

The radial has been selling for $92 per tire. This price was based on last year's unit data plus a 75 percent markup to cover operating costs and profit. The company's three main competitors have been charging about $87 for a tire of comparable quality. The company's process costing system adds all direct materials at the beginning of the process, and conversion costs are incurred uniformly throughout the process.

1. Identify what inaccuracies in costs, inventories, and selling prices result from the company's cost-charging error.
2. Prepare a revised process cost report for 2014. (Round total costs to whole dollars.)
3. What should have been the minimum selling price per tire this year?
4. Suggest ways of preventing such errors in the future.

LO 3, 4, 6

Interpreting Managerial Reports: Setting a Selling Price

C4. BUSINESS APPLICATION ▶ For the past four years, three companies have dominated the soft drink industry, holding a combined 85 percent of market share. Won Cola, Inc., ranks second nationally in soft drink sales. Its management is thinking about introducing a new low-calorie drink called Uncalorie Cola.

Won soft drinks are processed in a single department. All ingredients are added at the beginning of the process. At the end of the process, the beverage is poured into bottles that cost $0.24 per case produced. Direct labor and overhead costs are applied uniformly throughout the process.

Corporate controller Adam Daneen believes that costs for the new cola will be very much like those for the company's Cola Plus drink. Last year, he collected the data that follow about Cola Plus.

	Units*	Costs
Work in process inventory:		
January 1**	2,200	
Direct materials costs		$ 2,080
Conversion costs		620
December 31***	2,000	
Direct materials costs		1,880
Conversion costs		600
Units started during year	458,500	
Costs for year:		
Liquid materials added		430,990
Direct labor and overhead		229,400
Bottles		110,088

* Each unit is a 24-bottle case.
** 50% complete.
*** 60% complete.

The company's variable general administrative and selling costs are $1.10 per unit. Fixed administrative and selling costs are assigned to products at the rate of $0.50 per unit. Each of Won Cola's two main competitors is already marketing a diet cola. Company A's product sells for $4.10 per unit; Company B's, for $4.05. All costs are expected to increase by 10 percent in the next three years. Won Cola tries to earn a profit of at least 15 percent on the total unit cost.

1. What factors should Won Cola, Inc., consider in setting a unit selling price for a case of Uncalorie Cola?
2. Using the FIFO costing method, compute (a) equivalent units for direct materials, cases of bottles, and conversion costs; (b) the total production cost per unit; and (c) the total cost per unit of Cola Plus for the year.
3. What is the expected unit cost of Uncalorie Cola for the year? (Round unit costs to the nearest cent.)
4. Recommend a unit selling price range for Uncalorie Cola, and give the reason(s) for your choice. (Round to the nearest cent.)

LO **2, 3, 4, 6**

Business Communications: Using the Process Costing System

C5. BUSINESS APPLICATION ▶ You are the production manager for Breakfast Grain Corporation, a manufacturer of four cereal products. The company's best-selling product is Sugaroos, a sugar-coated puffed rice cereal. Yesterday, Clark Winslow, the controller, reported that the production cost for each box of Sugaroos has increased approximately 22 percent in the last four months. Because the company is unable to increase the selling price for a box of Sugaroos, the increased production costs will reduce profits significantly.

Today, you received a memo from Gilbert Rom, the company president, asking you to review your production process to identify inefficiencies or waste that can be eliminated. Once you have completed your analysis, you are to write a memo presenting your findings and suggesting ways to reduce or eliminate the problems. The president will use your information during a meeting with the top management team in ten days.

You are aware of previous problems in the Baking Department and the Packaging Department. Winslow has provided you with process cost reports for the two departments. He has also given you the following detailed summary of the cost per equivalent unit for a box of Sugaroos cereal:

(Continued)

	April	May	June	July
Baking Department:				
Direct materials	$1.25	$1.26	$1.24	$1.25
Direct labor	0.50	0.61	0.85	0.90
Overhead	0.25	0.31	0.34	0.40
Department totals	$2.00	$2.18	$2.43	$2.55
Packaging Department:				
Direct materials	$0.35	$0.34	$0.33	$0.33
Direct labor	0.05	0.05	0.04	0.06
Overhead	0.10	0.16	0.15	0.12
Department totals	$0.50	$0.55	$0.52	$0.51
Total cost per equivalent unit	$2.50	$2.73	$2.95	$3.06

1. In preparation for writing your memo, answer the following questions:
   a. For whom are you preparing the memo? Does this affect the length of the memo? Explain.
   b. Why are you preparing the memo?
   c. What actions should you take to gather information for the memo? What information is needed? Is the information that Winslow provided sufficient for analysis and reporting?
   d. When is the memo due? What can be done to provide accurate, reliable, and timely information?
2. Based on your analysis of the information that Winslow provided, where is the main problem in the production process?
3. Prepare an outline of the sections you would want in your memo.

Continuing Case: Cookie Company

C6. In this segment of our continuing case, you are considering whether process costing is more appropriate for your cookie company than job order costing. List reasons why your company may choose to use process costing instead of job order costing.

CHAPTER 18
Value-Based Systems: Activity-Based Costing and Lean Accounting

BUSINESS INSIGHT
La-Z-Boy, Inc.

La-Z-Boy, Inc., makes thousands of built-to-order sofas and chairs each week at its U.S. plants and generally delivers them in less than three weeks after customers have placed their orders with a retailer. Because of the efficiency with which it assembles and delivers its products, La-Z-Boy has a competitive advantage over its competitors. Critical factors in the company's success are the speed of its supply chain and its use of value-based systems.

1. **CONCEPT** ▶ *What underlying accounting concepts support the use of value-based systems like activity-based management and lean accounting?*

2. **ACCOUNTING APPLICATION** ▶ *How can activity-based costing and lean operations help businesses like La-Z-Boy improve business processes and eliminate waste?*

3. **BUSINESS APPLICATION** ▶ *How can managers of companies like La-Z-Boy plan to remain competitive in a challenging business environment?*

LEARNING OBJECTIVES

LO 1 **Describe value-based systems, and discuss their relationship to the supply chain and the value chain.**

LO 2 **Define *activity-based costing*, and explain how a cost hierarchy and a bill of activities are used.**

LO 3 **Define the elements of a lean operation, and identify the changes in inventory management that result when a firm adopts its just-in-time operating philosophy.**

LO 4 **Define and apply *backflush costing*, and compare the cost flows in traditional and backflush costing.**

LO 5 **Identify the management tools used for continuous improvement, and compare ABM and lean operations.**

SECTION 1 CONCEPTS

CONCEPTS
- Relevance
- Reliability

RELEVANT LEARNING OBJECTIVE

LO1 Describe value-based systems, and discuss their relationship to the supply chain and the value chain.

LO1 Concepts Underlying Value-Based Systems

Managers operating in volatile business environments that are strongly influenced by customer demands realize that value-based systems, instead of traditional cost-based systems, provide the *relevant* information they need. The information has more relevance because it is predictive and directly relates to the decisions made. **Value-based systems** provide customer-related, activity-based information. They focus on eliminating waste as companies produce and deliver quality products and services. *Reliability* also is important as it assures users that the value-based information is complete, neutral, and free from material error. It is all the information needed for a reliable decision. Managers can use value-based information reliably to compare the value created by products or services with the **full product cost**, which includes not only the costs of direct materials and direct labor, but also the costs of all production and nonproduction activities required to satisfy the customer. For example, the full product cost of a **La-Z-Boy** sofa includes the cost of the shredded foam and upholstery, as well as the costs of taking the sales order, processing the order, packaging and shipping the sofa, and providing subsequent customer service for warranty work.

Value Chain Analysis

Each step in making a product or delivering a service is a link in a chain that adds value to the product or service. This sequence of activities inside the organization that adds value to a company's product or service is known as the **value chain** (illustrated in Exhibit 1). The steps that add value to a product or service—which range from research and development to customer service—are known as **primary processes**. The sequence of primary processes varies, depending on such factors as the size of the company and the types of products or services offered.

The value chain also includes **support services**, such as legal services, human resources, information technology, and management accounting. These services facilitate the primary processes by providing business infrastructure but do not add value to the final product or service. Their roles are critical, however, to making the primary processes as efficient and effective as possible.

Value chain analysis allows a company to focus on its core competencies. A **core competency** is the activity that a company does best. It is what gives a company an advantage over its competitors. For example, **Wal-Mart**'s core competency is achieving the lowest prices, whereas **The Four Seasons Hotel** is known for providing exceptional guest service.

A common result of value chain analysis is outsourcing, which can also be of benefit to a business. **Outsourcing** is the engagement of other companies to perform a process or service in the value chain that is not among an organization's core competencies. For instance, **Wal-Mart** outsources its inventory management to its vendors, who monitor and stock Wal-Mart's stores and warehouses.

Supply Chains

Managers see their organization's internal value chain as part of a larger system. This larger system is the **supply chain** (or the *supply network*)—the path that leads from the suppliers of the materials from which a product is made to the final customer. The supply chain includes both suppliers and suppliers' suppliers, and customers and

Exhibit 1
The Value Chain in a Furniture Company

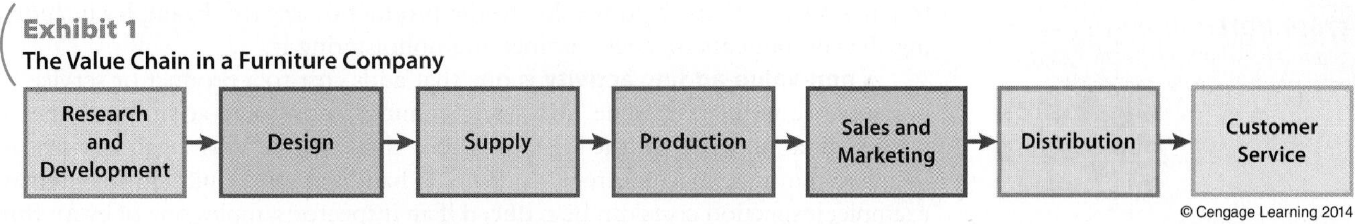

customers' customers. It links business to business to business and ultimately to the final consumer.

As Exhibit 2 shows, in the supply chain for a furniture company like **La-Z-Boy**, a farmer supplies cotton to the upholstery manufacturer, which supplies upholstery to the furniture manufacturer. The manufacturer supplies furniture to furniture stores, which in turn supply furniture to the final consumers. Each organization in this supply chain is a customer of an earlier supplier, and each has its own value chain.

Exhibit 2
The Supply Chain in a Furniture Company

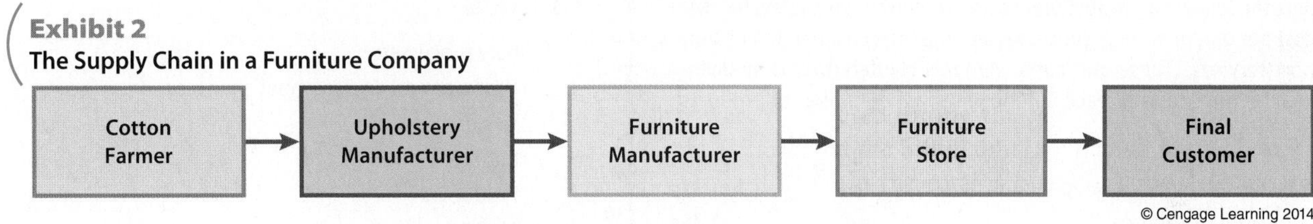

Using Information from Value Chains and Supply Chains

Understanding value chains and supply chains gives managers a better grasp of their company's internal and external operations. Managers who understand how their company's value-adding activities fit into their suppliers' and customers' value chains can see their company's role in the overall process of creating and delivering products or services. When organizations work cooperatively with others in their supply chain, they can develop new processes that reduce the total costs of their products or services. For example, **La-Z-Boy** places computers for online order entry in its sofa kiosks located in shopping malls. The computers streamline order processing and make the orders more accurate. Even though La-Z-Boy incurs the cost of the computers, the total cost of making and delivering furniture decreases because the cost of order processing decreases.

Each company in a supply chain is a customer of an earlier supplier. An upholstery company, for example, would be a customer of a cotton farmer and fabric supplier. Its customers might include furniture manufacturers or automobile companies.

Process Value Analysis

To improve the *relevance* and *reliability* of information for decision making, managers use **process value analysis (PVA)** to identify and link all the activities involved in the value chain. It analyzes business processes by relating activities to the events that prompt those activities and to the resources that the activities consume. PVA forces managers to look critically at all phases of their operations. PVA improves cost traceability and results in significantly more complete accurate product costs, which in turn improves management decisions and increases profitability. By using PVA to identify non-value-adding activities, companies can improve the relevance and reliability of their data to reduce their costs and redirect their resources to value-adding activities.

Value-Adding and Non-Value-Adding Activities

A **value-adding activity** is one that adds value to a product or service as perceived by the customer. In other words, if customers are willing

STUDY NOTE: *Customer perspective determines whether an activity adds value to a product or service.*

to pay for the activity, it adds value to the product or service. Examples include designing the components of a new recliner and upholstering it.

A **non-value-adding activity** is one that adds cost to a product or service but does not increase its market value. Managers eliminate non-value-adding activities that are not essential and reduce the costs of those that are, such as legal services, management accounting, machine repair, materials handling, and building maintenance. For example, inspection costs can be reduced if an inspector samples one of every three bolts of upholstery fabric received from a supplier rather than inspecting every one. If the supplier is a reliable source of high-quality upholstery, such a reduction in inspection activity is appropriate.

APPLY IT!

Sort the following product unit costs to determine the relevant total cost per unit of primary processes and the total cost per unit of support services. (These unit costs were reliably determined by dividing the total costs of each component by the number of products produced.)

Research and development	$ 1.25
Human resources	1.35
Design	0.15
Supply	1.10
Legal services	0.40
Production	4.00
Marketing	0.80
Distribution	0.90
Customer service	0.65
Information systems	0.75
Management accounting	0.10
Total cost per unit	$11.45

SOLUTION

Primary processes:	
Research and development	$1.25
Design	0.15
Supply	1.10
Production	4.00
Marketing	0.80
Distribution	0.90
Customer service	0.65
Total cost per unit	$8.85
Support services:	
Human resources	$1.35
Legal services	0.40
Information systems	0.75
Management accounting	0.10
Total cost per unit	$2.60

TRY IT! SE1, SE2, SE3, E1A, E2A, E3A, E4A, E5A, E1B, E2B, E3B, E4B, E5B

SECTION 2

ACCOUNTING APPLICATIONS

:OUNTING APPLICATIONS

- :lassify activities using a :ost hierarchy
- 'repare a bill of activities
- Jnderstand the elements of a lean operation
- \pply backflush costing

.EVANT
RNING OBJECTIVE

2 Define *activity-based costing,* and explain how a : hierarchy and a bill of vities are used.

3 Define the elements of a lean operation, and ntify the changes in inventory nagement that result when a adopts its just-in-time rating philosophy.

4 Define and apply *backflush costing,* and pare the cost flows in litional and backflush :ing.

LO 2 Activity-Based Management

Activity-based management (ABM) identifies all major operating activities, determines the resources consumed by each activity and the cause of the resource usage, and categorizes the activities as adding value to a product or service or not adding value. ABM focuses on reducing or eliminating non-value-adding activities.

Because it provides financial and performance information at the activity level, ABM is useful both for strategic planning and for making tactical and operational decisions about business segments, such as product lines, market segments, and customers. It also helps managers eliminate waste and inefficiencies and redirect resources to activities that add value to the product or service.

Activity-Based Costing

Activity-based costing (ABC) is the tool used in an ABM environment to assign activity costs to cost objects. As access to value chain data has improved, managers have refined the procedures for assigning costs fairly to determine unit costs. Traditional methods of allocating overhead costs to products use such cost drivers as direct labor hours, direct labor costs, or machine hours and one overhead rate. More than 20 years ago, organizations began realizing that these methods did not assign overhead costs accurately and that the resulting inaccuracy in unit costs was causing poor pricing decisions and poor control of overhead costs. In their search for more accurate product costing, many organizations embraced activity-based costing.

Activity-based costing (ABC) calculates a more accurate product cost than traditional methods. It does so by categorizing all indirect costs by activity, tracing the indirect costs to those activities, and assigning those costs to products or services using a cost driver related to the cause of the cost. In other words, ABC reflects the cause-and-effect relationships between costs and individual processes, products, services, or customers.

ABC improves the accuracy in allocating activity-driven costs to cost objects (i.e., products or services). To implement ABC, managers complete the following steps:

- **Step 1**. Identify and classify each activity.
- **Step 2**. Estimate the cost of resources for each activity.
- **Step 3**. Identify a cost driver for each activity, and estimate the quantity of each cost driver.
- **Step 4**. Calculate an activity cost rate for each activity.
- **Step 5**. Assign costs to cost objects based on the level of activity required to make the product or provide the service.

While ABC gives managers greater control over the costs they manage, it has limitations, including the following:

- High measurement costs of collecting accurate data from many activities instead of using just one overhead account may make ABC too costly.
- Some costs are difficult to assign to a specific activity or cost object since they benefit the business in general (e.g., the president's salary) and should not be arbitrarily allocated.
- ABC allocations may add undue complexity to controlling costs.

The Cost Hierarchy and the Bill of Activities

Two tools used in implementing ABC are cost hierarchy and the bill of activities.

Cost Hierarchy A **cost hierarchy** is a framework for classifying activities according to the level at which their costs are incurred. In a manufacturing company, the cost hierarchy typically has four levels, as shown in Exhibit 3.

- **Unit-level activities** are performed each time a unit is produced and are generally considered variable costs. For example, when a furniture manufacturer like **La-Z-Boy** installs a recliner mechanism in a chair, unit-level activities involve the direct material cost of the recliner mechanism, materials handling, and the direct labor cost incurred with connecting the mechanism to the chair frame. Because each chair contains only one mechanism, these activities have a direct correlation to the number of chairs produced.
- **Batch-level activities** are performed each time a batch or production run of goods is produced. Examples of batch-level activities include setup and moving and inspecting mechanisms for the production run of a certain style of furniture. These activities vary with the number of batches prepared or production runs completed.
- **Product-level activities** are performed to support a particular product line. Examples include implementing design, engineering, or marketing changes for a particular brand of product. These activities vary with the number of brands or product designs a company has.
- **Facility-level activities** are performed to support a facility's general manufacturing process and are generally fixed costs. Examples for a furniture manufacturer include maintaining, lighting, securing, and insuring the factory. These activities are generally a fixed amount for a certain time period.

Note that the frequency of activities varies across levels and that the cost hierarchy includes both value-adding and non-value-adding activities.

Exhibit 3
Sample Activities in Cost Hierarchies

	Unit Level Activities performed each time a unit is produced	**Examples** • Install mechanism • Test mechanism
	Batch Level Activities performed each time a batch or production run of goods is produced	**Examples** • Set up installation process • Move mechanisms • Inspect mechanisms
	Product Level Activities performed to support a particular product line	**Example** • Redesign installation process
	Facility Level Activities performed to support a facility's general manufacturing process	**Examples** • Provide facility maintenance • Provide lighting • Provide security

Service organizations can also use a cost hierarchy to group their activities. The four levels typically are the unit level, the batch level, the service level, and the operations level.

***STUDY NOTE:** A bill of activities summarizes costs relating to a product or service and supports the calculation of the product or service unit cost.*

Bill of Activities A **bill of activities** is a list of activities and related costs that is used to compute the costs assigned to activities and the product unit cost. More complex bills of activities group activities into activity pools and include activity cost rates and the cost driver levels used to assign costs to cost objects. A bill of activities may be used as the primary document or as a supporting schedule to calculate the product unit cost in both job order and process costing systems and in both manufacturing and service businesses. Exhibit 4 shows a bill of activities for a furniture manufacturer completing an order for 100 chairs.

Exhibit 4
Bill of Activities

Sample Furniture Corporation
Bill of Activities
Chair Order 1.1.12

Activity	Activity Cost Rate	Cost Driver Level	Activity Cost
Unit level:			
Parts production	$40 per machine hour	20 machine hours	$ 800
Assembly	$35 per direct labor hour	10 direct labor hours	350
Packaging and shipping	$10 per unit	100 units	1,000
Batch level:			
Setup	$100 per setup	5 setups	500
Product level:			
Product design	$60 per engineering hour	9 engineering hours	540
Product simulation	$30 per testing hour	3 testing hours	90
Facility level:			
Building occupancy	200% of assembly labor cost	$350 assembly labor cost	700
Total activity costs assigned to order			$3,980
Total units			÷ 100
Activity costs per unit (total activity costs ÷ total units)			$39.80
Cost summary:			
Direct materials			$2,000
Purchased parts			1,000
Activity costs			3,980
Total cost of order			$6,980
Product unit cost (total cost of order ÷ 100 units)			$69.80

Bean Bag Convertibles, Inc., has received an order for 100 bean bag sofa convertibles from Furniture Town, LLC. A partially complete bill of activities for that order follows. Fill in the missing data.

Bean Bag Convertibles, Inc.
Bill of Activities
Furniture Town, LLC, Order

Activity	Activity Cost Rate	Cost Driver Level	Activity Cost
Unit level:			
Parts production	$50 per machine hour	5 machine hours	$?
Assembly	$30 per DLH	10 DLH	?
Packing	$3.50 per unit	100 units	?
Batch level:			
Work setup	$25 per setup	4 setups	?
Product level:			
Product design	$160 per design hour	2 design hours	?
Facility level:			
Building occupancy	200% of assembly labor cost	?	?
Total activity costs assigned to job			$?
Total job units			100
Activity costs per unit (total activity costs ÷ total units)			$?
Cost summary:			
Direct materials			$1,000
Purchased parts			500
Activity costs			?
Total cost of order			$?
Product unit cost (total cost ÷ 100 units)			$?

SOLUTION

Bean Bag Convertibles, Inc.
Bill of Activities
Furniture Town, LLC Order

Activity	Activity Cost Rate	Cost Driver Level	Activity Cost
Unit level:			
Parts production	$50 per machine hour	5 machine hours	$ 250
Assembly	$30 per DLH	10 DLH	300
Packing	$3.50 per unit	100 units	350
Batch level:			
Work setup	$25 per setup	4 setups	100
Product level:			
Product design	$160 per design hour	2 design hours	320
Facility level:			
Building occupancy	200% of assembly labor cost	$300	600
Total activity costs assigned to job			$1,920
Total job units			÷ 100
Activity costs per unit (total activity costs ÷ total units)			$19.20
Cost summary:			
Direct materials			$1,000
Purchased parts			500
Activity costs			1,920
Total cost of order			$3,420
Product unit cost (total cost ÷ 100 units)			$34.20

TRY IT! SE4, SE5, E6A, E7A, E8A, E6B, E7B, E8B

LO3 The New Operating Environment and Lean Operations

A **lean operation** focuses on eliminating waste in an organization and on what a customer is willing to pay for. Lean operations emphasize waste that can be eliminated by management analysis of the actions of workers and machines in the process of making products and services.

STUDY NOTE: *ABM and lean operations focus on value-adding activities—not costs—to increase income.*

To achieve lean operations, a company must redesign its operating systems, plant layout, and basic management methods to conform to several basic concepts:

- Simple is better.
- The quality of the product or service is critical from product design to customer satisfaction.
- The work environment must emphasize continuous improvement.
- Maintaining large inventories wastes resources and may hide poor work.
- Activities or functions that do not add value to a product or service should be eliminated or reduced.
- Goods should be produced only when needed.
- Workers must be multiskilled and must participate in eliminating waste.
- Building and maintaining long-term relationships with suppliers is important.

Application of these lean elements creates a lean operation throughout the company's value chain and guides all employees' work. Piecemeal attempts at lean operations have proved disastrous when the implementation focused on a few lean tools and methodologies instead of understanding how to think lean throughout the organization.

STUDY NOTE: *Traditional environments emphasize* functional *departments that tend to group similar activities together (e.g., repairs and maintenance).*

Just-in-Time (JIT)

Managers determined that changes in how inventory was processed traditionally were necessary because:

- Large amounts of an organization's space and money were tied up in inventory.
- The source of poor-quality materials, products, or services was hard to pinpoint.
- The number of non-value-adding activities was growing.
- Accounting for the manufacturing process was becoming ever more complex.

Just-in-time (JIT) is one of the key strategies of a lean operation to reorganize production activities and manage inventory. In a lean operation, the **just-in-time (JIT) operating philosophy** requires that all resources—materials, personnel, and facilities—be acquired and used only as needed to create value for customers. A JIT environment reveals waste and eliminates it by using the principles discussed in the sections that follow.

Business Perspective
The Evolution to Lean Operations

- Eli Whitney perfected the concept of interchangeable parts in 1799, when he produced 10,000 muskets for the U.S. Army for the low price of $13.40 per musket.
- In the late 1890s, Frederick W. Taylor used his ideas of scientific management to standardize work through time studies.
- In the early twentieth century, Frank and Lillian Gilbreth (parents of the authors of *Cheaper by the Dozen*) focused on eliminating waste by studying worker motivation and using motion studies and process charting.
- Starting in 1910, Henry Ford and Charles E. Sorensen arranged all the elements of manufacturing into a continuous system called the *production line*.
- After World War II, Taiichi Ohno and Shigeo Shingo recognized the importance of inventory management, and they perfected the Toyota production system, from which lean operations developed.[1]

Minimum Inventory Levels In the traditional manufacturing environment, parts, materials, and supplies are purchased far in advance and stored until the production department needs them. In contrast, in a JIT environment, materials and parts are purchased and received only when they are needed. The JIT approach lowers costs by reducing the space needed for inventory storage, the amount of materials handling, and the amount of inventory obsolescence. It also reduces the need for inventory control facilities, personnel, and recordkeeping. In addition, it significantly decreases the amount of work in process inventory and the amount of working capital tied up in all inventories.

STUDY NOTE: *Pull-through production represents a change in concept. Instead of producing goods in anticipation of customers' needs, customers' orders trigger the production process.*

Pull-Through Production In **pull-through production**, a customer's order triggers the purchase of materials and the scheduling of production for the products that have been ordered. In contrast, with the **push-through production** method used in traditional manufacturing operations, products are manufactured in long production runs and stored in anticipation of customers' orders. With pull-through production, the size of a customer's order determines the size of a production run, and the company purchases materials and parts as needed. Inventory levels are kept low and machines must be set up more frequently as different jobs enter production.

Quick Setup and Flexible Work Cells By placing machines in more efficient locations and standardizing setups, setup time can be minimized in a JIT environment.

STUDY NOTE: *In the JIT environment, normal operating activities—setup, production, and maintenance—still take place. But the timing of those activities is altered to promote smoother operations and to minimize downtime.*

In a traditional factory layout, similar machines are grouped together, forming functional departments. Products are routed through these departments in sequence, so that all necessary operations are completed in order. This process can take several days or weeks, depending on the size and complexity of the job. By changing the factory layout so that all the machines needed for sequential processing are placed together, JIT may cut the manufacturing time of a product from days to hours, or from weeks to days. The new cluster of machinery forms a flexible **work cell**, an autonomous production line that can perform all required operations efficiently and continuously. The flexible work cell handles a "family of products"—that is, products of similar shape or size. Product families require minimal setup changes as workers move from one job to the next. The more flexible the work cell is, the greater its potential to minimize total production time.

A Multiskilled Workforce In flexible work cells, one worker may be required to operate several types of machines simultaneously. The worker may have to set up and retool the machines and even perform routine maintenance on them. Under a JIT operating philosophy, multiskilled workers have been very effective in contributing to high levels of productivity.

STUDY NOTE: *Although separate inspection costs are reduced in a JIT operating environment, some additional time is added to production because the machine operator is now performing the inspection function.*

High Levels of Product Quality A JIT environment results in high-quality products, since high-quality direct materials are used and inspections are made throughout the production process. In a JIT environment, inspection as a separate step does not add value to a product, so inspection is incorporated into ongoing operations. A JIT machine operator inspects the products as they pass through the manufacturing process. If the operator detects a flaw, he or she shuts down the work cell to prevent the production of similarly flawed products while the cause of the problem is being determined. The operator either fixes the problem or helps others find a way to correct it. This integrated inspection procedure, combined with high-quality materials, produces high-quality finished goods.

Effective Preventive Maintenance When a company rearranges its machinery into flexible work cells, each machine becomes an integral part of its cell. If one machine breaks down, the entire work cell stops functioning, and the product cannot easily be routed to another machine while the malfunctioning machine is being repaired. Continuous JIT operations therefore require an effective system of preventive maintenance. Preventing machine breakdowns is considered more important and more cost effective than keeping machines running continuously. Machine operators are trained to perform minor repairs when they detect problems. Machines are serviced regularly—much as

Business Perspective
Lean Operations Improve Hospital Safety and Efficiency

Many hospitals around the country use lean tools to enhance laboratory performance when drawing and processing blood samples, administering patient medications, or supplying sterile IV equipment to operating rooms. Staff participate in value stream mapping to optimize work flows, kaizen (meaning suggest improvements for) different processes to achieve rapid operations, and use JIT principles when managing inventory.

automobiles are—to help guarantee continued operation. The machine operator conducts routine maintenance during downtime periods between orders.

Continuous Improvement of the Work Environment

A JIT operating philosophy fosters loyalty among workers, who are likely to see themselves as part of a team that is deeply involved in the production process. Machine operators must have the skills to run several types of machines, detect defective products, suggest measures to correct problems, and maintain the machinery within their work cells. In addition, each worker is encouraged to suggest improvements to the production process. In Japanese, this is called **kaizen**, meaning "good change." Companies with a JIT operating philosophy receive thousands of employee suggestions and implement a high percentage of them, and they reward workers for suggestions that improve the process. Such an environment fosters workers' initiative and benefits the company.

Accounting for Product Costs in a JIT Operating Environment

When a firm like **La-Z-Boy** shifts to lean operations and adopts a JIT operating philosophy, the changes in the operations will affect how costs are determined and what measures are used to monitor performance. The work cells and the goal of reducing or eliminating non-value-adding activities change the way costs are classified and assigned.

Classifying Costs The traditional production process can be divided into five time frames:

- **Processing time:** The actual amount of time spent working on a product
- **Inspection time:** The time spent looking for product flaws or reworking defective units
- **Moving time:** The time spent moving a product from one operation or department to another
- **Queue time:** The time a product spends waiting to be worked on once it arrives at the next operation or department
- **Storage time:** The time a product spends in materials inventory, work in process inventory, or finished goods inventory

In product costing under JIT, costs associated with processing time are relevant, but costs associated with inspection, moving, queue, and storage time should be reduced or eliminated because they do not add value to the product.

Assigning Costs In a JIT operating environment, managers focus on **throughput time**, the time it takes to move a product through the entire production process. Sophisticated computer monitoring of the work cells allows many costs to be traced directly to the cells in which products are manufactured. As Exhibit 5 shows, several costs that in a traditional environment are treated as indirect costs and applied to products using an overhead rate are treated as the direct costs of a JIT work cell.

- The costs of repairs and maintenance, materials handling, operating supplies, utilities, employee benefits, and indirect labor and supervision can be traced directly to work cells as they are incurred.
- Depreciation charges on machinery are based on units of output, not on time, so depreciation can be charged directly to work cells based on the number of units produced.
- Building occupancy costs, insurance premiums, and property taxes remain indirect costs and must be assigned to the work cells.

Exhibit 5
Direct and Indirect Costs in Traditional and JIT Environments

	Costs in a Traditional Environment	Costs in a JIT Environment
Direct materials	Direct	Direct to work cell
Direct labor	Direct	Direct to work cell
Repairs and maintenance	Indirect	Direct to work cell
Materials handling	Indirect	Direct to work cell
Operating supplies	Indirect	Direct to work cell
Utilities costs	Indirect	Direct to work cell
Supervision	Indirect	Direct to work cell
Depreciation—machinery	Indirect	Direct to work cell
Depreciation—plant	Indirect	Indirect
Supporting service functions	Indirect	Mostly direct to work cell
Building occupancy	Indirect	Indirect
Insurance and taxes	Indirect	Indirect
President's salary	Indirect	Indirect

APPLY IT!

The cost categories in the following list are typical of a furniture manufacturer like Bean Bag Convertibles, Inc. Identify each cost as direct or indirect, assuming that it was incurred in (1) a traditional manufacturing setting and (2) a JIT environment.

a. Direct materials
b. Direct labor
c. Supervisory salaries
d. Electrical power
e. Operating supplies
f. Purchased parts
g. Employee benefits
h. Indirect labor
i. Insurance and taxes, plant

SOLUTION

	1. Traditional Setting	2. JIT Setting
a. Direct materials	Direct	Direct
b. Direct labor	Direct	Direct
c. Supervisory salaries	Indirect	Direct
d. Electrical power	Indirect	Direct
e. Operating supplies	Indirect	Direct
f. Purchased parts	Direct	Direct
g. Employee benefits	Indirect	Direct
h. Indirect labor	Indirect	Direct
i. Insurance and taxes—plant	Indirect	Indirect

TRY IT! SE6, SE9, E10A, E11A, E10B, E11B

LO4 Backflush Costing

We have focused on how managers can trim waste from operations. However, they can also reduce waste in other areas, including the accounting process. Because a lean operation reduces labor costs, the accounting system can combine the costs of direct labor and overhead into the single category of conversion costs. Also, because materials arrive just in time to be used in the production process, there is little reason to maintain a separate Materials Inventory account. Thus, by simplifying cost flows through the accounting records, it is possible to reduce the time it takes to record and account for the costs of the manufacturing process.

Cost Flows in Traditional and Backflush Costing

STUDY NOTE: *Backflush costing eliminates the need to make journal entries during the period to track cost flows through the production process.*

A lean organization can also streamline its accounting process by using backflush costing. In **backflush costing**, all product costs are first accumulated in the Cost of Goods Sold account. At the end of the period, they are "flushed back," or worked backward, into the appropriate inventory accounts. By having all product costs flow straight to a final destination and working back to determine the proper balances for the inventory accounts, this method saves recording time. As shown in Exhibit 6, it eliminates the need to record several transactions that must be recorded in traditional operating environments.

Exhibit 6
Comparison of Cost Flows in Traditional and Backflush Costing

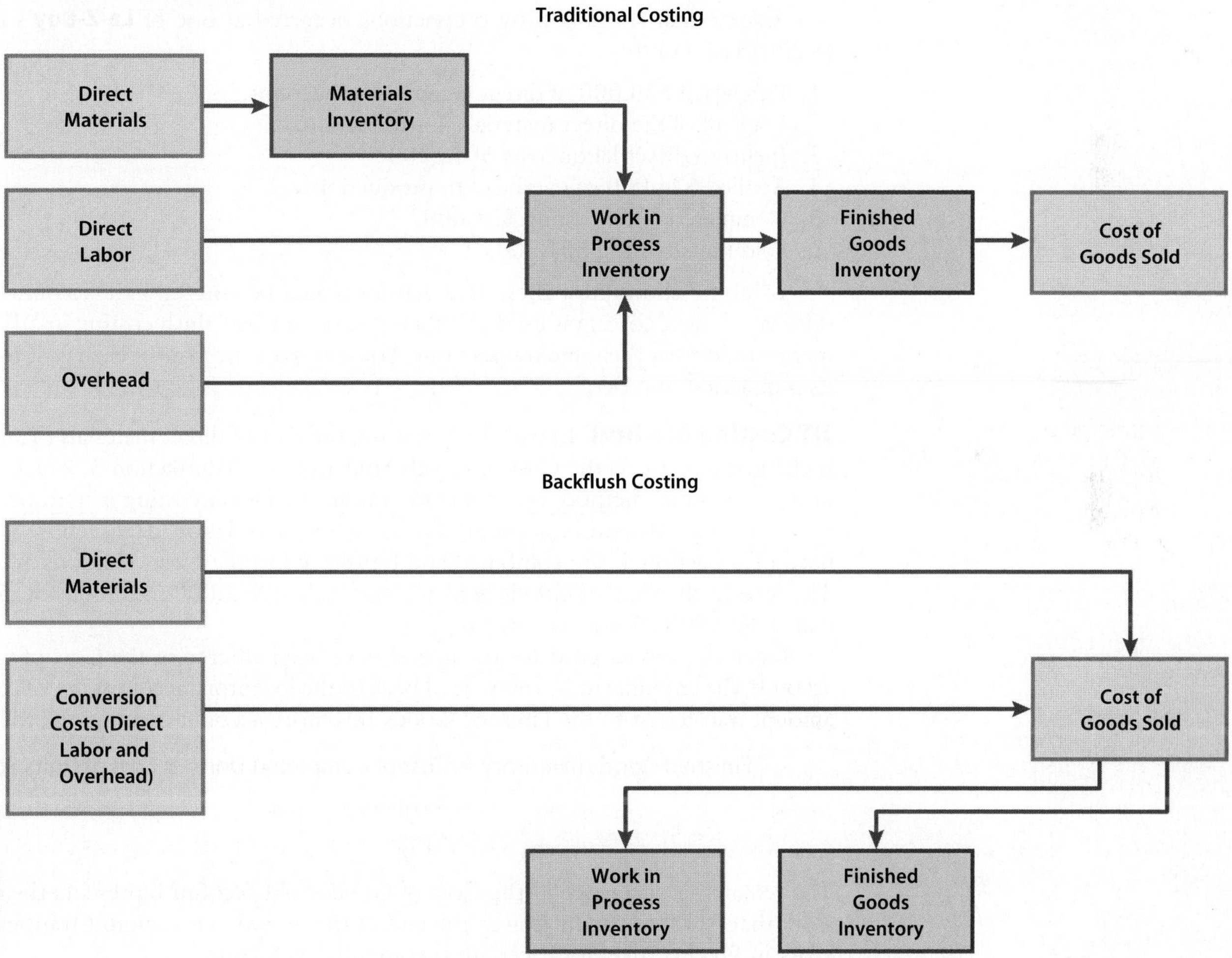

Cost flows differ depending on whether a company is using a traditional costing method or backflush costing.

Traditional Costing Method When a traditional costing method is used:

- Direct materials costs are entered into the Materials Inventory account upon arrival at the factory.
- Direct materials costs flow into the Work in Process Inventory account as materials are requisitioned into production. When direct labor is used, its costs are added to

the Work in Process Inventory account. Overhead is applied to production using a base like direct labor hours, machine hours, or number of units produced and is added to the other costs in the Work in Process Inventory account.

- The costs of the finished units are transferred to the Finished Goods Inventory account at the end of the manufacturing process. When the units are sold, their costs are transferred to the Cost of Goods Sold account.

Backflush Costing Method When the backflush costing method is used:

- Direct materials arrive just in time to be placed into production. The direct materials costs and the **conversion costs** (direct labor and overhead) are immediately charged to the Cost of Goods Sold account.
- The costs of goods in work in process inventory and in finished goods inventory are determined at the end of the period, and those costs are flushed back to the Work in Process Inventory account and the Finished Goods Inventory account. Once those costs have been flushed back, the Cost of Goods Sold account contains only the costs of units completed and sold during the period.

STUDY NOTE: *In backflush costing, entries to the Work in Process Inventory and Finished Goods Inventory accounts are made at the end of the period.*

Assume that the following transactions occurred at one of **La-Z-Boy**'s production facilities last month:

1. Purchased \$20,000 of direct materials on account.
2. Used all of the direct materials in production.
3. Incurred direct labor costs of \$8,000.
4. Applied \$24,000 of overhead to production.
5. Completed units costing \$51,600.
6. Sold units costing \$51,500.

Exhibit 7 shows how these transactions would be entered in T accounts when traditional product costing is used and then shows how backflush costing in a JIT environment would treat the same transactions. You can trace the flow of each cost by following its transaction number.

JIT Costing Method In backflush costing, the cost of direct materials (Transaction 1) is charged directly to the Cost of Goods Sold account. Transaction 2, which is included in the traditional method, is not included when backflush costing is used because there is no Materials Inventory account. The costs of direct labor (Transaction 3) and overhead (Transaction 4) are combined and transferred to the Cost of Goods Sold account. The total in the Cost of Goods Sold account is then \$52,000 (\$20,000 for direct materials + \$32,000 for conversion costs).

Once all product costs for the period have been entered in the Cost of Goods Sold account, the amounts to be transferred back to the inventory accounts are calculated. The amount transferred to the Finished Goods Inventory account is computed as follows.

$$\begin{aligned}\text{Finished Goods Inventory} &= \text{Cost of Completed Units} - \text{Cost of Units Sold}\\ &= \$51{,}600 - \$51{,}500\\ &= \$100\end{aligned}$$

The remaining difference in the Cost of Goods Sold account represents the cost of the work that is still in production at the end of the period. The amount transferred to the Work in Process Inventory account is computed as follows.

$$\begin{aligned}\text{Work in Process Inventory} &= \text{Costs Charged to Cost of Goods Sold} - \text{Cost of Completed Units}\\ &= (\$20{,}000 + \$8{,}000 + \$24{,}000) - \$51{,}600\\ &= \$400\end{aligned}$$

The ending balance in the Cost of Goods Sold account, \$51,500, is the same as the ending balance when traditional costing is used. The difference is that backflush costing uses fewer accounts and avoids recording several transactions.

Exhibit 7
Comparison of Cost Flows Through T Accounts with Traditional and Backflush Costing

Traditional Costing

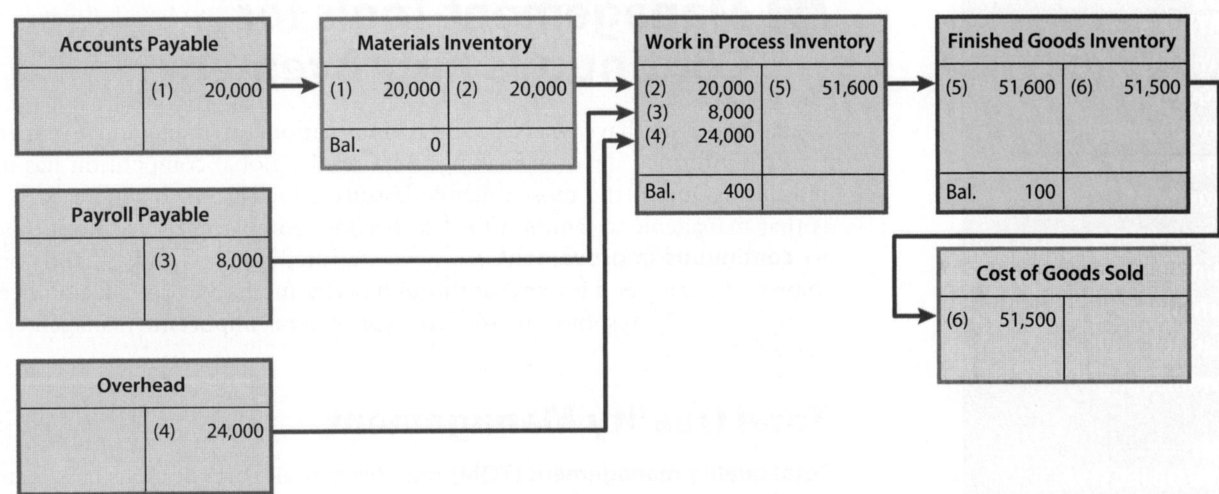

Backflush Costing

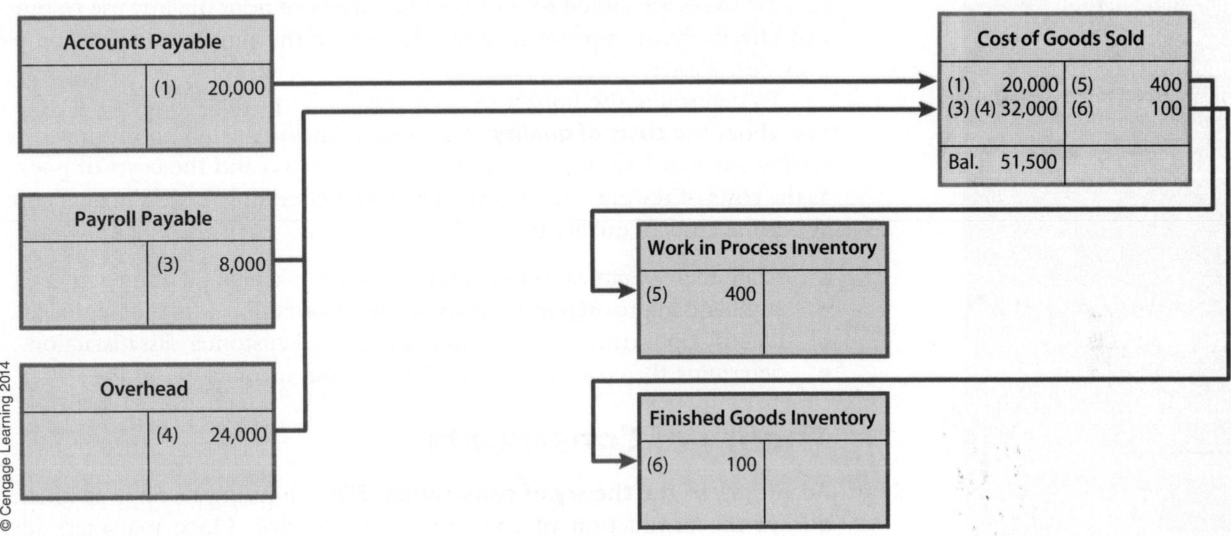

APPLY IT!

For work done during August, Bean Bag Convertibles incurred direct materials costs of $123,450 and conversion costs of $265,200. The company employs a just-in-time operating environment and backflush costing.

At the end of August, the Work in Process Inventory account had been assigned $980 of costs, and the ending balance of the Finished Goods Inventory account was $1,290. There were no beginning inventory balances.

1. How much was charged to the Cost of Goods Sold account during August?
2. What was the ending balance of the Cost of Goods Sold account?

SOLUTION

1. $123,450 + $265,200 = $388,650
2. $388,650 − $980 − $1,290 = $386,380

TRY IT! SE7, E12A, E13A, E12B, E13B

SECTION 3

BUSINESS APPLICATIONS

BUSINESS APPLICATIONS

- Total quality management
- Theory of constraints
- Activity-based management
- Lean accounting
- Planning
- Performing
- Evaluating
- Communicating

RELEVANT LEARNING OBJECTIVE

LO 5 Identify the management tools used for continuous improvement, and compare ABM and lean operations.

LO 5 Management Tools for Continuous Improvement

Today managers have ready access to international markets and to current information for informed decision making. As a result, global competition has increased significantly. One of the most valuable lessons gained from this increase in competition is that management cannot afford to become complacent. Organizations that adhere to **continuous improvement** are never satisfied with what is. They constantly seek improved quality and lower cost through better methods, products, services, processes, or resources. In response to this concept, several important management tools have emerged.

Total Quality Management

Total quality management (TQM) requires that all parts of a business focus on quality. TQM's goal is the improved quality of products or services and the work environment. Workers are empowered to make operating decisions that improve quality in both areas. All employees are tasked to spot possible causes of poor quality, use resources efficiently and effectively to improve quality, and reduce the time needed to complete a task or provide a service.

To determine the impact of poor quality on profits, TQM managers use information about the **costs of quality**. The costs of quality include both the costs of achieving quality (such as training costs and inspection costs) and the costs of poor quality (such as the costs of rework and of handling customer complaints). Managers use information about the costs of quality to:

- relate their organization's business plan to its daily operating activities.
- stimulate improvement by sharing this information with all employees.
- identify opportunities for reducing costs and customer dissatisfaction.
- determine the costs of quality relative to net income.

Theory of Constraints

According to the **theory of constraints (TOC)**, limiting factors, or bottlenecks, occur during the production of any product or service. Once managers identify such a constraint, they can focus their attention and resources on it and achieve significant improvements. TOC thus helps managers set priorities for how they spend their time and resources.

Comparison of ABM and Lean Operations

ABM and lean have several things in common as value-based systems:

- Both analyze processes and identify value-adding and non-value-adding activities.
- Both seek to eliminate waste and reduce non-value-adding activities to improve product or service quality, reduce costs, and improve an organization's efficiency and productivity.
- Both improve the quality of the information that managers use to make decisions about bidding, pricing, product lines, and outsourcing.

The two systems differ in their methods of costing and cost assignment. ABM's tool, ABC, calculates product or service cost by using cost drivers to assign the indirect costs of production to cost objects. ABC is often a fairly complex accounting method used with job order and process costing systems. Note that the ABC method can also be used to examine nonproduction-related activities, such as marketing and shipping.

A lean operation uses JIT and reorganizes many activities so that they are performed within work cells. The costs of those activities become direct costs of the work cell and of the products made in that cell. The total production costs within the cell can then be assigned by using simple cost drivers, such as process hours or direct materials cost. Companies that have implemented lean operations may use backflush costing rather than job order costing or process costing. This approach focuses on the output at the end of the production process and simplifies the accounting system.

STUDY NOTE: *ABM's primary goal is to calculate product or service cost accurately. The primary goal of lean operations is to eliminate waste in business processes.*

Exhibit 8 summarizes the characteristics of ABM and lean operations. A company can use both ABM and lean. ABM and ABC will improve the accuracy of the company's product or service costing and help it to reduce or eliminate business activities that do not add value for its customers. At the same time, the company can apply lean thinking to simplify processes, use resources effectively, and eliminate waste.

Exhibit 8
Comparison of ABM and Lean Operations

	ABM	Lean Operations
Primary purpose	To eliminate or reduce non-value-adding activities	To eliminate or reduce waste in all aspects of a business, including its processes and products or services
Cost assignment	Uses ABC to assign overhead costs to the product by using appropriate cost drivers	Uses JIT and reorganizes production activities into work cells; overhead costs incurred in the work cell become direct costs of the cell's products
Costing method	Integrates ABC with job order or process costing to calculate product costs	May use backflush costing to calculate product costs
Limitation	ABC can involve costly data collection and complex allocations	Requires management to think differently and use different performance measures

To remain competitive in today's business environment, companies have had to rethink their organizational processes and basic operating methods. Managers now focus on creating value for their customers as well as controlling costs throughout their management process. They design their internal value chain and external supply chain to provide customer-related, activity-based information; to track costs; and to eliminate waste and inefficiencies. In this chapter, two value-based systems that help managers improve operating processes and make better decisions as they plan, perform, evaluate, and report were discussed: activity-based management and lean operations. Exhibit 9 summarizes the steps managers take during the management process to manage for value and control costs.

Exhibit 9
Managing for Value and Controlling Costs

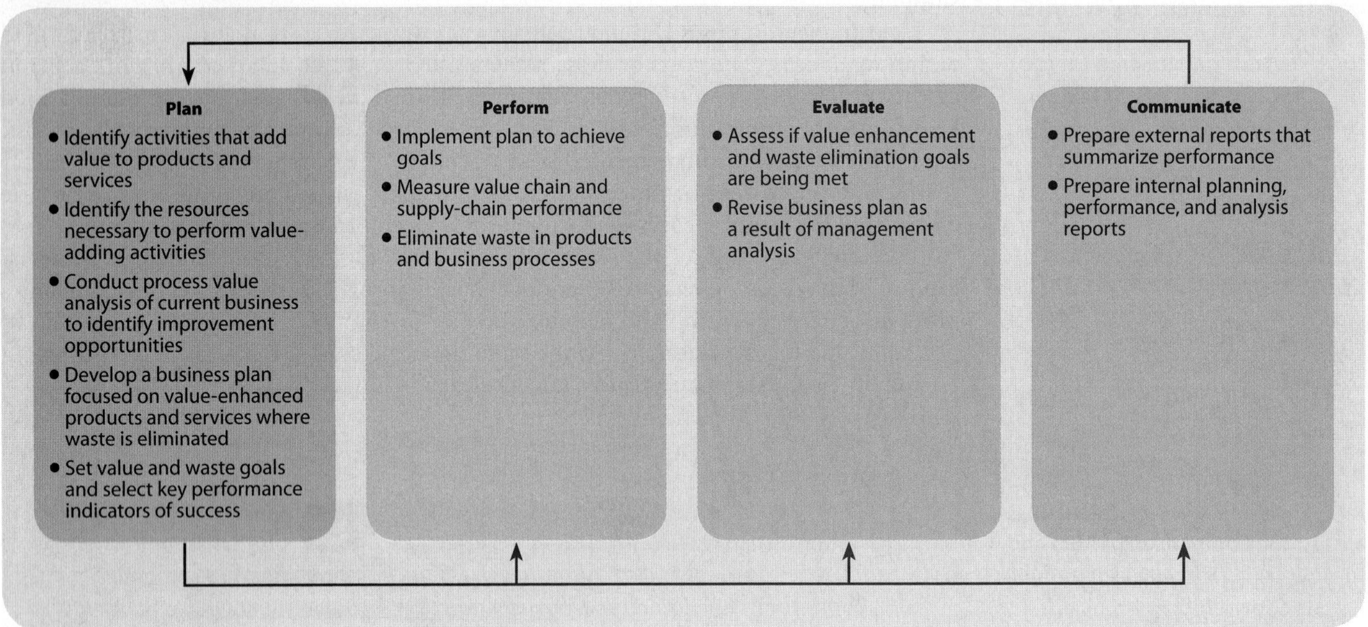

APPLY IT!

Recently, you had dinner with four chief financial officers (CFOs) who were attending a seminar on management tools and approaches to improving operations. The CFOs shared information about their organizations' current operating environments. Excerpts from the conversation appear below. Indicate whether each CFO describes activity-based management (ABM), lean operations, total quality management (TQM), or the theory of constraints (TOC).

- **CFO 1:** We think quality can be achieved through carefully designed production processes. We focus on minimizing the time needed to move, store, queue, and inspect our materials and products. We've reduced inventories by purchasing and using materials only when they're needed.
- **CFO 2:** Your approach is good. But we're more concerned with our total operating environment, so we have a strategy that asks all employees to contribute to the quality of both our products and our work environment. We focus on eliminating poor product quality by reducing waste and inefficiencies in our current operating methods.
- **CFO 3:** Our organization has adopted a strategy for producing high-quality products that incorporates many of your approaches. We also want to manage our resources effectively, and we do it by monitoring operating activities. We analyze all activities to eliminate or reduce the ones that don't add value to products.
- **CFO 4:** But how do you set priorities for your management efforts? We find that we achieve the greatest improvements by focusing our time and resources on the bottlenecks in our production processes.

SOLUTION
CFO 1: Lean operations; CFO 2: TQM; CFO 3: ABM; CFO 4: TOC

TRY IT! SE8, SE9, SE10, E14A, E15A, E14B, E15B

TriLevel Problem

sturti/iStockphoto

La-Z-Boy, Inc.

The beginning of this chapter focused on **La-Z-Boy, Inc.**, a company that makes built-to-order sofas and chairs. Complete the following requirements in order to answer the questions posed at the beginning of the chapter.

Section 1: Concepts

What underlying accounting concepts support the use of value-based systems like activity-based management and lean accounting?

Section 2: Accounting Applications

How can activity-based costing and lean operations help businesses like La-Z-Boy improve business processes and eliminate waste?

1. Assume that one of La-Z-Boy's production facilities produces more than a dozen styles of convertible sofas. The six-piece modular seating/sleeping style is the most difficult to produce and the most expensive. Campus Stores recently ordered 350 six-piece modular sets. Assume the production facility that received this order has been using a traditional costing system, but its controller is considering a shift to activity-based costing. He therefore wants to use the order from Campus Stores to compare ABC with traditional costing. Costs directly traceable to the order are as follows:

Direct materials	$57,290
Purchased parts	$76,410
Direct labor hours	1,320
Average direct labor pay rate per hour	$14.00

With the traditional costing approach, the controller applies overhead costs at a rate of 320 percent of direct labor costs.

For activity-based costing of the Campus Stores order, the controller uses the following data:

Activity	Cost Driver	Activity Cost Rate	Activity Usage
Product design	Engineering hours	$62 per engineering hour	76 engineering hours
Work cell setup	Number of setups	$90 per setup	16 setups
Parts production	Machine hours	$38 per machine hour	380 machine hours
Assembly	Assembly labor hours	$40 per assembly labor hour	500 assembly labor hours
Product simulation	Testing hours	$90 per testing hour	28 testing hours
Packaging and shipping	Product units	$13 per unit	350 units
Building occupancy	Direct labor cost	125% of direct labor cost	$18,480 direct labor cost

(a) Use the traditional costing approach to compute the total cost and product unit cost of the Campus Stores order.

(b) Using the cost hierarchy for manufacturing companies, classify each activity of the Campus Stores order according to the level at which it occurs.

(c) Prepare a bill of activities for the operating costs.

(d) Use ABC to compute the total cost and product unit cost. Round your answer to the nearest cent.

(e) What is the difference between the product unit cost you computed using the traditional approach and the one you computed using ABC? Does the use of ABC guarantee cost reduction for every order?

2. Assume that one of La-Z-Boy's production facilities is a lean operation and uses backflush costing in its management of reclining sofa inventory. At the beginning of the month, Work in Process Inventory and Finished Goods Inventory had zero balances. During the month, the following transactions took place:
   - Ordered, received, and used materials costing $11,000.
   - Direct labor costs incurred, $6,000.
   - Overhead costs incurred, $3,000.
   - Completed reclining sofas costing $19,000.
   - Sold reclining sofas costing $18,500.

Using backflush costing, calculate the ending balance in the Work in Process Inventory and Finished Goods Inventory accounts.

Section 3: Business Applications

How can managers of companies like La-Z-Boy plan to remain competitive in a challenging business environment? To answer this question, match this chapter's manager responsibilities with when they occur within the management process.

a. Plan
b. Perform
c. Evaluate
d. Communicate

1. Identify value-adding activities
2. Prepare external reports
3. Conduct process value analysis to identify improvement opportunities
4. Assess if value and waste goals are met.
5. Prepare internal reports
6. Identify the resources necessary to perform value-adding activities
7. Develop a business plan
8. Implement plan to achieve goals
9. Set value and waste goals and select key performance indicators of success
10. Revise business plan as a result of management analysis
11. Manage and measure value chain and supply chain performance
12. Eliminate waste in products and business processes

SOLUTION

Section 1: Concepts

The concepts of *relevance* and *reliability* underlie value-based systems like activity-based management and lean operations. Value-based systems add relevance since they categorize activities as either adding value to a product or service or not adding value. It enables managers to see their organization as a collection of value-creating activities (a value chain) that operates as part of a larger system that includes suppliers' and customers' value chains (a supply chain). This perspective has a direct bearing on a manager's ability to work with reliable information that is free from material error, complete, and neutral to reduce costs by eliminating waste and inefficiencies and by redirecting resources toward value-adding activities.

Section 2: Accounting Applications

1. (a)

Direct materials	$ 57,290
Purchased parts	76,410
Direct labor	18,480
Overhead (320% of direct labor cost)	59,136
Total cost of order	$211,316
Product unit cost (total costs ÷ 350 units)	$ 603.76

(b) Unit level: Parts production
Assembly
Packaging and shipping
Batch level: Work cell setup
Product level: Product design
Product simulation
Facility level: Building occupancy

(c) and (d)

La-Z-Boy, Inc.
Bill of Activities
Campus Stores Order

Activity	Activity Cost Rate	Cost Driver Level	Activity Cost
Unit level:			
Parts production	$38 per machine hour	380 machine hours	$ 14,440
Assembly	$40 per assembly labor hour	500 assembly labor hours	20,000
Packaging and shipping	$13 per unit	350 units	4,550
Batch level:			
Work cell setup	$90 per setup	16 setups	1,440
Product level:			
Product design	$62 per engineering hour	76 engineering hours	4,712
Product simulation	$90 per testing hour	28 testing hours	2,520
Facility level:			
Building occupancy	125% of direct labor cost	$18,480 direct labor cost	23,100
Total activity costs assigned to job			$ 70,762
Total job units			÷ 350
Activity costs per unit (total activity costs ÷ total units)			$ 202.18*
Cost summary:			
Direct materials			$ 57,290
Purchased parts			76,410
Activity costs (includes labor and overhead)			70,762
Total cost of order			$204,462
Product unit cost (total cost of order ÷ 350 units)			$ 584.18*

*Rounded

(e)

Product unit cost using traditional costing approach	$603.76
Product unit cost using activity-based costing approach	584.18
Difference	$ 19.58

Although the product unit cost computed using ABC is lower than the one computed using the traditional costing approach, ABC does not guarantee cost reduction for every product. It does improve cost traceability, which often identifies products that are "undercosted" or "overcosted" by a traditional product costing system.

2. Costs added to Cost of Goods Sold account:

Direct materials	$ 11,000
Conversion costs (direct labor and overhead)	9,000
Total manufacturing costs	$ 20,000
Less: Cost of goods completed	(19,000)
Ending balance of Work in Process Inventory	$ 1,000

Cost of goods completed	$ 19,000
Less: Cost of goods sold	(18,500)
Ending balance of Finished Goods Inventory	$ 500

SOLUTION•

Section 3: Business Applications

1. a
2. d
3. a
4. c
5. d
6. a
7. a
8. b
9. a
10. c
11. b
12. b

Chapter Review

Describe value-based systems, and discuss their relationship to the supply chain and the value chain. LO 1

Value-based systems add relevance and reliability since they categorize activities as either adding value to a product or service or not adding value. They enable managers to see their organization as a collection of value-creating activities (a value chain) that operates as part of a larger system that includes suppliers' and customers' value chains (a supply chain). This perspective helps managers work cooperatively both inside and outside their organizations to reduce costs by eliminating waste and inefficiencies and by redirecting resources toward value-adding activities. Process value analysis (PVA) is a technique for analyzing business processes by relating activities to the events that prompt the activities and to the resources that the activities consume. A value-adding activity adds value to a product or service as perceived by the customer. A non-value-adding activity adds cost to a product or service but does not increase its market value.

Define *activity-based costing*, and explain how a cost hierarchy and a bill of activities are used. LO 2

To implement activity-based costing (ABC), managers (1) identify and classify each activity, (2) estimate the cost of resources for each activity, (3) identify a cost driver for each activity and estimate the quantity of each cost driver, (4) calculate an activity cost rate for each activity, and (5) assign costs to cost objects based on the level of activity required to make the product or provide the service. ABC's primary disadvantage is that it is costly to implement.

A cost hierarchy and a bill of activities help in the implementation of ABC. To create a cost hierarchy, managers classify activities into four levels. Unit-level activities are performed each time a unit is produced. Batch-level activities are performed each time a batch of goods is produced. Product-level activities are performed to support a particular product line or brand. Facility-level activities are performed to support a facility's general manufacturing process. A bill of activities is then used to compute the costs assigned to activities and the product or service unit cost.

Define the elements of a lean operation, and identify the changes in inventory management that result when a firm adopts its just-in-time operating philosophy. LO 3

One of the primary elements of a lean operation is to produce on a just-in-time (JIT) basis. The elements of a JIT environment are minimum inventory levels, pull-through production, quick setup and flexible work cells, a multiskilled work force, high levels of product quality, effective preventive maintenance, and continuous improvement of the work environment.

In product costing under JIT, processing costs are classified as either direct materials costs or conversion costs. The costs associated with inspection time, moving time, queue time, and storage time are reduced or eliminated. With computerized monitoring of the work cells, many costs that are treated as indirect or overhead costs in traditional manufacturing settings become direct costs since they can be traced directly to work cells. The only costs that remain indirect costs and must be assigned to the work cells are those that cannot be linked to a specific work cell, such as building occupancy, insurance, and property taxes.

Define and apply *backflush costing*, and compare the cost flows in traditional and backflush costing. LO 4

In backflush costing, all product costs are first accumulated in the Cost of Goods Sold account. At the end of the period, they are "flushed back" into the appropriate inventory accounts. Backflush costing is commonly used to account for product costs in a JIT operating environment. It differs from the traditional costing approach, which records the costs of materials purchased in the Materials Inventory account and uses the Work in Process Inventory account to record the costs of direct materials, direct labor, and overhead during the production process. The objective of backflush costing is to save recording time, which cuts costs.

LO 5 Identify the management tools used for continuous improvement, and compare ABM and lean operations.

Management tools for continuous improvement include total quality management (TQM), the theory of constraints (TOC), activity-based management (ABM), and lean operations. These tools are designed to help businesses meet the demands of a challenging business environment by reducing resource waste and costs and by improving product or service quality, thereby increasing customer satisfaction. As value-based systems, both ABM and lean operations enhance the relevance and reliability of cost information as they seek to eliminate waste and reduce non-value-adding activities. However, ABM uses ABC to assign indirect costs to products using cost drivers, while lean uses JIT to reorganize activities so that they are performed within work cells. The overhead costs incurred in a work cell become direct costs of the products made in that cell. ABM uses job order or process costing to calculate product costs, whereas lean operations may use backflush costing.

Key Terms

activity-based costing (ABC) 835 (LO2)
activity-based management (ABM) 835 (LO2)
backflush costing 843 (LO4)
batch-level activities 836 (LO2)
bill of activities 837 (LO2)
continuous improvement 846 (LO5)
conversion costs 844 (LO4)
core competency 832 (LO1)
cost hierarchy 836 (LO2)
costs of quality 846 (LO5)
facility-level activities 836 (LO2)
full product cost 832 (LO1)
inspection time 841 (LO3)
just-in-time (JIT) operating philosophy 839 (LO3)
kaizen 841 (LO3)
lean operation 839 (LO3)
moving time 841 (LO3)
non-value-adding activity 834 (LO1)
outsourcing 832 (LO1)
primary processes 832 (LO1)
process value analysis (PVA) 833 (LO1)
processing time 841 (LO3)
product-level activities 836 (LO2)
pull-through production 840 (LO3)
push-through production 840 (LO3)
queue time 841 (LO3)
storage time 841 (LO3)
supply chain 832 (LO1)
support services 832 (LO1)
theory of constraints (TOC) 846 (LO5)
throughput time 841 (LO3)
total quality management (TQM) 846 (LO5)
unit-level activities 836 (LO2)
value-adding activity 833 (LO1)
value-based systems 832 (LO1)
value chain 832 (LO1)
work cell 840 (LO3)

Chapter Assignments

DISCUSSION QUESTIONS

LO 1 **DQ1. CONCEPT ▶** Discuss how differentiating between activities that add value and those that do not add value enhance the relevance and reliability of manager information.

LO 2 **DQ2. CONCEPT ▶** Why do the concepts of relevance and reliability underlie the five steps in implementing activity-based costing (ABC)?

LO 2 **DQ3. CONCEPT ▶** Describe how a cost hierarchy and a bill of activities can improve the relevance and reliability of an ABC implementation.

LO 3, 4 **DQ4. CONCEPT ▶** Why does the classification of costs in lean operations improve the relevance and reliability of product costs?

LO 1, 5 **DQ5. CONCEPT ▶ BUSINESS APPLICATION ▶** Why do value-based systems in the management process reinforce the concepts of relevance and reliability to lead to better business operations?

SHORT EXERCISES

LO 1

Concepts

SE1. CONCEPT ▶ Indicate whether each of the following pertains to the accounting concept of reliability or relevance.

a. Predictive value
b. Faithful representation
c. Free from material error
d. Has a direct bearing on a decision

LO 1

The Value Chain

SE2. The unit costs that follow were determined by dividing the total costs of each component by the number of products produced. From these unit costs, determine the total cost per unit of primary processes and the total cost per unit of support services.

Research and development	$ 1.00
Human resources	1.45
Design	0.55
Supply	1.10
Legal services	0.60
Production	4.00
Marketing	0.80
Distribution	0.90
Customer service	0.65
Information systems	0.75
Management accounting	0.20
Total cost per unit	$12.00

LO 1

Value-Adding and Non-Value-Adding Activities

SE3. Indicate whether the following activities of a gourmet sandwich shop are value-adding (VA) or non-value-adding (NVA).

a. Purchasing sandwich ingredients
b. Storing condiments
c. Making sandwiches
d. Cleaning up the shop
e. Making home deliveries
f. Accounting for sales and costs

LO 2

The Cost Hierarchy

SE4. Engineering design is an activity that is vital to the success of any motor vehicle manufacturer. Identify the level at which engineering design would be classified in the cost hierarchy used with ABC for each of the following:

a. A maker of unique editions of luxury automobiles
b. A maker of built-to-order city and county emergency vehicles (orders are usually placed for 10 to 12 identical vehicles)
c. A maker of a line of automobiles sold throughout the world

LO 2

The Cost Hierarchy

SE5. Match the four levels of the cost hierarchy to the following activities of a jeans manufacturer that uses activity-based management:

a. Routine maintenance of sewing machines
b. Designing a pattern for a new style
c. Sewing seams on a garment
d. Producing 100 jeans of a certain style in a certain size

LO 3 **Product Costing Changes in a JIT Environment**

SE6. Beauty Products Company is in the process of adopting the JIT operating environment for its lotion-making operations. Indicate which of the following overhead costs are non-value-adding costs (NVA) and which can be traced directly to the new lotion-making work cell (D):

a. Storage containers for work in process inventory
b. Insurance on the storage warehouse
c. Machine electricity
d. Machine repairs
e. Depreciation of the storage container moving equipment
f. Machine setup labor

LO 4 **Backflush Costing**

SE7. For work done during August, Ohir Company incurred direct materials costs of $120,000 and conversion costs of $260,000. The company employs a JIT operating philosophy and backflush costing. At the end of August, the Work in Process Inventory account had been assigned $900 of costs, and the ending balance of the Finished Goods Inventory account was $1,300. There were no beginning inventory balances. How much was charged to the Cost of Goods Sold account during August? What was the ending balance of that account?

LO 5 **Comparison of ABM and Lean**

SE8. ACCOUNTING CONNECTION ▶ Hong Corp. recently installed three just-in-time work cells in its screen-making division. The work cells will make large quantities of similar products for major window and door manufacturers. Should Hong use lean operations with JIT and backflush costing or ABM and ABC to account for product costs? Defend your choice of activity-based system.

LO 5 **TQM and Value**

SE9. Petal Dry Cleaners recently adopted total quality management. The owner has hired you as a consultant. Classify each of the following activities as either value-adding (VA) or non-value-adding (NVA):

a. Providing same-day service
b. Closing the store on weekends
c. Providing free delivery service
d. Having a seamstress on site
e. Making customers pay for parking

LO 5 **Activity-Based Systems**

SE10. ACCOUNTING CONNECTION ▶ Bob Lillie started a retail clothing business two years ago. Lillie's first year was very successful, but sales dropped 50 percent in the second year. A friend who is a business consultant analyzed Lillie's business and came up with two basic reasons for the decline in sales: (1) Lillie has been placing orders late in each season, and (2) shipments of clothing have been arriving late and in poor condition. What measures can Lillie take to improve his business and persuade customers to return?

EXERCISES: SET A

LO 1

The Supply Chain and Value Chain

E1A. Indicate which of the following items associated with a hotel are part of the supply chain (S) and which are part of the value chain (V):

a. Travel agency
b. Housekeeping supplies
c. Special events and promotions
d. Customer service
e. Travel bureau website
f. Tour agencies

LO 1

The Value Chain

E2A. As shown in the data that follow, a producer of ceiling fans has determined the unit cost of its most popular model. From these unit costs, determine the total cost per unit of primary processes and the total cost per unit of support services.

Research and development	$ 5.00
Human resources	4.50
Design	1.50
Supply	1.00
Legal services	0.50
Production	4.50
Marketing	2.00
Distribution	2.50
Customer service	6.50
Information systems	1.80
Management accounting	0.20
Total cost per unit	$30.00

LO 1

Management Reports

E3A. ACCOUNTING CONNECTION ▶ The reports that follow are from a grocery store. Which report would be used for financial purposes, and which would be used for activity-based decision making? Why?

Salaries	$ 1,000	Scan grocery purchases	$ 3,000
Equipment	2,200	Stock fruit	1,000
Freight	5,000	Bake rye bread	500
Supplies	800	Operate salad bar	2,500
Use and occupancy	1,000	Stock can goods	2,000
Total	$10,000	Collapse cardboard boxes	1,000
		Total	$10,000

LO 1

The Value Chain

E4A. Edwin Cortez recently opened his own company. In order to improve the business, he will be undertaking the following actions:

a. Engaging an accountant to help analyze progress in meeting the objectives of the company
b. Hiring a company to handle payroll records and employee benefits
c. Developing a logo for labeling and packaging the ceramics
d. Making gift packages by placing gourmet food products in ceramic pots and wrapping them in plastic
e. Engaging an attorney to write contracts
f. Traveling to Mexico himself to arrange for the purchase of products and their shipment back to the company
g. Arranging new ways of taking orders over the Internet and shipping the products
h. Keeping track of the characteristics of customers and the number and types of products they buy

i. Following up with customers to see if they received the products and if they are happy with them
j. Arranging for an outside firm to keep the accounting records
k. Distributing brochures that display the ceramics and refer to the website

1. Classify each of Cortez's actions as one of the value chain's primary processes—research and development, design, supply, production, marketing, distribution, or customer service—or as a support service—human resources, legal services, information systems, or management accounting.
2. **ACCOUNTING CONNECTION ▶** Of these actions, which are the most likely candidates for outsourcing? Why?

LO 1
Value-Adding and Non-Value-Adding Activities

E5A. When Cornelia Tyson prepared a process value analysis for her company, she identified the following primary activities. Identify the value-adding activities (VA) and the non-value-adding activities (NVA).

a. Engineering design
b. Product marketing
c. Product sales
d. Materials storage

LO 2
The Cost Hierarchy

E6A. Topa Electronics makes speaker systems. Its customers range from new hotels and restaurants that need specifically designed sound systems to nationwide retail outlets that order large quantities of similar products. The following activities are part of the company's operating process:

a. Retail sales commissions
b. Product design
c. Assembly labor
d. Assembly line setup
e. Building security
f. Facility supervision

Classify each activity as unit level (UL), batch level (BL), product level (PL), or facility level (FL).

LO 2
Bill of Activities

E7A. Ohfir Corporation has received an order for handheld computers from Townsend, LLC. A partially complete bill of activities for that order follows. Fill in the missing data.

Ohfir Corporation
Bill of Activities for Townsend, LLC
Handheld Computers Order

Activity	Activity Cost Rate	Cost Driver Level	Activity Cost
Unit level:			
Parts production	$50 per machine hour	200 machine hours	$?
Assembly	$20 per DLH	100 DLH	?
Packaging and shipping	$12.50 per unit	400 units	?
Batch level:			
Work cell setup	$100 per setup	16 setups	?
Product level:			
Product design	$60 per engineering hour	80 engineering hours	?
Product simulation	$80 per testing hour	30 testing hours	?
Facility level:			
Building occupancy	200% of direct labor cost	?	?
Total activity costs assigned to job			$?
Total job units			400
Activity costs per unit (total activity costs ÷ total units)			$?
Cost summary:			
Direct materials			$60,000
Purchased parts			80,000
Activity costs			?
Total cost of order			$?
Product unit cost (total cost of order ÷ 400 units)			$?

LO 2

Activity Cost Rates

E8A. Compute the activity cost rates for materials handling, assembly, and design based on the data that follow.

Materials:	
Cloth	$26,000
Fasteners	4,000
Purchased parts	40,000
Materials handling:	
Labor	8,000
Equipment depreciation	5,000
Electrical power	2,000
Maintenance	6,000
Assembly:	
Machine operators	5,000
Design:	
Labor	5,000
Electrical power	1,000
Overhead	8,000

Output totaled 40,000 units. Each unit requires three machine hours of effort. Materials handling costs are allocated to the products based on direct materials cost. Design costs are allocated based on units produced. Assembly costs are allocated based on 500 machine operator hours. (*Hint:* Activity cost rate = Total activity costs ÷ Total allocation base. Examples of an allocation base include total dollars of materials, total machine operator hours, or total units of output.)

LO 3

Elements of a Lean Operating Environment

E9A. The numbered items that follow are concepts that underlie value-based systems, such as ABM and lean operations. Match each concept to the related lettered element(s) of a lean operating environment.

1. Business processes are simplified.
2. The quality of the product or service is critical.
3. Employees are cross-trained.
4. Large inventories waste resources and may hide bad work.
5. Goods should be produced only when needed.
6. Equipment downtime is minimized.

a. Minimum inventory levels
b. Pull-through production
c. Quick machine setups and flexible work cells
d. A multiskilled work force
e. High levels of product quality
f. Effective preventive maintenance

LO 3

Comparison of Traditional and JIT Manufacturing Environments

E10A. Identify which of the following exist in a traditional manufacturing environment and which exist in a JIT operating environment:

a. Large amounts of inventory
b. Complex manufacturing processes
c. A multiskilled labor force
d. Flexible work cells
e. Push-through production methods
f. Materials purchased infrequently but in large lot sizes
g. Infrequent setups

LO 3 **Direct and Indirect Costs in JIT and Traditional Manufacturing Environments**

E11A. The cost categories in the following list are typical of many manufacturing operations:

a. Direct materials:
   (1) Sheet steel
   (2) Iron castings
b. Assembly parts:
   (1) Part 24
   (2) Part 15
c. Direct labor
d. Engineering labor
e. Indirect labor
f. Operating supplies
g. Small tools
h. Depreciation—plant
i. Depreciation—machinery
j. Supervisory salaries
k. Electrical power
l. Insurance and taxes—plant
m. President's salary
n. Employee benefits

Identify each cost as direct or indirect, assuming that it was incurred in (1) a traditional manufacturing setting and (2) a JIT environment.

LO 4 **Backflush Costing**

E12A. Telluride Products Company implemented a JIT work environment in its shovel division eight months ago, and the division has been operating at near capacity since then. At the beginning of May, Work in Process Inventory and Finished Goods Inventory had zero balances. The following transactions took place during the month:

- Ordered, received, and used handles and sheet metal costing $11,340.
- Direct labor costs incurred, $5,400.
- Overhead costs incurred, $8,100.
- Completed shovels costing $24,800.
- Sold shovels costing $24,000.

Using backflush costing, calculate the ending balance in the Work in Process Inventory and Finished Goods Inventory accounts.

LO 4 **Backflush Costing**

E13A. Morning Enterprises produces clocks. It has a JIT assembly process and uses backflush costing to record production costs. Overhead is assigned at a rate of $17 per assembly labor hour. There were no beginning inventories in March. During March, the following operating data were generated:

Cost of direct materials purchased and used	$53,200
Direct labor costs incurred	$27,300
Overhead costs assigned	?
Assembly hours worked	3,840 hours
Ending work in process inventory	$1,050
Ending finished goods inventory	$960

Using T accounts, show the flow of costs through the backflush costing system. What is the total cost of goods sold in March?

LO 5 **Comparison of ABM and Lean Operations**

E14A. Identify each of the following as a characteristic of ABM or lean operations:

a. Backflush costing
b. ABC used to assign overhead costs to the product cost
c. ABC integrated with job order or process costing systems
d. Complexity reduced by using work cells, minimizing inventories, and reducing or eliminating non-value-adding activities
e. Activities reorganized so that they are performed within work cells

LO 5 **Comparison of ABM and Lean Operations**

E15A. BUSINESS APPLICATION ▶ Excerpts from a conversation between two managers about their companies' management systems follow. Identify the manager who works for a company that emphasizes ABM and the one who works for a company that emphasizes a lean operating system.

- **Manager 1:** We try to manage our resources effectively by monitoring operating activities. We analyze all major operating activities, and we focus on reducing or eliminating the ones that don't add value to our products.
- **Manager 2:** We're very concerned with eliminating waste. We've designed our operations to reduce the time it takes to move, store, queue, and inspect materials. We've also reduced our inventories by buying and using materials only when we need them.

EXERCISES: SET B

Visit the textbook companion website at www.cengagebrain.com to access Exercise Set B for this chapter.

PROBLEMS

LO 1 **The Value Chain**

✔ 1: Total current cost per unit: $27.60
✔ 1: Total projected cost per unit: $22.25

P1. Reigle Electronics is a manufacturer of cell phones, a highly competitive business. Reigle's phones carry a price of $99, but competition forces the company to offer significant discounts and rebates. As a result, the average price of Reigle's cell phones has dropped to around $50, and the company is losing money. Management is applying value chain analysis to the company's operations in an effort to reduce costs and improve product quality. A study by the company's management accountant has determined the following per unit costs for primary processes:

Primary Process	Cost per Unit
Research and development	$ 2.50
Design	3.50
Supply	4.50
Production	6.70
Marketing	8.00
Distribution	1.90
Customer service	0.50
Total cost	$27.60

To generate a gross margin large enough for the company to cover its overhead costs and earn a profit, Reigle must lower its total cost per unit for primary processes to no more than $20. After analyzing operations, management reached the following conclusions about primary processes:

- Research and development and design are critical functions because the market and competition require constant development of new features with "cool" designs at lower cost. Nevertheless, management feels that the cost per unit of these processes must be reduced by 10 percent.
- Six different suppliers currently provide the components for the cell phones. Ordering these components from just two suppliers and negotiating lower prices could result in a savings of 15 percent.
- The cell phones are currently manufactured in Mexico. By shifting production to China, the unit cost of production can be lowered by 20 percent.
- Most cell phones are sold through wireless communication companies that are trying to attract new customers with low-priced cell phones. Management believes that

these companies should bear more of the marketing costs and that it is feasible to renegotiate its marketing arrangements with them so that they will bear 35 percent of the current marketing costs.

- Distribution costs are already very low, but management will set a target of reducing the cost per unit by 10 percent.
- Customer service is a weakness of the company and has resulted in lost sales. Management therefore proposes increasing the cost per unit of customer service by 50 percent.

REQUIRED

1. Prepare a table showing the current cost per unit of primary processes and the projected cost per unit based on management's proposals for cost reduction. (Round to the nearest cent.)
2. **ACCOUNTING CONNECTION ▶** Will management's proposals for cost reduction achieve the targeted total cost per unit? What further steps should management take to reduce costs? Which steps that management is proposing do you believe will be the most difficult to accomplish?
3. **ACCOUNTING CONNECTION ▶** What are the company's support services? What role should these services play in the value chain analysis?

LO 2

SPREADSHEET

✔ 1: Product unit cost: $90.00
✔ 4: Activity cost per unit: $21.47
✔ 4: Product unit cost: $93.49

Activity-Based Costing

P2. Printware Products, Inc., produces printers for wholesale distributors. It has just completed packaging an order from Hawes Company for 450 printers. Before the order is shipped, the controller wants to compare the unit costs computed under the company's new activity-based costing system with the unit costs computed under its traditional costing system. Printware's traditional costing system assigned overhead costs at a rate of 240 percent of direct labor cost.

Data for the Hawes order are as follows: direct materials, $17,552; purchased parts, $14,856; direct labor hours, 140; and average direct labor pay rate per hour, $17. Data for activity-based costing related to processing direct materials and purchased parts for the Hawes order follow.

Activity	Cost Driver	Activity Cost Rate	Activity Usage
Engineering systems design	Engineering hours	$28 per engineering hour	18 engineering hours
Setup	Number of setups	$36 per setup	12 setups
Parts production	Machine hours	$37 per machine hour	82 machine hours
Product assembly	Assembly hours	$42 per assembly hour	96 assembly hours
Packaging	Number of packages	$5.60 per package	150 packages
Building occupancy	Machine hours	$10 per machine hour	82 machine hours

REQUIRED

1. Use the traditional costing approach to compute the total cost and the product unit cost of the Hawes order.
2. Using the cost hierarchy, identify each activity as unit level, batch level, product level, or facility level.
3. Prepare a bill of activities for the activity costs.
4. Use ABC to compute the total cost and product unit cost of the Hawes order. (Round your answer to the nearest cent.)
5. **ACCOUNTING CONNECTION ▶** What is the difference between the product unit cost you computed using the traditional approach and the one you computed using ABC? Does the use of ABC guarantee cost reduction for every order?

LO 2

SPREADSHEET

✔ 3: Product unit cost: $8.67

Activity Cost Rates

P3. Tailgator Company produces four versions of its model J7-21 bicycle seat. The four versions have different shapes, but their processing operations and production costs are identical. During July, the following costs were incurred:

(Continued)

Direct materials:	
Leather	$25,430
Metal frame	39,180
Bolts	3,010
Materials handling:	
Labor	8,232
Equipment depreciation	4,410
Electrical power	2,460
Maintenance	5,184
Assembly:	
Direct labor	13,230
Engineering design:	
Labor	4,116
Electrical power	1,176
Engineering overhead	7,644
Overhead:	
Equipment depreciation	7,056
Indirect labor	30,870
Supervision	17,640
Operating supplies	4,410
Electrical power	10,584
Repairs and maintenance	21,168
Building occupancy overhead	52,920

July's output totaled 29,400 units. Each unit requires three machine hours of effort. Materials handling costs are allocated to the products based on direct materials cost, engineering design costs are allocated based on units produced, and overhead is allocated based on machine hours. Assembly costs are allocated based on direct labor hours, which are estimated at 882 for July.

During July, Tailgator completed 520 bicycle seats for Job 14. The activity usage for Job 14 was as follows: direct materials, $1,150; direct labor hours, 15.

REQUIRED

1. Compute the following activity cost rates: (a) materials handling cost rate, (b) assembly cost rate, (c) engineering design cost rate, and (d) overhead rate.
2. Prepare a bill of activities for Job 14.
3. Use activity-based costing to compute the job's total cost and product unit cost. (Round activity costs to the nearest dollar, and round unit costs to the nearest cent.)

LO 3 **Direct and Indirect Costs in Lean and Traditional Manufacturing Environments**

✓ 3: Direct cost per unit: $12

P4. Zunz Company, a producer of wooden toys, is about to adopt a lean operating environment. In anticipation of the change, Zunz's controller prepared the following list of costs for December:

Wood	$1,200	Insurance—plant	$ 324
Bolts	32	President's salary	4,000
Small tools	54	Engineering labor	2,700
Depreciation—plant	450	Utilities	1,250
Depreciation—machinery	275	Building occupancy	1,740
Direct labor	2,675	Supervision	2,686
Indirect labor	890	Operating supplies	254
Purchased parts	58	Repairs and maintenance	198
Materials handling	74	Employee benefits	2,654

REQUIRED

1. Identify each cost as direct or indirect, assuming that it was incurred in a traditional manufacturing setting.
2. Identify each cost as direct or indirect, assuming that it was incurred in a lean operating environment.
3. Assume that the costs incurred in the lean operating environment are for a work cell that completed 1,250 toy cars in December. Compute the total direct cost and the direct cost per unit for the cars produced.

LO 4

✔ 3: Total cost of goods sold: $564,400

Backflush Costing

P5. Auto Parts Company produces 12 parts for car bodies and sells them to four automobile assembly companies in Canada. The company implemented lean operating and costing procedures three years ago. Overhead is applied at a rate of $26 per work cell hour used. All direct materials and purchased parts are used as they are received.

One of the company's work cells produces automotive fenders that are completely detailed and ready to install when received by the customer. The cell is operated by four employees and involves a flexible manufacturing system with 14 workstations. Operating details for February for this cell follow.

Beginning work in process inventory	—
Beginning finished goods inventory	$420
Cost of direct materials purchased on account and used	$213,400
Cost of parts purchased on account and used	$111,250
Direct labor costs incurred	$26,450
Overhead costs assigned	?
Work cell hours used	8,260
Costs of goods completed during February	$564,650
Ending work in process inventory	$1,210
Ending finished goods inventory	$670

REQUIRED

1. Using T accounts, show the cost flows through a backflush costing system.
2. Using T accounts, show the cost flows through a traditional costing system.
3. What is the total cost of goods sold for the month?

ALTERNATE PROBLEMS

LO 1

Support Services:
✔ 1: Total current cost per unit: $8.00
✔ 1: Total projected cost per unit: $6.40

The Value Chain

P6. Comfy Spot is a manufacturer of futon mattresses. Comfy Spot's mattresses are priced at $60, but competition forces the company to offer significant discounts and rebates. As a result, the average price of the futon mattress has dropped to around $50, and the company is losing money. Management is applying value chain analysis to the company's operations in an effort to reduce costs and improve product quality. A study by the company's management accountant has determined the following per unit costs for primary processes and support services:

(Continued)

	Cost per Unit
Primary processes:	
Research and development	$ 5.00
Design	3.00
Supply	4.00
Production	16.00
Marketing	6.00
Distribution	7.00
Customer service	1.00
Total cost per unit	$42.00
Support services:	
Human resources	$ 2.00
Information services	5.00
Management accounting	1.00
Total cost per unit	$ 8.00

To generate a gross margin large enough for the company to cover its overhead costs and earn a profit, Comfy Spot must lower its total cost per unit for primary processes to no more than $32.00 and its support services to no more than $5.00. After analyzing operations, management reached the following conclusions about primary processes and support services:

- Research and development and design are critical functions because the market and competition require constant development of new features with "cool" designs at lower cost. Nevertheless, management feels that the cost per unit of these processes must be reduced by 20 percent.
- Ten different suppliers currently provide the components for the futons. Ordering these components from just two suppliers and negotiating lower prices could result in a savings of 15 percent.
- The futons are currently manufactured in Mali. By shifting production to China, the unit cost of production can be lowered by 40 percent.
- Management believes that by selling to large retailers like Wal-Mart, it is feasible to lower current marketing costs by 25 percent.
- Distribution costs are already very low, but management will set a target of reducing the cost per unit by 10 percent.
- Customer service and support to large customers are key to keeping their business. Management therefore proposes increasing the cost per unit of customer service by 20 percent.
- By outsourcing its support services, management projects a 20 percent drop in these costs.

REQUIRED

1. Prepare a table showing the current cost per unit of primary processes and support services and the projected cost per unit based on management's proposals.
2. **ACCOUNTING CONNECTION ▶** Will management's proposals achieve the targeted total cost per unit? What further steps should management take to reduce costs?
3. **ACCOUNTING CONNECTION ▶** What role should the company's support services play in the value chain analysis?

LO 2

Activity-Based Costing

✔ 1: Product unit cost traditional: $7.03
✔ 4: Activity cost per unit: $1.11
✔ 4: Product unit cost: $6.91

P7. Kall Company produces cellular phones. It has just completed an order for 10,000 phones placed by Connect, Ltd. Kall recently shifted to an activity-based costing system, and its controller is interested in the impact that the ABC system had on the Connect order. Data for that order are as follows: direct materials, $36,950; purchased parts, $21,100; direct labor hours, 220; and average direct labor pay rate per hour, $15.

Under Kall's traditional costing system, overhead costs were assigned at a rate of 270 percent of direct labor cost. Data for activity-based costing for the Connect order follow.

Activity	Cost Driver	Activity Cost Rate	Activity Usage
Electrical engineering design	Engineering hours	$19 per engineering hour	32 engineering hours
Setup	Number of setups	$29 per setup	11 setups
Parts production	Machine hours	$26 per machine hour	134 machine hours
Product testing	Number of tests	$32 per test	52 tests
Packaging	Number of packages	$0.0374 per package	10,000 packages
Building occupancy	Machine hours	$9.80 per machine hour	134 machine hours
Assembly	Direct labor hours	$15 per direct labor hour	220 direct labor hours

REQUIRED

1. Use the traditional costing approach to compute the total cost and the product unit cost of the Connect order. (Round unit costs to the nearest cent.)
2. Using the cost hierarchy, identify each activity as unit level, batch level, product level, or facility level.
3. Prepare a bill of activities for the activity costs.
4. Use ABC to compute the total cost and product unit cost of the Connect order. (Round activity costs to the nearest dollar, and round unit costs to the nearest cent.)
5. **ACCOUNTING CONNECTION ▶** What is the difference between the product unit cost you computed using the traditional approach and the one you computed using ABC? Does the use of ABC guarantee cost reduction for every order?

LO **2**

Activity Cost Rates

✓ 3: Product unit cost: $10.43

P8. Nifty Company produces three models of aluminum skateboards. The models have minor differences, but their processing operations and production costs are identical. During June, the following costs were incurred:

Direct materials:	
Aluminum frame	$162,524
Bolts	3,876
Purchased parts:	
Wheels	74,934
Decals	5,066
Materials handling *(assigned based on direct materials cost)*:	
Labor	17,068
Utilities	4,438
Maintenance	914
Depreciation	876
Assembly line *(assigned based on labor hours)*:	
Labor	46,080
Setup *(assigned based on number of setups)*:	
Labor	6,385
Supplies	762
Overhead	3,953
Product testing *(assigned based on number of tests)*:	
Labor	2,765
Supplies	435
Building occupancy *(assigned based on machine hours)*:	
Insurance	5,767
Depreciation	2,452
Repairs and maintenance	3,781

(Continued)

For June, output totaled 32,000 skateboards. Each board required 1.5 machine hours of effort. During June, Nifty's assembly line worked 2,304 hours, performed 370 setups and 64,000 product tests, and completed an order for 1,000 skateboards placed by Wow Toys Company. The job incurred costs of $5,200 for direct materials and $2,500 for purchased parts. It required 3 setups, 2,000 tests, and 72 assembly line hours.

REQUIRED

1. Compute the following activity cost rates: (a) materials handling cost rate, (b) assembly line cost rate, (c) setup cost rate, (d) product testing cost rate, and (e) building occupancy cost rate.
2. Prepare a bill of activities for the Wow Toys job.
3. Use activity-based costing to compute the job's total cost and product unit cost. (Round unit costs to the nearest cent.)

LO 3

Direct and Indirect Costs in JIT and Traditional Manufacturing Environments

✔ 3: Direct cost per unit: $2.19

P9. Peralto Company, which processes coffee beans into ground coffee, is about to adopt a JIT operating environment. In anticipation of the change, Peralto's controller prepared the following list of costs for the month:

Coffee beans	$5,000	Insurance—plant	$ 300
Bags	100	President's salary	4,000
Small tools	80	Engineering labor	1,700
Depreciation—plant	400	Utilities	1,250
Depreciation—grinder	200	Building occupancy	1,940
Direct labor	1,000	Supervision	400
Indirect labor	300	Operating supplies	205
Labels	20	Repairs and maintenance	120
Materials handling	75	Employee benefits	500

REQUIRED

1. Identify each cost as direct or indirect, assuming that it was incurred in a traditional manufacturing setting.
2. Identify each cost as direct or indirect, assuming that it was incurred in a just-in-time (JIT) environment.
3. Assume that the costs incurred in the JIT environment are for a work cell that completed 5,000 1-pound bags of coffee during the month. Compute the total direct cost and the direct cost per unit for the bags produced. (Carry unit cost to two decimal places.)

LO 4

Backflush Costing

✔ 3: Total cost of goods sold: $391,520

P10. Elly Corporation produces metal fasteners using six work cells, one for each of its product lines. It implemented JIT operations and costing methods two years ago. Overhead is assigned using a rate of $14 per machine hour for the Snap Work Cell. There were no beginning inventories on April 1. All direct materials and purchased parts are used as they are received. Operating details for April for the Snap Work Cell follow.

Cost of direct materials purchased on account and used	$104,500
Cost of parts purchased on account and used	$78,900
Direct labor costs incurred	$39,000
Overhead costs assigned	?
Machine hours used	12,220
Costs of goods completed during April	$392,540
Ending work in process inventory	$940
Ending finished goods inventory	$1,020

REQUIRED

1. Using T accounts, show the flow of costs through a backflush costing system.
2. Using T accounts, show the flow of costs through a traditional costing system.
3. What is the total cost of goods sold for April using a traditional costing system?

CASES

LO 2, 5 Group Activity: ABM and ABC in a Service Business

C1. MUF, a Chartered Accounting firm, has provided audit and tax services to businesses in the London area for over 50 years. Recently, the firm decided to use ABM and activity-based costing to assign its overhead costs to those service functions. Ginny Fior is interested in seeing how the change from the traditional to the activity-based costing approach affects the average cost per audit job. The following information has been provided to assist in the comparison:

Total direct labor costs	£400,000
Other direct costs	120,000
Total direct costs	£520,000

The traditional costing approach assigned overhead costs at a rate of 120 percent of direct labor costs.

Data for activity-based costing of the audit function follow.

Activity	Cost Driver	Activity Cost Rate	Activity Usage
Professional development	Number of employees	£2,000 per employee	50 employees
Administration	Number of jobs	£1,000 per job	50 jobs
Client development	Number of new clients	£5,000 per new client	29 new clients

Your instructor will divide the class into groups to work through the case. One student from each group should present the group's findings to the class.

1. Using traditional costing and direct labor cost as the cost driver, calculate the total costs for the audit function. What is the average cost per job?
2. Using activity-based costing to assign overhead, calculate the total costs for the audit function. What is the average cost per job?
3. Calculate the difference in total costs between the two approaches. Why would activity-based costing be the better approach for assigning overhead to the audit function?

LO 2, 5 Interpreting Management Reports: ABC and Selling and Administrative Expenses

C2. Star Kleymeyer, owner of Star Bakery, wants to know the profitability of each of her bakery's customer groups. She is especially interested in the State Institutions customer group, which is one of the company's largest. Currently, the bakery is selling doughnuts and snack foods to ten state institutions in three states. The controller has prepared the following income statement for the State Institutions customer group:

Star Bakery
Income Statement for State Institutions Customer Group
For the Year Ended December 31

Sales ($5 per case × 50,000 cases)	$250,000
Cost of goods sold ($3.50 per case × 50,000 cases)	175,000
Gross margin	$ 75,000
Less: Selling and administrative activity costs (see schedule below)	94,750
Operating income (loss) contributed by State Institutions customer group	$ (19,750)

(Continued)

Schedule of Selling and Administrative Activity Costs

Activity	Activity Cost Rate	Actual Cost Driver Level	Activity Cost
Make sales calls	$60 per sales call	60 sales calls	$ 3,600
Prepare sales orders	$10 per sales order	900 sales orders	9,000
Handle inquiries	$5 per minute	1,000 minutes	5,000
Ship products	$1 per case sold	50,000 cases	50,000
Process invoices	$20 per invoice	950 invoices	19,000
Process credits	$20 per notice	40 notices	800
Process billings and collections	$7 per billing	1,050 billings	7,350
Total selling and administrative activity costs			$94,750

The controller has also provided budget information about selling and administrative activities for the State Institutions customer group. For this year, the planned activity cost rates and the annual cost driver levels for each selling and administrative activity are as follows:

Activity	Planned Activity Cost Rate	Planned Annual Cost Driver Level
Make sales calls	$60 per sales call	59 sales calls
Prepare sales orders	$10 per sales order	850 sales orders
Handle inquiries	$5.10 per minute	1,000 minutes
Ship products	$0.60 per case sold	50,000 cases
Process invoices	$1 per invoice	500 invoices
Process credits	$10 per notice	5 notices
Process billings and collections	$4 per billing	600 billings

You have been called in as a consultant on the State Institutions customer group.

1. Calculate the planned activity cost for each activity.
2. Calculate the differences between the planned activity cost and the State Institutions customer group's activity costs for this year.
3. From your evaluation of the differences calculated in **2** and your review of the income statement, identify the non-value-adding activities and state which selling and administrative activities should be examined.
4. What actions might the company take to reduce the costs of non-value-adding selling and administrative activities?

LO **2, 5**

Decision Analysis: ABC in Planning and Control

C3. Refer to the income statement in **C2** for the State Institutions customer group for the year ended December 31, this year. Star Kleymeyer, owner of Star Bakery, is in the process of budgeting income for next year. She has asked the controller to prepare a budgeted income statement for the State Institutions customer group. She estimates that the selling price per case, the number of cases sold, the cost of goods sold per case, and the activity costs for making sales calls, preparing sales orders, and handling inquiries will remain the same for next year. She has contracted with a new freight company to ship the 50,000 cases at $0.60 per case sold. She has also analyzed the procedures for invoicing, processing credits, billing, and collecting and has decided that it would be less expensive for a customer service agency to do the work. The agency will charge the bakery 1.5 percent of the total sales revenue.

1. Prepare a budgeted income statement for the State Institutions customer group for next year; the year ends December 31.

2. Refer to the information in **C2.** Assuming that the planned activity cost rate and planned annual cost driver level for each selling and administrative activity remain the same next year, calculate the planned activity cost for each activity.
3. Calculate the differences between the planned activity costs (determined in **2**) and the State Institutions customer group's budgeted activity costs for next year (determined in **1**).
4. Evaluate the results of changing freight companies and outsourcing the customer service activities.

LO **3, 5**

Conceptual Understanding: Lean Operations in a Service Business

C4. At an initiation banquet for new members of your business club, you are talking with two college students who are majoring in marketing. In discussing the accounting course they are taking, they mention that they are having difficulty understanding lean operations. They have read that the elements of a company's operating system support the concepts of simplicity, continuous improvement, waste reduction, timeliness, and efficiency. They realize that to understand lean thinking in a complex manufacturing environment, they must first understand lean operations in a simpler service context. They ask you to explain the lean operating philosophy and provide an example.

Briefly explain lean operations. Apply the elements of a JIT operating system to the restaurant where the banquet is being held. Do you believe a lean operating philosophy applies in all restaurant operations? Explain your answer.

LO **3, 5**

Conceptual Understanding: Activities, Cost Drivers, and JIT

C5. Fifteen years ago, Bryce Stabele, together with several financial supporters, founded SA Corporation. Located in Atlanta, the company originally manufactured roller skates, but 12 years ago, on the advice of its marketing department, it switched to making skateboards. More than 4 million skateboards later, SA Corporation finds itself an industry leader in both volume and quality. To retain market share, it has decided to automate its manufacturing process. It has ordered flexible manufacturing systems for wheel assembly and board shaping. Manual operations will be retained for board decorating because some hand painting is involved. All operations will be converted to a JIT environment.

Bryce wants to know how the JIT approach will affect the company's product costing practices and has called you in as a consultant.

1. Summarize the elements of a JIT environment.
2. How will the automated systems change product costing?
3. What are some cost drivers that the company should employ? In what situations should it employ them?

Continuing Case: Cookie Company

C6. As we continue with this case, assume that your company has been using a continuous manufacturing process to make chocolate chip cookies. Demand has been so great that the company has built a special plant that makes only custom-ordered cookies. The cookies are shaped by machines but vary according to the customer's specific instructions. Ten basic sizes of cookies are produced and then customized. Slight variations in machine setup produce the different sizes.

In the past six months, several problems have developed. Even though a computer-controlled machine is used in the manufacturing process, the company's backlog is growing rapidly, and customers are complaining that delivery is too slow. Quality is declining because cookies are being pushed through production without proper inspection. Working capital is tied up in excessive amounts of inventory and storage space. Workers are complaining about the pressure to produce the backlogged orders. Machine breakdowns are increasing. Production control reports are not useful because they are not timely and contain irrelevant information. The company's profitability and cash flow are suffering.

(Continued)

Assume that you have been appointed CEO and that the company has asked you to analyze its problems. The board of directors asks that you complete your preliminary analysis quickly so that you can present it to the board at its midyear meeting.

1. In memo form, prepare a preliminary report recommending specific changes in the manufacturing processes.
2. In preparing the report, answer the following questions:
   a. Why are you preparing the report? What is its purpose?
   b. Who is the audience for this report?
   c. What kinds of information do you need to prepare the report, and where will you find it (i.e., what sources will you use)?
   d. When do you need to obtain the information?

CHAPTER 19
Cost-Volume-Profit Analysis

BUSINESS INSIGHT
Flickr

The types of products and services that a company offers often vary from year to year depending on customer preferences. For example, **Flickr**, which is today a popular website for sharing photos and videos online, evolved from an online game for multiple players called *Game Neverending* that was launched in 2002. The game was shelved in 2004, and the tools used in developing it were then focused on photo exchange capabilities. The site currently claims to host over five billion photos, and it not only provides public and private photo and video storage but also mobile apps and an online community platform. The ongoing challenge for Flickr's management is to offer a mix of services that appeal to customers and that allows the company to optimize its resources, cash, and profits. In this chapter, we describe how managers in any company make such an evaluation.

1. **CONCEPT** ▶ *Why is cost-volume-profit analysis useful for the purposes of comparability and understandability?*

2. **ACCOUNTING APPLICATION** ▶ *How will Flickr's managers decide which products and services to offer?*

3. **BUSINESS APPLICATION** ▶ *How can managers use cost behavior analysis to improve business performance?*

LEARNING OBJECTIVES

LO 1 **Define *cost behavior*, and identify variable, fixed, and mixed costs.**

LO 2 **Separate mixed costs into their variable and fixed components, and prepare a contribution margin income statement.**

LO 3 **Perform cost-volume-profit (CVP) analysis.**

LO 4 **Define *breakeven point*, and use contribution margin to determine a company's breakeven point for multiple products.**

LO 5 **Discuss how managers use CVP analysis in the management process and how they can project the profitability of products and services.**

SECTION 1 CONCEPTS

CONCEPTS
- Comparability
- Understandability

RELEVANT LEARNING OBJECTIVE

LO 1 Define *cost behavior*, and identify variable, fixed, and mixed costs.

LO1 Concepts Underlying Cost Behavior

Cost behavior—the way costs respond to changes in volume or activity—is a factor in almost every decision managers make. Two underlying accounting concepts support the usefulness of cost-volume-profit analysis in decision making: *understandability* and *comparability*. Knowing how costs will behave improves manager comprehension of the meaning of the information they receive, enhancing their *understanding* of it. Knowledge of cost behavior patterns enables managers to identify cost similarities and differences so *comparisons* of alternatives are possible. Thus, when evaluating operations, managers compare how changes in cost and sales affect the profitability of product lines, sales territories, customers, departments, and other segments. Service businesses like **Flickr**, **Facebook**, and **Google** find that understanding cost behavior is useful when planning the optimal mix of services to offer. For example, Google's managers analyze cost behavior of new features for products like Gmail in their online Google Labs and gather user data and feedback before officially deciding to add a new feature.

During the year, managers collect cost behavior data and use it in decision making. Managers must understand and anticipate cost behavior to determine the impact of their actions on operating income and resource optimization. For example, Google's managers must compare the changes in income that can result from buying new, more productive servers or launching an online advertising product like AdWords or AdSense.

Although our focus in this chapter is on cost behavior as it relates to products and services, it is also important to understand the cost behaviors of selling, administrative, and general activities, such as how increasing the number of shipments affects shipping costs, how the number of units sold or total sales revenue affects the cost of sales commissions, and how the number of customers billed affects total billing costs. If managers can predict how costs behave, and whether they are product- or service-related or are for selling, administrative, or general activities, then costs become manageable.

Cost Behavior

Some costs vary with volume or operating activity (variable costs). Others remain fixed as volume changes (fixed costs). Between those two extremes are costs that exhibit characteristics of each type (mixed costs). Exhibit 1 shows examples of each type of cost for different industries.

Variable Costs Total costs that change in direct proportion to changes in productive output (or any other measure of volume) are called **variable costs**. They are referred to as unit-level activities, since the cost is incurred each time a unit is produced or a service is delivered. For example, direct materials, direct labor, operating supplies, and gasoline are variable costs.

Total variable costs go up or down as volume increases or decreases, but the cost per unit remains unchanged. For example, as shown in Exhibit 2, for My Media Place, a hypothetical company that designs and sets up websites for small businesses and individuals, there is a linear relationship between direct labor (webpage designers) and units produced (completed webpages). Each webpage, or unit of output, requires $2.50 of labor cost. Total labor costs grow in direct proportion to the increase in units of output. For two units, total labor costs are $5.00; for six units, the organization incurs $15.00 in labor costs.

Exhibit 1
Examples of Variable, Fixed, and Mixed Costs

Costs	Manufacturing Company—Tire Manufacturer	Merchandising Company—Department Store	Service Company—Bank
Variable	• Direct materials • Direct labor (hourly) • Indirect labor (hourly) • Operating supplies • Small tools	• Merchandise to sell • Sales commissions • Shelf stockers (hourly)	• Computer equipment leasing (Based on usage) • Computer operators (hourly) • Operating supplies • Data storage disks

Fixed	• Depreciation, machinery and building (straight-line)
	• Insurance premiums
	• Labor (salaried)
	• Supervisory salaries
	• Property taxes (on machinery and building)
		• Depreciation, equipment and building (straight-line)
		• Insurance premiums
		• Buyers (salaried)
		• Supervisory salaries
		• Property taxes (on equipment and building)
			• Depreciation, furniture and fixtures (straight-line)
			• Insurance premiums
			• Salaries:
			  • Programmers
			  • Systems designers
			  • Bank administrators
			• Rent, buildings

Mixed	• Electrical power • Telephone • Heat	• Electrical power • Telephone • Heat	• Electrical power • Telephone • Heat

Exhibit 2
A Common Variable Cost Behavior Pattern: A Linear Relationship

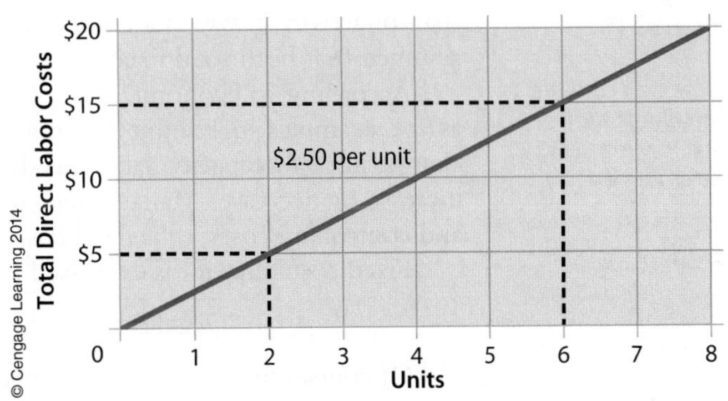

Variable cost can be computed using the following **variable cost formula**:

Total Variable Cost = Variable Rate × Units Produced

The cost formula for direct labor for My Media Place is computed as follows.

Total Direct Labor Costs = $2.50 × Units Produced

STUDY NOTE: *Variable costs change in direct proportion to changes in activity; that is, they increase in total with an increase in volume and decrease in total with a decrease in volume, but they remain the same on a per unit basis.*

Because variable costs increase or decrease in direct proportion to volume or output, it is important to know an organization's operating capacity. **Operating capacity** is the upper limit of an organization's productive output capability, given its existing resources. It describes what an organization can accomplish in a given period. In our discussions, we assume that operating capacity is constant and that all activity occurs within the limits of current operating capacity.

There are three common measures, or types, of operating capacity:

- **Theoretical capacity** (or *ideal capacity*) is the maximum productive output for a given period in which all machinery and equipment are operating at optimum speed, without interruption. No company ever actually operates at such an ideal level.
- **Practical capacity** (or *engineering capacity*) is theoretical capacity reduced by normal and expected work stoppages, such as machine breakdowns; downtime for retooling, repairs, and maintenance; and employee breaks. Practical capacity is used primarily as a planning goal of what could be produced if all went well; but no company ever actually operates at such a level.
- **Normal capacity** is the average annual level of operating capacity needed to meet expected sales demand. Normal capacity is the realistic measure of what an organization is *likely* to produce, not what it *can* produce. Thus, each variable cost should be related to an appropriate measure of normal capacity. For example, operating costs can be related to machine hours used or total units produced, and sales commissions usually vary in direct proportion to total sales dollars.

The basis for measuring the activity of variable costs should be carefully selected for two reasons:

- An appropriate activity base simplifies cost planning and control.
- Managers must combine (aggregate) many variable costs with the same activity base so that the costs can be analyzed in a reasonable way. Such aggregation also provides information that allows managers to predict future costs.

An **activity base** (or *denominator activity* or *cost driver*) is the activity for which relationships are established. The basic relationships should not change greatly if activity fluctuates around the level of denominator activity. The general guide for selecting an activity base is to relate costs to their most logical or causal factor. For example, direct material and direct labor costs should be considered variable in relation to the number of units produced.

Fixed Costs **Fixed costs**, referred to as facility-level activities, are total costs that remain constant within a relevant range of volume or activity. **Relevant range** is the span of activity in which a company expects to operate. Within the relevant range, it is assumed that both total fixed costs and per unit variable costs are constant.

STUDY NOTE: *Because fixed costs are expected to hold relatively constant over the entire relevant range of activity, they can be described as the costs of providing capacity.*

According to economic theory, all costs tend to be variable in the long run; thus, as the examples in Exhibit 1 suggest, a cost is fixed only within a limited period. A change in plant capacity, labor needs, or other production factors causes fixed costs to increase or decrease. Management usually considers a one-year period when planning and controlling costs; thus fixed costs are expected to be constant within that period.

Fixed cost behavior is expressed mathematically in the **fixed cost formula** as follows.

Total Fixed Cost = Fixed Cost in Relevant Range

Of course, fixed costs change when activity exceeds the relevant range. These costs are called *step costs* or *step-variable*, *step-fixed*, or *semifixed costs*. A **step cost** remains constant in a relevant range of activity and increases or decreases in a step-like manner when activity is outside the relevant range.

For example, assume that one Customer Support Team at My Media Place has the capacity to handle up to 500,000 customer incidents per 8-hour shift. The relevant range, then, is from 0 to 500,000 units. Unfortunately, volume has increased to more than 500,000 incidents per 8-hour shift, taxing current equipment capacity and the quality of customer care. My Media Place must add another Customer Support Team to handle the additional volume. Exhibit 3 shows this behavior pattern. The fixed costs for the first 500,000 units of production are $4,000. Thus, the fixed cost formula for up to 500,000 units is:

Total Fixed Cost = $4,000

But if output goes above 500,000 units, another team must be added, pushing this fixed cost to $8,000.

Exhibit 3
A Common Step-Like Fixed Cost Behavior Pattern

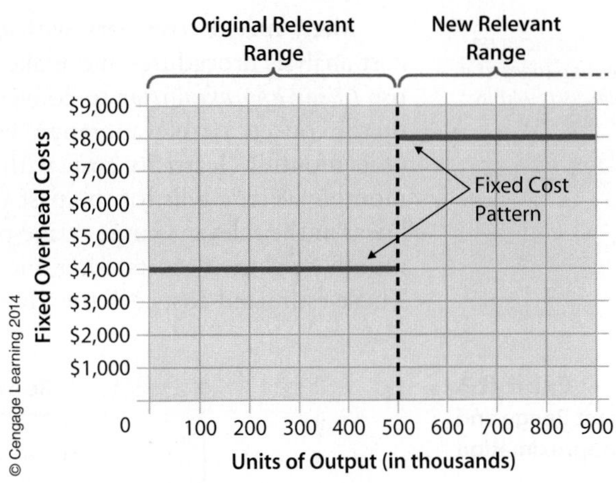

On a per unit basis, fixed costs go down as volume goes up, as long as a firm is operating within the relevant range of activity. Look at how the Customer Support Team cost per unit falls as the volume of activity increases within the relevant range:

Volume of Activity	*Support Team Cost per Unit*
100,000 units	$4,000 ÷ 100,000 = $0.0400
300,000 units	$4,000 ÷ 300,000 = $0.0133*
500,000 units	$4,000 ÷ 500,000 = $0.0080
600,000 units	$8,000 ÷ 600,000 = $0.0133*

*Rounded

At 600,000 units, the activity level is above the relevant range, which means another team must be added. Thus, the per unit cost changes to $0.0133.

Mixed Costs **Mixed costs** have both variable and fixed cost components. Part of a mixed cost changes with volume or usage, and part is fixed over a particular period. Electric, telephone, and heating costs are examples of mixed costs. Exhibit 4 depicts My Media Place's total electricity costs. Electric costs include charges per kilowatt-hour used plus a basic monthly service charge. The kilowatt-hour charges are variable because they depend on the amount of use; the monthly service charge is a fixed cost. Notice that the cost line does not start at $0 (compare to Exhibit 2). The cost line starts at the Y axis at the amount of fixed cost, and the variable cost rate determines the slope of the line from that point as kilowatt-hours are consumed.

Exhibit 4
Behavior Patterns of Mixed Costs

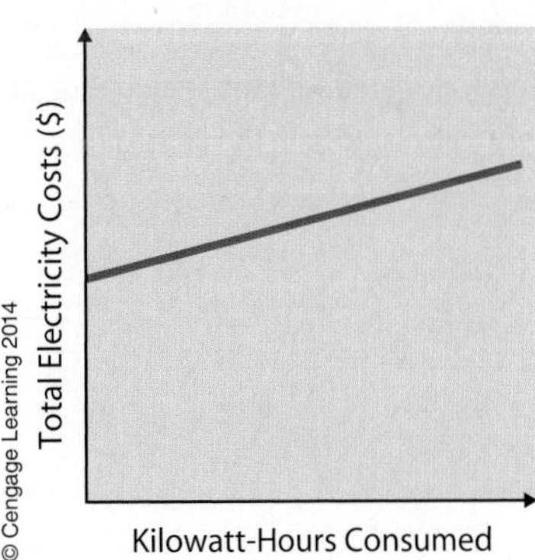

Mixed cost behavior is expressed mathematically in the **mixed cost formula** as follows.

Total Mixed Cost = (Variable Rate × Units Produced) + Fixed Cost

STUDY NOTE: Nonlinear costs can be roughly estimated by treating them as if they were linear (variable) costs within set limits of volume.

Many mixed costs vary with operating activity in a nonlinear fashion. To simplify cost analysis procedures and make mixed costs easier to use, managers and accountants use ***linear approximation*** to convert nonlinear costs into linear ones. This method relies on the concept of relevant range. For example, My Media Place can examine the linearity of its monthly electricity costs with machine hours worked (in thousands) by plotting its monthly electric bills for the past year as illustrated in Exhibit 5. Since the data appears linear in the relevant range of the past 12 months then a cost formula can be derived for monthly electricity costs using one of the methods explained in Section 2 of this chapter. Those estimated costs can then be treated as part of the other variable and fixed costs.

Exhibit 5
Relevant Range and Linear Approximation

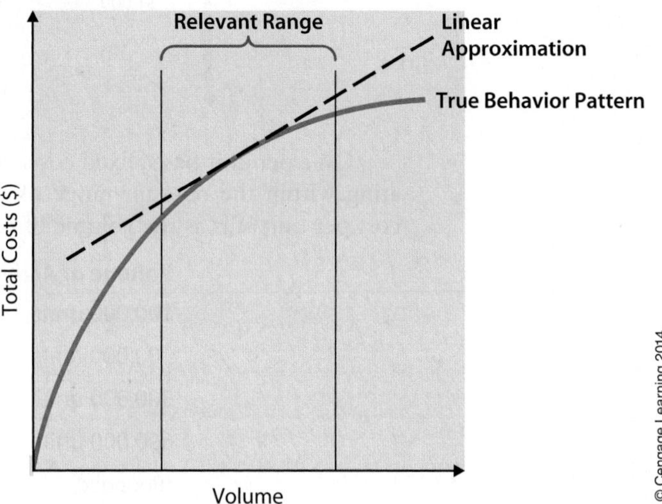

A linear approximation of a nonlinear cost is not a precise measure, but it allows the inclusion of nonlinear costs in cost behavior analysis, and the loss of accuracy is usually not significant. The goal is to help management estimate and control costs and to prepare budgets.

APPLY IT!

Indicate whether each of the following costs is usually variable (V) or fixed (F):

1. Operating supplies
2. Real estate taxes
3. Gasoline for a delivery truck
4. Property insurance
5. Depreciation expense of computers (calculated with the straight-line method)
6. Depreciation expense of machinery (calculated with the units-of-production method)

SOLUTION

1. V; 2. F; 3. V; 4. F; 5. F; 6. V

TRY IT! SE1, SE2, E1A, E2A, E1B, E2B

SECTION 2 ACCOUNTING APPLICATIONS

CCOUNTING PPLICATIONS

- Separate mixed costs into their variable and fixed components using the high-low method
- Separate mixed costs into their variable and fixed components using the scatter diagram method
- Prepare a contribution margin income statement
- Compute the breakeven point in sales units and sales dollars
- Compute the breakeven point for multiple products

ELEVANT EARNING OBJECTIVES

LO2 Separate mixed costs into their variable and xed components, and repare a contribution nargin income statement.

LO3 Perform cost-volume-profit (CVP) analysis.

LO4 Define *breakeven point*, and use ontribution margin to etermine a company's reakeven point for multiple roducts.

LO2 Mixed Costs and the Contribution Margin Income Statement

For cost planning and control purposes, mixed costs must be divided into their variable and fixed components. The separate components can then be grouped with other variable and fixed costs for analysis. Four methods are commonly used to separate mixed cost components. Because the results yielded by each of these methods often differ, managers usually use multiple approaches to find the best possible estimate for a mixed cost.

The Scatter Diagram Method

When there is doubt about the behavior pattern of a particular cost, especially a mixed cost, it helps to plot past costs and related measures of volume in a scatter diagram. A **scatter diagram** is a chart of plotted points that helps determine whether a linear relationship exists between a cost item and its related activity measure. It is a form of linear approximation. If the diagram suggests a linear relationship, a cost line can be imposed on the data by either visual means or statistical analysis. For example, suppose that My Media Place incurred the following machine hours and electricity costs last year:

Month	Machine Hours	Electricity Costs
January	6,250	$ 24,000
February	6,300	24,200
March	6,350	24,350
April	6,400	24,600
May	6,300	24,400
June	6,200	24,300
July	6,100	23,900
August	6,050	23,600
September	6,150	23,950
October	6,250	24,100
November	6,350	24,400
December	6,450	24,700
Totals	75,150	$290,500

Exhibit 6 shows a scatter diagram of these data. The diagram suggests a linear relationship between machine hours and the cost of electricity. If we were to add a line to the diagram to represent the linear relationship, the estimated fixed electricity cost would occur at the point at which the line intersects the vertical axis, or $23,200 of fixed monthly electric costs. The variable cost per machine hour can be estimated by determining the slope of the line, much as is done in Step 1 of the high-low method.

Exhibit 6
Scatter Diagram of Machine Hours and Electricity Costs

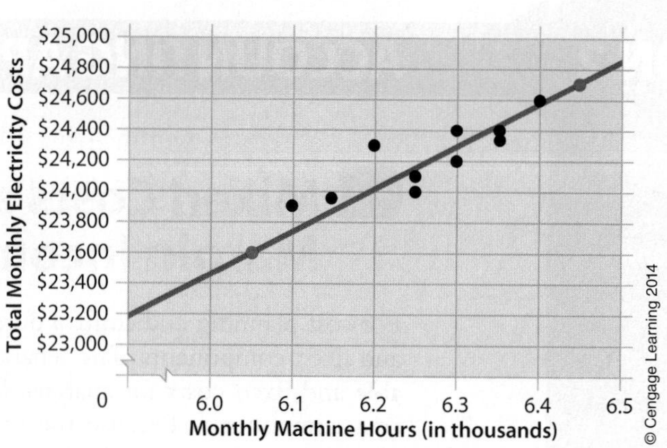

STUDY NOTE: *A scatter diagram shows how closely volume and costs are correlated. A tight, closely associated group of data is better suited to linear approximation than a random or circular pattern.*

The High-Low Method

The **high-low method** is another approach to determining the variable and fixed components of a mixed cost, which is based on the premise that only two data points are necessary to define a linear cost-volume relationship. The disadvantage of this method is that if the high or low data points are not representative of the remaining data set, the estimate of variable and fixed costs may not be accurate. Its advantage is that it can be used when only limited data are available. The example that follows illustrates how to use the high-low method for My Media Place.

Step 1. Find the variable rate. To determine the variable rate,

- Select the periods of highest and lowest activity within the accounting period. For My Media Place, the highest-volume machine-hour month was in December (6,450 hours) and the lowest was in August (6,050 hours).
- Find the difference between the highest and lowest amounts for both the machine hours and their related electricity costs.

$$6{,}450 \text{ hours} - 6{,}050 \text{ hours} = 400 \text{ hours}$$

$$\$24{,}700 - \$23{,}600 = \$1{,}100$$

- Compute the variable cost per machine hour by dividing the difference in cost by the difference in machine hours.

$$\text{Variable Cost per Machine Hour} = \$1{,}100 \div 400 \text{ Machine Hours}$$

$$= \$2.75 \text{ per Machine Hour}$$

Step 2. Find the total fixed costs. Compute total fixed costs for a month by putting the known variable rate and the information from the month with the highest volume into the cost formula and solve for the total fixed costs.

$$\text{Total Fixed Costs} = \text{Total Costs} - \text{Total Variable Costs}$$

$$\text{Total Fixed Costs for December} = \$24{,}700.00 - (6{,}450 \text{ Hours} \times \$2.75) = \$6{,}962.50$$

You can check your answer by recalculating total fixed costs using the month with the lowest activity.

$$\text{Total Fixed Costs for August} = \$23{,}600.00 - (6{,}050 \text{ Hours} \times \$2.75) = \$6{,}962.50$$

Step 3. Express the cost formula to estimate the total costs within the relevant range. For My Media Place, this is computed as follows.

$$\text{Total Mixed Cost} = (\text{Variable Rate} \times \text{Volume Level}) + \text{Fixed Costs}$$

$$\text{Total Electricity Costs per Month} = (\$2.75 \times \text{Machine Hours}) + \$6{,}962.50$$

Remember that the cost formula will work only within the relevant range. In this example, the formula would work for activity between 6,050 machine hours and 6,450 machine hours. To estimate the electricity costs for machine hours outside the relevant range (in this case, below 6,050 machine hours or above 6,450 machine hours), a new cost formula must be calculated.

Statistical Methods

Statistical methods, such as **regression analysis**, mathematically describe the relationship between costs and activities and are used to separate mixed costs into variable and fixed components. Because all data observations are used, the resulting linear equation is more representative of cost behavior than either the high-low or scatter diagram methods. Regression analysis can be performed using one or more activities to predict costs. For example, overhead costs can be predicted using only machine hours (a simple regression analysis), or they can be predicted using both machine hours and labor hours (a multiple regression analysis) because both activities affect overhead. We leave further description of regression analysis to statistics courses, which provide detailed coverage of this method.

The Engineering Method

The **engineering method** separates costs by performing a step-by-step analysis (sometimes called a *time and motion study*) of the tasks, costs, and processes involved. The engineering method is expensive because it is so detailed, and it is generally used to estimate the cost of activities or new products. For example, the U.S. Postal Service conducts periodic audits of how many letters a postal worker should be able to deliver on a particular mail route within a certain period.

Like most businesses, the U.S. Postal Service is concerned about delivery time. To determine how many deliveries a postal worker should be able to make within a certain period, it conducts periodic audits using the engineering method.

Richard Susanto/Shutterstock.com

Contribution Margin Income Statements

Once an organization's costs are classified as being either variable or fixed, the traditional income statement can be reorganized into a more useful format for internal operations and decision making. Exhibit 7 compares the structure of a traditional and a **contribution margin income statement** (or *variable costing income statement*). A contribution margin income statement emphasizes cost behavior rather than organizational functions. **Contribution margin (CM)** is the amount that remains after all variable costs are subtracted from sales. All variable costs related to production, selling, administration, and general expenses are subtracted from sales to determine the total contribution margin. All fixed costs related to production, selling, administration, and general expenses are subtracted from the total contribution margin to determine operating income.

Exhibit 7
Comparison of Income Statements

Traditional Income Statement	Contribution Margin Income Statement
Sales revenue	Sales revenue
– Cost of goods sold, variable	– Cost of goods sold, variable
– Cost of goods sold, fixed	– Operating expenses, variable
= Gross margin	= Contribution margin
– Operating expenses, variable	– Cost of goods sold, fixed
– Operating expenses, fixed	– Operating expenses, fixed
= Operating income	= Operating income

***STUDY NOTE:** Although both statements arrive at the same operating income, the traditional approach divides costs into product and period costs, whereas the contribution margin approach divides costs into variable and fixed costs.*

The contribution margin income statement enables managers to view revenue and cost relationships on a per unit basis or as a percentage of sales. If managers understand these relationships, they can determine:

- How many units they must sell to avoid losing money
- What the sales price per unit must be to cover costs
- What their profits will be for a certain dollar amount of sales revenue

Exhibit 8 shows the two ways a contribution margin income statement can be presented.

Exhibit 8
Contribution Margin Income Statement

	Per Unit Relationships	As a Percentage of Sales
Sales revenue	(Sales price per unit × Units sold)	(Sales revenue ÷ Sales revenue)
Less variable costs	(Variable rate per unit × Units sold)	(Variable costs ÷ Sales revenue)
Contribution margin	(Contribution margin per unit × Units sold)	Contribution margin ÷ Sales revenue
Less fixed costs	(Fixed costs)	(Fixed costs ÷ Sales revenue)
Operating income	(Operating income)	(Operating income ÷ Sales revenue)

APPLY IT!

Using the high-low method and the information that follows, compute the monthly variable cost per kilowatt-hour and the monthly fixed electricity cost for a local business. Finally, express the monthly electricity cost formula and its relevant range.

Month	Kilowatt-Hours Used	Electricity Costs
April	90	$450
May	80	430
June	70	420

SOLUTION

Volume	Month	Activity Level	Cost
High	April	90 hours	$450
Low	June	70 hours	420
Difference		20 hours	$ 30

Variable cost per kilowatt-hour = $30 ÷ 20 hours
= $1.50 per hour

Fixed costs for April: $450 − (90 × $1.50) = $315

Fixed costs for June: $420 − (70 × $1.50) = $315

Monthly electricity costs = ($1.50 × Hours) + $315

The cost formula can be used for hourly activity between 70 and 90 hours per month.

TRY IT! SE3, SE4, SE9, E3A, E4A, E5A, E3B, E4B, E5B

LO3 Cost-Volume-Profit Analysis

Cost-volume-profit (CVP) analysis is an examination of the relationships among cost, volume of output, and profit. CVP analysis usually applies to a single product, product line, or division of a company. For that reason, *profit* is the term used in the CVP equation. In the context of CVP analysis, however, profit and operating income mean the same thing. The CVP equation is expressed as:

Sales Revenue − Variable Costs − Fixed Costs = Profit

or as:

(Sales Price × Units Sold) − (Variable Rate × Units Sold) − Fixed Costs = Profit

For example, suppose My Media Place wants to make a profit of $50,000 on one of its services. Each service sells for $95.50 and has variable costs of $80. If 4,000 services are sold during the period, what are the fixed costs?

($95.50 × 4,000) − ($80 × 4,000) − Fixed Costs = $50,000

$382,000 − $320,000 − Fixed Costs = $50,000

Fixed Costs = $12,000

APPLY IT!

A local business wants to make a profit of $10,000 each month. It has variable costs of $5 per unit and fixed costs of $20,000 per month. How much must it charge per unit if 6,000 units are sold?

SOLUTION

(Sales Price × Units Sold) − (Variable Rate × Units Sold) − Fixed Costs = Profit

(Sales Price × 6,000) − ($5 × 6,000) − $20,000 = $10,000

$$\text{Sales Price} = \frac{(\$5 \times 6{,}000) + \$20{,}000 + \$10{,}000}{6{,}000 \text{ units}} = \frac{\$60{,}000}{6{,}000} = \$10 \text{ per unit}$$

TRY IT! SE4, SE10, E6A, E12A, E13A, E14A, E6B, E12B, E13B, E14B

LO4 Breakeven Analysis

The **breakeven point** is the point at which total revenues equal total costs. It is thus the point at which an organization can begin to earn a profit. When a new venture or product line is being planned, the likelihood of the project's success can be quickly measured by finding its breakeven point. If, for instance, the breakeven point is 24,000 units and the total market is only 25,000 units, the margin of safety would be very low, and the idea should be considered carefully. The **margin of safety** is the number of sales units or amount of sales dollars by which actual sales can fall below planned sales without resulting in a loss—in this example, 1,000 units.

The general equation for finding the breakeven point is expressed as:

Breakeven Point = Sales − Variable Costs − Fixed Costs

or as:

(Sales Price × Units Sold) − (Variable Rate × Units Sold) − Fixed Costs = Profit

Suppose, for example, that one of the services My Media Place sells is website setups. Variable costs are $50 per unit, and fixed costs average $20,000 per year. A unit is a basic website setup, which sells for $90.

Breakeven in Sales Units The breakeven point for website setup services in sales units is:

$$\text{Sales Price} - \text{Variable Cost} - \text{Fixed Cost} = \$0$$
$$(\$90 \times \text{Sales Units}) - (\$50 \times \text{Sales Units}) - \$20{,}000 = \$0$$
$$(\$40 \times \text{Sales Units}) = \$20{,}000$$
$$\text{Sales Units} = \$20{,}000 \div \$40$$
$$\text{Sales Units} = \underline{\underline{500}}$$

Breakeven in Sales Dollars The breakeven point in sales dollars is:

$$\$90 \times 500 \text{ units} = \underline{\underline{\$45{,}000}}$$

Breakeven by Scatter Diagram We can make a rough estimate of the breakeven point using a scatter diagram. Exhibit 9 shows My Media Place's breakeven graph, which has five parts:

- A horizontal axis for units of output
- A vertical axis for dollars
- A line running horizontally from the vertical axis at the level of fixed costs
- A total cost line that begins at the point where the fixed cost line crosses the vertical axis and slopes upward to the right (The slope of the line depends on the variable cost per unit.)
- A total revenue line that begins at the origin of the vertical and horizontal axes and slopes upward to the right (The slope depends on the selling price per unit.)

At the point at which the total revenue line crosses the total cost line, revenues equal total costs. The breakeven point, stated in either sales units or dollars of sales, is found by extending broken lines from this point to the axes. As Exhibit 9 shows, My Media Place will break even when it has sold 500 website setups for $45,000.

Exhibit 9
Graphic Breakeven Analysis

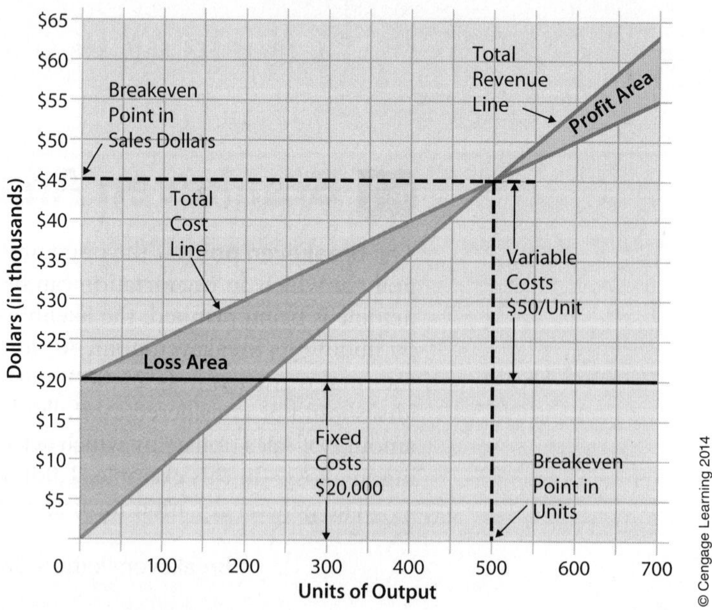

Using an Equation to Determine the Breakeven Point

A simpler method of determining the breakeven point uses contribution margin in an equation. You will recall from the contribution margin income statement that the contribution margin is the amount that remains after all variable costs are subtracted from sales:

$$\text{Sales} - \text{Variable Costs} = \text{Contribution Margin}$$

STUDY NOTE: *The maximum contribution a unit of product or service can make is its selling price. After paying for itself (variable costs), a product or service provides a contribution margin to help pay total fixed costs and then earn a profit.*

A product line's contribution margin represents its net contribution to paying off fixed costs and earning a profit. Profit is what remains after fixed costs are paid and subtracted from the contribution margin:

$$\text{Contribution Margin} - \text{Fixed Costs} = \text{Profit}$$

The example that follows uses the contribution margin income statement approach to determine the profitability of one of My Media Place's products.

		Units Produced and Sold		
Symbols		**250**	**500**	**750**
S	Sales revenue ($90 per unit)	$ 22,500	$45,000	$67,500
VC	Less variable costs ($50 per unit)	12,500	25,000	37,500
CM	Contribution margin ($40 per unit)	$ 10,000	$20,000	$30,000
FC	Less fixed costs	20,000	20,000	20,000
P	Profit (loss)	$(10,000)	$ 0	$10,000

The breakeven point (BE) can be expressed as the point at which contribution margin minus total fixed costs equals zero (or the point at which contribution margin equals total fixed costs).

Breakeven in Sales Units In terms of units of product, the equation for the breakeven point looks like this:

$$(\text{Contribution Margin per Unit} \times \text{Breakeven Point Units}) - \text{Fixed Costs} = \$0$$

It can also be expressed like this:

$$\text{Breakeven (BE) Point Units} = \frac{\text{Fixed Costs (FC)}}{\text{Contribution Margin (CM) per Unit}}$$

STUDY NOTE: *Remember that the breakeven point provides a rough estimate of the number of units that must be sold to cover the total costs.*

For My Media Place, the breakeven point would be computed as follows.

$$\text{Breakeven Point Units} = \frac{\text{Fixed Costs}}{\text{Contribution Margin per Unit}} = \frac{\$20{,}000}{\$90 - \$50} = \frac{\$20{,}000}{\$40} = 500 \text{ units}$$

Breakeven in Sales Dollars The breakeven point in total sales dollars may be determined as follows.

$$\begin{aligned}\text{Breakeven (BE) Point Dollars} &= \text{Selling Price (SP)} \times \text{Breakeven (BE) Point Units}\\ &= \$90 \times 500 \text{ units}\\ &= \underline{\underline{\$45{,}000}}\end{aligned}$$

RATIO

An alternative way of determining the breakeven point in total sales dollars is to divide the fixed costs by the contribution margin ratio. The contribution margin ratio is the contribution margin divided by the selling price:

$$\text{Contribution Margin Ratio} = \frac{\text{Contribution Margin}}{\text{Selling Price}} = \frac{\$40}{\$90} = 0.444^*, \text{ or } 4/9$$

$$\text{Breakeven Point Dollars} = \frac{\text{Fixed Costs}}{\text{Contribution Margin Ratio}} = \frac{\$20{,}000}{0.444} = \underline{\underline{\$45{,}045^*}}$$

*Rounded

The Breakeven Point for Multiple Products

To satisfy the needs of different customers, most companies sell a variety of products or services that often have different variable and fixed costs and different selling prices.

STUDY NOTE: A company's sales mix can be very dynamic. If the mix is constantly changing, an assumption of stability may undermine the CVP analysis.

To calculate the breakeven point for each product, its unit contribution margin must be weighted by the sales mix. The **sales mix** is the proportion of each product's unit sales relative to the company's total unit sales.

Assume that My Media Place sells two types of websites: standard and express. If the company sells 500 units, of which 300 units are standard and 200 are express, the sales mix would be 3:2. The sales mix can also be stated in percentages. Of the 500 units sold, 60 percent (300 ÷ 500) are standard sales, and 40 percent (200 ÷ 500) are express sales (see Exhibit 10).

Exhibit 10
Sales Mix

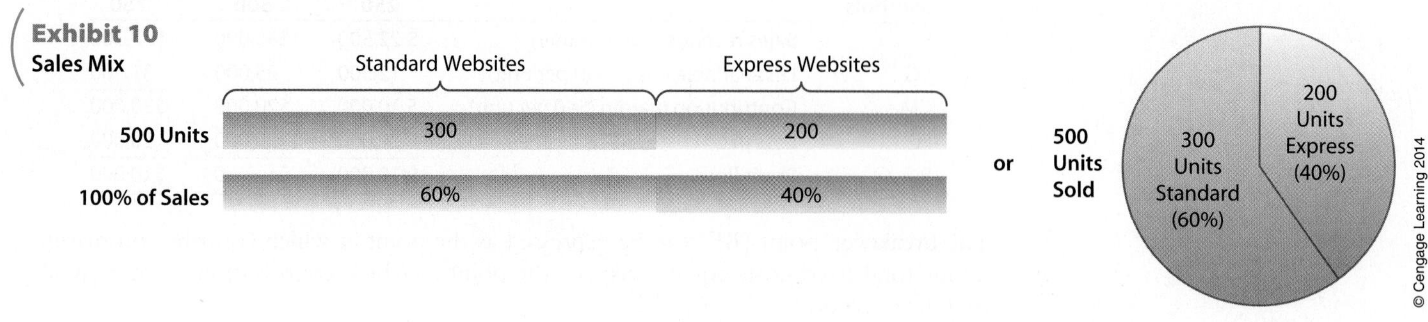

The example that follows illustrates how to compute the breakeven point for multiple products using My Media Place's sales mix of 60 percent standard websites to 40 percent express websites and total fixed costs of $32,000.

Step 1. Compute the weighted-average contribution margin. Multiply the contribution margin for each product by its percentage of the sales mix, as follows.

	Selling Price		Variable Costs		Contribution Margin (CM)		Percentage of Sales Mix		Weighted-Average CM
Standard	$90	–	$50	=	$40	×	60%	=	$24
Express	$40	–	$20	=	$20	×	40%	=	8
Weighted-average contribution margin									$32

Step 2. Calculate the weighted-average breakeven point. Divide total fixed costs by the weighted-average contribution margin:

Weighted-Average Breakeven Point Units = Total Fixed Costs ÷ Weighted Average Contribution Margin
= $32,000 ÷ $32
= 1,000 units

Step 3. Calculate the breakeven point for each product. Multiply the weighted-average breakeven point by each product's percentage of the sales mix:

	Weighted-Average Breakeven Point		Sales Mix		Breakeven Point
Standard	1,000 units	×	60%	=	600 units
Express	1,000 units	×	40%	=	400 units

Step 4. Verify results. To verify, determine the contribution margin of each product and subtract the total fixed costs:

Contribution margin:		
Standard	600 × $40	$24,000
Express	400 × $20	8,000
Total contribution margin		$32,000
Less fixed costs		32,000
Profit		$ 0

APPLY IT!

Using the contribution margin approach, find the breakeven point in units for a local business's two products. Product M's selling price per unit is $20, and its variable cost per unit is $11. Product N's selling price per unit is $12, and its variable cost per unit is $6. Fixed costs are $24,000, and the sales mix of Product M to Product N is 2:1.

SOLUTION

Step 1.

	Selling Price		Variable Costs		Contribution Margin (CM)		Percentage of Sales Mix		Weighted-Average CM*
M	$20	−	$11	=	$9	×	66.67%	=	$6
N	$12	−	$ 6	=	$6	×	33.33%	=	2
Weighted-average contribution margin									$8

*Rounded

Step 2.

Weighted-average breakeven point = $24,000 ÷ $8.00 = 3,000 units

Step 3. Breakeven point for each product line:

		Weighted-Average Breakeven Point		Sales Mix		Breakeven Point
M	=	3,000 units	×	0.6667	=	2,000 units
N	=	3,000 units	×	0.3333	=	1,000 units

Step 4. Check:

Contribution margin:						
Product M	=	2,000	×	$9	=	$18,000
Product N	=	1,000	×	$6	=	6,000
Total contribution margin						$24,000
Less fixed costs						24,000
Profit						$ 0

TRY IT! SE5, SE6, SE7, SE8, E5A, E6A, E7A, E8A, E9A, E10A, E11A, E15A, E5B, E6B, E7B, E8B, E9B, E10B, E11B, E15B

SECTION 3

BUSINESS APPLICATIONS

BUSINESS APPLICATIONS

- Planning
- Performing
- Evaluating
- Communicating

RELEVANT LEARNING OBJECTIVE

LO 5 Discuss how managers use CVP analysis in the management process and how they can project the profitability of products and services.

LO5 Using CVP Analysis to Plan Future Sales, Costs, and Profits

CVP analysis is a general model of financial activity. CVP analysis allows managers to adjust different variables and to evaluate how these changes affect profit. For planning, managers can use CVP analysis to calculate net income when sales volume is known, or they can determine the level of sales needed to reach a targeted amount of net income. CVP analysis is used extensively in budgeting as well, and is also a way of measuring how well an organization's departments are performing. At the end of a period, sales volume and related actual costs are analyzed to find actual net income. A department's performance is measured by comparing actual costs with expected costs, which have been computed by applying CVP analysis to actual sales volume. The result is a performance report on which managers can base the control of operations.

Managers use CVP analysis to measure the effects of alternative courses of action, such as changing variable or fixed costs, expanding or contracting sales volume, and increasing or decreasing selling prices. CVP analysis is useful in making decisions about:

- product pricing
- product mix (when an organization makes more than one product or offers more than one service)
- adding or dropping a product line
- accepting special orders.

Assumptions Underlying CVP Analysis

CVP analysis is useful only under certain conditions and only when the following assumptions hold true:

- The behavior of variable and fixed costs can be measured accurately.
- Costs and revenues have a close linear approximation throughout the relevant range. For example, if costs rise, revenues rise proportionately.
- Efficiency and productivity hold steady within the relevant range of activity.
- Cost and price variables also hold steady during the period being planned.
- The sales mix does not change during the period being planned.
- Production and sales volume are roughly equal.

If one or more of these conditions and assumptions are absent, the CVP analysis may be misleading.

Applying CVP to Target Profits

The primary goal of a business venture is not to break even, but to generate profits. CVP analysis adjusted for targeted profit can be used to estimate the profitability of a venture. This approach is excellent for "what-if" analysis, in which managers select several scenarios and compute the profit that may be anticipated from each. For instance, what if sales increase by 17,000 units? What effect will the increase have on profit? What if sales increase by only 6,000 units? What if fixed costs are reduced by $14,500? What if the variable unit cost increases by $1.40?

We will continue the My Media Place example to illustrate two ways a business can apply CVP analysis to target profits. Assuming that the company wants to make $4,000 in profit this year, how many website services must it sell to reach the targeted profit?

Contribution Margin Approach Using the contribution margin approach, the number of websites My Media Place must sell to obtain \$4,000 in profit would be computed as follows.

$$\text{Sales Revenue} = \text{Variable Costs} + \text{Fixed Costs} + \text{Profit}$$
$$(\$90 \times \text{Targeted Sales Units}) = (\$50 \times \text{Targeted Sales Units}) + \$20{,}000 + \$4{,}000$$
$$(\$40 \times \text{Targeted Sales Units}) = \$24{,}000$$
$$\text{Targeted Sales Units} = \underline{\underline{600}} \text{ units}$$

Equation Approach Using the equation approach, add the targeted profit to the numerator of the contribution margin breakeven equation and solve for targeted sales in units:

$$\text{Targeted Sales Units} = \frac{\text{Fixed Costs} + \text{Profit}}{\text{Contribution Margin per Unit}}$$

The number of sales units My Media Place needs to generate \$4,000 in profit is computed as follows.

$$\text{Targeted Sales Units} = \frac{\$20{,}000 + \$4{,}000}{\$40}$$
$$= \frac{\$24{,}000}{\$40}$$
$$= \underline{\underline{600}} \text{ units}$$

Contribution Margin Income Statement To summarize My Media Place's plans for the coming year, a contribution income statement can be used, as shown below. The focus of such a statement is on cost behavior, *not* cost function.

My Media Place
Contribution Income Statement
For the Year Ended December 31

	Per Unit	Total for 600 Units
Sales revenue	\$90	\$54,000
Less variable costs	50	30,000
Contribution margin	\$40	\$24,000
Less fixed costs		20,000
Operating income		\$ 4,000

Comparing Alternative Options Using CVP My Media Place's planning team wants to consider three alternatives to the original plan shown in the statement.

Alternative 1: Decrease Variable Costs, Increase Sales Volume What if website design labor were outsourced? Based on the planning team's research, the direct labor cost of a website would decrease by \$3 to \$47 and sales volume would increase by 10 percent to 660 units. How does this alternative affect operating income?

Alternative 1	Per Unit	Total for 660 Units
Sales revenue	\$90	\$59,400
Less variable costs	47	31,020
Contribution margin	\$43	\$28,380
Less fixed costs		20,000
Operating income		\$ 8,380
Increase in operating income (\$8,380 − \$4,000)		\$ 4,380

Alternative 2: Increase Fixed Costs, Increase Sales Volume What if the Marketing Department suggests that a $500 increase in advertising costs would increase sales volume by 5 percent to 630 units? How does this alternative affect operating income?

Aternative 2	Per Unit	Total for 630 Units
Sales revenue	$90	$56,700
Less variable costs	50	31,500
Contribution margin	$40	$25,200
Less fixed costs		20,500
Operating income		$ 4,700
Increase in operating income ($4,700 − $4,000)		$ 700

Alternative 3: Increase Selling Price, Decrease Sales Volume What is the impact of a $10 increase in selling price on the company's operating income? If the selling price is increased, the planning team estimates that the sales volume will decrease by 15 percent to 510 units. How does this alternative affect operating income?

Alternative 3	Per Unit	Total for 510 Units
Sales revenue	$100	$51,000
Less variable costs	50	25,500
Contribution margin	$ 50	$25,500
Less fixed costs		20,000
Operating income		$ 5,500
Increase in operating income ($5,500 − $4,000)		$ 1,500

Comparative Summary In preparation for a meeting, the planning team at My Media Place compiled the summary presented in Exhibit 11. It compares the three alternatives with the original plan and shows how changes in variable and fixed costs, selling price, and sales volume affect the breakeven point.

Exhibit 11
Comparative Summary of Alternatives

	Original Plan	Alternative 1	Alternative 2	Alternative 3
	Totals for 600 Units	Decrease Direct Materials Costs for 660 Units	Increase Advertising Costs for 630 Units	Increase Selling Price for 510 Units
Sales revenue	$54,000	$59,400	$56,700	$51,000
Less variable costs	30,000	31,020	31,500	25,500
Contribution margin	$24,000	$28,380	$25,200	$25,500
Less fixed costs	20,000	20,000	20,500	20,000
Operating income	$ 4,000	$ 8,380	$ 4,700	$ 5,500
Breakeven point in whole units (FC ÷ CM):				
$20,000 ÷ $40 =	500			
$20,000 ÷ $43 =		466*		
$20,500 ÷ $40 =			513*	
$20,000 ÷ $50 =				400

*Rounded up to next whole unit

The three alternatives differ as follows.

- The decrease in variable costs (direct materials) proposed in Alternative 1 increases the contribution margin per unit (from \$40 to \$43), which reduces the breakeven point. Because fewer sales dollars are required to cover variable costs, the breakeven point is reached sooner than in the original plan—at a sales volume of 466 units rather than at 500 units.
- In Alternative 2, the increase in fixed costs has no effect on the contribution margin per unit, but it does require the total contribution margin to cover more fixed costs before reaching the breakeven point. Thus, the breakeven point is higher than in the original plan—513 units, as opposed to 500.
- The increase in selling price in Alternative 3 increases the contribution margin per unit, which reduces the breakeven point. Because more sales dollars are available to cover fixed costs, the breakeven point of 400 units is lower than the breakeven point in the original plan.

From a strategic standpoint, which plan should the planning team choose? If they want the highest operating income, they will choose Alternative 1. If, however, they want the company to begin generating operating income more quickly, they will choose the plan with the lowest breakeven point, Alternative 3. Additional quantitative and qualitative information may help the planning team make a better decision. While quantitative information is essential for planning, managers must also be sensitive to qualitative factors, such as product quality, reliability and quality of suppliers, and availability of human and technical resources.

Besides using cost-volume-profit analysis for planning and evaluating purposes, it can be a useful tool in the performing stage of the management process for determining cost behavior and in the communicating stage for providing relevant information for internal decision makers and for summarizing performance in external reports. Exhibit 12 summarizes how CVP analysis relates to the management process.

Exhibit 12
CVP and the Management Process

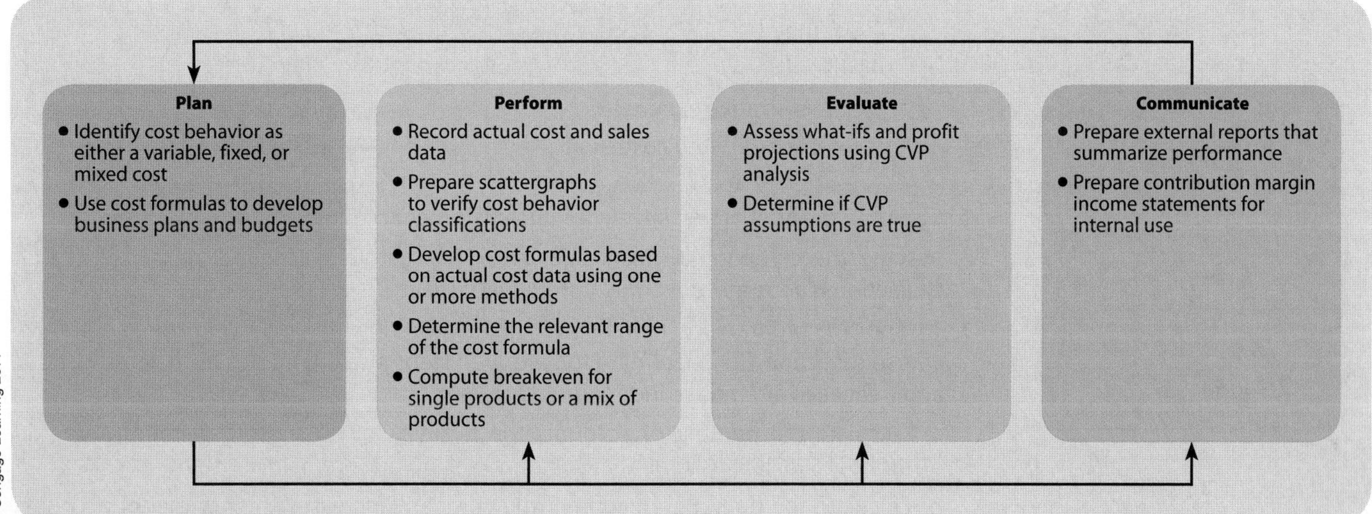

APPLY IT!

A local real estate appraisal business is planning its home appraisal activities for the coming year. The manager estimates that her variable costs per appraisal will be \$220, monthly fixed costs are \$16,200, and service fee revenue will be \$400 per appraisal. How many appraisals will the business have to perform each month to achieve a targeted profit of \$18,000 per month?

SOLUTION

Sales Revenue − Variable Costs − Fixed Costs = Profit

(\$400 × Targeted Sales Units) −
(\$220 × Targeted Sales Units) − \$16,200 = \$18,000
\$180 × Targeted Sales Units = \$34,200
Targeted Sales Units = 190 appraisals per month

TRY IT! SE9, SE10, E12A, E13A, E14A, E15A, E12B, E13B, E14B, E15B

TriLevel Problem

oliveromg/Shutterstock.com

Flickr

The beginning of this chapter focused on **Flickr**, a company whose business is continually evolving to meet changing customer preferences. Complete the following requirements in order to answer the questions posed at the beginning of the chapter.

Section 1: Concepts

Why is cost-volume-profit analysis useful for the purposes of comparability and understandability?

Section 2: Accounting Applications

How will Flickr's managers decide which products and services to offer? Suppose Flickr is considering entering the online digital lockbox business by renting server space to customers to store their movies, music, photos, and other computer files. Its managers believe this service has a large potential market as more individuals and small businesses are starting to move their backup files to secure online servers that can be accessed around the clock. A summary of the data projections for this potential service offering follows.

Selling price per year per customer account	$95
Variable costs per unit:	
Direct supplies	$23
Direct labor	8
Overhead	6
Selling expense	5
Total variable costs per unit	$42
Annual fixed costs:	
Overhead	$195,000
Advertising	55,000
Administrative expense	68,000
Total annual fixed costs	$318,000

1. Compute the annual breakeven point in customer accounts.
2. Assume the company projects sales to 6,500 customer accounts next year. If that projection is accurate, how much profit will it realize?
3. To improve profitability, management is considering the following four alternative courses of action. (In performing the required steps, use the figures from items **1** and **2**, and treat each alternative independently.)
   a. Calculate the number of accounts the business must sell to generate a targeted profit of $95,400. Assume that costs and selling price remain constant.
   b. Calculate the operating income if the company increases the number of accounts sold by 20 percent and cuts the selling price by $5 per account.
   c. Determine the number of accounts that must be sold to break even if advertising costs (fixed costs) increase by $47,700.
   d. Find the number of accounts that must be sold to generate a targeted profit of $120,000 if variable costs decrease by 10 percent.

Section 3: Business Applications

How can managers use cost behavior analysis to improve business performance? To answer this question, match this chapter's manager responsibilities with when they occur within the management process.

a. Plan
b. Perform
c. Evaluate
d. Communicate

1. Use actual data to develop cost formulas
2. Identify variable, fixed, or mixed costs
3. Assess what-ifs and profit projections
4. Use cost formulas to develop business plans and budgets
5. Record actual cost and sales data
6. Determine the relevant range of the cost formula
7. Prepare scatter diagrams to verify cost behavior classifications
8. Prepare external reports
9. Compute breakeven for single products or a mix of products
10. Prepare contribution margin income statements for internal use
11. Determine if CVP assumptions are true

SOLUTION

Concepts

Two underlying accounting concepts support the usefulness of cost-volume-profit analysis: *understandability* and *comparability*. Knowing how costs will behave improves a user's comprehension of the meaning of the information they have received, enhancing their understanding of it. Knowledge of cost behavior patterns enables users to identify cost similarities and differences so comparisons of alternatives are possible. As a result, managers commonly use cost behavior information when they select the course of action that will best generate income for an organization's owners, maintain liquidity for its creditors, and use the organization's resources responsibly. With an understanding of cost behavior patterns, managers can use cost-volume-profit (CVP) analysis to evaluate "what-if" scenarios and to determine selling prices that cover both fixed and variable costs and that take into account the variability of demand for their company's products or services.

Accounting Applications

1. Breakeven Point Units $= \dfrac{\text{Fixed Costs}}{\text{Contribution Margin per Unit}}$

$$= \frac{\$318{,}000}{\$95 - \$42} = \frac{\$318{,}000}{\$53} = \underline{\underline{6{,}000}} \text{ units}$$

2. Profit at 6,500 accounts:

Units sold	6,500
Units required to break even	6,000
Units over breakeven	500
Profit = \$53 per unit × 500 =	\$26,500

Contribution margin equals sales minus all variable costs. Contribution margin per account equals the amount left to cover fixed costs and earn a profit after variable costs have been subtracted from sales dollars. If all fixed costs have been absorbed by the time breakeven is reached, the entire contribution margin of each unit sold in excess of breakeven represents profit.

3. (a) $\text{Targeted Sales Units} = \dfrac{\text{Fixed Costs} + \text{Profit}}{\text{Contribution Margin per Unit}}$

$$= \frac{\$318{,}000 + \$95{,}400}{\$53} = \frac{\$413{,}400}{\$53}$$

$$= \underline{\underline{7{,}800}} \text{ units}$$

(b)

Sales revenue [(6,500 × 1.20) accounts at $90 per account]	$702,000
Less variable costs (7,800 units × $42)	327,600
Contribution margin	$374,400
Less fixed costs	318,000
Operating income	$ 56,400

(c) $\text{Breakeven Point Units} = \dfrac{\text{Fixed Costs}}{\text{Contribution Margin per Unit}}$

$$= \frac{\$318{,}000 + \$47{,}700}{\$53} = \frac{\$365{,}700}{\$53}$$

$$= \underline{\underline{6{,}900}} \text{ units*}$$

(d) $\text{Targeted Sales Units} = \dfrac{\text{Fixed Costs} + \text{Profit}}{\text{Contribution Margin per Unit}}$

$$= \frac{\$318{,}000 + \$120{,}000}{\$95 - (\$42 \times 0.9)} = \frac{\$438{,}000}{\$57.20}$$

$$= \underline{\underline{7{,}658}} \text{ units*}$$

*Rounded

Business Applications

1. b
2. a
3. c
4. a
5. b
6. b
7. b
8. d
9. b
10. d
11. c

Chapter Review

Define *cost behavior*, and identify variable, fixed, and mixed costs. LO 1

Cost behavior is the way costs respond to changes in volume or activity. Some costs vary in relation to volume or operating activity; other costs remain fixed as volume changes. Total costs that change in direct proportion to changes in productive output (or any other volume measure) are called variable costs. They include hourly wages, the cost of operating supplies, direct materials costs, and the cost of merchandise. Total fixed costs remain constant within a relevant range of volume or activity. They change only when volume or activity exceeds the relevant range—for example, when new equipment or new buildings must be purchased, higher insurance premiums and property taxes must be paid, or additional supervisory personnel must be hired to accommodate increased activity. A mixed cost, such as the cost of electricity, has both variable and fixed cost components.

Separate mixed costs into their variable and fixed components, and prepare a contribution margin income statement. LO 2

Mixed costs must be separated into their variable and fixed components, using a variety of methods, including the engineering, scatter diagram, high-low, and statistical methods. When preparing a contribution margin income statement, all variable costs related to production, selling, and administration are subtracted from sales to determine the total contribution margin. Then, all fixed costs are subtracted from the total contribution margin to determine operating income.

Perform cost-volume-profit (CVP) analysis. 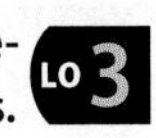

Cost-volume-profit analysis is an examination of the cost behavior patterns that underlie the relationships among cost, volume of output, and profit. It is a tool for both planning and control.

Define *breakeven point*, and use contribution margin to determine a company's breakeven point for multiple products. LO 4

The breakeven point is the point at which total revenues equal total costs—the point at which net sales equal variable costs plus fixed costs. Once the number of units needed to break even is known, the number can be multiplied by the product's selling price to determine the breakeven point in sales dollars. Contribution margin is the amount that remains after all variable costs have been subtracted from sales. A product's contribution margin represents its net contribution to paying off fixed costs and earning a profit. The breakeven point in units can be computed by using the following formula:

$$\text{Breakeven Point Units} = \frac{\text{Fixed Costs}}{\text{Contribution Margin per Unit}}$$

Sales mix is used to calculate the breakeven point for each product when a company sells more than one product.

Discuss how managers use CVP analysis in the management process and how they can project the profitability of products and services. LO 5

CVP relationships provide a general model of financial activity that management can use for short-range planning and for evaluating performance and analyzing alternatives. The addition of targeted profit to the breakeven equation makes it possible to plan levels of operation that yield the desired profit. The formula in terms of contribution margin is:

$$\text{Targeted Sales Units} = \frac{\text{Fixed Costs} - \text{Profit}}{\text{Contribution Margin per Unit}}$$

CVP analysis enables managers to select several "what-if" scenarios and evaluate the outcome of each to determine which will generate the desired results.

Key Terms

activity base 874 (LO1)
breakeven point 881 (LO4)
contribution margin (CM) 879 (LO2)
contribution margin income statement 879 (LO2)
cost behavior 872 (LO1)
cost-volume-profit (CVP) analysis 881 (LO3)
engineering method 879 (LO2)
fixed cost formula 874 (LO1)
fixed costs 874 (LO1)
high-low method 878 (LO2)
margin of safety 881 (LO4)
mixed cost formula 875 (LO1)
mixed costs 875 (LO1)
normal capacity 874 (LO1)
operating capacity 873 (LO1)
practical capacity 874 (LO1)
regression analysis 879 (LO2)
relevant range 874 (LO1)
sales mix 884 (LO4)
scatter diagram 877 (LO2)
step cost 874 (LO1)
theoretical capacity 874 (LO1)
variable cost formula 873 (LO1)
variable costs 872 (LO1)

Chapter Assignments

DISCUSSION QUESTIONS

LO 1 **DQ1. CONCEPT ▶** Describe how the identification of variable, fixed, and mixed costs increases cost comparability and understanding within the relevant range of volume or activity.

LO 2 **DQ2. CONCEPT ▶** What methods separate mixed costs into their fixed and variable components to better understand cost behavior?

LO 2 **DQ3. CONCEPT ▶** How does the preparation of a contribution margin income statement enhance cost behavior understanding and comparisons?

LO 3, 4 **DQ4. CONCEPT ▶** How does cost-volume-profit (CVP) analysis improve understanding and comparisons when using the contribution margin to determine a company's breakeven point for a single product or multiple products?

LO 5 **DQ5. CONCEPT ▶ BUSINESS APPLICATION ▶** Why does CVP analysis in the management process reinforce the concepts of comparability and understandability to better business profitability?

SHORT EXERCISES

LO 1 **Accounting Concepts**

SE1. CONCEPT ▶ Match the accounting concepts with why they support the decision usefulness of CVP analysis.

a. Understandability
b. Comparability

1. A quality that enables users to identify similarities and differences between alternatives
2. A quality that enables users to comprehend the meaning of the information they receive

LO 1 **Identification of Variable, Fixed, and Mixed Costs**

SE2. Identify the following as (a) fixed costs, (b) variable costs, or (c) mixed costs:

1. Direct materials
2. Electricity
3. Factory building rent
4. Manager's salary
5. Operating supplies

LO 2 **Mixed Costs: High-Low Method**

SE3. Using the high-low method, compute Soho Corporation's monthly variable cost per telephone hour and total fixed costs.

Month	Telephone Hours Used	Telephone Costs
April	95	$4,350
May	90	4,230
June	100	4,680

LO 2, 3 **Contribution Margin Income Statement**

SE4. Prepare a contribution margin income statement if Greenwich, Inc., wants to make a profit of $50,000. It has variable costs of $10 per unit and fixed costs of $20,000. How much must it charge per unit if 5,000 units are sold?

LO 4 **Breakeven Analysis in Units and Dollars**

SE5. How many units must Queens Company sell to break even if the selling price per unit is $9, variable costs are $5 per unit, and fixed costs are $6,000? What is the breakeven point in total dollars of sales?

LO 4 **Contribution Margin in Units**

SE6. Using the contribution margin approach, find the breakeven point in units for Staten Products if the selling price per unit is $11, the variable cost per unit is $4, and the fixed costs are $7,700.

LO 4 **Contribution Margin Ratio**

SE7. Compute the contribution margin ratio and the breakeven point in total sales dollars for Wall Street Products if the selling price per unit is $16, the variable cost per unit is $8, and the fixed costs are $6,250.

LO 4 **Breakeven Analysis for Multiple Products**

SE8. Using the contribution margin approach, find the breakeven point in units for Suffolk Company's two products. Product A's selling price per unit is $10, and its variable cost per unit is $4. Product B's selling price per unit is $8, and its variable cost per unit is $5. Fixed costs are $14,175, and the sales mix of Product A to Product B is 3:1.

LO 2, 5 **Monthly Costs and the High-Low Method**

SE9. Pup Noir, a private investigation firm, investigated 90 cases in December and had the following costs: direct labor, $190 per case; and service overhead of $20,840. Service overhead for October was $21,150; for November, it was $21,350. The number of cases investigated during October and November was 92 and 95, respectively. Compute the variable and fixed cost components of service overhead using the high-low method. Then determine the variable and fixed costs per case for December. (Round final answers to the nearest dollar where necessary.)

LO 3, 5 **CVP Analysis and Projected Profit**

SE10. If Bronx Watches sells 300 watches at $38 per watch and has variable costs of $18 per watch and fixed costs of $4,000, what is the projected profit?

EXERCISES: SET A

LO 1 **Identification of Variable and Fixed Costs**

E1A. Indicate whether each of the following costs of productive output is usually (a) variable or (b) fixed:

1. License fee for company car
2. Wiring used in radios
3. Machine helper's wages
4. Wood used in bookcases
5. City operating license
6. Machine depreciation based on machine hours used
7. Machine operator's hourly wages
8. Cost of required outside inspection of each unit produced

LO 1 **Variable Cost Analysis**

E2A. Zero Time Oil Change has been in business for six months. The company pays $0.75 per quart for the oil it uses in servicing cars. Each job requires an average of 4 quarts of oil. The company estimates that in the next three months, it will service 250, 280, and 360 cars.

1. Compute the cost of oil for each of the three months and the total cost for all three months.
2. Complete the following sentences by choosing the words that best describe the cost behavior at Zero Time:
   a. Cost per unit (increased, decreased, remained constant).
   b. Total variable cost per month (increased, decreased) as the quantity of oil used (increased, decreased).

LO 2 **Mixed Costs: High-Low Method**

E3A. Madison Company manufactures major appliances. Because of growing interest in its products, it has just had its most successful year. In preparing the budget for next year, its controller compiled the following information:

Month	Volume in Machine Hours	Electricity Cost
July	6,000	$ 60,000
August	5,000	53,000
September	4,500	49,500
October	4,000	46,000
November	3,500	42,500
December	3,000	36,000
Six-month total	26,000	$287,000

Using the high-low method, determine the variable electricity cost per machine hour and the monthly fixed electricity cost. Estimate the total variable electricity costs and fixed electricity costs if 4,800 machine hours are projected to be used next month.

LO 2 **Mixed Costs: High-Low Method**

E4A. When Jerome Company's monthly costs were $80,000, sales were $90,000. When its monthly costs were $60,000, sales were $50,000. Use the high-low method to develop a monthly cost formula for Jerome's coming year.

LO 2, 4 **Contribution Margin Income Statement and Ratio**

E5A. Bowery Company manufactures a single product that sells for $100 per unit. The company projects sales of 400 units per month. Projected costs follow.

Type of Cost	Manufacturing	Nonmanufacturing
Variable	$10,000	$6,000
Nonvariable	13,000	5,000

1. Prepare a contribution margin income statement for the month.
2. What is the contribution margin ratio?
3. What volume, in terms of units, must the company sell to break even?

LO 3, 4 **Contribution Margin Income Statement and Breakeven Analysis**

E6A. Using the data in the contribution margin income statement for Broadway, Inc., that follows, calculate (a) selling price per unit, (b) variable costs per unit, and (c) break-even point in units and in sales dollars.

Broadway, Inc.
Contribution Margin Income Statement
For the Year Ended December 31

Sales (20,000 units)		$16,000,000
Less variable costs:		
Cost of goods sold	$8,000,000	
Selling, administrative, and general	4,000,000	
Total variable costs		12,000,000
Contribution margin		$ 4,000,000
Less fixed costs:		
Overhead	$1,200,000	
Selling, administrative, and general	800,000	
Total fixed costs		2,000,000
Operating income		$ 2,000,000

LO 4 **Breakeven Analysis**

E7A. Meadowlands Design produces head covers for golf clubs. The company expects to generate a profit next year. It anticipates fixed manufacturing costs of $200,500 and fixed general and administrative expenses of $80,000 for the year. Variable manufacturing and selling costs per set of head covers will be $8 and $12, respectively. Each set will sell for $30.

1. Compute the breakeven point in sales units.
2. Compute the breakeven point in sales dollars.
3. If the selling price is increased to $34 per unit and fixed general and administrative expenses are cut to $37,500, what will the new breakeven point be in units?
4. Prepare a graph to illustrate the breakeven point computed in **3**.

LO 4 **Breakeven Point for Multiple Products**

E8A. Eastside Aquarium, Inc., manufactures and sells aquariums, water pumps, and air filters. The sales mix is 1:2:2 (i.e., for every one aquarium sold, two water pumps and two air filters are sold). Using the contribution margin approach, find the breakeven point in units for each product. The company's fixed costs are $52,000. Other information follows.

	Selling Price per Unit	Variable Costs per Unit
Aquariums	$60	$25
Water pumps	20	12
Air filters	10	3

LO 4 **Breakeven Point for Multiple Products**

E9A. Hamburgers and More, Inc., sells hamburgers, drinks, and fries. The sales mix is 1:3:2 (i.e., for every one hamburger sold, three drinks and two fries are sold). Using the contribution margin approach, find the breakeven point in units for each product. The company's fixed costs are $1,020. Other information follows.

	Selling Price per Unit	Variable Costs per Unit
Hamburgers	$0.99	$0.27
Drinks	0.99	0.09
Fries	0.99	0.15

LO 4 **Sales Mix Analysis**

E10A. Marj Plimpton is the owner of a hairdressing salon in New York City. Her salon provides three basic services: shampoo and set, permanent, and cut and blow dry. Its operating results from the past quarter follow.

Type of Service	Number of Customers	Total Sales	Contribution Margin in Dollars
Shampoo and set	1,200	$24,000	$14,700
Permanent	420	21,000	15,120
Cut and blow dry	1,000	15,000	10,000
	2,620	$60,000	$39,820
Total fixed costs			40,000
Profit (loss)			$ (180)

Compute the breakeven point in units based on the weighted-average contribution margin for the sales mix.

LO 2, 5

Cost Behavior in a Service Business

E11A. BUSINESS APPLICATION ▶ Jim Lucky, CPA, is the owner of a firm that provides payroll support services. The firm charges $40 per payroll return for the direct professional labor involved in preparing the payroll and submitting the required tax forms. In January, the firm prepared 50 such returns; in February, 100; and in March, 70. Service overhead (telephone and utilities, depreciation on equipment and building, tax forms, office supplies, and wages of clerical personnel) for January was $2,000; for February, $3,500; and for March, $2,700.

1. Using the high-low method, determine the variable and fixed cost components of the firm's Service Overhead account.
2. What would the estimated total cost per tax return be if the firm prepares 80 payroll forms in April?

LO 4, 5

CVP Analysis and Profit Planning

E12A. BUSINESS APPLICATION ▶ Cos Cob Systems, Inc., makes heat-seeking missiles. It has recently been offered a government contract from which it may realize a profit. The contract purchase price is $130,000 per missile, but the number of units to be purchased has not yet been decided. The company's fixed costs are budgeted at $4,035,000, and variable costs are $68,500 per unit.

1. Compute the number of units the company should agree to make at the stated contract price to earn a profit of $1,500,000.
2. Using a lighter material, the variable unit cost can be reduced by $1,730, but total fixed overhead will increase by $29,240. How many units must be produced to make $1,500,000 in profit?
3. Given the figures in **2**, how many additional units must be produced to increase profit by $1,264,600?

LO 4, 5

Planning Future Sales

E13A. BUSINESS APPLICATION ▶ Short-term automobile rentals are Snap Rentals, Inc.'s specialty. Average variable operating costs have been $20 per day per automobile. The company owns 50 automobiles. Fixed operating costs for the next year are expected to be $150,000. Average daily rental revenue per automobile is expected to be $40. Management would like to earn a profit of $50,000 during the year.

1. Calculate the total number of daily rentals the company must have during the year to earn the targeted profit.
2. On the basis of your answer to **1**, determine the average number of days each automobile must be rented.
3. Determine the total revenue needed to achieve the targeted profit of $50,000.
4. What would the total rental revenue be if fixed operating costs could be lowered by $5,000 and the targeted profit increased to $70,000?

LO 4, 5

CVP Analysis in a Service Business

E14A. BUSINESS APPLICATION ▶ Westport Inspection Service specializes in inspecting cars that have been returned to automobile leasing companies at the end of their leases. Westport's charge for each inspection is $60; its average cost per inspection is $15. The owner wants to expand his business by hiring another employee and purchasing an automobile. The fixed costs of the new employee and automobile would be $3,000 per month. How many inspections per month would the new employee have to perform to earn a profit of $1,500?

LO 3, 4, 5

CVP and Breakeven Analysis and Pricing

E15A. Americas Company has a plant capacity of 100,000 units per year, but its budget for this year indicates that only 60,000 units will be produced and sold. The entire budget for this year follows.

Sales (60,000 units at $3.75)		$225,000
Less cost of goods produced (based on production of 60,000 units):		
Direct materials (variable)	$60,000	
Direct labor (variable)	30,000	
Variable overhead costs	45,000	
Fixed overhead costs	75,000	
Total cost of goods produced		210,000
Gross margin		$ 15,000
Less selling and administrative expenses:		
Selling (fixed)	$24,000	
Administrative (fixed)	36,000	
Total selling and administrative expenses		60,000
Operating income (loss)		$(45,000)

1. Given the budgeted selling price and cost data, how many units would Americas have to sell to break even? (*Hint:* Be sure to consider selling and administrative expenses.)
2. **BUSINESS APPLICATION ▶** Market research indicates that if Americas were to drop its selling price to $3.70 per unit, it could sell 100,000 units. Would you recommend the drop in price? What would the new operating income or loss be?

EXERCISES: SET B

Visit the textbook companion website at www.cengagebrain.com to access Exercise Set B for this chapter.

PROBLEMS

LO 1, 2, 5

Cost Behavior and Projection for a Service Business

✔ 2: Fixed cost component of mixed cost: $1,145
✔ 3: Average cost per job: $907.76

P1. Wabash Company specializes in refurbishing exterior painted surfaces that have been hard hit by humidity and insect debris. It uses a special technique, called pressure cleaning, before priming and painting the surface. The refurbishing process involves the following steps:

1. Unskilled laborers trim all trees and bushes within two feet of the structure.
2. Skilled laborers clean the building with a high-pressure cleaning machine, using about 6 gallons of chlorine per job.
3. Unskilled laborers apply a coat of primer.
4. Skilled laborers apply oil-based exterior paint to the entire surface.

On average, skilled laborers work 12 hours per job, and unskilled laborers work 8 hours. The refurbishing process generated the following operating results during the year on 500 jobs:

Skilled labor	$20	per hour
Unskilled labor	$8	per hour
Gallons of chlorine used	3,000	gallons at $5.50 per gallon
Paint primer	7,536	gallons at $15.50 per gallon
Paint	6,280	gallons at $16.00 per gallon
Depreciation of paint-spraying equipment	$600	per month depreciation
Lease of two vans	$800	per month total
Rent on storage building	$421	per month

(Continued)

Data on utilities for the year follow:

Month	Number of Jobs	Cost	Hours Worked
January	42	$ 3,950	840
February	37	3,550	740
March	44	4,090	880
April	49	4,410	980
May	54	4,720	1,080
June	62	5,240	1,240
July	71	5,820	1,420
August	73	5,890	1,460
September	63	5,370	1,260
October	48	4,340	960
November	45	4,210	900
December	40	3,830	800
Totals	628	$55,420	12,560

REQUIRED

1. Classify the costs as variable, fixed, or mixed.
2. Using the high-low method, separate mixed costs into their variable and fixed components. Use total hours worked as the basis.
3. Compute the average cost per job for the year. (*Hint:* Divide the total of all costs for the year by the number of jobs completed.) Use estimated hours to determine utilities costs. (Round to two decimal places.)
4. **BUSINESS APPLICATION ▶** Project the average cost per job for next year if variable costs per job increase 20 percent. (Round to two decimal places.)
5. **ACCOUNTING CONNECTION ▶** Why can actual utilities costs vary from the amount computed using the utilities cost formula?

LO **4, 5**

Breakeven Analysis

✔ 1: Breakeven hours: 7,500 hours

P2. Park & Morgan, a law firm, is considering opening a legal clinic for middle- and low-income clients. The clinic would bill at a rate of $18 per hour. It would employ law students as paraprofessional help and pay them $9 per hour. Other variable costs are anticipated to be $5.40 per hour, and annual fixed costs are expected to total $27,000.

REQUIRED

1. Compute the breakeven point in billable hours.
2. Compute the breakeven point in total billings.
3. **BUSINESS APPLICATION ▶** Find the new breakeven point in total billings if fixed costs should go up by $2,340.
4. **BUSINESS APPLICATION ▶** Using the original figures, compute the breakeven point in total billings if the billing rate decreases by $1 per hour, other variable costs decrease by $0.40 per hour, and fixed costs go down by $3,600.

LO **3, 4, 5**

Planning Future Sales: Contribution Margin Approach

✔ 1a: Breakeven units: 3,500 units
✔ 3: Selling price: $51

P3. BUSINESS APPLICATION ▶ All Honors Industries is considering a new product for its Trophy Division. The product, which would feature an alligator, is expected to have global market appeal and to become the mascot for many high school and university athletic teams. Expected variable unit costs are as follows: direct materials, $18.50; direct labor, $4.25; production supplies, $1.10; selling costs, $2.80; and other, $1.95. Annual fixed costs are depreciation, building, and equipment, $36,000; advertising, $45,000; and other, $11,400. Plans are to sell the product for $55.

REQUIRED

1. Using the contribution margin approach, compute the number of units the company must sell to (a) break even and (b) earn a profit of $70,224.
2. Using the same data, compute the number of units that must be sold to earn a profit of $139,520 if advertising costs rise by $40,000.
3. Using the original information and sales of 10,000 units, compute the selling price the company must use to make a profit of $131,600. (*Hint:* Calculate contribution margin per unit first.)
4. According to the vice president of marketing, Flora Albert, the most optimistic annual sales estimate for the product would be 15,000 units, and the highest competitive selling price the company can charge is $52 per unit. How much more can be spent on fixed advertising costs if the selling price is $52, the variable costs cannot be reduced, and the targeted profit for 15,000 unit sales is $251,000?

LO **4, 5**

Breakeven Analysis and Planning Future Sales

✔ 1a: Breakeven units: 150,000 units
✔ 2: 190,000 units

P4. Marina Company has a maximum capacity of 200,000 units per year. Variable manufacturing costs are $12 per unit. Fixed overhead is $600,000 per year. Variable selling and administrative costs are $5 per unit, and fixed selling and administrative costs are $300,000 per year. The current sales price is $23 per unit.

REQUIRED

1. What is the breakeven point in (a) sales units and (b) sales dollars?
2. **BUSINESS APPLICATION ▶** How many units must Marina Company sell to earn a profit of $240,000 per year?
3. **BUSINESS APPLICATION ▶** A strike at one of the company's major suppliers has caused a shortage of materials, so the current year's production and sales are limited to 160,000 units. To partially offset the effect of the reduced sales on profit, management is planning to reduce fixed costs to $841,000. Variable costs per unit are the same as last year. The company has already sold 30,000 units at the regular selling price of $23 per unit.
   a. What amount of fixed costs was covered by the total contribution margin of the first 30,000 units sold?
   b. What contribution margin per unit will be needed on the remaining 130,000 units to cover the remaining fixed costs and to earn a profit of $210,000 this year?

LO **3, 4, 5**

Planning Future Sales for a Service Business

✔ 1a: 262 loans
✔ 3: Loan application fee: $255

P5. BUSINESS APPLICATION ▶ State Street Lending processes loan applications. The manager of the loan department has established a policy of charging a $250 fee for every loan application processed. Variable costs have been projected as follows: loan consultant's wages, $15.50 per hour (a loan application takes 5 hours to process); supplies, $2.40 per application; and other variable costs, $5.60 per application. Annual fixed costs include depreciation of equipment, $8,500; building rental, $14,000; promotional costs, $12,500; and other fixed costs, $8,099.

REQUIRED

1. Using the contribution margin approach, compute the number of loan applications the company must process to (a) break even and (b) earn a profit of $14,476.
2. Using the same approach and assuming promotional costs increase by $5,662, compute the number of applications the company must process to earn a profit of $20,000.
3. Assuming the original information and the processing of 500 applications, compute the loan application fee the company must charge if the targeted profit is $41,651.
4. The maximum number of loan applications that the department can process is 750. How much more can be spent on promotional costs if the highest fee tolerable to the customer is $280, if variable costs cannot be reduced, and if the targeted profit is $50,000?

ALTERNATE PROBLEMS

LO 1, 2, 5

Mixed Costs

✔ 1: Total fixed cost: $2,250
✔ 3: Total repairs and maintenance cost: $99,824

P6. Officials of the Oakbrook Hills Golf and Tennis Club are in the process of preparing a budget for the year ending December 31. Because the club treasurer has had difficulty with two expense items, the process has been delayed. The two items are mixed costs—expenses for electricity and for repairs and maintenance—and the treasurer has been having trouble breaking them down into their variable and fixed components.

An accountant friend has suggested that he use the high-low method to divide the costs into their variable and fixed parts. The spending patterns and activity measures related to each cost during the past year are as follows:

	Electricity Expense		Repairs and Maintenance	
Month	**Amount**	**Kilowatt-Hours**	**Amount**	**Labor Hours**
January	$ 7,500	210,000	$ 7,578	220
February	8,255	240,200	7,852	230
March	8,165	236,600	7,304	210
April	8,960	268,400	7,030	200
May	7,520	210,800	7,852	230
June	7,025	191,000	8,126	240
July	6,970	188,800	8,400	250
August	6,990	189,600	8,674	260
September	7,055	192,200	8,948	270
October	7,135	195,400	8,674	260
November	8,560	252,400	8,126	240
December	8,415	246,600	7,852	230
Totals	$92,550	2,622,000	$96,416	2,840

REQUIRED

1. Using the high-low method, compute the variable cost rates used last year for each expense. What was the monthly fixed cost for electricity and for repairs and maintenance? (Round variable cost rate answers to three decimal places.)
2. Compute the total variable cost and total fixed cost for each expense category for last year.
3. **BUSINESS APPLICATION ▶** The treasurer believes that in the coming year, the electricity rate will increase by $0.005 and the repairs rate, by $1.20. Usage of all items and their fixed cost amounts will remain constant. Compute the projected total cost for each category. How will the cost increases affect the club's profits and cash flow?

LO 4, 5

Breakeven Analysis

✔ 1: Breakeven units: 740 systems
✔ 4: Breakeven units: 790 systems

P7. At the beginning of each year, LED Lighting, Ltd.'s Accounting Department must find the point at which projected sales revenue will equal total budgeted variable and fixed costs. The company produces low-voltage outdoor lighting systems. Each system sells for an average of $435. Variable costs per unit are $210. Total fixed costs for the year are estimated to be $166,500.

REQUIRED

1. Compute the breakeven point in sales units.
2. Compute the breakeven point in sales dollars.
3. **BUSINESS APPLICATION ▶** Find the new breakeven point in sales units if the fixed costs go up by $10,125.
4. **BUSINESS APPLICATION ▶** Using the original figures, compute the breakeven point in sales units if the selling price decreases to $425 per unit, fixed costs go up by $15,200, and variable costs decrease by $15 per unit.

LO 3, 4, 5

✓ 1a: Breakeven units: 7,900 statues
✓ 2: Target sales units: 16,900 statues

Planning Future Sales: Contribution Margin Approach

P8. BUSINESS APPLICATION ▶ Lipsius Marbles manufactures birdbaths, statues, and other decorative items, which it sells to florists and retail home and garden centers. Its design department has proposed a new product, a frog statue, that it believes will be popular with home gardeners. Expected variable unit costs are direct materials, $9.25; direct labor, $4.00; production supplies, $0.55; selling costs, $2.40; and other, $3.05. The following are fixed costs: depreciation, $33,000; advertising, $40,000; and other, $6,000. Management plans to sell the product for $29.25.

REQUIRED

1. Using the contribution margin approach, compute the number of statues the company must sell to (a) break even and (b) earn a profit of $50,000.
2. Using the same data, compute the number of statues that must be sold to earn a profit of $70,000 if advertising costs rise by $20,000.
3. Using the original data and sales of 15,000 units, compute the selling price the company must charge to make a profit of $101,000.
4. According to the vice president of marketing, if the price of the statues is reduced and advertising is increased, the most optimistic annual sales estimate is 25,000 units. How much more can be spent on fixed advertising costs if the selling price is reduced to $28.00 per statue, the variable costs cannot be reduced, and the targeted profit for sales of 25,000 statues is $120,000?

LO 4, 5

✓ 1a: Breakeven units: 200,000 units
✓ 2: Sales units: 300,000 units

Breakeven Analysis and Planning Future Sales

P9. Bar Company has a maximum capacity of 500,000 units per year. Variable manufacturing costs are $25 per unit. Fixed overhead is $900,000 per year. Variable selling and administrative costs are $5 per unit, and fixed selling and administrative costs are $300,000 per year. The current sales price is $36 per unit.

REQUIRED

1. What is the breakeven point in (a) sales units and (b) sales dollars?
2. **BUSINESS APPLICATION ▶** How many units must Bar Company sell to earn a profit of $600,000 per year?
3. **BUSINESS APPLICATION ▶** A strike at one of the company's major suppliers has caused a shortage of materials, so the current year's production and sales are limited to 400,000 units. To partially offset the effect of the reduced sales on profit, management is planning to reduce fixed costs to $1,000,000. Variable cost per unit is the same as last year. The company has already sold 30,000 units at the regular selling price of $36 per unit.
   a. What amount of fixed costs was covered by the total contribution margin of the first 30,000 units sold?
   b. What contribution margin per unit will be needed on the remaining 370,000 units to cover the remaining fixed costs and to earn a profit of $290,000 this year?

LO 3, 4, 5

✓ 1a: Breakeven units: 270 loans
✓ 3: Loan application fee: $403

Planning Future Sales for a Service Business

P10. BUSINESS APPLICATION ▶ Last Mortgage, Inc.'s primary business is processing mortgage loan applications. Last year, the manager of the mortgage application department established a policy of charging a $500 fee for every loan application processed. Next year's variable costs have been projected as follows: mortgage processor wages, $30 per hour (a mortgage application takes 3 hours to process); supplies, $10 per application; and other variable costs, $15 per application. Annual fixed costs include depreciation of equipment, $4,950; building rental, $34,000; promotional costs, $45,000; and other fixed costs, $20,000.

(Continued)

REQUIRED

1. Using the contribution margin approach, compute the number of loan applications the company must process to (a) break even and (b) earn a profit of $50,050.
2. Using the same approach and assuming promotional costs increase by $5,450, compute the number of applications the company must process to earn a profit of $60,000.
3. Assuming the original information and the processing of 500 applications, compute the loan application fee the company must charge if the targeted profit is $40,050.
4. The mortgage department can handle a maximum of 750 loan applications. How much more can be spent on promotional costs if the highest fee tolerable to the customer is $400, if variable costs cannot be reduced, and if the targeted profit for the loan applications is $50,000?

CASES

LO 4 Ethical Dilemma: Breaking Even and Ethics

C1. Les Pulaski is the supervisor of a new division of Innovation Corporation. Her annual bonus is based on the success of new products and is computed on the number of sales that exceed each new product's projected breakeven point. In reviewing the computations supporting her most recent bonus, Pulaski found that although an order for 7,500 units of a new product called R56 had been refused by a customer and returned to the company, the order had been included in the bonus calculations. She later discovered that the company's accountant had labeled the return an overhead expense and had charged the entire cost of the returned order to the plantwide Overhead account. The result was that product R56 appeared to exceed breakeven by more than 5,000 units and Pulaski's bonus from this product amounted to over $1,000. What actions should Pulaski take? Be prepared to discuss your response in class.

LO 1, 4 Group Activity: Cost Behavior and Contribution Margin

C2. Visit a local fast-food restaurant. Observe all aspects of the operation and take notes on the entire process. Describe the procedures used to take, process, and fill an order and deliver the order to the customer. Based on your observations, make a list of the costs incurred by the operation. Identify at least three variable costs and three fixed costs. Can you identify any potential mixed costs? Why is the restaurant willing to sell a large drink for only a few cents more than a medium drink? How is the restaurant able to offer a "value meal" (e.g., sandwich, drink, and fries) for considerably less than those items would cost if they were bought separately? Bring your notes to class and be prepared to discuss your findings.

Your instructor will divide the class into groups to discuss the case. Summarize your group's discussion, and ask one member of the group to present the summary to the rest of the class.

LO 3, 4 Conceptual Understanding: CVP Analysis

C3. Based in Italy, Datura, Ltd., is an international importer-exporter of pottery with distribution centers in the United States, Europe, and Australia. The company was very successful in its early years, but its profitability has since declined. As a member of a management team selected to gather information for Datura's next strategic planning meeting, you have been asked to review its most recent contribution margin income statement for the year ended December 31, 2014, which follows.

Datura, Ltd.
Contribution Margin Income Statement
For the Year Ended December 31, 2014

Sales revenue		€13,500,000
Less variable costs:		
Purchases	€6,000,000	
Distribution	2,115,000	
Sales commissions	1,410,000	
Total variable costs		9,525,000
Contribution margin		€ 3,975,000
Less fixed costs:		
Distribution	€ 985,000	
Selling	1,184,000	
General and administrative	871,875	
Total fixed costs		3,040,875
Operating income		€ 934,125

In 2014, Datura sold 15,000 sets of pottery.

1. For each set of pottery sold in 2014, calculate the (a) selling price, (b) variable purchases cost, (c) variable distribution cost, (d) variable sales commission, and (e) contribution margin.
2. Calculate the breakeven point in units and in sales euros.
3. Historically, Datura's variable costs have been about 60 percent of sales. What was the ratio of variable costs to sales in 2014? (Round to two decimal places.) List three actions Datura could take to correct the difference.
4. How would fixed costs have been affected if Datura had sold only 14,000 sets of pottery in 2014?

LO 5 **Business Communications: CVP Analysis Applied**

C4. Refer to the information in **C3**. In January 2015, the president of Datura, Ltd., conducted a strategic planning meeting. During the meeting, the vice president of distribution noted that because of a new contract with an international shipping line, the company's fixed distribution costs for 2015 would be reduced by 10 percent and its variable distribution costs by 4 percent. The vice president of sales offered the following information:

> *We plan to sell 15,000 sets of pottery again in 2015, but based on review of the competition, we are going to lower the selling price to €890 per set. To encourage increased sales, we will raise sales commissions to 12 percent of the selling price.*

The president is concerned that the changes described by the vice presidents may not improve operating income sufficiently in 2015. If operating income does not increase by at least 10 percent, she will want to find other ways to reduce the company's costs. She asks you to evaluate the situation in a written report. Because it is already January 2015 and changes need to be made quickly, she requests your report within five days.

1. Prepare a budgeted contribution margin income statement for 2015. Your report should show the budgeted (estimated) operating income based on the information provided above and in **C3**. Will the changes improve operating income sufficiently? Explain.
2. In preparation for writing your report, answer the following questions:
   a. Why are you preparing the report?
   b. Who needs the report?
   c. What sources of information will you use?
   d. When is the report due?

LO 5

Decision Analysis: Planning Future Sales

C5. As noted in **C3** and **C4**, Datura, Ltd., sold 15,000 sets of pottery in 2014. For the next year, 2015, Datura's strategic planning team targeted sales of 15,000 sets of pottery, reduced the selling price to €890 per set, increased sales commissions to 12 percent of the selling price, and decreased fixed distribution costs by 10 percent and variable distribution costs by 4 percent. It was assumed that all other costs would stay the same.

Based on an analysis of these changes, Datura's president is concerned that the proposed strategic plan will not meet her goal of increasing Datura's operating income by 10 percent over last year's income and that the operating income will be less than last year's income. She has come to you for spreadsheet analysis of the proposed strategic plan and for analysis of a special order she just received from an Australian distributor for 4,500 sets of pottery. The order's selling price, variable purchases cost per unit, sales commission, and total fixed costs will be the same as for the rest of the business, but the variable distribution costs will be €160 per unit.

Using a spreadsheet, complete the following tasks:

1. Calculate the targeted operating income for 2015 using just the proposed strategic plan. (Round to the nearest whole number.)
2. Prepare a budgeted contribution margin income statement for 2015 based on just the strategic plan. Do you agree with Datura's president that the company's projected operating income for 2015 will be less than the operating income for 2014? Explain your answer.
3. Calculate the total contribution margin from the Australian sales.
4. Prepare a revised budgeted contribution margin income statement for 2015 that includes the Australian order. (*Hint:* Combine the information from **2** and **3** above.)
5. Does Datura need the Australian sales to achieve its targeted operating income for 2015?

Continuing Case: Cookie Company

C6. In this segment of our continuing cookie company case, you will classify the costs of the business as variable, fixed, or mixed; use the high-low method to evaluate utility costs; and prepare a contribution margin income statement.

1. Review your cookie recipe and the overhead costs you identified in previous chapters, and classify the costs as variable, fixed, or mixed costs.
2. Obtain your electric bills for three months, and use the high-low method's cost formula to determine the monthly cost of electricity—that is, monthly electric cost = variable rate per kilowatt-hour + monthly fixed cost. If you do not receive an electric bill, use the following information:

Month	Kilowatt-Hours Used	Electric Costs
August	1,439	$202
September	1,866	230
October	1,146	158

3. a. Prepare a daily contribution margin income statement based on the following assumptions:

   My Cookie Company makes only one kind of cookie and sells it for $1.00 per unit. The company projects sales of 500 units per day. Projected daily costs are as follows:

Type of Cost	Manufacturing	Nonmanufacturing
Variable	$100	$50
Nonvariable	120	60

   b. What is the contribution margin ratio?

   c. What volume, in terms of units, must the company sell to break even each day? (Round to the nearest dollar.)

CHAPTER 20
The Budgeting Process

BUSINESS INSIGHT
Framerica Corporation

Framerica Corporation is one of the leading manufacturers of picture frames in North America. Because the company believes its work force is its most valuable asset, one of its priorities is to help employees attain their personal goals. One highly effective way of achieving congruence between a company's goals and its employees' personal aspirations is through a participatory budgeting process—an ongoing dialogue that involves personnel at all levels of the company in making budgeting decisions. This ongoing dialogue provides both managers and lower-level employees with insight into the company's current activities and future direction and motivates them to improve their performance, which, in turn, improves the company's performance.

1. CONCEPT ▶ *What concepts underlie the usefulness of the budgeting process?*

2. ACCOUNTING APPLICATION ▶ *How does the budgeting process translate long-term goals into operating objectives?*

3. BUSINESS APPLICATION ▶ *Why are budgets an essential part of planning, controlling, evaluating, and reporting on business?*

LEARNING OBJECTIVES

LO 1 **Define *budgeting* and describe how it relates to the concepts of comparability and understandability.**

LO 2 **Identify the elements of a master budget in different types of organizations and the guidelines for preparing budgets.**

LO 3 **Prepare the operating budgets that support the financial budgets.**

LO 4 **Prepare a budgeted income statement, a cash budget, and a budgeted balance sheet.**

LO 5 **Explain why budgeting is essential to the management process.**

SECTION 1 CONCEPTS

CONCEPTS
- Comparability
- Understandability

RELEVANT LEARNING OBJECTIVE

LO 1 Define *budgeting* and describe how it relates to the concepts of comparability and understandability.

LO 1 Concepts Underlying the Budgeting Process

Budgeting is the process of identifying, gathering, summarizing, and communicating financial and nonfinancial information about an organization's future activities. The budgeting process provides managers of all types of organizations the opportunity to match their organizational goals with the resources necessary to accomplish those goals. Budgeting empowers all in the organization to understand organizational goals in terms of their responsibilities and be held accountable for budget plans and results since they can be compared. Budgeting is synonymous with managing an organization. **Budgets** are plans of action based on forecasted transactions, activities, and events.

The concepts of *understandability* and *comparability* underlie the power of budgeting. Budgeting enhances *understandability*, since managers and employees will understand their organizational roles and responsibilities based on how the budget links the organization's strategic plans to its annual plans. Because the budget expresses these plans and objectives in concrete monetary terms, managers and employees are able to understand and act in ways that will achieve them. Budgeting enhances *comparability*, since budget-to-actual comparisons give managers and employees a means of monitoring the results of their actions. As you will see in this chapter, budgeting is not only an essential part of planning; it also helps managers command, control, evaluate, and report on operations.

The Master Budget

A **master budget** consists of a set of operating budgets and a set of financial budgets that detail an organization's financial plans for a specific period, generally a year. When a master budget covers an entire year, some of the operating and financial budgets may show planned results by month or by quarter. As the term implies, **operating budgets** are plans used in daily operations.

Operating budgets include:

- sales budget
- production budget
- direct materials purchases budget
- direct labor budget
- overhead budget
- selling and administrative expenses budget
- cost of goods manufactured budget

The sales budget is prepared first because it is used to estimate sales volume and revenues. Once managers know the quantity of products or services to be sold and how many sales dollars to expect, they can develop other budgets that will enable them to manage their resources so that they generate profits on those sales.

Operating budgets are also the basis for preparing the **financial budgets**, which are projections of financial results for the period.

Financial budgets include:

- a budgeted income statement
- a capital expenditures budget
- a cash budget
- a budgeted balance sheet

STUDY NOTE: *Budgeted financial statements are often referred to as* forecasted financial statements, pro forma financial statements, *or* forward-looking financial statements.

The budgeted income statement and budgeted balance sheet are also called **pro forma financial statements**, meaning that they show projections rather than actual results. Pro forma financial statements are often used to communicate business plans to external parties. For example, if you apply for a bank loan to start a new business, you would have to present a pro forma income statement and balance sheet showing that you could repay the loan with cash generated by profitable operations.

APPLY IT!

A master budget is a compilation of forecasts for the coming year or operating cycle made by various departments or functions within an organization. What is the most important forecast made in a master budget? List the reasons for your answer.

a. Direct materials purchases in units

b. Sales in units

c. Cash outflows

d. Selling expenses

SOLUTION

b. The amount of estimated sales in units is the most important forecast. It is the key to an accurate master budget. The entire master budget is based on the unit sales forecast.

TRY IT! SE1

SECTION 2 ACCOUNTING APPLICATIONS

ACCOUNTING APPLICATIONS

- Prepare operating budgets
  - Sales budget
  - Production budget
  - Direct materials purchases budget
  - Direct labor budget
  - Overhead budget
  - Selling and administrative expenses budget
  - Cost of goods manufactured budget
- Prepare financial budgets
  - Budgeted income statement
  - Cash budget
  - Budgeted balance sheet

RELEVANT LEARNING OBJECTIVES

LO2 Identify the elements of a master budget in different types of organizations and the guidelines for preparing budgets.

LO3 Prepare the operating budgets that support the financial budgets.

LO4 Prepare a budgeted income statement, a cash budget, and a budgeted balance sheet.

LO2 Preparation of a Master Budget

Exhibits 1, 2, and 3 display the elements of a master budget for a manufacturing organization, a retail organization, and a service organization, respectively. As these illustrations indicate, the process of preparing a master budget is similar in all three types of organizations in that each prepares a set of operating budgets that serve as the basis for preparing the financial budgets. The sales budget (or, in service organizations, the service revenue budget) is prepared first because it is used to estimate sales volume and revenues. Once managers know the quantity of products or services to be sold and how many sales dollars to expect, they can develop other budgets that will enable them to manage their resources so that they generate profits on those sales.

Exhibit 1
Preparation of a Master Budget for a Manufacturing Organization

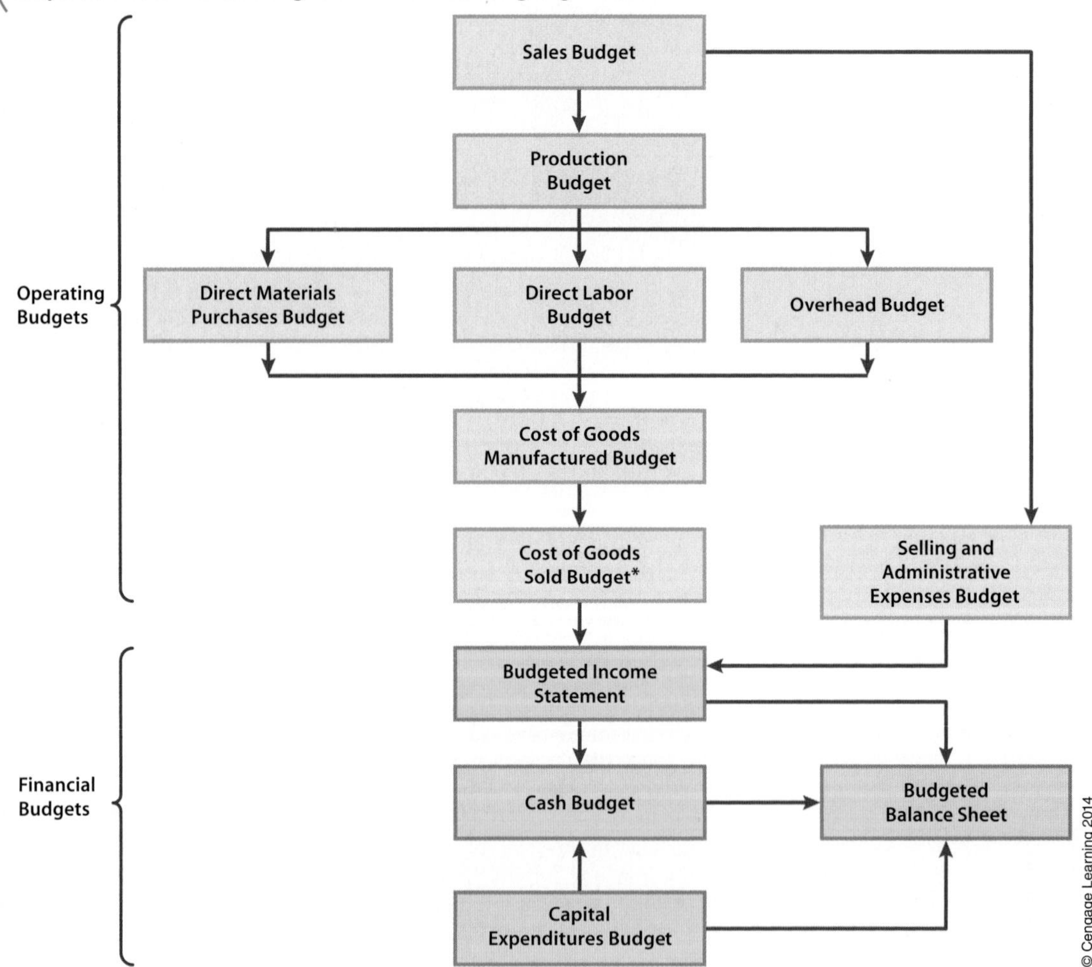

*Some organizations choose to include the cost of goods sold budget in the budgeted income statement.

Exhibit 2
Preparation of a Master Budget for a Retail Organization

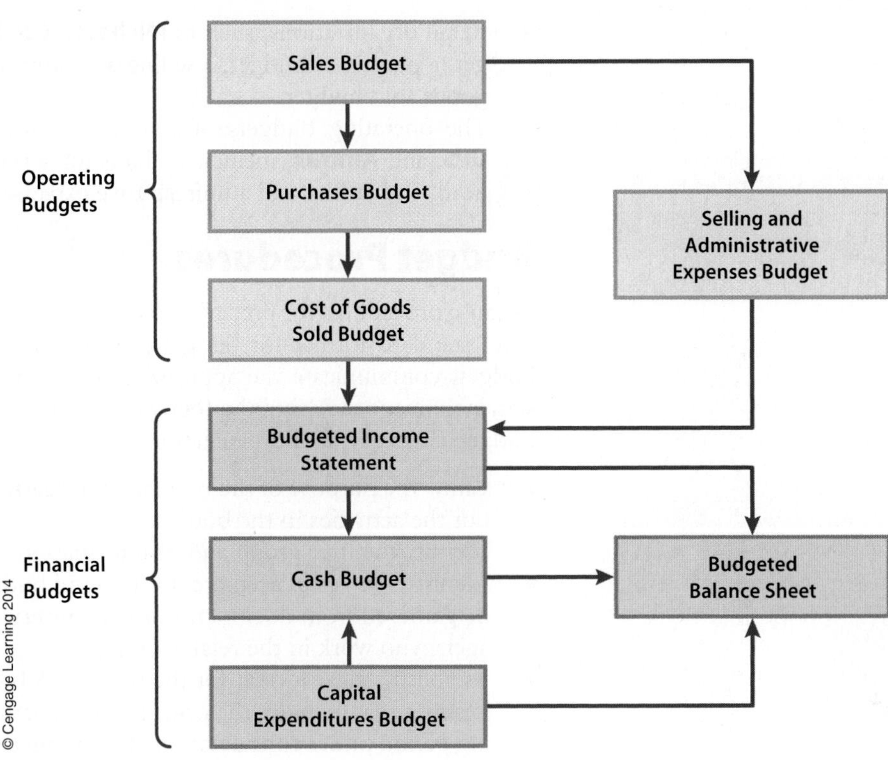

Exhibit 3
Preparation of a Master Budget for a Service Organization

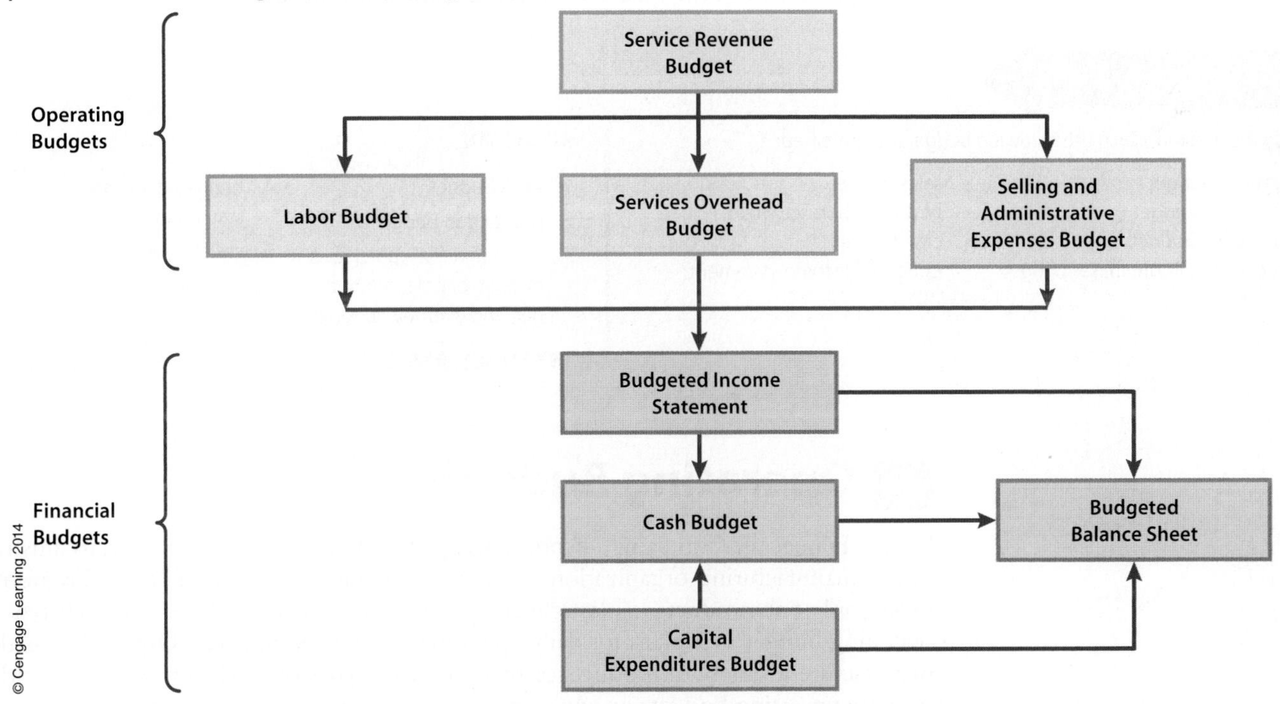

The process differs mainly in the kinds of operating budgets that each type of organization prepares.

- The operating budgets of manufacturing organizations, such as **Framerica**, **GM**, and **Harley-Davidson**, include budgets for sales, production, direct materials, direct labor, overhead, selling and administrative expenses, and cost of goods manufactured.

- Retail organizations, such as **Michaels**, **Old Navy**, and **Lowe's**, prepare a sales budget, a purchases budget, a selling and administrative expenses budget, and a cost of goods sold budget.
- The operating budgets of service organizations, such as **Enterprise Rent-A-Car**, **UPS**, and **Amtrak**, include budgets for service revenue (sales), labor, services overhead, and selling and administrative expenses.

Budget Procedures

Because procedures for preparing budgets vary from organization to organization, there is no standard format for budget preparation. The only universal requirement is that budgets communicate the appropriate information to the reader in a clear and understandable manner. Using the following guidelines, managers can improve the quality of budgets in any type of organization:

- Know the purpose of the budget, and clearly identify who is responsible for carrying out the activities in the budget.
- Identify the user group and its information needs.
- Identify sources of accurate, meaningful budget information. Such information may be gathered from documents or from interviews with employees, suppliers, or managers who work in the related areas.
- Establish a clear format for the budget. A budget should begin with a clearly stated heading that includes the organization's name, the type of budget, and the accounting period under consideration. The budget's components should be clearly labeled, and the unit and financial data should be listed in an orderly manner.
- Use appropriate formulas and calculations in deriving the quantitative information.
- Revise the budget until it includes all planning decisions. Several revisions may be required before the final version is ready for distribution.

APPLY IT!

Identify the order in which the following budgets are prepared:

- overhead budget
- production budget
- direct labor budget
- direct materials purchases budget
- sales budget
- budgeted balance sheet
- cash budget
- budgeted income statement

SOLUTION

1. sales budget
2. production budget
3. direct materials purchases budget, direct labor budget, and overhead budget
4. budgeted income statement
5. cash budget
6. budgeted balance sheet

TRY IT! SE1, E1A, E1B

LO3 Operating Budgets

We use Framecraft Company, a hypothetical picture frame making company, to illustrate how a manufacturing organization prepares its operating budgets. Because Framecraft makes only one product—a plastic picture frame—it prepares only one of each type of operating budget as it plans for daily operations in the coming year. Organizations that manufacture a variety of products or provide many types of services may prepare either separate operating budgets or one comprehensive budget for each product or service.

The Sales Budget

The first step in preparing a master budget is to prepare a sales budget. A **sales budget** shows expected sales during a period, expressed in both units and dollars. Sales managers use this information to plan sales- and marketing-related activities and to determine

STUDY NOTE: The sales budget is the only budget based on an estimate of customer demand. Other budgets for the period are based on the sales numbers.

their human, physical, and technical resource needs. Accountants use the information to determine estimated cash receipts for the cash budget.

The following equation is used to determine the total budgeted sales:

Total Budgeted Sales = Estimated Selling Price per Unit × Estimated Sales in Units

Although the calculation is easy, selecting the best estimates for the selling price per unit and the sales demand in units can be difficult. An estimated selling price below the current selling price may be needed if competitors are currently selling the same product or service at lower prices or if the organization wants to increase its share of the market. On the other hand, if the organization has improved the quality of its product or service by using more expensive materials or processes, the estimated selling price may have to be higher than the current price.

The estimated sales volume is very important because it will affect the level of operating activities and the amount of resources needed for operations. To help estimate sales volume, managers often use a **sales forecast**, which is a projection of the estimated sales in units, based on an analysis of external and internal factors.

External factors include:

- the state of the local and national economies
- the state of the industry's economy
- the nature of the competition and its sales volume and selling price

Internal factors include:

- the number of units sold in prior periods
- the organization's credit policies
- the organization's collection policies
- the organization's pricing policies
- any new products that the organization plans to introduce to the market
- the capacity of the organization's manufacturing facilities

Exhibit 4 shows Framecraft's sales budget for the year. The budget shows the estimated number of unit sales and dollar revenue amounts for each quarter and for the entire year. Because the sales forecast indicated a highly competitive marketplace, Framecraft's managers have estimated a selling price of $5 per unit. The sales forecast also indicated highly seasonal sales activity. The estimated sales volume therefore varies from 10,000 to 40,000 per quarter.

Exhibit 4
Sales Budget

Framecraft Company
Sales Budget
For the Year Ended December 31

	Quarter 1	2	3	4	Year
Sales in units	10,000	30,000	10,000	40,000	90,000
Selling price per unit	× $5	× $5	× $5	× $5	× $5
Total sales	$50,000	$150,000	$50,000	$200,000	$450,000

The Production Budget

A **production budget** shows the number of units that a company must produce to meet budgeted sales and inventory needs. Production managers use this information to plan for the materials and human resources that production-related activities will require. To prepare a production budget, managers must know the budgeted number of unit sales (which is specified in the sales budget) and the desired level of ending finished goods inventory for each period in the budget year. That level is often stated as a percentage of the next period's budgeted unit sales.

For example, Framecraft's desired level of ending finished goods inventory is 10 percent of the next quarter's budgeted unit sales. (Its desired level of beginning finished goods inventory is 10 percent of the current quarter's budgeted unit sales.)

The following formula identifies the production needs for each period:

$$\text{Total Production Units} = \text{Budgeted Sales in Units} + \text{Desired Units of Ending Finished Goods Inventory} - \text{Desired Units of Beginning Finished Goods Inventory}$$

Exhibit 5 shows Framecraft's production budget for the year. Notice that each quarter's desired total units of ending finished goods inventory become the next quarter's desired total units of beginning finished goods inventory.

Exhibit 5
Production Budget

Framecraft Company
Production Budget (Units)
For the Year Ended December 31

	Quarter				
	1	**2**	**3**	**4**	**Year**
Sales in units	10,000	30,000	10,000	40,000	90,000
Plus desired units of ending finished goods inventory	3,000	1,000	4,000	1,500	1,500
Desired total units	13,000	31,000	14,000	41,500	91,500
Less desired units of beginning finished goods inventory	1,000	3,000	1,000	4,000	1,000
Total production units	12,000	28,000	13,000	37,500	90,500

Because unit sales of 15,000 are budgeted for the first quarter of next year, the ending finished goods inventory for the fourth quarter of the year is 1,500 units (0.10 × 15,000 units), which is the same as the desired number of units of ending finished goods inventory for the entire year.

The Direct Materials Purchases Budget

A **direct materials purchases budget** identifies the quantity of purchases required to meet budgeted production and inventory needs and the costs associated with those purchases. A purchasing department uses this information to plan purchases of direct materials. Accountants use the same information to estimate cash payments to suppliers.

To prepare a direct materials purchases budget, managers must know what production needs will be in each period. This information is provided by the production budget. They must also know the desired level of the direct materials inventory for each period and the per-unit cost of direct materials. The desired level of ending direct materials inventory is usually stated as a percentage of the next period's production needs.

For example, Framecraft's desired level of ending direct materials inventory is 20 percent of the next quarter's budgeted production needs. (Its desired level of beginning direct materials inventory is 20 percent of the current quarter's budgeted production needs.)

The following steps are involved in preparing a direct materials purchases budget:

- **Step 1.** Calculate each period's total production needs in units of direct materials using the following formula:

  Total Production Needs in Units of Direct Materials = Total Production Units × Required Amount of Direct Materials per Unit

  Plastic is the only direct material used in Framecraft's picture frames. Framecraft's managers calculate units of production needs in ounces by multiplying the number of frames budgeted for production by the 10 ounces of plastic that each frame requires.

- **Step 2.** Determine the quantity of direct materials to be purchased during each accounting period in the budget using the following formula:

  Total Units of Direct Materials to Be Purchased = Total Production Needs in Units of Direct Materials + Desired Units of Ending Direct Materials Inventory − Desired Units of Beginning Direct Materials Inventory

  As shown in Exhibit 6, Framecraft's total ounces of direct materials to be purchased in the first quarter are 152,000 ounces and for the year are 911,000 ounces.

- **Step 3.** Calculate the cost of the direct materials purchases using the following formula:

  Cost of Direct Materials Purchased = Total Units to Be Purchased × Direct Materials Cost per Unit

  Framecraft's Purchasing Department has estimated the cost of the plastic used in the picture frames at $0.05 per ounce.

Exhibit 6 shows Framecraft's direct materials purchases budget for the year. Notice that each quarter's desired units of ending direct materials inventory become the next quarter's desired units of beginning direct materials inventory.

Exhibit 6
Direct Materials Purchases Budget

Framecraft Company
Direct Materials Purchases Budget
For the Year Ended December 31

	Quarter				
	1	**2**	**3**	**4**	**Year**
Total production units	12,000	28,000	13,000	37,500	90,500
Ounces per unit	× 10	× 10	× 10	× 10	× 10
Total production needs in ounces	120,000	280,000	130,000	375,000	905,000
Plus desired ounces of ending direct materials inventory	56,000	26,000	75,000	30,000	30,000
	176,000	306,000	205,000	405,000	935,000
Less desired ounces of beginning direct materials inventory	24,000	56,000	26,000	75,000	24,000
Total ounces of direct materials to be purchased	152,000	250,000	179,000	330,000	911,000
Cost per ounce	× $0.05	× $0.05	× $0.05	× $0.05	× $0.05
Total cost of direct materials purchases	$ 7,600	$12,500	$ 8,950	$16,500	$ 45,550

Framecraft's budgeted number of units for the first quarter of the following year is 150,000 ounces; its ending direct materials inventory for the fourth quarter of this year is therefore 30,000 ounces (0.20 × 150,000 ounces), which is the same as the number of desired units of ending direct materials inventory for the entire year.

The Direct Labor Budget

A **direct labor budget** shows the direct labor hours needed during a period and the associated costs. Production managers use estimated direct labor hours to plan how many employees will be required during the period and the hours that each will work. Accountants use estimated direct labor costs to plan for cash payments to the workers. Managers of human resources use the direct labor budget in deciding whether to hire new employees or reduce the existing work force. The direct labor budget also serves as a guide in assessing employee training needs and preparing schedules of employee benefits.

The following two steps are used to prepare a direct labor budget:

- **Step 1.** Estimate the total direct labor hours using the following formula:

$$\text{Total Direct Labor Hours} = \text{Estimated Direct Labor Hours per Unit} \times \text{Total Production Units}$$

  Framecraft's Production Department needs an estimated one-tenth (0.10) of a direct labor hour to complete one unit.

- **Step 2.** Calculate the total budgeted direct labor cost using the following formula:

$$\text{Total Budgeted Direct Labor Costs} = \text{Total Direct Labor Hours} \times \text{Estimated Direct Labor Cost per Hour}$$

  A company's human resources department provides an estimate of the hourly labor wage. Framecraft's Human Resources Department estimates a direct labor cost of $6 per hour.

Exhibit 7 shows how Framecraft uses these data and formulas to estimate the total direct labor cost.

Exhibit 7
Direct Labor Budget

Framecraft Company
Direct Labor Budget
For the Year Ended December 31

	Quarter				
	1	**2**	**3**	**4**	**Year**
Total production units	12,000	28,000	13,000	37,500	90,500
Direct labor hours per unit	× 0.10	× 0.10	× 0.10	× 0.10	× 0.10
Total direct labor hours	1,200	2,800	1,300	3,750	9,050
Direct labor cost per hour	× $6	× $6	× $6	× $6	× $6
Total direct labor cost	$7,200	$16,800	$7,800	$22,500	$54,300

The Overhead Budget

An **overhead budget** shows the anticipated manufacturing costs, other than direct materials and direct labor costs, that must be incurred to meet budgeted production needs. It has two purposes:

- To integrate the overhead cost budgets developed by the managers of production and production-related departments.
- To group information for the calculation of overhead rates for the next accounting period.

The format for presenting information in an overhead budget is flexible. Grouping information by activities is useful for organizations that use activity-based costing. This approach makes it easier for accountants to determine the application rates for each cost pool.

Exhibit 8
Overhead Budget

Framecraft Company
Overhead Budget
For the Year Ended December 31

	Quarter				
	1	**2**	**3**	**4**	**Year**
Total production units	**12,000**	**28,000**	**13,000**	**37,500**	**90,500**
Variable overhead costs:*					
Factory supplies ($0.18)	$ 2,160	$ 5,040	$ 2,340	$ 6,750	$ 16,290
Employee benefits ($0.24)	2,880	6,720	3,120	9,000	21,720
Inspection ($0.09)	1,080	2,520	1,170	3,375	8,145
Maintenance and repairs ($0.16)	1,920	4,480	2,080	6,000	14,480
Utilities ($0.30)	3,600	8,400	3,900	11,250	27,150
Total variable overhead costs	$11,640	$27,160	$12,610	$36,375	$ 87,785
Fixed overhead costs:					
Depreciation—machinery	$ 2,810	$ 2,810	$ 2,810	$ 2,810	$ 11,240
Depreciation—building	3,225	3,225	3,225	3,225	12,900
Supervision	9,000	9,000	9,000	9,000	36,000
Maintenance and repairs	2,150	2,150	2,150	2,150	8,600
Other overhead expenses	3,630	3,630	3,630	3,630	14,520
Total fixed overhead costs	$20,815	$20,815	$20,815	$20,815	$ 83,260
Total overhead costs	$32,455	$47,975	$33,425	$57,190	$171,045

*Amounts in parentheses are unit variable costs.

As Exhibit 8 shows, Framecraft prefers to group overhead information into variable and fixed costs to facilitate CVP analysis. The single overhead rate is computed using the following formula:

Single Overhead Rate = Estimated Total Overhead Costs ÷ Estimated Total Direct Labor Hours

Framecraft's predetermined overhead rate is:

$171,045 ÷ 9,050 direct labor hours = $18.90 per direct labor hour

or

$18.90 per direct labor hour × 0.10 direct labor hour per unit = $1.89 per unit produced

The Selling and Administrative Expenses Budget

STUDY NOTE: Selling and administrative expenses are period costs, not product costs.

A **selling and administrative expenses budget** shows the operating expenses, other than those related to production, that are needed to support sales and overall operations during a period. Accountants use this budget to estimate cash payments for products or services not used in production-related activities.

Framecraft's selling and administrative expenses budget appears in Exhibit 9. The company groups its selling and administrative expenses into variable and fixed

Exhibit 9
Selling and Administratives Expenses Budget

Framecraft Company
Selling and Administrative Expenses Budget
For the Year Ended December 31

	Quarter				
	1	**2**	**3**	**4**	**Year**
Total sales units	**10,000**	**30,000**	**10,000**	**40,000**	**90,000**
Variable selling and administrative expenses:*					
Delivery expenses ($0.08)	$ 800	$ 2,400	$ 800	$ 3,200	$ 7,200
Sales commissions ($0.10)	1,000	3,000	1,000	4,000	9,000
Accounting ($0.07)	700	2,100	700	2,800	6,300
Other administrative Expenses ($0.04)	400	1,200	400	1,600	3,600
Total variable selling and administrative expenses	$ 2,900	$ 8,700	$ 2,900	$11,600	$ 26,100
Fixed selling and administrative expenses:					
Sales salaries	$ 4,500	$ 4,500	$ 4,500	$ 4,500	$ 18,000
Executive salaries	12,750	12,750	12,750	12,750	51,000
Depreciation—office equipment	925	925	925	925	3,700
Taxes and insurance	1,700	1,700	1,700	1,700	6,800
Total fixed selling and administrative expenses	$19,875	$19,875	$19,875	$19,875	$ 79,500
Total selling and administrative expenses	$22,775	$28,575	$22,775	$31,475	$105,600

*Amounts in parentheses are unit variable costs.

components for purposes of cost behavior analysis, CVP analysis, and profit planning. The number of units sold, not produced, are used to compute this budget since selling and administrative costs are triggered by sales, not production.

The Cost of Goods Manufactured Budget

A **cost of goods manufactured budget** summarizes the estimated costs of production during a period. The sources of information for total manufacturing costs are the direct materials, direct labor, and overhead budgets. Most manufacturing organizations anticipate some work in process at the beginning or end of a period. However, Framecraft has a policy of no work in process on December 31 of any year.

Exhibit 10 summarizes the company's estimated costs of production for the year. (The right-hand column of the exhibit shows the sources of key data.) The budgeted, or standard, product unit cost for one picture frame is computed as follows.

Budgeted Product Unit Cost = Cost of Goods Manufactured ÷ Units Produced
= $270,595 ÷ 90,500 units
= $2.99

Exhibit 10
Cost of Goods Manufactured Budget

Framecraft Company
Cost of Goods Manufactured Budget
For the Year Ended December 31

			Source of Data
Direct materials used:			
Direct materials inventory, beginning	$ 1,200*		Direct materials purchases budget
Purchases	45,550		Direct materials purchases budget
Cost of direct materials available for use	$46,750		
Less direct materials inventory, ending	1,500*		Direct materials purchases budget
Cost of direct materials used		$ 45,250	
Direct labor costs		54,300	Direct labor budget
Overhead costs		171,045	Overhead budget
Total manufacturing costs		$270,595	
Work in process inventory, beginning		—**	
Less work in process inventory, ending		—**	
Cost of goods manufactured		$270,595	

*The desired direct materials inventory balance at the beginning of the year is $1,200 (24,000 ounces × $0.05 per ounce); at year end, it is $1,500 (30,000 ounces × $0.05 per ounce).
** It is the company's policy to have no units in process at the beginning or end of the year.

APPLY IT!

Sample Company is preparing a production budget for the year. The company's policy is to maintain a finished goods inventory equal to one-half of the next month's sales. Sales of 4,000 units are budgeted for April. Complete the following monthly production budget for the first quarter to determine how many units should be produced in January, February, and March:

	January	February	March
Sales in units	3,000	2,400	6,000
Add desired units in ending finished goods inventory	?	?	?
Desired total units	?	?	?
Less desired units of beginning finished goods inventory	?	?	?
Total production units	?	?	?

SOLUTION

	January	February	March
Sales in units	3,000	2,400	6,000
Add desired units of ending finished goods inventory	1,200	3,000	2,000
Desired total units	4,200	5,400	8,000
Less desired units of beginning finished goods inventory	1,500	1,200	3,000
Total production units	2,700	4,200	5,000

TRY IT! SE2, SE3, SE4, E2A, E3A, E4A, E5A, E6A, E7A, E2B, E3B, E4B, E5B, E6B, E7B

LO 4 Financial Budgets

With revenues and expenses itemized in the operating budgets, an organization is able to prepare the financial budgets, which are projections of financial results for the period. Financial budgets include a budgeted income statement, a capital expenditures budget, a cash budget, and a budgeted balance sheet.

The Budgeted Income Statement

A **budgeted income statement** projects an organization's net income for a period based on the revenues and expenses estimated for that period. Exhibit 11 shows Framecraft's budgeted income statement for the year. The company's expenses include 8 percent interest paid on a $70,000 note payable and income taxes paid at a rate of 30 percent. Information about projected sales and costs comes from several operating budgets. (The right-hand column of the exhibit shows the sources of key data.)

At this point, you can review the overall preparation of the operating budgets and the budgeted income statement by comparing the preparation flow in Exhibit 1 with the budgets in Exhibits 4 through 11. Framecraft has no separate budget for cost of goods sold since it is embedded in its budgeted income statement.

Exhibit 11
Budgeted Income Statement

Framecraft Company
Budgeted Income Statement
For the Year Ended December 31

			Source of Data
Sales		$450,000	Sales budget
Cost of goods sold:			
Finished goods inventory, beginning	$ 2,990*		Production budget
Cost of goods manufactured	270,595		Cost of goods manufactured budget
Cost of goods available for sale	$273,585		
Less finished goods inventory, ending	4,485**		Production budget
Cost of goods sold		269,100	
Gross margin		$180,900	
Selling and administrative expenses		105,600	Selling and admin. expenses budget
Income from operations		$ 75,300	
Interest expense (8% × $70,000)		5,600	
Income before income taxes		$ 69,700	
Income taxes expense (30%)		20,910	
Net income		$ 48,790	

Note: Finished goods inventory balances assume that product unit costs were the same in both years:

*Beginning	**Ending
1,000 units[a]	1,500 units[a]
× $2.99[b]	×$2.99[b]
$2,990	$ 4,485

[a]Production budget (Exhibit 5)
[b]$270,595 ÷ 90,500 units (Exhibits 10 and 5) = $2.99

The Capital Expenditures Budget

A **capital expenditures budget** outlines the anticipated amount and timing of capital outlays for long-term assets during a period. Managers rely on the information in a capital expenditures budget when making decisions about such matters as buying equipment, building a new plant, purchasing and installing a materials handling system, or acquiring another business. Framecraft's capital expenditures budget for the year includes $30,000 for the purchase of a new framemaking machine. The company plans to pay $15,000 in the first quarter of the year, when the order is placed, and $15,000 in the second quarter of the year, when it receives the machine. This information is necessary for preparing the company's cash budget.*

The Cash Budget

A **cash budget** is a projection of the cash that an organization will receive and pay out during a period. It summarizes the cash flow prospects of all transactions considered in the master budget. Exhibit 12 shows how the elements of a cash budget relate to operating, investing, and financing activities.

A cash budget excludes planned noncash transactions, such as depreciation expense, amortization expense, issuance and receipt of stock dividends, uncollectible accounts expense, and gains and losses on sales of assets. Some organizations also exclude deferred taxes and accrued interest from the cash budget.

The following formula is useful in preparing a cash budget:

$$\text{Estimated Ending Cash Balance} = \text{Total Estimated Cash Receipts} - \text{Total Estimated Cash Payments} + \text{Estimated Beginning Cash Balance}$$

Exhibit 12
Elements of a Cash Budget

Activities	Cash Receipts From	Cash Payments For
Operating	• Cash sales • Cash collections on credit sales • Interest income from investments • Cash dividends from investments	• Purchases of materials • Direct labor • Overhead expenses • Selling and administrative expenses • Interest expense • Income taxes
Investing	• Sale of investments • Sale of long-term assets	• Purchases of investments • Purchases of long-term assets
Financing	• Proceeds from loans • Proceeds from issue of stock • Proceeds from issue of bonds	• Loan repayments • Cash dividends to stockholders • Retirement of bonds • Purchases of treasury stock

Note: Classifications of cash receipts and cash payments correspond to those in a statement of cash flows.

In estimating cash receipts and cash payments for the cash budget, many organizations prepare supporting schedules. For example, Framecraft's controller converts credit sales to cash inflows and purchases made on credit to cash outflows and then discloses those conversions to support the cash budget.

*We discuss capital expenditures in more detail in a later chapter.

Cash Collections The schedule in Exhibit 13 shows the cash that Framecraft expects to collect from customers during the year. Cash sales represent 20 percent of the company's expected sales; the other 80 percent are credit sales. Experience has shown that Framecraft collects payments for 60 percent of all credit sales in the quarter of sale, 30 percent in the quarter following sale, and 10 percent in the second quarter following sale.

Exhibit 13
Schedule of Expected Cash Collections from Customers

Framecraft Company
Schedule of Expected Cash Collections from Customers
For the Year Ended December 31

	Quarter				
	1	**2**	**3**	**4**	**Year**
Accounts receivable, beginning	$38,000	$ 10,000	$ —	$ —	$ 48,000
Cash sales	10,000	30,000	10,000	40,000	90,000
Collections of credit sales:					
First quarter ($40,000)	24,000	12,000	4,000	—	40,000
Second quarter ($120,000)	—	72,000	36,000	12,000	120,000
Third quarter ($40,000)	—	—	24,000	12,000	36,000
Fourth quarter ($160,000)	—	—	—	96,000	96,000
Total cash to be collected from customers	$72,000	$124,000	$74,000	$160,000	$430,000

As you can see in Exhibit 13, Framecraft's balance of accounts receivable was $48,000 at the beginning of the budget year. The company expects to collect $38,000 of that amount in the first quarter and the remaining $10,000 in the second quarter. At the end of the budget year, the estimated ending balance of accounts receivable is $68,000 comprised of $ 4,000 from the third quarter's credit sales [($50,000 × 0.80) × 0.10] and $64,000 from the fourth quarter's sales [($200,000 × 0.80) × 0.40]

The expected cash collections for each quarter and for the year appear in the total cash receipts section of the cash budget.

Cash Payments Exhibit 14 shows Framecraft's schedule of expected cash payments for direct materials during the year. This information is summarized in the first line of the cash payments section of the company's cash budget. Framecraft pays 50 percent of the invoices it receives in the quarter of purchase and the other 50 percent in the following quarter.

Exhibit 14
Schedule of Expected Cash Payments for Direct Materials

Framecraft Company
Schedule of Expected Cash Payments for Direct Materials
For the Year Ended December 31

	Quarter				
	1	**2**	**3**	**4**	**Year**
Accounts payable, beginning	$4,200	$ —	$ —	$ —	$ 4,200
First quarter ($7,600)	3,800	3,800	—	—	7,600
Second quarter ($12,500)	—	6,250	6,250	—	12,500
Third quarter ($8,950)	—	—	4,475	4,475	8,950
Fourth quarter ($16,500)	—	—	—	8,250	8,250
Total cash payments for direct materials	$8,000	$10,050	$10,725	$12,725	$41,500

The beginning balance of accounts payable for the first quarter is given at $4,200. At the end of the budget year, the estimated ending balance of accounts payable is $8,250 (50 percent of the $16,500 of direct materials purchases in the fourth quarter).

Exhibit 15
Cash Budget

Cash Budget Framecraft's cash budget for the year appears in Exhibit 15. (The right-hand column of the exhibit shows the sources of key data.) It shows the estimated cash

Framecraft Company
Cash Budget
For the Year Ended December 31

	Quarter					
	1	2	3	4	Year	Source of Data
Cash receipts:						
Cash collections from customers	$ 72,000	$124,000	$74,000	$160,000	$430,000	Schedule of expected cash collections from customers
Total cash receipts	$ 72,000	$124,000	$74,000	$160,000	$430,000	
Cash payments:						
Direct materials	$ 8,000	$ 10,050	$10,725	$ 12,725	$ 41,500	Schedule of expected cash payments for direct materials
Direct labor	7,200	16,800	7,800	22,500	54,300	Direct labor budget
Factory supplies	2,160	5,040	2,340	6,750	16,290	Overhead budget
Employee benefits	2,880	6,720	3,120	9,000	21,720	Overhead budget
Inspection	1,080	2,520	1,170	3,375	8,145	Overhead budget
Variable maintenance and repairs	1,920	4,480	2,080	6,000	14,480	Overhead budget
Utilities	3,600	8,400	3,900	11,250	27,150	Overhead budget
Supervision	9,000	9,000	9,000	9,000	36,000	Overhead budget
Fixed maintenance and repairs	2,150	2,150	2,150	2,150	8,600	Overhead budget
Other overhead expenses	3,630	3,630	3,630	3,630	14,520	Overhead budget
Delivery expenses	800	2,400	800	3,200	7,200	Selling and admin. expenses budget
Sales commissions	1,000	3,000	1,000	4,000	9,000	Selling and admin. expenses budget
Accounting	700	2,100	700	2,800	6,300	Selling and admin. expenses budget
Other administrative expenses	400	1,200	400	1,600	3,600	Selling and admin. expenses budget
Sales salaries	4,500	4,500	4,500	4,500	18,000	Selling and admin. expenses budget
Executive salaries	12,750	12,750	12,750	12,750	51,000	Selling and admin. expenses budget
Taxes and insurance	1,700	1,700	1,700	1,700	6,800	Selling and admin. expenses budget
Capital expenditures*	15,000	15,000			30,000	Budgeted income statement
Interest expense	1,400	1,400	1,400	1,400	5,600	Budgeted income statement
Income taxes	5,228	5,227	5,228	5,227	20,910	Budgeted income statement
Total cash payments	$ 85,098	$118,067	$74,393	$123,557	$401,115	
Cash increase (decrease)	$(13,098)	$ 5,933	$ (393)	$ 36,443	$ 28,885	
Beginning cash balance	20,000	6,902	12,835	12,442	20,000	
Ending cash balance	$ 6,902	$ 12,835	$12,442	$ 48,885	$ 48,885	

*The company plans to purchase a machine costing $30,000 and to pay for it in two installments of $15,000 each in the first and second quarters of the year.

receipts and cash payments for the period, as well as the cash increase or decrease. The cash increase or decrease plus the period's beginning cash balance equals the ending cash balance anticipated for the period. As you can see in Exhibit 15, the beginning cash balance for the first quarter is $20,000. Note that each quarter's budgeted ending cash balance becomes the next quarter's beginning cash balance. Also note that equal income tax payments are made quarterly.

Minimum Cash Balance Many organizations maintain a minimum cash balance to provide a margin of safety against uncertainty. If the ending cash balance on the cash budget falls below the minimum level required, short-term borrowing may be necessary to cover planned cash payments during the year. If the ending cash balance is significantly larger than the organization needs, it may invest the excess cash in short-term securities to generate additional income.

For example, if Framecraft wants a minimum of $10,000 cash available at the end of each quarter, its balance of $6,902 at the end of the first quarter indicates that there is a problem. Framecraft can borrow cash to cover the first quarter's cash needs, delay purchasing the new machine until the second quarter, or reduce some of the operating expenses. On the other hand, the balance at the end of the fourth quarter may be higher than the company wants, in which case management might invest a portion of the idle cash in short-term securities.

The Budgeted Balance Sheet

A **budgeted balance sheet** projects an organization's financial position at the end of a period. It uses all estimated data compiled in preparing a master budget and is the final step in the budgeting process. Exhibit 16 presents Framecraft Company's budgeted balance sheet at the end of the year. (The right-hand column of the exhibit shows the sources of key data.) The beginning balances for Land, Notes Payable, Common Stock, and Retained Earnings were $50,000, $70,000, $150,000, and $52,107, respectively.

APPLY IT!

Sample Corporation's budgeted balance sheet for the beginning of the coming year shows total assets of $5,000,000 and total liabilities of $2,000,000. Common stock and retained earnings make up the entire stockholders' equity section of the balance sheet. Common stock remains at its beginning balance of $1,500,000. The projected net income for the year is $350,000. The company plans to pay no cash dividends. What is the balance of retained earnings at the beginning and end of the year?

SOLUTION

Using the accounting equation A = L + SE, knowing that common stock + retained earnings make up the entire SE, and the information given:

Beginning retained earnings:

$5,000,000 = $2,000,000 + $1,500,000 + Beginning RE

Thus, the beginning balance of retained earnings is $1,500,000.

Ending retained earnings:

Beginning retained earnings	$1,500,000
+ Net income	350,000
− Dividends	0
Ending retained earnings	$1,850,000

TRY IT! SE4, SE5, SE6, SE7, SE8, E8A, E9A, E10A, E11A, E12A, E8B, E9B, E10B, E11B, E12B

Exhibit 16
Budgeted Balance Sheet

Framecraft Company Budgeted Balance Sheet December 31				Source of Data
Assets				
Current assets:				
Cash		$ 48,885		Cash budget
Accounts receivable		68,000[a]		Schedule of expected cash collections from customers
Direct materials inventory		1,500		Cost of goods manufactured budget
Work in process inventory		—		Cost of goods manufactured budget (note)
Finished goods inventory		4,485		Budgeted income statement (note)
Total current assets			$122,870	
Property, plant, and equipment:				
Land		$ 50,000		
Plant and equipment[b]	$200,000			
Less accumulated depreciation[c]	45,000	155,000		
Total property, plant, and equipment			205,000	
Total assets			$327,870	
Liabilities				
Current liabilities:				
Accounts payable			$ 8,250[d]	Schedule of expected cash payments for direct materials
Long-term liabilities:				
Notes payable			70,000	
Total liabilities			$ 78,250	
Stockholders' Equity				
Common stock		$150,000		
Retained earnings[e]		99,620		
Total stockholders' equity			249,620	
Total liabilities and stockholders' equity			$327,870	

[a]The accounts receivable balance at year end is $68,000: $4,000 from the third quarter's sales [($50,000 × 0.80) × 0.10] plus $64,000 from the fourth quarter's sales [($200,000 × 0.80) × 0.40].
[b]The plant and equipment balance includes the $30,000 purchase of a machine.
[c]The accumulated depreciation balance includes depreciation expense of $27,840 for machinery, building, and office equipment ($11,240, $12,900, and $3,700, respectively).
[d]At year end, the estimated ending balance of accounts payable is $8,250 (50 percent of the $16,500 of direct materials purchases in the fourth quarter).
[e]The retained earnings balance at December 31 equals the beginning retained earnings balance plus the net income projected for the year ($50,830 and $48,790, respectively).

SECTION 3 BUSINESS APPLICATIONS

BUSINESS APPLICATIONS
- Planning
- Performing
- Evaluating
- Communicating

RELEVANT LEARNING OBJECTIVE

LO5 Explain why budgeting is essential to the management process.

LO5 Budgeting and the Management Process

Budgets are essential to accomplishing an organization's strategic plan. They are used to communicate understandable information, coordinate activities and resource usage, motivate employees, and provide comparative information to evaluate performance. For example, a board of directors may use budgets to determine managers' areas of responsibility and to measure managers' performance in those areas. Budgets are also used to manage and account for cash.

Advantages of Budgeting

Budgeting is advantageous for organizations, because budgets:

- foster organizational communication
- ensure a focus both on future events and on resolving day-to-day issues
- assign resources and the responsibility to use them wisely to managers who are held accountable for their results
- can identify potential constraints before they become problems
- facilitate congruence between organizational and personal goals
- define organizational goals and objectives numerically, against which actual performance results can be evaluated

Budgeting and Goals

Budgeting helps managers achieve both long-term and short-term goals.

Long-Term Goals **Strategic planning** is the process by which management establishes an organization's long-term goals. These goals define the direction that an organization will take and are the basis for making annual operating plans and preparing budgets. Long-term goals cannot be vague. They must set specific tactical targets and timetables and assign responsibility to specific personnel. For example, a long-term goal for a company that currently holds only 4 percent of its product's market share might specify that the vice president of marketing is to develop strategies to ensure that the company controls 10 percent of the market in five years and 15 percent by the end of ten years.

Business Perspective
What Can Cause the Planning Process to Fail?

When chief financial officers were asked what caused their planning process to fail, the six factors they most commonly cited were:[1]

- An inadequately defined strategy
- No clear link between strategy and the operational budget
- Lack of individual accountability for results
- Lack of meaningful performance measures
- Inadequate pay for performance
- Lack of appropriate data

STUDY NOTE: As plans are formulated for time periods closer to the current date, they become more specific and quantified. The annual budget is a very specific plan of action.

Short-Term Goals Annual operating plans involve every part of an enterprise and are much more detailed than long-term strategic plans. To formulate an annual operating plan, an organization must restate its long-term goals in terms of what it needs to accomplish during the next year. The process entails making decisions about sales and profit targets, human resource needs, and the introduction of new products or services. The short-term goals identified in an annual operating plan are the basis of an organization's operating budgets for the year.

Budgeting Basics

Once long- and short-term goals have been decided, the organization's management plays a central role in coordinating the budgeting process. Managers set the basics of the budgeting process, including assigning budget authority, inviting employee participation, selecting the budget period, and implementing the budget.

Assigning Budget Authority Every budget and budget line item is associated with a specific role or job in an organization. For example, a department manager is responsible for the department's budget, and the marketing vice president is responsible for what is spent on advertising.

Since manager responsibilities and budget authority are linked, managers must explain or take corrective action for any deviations between budget and actual results. Responsibility accounting (which will be discussed in greater detail in the next chapter) authorizes managers to command and be held accountable for the revenues and expenses in their budgets. If managers do not have budget authority over what they need to accomplish their job responsibilities, they lack the control necessary to accomplish their duties and cannot be held accountable for results.

Inviting Employee Participation Because an organization's main activities—such as production, sales, and employee training—take place at its lower levels, the information necessary for establishing a budget flows from the employees and supervisors of those activities through middle managers to senior executives. Each person in this chain of communication thus plays a role in developing a budget, as well as in implementing it. If these individuals have a voice in setting the budget targets, they will be motivated to ensure that their departments attain those targets and stay within the budget. If they do not have a role in the budgeting process, motivation will suffer. The key to a successful budget is therefore **participative budgeting**, a process in which personnel at all levels of an organization actively engage in making decisions about the budget. Participative budgeting depends on joint decision making. Without it, the budgeting process will be authoritative rather than participative, and the budget targets may be unrealistic and impossible to attain.

Selecting the Budget Period Budgets, like the company's fiscal period, generally cover a one-year period of time. An annual operating budget may be divided further into monthly or quarterly periods, depending on the detail of information needed.

The organization's management will decide if they will use a static or continuous budgeting process. **Static budgets** are prepared once a year and do not change during

Business Perspective
Can Budgeting Lead to a Breakdown in Corporate Ethics?

When budgets are used to force performance results, as they were at **WorldCom**, breaches in corporate ethics can occur. One former WorldCom employee described the situation at that company as follows: "You would have a budget, and he [WorldCom CEO Bernard Ebbers] would mandate that you had to be 2% under budget. Nothing else was acceptable."[2] This type of restrictive budget policy appears to have been a factor in many corporate scandals.

the annual budget period. To ensure that its managers have continuously updated operating data against which to measure performance, an organization may select an ongoing budgeting process, called a continuous budget. A **continuous budget** is a 12-month forward-rolling budget that summarizes budgets for the next 12 months. Each month managers prepare a budget for that month, 12 months hence.

Traditional budgeting approaches require managers to justify only budget changes over the past year. An alternative to traditional budgeting is **zero-based budgeting**, which requires that every budget item be justified annually. So each year the budget is built from scratch.

Implementing the Budget The **budget committee,** which includes the controller and many of the organization's top management, has overall responsibility for budget implementation. The budget committee:

- Oversees each stage in the preparation of the organization's overall budget
- Mediates any departmental disputes that may arise in the process
- Gives final approval to the budget

A budget may go through many revisions before it includes all planning decisions and has the approval of the committee. Once approved, periodic reports from department managers allow the committee to monitor the company's progress in attaining budget targets.

Successful budget implementation depends on two factors—clear communication and the support of top management. To ensure their cooperation in implementing the budget, all key persons involved must know what roles they are expected to play and must have specific directions on how to achieve their performance goals. Thus, the budget committee must communicate clearly the performance expectations and budget targets. Equally important, top management must show support for the budget and encourage its implementation. The process will succeed only if middle- and lower-level managers are confident that top management is truly interested in the outcome and is willing to reward personnel for meeting the budget targets. Today, many organizations have employee incentive plans that tie the achievement of budget targets to bonuses or other types of compensation.

As you have seen in this chapter, budgeting is not only an essential part of planning; it also helps managers command, control, evaluate, and report on operations. Exhibit 17 summarizes how budgeting is an integral part of the management process.

Exhibit 17
Budgeting and the Management Process

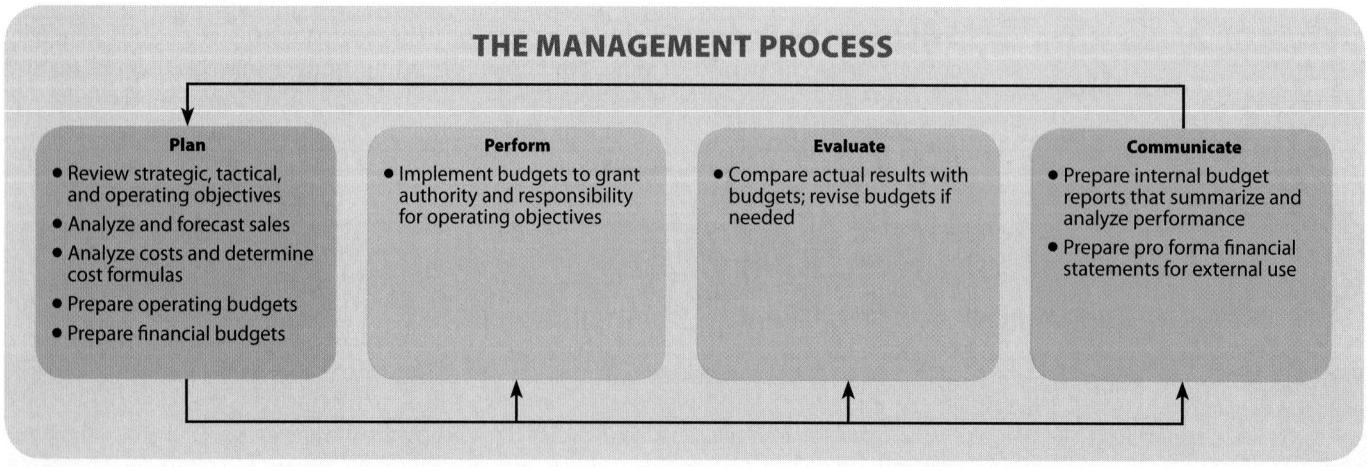

THE MANAGEMENT PROCESS
Plan
• Review strategic, tactical, and operating objectives
• Analyze and forecast sales
• Analyze costs and determine cost formulas
• Prepare operating budgets
• Prepare financial budgets
Perform
• Implement budgets to grant authority and responsibility for operating objectives
Evaluate
• Compare actual results with budgets; revise budgets if needed
Communicate
• Prepare internal budget reports that summarize and analyze performance
• Prepare pro forma financial statements for external use

APPLY IT!

Randi Quelle is the manager of the electronics department in a large discount store. During a recent meeting, Quelle and her supervisor agreed that Quelle's goal for the next year would be to increase the number of flat-screen televisions sold by 20 percent. The department sold 500 TV sets last year. Two salespersons currently work for Quelle. What types of budgets should Quelle use to help her achieve her sales goal? What kinds of information should those budgets provide?

SOLUTION

Budgets and information that might be useful include:

- Breakdown by month of last year's sales to use as a guide to build this year's monthly targets. This would include seasonal sales information.
- Budgets by salesperson, which may indicate a need for a third salesperson.
- Inventory and purchasing information.
- Budgets of sales promotion and advertising.
- Information on customer flow and the best times to sell.

TRY IT! SE9, SE10, E12A, E13A, E14A, E15A, E12B, E13B, E14B, E15B

TriLevel Problem

Jeremy Hoare/Photoshot

Framerica Corporation

The beginning of this chapter focused on **Framerica Corporation**. One of Framerica's priorities is to help employees attain personal goals. A participatory budgeting process is a highly effective way to achieve goal congruence between a company's goals and objectives and employee personal aspirations. Complete the following requirements in order to answer the questions posed at the beginning of the chapter.

Section 1: Concepts

What concepts underlie the usefulness of the budgeting process?

Section 2: Accounting Applications

How does the budgeting process translate long-term goals into operating objectives?

Assume Framerica has an Information Processing Division that provides database management services for the professional photographers and artists who buy its frames. Suppose the division uses state-of-the-art equipment and employs five information specialists. Each specialist works an average of 160 hours a month. Assume the division's controller has compiled the following information:

	Actual Data for Past Year		Forecasted Data for This Year		
	November	**December**	**January**	**February**	**March**
Client billings (sales)	$25,000	$35,000	$25,000	$20,000	$40,000
Selling and administrative expenses	12,000	13,000	12,000	11,000	12,500
Operating supplies	2,500	3,500	2,500	2,500	4,000
Processing overhead	3,200	3,500	3,000	2,500	3,500

Of the client billings, 60 percent are cash sales collected during the month of sale, 30 percent are collected in the first month following sale, and 10 percent are collected in the second month following sale. Operating supplies are paid for in the month of purchase. Selling and administrative expenses and processing overhead are paid in the month following the cost's incurrence.

The division has a bank loan of $12,000 with a 12 percent annual interest rate. Interest is paid monthly, and $2,000 of the loan principal is due on February 28 of next year. Income taxes of $4,550 for this calendar year are due and payable on March 15 of next year. The information specialists earn $8.50 an hour, and all payroll-related employee benefit costs are included in processing overhead. The division anticipates no capital expenditures for the first quarter of the coming year. It expects its cash balance on December 31 of this year to be $13,840.

Prepare a monthly cash budget for the Information Processing Division for the three-month period ending March 31 of this year. Comment on whether the ending cash balances are adequate for the division's cash needs.

Section 3: Business Applications

Why are budgets an essential part of planning, controlling, evaluating, and reporting on business? To answer this question, match this chapter's manager responsibilities with when they occur within the management process.

a. Plan
b. Perform
c. Evaluate
d. Communicate

1. Prepare internal budget reports that summarize and analyze performance
2. Develop operating budgets
3. Grant authority and responsibility of operating objectives by implementing budgets
4. Review strategic, tactical, and operating objectives
5. Compare actual results with budgets
6. Develop financial budgets
7. Prepare pro forma financial statements
8. Analyze and forecast sales
9. Analyze costs and determine cost formulas
10. Revise budgets as needed

SOLUTION

Section 1: Concepts

The budgeting process can be a highly effective way of linking strategic planning to operations. Because the budgets express these goals and objectives in concrete terms, managers and employees are more likely to understand them and are able to act in ways that will achieve them. Budgets give managers and employees a means of monitoring the results of their actions because they can compare operating and financial budgets with actual results. The concepts of *comparability* and *understandability* assure budget accountability, especially when it involves all employees in an ongoing dialogue about a company's activities and direction and engages them in making budgeting decisions.

Section 2: Accounting Applications

Information Processing Division
Monthly Cash Budgets
For the Quarter Ended March 31

	January	February	March	Quarter
Total cash receipts	$28,000	$23,000	$32,500	$83,500
Cash payments:				
Operating supplies	$ 2,500	$ 2,500	$ 4,000	$ 9,000
Direct labor	6,800	6,800	6,800	20,400
Selling & admin. expenses	13,000	12,000	11,000	36,000
Processing overhead	3,500	3,000	2,500	9,000
Interest expense	120	120	100	340
Loan payment	—	2,000	—	2,000
Income tax payment	—	—	4,550	4,550
Total cash payments	$25,920	$26,420	$28,950	$81,290
Cash increase (decrease)	$ 2,080	$ (3,420)	$ 3,550	$ 2,210
Beginning cash balance	13,840	15,920	12,500	13,840
Ending cash balance	$15,920	$12,500	$16,050	$16,050

The details supporting the individual computations in this cash budget are as follows:

	January	February	March
Client billings:			
November	$ 2,500	$ —	$ —
December	10,500	3,500	—
January	15,000	7,500	2,500
February	—	12,000	6,000
March	—	—	24,000
	$28,000	$23,000	$32,500
Operating supplies:			
Paid for in the month purchased	$ 2,500	$ 2,500	$ 4,000
Direct labor:			
5 employees × 160 hours a month × $8.50 an hour	6,800	6,800	6,800
Selling and administrative expenses:			
Paid in the month following incurrence	13,000	12,000	11,000
Processing overhead:			
Paid in the month following incurrence	3,500	3,000	2,500
Interest expense:			
January and February = 1% of $12,000	120	120	—
March = 1% of $10,000	—	—	100
Loan payment	—	2,000	—
Income tax payment	—	—	4,550

The ending cash balances of $15,920, $12,500, and $16,050 for January, February, and March, respectively, appear to be comfortable and not too large for the Information Processing Division.

Section 3: Business Applications

1. d
2. a
3. c
4. a
5. c
6. a
7. d
8. a
9. a
10. c

Chapter Review

LO 1 Define *budgeting*, and describe how it relates to the concepts of comparability and understandability.

Budgeting is the process of identifying, gathering, summarizing, and communicating financial and nonfinancial information about an organization's future activities. A master budget consists of a set of operating budgets and a set of financial budgets that detail an organization's financial plans for a specific period. The operating budgets serve as the basis for preparing the budgeted income statement, a capital expenditures budget, a cash budget, and a budgeted balance sheet. The concepts of understandability and comparability underlie the power of the budgeting process. Budgeting enhances understandability, since managers and employees understand their organizational roles and responsibilities based on how the master budget links the organization's strategic plans to its annual budget. Budgeting enhances comparability, since budget to actual comparisons gives managers and employees a means of monitoring the results of their actions.

Identify the elements of a master budget in different types of organizations and the guidelines for preparing budgets. LO 2

The operating budgets of a manufacturing organization include budgets for sales, production, direct materials purchases, direct labor, overhead, selling and administrative expenses, and cost of goods manufactured. The operating budgets of a retail organization include budgets for sales, purchases, selling and administrative expenses, and cost of goods sold. The operating budgets of a service organization include budgets for service revenue, labor, services overhead, and selling and administrative expenses.

The guidelines for preparing budgets include identifying the purpose of the budget, the user group and its information needs, and the sources of budget information; establishing a clear format for the budget; and using appropriate formulas and calculations to derive the quantitative information.

Prepare the operating budgets that support the financial budgets. LO 3

The initial step in preparing a master budget in any type of organization is to prepare a sales budget. Once sales have been estimated, the manager of a manufacturing organization's production department is able to prepare a budget that shows how many units of products must be manufactured to meet the projected sales volume. With that information, other managers are able to prepare budgets for direct materials purchases, direct labor, overhead, selling and administrative expenses, and cost of goods manufactured. A cost of goods sold budget may be prepared separately, or it may be included in the cost of goods manufactured budget for a manufacturing organization. The operating budgets supply the information needed to prepare the financial budgets.

Prepare a budgeted income statement, a cash budget, and a budgeted balance sheet. LO 4

With estimated revenues and expenses itemized in the operating budgets, a controller is able to prepare the financial budgets. A budgeted income statement projects an organization's net income for a specific accounting period. A capital expenditures budget estimates the amount and timing of the organization's capital outlays during the period. A cash budget projects its cash receipts and cash payments for the period. Information about cash receipts comes from several sources, including the sales budget, the budgeted income statement, and various financial records. Sources of information about cash payments include the operating budgets, the budgeted income statement, and the capital expenditures budget. The difference between the total estimated cash receipts and total estimated cash payments is the cash increase or decrease anticipated for the period. That total plus the period's beginning cash balance equals the ending cash balance. The final step in developing a master budget is to prepare a budgeted balance sheet, which projects the organization's financial position at the end of the period.

Explain why budgeting is an essential part of the management process. LO 5

Budgeting helps managers plan, command, control, evaluate, and report on operations. When managers develop budgets, they match their organizational goals with the resources necessary to accomplish those goals. During the budgeting process, they evaluate operational, tactical, value chain, and capacity issues; assess how resources can be efficiently used; and develop contingency budgets as business conditions change. During the budget period, budgets authorize managers to use resources and provide guidelines to control costs. When managers assess performance, they can compare actual operating results to budget plans and evaluate the variances. In participative budgeting, personnel at all levels actively engage in making decisions about the budget.

Budgets can be static, meaning they do not change during the annual budget period, or continuous, meaning they are forward-moving for the next 12 months. An alternative to traditional budgeting is zero-based budgeting, which requires every budget item to be justified, not just the changes over the past year.

A budget committee made up of the company's controller and top managers has overall responsibility for budget implementation. The committee oversees each stage in the preparation of the master budget, mediates any departmental disputes that may arise during the process, and gives final approval to the budget. After the master budget is approved, periodic reports from department managers enable the committee to monitor the progress in attaining budget targets.

Key Terms

budget committee 928 (LO5)
budgeted balance sheet 924 (LO4)
budgeted income statement 920 (LO4)
budgeting 908 (LO1)
budgets 908 (LO1)
capital expenditures budget 921 (LO4)
cash budget 921 (LO4)
continuous budget 928 (LO5)
cost of goods manufactured budget 918 (LO3)
direct labor budget 916 (LO3)
direct materials purchases budget 914 (LO3)
financial budgets 908 (LO1)
master budget 908 (LO1)
operating budgets 908 (LO1)
overhead budget 916 (LO3)
participative budgeting 927 (LO5)
pro forma financial statements 909 (LO1)
production budget 913 (LO3)
sales budget 912 (LO3)
sales forecast 913 (LO3)
selling and administrative expenses budget 917 (LO3)
static budgets 927 (LO5)
strategic planning 926 (LO5)
zero-based budgeting 928 (LO5)

Chapter Assignments

DISCUSSION QUESTIONS

LO 1, 2 **DQ1. CONCEPT ▶** What is a master budget and what are the guidelines that enhance its understandability and comparability?

LO 3, 4 **DQ2.** Why does the preparation of operating budgets before financial budgets increase the usefulness of the budget process?

LO 5 **DQ3. BUSINESS APPLICATION ▶** Why is the difference between a static budget and a continuous budget important in understanding budgets?

LO 5 **DQ4. CONCEPT ▶ BUSINESS APPLICATION ▶** How are understandability and comparability enhanced when knowing who is responsible for the budgeting process?

LO 5 **DQ5. CONCEPT ▶ BUSINESS APPLICATION ▶** Why does the use of budgets in the management process reinforce the concepts of comparability and understandability to better business performance?

SHORT EXERCISES

LO 1, 2 **Budget Usefulness**

SE1. CONCEPT ▶ Budgeting is not only an essential part of planning; but it also helps managers command, control, evaluate, and report on operations. Why are the concepts of understandability and comparability important in budgeting? List the reasons for your answer.

LO 3 **Production Budget**

SE2. Windsor Lock Company's controller is preparing a production budget for the year. The company's policy is to maintain a finished goods inventory equal to one-half of the following month's sales. Sales of 5,000 locks are budgeted for April. Complete the monthly production budget for the first quarter:

	January	February	March
Sales in units	5,000	4,000	6,000
Add desired units of ending finished goods inventory	2,000	?	?
Desired total units	7,000	?	?
Less desired units of beginning finished goods inventory	?	?	?
Total production units	4,500	?	?

LO 3

Preparing an Operating Budget

SE3. Hartford Company expects to sell 50,000 units of its product in the coming year. Each unit sells for $50. Sales brochures and supplies for the year are expected to cost $9,000. Two sales representatives cover the southeast region. Each representative's base salary is $20,000, and each earns a sales commission of 5 percent of the selling price of the units he or she sells. The sales representatives supply their own transportation; they are reimbursed for travel at a rate of $0.60 per mile. The company estimates that the sales representatives will drive a total of 70,000 miles next year. Calculate Hartford's budgeted selling expenses for the coming year.

LO 3, 4

Budgeted Gross Margin

SE4. Eastport Company's operating budgets reveal the following information: net sales, $400,000; beginning materials inventory, $23,000; materials purchased, $185,000; beginning work in process inventory, $64,700; beginning finished goods inventory, $21,600; direct labor costs, $34,000; overhead applied, $67,000; ending work in process inventory, $61,200; ending materials inventory, $20,000; and ending finished goods inventory, $18,000. Compute Eastport's budgeted gross margin.

LO 4

Estimating Cash Collections

SE5. Standard Insurance Company specializes in term life insurance contracts. Cash collection experience shows that 40 percent of billed premiums are collected in the month in which they are billed, 50 percent are paid in the first month after they are billed, and 6 percent are paid in the second month after they are billed. Four percent of the billed premiums are paid late (in the third month after they are billed) and include a 10 percent penalty payment. Total billing notices in January were $58,000; in February, $62,000; in March, $66,000; in April, $65,000; in May, $60,000; and in June, $62,000. How much cash does the company expect to collect in May?

LO 4

Cash Budget

SE6. The projections of direct materials purchases that follow are for Creek Corporation.

	Purchases on Account	Cash Purchases
December 2014	$50,000	$20,000
January 2015	70,000	30,000
February 2015	60,000	25,000
March 2015	70,000	35,000

The company pays for 60 percent of purchases on account in the month of purchase and 40 percent in the month following the purchase. Prepare a monthly schedule of expected cash payments for direct materials for the first quarter of 2015.

LO 4

Cash Budget

SE7. Eagles Limited needs a cash budget for the month of November. The following information is available:

- The cash balance on November 1 is $5,000.
- Sales for October and November are $80,000 and $60,000, respectively. Cash collections on sales are 30 percent in the month of sale and 68 percent in the month after the sale; 2 percent of sales are uncollectible.
- General expenses budgeted for November are $26,000 (depreciation represents $2,000 of this amount).
- Inventory purchases will total $30,000 in October and $40,000 in November. The company pays for half of its inventory purchases in the month of purchase and for the other half the month after purchase.

- The company will pay $4,000 in cash for office furniture in November. Sales commissions for November are budgeted at $13,000.
- The company maintains a minimum ending cash balance of $4,000 and can borrow from the bank in multiples of $100. All loans are repaid after 60 days.

Prepare a cash budget for Eagles Limited for the month of November.

LO 4 **Budgeted Balance Sheet**

SE8. Bulldog Corporation's budgeted balance sheet for the coming year shows total assets of $4,000,000 and total liabilities of $1,900,000. Common stock and retained earnings make up the entire stockholders' equity section of the balance sheet. Common stock remains at its beginning balance of $1,500,000. The projected net income for the year is $350,000. The company pays no cash dividends. What is the balance of retained earnings at the beginning of the budget period?

LO 5 **Budgeting in a Retail Organization**

SE9. BUSINESS APPLICATION ▶ In a discount department store, the shoe department manager's goal for the next year is to increase the number of pairs of shoes sold by 20 percent. The department sold 8,000 pairs of shoes last year. Two salespeople currently work in the department. What types of budgets should the manager use to help him achieve his sales goal? What kinds of information should those budgets provide?

LO 5 **Budgetary Control**

SE10. BUSINESS APPLICATION ▶ The owner of a tree nursery analyzes her business's results by comparing actual operating results with figures budgeted at the beginning of the year. When the business generates large profits, she often overlooks the differences between actual and budgeted data. But when profits are low, she spends many hours analyzing the differences. If you owned the business, would you use her approach to budgetary control? If not, what changes would you make?

EXERCISES: SET A

LO 2 **Components of a Master Budget**

E1A. Assigning the numbers 1 through 7, identify the order in which the following budgets are prepared.

- direct labor budget
- production budget
- selling, administrative, and general expenses budget
- budgeted income statement
- sales budget
- budgeted balance sheet
- cash budget

LO 3 **Sales Budget**

E2A. Outside Company's quarterly and annual sales for this year follow. Prepare a sales budget for next year based on the estimated percentage increases shown by product class. Show both quarterly and annual totals for each product class.

(Continued)

Outside Company
Actual Sales Revenue
For the Year Ended December 31

Product Class	January–March	April–June	July–September	October–December	Annual Totals	Estimated Percent Increases by Product Class
Backcountry products	$ 44,500	$ 45,500	$ 48,200	$ 47,900	$ 186,100	20%
Marine products	36,900	32,600	34,100	37,200	140,800	5%
Walking products	29,800	29,700	29,100	27,500	116,100	30%
Hiking products	38,800	37,600	36,900	39,700	153,000	10%
Running products	47,700	48,200	49,400	49,900	195,200	25%
Biking products	65,400	65,900	66,600	67,300	265,200	20%
Totals	$263,100	$259,500	$264,300	$269,500	$1,056,400	

LO 3

Production Budget

E3A. Southside Corporation produces and sells a single product. Expected sales for September are 13,000 units; for October, 14,000 units; for November, 9,000 units; for December, 10,000 units; and for January, 15,000 units. The company's desired level of ending finished goods inventory at the end of a month is 10 percent of the following month's expected sales in units. At the end of August, 1,200 units were on hand. How many units need to be produced in the fourth quarter?

LO 3

Direct Materials Purchases Budget

E4A. Eco Door Company manufactures garage door units. The units include hinges, door panels, and other hardware. The controller has provided the information that follows.

Part	Units Needed	Cost
Hinges	4 sets per door	$6.00 per set
Door panels	4 panels per door	$27.00 per panel
Other hardware	1 lock per door	$31.00 per lock
	1 handle per door	$22.50 per handle
	2 roller tracks per door	$16.00 per set of 2 roller tracks
	8 rollers per door	$4.00 per roller

Prepare a direct materials purchases budget for the first quarter of the year based on the budgeted production of 25,000 garage door units. Assume no beginning or ending quantities of direct materials inventory.

LO 2, 3

Purchases Budget

E5A. Spartan Corporation projects the dollar value of the company's cost of goods sold to be $160,000 in June, $169,000 in July, and $154,000 in August. The dollar value of its desired ending inventory is 25 percent of the following month's cost of goods sold.

Compute the total purchases in dollars budgeted for June and the total purchases in dollars budgeted for July.

LO 3

Direct Labor Budget

E6A. Crimson Company has two departments—Dye and Dry—and manufactures three products. Budgeted unit production for the coming year is 21,000 of Product J, 36,000 of Product C, and 30,000 of Product B. The company is currently analyzing direct labor hour requirements for the coming year. Data for each department follow.

	Dye	Dry
Estimated hours per unit:		
Product J	2.0	3.0
Product C	1.0	4.0
Product B	2.5	5.0
Hourly labor rate	$10	$4

Prepare a direct labor budget for the coming year that shows the budgeted direct labor costs for each department and for the company as a whole.

LO 3 **Overhead Budget**

E7A. As part of the budgeting process, Northview Corporation's CFO is developing the overhead budget for next year for its Evans Division. The division estimates that it will manufacture 150,000 units during the year. The budgeted cost information follows.

	Variable Rate per Unit	Fixed Costs
Indirect materials	$1.00	
Indirect labor	4.00	
Supplies	0.40	
Repairs and maintenance	3.00	$ 50,000
Electricity	0.10	120,000
Factory supervision		160,000
Insurance		25,000
Property taxes		25,000
Depreciation—machinery		82,000
Depreciation—building		72,000

Prepare the division's overhead budget for next year.

LO 4 **Cash Collections**

E8A. Five Bros., Inc., is an automobile maintenance and repair company with outlets throughout the western United States. The company controller is starting to assemble the cash budget for the fourth quarter. Projected sales for the quarter follow.

	On Account	Cash
October	$400,000	$190,000
November	690,000	220,000
December	750,000	245,000

Cash collection records pertaining to sales on account indicate the following collection pattern:

Month of sale	40%
First month following sale	30%
Second month following sale	28%
Uncollectible	2%

Sales on account during August were $346,000. During September, sales on account were $390,000.

Compute the amount of cash to be collected from customers during each month of the fourth quarter.

LO 4 **Cash Collections**

E9A. NSW Company collects payment on 50 percent of credit sales in the month of sale, 40 percent in the month following the sale, and 5 percent in the second month following the sale. Its sales budget follows.

(Continued)

Month	Cash Sales	Credit Sales
May	$24,000	$ 40,000
June	30,000	60,000
July	50,000	80,000
August	70,000	100,000

Compute NSW's total cash collections in July and its total cash collections in August.

LO 4

Cash Budget

E10A. Queensland Enterprises needs a cash budget for the month of June. The following information is available:

- The cash balance on June 1 is $13,000.
- Sales for May and June are $40,000 and $50,000, respectively. Cash collections on sales are 45 percent in the month of sale and 50 percent in the month after the sale; 5 percent of sales are uncollectible.
- General expenses budgeted for June are $20,000 (depreciation represents $1,000 of this amount).
- Inventory purchases will total $40,000 in May and $30,000 in June. The company pays for half of its inventory purchases in the month of purchase and for the other half the month after purchase.
- The company will pay $5,000 in cash for office furniture in June. Sales commissions for June are budgeted at $3,000.
- The company maintains a minimum ending cash balance of $5,000 and can borrow from the bank in multiples of $100. All loans are repaid after 60 days.

Prepare a cash budget for Queensland for the month of June.

LO 4

Cash Budget

E11A. Citizens Produce Co-op is one of the biggest produce operations in northern Texas. Credit sales to retailers in the area constitute 80 percent of Citizens Produce's business; cash sales to customers at the company's retail outlet make up the other 20 percent. Collection records indicate that Citizens Produce collects payment on 50 percent of all credit sales during the month of sale, 30 percent in the month after the sale, and 20 percent in the second month after the sale.

The company's total sales in May were $60,000; in June, they were $70,000. Anticipated sales in July are $75,000; in August, $80,000; and in September, $90,000. The company's produce purchases are expected to total $45,000 in July, $51,000 in August, and $60,000 in September. The company pays for all purchases in cash.

Projected monthly costs for the quarter include $1,000 for heat, light, and power; $400 for bank fees; $2,000 for rent; $1,120 for supplies; $1,705 for depreciation of equipment; $1,285 for equipment repairs; and $500 for miscellaneous expenses. Other projected costs for the quarter are salaries and wages of $18,700 in July, $19,500 in August, and $20,600 in September.

The company's cash balance at June 30 was $2,000. Effective July 1, the company has a new policy of maintaining a minimum monthly cash balance of $3,000 and can borrow from the bank in multiples of $100.

1. Prepare a monthly cash budget for Citizens Produce Co-op for the quarter ended September 30.
2. **ACCOUNTING CONNECTION ▶** Should Citizens Produce anticipate taking out a loan during the quarter? If so, how much should it borrow, and when?

LO 4, 5

Budgeted Income Statement

E12A. Plenair, Inc., is located in France and organizes and coordinates art shows and auctions throughout the world. Its budgeted and actual costs for last year follow.

	Budgeted Cost	Actual Cost
Total operating expenses	€3,140,000	€3,176,868
Net receipts	6,200,000	6,369,200

Because the company sells only services, there is no cost of goods sold (net receipts equal gross margin). Plenair has budgeted the following fixed costs for the coming year: salaries, €1,000,000; advertising expense, €190,000; insurance, €150,000; and space rental costs, €300,000.

Additional information:

a. Net receipts are estimated at €6,400,000.
b. Travel costs are expected to be 11 percent of net receipts.
c. Auctioneer services will be billed at 15 percent of net receipts.
d. Printing costs are expected to be €190,000.
e. Home office costs are budgeted for €30,000.
f. Shipping costs are expected to be 20 percent higher than the €105,000 budgeted in the last year.
g. Miscellaneous expenses for the coming year will be budgeted at €8,000.

1. Prepare the company's budgeted income statement for the coming year using a 40 percent income tax rate,
2. **ACCOUNTING CONNECTION** ▶ Should the budget committee be worried about the trend in the company's operations? Explain your answer.

LO **5**

Characteristics of Budgets

E13A. BUSINESS APPLICATION ▶ You recently attended a workshop on budgeting and overheard the following comments as you walked to the refreshment table:

a. "Budgets are the same regardless of the size of an organization or management's role in the budgeting process."
b. "Budgets can include financial or nonfinancial data. In our organization, we plan the number of hours to be worked and the number of customer contacts we want our salespeople to make."

Do you agree or disagree with each comment? Explain your answers.

LO **5**

Budgeting and Goals

E14A. BUSINESS APPLICATION ▶ Effective planning of long- and short-term goals has contributed to the success of Multitasker Calendars, Inc. Described below are the actions that the company's management team took during a recent planning meeting. Indicate whether the goals related to those actions are short-term or long-term.

1. Based on the 10-year forecast, the management team made decisions about next year's sales, personnel, material purchases, and profit targets.
2. In forecasting the next 10-year period, the management team considered economic and industry forecasts, product and service projections, and the long-term capital needs of the business.

LO **5**

Budgeting and Goals

E15A. BUSINESS APPLICATION ▶ Assume that you work in the accounting department of a small shipping services company. Inspired by a recent seminar on budgeting, the company's president wants to develop a budgeting system and has asked you to direct it. Identify the points concerning the initial steps in the budgeting process that you should communicate to the president. Concentrate on principles related to long-term goals and short-term goals.

EXERCISES: SET B

Visit the textbook companion website at www.cengagebrain.com to access Exercise Set B for this chapter.

PROBLEMS

LO 3

✔ 2: October total manufacturing costs budgeted: $1,486,080
✔ 2: Quarter cost of goods manufactured budget: $4,293,120

Preparing Operating Budgets

P1. Enterprises, Inc.'s principal product is a hammer that carries a lifetime guarantee. Cost and production data for the hammer follow.

Direct materials:
 Anodized steel: 1 kilograms per hammer at $2 per kilogram
 Leather strapping for the handle: 0.5 square meter per hammer at $4 per square meter

Direct labor:
 Forging operation: $24 per labor hour; 6 minutes per hammer
 Leather-wrapping operation: $20 per direct labor hour; 12 minutes per hammer

Overhead:
 Forging operation: rate equals 40 percent of department's direct labor dollars
 Leather-wrapping operation: rate equals 60 percent of department's direct labor dollars

In October, November, and December, Enterprises expects to produce 108,000, 104,000, and 100,000 hammers, respectively. The company has no beginning or ending balances of direct materials inventory or work in process inventory for the year.

REQUIRED

1. For the three-month period ending December 31, prepare monthly production cost information for the hammer. Classify the costs as direct materials, direct labor, or overhead, and show your computations.
2. Prepare a cost of goods manufactured budget for the hammer. Show monthly cost data and combined totals for the quarter for each cost category.

LO 3, 4

SPREADSHEET

✔ 1: Total annual sales: $102,000
✔ 3: Total annual cost of direct materials purchases: $6,928

Preparing a Comprehensive Budget

P2. Bathworks produces hair and bath products. Bathworks' owner would like to have an estimate of the company's net income in the coming year.

REQUIRED

Project Bathworks's net income next year by completing the operating budgets and budgeted income statement that follows. Assume that the selling price will remain constant.

1. Sales budget:

Bathworks
Sales Budget
For the Year Ended December 31

	Quarter				
	1	2	3	4	Year
Sales in units	4,000	3,000	5,000	5,000	17,000
Selling price per unit	× $6	× ?	× ?	× ?	× ?
Total sales	$24,000	?	?	?	?

2. Production budget:

Bathworks
Production Budget
For the Year Ended December 31

	Quarter				
	1	**2**	**3**	**4**	**Year**
Sales in units	4,000	?	?	?	?
Plus desired units of ending finished goods inventory[a]	300	?	?	600	600
Desired total units	4,300	?	?	?	?
Less desired units of beginning finished goods inventory[b]	400	?	?	?	400
Total production units	3,900	?	?	?	?

[a]Desired units of ending finished goods inventory = 10% of next quarter's budgeted sales.
[b]Desired units of beginning finished goods inventory = 10% of current quarter's budgeted sales.

3. Direct materials purchases budget:

Bathworks
Direct Materials Purchases Budget
For the Year Ended December 31

	Quarter				
	1	**2**	**3**	**4**	**Year**
Total production units	3,900	3,200	5,000	5,100	17,200
Ounces per unit	× 4	× 4	× 4	× 4	× 4
Total production needs in ounces	15,600	?	?	?	?
Plus desired ounces of ending direct materials inventory[a]	2,560	?	?	3,600	3,600
	18,160	?	?	?	?
Less desired ounces of beginning direct materials inventory[b]	3,120	?	?	?	3,120
Total ounces of direct materials to be purchased	15,040	?	?	?	?
Cost per ounce	× $0.10	× ?	× ?	× ?	× ?
Total cost of direct materials purchases	$ 1,504	?	?	?	?

[a]Desired ounces of ending direct materials inventory = 20% of next quarter's budgeted production needs in ounces.
[b]Desired ounces of beginning direct materials inventory = 20% of current quarter's budgeted production needs in ounces.

4. Direct labor budget:

Bathworks
Direct Labor Budget
For the Year Ended December 31

	Quarter				
	1	**2**	**3**	**4**	**Year**
Total production units	3,900	?	?	?	?
Direct labor hours per unit	× 0.10	× ?	× ?	× ?	× ?
Total direct labor hours	390	?	?	?	?
Direct labor cost per hour	× $20	× ?	× ?	× ?	× ?
Total direct labor cost	$7,800	?	?	?	?

(Continued)

5. Overhead budget:

Bathworks
Overhead Budget
For the Year Ended December 31

	Quarter				
	1	**2**	**3**	**4**	**Year**
Variable overhead costs:					
Factory supplies ($0.05)	$ 195	$?	$?	$?	$?
Employee benefits ($0.25)	975	?	?	?	?
Inspection ($0.10)	390	?	?	?	?
Maintenance and repairs ($0.15)	585	?	?	?	?
Utilities ($0.05)	195	?	?	?	?
Total variable overhead costs	$2,340	$?	$?	$?	$?
Total fixed overhead costs	4,300	?	?	?	?
Total overhead costs	$6,640	$?	$?	$?	$?

Note: The figures in parentheses are variable costs per unit.

6. Selling and administrative expenses budget:

Bathworks
Selling and Administrative Expenses Budget
For the Year Ended December 31

	Quarter				
	1	**2**	**3**	**4**	**Year**
Variable selling and administrative expenses:					
Delivery expenses ($0.10)	$ 400	$?	$?	$?	$?
Sales commissions ($0.15)	600	?	?	?	?
Accounting ($0.05)	200	?	?	?	?
Other administrative expenses ($0.20)	800	?	?	?	?
Total variable selling and administrative expenses	$2,000	$?	$?	$?	$?
Total fixed selling and administrative expenses	5,000	?	?	?	?
Total selling and administrative expenses	$7,000	$?	$?	$?	$?

Note: The figures in parentheses are variable costs per unit.

7. Cost of goods manufactured budget:

Bathworks
Cost of Goods Manufactured Budget
For the Year Ended December 31

Direct materials used:		
Direct materials inventory, beginning	$?	
Purchases	?	
Cost of direct materials available for use	$?	
Less direct materials inventory, ending	?	
Cost of direct materials used		$?
Direct labor costs		?
Overhead costs		?
Total manufacturing costs		$?
Work in process inventory, beginning		?
Less work in process inventory, ending*		?
Cost of goods manufactured		$?
Units produced		÷ ?
Manufactured cost per unit		$?

* It is the company's policy to have no units in process at the end of the year.

8. Budgeted income statement:

Bathworks
Budgeted Income Statement
For the Year Ended December 31

Sales		$?
Cost of goods sold:		
Finished goods inventory, beginning	$?	
Cost of goods manufactured	?	
Cost of goods available for sale	$?	
Less finished goods inventory, ending	?	
Cost of goods sold		?
Gross margin		$?
Selling and administrative expenses		?
Income from operations		$?
Income taxes expense (30% tax rate)		?
Net income		$?

LO 4

SPREADSHEET

✔ Ending cash balance: $11,260

Cash Budget

P3. All Eyes Security Services Company provides security monitoring services. It employs four security specialists. Each specialist works an average of 180 hours a month. The company's controller has compiled the information that follows.

	Actual Data for Last Year		Forecasted Data for Current Year		
	November	**December**	**January**	**February**	**March**
Security billings (sales)	$30,000	$35,000	$25,000	$20,000	$30,000
Selling and admin. expenses	10,000	11,000	9,000	8,000	10,500
Operating supplies	2,500	3,500	2,500	2,000	3,000
Service overhead	3,000	3,500	3,000	2,500	3,000

Sixty percent of the client billings are cash sales collected during the month of sale; 30 percent are collected in the first month following the sale; and 10 percent are collected in the second month following the sale. Operating supplies are paid for in the month of purchase. Selling and administrative expenses and service overhead are paid in the month following the cost's incurrence.

The company has a bank loan of $12,000 at a 12 percent annual interest rate. Interest is paid monthly, and $2,000 of the loan principal is due on February 28. Income taxes of $2,500 for the last calendar year are due and payable on March 15. The four security specialists each earn $15 an hour, and all payroll-related employee benefit costs are included in service overhead. The company anticipates no capital expenditures for the first quarter of the coming year. It expects its cash balance on December 31 to be $15,000.

REQUIRED

Prepare a monthly cash budget for All Eyes for the three-month period ended March 31.

LO 4

✔ 2: Net income: $107,982
✔ 3: Total assets: $742,288

Budgeted Income Statement and Budgeted Balance Sheet

P4. Local Bank has asked Wonderware Products, Inc.'s president for a budgeted income statement and budgeted balance sheet for the quarter ended June 30. These pro forma financial statements are needed to support Wonderware's request for a loan.

Wonderware routinely prepares a quarterly master budget. The operating budgets prepared for the quarter ending June 30 have provided the following information:

(Continued)

Projected sales for April are $220,400; for May, $164,220; and for June, $165,980. Direct materials purchases for the period are estimated at $96,840; direct materials usage, at $102,710; direct labor expenses, at $71,460; overhead, at $79,940; selling and administrative expenses, at $143,740; capital expenditures, at $125,000 (to be spent on June 29); cost of goods manufactured, at $252,880; and cost of goods sold, at $251,700.

Balance sheet account balances at March 31 were as follows: Accounts Receivable, $26,500; Materials Inventory, $23,910; Work in Process Inventory, $31,620; Finished Goods Inventory, $36,220; Prepaid Expenses, $7,200; Plant, Furniture, and Fixtures, $498,600; Accumulated Depreciation—Plant, Furniture, and Fixtures, $141,162; Patents, $90,600; Accounts Payable, $39,600; Notes Payable, $105,500; Common Stock, $250,000; and Retained Earnings, $200,988.

Projected monthly cash balances for the second quarter are as follows: April 30, $20,490; May 31, $35,610; and June 30, $39,320. During the quarter, accounts receivable are expected to increase by 30 percent, patents to go up by $6,500, prepaid expenses to remain constant, and accounts payable to go down by 10 percent (Wonderware will make a $5,000 payment on a note payable, $4,100 of which is principal reduction). The federal income tax rate is 30 percent, and the second quarter's tax is paid in July. Depreciation for the quarter will be $6,420, which is included in the overhead budget. The company will pay no dividends.

REQUIRED

1. Determine the June 30 ending balances for Materials Inventory, Work in Process Inventory, and Finished Goods Inventory.
2. Prepare a budgeted income statement for the quarter ended June 30.
3. Prepare a budgeted balance sheet as of June 30.

LO **4, 5**

Basic Cash Budget

✔ March cash receipts from sales on account: $87,360
✔ 1: Ending cash balance: $10,020

P5. Xeriscape Nurseries, Inc., has four divisions. The corporation's controller has been asked to prepare a cash budget for the Northern Division for the first quarter. Projected data supporting this budget follow.

Sales (60% on credit)		Purchases	
November	$160,000	December	$ 90,000
December	200,000	January	98,000
January	120,000	February	100,000
February	160,000	March	104,000
March	140,000		

Collection records of accounts receivable have shown that 40 percent of all credit sales are collected in the month of sale, 50 percent in the month following the sale, and 8 percent in the second month following the sale; 2 percent of the sales are uncollectible. All purchases are paid for in the month of the purchase. Salaries and wages are projected to be $25,000 in January, $33,000 in February, and $21,000 in March. Estimated monthly costs are utilities, $4,220; collection fees, $1,700; rent, $5,300; equipment depreciation, $5,440; supplies, $2,480; small tools, $3,140; and miscellaneous, $1,900. Each of the corporation's divisions maintains a $10,000 minimum cash balance and can borrow from the bank in multiples of $100, as needed. As of December 31, the Southern Division had a cash balance of $10,000.

REQUIRED

1. Prepare a monthly cash budget for Xeriscape Nurseries' Northern Division for the first quarter.
2. **ACCOUNTING CONNECTION ▶** Should Xeriscape Nurseries anticipate taking out a loan for the Northern Division during the quarter? If so, how much should it borrow, and when?

ALTERNATE PROBLEMS

LO 3

Preparing Operating Budgets

✔ 1: January total manufacturing costs budgeted: $780,000
✔ 2: Quarter cost of goods manufactured budget: $2,242,500

P6. Bobble, Inc.'s principal product is a stainless steel water bottle that carries a lifetime guarantee. Cost and production data for the water bottle follow.

Direct materials:
Stainless steel: 0.25 kilogram per bottle at $8.00 per kilogram
Clip for the handle: 1 per bottle at $0.10 each

Direct labor:
Stamping operation: $30 per labor hour; 2 minutes per bottle

Overhead:
Stamping operation: rate equals 80 percent of department's direct labor dollars

In January, February, and March, Waterworks expects to produce 200,000, 225,000, and 150,000 bottles, respectively. The company has no beginning or ending balances of direct materials inventory or work in process inventory for the year.

REQUIRED

1. For the three-month period ending March 31, prepare monthly production cost information for the metal water bottle. Classify the costs as direct materials, direct labor, or overhead, and show your computations. (Round to the nearest dollar.)
2. Prepare a cost of goods manufactured budget for the water bottle. Show monthly cost data and combined totals for the quarter for each cost category.

LO 3, 4

SPREADSHEET

✔ 1: Total annual sales: $175,000
✔ 3: Total annual cost of direct materials purchases: $36,240
✔ 8: Net income: $60,725

Preparing a Comprehensive Budget

P7. Ginnie Springs Company has been bottling and selling water since 1940. The company's current owner would like to know how a new product would affect the company's net income in the coming year.

REQUIRED

Calculate Ginnie Springs' net income for the new product in the coming year by completing the operating budgets and budgeted income statement that follow. Assume that the selling price will remain constant.

1. Sales budget:

Ginnie Springs Company
Sales Budget
For the Year Ended December 31

	Quarter				
	1	**2**	**3**	**4**	**Year**
Sales in units	40,000	30,000	50,000	55,000	175,000
Selling price per unit	× $1	× ?	× ?	× ?	× ?
Total sales	$40,000	$?	$?	$?	$?

(Continued)

2. Production budget:

Ginnie Springs Company
Production Budget
For the Year Ended December 31

	Quarter				
	1	2	3	4	Year
Sales in units	40,000	?	?	?	?
Plus desired units of ending finished goods inventory[a]	3,000	?	?	6,000	6,000
Desired total units	43,000	?	?	?	?
Less desired units of beginning finished goods inventory[b]	4,000	?	?	?	4,000
Total production units	39,000	?	?	?	?

[a]Desired units of ending finished goods inventory = 10% of next quarter's budgeted sales.
[b]Desired units of beginning finished goods inventory = 10% of current quarter's budgeted sales.

3. Direct materials purchases budget:

Ginnie Springs Company
Direct Materials Purchases Budget
For the Year Ended December 31

	Quarter				
	1	2	3	4	Year
Total production units	39,000	32,000	50,500	55,500	?
Ounces per unit	× 20	× 20	× 20	× 20	× 20
Total production needs in ounces	780,000	?	?	?	?
Plus desired ounces of ending direct materials inventory[a]	128,000	?	?	240,000	240,000
	908,000	?	?	?	?
Less desired ounces of beginning direct materials inventory[b]	156,000	?	?	?	156,000
Total ounces of direct materials to be purchased	752,000	?	?	?	?
Cost per ounce	× $0.01	× ?	× ?	× ?	× ?
Total cost of direct materials purchases	$ 7,520	?	?	?	?

[a]Desired ounces of ending direct materials inventory = 20% of next quarter's budgeted production needs in ounces.
[b]Desired ounces of beginning direct materials inventory = 20% of current quarter's budgeted production needs in ounces.

4. Direct labor budget:

Ginnie Springs Company
Direct Labor Budget
For the Year Ended December 31

	Quarter				
	1	2	3	4	Year
Total production units	39,000	?	?	?	?
Direct labor hours per unit	×0.001	× ?	× ?	× ?	× ?
Total direct labor hours	39.0	?	?	?	?
Direct labor cost per hour	× $8	× ?	× ?	× ?	× ?
Total direct labor cost	$ 312	$?	$?	$?	$?

5. Overhead budget:

Ginnie Springs Company
Overhead Budget
For the Year Ended December 31

	Quarter 1	Quarter 2	Quarter 3	Quarter 4	Year
Variable overhead costs:					
Factory supplies ($0.01)	$ 390	$?	$?	$?	$?
Employee benefits ($0.05)	1,950	?	?	?	?
Inspection ($0.01)	390	?	?	?	?
Maintenance and repairs ($0.02)	780	?	?	?	?
Utilities ($0.01)	390	?	?	?	?
Total variable overhead costs	$3,900	$?	$?	$?	$?
Total fixed overhead costs	1,416	?	?	?	?
Total overhead costs	$5,316	$?	$?	$?	$?

Note: The figures in parentheses are variable costs per unit.

6. Selling and administrative expenses budget:

Ginnie Springs Company
Selling and Administrative Expenses Budget
For the Year Ended December 31

	Quarter 1	Quarter 2	Quarter 3	Quarter 4	Year
Variable selling and administrative expenses:					
Delivery expenses ($0.01)	$ 400	$?	$?	$?	$?
Sales commissions ($0.02)	800	?	?	?	?
Accounting ($0.01)	400	?	?	?	?
Other administrative expenses ($0.01)	400	?	?	?	?
Total variable selling and administrative expenses	$2,000	$?	$?	$?	$?
Total fixed selling and administrative expenses	5,000	?	?	?	?
Total selling and administrative expenses	$7,000	$?	$?	$?	$?

Note: The figures in parentheses are variable costs per unit.

7. Cost of goods manufactured budget:

Ginnie Springs Company
Cost of Goods Manufactured Budget
For the Year Ended December 31

Direct materials used:		
Direct materials inventory, beginning	$?	
Purchases	?	
Cost of direct materials available for use	$?	
Less direct materials inventory, ending	?	
Cost of direct materials used		$?
Direct labor costs		?
Overhead costs		?
Total manufacturing costs		$?
Work in process inventory, beginning*		?
Less work in process inventory, ending*		?
Cost of goods manufactured		$?
Units produced		÷ ?
Manufactured cost per unit		$?

* It is the company's policy to have no units in process at the end of the year.

(Continued)

8. Budgeted income statement:

Ginnie Springs Company
Budgeted Income Statement
For the Year Ended December 31

Sales		$?
Cost of goods sold:		
Finished goods inventory, beginning	$?	
Cost of goods manufactured	?	
Cost of goods available for sale	$?	
Less finished goods inventory, ending	?	
Cost of goods sold		?
Gross margin		$?
Selling and administrative expenses		?
Income from operations		$?
Income taxes expense (30% tax rate)		?
Net income		$?

LO 4

Cash Budget

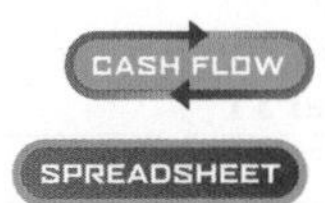

✔ Ending cash balance: $41,330

P8. Forensics Company provides fraud monitoring services. It employs five fraud specialists. Each specialist works an average of 200 hours a month. The company's controller has compiled the information that follows.

	Actual Data for Last Year		Forecasted Data for the Current Year		
	November	**December**	**January**	**February**	**March**
Billings (sales)	$100,000	$80,000	$60,000	$50,000	$70,000
Selling and administrative expenses	15,000	12,000	8,000	7,000	10,000
Operating supplies	2,500	3,500	2,500	2,000	3,000
Service overhead	14,000	13,500	13,000	12,500	13,000

Of the client billings, 70 percent are cash sales collected during the month of sale; 20 percent are collected in the first month following the sale; and 10 percent are collected in the second month following the sale. Operating supplies are paid in the month of purchase. Selling and administrative expenses and service overhead are paid in the month the cost is incurred.

The company has a bank loan of $12,000 at a 6 percent annual interest rate. Interest is paid monthly, and $2,000 of the loan principal is due on February 28. Income taxes of $6,500 for last calendar year are due and payable on March 15. The five security specialists each earn $24.00 an hour, and all payroll-related employee benefit costs are included in service overhead. The company anticipates no capital expenditures for the first quarter of the coming year. It expects its cash balance on December 31 to be $5,000.

REQUIRED

Prepare a monthly cash budget for Forensics for the three-month period ended March 31.

LO 4

Budgeted Income Statement and Budgeted Balance Sheet

✔ 2: Net income: $55,580
✔ 3: Total assets: $385,316

P9. Video Company, Inc., produces and markets two popular video games, *High Ranger* and *Star Bounder*. The closing account balances on the company's balance sheet for last year are as follows: Cash, $18,735; Accounts Receivable, $19,900; Materials Inventory, $18,510; Work in Process Inventory, $24,680; Finished Goods Inventory, $21,940; Prepaid Expenses, $3,420; Plant and Equipment, $262,800; Accumulated Depreciation—Plant and Equipment, $55,845; Other Assets, $9,480; Accounts Payable,

$52,640; Mortgage Payable, $70,000; Common Stock, $90,000; and Retained Earnings, $107,804.

Operating budgets for the first quarter of the coming year show the following estimated costs: direct materials purchases, $58,100; direct materials usage, $62,400; direct labor expense, $42,880; overhead, $51,910; selling expenses, $35,820; general and administrative expenses, $60,240; cost of goods manufactured, $163,990; and cost of goods sold, $165,440. Estimated ending cash balances are as follows: January, $34,610; February, $60,190; and March, $51,626. The company will have no capital expenditures during the quarter.

Sales are projected to be $125,200 in January, $105,100 in February, and $112,600 in March. Accounts receivable are expected to double during the quarter, and accounts payable are expected to decrease by 20 percent. Mortgage payments for the quarter will total $6,000, of which $2,000 will be interest expense. Prepaid expenses are expected to go up by $20,000, and other assets are projected to increase by 50 percent over the budget period. Depreciation for plant and equipment (already included in the overhead budget) averages 5 percent of total plant and equipment per year. Federal income taxes (30 percent of profits) are payable in April. The company pays no dividends.

REQUIRED

1. Determine the March 31 ending balances for Materials Inventory, Work in Process Inventory, and Finished Goods Inventory.
2. Prepare a budgeted income statement for the quarter ended March 31.
3. Prepare a budgeted balance sheet as of March 31.

LO **4**

Comprehensive Cash Budget

✔ Ending cash balance: $36,105

P10. Pur Centers, Inc., operates three fully equipped fitness centers, as well as a medical center that specializes in preventive medicine. The data that follow pertain to the corporation's first quarter.

Cash receipts:
- Memberships: December, 870; January, 880; February, 910; March, 1,030
- Membership dues: $100 per month, payable on the 10th of the month (80 percent collected on time; 20 percent collected one month late)
- Medical examinations: January, $35,610; February, $41,840; March, $45,610
- Special aerobics classes: January, $4,020; February, $5,130; March, $7,130
- High-protein food sales: January, $4,890; February, $5,130; March, $6,280

Cash payments:
- Salaries and wages:
  - Corporate officers: 2 at $18,000 per month
  - Physicians: 2 at $7,000 per month
  - Nurses: 3 at $2,900 per month
  - Clerical staff: 2 at $1,500 per month
  - Aerobics instructors: 3 at $1,100 per month
  - Clinic staff: 6 at $1,700 per month
  - Maintenance staff: 3 at $900 per month
  - Health-food servers: 3 at $750 per month
- Purchases:
  - Muscle-toning machines: January, $14,400; February, $13,800 (no purchases in March)
  - Pool supplies: $520 per month
  - Health food: January, $3,290; February, $3,460; March, $3,720
  - Medical supplies: January, $10,400; February, $11,250; March, $12,640
  - Medical uniforms and disposable garments: January, $7,410; February, $3,900; March, $3,450

(Continued)

Medical equipment: January, $11,200; February, $3,400; March $5,900
Advertising: January, $2,250; February, $1,190; March, $2,450
Utilities expense: January, $5,450; February, $5,890; March, $6,090

Insurance:
Fire: January, $3,470
Liability: March, $3,980

Property taxes: $3,760 due in January
Federal income taxes: Last year's taxes of $21,000 due in March
Miscellaneous: January, $2,625; February, $2,800; March, $1,150

Pur Centers' controller anticipates that the beginning cash balance on January 1 will be $14,000.

REQUIRED

Prepare a cash budget for Pur Centers for the first quarter of the year. Use January, February, March, and Quarter as the column headings.

CASES

LO 1, 2, 4, 5

Conceptual Understanding: Policies for Budget Development

C1. BUSINESS APPLICATION ▶ Raiders Corporation is a company with annual sales of $50 million. Its budget committee has created the following policy that the company uses each year in developing its master budget for the following calendar year:

May — The company's controller and other members of the budget committee meet to discuss plans and objectives for next year. The controller conveys all relevant information from this meeting to division managers and department heads.

June — Division managers, department heads, and the controller meet to discuss the corporate plans and objectives for next year. They develop a timetable for developing next year's budget data.

July — Division managers and department heads develop budget data. The vice president of sales provides them with final sales estimates, and they complete monthly sales estimates for each product line.

Aug. — Estimates of next year's monthly production activity and inventory levels are completed. Division managers and department heads communicate these estimates to the controller, who distributes them to other operating areas.

Sept. — All operating areas submit their revised budget data. The controller integrates their labor requirements, direct materials requirements, unit cost estimates, cash requirements, and profit estimates into a preliminary master budget.

Oct. — The budget committee meets to discuss the preliminary master budget and to make any necessary corrections, additions, or deletions. The controller incorporates all authorized changes into a final draft of the master budget.

Nov. — The controller submits the final draft to the budget committee for approval. If the committee approves it, it is distributed to all corporate officers, division managers, and department heads.

1. Comment on this policy.
2. What changes would you recommend?

LO 3, 5

Ethical Dilemma: Ethical Considerations in Budgeting

C2. BUSINESS APPLICATION ▶ Joakim Keynes is the manager of the Repairs and Maintenance Department of JB Industries. He is responsible for preparing his department's annual budget. Most managers in the company inflate their budget numbers by at least 10 percent because their bonuses depend upon how much below budget their departments operate. Keynes turned in the following information for his department's budget for next year to the company's budget committee:

	Budget This Year	Actual This Year	Budget Next Year
Supplies	$ 20,000	$ 16,000	$ 24,000
Labor	80,000	82,000	96,000
Utilities	8,500	8,000	10,200
Tools	12,500	9,000	15,000
Hand-carried equipment	25,000	16,400	30,000
Cleaning materials	4,600	4,200	5,520
Miscellaneous	2,000	2,100	2,400
Totals	$152,600	$137,700	$183,120

Because the figures for next year are 20 percent above those in this year's budget, the budget committee questioned them. Keynes defended them by saying that he expects a significant increase in activity in his department next year.

What do you think are the real reasons for the increase in the budgeted amounts? What ethical considerations enter into this situation?

LO 4

Conceptual Understanding: Budgeting for Cash Flows

CASH FLOW

C3. The nature of a company's business affects its need to budget for cash flows.

- **H&R Block** is a service company whose main business is preparing tax returns. Most tax returns are prepared after January 31 and before April 15. For a fee and interest, the company will advance cash to clients who are due refunds. The clients are expected to repay the cash advances when they receive their refunds. Although H&R Block has some revenues throughout the year, it devotes most of the nontax season to training potential employees in tax preparation procedures and to laying the groundwork for the next tax season.
- **Toys"R"Us** is a toy retailer whose sales are concentrated in October, November, and December of one year and January of the next year. Sales continue at a steady but low level during the rest of the year. The company purchases most of its inventory between July and September.
- **Johnson & Johnson** sells the many health care products that it manufactures to retailers, and the retailers sell them to the final customer. Johnson & Johnson offers retailers credit terms.

Discuss the nature of cash receipts and cash disbursements over a calendar year in the three companies we have just described. What are some key estimates that the management of these companies must make when preparing a cash budget?

LO 4, 5

Interpreting Management Reports: Budgeting Procedures

C4. BUSINESS APPLICATION ▶ Since Smart Enterprises inaugurated participative budgeting 10 years ago, everyone in the organization—from maintenance personnel to the president's staff—has had a voice in the budgeting process. Until recently, participative budgeting has worked in the best interests of the company as a whole. Now, however, it is becoming evident that some managers are using the practice solely to benefit their own divisions. The budget committee has therefore asked you, the company's controller, to analyze this year's divisional budgets carefully before incorporating them into the company's master budget.

The Gadget Division was the first of the company's six divisions to submit its budget request for next year. The division's budgeted income statement follows.

(Continued)

Smart Enterprises
Gadget Division
Budgeted Income Statement
For the Years Ended December 31

	Budget for This Year	Budget for Next Year	Increase (Decrease)
Net sales:			
Radios	$ 850,000	$ 910,000	$ 60,000
Appliances	680,000	740,000	60,000
Telephones	270,000	305,000	35,000
Miscellaneous	84,400	90,000	5,600
Net sales	$1,884,400	$2,045,000	$160,600
Less cost of goods sold	750,960	717,500[a]	(33,460)
Gross margin	$1,133,440	$1,327,500	$194,060
Operating expenses:			
Wages			
Warehouse	$ 94,500	$ 102,250	$ 7,750
Purchasing	77,800	84,000	6,200
Delivery/shipping	69,400	74,400	5,000
Maintenance	42,650	45,670	3,020
Salaries:			
Supervisory	60,000	92,250	32,250
Executive	130,000	164,000	34,000
Purchases, supplies	17,400	20,500	3,100
Maintenance	72,400	82,000	9,600
Depreciation	62,000	74,000[b]	12,000
Building rent	96,000	102,500	6,500
Sales commissions	188,440	204,500	16,060
Insurance:			
Fire	12,670	20,500	7,830
Liability	18,200	20,500	2,300
Utilities	14,100	15,375	1,275
Taxes			
Property	16,600	18,450	1,850
Payroll	26,520	41,000	14,480
Miscellaneous	4,610	10,250	5,640
Total operating expenses	$1,003,290	$1,172,145	$168,855
Income from operations	$ 130,150	$ 155,355	$ 25,205

[a] Less expensive merchandise will be purchased in the next year to boost profits.
[b] Depreciation is increased because additional equipment must be bought to handle increased sales.

1. Recast the Gadget Division's budgeted income statement in the following format (round percentages to two decimal places):

	Budget for This Year		Budget for Next Year	
Account	Amount	Percentage of Net Sales	Amount	Percentage of Net Sales

2. Actual results for this year revealed the following information about revenues and cost of goods sold:

	Amount	Percentage of Net Sales
Net sales:		
Radios	$ 780,000	43.94%
Appliances	640,000	36.06
Telephones	280,000	15.77
Miscellaneous	75,000	4.23
Net sales	$1,775,000	100.00%
Less cost of goods sold	763,425	43.01
Gross margin	$1,011,575	56.99%

On the basis of this information and your analysis in **1**, what do you think the budget committee should say to the Gadget Division's managers? Identify any specific areas of the budget that may need to be revised, and explain why the revision is needed.

LO **3, 4**

The Budgeting Process

SPREADSHEET

C5. Refer to our development of Framecraft Company's master budget in this chapter. Suppose that because of a new customer in Canada, the company management has decided to increase budgeted sales in the first quarter by 5,000 units. The expenses for this sale will include direct materials, direct labor, variable overhead, and variable selling and administrative expenses. The delivery expense for the Canadian customer will be $0.18 per unit rather than the regular $0.08 per unit. The desired units of beginning finished goods inventory will remain at 1,000 units.

1. Using a spreadsheet, revise Framecraft's budgeted income statement and the operating budgets that support it to reflect the changes described above. (Round manufactured cost per unit to three decimal places, and round income tax expense to the nearest dollar.)
2. What is the change in income from operations? Would you recommend accepting the order from the Canadian customer? If so, why?

Continuing Case: Cookie Company

C6. In this segment of our continuing case, you have decided to open a store where you will sell your company's cookies, as well as coffee, tea, and other beverages. You believe that the store will be able to provide excellent service and undersell the local competition. To fund operations, you are applying for a loan from the Small Business Administration. The loan application requires you to submit two financial budgets—a pro forma income statement and a pro forma balance sheet—within six weeks.

How do the four *w*'s of preparing an accounting report apply in this situation—that is, *why* are you preparing these financial budgets, *who* needs them, *what* information do you need to prepare them, and *when* are they due?

CHAPTER 21
Flexible Budgets and Performance Analysis

BUSINESS INSIGHT
Vail Resorts

Vail Resorts includes vacation spots like Vail, Breckenridge, Keystone, Heavenly, and Beaver Creek. To help guests enjoy all the activities that these places offer, Vail Resorts instituted an "all-in-one" charge card, which guests can use to pay for anything they might buy at the resort, including meals or snacks, skiing or snowboarding lessons, lift tickets, treatments at the spa, or merchandise from one of the resort's retail shops.

Guests like the all-in-one card because of its convenience, and they can earn points toward free lodging, meals, or lift tickets. The resort's managers like the card system because it is a simple way of collecting vast amounts of both financial and nonfinancial information. Each time a guest makes a purchase, the all-in-one card is electronically scanned. The new data then become part of an integrated management information system, which managers use in a variety of ways to measure and evaluate the resort's performance.

1. **CONCEPT** ▶ *What concepts guide managers when they evaluate performance?*

2. **ACCOUNTING APPLICATION** ▶ *How will managers use flexible budgets and other performance measures to analyze the financial and nonfinancial performance of responsibility centers?*

3. **BUSINESS APPLICATION** ▶ *How can managers achieve a balanced view of a business's well-being and how to improve it?*

LEARNING OBJECTIVES

LO1 **Define a *performance management and evaluation system* and *responsibility accounting*, and describe the roles they play in performance analysis.**

LO2 **Use flexible budgets and variable costing to analyze cost center and profit center performance.**

LO3 **Analyze investment centers using return on investment, residual income, and economic value added.**

LO4 **Describe how the balanced scorecard aligns performance with organizational goals.**

LO5 **Explain how properly linked performance incentives and measures add value for all stakeholders in performance management and evaluation.**

Blend Images/Fotolia LLC

SECTION 1

CONCEPTS

CONCEPTS
- Comparability
- Understandability

RELEVANT LEARNING OBJECTIVE

LO1 Define a *performance management and evaluation system* and *responsibility accounting*, and describe the roles they play in performance analysis.

LO1 Concepts Underlying Performance Analysis

Managers use the concepts of *understandability* and *comparability* as they manage a wide range of financial and nonfinancial data to guide and evaluate performance. If they want satisfactory results, managers must understand the cause-and-effect relationships between their actions and their performance. By measuring and tracking the causal relationships for which they are accountable, managers can improve performance as they command, control, and evaluate the organization.

A **performance management and evaluation system** is a set of procedures that account for and report on both financial and nonfinancial performance so that a company can *understand* how well it is doing, where it is going, and what improvements will make it more profitable. **Performance measures** are quantitative tools that gauge and *compare* an organization's performance in relation to a specific goal or an expected outcome.

- Financial performance measures use monetary information to measure and *compare* the performance of a profit-generating organization or its divisions, departments, product lines, sales territories, or operating activities. Examples include return on investment, net income as a percentage of sales, and the costs of poor quality as a percentage of sales.
- Nonfinancial performance measures use statistics to *understand* how to reduce or eliminate waste and inefficiencies in operating activities. Examples include the number of times an activity occurs or the time taken to perform a task, such as the number of customer complaints; number of orders shipped the same day; or the time taken to fill an order.

What to Measure, How to Measure

Performance measurement is the use of quantitative tools to *understand* an organization's performance in relation to a specific goal or an expected outcome. For performance measurement to succeed, managers must be able to distinguish between what is being measured and the actual measures used to monitor performance and *compare* results. For instance, product or service quality is not a performance measure. It is part of management's strategy to produce the highest-quality product or service possible, given the resources available. Product or service quality thus is what management wants to measure and compare.

As part of their performance management systems, organizations assign resources to specific areas of responsibility and track how the managers of those areas use those resources. For example, **Vail Resorts** assigns resources to its Lodging, Dining, Retail and Rental, Ski School, and Real Estate divisions and holds the managers of those divisions responsible for generating revenue and managing costs. Within each division, other managers are assigned responsibility for such areas as Children and Adult Ski School, Snowboard School, or Private Lessons.

All managers at all levels are then evaluated in terms of their ability to manage their areas of responsibility. To assist in performance management and evaluation, many organizations use responsibility accounting. **Responsibility accounting** is an information system that classifies data according to areas of responsibility and reports each area's activities by including only the revenue, cost, and resource categories that the assigned manager can control. A **responsibility center** is an organizational unit whose manager has been assigned the responsibility of managing a portion of the organization's resources. The activities of a responsibility center dictate the extent of a manager's responsibility. Thus, responsibility accounting establishes accountability—the foundation of performance analysis—by grounding user *comparisons* and *understanding* of an organization.

A report for a responsibility center should contain only the costs, revenues, and resources that the manager of that center can control. Such costs and revenues are called **controllable costs and revenues**, because they are the result of a manager's actions, influence, or decisions. A responsibility accounting system ensures that managers will not be held responsible for items that they cannot change.

Types of Responsibility Centers

There are five types of responsibility centers:

- cost center
- discretionary cost center
- revenue center
- profit center
- investment center

The key characteristics of each type of responsibility center are summarized in Exhibit 1.

Exhibit 1
Types of Responsibility Centers

Responsibility Center	Manager Responsibility	Performance Measures	Examples
Cost center	Only controllable costs, where there are well-defined links between the costs of resources and the resulting products or services	• Comparison of actual costs with flexible and master budget costs • Analysis of resulting variances	**Product:** Manufacturing assembly plants **Service:** Food service for hospital patients
Discretionary cost center	Only controllable costs; the links between the costs of resources and the resulting products or services are *not* well defined	• Comparison of actual noncost-based measures with targets • Determination of compliance with preapproved budgeted spending limits	**Product or service:** Administrative activities such as accounting, human resources, and research and development
Revenue center	Revenue generation	• Comparison of actual revenue with budgeted revenue • Analysis of resulting variances	**Product:** Phone or e-commerce sales for pizza delivery **Service:** Reservation center on Internet
Profit center	Operating income resulting from controllable revenues and costs	• Comparison of actual variable costing income statement with the budgeted income statement	**Product or service:** Local store of a national chain
Investment center	Controllable revenues, costs, and the investment of resources to achieve organizational goals	• Return on investment • Residual income • Economic value added	**Product:** A division of a multinational corporation **Service:** A national office of a multinational consulting firm

Cost Center A responsibility center whose manager is accountable only for controllable costs that have well-defined relationships between the center's resources and certain products or services is called a **cost center**. Manufacturing companies like **Apple** use cost centers to manage assembly plants, where the causal relationship between the costs of resources (direct material, direct labor) and the resulting products is well defined. Service organizations use cost centers to manage activities in which resources are clearly linked with a service that is provided at no additional charge. For example, in nursing homes and hospitals, there is a clear relationship between the costs of food and direct labor and the number of inpatient meals served.

The performance of a cost center is usually evaluated by *comparing* an activity's actual cost with its budgeted cost and analyzing the resulting variances. You will learn more about this performance evaluation process in the chapter on standard costing.

Discretionary Cost Center A responsibility center whose manager is accountable for costs only and in which the relationship between resources and the products or services produced is not well defined is called a **discretionary cost center**. Departments that perform administrative activities, such as accounting, human resources, and legal services, are typical examples of discretionary cost centers. These centers, like cost centers, have approved budgets that set spending limits.

Because the spending and use of resources in discretionary cost centers are not clearly linked to the production of a product or service, cost-based measures usually cannot be used to evaluate performance (although such centers are penalized if they exceed their approved budgets). For example, among the performance measures used to evaluate the research and development activities are the number of patents obtained and the number of cost-saving innovations that are developed. At service organizations, such as **United Way**, a common measure of administrative activities is how low their costs are as a percentage of total contributions.

Research and development units are a type of discretionary cost center in which a manager is accountable for costs only and the relationship between resources and products or services produced is not well defined. A common performance measure used to evaluate research and development activities is the number of patents obtained.

Otnaydur/Dreamstime.com

Revenue Center A responsibility center whose manager is accountable primarily for revenue and whose success is based on its ability to generate revenue is called a **revenue center**. Examples of revenue centers are **Hertz**'s national car reservation center and **Amazon**'s ecommerce order department.

A revenue center's performance is usually evaluated by *comparing* its actual revenue with its budgeted revenue and analyzing the resulting variances. Performance measures may include sales dollars, number of customer sales, or sales revenue per minute.

Profit Center A responsibility center whose manager is accountable for both revenue and costs and for the resulting operating income is called a **profit center**. A good example is a local store of a national chain, such as **Wal-Mart** or **Jiffy Lube**.

The performance of a profit center is usually evaluated by *comparing* the figures on its actual income statement with the figures on its master or flexible budget income statement.

Investment Center A responsibility center whose manager is accountable for profit generation and who can also make significant decisions about the resources that the center uses is called an **investment center**. For example, the president of **Harley-Davidson**'s Buell subsidiary and the president of **Brinker International**'s Chili's Grill and Bar can control revenues, costs, and the investment of assets to achieve organizational goals.

The performance of these centers is evaluated using such measures as return on investment, residual income, and economic value added, (which will be discussed later in the chapter). These measures are used in all types of organizations, both manufacturing and service.

Organizational Structure and Performance Reports

Much can be learned about an organization by examining how its managers organize activities and resources. A company's organizational structure formalizes its lines of managerial authority and control. An **organization chart** is a visual representation of an organization's hierarchy of responsibility for the purposes of management control. Within an organization chart, the five types of responsibility centers are arranged by level of management authority and control.

Exhibit 2 shows a typical corporate organization chart for part of the management structure for the Restaurant Division of a hospitality corporation like **Vail Resorts**. Notice that all five types of responsibility centers are represented.

Exhibit 2
Partial Organization Chart of the Restaurant Division

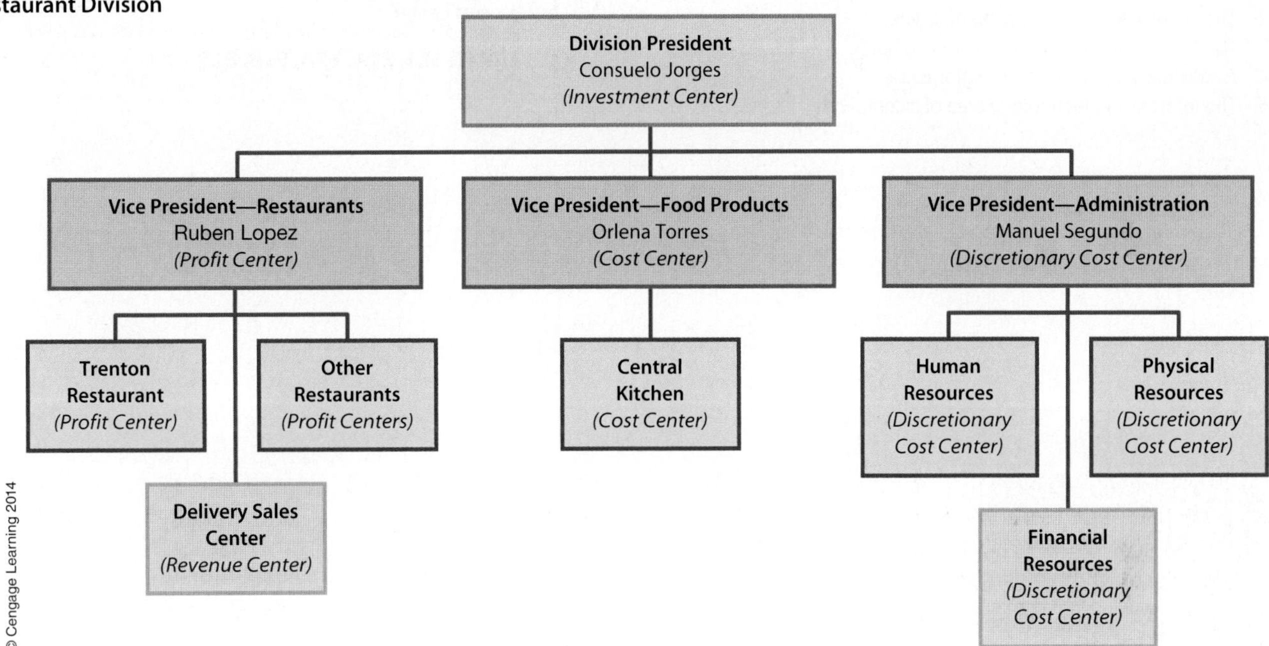

In a responsibility accounting system, the performance reports for each level of management are tailored to each manager's individual needs for information. As information moves up the organizational chart, it is usually condensed. Performance reporting by responsibility level enables an organization to trace the source of a cost, revenue, or resource to the manager who controls it and to evaluate that manager's performance accordingly.

STUDY NOTE: *Only controllable items should be included on a manager's performance report.*

Because performance reports contain information about costs, revenues, and resources, they allow *comparisons* between actual performance and budget expectations. Such comparisons allow management to *understand* and evaluate an individual's performance with respect to responsibility center and company-wide objectives and to recommend changes. Performance reports should contain only costs, revenues, and resources that the manager can control. If a performance report includes items that the manager cannot control, the credibility of the entire responsibility accounting system can be called into question. The content and format of a performance report depend on the nature of the responsibility center. It is up to management to structure and interpret them fairly.

Although performance reports vary in format, they have some common themes:

- All responsibility center reports compare actual results to budgeted figures and focus on the differences.
- Often, comparisons are made to a flexible budget (to be discussed in the next section) as well as to the master budget.
- Only the items that the manager can control are included in the performance report.
- Nonfinancial measures are also examined to achieve a more balanced view of the manager's responsibilities.

APPLY IT!

Identify the most appropriate type of responsibility center for each of the following organizational units:

1. A pizza store in a pizza chain
2. The ticket sales center of a major airline
3. The food service function at a nursing home
4. A subsidiary of a business conglomerate
5. The information technology area of a company

SOLUTION

1. profit center
2. revenue center
3. cost center
4. investment center
5. discretionary cost center

TRY IT! SE1, E1A, E2A, E1B, E2B

SECTION 2

ACCOUNTING APPLICATIONS

ACCOUNTING APPLICATIONS
- Create a flexible budget
- Create a variable costing income statement
- Compute return on investment (ROI)
- Compute residual income (RI)
- Compute economic value added (EVA)

RELEVANT LEARNING OBJECTIVES

LO2 Use flexible budgets and variable costing to analyze cost center and profit center performance.

LO3 Analyze investment centers using return on investment, residual income, and economic value added.

LO2 Performance Evaluation of Cost Centers and Profit Centers

The accuracy of performance analysis depends to a large extent on the type of budget that managers use when *comparing* actual results to a budget. Static, or fixed, budgets forecast revenues and expenses for just one level of sales and just one level of output. The budgets that make up a master budget are usually based on a single level of output; but many things can cause actual output to differ from the estimated output. If a company produces more products than predicted, total production costs will almost always be greater than predicted. Thus, a comparison of actual production costs with master budgeted costs will inevitably show variances.

Flexible Budgets and Performance Analysis

To judge a product or division's performance accurately, the company's managers can use a **flexible budget** (or *variable budget*), which is a summary of expected costs for a range of activity levels. Unlike a static budget, a flexible budget provides forecasted data that can be adjusted for changes in the level of output. In terms of *comparability*, flexible budgets allow managers to compare budgeted and actual costs at any level of output. An important element in preparing a flexible budget is the **flexible budget formula**, an equation that determines the expected, or budgeted, cost for any level of output. The flexible budget formula can be used to create a budget for any level of output in the range of levels given and is computed as follows.

$$\text{Flexible Budgeted Costs} = \left(\text{Variable Cost per Unit} \times \text{Number of Units Produced}\right) + \text{Budgeted Fixed Costs}$$

We will use Winter Wonderland Resort, a hypothetical company, to illustrate how managers use flexible budgets. In the Restaurant Division of Winter Wonderland, the central kitchen evaluates the performance of each food item produced. The flexible budget formula for one of its products, House Dressing, would be computed as follows.

$$\text{House Dressing Flexible Budget Formula} = (\$0.33 \times \text{Gallons Produced}) + \$5$$

A flexible budget for Winter Wonderland's House Dressing appears in Exhibit 3, which shows the estimated costs for 1,000, 1,200, and 1,500 gallons of salad dressing output.

Exhibit 3
Flexible Budget for House Dressing

Winter Wonderland—Restaurant Division
House Dressing Flexible Budget
Current Year

	Units Produced		
Cost Category	**1,000**	**1,200**	**1,500**
Direct materials ($0.25 per gallon)	$250	$300	$375
Direct labor ($0.05 per gallon)	50	60	75
Variable overhead ($0.03 per gallon)	30	36	45
Total variable costs ($0.33 per gallon)	$330	$396	$495
Fixed overhead costs	5	5	5
Total costs	$335	$401	$500

Evaluating Cost Center Performance Using Flexible Budgeting

In the Restaurant Division of a major hospitality company like Winter Wonderland, the central kitchen is where the food products that the restaurants sell are prepared. It is a cost center because its costs have well-defined relationships with the resulting products, which are then transferred to the restaurants for further processing and sale. To ensure each food item is meeting its performance goals, the manager will evaluate each product by *comparing* its actual costs with the corresponding amounts from the budget.

The performance report on House Dressing presented in Exhibit 4 compares data from Winter Wonderland's master budget (prepared at the beginning of the period) and flexible budget (prepared at the end of the period) with the actual results for the period. As you can see, actual costs exceeded budgeted costs. Most managers would consider such a cost overrun significant. But was there really a cost overrun if the amounts budgeted in the master budget are based on an output of 1,000 units of dressing and the actual output was 1,200 units of dressing?

To judge the central kitchen's performance accurately, the company needs to change the budgeted data in the master budget to reflect an output of 1,200 units, as illustrated in Exhibit 4. The flexible budget is used primarily as an evaluation tool at the end of a period. Favorable (positive, or F) and unfavorable (negative, or U) variances between actual costs and the flexible budget can be further examined by using standard costing to compute specific variances for direct materials, direct labor, and variable and fixed overhead.*

Exhibit 4
Central Kitchen's Performance Report on House Dressing

	Actual Results	Variance	Flexible Budget	Variance	Master Budget
Gallons produced	**1,200**	**0**	**1,200**	**200 (F)**	**1,000**
Center costs:					
Direct materials ($0.25 per gallon)	$312	$(12) (U)	$300	$(50) (U)	$250
Direct labor ($0.05 per gallon)	72	(12) (U)	60	(10) (U)	50
Variable overhead ($0.03 per gallon)	33	3 (F)	36	(6) (U)	30
Fixed overhead	2	3 (F)	5	0	5
Total cost	$419	$(18) (U)	$401	$(66) (U)	$335
Performance measures:					
Defect-free gallons to total produced	0.98	(0.01) (U)	N/A	N/A	0.99
Average throughput minutes per gallon	11	1 (F)	N/A	N/A	12

Note: In this exhibit and others that appear later in this chapter, (F) indicates a favorable variance, and (U) indicates an unfavorable variance.

Evaluating Profit Center Performance Using Variable Costing

Restaurants are profit centers, since each is accountable for its own revenues and costs and for the resulting operating income. A profit center's performance is usually evaluated by *comparing* its actual income statement results to its budgeted income statement.

STUDY NOTE: *A variable costing income statement has a similar format to the contribution margin income statement used in cost-volume-profit analysis.*

One method of preparing profit center performance reports is **variable costing**, which classifies a manager's controllable costs as either variable or fixed. Variable costing produces a variable costing income statement instead of a traditional income statement (also called a *full costing* or *absorption costing income statement*), which is used for external reporting purposes. It is an internally prepared income statement that is useful in performance management and evaluation because it focuses on cost variability and the

* Refer to the chapter on standard costing for further information on performance evaluation using variances or the flexible budget.

profit center's contribution to operating income. Under variable costing, variable costs include direct materials costs, direct labor costs, variable overhead costs, and variable selling, administrative, and general costs. Fixed costs include fixed manufacturing costs, like fixed overhead, and fixed selling, administrative, and general costs. The format of a variable costing income statement follows.

Sales
– Variable costs
Contribution margin
– Fixed costs
Operating income

The variable costing income statement differs from the traditional income statement prepared for financial reporting, as shown by the two income statements in Exhibit 5 for Trenton Restaurant, which is part of Winter Wonderland's Restaurant Division. In the traditional income statement, all manufacturing costs are assigned to the cost of goods sold. In the variable costing income statement, only the variable manufacturing costs are included in the variable cost of goods sold. Fixed manufacturing costs are considered costs of the current period and are listed with fixed selling expenses after the contribution margin has been computed.

Exhibit 5
Variable Costing Income Statement Versus Traditional Income Statement for Trenton Restaurant (Amounts in Thousands)

Variable Costing Income Statement		Traditional Income Statement	
Sales	$ 2,500	Sales	$ 2,500
Variable cost of goods sold	(1,575)	Cost of goods sold	
Variable selling expenses	(325)	($1,575 + $170)	(1,745)
Contribution margin	$ 600	Gross margin	$ 755
Fixed manufacturing costs	(170)	Variable selling expenses	(325)
Fixed selling expenses	(230)	Fixed selling expenses	(230)
Profit center operating income	$ 200	Profit center operating income	$ 200

In addition to tracking financial performance measures, a manager of a profit center may also want to measure and evaluate nonfinancial information, such as the number of food orders processed and the average amount of a sales order at Trenton Restaurant. The resulting report, based on variable costing and flexible budgeting, is shown in Exhibit 6.

Exhibit 6
Performance Report Based on Variable Costing and Flexible Budgeting for Trenton Restaurant (Amounts in Thousands)

	Actual Results	Variance	Flexible Budget	Variance	Master Budget
Meals served	**750**	**0**	**750**	**250 (U)**	**1,000**
Sales (average meal $2.85)	$ 2,500.00	$ 362.50 (F)	$ 2,137.50	$ 712.50 (U)	$ 2,850.00
Controllable variable costs:					
Variable cost of goods sold ($1.50)	(1,575.00)	(450.00) (U)	(1,125.00)	(375.00) (F)	(1,500.00)
Variable selling expenses ($0.40)	(325.00)	(25.00) (U)	(300.00)	(100.00) (F)	(400.00)
Contribution margin	$ 600.00	$ 112.50 (U)	$ 712.50	$ 237.50 (U)	$ 950.00
Controllable fixed costs:					
Fixed manufacturing expenses	(170.00)	(30.00) (F)	(200.00)	0.00	(200.00)
Fixed selling expenses	(230.00)	(20.00) (F)	(250.00)	0.00	(250.00)
Profit center operating income	$ 200.00	$ 62.50 (U)	$ 262.50	$ 237.50 (U)	$ 500.00
Nonfinancial performance measures:					
Number of orders processed	300	50 (F)	N/A	N/A	250
Average sales order	$8.34	$3.06 (U)	N/A	N/A	$11.40

Complete the following performance report for a profit center for the month ended December 31:

	Actual Results	Variance	Master Budget
Sales	$?	$ 20 (F)	$ 120
Controllable variable costs:			
Variable cost of goods sold	(25)	(10) (U)	?
Variable selling and administrative expenses	(15)	? (?)	(5)
Contribution margin	$100	$? (?)	$ 100
Controllable fixed costs	?	10 (F)	60
Profit center income	$ 50	$ 10 (F)	$?
Nonfinancial performance measures:			
Number of orders processed	50	20 (F)	?
Average daily sales	$?	$0.66 (F)	$4.00
Number of units sold	100	40 (F)	?

SOLUTION

Profit Center
Performance Report
For the Month Ended December 31

	Actual Results	Variance	Master Budget
Sales	$140	$ 20 (F)	$120
Controllable variable costs:			
Variable cost of goods sold	(25)	(10) (U)	(15)
Variable selling and administrative expenses	(15)	(10) (U)	(5)
Contribution margin	$100	$ 0	$100
Controllable fixed costs	50	10 (F)	60
Profit center operating income	$ 50	$ 10 (F)	$ 40
Nonfinancial performance measures:			
Number of orders processed	50	20 (F)	30
Average daily sales	$4.66	$0.66 (F)	$4.00
Number of units sold	100	40 (F)	60

TRY IT! SE2, SE3, SE4, E3A, E4A, E5A, E6A, E3B, E4B, E5B, E6B

LO3 Performance Evaluation of Investment Centers

The evaluation of an investment center's performance requires more than a comparison of controllable revenues and costs with budgeted amounts. Because the managers of investment centers also control resources and invest in assets, other performance measures must be used to hold them accountable for revenues, costs, and the capital investments that they control. In this section, we focus on the traditional performance evaluation measures of return on investment and residual income and the relatively new performance measure of economic value added.

Return on Investment

Traditionally, the most common performance measure that takes into account both operating income and the assets invested to earn that income is **return on investment (ROI)**, which is computed as follows.

Computing Return on Investment (ROI)

Formula

$$\text{Return on Investment (ROI)} = \frac{\text{Operating Income}}{\text{Assets Invested}}$$

In this formula, assets invested is the average of the beginning and ending asset balances for the period.

Properly measuring the income and the assets specifically controlled by a manager is critical to the quality of this performance measure. Using ROI, it is possible to evaluate the manager of any investment center, whether it is an entire company or a unit within a company, such as a subsidiary, division, or other business segment.

Example Winter Wonderland's Restaurant Division had actual operating income of $610, and the average assets invested were $800. The master budget called for $890 in operating income and $1,000 in invested assets. As shown in Exhibit 7, the budgeted

Exhibit 7
Performance Report Based on Return on Investment for the Restaurant Division

	Actual Results	Variance	Master Budget
Operating income	\$610	\$(280) (U)	\$890
Assets invested	\$800	\$200 (F)	\$1,000
Performance measure:			
ROI*	76%	(13%) (U)	89%

*ROI = Operating Income ÷ Assets Invested
Actual = \$890 ÷ \$1,000
= 0.89 = 89%
Master = \$610 ÷ \$800
= 0.7625 = 76% (rounded)

ROI for the division would be 89 percent, and the actual ROI would be 76 percent. The actual ROI was lower than the budgeted ROI because the division's actual operating income was lower than expected relative to the actual assets invested.

***STUDY NOTE:** Profit margin focuses on the income statement, and asset turnover focuses on the balance sheet aspects of ROI.*

The basic ROI equation, Operating Income ÷ Assets Invested, can be rewritten to show the many elements within the aggregate ROI number that a manager can influence. Two important indicators of performance are profit margin and asset turnover.

- **Profit margin** is the ratio of operating income to sales. It represents the percentage of each sales dollar that results in profit.
- **Asset turnover** is the ratio of sales to average assets invested. It indicates the productivity of assets, or the number of sales dollars generated by each dollar invested in assets.

A single ROI number is a composite index of many cause-and-effect relationships and interdependent financial elements. The following formula recognizes the many interrelationships that affect ROI:

$$\text{ROI} = \frac{\text{Operating Income}}{\text{Sales}} \times \frac{\text{Sales}}{\text{Assets Invested}} = \frac{\text{Operating Income}}{\text{Assets Invested}}$$

$$\text{ROI} = \text{Profit Margin} \times \text{Asset Turnover}$$

Profit margin and asset turnover help explain changes in return on investment for a single investment center or differences in return on investment among investment centers. Therefore, the formula ROI = Profit Margin × Asset Turnover is useful for analyzing and interpreting the elements that make up a business's overall return on investment.

ROI is affected by a manager's decisions about pricing, product sales mix, capital budgeting for new facilities, product sales volume, and other financial matters. A manager can improve ROI by increasing sales, decreasing costs, or decreasing assets.

Business Application If ROI is overemphasized, investment center managers may react by making business decisions that favor their personal ROI performance at the expense of company-wide profits or the long-term success of other investment centers. To avoid such problems, other performance measures should always be used in conjunction with ROI—for example, *comparisons* of revenues, costs, and operating income with budget amounts or past trends; sales growth percentages; market share percentages; or other key variables in the organization's activity. ROI should also be compared with budgeted goals and with past ROI trends because changes in this ratio over time can be more revealing than any single number.

Residual Income

Because of the pitfalls of using ROI as a performance measure, **residual income (RI)** is another approach to evaluating investment centers. Residual income is the operating income that an investment center earns above a minimum desired return on invested assets. Residual income is not a ratio but a dollar amount—the amount of profit left after subtracting a predetermined desired income target for an investment center.

Computing Residual Income (RI)

Formula

Residual Income = Operating Income − (Desired ROI × Assets Invested)

STUDY NOTE: *ROI is expressed as a percentage, and residual income is expressed in dollars.*

As in the computation of ROI, assets invested is the average of the center's beginning and ending asset balances for the period.

The desired RI will vary from investment center to investment center depending on the type of business and the level of risk assumed.

Example Exhibit 8 shows Winter Wonderland's Restaurant Division's performance report based on residual income. The residual income performance target is to exceed a 20 percent return on assets invested in the division.

Exhibit 8
Performance Report Based on Residual Income for the Restaurant Division

	Actual Results	Variance	Master Budget
Operating income	$610	$(280) (U)	$890
Assets invested	$800	$200 (F)	$1,000
Desired ROI			20%
Performance measures:			
ROI	76%	(13%) (U)	89%
Residual income*	$450	$(240) (U)	$690

*Residual Income = Operating Income − (Desired ROI × Assets Invested)

Actual = $610 − (20% × $800)
= $450

Master = $890 − (20% × $1,000)
= $690

Note that the division's residual income is $450, which was lower than the $690 that was projected in the master budget.

Comparisons with other residual income figures will strengthen the analysis. To add context to the analysis of the division and its manager, questions such as the following need to be answered:

- How did the division's residual income this year compare with its residual income in previous years?
- Did the actual residual income exceed the budgeted residual income?
- How did this division's residual income compare with the amounts generated by other investment centers of the company?

Concept For their residual income figures to be *comparable*, all investment centers must have equal access to resources and similar asset investment bases. Some managers may be able to produce larger residual incomes simply because their investment centers are larger rather than because their performance is better.

Economic Value Added

More and more businesses are using the shareholder wealth created by an investment center, or the **economic value added (EVA™)**, as an indicator of performance.[1] The calculation of EVA can be quite complex because it makes various cost of capital and accounting principles adjustments. The **cost of capital** is the minimum desired rate of return on an investment, such as the assets invested in an investment center.

STUDY NOTE: *The EVA number is a composite index drawn from many cause-and-effect relationships and interdependent financial elements.*

Basically, the computation of EVA is similar to that of RI, except that after-tax operating income is used instead of pretax operating income. Also, a cost of capital percentage is multiplied by the center's invested assets less current liabilities instead of a desired ROI percentage being multiplied by invested assets. Like RI, EVA is expressed in dollars. EVA is computed as follows.

Computing Economic Value Added (EVA)

Formula

EVA = After-Tax Operating Income − [Cost of Capital × (Total Assets − Current Liabilities)]

Example Exhibit 9 shows a basic computation of EVA for Winter Wonderland's Restaurant Division. The division's after-tax operating income is \$400, its cost of capital is 12 percent, its total assets are \$800, and its current liabilities are \$250. The report shows that the division has added \$334 to its economic value after taxes and cost of capital. In other words, the division produced after-tax profits of \$334 in excess of the cost of capital required to generate those profits.

Exhibit 9
Performance Report Based on Economic Value Added for the Restaurant Division

	Actual Results	Variance	Master Budget
Performance measures:			
ROI	76%	(13%) (U)	89%
Residual income	\$450	\$(240) (U)	\$690
Economic value added*	\$334		

*EVA = After-Tax Operating Income − [Cost of Capital × (Total Assets − Current Liabilities)]
= \$400 − [12% × (\$800 − \$250)]
= \$334

The factors that affect the computation of EVA are the managers' decisions on pricing, product sales volume, taxes, cost of capital, capital investments, and other financial matters. A manager can improve the economic value of an investment center by increasing sales, decreasing costs, decreasing assets, or lowering the cost of capital.

Concept The economic value of an investment center and its cost of capital will be more meaningful if the current economic value added is *compared* to EVAs from previous periods, target EVAs, and EVAs from other investment centers.

APPLY IT!

Brew Mountain Company sells coffee and hot beverages. Its Coffee Cart Division sells to skiers as they come off the mountain. The Coffee Cart Division's balance sheet showed that the company had invested assets of \$30,000 at the beginning of the year and \$50,000 at the end of the year. During the year, the division's operating income was \$80,000 on sales of \$120,000.

1. Compute the division's residual income if the desired ROI is 20 percent.
2. Compute the return on investment for the division.
3. Compute the economic value added for the company if total corporate assets are \$600,000, current liabilities are \$80,000, after-tax operating income is \$70,000, and the cost of capital is 12 percent.

SOLUTION

1. \$80,000 − {20% × [(\$30,000 + \$50,000) ÷ 2]} = \$72,000
2. \$80,000 ÷ [(\$30,000 + \$50,000) ÷ 2] = 200%
3. \$70,000 − [12% × (\$600,000 − \$80,000)] = \$7,600

TRY IT! SE5, SE6, SE7, E7A, E8A, E9A, E7B, E8B, E9B

SECTION 3 BUSINESS APPLICATIONS

BUSINESS APPLICATIONS

- Balanced scorecard
- Benchmarking
- Planning
- Performing
- Evaluating
- Communicating

RELEVANT LEARNING OBJECTIVES

LO 4 Describe how the balanced scorecard aligns performance with organizational goals.

LO 5 Explain how properly linked performance incentives and measures add value for all stakeholders in performance management and evaluation.

LO 4 Performance Measurement

To be effective, a performance management system must consider both operating results and multiple performance measures, such as return on investment, residual income, and economic value added. Comparing actual results to budgeted figures adds meaning to the evaluation. Performance measures such as ROI, RI, and EVA indicate whether an investment center is effective in coordinating its own goals with company-wide goals because these measures take into account both operating income and the assets used to produce that income. However, all three measures are limited by their focus on short-term financial performance. To obtain a fuller picture, management needs to *understand* and *compare* all stakeholders' performance perspectives to ensure a more balanced view of a business's well-being and how to improve it. To do this, managers must collaborate with other managers to develop a group of measures, such as the balanced scorecard.

Organizational Goals and the Balanced Scorecard

The **balanced scorecard** is a framework that links the perspectives of an organization's four basic stakeholder groups—financial (investor), learning and growth (employee), internal business processes, and customer—with the organization's mission and vision, performance measures, strategic and tactical plans, and resources. To succeed, an organization must add value for all groups in both the short and the long term. Thus, an organization will determine each group's objectives and translate them into performance measures that have specific, quantifiable performance targets. Ideally, managers should be able to see how their actions contribute to the achievement of organizational goals and understand how their compensation is related to their actions. The balanced scorecard assumes that an organization will get only what it measures. The balanced scorecard adds dimension to the management process. Managers plan, perform, evaluate, and communicate the organization's performance from multiple perspectives. By balancing the needs of all stakeholders, managers are more likely to achieve their objectives in both the short and the long term. We will use Winter Wonderland to illustrate how managers use the balanced scorecard.

Planning During the planning stage, the balanced scorecard provides a framework that enables managers to translate their organization's vision and strategy into operational terms. Managers evaluate the company's vision from the perspective of each stakeholder group and seek to answer one key question for each group:

- **Financial (investor):** To achieve our organization's vision, how should we appear to our shareholders?
- **Learning and growth (employee):** To achieve our organization's vision, how should we sustain our ability to improve and change?
- **Internal business processes:** To succeed, in which business processes must our organization excel?
- **Customer:** To achieve our organization's vision, how should we appeal to our customers?

These key questions align the organization's strategy from all perspectives.

The answers to the questions result in performance objectives that are mutually beneficial to all stakeholders. Once the organization's objectives are set, managers can select performance measures and set performance targets to translate the objectives into

Business Perspective
"Tableau de Bord and the Balanced Scorecard"

The *tableau de bord*, or "dashboard," was developed by French engineers around 1900 as a concise performance measurement system that helped managers understand the cause-and-effect relationships between their decisions and the resulting performance. The indicators, both financial and nonfinancial, allowed managers at all levels to monitor their progress in terms of the mission and objectives of their unit and of their company overall. The dashboard focuses on and supports an organization's strategic plan.

Source: A. Bourguignon, "The American Balanced Scorecard versus the French Tableau de Bord: The Ideological Dimension," *Management Accounting Research,* Jan. 2004, Vol. 15, Issue 2 (Elsevier), pp. 107–134.

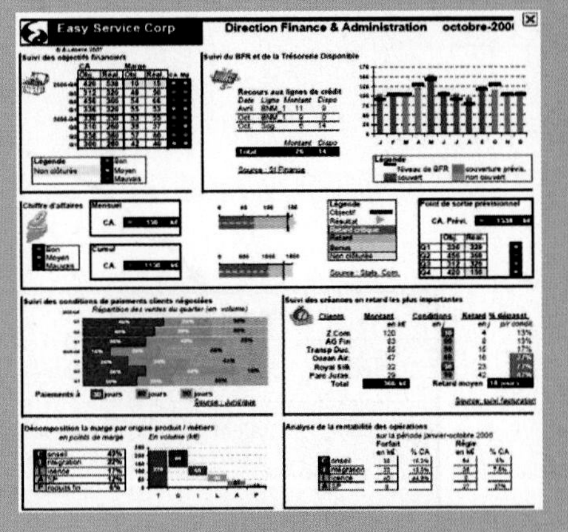

an action plan. For example, if Winter Wonderland's collective vision and strategy is to please guests, its managers might establish the following overall objectives:

Perspective	Objective
Financial (investor)	Increase guests' spending at the resort.
Learning and growth (employee)	Continually cross-train employees in each other's duties to sustain premium-quality service for guests.
Internal business processes	Leverage market position by introducing and improving innovative marketing and technology-driven advances that clearly benefit guests.
Customer	Create new premium-price experiences and facilities for vacations in all seasons.

These overall objectives are then translated into specific performance objectives and measures for specific managers. Exhibit 10 summarizes how Winter Wonderland's managers might link their organization's vision and strategy to objectives, then link the objectives to logical performance measures, and, finally, set performance targets for a ski lift manager. As a result, a ski lift manager will have a variety of performance measures that balance the perspectives and needs of all stakeholders.

STUDY NOTE: *Although their perspectives differ, stakeholder groups may be interested in the same measurable performance goals. For example, both the customer and internal business processes perspectives desire high-quality products.*

Performing Managers use the mutually agreed-upon strategic and tactical objectives for the entire organization as the basis for decision making within their individual areas of responsibility. This practice ensures that they consider the needs of all stakeholder groups and shows how measuring and managing performance for some stakeholder groups can lead to improved performance for another stakeholder group. Specifically, improving the performance of leading indicators like internal business processes and learning and growth will create improvements for customers, which in turn will result in improved financial performance (a lagging indicator). For example, when making decisions about available ski lift capacity, the ski lift manager will balance such factors as lift ticket sales, snow conditions, equipment reliability, trained staff availability, and length of wait for ski lifts.

The balanced scorecard provides a way of linking the lead performance indicators of employees, internal business processes, and customer needs to the lag performance indicator of external financial results. In other words, if managers can foster excellent

Exhibit 10
Sample Balanced Scorecard of Linked Objectives, Performance Measures, and Targets

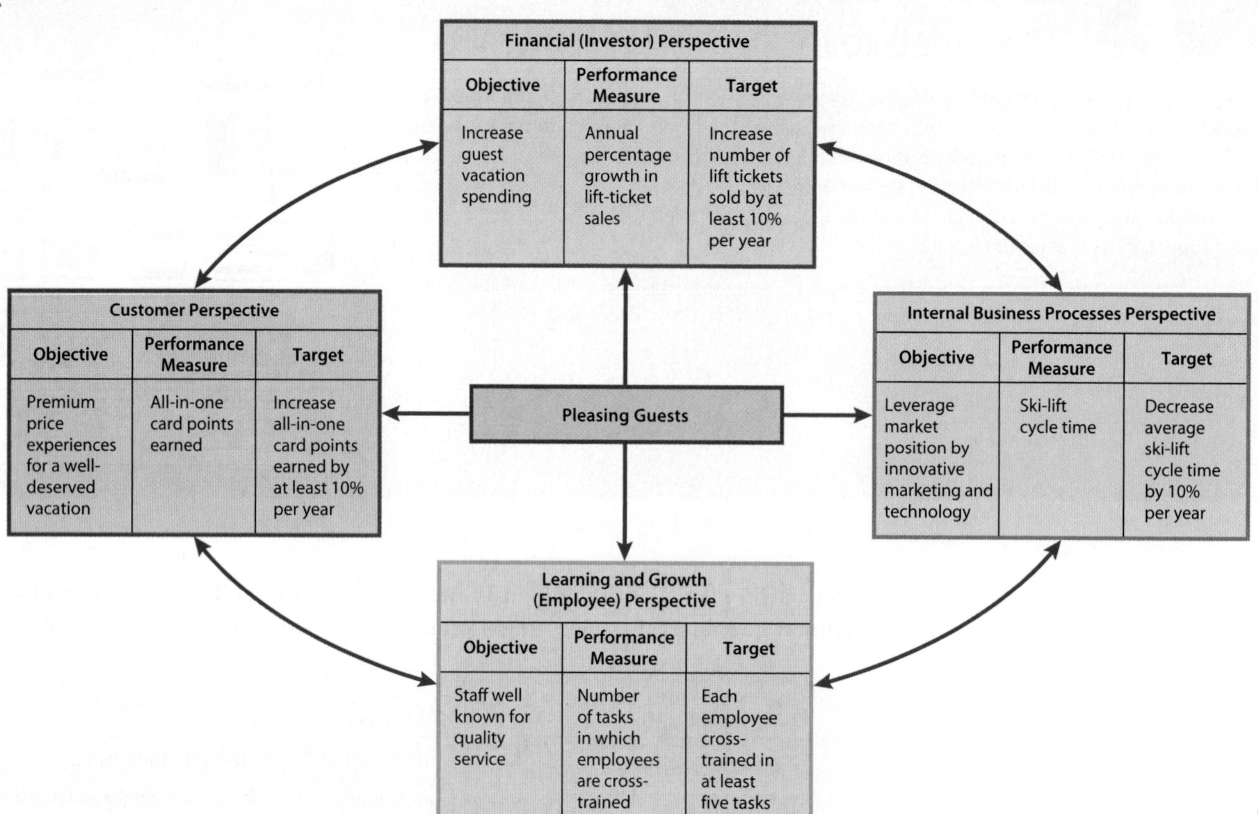

Source: Adapted from Robert S. Kaplan and David P. Norton, "Using the Balanced Scorecard as a Strategic Management System," *Harvard Business Review*, January–February 1996.

performance for three of the stakeholder groups, good financial results will occur for the investor stakeholder group. When managers understand the causal and linked relationship between their actions and their company's overall performance, they can see new ways to be more effective. For example, a ski lift manager may hypothesize that shorter waiting lines for the ski lifts would improve customer satisfaction and lead to more visits to the ski lift. The manager could test this possible cause-and-effect relationship by measuring and tracking the length of ski lift waiting lines and the number of visits to the ski lift. If a causal relationship exists, the manager can improve the performance of the ski lift operation by doing everything possible to ensure that waiting lines are short because a quicker ride to the top will result in improved results for the operation and for other perspectives as well.

Evaluating The balanced scorecard enables a company to determine whether it is making continuous improvement in its operations. Managers *compare* performance objectives and targets with actual results to determine if the targets were met, what measures need to be changed, and what strategies or objectives need revision. For example, the ski lift manager would analyze the reasons for performance gaps and make recommendations to improve the performance of the ski lift area.

A company will also *compare* its performance with that of similar companies in the same industry. **Benchmarking** determines a company's competitive advantage by comparing its performance with that of its closest competitors. **Benchmarks** are measures of the best practices in an industry.

Communicating A variety of reports enable managers to monitor and evaluate performance measures that add value for stakeholder groups. For example, a database makes it possible to prepare financial performance reports, customer statements, internal business process reports for targeted performance measures and results, and performance appraisals of individual employees.

Performance Evaluation and the Management Process

Exhibit 11 summarizes the ways in which performance measures and evaluation support and inform the management process.

Exhibit 11
Performance Evaluation and the Management Process

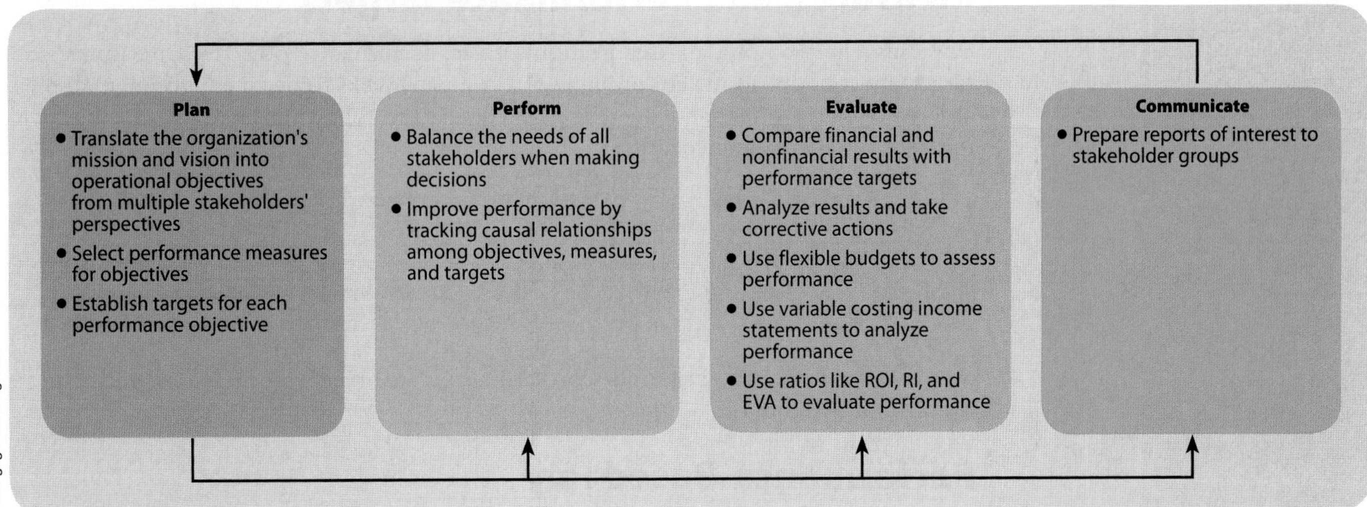

Plan
• Translate the organization's mission and vision into operational objectives from multiple stakeholders' perspectives
• Select performance measures for objectives
• Establish targets for each performance objective
Perform
• Balance the needs of all stakeholders when making decisions
• Improve performance by tracking causal relationships among objectives, measures, and targets
Evaluate
• Compare financial and nonfinancial results with performance targets
• Analyze results and take corrective actions
• Use flexible budgets to assess performance
• Use variable costing income statements to analyze performance
• Use ratios like ROI, RI, and EVA to evaluate performance
Communicate
• Prepare reports of interest to stakeholder groups

APPLY IT!

Connie's Takeout caters to resort employees who want a good meal at home but do not have time to prepare it. Connie's has developed the following business objectives:

1. To provide fast, courteous service
2. To manage the inventory of food carefully
3. To have repeat customers
4. To be profitable and grow

Connie's has also developed the following performance measures:

5. Growth in revenues per quarter and net income
6. Average unsold food at the end of the business day as a percentage of the total food purchased that day
7. Average customer time at the counter before being waited on
8. Percentage of customers providing repeat business

Match each of these objectives and performance measures with the four perspectives of the balanced scorecard: financial perspective, learning and growth perspective, internal business processes perspective, and customer perspective.

SOLUTION

Financial perspective: 4, 5; learning and growth perspective: 1, 7; internal business processes perspective: 2, 6; customer perspective: 3, 8

TRY IT! SE8, SE9, E10A, E11A, E12A, E13A, E10B, E11B, E12B, E13B

LO 5 Performance Incentives and Goals

The effectiveness of a performance management and evaluation system depends on how well it coordinates the goals of responsibility centers, managers, and the entire company. Two factors are key to the successful coordination of goals:

- The logical linking of goals to measurable objectives and targets
- The tying of appropriate compensation incentives to the achievement of the targets—that is, performance-based pay

Linking Goals, Performance Objectives, Measures, and Performance Targets

The causal links among an organization's goals, performance objectives, measures, and targets must be apparent. For example, if a company seeks to be an environmental steward, as Winter Wonderland does, it may choose the following linked goal, objective, measure, and performance target:

Goal	Objective	Measure	Performance Target
To be an environmental steward	To reduce, reuse, and recycle	Number of tons recycled per year	To recycle at least one pound per guest

You may recall that the balanced scorecard also links objectives, measures, and targets, as shown in Exhibit 10.

Performance-Based Pay

The tying of appropriate compensation incentives to performance targets increases the likelihood that the goals of responsibility centers, managers, and the entire organization will be well coordinated. Unfortunately, this linkage does not always happen. Responsibility center managers are more likely to achieve their performance targets if their compensation depends on it. **Performance-based pay** is the linking of employee compensation to the achievement of measurable business targets.

Cash bonuses, awards, profit-sharing plans, and stock options are common types of incentive compensation. Cash bonuses are usually given to reward an individual's short-term performance. A bonus may be stated as a fixed dollar amount or as a percentage of a target figure, such as 5 percent of operating income or 10 percent of the dollar increase in operating income. An award may be a trip or some other form of recognition for desirable individual or group performance. For example, many companies sponsor a trip for all managers who have met their performance targets during a specified period. Other companies award incentive points that employees may redeem for goods or services. (Awards can be used to encourage both short-term and long-term performance.) Profit-sharing plans reward employees with a share of the company's profits. Employees often receive company stock as recognition of their contribution to a profitable period. Using stock as a reward encourages employees to think and act as both investors and employees and encourages a stable work force. In terms of the balanced scorecard, employees assume two stakeholder perspectives and take both a short- and a long-term viewpoint. Companies use stock to motivate employees to achieve financial targets that increase the company's stock price.

The Coordination of Goals

What performance incentives and measures should a company use to manage and evaluate performance? What actions and behaviors should an organization reward? Which incentive compensation plans work best? The answers to such questions depend on the facts and circumstances of each organization. To determine the right performance incentives for their organization, employees and managers must answer several questions:

- When should the reward be given—now or sometime in the future?
- Whose performance should be rewarded—that of responsibility centers, individual managers, or the entire company?
- How should the reward be computed?
- On what should the reward be based?
- What performance criteria should be used?
- Does the performance incentive plan address the interests of all stakeholders?

The effectiveness of a performance management and evaluation system relies on the coordination of responsibility center, managerial, and company goals. Performance can be optimized by linking goals to measurable objectives and targets and by tying appropriate compensation incentives to the achievement of the targets. Each organization's unique circumstances will determine the correct mix of measures and compensation incentives for that organization. If management values the perspectives of all of its stakeholder groups, its performance management and evaluation system will balance and benefit all interests.

APPLY IT!

Necessary Toys, Inc., has adopted the balanced scorecard to motivate its managers to work toward the companywide goal of leading its industry in innovation. Identify the four stakeholder perspectives that would link to the following objectives, measures, and targets:

Perspective	Objective	Measure	Target
	Successful product introductions	New-product market share	Capture 80 percent of new-product market within one year
	Agile product design and production processes	Time to market (the time between a product idea and its first sales)	Time to market less than one year for 80 percent of product introductions
	Workforce with cutting-edge skills	Percentage of employees cross-trained on work- group tasks	100 percent of work group cross-trained on new tasks within 30 days
	Profitable new products	New-product ROI	New-product ROI of at least 75 percent

SOLUTION

Goal: To lead the industry in innovation

Perspective	Objective	Measure	Target
Customer	Successful product introductions	New-product market share	Capture 80 percent of new-product market within one year
Internal business processes	Agile product design and production processes	Time to market (the time between a product idea and its first sales)	Time to market less than one year for 80 percent of product introductions
Learning and growth (employee)	Workforce with cutting-edge skills	Percentage of employees cross-trained on work- group tasks	100 percent of work group cross-trained on new tasks within 30 days
Financial (investor)	Profitable new products	New-product ROI	New-product ROI of at least 75 percent

TRY IT! SE10, E14A, E15A, E14B, E15B

TriLevel Problem

Blend Images/Fotolia LLC

Vail Resorts

The beginning of this chapter focused on **Vail Resorts**, a well-known vacation destination for skiers. Complete the following requirements in order to answer the questions posed at the beginning of the chapter.

Section 1: Concepts

What concepts guide managers when they evaluate performance?

Section 2: Accounting Applications

How will managers use flexible budgets and other performance measures to analyze the financial and nonfinancial performance of responsibility centers?

Winter Wonderland Resorts is a major hospitality company like Vail Resorts. Winter Wonderland's general manager is responsible for guest activities, administration, and food and lodging and is also solely responsible for Winter Wonderland's capital investments. The following organization chart shows the resort's various activities and the levels of authority that the general manager has established:

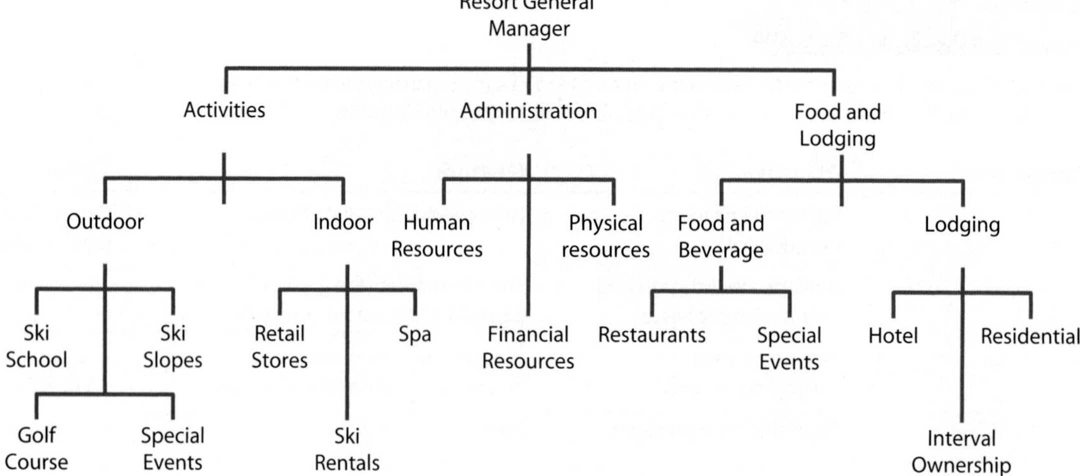

Three divisional managers receive compensation based on their division's performance and have the authority to make employee compensation decisions for their division. Alexandra Patel manages the Food and Lodging Division. The Food and Lodging Division's master budget and actual results for the year ended June 30 follow.

	A	B	C
1	**Winter Wonderland Resort**		
2	**Food and Lodging Division**		
3	**For the Year Ended June 30**		
4	(Dollar amounts in thousands)		
5		**Master**	**Actual**
6		**Budget**	**Results**
7	Guest days	4,000	4,100
8	Sales	$38,000	$40,000
9	Variable cost of sales	24,000	25,000
10	Variable selling and administrative expenses	4,000	4,250
11	Fixed cost of sales	2,000	1,800
12	Fixed selling and administrative expenses	2,500	2,500
13			

1. What types of responsibility centers are (a) Administration, (b) Food and Lodging, and (c) Resort General Manager?
2. Assume that Food and Lodging is a profit center. Prepare a performance report using variable costing and flexible budgeting. Determine the variances between actual results and the corresponding figures in the flexible budget and the master budget.
3. Assume that the divisional managers have been assigned responsibility for capital expenditures and that their divisions are thus investment centers. Food and Lodging is expected to generate a desired ROI of at least 30 percent on average assets invested of $10,000,000.
   (a) Compute the division's return on investment and residual income using the average assets invested in both the actual and budget calculations.
   (b) Using the ROI and residual income, evaluate Alexandra Patel's performance as divisional manager.
4. Compute the division's actual economic value added if the division's assets are $12,000,000, current liabilities are $3,000,000, after-tax operating income is $4,500,000, and the cost of capital is 20 percent.

Section 3: Business Applications

How can managers achieve a balanced view of a business's well-being and how to improve it? To answer this question, match this chapter's manager responsibilities with when they occur within the management process.

a. Plan
b. Perform
c. Evaluate
d. Communicate

1. Establish performance targets of each objective
2. Track causal relationships to improve performance
3. Use flexible budgets to assess performance
4. Translate the organization's mission and vision into objectives from multiple stakeholder perspectives
5. Use variable costing income statements to analyze performance
6. Prepare reports
7. When making decisions, balance all stakeholder needs
8. Use ratios like ROI, RI, and EVA to evaluate performance
9. Compare results with performance targets
10. Analyze results and take corrective actions
11. Select performance measures for objectives

SOLUTION

Section 1: Concepts

Managers use the concepts of *understandability* and *comparability* as they manage a wide range of financial and nonfinancial data to guide and evaluate performance. If they want satisfactory results for their responsibility centers, managers must understand the cause-and-effect relationships between their actions and their responsibility center's performance. To do this, managers use performance analysis tools like flexible budgets; variable costing income statements; and ROI, RI, and EVA ratio analyses to compare plans, actions, and results. By measuring and tracking the causal relationships that they are accountable for, managers can improve performance and thereby add value for all of their organization's stakeholders. A balanced scorecard approach enables managers to understand and compare the perspectives of all the organization's stakeholders: financial (investors), learning and growth (employees), internal business processes, and customers as they command, control, and evaluate the organization.

Section 2: Accounting Applications

1. (a) discretionary cost center
   (b) profit center
   (c) investment center

2.

	A					B		C
1	Winter Wonderland Resort							
2	Food and Lodging Division							
3	For the Year Ended June 30							
4	(Dollar amounts in thousands)							
5		Actual			Flexible			Master
6		Results	Variance		Budget	Variance		Budget
7	Guest days	4,100	—		4,100	100	(F)	4,000
8	Sales	$40,000	$1,050	(F)	$38,950	$950	(F)	$38,000
9	Controllable variable costs							
10	Variable cost of sales	25,000	400	(U)	24,600	600	(U)	24,000
11	Variable selling and							
12	administrative							
13	expenses	4,250	150	(U)	4,100	100	(U)	4,000
14	Contribution margin	$10,750	$ 500	(F)	$10,250	$250	(F)	$10,000
15	Controllable fixed costs							
16	Fixed cost of sales	1,800	200	(F)	2,000	—		2,000
17	Fixed selling and							
18	administrative							
19	expenses	2,500	—		2,500	—		2,500
20	Division operating income	$ 6,450	$ 700	(F)	$ 5,750	$250	(F)	$ 5,500
21								

3. (a) Return on investment:

   Actual results: $6,450,000 ÷ $10,000,000 = 64.50%
   Flexible budget: $5,750,000 ÷ $10,000,000 = 57.50%
   Master budget: $5,500,000 ÷ $10,000,000 = 55.00%

   Residual income:

   Actual results: $6,450,000 − (30% × $10,000,000) = $3,450,000
   Flexible budget: $5,750,000 − (30% × $10,000,000) = $2,750,000
   Master budget: $5,500,000 − (30% × $10,000,000) = $2,500,000

(b) Alexandra Patel's performance as the divisional manager of Food and Lodging exceeds company performance expectations. Actual ROI was 64.5 percent, whereas the company expected an ROI of 30 percent, and the flexible budget and the master budget showed projections of 57.5 percent and 55.0 percent, respectively. Residual income also exceeded expectations. The Food and Lodging Division generated \$3,450,000 in residual income when the flexible budget and master budget had projected RIs of \$2,750,000 and \$2,500,000, respectively. The performance report for the division shows 100 more guest days than had been anticipated and a favorable controllable fixed cost variance. As a manager, Patel will investigate the unfavorable variances associated with her controllable variable costs.

4. Economic value added:

$$\$4{,}500{,}000 - [20\% \times (\$12{,}000{,}000 - \$3{,}000{,}000)] = \underline{\underline{\$2{,}700{,}000}}$$

Section 3: Business Applications

1. a
2. b
3. c
4. a
5. c
6. d
7. b
8. c
9. c
10. c
11. a

Chapter Review

Define a *performance management and evaluation system* and *responsibility accounting*, and describe the roles they play in performance analysis. LO 1

An effective performance management and evaluation system accounts for and reports on both financial and nonfinancial performance so that an organization can understand how well it is doing, where it is going, and what improvements will make it more profitable. Each organization must develop a unique set of performance measures to compare and evaluate based on areas of responsibility that are appropriate to its specific situation. Responsibility accounting classifies data according to areas of responsibility and reports each area's activities by including only the revenue, cost, and resource categories that the assigned manager can control. There are five types of responsibility centers: cost, discretionary cost, revenue, profit, and investment. Performance reporting by responsibility center allows the source of a cost, revenue, or resource to be traced to the manager who controls it and thus makes it easier to understand, compare, and evaluate a manager's performance. The content and format of a performance report depend on the nature of the responsibility center.

Use flexible budgets and variable costing to analyze cost center and profit center performance. LO 2

The performance of a cost center can be evaluated by comparing its actual costs with the corresponding amounts in the flexible and master budgets. A flexible budget is a summary of anticipated costs for a range of activity levels. It provides forecasted cost data that can be adjusted for changes in the level of output. A flexible budget is derived by multiplying actual unit output by predetermined standard unit costs for each cost item in the report. The resulting variances between actual costs and the flexible budget can be examined further by using standard costing to compute specific variances for direct materials, direct labor, and overhead.

The performance of a profit center is usually evaluated by comparing the profit center's actual income statement results with its budgeted income statement. When variable costing is used, the controllable costs of the profit center's manager are classified as variable or fixed. The resulting performance report takes the form of a contribution margin income statement instead of a traditional income statement. The variable costing income statement is useful because it focuses on cost variability and the profit center's contribution to operating income.

Analyze investment centers using return on investment, residual income, and economic value added. **LO 3**

Traditionally, the most common performance measure has been return on investment (ROI). The basic formula is ROI = Operating Income ÷ Assets Invested. Return on investment can also be examined in terms of profit margin and asset turnover. In this case, ROI = Profit Margin × Asset Turnover, where Profit Margin = Operating Income ÷ Sales, and Asset Turnover = Sales ÷ Assets Invested. Residual income (RI) is the operating income that an investment center earns above a minimum desired return on invested assets. It is expressed as a dollar amount: Residual Income = Operating Income − (Desired ROI × Assets Invested). It is the amount of profit left after subtracting a predetermined desired income target for an investment. Today, businesses are increasingly using the shareholder wealth created by an investment center, or economic value added (EVA), as a performance measure. The calculation of economic value added can be quite complex because of the various adjustments it involves. Basically, it is similar to the calculation of residual income: EVA = After-Tax Operating Income − [Cost of Capital × (Total Assets − Current Liabilities)]. A manager can improve the economic value of an investment center by increasing sales, decreasing costs, decreasing assets, or lowering the cost of capital.

Describe how the balanced scorecard aligns performance with organizational goals. **LO 4**

Besides answering basic questions about what to measure and how to measure, management must collaborate to develop a group of measures, such as the balanced scorecard, that will help them determine how to improve performance. The balanced scorecard is a framework that links the perspectives of an organization's four basic stakeholder groups—financial (investor), learning and growth (employee), internal business processes, and customer—with its mission and vision, performance measures, strategic and tactical plans, and resources. The balanced scorecard assumes that an organization will get what it measures. Ideally, managers should see how their actions help to achieve organizational goals and understand how their compensation is linked to their actions. Managers may use benchmarking to determine a company's competitive advantage by comparing its performance with that of its industry peers.

Explain how properly linked performance incentives and measures add value for all stakeholders in performance management and evaluation. **LO 5**

The effectiveness of a performance management and evaluation system depends on how well it coordinates the goals of responsibility centers, managers, and the entire company. Performance can be optimized by linking goals to measurable objectives and targets and tying appropriate compensation incentives to the achievement of those targets. Common types of incentive compensation are cash bonuses, awards, profit-sharing plans, and stock options. If management values the perspectives of all of its stakeholder groups, its performance management and evaluation system will balance and benefit all interests.

Key Terms and Ratios

balanced scorecard 968 (LO4)
benchmarking 970 (LO4)
benchmarks 970 (LO4)
controllable costs and revenues 957 (LO1)
cost center 958 (LO1)
cost of capital 967 (LO3)
discretionary cost center 958 (LO1)
economic value added (EVA) 967 (LO3)
flexible budget 961 (LO2)
flexible budget formula 961 (LO2)
investment center 958 (LO1)
organization chart 959 (LO1)
performance-based pay 972 (LO5)
performance management and evaluation system 956 (LO1)
performance measurement 956 (LO1)
performance measures 956 (LO1)
profit center 958 (LO1)
residual income (RI) 966 (LO3)
responsibility accounting 956 (LO1)
responsibility center 956 (LO1)
revenue center 958 (LO1)
variable costing 962 (LO2)

RATIOS

asset turnover 965 (LO3)
profit margin 965 (LO3)
return on investment (ROI) 964 (LO3)

Chapter Assignments

DISCUSSION QUESTIONS

LO 1 **DQ1. CONCEPT ▶** Jackie Jefferson, a new employee at Foster, Inc., is learning about the various types of performance reports. Describe the typical contents of a performance report for each type of responsibility center. Why do these reports enhance the understandability and comparability of the data presented?

LO 2, 3, 4 **DQ2. CONCEPT ▶** What tools can managers use to enhance the understandability and comparability of performance analysis?

LO 2 **DQ3. CONCEPT ▶** How does the flexible budget formula enhance understandability and comparability when preparing a flexible budget?

LO 2 **DQ4. CONCEPT ▶** Why is a variable costing income statement more useful than a traditional income statement for understanding and evaluating a profit center's performance?

LO 4, 5 **DQ5. CONCEPT ▶ BUSINESS APPLICATION ▶** How does the balanced scorecard empower managers to understand and compare the interests of all the organization's stakeholders?

SHORT EXERCISES

LO 1 **Responsibility Centers**

SE1. Identify each of the following as a cost center, a discretionary cost center, a revenue center, a profit center, or an investment center:

a. Center A's manager is responsible for generating cash inflows and incurring costs with the goal of making money for the company. The manager has no responsibility for assets.
b. Center B produces a product that is not sold to an external party but transferred to another center for further processing.
c. Center C's manager is responsible for the telephone order operations of a large retailer.
d. Center D designs, produces, and sells products to external parties. The manager makes both long-term and short-term decisions.
e. Center E provides human resource support for the other centers in the company.

LO 2 **Preparing a Flexible Budget**

SE2. Prepare a flexible budget for 20,000, 22,000, and 24,000 units of output, using the information that follows.

Variable costs:	
Direct materials	$1.00 per unit
Direct labor	$4.00 per unit
Variable overhead	$8.00 per unit
Total budgeted fixed overhead	$180,800

LO 2 **Cost Center Performance Report**

SE3. Complete the following performance report for cost center S for the month ended September 30:

(Continued)

	Actual Results	Variance	Flexible Budget	Variance	Master Budget
Units produced	80	0	?	(20) (U)	100
Center costs:					
Direct materials	$ 84	$?	$ 80	$?	$100
Direct labor	150	?	?	40 (F)	200
Variable overhead	?	(20) (U)	240	?	300
Fixed overhead	270	?	250	?	250
Total cost	$?	$(34) (U)	$?	$120 (F)	$850
Performance measures:					
Defect-free units to total produced	80%	?	N/A	N/A	90%
Average throughput minutes per unit	11	?	N/A	N/A	10

LO 2 **Profit Center Performance Report**

SE4. Complete the following performance report for profit center P for the month ended December 31:

	Actual Results	Variance	Master Budget
Sales	$?	$ 20 (F)	$120
Controllable variable costs:			
Variable cost of goods sold	(25)	(10) (U)	?
Variable selling and administrative expenses	(15)	? (?)	(5)
Contribution margin	$100	$? (?)	$100
Controllable fixed costs	?	20 (F)	60
Profit center operating income	$ 60	$ 20 (F)	$?
Performance measures:			
Number of orders processed	50	20 (F)	?
Average daily sales	$?	$0.68 (F)	$4.00
Number of units sold	100	40 (F)	?

LO 3 **Return on Investment**

SE5. Complete the profit margin, asset turnover, and return on investment calculations for investment centers D and V. (Round to two decimal places.)

	Center D	Center V
Sales	$1,600	$2,000
Operating income	$400	$200
Average assets invested	$3,200	$1,250
Profit margin	?	?
Asset turnover	?	?
ROI	?	?

LO 3 **Residual Income**

SE6. Complete the operating income, ending assets invested, average assets invested, and residual income calculations for investment centers H and F.

	Center H	Center F
Sales	$20,000	$25,000
Operating income	$1,500	$?
Beginning assets invested	$4,000	$ 500
Ending assets invested	$6,000	$?
Average assets invested	$?	$1,000
Desired ROI	20%	20%
Residual income	$?	$600

LO 3

Economic Value Added

SE7. Complete the current liabilities, total assets − current liabilities, and economic value added calculations for investment centers M and N.

	Center M	Center N
Sales	$15,000	$18,000
After-tax operating income	$1,000	$1,100
Total assets	$4,000	$5,000
Current liabilities	$1,000	$?
Total assets − current liabilities	$?	$3,500
Cost of capital	15%	15%
Economic value added	$?	$?

LO 4

The Balanced Scorecard: Stakeholder Values

SE8. BUSINESS APPLICATION ▶ In the balanced scorecard approach, stakeholder groups with different perspectives value different performance goals. Sometimes, however, they may be interested in the same goal. Indicate which stakeholder groups—financial (F), learning and growth (L), internal business processes (P), and customer (C)—value the performance goals that follow.

a. high wages
b. safe products
c. low-priced products
d. improved return on investment
e. job security
f. cost-effective production processes

LO 4

Balanced Scorecard

SE9. BUSINESS APPLICATION ▶ One of your college's overall goals is customer satisfaction. In light of that goal, match each of the stakeholders' perspectives that follow with the appropriate objective.

Perspective	Objective
a. Financial (investor)	1. Customer satisfaction means that the faculty (employees) engages in cutting-edge research.
b. Learning and growth (employee)	2. Customer satisfaction means that students receive their degrees in four years.
c. Internal business processes	3. Customer satisfaction means that the college has a winning athletics program.
d. Customer	4. Customer satisfaction means that fund-raising campaigns are successful.

LO 5

Coordination of Goals

SE10. BUSINESS APPLICATION ▶ One of your college's goals is customer satisfaction. In view of that goal, identify each of the following as a linked objective, a measure, or a performance target.

1. To have successful fund-raising campaigns
2. Number of publications per year per tenure-track faculty
3. To increase the average donation by 10 percent
4. Average number of dollars raised per donor
5. To have faculty engage in cutting-edge research
6. To increase the number of publications per faculty member by at least one per year

EXERCISES: SET A

LO 1 Responsibility Centers

E1A. Identify the most appropriate type of responsibility center for each of the organizational units that follow.

a. The sheets and towels laundry facility of a large hotel chain
b. The online order department of a retailer
c. A manufacturing department of a large corporation
d. An urgent care clinic in a community hospital
e. A famous brand of a large corporation

LO 1 Organization Chart

E2A. Higgly Industries wants to formalize its management structure by designing an organization chart. The company has a president, a board of directors, and two vice presidents. Four discretionary cost centers—Business Office, Personnel, Technology Services, and Physical Plant—report to one of the vice presidents. The other vice president has one production facility with three cost centers reporting to her. Draw the company's organization chart.

LO 2 Preparing a Flexible Budget

E3A. Bexar Company's fixed overhead costs for the year are expected to be as follows: depreciation, $80,000; supervisory salaries, $90,000; property taxes and insurance, $25,000; and other fixed overhead, $15,000. Total fixed overhead is thus expected to be $210,000. Variable costs per unit are expected to be as follows: direct materials, $15.00; direct labor, $10.00; operating supplies, $2.00; indirect labor, $3.50; and other variable overhead costs, $2.50. Prepare a flexible budget for the following levels of production: 25,000 units, 30,000 units, and 35,000 units. What is the flexible budget formula for the year ended December 31?

LO 2 Performance Report for a Cost Center

E4A. Keystone, LLC, owns a peach processing plant. Last month, the plant generated the following information: peaches processed, 60,000 pounds; direct materials, $6,200; direct labor, $12,500; variable overhead, $17,600; and fixed overhead, $15,000. There were no beginning or ending inventories. Average daily pounds processed (25 business days) were 2,400. Average rate of processing was 300 pounds per hour.

At the beginning of the month, Keystone had budgeted costs of peaches, $5,000; direct labor, $10,000; variable overhead, $15,000; and fixed overhead, $14,000. The monthly master budget was based on producing 50,000 pounds of peaches each month. This means that the plant had been projected to process 2,000 pounds daily at the rate of 250 pounds per hour.

Prepare a performance report for the month for the peach processing plant. Include a flexible budget and the computation of variances in your report. Indicate whether the variances are favorable (F) or unfavorable (U) to the performance of the plant.

LO 2 Variable Costing Income Statement

E5A. Vegan, LLC, owns a chain of gourmet vegetarian take-out markets. Vegan's income statement in the traditional reporting format for the month follows.

Vegan, LLC
Income Statement
For the Month

Sales	$890,000
Cost of goods sold	607,000
Gross margin	$283,000
Selling and administrative expenses:	
Variable	(44,500)
Fixed	(72,300)
Operating income	$166,200

Total fixed production costs for the month were $140,000.

Prepare an income statement for Vegan, LLC, for the month, using the variable costing format.

LO 2 **Traditional and Variable Costing Income Statements**

E6A. Roofing tile is Tops Corporation's major product. It sold 88,400 cases of tile during the year. Variable cost of goods sold was $848,640; variable selling expenses were $132,600; fixed overhead was $166,680; fixed selling expenses were $152,048; and fixed administrative expenses were $96,450. The selling price was $18 per case. There were no partially completed jobs in process at the beginning or the end of the year. Finished goods inventory had been used up at the end of the previous year. Prepare the calendar year-end income statement for Tops using:

1. the traditional reporting format
2. the variable costing format

LO 3 **Investment Center Performance**

E7A. ACCOUNTING CONNECTION ▶ Flowers Associates is evaluating the performance of three divisions: Daisies, Pansies, and Tulips. Using the data that follow, compute the return on investment and residual income for each division, compare the divisions' performance, and comment on the factors that influenced performance.

	Daisies	Pansies	Tulips
Sales	$50,000	$50,000	$50,000
Operating income	$10,000	$10,000	$20,000
Assets invested	$25,000	$12,500	$25,000
Desired ROI	30%	30%	30%

LO 3 **Economic Value Added**

E8A. ACCOUNTING CONNECTION ▶ Game, LLP, is evaluating the performance of three divisions: Rock, Scissors, and Paper. Using the data that follow, compute the economic value added by each division, and comment on each division's performance.

	Rock	Scissors	Paper
Sales	$50,000	$50,000	$50,000
After-tax operating income	$5,000	$5,000	$20,000
Total assets	$25,000	$12,500	$25,000
Current liabilities	$5,000	$5,000	$5,000
Cost of capital	15%	15%	15%

LO 3 **Return on Investment and Economic Value Added**

E9A. The balance sheet for NuBone Corporation's New Products Division showed invested assets of $200,000 at the beginning of the year and $300,000 at the end of the year. During the year, the division's operating income was $12,500 on sales of $500,000.

(Continued)

1. Compute the division's residual income if the desired ROI is 6 percent.
2. Compute the following performance measures for the division: (a) profit margin, (b) asset turnover, and (c) return on investment. (Round profit margin percentage to one decimal place.)
3. Recompute the division's ROI under each of the following independent assumptions.
   a. Sales increase from $500,000 to $600,000, causing operating income to rise from $12,500 to $30,000.
   b. Invested assets at the beginning of the year are reduced from $200,000 to $100,000. (Round percentage to two decimal places.)
   c. Operating expenses are reduced, causing operating income to rise from $12,500 to $20,000.
4. Compute the company's EVA if total corporate assets are $500,000, current liabilities are $80,000, after-tax operating income is $50,000, and the cost of capital is 8 percent.

LO 4

Balanced Scorecard

E10A. BUSINESS APPLICATION ▶ Online Products is considering adopting the balanced scorecard and has compiled the following list of possible performance measures. Select the balanced scorecard perspective that best matches each performance measure.

Balanced Scorecard Perspective	Performance Measure
a. Financial (investor)	1. Economic value added
b. Learning and growth (employee)	2. Employee turnover
c. Internal business processes	3. Average daily sales
d. Customer	4. Defect-free units
	5. Number of repeat customer visits
	6. Employee training hours

LO 4

Performance Measures

E11A. BUSINESS APPLICATION ▶ Wendy Jefferson wants to measure her division's product quality. Link an appropriate performance measure with each balanced scorecard perspective.

Product Quality	Possible Performance Measures
a. Financial (investor)	1. Number of defective products returned
b. Learning and growth (employee)	2. Number of products failing inspection
c. Internal business processes	3. Increased market share
d. Customer	4. Savings from employee suggestions

LO 4

The Balanced Scorecard

E12A. BUSINESS APPLICATION ▶ Unique Exclusive sells antiques to discerning clients. The business has developed the following business objectives:

1. To buy only the antiques that sell
2. To have repeat customers
3. To be profitable and grow
4. To keep employee turnover low

The business also developed the following performance measures:

5. Growth in revenues and net income per quarter
6. Average unsold antiques at the end of the month as a percentage of the total antiques purchased that month
7. Number of unemployment claims
8. Percentage of repeat customers

Match each of these objectives and performance measures with the four perspectives of the balanced scorecard: financial perspective, learning and growth perspective, internal business processes perspective, and customer perspective.

LO 4 **The Balanced Scorecard**

E13A. BUSINESS APPLICATION ▶ Your college's overall goal is to add value to the communities it serves. In light of that goal, match each of the stakeholders' perspectives that follow with the appropriate objective.

Perspective	Objective
a. Financial (investor)	1. Adding value means that the annual operating budget balances.
b. Learning and growth (employee)	2. Adding value means that students can enroll in courses of their choice.
c. Internal business processes	3. Adding value means that the college has winning interscholastic teams.
d. Customer	4. Adding value means that the faculty engages in meaningful teaching and research.

LO 5 **Performance Incentives**

E14A. BUSINESS APPLICATION ▶ MOG Consulting is advising Triangle Industries on the short-term and long-term effectiveness of cash bonuses, awards, profit sharing, and stock as performance incentives. Prepare a chart identifying the effectiveness of each incentive as either long-term or short-term or both.

LO 5 **Goal Congruence**

E15A. BUSINESS APPLICATION ▶ Tech Toys, Inc., has adopted the balanced scorecard to motivate its managers to work toward the companywide goal of leading its industry in innovation. Identify the four stakeholder perspectives that would link to the following objectives, measures, and targets:

Perspective	Objective	Measure	Target
	Agile production processes	Time to market (the time between a product idea and its first sales)	Time to market less than 8 months for 70 percent of product introductions
	Profitable new products	New-product RI	New-product RI of at least $50,000
	Successful product introductions	New-product market share	Capture 65 percent of new-product market within 8 months
	Workforce with cutting-edge skills	Percentage of employees cross-trained on work-group tasks	80 percent of work group cross-trained on new tasks within 20 days

EXERCISES: SET B

Visit the textbook companion website at www.cengagebrain.com to access Exercise Set B for this chapter.

PROBLEMS

LO 2 **Preparing a Flexible Budget and Evaluating Performance**

✔ 1: Total variable overhead cost per unit: $0.35
✔ 1: Total costs using 55,000 units: $29,750
✔ 3: Total variable overhead costs over budget: $794.00

P1. Beverage Products Company specializes in 12-ounce drinking glasses. The president asks the controller to prepare a performance report for April. The following report was handed to her a few days later:

(Continued)

Cost Category (Variable Unit Cost)	Budgeted Costs*	Actual Costs	Difference Under (Over) Budget
Direct materials ($0.10)	$ 5,000	$ 4,975	$ 25
Direct labor ($0.12)	6,000	5,850	150
Variable overhead:			
Indirect labor ($0.03)	1,500	1,290	210
Supplies ($0.02)	1,000	960	40
Heat and power ($0.03)	1,500	1,325	175
Other ($0.05)	2,500	2,340	160
Fixed overhead:			
Heat and power	3,500	3,500	—
Depreciation	4,200	4,200	—
Insurance and taxes	1,200	1,200	—
Other	1,600	1,600	—
Totals	$28,000	$27,240	$760

*Based on normal capacity of 50,000 units.

In discussing the report with the controller, the president stated, "Profits have been decreasing in recent months, but this report indicates that our production process is operating efficiently."

REQUIRED

1. Prepare a flexible budget for the company using production levels of 45,000 units, 50,000 units, and 55,000 units.
2. What is the flexible budget formula?
3. Assume that the company produced 45,560 units in April and that all fixed costs remained constant. Prepare a revised performance report similar to the one above, using actual production in units as a basis for the budget column. (Do not round your answers.)
4. **ACCOUNTING CONNECTION ▶** Which report is more meaningful for performance evaluation, the original one or the revised one? Why?

LO 1, 2

Evaluating Cost Center Performance

SPREADSHEET

East Coast plant:
✔ 1: Total variance between actual results and flexible budget: $0
✔ 1: Total variance between flexible budget and master budget: $752,000F
✔ 1: Performance measure: Cans processed per hour: 4,566U

P2. Metal Products, LLC, manufactures metal beverage containers. The division that manufactures soft-drink beverage cans for the North American market has two plants that operate 24 hours a day, 365 days a year. The plants are evaluated as cost centers. Small tools and supplies are considered variable overhead. Depreciation and rent are considered fixed overhead. For the month, the master budget for a plant and the actual operating results of the two North American plants, East Coast and West Coast, follow.

	Master Budget	East Coast Actual	West Coast Actual
Center costs:			
Rolled aluminum ($0.01)	$4,000,000	$3,492,000	$5,040,000
Lids ($0.005)	2,000,000	1,980,000	2,016,000
Direct labor ($0.0025)	1,000,000	864,000	1,260,000
Small tools and supplies ($0.0013)	520,000	432,000	588,000
Depreciation and rent	480,000	480,000	480,000
Total cost	$8,000,000	$7,248,000	$9,384,000
Performance measures:			
Cans processed per hour	45,662	41,096	47,945
Average daily pounds of scrap metal	5	6	7
Cans processed (in millions)	400	360	420

REQUIRED

1. Prepare a performance report for the East Coast plant. Include a flexible budget and variance analysis.
2. Prepare a performance report for the West Coast plant. Include a flexible budget and variance analysis.
3. **ACCOUNTING CONNECTION ▶** Compare the two plants, and comment on their performance.
4. **ACCOUNTING CONNECTION ▶** Explain why a flexible budget should be prepared.

LO **1, 2, 3**

SPREADSHEET

✔ 1: Total variance between actual and flexible budget operating income: $1,900U
✔ 1: Total variance between flexible and master budget operating income: $1,800U

Evaluating Profit and Investment Center Performance

P3. The managing partner of the law firm Sewell, Bagan, and Clark, LLP, makes asset acquisition and disposal decisions for the firm. As managing partner, she supervises the partners in charge of the firm's three branch offices. Those partners have the authority to make employee compensation decisions. The partners' compensation depends on the profitability of their branch office. Vanessa Smith manages the City Branch, which has the following master budget and actual results for the year ended December 31.

	Master Budget	Actual Results
Billed hours	5,000	4,900
Revenue	$ 250,000	$ 254,800
Controllable variable costs:		
Direct labor	(120,000)	(137,200)
Variable overhead	(90,000)	(34,300)
Contribution margin	$ 90,000	$ 83,300
Controllable fixed costs:		
Rent	(30,000)	(30,000)
Other administrative expenses	(45,000)	(42,000)
Branch operating income	$ 15,000	$ 11,300

REQUIRED

1. Assume that the City Branch is a profit center. Prepare a performance report that includes a flexible budget. Determine the variances between actual results, the flexible budget, and the master budget.
2. **ACCOUNTING CONNECTION ▶** Evaluate Vanessa Smith's performance as manager of the City Branch.
3. Assume that the branch managers are assigned responsibility for capital expenditures and that the branches are thus investment centers. City Branch is expected to generate a desired ROI of at least 30 percent on average invested assets of $40,000.
   a. Compute the branch's return on investment and residual income. (Round percentages to two decimal places.)
   b. **ACCOUNTING CONNECTION ▶** Using the ROI and residual income, evaluate Vanessa Smith's performance as branch manager.

LO **3**

✔ 1: This year return on investment: 31.08%
✔ 2: This year residual income: $32,232

Return on Investment and Residual Income

P4. The financial results for the past two years for Ornamental Iron, a division of Iron Horse Company, follow.

(Continued)

Iron Horse Company
Ornamental Iron Division
Balance Sheet
December 31

	This Year	Last Year
Assets		
Cash	$ 5,000	$ 3,000
Accounts receivable	10,000	8,000
Inventory	30,000	32,000
Other current assets	600	600
Plant assets	128,300	120,300
Total assets	$173,900	$163,900
Liabilities and Stockholders' Equity		
Current liabilities	$ 13,900	$ 10,000
Long-term liabilities	90,000	93,900
Stockholders' equity	70,000	60,000
Total liabilities and stockholders' equity	$173,900	$163,900

Iron Horse Company
Ornamental Iron Division
Income Statement
For the Years Ended December 31

	This Year	Last Year
Sales	$ 180,000	$160,000
Cost of goods sold	(100,000)	(90,000)
Selling and administrative expenses	(27,500)	(26,500)
Operating income	$ 52,500	$ 43,500
Income taxes	17,850	14,790
After-tax operating income	$ 34,650	$ 28,710

REQUIRED

1. Compute the division's profit margin, asset turnover, and return on investment for this year and last year. Beginning total assets for last year were $157,900. Round to two decimal places.
2. The desired return on investment for the division has been set at 12 percent. Compute the division's residual income for this year and last year.
3. The cost of capital for the division is 8 percent. Compute the division's economic value added for this year and last year.
4. **ACCOUNTING CONNECTION ▶** Before drawing conclusions about this division's performance, what additional information would you want?

LO 4

The Balanced Scorecard and Benchmarking

P5. BUSINESS APPLICATION ▶ Howski Associates is an independent insurance agency that sells business, automobile, home, and life insurance. Maya Doyle, senior partner of the agency, recently attended a workshop at the local university in which the balanced scorecard was presented as a way of focusing all of a company's functions on its mission. After the workshop, she met with her managers in a weekend brainstorming session. The group determined that Howski's mission was to provide high-quality, innovative, risk-protection services to individuals and businesses. To ensure that the agency would fulfill this mission, the group established the following objectives:

- To provide a sufficient return on investment by increasing sales and maintaining the liquidity needed to support operations
- To add value to the agency's services by training employees to be knowledgeable and competent
- To retain customers and attract new customers
- To operate an efficient and cost-effective office support system for customer agents

To determine the agency's progress in meeting these objectives, the group established the following performance measures:

- Number of new ideas for customer insurance
- Percentage of customers who rate services as excellent
- Average time for processing insurance applications
- Number of dollars spent on training
- Growth in revenues for each type of insurance
- Average time for processing claims
- Percentage of employees who complete 40 hours of training during the year
- Percentage of new customer leads that result in sales
- Cash flow
- Number of customer complaints
- Return on assets
- Percentage of customers who renew policies
- Percentage of revenue devoted to office support system (information systems, accounting, orders, and claims processing)

REQUIRED

1. Prepare a balanced scorecard for Howski by stating the agency's mission and matching its four objectives to the four stakeholder perspectives: the financial, learning and growth, internal business processes, and customer. Indicate which of the agency's performance measures would be appropriate for each objective.
2. Howski is a member of an association of independent insurance agents that provides industry statistics about many aspects of operating an insurance agency. What is benchmarking, and in what ways would the industry statistics assist Howski in further developing its balanced scorecard?

ALTERNATE PROBLEMS

LO 2

Flexible Budgets and Performance Evaluation

✔ 2: Budgeted variable cost per home: $10,922.50
✔ 3: Operating income under budget: $10,003

P6. Realtors, Inc., specializes in the sale of residential properties. It earns its revenue by charging a percentage of the sales price. Commissions for sales persons, listing agents, and listing companies are its main costs. Business has improved steadily over the last 10 years. The managing partner of Realtors, Inc., receives a report summarizing the company's performance each year. The report for the most recent year follows.

Realtors, Inc.
Performance Report
For the Year Ended December 31

	Budget*	Actual**	Difference Under (Over) Budgeted
Total selling fees	$2,052,000	$2,242,200	$(190,200)
Variable costs:			
Sales commissions	$1,102,950	$1,205,183	$(102,233)
Automobile	36,000	39,560	(3,560)
Advertising	93,600	103,450	(9,850)
Home repairs	77,400	89,240	(11,840)
General overhead	656,100	716,970	(60,870)
Total variable costs	$1,966,050	$2,154,403	$(188,353)
Fixed costs:			
General overhead	60,000	62,300	(2,300)
Total costs	$2,026,050	$2,216,703	$(190,653)
Operating income	$ 25,950	$ 25,497	$ 453

*Budgeted data are based on 180 units sold.
**Actual data for 200 units sold.

(Continued)

REQUIRED

1. **ACCOUNTING CONNECTION ▶** Analyze the performance report. What does it say about the company's performance? Is the performance report reliable? Explain your answer.
2. Calculate the budgeted selling fee and budgeted variable costs per home sale.
3. Prepare a performance report using a flexible budget based on the actual number of home sales.
4. **ACCOUNTING CONNECTION ▶** Analyze the report you prepared in requirement 3. What does it say about the company's performance? Is the report reliable? Explain your answer.
5. **ACCOUNTING CONNECTION ▶** What recommendations would you make to improve the company's performance next year?

LO **1, 2**

SPREADSHEET

North plant:
✔ 1: Total variance between actual results and flexible budget: $52,000F
✔ 1: Total variance between flexible budget and master budget: $775,000F
✔ 1: Performance measure: Bottles processed per hour: 7,450U

Evaluating Cost Center Performance

P7. Reuse Products, LLC, manufactures plastic beverage bottles. The division that manufactures water bottles for the North American market has two plants that operate 24 hours a day, 365 days a year. The plants are evaluated as cost centers. Small tools and supplies are considered variable overhead. Depreciation and rent are considered fixed overhead. For the month, the master budget for a plant and the actual operating results of the two North American plants, North and South, follow.

Cost Category (Variable Unit Cost)	Master Budget	North Actual	South Actual
Center costs:			
Plastic pellets ($0.009)	$4,500,000	$3,880,000	$5,500,000
Caps ($0.004)	2,000,000	1,990,000	2,000,000
Direct labor ($0.002)	1,000,000	865,000	1,240,000
Small tools and supplies ($0.0005)	250,000	198,000	280,000
Depreciation and rent	450,000	440,000	480,000
Total cost	$8,200,000	$7,373,000	$9,500,000
Performance measures:			
Bottles processed per hour	69,450	62,000	70,250
Average daily pounds of scrap	5	6	7
Bottles processed (in millions)	500	450	520

REQUIRED

1. Prepare a performance report for the North plant. Include a flexible budget and variance analysis.
2. Prepare a performance report for the South plant. Include a flexible budget and variance analysis.
3. **ACCOUNTING CONNECTION ▶** Compare the two plants, and comment on their performance.
4. **ACCOUNTING CONNECTION ▶** Explain why a flexible budget should be prepared.

LO **1, 2, 3**

RATIO

SPREADSHEET

✔ 1: Total variance between actual and flexible budget operating income: $6,000F
✔ 1: Total variance between flexible and master budget operating income: $20,000U

Evaluating Profit and Investment Center Performance

P8. Thomas Carter is the president of a company that owns six multiplex movie theaters. Carter has delegated decision-making authority to the theater managers for all decisions except those relating to capital expenditures and film selection. The theater managers' compensation depends on the profitability of their theaters. Morris Burgman, the manager of the Park Theater, had the following master budget and actual results for the month:

	Master Budget	Actual Results
Tickets sold	120,000	110,000
Revenue—tickets	$ 840,000	$ 880,000
Revenue—concessions	480,000	330,000
Total revenue	$1,320,000	$1,210,000
Controllable variable costs:		
Concessions	(120,000)	(99,000)
Direct labor	(420,000)	(330,000)
Variable overhead	(540,000)	(550,000)
Contribution margin	$ 240,000	$ 231,000
Controllable fixed costs:		
Rent	(55,000)	(55,000)
Other administrative expenses	(45,000)	(50,000)
Theater operating income	$ 140,000	$ 126,000

REQUIRED

1. Assuming that the theaters are profit centers, prepare a performance report for the Park Theater. Include a flexible budget. Determine the variances between actual results, the flexible budget, and the master budget.
2. **ACCOUNTING CONNECTION ▶** Evaluate Burgman's performance as manager of the Park Theater.
3. Assume that the managers are assigned responsibility for capital expenditures and that the theaters are thus investment centers. Park Theater is expected to generate a desired ROI of at least 6 percent on average invested assets of $2,000,000.
   a. Compute the theater's return on investment and residual income. (Round percentages to one decimal place.)
   b. **ACCOUNTING CONNECTION ▶** Using the ROI and residual income, evaluate Burgman's performance as manager.

LO **3**

RATIO

✔ 1: This year return on investment: 36.40%
✔ 2: This year residual income: $50,160

Return on Investment and Residual Income

P9. LET Company's financial results for the past two years follow.

LET Company
Balance Sheet
December 31

	This Year	Last Year
Assets		
Cash	$ 9,000	$ 4,000
Accounts receivable	40,000	50,000
Inventory	30,000	25,000
Other current assets	1,000	1,000
Plant assets	120,000	100,000
Total assets	$200,000	$180,000
Liabilities and Stockholders' Equity		
Current liabilities	$ 10,000	$ 10,000
Long-term liabilities	20,000	10,000
Stockholders' equity	170,000	160,000
Total liabilities and stockholders' equity	$200,000	$180,000

(Continued)

LET Company
Income Statement
For the Years Ended December 31

	This Year	Last Year
Sales	$ 247,000	$ 204,000
Cost of goods sold	(150,000)	(115,000)
Selling and administrative expenses	(27,840)	(17,600)
Operating income	$ 69,160	$ 71,400
Income taxes	20,160	29,400
After-tax operating income	$ 49,000	$ 42,000

REQUIRED

1. Compute the company's profit margin, asset turnover, and return on investment for this year and last year. Beginning total assets for last year were $160,000. (Round percentages to two decimal places.)
2. The desired return on investment for the company has been set at 10 percent. Compute LET's residual income for this year and last year.
3. The cost of capital for the company is 5 percent. Compute the company's economic value added for this year and last year.
4. **ACCOUNTING CONNECTION ▶** Before drawing conclusions about this company's performance, what additional information would you want?

LO 4

The Balanced Scorecard and Benchmarking

P10. BUSINESS APPLICATION ▶ Resource College is a liberal arts school that provides local residents the opportunity to take college courses and earn bachelor's degrees. Yolanda Howard, the school's provost, recently attended a workshop in which the balanced scorecard was presented as a way of focusing all of an organization's functions on its mission. After the workshop, she met with her administrative staff and college deans in a weekend brainstorming session. The group determined that the college's mission was to provide high-quality courses and degrees to individuals to add value to their lives. To ensure that the college would fulfill this mission, the group established the following objectives:

- To provide a sufficient return on investment by increasing tuition revenues and maintaining the liquidity needed to support operations
- To add value to the college's courses by encouraging faculty to be lifelong learners
- To retain students and attract new students
- To operate efficient and cost-effective student support systems

To determine the college's progress in meeting these objectives, the group established the following performance measures:

- Number of faculty publications
- Percentage of students who rate college as excellent
- Average time for processing student applications
- Number of dollars spent on professional development
- Growth in revenues for each department
- Average time for processing transcript requests
- Percentage of faculty who annually do 40 hours of professional development
- Percentage of new student leads that result in enrollment
- Cash flow
- Number of student complaints
- Return on assets
- Percentage of returning students
- Percentage of revenue devoted to student services systems (registrar, computer services, financial aid, and student health)

REQUIRED

1. Prepare a balanced scorecard for Resource by stating the college's mission and matching its four objectives to the four stakeholder perspectives: the financial, learning and growth, internal business processes, and customer perspectives. Indicate which of the college's performance measures would be appropriate for each objective.
2. Resource College is a member of an association of independent liberal arts schools that provides industry statistics about many aspects of operating a college. What is benchmarking, and in what ways would the association's statistics assist Resource College in further developing its balanced scorecard?

CASES

LO 1

Interpreting Management Reports: Responsibility Centers

C1. Wood4Fun makes wooden playground equipment for the institutional and consumer markets. The company strives for low-cost, high-quality production because it operates in a highly competitive market in which product price is set by the marketplace and is not based on production costs. The company is organized into responsibility centers. The vice president of manufacturing is responsible for three manufacturing plants. The vice president of sales is responsible for four sales regions. Recently, these two vice presidents began to disagree about whether the manufacturing plants are cost centers or profit centers. The vice president of manufacturing views the plants as cost centers because the managers of the plants control only product-related costs. The vice president of sales believes the plants are profit centers because product quality and product cost strongly affect company profits.

1. Identify the controllable performance that Wood4Fun values and wants to measure. Give at least three examples of performance measures that Wood4Fun could use to monitor such performance.
2. For the manufacturing plants, what type of responsibility center is most consistent with the controllable performance Wood4Fun wants to measure?
3. For the sales regions, what type of responsibility center is most appropriate?

LO 1, 2

Conceptual Understanding: Types of Responsibility Centers

C2. Yuma Foods acquired Aldo's Tortillas several years ago. Aldo's has continued to operate as an independent company, except that Yuma Foods has exclusive authority over capital investments, production quantity, and pricing decisions because Yuma has been Aldo's only customer since the acquisition. Yuma uses return on investment to evaluate the performance of Aldo's manager. The most recent performance report follows.

Yuma Foods
Performance Report for Aldo's Tortillas
For the Year Ended June 30

Sales	$6,000
Variable cost of goods sold	(3,000)
Variable administrative expenses	(1,000)
Variable corporate expenses (% of sales)	(600)
Contribution margin	$1,400
Fixed overhead (includes depreciation of $100)	(400)
Fixed administrative expenses	(500)
Operating income	$ 500
Average assets invested	$5,500
Return on investment	9.09%*

*Rounded

(Continued)

1. Analyze the items listed in the performance report, and identify the items that Aldo controls and those that Yuma controls. In your opinion, what type of responsibility center is Aldo's Tortillas? Explain your response. (Round to two decimal places.)
2. Prepare a revised performance report for Aldo's Tortillas and an accompanying memo to the president of Yuma Foods that explains why it is important to change the content of the report. Cite some basic principles of responsibility accounting to support your recommendation.

LO **3**

Decision Analysis: Return on Investment and Residual Income

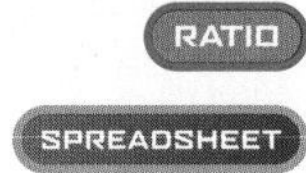

C3. Suppose Alexandra Patel, the manager of the Food and Lodging Division at Winter Wonderland Resort, has hired you as a consultant to help her examine her division's performance under several different circumstances.

1. Type the data that follow into a spreadsheet to compute the division's actual return on investment and residual income. (Data are from parts **3** and **4** of this chapter's TriLevel Problem.) Match your data entries to the rows and columns shown below. (*Hint:* Remember to format each cell for the type of numbers it holds, such as percentage, currency, or general. Round profit margin to two decimal places.)

	A	B	C	D
1				**Investment Center**
2				**Food and Lodging Division**
3				**Actual Results**
4	Sales			$40,000,000
5	Operating income			$ 6,450,000
6	Average assets invested			$10,000,000
7	Desired ROI			30%
8	Return on investment			=(D5/D6)
9	Profit margin			=(D5/D4)
10	Asset turnover			=(D4/D6)
11	Residual income			=(D5–(D7*D6))
12				

2. Patel would like to know how the figures would change if Food and Lodging had a desired ROI of 40 percent and average assets invested of $10,000,000. Revise your spreadsheet from **1** to compute the division's return on investment and residual income under those conditions.
3. Patel also wants to know how the figures would change if Food and Lodging had a desired ROI of 30 percent and average assets invested of $12,000,000. Revise your spreadsheet from **1** to compute the division's return on investment and residual income under those conditions.
4. Does the use of formatted spreadsheets simplify the computation of ROI and residual income? Do such spreadsheets make it easier to perform "what-if" analyses?

LO **3, 5**

Conceptual Understanding: Economic Value Added and Performance

C4. Sevilla Consulting offers environmental consulting services worldwide. The managers of branch offices are rewarded for superior performance with bonuses based on the economic value that the office adds to the company. Last year's operating results for the entire company and for its three offices, expressed in millions of U.S. dollars, follow.

	Worldwide	**Europe**	**Americas**	**Asia**
Cost of capital	9%	10%	8%	12%
Total assets	$210	$70	$70	$70
Current liabilities	80	10	40	30
After-tax operating income	15	5	5	5

1. Compute the economic value added for each office worldwide. What factors affect each office's economic value added? How can an office improve its economic value added? (Round to two decimal places.)
2. **BUSINESS APPLICATION ▶** If managers' bonuses are based on economic value added to office performance, what specific actions will managers be motivated to take?
3. Is economic value added the only performance measure needed to evaluate investment centers adequately? Explain your response.

LO 4, 5

Group Activity: Performance Measures and the Balanced Scorecard

C5. BUSINESS APPLICATION ▶ Working in a group of four to six students, select a local business. The group should become familiar with the background of the business by interviewing its manager or accountant. Each group member should identify several performance objectives for the business and link each objective with a specific stakeholder's perspective from the balanced scorecard. (Select at least one performance objective for each perspective.) For each objective, ask yourself, "If I were the manager of the business, how would I set performance measures for each objective?" Then prepare an email stating the business's name, location, and activities and your linked performance objectives and perspectives. Also list possible measures for each performance objective.

In class, members of the group should compare their individual emails and compile them into a group report by having each group member assume a different stakeholder perspective (add government and community if you want more than four perspectives). Each group should be ready to present all perspectives and the group's report on performance objectives and measures in class.

Continuing Case: Cookie Company

C6. As we continue with this case, assume that your cookie store is now part of a national chain. The store has been consistently profitable, and sales remain satisfactory despite a temporary economic downturn in your area.

At the first of the year, corporate headquarters set a targeted return on investment of 20 percent for your store. The store currently averages \$140,000 in invested assets (beginning invested assets, \$130,000; ending invested assets, \$150,000) and is projected to have an operating income of \$30,800. You are considering whether to take one or both of the following actions before the end of the year:

- Hold off recording and paying \$5,000 in bills owed until the start of the next fiscal year.
- Write down to zero value \$3,000 in store inventory (nonperishable containers) that you have been unable to sell.

Currently, your bonus is based on store profits. Next year, corporate headquarters is changing its performance incentive program so that bonuses will be based on a store's actual return on investment.

1. What effect would each of the actions that you are considering have on the store's operating income this year? In your opinion, is either action unethical?
2. Independent of question 1, how would the inventory write-down affect next year's income and return on investment if the inventory is sold for \$4,000 next year, when corporate headquarters changes its performance incentive plan for store managers? In your opinion, do you have an ethical dilemma? (Round ROI to the nearest whole percentage.)

CHAPTER 22
Standard Costing and Variance Analysis

BUSINESS INSIGHT
iRobot Corporation

Known for its floor-cleaning home robots, Roomba and Scooba, **iRobot** is a leader in the emerging robotics industry. Its PackBot, a combat-proven mobile robot, has saved many lives by performing hazardous reconnaissance, search, and bomb disposal duties in battle zones worldwide.

As iRobot develops the next generation of robots for military, industrial, and home use, its managers will continue to keep the business highly profitable by using design specifications to set standard costs for the company product lines. Managers in all types of companies use these figures as performance targets and as benchmarks against which to measure actual spending trends and monitor changes in business conditions.

1. **CONCEPT** ▶ *Why is standard costing and variance analysis useful?*

2. **ACCOUNTING APPLICATION** ▶ *How can iRobot's managers evaluate the performance of its cost centers?*

3. **BUSINESS APPLICATION** ▶ *Why does the setting of performance standards help managers control costs and improve performance?*

LEARNING OBJECTIVES

LO1 **Define *standard costs*, and explain why standard costing is useful.**

LO2 **Compute standard unit costs, and describe the role of flexible budgets in variance analysis to control costs.**

LO3 **Compute and analyze direct materials variances.**

LO4 **Compute and analyze direct labor variances.**

LO5 **Compute and analyze overhead variances.**

LO6 **Explain how variances are used to evaluate a business's performance.**

Vaughn Youtz/Newscom

SECTION 1 CONCEPTS

CONCEPTS
- Comparability
- Understandability

RELEVANT LEARNING OBJECTIVE

LO 1 Define *standard costs*, and explain why standard costing is useful.

LO 1 Concepts Underlying Standard Costing

Managers find standard costing useful due to the concepts of understandability and comparability. *Understandability* applies because the **standard costs** are realistic estimates of costs based on analyses of both past and projected operating costs and conditions. They are usually stated in terms of cost per unit. They provide a standard, or predetermined performance level for use in standard costing. *Comparability* applies because **standard costing** is a method of cost control that is used to compare the difference, or **variance**, between standard and actual performance. This method differs from actual and normal costing methods in that it uses estimated costs exclusively to compute all three elements of product cost—direct materials, direct labor, and overhead.

Standard costing is especially effective for understanding and managing cost centers. Recall that a *cost center* is a responsibility center in which there are well-defined links between the cost of the resources (direct materials, direct labor, and overhead) and the resulting products or services.

Managers find standard costing and variance analysis useful to develop budgets, to control costs, and to prepare reports. Managers set standard costs based on realistic estimates of operating costs and then use the standards to prepare flexible budgets. Flexible budgets improve the understanding and accuracy of their variance analysis since these budgets compare actual costs and a budget based on the same amount of output. By analyzing variances between standard and actual costs, managers gain insight into the causes of those differences. Once they have identified an operating problem that is causing a cost variance, they can devise a solution that results in better control of costs.

Standard costing can be used in any type of business. Both manufacturers and service businesses can use standard costing in conjunction with a job order costing, process costing, or activity-based costing system to compare actual performance results for materials, labor, and overhead with their predetermined performance standards. However, a disadvantage to using standard costing is that it can be expensive and time-consuming to gather all the needed information. The estimated costs are based not just on past costs, but also on engineering estimates, forecasted demand, worker input, time and motion studies, and type and quality of direct materials.

In the next section, we describe how standard unit costs are computed and used to prepare flexible budgets and how managers use the variance between standard and actual costs to evaluate performance and control costs.

APPLY IT!

Kellman Corporation is considering adopting the standard costing method. Dan Osterheld, the Midwest Division's manager, attended a corporate meeting at which the controller discussed the proposal. Osterheld asked, "How will this new method help me understand my division's performance? Does performance comparability improve if my division uses this new method?" Help prepare the controller's response to Osterheld by deciding whether the following statements are true or false. If false, make the statement true.

1. Standard costing helps managers compare actual cost results to a standard or predetermined performance level.
2. At the end of the period, variance analysis will only identify areas of cost efficiency.
3. Standard costing helps managers understand where to focus efforts for improvement.

SOLUTION

1. True
2. False

   At the end of the period, variance analysis will identify areas of cost efficiency and inefficiency.
3. True

TRY IT! SE1, SE2, E1A, E1B

SECTION 2

ACCOUNTING APPLICATIONS

COUNTING PLICATIONS
Compute standard unit costs
Compute total flexible budget costs
Compute and analyze direct materials variances
- Direct materials price variance
- Direct materials quantity variance

Compute and analyze direct labor variances
- Direct labor rate variance
- Direct labor efficiency variance

Compute and analyze overhead variances
- Variable overhead spending variance
- Variable overhead efficiency variance
- Fixed overhead budget variance
- Fixed overhead volume variance

LEVANT ARNING OBJECTIVES

2 Compute standard unit costs, and scribe the role of flexible dgets in variance analysis control costs.

3 Compute and analyze direct materials iances.

4 Compute and analyze direct labor variances.

5 Compute and analyze overhead variances.

LO 2 Variance Analysis

Variance analysis is the process of computing the differences between standard costs and actual costs and identifying the causes of those differences. By examining the differences, or variances, between standard and actual costs, managers can gather valuable information about improving the accuracy of variance analysis and controlling costs.

Computing Standard Costs

A fully integrated standard costing system uses standard costs for all the elements of product cost: direct materials, direct labor, and overhead. Standard costs are recorded in inventory accounts for materials, work in process, and finished goods, as well as the Cost of Goods Sold account. Actual costs are recorded separately so that managers can compare what should have been spent (the standard costs) with the actual costs incurred in the cost center.

A standard unit cost for a manufactured product has the following six elements:

- Direct materials price standard
- Direct labor rate standard
- Variable overhead rate standard
- Direct materials quantity standard
- Direct labor time standard
- Fixed overhead rate standard

To compute a standard unit cost, it is necessary to identify and analyze each of these elements. (Note that a standard unit cost for a service includes only the elements that relate to direct labor and overhead.)

Standard Direct Materials Cost

The **standard direct materials cost** is the price that should be paid for the materials and is computed as follows.

$$\text{Standard Direct Materials Cost} = \text{Direct Materials Price Standard} \times \text{Direct Materials Quantity Standard}$$

In this equation, the **direct materials price standard** is a careful estimate of the cost of a specific direct material in the next period. An organization's purchasing department is responsible for developing price standards for all direct materials and for making the actual purchases. When estimating a direct materials price standard, the purchasing department must take into account all possible price increases, changes in available quantities, and new sources of supply.

The **direct materials quantity standard** is an estimate of the amount of direct materials, including scrap and waste, that will be used in a period. It is influenced by product engineering specifications, the quality of direct materials, the age and productivity of machinery, and the quality and experience of the work force. Production managers or managerial accountants usually establish and monitor standards for direct materials quantity, but engineers, purchasing agents, and machine operators may also contribute to the development of these standards.

We will use ICU, which makes surveillance robots, to illustrate how standard costs are used to compute total unit cost. ICU has recently updated the standards for its Watch Dog product. Direct materials price standards are now $9.20 per square foot for casing materials and $20.17 for each mechanism. Direct materials quantity standards are 0.025 square foot of casing materials per robot and one mechanism per robot. Thus, the direct materials costs of making one robot are:

Direct materials costs:	
Casing ($9.20 per sq. ft. × 0.025 sq. ft.)	$ 0.23
One mechanism	20.17

Standard Direct Labor Cost

The **standard direct labor cost** for a product, task, or job order is the cost necessary to produce that product, task, or job order and is computed as follows.

$$\text{Standard Direct Labor Cost} = \text{Direct Labor Rate Standard} \times \text{Direct Labor Time Standard}$$

In this equation, the **direct labor rate standard** is the hourly direct labor rate that is expected to prevail during the next period for each function or job classification. Although rate ranges are established for each type of worker and rates vary within those ranges according to each worker's experience and length of service, an average standard rate is developed for each task. Even if the person making the product is paid more or less than the standard rate, the standard rate is used to calculate the standard direct labor cost.

STUDY NOTE: *Both the direct labor rate standard and the direct labor time standard are based on an average of the different levels of skilled workers, and both are related to the production of one unit or batch.*

The **direct labor time standard** is the expected labor time required for each department, machine, or process to complete the production of one unit or one batch of output. In many cases, standard time per unit is a small fraction of an hour. Current time and motion studies of workers and machines, as well as records of their past performance, provide the data for developing this standard. The direct labor time standard should be revised whenever a machine is replaced or the quality of the labor force changes.

For ICU, for example, direct labor time standards are 0.01 hour per robot for the Case Stamping Department and 0.05 hour per robot for the Assembly Department. Direct labor rate standards are $8.00 per hour for the Case Stamping Department and $10.20 per hour for the Assembly Department. Thus, the direct labor costs of making one robot in each department are:

Direct labor costs:	
Case Stamping Department ($8.00 per hour × 0.01 hour per robot)	$0.08
Assembly Department ($10.20 per hour × 0.05 hour per robot)	0.51

Standard Overhead Cost

The **standard overhead cost** is the sum of the estimates of variable and fixed overhead costs in the next period. It is based on standard overhead rates that are computed in much the same way as the predetermined overhead rate discussed in an earlier chapter. Unlike that rate, however, the standard overhead rate has two parts:

- variable costs
- fixed costs

The reason for computing the standard variable and fixed overhead rates separately is that their cost behavior differs.

The **standard variable overhead rate** is computed by dividing the total budgeted variable overhead costs by an expression of capacity, such as the budgeted number of standard machine hours or standard direct labor hours.* Using standard direct labor hours as the base, the formula is as follows.

$$\text{Standard Variable Overhead Rate} = \frac{\text{Total Budgeted Variable Overhead Costs}}{\text{Total Budgeted Number of Standard Direct Labor Hours}}$$

For ICU, for example, the standard variable overhead rate is $12.00 per direct labor hour. Thus, the variable overhead cost of making one robot is:

Variable overhead cost ($12.00 per hour × 0.06 hour per robot)	$0.72

The **standard fixed overhead rate** is computed by dividing the total budgeted fixed overhead costs by an expression of capacity, usually normal capacity in terms of standard

*Other bases may be used if machine hours or direct labor hours are not good predictors, or drivers, of variable overhead costs.

hours or units. The denominator is expressed in the same terms as the variable overhead rate. Using normal capacity in terms of standard direct labor hours as the denominator, the formula is as follows.

$$\text{Standard Fixed Overhead Rate} = \frac{\text{Total Budgeted Fixed Overhead Costs}}{\text{Normal Capacity in Terms of Standard Direct Labor Hours}}$$

For ICU, for example, the standard fixed overhead rate is $9.00 per direct labor hour. Thus, the fixed overhead cost of making one robot is:

Fixed overhead cost ($9.00 per hour × 0.06 hour per robot)	$0.54

Recall that *normal capacity* is the level of operating capacity needed to meet expected sales demand. Using it as the application base ensures that all fixed overhead costs have been applied to units produced by the time normal capacity is reached.

Total Standard Unit Cost

Using standard costs eliminates the need to calculate unit costs from actual cost data every week or month or for each batch of goods produced. Once standard costs for direct materials, direct labor, and variable and fixed overhead have been developed, a total standard unit cost can be computed at any time. We used ICU to illustrate how standard costs are used to compute total unit cost. The standard cost of making one robot would be computed as follows.

STUDY NOTE: *The total standard unit cost of $22.25 represents the* desired *cost of producing one robot.*

Direct materials costs:	
Casing ($9.20 per sq. ft. × 0.025 sq. ft.)	$ 0.23
One mechanism	20.17
Direct labor costs:	
Case Stamping Department ($8.00 per hour × 0.01 hour per robot)	0.08
Assembly Department ($10.20 per hour × 0.05 hour per robot)	0.51
Variable overhead ($12.00 per hour × 0.06 hour per robot)	0.72
Total standard variable cost of one robot	$21.71
Fixed overhead ($9.00 per hour × 0.06 hour per robot)	0.54
Total standard unit cost	$22.25

The Role of Flexible Budgets in Variance Analysis

The accuracy of variance analysis depends to a large extent on the type of budget that managers use when comparing variances. Static, or fixed, budgets forecast revenues and expenses for just one level of sales and just one level of output. The budgets that make up a master budget are usually based on a single level of output; but many things can cause actual output to differ from the estimated output. If a company produces more products than predicted, total production costs will almost always be greater than predicted. Thus, a comparison of actual production costs with fixed budgeted costs will inevitably show variances.

The performance report in Exhibit 1 compares data from ICU's static master budget with the actual costs of the company's Watch Division, the division responsible for manufacturing the Watch Dog. As you can see, actual costs exceeded budgeted costs by $5,539. Most managers would consider such a cost overrun significant. But was there really a cost overrun? The budgeted amounts are based on an output of 17,500 units when the actual output was 19,100 units.

The total standard unit cost of producing a video game controller or a robot like the Watch Dog represents the desired production cost. It is based on the standards established for direct materials costs, direct labor costs, and variable and fixed overhead.

Beyond Fotomedia GmbH / Alamy

Exhibit 1
Performance Report Using Data from a Static Budget

ICU, Inc.
Performance Report—Watch Division
For the Year Ended December 31

Cost Category	Master Budgeted Costs*	Actual Costs**	Difference Under (Over) Budget
Direct materials	$357,000	$361,000	$(4,000)
Direct labor	10,325	11,779	(1,454)
Variable overhead:			
Indirect materials	3,500	3,600	(100)
Indirect labor	5,250	5,375	(125)
Utilities	1,750	1,810	(60)
Other	2,100	2,200	(100)
Fixed overhead:			
Supervisory salaries	4,000	3,500	500
Depreciation	2,000	2,000	—
Utilities	450	450	—
Other	3,000	3,200	(200)
Totals	$389,375	$394,914	$(5,539)

*Budgeted costs are based on an output of 17,500 units.
**Actual output was 19,100 units.

To judge the division's performance accurately, ICU's managers can use a flexible budget. Recall that a *flexible* (or *variable*) *budget* is a summary of expected costs for a range of activity levels. Unlike a static budget, a flexible budget provides forecasted data that can be adjusted for changes in the level of output. The flexible budget in Exhibit 2 is based on standard unit cost data from the static master budget in Exhibit 1. Variable unit costs have been multiplied by the 19,100 units actually produced to arrive at the

Exhibit 2
Performance Report Using Data from a Flexible Budget

ICU, Inc.
Performance Report—Watch Division
For the Year Ended December 31

Cost Category	Flexible Budgeted Costs*	Actual Costs	Difference Under (Over) Budget
Direct materials ($20.40)**	$389,640	$361,000	$28,640
Direct labor ($0.59)	11,269	11,779	(510)
Variable overhead:			
Indirect materials ($0.20)	3,820	3,600	220
Indirect labor ($0.30)	5,730	5,375	355
Utilities ($0.10)	1,910	1,810	100
Other ($0.12)	2,292	2,200	92
Fixed overhead:			
Supervisory salaries	4,000	3,500	500
Depreciation	2,000	2,000	—
Utilities	450	450	—
Other	3,000	3,200	(200)
Totals	$424,111	$394,914	$29,197

*Budgeted costs are based on actual output of 19,100 units.
**Amounts in parentheses in the Cost Category column are variable unit costs.

total flexible budgeted costs, and fixed overhead information has been carried over from Exhibit 1. In this report, actual costs are $29,197 less than the amount budgeted. In other words, the flexible budget shows that the Watch Division's performance in this period actually exceeded budget targets by $29,197.

The rest of this chapter will discuss how to explain the variances between actual costs and the flexible budget by using standard costing to analyze specific variances for direct materials, direct labor, variable overhead, and fixed overhead.

Using Variance Analysis to Control Costs

As Exhibit 3 shows, using variance analysis to control costs is a four-step process:

- **Step 1.** Managers compute the amount of the variance. If the amount is insignificant—actual operating results are close to those anticipated—no corrective action is needed.
- **Step 2.** If the variance is significant, managers analyze the variance to identify its cause.
- **Step 3.** In identifying the cause, they then select performance measures that will enable them to track the activities that need to be monitored, analyze the results, and determine the action needed to correct the problem.
- **Step 4.** The final step is to take the appropriate corrective action.

Exhibit 3
Variance Analysis: A Four-Step Approach to Controlling Costs

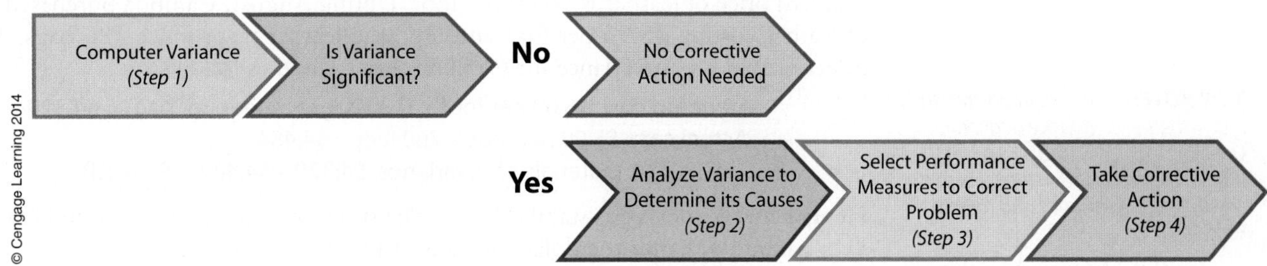

Although computing the amount of a variance is important, it does nothing to prevent the variance from recurring. To control costs, managers must determine the cause of the variance and select performance measures that will help them track the problem and find the best solution for it.

APPLY IT!

Using the information that follows, compute the total standard unit cost of a 5-pound bag of sugar.

Direct materials quantity standard	5 pounds per unit
Direct materials price standard	$0.05 per pound
Direct labor time standard	0.01 hour per unit
Direct labor rate standard	$10.00 per hour
Variable overhead rate standard	$0.15 per machine hour
Fixed overhead rate standard	$0.10 per machine hour
Machine hour standard	0.5 hour per unit

SOLUTION

Direct materials cost ($0.05 × 5 pounds)	$0.25
Direct labor cost ($10.00 × 0.01 hour)	0.10
Variable overhead ($0.15 × 0.5 machine hour)	0.08*
Fixed overhead ($0.10 × 0.5 machine hour)	0.05
Total standard unit cost	$0.48

*Rounded

TRY IT! SE3, SE4, E2A, E3A, E2B, E3B

LO3 Computing and Analyzing Direct Materials Variances

To control cost center operations, managers compute and analyze variances for whole cost categories, such as total direct materials costs, as well as variances for elements of those categories, such as the price and quantity of each direct material. The more detailed their analysis of direct materials variances, the more effective they will be in controlling costs.

Computing Total Direct Materials Cost Variance

Total Direct Materials Cost Variance

Performance Measure The **total direct materials cost variance** measures the difference between what the actual total materials cost and what they should have cost according to the flexible budget for the good units produced. *Good units* are the total units produced less units that are scrapped or need to be reworked—in other words, the salable units.

Formula

Total Direct Materials Cost Variance = Standard Cost* − Actual Cost**

*Standard Cost = Standard Price × Standard Quantity
**Actual Cost = Actual Price × Actual Quantity

Example Cambria Company is a manufacturer that makes leather bags to carry the Watch Dog robots. Each bag should use 4 feet of leather (standard quantity), and the standard price of leather is $6.00 per foot. During August, Cambria purchased 760 feet of leather costing $5.90 per foot and used the leather to produce 180 bags. The total direct materials cost variance for Cambria is calculated as follows.

Standard cost: $6.00 per foot × (180 bags × 4 feet per bag) = $4,320
Actual cost: $5.90 per foot × 760 feet = $4,484
Total direct materials cost variance: $4,320 − $4,484 = $164 (U)

STUDY NOTE: *It is just as important to identify whether a variance is favorable or unfavorable as it is to compute the variance. This information is necessary for analyzing the variance and taking corrective action.*

Here, actual cost exceeds standard cost. The situation is unfavorable, as indicated by the U in parentheses after the dollar amount. An F means a favorable situation.

Computing Total Direct Materials Price Variance

To find the area or people responsible for the variance, the total direct materials cost variance must be broken down into two parts: the direct materials price variance and the direct materials quantity variance.

Direct Materials Price Variance

Performance Measure The **direct materials price variance** (or *direct materials spending* or *rate variance*) measures the difference between what the purchased materials actually cost and what they should have cost according to the flexible budget standard.

Formula

Direct Materials Price Variance = (Standard Price − Actual Price) × Actual Quantity

Example For Cambria, the direct materials price variance is computed as follows.

Direct Materials Price Variance = ($6.00 − $5.90) × 760 feet = $76 (F)

Because the price that the company paid for the direct materials was less than the standard price, the variance is favorable.

Computing Total Direct Materials Quantity Variance

Direct Materials Quantity Variance

Performance Measure The **direct materials quantity variance** (or *direct materials efficiency* or *usage variance*) measures the difference between the quantity of materials actually used to make the product and what the design standard called for.

Formula

Direct Materials Quantity Variance = Standard Price × (Standard Quantity − Actual Quantity)

Example For Cambria, it is computed as follows.

Direct Materials Quantity Variance = \$6 × [(180 bags × 4 feet) − 760 feet] = \$240 (U)

Because more leather than the standard quantity was used in the production process, the direct materials quantity variance is unfavorable.

Summary of Direct Materials Variances

The net of the direct materials price variance and the direct materials quantity variance should equal the total direct materials cost variance. The following check shows that the variances for Cambria were computed correctly:

Direct materials price variance	\$ 76 (F)
Direct materials quantity variance	240 (U)
Total direct materials cost variance	\$164 (U)

Variance analyses are sometimes easier to interpret in diagram form, as shown for Cambria in Exhibit 4. Notice that although direct materials are purchased at actual cost, they are entered in the Materials Inventory account at standard price. Thus, the direct materials price variance of \$76 (F) is obvious when the costs are recorded. As Exhibit 4 shows, the standard price multiplied by the standard quantity is the amount entered in the Work in Process Inventory account.

Exhibit 4
Diagram of Direct Materials Variance Analysis

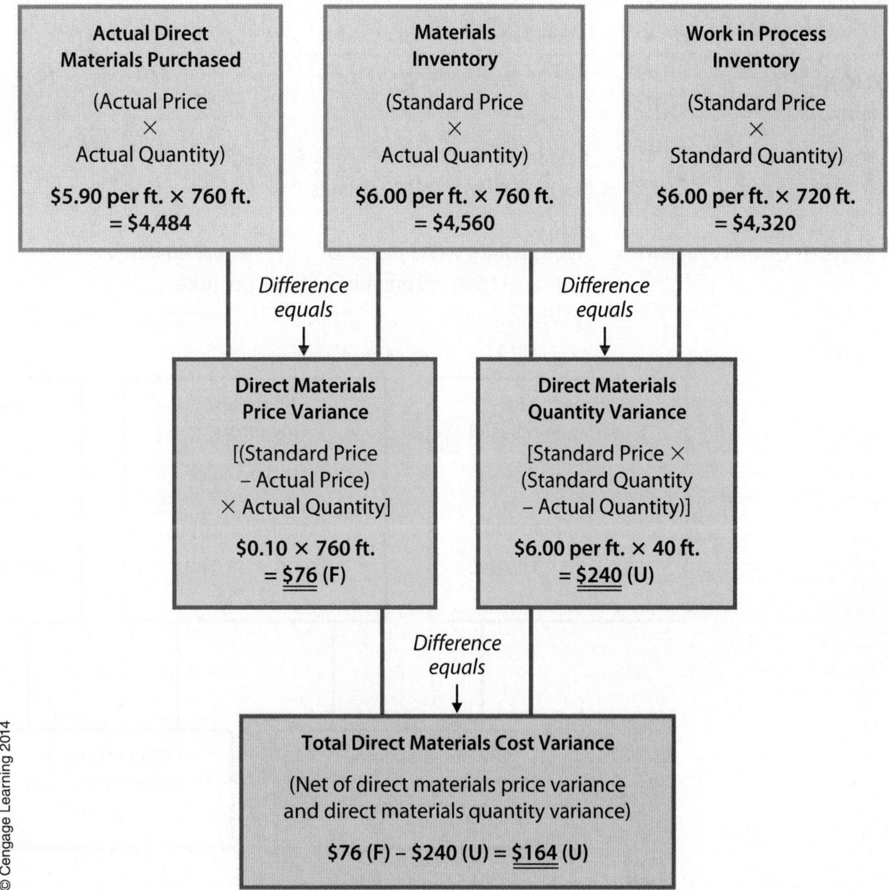

Business Application

Cambria's managers were concerned because the company had been experiencing direct materials price and quantity variances for some time. Moreover, as our analysis shows, the price variances were always favorable and the quantity variances were always unfavorable. By tracking the purchasing activity for three months, the managers discovered that the company's purchasing agent, without any authorization, had been purchasing a lower grade of leather at a reduced price. After careful analysis, the engineering manager determined that the substitute leather was not appropriate and that the company should resume purchasing the grade of leather originally specified. In addition, an analysis of scrap and rework revealed that the inferior quality of the substitute leather was causing the unfavorable quantity variance. By tracking the purchasing activity, Cambria's managers were able to solve the problems.

APPLY IT!

Using the information that follows, compare the actual and standard cost and usage data for the production of 5-pound bags of sugar, and compute the direct materials price and direct materials quantity variances using formulas or diagram form.

Direct materials quantity standard	5 pounds per unit
Direct materials price standard	\$0.05 per pound
Direct materials purchased and used	55,100 pounds
Price paid for direct materials	\$0.04 per pound
Number of good units produced	11,000 units

SOLUTION

Using formulas:

Direct Materials Price Variance = (Standard Price − Actual Price) × Actual Quantity
= (\$0.05 − \$0.04) × 55,100 pounds
= \$551 (F)

Direct Materials Quantity Variance = Standard Price × (Standard Quantity − Actual Quantity)
= \$0.05 × [(11,000 × 5 pounds) − 55,100 pounds]
= \$5 (U)

In diagram form:

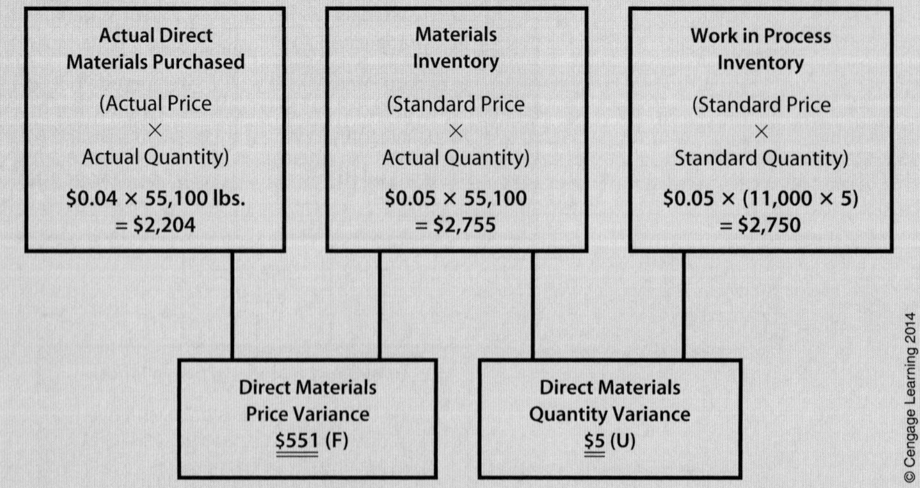

TRY IT! SE5, SE6, E4A, E5A, E6A, E4B, E5B, E6B

LO 4 Computing and Analyzing Direct Labor Variances

The procedure for computing and analyzing direct labor cost variances parallels the procedure for finding direct materials variances. Again, the more detailed the analysis, the more effective managers will be in controlling costs.

Computing Total Direct Labor Cost Variance

Total Direct Labor Cost Variance

Performance Measure The **total direct labor cost variance** measures the difference between what the actual total labor cost and what it should have cost according to the flexible budget for the good units produced.

Formula

Total Direct Labor Cost Variance = Standard Cost* − Actual Cost**

*Standard Cost = Standard Price × Standard Quantity
**Actual Cost = Actual Price × Actual Quantity

Example At Cambria, each leather bag requires 2.4 standard direct labor hours, and the standard direct labor rate is $8.50 per hour. During August, 450 direct labor hours were used to make 180 bags at an average pay rate of $9.20 per hour. Cambria's total direct labor cost variance is computed as follows.

Standard cost: $8.50 per hour × (180 bags × 2.4 hours per bag) = $3,672
Actual cost: $9.20 per hour × 450 hours = $4,140
Total direct labor cost variance: $3,672 − $4,140 = $468 (U)

Both the actual direct labor hours per bag and the actual direct labor rate varied from the standard.

For effective performance evaluation, management must know how much of the total cost arose from different direct labor rates and how much from different numbers of direct labor hours. This information is found by computing the direct labor rate variance and the direct labor efficiency variance.

Computing Direct Labor Rate Variance

Direct Labor Rate Variance

Performance Measure The **direct labor rate variance** (or *direct labor spending variance*) measures the difference between what the direct labor actually cost and what it should have cost according to the flexible budget standard.

Formula

Direct Labor Rate Variance = (Standard Rate − Actual Rate) × Actual Hours

Example For Cambria, it is computed as follows.

Direct Labor Rate Variance = ($8.50 − $9.20) × 450 hours = $315 (U)

Computing Direct Labor Efficiency Variance

Direct Labor Efficiency Variance

Performance Measure The **direct labor efficiency variance** (or *direct labor quantity* or *usage variance*) measures the difference between the labor quantity actually used to make the product and what the design standard called for. It is computed as follows.

Formula

$$\text{Direct Labor Efficiency Variance} = \text{Standard Rate} \times (\text{Standard Hours Allowed} - \text{Actual Hours})$$

Example For Cambria, it is computed this way:

$$\text{Direct Labor Efficiency Variance} = \$8.50 \times [(180 \text{ bags} \times 2.4 \text{ hours}) - 450 \text{ hours}] = \underline{\underline{\$153}} \text{ (U)}$$

Summary of Direct Labor Variances The net of the direct labor rate variance and the direct labor efficiency variance should equal the total direct labor cost variance. The following check shows that the variances were computed correctly:

Direct labor rate variance	$315 (U)
Direct labor efficiency variance	153 (U)
Total direct labor cost variance	$468 (U)

Exhibit 5 summarizes Cambria's direct labor variances. Unlike direct materials variances, the direct labor rate and efficiency variances are usually computed and recorded at the same time.

Exhibit 5
Diagram of Direct Labor Variance Analysis

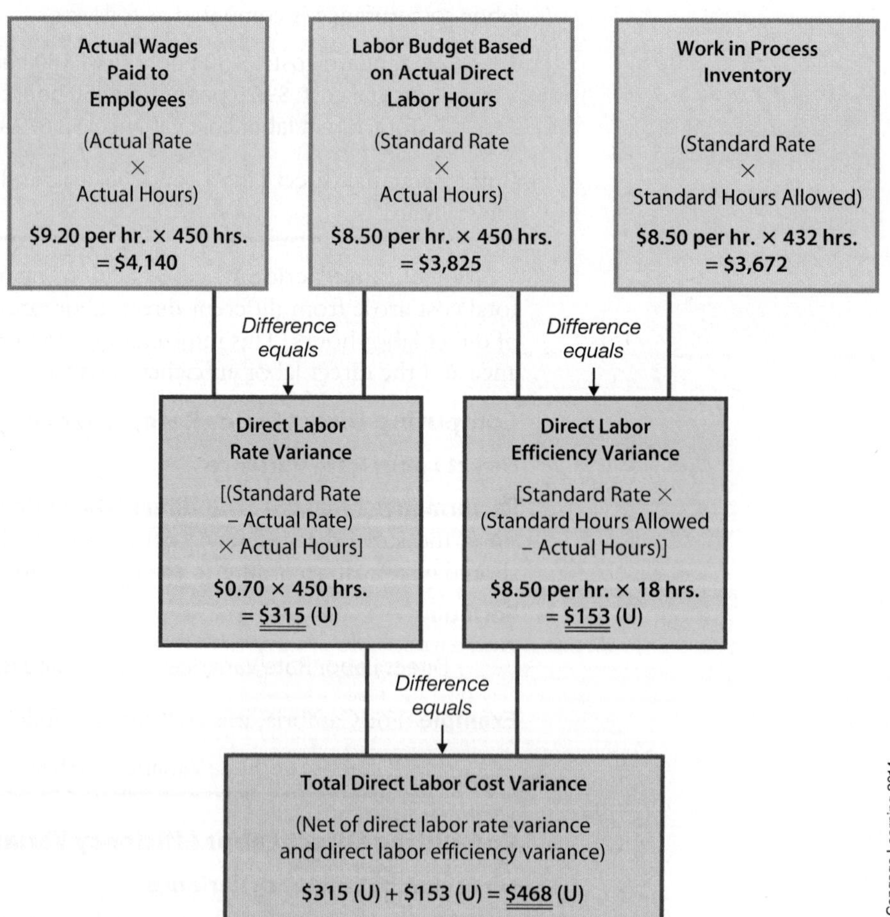

Business Perspective

What Do You Get When You Cross a Vacuum Cleaner with a Gam

The transfer of technology ideas developed for government purposes to everyday consumer use is common—for ers. But what about transferring technology from home use to the battlefield? **iRobot Corporation**[1] applied t vacuum cleaner to create Small Unmanned Ground Vehicles (SUGVs). These robots, such as the PackBot, have camer at night, flexible treads that allow them to climb stairs, and radio links that connect them to an operator at a gam command center.

Business Application

Because Cambria's direct labor rate variance and direct labor efficiency variance were unfavorable, its managers investigated the causes of these variances. An analysis of employee time cards revealed that the Bag Assembly Department had replaced an assembly worker who was ill with a machine operator from another department. The machine operator made $9.20 per hour, whereas the assembly worker earned the standard $8.50 per hour rate. When questioned about the unfavorable efficiency variance, the assembly supervisor identified two causes. First, the machine operator had to learn assembly skills on the job, so his assembly time was longer than the standard time per bag. Second, the materials handling people were partially responsible because they delivered parts late on five different occasions. Because the machine operator was a temporary replacement, Cambria's managers took no corrective action; but they decided to keep a close eye on the materials handling function by tracking delivery times and the number of delays for the next three months. Once they have collected and analyzed the new data, they will take whatever action is needed to correct the scheduling problem.

APPLY IT!

Using the information that follows, compare the standard cost and usage data for the production of 5-pound bags of sugar, and compute the direct labor rate and direct labor efficiency variances using formulas or diagram form.

Direct labor time standard	0.01 hour per unit
Direct labor rate standard	$10.00 per hour
Direct labor hours used (actual)	100 hours
Total cost of direct labor	$1,010
Number of good units produced	11,000 units

SOLUTION

Using formulas:

Direct Labor Rate Variance = (Standard Rate − Actual Rate) × Actual Hours
= [$10.00 − ($1,010 ÷ 100 hours)] × 100 hours
= $10 (U)

Direct Labor Efficiency Variance = Standard Rate × (Standard Hours Allowed − Actual Hours)
= $10 × [(11,000 × 0.01 hour) − 100 hours]
= $100 (F)

(Continued)

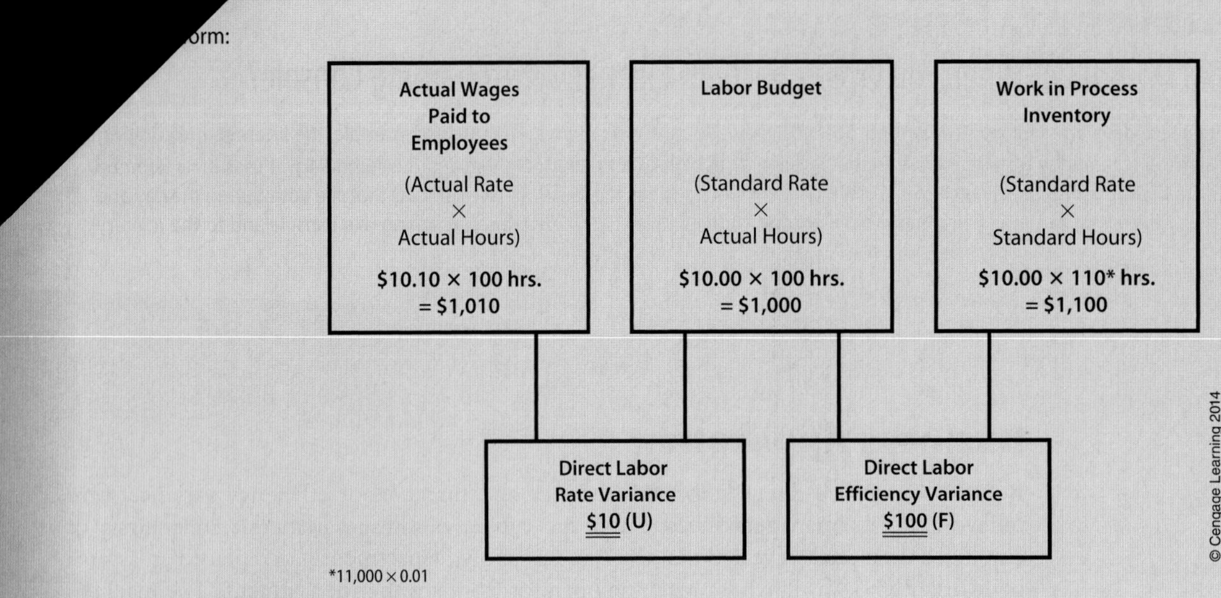

TRY IT! SE7, E7A, E8A, E7B, E8B

LO5 Computing and Analyzing Overhead Variances

Controlling variable and fixed overhead costs is more difficult than controlling direct materials and direct labor costs because the responsibility for overhead costs is hard to assign. Fixed overhead costs may be unavoidable past costs, such as depreciation and lease expenses, which are not under the control of any department manager. If variable overhead costs can be related to departments or activities, however, some control is possible.

Computing Total Overhead Cost Variance

Total Overhead Cost Variance

Performance Measure Analyses of overhead variances differ in degree of detail. The basic approach is to compute the **total overhead cost variance**, which is the difference between what actual overhead cost and what it should have cost according to the flexible budget for the good units produced.

Formula

Total Overhead Cost Variance = Standard Cost* − Actual Cost**

*Standard Cost = Standard Rate × Standard Hours for the Good Units Produced
**Actual cost is given.

Example Recall how overhead is applied to production using a standard or predetermined overhead rate. A standard overhead rate has two parts: a variable rate and a fixed rate. For Cambria, these standard overhead rates are as follows.

Variable overhead rate (from the flexible budget)	$5.75 per direct labor hour
Standard fixed overhead rate [$1,300 total budgeted fixed overhead ÷ 400 direct labor hours (normal capacity)]	3.25 per direct labor hour
Total standard overhead rate	$9.00 per direct labor hour

Cambria's total overhead cost variance would therefore be computed as follows.

Standard cost: \$9.00 per hour × (180 bags × 2.4 hours per bag) = \$3,888
Actual cost (given): Variable \$2,500 + Fixed \$1,600 = \$4,100
Total direct materials cost variance: \$3,888 – \$4,100 = \$212 (U)

This amount can be divided into a variable overhead variance and a fixed overhead variance.

Variable Overhead Variances

Total Variable Overhead Cost Variance

Performance Measure The **total variable overhead cost variance** measures the difference between what the actual variable overhead cost and what it should have cost according to the flexible budget for the good units produced.

Formula

Total Variable Overhead Cost Variance = Overhead Applied* – Actual Overhead

*Overhead Applied = Standard Rate × Standard Hours for the Good Units Produced

Example At Cambria, each leather bag requires 2.4 standard direct labor hours, and the standard variable overhead rate is \$5.75 per direct labor hour. For the month, the company incurred \$2,500 of actual variable overhead costs. The total variable overhead cost variance is computed as follows.

Overhead applied: \$5.75 per hour × (180 bags × 2.4 hours per bag) = \$2,484
Total variable overhead cost variance: \$2,484 – \$2,500 = \$16 (U)

Exhibit 6 shows an analysis of Cambria's variable overhead variances.

Exhibit 6
Diagram of Variable Overhead Variance Analysis

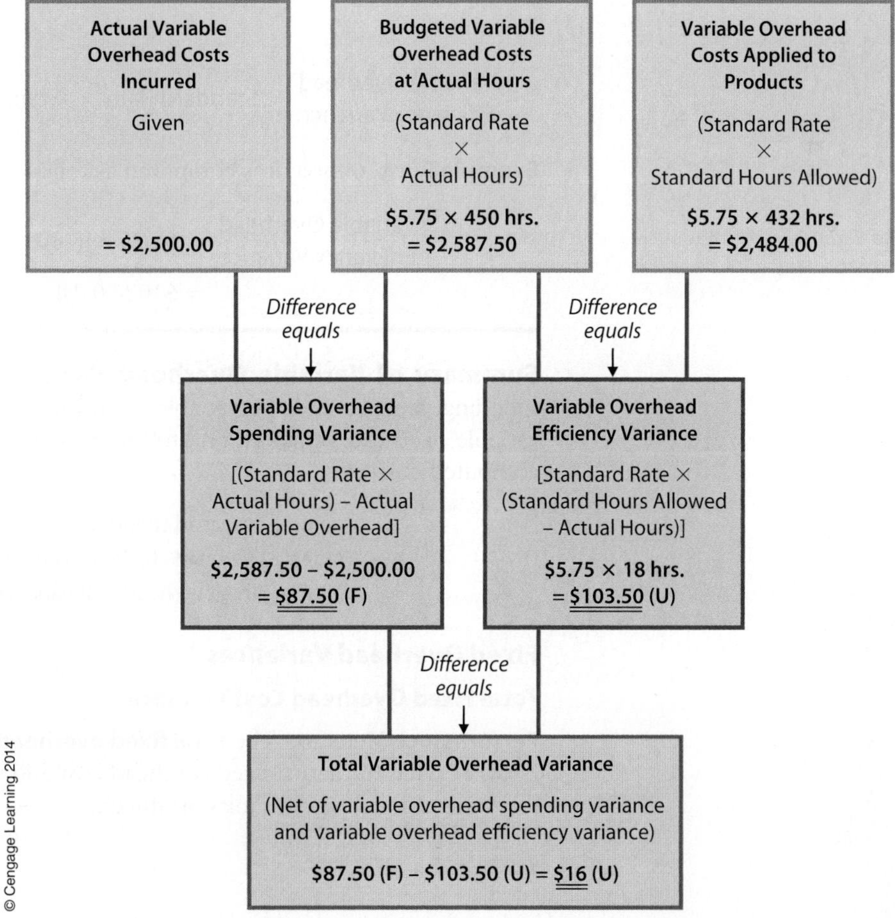

For effective performance evaluation, managers must know how much of the total cost arose from variable overhead spending deviations and how much from variable overhead application deviations (i.e., applied and actual direct labor hours). This information is found by computing the variable overhead spending variance and the variable overhead efficiency variance.

Computing Variable Overhead Spending Variance

Variable Overhead Spending Variance

Performance Measure The **variable overhead spending variance** (or *variable overhead rate variance*) measures the difference between what variable overhead actually cost and what it should have cost according to the flexible budget standard.

Formula

$$\text{Variable Overhead Spending Variance} = (\text{Standard Rate} \times \text{Actual Hours}) - \text{Actual Variable Overhead Cost}$$

Example For Cambria, it is computed as follows:

$$\text{Variable Overhead Spending Variance} = (\$5.75 \times 450 \text{ hours}) - \$2,500$$
$$= \underline{\underline{\$87.50}} \text{ (F)}$$

Computing Variable Overhead Efficiency Variance

Variable Overhead Efficiency Variance

Performance Measure The **variable overhead efficiency variance** measures the difference between the labor hours actually worked to make the product and the labor hours that should have been worked to produce the number of products made.

Formula

$$\text{Variable Overhead Efficiency Variance} = \text{Standard Rate} \times (\text{Standard Hours Allowed} - \text{Actual Hours})$$

Example For Cambria, it is computed as follows.

$$\text{Variable Overhead Efficiency Variance} = \$5.75 \times [(180 \text{ bags} \times 2.4 \text{ hours}) - 450 \text{ hours}]$$
$$= \underline{\underline{\$103.50}} \text{ (U)}$$

Summary of Variable Overhead Variances The net of the variable overhead spending variance and the variable overhead efficiency variance should equal the total variable overhead variance. The following check shows that these variances have been computed correctly:

Variable overhead spending variance	$ 87.50 (F)
Variable overhead efficiency variance	103.50 (U)
Total variable overhead cost variance	$ 16.00 (U)

Fixed Overhead Variances

Total Fixed Overhead Cost Variance

Performance Measure The **total fixed overhead cost variance** measures the difference between what the actual fixed overhead cost and what was applied according to the flexible budget for the good units produced.

Formula

$$\text{Total Fixed Overhead Cost Variance} = \text{Fixed Overhead Applied*} - \text{Actual Fixed Overhead}$$

*Fixed Overhead Applied = Standard Rate × Standard Hours for the Good Units Produced

STUDY NOTE: *The procedure for finding the total fixed overhead cost variance differs from the procedure used for finding direct materials, direct labor, and variable overhead variances.*

Example At Cambria, each bag requires 2.4 standard direct labor hours, and the standard fixed overhead rate is $3.25 per direct labor hour. As we noted earlier, the standard fixed overhead rate is found by dividing budgeted fixed overhead ($1,300) by normal capacity, which was set by the master budget at the beginning of the period. In this case, because normal capacity is 400 direct labor hours, the fixed overhead rate is $3.25 per direct labor hour ($1,300 ÷ 400 hours). For the month, Cambria incurred $1,600 of actual fixed overhead costs. The total fixed overhead variance is computed as follows.

Fixed overhead applied: $3.25 per hour × (180 bags × 2.4 hours per bag) = $1,404
Total fixed overhead variance: $1,404 – $1,600 = $196 (U)

Exhibit 7 shows an analysis of Cambria's fixed overhead variances.

Exhibit 7
Diagram of Fixed Overhead Variance Analysis

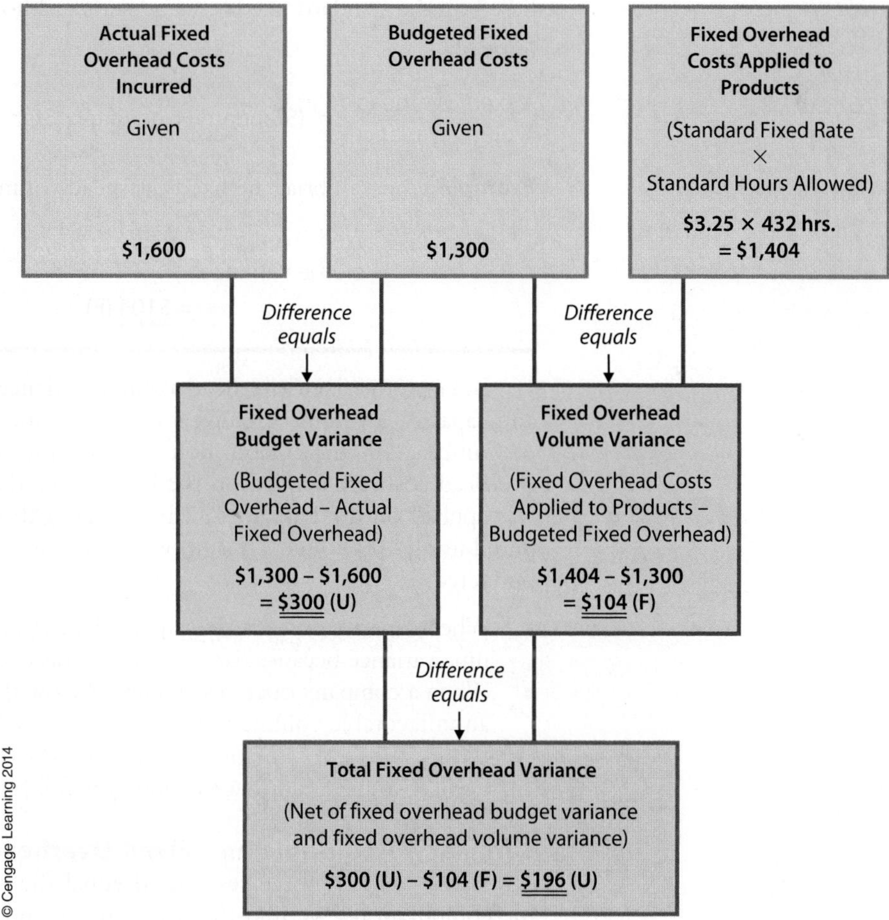

For effective performance evaluation, managers break down the total fixed overhead cost variance into two additional variances: the fixed overhead budget variance and the fixed overhead volume variance.

Computing Fixed Overhead Budget Variance

Fixed Overhead Budget Variance

Performance Measure The **fixed overhead budget variance** (or *budgeted fixed overhead variance*) measures the difference between what fixed overhead actually cost and what was budgeted.

Formula

$$\text{Fixed Overhead Budget Variance} = \text{Budgeted Fixed Overhead} - \text{Actual Fixed Overhead}$$

Example For Cambria, it is computed as follows.

$$\text{Fixed Overhead Budget Variance} = \$1{,}300 - \$1{,}600 = \underline{\underline{\$300}}\text{ (U)}$$

Computing Fixed Overhead Volume Variance

Fixed Overhead Volume Variance

Performance Measure The **fixed overhead volume variance** measures the difference between budgeted fixed overhead costs and the fixed overhead costs applied to products based on the standard fixed rate and standard hours allowed.

Formula

$$\text{Fixed Overhead Volume Variance} = (\text{Standard Fixed Rate} \times \text{Standard Hours Allowed}) - \text{Budgeted Fixed Overhead}$$

Example For Cambria, the fixed overhead volume variance is computed as follows.

$$\text{Fixed Overhead Volume Variance} = [\$3.25 \times (180\text{ bags} \times 2.4\text{ hours})] - \$1{,}300$$
$$= \underline{\underline{\$104}}\text{ (F)}$$

Because the fixed overhead volume variance measures the use of existing facilities and capacity, a volume variance will occur if more or less than normal capacity is used. At Cambria, 400 direct labor hours are considered normal use of facilities. Because fixed overhead costs are applied on the basis of standard hours allowed, Cambria's overhead was applied on the basis of 432 hours, even though the fixed overhead rate was computed using 400 hours. Thus, more fixed costs would be applied to products than were budgeted.

- When capacity exceeds the expected amount, the result is a favorable overhead volume variance because fixed overhead was overapplied.
- When a company operates at a level below the normal capacity in units, the result is an unfavorable volume variance. Not all of the fixed overhead costs will be applied to units produced. In other words, fixed overhead is underapplied, and the cost of goods produced does not include the full budgeted cost of fixed overhead.

Summary of Variable and Fixed Overhead Variances The net of the variable and fixed overhead variances should equal the total overhead cost variance. Checking the computations, we find that the variable and fixed overhead variances do equal the total overhead cost variance:

Variable overhead spending variance	$ 87.50 (F)
Variable overhead efficiency variance	103.50 (U)
Fixed overhead budget variance	300.00 (U)
Fixed overhead volume variance	104.00 (F)
Total overhead cost variance	$212.00 (U)

Exhibits 6 and 7 summarize the analysis of overhead varia
cost variance is also the amount of overapplied or underappli
actual variable and fixed overhead costs are recorded as they
fixed overhead are applied to products as they are produced, ar
underapplied overhead is computed and reconciled at the end
ing down the total overhead cost variance into its variable and
agers can more accurately control costs and reconcile their ca
two overhead variances will help explain why the amount of overhead applied to units produced is different from the actual overhead costs incurred.

Business Application

In analyzing the unfavorable total overhead cost variance of $212, the manager of Cambria's Bag Assembly Department found the following causes for the variances that contributed to it.

- Although the variable overhead spending variance was favorable ($87.50 less than expected because of savings on purchases), the inefficiency of the machine operator who substituted for an assembly worker created unfavorable variances for both direct labor efficiency and variable overhead efficiency. As a result, the manager is going to consider the feasibility of implementing a program for cross-training employees.
- After reviewing the fixed overhead costs, the Bag Assembly Department's manager concluded that higher-than-anticipated factory insurance premiums were the reason for the unfavorable fixed overhead budget variance and were the result of an increase in the number of insurance claims filed by employees. To obtain more specific information, the manager will study the insurance claims filed over a three-month period.
- Finally, since the 432 standard hours were well above the normal capacity of 400 direct labor hours, fixed overhead was overapplied, and it resulted in a $104 (F) volume variance. The overutilization of capacity was traced to high demand that pressed the company to use almost all its capacity. Management decided not to do anything about the fixed overhead volume variance because it fell within an anticipated seasonal range.

APPLY IT!

Sutherland Products uses standard costing. The following information about overhead was generated during August:

Standard variable overhead rate	$2 per machine hour
Standard fixed overhead rate	$3 per machine hour
Actual variable overhead costs	$443,200
Actual fixed overhead costs	$698,800
Budgeted fixed overhead costs	$700,000
Standard machine hours per unit produced	12
Good units produced	18,940
Actual machine hours	228,400

Compute the variable overhead spending and efficiency variances and the fixed overhead budget and volume variances using formulas or diagram form.

(Continued)

LUTION

Using formulas:

Variable Overhead Spending Variance = (Standard Rate × Actual Hours) − Actual Variable Overhead Cost
= ($2 × 228,400 hours) − $443,200
= $13,600 (F)

Variable Overhead Efficiency Variance = Standard Rate × (Standard Hours Allowed − Actual Hours)
= $2 × [(18,940 × 12) − 228,400 hours]
= $2,240 (U)

Fixed Overhead Budget Variance = Budgeted Fixed Overhead − Actual Fixed Overhead
= $700,000 − $698,800
= $1,200 (F)

Fixed Overhead Volume Variance = (Standard Rate × Standard Hours Allowed) − Budgeted Fixed Overhead
= [$3 × (18,940 × 12)] − $700,000
= $18,160 (U)

In diagram form:

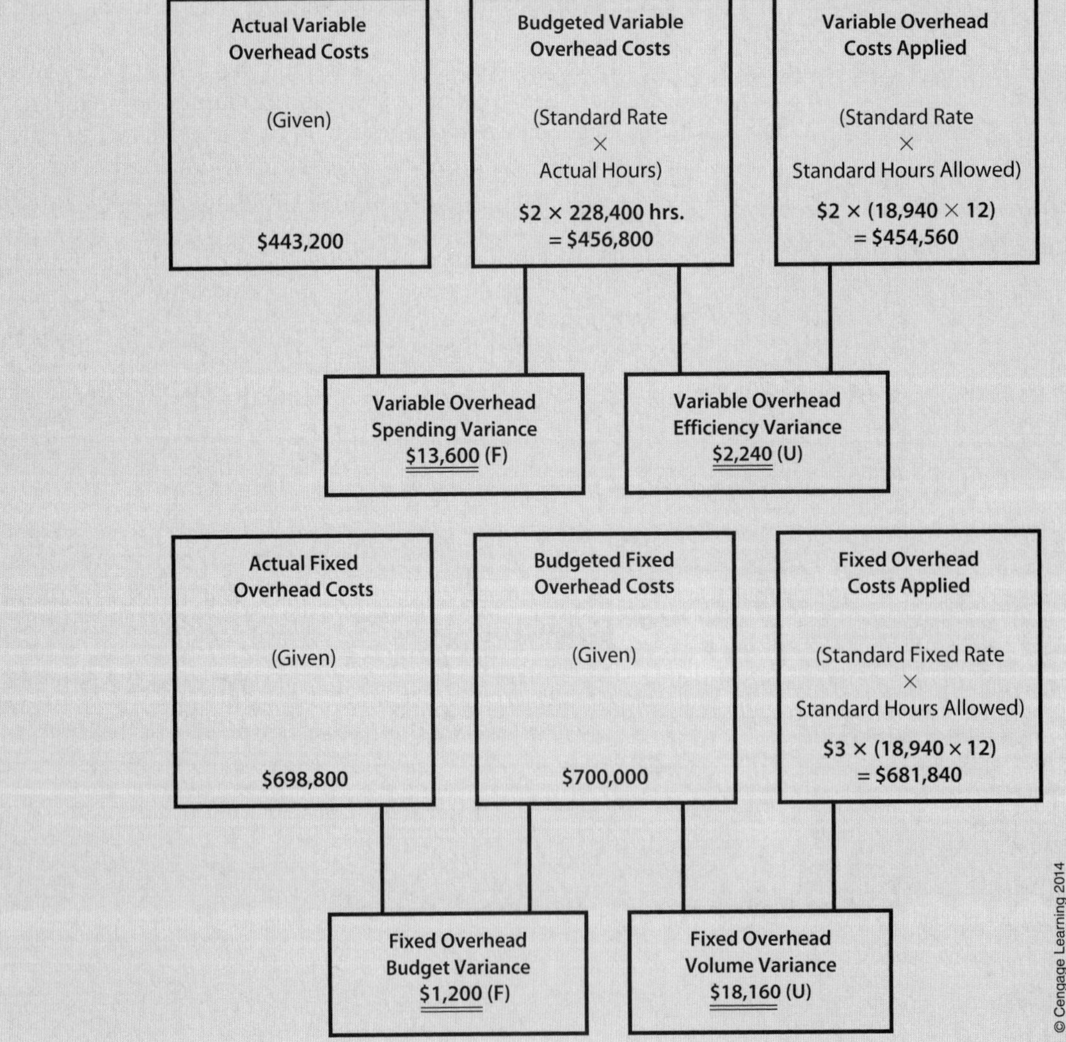

TRY IT! SE8, SE9, E9A, E10A, E11A, E12A, E13A, E14A, E9B, E10B, E11B, E12B, E13B, E14B

SECTION 3 BUSINESS APPLICATIONS

SINESS
PLICATIONS
Planning
Performing
Evaluating
Communicating

EVANT
ARNING OBJECTIVE

6 Explain how variances are used to evaluate a iness's performance.

LO 6 Using Cost Variances to Evaluate Managers' Performance

To ensure that the evaluation of a business's performance is effective and fair, a company's policies should be based on input from managers and employees and should specify the procedures that managers are to use when doing the following:

- Preparing operational plans
- Assigning responsibility for carrying out the operational plans
- Communicating the operational plans to key personnel
- Evaluating performance in each area of responsibility
- Identifying the causes of significant variances from the operational plan
- Taking corrective action to eliminate problems

Exhibit 8 frames these manager responsibilities for standard costing and variance analysis within the management process of planning, performing, evaluating and reporting on cost center operations.

Exhibit 8
Variance Analysis and The Management Process

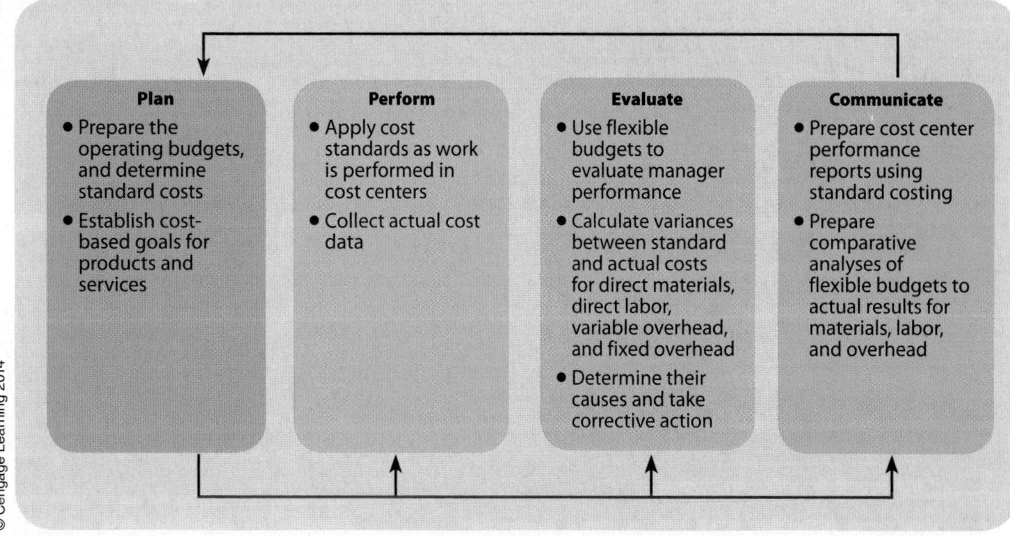

Variance analysis is usually more effective at pinpointing efficient and inefficient operating areas than are basic comparisons of budgeted and actual data. A managerial performance report based on standard costs and related variances should identify the causes of each significant variance, the personnel involved, and the corrective actions taken. It should be tailored to the cost center manager's specific areas of responsibility and explain clearly how the manager's department met or did not meet operating expectations. Managers should be held accountable only for the cost areas under their control.

Exhibit 9 shows a performance report for the manager of Cambria's Bag Assembly Department. The report summarizes all cost data and variances for direct materials, direct labor, and overhead. In addition, it identifies the causes of the variances and the corrective actions taken.

Exhibit 9
Managerial Performance Report Using Variance Analysis

Cambria Company
Managerial Performance Report—Bag Assembly Department
For the Month Ended August 31

Productivity Summary:

Normal capacity in units	167 bags
Normal capacity in direct labor hours (DLH)	400* DLH
Good units produced (actual)	180 bags
Performance level (standard hours allowed for good units produced)	432 DLH

*Rounded

Cost and Variance Analysis:

	Standard Costs	Actual Costs	Total Variance	Variance Breakdown Amount	Variance Breakdown Type
Direct materials	$ 4,320	$ 4,484	$164 (U)	$ 76.00 (F)	Direct materials price variance
				240.00 (U)	Direct materials quantity variance
Direct labor	3,672	4,140	468 (U)	315.00 (U)	Direct labor rate variance
				153.00 (U)	Direct labor efficiency variance
Variable overhead	2,484	2,500	16 (U)	87.50 (F)	Variable overhead spending variance
				103.50 (U)	Variable overhead efficiency variance
Fixed overhead	1,404	1,600	196 (U)	300.00 (U)	Fixed overhead budget variance
				104.00 (F)	Fixed overhead volume variance
Totals	$11,880	$12,724	$844 (U)	$844.00 (U)	

Causes of Variances	Actions Taken
Direct materials price variance:	
New direct materials purchased at reduced price	New direct materials deemed inappropriate; resumed purchasing materials originally specified
Direct materials quantity variance:	
Poor quality of new direct materials	New direct materials deemed inappropriate; resumed using direct materials originally specified
Direct labor rate variance:	
Machine operator who had to learn assembly	Temporary replacement; no action taken on the job skills
Direct labor efficiency variance:	
Machine operator who had to learn assembly	Temporary replacement; no action taken on the job skills
Late delivery of parts to assembly floor	Material delivery times and number of delays being tracked
Variable overhead spending variance:	
Cost savings on purchases	No action necessary
Variable overhead efficiency variance:	
Machine operator who had to learn assembly	A cross-training program for employees is under consideration
Fixed overhead budget variance:	
Large number of factory insurance claims	Study of insurance claims being conducted
Fixed overhead volume variance:	
High number of orders caused by demand	No action necessary

Remember that the mere occurrence of a variance does not indicate that a manager of a cost center has performed poorly. However, if a variance occurs consistently, and no cause is identified and no corrective action is taken, it may well indicate poor managerial performance. Exhibit 9 shows that the causes of the variances have been identified and corrective actions are being taken, indicating that the manager of Cambria's Bag Assembly Department has the operation under control.

APPLY IT!

Jayson Dunn, the production manager at Sample Industries, recently received his performance report from the company's controller. The report contained the following information:

	Actual Cost	Standard Cost	Variance
Direct materials	$38,200	$36,600	$1,600 (U)
Direct labor	19,450	19,000	450 (U)
Variable overhead	62,890	60,000	2,890 (U)

The controller asked Dunn to respond to his performance report. Help Dunn prepare his response by deciding whether the following statements are true or false. If false, make the statement true.

1. Dunn is responsible for all the variances listed on his performance report.
2. Before Dunn can answer the controller's query, the total variances given to him need to be broken down into their component parts. Then, and only then, will Dunn find out how well or poorly he performed.

SOLUTION

1. False
   Dunn is responsible only for the direct materials quantity variance, the direct labor efficiency variance, and the variable overhead efficiency variance listed on his performance report.
2. True

TRY IT! SE10, E15A, E15B

TriLevel Problem

Vaughn Youtz/Newscom

iRobot Corporation

The beginning of this chapter focused on **iRobot Corporation**, a manufacturer of robots for military, industrial, and home use. Complete the following requirements in order to answer the questions posed at the beginning of the chapter.

Section 1: Concepts

Why is standard costing and variance analysis useful?

Section 2: Accounting Applications

How can iRobot's managers evaluate the performance of its cost centers? Assume iRobot has begun producing carrier bags for its robots. Suppose these high-quality, heavy-duty bags are made in a single cost center using a standard costing system. Assume the standard variable costs for one bag (a unit) are as follows.

Direct materials (3 sq. meters @ $12.50 per sq. meter)	$37.50
Direct labor (1.2 hours @ $9.00 per hour)	10.80
Variable overhead (1.2 hours @ $5.00 per direct labor hour)	6.00
Total standard variable cost per unit	$54.30

The center's master budget was based on its normal capacity of 15,000 direct labor hours. Its budgeted fixed overhead costs for the year were $54,000. During the year, the company produced and sold 12,200 bags, and it purchased and used 37,500 square meters of direct materials; the purchase cost was $12.40 per square meter. The average labor rate was $9.20 per hour, and 15,250 direct labor hours were worked. The center's actual variable overhead costs for the year were $73,200, and its fixed overhead costs were $55,000.

Using the data given, compute the following using formulas or diagram form:

1. Standard hours allowed for good output
2. Standard fixed overhead rate
3. Direct materials cost variances:
   (a) Direct materials price variance
   (b) Direct materials quantity variance
   (c) Total direct materials cost variance
4. Direct labor cost variances:
   (a) Direct labor rate variance
   (b) Direct labor efficiency variance
   (c) Total direct labor cost variance
5. Variable overhead cost variances:
   (a) Variable overhead spending variance
   (b) Variable overhead efficiency variance
   (c) Total variable overhead cost variance
6. Fixed overhead cost variances:
   (a) Fixed overhead budget variance
   (b) Fixed overhead volume variance
   (c) Total fixed overhead cost variance

Section 3: Business Applications

Why does the setting of performance standards help managers control costs and improve performance? To answer this question, match this chapter's manager responsibilities with when they occur within the management process.

a. Plan	1. Prepare operating budgets
b. Perform	2. Apply cost standards as work is performed in cost centers
c. Evaluate	3. Establish product and service cost goals
d. Communicate	4. Collect actual cost data
	5. Determine standard costs
	6. Calculate variances
	7. Use flexible budgets to evaluate performance
	8. Prepare comparative reports using flexible budgets
	9. Determine cause of variances and take corrective action
	10. Prepare cost center performance reports using standard costing

SOLUTION

Section 1: Concepts

Managers find standard costing and variance analysis useful because they enhance *comparability* and *understandability*. When evaluating cost centers, managers use standard costs to prepare a flexible budget, which will improve the accuracy of their cost comparisons and variance analysis. This comparison of actual costs and a budget based on the same amount of output can provide managers with understandable objective data that they can use to assess the center's performance in terms of its key success factor—cost. By analyzing variances between standard and actual costs, they gain insight into the causes of those differences. Once they understand the operating problem that is causing a cost variance, they can devise a solution that results in better control of costs.

Section 2: Accounting Applications

1. Standard Hours Allowed = Good Units Produced × Standard Direct Labor Hours per Unit
   = 12,200 units × 1.2 hours
   = 14,640 hours

2. Standard Fixed Overhead Rate $= \dfrac{\text{Budgeted Fixed Overhead Cost}}{\text{Normal Capacity}}$

   $= \dfrac{\$54{,}000}{\text{15,000 Direct Labor Hours}}$

   = $3.60 per Direct Labor Hour

3. Direct Materials Cost Variances:
   Using formulas:

   (a) Direct Materials Price Variance = (Standard Price – Actual Price) × Actual Quantity
   = ($12.50 – 12.40) × 37,500 sq. meters
   = $3,750 (F)

   (b) Direct Materials Quantity Variance = Standard Price × (Standard Quantity Allowed – Actual Quantity)
   = $12.50 × [(12,200 × 3) – 37,500]
   = $11,250 (U)

   (c) Total Direct Materials Cost Variance = Direct Materials Price Variance + Direct Materials Quantity Variance
   = $3,750 (F) + $11,250 (U)
   = $7,500 (U)

In diagram form:

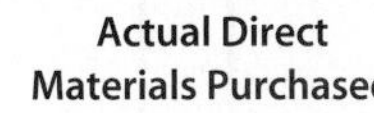

Actual Direct Materials Purchased	Materials Inventory	Work in Process Inventory
(Actual Price × Actual Quantity)	(Standard Price × Actual Quantity)	(Standard Price × Standard Quantity)
$12.40 × 37,500 = $465,000	**$12.50 × 37,500 = $468,750**	**$12.50 × (12,200 × 3) = $457,500**

(a) Direct Materials Price Variance	(b) Direct Materials Quantity Variance
$3,750 (F)	**$11,250 (U)**

(c) Total Direct Materials Cost Variance
$7,500 (U)

4. Direct Labor Cost Variances:

Using formulas:

(a) Direct Labor Rate Variance = (Standard Rate – Actual Rate) × Actual Hours

= ($9.00 – $9.20) × 15,250 hours

= $3,050 (U)

(b) Direct Labor Efficiency Variance = Standard Rate × (Standard Hours Allowed – Actual Hours)

= $9.00 × [(12,200 units produced × 1.2 hours) – 15,250]

= $5,490 (U)

(c) Total Direct Labor Cost Variance = Direct Labor Rate Variance + Direct Labor Efficiency Variance

= $3,050 (U) + $5,490 (U)

= $8,540 (U)

In diagram form:

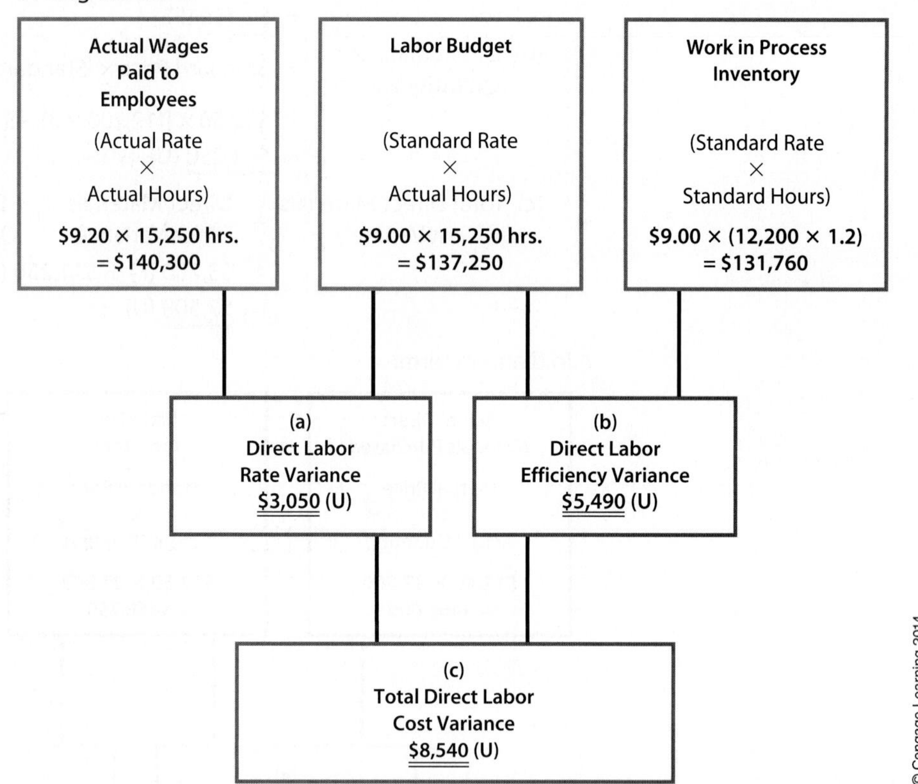

5. Variable Overhead Cost Variances:
   Using formulas:

   (a) Variable Overhead Spending Variance = (Standard Rate × Actual Hours) − Actual Variable Overhead Cost
   = (\$5 × 15,250) − \$73,200
   = \$3,050 (F)

   (b) Variable Overhead Efficiency Variance = Standard Rate × (Standard Hours Allowed − Actual Hours)
   = \$5 × [(12,200 units produced × 1.2 hours) − 15,250 hours]
   = \$3,050 (U)

   (c) Total Variable Overhead Cost Variance = Variable Overhead Spending Variance + Variable Overhead Efficiency Variance
   = \$3,050 (F) + \$3,050 (U)
   = \$0

In diagram form:

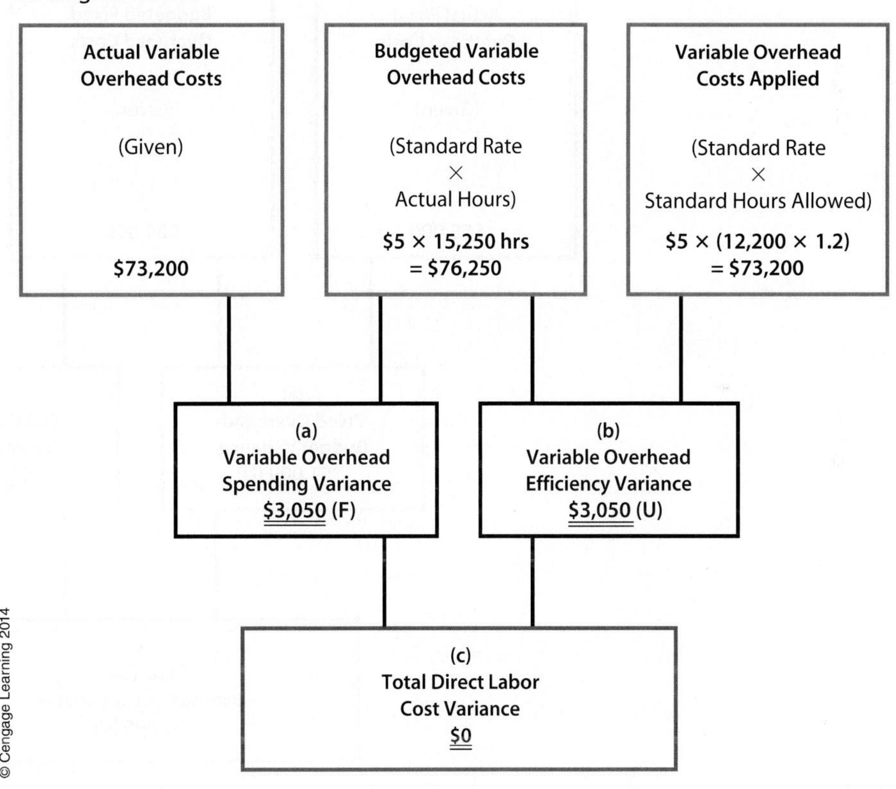

6. Fixed Overhead Cost Variances:
   Using formulas:

   (a) Fixed Overhead Budget Variance = Budgeted Fixed Overhead − Actual Fixed Overhead
   = $54,000 – $55,000
   = $1,000 (U)

   (b) Fixed Overhead Volume Variance = (Standard Rate × Standard Hours Allowed) − Budgeted Fixed Overhead
   = [$3.60 × (12,200 units produced × 1.2)] – $54,000
   = $1,296 (U)

   (c) Total Fixed Overhead Cost Variance = Fixed Overhead Budget Variance + Fixed Overhead Volume Variance
   = $1,000 (U) + $1,296 (U)
   = $2,296 (U)

In diagram form:

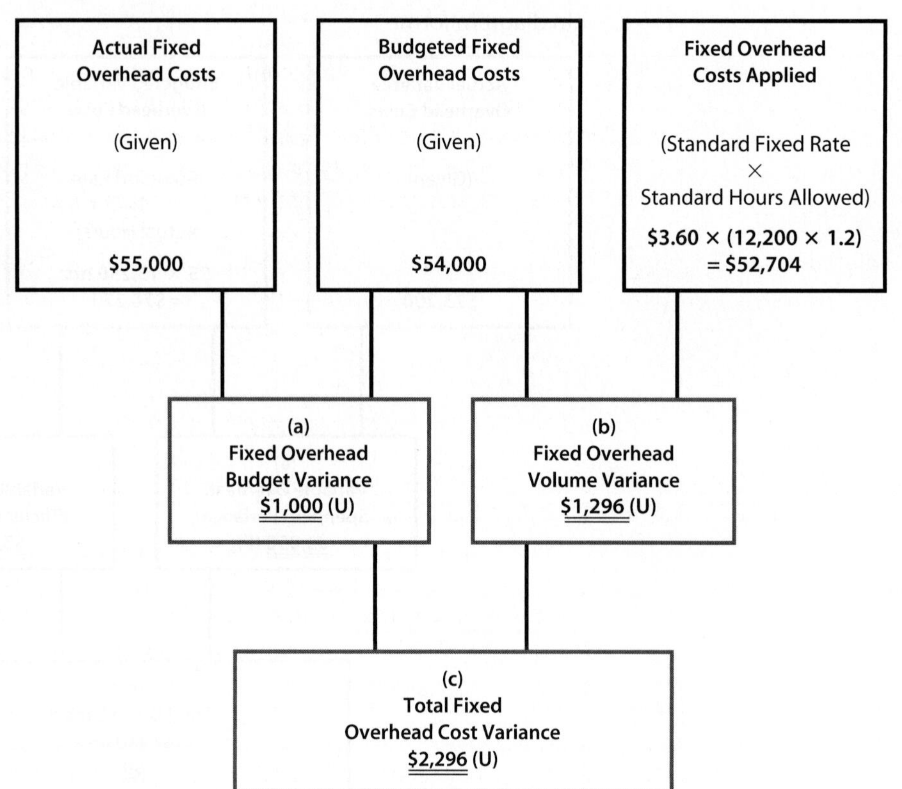

Section 3: Business Applications

1. a
2. b
3. a
4. b
5. a
6. c
7. c
8. d
9. c
10. d

Chapter Review

Define *standard costs*, and explain why standard costing is useful. LO 1

Standard costs are realistic estimates of costs based on analyses of both past and projected operating costs and conditions. They provide an understandable standard, or predetermined, performance level for use in standard costing, which includes a comparison measure of the variance between standard and actual performance.

Compute standard unit costs, and describe the role of flexible budgets in variance analysis to control costs. LO 2

A standard unit cost has six elements. A total standard unit cost is computed by adding the following costs: direct materials costs (direct materials price standard times direct materials quantity standard), direct labor costs (direct labor rate standard times direct labor time standard), and overhead costs (standard variable and standard fixed overhead rates times standard direct labor hours allowed per unit). Standard unit costs are used to develop a flexible budget. A flexible budget is a summary of anticipated costs for a range of activity levels. It provides forecasted cost data that can be adjusted for changes in level of output. The variable cost per unit and total fixed costs presented in a flexible budget are components of the flexible budget formula, which determines the budgeted cost for any level of output. A flexible budget improves the accuracy of variance analysis, which is a four-step approach to controlling costs. First, managers compute the amount of the variance. If the amount is significant, managers then analyze the variance to identify its cause. They then select performance measures that will enable them to track those activities, analyze the results, and determine the action needed to correct the problem. Their final step is to take the appropriate corrective action.

Compute and analyze direct materials variances. 

The direct materials price variance is computed by finding the difference between the standard price and the actual price per unit and multiplying it by the actual quantity purchased. The direct materials quantity variance is the difference between the standard quantity that should have been used and the actual quantity used, multiplied by the standard price. An analysis of these variances enables managers to identify what is causing them and to formulate plans for correcting related operating problems.

Compute and analyze direct labor variances. LO 4

The direct labor rate variance is computed by determining the difference between the standard direct labor rate and the actual rate and multiplying it by the actual direct labor hours worked. The direct labor efficiency variance is the difference between the standard hours allowed for the number of good units produced and the actual hours worked multiplied by the standard direct labor rate. Managers analyze these variances to find the causes of differences between standard direct labor costs and actual direct labor costs.

Compute and analyze overhead variances. 

The total overhead variance is equal to the amount of under- or overapplied overhead costs for an accounting period. An analysis of the variable and fixed overhead variances will help explain why the amount of overhead applied to units produced differs from the actual overhead costs incurred. The total overhead cost variance can be broken down into a variable overhead spending variance, a variable overhead efficiency variance, a fixed overhead budget variance, and a fixed overhead volume variance.

Explain how variances are used to evaluate a business's performance. LO 6

To ensure that performance evaluation is effective and fair, a company's evaluation policies should be based on input from managers and employees and should be specific about the procedures that managers are to follow. The evaluation process becomes more accurate when performance reports for cost centers include variances from standard costs. A performance report based on standard costs and related variances should identify the causes of each significant variance, along with the personnel involved and the corrective actions taken. It should be tailored to the cost center manager's specific areas of responsibility.

Key Terms

direct labor efficiency variance 1007 (LO4)
direct labor rate standard 1000 (LO2)
direct labor rate variance 1007 (LO4)
direct labor time standard 1000 (LO2)
direct materials price standard 999 (LO2)
direct materials price variance 1004 (LO3)
direct materials quantity standard 999 (LO2)
direct materials quantity variance 1004 (LO3)
fixed overhead budget variance 1014 (LO5)
fixed overhead volume variance 1014 (LO5)
standard costing 998 (LO1)
standard costs 998 (LO1)
standard direct labor cost 1000 (LO2)
standard direct materials cost 999 (LO2)
standard fixed overhead rate 1000 (LO2)
standard overhead cost 1000 (LO2)
standard variable overhead rate 1000 (LO2)
total direct labor cost variance 1007 (LO4)
total direct materials cost variance 1004 (LO3)
total fixed overhead cost variance 1012 (LO5)
total overhead cost variance 1010 (LO5)
total variable overhead cost variance 1011 (LO5)
variable overhead efficiency variance 1012 (LO5)
variable overhead spending variance 1012 (LO5)
variance 998 (LO1)
variance analysis 999 (LO2)

Chapter Assignments

DISCUSSION QUESTIONS

LO 1, 2 **DQ1. CONCEPT ▶** Describe how the six elements of a standard unit cost increase cost comparability and understandability.

LO 2 **DQ2.** What role do flexible budgets play in improving the understanding of variance analysis?

LO 2, 3, 4, 5 **DQ3.** Why does the four-step process of variance analysis enhance a cost center's ability to control costs?

LO 6 **DQ4. CONCEPT ▶ BUSINESS APPLICATION ▶** What should be included in a management report to further understandability and comparability when evaluating a cost center?

LO 6 **DQ5. CONCEPT ▶ BUSINESS APPLICATION ▶** Why does the use of standard costing and variance analysis in the management process reinforce the concepts of comparability and understandability to better business performance?

SHORT EXERCISES

LO 1 **Standard Costing Concepts**

SE1. CONCEPT ▶ Columbus Corporation is considering adopting the standard costing method to enhance the understandability and comparability of accounting information. Prepare several reasons in support of why understandability and comparability will be enhanced.

LO 1 **Purposes of Standard Costs**

SE2. ACCOUNTING CONNECTION ▶ Suppose you are a management consultant and a client asks you the advantages and disadvantages of using standard costs in cost accounting systems. Prepare your response, listing the advantages and disadvantages of using standard costs.

LO 2

Computing a Standard Unit Cost

SE3. Using the information that follows, compute the total standard unit cost of Product WW+.

Direct materials quantity standard	1 pound per unit
Direct materials price standard	$10.00 per pound
Direct labor time standard	0.5 hour per unit
Direct labor rate standard	$12.00 per hour
Variable overhead rate standard	$6.00 per machine hour
Fixed overhead rate standard	$11.00 per machine hour
Machine hour standard	4 hours per unit

LO 2

Analyzing Cost Variances

SE4. ACCOUNTING CONNECTION ▶ Dancing Waters produces fountains. The company analyzes only variances that differ by more than 5 percent from the standard cost. The controller computed the following direct labor efficiency variances for May:

	Direct Labor Efficiency Variance	Standard Direct Labor Cost
Product 4	$1,200 (U)	$24,000
Product 6	3,200 (F)	42,800
Product 7	2,000 (U)	42,000
Product 9	1,600 (F)	34,000
Product 12	2,800 (U)	50,000

For each product, determine the variance as a percentage of the standard cost (round to one decimal place). Then identify the products for which variances should be analyzed and suggest possible causes for the variances.

LO 3

Direct Materials Variances

SE5. Clean Plate Company produces placemats. Each placemat calls for 0.2 meters of vinyl material; the material should cost $1 per meter. In June, the company manufactured and sold 100,000 placemats. During the month, it used 20,200 meters of vinyl material. The total cost of the material was $19,796. Compute the direct materials price and direct materials quantity variances for June.

LO 3

Direct Materials Variances

SE6. Using the standard unit costs that you computed in **SE3** and the actual cost and usage data that follow, compute the direct materials price and direct materials quantity variances.

Direct materials purchased and used (pounds)	21,800
Price paid for direct materials	$10.10 per pound
Number of good units produced	21,000 units

LO 4

Direct Labor Variances

SE7. Using the standard unit costs that you computed in **SE3** and the actual cost and usage data that follow, compute the direct labor rate and direct labor efficiency variances.

Direct labor hours used	11,000 hours
Total cost of direct labor	$134,200
Number of good units produced	21,000 units

LO 5 **Overhead Variances**

SE8. Meanwhile Products uses standard costing. The following information about overhead was generated during August:

Standard variable overhead rate	$2.50 per machine hour
Standard fixed overhead rate	$3.00 per machine hour
Actual variable overhead costs	$60,100
Actual fixed overhead costs	$68,800
Budgeted fixed overhead costs	$70,000
Standard machine hours per unit produced	2.8
Good units produced	8,000
Actual machine hours	24,200

Compute the variable overhead spending and efficiency variances and the fixed overhead budget and volume variances.

LO 5 **Fixed Overhead Rate and Variances**

SE9. Point Manufacturing Company uses the standard costing method. The company's main product is a fine-quality pen that normally takes 5.1 hours to produce. Normal annual capacity is 20,000 direct labor hours, and budgeted fixed overhead costs for the year were $10,000. During the year, the company produced and sold 4,000 units. Actual fixed overhead costs were $10,200. Compute the fixed overhead rate per direct labor hour, and determine the fixed overhead budget and volume variances.

LO 6 **Evaluating Managerial Performance**

SE10. BUSINESS APPLICATION ▶ ZMT Products' controller gave the production manager a report containing the following information:

	Actual Cost	Standard Cost	Variance
Direct materials	$50,000	$48,200	$1,800 (U)
Direct labor	7,550	7,000	550 (U)
Variable overhead	52,000	50,000	2,000 (U)

The controller asked for a response. How would you respond? What additional information might you need to prepare your response?

EXERCISES: SET A

LO 1 **Uses of Standard Costs**

E1A. ACCOUNTING CONNECTION ▶ Asa Wentz, the new controller at Market Research Company, is concerned that the company's methods of cost control do not accurately track the operations of the business. She plans to suggest to Tyson Getz, the company's president, that the company start using standard costing for budgeting and cost control. The new method could be incorporated into the existing accounting system. The anticipated cost of adopting it and training managers is around $80,000. Prepare a memo from Wentz to Getz that defines standard costing and outlines its uses and benefits.

LO 2 **Computing Standard Costs**

E2A. Flossmoor Corporation uses standard costing and is in the process of updating its direct materials and direct labor standards for Product 2B. The following data have been accumulated:

Direct materials: In the previous period, 20,000 units were produced, and 32,000 square yards of direct materials at a cost of $128,000 were used to produce them.

Direct labor: In the previous period, 20,000 units were produced and 58,000 direct labor hours were worked—34,000 hours on machine H and 24,000 hours on machine K. Machine H operators earned $10 per hour, and machine K operators earned $9 per hour last period. A new labor union contract calls for a 10 percent increase in labor rates for the coming period.

Using this information as the basis for the new standards, compute the direct materials quantity and price standards and the direct labor time and rate standards for each machine for the coming accounting period.

LO 2 **Computing a Total Standard Unit Cost**

E3A. Weather Balloons, Inc., makes reusable weather-detecting balloons. Because of a recent recession, management has ordered that standard costs be recomputed. New direct materials price standards are $600 per set for electronic components and $13 per square meter for heavy-duty canvas. Direct materials quantity standards include one set of electronic components and 100 square meters of heavy-duty canvas per balloon. Direct labor time standards are 26 hours per balloon for the Electronics Department and 21 hours per balloon for the Assembly Department. Direct labor rate standards are $20 per hour for the Electronics Department and $15 per hour for the Assembly Department. Standard overhead rates are $18 per direct labor hour for the standard variable overhead rate and $10 per direct labor hour for the standard fixed overhead rate. Compute the total standard unit cost of one weather balloon.

LO 3 **Direct Materials Price and Quantity Variances**

E4A. Natural Company produces organic twig brooms. Each broom calls for 1 pound of wood; the wood should cost $0.25 per pound. In July, the division manufactured and sold 500,000 brooms. During the month, it used 495,000 pounds of wood, and the total cost of the material was $128,700. Normal monthly capacity was set at 580,000 brooms. Calculate Natural's material price and quantity variances for wood for the month.

LO 3 **Direct Materials Price and Quantity Variances**

E5A. LIFT Elevator Company manufactures small hydroelectric elevators. One of the direct materials used is heavy-duty carpeting for the floor of the elevator. The direct materials quantity standard for May was 6 square yards per elevator. During May, the purchasing agent purchased this carpeting at $20 per square yard; the standard price for the period was $22. Fifty elevators were completed and sold during the month; the Production Department used an average of 6.5 square yards of carpet per elevator. Calculate the company's direct materials price and quantity variances for carpeting for May.

LO 3 **Direct Materials Variances**

E6A. Creative Productions manufactured and sold 800 products at $10,000 each during the past year. At the beginning of the year, production had been set at 1,000 products, and direct materials standards had been set at 10 pounds of direct materials at $12 per pound for each product produced. During the year, the company purchased and used 7,900 pounds of direct materials with a cost of $12.02 per pound. Calculate the company's direct materials price and quantity variances for the year.

LO 4 **Direct Labor Variances**

E7A. At the beginning of last year, Creative Productions set direct labor standards of 2 hours at $25 per hour for each product produced. During the year, 1,700 direct labor hours were actually worked at an average cost of $26 per hour. Using this information and the applicable information in **E6A**, calculate the company's direct labor rate and efficiency variances for the year.

LO 4 **Direct Labor Rate and Efficiency Variances**

E8A. For the past two years, NE Company's best-selling product has been a titanium engine block. Standard direct labor hours per block are 2.0 hours. All direct labor employees are paid $24 per hour. During July, NE produced 16,000 blocks. Actual direct labor hours and costs for the month were 31,000 hours and $775,000, respectively.

1. Compute the direct labor rate variance for blocks during July.
2. Using the same data, compute the direct labor efficiency variance for engine blocks during July. Check your answer, assuming that the total direct labor cost variance is $7,000 (U).

LO 5 **Variable Overhead Variances**

E9A. At the beginning of last year, Creative Productions set variable overhead standards of 5 machine hours at a rate of $15 per hour for each product produced. During the year, 4,800 machine hours were used at a cost of $15.10 per hour. Using this information and the applicable information in **E6A**, calculate the company's variable overhead spending and efficiency variances for the year.

LO 5 **Fixed Overhead Variances**

E10A. At the beginning of last year, Creative Productions set budgeted fixed overhead costs at $46,000 and budgeted production at 1,000 products. During the year, actual fixed overhead costs were $50,000. Using this information and the applicable information in **E6A**, calculate the company's fixed overhead budget and volume variances for the year. Assume that fixed overhead is applied based on units of product.

LO 5 **Variable Overhead Variances for a Service Business**

E11A. MUF Architects, LLP, billed clients for 6,000 hours of design work for the month. Actual variable overhead costs for the month were $910,000, and 6,050 hours were worked. At the beginning of the year, a variable overhead standard of $150 per design hour had been developed based on a budget of 5,000 design hours each month. Calculate the company's variable overhead spending and efficiency variances for the month.

LO 5 **Fixed Overhead Variances for a Service Business**

E12A. Engineering Associates billed clients for 10,000 hours of engineering work for the month. Actual fixed overhead costs for the month were $1,450,000. At the beginning of the year, a fixed overhead standard of $140 per engineering hour had been developed based on a budget of 10,500 engineering hours each month. Calculate the company's fixed overhead budget and volume variances for the month.

LO 5 **Overhead Variances**

E13A. Quay Company produces handmade scallop buckets and sells them to distributors along Florida's Gulf Coast. The company incurred $10,500 of actual overhead costs ($9,500 variable; $1,000 fixed) in March. Budgeted standard overhead costs for March were $1 of variable overhead costs per direct labor hour and $1,200 of fixed overhead costs. Normal capacity was set at 10,000 direct labor hours per month. In March, the company produced 8,100 clamming buckets by working 9,000 direct labor hours. The time standard is 0.9 direct labor hour per bucket. Compute (a) the variable overhead spending and efficiency variances and (b) the fixed overhead budget and volume variances for March. (Round to the nearest dollar.)

LO 5 **Overhead Variances**

E14A. Goldencoast Industries uses standard costing and a flexible budget for cost planning and control. Its monthly budget for overhead costs is $100,000 of fixed costs plus $5 per machine hour. Monthly normal capacity of 100,000 machine hours is used to compute the standard fixed overhead rate. During the month, 104,000 machine hours were used. Only 102,500 standard machine hours were allowed for good units produced during the month. Actual overhead costs incurred during the month totaled $511,000 of variable costs and $94,500 of fixed costs. Compute (a) the under- or overapplied overhead for the month and (b) the variable overhead spending and efficiency variances and the fixed overhead budget and volume variances.

LO 6

Evaluating Managerial Performance

E15A. BUSINESS APPLICATION ▶ Layton Davis oversees projects for Pace Construction Company. Recently, the company's controller sent him a performance report regarding the construction of the Highlands Bank, a project that Davis supervised. Included in the report was an unfavorable direct labor efficiency variance of $900 for roof structures. What types of information does Davis need to analyze before he can respond to this report?

EXERCISES: SET B

Visit the textbook companion website at www.cengagebrain.com to access Exercise Set B for this chapter.

PROBLEMS

LO 2

SPREADSHEET

✔ 2: Total standard unit cost per entrance last year: $9,542

Computing and Using Standard Costs

P1. Modular houses are Homes, Inc.'s specialty. The company's best-selling model is a three-bedroom, 1,400-square-foot house with an impressive front entrance. Last year, the standard costs for the six basic direct materials used in manufacturing the entrance were as follows: wood framing materials, $2,140; deluxe front door, $480; door hardware, $260; exterior siding, $710; electrical materials, $580; and interior finishing materials, $1,520. Three types of direct labor are used to build the entrance: carpenter, 30 hours at $36 per hour; door specialist, 4 hours at $24 per hour; and electrician, 8 hours at $50 per hour. Last year, the company used an overhead rate of 40 percent of total direct materials cost.

This year, the cost of wood framing materials is expected to increase by 20 percent, and a deluxe front door will cost $496. The cost of the door hardware will increase by 10 percent, and the cost of electrical materials will increase by 20 percent. Exterior siding cost should decrease by $15 per unit. The cost of interior finishing materials is expected to remain the same. The carpenter's wages will increase by $1 per hour, and the door specialist's wages should remain the same. The electrician's wages will increase by $0.50 per hour. Finally, the overhead rate will decrease to 30 percent of total direct materials cost.

REQUIRED

1. Compute the total standard cost of direct materials per entrance for last year.
2. Using your answer to requirement **1**, compute the total standard unit cost per entrance for last year.
3. Compute the total standard unit cost per entrance for this year. (Round to the nearest dollar.)

LO 3, 4

✔ 1: Direct materials price variance, $1,204 (F)
✔ 1: Direct materials quantity variance, $6 (U)
✔ 2: Direct labor rate variance, $1,000 (U)
✔ 2: Direct labor efficiency variance, $108 (F)

Direct Materials and Direct Labor Variances

P2. Party Balloons Company produces mylar balloons. The company's direct materials standards for its deluxe balloon include 3 ounces of mylar. Standard prices for the year were $0.030 per ounce. Direct labor standards for the deluxe balloon specify 0.01 hour of direct labor at a standard direct labor rate of $18 per hour.

During January, the company made 200,600 deluxe balloons. Actual production data follow.

Direct materials	602,000 ounces @ $0.028 per ounce
Direct labor	2,000 hours @ $18.50 per hour

REQUIRED

1. Compute the direct materials price and quantity variances.
2. Compute the direct labor rate and efficiency variances.

LO 3, 4

Direct Materials and Direct Labor Variances

✔ 1: Wood: Direct materials price variance, $4,932 (U)
✔ 1: Wood: Direct materials quantity variance, $180 (U)
✔ 2: Molding: Direct labor rate variance, $680 (F)
✔ 2: Molding: Direct labor efficiency variance, $2,400 (U)

P3. Winners Trophy Company produces trophies. The company's direct materials standards for its deluxe trophy include 1 pound of metal and 10 ounces of wood for the base. Standard prices for the year were $3 per pound of metal and $0.45 per ounce of wood. Direct labor standards for the deluxe trophy specify 0.2 hour of direct labor in the Molding Department and 0.4 hour in the Trimming/Finishing Department. Standard direct labor rates are $20 per hour in the Molding Department and $18.00 per hour in the Trimming/Finishing Department.

During January, the company made 16,400 deluxe trophies. Actual production data follow.

Direct materials:	
Metal	16,640 pounds @ $2.95 per pound
Wood	164,400 ounces @ $0.48 per ounce
Direct labor:	
Molding	3,400 hours @ $19.80 per hour
Trimming/Finishing	6,540 hours @ $18.10 per hour

REQUIRED

1. Compute the direct materials price and quantity variances for metal and wood.
2. Compute the direct labor rate and efficiency variances for the Molding and Trimming/Finishing Departments.

LO 5

Overhead Variances

✔ b: Variable overhead efficiency variance, $1,000 (F)
✔ d: Normal capacity in machine hours, 17,000 hours
✔ f: Fixed overhead applied, $157,500

P4. Copa Corporation's accountant left for vacation before completing the monthly cost variance report. The corporation's president has asked you to complete the report. The following data are available (capacities are expressed in machine hours):

Actual machine hours	17,100
Standard machine hours allowed	17,500
Actual variable overhead	(a)
Standard variable overhead rate	$2.50
Variable overhead spending variance	$750 (F)
Variable overhead efficiency variance	(b)
Actual fixed overhead	(c)
Budgeted fixed overhead	$153,000
Fixed overhead budget variance	$1,300 (U)
Fixed overhead volume variance	$4,500 (F)
Normal capacity in machine hours	(d)
Standard fixed overhead rate	(e)
Fixed overhead applied	(f)

REQUIRED

Analyze the data and fill in the missing amounts. [*Hint:* Use the structure of Exhibits 6 and 7 to guide your analysis. Solve for (f) before solving for (e) and (d).]

LO 3, 4, 5, 6

Computing Variances and Evaluating Performance

SPREADSHEET

P5. Clean Sweep Company produces all-vinyl mats. Each doormat calls for 0.5 meter of vinyl material; the material should cost $3 per meter. Standard direct labor hours and labor cost per doormat are 0.3 hour and $6 (0.3 hour × $20 per hour), respectively. Currently, the division's standard variable overhead rate is $1.50 per direct labor hour, and its standard fixed overhead rate is $0.80 per direct labor hour.

✔ 1a: Direct materials price variance, $2,520 (F)
✔ 1d: Direct labor efficiency variance, $84,000 (F)
✔ 1e: Variable overhead spending variance, $2,000 (U)
✔ 1f: Variable overhead efficiency variance, $6,300 (F)
✔ 1g: Fixed overhead budget variance, $720 (U)
✔ 1h: Fixed overhead volume variance, $2,720 (F)

In August, the division manufactured and sold 50,000 doormats. During the month, it used 25,200 meters of vinyl material; the total cost of the material was $73,080. The total actual overhead costs for August were $28,200, of which $18,200 was variable. The total number of direct labor hours worked was 10,800, and the factory payroll for direct labor for the month was $214,920. Budgeted fixed overhead for August was $9,280. Normal monthly capacity for the year was set at 58,000 doormats.

REQUIRED

1. Compute for August the (a) direct materials price variance, (b) direct materials quantity variance, (c) direct labor rate variance, (d) direct labor efficiency variance, (e) variable overhead spending variance, (f) variable overhead efficiency variance, (g) fixed overhead budget variance, and (h) fixed overhead volume variance.
2. **BUSINESS APPLICATION ▶** Prepare a performance report based on your variance analysis, and suggest possible causes for each variance.

ALTERNATE PROBLEMS

LO 2

Computing Standard Costs for Direct Materials

SPREADSHEET

✔ 1: Total standard direct materials cost per unit for next year: $167.52

P6. BUSINESS APPLICATION ▶ Old Hands, Ltd., assembles clock movements for grandfather clocks. Each movement has four components: the clock facing, the clock hands, the time movement, and the spring assembly. For the current year, the company used the following standard costs: clock facing, $15.90; clock hands, $12.70; time movement, $66.10; and spring assembly, $52.50.

Prices of materials are expected to change next year. Old Hands will purchase 60 percent of the facings from Company A at $18.50 each and the other 40 percent from Company B at $18.80 each. The clock hands are purchased from Hardware, Inc., and will cost $15.50 per set next year. Old Hands will purchase 30 percent of the time movements from Company Q at $68.50 each, 20 percent from Company R at $69.50 each, and 50 percent from Company S at $71.90 each. The manufacturer that supplies Old Hands with spring assemblies has announced that it will increase its prices by 20 percent.

REQUIRED

1. Determine the total standard direct materials cost per unit for next year.
2. Suppose that because Old Hands has guaranteed Hardware that it will purchase 2,500 sets of clock hands next year, the cost of a set of clock hands has been reduced by 20 percent. Find the total standard direct materials cost per clock.
3. Suppose that to avoid the increase in the cost of spring assemblies, Old Hands purchased substandard ones from a different manufacturer at $50 each; 20 percent of them turned out to be unusable and could not be returned. Assuming that all other data remain the same, compute the total standard direct materials unit cost. Spread the cost of the defective materials over the good units produced.

LO 3, 4

Direct Materials and Direct Labor Variances

✔ 1: Direct materials price variance, $500.10 (U)
✔ 1: Direct materials quantity variance, $1.10 (U)
✔ 2: Direct labor rate variance, $1,995 (U)
✔ 2: Direct labor efficiency variance, $200 (F)

P7. Flat Cups Company produces collapsible beverage containers. The company's direct materials standards for its 16-ounce beverage bottle include 5 ounces of biodegradable plastic. Standard prices for the year were $0.011 per ounce. Direct labor standards for the beverage bottle specify 0.04 hours of direct labor at a standard direct labor rate of $20 per hour.

During January, the company made 100,000 16-ounce beverage bottles. Actual production data follow.

Direct materials	500,100 ounces @ $0.012 per ounce
Direct labor	3,990 hours @ $20.50 per hour

(Continued)

REQUIRED

1. Compute the direct materials price and quantity variances.
2. Compute the direct labor rate and efficiency variances.

LO 3, 4

Direct Materials and Direct Labor Variances

✔ 1: Material G: Direct materials price variance, $386 (F)
✔ 1: Material G: Direct materials quantity variance, $30 (U)
✔ 2: Molding: Direct labor rate variance, $96 (F)
✔ 2: Molding: Direct labor efficiency variance, $0

P8. Green Packaging Company makes plant-based baskets for food wholesalers. Each basket requires 0.8 gram of material G and 0.6 gram of an additive that includes color and hardening agents. The standard prices are $0.15 per gram of material G and $0.09 per gram of additive. Two kinds of direct labor—molding and trimming/packing—are required to make the baskets. The direct labor time and rate standards for a batch of 100 baskets are as follows: molding, 1.0 hour per batch at an hourly rate of $12; and trimming/packing, 1.2 hours per batch at $10 per hour.

During the year, the company produced 48,000 baskets. It used 38,600 grams of material G at a total cost of $5,404 and 28,950 grams of additive at $2,895. Actual direct labor included 480 hours for molding at a total cost of $5,664 and 560 hours for trimming/packing at $5,656.

REQUIRED

1. Compute the direct materials price and quantity variances for both material G and the additive.
2. Compute the direct labor rate and efficiency variances for the molding and trimming/packing processes.

LO 5

Overhead Variances

✔ b: Variable overhead efficiency variance, $800 (F)
✔ d: Normal capacity in machine hours, 20,400 hours
✔ f: Fixed overhead applied, $153,750

P9. Exact Corporation's accountant left for vacation before completing the monthly cost variance report. The corporation's president has asked you to complete the report. The following data are available (capacities are expressed in machine hours):

Actual machine hours	20,100
Standard machine hours allowed	20,500
Actual variable overhead	(a)
Standard variable overhead rate	$2.00
Variable overhead spending variance	$250 (F)
Variable overhead efficiency variance	(b)
Actual fixed overhead	(c)
Budgeted fixed overhead	$153,000
Fixed overhead budget variance	$500 (U)
Fixed overhead volume variance	$750 (F)
Normal capacity in machine hours	(d)
Standard fixed overhead rate	(e)
Fixed overhead applied	(f)

REQUIRED

Analyze the data and fill in the missing amounts. [*Hint:* Use the structure of Exhibits 6 and 7 to guide your analysis. Solve for (f) before solving for (e) and (d).]

LO 3, 4, 5, 6

SPREADSHEET

Computing Variances and Evaluating Performance

P10. Last year, Panacea Laboratories, Inc., researched and perfected a cure for the common cold. Called Cold-Gone, the product sells for $28.00 per package, each of which contains five tablets. Standard unit costs for this product were developed late last year for use this year. Per package, the standard unit costs were as follows: chemical ingredients, 6 ounces at $1.00 per ounce; packaging, $1.20; direct labor, 0.8 hour at $14.00 per hour; standard variable overhead, $4.00 per direct labor hour; and standard fixed overhead, $6.40 per direct labor hour. Normal capacity is 46,875 units per week.

✔ 1a: Chemicals direct materials price variance, $12,200 (F)
✔ 1d: Direct labor efficiency variance, $3,500 (U)
✔ 1e: Variable overhead spending variance, $100 (U)
✔ 1f: Variable overhead efficiency variance, $1,000 (U)
✔ 1g: Fixed overhead budget variance, $2,000 (U)
✔ 1h: Fixed overhead volume variance, $16,000 (F)

In the first quarter of this year, demand for the new product rose well beyond the expectations of management. During those three months, the peak season for colds, the company produced and sold over 500,000 packages of Cold-Gone. During the first week in April, it produced 50,000 packages but used materials for 50,200 packages costing $60,240. It also used 305,000 ounces of chemical ingredients costing $292,800. The total cost of direct labor for the week was $579,600; direct labor hours totaled 40,250. Total variable overhead was $161,100, and total fixed overhead was $242,000. Budgeted fixed overhead for the week was $240,000.

REQUIRED

1. Compute for the first week of April (a) all direct materials price variances, (b) all direct materials quantity variances, (c) the direct labor rate variance, (d) the direct labor efficiency variance, (e) the variable overhead spending variance, (f) the variable overhead efficiency variance, (g) the fixed overhead budget variance, and (h) the fixed overhead volume variance.
2. **BUSINESS APPLICATION ▶** Prepare a performance report based on your variance analysis, and suggest possible causes for each significant variance.

CASES

LO 2

Ethical Dilemma: An Ethical Question Involving Standard Costs

C1. Lopez Industries, Inc., develops standard costs for all its direct materials, direct labor, and overhead costs. It uses these costs to price products, cost inventories, and evaluate the performance of purchasing and production managers. It updates the standard costs whenever costs, prices, or rates change by 3 percent or more. It also reviews and updates all standard costs each December; this practice provides current standards that are appropriate for use in valuing year-end inventories on the company's financial statements.

Jaye Elgar is in charge of standard costing at Lopez. On November 30, she received a memo from the chief financial officer informing her that Lopez was considering purchasing another company and that she and her staff were to postpone adjusting standard costs until late February; they were instead to concentrate on analyzing the proposed purchase.

In the third week of November, prices on more than 20 of Lopez's direct materials had been reduced by 10 percent or more, and a new labor union contract had reduced several categories of labor rates. A revision of standard costs in December would have resulted in lower valuations of inventories, higher cost of goods sold because of inventory write-downs, and lower net income for the year. Elgar believed that the company was facing an operating loss and that the assignment to evaluate the proposed purchase was designed primarily to keep her staff from revising and lowering standard costs. She questioned the chief financial officer about the assignment and reiterated the need for updating the standard costs, but she was again told to ignore the update and concentrate on the proposed purchase. Elgar and her staff were relieved of the evaluation assignment in early February. The purchase never materialized.

Assess Elgar's actions in this situation. Did she follow all ethical paths to solving the problem? What are the consequences of failing to adjust the standard costs?

LO 1, 2

Group Activity: Standard Costs and Variance Analysis

C2. Domino's Pizza is a major purveyor of home-delivered pizzas. Although customers can pick up their orders at the shops where Domino's makes its pizzas, employees deliver most orders to customers' homes, and they use their own cars to do it.

Specify what standard costing for a Domino's pizza shop would entail. Where would you obtain the information for determining the cost standards? In what ways would the standards help in managing a pizza shop? If necessary to gain a better understanding of the operation, visit a pizzeria (it does not have to be a Domino's).

(Continued)

Your instructor will divide the class into groups to discuss the case. Summarize your group's discussion, and select one person from your group to report the group's findings to the class.

LO 2, 4, 5, 6

Business Communication: Preparing Performance Reports

C3. BUSINESS APPLICATION ▶ Terry Correy, Pine Valley Spa's president, is concerned about the spa's operating performance during March. He budgeted his costs carefully so that he could reduce the annual membership fees. He now needs to evaluate those costs to make sure that the spa's profits are at the level he expected.

He has asked you, the spa's controller, to prepare a performance report on labor and overhead costs for March. He also wants you to analyze the report and suggest possible causes for any problems that you find. He wants to attend to any problems quickly, so he has asked you to submit your report as soon as possible. The following information for the month is available:

	Budgeted Costs	Actual Costs
Variable costs:		
Operating labor	$10,880	$12,150
Utilities	2,880	3,360
Repairs and maintenance	5,760	7,140
Fixed overhead costs:		
Depreciation, equipment	2,600	2,680
Rent	3,280	3,280
Other	1,704	1,860
Totals	$27,104	$30,470

Correy's budget allows for eight employees to work 160 hours each per month. During March, nine employees worked an average of 150 hours each.

1. Answer the following questions:
   a. Why are you preparing this performance report?
   b. Who will use the report?
   c. What information do you need to develop the report? How will you obtain that information?
   d. When are the performance report and the analysis needed?
2. With the limited information available to you, compute the labor rate variance, the labor efficiency variance, and the variable and fixed overhead variances.
3. Prepare a performance report for the spa for March. Analyze the report, and suggest causes for any problems that you find.

LO 2, 5, 6

Decision Analysis: Developing a Flexible Budget and Analyzing Overhead Variances

C4. BUSINESS APPLICATION ▶ The controller at FT Industries has asked you, her new assistant, to analyze the following data related to projected and actual overhead costs for October:

Variable Overhead Costs	Standard Variable Costs per Machine Hour (MH)	Actual Variable Costs in October
Indirect materials and supplies	$1.10	$ 2,380
Indirect machine setup labor	2.50	5,090
Materials handling	1.40	3,950
Maintenance and repairs	1.50	2,980
Utilities	0.80	1,490
Miscellaneous	0.10	200
Totals	$7.40	$16,090

Fixed Overhead Costs	Budgeted Fixed Overhead	Actual Fixed Overhead in October
Supervisory salaries	$ 3,630	$ 3,630
Machine depreciation	8,360	8,580
Other	1,210	1,220
Totals	$13,200	$13,430

For October, the number of good units produced was used to compute the 2,100 standard machine hours allowed.

1. Prepare a monthly flexible budget for operating activity at 2,000 machine hours, 2,200 machine hours, and 2,500 machine hours.
2. Develop a flexible budget formula.
3. The company's normal operating capacity is 2,200 machine hours per month. Compute the fixed overhead rate at this level of activity. Then break the rate down into rates for each element of fixed overhead.
4. Prepare a detailed comparative cost analysis for October. Include all variable and fixed overhead costs. Format your analysis by using columns for the following five elements: cost category, cost per machine hour, costs applied, actual costs incurred, and variance.
5. Develop an overhead variance analysis for October that identifies the variable overhead spending and efficiency variances and the fixed overhead budget and volume variances.
6. Prepare an analysis of the variances. Could a manager control some of the fixed costs? Defend your answer.

LO 4, 5

Conceptual Understanding: Standard Costing in a Service Company

C5. AAA Life Insurance Company's (ALIC) most popular life insurance policy is P20A—a permanent, 20-year life annuity policy. This policy sells in $10,000 increments depending on the policyholder's needs and age. ALIC devotes an entire department to supporting and marketing the P20A policy. Because both the support staff and the salespersons contribute to each P20A policy, ALIC categorizes them as direct labor for purposes of variance analysis, cost control, and performance evaluation. For unit costing, each $10,000 increment is considered one unit; thus, a $90,000 policy is counted as nine units. Standard unit cost information for January is as follows.

Direct labor:	
Policy support staff (3 hours at $12.00 per hour)	$ 36.00
Policy salespersons (8.5 hours at $14.20 per hour)	120.70
Operating overhead:	
Variable operating overhead (11.5 hours at $26.00 per hour)	299.00
Fixed operating overhead (11.5 hours at $18.00 per hour)	207.00
Standard unit cost	$662.70

Actual costs incurred for the 265 units sold during January were as follows.

Direct labor:	
Policy support staff (848 hours at $12.50 per hour)	$10,600
Policy salespersons (2,252.5 hours at $14.00 per hour)	31,535
Operating overhead:	
Variable operating overhead	78,440
Fixed operating overhead	53,400

Normal monthly capacity is 260 units, and the budgeted fixed operating overhead for January was $53,820.

1. Compute the standard hours allowed in January for policy support staff and policy salespersons.
2. What should the total standard costs for January have been? What were the total actual costs that the company incurred in January? Compute the total cost variance for the month.

(Continued)

3. Compute the direct labor rate and efficiency variances for policy support staff and policy salespersons.
4. Compute the variable and fixed operating overhead variances for January.
5. Identify possible causes for each variance and suggest possible solutions.

Continuing Case: Cookie Company

C6. In this segment of our continuing case, assume that you have been using standard costing to plan and control costs at your cookie store. In a meeting with your budget team, which includes managers and employees from the Purchasing, Product Design, and Production departments, you ask all team members to describe any operating problems they encountered in the last quarter. You explain that you will use this information to analyze the causes of significant cost variances that occurred during the quarter.

For each of the following situations, identify the direct materials and/or direct labor variance(s) that could be affected, and indicate whether the variances are favorable or unfavorable.

1. The production department uses highly skilled, highly paid workers.
2. Machines were improperly adjusted.
3. Direct labor personnel worked more carefully than they had in the past to manufacture the product.
4. The Product Design Department replaced a direct material with one that was less expensive and of lower quality.
5. The Purchasing Department bought higher-quality materials at a higher price.
6. A major supplier used a less-expensive mode of transportation to deliver the raw materials.
7. Work was halted for 2 hours because of a power failure.

CHAPTER 23
Short-Run Decision Analysis

BUSINESS INSIGHT
Bank of America

Bank of America is one of the world's largest financial institutions. It has received many awards for its online services and initiatives in preventing online fraud and identity theft. Bank of America's managers believe the trend to online commerce is good for business, and as customers gain confidence in dealing with their finances online, they plan to offer more online products and services. In looking for safe and innovative ways to meet customers' needs, the managers will make short-run decisions that will affect the bank's profits, resources, and opportunities.

1. **CONCEPT ▶** Why is the concept of cost-benefit important when making short-run decisions?
2. **ACCOUNTING APPLICATION ▶** How does incremental analysis ensure a wise allocation of resources involved in short-run decisions?
3. **BUSINESS APPLICATION ▶** How can incremental analysis help managers improve performance and take advantage of business opportunities?

LEARNING OBJECTIVES

LO1 Describe how the concept of cost-benefit is useful when making short-run decisions.

LO2 Perform incremental analysis for outsourcing decisions.

LO3 Perform incremental analysis for special order decisions.

LO4 Perform incremental analysis for segment profitability decisions.

LO5 Perform incremental analysis for sales mix decisions involving constrained resources.

LO6 Perform incremental analysis for sell-or-process-further decisions.

LO7 Describe why short-run decision analysis is critical for business success.

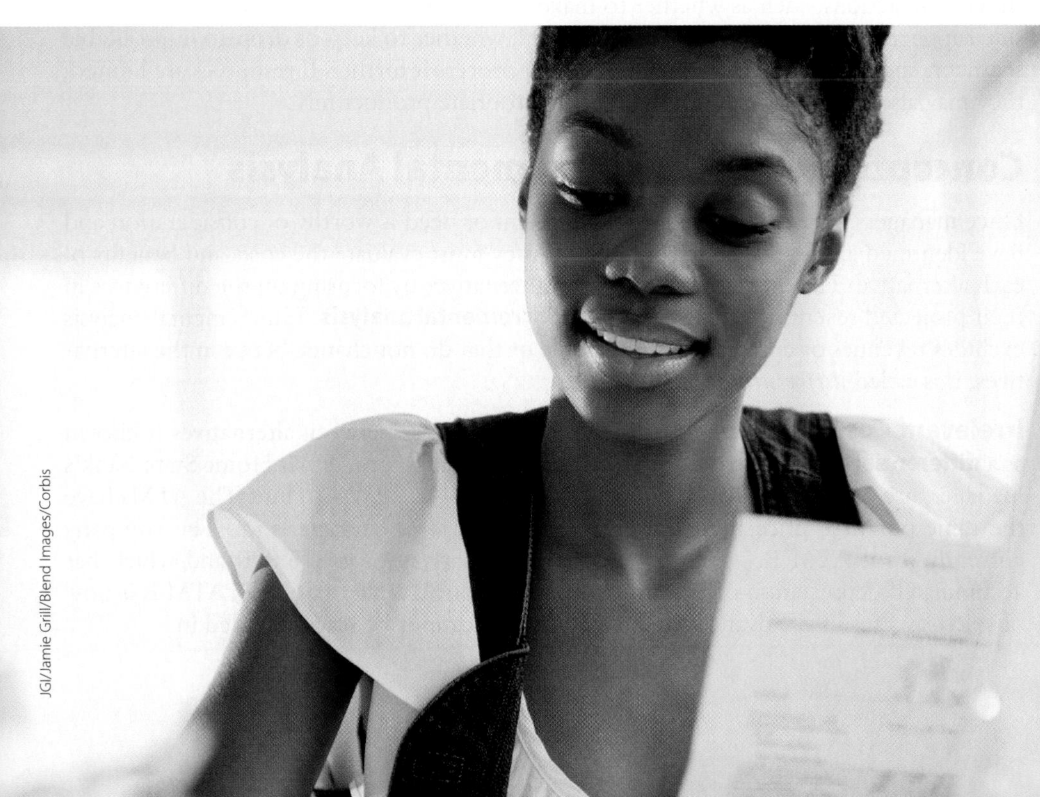

JGI/Jamie Grill/Blend Images/Corbis

SECTION 1 CONCEPTS

CONCEPT

- Cost-benefit

RELEVANT LEARNING OBJECTIVE

LO 1 Describe how the concept of cost-benefit is useful when making short-run decisions.

LO 1 Concepts Underlying Decision Analysis

The concept of *cost-benefit* holds that the benefits to be gained from a course of action or alternative should be greater than the costs of implementing it. Cost-benefit is an accounting convention or rule of thumb that supports both short-run and long-run decision making. It considers both quantitative and qualitative cost and benefit measures to facilitate cost-benefit comparisons between alternatives for sound business decisions. Managers frequently take the following actions when applying the cost-benefit concept to short-run decisions:

- **Step 1.** Discover a problem or need.
- **Step 2.** Identify all reasonable courses of action that can solve the problem or meet the need.
- **Step 3.** Prepare a thorough analysis of each possible solution, identifying its total costs, savings, benefits, other financial effects, and any qualitative factors.
- **Step 4.** Select the best course of action.

Later, each decision is reviewed to determine whether it produced the forecasted results by examining how each decision was carried out and how its actual costs and benefits affected the organization. If results fell short, managers identify and prescribe corrective action. This post-decision audit supplies feedback about the results of the decision. If the solution is not completely satisfactory or if the problem remains, the process of evaluating costs and benefits of alternatives begins again.

Short-run decision analysis is the systematic examination of any decision whose effects will be felt over the course of the next year or less. In making such decisions, managers analyze not only quantitative cost and benefit factors relating to profitability and liquidity, they also analyze qualitative factors. In the course of a year, managers may make many short-run decisions that involve the evaluation of the costs and benefits of short-term actions, such as whether to make a product or service or buy it from an outside supplier, whether to accept a special order, whether to keep or drop an unprofitable segment, and whether to sell a product as is or process it further. If resources are limited, they may also have to decide on the most appropriate product mix.

Concepts Underlying Incremental Analysis

Once managers have determined that a problem or need is worthy of consideration and have identified alternative courses of action, they must evaluate the costs and benefits of each alternative. The method of comparing alternatives by focusing on the differences in their projected revenues and costs is called **incremental analysis**. If incremental analysis excludes revenues or costs that stay the same or that do not change between the alternatives, it is called *differential analysis.*

Irrelevant Costs and Revenues A cost that changes between alternatives is known as a **differential cost** (or *incremental cost*). For example, suppose that Home State Bank's managers are deciding which of two ATM machines—C or W—to buy. The ATMs have the same purchase price but different revenue and cost characteristics. The company currently owns ATM B, which it bought three years ago for $15,000 and which has accumulated depreciation of $9,000, and carries a book value of $6,000. ATM B is now obsolete as a result of advances in technology and cannot be sold or traded in.

A manager has prepared the following comparison of the annual revenue and operating cost estimates for the two new machines:

	ATM C	ATM W
Increase in revenue	$16,200	$19,800
Increase in annual operating costs:		
Direct materials	4,800	4,800
Direct labor	2,200	4,100
Variable overhead	2,100	3,050
Fixed overhead (depreciation included)	5,000	5,000

***STUDY NOTE:** Sunk costs cannot be recovered and are irrelevant in short-run decision making.*

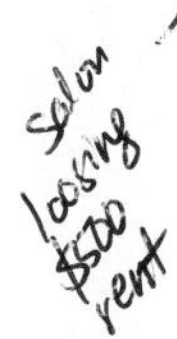

Incremental Analysis The first step in the incremental analysis is to eliminate any irrelevant revenues and costs. *Irrelevant revenues* are those that will not differ between the alternatives. *Irrelevant costs* include costs that will not differ between the alternatives and sunk costs. A **sunk cost** is a cost that was incurred because of a previous decision and cannot be recovered through the current decision. For Home State Bank, the costs of direct materials and fixed overhead (depreciation included) are irrelevant costs because they are the same under both alternatives. In addition, ATM B's book value is a sunk cost because it represents money that was spent in the past and so does not affect the decision about whether to replace ATM B with a new one. ATM B would be of interest only if it could be sold or traded in, and if the amount received for it would be different, depending on which new ATM was chosen. In that case, the amount of the sale or trade-in value would be relevant to the decision because it would affect the future cash flows of the alternatives.

Once the irrelevant revenues and costs have been identified, the incremental analysis can be prepared using only the differential revenues and costs that will change between the alternative ATMs, as shown in Exhibit 1. The analysis shows that ATM W would produce $750 more in operating income than ATM C. Because the costs of buying the two ATMs are the same, this report would favor the purchase of ATM W.

Exhibit 1
Incremental Analysis

Home State Bank
Incremental Analysis

	ATM C	ATM W	Difference in Favor of ATM W
Increase in revenue	$16,200	$19,800	$ 3,600
Increase in annual operating costs that differ between alternatives:			
Direct labor	$ 2,200	$ 4,100	$(1,900)
Variable overhead	2,100	3,050	(950)
Total increase in operating costs	$ 4,300	$ 7,150	$(2,850)
Resulting change in operating income	$11,900	$12,650	$ 750

Opportunity Costs Because incremental analysis focuses on only the quantitative differences among the alternatives, it simplifies management's evaluation of a decision and reduces the time needed to choose the best course of action. However, incremental analysis is only one input to the final decision. Management needs to consider qualitative issues. For instance, the manufacturer of ATM C might have a reputation for better quality or service than the manufacturer of ATM W.

Operating Central Park in New York city involves maintenance, employee, and equipment costs. But the largest cost is actually the opportunity cost of the tens of billions of dollars the city could get by leasing the land to real estate developers.

Opportunity costs are the benefits that are forfeited or lost when one alternative is chosen over another. In other words, opportunity costs arise when the choice of one course of action eliminates the possibility of another course of action. Opportunity costs often come into play when a company is operating at or near capacity and must choose which products or services to offer. For example, suppose that Home State Bank, which currently services 20,000 debit cards, has the option of offering 15,000 premium debit cards, which is a higher-priced product, but it cannot do both. The amount of income from the 20,000 debit cards is an opportunity cost of the premium debit cards.

APPLY IT!

Credit Bank has assembled the following monthly information related to the purchase of a new automated teller machine:

	Machine A	Machine B
Increase in revenue	$4,200	$5,100
Increase in annual operating costs:		
Direct materials	1,200	1,200
Direct labor	1,200	1,600
Variable overhead	2,500	2,900
Fixed overhead (including depreciation)	1,400	1,400

Use incremental analysis to determine the cost-benefit difference in favor of Machine B.

SOLUTION

Credit Bank
Incremental Analysis

	Machine A	Machine B	Difference in Favor of Machine B
Increase in revenue	$4,200	$5,100	$ 900
Increase in operating costs that differ between alternatives:			
Direct labor	$1,200	$1,600	$(400)
Variable overhead	2,500	2,900	(400)
Total increase in operating costs	$3,700	$4,500	$(800)
Resulting change in operating income	$ 500	$ 600	$ 100

TRY IT! SE1, SE2, E1A, E1B

SECTION 2 ACCOUNTING APPLICATIONS

COUNTING
PLICATIONS
Perform incremental analysis for
- Outsourcing decisions
- Special order decisions
- Segment profitability decisions
- Sales mix decisions
- Sell-or-process-further decisions

LEVANT
ARNING OBJECTIVES

2 Perform incremental analysis for sourcing decisions.

3 Perform incremental analysis for special er decisions.

4 Perform incremental analysis for segment fitability decisions.

5 Perform incremental analysis for sales mix isions involving strained resources.

6 Perform incremental analysis for sell-or-cess- further decisions.

LO2 Incremental Analysis for Outsourcing Decisions

Outsourcing is the use of suppliers outside the organization to perform services or produce goods that could be performed or produced internally. **Make-or-buy decisions**, which are decisions about whether to make a part internally or buy it from an external supplier, may lead to outsourcing. A company may decide to outsource entire operating activities, such as warehousing or human resources, that have traditionally been performed in-house. Outsourcing can reduce a company's investment in physical assets and human resources, which can improve cash flow. It can also help a company reduce its operating costs and improve operating income. For example, because **Amazon.com** outsources the distribution of most of its products, it has been able to reduce its storage and distribution costs enough to offer product discounts of up to 40 percent off the list price.

Outsourcing Analysis

In manufacturing companies, a common decision facing managers is whether to make or buy some or all of the parts used in product assembly. The goal is to select the more profitable choice by identifying the costs of each alternative and their effects on revenues and existing costs. Managers need the following information for this analysis:

Information About Making
- Variable costs of making the item
- Need for additional machinery
- Incremental fixed costs

Information About Buying
- Purchase price of item
- Rent or cash flow to be generated from vacated space in the factory
- Salvage value of unused machinery

For example, for the past five years, Box Company has purchased packing cartons from Pappe, Inc., an outside supplier, at a cost of $1.25 per carton. Effective immediately, Pappe is raising the price 20 percent, to $1.50 per carton. Box has space and idle machinery that could be adjusted to produce the cartons. Annual production and usage would be 20,000 cartons. Box estimates the cost of direct materials at $0.84 per carton. Workers, who will be paid $8.00 per hour, can process 20 cartons per hour ($0.40 per carton). The cost of variable overhead will be $4 per direct labor hour, and 1,000 direct labor hours will be required. Fixed overhead includes $4,000 of depreciation per year and $6,000 of other fixed costs. The idle machines will continue to be idle if the cartons are purchased. Should Box continue to outsource the cartons?

Exhibit 2 presents an incremental analysis of the two alternatives. All relevant costs are listed. Because the machinery has already been purchased, and neither the

Exhibit 2
Incremental Analysis: Outsourcing Decision

Box Company
Outsourcing Decision
Incremental Analysis

	Make	Outsource	Difference in Favor of Make
Direct materials (20,000 × $0.84)	$16,800	$ —	$(16,800)
Direct labor (20,000 × $0.40)	8,000	—	(8,000)
Variable overhead (1,000 hours × $4)	4,000	—	(4,000)
Purchase price (20,000 × $1.50)	—	30,000	30,000
Totals	$28,800	$30,000	$ 1,200

STUDY NOTE: *Remember to exclude irrelevant information (such as depreciation and other fixed costs). Only costs that change between the alternatives should be used in incremental analysis.*

machinery nor the required factory space has any other use, the depreciation costs and other fixed overhead costs are the same for both alternatives. Therefore, they are not relevant to the decision. The cost of making the needed cartons is $28,800. The cost of buying 20,000 cartons at the increased purchase price will be $30,000. Since the company would save $1,200 by making the cartons, management should decide to make the cartons.

APPLY IT!

Office Associates, Inc., is currently operating at less than capacity. The company thinks it could cut costs by outsourcing office cleaning to an independent cleaning service for $75 a week. Currently, a general office worker is employed for $10 an hour to do light cleaning and other general office duties. Cleaning the office usually takes one hour a day to perform and consumes $10 of supplies, $2 of variable overhead, and $18 of fixed overhead each week. Should Office Associates continue to perform office cleanings, or should it outsource them?

SOLUTION

Costs per Cleaning	Continue to Perform Cleanings	Outsource Cleanings	Difference in Favor of Continuing to Perform Cleanings
Employee labor	$50	$—	$(50)
Supplies	10	—	(10)
Variable overhead	2	—	(2)
Outside cleaning service	—	75	75
Totals	$62	$75	$ 13

Office Associates should continue to perform office cleanings itself.

TRY IT! **SE3, SE4, E2A, E3A, E2B, E3B**

LO 3 Incremental Analysis for Special Order Decisions

Managers are often faced with **special order decisions**, which are decisions about whether to accept or reject special orders at prices below the normal market prices. Special order decisions must be consistent with the company's strategic plan and tactical objectives and must take into account not only costs and revenues but also relevant qualitative factors, such as the impact of the special order on regular customers, the potential of the special order to lead into new sales areas, and the customer's ability to maintain an ongoing relationship that includes good ordering and paying practices.

Before a company accepts a special product order, it must be sure that excess capacity exists to complete the order and that the order will not reduce unit sales from its full-priced regular product line. In addition, a special order should be accepted only if it maximizes operating income. In many situations, sales commission expenses are excluded from a special order decision analysis because the customer approached the company directly. In addition, the fixed costs of existing facilities usually do not change if a company accepts a special order, and therefore these costs are usually irrelevant to the decision. If additional fixed costs must be incurred to fill the special order, they would be relevant to the decision. Examples of relevant fixed costs are the purchase of additional machinery, an increase in supervisory help, and an increase in insurance premiums required by a specific order.

Special Order Analysis: Price and Relevant Cost Comparison

One approach to a special order decision is to compare the price of the special order with the relevant costs of producing, packaging, and shipping the order. The relevant costs include the variable costs, variable selling costs (if any), and other costs directly associated with the special order (e.g., freight, insurance, and packaging and labeling the product). For example, suppose Home State Bank has been approved to provide and service four ATMs at a special event. The event sponsors want the fee reduced to $0.50 per ATM transaction. At past special events, ATM use has averaged 2,000 transactions per machine. Home State Bank has four idle ATMs and determined the following additional information:

ATM Cost Data for Annual Use of One Machine (400,000 Transactions)	
Direct materials	$0.10
Direct labor	0.05
Variable overhead	0.20
Fixed overhead ($100,000 ÷ 400,000)	0.25
Advertising ($60,000 ÷ 400,000)	0.15
Other fixed selling and administrative expenses ($120,000 ÷ 400,000)	0.30
Cost per transaction	$1.05
Regular fee per transaction	$1.50

Should Home State Bank accept the special event offer?

An incremental analysis of the decision appears in Exhibit 3. The report shows the contribution margin for Home State Bank's operations both with and without the special order for the four machines. Fixed costs are not included because the only costs affected by the order are direct materials, direct labor, and variable overhead. The net result of accepting the special order is a $1,200 increase in contribution margin (and, correspondingly, in operating income). The analysis reveals that Home State Bank should accept the special order. The $1,200 increase is verified by the following contribution margin calculation:

Special order sales [(2,000 transactions × 4 machines) × $0.50]		$4,000
Less variable costs:		
Direct materials (8,000 transactions × $0.10)	$ 800	
Direct labor (8,000 transactions × $0.05)	400	
Variable overhead (8,000 transactions × $0.20)	1,600	
Total variable costs		2,800
Special order contribution margin		$1,200

Exhibit 3
Incremental Analysis: Special Order Decision

Home State Bank
Special Order Decision
Incremental Analysis

	Without Order	With Order	Difference in Favor of Accepting Order
Sales	$2,400,000	$2,404,000	$ 4,000
Less variable costs:			
Direct materials	$ 160,000	$ 160,800	$ (800)
Direct labor	80,000	80,400	(400)
Variable overhead	320,000	321,600	(1,600)
Total variable costs	$ 560,000	$ 562,800	$(2,800)
Contribution margin	$1,840,000	$1,841,200	$ 1,200

Special Order Analysis: Minimum Bid Price for Special Order

Another approach to this kind of decision is to prepare a special order bid price by calculating a minimum selling price for the special order. The bid price must cover the relevant costs and an estimated profit. For example, assume that the event sponsor asks Home State Bank what its minimum special order price is. If the incremental costs for the special order are $2,800, the relevant cost per transaction is $0.35 ($2,800 ÷ 8,000). The special order price should cover this cost and generate a profit. If Home State Bank would like to earn $800 from the special order, the special order price should be $0.45 [$0.35 cost per transaction plus $0.10 profit per transaction ($800 ÷ 8,000 transactions)].

APPLY IT!

Sample Company has received an order for Product EZ at a special selling price of $26 per unit (suggested retail price is $30). This order is over and above normal production, and budgeted production and sales targets for the year have already been exceeded. Capacity exists to satisfy the special order. No selling costs will be incurred in connection with this order. Unit costs to manufacture and sell Product EZ are as follows: direct materials, $7.00; direct labor, $10.00; variable overhead, $8.00; fixed manufacturing costs, $5.00; variable selling costs, $3.00; and fixed general and administrative costs, $9.00. Should Sample accept the order?

SOLUTION

Variable costs to produce Product EZ:

Direct materials	$ 7.00
Direct labor	10.00
Variable overhead	8.00
Total variable costs to produce	$25.00

Sample should accept the special order, because the offered price of $26 exceeds the variable manufacturing costs of $25.

TRY IT! SE5, SE6, E4A, E5A, E4B, E5B

LO4 Incremental Analysis for Segment Profitability Decisions

Another type of operating decision that management must make is whether to keep or drop unprofitable segments, such as product lines, services, sales territories, divisions, departments, stores, or outlets. Management must select the alternative that maximizes operating income. The objective of the decision analysis is to identify the segments that have a negative segment margin so that managers can drop them or take corrective action.

A **segment margin** is a segment's sales revenue minus its direct costs (direct variable costs and direct fixed costs traceable to the segment). Such costs are assumed to be **avoidable costs**. An avoidable cost could be eliminated if management were to drop the segment.

- ▲ If a segment has a positive segment margin—that is, the segment's revenue is greater than its direct costs—it is able to cover its own direct costs and contribute a portion of its revenue to cover common costs and add to operating income. In that case, management should keep the segment.
- ▼ If a segment has a negative segment margin—that is, the segment's revenue is less than its direct costs—management should eliminate the segment.

However, certain common costs will be incurred regardless of the decision. Those are unavoidable costs, and the remaining segments must have sufficient contribution margin to cover their own direct costs and the common costs.

Segment Profitability Analysis

An analysis of segment profitability includes the preparation of a segmented income statement using variable costing to identify variable and fixed costs. The fixed costs that are traceable to the segments are called *direct fixed costs*. The remaining fixed costs are *common costs* and are not assigned to segments.

Business Perspective

Why Banks Prefer e-Banking

After performing segment analysis of online banking and face-to-face banking, bank managers worldwide are encouraging customers to do their banking over the Internet. Banks have found that linking global Internet access with customer relationship management (CRM), customer-friendly financial software, and online bill payment in a secure banking environment can reduce costs, increase service and product availability, and boost earnings.[1]

Suppose Home State Bank wants to determine if it should eliminate its Safe Deposit Division. Managers prepare a segmented income statement, separating variable and fixed costs to calculate the contribution margin. They separate the total fixed costs of $84,000 further by directly tracing $55,500 to Bank Operations and $16,500 to the Safe Deposit Division. The remaining $12,000 are common fixed costs. Exhibit 4 shows the segment margins for Bank Operations and the Safe Deposit Division and the operating income for the total company.

Exhibit 4
Segmented Income Statement

Home State Bank
Segmented Income Statement
For the Year Ended December 31, 2014

	Bank Operations	Safe Deposit Division	Total Company
Sales	$135,000	$15,000	$150,000
Less variable costs	52,500	7,500	60,000
Contribution margin	$ 82,500	$ 7,500	$ 90,000
Less direct fixed costs	55,500	16,500	72,000
Segment margin	$ 27,000	$ (9,000)	$ 18,000
Less common fixed costs			12,000
Operating income			$ 6,000

Situation 1 Exhibit 5 demonstrates that dropping the Safe Deposit Division will increase operating income by $9,000. Unless the bank can increase the division's segment margin by increasing sales revenue or by reducing direct costs, management should drop the segment. The incremental approach to analyzing this decision isolates the segment and focuses on its segment margin, as shown in the last column of Exhibit 5. The decision to drop a segment also requires a careful review of the other segments to see whether they will be affected.

Situation 2 Exhibit 6 assumes that the Bank Operations' sales volume and variable costs will decrease 20 percent if management eliminates the Safe Deposit Division. The reduction in sales volume stems from the loss of customers who purchase products from both divisions. The analysis shows that dropping the division would reduce both the segment margin and the bank's operating income by $7,500. In this situation, Home State Bank would want to keep the Safe Deposit Division.

Exhibit 5
Incremental Analysis: Segment Profitability Decision (Situation 1)

Home State Bank
Segment Profitability Decision
Incremental Analysis—Situation 1

	Keep Safe Deposit Division	Drop Safe Deposit Division	Difference in Favor of Dropping Safe Deposit Division
Sales	$150,000	$135,000	$(15,000)
Less variable costs	60,000	52,500	7,500
Contribution margin	$ 90,000	$ 82,500	$ (7,500)
Less direct fixed costs	72,000	55,500	16,500
Segment margin	$ 18,000	$ 27,000	$ 9,000
Less common fixed costs	12,000	12,000	0
Operating income	$ 6,000	$ 15,000	$ 9,000

Exhibit 6
Incremental Analysis: Segment Profitability Decision (Situation 2)

Home State Bank
Segment Profitability Decision
Incremental Analysis—Situation 2

	Keep Safe Deposit Division	Drop Safe Deposit Division	Difference in Favor of Keeping Safe Deposit Division
Sales	$150,000	$108,000	$(42,000)
Less variable costs	60,000	42,000	18,000
Contribution margin	$ 90,000	$ 66,000	$(24,000)
Less direct fixed costs	72,000	55,500	16,500
Segment margin	$ 18,000	$ 10,500	$ (7,500)
Less common fixed costs	12,000	12,000	0
Operating income	$ 6,000	$ (1,500)	$ (7,500)

APPLY IT!

Sample Company is evaluating its two divisions, East Division and West Division. Data for East Division include sales of $500,000, variable costs of $250,000, and fixed costs of $400,000, 50 percent of which are traceable to the division. West Division's data for the same period include sales of $600,000, variable costs of $350,000, and fixed costs of $450,000, 60 percent of which are traceable to the division. Should either division be considered for elimination?

SOLUTION

	East Division	West Division	Total Company
Sales	$500,000	$600,000	$1,100,000
Less variable costs	250,000	350,000	600,000
Contribution margin	$250,000	$250,000	$ 500,000
Less direct fixed costs	200,000	270,000	470,000
Divisional income	$ 50,000	$ (20,000)	$ 30,000
Less common fixed costs			380,000
Operating income (loss)			$ (350,000)

The company should keep East Division because it is profitable. West Division does not seem to be profitable and should be considered for elimination. The home office and its very heavy overhead costs are causing the company's loss.

TRY IT! SE7, E6A, E6B

LO5 Incremental Analysis for Sales Mix Decisions

Limits on resources like machine time or available labor may restrict the types or quantities of products or services that a company can provide. The question is, which products or services contribute the most to profitability in relation to the amount of capital assets or other constrained resources needed to offer those items? To satisfy customers' demands and maximize operating income, management will make a **sales mix decision** to offer the most profitable combination of products and services. To decide on the optimal sales mix of products or services, managers calculate the contribution margin per constrained resource (such as labor hours or machine hours) for each product or service.

Sales Mix Analysis

The objective of a sales mix decision is to select the alternative that maximizes the contribution margin per constrained resource. The decision analysis, which uses incremental analysis to identify the relevant costs and revenues, consists of two steps.

- **Step 1.** Calculate the contribution margin per unit for each product or service affected by the constrained resource as follows.

Contribution Margin per Unit = Selling Price per Unit − Variable Costs per Unit

- **Step 2.** Calculate the contribution margin per unit of the constrained resource as follows.

STUDY NOTE: *When resources like direct materials, direct labor, or time are scarce, the goal is to maximize the contribution margin per unit of scarce resource.*

$$\text{Contribution Margin per Unit of Constrained Resources} = \frac{\text{Contribution Margin per Unit}}{\text{Quantity of the Constrained Resource Required per Unit}}$$

Suppose Home State Bank offers three types of loans: commercial loans, auto loans, and home loans. The product line data follows.

	Commercial Loans	Auto Loans	Home Loans
Current loan application demand	20,000	30,000	18,000
Processing hours per loan application	2.0	1.0	2.5
Loan origination fee	$24.00	$18.00	$32.00
Variable processing costs	$12.50	$10.00	$18.75
Variable selling costs	$6.50	$5.00	$6.25

The current loan application capacity is 100,000 processing hours.

Ranking the Order Which loan type should be advertised and promoted first because it is the most profitable for the bank? Which should be second? Which last? Exhibit 7 shows the sales mix analysis. It indicates that the auto loans should be promoted first because they provide the highest contribution margin per processing hour. Home loans should be second, and commercial loans should be last.

Number of Units How many of each type of loan should the bank sell to maximize its contribution margin based on the current loan application capacity of 100,000 processing hours? What is the total contribution margin for that combination? To begin the analysis, compare the current loan application capacity with the total capacity required to meet the current loan demand. The company needs 115,000 processing hours to meet the current loan demand, calculated as follows.

Processing hours for commercial loans (20,000 loans × 2 processing hours per loan)	40,000
Processing hours for auto loans (30,000 loans × 1 processing hour per loan)	30,000
Processing hours for home loans (18,000 × 2.5 processing hours per loan)	45,000
Total processing hours	115,000

Because the 115,000 processing hours needed exceeds the current capacity of 100,000 processing hours, management must determine the sales mix that maximizes the company's contribution margin, which will also maximize its operating income.

The calculations in Exhibit 8 show that Home State Bank should sell 30,000 auto loans, 18,000 home loans, and 12,500 commercial loans. The total contribution margin is as follows.

Auto loans (30,000 loans × $3.00 per loan)	$ 90,000
Home loans (18,000 loans × $7.00 per loan)	126,000
Commercial loans (12,500 loans × $5.00 per loan)	62,500
Total contribution margin	$278,500

Exhibit 7
Incremental Analysis: Sales Mix Decision Involving Constrained Resources (Ranking the Order)

Home State Bank
Sales Mix Decision: Ranking the Order of Loans
Incremental Analysis

	Commercial Loans	Auto Loans	Home Loans
Loan origination fee per loan	$24.00	$18.00	$32.00
Less variable costs:			
Processing	$12.50	$10.00	$18.75
Selling	6.50	5.00	6.25
Total variable costs	$19.00	$15.00	$25.00
Contribution margin per loan	$ 5.00	$ 3.00	$ 7.00
Processing hours per loan	÷ 2.0	÷ 1.0	÷ 2.5
Contribution margin per processing hour	$ 2.50	$ 3.00	$ 2.80

Exhibit 8
Incremental Analysis: Sales Mix Decision Involving Constrained Resources (Number of Units)

Home State Bank
Sales Mix Decision: Number of Units to Make
Incremental Analysis

	Processing Hours
Total processing hours available	100,000
Less processing hours to produce auto loans (30,000 loans × 1 processing hour per loan)	30,000
Balance of processing hours available	70,000
Less processing hours to produce home loans (18,000 loans × 2.5 processing hours per loan)	45,000
Balance of processing hours available	25,000
Less processing hours to produce commercial loans (12,500 loans × 2 processing hours per loan)	25,000
Balance of processing hours available	0

APPLY IT!

Surf, Inc., makes three kinds of surfboards, but it has a limited number of machine hours available to make them. Product line data are as follows. In what order should the surfboard product lines be produced?

	Fiberglass	Plastic	Graphite
Machine hours per unit	4	1	2
Selling price per unit	$1,500	$800	$1,300
Variable manufacturing cost per unit	500	200	800
Variable selling costs per unit	200	350	200

SOLUTION

	Fiberglass	Plastic	Graphite
Selling price per unit	$1,500	$800	$1,300
Less variable costs:			
Manufacturing	$ 500	$200	$ 800
Selling	200	350	200
Total unit variable costs	$ 700	$550	$1,000
Contribution margin per unit	$ 800	$250	$ 300
Machine hours per unit	÷ 4	÷ 1	÷ 2
Contribution margin per machine hour	$ 200	$250	$ 150

Surf should produce plastic first, then fiberglass, and finally graphite surfboards.

TRY IT! SE8, E7A, E8A, E9A, E7B, E8B, E9B

LO 6 Incremental Analysis for Sell-or-Process-Further Decisions

STUDY NOTE: *Products are made by combining materials or by dividing materials, as in oil refining or ore extraction.*

Some companies offer products or services that can either be sold in a basic form or be processed further and sold as a more refined product or service to a different market. A **sell-or-process-further decision** is a decision about whether to sell a joint product at the split-off point or sell it after further processing. **Joint products** are two or more products made from a common material or process that cannot be identified as separate products or services during some or all of the processing. Only at a specific point, called the **split-off point**, do joint products or services become separate and identifiable. At that point, a company may choose to sell the product or service as is or to process it into another form for sale to a different market.

Sell-or-Process-Further Analysis

The objective of a sell-or-process-further decision is to select the alternative that maximizes operating income. The decision analysis entails calculating the **incremental revenue** as follows.

$$\text{Incremental Revenue} = \text{Total Revenue if Product/Service Is Sold at Split-Off Point} - \text{Total Revenue if Product/Service Is Sold after Further Processing}$$

- ▲ If the incremental *revenue* is greater than the incremental costs of processing further, a decision to process the product or service further would be justified.
- ▲ If the incremental *costs* are greater than the incremental revenue, a decision to sell the product or service at the split-off point would be in order.

STUDY NOTE: *Joint costs are irrelevant in a sell-or-process-further decision.*

The common costs shared by two or more products before they are split off are called **joint costs** (or *common costs*). Although accountants assign joint costs to products or services when valuing inventories and calculating cost of goods sold, joint costs are not relevant to a sell-or-process-further decision because they are incurred *before* the split-off point and do not change if further processing occurs.

For example, as part of the company's strategic plan, Home State Bank's management is looking for new markets for banking services, and management is considering whether it would be profitable to bundle banking services. The bank is considering adding two levels of service beyond its current Basic Checking account services: Premier Checking and Personal Banker. The three levels have the following bundled features:

- **Basic Checking:** Online checking account, debit card, and online bill payment with a required minimum average balance of $500
- **Premier Checking:** Paper and online checking, a debit card, a credit card, and a small life insurance policy equal to the maximum credit limit on the credit card for customers who maintain a minimum average balance of $1,000
- **Personal Banker:** All of the features of Premier Checking plus a safe deposit box, a $5,000 personal line of credit at the prime interest rate, financial investment advice, and a toaster upon opening the account for customers who maintain a minimum average balance of $5,000

Assume that the bank can earn sales revenue of 5 percent on its checking account balances and that the total cost of offering basic checking services is currently $50,000. The bank's accountant provided these data for each level of service:

Product	Sales Revenue	Additional Costs
Basic Checking	$ 25	$ 0
Premier Checking	50	30
Personal Banker	250	200

Should the bank offer any additional services? The decision analysis in Exhibit 9 indicates that the bank should offer Personal Banker services in addition to Basic Checking accounts. Notice that the $50,000 joint costs of Basic Checking were ignored because they are sunk costs that will not influence the decision.

Exhibit 9
Incremental Analysis: Sell-or-Process-Further Decision

Home State Bank
Sell-or-Process-Further Decision
Incremental Analysis

	Premier Checking	Personal Banker
Incremental revenue per account if processed further:		
Process further	$50	$250
Split-off—Basic Checking	25	25
Incremental revenue	$25	$225
Less incremental costs	30	200
Operating income (loss) from processing further	$ (5)	$ 25

APPLY IT!

In an attempt to provide superb customer service, Anytime Movie Access is considering expanding its product offerings from single movie or game pay-per-view to complete movie or game evenings. Each evening would include unlimited online access to movies or games and a coupon for candy, popcorn, and drinks. The company's accountant has compiled the information that follows. Determine which products Anytime Movie Access should offer.

Product	Sales Revenue if No Additional Services	Sales Revenue if Processed Further into Unlimited Evening	Additional Processing Costs
Movie	$2	$10	$5
Game	1	6	5

SOLUTION

	Movie Evening	Game Evening
Incremental revenue if processed further:		
Process further	$10	$6
Split-off	2	1
Incremental revenue	$ 8	$5
Less incremental costs	5	5
Operating income from further processing	$ 3	$0

Anytime Movie Access should promote movie evenings first, then movies, and finally games or game evenings. There is no difference in profitability between the sale of games and the sale of game evenings.

TRY IT! SE9, E10A, E11A, E10B, E11B

SECTION 3

SINESS PLICATIONS
Planning
Performing
Evaluating
Communicating

LEVANT ARNING OBJECTIVE

7 Describe why short-run decision analysis is ical for business success.

BUSINESS APPLICATIONS

LO 7 The Management Process

Managers use both financial and nonfinancial quantitative and qualitative information to analyze the effects of past and potential business actions on their organization's resources and profits. Although many business problems are unique and cannot be solved by following strict rules, managers often use a suite of short-run decision-making methods and tools. Those decision methods and tools were the focus of this chapter. Exhibit 10 summarizes the tools and methods managers use to ensure a wise allocation of resources and at the same time minimize the business risks involved.

Exhibit 10
Short-Run Decisions and the Management Process

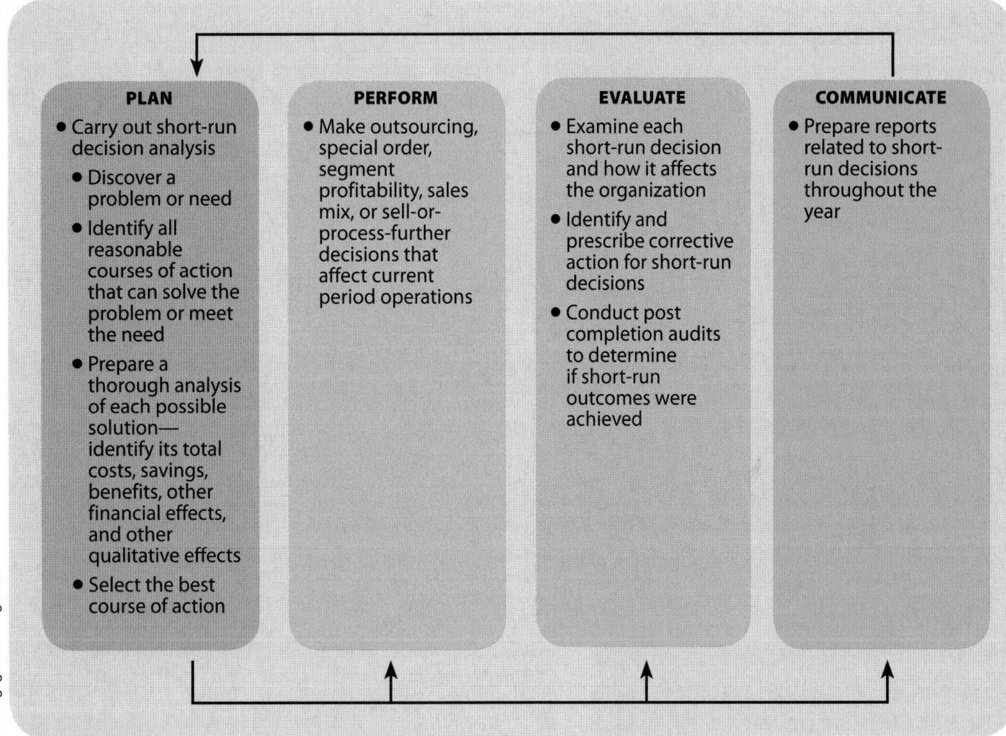

PLAN
• Carry out short-run decision analysis
• Discover a problem or need
• Identify all reasonable courses of action that can solve the problem or meet the need
• Prepare a thorough analysis of each possible solution—identify its total costs, savings, benefits, other financial effects, and other qualitative effects
• Select the best course of action
PERFORM
• Make outsourcing, special order, segment profitability, sales mix, or sell-or-process-further decisions that affect current period operations
EVALUATE
• Examine each short-run decision and how it affects the organization
• Identify and prescribe corrective action for short-run decisions
• Conduct post completion audits to determine if short-run outcomes were achieved
COMMUNICATE
• Prepare reports related to short-run decisions throughout the year
© Cengage Learning 2014

APPLY IT!

When managers make short-run decisions that are critical to their business, they ask questions. From the list that follows, select the questions a manager might ask.

1. When should products and services be outsourced?
2. Which capital budget proposal should be accepted?
3. When is a business segment profitable?
4. When resource constraints exist, what is the best sales mix?
5. When should products or services be sold as is or processed further into different products or services?
6. When should a special order for service or products be accepted?

SOLUTION

All are examples of questions managers might ask when making short-term decisions that are critical to their business's success.

TriLevel Problem

JGI/Jamie Grill/Blend Images/Corbis

Bank of America

The beginning of this chapter focused on **Bank of America**. Complete the following requirements in order to answer the questions posed at the beginning of the chapter.

Section 1: Concepts
Why is the concept of cost-benefit important when making short-run decisions?

Section 2: Accounting Applications
How does incremental analysis ensure a wise allocation of resources involved in short-run decisions?

Suppose a loan officer at a bank like Bank of America has been analyzing Home Services, Inc., to determine whether the bank should grant it a loan. Home Services has been in business for ten years, and its services now include tree trimming and auto, boat, and tile floor repair. The following data pertaining to those services were available for analysis:

	A	B	C	D	E	F	G
1	Home Services, Inc.						
2	Segmented Income Statement						
3	For the Year Ended December 31, 2014						
4							
5					Tile		
6			Auto	Boat	Floor	Tree	Total
7			Repair	Repair	Repair	Trimming	Impact
8	Sales		$297,500	$114,300	$126,400	$97,600	$635,800
9	Less variable costs						
10		Direct labor	$119,000	$ 40,005	$ 44,240	$34,160	$237,405
11		Operating supplies	14,875	5,715	6,320	4,880	31,790
12		Small tools	11,900	4,572	5,056	7,808	29,336
13		Replacement parts	59,500	22,860	25,280	—	107,640
14		Truck costs	—	11,430	12,640	14,640	38,710
15		Selling costs	44,625	17,145	18,960	9,760	90,490
16		Other variable costs	5,950	2,286	2,528	1,952	12,716
17	Total variable costs		$255,850	$104,013	$115,024	$73,200	$548,087
18	Contribution margin		$ 41,650	$ 10,287	$ 11,376	$24,400	$ 87,713
19	Less direct fixed costs		35,800	16,300	24,100	5,200	81,400
20	Segment margin		$ 5,850	$ (6,013)	$ (12,724)	$19,200	$ 6,313
21	Less common fixed						
22		costs					32,100
23	Operating income						
24		(loss)					$ (25,787)
25							

Home Services' profitability has decreased over the past two years, and to increase the likelihood that the company will qualify for a loan, the loan officer has advised its owner, Dale Bandy, to determine which service lines are not meeting the company's profit targets. Once Bandy has identified the unprofitable service lines, he can either eliminate them or set higher prices. If he sets higher prices, those prices will have to cover all variable and fixed operating, selling, and general administration costs.

1. Analyze the performance of the four service lines. Should Dale Bandy eliminate any of them? Explain your answer.
2. Why might Bandy want to continue providing unprofitable service lines?
3. Identify possible causes of a service's poor performance. What actions do you think Bandy should take to make his company a better loan candidate?

Section 3: Business Applications

How can incremental analysis help managers improve performance and take advantage of business opportunities?

To answer this question, match this chapter's managerial responsibilities with when they occur within the management process.

a. Plan
b. Perform
c. Evaluate
d. Communicate

1. Carry out short-run decision analysis: discover a problem or need
2. Prepare reports related to short-run decisions throughout the year.
3. Examine each short-run decision and how it affects the organization.
4. Identify and prescribe corrective action for short-run decisions.
5. Make outsourcing, special order, segment profitability, sales mix, or sell-or-process-further decisions that affect current period operations.
6. Conduct post completion audits to determine if short-run outcomes were achieved.

SOLUTION

Section 1: Concepts

The concept of *cost-benefit* is used to evaluate short-run decisions so that the benefits to be gained from a course of action or alternative can be compared to the costs of implementing it. For an alternative to be feasible, its benefits must outweigh its costs. Cost-benefit is an accounting convention or rule of thumb that considers both quantitative and qualitative cost and benefit measures to facilitate comparisons between alternatives for sound business decisions. Managers frequently take the following actions when applying the cost-benefit concept:

- **Step 1.** Discover a problem or need.
- **Step 2.** Identify all reasonable courses of action that can solve the problem or meet the need.
- **Step 3.** Prepare a thorough analysis of each possible solution, identifying its total costs, savings, benefits, other financial effects, and any qualitative factors.
- **Step 4.** Select the best course of action.

Section 2: Accounting Applications

1. In deciding whether to eliminate any of the four service lines, Dale Bandy should concentrate on those that have a negative segment margin. If the revenues from a service line are less than the sum of its variable and direct fixed costs, then other service lines must cover some of the losing line's costs and carry the burden of the common fixed costs.

   By looking at the segmented income statement, Dale Bandy can see that the company will improve its operating income by $18,737 ($6,013 + $12,724) if he eliminates the boat and tile floor repair services, both of which have a negative segment margin. Bandy's decision can also be supported by the following analysis:

	A	B	C	D	E
1		Home Services, Inc.			
2		Segment Profitability Decision			
3					
4					Difference in
5					Favor of
6			Keep	Drop	Dropping
7			Boat Repair	Boat Repair	Boat Repair
8			and	and	and
9			Tile Floor Repair	Tile Floor Repair	Tile Floor Repair
10	Sales		$635,800	$395,100	$(240,700)
11	Less variable costs		548,087	329,050	219,037
12	Contribution margin		$ 87,713	$ 66,050	$ (21,663)
13	Less direct fixed costs		81,400	41,000	40,400
14	Segment margin		$ 6,313	$ 25,050	$ 18,737
15	Less common fixed costs		32,100	32,100	—
16	Operating income (loss)		$ (25,787)	$ (7,050)	$ 18,737

2. Bandy may want to continue offering the unprofitable service lines if their elimination would have a negative effect on the sale of the auto repair or tree trimming services.
3. The following are among the possible causes of a service's poor performance:
   a. Service fees set too low
   b. Inadequate advertising
   c. Excessively high direct labor costs
   d. Other variable costs
   e. Poor management of fixed costs
   f. Excessive supervision costs

   To improve profitability and make the company a better candidate for a bank loan, Bandy should eliminate non-value-adding costs, increase service fees, or increase the volume of services provided to customers.

Section 3: Business Applications

1. a
2. d
3. c
4. c
5. b
6. c

Chapter Review

Describe how the concept of cost-benefit is useful when making short-run decisions. LO 1

The concept of cost-benefit considers both quantitative and qualitative cost and benefit measures to facilitate comparisons between alternatives for sound business decisions. Managers apply the cost-benefit concept when following the four decision-making steps: (1) discover a problem or need; (2) identify all reasonable courses of action that can solve the problem or meet the need; (3) prepare a thorough analysis of each possible solution, identifying its total costs, savings, benefits, other financial effects, and any qualitative factors; and (4) select the best course of action.

Incremental analysis helps managers compare alternative courses of action by focusing on the cost and benefit differences in projected revenues and costs. Any data that relate to future costs, revenues, or uses of resources and that will differ among alternative courses of action are considered relevant decision information. Examples of relevant information are projected sales or estimated costs, such as the costs of direct materials or direct labor, which differ for each alternative. The manager analyzes relevant information to determine which alternative contributes the most to profits or incurs the lowest costs. Only data that differ for each alternative are considered. Differential or incremental costs are costs that vary among alternatives and thus are relevant to the decision. Sunk costs are past costs that cannot be recovered. They are irrelevant to the decision process. Opportunity costs are revenue or income forgone as a result of choosing an alternative.

Perform incremental analysis for outsourcing decisions. LO 2

Outsourcing (including make-or-buy) decision analysis helps managers decide whether to use suppliers from outside the organization to perform services or provide goods that could be performed or produced internally. An incremental analysis of the expected costs and revenues for each alternative is used to identify the best alternative.

Perform incremental analysis for special order decisions. LO 3

A special order decision is a decision about whether to accept or reject a special order at a price below the normal market price. One approach is to compare the special order price with the relevant costs to see if a profit can be generated. Another approach is to prepare a special order bid price by calculating a minimum selling price for the special order. Generally, fixed costs are irrelevant to a special order decision because such costs are covered by regular sales activity and do not differ among alternatives.

Perform incremental analysis for segment profitability decisions. LO 4

Segment profitability decisions involve the review of product lines, services, sales territories, divisions, or departments. Managers often must decide whether to add or drop a segment. A segment with a negative segment margin may be dropped. A segment margin is a segment's sales revenue minus its direct costs, which include variable costs and avoidable fixed costs. Avoidable costs are traceable to a specific segment. If the segment is eliminated, the avoidable costs will also be eliminated.

Perform incremental analysis for sales mix decisions involving constrained resources. LO 5

Sales mix decisions require the selection of the most profitable combination of sales items when a company makes more than one product or service using a common constrained resource. The product or service generating the highest contribution margin per constrained resource is offered and sold first.

Perform incremental analysis for sell-or-process-further decisions. LO 6

Sell-or-process-further decisions require managers to choose between selling a joint product at its split-off point or processing it into a more refined product. Managers compare the incremental revenues and costs of the two alternatives. Joint processing costs are irrelevant to the decision because they are identical for both alternatives. A product should be processed further only if the incremental revenues generated exceed the incremental costs incurred.

Describe why short-run decision analysis is critical for business success. LO 7

Managers use both financial and nonfinancial quantitative and qualitative information to analyze the effects of past and potential business actions on their organization's resources and profits on a daily basis. Although many business problems are unique and cannot be solved by following strict rules, managers often use a suite of short-run decision-making methods and tools. Those decision methods and tools were the focus of this chapter. During the management process, as managers plan, perform, evaluate, and report on business operations, they utilize these tools and methods to ensure a wise allocation of resources and, at the same time, minimize the daily business risks involved.

Key Terms and Ratios

avoidable costs 1046 (LO4)
differential cost 1040 (LO1)
incremental analysis 1040 (LO1)
incremental revenue 1051 (LO6)
joint costs 1051 (LO6)
joint products 1051 (LO6)
make-or-buy decisions 1043 (LO2)
opportunity costs 1042 (LO1)
outsourcing 1043 (LO2)
sales mix decision 1048 (LO5)
segment margin 1046 (LO4)
sell-or-process-further decision 1051 (LO6)
short-run decision analysis 1040 (LO1)
special order decisions 1044 (LO3)
split-off point 1051 (LO6)
sunk cost 1041 (LO1)

Chapter Assignments

DISCUSSION QUESTIONS

LO 1, 7 **DQ1. CONCEPT ▶ BUSINESS APPLICATION ▶** How do managers use the concept of cost-benefit for short-run decisions during the planning phase of the management process?

LO 1, 7 **DQ2. CONCEPT ▶ BUSINESS APPLICATION ▶** How do managers use the concept of cost-benefit for short-run decisions during the performing phase of the management process?

LO 1, 7 **DQ3. CONCEPT ▶ BUSINESS APPLICATION ▶** How do managers use the concept of cost-benefit for short-run decisions during the evaluating phase of the management process?

LO 1, 7 **DQ4. CONCEPT ▶ BUSINESS APPLICATION ▶** How do managers use the concept of cost-benefit for short-run decisions during the communicating phase of the management process?

SHORT EXERCISES

LO 1 **Qualitative and Quantitative Information in Short-Run Decision Analysis**

SE1. The owner of a Mexican restaurant is deciding whether to take fish tacos off the menu. State whether each item of decision information that follows is qualitative or quantitative. If the information is quantitative, specify whether it is financial or nonfinancial.

1. The time needed to prepare the fish
2. The daily number of customers who order the tacos
3. Whether competing Mexican restaurants have this entrée on the menu
4. The labor cost of the chef who prepares the fish tacos
5. The fact that the president of a nearby company who brings ten guests with him each week always orders fish tacos

LO 1 **Using Incremental Analysis**

SE2. Fortress Hill Corporation has assembled the following information related to the purchase of a new cable car:

	Peaks Machine	Valley Machine
Increase in revenue	$44,200	$49,300
Increase in annual operating costs:		
Direct materials	12,200	12,200
Direct labor	10,200	10,600
Variable overhead	24,500	26,900
Fixed overhead (including depreciation)	12,400	12,400

Using incremental analysis and only relevant information, compute the difference in favor of the Valley machine.

LO 2 **Outsourcing Decision**

SE3. Will Company assembles products from a group of interconnecting parts. The company produces some of the parts and buys some from outside vendors. The vendor for Part X has just increased its price by 35 percent, to $10 per unit for the first 5,000 units and $9 per additional unit ordered each year. The company uses 7,500 units of Part X each year. Unit costs if the company makes the part are as follows.

Direct materials	$3.50
Direct labor	2.00
Variable overhead	4.00
Variable selling costs for the assembled product	3.75

Should Will Company continue to purchase Part X or begin making it?

LO 2 **Outsourcing Decision**

SE4. Dental Associates, Inc., is currently operating at less than capacity. The company thinks it could cut costs by outsourcing dental cleaning to an independent dental hygienist for $50 per cleaning. Currently, a dental hygienist is employed for $30 an hour. A dental cleaning usually takes one hour to perform and consumes $10 of dental supplies, $8 of variable overhead, and $16 of fixed overhead. Should Dental Associates continue to perform dental cleanings, or should it begin to outsource them?

LO 3 **Special Order Decision**

SE5. Hadley Company has received a special order request for Product R3P at a selling price of $20 per unit. This order is over and above normal production, and budgeted production and sales targets for the year have already been exceeded. Capacity exists to satisfy the special order. No selling costs will be incurred in connection with this order. Unit costs to manufacture and sell Product R3P are as follows: direct materials, $7.60; direct labor, $3.75; variable overhead, $9.25; fixed overhead, $4.85; variable selling costs, $2.75; and fixed general and administrative costs, $6.75. Should Hadley accept the order?

LO 3 **Special Order Decision**

SE6. Wong Accounting Services is considering a special order that it received from one of its corporate clients. The special order calls for Wong to prepare the individual tax returns of the corporation's four largest shareholders. The company has idle capacity

(Continued)

that could be used to complete the special order. The following data have been gathered about the preparation of individual tax returns:

Materials cost per page	$1
Average hourly labor rate	$60
Standard hours per return	4
Standard pages per return	10
Variable overhead cost per page	$0.50
Fixed overhead cost per page	$0.50

Wong would be satisfied with a $40 gross profit per return. Compute the minimum bid price for the entire order.

LO 4 **Segment Profitability Decision**

SE7. ACCOUNTING CONNECTION ▶ Peruna Company is evaluating its two divisions, North Division and South Division. Data for North Division include sales of $530,000, variable costs of $290,000, and fixed costs of $260,000, 50 percent of which are traceable to the division. South Division's efforts for the same period include sales of $610,000, variable costs of $340,000, and fixed costs of $290,000, 60 percent of which are traceable to the division. Should Peruna consider eliminating either division? Is there any other problem that needs attention? Explain your answer.

LO 5 **Sales Mix Decision**

SE8. Blizzard, Inc., makes three kinds of snowboards, but it has a limited number of machine hours available to make them. Product line data are as follows:

	Wood	Plastic	Graphite
Machine hours per unit	1.25	1.0	1.5
Selling price per unit	$100	$120	$200
Variable manufacturing cost per unit	$45	$50	$100
Variable selling costs per unit	$15	$26	$37

In what order should the snowboard product lines be produced?

LO 6 **Sell-or-Process-Further Decision**

SE9. Gomez Industries produces three products from a single operation. Product A sells for $4 per unit, Product B for $6 per unit, and Product C for $10 per unit. When B is processed further, there are additional unit costs of $3, and its new selling price is $10 per unit. Each product is allocated $2 of joint costs from the initial production operation. Should Product B be processed further, or should it be sold at the end of the initial operation?

LO 6 **Sell-or-Process-Further Decision**

SE10. In an attempt to provide superb customer service, Richard V. Meats is considering the expansion of its product offerings from whole hams and turkeys to complete ham and turkey dinners. Each dinner would include a carved ham or turkey, two side dishes, and six rolls or cornbread. The company's accountant has compiled the following relevant information:

Product	Sales Revenue if No Additional Service	Sales Revenue if Processed Further	Additional Processing Costs
Ham	$30	$50	$15
Turkey	20	35	15

A cooked, uncarved ham costs the company $20 to prepare. A cooked, uncarved turkey costs $15 to prepare. Use incremental analysis to determine which products the company should offer.

EXERCISES: SET A

LO 1 **Incremental Analysis**

E1A. Coffee Culture Company's managers must decide which of two coffee grinders—Y or Z—to buy. The grinders have the same purchase price but different revenue and cost characteristics. The company currently owns Grinder X, which it bought three years ago for $10,000 and which has accumulated depreciation of $9,000 and a book value of $1,000. Grinder X is now obsolete as a result of advances in technology and cannot be sold or traded in.

The accountant has collected the following annual revenue and operating cost estimates for the two new machines:

	Grinder Y	Grinder Z
Increase in revenue	$15,000	$18,000
Increase in annual operating costs:		
Direct materials	4,500	4,500
Direct labor	3,000	4,000
Variable overhead	2,000	3,000
Fixed overhead (depreciation included)	4,000	4,000

1. Identify the relevant data in this problem.
2. Prepare an incremental analysis to aid the managers in their decision.
3. **ACCOUNTING CONNECTION** ▶ Should the company purchase Grinder Y or Grinder Z? Explain your answer.

LO 2 **Outsourcing Decision**

E2A. ACCOUNTING CONNECTION ▶ Cyber Queen Services' manager must decide whether to hire a new employee or to outsource some of the web design work to Kai Yu, a freelance graphic designer. If she hires a new employee, she will pay $30 per design hour for the employee to work 500 hours and incur service overhead costs of $2 per design hour. She will also redirect the use of a computer and server to generate $4,000 in additional revenue from web page maintenance work. If she outsources the work to Kai Yu, she will pay $34 per design hour for 500 hours of work. Should Cyber Queen Services hire a new designer or outsource the work to Kai Yu? Explain your answer.

LO 2 **Outsourcing Decision**

E3A. One component of a radio produced by Audio Systems, Inc., is currently being purchased for $225 per 100 parts. Management is studying the possibility of manufacturing that component. Annual production (usage) at Audio is 70,000 units; fixed costs (all of which remain unchanged whether the part is made or purchased) are $38,500; and variable costs are $0.95 per unit for direct materials, $0.55 per unit for direct labor, and $0.60 per unit for variable overhead. Using incremental analysis, decide whether Audio Systems should manufacture the part or continue to purchase it from an outside vendor.

LO 3 **Special Order Decision**

E4A. Antiquities, Inc., produces antique-looking books. Management has just received a request for a special order of 2,000 books and must decide whether to accept it. Venus Company, the purchaser, is offering to pay $22.00 per book, plus $3.00 per book for shipping costs.

The variable production costs per book include $9.20 for direct materials, $4.00 for direct labor, and $3.80 for variable overhead. The current year's production is 22,000 books, and maximum capacity is 25,000 books. Fixed costs, including overhead, advertising, and selling and administrative costs, total $80,000. The usual selling price is $25.00 per book. Shipping costs, which are additional, average $3.00 per book.

Determine whether Antiquities should accept the special order.

LO 3 **Special Order Decision**

E5A. Fun Sporting Goods, Inc., manufactures a complete line of sporting equipment. Lei Enterprises operates a large chain of discount stores. Lei has approached Fun with a special order for 20,000 deluxe baseballs. Instead of being packaged separately, the balls are to be packed in boxes containing 500 baseballs each. Lei is willing to pay $2.50 per baseball. Fun's standard annual expected production is 400,000 baseballs, but Fun is on track to produce 410,000 baseballs as the current year's production. Fun's maximum production capacity is 450,000 baseballs. The following additional information is available:

Standard unit cost data for 400,000 baseballs:	
Direct materials	$ 1.00
Direct labor	0.50
Overhead:	
Variable	0.60
Fixed ($100,000 ÷ 400,000)	0.25
Packaging per unit	0.20
Advertising ($60,000 ÷ 400,000)	0.15
Other fixed selling and administrative expenses ($120,000 ÷ 400,000)	0.30
Product unit cost	$ 3.00
Unit selling price	$ 4.00
Total estimated bulk packaging costs for special order (20,000 baseballs: 500 per box)	$2,000

1. Should Fun Sporting Goods accept Lei's offer?
2. What would be the minimum order price per baseball if Fun would like to earn a profit of $3,000 from the special order?

LO 4 **Elimination of Unprofitable Segment Decision**

E6A. Gold's Glass, Inc., has three divisions: Commercial, Nonprofit, and Residential. The segmented income statement for last year revealed the following:

Gold's Glass, Inc.
Divisional Profit Summary and Decision Analysis

	Commercial Division	Nonprofit Division	Residential Division	Total Company
Sales	$300,000	$523,000	$837,000	$1,660,000
Less variable costs	157,000	425,000	472,000	1,054,000
Contribution margin	$143,000	$ 98,000	$365,000	$ 606,000
Less direct fixed costs	114,000	116,000	139,000	369,000
Segment margin	$ 29,000	$ (18,000)	$226,000	$ 237,000
Less common fixed costs				168,000
Operating income				$ 69,000

1. How will Gold's Glass be affected if the Nonprofit Division is dropped?
2. Assume the elimination of the Nonprofit Division causes the sales of the Residential Division to decrease by 10 percent. How will Gold's Glass be affected if the Nonprofit Division is dropped?

LO 5 **Constrained Resource Usage**

E7A. ZE, Inc., manufactures two products that require both machine processing and labor operations. Although there is unlimited demand for both products, ZE could devote all its capacities to a single product. Unit prices, cost data, and processing requirements follow.

	Product E	Product Z
Unit selling price	$75	$200
Unit variable costs	$25	$80
Machine hours per unit	0.4	1.2
Labor hours per unit	2.0	6.0

Next year, the company will be limited to 160,000 machine hours and 120,000 labor hours. Fixed costs for the year are $1,000,000.

1. **ACCOUNTING CONNECTION ▶** Compute the most profitable combination of products to be produced next year. Explain your answer.
2. Prepare an income statement using the contribution margin format for the product volume computed in **1**.

LO 5 **Sales Mix Decision**

E8A. GAME Enterprises manufactures three computer games called Rocket Star, Game Master, and Rock Warrior. The product line data follow.

	Rocket Star	Game Master	Rock Warrior
Current unit sales demand	20,000	30,000	18,000
Machine hours per unit	2.0	1.0	2.5
Selling price per unit	$20.00	$16.00	$30.00
Unit variable manufacturing costs	$12.50	$10.00	$18.75
Unit variable selling costs	$6.50	$5.00	$6.25

The current production capacity is 100,000 machine hours.

1. Which computer game should be manufactured first? Which should be manufactured second? Which last?
2. How many of each type of computer game should be manufactured and sold to maximize the company's contribution margin based on the current production activity of 100,000 machine hours? What is the total contribution margin for that combination?

LO 5 **Sales Mix Decision**

E9A. ACCOUNTING CONNECTION ▶ Web Services, a small company owned by Simon Orozco, provides web page services to small businesses. His services include the preparation of basic pages and custom pages. The following summary of information will be used to make several short-run decisions for Web Services:

	Basic Pages	Custom Pages
Service revenue per page	$200	$750
Variable costs per page	77	600
Contribution margin per page	$123	$150

Total annual fixed costs are $78,000.

One of Web Services' two graphic designers, Taylor Campbell, is planning to take maternity leave in July and August. As a result, there will only be one designer available to perform the work, and design labor hours will be a resource constraint. Orozco plans to help the other designer complete the projected 160 orders for basic pages and 30 orders for custom pages for those two months. However, he wants to know which type of page Web Services should advertise and market. Although custom pages have a higher contribution margin per service, each custom page requires 12.5 design hours, whereas basic pages require only 1 design hour per page. On which page type should his company focus? Explain your answer.

LO 6 **Sell-or-Process-Further Decision**

E10A. ACCOUNTING CONNECTION ▶ Beef Products, Inc., processes cattle. It can sell the meat as sides of beef or process it further into final cuts (steaks, roasts, and hamburger). As part of the company's strategic plan, management is looking for new markets for meat or meat by-products. The production process currently separates hides and bones for sale to other manufacturers. However, management is considering whether it would be profitable to process the hides into leather and the bones into fertilizer. The costs of the cattle and of transporting, hanging, storing, and cutting sides of beef are $100,000. The company's accountant provided these data:

Product	Sales Revenue if Sold at Split-Off	Sales Revenue if Sold After Further Processing	Additional Processing Costs
Meat	$100,000	$200,000	$80,000
Bones	20,000	40,000	25,000
Hides	50,000	60,000	5,000

Should the products be processed further? Explain your answer.

LO 6 **Sell-or-Process-Further Decision**

E11A. ACCOUNTING CONNECTION ▶ Four Star Pizza manufactures make-at-home frozen pizza and calzone kits and sells them for $5 each. It is currently considering a proposal to manufacture and sell fully prepared products. The following relevant information has been gathered by management:

Product	Sales Revenue if No Additional Processing	Sales Revenue if Processed Further	Additional Processing Costs
Pizza	$5	$15	$6
Calzone	5	10	6

Use incremental analysis to determine which products Four Star should offer. Explain your answer.

EXERCISES: SET B

Visit the textbook companion website at www.cengagebrain.com to access Exercise Set B for this chapter.

PROBLEMS

LO 2 **Outsourcing Decision**

✔ 1: Incremental cost to make: $93,750
✔ 2: Variable unit cost to make: $16

P1. Freeze Refrigerator Company purchases ice makers and installs them in its products. The ice makers cost $138 per case, and each case contains 12 ice makers. The supplier recently gave advance notice that the price will rise by 50 percent immediately. Freeze Refrigerator Company has idle equipment that with only a few minor changes could be used to produce similar ice makers.

Cost estimates have been prepared under the assumption that the company could make the product itself. Direct materials would cost $100.80 per 12 ice makers. Direct labor required would be 10 minutes per ice maker at a labor rate of $18.00 per hour. Variable overhead would be $4.60 per ice maker. Fixed overhead, which would be incurred under either decision alternative, would be $32,420 a year for depreciation and $234,000 a year for other costs. Production and usage are estimated at 75,000 ice makers a year. (Assume that any idle equipment cannot be used for any other purpose.)

REQUIRED

1. Prepare an incremental analysis to determine whether the ice makers should be made within the company or purchased from the outside supplier at the higher price.
2. Compute the variable unit cost to (a) make one ice maker and (b) buy one ice maker.

LO 3

Special Order Decision

✔ 1: Contribution margin from order: $6,420
✔ 2: Total variable costs per unit: $621.50

P2. On March 26, Buoy Industries received a special order request for 120 ten-foot aluminum fishing boats. Operating on a fiscal year ending May 31, the company already has orders that will allow it to produce at budget levels for the period. However, extra capacity exists to produce the 120 additional boats.

The terms of the special order call for a selling price of $675 per boat, and the customer will pay all shipping costs. No sales personnel were involved in soliciting the order.

The ten-foot fishing boat has the following cost estimates:

- Direct materials, aluminum, two 49 × 89 sheets at $155 per sheet
- Direct labor, 14 hours at $15.00 per hour
- Variable overhead, $7.25 per direct labor hour
- Fixed overhead, $4.50 per direct labor hour
- Variable selling expenses, $46.50 per boat
- Variable shipping expenses, $57.50 per boat

REQUIRED

1. Prepare an analysis for Buoy's management to use in deciding whether to accept or reject the special order. What decision should be made?
2. To make an $8,000 profit on this order, what would be the lowest possible price that Buoy could charge per boat?

LO 4

Elimination of Unprofitable Segment Decision

SPREADSHEET

✔ 1: Revised operating income: $77,000
✔ 2: URL Services segment margin: $131,000

P3. URL Services has two divisions: Basic Webpages and Custom Webpages. Ricky Vega, Custom's manager, wants to find out why Custom is not profitable. He has prepared the reports that follow.

URL Services
Segmented Income Statement
For the Year Ended December 31

	Basic Webpages (1,000 units)	Custom Webpages (200 units)	Total Company
Service revenue	$200,000	$150,000	$350,000
Less variable costs:			
Direct professional labor: design	$ 32,000	$ 80,000	$112,000
Direct professional labor: install	30,000	4,000	34,000
Direct professional labor: maintain	15,000	36,000	51,000
Total variable costs	$ 77,000	$120,000	$197,000
Contribution margin	$123,000	$ 30,000	$153,000
Less direct fixed costs:			
Depreciation on computer equipment	$ 6,000	$ 12,000	$ 18,000
Depreciation on servers	10,000	20,000	30,000
Total direct fixed costs	$ 16,000	$ 32,000	$ 48,000
Segment margin	$107,000	$ (2,000)	$105,000
Less common fixed costs:			
Building rent			$ 24,000
Supplies			1,000
Insurance			3,000
Telephone			1,500
Website rental			500
Total common fixed costs			$ 30,000
Operating income			$ 75,000

(Continued)

URL Services
Custom Webpages Division
Segment Profitability Decision
Incremental Analysis

	Design	Install	Maintain	Total
Service revenue	$ 60,000	$25,000	$65,000	$150,000
Less variable costs	80,000	4,000	36,000	120,000
Contribution margin	$(20,000)	$21,000	$29,000	$ 30,000
Less direct fixed costs	6,000	13,000	13,000	32,000
Segment margin	$(26,000)	$ 8,000	$16,000	$ (2,000)

1. How will URL Services be affected if the Custom Webpages Division is eliminated?
2. How will URL Services be affected if the Design segment of Custom Webpages is eliminated?
3. **ACCOUNTING CONNECTION ▶** What should Ricky Vega do? What additional information would be helpful to him in making the decision?

LO **5, 7**

Sales Mix Decision

SPREADSHEET

✔ 2: Product C5 contribution margin per machine hour: $2.50

P4. Common Chemical Company's management is evaluating its product mix in an attempt to maximize profits. For the past two years, Common has produced four products, and all have large markets in which to expand market share. Common's controller has gathered data from current operations and wants you to analyze them for him. Sales and operating data are as follows.

	Product A1	Product B7	Product C5	Product D9
Variable production costs	$71,000	$91,000	$91,920	$97,440
Variable selling costs	$10,200	$5,400	$12,480	$30,160
Fixed production costs	$20,400	$21,600	$29,120	$18,480
Fixed administrative costs	$3,400	$5,400	$6,240	$10,080
Total sales	$122,000	$136,000	$156,400	$161,200
Units produced and sold	85,000	45,000	26,000	14,000
Machine hours used*	17,000	18,000	20,800	16,800

*Common's scarce resource, machine hours, is being used to full capacity.

REQUIRED

1. Compute the machine hours needed to produce one unit of each product.
2. Determine the contribution margin per machine hour for each product.
3. Which product line(s) should be targeted for market share expansion?

LO **6, 7**

Sell-or-Process-Further Decision

✔ 1: Incremental contribution margin for bagels with cream cheese: $1.50
✔ 1: Incremental contribution margin for bagel sandwiches: $2.00
✔ 3: Operating income from further processing bagel sandwiches with cheese: $0.50

P5. Bakers Bagels, Inc., produces and sells 20 types of bagels by the dozen. Bagels are priced at $6.00 per dozen (or $0.50 each) and cost $0.20 per unit to produce. The company is considering processing the bagels further into two products: bagels with cream cheese and bagel sandwiches. It would cost an additional $0.50 per unit to produce bagels with cream cheese, and the new selling price would be $2.50 each. It would cost an additional $1.00 per sandwich to produce bagel sandwiches, and the new selling price would be $3.50 each.

REQUIRED

1. Identify the relevant per-unit costs and revenues for the alternatives. Are there any sunk costs?
2. Based on the information in requirement **1**, should Bakers Bagels expand its product offerings?
3. **ACCOUNTING CONNECTION ▶** Suppose that Bakers Bagels did expand its product line to include bagels with cream cheese and bagel sandwiches. Based on customer feedback, the company determined that it could further process those two products

into bagels with cream cheese and fruit and bagel sandwiches with cheese. The company's accountant compiled the following information:

Product (per unit)	Sales Revenue if Sold without Further Processing	Sales Revenue if Processed Further	Additional Processing Costs
Bagels with cream cheese	$2.50	$3.50	Fruit: $1.00
Bagel sandwiches	3.50	4.50	Cheese: 0.50

Perform an incremental analysis to determine if Bakers Bagels should process its products further. Explain your findings.

ALTERNATE PROBLEMS

LO 2

Outsourcing Decision

✔ 2: Variable unit cost to make: $28.00

P6. Sisters Restaurant purchases cheesecakes and offers them as dessert items on its menu. The cheesecakes cost $24 each, and a cake contains 8 pieces. The supplier recently gave notice that the price will rise by 20 percent immediately. Sisters has idle equipment that, with only a few minor changes, could be used to produce similar cheesecakes.

Cost estimates have been prepared under the assumption that the company could make the product itself. Direct materials would cost $7.00 per cheesecake. Direct labor required would be 0.5 hour per cheesecake at a labor rate of $24.00 per hour. Variable overhead would be $9.00 per cheesecake. Fixed overhead, which would be incurred under either decision alternative, would be $35,200 a year for depreciation and $230,000 a year for other costs. Production and usage are estimated at 3,600 cheesecakes a year. (Assume that any idle equipment cannot be used for any other purpose.)

REQUIRED

1. Prepare an incremental analysis to determine whether the cheesecakes should be made within the company or purchased from the outside supplier at the higher price.
2. Compute the variable unit cost to (a) make one cheesecake and (b) buy one cheesecake.

LO 3

Special Order Decision

✔ 1: Total variable costs per thousand: $48.50

P7. Leisure Resorts, Ltd., has approached EZ Printers, Inc., with a special order to produce 300,000 two-page brochures. Most of EZ's work consists of recurring short-run orders. Leisure Resorts is offering a one-time order, and EZ has the capacity to handle the order over a two-month period.

Leisure Resorts' management has stated that the company would be unwilling to pay more than $48 per 1,000 brochures. EZ's controller assembled the following cost data for this decision analysis:

Direct materials (paper)	$26.80 per 1,000 brochures
Direct labor costs	$6.80 per 1,000 brochures
Direct materials (ink)	$4.40 per 1,000 brochures
Variable production overhead	$6.20 per 1,000 brochures
Machine maintenance (fixed cost)	$1.00 per direct labor dollar
Other fixed production overhead	$2.40 per direct labor dollar
Variable packing costs	$4.30 per 1,000 brochures
General and administrative expenses (fixed costs) to be allocated	$5.25 per direct labor dollar

REQUIRED

1. Prepare an analysis for EZ's management to use in deciding whether to accept or reject Leisure Resorts' offer. What decision should be made?
2. What is the lowest possible price EZ can charge per thousand and still make a $6,000 profit on the order?

LO 4

Elimination of Unprofitable Segment Decision

SPREADSHEET

✔ 1: Revised operating income: $94,000
✔ 2: Security Services segment margin: $148,000

P8. Security Services has two divisions: Basic Monitoring and Custom Monitoring. Rachel Sims, Custom's manager, wants to find out why the Custom Monitoring Division is not profitable. She has prepared the reports that follow.

Security Services
Segmented Income Statement
For the Year Ended December 31

	Basic Monitoring (1,000 locations)	Custom Monitoring (200 locations)	Total Company
Service revenue	$250,000	$100,000	$350,000
Less variable costs:			
Direct professional labor: design	$ 25,000	$ 40,000	$ 65,000
Direct professional labor: install	20,000	14,000	34,000
Direct professional labor: maintain	5,000	16,000	21,000
Total variable costs	$ 50,000	$ 70,000	$120,000
Contribution margin	$200,000	$ 30,000	$230,000
Less direct fixed costs:			
Depreciation on computer equipment	$ 6,000	$ 14,000	$ 20,000
Depreciation on servers	50,000	20,000	70,000
Total direct fixed costs	$ 56,000	$ 34,000	$ 90,000
Segment margin	$144,000	$ (4,000)	$140,000
Less common fixed costs:			
Building rent			$ 34,000
Supplies			2,000
Insurance			6,000
Telephone			2,500
Equipment rental			5,500
Total common fixed costs			$ 50,000
Operating income			$ 90,000

Security Services
Custom Monitoring Division
Segment Profitability Decision
Incremental Analysis

	Design	Install	Maintain	Total
Service revenue	$50,000	$25,000	$25,000	$100,000
Less variable costs	50,000	10,000	10,000	70,000
Contribution margin	$ 0.00	$15,000	$15,000	$ 30,000
Less direct fixed costs	8,000	13,000	13,000	34,000
Segment margin	$(8,000)	$ 2,000	$ 2,000	$ (4,000)

1. How will Security Services be affected if the Custom Monitoring Division is eliminated?
2. How will Security Services be affected if the Design segment of Custom Monitoring is eliminated?
3. **ACCOUNTING CONNECTION ▶** What should Rachel Sims do? What additional information would be helpful to her in making the decision?

LO 5, 7

Sales Mix Decision

SPREADSHEET

P9. Dr. Stott, who specializes in internal medicine, wants to analyze his sales mix to find out how the time of his physician assistant, Connie Mortiz, can be used to generate the highest operating income.

✔ 1: Office visits contribution margin per hour: $100
✔ 2: Three hours for office visits
✔ 2: Total daily contribution margin: $820

Mortiz sees patients in Dr. Stott's office, consults with patients over the telephone, and conducts one daily weight-loss support group attended by up to 50 patients. Statistics for the three services are as follows.

	Office Visits	Phone Calls	Weight-Loss Support Group
Maximum number of patient billings per day	20	40	50
Hours per billing	0.25	0.10	1.0
Billing rate	$50	$25	$10
Variable costs	$25	$12	$5

Mortiz works seven hours a day.

REQUIRED

1. Determine the best sales mix. Rank the services offered in order of their profitability.
2. Based on the ranking in requirement 1, how much time should Mortiz spend on each service in a day? (*Hint:* Remember to consider the maximum number of patient billings per day.) What would be the daily total contribution margin generated by Mortiz?
3. Dr. Stott believes the ranking is incorrect. He knows that the daily 60-minute meeting of the weight-loss support group has 50 patients and should continue to be offered. If the new ranking for the services is (1) weight-loss support group, (2) phone calls, and (3) office visits, how much time should Mortiz spend on each service in a day? What would be the total contribution margin generated by Mortiz, assuming the weight-loss support group has the maximum number of patient billings?
4. **ACCOUNTING CONNECTION ▶** Which ranking would you recommend? What additional amount of total contribution margin would be generated if your recommendation were to be accepted?

LO 6, 7

Sell-or-Process-Further Decision

✔ 1: Total costs for brochures: $26,200
✔ 2: Incremental loss to income: $2,400

P10. CU, Inc., developed a promotional program for a local shopping center a few years ago. Having invested $360,000 in developing the original promotion campaign, the firm is ready to present its client with an add-on contract offer that includes the original promotion areas of (1) a TV advertising campaign, (2) a series of brochures for mass mailing, and (3) a special rotating BIG SALE schedule for 10 of the 28 tenants in the shopping center. The revenue terms from the original contract with the shopping center and the offer for the add-on contract, which extends the original contract terms, follow.

	Original Contract Terms	Extended Contract Including Add-On Terms
TV advertising campaign	$520,000	$ 580,000
Brochure series	210,000	230,000
Rotating BIG SALE schedule	170,000	190,000
Totals	$900,000	$1,000,000

CU estimates that the following additional costs will be incurred by extending the contract:

	TV Campaign	Brochures	BIG SALE Schedule
Direct labor	$30,000	$ 9,000	$7,000
Variable overhead costs	22,000	14,000	6,000
Fixed overhead costs*	12,000	4,000	2,000

*80 percent are direct fixed costs applied to this contract.

(*Continued*)

REQUIRED

1. Compute the costs that will be incurred for each part of the add-on portion of the contract.
2. **ACCOUNTING CONNECTION ▶** Should CU offer the add-on contract, or should it ask for a final settlement check based on the original contract only? Defend your answer.
3. **ACCOUNTING CONNECTION ▶** If management of the shopping center indicates that the terms of the add-on contract are negotiable, how should CU respond?

CASES

LO 1, 7

Conceptual Understanding: Defining and Identifying Relevant Information

C1. BUSINESS APPLICATION ▶ Big Burgers is in the fast-food restaurant business. One component of its marketing strategy is to increase sales by expanding in foreign markets. It uses both financial and nonfinancial quantitative and qualitative information when deciding whether to open restaurants abroad. Big decided to open a restaurant in Prague (Czech Republic) five years ago. The following information helped the managers in making that decision:

Financial Quantitative Information

- Operating information
- Estimated food, labor, and other operating costs (e.g., taxes, insurance, utilities, and supplies)
- Estimated selling price for each food item
- Capital investment information
- Cost of land, building, equipment, and furniture
- Financing options and amounts

Nonfinancial Quantitative Information

- Estimated daily number of customers, hamburgers to be sold, employees to work
- High-traffic time periods
- Income of people living in the area
- Ratio of population to number of restaurants in the market area
- Traffic counts in front of similar restaurants in the area

Qualitative Information

- Government regulations, taxes, duties, tariffs, political involvement in business operations
- Property ownership restrictions
- Site visibility
- Accessibility of store location
- Training process for local managers
- Hiring process for employees
- Local customs and practices

Big Burgers has hired you as a consultant and given you an income statement comparing the operating incomes of its five restaurants in Eastern Europe. You have noticed that the Prague location is operating at a loss (including unallocated fixed costs) and must decide whether to recommend closing that restaurant.

Review the information used in making the decision to open the restaurant. Identify the types of information that would also be relevant in deciding whether to close the restaurant. What additional information would be relevant in making your decision?

LO 1, 7

Group Activity: Identifying Relevant Decision Information

C2. BUSINESS APPLICATION ▶ Select two destinations for a one-week vacation, and gather information about them from brochures, magazines, travel agents, the Internet, and friends. Then list the relevant quantitative and qualitative information in order of its importance to your decision. Analyze the information, and select a destination.

Which factors were most important to your decision? Why? Which were least important? Why? How would the process of identifying relevant information differ if the president of your company asked you to prepare a budget for the next training meeting, to be held at a location of your choice?

Your instructor will divide the class into groups and ask each group to discuss this case. One student from each group will summarize his or her group's findings and debrief the entire class.

LO **6, 7**

Conceptual Understanding: Decision to Add a New Department

C3. *(CMA adapted)* Cakes Company's management is considering a proposal to install a third production department in its factory building. With the company's existing production setup, direct materials are processed through the Mixing Department to produce Materials A and B in equal proportions. The Shaping Department then processes Material A to yield Product C. Material B is sold as is at $20.25 per pound. Product C has a selling price of $100.00 per pound. There is a proposal to add a Baking Department to process Material B into Product D. It is expected that any quantity of Product D can be sold for $30.00 per pound.

Costs per pound under this proposal appear here.

	Mixing Department (Materials A and B)	Shaping Department (Product C)	Baking Department (Product D)
Costs from Mixing Department	—	$52.80	$13.20
Direct materials	$20.00	—	—
Direct labor	6.00	9.00	3.50
Variable overhead	4.00	8.00	4.00
Fixed overhead:			
Traceable (direct, avoidable)	2.25	2.25	1.80
Allocated (common, unavoidable)	0.75	0.75	0.75
Totals	$33.00	$72.80	$23.25

1. If sales and production levels are expected to remain constant in the foreseeable future, and there are no foreseeable alternative uses for the factory space, should Cakes Company add a Baking Department and produce Product D, if 100,000 pounds of D can be sold? Show calculations of incremental revenues and costs to support your answer.
2. **BUSINESS APPLICATION** ▶ List at least two qualitative reasons why Cakes Company may not want to install a Baking Department and produce Product D, even if this decision appears profitable.
3. **BUSINESS APPLICATION** ▶ List at least two qualitative reasons why Cakes Company may want to install a Baking Department and produce Product D, even if it appears that this decision is unprofitable.

Continuing Case: Cookie Company

C4. As the CEO of your cookie company, you are interested in how public companies with a segment that includes cookies report their operating results. Because public companies are required to report on their segments, it is possible to evaluate the performance of comparable segments of different companies.

Access the website of **Kraft Foods, Inc.,** which markets Nabisco cookies (www.kraftfoodscompany.com/About), and the website of **Kellogg Company,** which markets Keebler cookies (www.kelloggcompany.com). Find information about these companies' major segments. Which segments are comparable, and which are not comparable? Which segments of these companies do you think include their brand of cookies?

CHAPTER 24
Capital Investment Analysis

BUSINESS INSIGHT
Air Products and Chemicals, Inc.

Air Products and Chemicals, Inc., is an industrial producer of gases that are piped directly to steel mills and other factories from small unmanned gas plants located near customers. What makes Air Products and Chemicals competitive is its use of "lights-out" systems, which link the unmanned plants to the Internet so that managers can monitor operations at any time and from anywhere. Automated systems of this kind are expensive, and managers must carefully weigh the risks and rewards of investing in them.

1. **CONCEPT** ▶ Why is the concept of cost-benefit important when making capital budgeting decisions?
2. **ACCOUNTING APPLICATION** ▶ How does capital budgeting ensure a wise allocation of resources and minimize the risks involved in long-run decisions?
3. **BUSINESS APPLICATION** ▶ Why is capital investment analysis critical for the business performance of a company like Air Products and Chemicals?

LEARNING OBJECTIVES

LO 1 **Define *capital investment analysis*, and state why the concept of cost-benefit is important when making long-term investment decisions.**

LO 2 **Identify the types of projected costs and revenues used to evaluate alternatives for capital investment.**

LO 3 **Analyze capital investment proposals using the net present value method.**

LO 4 **Analyze capital investment proposals using the payback period method and the accounting rate-of-return method.**

LO 5 **Describe why capital investment analysis is critical for business success.**

Keith Wood/Corbis

SECTION 1 CONCEPTS

CONCEPT

- Cost-benefit

RELEVANT LEARNING OBJECTIVE

LO 1 Define *capital investment analysis,* and state why the concept of cost-benefit is important when making long-term investment decisions.

LO 1 Concepts Underlying Long-Term Decision Analysis

The concept of *cost-benefit* holds that the benefits to be gained from a course of action or alternative should be greater than the costs of providing it. Cost-benefit is an accounting convention or rule of thumb that supports long-run decision making. It considers both quantitative and qualitative cost and benefit measures to facilitate cost-benefit comparisons between alternatives for sound business decisions.

Capital investment decisions are decisions about when and how much to spend on capital facilities and other long-term projects. For example, **Air Products and Chemicals, Inc.**, will make decisions about installing new equipment, replacing old equipment, expanding service by renovating or adding to existing equipment, buying a building, or acquiring another company.

Capital Investment Analysis

Each decision made about a capital investment is vitally important because it involves a large amount of money and commits a company to a course of action for years to come. **Capital investment analysis** (or *capital budgeting*) involves the evaluation of alternative proposals for large capital investments, including considerations for financing the projects. Managers frequently follow six key steps when applying the cost-benefit concept to the capital budgeting process.

Step 1. Identify Capital Investment Needs Managers identify capital investment opportunities from past sales experience, changes in sources and quality of materials, employees' suggestions, bottlenecks caused by obsolete equipment, new production or distribution methods, or customer complaints. In addition, capital investment needs are identified through proposals to add new products to the product line, expand capacity in existing product lines, reduce production costs of existing products without altering operating levels, or automate existing production processes.

Step 2. Prepare Formal Requests for Capital Investments Each request includes a complete description of the investment under review; the reasons a new investment is needed; the alternative means of satisfying the need; the timing, estimated costs, and related cost savings of each alternative; and the investment's engineering specifications, if necessary.

Step 3. Conduct a Preliminary Screening Organizations that have a highly developed system for capital investment analysis require that all proposals go through preliminary screening. The purpose of preliminary screening is to ensure that the only proposals to receive serious review are those that both meet company strategic goals and produce the minimum rate of return set by management.

Step 4. Establish the Acceptance-Rejection Standard An acceptance-rejection standard may be expressed as a minimum rate of return or a minimum cash flow payback period. If the number of acceptable requests exceeds the funds available for capital investments, the proposals must be ranked according to their rates of return. Acceptance-rejection standards are used to identify projects that are expected to yield inadequate or marginal returns. They also identify proposed projects for which high product demand and high financial returns are expected.

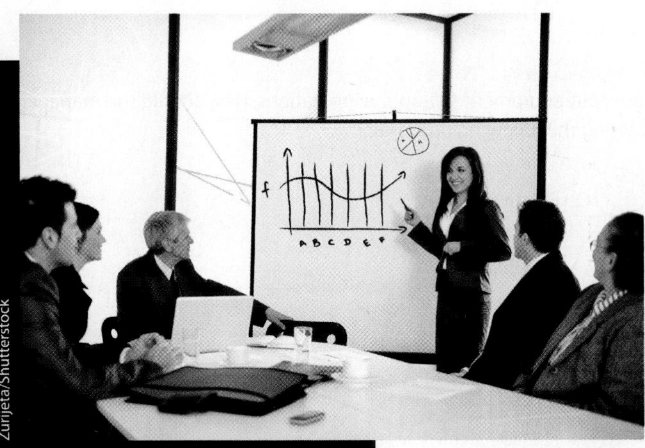

Zurijeta/Shutterstock

Management can evaluate proposed capital investments using the net present value method, payback period method, and/or accounting rate-of-return method to determine whether the projects meet the minimum acceptance-rejection standard.

Step 5. Evaluate Proposals Proposals are evaluated by verifying decision variables and applying established proposal evaluation methods. The key decision variables are expected life, estimated cash flow, and investment cost. Three commonly used methods of evaluating proposed capital investments are: net present value method, payback period method, and accounting rate-of-return method. Using one or more evaluation methods and the minimum acceptance-rejection standard, management evaluates all proposals. Management will also consider qualitative factors, such as availability and training of employees, competition, anticipated future technological improvements, and the proposal's impact on other company operations.

Step 6. Make Capital Investment Decisions The proposals that meet the standards of the evaluation process are given to the appropriate manager for final review. When deciding which requests to implement, the manager must consider the funds available. The acceptable proposals are ranked, and the highest-ranking proposals are funded first. Often there will not be enough money to fund all proposals. The final capital investment budget is then prepared by allocating funds to the selected proposals.

The Minimum Rate of Return on Investment

Most companies set a **minimum rate of return** to guard their profitability, and any capital expenditure proposal that fails to produce that rate of return is automatically refused. The minimum rate of return is often referred to as a *hurdle rate*, because it is the rate that must be exceeded, or hurdled. If the return from a capital investment falls below the minimum rate of return, the funds can be used more profitably in another part of the organization. Projects that produce poor returns will ultimately have a negative effect on an organization's profitability.

Ranking Capital Investment Proposals Even after management evaluates and selects proposals under the minimum acceptance-rejection standard, there are often too many proposals to fund adequately. At that point, managers must rank the proposals according to their rates of return, or profitability, and begin a second selection process.

Suppose that **Air Products and Chemicals, Inc.**, has $4,500,000 to spend this year for capital improvements and that five acceptable proposals are competing for those funds. The company's current minimum rate of return is 18 percent, and it is considering the following proposals:

Project	Rate of Return	Capital Investment	Cumulative Investment
A	32%	$1,460,000	$1,460,000
B	30%	1,890,000	3,350,000
C	28%	460,000	3,810,000
D	24%	840,000	4,650,000
E	22%	580,000	5,230,000
Total		$5,230,000	

The proposals are listed in the order of their rates of return. As you can see, Projects A, B, and C have the highest rates of return and together will cost a total of $3,810,000. That leaves $690,000 in capital funds for other projects. Project D should be examined first to see if it could be implemented for $150,000 less. If not, then Project E should be selected. The selection of Projects A, B, C, and E means that $110,000 in capital funds will be uncommitted for the year.

APPLY IT!

The supervisor of one of the "lights out" facilities has $1,000,000 to spend on new lights out equipment to improve operations. How should the manager proceed if the company's current minimum rate of return is 16 percent and it is considering the following proposals?

Proposal	Rate of Return	Capital Investment
L	12%	$ 600,000
M	20%	900,000
N	18%	100,000
O	14%	800,000
P	15%	800,000
Total		$3,200,000

SOLUTION

The manager should proceed with proposals M and N since they have the highest rates of return over the 16% minimum and together will cost a total of $1,000,000.

TRY IT! SE1, SE2, E1A, E14A, E1B, E14B

SECTION 2

OUNTING PLICATIONS

- stimate costs and enefits related to apital investment lternatives
- nalyze capital nvestment roposals using
  - net present value method
  - payback period method
  - accounting rate-of-return method

EVANT RNING OBJECTIVES

2 Identify the types of projected costs and nues used to evaluate rnatives for capital stment.

3 Analyze capital investment proposals g the net present value hod.

4 Analyze capital investment proposals g the payback period hod and the accounting -of-return method.

ACCOUNTING APPLICATIONS

CASH FLOW LO2 Capital Investment Analysis Measures and Methods

When evaluating a proposed capital investment, managers must predict how the new asset will perform and how it will benefit the company.

Expected Benefits from a Capital Investment

Managers must measure and evaluate all the investment alternatives consistently. The measure of expected benefit depends on the method of analyzing capital investment alternatives. The benefits from a capital investment can be measured by net income and net cash flows and cost savings.

Net Income Net income is calculated in the usual way:

Revenue − Expenses = Net Income

Managers must determine the increases in net income that will result from each capital investment alternative.

Net Cash Flows and Cost Savings A more widely used measure of expected benefit is projected cash flows. **Net cash inflows** are the balance of increases in projected cash receipts over increases in projected cash payments resulting from a capital investment, computed as follows.

Projected Capital Investment Cash Receipts − Projected Capital Investment Cash Payments = Net Cash Inflows

In some cases, equipment replacement decisions involve situations in which revenues are the same among alternatives. In such cases, the benefits are measured by the **cost savings**, or the decrease in operating costs that will result from the proposed capital investments. Either net cash inflows or cost savings can be used as the basis for an evaluation, but the two measures should not be confused.

- If the analysis involves cash receipts, net cash inflows are used.
- If the analysis involves only cash outlays, cost savings are used.

Equal Versus Unequal Cash Flows

Projected cash flows may be the same for each year of an asset's life, or they may vary from year to year. Unequal annual cash flows are common and must be analyzed for each year of an asset's life. Proposed projects with equal annual cash flows require less detailed analysis.

Carrying Value of Assets

Carrying value (or *book value*) is the undepreciated portion of the original cost of a fixed asset—that is, the asset's cost less its accumulated depreciation. When a decision to replace an asset is being evaluated, the carrying value of the old asset is irrelevant because it is a past, or historical, cost and will not be altered by the decision. Net proceeds from the asset's sale or disposal are relevant, however, because the proceeds affect cash flows and may differ for each alternative.

Depreciation Expense and Income Taxes

Income taxes alter the amount and timing of cash flows of projects under consideration by for-profit companies. To assess the benefits of a capital project, a company must include the effects of taxes in its capital investment analyses. Corporate income tax rates vary and can change yearly.

Depreciation expense is deductible when determining income taxes.* Thus, depreciation expense influences the amount of income taxes that a company pays and can lead to significant tax savings.

To examine how taxes affect capital investment analysis, assume that **Air Products and Chemicals, Inc.**, has a tax rate of 30 percent. It is considering a capital project that will make the following annual contribution to operating income:

Cash revenues	$ 400,000
Cash expenses	(200,000)
Depreciation	(100,000)
Operating income before income taxes	$ 100,000
Income taxes at 30%	(30,000)
Operating income	$ 70,000

The net cash inflows for this project can be determined in either of two ways:

1. Net cash inflows—receipts and disbursements:

Revenues (cash inflows)	$400,000
Cash expenses (outflows)	(200,000)
Income taxes (outflows)	(30,000)
Net cash inflows	$170,000

2. Net cash inflows—income adjustment procedure:

Income after income taxes	$ 70,000
Add back noncash expenses (depreciation)	100,000
Less noncash revenues	—
Net cash inflows	$170,000

In both computations, the net cash inflows are $170,000, and the total effect of income taxes is to lower the net cash inflows by $30,000.

Disposal or Residual Values

Proceeds from the sale of an old asset are current cash inflows and are relevant to evaluating a proposed capital investment. Projected disposal or residual values of replacement equipment are also relevant because they represent future cash inflows and usually differ among alternatives. Remember that the *residual value* (or *disposal* or *salvage value*) of an asset will be received at the end of the asset's estimated life.

APPLY IT!

Palmer Company has a tax rate of 25 percent. It is considering a capital project that will make the following annual contribution to operating income:

Cash revenues	$ 500,000
Cash expenses	(300,000)
Depreciation	(150,000)
Operating income before income taxes	$ 50,000
Income taxes at 25%	(12,500)
Operating income	$ 37,500

1. Determine the net cash inflows for this project in two different ways. Are net cash flows the same under either approach?
2. What is the impact of income taxes on net cash flows?

SOLUTION

1. The net cash inflows for this project can be determined in two ways:

(a) Net cash inflows—receipts and disbursements:

Revenues (cash inflows)	$500,000
Cash expenses (outflows)	(300,000)
Income taxes (outflows)	(12,500)
Net cash inflows	$187,500

(b) Net cash inflows—income adjustment procedure

Income after income taxes	$ 37,500
Add back noncash expenses (depreciation)	150,000
Less noncash revenues	—
Net cash inflows	$187,500

In both computations, the net cash inflows are $187,500.

2. The total effect of income taxes is to lower the net cash inflows by $12,500.

TRY IT! SE3, E2A, E2B

* You may recall that the annual depreciation expense computation using the straight-line method is the asset's cost less its residual value, divided by the asset's useful life.

LO 3 The Net Present Value Method

STUDY NOTE: *Because it is based on cash flow, the net present value method is widely used not only in business but also by individuals.*

A variety of methods can help managers make cost-benefit decisions about when and how much to spend on capital facilities and other long-term projects. One of the most popular methods is the *net present value method*. The net present value method incorporates the time value of money, which is discussed in Appendix C. You may wish to review this material prior to reading further.

The **net present value method** evaluates a capital investment by discounting its future cash flows to their present values and subtracting the amount of the initial investment from their sum, as follows.

Net Present Value = Present Value of Future Net Cash Inflows − Cost of Investment

All proposed capital investments are evaluated in the same way, and the projects with the highest net present value—the amount that exceeds the initial investment—are selected for implementation.

Advantages of the Net Present Value Method

A significant advantage of the net present value method is that it incorporates the time value of money into the analysis of proposed capital investments. Future cash inflows and outflows are discounted by the company's minimum rate of return to determine their present values. The minimum rate of return should at least equal the company's average cost of capital.

When dealing with the time value of money, use discounting to find the present value of an amount to be received in the future. To determine the present values of future amounts of money, use Tables 1 and 2 in Appendix C. Remember that Table 1 deals with a single payment or amount and Table 2 is used for a series of equal periodic amounts. Tables 1 and 2 are used to discount each future cash inflow and cash outflow over the life of the asset to the present.

- If the net present value is positive (the total of the discounted net cash inflows exceeds the cash investment at the beginning), the rate of return on the investment will exceed the company's minimum rate of return, or hurdle rate, and the project can be accepted.
- If the net present value is negative (the cash investment at the beginning exceeds the discounted net cash inflows), the return on the investment is less than the minimum rate of return and the project should be rejected.
- If the net present value is zero (if discounted cash inflows equal discounted cash outflows), the project meets the minimum rate of return and can be accepted.

STUDY NOTE: *If the net present value is zero, the investment will earn the minimum rate of return.*

The Net Present Value Method Illustrated

Suppose that **Air Products and Chemicals, Inc.**, is considering the purchase of a new "lights out" unit. The company's minimum rate of return is 16 percent. Management must decide between two models.

- Model M costs $17,500 and will have an estimated residual value of $2,000 after five years. It is projected to produce cash inflows of $6,000, $5,500, $5,000, $4,500, and $4,000 during its five-year life.
- Model N costs $21,000 and will have an estimated residual value of $2,000. It is projected to produce cash inflows of $6,000 per year for five years.

STUDY NOTE: *When using the net present value method, remember to consider the present value of the residual or disposal value.*

Model M Analysis Because Model M is expected to produce unequal cash inflows, Table 1 in Appendix C is used to determine the present value of each cash inflow from each year of the machine's life. The net present value of Model M is determined as follows.

Model M

Year	Net Cash Inflows	16% Factor	Present Value
1	$6,000	0.862	$ 5,172.00
2	5,500	0.743	4,086.50
3	5,000	0.641	3,205.00
4	4,500	0.552	2,484.00
5	4,000	0.476	1,904.00
Residual value	2,000	0.476	952.00
Total present value of cash inflows			$17,803.50
Less purchase price of Model M			17,500.00
Net present value			$ 303.50

All the factors for this analysis can be found in the column for 16 percent in Table 1. The factors are used to discount the individual cash flows, including the expected residual value, to the present. The amount of the investment in Model M is deducted from the total present value of the cash inflows to arrive at the net present value of $303.50. Since the entire investment of $17,500 in Model M is a cash outflow at the beginning—that is, at time zero—no discounting of the $17,500 purchase price is necessary. Because the net present value is positive, the proposed investment in Model M will achieve at least the minimum rate of return.

Model N Analysis Because Model N is expected to produce equal cash receipts in each year of its useful life, Table 2 in Appendix C is used to determine the combined present value of those future cash inflows. However, Table 1 is used to determine the present value of the machine's residual value because it represents a single payment, not an annuity. The net present value of Model N is calculated as follows.

Model N

Year	Net Cash Inflows	16% Factor	Present Value
1–5	$6,000	3.274	$19,644.00
Residual value	2,000	0.476	952.00
Total present value of cash inflows			$20,596.00
Less purchase price of Model N			21,000.00
Net present value			$ (404.00)

Table 2 is used to determine the factor of 3.274 (found in the column for 16 percent and the row for five periods). Because the residual value is a single inflow in the fifth year, the factor of 0.476 must be taken from Table 1 (the column for 16 percent and the row for five periods). The result is a net present value of ($404). Because the net present value is negative, the proposed investment in Model N will not achieve the minimum rate of return and should be rejected.

Analysis Recap The two analyses show that Model M should be chosen because it has a positive net present value and would exceed the company's minimum rate of return. Model M is the better choice because it is expected to produce cash inflows sooner and will thus produce a proportionately greater present value.

Business Perspective

What Is Total Cost of Ownership, and Why Is It Important?

The concept of total cost of ownership (TCO) was developed to determine the total lifetime costs of owning an information technology (IT) asset, such as a computer system. TCO includes both the direct and indirect costs associated with the acquisition, deployment, operation, support, and retirement of the asset. Today, TCO is the industry standard for evaluating and comparing the costs associated with long-lived asset acquisitions. For example, if you buy a printer, TCO includes the direct costs of buying the printer, the annual supplies costs of ink and paper, and the indirect costs of maintaining it. Thus, the decision about which printer to buy is not based solely on the cost of the printer, but on all costs related to it over its useful lifetime.

Woods Communications, Inc., is considering purchasing a new piece of data transmission equipment. Estimated annual net cash inflows for the new equipment are $575,000. The equipment costs $2 million, has a five-year life, and will have no residual value at the end of the five years. The company's minimum rate of return is 12 percent. Compute the net present value of the equipment. Should the company purchase it?

SOLUTION

Net Present Value = Present Value of Future Net Cash Inflows − Cost of Equipment
= ($575,000 × 3.605*) − $2,000,000
= $2,072,875 − $2,000,000
= $72,875

*From Table 1 in Appendix C.

The solution is positive, so the company should purchase the equipment. A positive answer means that the investment will yield more than the minimum 12 percent return required by the company.

TRY IT! SE4, SE5, SE6, SE7, E3A, E4A, E5A, E6A, E7A, E8A, E3B, E4B, E5B, E6B, E7B, E8B

LO 4 Other Methods of Capital Investment Analysis

STUDY NOTE: Payback period is expressed in time, net present value is expressed in money, and accounting rate of return is expressed as a percentage.

The net present value method is the best method for capital investment analysis. However, two other commonly used methods are the payback period method and the accounting rate-of-return method.

The Payback Period Method

STUDY NOTE: The payback period method measures the estimated length of time necessary to recover in cash the cost of an investment.

Because cash is an essential measure of a business's health, many managers estimate the cash flow that an investment will generate. Their goal is to determine the minimum time it will take to recover the initial investment. If two investment alternatives are being studied, management should choose the investment that pays back its initial cost in the shorter time. That period of time is known as the *payback period*, and the method of evaluation is called the **payback period method**. The payback period method is simple to use, but it does not consider the time value of money.

Payback Calculation The payback period is computed as follows.

$$\text{Payback Period} = \frac{\text{Cost of Investment}}{\text{Annual Net Cash Inflows}}$$

Suppose that **Air Products and Chemicals, Inc.**, is interested in purchasing a new server that costs $51,000 and has a residual value of $3,000. Assume that estimates for the proposal include revenue increases of $17,900 a year and operating cost increases of $11,696 a year (including depreciation and taxes). To evaluate this proposed capital investment, use the following steps.

Step 1 Determine the cost of the investment. For Air Products and Chemicals, it is $51,000.

Step 2 Determine the annual net cash inflows, which are the annual cash revenues minus the cash expenses. Eliminate the effects of all noncash revenue and expense items included in the analysis of net income to determine cash revenues and cash expenses. In this case, the only noncash expense or revenue is machine depreciation. To eliminate it from operating expenses, you must first calculate depreciation expense. To calculate this amount, you must know the asset's life and the depreciation method. Suppose Air Products and Chemicals uses the straight-line method of depreciation, and the new server will have a ten-year service life. The annual depreciation is computed as follows.

$$\text{Annual Depreciation} = \frac{\text{Cost} - \text{Residual Value}}{\text{Years}}$$

$$= \frac{\$51{,}000 - \$3{,}000}{\text{10 Years}}$$

$$= \underline{\underline{\$4{,}800}} \text{ per year}$$

Thus, cash expenses are equal to the operating cost of $11,696 reduced by the depreciation expense of $4,800, or $6,896. The annual net cash inflows are $11,004, or cash revenue increases of $17,900 less cash expenses of $6,896.

STUDY NOTE: *In computing the payback period, depreciation is omitted because it is a noncash expense.*

Step 3 Compute the payback period.

$$\text{Payback Period} = \frac{\text{Cost of Machine}}{\text{Cash Revenue} - \text{Cash Expenses}}$$

$$= \frac{\$51{,}000}{\$17{,}900 - (\$11{,}696 - \$4{,}800)}$$

$$= \frac{\$51{,}000}{\$11{,}004}$$

$$= \underline{\underline{4.6}} \text{ years*}$$

*Rounded

If the company's desired payback period is five years or less, this proposal would be approved.

Unequal Annual Net Cash Inflows If a proposed capital investment has unequal annual net cash inflows, the payback period is determined as follows.

Payback Period = Cost of Investment − Unequal Annual Net Cash Inflows*

*In chronological order until a zero balance is reached.

When a zero balance is reached, the payback period has been determined. This will often occur in the middle of a year. The portion of the final year is computed by dividing the amount needed to reach zero (the unrecovered portion of the investment) by the entire year's estimated cash inflow.

Advantages and Disadvantages The payback period method is especially useful in areas in which technology changes rapidly, such as in Internet companies, and when risk is high, such as when investing in emerging countries. However, this approach has several disadvantages:

- The payback period method does not measure profitability.
- It ignores differences in the present values of cash flows from different periods; thus, it does not adjust cash flows for the time value of money.
- The payback period method emphasizes the time it takes to recover the investment rather than the long-term return on the investment.
- It ignores all future cash flows after the payback period is reached.

The Accounting Rate-of-Return Method

The **accounting rate-of-return method** is an imprecise but easy way to measure the estimated performance of a capital investment, since it uses financial statement information.

This method does not use an investment's cash flows but considers the financial reporting effects of the investment instead. The accounting rate-of-return method measures expected performance using two variables: the estimated annual net income from the project and average investment cost.

Accounting Rate-of-Return Calculation The basic equation follows.

$$\text{Accounting Rate of Return} = \frac{\text{Average Annual Net Income}}{\text{Average Investment Cost}}$$

Step 1 Compute the average annual net income. Use the cost and revenue data prepared for evaluating the project—that is, revenues minus operating expenses (including depreciation and taxes).

Step 2 Compute the average investment cost in a proposed capital facility as follows.

$$\text{Average Investment Cost} = \left(\frac{\text{Total Investment} - \text{Residual Value}}{2}\right) + \text{Residual Value}$$

Step 3 Compute the accounting rate of return. For example, assume the same facts as before for Air Products and Chemicals' interest in purchasing a server. Also assume that the company's management will consider only projects that promise to yield more than a 16 percent return. To determine if the company should invest in the machine, compute the accounting rate of return as follows.

$$\text{Accounting Rate of Return} = \frac{\$17{,}900 - \$11{,}696}{\left(\frac{\$51{,}000 - \$3{,}000}{2}\right) + \$3{,}000}$$

$$= \underline{\underline{23\%}}^{*}$$

*Rounded

The projected rate of return is higher than the 16 percent minimum, so management should think seriously about making the investment.

Advantages and Disadvantages The accounting rate-of-return method is easy to understand and apply. However, it has several disadvantages.

- Because net income is averaged over the life of the investment, it is not a reliable figure, as actual net income may vary considerably from the estimates.
- It ignores cash flows.
- It does not consider the time value of money; thus, future and present dollars are treated as equal.

APPLY IT!

Part One: Payback Period Method

Segovia, Inc., is considering purchasing new data transmission equipment. Estimated annual net cash inflows from the new equipment are $575,000. The equipment costs $2 million and will have no residual value at the end of its five-year life. Compute the payback period for the equipment. Does this method yield a positive or negative response to the proposal to buy the equipment, assuming that the company has set a maximum payback period of four years?

Part Two: Accounting Rate-of-Return Method

Conaton, Inc., is considering whether to purchase a delivery truck that will cost $26,000, last six years, and have an estimated residual value of $6,000. Average annual net income from the delivery truck is estimated at $4,000. The company's owners want to earn an accounting rate of return of 20 percent. Compute the average investment cost and the accounting rate of return. Should the company make the investment?

SOLUTION

Part One: Payback Period Method

$$\begin{aligned}\text{Payback Period} &= \text{Cost of Investment} \div \text{Annual Net Cash Inflows}\\ &= \$2{,}000{,}000 \div \$575{,}000\\ &= \underline{\underline{3.5}}\text{ years*}\end{aligned}$$

*Rounded

The piece of equipment should be purchased because its payback period is less than the company's maximum payback period of 4 years.

TRY IT! SE8, SE9, E9A, E9B

Part Two: Accounting Rate-of-Return Method

$$\text{Average Investment Cost} = \left(\frac{\text{Total Investment} - \text{Residual Value}}{2}\right) + \text{Residual Value}$$

$$= \left(\frac{\$26{,}000 - \$6{,}000}{2}\right) + \$6{,}000$$

$$= \$16{,}000$$

$$\text{Accounting Rate of Return} = \frac{\text{Average Annual Net Income}}{\text{Average Investment Cost}}$$

$$= \frac{\$4{,}000}{\$16{,}000}$$

$$= \underline{\underline{25\%}}$$

The project will exceed the desired return of 20% and should be undertaken.

TRY IT! SE10, E10A, E11A, E12A, E13A, E10B, E11B, E12B, E13B

SECTION 3 BUSINESS APPLICATIONS

BUSINESS APPLICATIONS
- Planning
- Performing
- Evaluating
- Communicating

RELEVANT LEARNING OBJECTIVE

LO5 Describe why capital investment analysis is critical for business success.

LO5 The Management Process

Once a capital investment decision has been made, the implementation of the project is critical to its success. A project must be scheduled, and its development, construction, or purchase must be overseen. Controls must be established to make sure the project is completed on time, within budget, and at the desired level of quality. Upon completion, the project should be audited to determine if it is meeting the company's goals and targets set forth in the planning phase. Finally, to communicate results, project reports should be prepared and distributed within the organization. These reports should include comparisons of budgeted expenditures and actual expenditures.

Managers use quantitative and qualitative information to analyze the effects of capital investment decisions on their organization's resources and profits. Although many capital budgeting problems are unique and cannot be solved by following strict rules, managers often use the present value, payback, and accounting rate-of-return methods. Exhibit 1 summarizes the tools and methods managers use to ensure a wise allocation of resources, to make sound, ethical decisions that will enhance customers' and other stakeholders' value, to earn a profit, and to minimize business risks.

Exhibit 1
Capital Investment Analysis and the Management Process

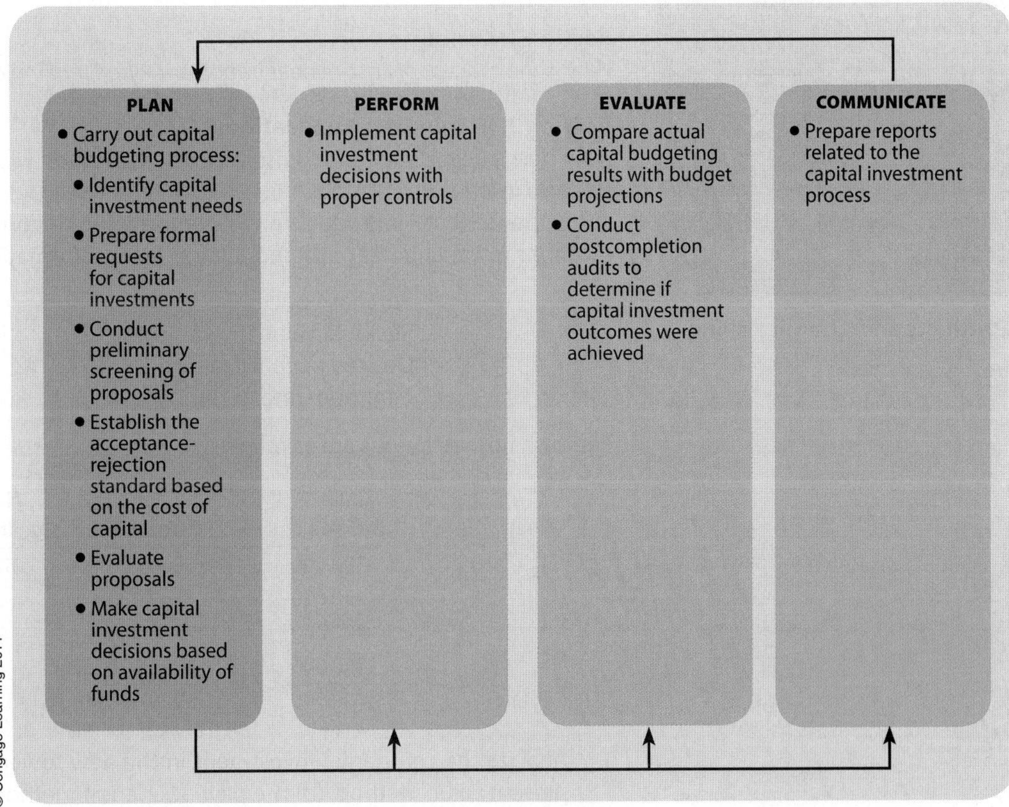

PLAN
• Carry out capital budgeting process:
• Identify capital investment needs
• Prepare formal requests for capital investments
• Conduct preliminary screening of proposals
• Establish the acceptance-rejection standard based on the cost of capital
• Evaluate proposals
• Make capital investment decisions based on availability of funds
PERFORM
• Implement capital investment decisions with proper controls
EVALUATE
• Compare actual capital budgeting results with budget projections
• Conduct postcompletion audits to determine if capital investment outcomes were achieved
COMMUNICATE
• Prepare reports related to the capital investment process
© Cengage Learning 2014

APPLY IT!

Arrange the steps of the capital budgeting process in their proper order:

a. Identify capital investment needs
b. Conduct preliminary screening of proposals
c. Evaluate proposals
d. Prepare formal requests for capital investments
e. Make decisions based on availability of funds
f. Establish the acceptance-rejection standard based on the cost of capital

SOLUTION

1. a; 2. d; 3. b; 4. f; 5. c; and 6. e

TRY IT! E14A, E14B

TriLevel Problem

Keith Wood/Corbis

Air Products and Chemicals, Inc.

The beginning of this chapter focused on **Air Products and Chemicals, Inc.**, Complete the following requirements in order to answer the questions posed at the beginning of the chapter.

Section 1: Concepts

Why is the concept of cost-benefit important when making capital budgeting decisions?

Section 2: Accounting Applications

How does capital budgeting ensure a wise allocation of resources and minimize the risks involved in long-run decisions?

Suppose that Air Products and Chemicals, Inc., is considering building a new communications tower and has gathered the following information:

Purchase price	$600,000
Residual value	$100,000
Desired payback period	3 years
Minimum rate of return	15%

The cash flow estimates are as follows.

Year	Cash Inflows	Cash Outflows	Net Cash Inflows	Projected Net Income
1	$ 500,000	$260,000	$240,000	$115,000
2	450,000	240,000	210,000	85,000
3	400,000	220,000	180,000	55,000
4	350,000	200,000	150,000	25,000
Totals	$1,700,000	$920,000	$780,000	$280,000

1. Analyze the company's investment in the new tower. In your analysis, use (a) the net present value method, (b) the payback period method, and (c) the accounting rate-of-return method.
2. Summarize your findings from requirement 1, and recommend a course of action.

Section 3: Business Applications

Why is capital investment analysis critical for the business performance of a company like Air Products and Chemicals?

To answer this question, match this chapter's managerial responsibilities with when they occur within the management process.

a. Plan	1. Implement capital investment decision with proper controls
b. Perform	2. Carry out capital budgeting process
c. Evaluate	3. Compare actual capital budgeting results with budget projections
d. Communicate	4. Prepare reports related to the capital investment process
	5. Conduct postcompletion audits to determine if capital investment outcomes were achieved

SOLUTION

Section 1: Concepts

The concept of *cost-benefit* is used to evaluate long-run decisions so that the benefits to be gained from a course of action or alternative can be compared to the costs of providing it. For an alternative to be feasible, its benefits must outweigh its costs. Cost-benefit is an accounting convention or rule of thumb that considers both quantitative and qualitative cost and benefit measures to facilitate comparisons between alternatives for sound business decisions.

Section 2: Accounting Applications

1. (a) Net present value method (factors are from Table 1 in Appendix C):

Year	Net Cash Inflows	Present Value Factor	Present Value
1	$240,000	0.870	$208,800
2	210,000	0.756	158,760
3	180,000	0.658	118,440
4	150,000	0.572	85,800
4	100,000 (residual value)	0.572	57,200
Total present value			$629,000
Less cost of original investment			600,000
Net present value			$ 29,000

(b) Payback period method:

Total cash investment		$ 600,000
Less cash flow recovery:		
Year 1	$240,000	
Year 2	210,000	
Year 3 (10/12 of $180,000)	150,000	(600,000)
Unrecovered investment		$ 0

Payback period: 2 years, 10 months, or 2.833 years

(c) Accounting rate-of-return method:

$$\text{Accounting Rate of Return} = \frac{\text{Average Annual Net Income}}{\text{Average Investment Cost}}$$

$$= \frac{\$280{,}000 \div 4}{\left(\dfrac{\$600{,}000 - \$100{,}000}{2}\right) + \$100{,}000}$$

$$= \frac{\$70{,}000}{\$350{,}000}$$

$$= 0.20 = 20\%$$

SOLUTION • SOLUTION • SOLUTION • SOLUTION • SOLUTION • SOLUTION • SOLUTION • SOLUTION

2. Summary of decision analysis:

	Decision Measures	
	Desired	**Calculated**
Net present value	—	$29,000
Accounting rate of return	15%	20%
Payback period	3 years	2.833 years

Based on the calculations in requirement **1**, the company should invest in the communication tower.

Section 3: Business Applications

1. b
2. a
3. c
4. d
5. c

Chapter Review

Define *capital investment analysis*, and state why the concept of cost-benefit is important when making long-term investment decisions. LO1

The concept of cost-benefit considers both quantitative and qualitative cost and benefit measures to facilitate comparisons between alternatives for sound business decisions. Capital investment analysis, or capital budgeting, consists of identifying the need for a capital investment, analyzing courses of action to meet that need, preparing reports for management, choosing the best alternative, and dividing funds among competing resource needs. The minimum rate of return, or hurdle rate, is used as a screening mechanism to eliminate from further consideration capital investment requests with anticipated inadequate returns.

Identify the types of projected costs and revenues used to evaluate alternatives for capital investment. LO2

The accounting rate-of-return method requires measures of net income. Other methods evaluate net cash inflows or cost savings. The analysis process must take into consideration whether each period's cash flows will be equal or unequal. Unless the after-income-tax effects on cash flows are being considered, carrying values and depreciation expense of assets awaiting replacement are irrelevant. Net proceeds from the sale of an old asset and estimated residual value of a new facility represent future cash flows and must be a part of the estimated benefit of a project. Depreciation expense on replacement equipment is relevant to evaluations based on after-income-tax cash flows.

Analyze capital investment proposals using the net present value method. LO3

The net present value method incorporates the time value of money into the analysis of a proposed capital investment. A minimum required rate of return is used to discount an investment's expected future cash flows to their present values. The present values are added together, and the amount of the initial investment is subtracted from their total. If the resulting amount, called the net present value, is positive, the rate of return on the investment will exceed the required rate of return, and the investment should be accepted. If the net present value is negative, the return on the investment will be less than the minimum rate of return, and the investment should be rejected.

Analyze capital investment proposals using the payback period method and the accounting rate-of-return method. LO4

The payback period method of evaluating a capital investment focuses on the minimum length of time needed to get the amount of the initial investment back in cash. The accounting rate-of-return method requires measures of net income. With the accounting rate-of-return method, managers evaluate two or more capital investment proposals and then select the alternative that yields the highest ratio of average annual net income to average cost of investment. Both of these methods are very rough measures that do not consider the time value of money. As a result, the net present value method is preferred.

Describe why capital investment analysis is critical for business success. LO 5

Managers often use the present value, payback, and accounting rate-of-return methods during the management process as they plan, perform, evaluate, and report on business operations. They utilize these capital budgeting tools to ensure a wise allocation of resources, to make sound, ethical decisions that will enhance customers' and other stakeholders' value, to earn a profit, and to minimize business risks.

Key Terms and Ratios

Chapter Assignments

DISCUSSION QUESTIONS

LO 1, 5 **DQ1. CONCEPT ▶ BUSINESS APPLICATION ▶** How do managers use the concept of cost-benefit for capital budgeting decisions during the planning phase of the management process?

LO 1, 5 **DQ2. CONCEPT ▶ BUSINESS APPLICATION ▶** How do managers use the concept of cost-benefit for capital budgeting decisions during the performing phase of the management process?

LO 1, 5 **DQ3. CONCEPT ▶ BUSINESS APPLICATION ▶** How do managers use the concept of cost-benefit for capital budgeting decisions during the evaluating phase of the management process?

LO 1, 5 **DQ4. CONCEPT ▶ BUSINESS APPLICATION ▶** How do managers use the concept of cost-benefit for capital budgeting decisions during the communicating phase of the management process?

SHORT EXERCISES

LO 1 **Manager's Role in Capital Investment Decisions**

SE1. The Logistics Department's supervisor has suggested to the plant manager that a new machine costing $285,000 be purchased to improve material handling operations for the plant's newest product line. How should the plant manager proceed with this request?

LO 1 **Ranking Capital Investment Proposals**

SE2. ACCOUNTING CONNECTION ▶ Zelolo Corp. has the following capital investment requests pending from its three divisions:

Project Request	Capital Investment	Projected Rate of Return
Request 1	$ 60,000	11%
Request 2	110,000	14%
Request 3	130,000	16%
Request 4	160,000	13%
Request 5	175,000	12%
Request 6	230,000	15%

(Continued)

Zelolo's minimum rate of return is 13 percent, and $500,000 is available for capital investment this year. Which requests will be honored, and in what order? Explain your answer.

LO 2 **Capital Investment Analysis and Revenue Measures**

SE3. ACCOUNTING CONNECTION ▶ Admiralty Corporation is analyzing a proposal to switch its factory over to a lights-out operation. To do so, it must acquire a fully automated machine. The machine will be able to produce an entire product line in a single operation. Projected annual net cash inflows from the machine are $180,000, and projected net income is $120,000. Why is the projected net income lower than the projected net cash inflows? Identify possible causes for the $60,000 difference.

LO 3 **Net Present Value Method**

SE4. ACCOUNTING CONNECTION ▶ Sandcastles, Inc.'s management has recently been looking at a proposal to purchase a new brick molding machine. With the new machine, the company would not have to buy bricks. The estimated useful life of the machine is 15 years, and the purchase price, including all setup charges, is $400,000. The residual value is estimated to be $40,000. The net addition to the company's cash inflow as a result of the savings from making the bricks is estimated to be $70,000 a year. Sandcastle's management has decided on a minimum rate of return of 14 percent. Using the net present value method to evaluate this capital investment, determine whether the company should purchase the machine. Support your answer. (*Hint:* Use Tables 1 and 2 in Appendix C.)

LO 3 **Net Present Value Method**

SE5. ACCOUNTING CONNECTION ▶ Noway Jose Communications, Inc., is considering purchasing a new piece of computerized data transmission equipment. Estimated annual net cash inflows for the new equipment are $590,000. The equipment costs $2 million, it has a five-year life, and it will have no residual value at the end of the five years. The company has a minimum rate of return of 12 percent. Compute the net present value of the piece of equipment. Should the company purchase it? Why?. (*Hint:* Use Table 2 in Appendix C.)

LO 4 **Payback Period Method**

SE6. Refer to the information in **SE5** for Noway Jose Communications, Inc. Compute the payback period for the piece of equipment. (Round to one decimal place.) Does this method yield a positive or a negative response to the proposal to buy the equipment, assuming that the company sets a maximum payback period of four years?

LO 4 **Payback Period Method**

SE7. ACCOUNTING CONNECTION ▶ Territories Cable, Inc., is considering purchasing new data transmission equipment. Estimated annual cash revenues for the new equipment are $1 million, and operating costs (including depreciation of $400,000) are $825,000. The equipment costs $2 million, it has a five-year life, and it will have no residual value at the end of the five years. Compute the payback period for the piece of equipment. (Round to one decimal place.) Does this method yield a positive or a negative response to the proposal to buy the equipment if the company has set a maximum payback period of four years? Explain your answer.

LO 4 **Accounting Rate-of-Return Method**

SE8. Doorstep Cleaners is considering whether to purchase a delivery truck that will cost $50,000, last six years, and have an estimated residual value of $5,000. Average annual net income from the delivery service is estimated to be $4,000. Doorstep Cleaners' owners seek to earn an accounting rate of return of 10 percent. Compute the average investment cost and the accounting rate of return. (Round percentages to one decimal place.) Should the investment be made?

LO 3

Residual Value and Present Value

SE9. Annelle Coiner is developing a capital investment analysis for her supervisor. The proposed capital investment has an estimated residual value of $5,500 at the end of its five-year life. The company uses an 8 percent minimum rate of return. What is the present value of the residual value? (Round to the nearest dollar.) (*Hint:* Use Table 1 in Appendix C.)

LO 3

Time Value of Money

SE10. ACCOUNTING CONNECTION ▶ Sherry Rudd recently inherited a trust fund from a distant relative. On January 2, the bank managing the trust fund notified Rudd that she has the option of receiving a lump-sum check for $200,000 or leaving the money in the trust fund and receiving an annual year-end check for $20,000 for each of the next 20 years. Rudd likes to earn at least a 5 percent return on her investments. What should she do?

EXERCISES: SET A

LO 1

Ranking Capital Investment Proposals

E1A. Emerald Bay Furniture Company's managers have gathered all of the capital investment proposals for the year, and they are ready to make their final selections. The following proposals and related rate-of-return amounts were received during the period:

Project	Capital Investment	Rate of Return
AB	$ 450,000	19%
CD	500,000	28%
EF	654,000	12%
GH	800,000	32%
IJ	320,000	23%
KL	240,000	18%
MN	180,000	16%
OP	400,000	26%
QR	560,000	14%
ST	1,200,000	22%
UV	1,600,000	20%

Assume that the company's minimum rate of return is 15 percent and that $5,000,000 is available for capital investments during the year.

1. List the acceptable capital investment proposals in order of profitability.
2. **ACCOUNTING CONNECTION ▶** Which proposals should be selected for this year? Why?

LO 2

Income Taxes and Net Cash Flow

E2A. Santa Rita Company has a tax rate of 20 percent on taxable income. It is considering a capital project that will make the following annual contribution to operating income:

Cash revenues	$ 360,000
Cash expenses	(160,000)
Depreciation	(140,000)
Operating income before income taxes	$ 60,000
Income taxes at 20%	(12,000)
Operating income	$ 48,000

1. Determine the net cash inflows for this project in two different ways. Are net cash inflows the same under either approach?
2. What is the impact of income taxes on net cash inflows?

LO 3 **Using the Present Value Tables**

E3A. For each of the following situations, identify the correct factor to use from Tables 1 or 2 in Appendix C. Also, compute the appropriate present value.

1. Annual net cash inflows of $10,000 for five years, discounted at 6 percent
2. An amount of $20,000 to be received at the end of ten years, discounted at 4 percent
3. The amount of $10,000 to be received at the end of two years, and $7,000 to be received at the end of years 4, 5, and 6, discounted at 10 percent

LO 3 **Using the Present Value Tables**

E4A. For each of the following situations, identify the correct factor to use from Tables 1 or 2 in Appendix C. Also, compute the appropriate present value.

1. Annual net cash inflows of $22,500 for a period of twelve years, discounted at 14 percent
2. The following five years of cash inflows, discounted at 10 percent:

Year 1	$35,000	Year 4	$40,000
Year 2	20,000	Year 5	50,000
Year 3	30,000		

3. The amount of $70,000 to be received at the beginning of year 7, discounted at 14 percent

LO 3 **Net Present Value Method**

E5A. Tuen and Associates wants to buy an automated coffee roaster/grinder/brewer. This piece of equipment would have a useful life of six years, would cost $190,000, and would increase annual net cash inflows by $50,000. Assume that there is no residual value at the end of six years. The company's minimum rate of return is 14 percent. Using the net present value method, prepare an analysis to determine whether the company should purchase the machine. (*Hint:* Use Tables 1 and 2 in Appendix C.)

LO 3 **Net Present Value Method**

E6A. ACCOUNTING CONNECTION ▶ Full Service Station is planning to invest in automatic car wash equipment valued at $210,000. The owner estimates that the equipment will increase annual net cash inflows by $40,000. The equipment is expected to have a ten-year useful life with an estimated residual value of $20,000. The company requires a 14 percent minimum rate of return. Using the net present value method, prepare an analysis to determine whether the company should purchase the equipment. How important is the estimate of residual value to this decision? (*Hint:* Use Tables 1 and 2 in Appendix C.)

LO 3 **Net Present Value Method**

E7A. Assume the same facts for Full Service Station as in **E6A**, except that the company requires a 20 percent minimum rate of return. Using the net present value method, prepare an analysis to determine whether the company should purchase the equipment. (*Hint*: Use Tables 1 and 2 in the Appendix C.)

LO 3 **Present Value Computations**

E8A. Two machines—Machine M and Machine P—are being considered in a replacement decision. Both machines have about the same purchase price and an estimated ten-year life. The company uses a 12 percent minimum rate of return as its acceptance-rejection standard. The estimated net cash inflows for each machine follow.

Year	Machine M	Machine P
1	$12,000	$17,500
2	12,000	17,500
3	14,000	17,500
4	19,000	17,500
5	20,000	17,500
6	22,000	17,500
7	23,000	17,500
8	24,000	17,500
9	25,000	17,500
10	20,000	17,500
Residual value	14,000	12,000

1. Compute the present value of future cash flows for each machine, using Tables 1 and 2 in Appendix C.
2. Which machine should the company purchase, assuming that both involve the same capital investment?

LO 4 **Payback Period Method**

E9A. Eco Wet, Inc., a manufacturer of gears for lawn sprinklers, is thinking about adding a new fully automated machine. This machine can produce gears that the company now produces on its third shift. The machine has an estimated useful life of ten years and will cost $500,000. The residual value of the new machine is $50,000. Gross cash revenue from the machine will be about $420,000 per year, and related operating expenses, including depreciation, should total $400,000. Depreciation is estimated to be $80,000 annually. The payback period should be five years or less. Use the payback period method to determine whether the company should invest in the new machine. Show the computations that support your answer.

LO 4 **Accounting Rate-of-Return Method**

E10A. Assume the same facts as in **E9A** for Eco Wet, Inc. Management has decided that only capital investments that yield at least an 8 percent return will be accepted. Using the accounting rate-of-return method, decide whether the company should invest in the machine. (Round percentages to one decimal place.) Show the computations that support your decision.

LO 4 **Accounting Rate-of-Return Method**

E11A. Sound Perfection, Inc., a manufacturer of stereo speakers, is thinking about adding a new machine. This machine can produce speaker parts that the company now buys from outsiders. The machine has an estimated useful life of 14 years and will cost $450,000. The residual value of the new machine is $50,000. Gross cash revenue from the machine will be about $300,000 per year, and related cash expenses should total $210,000. Depreciation is estimated to be $30,000 annually. Sound Perfection's management has decided that only capital investments that yield at least a 20 percent return will be accepted. Using the accounting rate-of-return method, decide whether the company should invest in the machine. Show the computations that support your decision.

LO 4 **Accounting Rate-of-Return Method**

E12A. Assume the same facts as in **E11A** for Sound Perfection, Inc. Management has decided that only capital investments that yield at least a 25 percent return will be

(Continued)

accepted. Using the accounting rate-of-return method, decide whether the company should invest in the machine. Show the computations that support your decision.

LO 4

Accounting Rate-of-Return Method

E13A. Boink Corporation manufactures metal hard hats for on-site construction workers. Recently, management has tried to raise productivity to meet the growing demand from the real estate industry. The company is now thinking about buying a new stamping machine. Management has decided that only capital investments that yield at least a 14 percent return will be accepted. The new machine would cost $325,000, revenue would increase by $98,400 per year, the residual value of the new machine would be $32,500, and operating cost increases (including depreciation) would be $75,000. Using the accounting rate-of-return method, decide whether the company should invest in the machine. (Round percentages to one decimal place.) Show the computations that support your decision.

LO 1, 5

Capital Investment Analysis

E14A. BUSINESS APPLICATION ▶ Genette Henderson was just promoted to supervisor of building maintenance for Ford Valley Theater complex. Allpoints Entertainment, Inc., Henderson's employer, uses a company-wide system for evaluating capital investment requests from its 22 supervisors. Henderson has approached you, the corporate controller, for advice on preparing her first proposal. She would also like to become familiar with the entire decision-making process.

1. What advice would you give Henderson before she prepares her first capital investment proposal?
2. Explain the role of capital investment analysis in the management process, including the key steps taken during planning.

EXERCISES: SET B

Visit the textbook companion website at www.cengagebrain.com to access Exercise Set B for this chapter.

PROBLEMS

LO 3, 5

Net Present Value Method

✔ 1: Present value of future cash flows: $99,672
✔ 2: Net present value: $112,465

P1. Sonja and Sons, Inc., owns and operates a group of apartment buildings. Management wants to sell one of its older four-family buildings and buy a new building. The old building, which was purchased 25 years ago for $100,000, has a 40-year estimated life. The current market value is $80,000, and if it is sold, the cash inflow will be $67,675. Annual net cash inflows from the old building are expected to average $16,000 for the remainder of its estimated useful life.

The new building will cost $300,000. It has an estimated useful life of 25 years. Net cash inflows are expected to be $50,000 annually.

Assume that (1) all cash flows occur at year end, (2) the company uses straight-line depreciation, (3) the buildings will have a residual value equal to 10 percent of their purchase price, and (4) the minimum rate of return is 14 percent. (*Hint:* Use Tables 1 and 2 in Appendix C.)

REQUIRED

1. Compute the present value of future cash flows from the old building.
2. What will the net present value of cash flows be if the company purchases the new building?
3. **ACCOUNTING CONNECTION ▶** Should the company keep the old building or purchase the new one? Why?

LO 3, 5

✔ 1: Net present value: $35,540
✔ 2: Net present value: ($5,430)

Net Present Value Method

P2. Better Plastics' management has recently been looking at a proposal to purchase a new plastic-injection-style molding machine. With the new machine, the company would not have to buy small plastic parts to use in production. The estimated useful life of the machine is 15 years, and the purchase price, including all setup charges, is $400,000. The residual value is estimated to be $40,000. The net addition to the company's cash inflow as a result of the savings from making the parts is estimated to be $70,000 a year. Better Plastics' management has decided on a minimum rate of return of 14 percent. (*Hint:* Use Tables 1 and 2 in Appendix C.)

REQUIRED

1. Using the net present value method to evaluate this capital investment, determine whether the company should purchase the machine. Support your answer.
2. If management had decided on a minimum rate of return of 16 percent, should the machine be purchased? Show computations to support your answer.

LO 4, 5

SPREADSHEET

✔ 1: Accounting rate of return for HZT machine: 13.4%
✔ 2: Payback period for HZT machine: 6.1 years

Accounting Rate-of-Return and Payback Period Methods

P3. Raab Company is expanding its production facilities to include a new product line, a sporty automotive tire rim. Tire rims can now be produced with little labor cost using new computerized machinery. The controller has advised management about two such machines. Details about each machine follow.

	XJS Machine	HZT Machine
Cost of machine	$500,000	$550,000
Residual value	50,000	55,000
Net income	34,965	40,670
Annual net cash inflows	91,215	90,170

The company's minimum rate of return is 12 percent. The maximum payback period is six years.

REQUIRED

1. For each machine, compute the projected accounting rate of return. (Round percentages to one decimal place.)
2. Compute the payback period for each machine. (Round to one decimal place.)
3. **ACCOUNTING CONNECTION ▶** Based on the information from requirements **1** and **2**, which machine should be purchased? Why?

LO 2, 3, 4, 5

SPREADSHEET

✔ 1a: Net present value: ($26,895)
✔ 1b: Accounting rate of return: 8.2%
✔ 1c: Payback period: 3.7 years

Capital Investment Decision: Comprehensive

P4. Edge Company's production vice president believes keeping up-to-date with technological changes is what makes the company successful and feels that a machine introduced recently would fill an important need. The machine has an estimated useful life of four years, a purchase price of $250,000, and a residual value of $25,000. The company controller has estimated average annual net income of $11,250 and the following cash flows for the new machine:

Cash Flow Estimates

Year	Cash Inflows	Cash Outflows	Net Cash Inflows
1	$325,000	$250,000	$75,000
2	320,000	250,000	70,000
3	315,000	250,000	65,000
4	310,000	250,000	60,000

The company uses a 12 percent minimum rate of return and a three-year payback period for capital investment evaluation purposes.

(Continued)

REQUIRED

1. Analyze the data about the machine. Use the following evaluation approaches in your analysis:
   a. the net present value method (Round to the nearest dollar.)
   b. the accounting rate-of-return method. (Round percentage to one decimal place.)
   c. the payback period method (Round to one decimal place.)
   (*Hint:* Use Tables 1 and 2 in Appendix C.)
2. **ACCOUNTING CONNECTION ▶** Summarize the information generated in requirement 1, and make a recommendation.

ALTERNATE PROBLEMS

LO **3, 5**

✔ 1: Present value of future cash flows: $92,536.50
✔ 2: Net present value: $222,646

Comparison of Alternatives: Net Present Value Method

P5. City Sights, Ltd., operates a tour and sightseeing business. Its trademark is the use of trolley buses. Each vehicle has its own identity and is specially made for the company. Gridlock, the oldest bus, was purchased 15 years ago and has 5 years of its estimated useful life remaining. The company paid $25,000 for Gridlock, and the bus could be sold today for $20,000. Gridlock is expected to generate average annual net cash inflows of $24,000 for the remainder of its estimated useful life.

Management wants to replace Gridlock with a modern-looking vehicle called Phantom. Phantom has a purchase price of $140,000 and an estimated useful life of 20 years. Net cash inflows for Phantom are projected to be $40,000 per year.

Assume that (1) all cash flows occur at year end, (2) each vehicle's residual value equals 10 percent of its purchase price, and (3) the minimum rate of return is 10 percent. (*Hint:* Use Tables 1 and 2 in Appendix C.)

REQUIRED

1. Compute the present value of the future cash flows from Gridlock.
2. Compute the net present value of cash flows if Phantom were purchased.
3. **ACCOUNTING CONNECTION ▶** Should City Sights keep Gridlock or purchase Phantom?

LO **3, 5**

✔ 1: Net present value: $16,573
✔ 2: Net present value: ($7,080)

Net Present Value Method

P6. Mansion is a famous restaurant in the French Quarter of New Orleans. Bouillabaisse Sophie is Mansion's house specialty. Management is considering purchasing a machine that would prepare all the ingredients, mix them automatically, and cook the dish to the restaurant's specifications. The machine will function for an estimated 12 years, and the purchase price, including installation, is $250,000. Estimated residual value is $25,000. This labor-saving device is expected to increase net cash inflows by an average of $42,000 per year during its estimated useful life. For capital investment decisions, the restaurant uses a 12 percent minimum rate of return. (*Hint:* Use Tables 1 and 2 in Appendix C.)

REQUIRED

1. Using the net present value method, determine if the company should purchase the machine. Support your answer.
2. If management had decided on a minimum rate of return of 14 percent, should the machine be purchased? Show computations to support your answer.

LO **4, 5**

SPREADSHEET

✔ 1: Accounting rate of return for Autom machine: 16.8%
✔ 2: Payback period for Autom machine: 6.5 years

Accounting Rate-of-Return and Payback Period Methods

P7. Cute Car Company is expanding its production facilities to include a new product line, an energy-efficient sporty convertible. The car can be produced with little labor cost using computerized machinery. There are two such machines to choose from. Details about each machine follow.

	GoGo Machine	Autom Machine
Cost of machine	$300,000	$325,000
Residual value	30,000	32,500
Net income	25,000	30,000
Annual net cash inflows	60,000	50,000

The company's minimum rate of return is 15 percent. The maximum payback period is six years. (Round to one decimal place.)

REQUIRED

1. For each machine, compute the projected accounting rate of return.
2, Compute the payback period for each machine.
3. Based on the information from requirements **1** and **2**, which machine should be purchased?

LO **2, 3, 4, 5**

Capital Investment Decision: Comprehensive

✔ 1: Net present value for LKR machine: $4,658
✔ 2: Accounting rate of return for LKR machine: 23.7%
✔ 3: Payback period for LKR machine: 4.9 years

P8. Express Corporation wants to buy a new stamping machine. The machine will provide the company with a new product line: pressed food trays for kitchens. Two machines are being considered; the data for each machine follows.

	ETZ Machine	LKR Machine
Cost of machine	$350,000	$370,000
Net income	$39,204	$48,642
Annual net cash inflows	$64,404	$75,642
Residual value	$28,000	$40,000
Estimated useful life in years	10	10

The company's minimum rate of return is 16 percent, and the maximum allowable payback period is 5.0 years.

REQUIRED

1. Compute the net present value for each machine. (Round to the nearest dollar.)
2. Compute the accounting rate of return for each machine. (Round percentages to one decimal place.)
3. Compute the payback period for each machine. (Round to one decimal place.)
4. **ACCOUNTING CONNECTION ▶** From the information generated in requirements **1**, **2**, and **3**, decide which machine should be purchased. Why?

CASES

LO **1, 5**

Evaluation of Proposed Capital Investments

C1. Tanashi Corporation's board of directors met to review a number of proposed capital investments that would improve the quality of company products. One production-line manager requested purchasing new computer-integrated machines to replace the older machines in one of the ten production departments at the Tokyo plant. Although the manager had presented quantitative information to support the purchase of the new machines, the board members asked the following important questions:

1. Why do we want to replace the old machines? Have they deteriorated? Are they obsolete?
2. Will the new machines require less cycle time?
3. Can we reduce inventory levels or save floor space by replacing the old machines?
4. How expensive is the software used with the new machines?

5. Will we be able to find highly skilled employees to maintain the new machines? Or can we find workers who are trainable? What would it cost to train workers? Would the training disrupt the staff by causing relocations?
6. Would the implementation of the machines be delayed because of the time required to recruit and train new workers?
7. How would the new machines affect the other parts of the manufacturing systems? Would the company lose some of the flexibility in its manufacturing systems if it introduced the new machines?

The board members believe that the qualitative information needed to answer their questions could lead to the rejection of the project, even though it would have been accepted based on the quantitative information.

1. Identify the questions that can be answered with quantitative information. Give an example of the quantitative information that could be used.
2. Identify the questions that can be answered with qualitative information. Explain why this information could negatively influence the capital investment decision even though the quantitative information suggests a positive outcome.

LO 3

Using Net Present Value

C2. McCall Syndicate owns four resort hotels in Europe. Because the Paris operation (Hotel 1) has been booming over the past five years, management has decided to build an addition to the hotel. This addition will increase the hotel's capacity by 20 percent. A construction company has bid to build the addition at a cost of $30,000,000. The building will have an increased residual value of $3,000,000.

Daj Van Dyke, the controller, has started an analysis of the net present value for the project. She has calculated the annual net cash inflows by subtracting the increase in cash operating expenses from the increase in cash inflows from room rentals. Her partially completed schedule follows:

Year	Net Cash Inflows
1–20 (each year)	$3,900,000

Capital investment projects must generate a 12 percent minimum rate of return to qualify for consideration.

Using net present value analysis, evaluate the proposal and make a recommendation to management. Explain how your recommendation would change if management were willing to accept a 10 percent minimum rate of return. (*Hint:* Use Tables 1 and 2 in Appendix C.)

LO 3, 5

Net Present Value of Cash Flows

SPREADSHEET

C3. CPC Corporation is an international plumbing equipment and supply company located in southern California. The Pipe Division's manager is considering purchasing a computerized copper pipe machine that costs $120,000.

The machine has a six-year life, and its expected residual value after six years of use will be 10 percent of its original cost. Cash revenue generated by the new machine is projected to be $50,000 in year 1 and will increase by $10,000 each year for the next five years. Variable cash operating costs will be materials and parts, 25 percent of revenue; machine labor, 5 percent of revenue; and overhead, 15 percent of revenue. First-year sales and marketing cash outflows are expected to be $10,500 and will decrease by 10 percent each year over the life of the new machine. Anticipated cash administrative expenses will be $2,500 per year. The company uses a 15 percent minimum rate of return for all capital investment analyses.

1. Prepare a spreadsheet to compute the net present value of the anticipated cash flows for the life of the proposed new machine. (Round to the nearest dollar.) Use the following format:

	A	B	C	D	E	F	G	H	I	J
1			Projected Cash Outflows							
2	Future Time Period	Projected Cash Revenue	Materials and Parts	Machine Labor	Overhead	Sales and Marketing	Adminis-trative Expenses	Projected Net Cash Inflows	15% Factor	Present Value
3										

Should the company invest in the new machine?

2. After careful analysis, the controller has determined that the variable rate for materials and parts can be reduced to 22 percent of revenue. Will this reduction in cash outflow change the decision about investing in the new machine? Explain your answer. (Round to the nearest dollar.)
3. The marketing manager has determined that the initial estimate of sales and marketing cash expenses was too high and has reduced that estimate by $1,000. The 10 percent annual reductions are still expected to occur. Together with the change in 2, will this reduction affect the initial investment decision? Explain your answer. (Round to the nearest dollar.)

LO 2, 3, 5

Interpreting Management Reports: Capital Investment Analysis

C4. Angelo Bank is planning to replace some old ATM machines and has decided to use the York Machine. Anita Chavez, the controller, has prepared the analysis shown here. She has recommended purchasing the machine based on the positive net present value shown in the analysis.

The York Machine has an estimated useful life of five years and an expected residual value of $35,000. Its purchase price is $385,000. Two existing ATMs, each having a carrying value of $25,000, can be sold to a neighboring bank for a total of $50,000. Annual operating cash inflows are expected to increase in the following manner:

Year 1	$79,900
Year 2	76,600
Year 3	79,900
Year 4	83,200
Year 5	86,500

Angelo Bank uses straight-line depreciation. The minimum rate of return is 12 percent.

Angelo Bank
Capital Investment Analysis
Net Present Value Method

Year	Net Cash Inflows	Present Value Factor	Present Value
1	$85,000	0.909	$ 77,265
2	80,000	0.826	66,080
3	85,000	0.751	63,835
4	90,000	0.683	61,470
5	95,000	0.621	58,995
5 (residual value)	35,000	0.621	21,735
Total present value			$ 349,380
Initial investment		$385,000	
Less proceeds from the sale of existing ATM machines		50,000	
Net capital investment			335,000
Net present value			$ 14,380

1. Analyze Chavez's work. (Round to the nearest dollar.) What changes need to be made in her capital investment analysis?
2. What would be your recommendation to bank management about the purchase of the York Machine?

LO 5

Ethical Understanding: Capital Investment Decisions and the Globally Competitive Business Environment

C5. Bramer Corporation's controller, Mara Jossen, was asked to prepare a capital investment analysis for a robot-guided aluminum window machine. This machine would automate the entire window-casing manufacturing line. She has just returned from an international seminar on the subject of qualitative inputs into the capital investment decision process and is eager to incorporate those new ideas into the analysis. In addition to the normal net present value analysis (which produced a significant negative result), Jossen factored in figures for customer satisfaction, scrap reduction, reduced inventory needs, and reputation for quality. With the additional information included, the analysis produced a positive response to the decision question.

1. When the chief financial officer finished reviewing Jossen's work, he threw the papers on the floor and said, "What kind of garbage is this! You know it's impossible to quantify such things as customer satisfaction and reputation for quality. How do you expect me to go to the board of directors and explain your work? I want you to redo the entire analysis and follow only the traditional approach to net present value. Get it back to me in two hours!"
2. What is Jossen's dilemma? What ethical courses of action are available to her?

LO 2, 3, 4, 5

Continuing Case: Cookie Company

C6. Suppose your cookie company is now a corporation that has granted franchises to more than 50 stores. Currently, only 10 of the 50 stores have computerized machines for mixing cookie dough. Because of a tremendous increase in demand for cookie dough, you, as the corporation's president, are considering purchasing 10 more computerized mixing machines by the end of this month. You are writing a memo evaluating this purchase that you will present at the board of directors' meeting next week.

According to your research, the 10 new machines will cost a total of $320,000. They will function for an estimated five years and should have a total residual value of $32,000. All of your corporation's capital investments are expected to produce a 20 percent minimum rate of return, and they should be recovered in three years or less. All fixed assets are depreciated using the straight-line method. The forecasted increase in operating results for the aggregate of the 10 new machines follows.

	Cash Flow Estimates	
Year	**Cash Inflows**	**Cash Outflows**
1	$310,000	$210,000
2	325,000	220,000
3	340,000	230,000
4	300,000	210,000
5	260,000	180,000

1. In preparation for writing your memo, answer the following questions:
   a. What kinds of information do you need to prepare this memo?
   b. Why is the information relevant?
   c. Where would you find the information?
   d. When would you want to obtain the information?
2. Using the following methods, analyze the purchase of the machines and decide if your corporation should purchase them.
   a. the net present value method
   b. the accounting rate-of-return method (Round percentages to one decimal place.)
   c. the payback period method (Round to one decimal place.)

CHAPTER 25
Pricing Decisions, Including Target Costing and Transfer Pricing

BUSINESS INSIGHT
Lab 126

Lab 126, a subsidiary of **Amazon.com**, dominates the e-book market with its Kindle readers and applications for other handheld devices. Competition between Lab 126 and its competitors is very keen, and there is constant pressure to offer more technology-rich features. Lab 126 managers are expected to make money, use resources wisely, and operate profitably. To fulfill these expectations, managers must know a lot about how to price products or services.

1. CONCEPT ▶ *How are pricing and the concept of revenue recognition related?*

2. ACCOUNTING APPLICATION ▶ *How do companies determine the price of products?*

3. BUSINESS APPLICATION ▶ *How does managerial accounting help managers during the management process with pricing decisions?*

LEARNING OBJECTIVES

LO1 Explain how the pricing of goods and services relates to the concept of revenue recognition.

LO2 Describe economic pricing concepts, including the auction-based pricing method used on the Internet.

LO3 Use cost-based pricing methods to develop prices.

LO4 Describe target costing, and use it to analyze pricing decisions and evaluate a new product opportunity.

LO5 Describe how transfer pricing is used for transferring goods and services and evaluating performance within a division or segment.

LO6 Relate pricing issues to the management process.

sturti/iStockphoto.com

SECTION 1 CONCEPTS

CONCEPTS

- Recognition
- Matching rule (accrual accounting)

RELEVANT LEARNING OBJECTIVES

LO1 Explain how the pricing of goods and services relates to the concept of revenue recognition.

LO2 Describe economic pricing concepts, including the auction-based pricing method used on the Internet.

LO1 Concepts Underlying Pricing Decisions

Establishing a product or service price depends on a manager's ability to analyze the marketplace for customers' price reactions and to know when to apply various cost-based or market-based approaches to pricing. Setting appropriate prices is one of the most difficult decisions that managers must make, and managers rely on managerial accounting information to make these decisions.

Revenue Recognition and Pricing Policies

The prices managers set have a significant impact on business operations, both externally and internally, since revenue is computed by multiplying the product or service price by the quantity sold. On the income statement, these revenues are generally *recognized* when goods are transferred or services are rendered, and they are *matched* with the costs incurred to generate them. The resulting difference is a net profit or loss, the fundamental measure of an organization's profitability. Thus, a manager's ability to set prices is essential to the long-term survival of any profit-oriented enterprise.

Organizational goals, objectives, and strategic plans that guide and control an organization's activities should include a pricing policy. A pricing policy is one way in which companies differentiate themselves from their competitors. Compare, for example, the pricing policies of luxury brands like **Lexus** and **Nordstrom** with those of cost-driven companies like **Toyota** or **Wal-Mart**. Consider also how prices are set on **eBay** and **Priceline.com**. Although all these companies are successful, their pricing policies differ significantly because each company has different pricing objectives.

Companies may also use pricing policies to differentiate among their own brands. For example, **Gap, Inc.**, uses price to differentiate the Gap brand from the brand of its subsidiary, **Old Navy**. **Mercedes-Benz** uses price to differentiate the Smart Car from the Mercedes. Thus, for each product brand, the company has identified the market segment that it intends to serve and has developed pricing objectives to meet the needs of that market.

Pricing Policy Objectives

Possible objectives of a pricing policy include the following:

- **Identifying and adhering to both short-run and long-run pricing strategies.** The pricing strategies of companies that produce standard items or commodities for a competitive marketplace will differ from the pricing strategies of companies that make custom-designed items. In a competitive market, companies can reduce prices to draw sales away from competing companies. They can also continuously add value-enhancing features and upgrades to their products and services to create the impression that customers are receiving more for their money. In contrast, a company that makes custom-designed items can be more conservative in its pricing strategy.
- **Maximizing profits.** Maximizing profits has traditionally been the underlying objective of any pricing policy.
- **Maintaining or gaining market share.** One key indicator of profit potential is an increasing share of the market. Maintaining or gaining market share is closely related to pricing strategies. However, market share is important only if sales are profitable. To increase market share by reducing prices below cost can be economically disastrous unless such a move is accompanied by strategies that compensate for the lost revenues.
- **Setting socially responsible prices.** To enhance their standing with the public and thus ensure their long-term survival, companies also consider whether their prices are socially responsible. The pricing policies of many companies now take into consideration a variety of social concerns, including environmental factors, the influence of an aging population, legal constraints, and ethical issues.

- **Maintaining a minimum rate of return on investment.** Organizations view each product or service as an investment. They will not invest in making a product or providing a service unless it will provide a minimum return. When setting prices, an organization adds a markup percentage to each product's costs of production in order to maintain a minimum return on investment. This markup percentage is closely related to the objective of profit maximization.
- **Being customer focused.** Taking customers' needs into consideration when setting prices or increasing a product's value to customers is important for at least three reasons:
  - Sensitivity to customers is necessary to sustain sales growth.
  - Customers' acceptance is crucial to success in a competitive market.
  - Prices should reflect the enhanced value that the company adds to the product or service, which is another way of saying that prices are customer-driven.

External and Internal Pricing Factors

When making and evaluating pricing decisions, managers must consider many factors. As shown in Exhibit 1, some of those factors relate to the external market, and others relate to internal constraints.

- The external factors include demand for the product, customer needs, competition, and quantity and quality of competing products or services.
- The internal factors include constraints caused by costs, desired return on investment, quality and quantity of materials and labor, and allocation of scarce resources.

Exhibit 1
External and Internal Factors Affecting Pricing Decisions

When Making and Evaluating Pricing Decisions

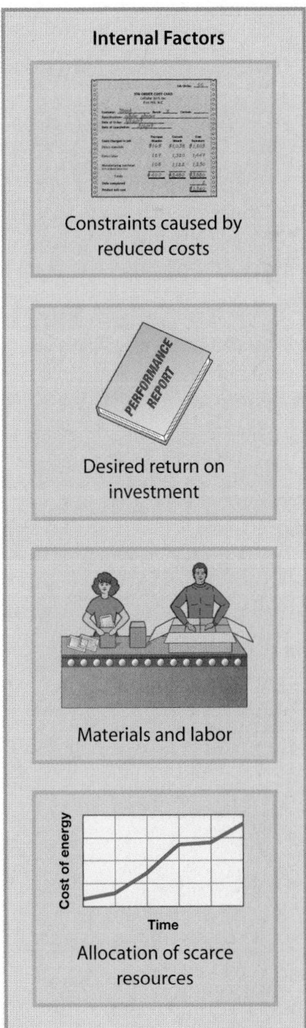

APPLY IT!

Towne's Tire Outlet features more than a dozen brands of tires. Information about two of the brands—Gripper and Roadster—follows.

	Gripper	Roadster
Selling price:		
Single tire, installed	$125	$110
Set of four tires, installed	460	400
Cost per tire	90	60

Selling prices include installation costs, which are $20 per tire.

1. Compute each brand's net unit selling price after installation for both a single tire and a set of four.
2. Was cost the main consideration in setting those prices?
3. What other factors could have influenced those prices?

SOLUTION

1.

	Gripper		Roadster	
	One Tire	Four Tires	One Tire	Four Tires
Selling price	$125	$460	$110	$400
Less installation cost	20	80	20	80
Net selling price	$105	$380	$ 90	$320
Unit selling price	$105	$ 95	$ 90	$ 80

2. The Gripper tire costs the company $30 more than the Roadster tire, but there is only a $15 difference between the two selling prices. The low cost of the Roadster allows the company to sell it at a significantly lower price than the higher-cost Gripper. Therefore, customers perceive the Roadster to be a better purchase value than the Gripper. The company is not using cost as a major consideration in its pricing decisions.
3. Other pricing considerations include local competition, quality versus price, and demand for the tires.

TRY IT! SE1, E1A, E1B

LO2 Economic Pricing Concepts

The economic approach to pricing is based on microeconomic theory. Although each product has its own set of revenues and costs, microeconomic theory states that profit will be greatest when the difference between total revenue and total cost is the greatest.

Total Revenue and Total Cost Curves

It may seem that if a company could produce an infinite number of products, it would realize the maximum profit. But this is not the case, and microeconomic theory explains why. Exhibit 2 shows the economist's view of a break-even chart. It contains two break-even points, between which is a large space labeled "profit area."

Total Revenues Notice that the total revenue line is curved rather than straight. The theory behind this is that as a product is marketed, because of competition and other factors, price reductions will be necessary if the firm is to sell additional units. Total revenue will continue to increase, but the rate of increase will diminish as more units are sold. Therefore, the slope of the total revenue line declines, and the line curves toward the right.

Total Costs Costs react in an opposite way. Over the assumed relevant range, variable and fixed costs are fairly predictable, with fixed costs remaining constant and variable costs being the same per unit. The result is a straight line for total costs. However, following microeconomic theory, costs per unit will increase as more units are sold because fixed costs, such as supervision and depreciation, will increase. Competition causes marketing costs to rise. As the company pushes for more and more products from limited facilities, repair and maintenance costs also increase. As the push from management increases, total costs per unit rise at an accelerating rate. The result is that the slope of the total cost line in Exhibit 2A increases, and the line begins curving upward. The total revenue line and the total cost line then cross again. Beyond that point, the company suffers a loss on additional sales.

Profit Maximization Profits are maximized at the point where the difference between total revenue and total cost is the greatest. In Exhibit 2A, this point is 6,000 units of sales.

Exhibit 2
Microeconomic Pricing Theory

A. Total Revenue and Total Cost Curves

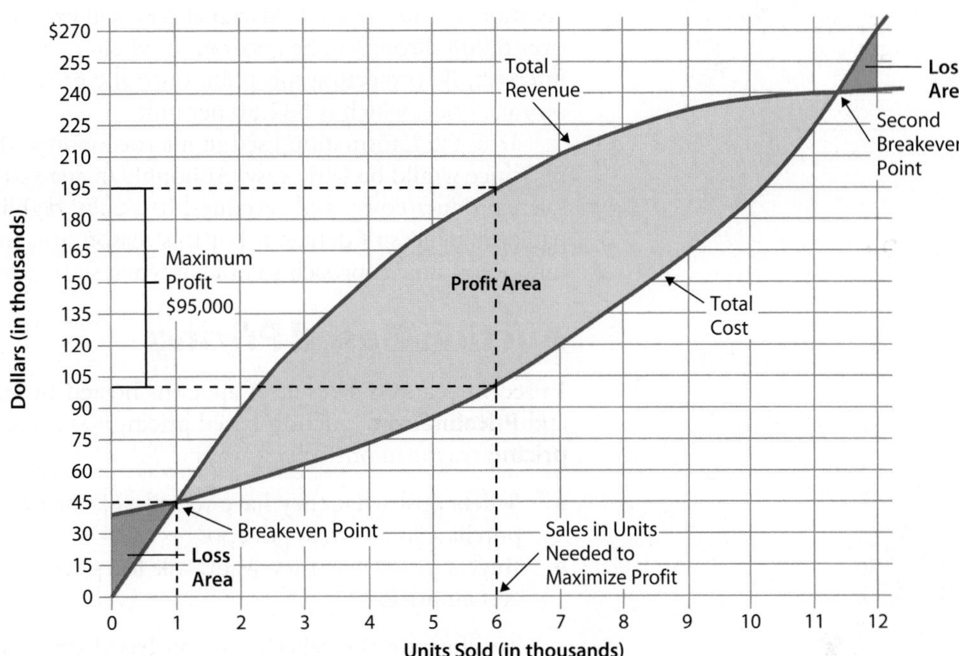

B. Marginal Revenue and Marginal Cost Curves

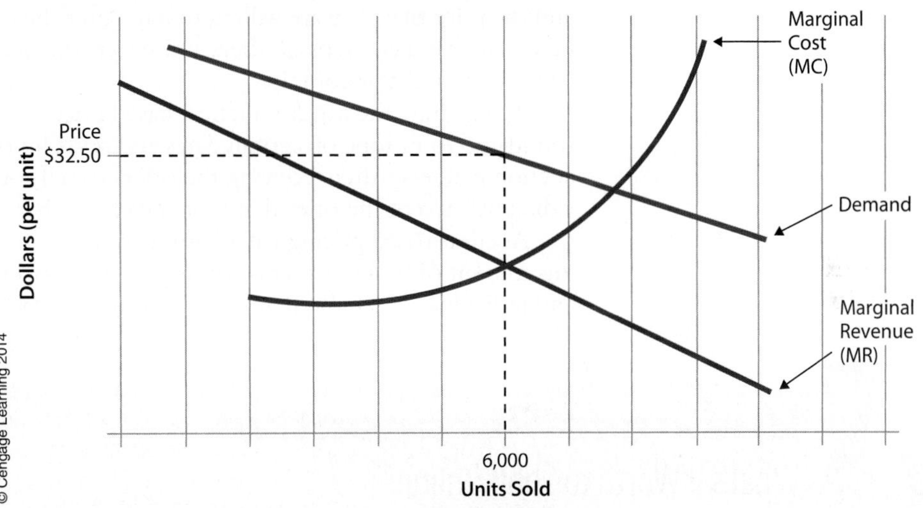

At that sales level, total revenue will be $195,000; total cost, $100,000; and profit, $95,000. In theory, if one additional unit is sold, profit per unit will drop because total cost is rising at a faster rate than total revenues. As you can see, if the company sells 11,000 units, total profits will be almost entirely depleted by the rising costs. Therefore, 6,000 sales units is the optimal operating level, and the price charged at that level is the optimal price.

Marginal Revenue and Marginal Cost Curves

Economists use marginal revenue and marginal cost to help determine the optimal price for a product or service. **Marginal revenue** is the change in total revenue caused by a one-unit change in output. **Marginal cost** is the change in total cost caused by a one-unit change in output. Graphic curves for marginal revenue and marginal cost are created by measuring and plotting the rate of change in total revenue and total cost at various activity levels.

If marginal revenue and marginal cost for each unit sold were plotted on a graph, the lines would resemble those in Exhibit 2B. Notice that the marginal cost line crosses the marginal revenue line at 6,000 units. After that point, profit per unit will decrease as additional units are sold. Marginal cost will exceed marginal revenue for each unit sold over 6,000. Profit will be maximized when the marginal revenue and marginal cost lines intersect. By projecting this point onto the product's demand curve, you can locate the optimal price, which is $32.50 per unit.

If all the information used in microeconomic theory were certain, picking the optimal price would be fairly easy. Although an analysis relies on projected amounts for unit sales, product costs, and revenues, it usually highlights cost patterns and the unanticipated influences of demand. For this reason, it is important that managers consider the microeconomic approach to pricing when setting product prices.

Auction-Based Pricing

In recent years, as a result of auctions hosted by Internet companies like **eBay**, **Yahoo**, and **Priceline.com**, auction-based pricing has skyrocketed in popularity. **Auction-based pricing** occurs in one of two ways:

- Sellers post what they have to sell, ask for price bids, and accept a buyer's offer to purchase at a certain price, or
- Buyers post what they want, ask for prices, and accept a seller's offer to sell at a certain price.

To illustrate the seller's auction-based price, suppose a corporation like **Intel** has an excess of silicon chips after a production run. The company posts a message on the Internet asking for the quantity of silicon chips that prospective buyers are willing to buy and the price that they are willing to pay. After the offers are received, the company prepares a demand curve of all offers and selects the one that best fits the quantity of silicon chips it has available for sale.

To illustrate the buyer's auction-based price, consider an individual who wants to fly round-trip to Europe on certain dates and posts his or her needs on one of the Internet's auction markets. After receiving the offers to sell round-trip tickets to Europe, the individual will accept the offer that best suits his or her needs.

Auction-based pricing will continue to grow in importance as a result of the escalating amount of business that is being conducted over the Internet by both organizations and individuals. Just about anything can be bought or sold via the Internet.

Business Perspective

What's It Worth to Shop Online?

The Internet makes it possible to price efficiently at the level of marginal costs. For instance, at websites like **Priceline.com**, travelers pick a destination and a price they are willing to pay for air or hotel reservations. The price must be guaranteed by credit card. An airline or hotel has a limited amount of time to accept or reject the bid. If the bid is accepted, the buyer is obligated to pay for the air or hotel reservation. The hotels and airlines are often willing to accept the low bid prices because the marginal cost of filling an additional seat on an airplane or an extra room in a hotel is very low.

APPLY IT!

Assume that a product has the total cost and total revenue curves pictured in Exhibit 2A. The difference between total revenue and total cost is the same at the 4,000- and 9,000-unit levels. Which of these two levels of activity would you chose as goals for total sales over the life of the product?

SOLUTION

4,000. If the same total profit will be made at both the 4,000- and the 9,000-unit levels, it does not make economic sense to produce the additional 5,000 units.

TRY IT! SE2, E2A, E2B

SECTION 2

ACCOUNTING APPLICATIONS

OUNTING
LICATIONS
ompute cost-based
xternal prices
- Gross margin pricing
- Return on assets pricing
- Time and materials pricing

ompute market-
ased external prices
- Target costing

ompute internal
ransfer prices
- Cost-plus transfer prices
- Market-based transfer prices
- Negotiated transfer prices

EVANT
RNING OBJECTIVES

3 Use cost-based pricing methods to develop
es.

4 Describe target costing, and use it to
yze pricing decisions and
uate a new product
ortunity.

5 Describe how transfer pricing is used for
sferring goods and
ices and evaluating
ormance within a division
egment.

LO3 Cost-Based Pricing Methods

In some areas of the economy, such as government contracts, cost-based pricing is widely used because a good starting point for developing a price is to base it on the cost of producing a good or service. Two pricing methods based on cost are gross margin pricing and return on assets pricing. Remember that in a competitive environment, market prices and conditions also influence price. However, if prices do not cover a company's costs, the company will eventually fail.

To illustrate the two methods of cost-based pricing, we will use Bookit Company. Bookit buys parts from outside vendors and assembles them into basic e-book readers. In the previous accounting period, the company produced 14,750 readers. The total costs and unit costs incurred follow.

	Total Costs	Unit Costs
Variable production costs:		
Direct materials and parts	$ 88,500	$ 6.00
Direct labor	66,375	4.50
Variable overhead	44,250	3.00
Total variable production costs	$199,125	$13.50
Fixed overhead	154,875	10.50
Total production costs	$354,000	$24.00
Selling, general, and administrative expenses:		
Selling expenses	$ 73,750	$ 5.00
General expenses	36,875	2.50
Administrative expenses	22,125	1.50
Total selling, general, and administrative expenses	$132,750	$ 9.00
Total costs and expenses	$486,750	$33.00

No changes in unit costs are expected this period. The desired profit for the period is $110,625. The company uses assets totaling $921,875 in producing the e-book readers and expects a 14 percent return on those assets.

Gross Margin Pricing

The **gross margin pricing method** (or the *income statement method*) emphasizes the use of income statement information to determine a selling price. (Gross margin is the difference between sales and the total production costs of those sales.) In gross margin pricing, the price is computed using a markup percentage based on a product's total production costs. The markup percentage is designed to include all costs other than those used in the computation of gross margin. Therefore, the gross margin markup percentage covers selling, general, and administrative expenses and the desired profit. Because an accounting system often provides management with unit production cost data, both variable and fixed, this method of determining selling price can be easily applied.

Gross Margin Calculations With gross margin pricing, there are three ways of determining a price.

1. The first approach uses the two formulas that follow.

$$\text{Markup Percentage} = \frac{\text{Desired Profit} + \text{Total Selling, General, and Administrative Expenses}}{\text{Total Production Costs}}$$

$$\text{Gross Margin-Based Price} = \text{Total Production Costs per Unit} + \left(\text{Markup Percentage} \times \text{Total Production Costs per Unit}\right)$$

For Bookit, the markup percentage and selling price are computed as follows.

$$\text{Markup Percentage} = \frac{\$110{,}625 + \$132{,}750}{\$354{,}000}$$

$$= 68.75\%$$

$$\text{Gross Margin-Based Price} = \$24.00 + (68.75\% \times \$24.00)$$

$$= \underline{\underline{\$40.50}}$$

The numerator in the markup percentage formula is the sum of the desired profit (\$110,625) and the total selling, general, and administrative expenses (\$132,750). The denominator contains all production costs: variable costs of \$199,125 and fixed production costs of \$154,875. The gross margin markup is 68.75 percent of total production costs, or \$16.50. Adding \$16.50 to the total production costs per unit yields a selling price of \$40.50.

STUDY NOTE: *Gross margin-based price per unit equals total production, selling, general, and administrative costs per unit plus a desired profit per unit.*

2. The second way to express the gross margin-based price is to state the formula in terms of a company's desire to recover all of its costs and make a profit. This approach ignores the computation of the markup percentage, achieves the same gross margin-based price, and is stated as follows.

$$\text{Gross Margin-Based Price} = \frac{\text{Total Production Costs} + \text{Total Selling, General, and Administrative Expenses} + \text{Desired Profit}}{\text{Total Units Produced}}$$

Using this formula, the gross margin-based price for Bookit is computed as follows.

$$\text{Gross Margin-Based Price} = \frac{\$354{,}000 + \$132{,}750 + \$110{,}625}{14{,}750 \text{ Units}}$$

$$= \$597{,}375 \div 14{,}750$$

$$= \underline{\underline{\$40.50}}$$

3. The third way the gross margin-based price can be determined is on a per-unit basis.

$$\begin{aligned}\text{Gross Margin-Based Price} = {} & \text{Direct Materials} + \text{Direct Labor} \\ & + \text{Variable Overhead} + \text{Fixed Overhead} \\ & + \text{Selling, General, and Administrative Expenses} \\ & + \text{Desired Profit per Unit}\end{aligned}$$

Applying this formula to Bookit's data, the computations are as follows.

$$\begin{aligned}\text{Gross Margin-Based Price} = {} & \$6.00 + \$4.50 + \$3.00 + \$10.50 + \$5.00 \\ & + \$2.50 + \$1.50 + (\$110{,}625 \div 14{,}750) \\ = {} & \underline{\underline{\$40.50}}\end{aligned}$$

Return on Assets Pricing

The **return on assets pricing method** (or *balance sheet method*) focuses on earning a specified rate of return on the assets employed in the operation. This changes the objective of the price determination process from earning a return on the income statement to earning a return on the business's resources on the balance sheet. Because this approach focuses on a desired minimum rate of return on assets, it is also known as the *balance sheet approach to pricing*.

Return on Assets Calculations There are two formulas for finding the return on assets price.

1. Return on Assets-Based Price = Total Costs and Expenses per Unit + (Desired Rate of Return × Cost of Assets Employed per Unit)

2. $$\text{Return on Assets-Based Price} = \left(\frac{\text{Total Production Costs} + \text{Total Selling, General, and Administrative Expenses}}{\text{Units to Be Produced}}\right) + \left(\frac{\text{Desired Rate of Return} \times \text{Total Cost of Assets Employed}}{\text{Units to Be Produced}}\right)$$

Recall that Bookit has an asset base of \$921,875. It plans to produce 14,750 units and would like to earn a 14 percent return on assets. If the company uses return on assets pricing, the selling price per unit would be calculated as follows.

$$\begin{aligned}\text{Return on Assets-Based Price} &= \$24.00 + \$9.00 \\ &\quad + [14\% \times (\$921,875 \div 14,750)] \\ &= \underline{\underline{\$41.75}}\end{aligned}$$

or as

$$\begin{aligned}\text{Return on Assets-Based Price} &= [(\$354,000 + \$132,750) \div 14,750] \\ &\quad + [14\% \times (\$921,875 \div 14,750)] \\ &= \$33.00 + \$8.75 \\ &= \underline{\underline{\$41.75}}\end{aligned}$$

Summary of Cost-Based Pricing Methods

Exhibit 3 summarizes the two cost-based pricing methods. If Bookit Company uses return on assets pricing and has a desired rate of return of 14 percent, it will need to set a higher selling price (\$41.75) than it would under the gross margin method (\$40.50).

Companies select their pricing methods based on their degree of trust in a cost base. The cost bases from which they can choose are (1) total product costs per unit and (2) total costs and expenses per unit.

- Often, total product costs per unit are readily available, which makes gross margin pricing a good way to compute selling prices. However, gross margin pricing depends on an accurate forecast of units because the fixed cost per-unit portion of total production costs will vary if the actual number of units produced differs from the estimated number of units.
- Return on assets pricing is also a good pricing method if the assets used to manufacture a product can be identified and their cost determined. If this is not the case, the method yields inaccurate results.

Business Perspective

Pricing a Six-Pack

The average cost of a six-pack of beer continues to rise. That's because **Anheuser-Busch**, maker of Bud Light and Budweiser—the world's largest-selling brands of beer—generally raises prices to keep pace with the consumer price index, and competitors have historically followed the company's price lead.[1]

Exhibit 3
Cost-Based Pricing Methods: Bookit Company

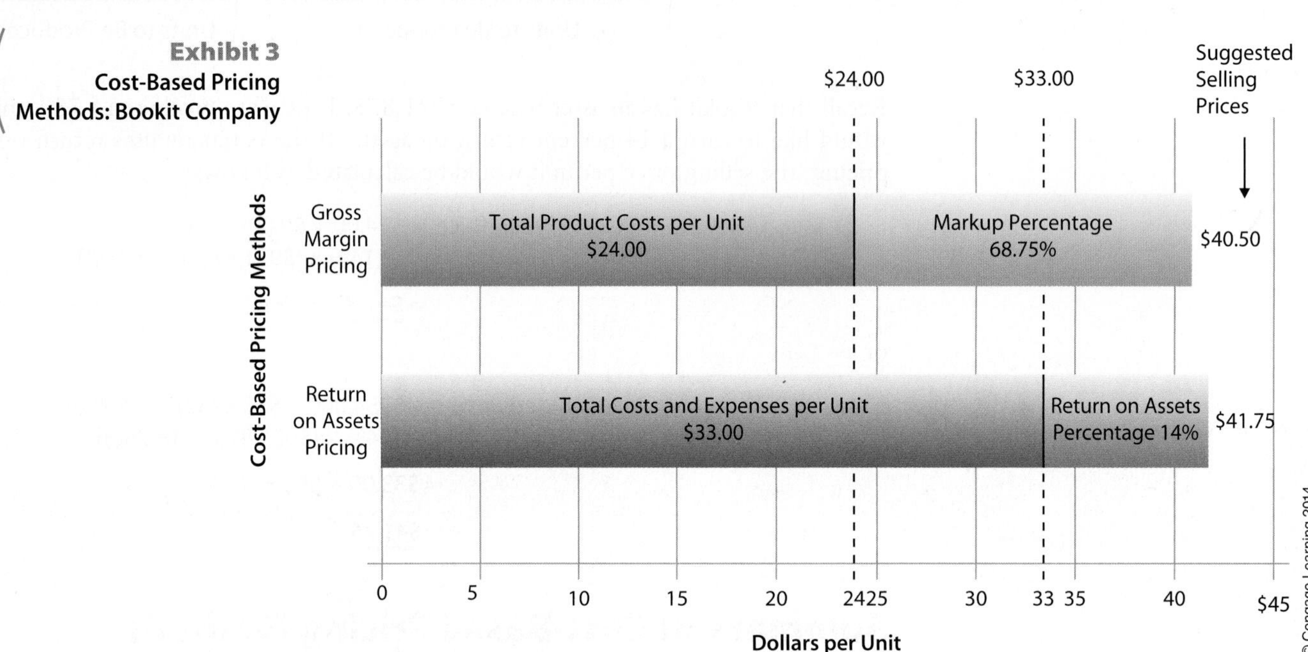

Pricing Services

A service business's approach to pricing differs from that of a manufacturer. Although a service has no physical substance, it must still be priced and billed to the customer. Most service organizations use a form of **time and materials pricing** (or *parts and labor pricing*) to arrive at the price of a service. With this method, service companies, such as appliance repair shops, home-remodeling specialists, and automobile repair shops, arrive at prices by using two computations: one for direct labor and one for materials and parts. Markup percentages are added to the costs of materials and labor to cover the cost of overhead and provide a profit factor. If the service does not require materials and parts, then only direct labor costs are used in developing the price. Professionals, such as attorneys, accountants, and consultants, apply a factor representing all overhead costs to the base labor costs to establish a price for their services.

Time and Materials Price Calculation The formula used in time and materials pricing follows.

$$\text{Time and Materials Price} = \text{Material Cost per Unit} + (\text{Markup \%} \times \text{Material Cost per Unit}) + \text{Labor Cost per Unit} + (\text{Markup \%} \times \text{Labor Cost per Unit})$$

To illustrate, suppose that the owner of an auto repair shop has just completed work on a customer's car. The parts used to repair the vehicle cost $840. The company's 40 percent markup rate on parts covers parts-related overhead costs and profit. The repairs required 4 hours of labor by a certified repair specialist, whose wages are $35 per hour. The company's overhead markup rate on labor is 80 percent. The repair shop will compute the bill as follows.

Repair parts used	$840	
Overhead charges: $840 × 40%	336	
Total parts charges		$1,176
Labor charges: 4 hours @ $35 per hour	$140	
Overhead charges: $140 × 80%	112	
Total labor charges		252
Total billing		$1,428

Factors Affecting Cost-Based Pricing Methods

Once a cost-based price has been determined, the decision maker must also consider such factors as competitors' prices, customers' expectations, and the cost of substitute products and services. Pricing is a risky part of operating a business, and care must be taken when establishing the selling price.

APPLY IT!

Gillson Industries has just patented a new product called Shine, an automobile wax for lasting protection against the elements. The company's controller has developed the following annual information:

Variable production costs	$1,110,000
Fixed overhead	540,000
Selling expenses	225,000
General and administrative expenses	350,000
Desired profit	250,000
Cost of assets employed	1,000,000

Annual demand for the product is expected to be 250,000 cans. On average, the company now earns a 10 percent return on assets.

1. Compute the projected unit cost for one can of Shine.
2. Using gross margin pricing, compute the markup percentage and selling price for one can.
3. Using return on assets pricing, compute the unit price for one can.

SOLUTION

1.

Costs Categories	**Total Projected Cost**
Variable production costs	$1,110,000
Fixed overhead	540,000
Total production costs	$1,650,000
Selling expenses	$ 225,000
General and administrative expenses	350,000
Total selling, general, and administrative expenses	$ 575,000
Total costs and expenses	$2,225,000
Total cost per unit ($2,225,000 ÷ 250,000 units)	$ 8.90

(Continued)

2.

$$\text{Markup Percentage} = \frac{\text{Desired Profit} + \text{Total Selling, General, and Administrative Expenses}}{\text{Total Production Costs}}$$

$$= \frac{\$250{,}000 + \$575{,}000}{\$1{,}650{,}000} = 50.0\%$$

Gross Margin-Based Price = Total Production Costs per Unit + (Markup Percentage × Total Production Costs per Unit)

= (\$1,650,000 ÷ 250,000) + [50.0% × (\$1,650,000 ÷ 250,000)]

= \$9.90

3.

Return on Assets-Based Price = Total Costs and Expenses per Unit + (Desired Rate of Return × Cost of Assets Employed per Unit)

= \$8.90 + [10% × (\$1,000,000 ÷ 250,000)]

= \$8.90 + \$0.40

= \$9.30

TRY IT! SE3, SE4, E3A, E4A, E5A, E6A, E7A, E3B, E4B, E5B, E6B, E7B

LO 4 Pricing Based on Target Costing

Target costing (or *target pricing*) is a pricing method designed to enhance a company's ability to compete, especially in markets for new or emerging products, such as the e-book readers described in this chapter's Business Insight. Target costing reverses the procedure used by the cost-based methods. Target costing:

- identifies the price at which a product will be competitive in the marketplace
- defines the desired profit to be made on the product
- computes the target cost for the product by subtracting the desired profit from the competitive market price

Target Costing Calculation The formula used in target costing follows.

Target Price – Desired Profit = Target Cost

Once the target cost has been established, the company's engineers and product designers use it as the maximum cost to be incurred for the materials and other resources needed to design and manufacture the product. It is their responsibility to create the product at or below its target cost.

Pricing based on target costing may not seem revolutionary, but a detailed look at its underlying principles reveals its strategic superiority:

- Target costing gives managers the ability to control or dictate the costs of a new product at the planning stage of the product's life cycle.
- In a competitive environment, the use of target costing enables managers to analyze a product's potential before they commit resources to its production.

Exhibit 4 compares the timing of a pricing decision that uses a traditional approach with one that uses target costing. The stages of the product life cycle, from the generation

Exhibit 4
Comparison of Price Decision Timing

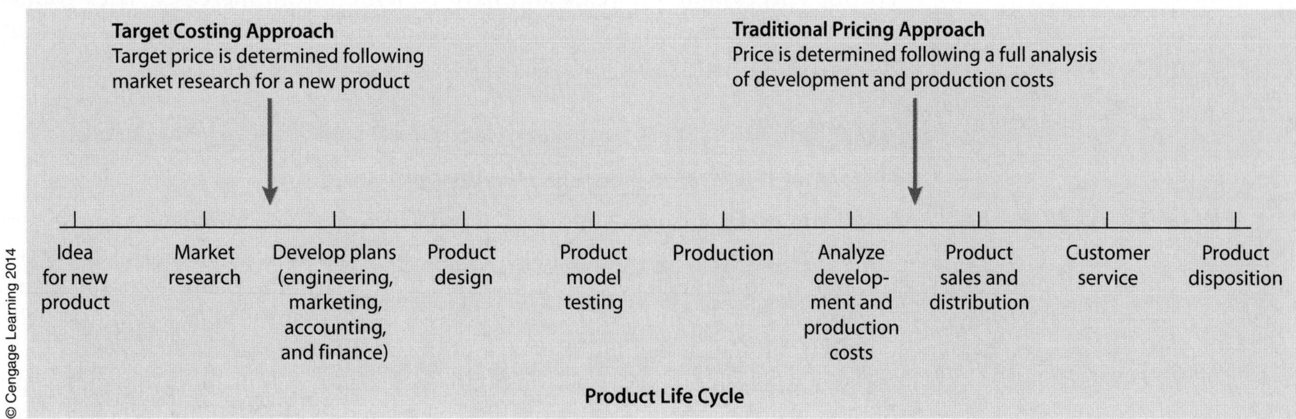

of the product idea to the final disposition of the product, are identified at the base of the figure.

STUDY NOTE: Remember that when desired profit is defined as a percentage of target cost, target price is equal to 100 percent of target cost plus the percentage of target cost desired as profit.

- When traditional cost-based pricing practices are used, prices cannot be set until production has taken place and costs have been incurred and analyzed. At that point, a profit factor is added to the product's cost, and the product is ready to be offered to customers.
- In contrast, under target costing, the pricing decision takes place immediately after the market research for a new product has been completed. The market research not only reveals the potential demand for the product but also identifies the maximum price that a customer would be willing to pay for it. Once the price is determined, target costing enables the company's engineers to design the product with a fixed maximum target cost on which to base the product's features.

Differences Between Cost-Based Pricing and Target Costing

The increased emphasis on product design allows a company to engineer the target cost into the product before manufacturing begins. A new product is designed only if its projected costs are equal to or lower than its target cost. The company can thus focus on holding costs down while it plans and designs the product, before the costs are actually committed and incurred.

Target costing enables IKEA to offer its products at competitive prices and ensures that a product will earn a profit as soon as it is introduced. This method identifies the price at which a product will be competitive in the marketplace, defines the desired profit to be made on the product, and computes the target cost by subtracting the desired profit from the competitive market price.

Adriano Castelli/Shutterstock.com

- **Committed costs** are the costs of design, development, engineering, testing, and production that are engineered into a product or service at the design stage of development.
- **Incurred costs** are the actual costs incurred in making the product.

When cost-based pricing is used, it is very difficult to control costs from the planning phase through the production phase. Under that approach, concern about reducing costs begins only after the product has been produced. This often leads to random efforts to cut costs, which can reduce product quality and further erode the customer base. Under target costing, the product is expected to produce a profit as soon as it is marketed. Cost-cutting improvements in a product's design and production methods can still be made, but profitability is built into the selling price from the beginning. Companies like **Sony** and **IKEA** have used target costing successfully for years and have benefited from increased sales volume each time they have cut prices because of production improvements. These companies never sacrifice product quality.

Target Costing Analysis in an Activity-Based Management Environment

To see how a company that uses activity-based management implements target costing, consider Elsinore Company's approach to new product decisions. A customer is seeking price quotations for a special-purpose router and a wireless palm-sized tablet computer. The current market-price ranges for the two products are as follows: router, \$320–\$380 per unit; and tablet computer, \$750–\$850 per unit.

One of Elsinore's salespersons thinks that if the company could quote prices of \$300 for the router and \$725 for the tablet computer, it would get the order and gain a significant share of the market for those products. Elsinore's usual profit markup is 25 percent of total unit cost.

The company's design engineers and accountants put together the following specifications and costs for the new products:

Activity-based cost rates:		
Materials handling	\$ 1.30 per dollar of direct materials and purchased parts cost	
Production	\$ 3.50 per machine hour	
Product delivery	\$24.00 per router	
	\$30.00 per computer	
	Router	**Computer**
Projected unit demand	26,000	18,000
Per-unit data:		
Direct materials cost	\$25.00	\$65.00
Purchased parts cost	\$15.00	\$45.00
Manufacturing labor:		
Hours	2.6	4.8
Hourly labor rate	\$12.00	\$15.00
Assembly labor:		
Hours	3.4	8.2
Hourly labor rate	\$14.00	\$16.00
Machine hours	12.8	28.4

The three steps used in arriving at the target cost follow.

- **Step 1. Find the target cost per unit.** The target cost for each product is computed as follows.

$$\text{Router} = \$300.00 \div 1.25 = \$240.00^*$$
$$\text{Computer} = \$725.00 \div 1.25 = \$580.00$$

*Target Price – Desired Profit = Target Cost

$$\$300.00 - 0.25X = X$$
$$\$300.00 = 1.25X$$
$$X = \frac{\$300.00}{1.25} = \underline{\underline{\$240.00}}$$

- **Step 2. Find the projected unit cost.** The projected total unit cost of production and delivery is as follows.

	Router	Computer
Direct materials cost	$ 25.00	$ 65.00
Purchased parts cost	15.00	45.00
Total cost of direct materials and parts	$ 40.00	$110.00
Manufacturing labor:		
Router (2.6 hours × $12.00)	31.20	
Computer (4.8 hours × $15.00)		72.00
Assembly labor:		
Router (3.4 hours × $14.00)	47.60	
Computer (8.2 hours × $16.00)		131.20
Activity-based costs:		
Materials handling:		
Router ($40.00 × $1.30)	52.00	
Computer ($110.00 × $1.30)		143.00
Production:		
Router (12.8 machine hours × $3.50)	44.80	
Computer (28.4 machine hours × $3.50)		99.40
Product delivery:		
Router	24.00	
Computer		30.00
Projected total unit cost	$239.60	$585.60

- **Step 3. Make a decision.** Using the target costing approach and the following data, we can determine whether Elsinore should produce the new products:

	Router	Computer
Target unit cost	$240.00	$580.00
Less projected unit cost	239.60	585.60
Difference	$ 0.40	$ (5.60)

The router can be produced below its target cost, so it should be produced. As currently designed, the tablet computer cannot be produced at or below its target cost, so Elsinore should either redesign it or drop plans to produce it.

APPLY IT!

Success Ltd. is considering a new product and must make a go or no-go decision when its planning team meets tomorrow. Market research shows that the unit selling price that would be agreeable to potential customers is $1,000, and the company's desired profit is 25 percent of target cost. The design engineer's preliminary estimate of the product's design, production, and distribution costs is $775 per unit. Using target costing, should the company market the new product?

SOLUTION

Yes. The company should market the new product. The target cost for the product is $800 ($1,000 ÷ 1.25). The engineer's projected cost is $775, or $25 below the amount needed to earn the desired profit.

TRY IT! SE5, SE6, E8A, E9A, E10A, E11A, E8B, E9B, E10B, E11B

LO 5 Pricing for Internal Providers of Goods and Services

So far, we have focused on how a company sets prices for consumers outside the organization. We now look at how an organization prices its products and services for internal transfers between divisions or segments.

As a business grows, its day to day operations may be more manageable if it is organized into divisions or operating segments. A separate manager is assigned to control the operations of each segment. Such a business is called a **decentralized organization**. Each division or segment often sells its goods and services both inside and outside the organization.

For example, the beverage division of **Pepsico** sells its drink products to internal customers like **KFC** and **Taco Bell** restaurants. It also sells to external customers like **Safeway** and **Wal-Mart**. **Anheuser-Busch**'s beer segment produces and sells its products internally to **Sea World** amusement parks, as well as externally to unrelated entities like airlines and grocery stores.

Transfer Pricing

When divisions or segments within a company exchange goods or services and assume the role of customer or supplier for each other, they use transfer prices. A **transfer price** is the price at which goods and services are charged and exchanged between a company's divisions or segments.

- Transfer prices affect the revenues and costs of the divisions involved.
- They do not affect the revenues and costs of the company as a whole.

STUDY NOTE: *Transfer pricing is not used for external pricing; it is used to set prices for transfers among a company's departments, divisions, or segments.*

The transfer price shifts part of the profits from the divisions or centers that externally charge for their goods or services to the divisions or centers that do not externally bill for their services and products. Transfer pricing enables a business to assess both the internal and the external profitability of its products or services. The three basic kinds of transfer prices are:

- Cost-plus transfer prices
- Market transfer prices
- Negotiated transfer prices

STUDY NOTE: *Cost-plus transfer pricing is similar to the gross margin pricing method.*

Cost-Plus Transfer Price A **cost-plus transfer price** is based on either the full cost or the variable costs incurred by the producing division plus an agreed-on profit percentage. The weakness of the cost-plus pricing method is that cost recovery is guaranteed to the selling division. Guaranteed cost recovery prevents the company from detecting inefficient operating conditions and the incurrence of excessive costs, and it may even inappropriately reward inefficient divisions that incur excessive costs. This reduces overall company profitability and shareholder value.

Market Transfer Price A **market transfer price** (or *external market price*) is based on the price that could be charged if a segment could buy from or sell to an external party. Some experts believe that the use of a market transfer price is preferable to the other methods. It forces the division that is "selling" or transferring the product or service to another division to be competitive with market conditions, and it does not penalize the "buying" or receiving division by charging it a higher price than it would have to pay if it bought from outside the firm.

However, using market prices may lead the selling division to ignore negotiation attempts from the buying division manager and to sell directly to outside customers. If this causes an internal shortage of materials and forces the buying division to purchase materials from the outside, overall company profits may decline even if the selling division makes a profit. Such use of market prices works against a company's overall operating objectives. Therefore, when market prices are used to develop transfer prices, they are usually used only as a basis for negotiation.

Negotiated Transfer Price A **negotiated transfer price** is arrived at through bargaining between the managers of the buying and selling divisions or segments. Such a transfer price may be based on an agreement to use a cost plus a profit percentage. The negotiated price will be between the negotiation floor (the selling division's variable cost) and the negotiation ceiling (the market price). This approach allows for cost recovery while still allowing the selling division to return a profit.

Developing a Transfer Price

To illustrate the development of the three kinds of transfer prices, we will use Simple Box Company, which makes cardboard boxes. As shown in Exhibit 5, this company has two divisions: the Pulp Division and the Cardboard Division. The Pulp Division produces pulp for the Cardboard Division. The Cardboard Division may also purchase pulp from outside suppliers.

Exhibit 5
Transfer Price Alternatives at Simple Box Company

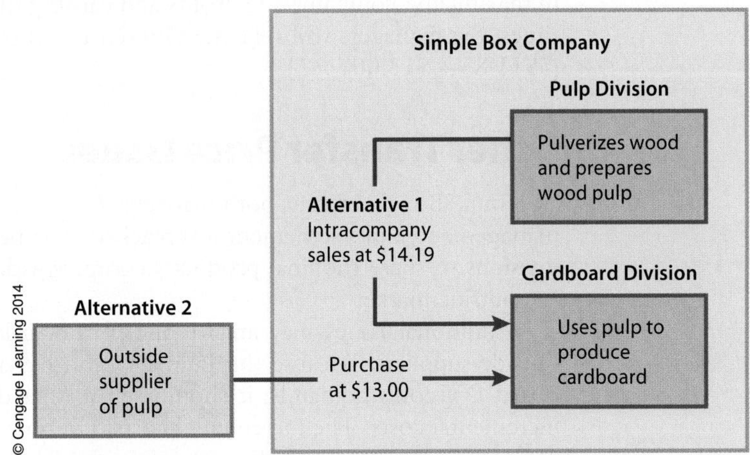

Exhibit 6 shows the development of a cost-plus transfer price for the Pulp Division. The Pulp Division's manager has created a one-year budget based on the expectation that the Cardboard Division will require 480,000 pounds of pulp. Unit costs appear in the last column.

Exhibit 6
Transfer Price Computation

Simple Box Company
Pulp Division—Transfer Price Computation

Cost Categories	Budgeted Costs	Cost per Unit
Direct materials:		
Wood	$1,584,000	$ 3.30
Scrap wood	336,000	0.70
Direct labor:		
Shaving/cleaning	768,000	1.60
Pulverizing	1,152,000	2.40
Blending	912,000	1.90
Overhead:		
Variable	936,000	1.95
Fixed	504,000	1.05
Subtotals	$6,192,000	$12.90
Costs allocated from corporate office	144,000	
Target profit, 10% of division's costs	619,200	1.29
Total costs and profit	$6,955,200	
Cost-plus transfer price		$14.19

Cost-Plus Transfer Price Notice that allocated corporate overhead is not included in the computation of the transfer price. Only the variable costs of $11.85 ($3.30 + $0.70 + $1.60 + $2.40 + $1.90 + $1.95) and the fixed cost of $1.05 related to the Pulp Division are included. The profit markup of 10 percent adds $1.29, producing the final cost-plus transfer price of $14.19.

Market Price Management could now dictate that the $14.19 price be used. However, the Cardboard Division's manager could point out that it is possible to purchase pulp from an outside supplier for $13.00 per pound. Use of the $13.00 price would represent a market-based approach.

Negotiated Transfer Price The best solution might be to agree on a negotiated transfer price between the variable costs of $11.85, the floor, and the outside market price of $13.00, the ceiling. The negotiation process will facilitate each manager's role in maximizing companywide profits and earning the 10 percent minimum return. Many times, the managers will split the difference and negotiate a price of $12.43 (rounded) [($11.85 + $13.00) ÷ 2].

Other Transfer Price Issues

At Simple Box Company, both managers brought their concerns to the attention of top management, and a settlement was reached. The negotiated transfer price allows the two divisions to share the final product's companywide profits when the boxes are sold on the outside market.

STUDY NOTE: *The use of transfer pricing encourages accountability for seller-customer relationships.*

Additional issues may arise if the Cardboard Division chooses to purchase from outside suppliers. Because the Pulp Division has adequate capacity to fulfill the Cardboard Division's demands, it should sell to that division at any price that recovers its incremental costs. The incremental costs of intracompany sales include all variable costs of production and distribution plus any avoidable fixed costs that are directly traceable to intracompany sales. If the Cardboard Division can acquire products from outside suppliers at an annual cost that is less than the Pulp Division's incremental costs, then purchases should be made from the outside supplier because it will enhance the company's overall profits. Before making such a decision, a thorough analysis of the Pulp Division's operations should be conducted.

Using Transfer Prices to Measure Performance

Because a transfer price contains an estimated amount of profit, a manager's ability to meet a targeted profit can be measured. Although transfer prices are often called *artificial* or *created* prices, they and their related policies are closely connected with performance evaluation.

When transfer prices are used, a division can be evaluated as a profit center, even if it does not sell to outsiders, because using transfer prices to value the division's output creates simulated revenues for the division. Although the operating income is not based on real sales to outsiders, it is a valuable performance measure if the transfer prices are realistic.

Exhibit 7 shows a performance report for Simple Box Company's Pulp Division. The Pulp Division produced and transferred 42,000 pounds as budgeted at a negotiated transfer price of $13.00 per pound. (The budgeted costs are based on the costs per unit in Exhibit 6.) The performance report shows that the Pulp Division's actual gross margin was ($1,725), whereas the budgeted gross margin was $4,200. The difference of $5,925 stems from cost overages in various materials, labor, and variable overhead accounts. Those differences will need to be investigated, as they would be for any division.

Exhibit 7
Performance Report Using Transfer Prices

Simple Box Company
Pulp Division—Performance Report
For March

	Budget	Actual	Difference Under/(Over) Budget
Sales to Carboard Division (42,000 lbs.)	$546,000	$546,000	$ 0
Costs Controllable by Manager			
Cost of goods sold:			
Direct materials:			
Wood	$138,600	$140,250	$(1,650)
Scrap wood	29,400	29,750	(350)
Direct labor:			
Shaving/cleaning	67,200	68,000	(800)
Pulverizing	100,800	102,000	(1,200)
Blending	79,800	80,750	(950)
Overhead:			
Variable	81,900	82,875	(975)
Fixed	44,100	44,100	—
Total cost of goods sold	$541,800	$547,725	$(5,925)
Gross margin from sales	$ 4,200	$ (1,725)	$ 5,925
Costs Uncontrollable by Manager			
Cost allocated from corporate office	12,600	12,600	—
Operating (loss)	$ (8,400)	$ (14,325)	$ 5,925

The use of transfer prices to simulate revenues allows further evaluation. For instance, the measures of operating income (loss) can be compared with the amount of capital the company has invested in the Pulp Division to determine whether the division is making an adequate return on the company's investment. The impact on the division of uncontrollable costs from the corporate office can also be assessed.

APPLY IT!

The Molding Process Division at Trophy Products has been treated as a cost center since the company was founded in 1968. Recently, management decided to change the performance evaluation approach and treat the company's processing divisions as profit centers. Each division is expected to earn a 20 percent profit on its total production costs. One of Trophy's products is a plastic base for a display chest. The Molding Process Division supplies this base to the Cabinet Process Division, and it also sells the base to another company. Molding's total production cost for the base is $27.40. It sells the base to the other company for $38.00. What should the transfer price for the plastic base be?

SOLUTION

In addition to the traditional approaches of transferring the product from one process to the next at variable or full cost, management should consider the following three options when setting the transfer price for the plastic base:

Cost plus profit:	$27.40 + ($27.40 × 20%) = $32.88
Market price:	$38.00
Negotiated price:	Any price between $27.40 and $38.00

Managers of the Molding Process Division have the option of selling the division's output to the outside company and earning more than the 20 percent minimum return. They should also be able to earn more than 20 percent internally. A price at the midpoint of the negotiated price range, $32.70, seems fair.

TRY IT! SE7, SE8, SE9, E12A, E13A, E12B, E13B

SECTION 3

BUSINESS APPLICATIONS

BUSINESS APPLICATIONS
- Planning
- Performing
- Evaluating
- Communicating

RELEVANT LEARNING OBJECTIVE

LO 6 Relate pricing issues to the management process.

LO 6 Pricing and the Management Process

For an organization to stay in business, its selling price must:

- be competitive with the competition's price
- be acceptable to customers
- recover all costs incurred in bringing the product or service to market
- return a profit

If a manager deviates from any of these four pricing rules, there must be a specific short-run objective that accounts for the change. Breaking those pricing rules for a long period will force a company into bankruptcy. Exhibit 8 illustrates the elements of pricing that managers need to consider at each step in the management process.

Exhibit 8
Pricing and the Management Process

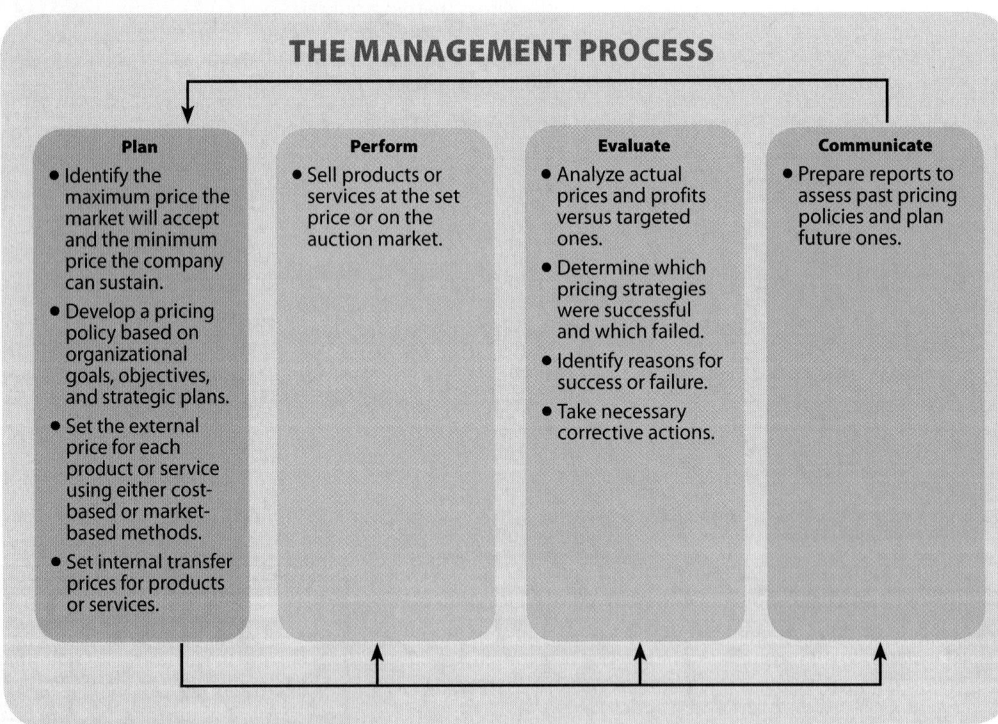

APPLY IT!

For an organization to stay in business, which of the following is *not true* when setting its selling price? The selling price must

a. return a profit
b. be acceptable to customers
c. be acceptable to competitors
d. be competitive with the competition's price
e. recover all costs incurred in bringing the product or service to market

SOLUTION

c.

TRY IT! SE10, E14A, E14B

TriLevel Problem

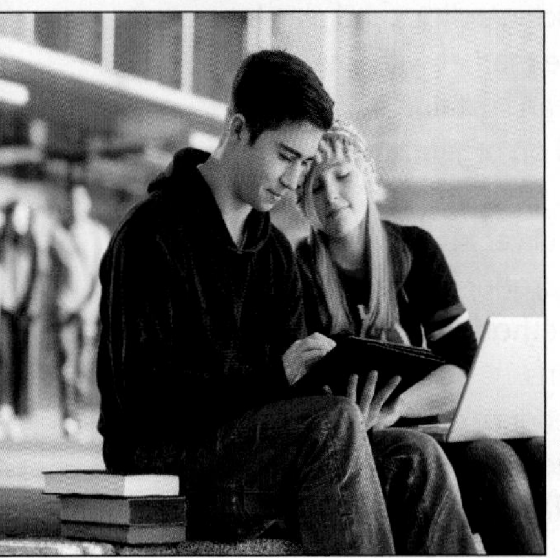
sturti/iStockphoto.com

Lab 126

The beginning of this chapter focused on **Lab 126**, an Amazon subsidiary that makes Kindle e-readers and e-reader applications for other handheld devices. Complete the following requirements in order to answer the questions posed at the beginning of the chapter.

Section 1: Concepts

How are pricing and the concept of revenue recognition related?

Section 2: Accounting Applications

How do companies determine the price of products?

Suppose that Undercovers Company makes a complete line of covers (a plain cover, a deluxe cover, and a trendy cover) for e-book readers like the Kindle. The covers are produced on an assembly line, beginning with the Stamping Department and continuing through the Sewing, Detailing, and Packaging departments. The projected costs of each cover and the percentages for assigning unavoidable fixed and common costs follow.

Cost Categories	Total Projected Costs	Plain Cover	Deluxe Cover	Trendy Cover
Direct materials:				
Leather	$137,000	$62,500	$29,000	$45,500
Magnet	5,250	2,500	1,000	1,750
Clip	9,250	3,750	2,000	3,500
Package	70,500	30,000	16,000	24,500
Direct labor:				
Stamping	53,750	22,500	12,000	19,250
Sewing	94,000	42,500	20,000	31,500
Detailing	107,500	45,000	24,000	38,500
Packaging	44,250	17,500	11,000	15,750
Indirect labor	173,000	77,500	36,000	59,500
Operating supplies	30,000	12,500	7,000	10,500
Variable overhead	90,500	40,000	19,000	31,500
Fixed overhead	120,000	45%	25%	30%
Distribution expenses	105,000	40%	20%	40%
Variable marketing expenses	123,000	$55,000	$26,000	$42,000
Fixed marketing expenses	85,400	40%	25%	35%
General and administrative expenses	47,600	40%	25%	35%

Undercovers' policy is to earn a minimum of 30 percent over total cost on each type of cover produced. Expected sales for the year are: plain, 50,000 units; deluxe, 20,000 units; and trendy, 35,000 units. Assume no change in inventory levels, and round all answers to two decimal places.

1. Using the gross margin pricing method, compute the selling price for each kind of cover.
2. The competition is selling a similar plain cover for around $14. Should this influence Undercovers' pricing decision? Give reasons for your answer.

Section 3: Business Applications

How does managerial accounting help managers during the management process with pricing decisions? To answer this question, match this chapter's manager responsibilities with when they occur within the management process.

a. Plan
b. Perform
c. Evaluate
d. Communicate

1. Prepare reports to assess past pricing policies and plan future ones.
2. Identify the maximum price the market will accept and the minimum price the company can sustain.
3. Develop a pricing policy based on organizational goals, objectives, and strategic plans.
4. Analyze actual prices and profits versus targeted ones.
5. Set the external price for each product or service using either cost-based or market-based methods.
6. Take necessary corrective actions.
7. Sell products or services at the set price or on the auction market.
8. Determine which pricing strategies were successful and which failed.
9. Identify reasons for success or failure.
10. Set internal transfer prices for products or services.

SOLUTION

Section 1: Concepts

The prices managers set have a significant impact on business operations, since revenue is computed by multiplying the product or service price by the quantity sold. Revenues are generally *recognized* when goods are transferred or services are rendered. On the income statement, the recognition of revenues is *matched* with the costs incurred to generate those revenues, resulting in the recognition of a net profit or loss, the fundamental measure of an organization's profitability. Thus, a manager's ability to set prices is essential to the long-term survival of any profit-oriented enterprise. There are various approaches that managers use to establish the prices of goods and services. Each approach may very well produce a different price for the same product or service. The process of establishing a correct price is, in fact, more of an art than a science. No one pricing method is superior because each business and market segment differs. Successful managers, like those at Lab 126, generally use several pricing approaches.

Early in the e-book reader market, there was little competition, and new models may have been priced to recover the product's cost and earn a certain amount of profit. Now that new products with desirable features, such as text-to-speech, are being introduced and the market has become very competitive, Lab 126's managers might use target costing to set a price for a new reader. To do so, they would subtract their desired profit from the proposed market price to arrive at the maximum target cost. A team of engineering, accounting, and sales managers would then analyze each proposed product feature to verify that the product could be designed and manufactured at or below the target cost.

Section 2: Accounting Applications

Before the selling prices are computed, the cost analysis must be completed and restructured to supply the information that is required for the pricing computations.

Cost Categories	Total Projected Costs	Plain Cover	Deluxe Cover	Trendy Cover
Total direct materials	$ 222,000	$ 98,750	$ 48,000	$ 75,250
Total direct labor	299,500	127,500	67,000	105,000
Indirect labor	173,000	77,500	36,000	59,500
Operating supplies	30,000	12,500	7,000	10,500
Variable overhead	90,500	40,000	19,000	31,500
Fixed overhead	120,000	54,000	30,000	36,000
Total production costs	$ 935,000	$410,250	$207,000	$317,750
Distribution expenses	$ 105,000	$ 42,000	$ 21,000	$ 42,000
Variable marketing expenses	123,000	55,000	26,000	42,000
Fixed marketing expenses	85,400	34,160	21,350	29,890
General and administrative expenses	47,600	19,040	11,900	16,660
Total selling, general, and administrative expenses	$ 361,000	$150,200	$ 80,250	$130,550
Total costs	$1,296,000	$560,450	$287,250	$448,300
Desired profit (30%)	$ 388,800	$168,135	$ 86,175	$134,490

1.
Markup percentage formula:

$$\text{Markup Percentage} = \frac{\text{Desired Profit} + \text{Total Selling, General, and Administrative Expenses}}{\text{Total Production Costs}}$$

Gross margin pricing formula:

Gross Margin-Based Price = Total Production Costs per Unit + (Markup Percentage × Total Production Costs per Unit)

Plain: $\text{Markup Percentage} = \frac{\$168,135 + \$150,200}{\$410,250} = 77.60\%$*

Gross Margin-Based Price = ($410,250 ÷ 50,000) + [77.60% × ($410,250 ÷ 50,000)] = $14.57*

Deluxe: $\text{Markup Percentage} = \frac{\$86,175 + \$80,250}{\$207,000} = 80.40\%$*

Gross Margin-Based Price = ($207,000 ÷ 20,000) + [80.40% × ($207,000 ÷ 20,000)] = $18.67*

Trendy: $\text{Markup Percentage} = \frac{\$134,490 + \$130,550}{\$317,750} = 83.41\%$*

Gross Margin-Based Price = ($317,750 ÷ 35,000) + [83.41% × ($317,750 ÷ 35,000)] = $16.65*

*Rounded

2. If the quality and design of the competition's plain cover are similar to those of Undercovers' plain cover, Undercovers' management should consider reducing the price of its cover to the $14.00 range. At $14.57, Undercovers has a 30 percent profit built into its price. The plain cover's break-even is at $11.21 (rounded, $14.57 ÷ 1.3). Therefore, the company could reduce its price below the competitor's price and still make a significant profit.

• SOLUTION

Section 3: Business Applications

1. d
2. a
3. a
4. c
5. a
6. c
7. b
8. c
9. c
10. a

Chapter Review

LO 1 Explain how the pricing of goods and services relates to the concept of revenue recognition.

The prices managers set have a strong relationship with revenue recognition since revenue is computed by multiplying the product or service price by the quantity sold. When goods are transferred or services are rendered is generally when revenue is recognized. Costs are then matched with the revenues they generated and the difference is shown on the income statement as a net profit or loss, the fundamental measure of an organization's profitability. Thus, it is important that an organization's activities be guided by a pricing policy. A pricing policy is one way companies differentiate themselves from their competitors. Possible pricing policy objectives include (1) identifying and adhering to both short-run and long-run pricing strategies, (2) maximizing profits, (3) maintaining or gaining market share, (4) setting socially responsible prices, (5) maintaining a minimum rate of return on investment, and (6) being customer focused.

LO 2 Describe economic pricing concepts, including the auction-based pricing method used on the Internet.

Microeconomic theory states that profits will be maximized when the difference between total revenue and total cost is greatest. Total revenue then increases more slowly, because as a product is marketed, price reductions are necessary to sell more units. Total cost increases when larger quantities are produced because fixed costs change. Profit is maximized at the point where the marginal revenue and marginal cost curves intersect. Auction-based pricing is growing in importance as a pricing mechanism as more companies and individuals are conducting business over the Internet. Basically, the Internet allows sellers and buyers to solicit bids and transact exchanges in an open market environment.

LO 3 Use cost-based pricing methods to develop prices.

Cost-based pricing methods include gross margin pricing and return on assets pricing. Under these two methods, a markup representing a percentage of production costs or a desired rate of return is added to the total costs. A pricing method often used by service businesses is time and materials pricing.

LO 4 Describe target costing, and use it to analyze pricing decisions and evaluate a new product opportunity.

Target costing (1) identifies the price at which a product will be competitive in the marketplace, (2) defines the desired profit to be made on the product, and (3) computes the target cost for the product by subtracting the desired profit from the competitive market price. Target costing gives managers the ability to control or dictate the costs of a new product at the planning stage. Under a traditional pricing system, managers cannot control costs until after the product has been manufactured. To identify a new product's target cost, the following formula is applied:

$$\text{Target Price} - \text{Desired Profit} = \text{Target Cost}$$

The target cost is then given to the engineers and product designers, who use it as a maximum cost to be incurred for materials and other resources needed to design and manufacture the product. It is their responsibility to create the product at or below its target cost. Sometimes, the cost requirements cannot be met. In such a case, the organization should try to adjust the product's design and the approach to production. If those attempts fail, the organization should either invest in new equipment and procedures or abandon its plans to market the product.

Describe how transfer pricing is used for transferring goods and services and evaluating performance within a division or segment. LO 5

A transfer price is the price at which goods and services are charged and exchanged between a company's divisions or segments. There are three primary approaches to developing transfer prices: (1) the price may be based on the cost of the item up to the point at which it is transferred to the next department or process; (2) the price may be based on market value if the item has an existing external market; or (3) the price may be negotiated by the managers of the buying and selling divisions. A cost-plus transfer price is the sum of costs incurred by the producing division plus an agreed-on profit percentage. A market-based transfer price is based on external market prices. In most cases, a negotiated transfer price is used; that is, a price is reached through bargaining between the managers of the selling and buying divisions. A division's performance may be evaluated by using transfer prices as the basis for determining revenues.

Relate pricing issues to the management process. LO 6

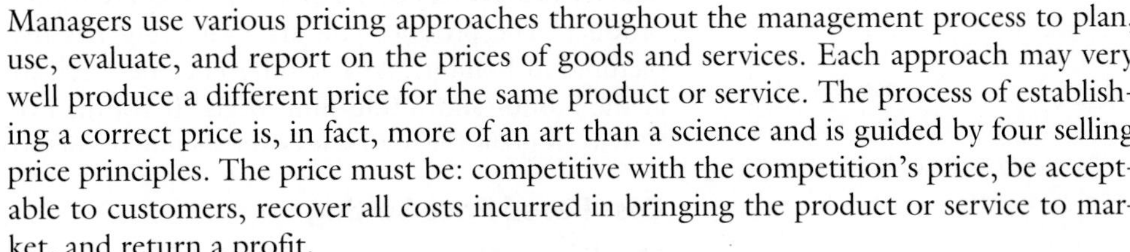

Managers use various pricing approaches throughout the management process to plan, use, evaluate, and report on the prices of goods and services. Each approach may very well produce a different price for the same product or service. The process of establishing a correct price is, in fact, more of an art than a science and is guided by four selling price principles. The price must be: competitive with the competition's price, be acceptable to customers, recover all costs incurred in bringing the product or service to market, and return a profit.

Key Terms

auction-based pricing 1106 (LO2)
committed costs 1113 (LO4)
cost-plus transfer price 1116 (LO5)
decentralized organization 1116 (LO5)
gross margin pricing method 1107 (LO3)
incurred costs 1113 (LO4)
marginal cost 1105 (LO2)
marginal revenue 1105 (LO2)
market transfer price 1116 (LO5)
negotiated transfer price 1116 (LO5)
return on assets pricing method 1108 (LO3)
target costing 1112 (LO4)
time and materials pricing 1110 (LO3)
transfer price 1116 (LO5)

Chapter Assignments

DISCUSSION QUESTIONS

LO 1 **DQ1. CONCEPT ▶** How do product or service prices set by managers impact the revenue recognized by an organization?

LO 1 **DQ2.** Why is setting an appropriate price one of the most difficult decisions a manager makes?

LO 1, 6 **DQ3. BUSINESS APPLICATION ▶** How does a pricing policy help companies differentiate their brands from their competitors?

LO 1, 6 **DQ4. BUSINESS APPLICATION ▶** List some of the objectives of a pricing policy.

LO 1, 6 **DQ5. BUSINESS APPLICATION ▶** What are some of the internal and external factors that affect pricing decisions?

SHORT EXERCISES

LO 1 External Factors That Influence Prices

SE1. ACCOUNTING CONNECTION ▶ Your client is about to introduce a very high-quality product that will remove an invasive form of pepper plant in the southern United States. The Marketing Department has established a price of $37 per gallon, and the company controller has projected total production, selling, and distribution costs of $26 per gallon. What other factors should your client consider before introducing the product into the marketplace?

LO 2 Traditional Economic Pricing Concept

SE2. ACCOUNTING CONNECTION ▶ You are to decide the total demand for a particular product. The product you are evaluating has the total cost and total revenue curves pictured in Exhibit 2A. The difference between total revenue and total cost is the same at the 5,000- and 8,000-unit levels. If you had to choose between those two levels of activity as goals for total sales over the life of the product, which would you prefer? Why?

LO 3 Cost-Based Price Setting

SE3. Kinder Company has collected the following data for one of its product lines: total production costs, $300,000; total selling, general, and administrative expenses, $112,600; desired profit, $67,400; and production costs per unit, $40. Using the gross margin pricing method, compute a suggested selling price for this product that would yield the desired profit.

LO 3 Pricing a Service

SE4. Eileen van Gelder runs a home repair business. Recently she gathered the following cost information about the repair of a client's deck: replacement wood, $650; deck screws and supplies, $112; and labor, 12 hours at $14 per hour. Van Gelder applies a 40 percent overhead rate to all direct costs of a job. Compute the total billing price for the repair of the deck.

LO 4 Committed Costs and Target Costing

SE5. ACCOUNTING CONNECTION ▶ Nat Osborn is a designer for Base Enterprises. In a discussion about a proposed new product, Osborn stated that the product's projected target cost was $6.50 below the committed costs identified by design estimates. Should the company proceed with the new product? Explain your answer, and include a definition of committed cost in your analysis.

LO 4 Pricing Using Target Costing

SE6. ACCOUNTING CONNECTION ▶ MTZ Furniture is considering a new product and must make a go or no-go decision before tomorrow's planning team meeting. Market research shows that the unit selling price agreeable to potential customers is $1,600, and the company's desired profit is 22 percent of target cost. The designer's preliminary estimate of the product's design, production, and distribution costs is $1,380 per unit. Using target costing, determine whether the company should market the new product. (Round to the nearest dollar.)

LO 5 Decision to Use Transfer Prices

SE7. ACCOUNTING CONNECTION ▶ The production process at Premium Castings includes eight processes, each of which is currently treated as a cost center with a specific set of operations to perform on each casting produced. Following the fourth process's operations, the rough castings have an external market. The fourth process must also supply the fifth process with its direct materials. Premium's management wants to develop a new approach to measuring process performance. Is Premium a candidate for using transfer prices? Explain your answer.

LO 5 **Cost-Based Versus Market-Based Transfer Prices**

SE8. ACCOUNTING CONNECTION ▶ Refer to the information in SE7. Should Premium Castings use cost-based, market-based, or negotiated transfer prices? Why?

LO 5 **Developing a Negotiated Transfer Price**

SE9. The Cookie Division at Sweet Products has been treated as a cost center since the company was founded. Recently, management decided to change the performance evaluation approach and treat its processing divisions as profit centers. Each division is expected to earn a 20 percent profit on its total production costs. One of Sweet's products is chocolate chip cookie dough. The Cookie Division supplies this dough to the Packaged Cookies Division, and it also sells it to another company. Cookie Division's total production cost for the dough is $2.40 per pound. It sells the dough to the other company for $5.00 a pound. What should the transfer price for a pound of cookie dough be?

LO 6 **Rules for Establishing Prices**

SE10. BUSINESS APPLICATION ▶ Jay Patel is planning to open a pizza restaurant next month in Flora, Alabama. He plans to sell his large pizzas for a base price of $18 plus $2 for each topping selected. When asked how he arrived at the base price, he said that his cousin developed that price for his pizza restaurant in New York City. What pricing rules has Patel not followed?

EXERCISES: SET A

LO 1 **External and Internal Pricing Factors**

E1A. Ready Tires features more than a dozen brands of tires in many sizes. Two of the brands are RoadPlus and RoadPower. Information about the two brands follows.

	RoadPlus	RoadPower
Selling price:		
Tire, installed	$180	$170
Cost per tire	120	80

As shown, selling prices include installation costs. Each tire costs $20 to install.

1. Compute each brand's net unit selling price after installation.
2. **ACCOUNTING CONNECTION ▶** Was cost the main consideration in setting those prices?
3. **ACCOUNTING CONNECTION ▶** What other factors could have influenced those prices?

LO 2 **Traditional Economic Pricing Theory**

E2A. InStyle, a product design firm, has just completed a contract to develop a wireless entry system. The wireless key fob needs to be recharged only once a week and can be used worldwide. Initial fixed costs for this product are $4,000. The designers estimate that the product will break even at the $5,000/100-unit mark. Total revenues will again equal total costs at the $25,000/900-unit point. Marginal cost is expected to equal marginal revenue when 550 units are sold.

1. Sketch total revenue and total cost curves for this product. Mark the vertical axis at each $5,000 increment and the horizontal axis at each 100-unit increment.
2. Based on your total revenue and total cost curves in **1**, at what unit selling price will profits be maximized? (Round to the nearest cent.)

LO 3 **Price Determination**

E3A. Soft Industries has just patented a new lotion with lasting sun protection. The company's controller has developed the following annual information for use in price determination meetings:

Variable production costs	$ 450,000
Fixed overhead	250,000
Selling expenses	100,000
General and administrative expenses	75,000
Desired profit	315,000
Cost of assets employed	1,000,000

Annual demand for the product is expected to be 500,000 tubes. On average, the company now earns an 8 percent return on assets.

1. Compute the projected unit cost for one tube of lotion.
2. Using gross margin pricing, compute the markup percentage and selling price for one tube.
3. Using return on assets pricing, compute the unit price for one tube of lotion.

LO 3 **Pricing a Service**

E4A. Iowa has just passed a law making it mandatory to have every chicken inspected at least once a year for a variety of communicable diseases. Cluck Enterprises is considering entering this inspection business. After extensive studies, Cluck's owner has developed the following annual projections:

Direct service labor	$275,000
Variable service overhead costs	25,000
Fixed service overhead costs	200,000
Selling expenses	100,500
General and administrative expenses	59,500
Minimum desired profit	100,000
Cost of assets employed	800,000

The owner believes his company could inspect 2,000,000 chickens per year. On average, the company now earns a 6 percent return on assets.

1. Compute the projected cost of inspecting each chicken.
2. Using gross margin pricing, determine the price to charge for inspecting each chicken.
3. Using return on assets pricing, compute the unit price to charge for this inspection service. (Round to two decimal places.)

LO 3 **Cost-Based Pricing**

E5A. Metro Transit is determining the price for its newest prepaid fare card. The fare card can be used at any transportation station or retail outlet—no PIN number or signature is required. The following annual information has been developed for use in upcoming price determination meetings:

Variable processing costs	$40 million
Fixed processing costs	4 million
Selling expenses (fixed)	4 million
General and administrative expenses (fixed)	2 million
Desired profit	90 million
Cost of assets employed	5 billion

Annual usage is expected to be 5 billion transactions. On average, the company now earns a 5 percent return on assets.

1. Compute the projected cost of one transaction.
2. Using gross margin pricing, compute the price to charge per transaction. (Round to three decimal places.)
3. Using return on assets pricing, compute the price to charge per transaction.

LO 3 **Pricing Services**

E6A. Watt Car Repair specializes in repairing electric cars. The company uses a 60 percent markup rate on parts to cover parts-related overhead costs and profit margin. It uses a 200 percent markup rate on labor to cover labor-related overhead costs and profit margin. Compute the bill for a recent job that used the following parts and labor:

Material and repair parts used	$300
Labor used	5 hours at $40 per hour

LO 3 **Time and Materials Pricing**

E7A. Orange Remodeling Service specializes in renovating older homes. Last week the company was asked to bid on the following remodeling job. The list of materials and labor needed to complete the job follows.

Materials		Labor	
Lumber	$ 5,000	Carpenter	$ 4,000
Nails/bolts	200	Floor specialist	2,000
Paint	1,800	Painter	2,000
Glass	3,000	Supervisor	1,000
Doors	500	Helpers	3,000
Hardware	500	Total	$12,000
Supplies	1,000		
Total	$12,000		

Orange uses an overhead markup percentage for materials (50 percent) and for labor (60 percent). Those markups cover all operating costs. In addition, Orange expects to make at least a 30 percent profit on all jobs. Compute the price that Orange should quote for the job.

LO 4 **Target Costing and Pricing**

E8A. Lovebug Company has determined that its new automotive hood screen would gain widespread customer acceptance if the company could price it at or under $30. Anticipated labor hours and costs for each unit of the new product follow.

Direct materials cost	$5
Direct labor cost	
Manufacturing labor:	
Hours	0.2
Hourly labor rate	$10
Assembly labor:	
Hours	0.5
Hourly labor rate	$15
Machine hours	1

The company currently uses the following three activity-based cost rates:

Materials handling	$0.30 per dollar of direct materials
Production	$5.00 per machine hour
Product delivery	$0.50 per unit

ACCOUNTING CONNECTION ▶ The company's minimum desired profit is 40 percent over total production and delivery cost. Compute the target cost for the new hood screen, and determine if the company should market it. (Round to two decimal places.)

LO 4 **Target Costing**

E9A. ACCOUNTING CONNECTION ▶ Assume the same facts as in **E8A** except that the company's minimum desired profit has been revised to 20 percent over production and delivery costs as a result of a recent economic downturn. Compute the revised target cost for the new hood screen, and determine if the company should market it.

LO 4 **Target Costing**

E10A. Suppose that Sleek Manufacturing is developing a new table targeted to sell for less than $10 and that it is considering the two production alternatives that follow. Rank the alternatives, assuming that the company's minimum desired profit is 40 percent over total production costs. (Round to two decimal places.)

	Alternative A	Alternative B
Direct material costs	$2	$2
Direct labor cost	0.25 hour at $10 per hour	0.20 hour at $12 per hour
Overhead costs	50 percent of direct labor costs	$0.40 per dollar of direct materials

LO 4 **Target Costing**

E11A. Management at Pew Co. is considering the development of an automated machine called the AutoMate. After conferring with the design engineers, the controller's staff assembled the following data about this product:

Target selling price	$500 per unit
Desired profit percentage	50% of total unit cost
Projected unit demand	5,000 units
Activity-based cost rates:	
Materials handling	1% of direct materials and purchased parts cost
Engineering	$20 per unit
Production and assembly	$10 per machine hour
Delivery	$7 per unit
Marketing	$4 per unit
Per-unit data:	
Direct materials cost	$160
Purchased parts cost	$40
Manufacturing labor:	
Hours	2
Hourly labor rate	$15
Assembly labor:	
Hours	3
Hourly labor rate	$10
Machine hours	4

1. Compute the product's target cost. (Round to the nearest dollar.)
2. Compute the product's projected unit cost based on the design engineers' estimates.
3. **ACCOUNTING CONNECTION ▶** Should management produce and market the Auto-Mate? Defend your answer.

LO 5 **Transfer Price Comparison**

E12A. Michelle Nicholas is developing a transfer price for the housing section of an automatic garage door opener. The housing for the opener is made in Department H. It is then passed on to Department G, where final assembly occurs. Unit costs for the housing follow.

Cost Categories	Unit Costs
Direct materials	$3.00
Direct labor	2.00
Variable overhead	1.00
Fixed overhead	2.50
Profit markup, 25% of cost	?

An outside vendor can supply the housing for $10.00 per unit.

1. Develop a cost-plus transfer price for the housing. (Round to two decimal places.)
2. **ACCOUNTING CONNECTION ▶** What should the transfer price be? Support your answer.

LO 5 **Transfer Pricing**

E13A. Quality Company's Seconds Store offers refurbished or factory seconds products to the public at substantially reduced prices. The controller is developing transfer price alternatives to present to management to determine the best price to use when transferring products from the factory to the store, using the following data:

Unit price if sold to outside retailers	$20
Variable product cost per unit	$8
Fixed product cost per unit	$6
Seconds Store profit markup	50%

1. What is the market-based transfer price alternative?
2. What is the minimum transfer price alternative?
3. Compute the cost-plus transfer price alternative assuming cost includes variable costs only.

LO 6 **Pricing Policy Objectives**

E14A. BUSINESS APPLICATION ▶ Bulls Eye, Ltd., is an international merchandising company that retails medium-priced goods. Its retail outlets are located throughout the United States, France, Germany, and Great Britain. Management wants to maintain the company's image of providing the highest possible quality at the lowest possible prices. Selling prices are developed to draw customers away from competitors' stores. First-of-the-month sales are regularly held at all stores, and customers are accustomed to this practice. Company buyers are carefully trained to seek out quality goods at inexpensive prices. Sales are targeted to increase a minimum of 5 percent per year. All sales should yield a 15 percent return on assets. Sales personnel are expected to wear a uniform while working. All stores are required to be clean and well organized. Competitors' prices are checked daily. Identify Bulls Eye's pricing policy objectives.

EXERCISES: SET B

Visit the textbook companion website at www.cengagebrain.com to access Exercise Set B for this chapter.

PROBLEMS

LO 3 **Pricing Decision**

✔ 1: Total costs and expenses: $12,492,000
✔ 2: Gross margin-based price: $24.03

P1. Chill Industries specializes in the assembly of home appliances. One division focuses most of its efforts on assembling a convection toaster. Projected costs of this product follow.

Cost Description	Budgeted Costs
Toaster casings	$ 960,000
Electrical components	2,220,000
Direct labor	3,600,000
Variable indirect assembly costs	780,000
Fixed indirect assembly costs	1,740,000
Selling expenses	1,536,000
General operating expenses	840,000
Administrative expenses	816,000

(Continued)

The projected costs are based on an estimated demand of 600,000 convection toasters per year. The company wants to make a $1,923,000 profit.

Competitors have just published their wholesale prices for the coming year. They range from $21.60 to $22.64 per toaster. The Chill convection toaster is known for its high quality and modern look. It competes with products at the top end of the price range. Even with its reputation, however, every $0.20 increase above the top competitor's price causes a drop in demand of 60,000 units below the original estimate. Assume that all price changes are in $0.20 increments.

REQUIRED

1. Prepare a schedule of total projected costs and unit costs.
2. Use gross margin pricing to compute the anticipated selling price. (Round to two decimal places.)
3. **ACCOUNTING CONNECTION ▶** Based on competitors' prices, what should the Chill toaster sell for (assume a constant unit cost)? Defend your answer. (*Hint:* Determine the total profit at various sales levels.)
4. **ACCOUNTING CONNECTION ▶** Would your pricing structure in requirement **3** change if the company had only limited competition at its quality level? If so, in what direction? Explain why.

LO **3**

Pricing Decisions

✔ 1a: Lawn mower return on assets-based price: $114.60
✔ 1b: Lawn edger gross margin-based price: $54

P2. *(CMA adapted)* Cutting Edge Company manufactures lawn equipment for retail stores. Ron Ellington, the vice president of marketing, has proposed that the company introduce two new products: a GPS lawn mower and a laser-guided lawn edger. Ellington has requested that the Profit Planning Department develop preliminary selling prices for the two new products for his review.

Profit Planning has followed the company's standard policy for developing potential selling prices. It has used all data available for each product. The data accumulated by Profit Planning follows.

	Lawn Mower	Lawn Edger
Estimated annual demand in units	20,000	18,000
Estimated unit manufacturing costs	$100.00	$30.00
Estimated unit selling and administrative expenses	$5.00	Not available
Assets employed in manufacturing	$480,000	Not available

Cutting Edge plans to use an average of $1,200,000 in assets to support operations in the current year. The condensed budgeted income statement that follows reflects the planned return on assets of 40 percent ($480,000 ÷ $1,200,000) for the entire company for all products.

Cutting Edge Company
Budgeted Income Statement
For the Year Ended May 31
(in thousands)

Revenue	$2,880
Cost of goods sold	1,600
Gross margin	$1,280
Selling and administrative expenses	800
Operating income	$ 480

REQUIRED

1. Use the budgeted income statement to calculate a potential selling price for (a) the lawn mower, using return on assets pricing, and (b) the lawn edger, using gross margin pricing.
2. **ACCOUNTING CONNECTION ▶** Could a selling price for the lawn mower be calculated using return on assets pricing? Explain your answer.

3. **ACCOUNTING CONNECTION ▶** Which of the two pricing methods—return on assets pricing or gross margin pricing—is more appropriate for decision analysis? Explain your answer.
4. **ACCOUNTING CONNECTION ▶** Discuss the additional steps Ron Ellington is likely to take in setting an actual selling price for each of the two products after he receives their potential selling prices (as calculated in requirement **1**.)

LO **3**

Time and Materials Pricing in a Service Business

✔ 3: Total materials and parts: $4,966.50
Materials overhead: $6,456.45
✔ Direct labor: $1,412.40
✔ Direct labor overhead: $1,977.36

P3. Acme Maintenance, Inc., repairs heavy construction equipment and vehicles. Recently, Turnkey Construction Company had one of its giant earthmovers overhauled and its tires replaced. Repair work for a vehicle of that size usually takes from one week to ten days. The vehicle must be lifted up so that maintenance workers can gain access to the engine. Parts are normally so large that a crane must be used to put them into place.

The company uses the time and materials pricing system and data from the previous year to compute markup percentages for overhead related to parts and materials and overhead related to direct labor. It adds markups of 130 percent to the cost of materials and parts and 140 percent to the cost of direct labor to cover overhead and profit. The following materials, parts, and direct labor are needed to repair the giant earthmover:

Quantity	Unit Price	Hours	Hourly Rate
Materials and parts:		Direct labor:	
24 Spark plugs	$ 3.40	42 Mechanic hours	$18.20
20 Oil, quarts	2.90	54 Assistant mechanic hours	12.00
12 Hoses	11.60		
1 Water pump	764.00		
30 Coolant, quarts	6.50		
18 Clamps	5.90		
1 Distributor cap	128.40		
1 Carburetor	214.10		
4 Tires	820.00		

REQUIRED

Prepare a complete billing for this job. Include itemized amounts for each type of materials, parts, and direct labor. Follow the time and materials pricing approach, and show the total price for the job.

LO **4**

Pricing Using Target Costing

✔ 1: Target cost for Speed-Calc 5: $88 .00
2: Projected total unit cost for Speed-Calc 4: $74.22
✔ 2: Projected total unit cost for Speed-Calc 5: $84.84

SPREADSHEET

P4. Yuan Hwang Corp. is considering marketing two new graphing calculators, named Speed-Calc 4 and Speed-Calc 5. According to recent market research, the two products will surpass the current competition in both speed and quality and would be welcomed in the market. Customers would be willing to pay $98 for Speed-Calc 4 and $110 for Speed-Calc 5, based on their projected design capabilities. Both products have many uses, but the primary market interest comes from college students. Current production capacity exists for the manufacture and assembly of the two products. The company has a minimum desired profit of 25 percent above all costs for all of its products. Current activity-based cost rates follow.

Materials/parts handling	$1.20 per dollar of direct materials and purchased parts cost
Production	$8.00 per machine hour
Marketing/delivery	$4.40 per unit of Speed-Calc 4
	$6.20 per unit of Speed-Calc 5

(Continued)

Design engineering and accounting estimates to produce the two new products follow.

	Speed-Calc 4	Speed-Calc 5
Projected unit demand	100,000	80,000
Per-unit data:		
Direct materials cost	$5.50	$7.50
Computer chip cost	$10.60	$11.70
Production labor:		
Hours	1.2	1.3
Hourly labor rate	$16.00	$16.00
Assembly labor:		
Hours	0.6	0.5
Hourly labor rate	$12.00	$12.00
Machine hours	1	1.2

REQUIRED

1. Compute the target costs for each product.
2. Compute the projected total unit cost of production and delivery.
3. **ACCOUNTING CONNECTION ▶** Using the target costing approach, decide whether the products should be produced.

LO 5

Developing Transfer Prices

✔ 1: Cost-plus transfer price: $19.20

P5. BUSINESS APPLICATION ▶ Sand Company has two divisions, Glass Division and Instrument Division. For several years, Glass Division has manufactured a special glass container, which it sells to Instrument Division at the prevailing market price of $20. Glass Division produces the glass containers only for Instrument Division and does not sell the product to outside customers. Annual production and sales volume is 20,000 containers. A unit cost analysis for Glass Division follows.

Cost Categories	Costs per Container
Direct materials	$ 3.50
Direct labor, 1/4 hour	2.30
Variable overhead	7.50
Avoidable fixed costs: $30,000 ÷ 20,000 units	1.50
Corporate overhead: $3.60 per direct labor hour	4.50
Variable shipping costs	1.20
Unit cost	$20.50

Corporate overhead represents the allocated joint fixed costs of production—building depreciation, property taxes, insurance, and executives' salaries. A profit markup of 20 percent is used to determine transfer prices.

REQUIRED

1. What would be the appropriate transfer price for Glass Division to use in billing its transactions with Instrument Division?
2. If Glass Division decided to sell some containers to outside customers, would your answer to requirement **1** change? Defend your response.
3. What factors concerning transfer price should management consider when transferring products between divisions?

ALTERNATE PROBLEMS

LO 3

Pricing Decision

✔ 1: Total costs and expenses: $5,658,800
✔ 2: Gross margin-based price: $27.68

P6. Connect, Ltd., designs and assembles low-priced portable Internet devices. It estimates that there will be 235,000 requests for its most popular model. Budgeted costs for this product for the year follow.

Description	Budgeted Costs
Casing	$ 432,400
Battery chamber	545,200
Electronics	1,151,500
Direct labor	1,598,000
Variable indirect assembly costs	789,600
Fixed indirect assembly costs	338,400
Selling expenses	493,500
General operating expenses	183,300
Administrative expenses	126,900

The budget is based on the demand previously stated. The company wants to earn an annual operating income of $846,000.

Last week, four competitors released the following wholesale prices for the year: Competitor A, $25.68; Competitor B, $24.58; Competitor C, $23.96; Competitor D, $25.30.

Connect's portable devices are known for their high quality. However, every $1 price increase above the top competitor's price causes a 55,000-unit drop in demand from the original estimate. (Assume all price changes occur in $1 increments.)

REQUIRED

1. Prepare a schedule of total projected costs and unit costs.
2. Use gross margin pricing to compute the anticipated selling price. (Round to two decimal places.)
3. **ACCOUNTING CONNECTION ▶** Based on competitors' prices, what should Connect's portable device sell for (assume a constant unit cost)? Defend your answer. (*Hint:* Determine the total operating income at various sales levels.)
4. **ACCOUNTING CONNECTION ▶** Would your pricing structure in requirement 3 change if the company had only limited competition at this quality level? If so, in what direction? Explain why.

LO 3

Pricing Decisions

✔ 1a: Electric stapler return on assets-based price: $20
✔ 1b: Electric pencil sharpener gross margin-based price: $25.00

P7. *(CMA adapted)* Offix Company manufactures office equipment for retail stores. Carole Windsor, the vice president of marketing, has proposed that Offix introduce two new products: an electric stapler and an electric pencil sharpener. Windsor has requested that the Profit Planning Department develop preliminary selling prices for the two new products for her review.

Profit Planning has followed the company's standard policy for developing potential selling prices. It has used all data available for each product. The data accumulated by Profit Planning follows.

	Electric Stapler	Electric Pencil Sharpener
Estimated annual demand in units	16,000	12,000
Estimated unit manufacturing costs	$14.00	$15.00
Estimated unit selling and administrative expenses	$3.00	Not available
Assets employed in manufacturing	$240,000	Not available

Offix plans to use an average of $1,200,000 in assets to support operations in the current year. The condensed budgeted income statement that follows reflects the planned return on assets of 20 percent ($240,000 ÷ $1,200,000) for the entire company for all products.

Offix Company
Budgeted Income Statement
For the Year Ended May 31
(in thousands)

Revenue	$2,400
Cost of goods sold	1,440
Gross margin	$ 960
Selling and administrative expenses	720
Operating income	$ 240

(Continued)

REQUIRED

1. Use the budgeted income statement to calculate a potential selling price for (a) the stapler, using return on assets pricing, and (b) the pencil sharpener, using gross margin pricing. (Round to two decimal places.)
2. **ACCOUNTING CONNECTION ▶** Could a selling price for the electric pencil sharpener be calculated using return on assets pricing? Explain your answer.
3. **ACCOUNTING CONNECTION ▶** Which of the two pricing methods—return on assets pricing or gross margin pricing—is more appropriate for decision analysis? Explain your answer.
4. **ACCOUNTING CONNECTION ▶** Discuss the additional steps Carole Windsor is likely to take in setting an actual selling price for each of the two products after she receives their potential selling prices (as calculated in requirement **1**.)

LO **3**

✔ 8: Total materials and parts: $1,852.90
✔ Materials overhead: $1,852.90
✔ Direct labor: $1,925.60
✔ Direct labor overhead: $2,310.72

Time and Materials Pricing in a Service Business

P8. Route 66 Car Repair performs routine maintenance on rental vehicles. Recently, the local auto rental business had its fleet serviced. The company uses the time and materials pricing system and data from the previous year to compute markup percentages for overhead related to parts and materials and overhead related to direct labor. It adds markups of 100 percent to the cost of materials and parts and 120 percent to the cost of direct labor to cover overhead and profit. The following materials, parts, and direct labor are needed to repair the rental fleet:

Quantity	Unit Price	Hours	Hourly Rate
Materials and parts:		Direct labor:	
24 Spark plugs	$ 0.50	38 Mechanic hours	$28.20
50 Oil, quarts	2.50	61 Assistant mechanic hours	14.00
12 Hoses	11.20		
1 Sun visor	13.50		
36 Coolant, quarts	6.50		
4 Clamps	5.50		
5 Emergency kits	12.40		
40 Washer fluid	1.25		
4 Tires	300.00		

REQUIRED

Prepare a complete billing for this job. Include itemized amounts for each type of materials, parts, and direct labor. Follow the time and materials pricing approach, and show the total price for the job.

LO **4**

✔ 1: Target cost for product Y14: $520 .00
✔ 2: Projected total unit cost for product Y14: $502.10
✔ 2: Projected total unit cost for product Z33: $623.40

Pricing Using Target Costing

P9. Queen Tool Company designs and produces a line of high-quality machine tools and markets them throughout the world. Its main competition comes from French, British, and Korean companies. Five competitors have recently introduced two highly specialized machine tools, Y14 and Z33. The prices charged for Y14 range from $625 to $675 per tool, and the price range for Z33 is from $800 to $840 per tool. Queen is contemplating entering the market for these two products. Market research has indicated that if Queen can sell Y14 for $650 per tool and Z33 for $750 per tool, it will be successful in marketing the products worldwide. The company's profit markup is 25 percent over all costs to produce and deliver a product. Current activity-based cost rates follow.

Materials handling	$1.30 per dollar of direct materials and purchased parts cost
Production	$4.40 per machine hour
Product delivery	$34.00 per unit of Y14
	$40.00 per unit of Z33

Design engineering and accounting estimates for the production of the two new products follow.

	Product Y14	Product Z33
Projected unit demand	75,000	95,000
Per-unit data:		
Direct materials cost	$50.00	$60.00
Purchased parts cost	$65.00	$70.00
Manufacturing labor:		
Hours	6.2	7.4
Hourly labor rate	$14.00	$14.00
Assembly labor:		
Hours	4.6	9.2
Hourly labor rate	$12.00	$12.00
Machine hours	14	16

REQUIRED

1. Compute the target cost for each product.
2. Compute the total projected unit cost of producing and delivering each product.
3. **ACCOUNTING CONNECTION ▶** Using target costing, decide whether the products should be produced.

LO 5

Developing Transfer Prices

✔ 1 Cost-plus transfer price: $34.08

P10. BUSINESS APPLICATION ▶ Tim Corporation produces sound equipment for home use. The Research and Development (R&D) Division is responsible for continually evaluating and updating critical electronic parts used in the corporation's products. Two years ago, R&D took on the added responsibility of producing all microchip circuit boards for the company's sound equipment. One of Tim's specialties is a sound dissemination board (SDB) that greatly enhances the quality of Tim's speakers.

Demand for the SDB has increased significantly in the past year. As a result, R&D has increased its production and assembly labor force. Three outside customers now want to purchase the SDB. To date, R&D has been producing SDBs for internal use only.

The R&D controller wants to create a transfer price for the SDBs that will apply to all intracompany transfers. Estimated demand over the next six months is 235,000 SDBs for internal use and 165,000 SDBs for external customers, for a total of 400,000 units. The following data show cost projections for the next six months:

Materials and parts	$2,600,000
Direct labor	1,920,000
Supplies	100,000
Indirect labor	580,000
Other variable overhead costs	200,000
Fixed overhead, SDBs	1,840,000
Other fixed overhead, corporate	560,000
Variable selling expenses, SDBs	1,480,000
Fixed selling expenses, corporate	520,000
General corporate operating expenses	880,000
Corporate administrative expenses	680,000

A profit markup of at least 20 percent must be added to total unit cost for internal transfer purposes. Outside customers are willing to pay $35 for each SDB. All categories of fixed costs are assumed to be unavoidable.

REQUIRED

1. Prepare a table that shows the total budgeted costs and the cost per unit for each component of the budget. Also show the profit markup and the cost-plus transfer price.
2. Should R&D use the computed transfer price? Explain the factors that influenced your decision.

CASES

LO 1, 6

Conceptual Understanding: Ethics in Pricing

C1. BUSINESS APPLICATION ▶ Karnes Company has been doing business in Shanghai for the past three years. The company produces leather handbags that are in great demand there. When Karnes's sales person Harriet Pakay was recently in Shanghai, Kai Choy, the purchasing agent for Chen Enterprises, approached her to arrange for a purchase of 2,500 handbags. Karnes's usual price is $75 per bag. Kai Choy wanted to purchase the handbags at $65 per bag. After an hour of haggling, they agreed to a final price of $68 per item. When Pakay returned to her hotel room after dinner, she found an envelope containing five new $100 bills and a note that said, "Thank you for agreeing to our order of 2,500 handbags at $68 per bag. My company's president wants you to have the enclosed gift for your fine service." Pakay later learned that Kai Choy was following her company's normal business practice. What should Harriet Pakay do? Is the gift hers to keep? Be prepared to justify your opinion.

LO 3, 4

Conceptual Understanding: Product Pricing in a Foreign Market

C2. Torner, Inc., is an international corporation that manufactures and sells home care products. Today a meeting is being held at corporate headquarters in New York City. The purpose of the meeting is to discuss changing the price of the laundry detergent the company manufactures and sells in Brazil. During the meeting, a conflict develops between Karl Mickleson, the corporate sales manager, and José Tapral, the Brazilian Division's sales manager.

Mickleson insists that the selling price of the laundry detergent should be increased to the equivalent of U.S. $3. This increase is necessary because the Brazilian Division's costs are higher than those of other international divisions. The Brazilian Division is paying high interest rates on notes payable for the acquisition of a new manufacturing plant. In addition, a stronger, more expensive ingredient has been introduced into the laundry detergent, which has caused the product cost to increase by $0.20.

Tapral believes that the laundry detergent's selling price should remain at $2.50 for several reasons. He argues that the market for laundry detergent in Brazil is highly competitive. Labor costs are low, and the costs of distribution are small because the target market is limited to the Rio de Janeiro metropolitan area. Inflation is extremely high in Brazil, and the Brazilian government continues to impose policies to control inflation. Because of these controls, Tapral insists, buyers will resist any price hikes.

1. What selling price do you believe Torner, Inc., should set for the laundry detergent? Explain your answer. Do you believe Torner should let the Brazilian Division set the selling price for laundry detergent in the future? When should corporate headquarters set prices?
2. Based on the information given, should cost-based pricing or target costing be used to set the selling price for laundry detergent in Brazil? Explain your answer.

LO 4

Internet Case: Target Costing and the Internet

C3. Assume that you work for a company that wants to develop a product to compete with the Kindle. You have been assigned the task of using target costing to help in its development. Do a search for Kindle product reviews and product specifications and get price quotes. Why would your company's management want to use target costing to help in its development of a competitive e-book reader? What retail price would you suggest be used as a basis for target costing? Assuming a desired profit of 25 percent of selling price, what is the resulting target cost? What actions should the company take now?

LO 4 **Decision Analysis: Target Costing**

C4. Treadwell Electronics, Inc., produces circuit boards for electronic devices that are made by more than a dozen customers. Competition among the producers of circuit boards is keen, with over 30 companies bidding on every job request from those customers. The circuit boards can vary widely in their complexity, and their unit prices can range from $250 to more than $500.

Treadwell's controller is concerned that the cost planning projection for a new complex circuit board, the CX35, is almost 6 percent above its target cost. The controller has asked the Engineering Design Department to review its design and projections and come up with alternatives that will reduce the proposed product's costs to equal to or below the target cost. The following information was used to develop the initial cost projections:

Target selling price	$590.00 per unit
Desired profit percentage	25% of total unit cost
Projected unit demand	13,600 units
Per-unit data:	
Direct materials cost	$56.00
Purchased parts cost	$37.00
Manufacturing labor:	
Hours	4.5
Hourly labor rate	$14.00
Assembly labor:	
Hours	5.2
Hourly labor rate	$15.00
Machine hours	26
Activity-based cost rates:	
Materials handling	10% of direct materials and purchased parts cost
Engineering	$13.50 per unit
Production	$8.20 per machine hour
Product delivery	$24.00 per unit
Marketing	$6.00 per unit

1. Compute the product's target cost.
2. Compute the product cost of the original estimate to verify that the controller's calculations were correct.
3. Rework the product cost calculations for each of the following alternatives recommended by the design engineers:
   a. Cut product quality, which will reduce direct materials cost by 20 percent and purchased parts cost by 15 percent.
   b. Increase the quality of direct materials, which will increase direct materials cost by 20 percent but will reduce machine hours by 10 percent, manufacturing labor hours by 16 percent, and assembly labor hours by 20 percent.
4. What decision should Treadwell's management make about the new product? Defend your answer.

LO 5 **Interpreting Managerial Reports: Transfer Pricing**

C5. BUSINESS APPLICATION ▶ Dalton Industries, Inc., has two major operating divisions, the Furniture Division and the Electronics Division. The company's main product is a deluxe entertainment center. The centers' components (shelving, drawers, and glass cabinet doors) are manufactured by the Furniture Division, and the Electronics Division produces all electronic components (HDTV receivers, portable electronics docking stations, speakers, etc.) and assembles the sets. The company has a decentralized organizational structure.

(Continued)

The Furniture Division not only supplies entertainment centers to the Electronics Division but also sells shelving, drawers, and cabinet doors to other manufacturers. The following unit cost breakdown for a deluxe entertainment center was developed based on a typical sales order of 40 entertainment centers:

Direct materials	$ 32.00
Direct labor	15.00
Variable overhead	12.00
Fixed overhead	18.00
Variable selling expenses	9.00
Fixed selling expenses	6.00
Fixed general and administrative expenses	8.00
Total unit cost	$100.00

The Furniture Division's usual profit margin is 20 percent, and the regular selling price of a deluxe entertainment center is $120. The division's managers recently decided that $120 will also be the transfer price for all intracompany transactions.

Managers at the Electronics Division are unhappy with that decision. They claim that the Furniture Division will show superior performance at the expense of the Electronics Division. Competition recently forced the company to lower its prices. Because of the newly established transfer price for the cabinet, the Electronics Division's portion of the profit margin on deluxe entertainment centers was lowered to 18 percent. To counteract the new intracompany transfer price, the managers of the Electronics Division announced that effective immediately, all furniture components of each center (shelving, drawers, and glass cabinet doors) will be purchased from an outside supplier, in lots of 200 entertainment centers at a unit price of $110 per center. The company president, Jack Dalton, has called a meeting of both divisions to negotiate a fair intracompany transfer price. The following prices were listed as possible alternatives:

Current market price	$120 per entertainment center
Current outside purchase price (This price is based on a large-quantity purchase discount. It will cause increased storage costs for the Electronics Division.)	$110 per entertainment center
Total unit manufacturing costs plus a 20 percent profit margin: $77.00 + $15.40	$92.40 per entertainment center
Total unit costs excluding variable selling expenses plus a 20 percent profit margin: $91.00 + $18.20	$109.20 per entertainment center

1. What price should be established for intracompany transactions? Defend your answer by showing the shortcomings of each alternative.
2. If there were an outside market for all units produced by the Furniture Division at the $120 price, would you change your answer to **1**? Why?

Continuing Case: Cookie Company

C6. Your company produces cookies in a two-step process. The Mixing Division prepares the cookie dough and transfers it to the Baking Division, which bakes the cookies and packs all finished cookies for shipment.

At a recent meeting of your company's board of directors, the manager of the Baking Division made this statement: "That Mixing Division is robbing us blind!" Because of the board's concern about this statement, the company controller gathered the following data for the past year:

	Mixing Division	Baking Division
Sales:		
Regular	$700,000	$1,720,000
Deluxe	900,000	3,300,000
Direct materials:		
Cookie dough (from Mixing Division)	—	1,600,000
Cookie ingredients	360,000	—
Box inserts	—	660,000
Boxes	—	1,560,000
Direct labor	480,000	540,000
Variable overhead	90,000	240,000
Fixed divisional overhead—avoidable	150,000	210,000
Selling and general operating expenses	132,000	372,000
Company administrative expenses	84,000	108,000

During the year, the two divisions completed and transferred or shipped 200,000 regular cookie boxes and 150,000 deluxe cookie boxes. Transfer prices used by the Mixing Division follow.

Regular	$3.50
Deluxe	6.00

The regular box wholesales for $8.60 and the deluxe box for $22.00. The company uses a predetermined formula to allocate administrative costs to the divisions. Management has indicated that the transfer price should include a 20 percent profit factor on total division costs.

1. Prepare a performance report on the Mixing Division.
2. Prepare a performance report on the Baking Division.
3. Compute each division's rate of return on controllable cost (cost of goods sold) and on total division costs. (Round percentages to two decimal places.)
4. Do you agree with the statement made by the manager of the Baking Division? Explain your response.
5. What procedures would you recommend to the board of directors?

CHAPTER 26
Quality Management and Measurement

BUSINESS INSIGHT
Facebook

Through its innovative approach to social networking, **Facebook** has changed the rules of human interactions. To maintain a competitive advantage, the company utilizes a system that can capture all kinds of information in huge, secure databases. The quality of a Facebook user's experience has many dimensions. Not only must service be defect-free and dependable, but it must also embody such quality intangibles as prestige and good taste. Facebook managers must meet or exceed a variety of user expectations and create innovative new products and services for their ever-evolving social utility and ecommerce business model. In this chapter, we describe measures of quality and how managers can use these measures to evaluate operating performance.

1. CONCEPT ▶ *What underlying accounting concepts support quality management and measurement?*

2. ACCOUNTING APPLICATION ▶ *What measures of quality can be used to evaluate operating performance?*

3. BUSINESS APPLICATION ▶ *Why does quality help managers improve company performance and maintain a competitive edge?*

LEARNING OBJECTIVES

LO 1 **Discuss quality and how it relates to the accounting concepts of relevance and understandability.**

LO 2 **Identify the awards and organizations that promote quality.**

LO 3 **Describe total quality management (TQM), and identify financial and nonfinancial measures of quality.**

LO 4 **Use measures of quality to evaluate operating performance.**

LO 5 **Describe a management information system, and explain how it enhances management decision making.**

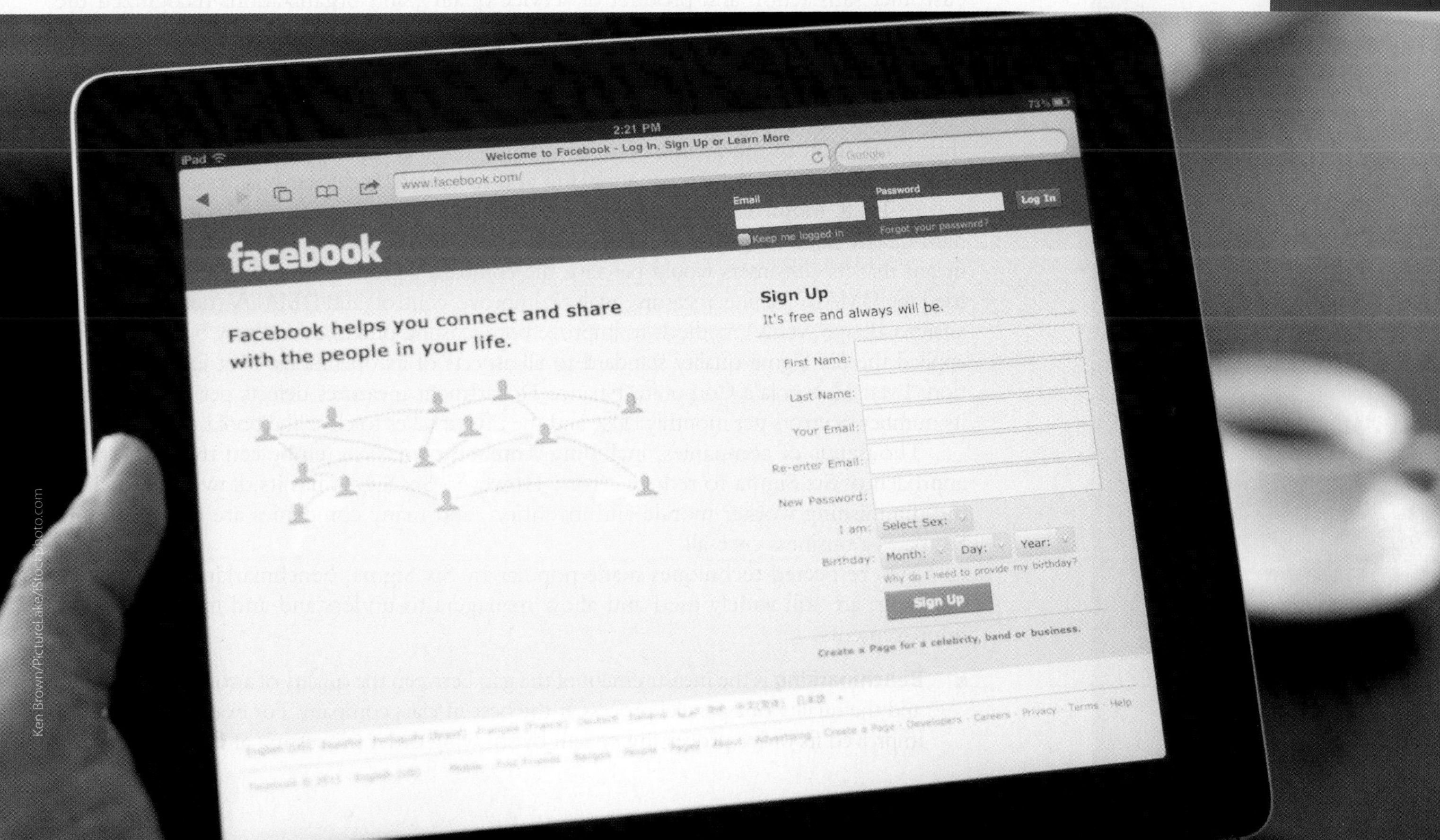

Ken Brown/PictureLake/iStockphoto.com

SECTION 1 CONCEPTS

CONCEPTS
- Relevance
- Understandability

RELEVANT LEARNING OBJECTIVES

LO1 Discuss quality and how it relates to the accounting concepts of relevance and understandability.

LO2 Identify the awards and organizations that promote quality.

LO1 Concepts Underlying Quality

To the average person, *quality* means that one product or service is better than another—perhaps because of its design, its durability, or some other attribute. In a business setting, however, **quality** is the result of an operating environment in which a product or service meets or conforms to a customer's specifications the first time it is produced or delivered.

Managers operating in volatile business environments that are strongly influenced by customer demands realize that value-based systems, instead of traditional cost-based systems, provide the relevant information they need. The information has more *relevance* because it is predictive and directly relates to the decisions made. This relevance enhances a manager's *understandability* of the environment in which their business operates, including the ever-changing e-business environment. Managers must understand both their customers and the responsiveness of their company's value chain as they make decisions to improve quality.

Before the advent of TQM over 20 years ago, managers assumed that there was a trade-off between the costs and the benefits of improving quality. **Total quality management (TQM)** is an organizational environment in which all business functions work together to build quality into the firm's products or services. In economic terms, a **return on quality (ROQ)** results when the marginal revenues possible from a higher-quality good or service exceed the marginal costs of providing that higher quality. In other words, managers must weigh the high costs of consistent quality against the resulting higher revenues, and they must base the quality standards for a good or service on the expected return on quality.

In the 1980s, quality gave organizations a competitive edge in the global marketplace. Managers realized they needed more than data from cost-based systems and ROQ to understand the business environment. This need for more relevant information led W. Edwards Deming and other advocates of TQM to stress quality as a means of enhancing an organization's efficiency and profits. As a result, managers focused on increasing customer satisfaction and product or service quality, and organizations recognized the value of producing highly reliable products. Companies emphasized **kaizen**, or the gradual and ongoing improvement of products and processes while reducing costs. Quality control methods such as statistical analysis, computer-aided design, and Six Sigma (discussed next) eliminated defects in the design and manufacture of products. Today more than 90 percent of the *Fortune* 500 companies use a combination of those methods for relevant information for decision making and to understand their businesses.

In 1978, **Motorola** was losing market share as a result of aggressive competition from high-quality Japanese goods. In response, Motorola set the goal of **Six Sigma** quality, which meant that its customers would perceive the company's products and services as perfect. It used the DMAIC (define, measure, analyze, improve, control) and DMADV (define, measure, analyze, design, verify) methods to improve both existing processes and new ones. Motorola applied the Six Sigma quality standard to all aspects of its operations—not just to production. Even Motorola's Corporate Finance Department measures defects per unit, tracking its number of errors per monthly close and the time it takes to close the books each month.

Thousands of companies, including **Amazon.com**, have embraced the data-driven approach of Six Sigma to reduce errors. However, Six Sigma has its drawbacks, including diminishing worker morale and invention, and many companies are rethinking Six Sigma as a business cure-all.

Two respected techniques made popular by Six Sigma, benchmarking and process mapping, are still widely used and allow managers to understand and measure quality improvements.

- **Benchmarking** is the measurement of the gap between the quality of a company's process and the quality of a parallel process at the best-in-class company. For example, **Motorola** improved its order-processing system by studying order processing at **Lands' End**.

- **Process mapping** is a method of using a visual diagram to indicate process inputs, outputs, constraints, and flows to help managers identify unnecessary efforts and inefficiencies in a business process. Quality problems and their causes are visually tracked using charts and diagrams. As a result, customer satisfaction with a product or service and with the buying experience, both before and after the sale, is enhanced.

Service businesses also recognize the importance of quality and seek to maximize customers' satisfaction with their services. For example, **Disney** theme parks minimize customers' impatience as they wait in long lines by having Disney characters interact and play with the crowd. A potential customer problem becomes another opportunity to deliver Disney magic.

In summary, a manager's concept of quality must continuously evolve to add information *relevance* to both long-term and short-term decision making. Quality performance measures aid managers in understanding the dynamic business environment. Quality has many dimensions. A product or service must not only be defect-free and dependable, but it must also embody such intangibles as brand prestige and life style. The accounting concepts of relevance and *understandability* help managers meet or exceed a variety of expectations about customer service and the creation of innovative new products and services.

APPLY IT!

Match the abbreviations that follow with the words they represent.

1. TQM	a. Return on quality
2. DMADV	b. Total quality management
3. ROQ	c. Define, measure, analyze, improve, control
4. DMAIC	d. Define, measure, analyze, design, verify

SOLUTION

1. b; 2. d; 3. a; 4. c

TRY IT! SE1, SE2

LO2 Recognition of Quality

Many awards and organizations have been established to recognize and promote the importance of quality. Three of the most prestigious awards are the Deming prizes, the EFQM Excellence Award, and the Malcolm Baldrige Quality Award. In addition, the International Organization for Standardization works to promote quality standards worldwide.

Deming Prizes

In the early 1950s, the Japanese Union of Scientists and Engineers established the **Deming Prize** to honor individuals or groups who have contributed to the development and dissemination of total quality control. Consideration for the prize was originally limited to Japanese companies, but interest in it was so great that the rules were revised to allow the participation of companies outside Japan who operate in Japan. Today, the organization awards several Deming Prizes to companies and individuals who achieve distinctive results by carrying out total quality control.

EFQM Excellence Award

Since the 1990s, the nonprofit European Foundation for Quality Management has presented the **EFQM Excellence Award** annually to businesses and organizations operating in Europe that excel in quality management. The EFQM has also developed a quality framework, called the EFQM Excellence Model, about what an organization does, how they do it, and what an organization achieves. Managers can use the model as a diagnostic tool to analyze the cause-and-effect relationships between the model's enabling and the results criteria to self-assess their organizations. The enablers and the results criteria follow:

- Enablers: Leadership; Strategy; People; Partnerships and Resources; and Processes, Products, and Services
- Results: Customer, People, Society, and Key

Malcolm Baldrige National Quality Award

In 1987, the U.S. Congress created the **Malcolm Baldrige National Quality Award** to recognize U.S. organizations for their achievements in quality and business performance and to raise awareness of the importance of quality and performance excellence. Organizations are evaluated on the basis of the Baldrige performance excellence criteria, which are divided into the following seven categories:

- Leadership
- Strategic planning
- Customer focus
- Measurement, analysis, and knowledge management
- Workforce focus
- Operations focus
- Results

Thousands of organizations throughout the world accept the Baldrige criteria as the standards for performance excellence and use them for training and self-assessment. Award winners are showcased annually on the Internet and are encouraged to share their best practices with others.[1]

ISO Standards

The International Organization for Standardization (ISO) is a worldwide federation of national standards bodies.[2] It promotes standardization with a view to facilitating the international exchange of goods and services. For example, by developing a standard format for credit cards, standard film speed codes, and standard graphical symbols for use on equipment and diagrams, the ISO has saved time and money for both individuals and businesses worldwide.

To standardize quality management and quality assurance, the ISO developed the **ISO 9000** series. The ISO 9000 series guidelines cover the design, development, production, final inspection and testing, installation, and servicing of products, processes, and services. Because many organizations do business only with ISO-certified companies, these guidelines have been adopted worldwide. To become ISO certified, an organization must pass a rigorous third-party audit of its manufacturing and service processes. As a result, certified companies have detailed documentation of their operations. The eight quality management principles of ISO 9000 follow.

- Customer focus
- Leadership
- Involvement of people
- Process approach
- System approach to management
- Continual involvement
- Factual approach to decision making
- Mutually beneficial supplier relationships

STUDY NOTE: *Some ISO standards vary between countries. For example, the standard size of computer paper in the United States is different from the standard size in European countries.*

Other popular standards include ISO 14000, ISO 26000, and ISO 31000.

- The **ISO 14000** series provides a management framework to minimize the harmful environmental effects of business activities and continually improve environmental performance.
- **ISO 26000** provides social responsibility guidance.
- **ISO 31000** outlines risk management principles and guidelines.

APPLY IT!

Match the organizations that follow with the quality principles or criteria they use. (*Hint:* Some principles or criteria may be used more than once.)

1. European Foundation for Quality Management
2. Baldrige Performance Excellence Program
3. International Organization for Standardization 9000

a. Leadership
b. Strategy or Strategic planning
c. People or Involvement of people
d. Customer focus or Customer results
e. Mutually beneficial supplier relationships or Partnerships and resources
f. Results or Key results

SOLUTION

1. a. b. c. d. e. f.
2. a. b. d. f.
3. a. c. d. e.

TRY IT! SE3, E1A, E1B

SECTION 2

ACCOUNTING APPLICATIONS

ACCOUNTING APPLICATIONS

- Financial measures of quality
  - Conformance costs
  - Nonconformance costs
  - Quality ratios
- Nonfinancial measures of quality
  - Delivery cycle time
  - Waste time

RELEVANT LEARNING OBJECTIVES

LO3 Describe total quality management (TQM), and identify financial and nonfinancial measures of quality.

LO4 Use measures of quality to evaluate operating performance.

LO3 Financial and Nonfinancial Measures of Quality

Over the past two decades, organizations have defined quality in terms of what their customers value. Organizations believe that customers want the highest-quality goods and services and that customers' willingness to pay for high quality will result in improved profits. As a result, organizations strive to exceed customers' expectations and improve the quality of their products or services. Quality is not something that a company can simply add at some point in the production process or assume will happen automatically. Inspections can detect bad products, but they do not ensure quality. Managers need to create a total quality management (TQM) environment to help them meet the goal of producing high-quality, reasonably priced products or services.

To create a TQM environment, managers take the following steps:

- **Step 1.** Identify and manage the financial measures of quality, or the costs of quality.
- **Step 2.** Analyze operating performance using nonfinancial measures.
- **Step 3.** Require that all processes and products or services be improved continuously.

Financial Measures of Quality

The **costs of quality** are the costs that are specifically associated with the achievement or nonachievement of product or service quality. They can make up a significant portion of a product's or service's total cost. Therefore, controlling the costs of quality strongly affects profitability. Today's managers should be able to identify the activities associated with improving quality and should be aware of the cost of resources used to achieve high quality.

The costs of quality have the following two components:

- **Costs of conformance:** The costs of good quality that are incurred to ensure the successful development of a product or service. In other words, the costs of building quality into products and services by doing it right the first time.
- **Costs of nonconformance:** The costs of poor quality that are incurred to correct defects in a product or service.

The costs of conformance are made up of prevention costs and appraisal costs.

- **Prevention costs:** The costs associated with the prevention of defects and failures in products and services.
- **Appraisal costs:** The costs of activities that measure, evaluate, or audit products, processes, or services to ensure their conformance to quality standards and performance requirements.

The costs of nonconformance include internal failure costs and external failure costs.

- **Internal failure costs:** Costs incurred to correct mistakes found by the company when defects are discovered before a product or service is delivered to a customer.
- **External failure costs:** Costs incurred to correct mistakes discovered by customers after the delivery of a defective product or service.

Exhibit 1 gives examples of each cost category. Note that there is an inverse relationship between the costs of conformance and the costs of nonconformance. For example, if a company spends money on the costs of conformance, the costs of nonconformance should be reduced. However, if little attention is paid to the costs of conformance, the costs of nonconformance may escalate.

Exhibit 1
Costs of Conformance and Nonconformance

Costs of Conformance to Customer Standards

Prevention Costs:

- Technical support for vendors
- Integrated system development
- Quality improvement projects
- Quality training of employees
- Design review of products and processes
- Quality-certified suppliers
- Quality circles
- Preventive maintenance
- Statistical process control
- Process engineering

Appraisal Costs:

- Inspection of materials, processes, and machines
- End-of-process sampling and testing
- Vendor audits and sample testing
- Maintenance of test equipment
- Quality audits of products and processes
- Field testing

Costs of Nonconformance to Customer Standards

Internal Failure Costs:

- Scrap and rework
- Reinspection and retesting of rework
- Quality-related downtime
- Scrap disposal losses
- Failure analysis
- Inventory control and scheduling
- Downgrading because of defects

External Failure Costs:

- Lost sales
- Restoration of reputation
- Warranty claims and adjustments
- Customer complaint processing
- Returned goods and replacements
- Investigation of defects
- Product recalls
- Product-liability settlements

An organization's overall goal is to avoid costs of nonconformance because both internal and external failures affect customers' satisfaction and the organization's profitability. High initial costs of conformance are justified when they minimize the total costs of quality over the life of a product or service.

Quality Ratios

Common quality ratios and the formulas showing how to compute them follow.

Total Costs of Quality as a Percentage of Net Sales	=	(Costs of Conformance + Costs of Nonconformance) ÷ Net Sales
Ratio of Costs of Conformance to Total Costs of Quality	=	Costs of Conformance ÷ (Costs of Conformance + Costs of Nonconformance)
Ratio of Costs of Nonconformance to Total Costs of Quality	=	Costs of Nonconformance ÷ (Costs of Conformance + Costs of Nonconformance)
Costs of Nonconformance as a Percentage of Net Sales	=	Costs of Nonconformance ÷ Net Sales

For example, consider the data for Garin's Cycle Shop that follow.

Total sales	$7,000
Costs of quality:	
Prevention	$ 400
Appraisal	500
Internal failure	200
External failure	300

The quality ratios for Garin's would be computed as follows.

Costs of Conformance	= Prevention Costs + Appraisal Costs
	= $400 + $500 = $900
Costs of Nonconformance	= Internal Failure Costs + External Failure Costs
	= $200 + $300 = $500
Total Costs of Quality as a Percentage of Net Sales	= (Costs of Conformance + Costs of Nonconformance) / Net Sales
	= ($900 + $500) ÷ $7,000
	= 20%
Ratio of Costs of Conformance to Total Costs of Quality	= Costs of Conformance ÷ (Costs of Conformance + Costs of Nonconformance)
	= $900 ÷ ($900 + $500)
	= 0.64 to 1
Ratio of Costs of Nonconformance to Total Costs of Quality	= Costs of Nonconformance ÷ (Costs of Conformance + Costs of Nonconformance)
	= $500 ÷ ($900 + $500)
	= 0.36 to 1
Costs of Nonconformance as a Percentage of Net Sales	= $500 ÷ $7,000 = 7.14%

Nonfinancial Measures of Quality

STUDY NOTE: *Nonfinancial measures gauge quality and the value created throughout the supply and value chains.*

By measuring the costs of quality, a company learns how much it has spent in its efforts to improve product or service quality. But critics say that tracking historical data to monitor quality performance does little to enhance quality. What managers need is a measurement and evaluation system that signals poor quality early enough to allow problems to be corrected before a defective product or service reaches the customer. Implementing a policy of continuous improvement satisfies this need for and is the second stage of total quality management.

Nonfinancial measures of performance are used to supplement cost-based measures. Although cost control is still an important consideration, a commitment to ongoing improvement encourages activities that enhance quality at every stage, from design to delivery. By controlling the leading nonfinancial performance measures of activities, managers can ultimately maximize the resulting financial return from operations. Five categories of nonfinancial measures of quality are discussed in the sections that follow:

- Product design
- Vendor performance
- Production performance
- Delivery cycle time
- Customer satisfaction

Product Design Problems with quality often are the result of poor design. Most automated production operations use **computer-aided design (CAD)**, a computer-based engineering system with a built-in program to identify poorly designed parts or manufacturing processes, which means that engineers can correct these problems before production begins. Among the measures that managers consider are:

- number and types of design defects detected
- average time between defect detection and correction
- number of unresolved design defects at the time of product introduction

Vendor Performance Instead of dealing with dozens of suppliers in a quest for the lowest cost, companies now analyze their vendors to determine which ones are most reliable, furnish high-quality goods, have a record of timely deliveries, and charge competitive prices. Once a company has identified such vendors, they become an integral part of the production team's effort to ensure a continuing supply of high-quality materials. Vendors may even contribute to product design to ensure that the correct materials are being used.

Managers use measures of quality (such as defect-free materials as a percentage of total materials received) and measures of delivery (such as timely deliveries as a percentage of total deliveries) to identify reliable vendors and monitor their performance.

Production Performance Management must always be concerned about the wasted time and money that can be traced to defective products, scrapped parts, machine maintenance, and downtime. To minimize such concerns, more and more companies have adopted **computer-integrated manufacturing (CIM) systems**, in which production and its support operations are coordinated by computers. Within a CIM system, computer-aided manufacturing (CAM) may be used to coordinate and control production activities, or a flexible manufacturing system (FMS) may be used to link together automated equipment into a flexible production network.

In CIM systems, most direct labor hours are replaced by machine hours, and very little direct labor cost is incurred. In addition, a significant part of variable product cost is replaced by the cost of expensive machinery, a fixed cost. Today, the largest item on a company's balance sheet is often automated machinery and equipment. Each piece of equipment has a specific capacity, above which continuous operation is threatened. When managers evaluate such machines, their measures have two objectives:

- To evaluate the performance of each piece of equipment in relation to its capacity
- To evaluate the performance of maintenance personnel in following a prescribed maintenance program

Measures of production quality, parts scrapped, equipment utilization, machine downtime, and machine maintenance time help managers monitor production performance.

Delivery Cycle Time To evaluate their responsiveness to customers, companies examine their **delivery cycle time**, which is the time between the acceptance of an order and the final delivery of the product or service. When a customer places an order, it is important for a salesperson to be able to promise an accurate delivery date. On-time delivery is important not only to customers but also to companies, because a decrease in delivery cycle time can lead to a significant increase in income from operations.

The formula to compute delivery cycle time follows.

Delivery Cycle Time = Purchase-Order Lead Time + Production Cycle Time + Delivery Time

- **Purchase-order lead time** is the time it takes a company to take and process an order and organize so that production can begin.
- **Production cycle time** is the time it takes to make a product.
- **Delivery time** is the time between the completion of a product and its receipt by the customer.

As a way of enhancing customer satisfaction for those waiting in line at Walt Disney World theme parks, characters interact with and entertain guests.

Shanghai Daily/AP Images

Managers should establish measures that emphasize the importance of minimizing the delivery cycle time for each order. They should also track the average purchase-order lead time, production cycle time, and delivery time for all orders. Trends should be highlighted, and reports should be readily available. Other measures designed to monitor delivery cycle time include order backlogs, on-time delivery performance, percentage of orders filled, and waste time. The formula to compute waste time follows.

Waste Time = Production Cycle Time − (Average Process Time + Average Setup Time)

Customer Satisfaction The sale and shipment of a product does not mark the end of performance measurement. Measures used to determine the degree of customer satisfaction include the following:

- the number and types of customer complaints
- the number and causes of warranty claims
- the percentage of shipments returned by customers (or the percentage of shipments accepted by customers)

Several companies have developed their own customer satisfaction indexes from these measures so that they can compare different product lines over different time periods.

Overview Exhibit 2 lists the nonfinancial measures used to monitor quality. These measures help a company continuously produce higher-quality products, improve production processes, and reduce throughput time and costs.

Exhibit 2
Nonfinancial Measures of Quality

Measure of Product Design Quality	
• Product design flaws	Number and types of design defects detected
	Average time between defect detection and correction
	Number of unresolved design defects at time of product introduction
Measures of Vendor Performance	
• Vendor quality	Defect-free materials as a percentage of total materials received; prepared for each vendor
• Vendor delivery	Timely deliveries of materials as a percentage of total deliveries; prepared for each vendor
Measures of Production Performance	
• Production quality	Number of defective products per thousand produced
• Parts scrapped	Number and type of materials spoiled during production
• Equipment utilization rate	Productive machine time as a percentage of total time available for production
• Machine downtime	Amount of time each machine is idle
• Machine maintenance time	Amount of time each machine is idle for maintenance and upgrades
Measures of Delivery Cycle Time	
• On-time deliveries	Shipments received by promised date as a percentage of total shipments
• Orders filled	Orders filled as a percentage of total orders received
• Average process time	Average time required to make a product available for shipment
• Average setup time	Average amount of time elapsed between the acceptance of an order and the beginning of production
• Purchase-order lead time	Time it takes a company to process an order and organize so that production can begin
• Production cycle time	Time it takes to make a product
• Delivery time	Time between a product's completion and its receipt by customer
• Delivery cycle time	Time between the acceptance of an order and the final delivery of the product or service (purchase-order lead time + production cycle time + delivery time)
• Waste time	Production cycle time − (average process time + average setup time)
• Production backlog	Number and type of units waiting to begin processing
Measures of Customer Satisfaction	
• Customer complaints	Number and types of customer complaints
• Warranty claims	Number and causes of claims
• Returned orders	Shipments returned as a percentage of total shipments

Measuring Service Quality

Many of the costs-of-quality categories and several of the nonfinancial measures of quality can be applied directly to services and can be adopted by any type of service company.

- Flaws in service design lead to poor-quality services.
- Timely service delivery is as important as timely product shipments.
- Customer satisfaction in a service business can be measured by services accepted or rejected, the number of complaints, and the number of returning customers.
- Poor service development leads to internal and external failure costs.

APPLY IT!

Internal reports on quality at Social Utility Company generated the following information for the Apps Division for the first three months of the year:

Total sales	$60,000,000
Costs of quality:	
Prevention	$ 523,000
Appraisal	477,000
Internal failure	1,360,000
External failure	640,000

Compute the following:

1. Total costs of quality as a percentage of sales
2. Ratio of costs of conformance to total costs of quality
3. Ratio of costs of nonconformance to total costs of quality
4. Costs of nonconformance as a percentage of total sales

SOLUTION

Costs of Conformance	= Prevention Costs + Appraisal Costs = $523,000 + $477,000 = $1,000,000
Costs of Nonconformance	= Internal Failure Costs + External Failure Costs = $1,360,000 + $640,000 = $2,000,000
1. Total Costs of Quality as a Percentage of Sales	= $3,000,000 ÷ $60,000,000 = 5%
2. Ratio of Costs of Conformance to Total Costs of Quality	= Costs of Conformance ÷ (Costs of Conformance + Costs of Nonconformance) = $1,000,000 ÷ ($1,000,000 + $2,000,000) = 0.33 to 1
3. Ratio of Costs of Nonconformance to Total Costs of Quality	= Costs of Nonconformance ÷ (Costs of Conformance + Costs of Nonconformance) = $2,000,000 ÷ ($1,000,000 + $2,000,000) = 0.67 to 1
4. Costs of Nonconformance as a Percentage of Total Sales	= $2,000,000 ÷ $60,000,000 = 3.33%

TRY IT! SE4, SE5, SE6, SE7, E2A, E3A, E4A, E5A, E6A, E2B, E3B, E4B, E5B, E6B

LO4 Measuring Quality: An Illustration

Using many of the examples of the costs of quality identified in Exhibit 1 and the nonfinancial measures of quality listed in Exhibit 2, the sections that follow demonstrate how a company measures and evaluates its progress toward the goal of achieving total quality management.

Evaluating the Costs of Quality

As demonstrated in Exhibit 3, three companies—Able, Baker, and Cane—have taken different approaches to achieving product quality. All three companies are the same size, each having generated $15 million in sales last year. Each company spent between 10.22 and 10.48 percent of its sales dollars on quality costs.

Key Quality Performance Questions Using the information in Exhibit 3, we can evaluate each company's approach to quality enhancement by analyzing the costs of quality and by answering the questions that follow.

- **Which company is most likely to succeed in the competitive marketplace?**

  Able spent the most money on costs of quality. What is more important, however, is that the company spent 80 percent of that money on costs of conformance, which

Exhibit 3
Analysis of the Costs of Quality

	Able Co.	Baker Co.	Cane Co.
Annual Sales	$15,000,000	$15,000,000	$15,000,000
Costs of conformance to customer standards			
Prevention Costs			
Quality training of employees	$ 210,000	$ 73,500	$ 136,500
Process engineering	262,500	115,500	189,000
Design review of products	105,000	42,000	84,000
Preventive maintenance	157,500	84,000	115,500
Subtotal	$ 735,000	$ 315,000	$ 525,000
Appraisal Costs			
End-of-process sampling and testing	$ 126,000	$ 63,000	$ 73,500
Inspection of materials	199,500	31,500	115,500
Quality audits of products	84,000	21,000	42,000
Vendor audits and sample testing	112,500	52,500	63,000
Subtotal	$ 522,000	$ 168,000	$ 294,000
Total costs of conformance	$ 1,257,000	$ 483,000	$ 819,000
Costs of nonconformance to customer standards			
Internal Failure Costs			
Scrap and rework	$ 21,000	$ 189,000	$ 126,000
Reinspection of rework	15,750	126,000	73,500
Quality-related downtime	42,000	231,000	178,500
Scrap disposal losses	26,250	84,000	52,500
Subtotal	$ 105,000	$ 630,000	$ 430,500
External Failure Costs			
Warranty claims	$ 47,250	$ 94,500	$ 84,000
Returned goods and replacements	15,750	68,250	36,750
Investigation of defects	26,250	78,750	57,750
Customer complaint processing	120,750	178,500	126,000
Subtotal	$ 210,000	$ 420,000	$ 304,500
Total costs of nonconformance	$ 315,000	$ 1,050,000	$ 735,000
Total costs of quality	$ 1,572,000	$ 1,533,000	$ 1,554,000
Total costs of quality as a percentage of sales	10.48%	10.22%	10.36%
Ratio of costs of conformance to total costs of quality	0.80 to 1	0.32 to 1	0.53 to 1
Ratio of costs of nonconformance to total costs of quality	0.20 to 1	0.68 to 1	0.47 to 1
Costs of nonconformance as a percentage of sales	2.10%	7.00%	4.90%

will reap benefits in years to come. The company's focus on the costs of conformance means that only a small amount had to be spent on internal and external failure costs. The resulting high-quality products will lead to high customer satisfaction.

- **Which company has serious problems with its product quality?**

  Baker spent the least on costs of quality. However, over 68 percent of its costs of quality ($1,050,000 of a total of $1,533,000) was spent on internal and external failure costs. Scrap costs, reinspection costs, the cost of downtime, warranty costs, and customer complaint costs were all high. Baker's products are very low in quality, which will lead to hard times in the future.

- **What do you think will happen to the total costs of quality for each company over the next five years? Why?**

  Able: When money is spent on costs of conformance early in a product's life cycle, quality is integrated into the development and production processes. Once a high level of quality has been established, total costs of quality should be lower in future years.

Baker: Baker's costs of conformance will have to increase significantly if the company expects to stay in business. It is spending 7 percent of its sales revenue on internal and external failure costs. Because the marketplace is not accepting its products, its competitors have the upper hand and the company is in a weak position.

Cane: Cane is taking a middle road. This company is spending a little more than half (53 percent) of its cost-of-quality dollars on conformance, so product quality should be increasing. However, the company is still incurring high internal and external failure costs. Cane's managers must learn to prevent such costs if they expect the company to remain competitive.

Evaluating Nonfinancial Measures of Quality

Exhibit 4 presents nonfinancial measures for each company for three years—2013, 2014, and 2015.

Exhibit 4
Analysis of Nonfinancial Measures of Quality

	Able Co.	Baker Co.	Cane Co.
Vendor Performance			
Percentage of defect-free materials			
2013	98.20%	94.40%	95.20%
2014	98.40%	93.20%	95.30%
2015	98.60%	93.10%	95.20%
Production Performance			
Production quality level (product defects per million)			
2013	1,400	4,120	2,710
2014	1,340	4,236	2,720
2015	1,210	4,340	2,680
Delivery Cycle Time			
Percentage of on-time deliveries			
2013	94.20%	76.20%	84.10%
2014	94.60%	75.40%	84.00%
2015	95.40%	73.10%	83.90%
Customer Satisfaction			
Percentage of returned orders			
2013	1.30%	6.90%	4.20%
2014	1.10%	7.20%	4.10%
2015	0.80%	7.60%	4.00%
Number of customer complaints			
2013	22	189	52
2014	18	194	50
2015	12	206	46

From the information in Exhibit 4, we can evaluate each company's experience in its pursuit of total quality management. The trends shown tend to support the findings in the analysis of the costs of quality in Exhibit 3.

- **Able:** For Able, 98.2 percent of the materials received from suppliers in 2013 were of high quality, and the quality has been increasing over the three years. The product defect rate, measured in number of defects per million, has been decreasing rapidly, proof that the costs of conformance are having a positive effect. The percentage of on-time deliveries has been increasing, and both the percentage of returned orders and the number of customer complaints have been decreasing, which means that customer acceptance and satisfaction have been increasing.

- **Baker:** Baker's experience is not encouraging. The number of high-quality shipments of materials from vendors has been decreasing, the product defect rate has been increasing (it seems to be out of control), on-time deliveries were bad to begin with and have been getting worse, more goods have been returned each year, and customer complaints have been on the rise. All these signs reflect the company's high costs of nonconformance.
- **Cane:** Cane is making progress toward higher quality, but its progress is very slow. Most of the nonfinancial measures show a very slight positive trend. More money needs to be spent on the costs of conformance.

A graphic analysis can be very useful when a manager is comparing the performance of several operating units. Mere columns of numbers do not always adequately depict differences in operating performance and may be difficult to interpret. In such cases, a chart or graph can help managers see what the data are saying. For example, the bar graph in Exhibit 5 illustrates the amounts that Able, Baker, and Cane are spending on costs of quality. It clearly shows that

- Able is focusing on costs of conformance and has low costs of nonconformance.
- Baker, in contrast, is paying over $1,000,000 in costs of nonconformance because it has not tried to increase spending on prevention and appraisal.
- Cane spends slightly more on costs of conformance than on costs of nonconformance, but, like Baker, it is spending too much on failure costs.

Exhibit 5
Comparison of Costs of Quality: Conformance Versus Nonconformance

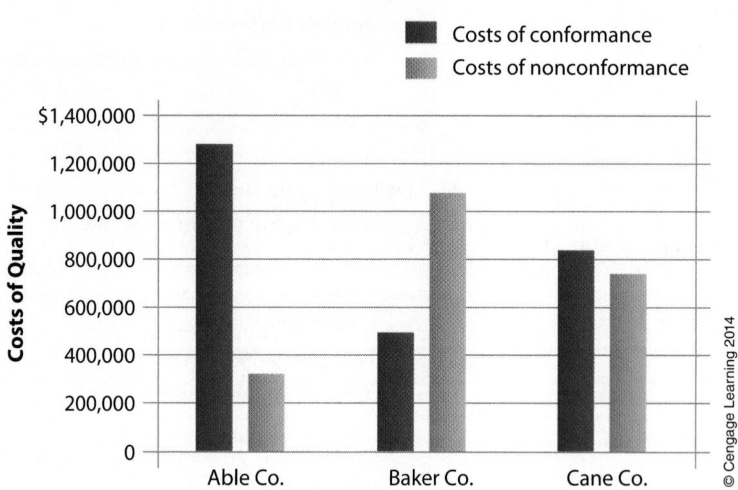

APPLY IT!

Essex Corporation has two departments, C and D, which produce two separate product lines. Essex has been implementing total quality management over the past year. Conformance and nonconformance cost ratios of quality for the year for each department are presented below. Which department is committed to TQM?

	Dept. C	Dept. D	Totals
Total costs of quality as a percentage of sales	5.00%	5.00%	5.00%
Ratio of costs of conformance to total costs of quality	0.70 to 1	0.35 to 1	0.51 to 1
Ratio of costs of nonconformance to total costs of quality	0.30 to 1	0.65 to 1	0.49 to 1
Costs of nonconformance as a percentage of sales	1.50%	3.25%	2.45%

SOLUTION

Department C is taking a more serious approach to implementing TQM. It is spending more than twice as much on costs of conformance as on costs of nonconformance. Department D is doing almost the opposite.

TRY IT! SE8, E7A, E8A, E9A, E10A, E11A, E12A, E13A, E7B, E8B, E9B, E10B, E11B, E12B, E13B

SECTION 3 BUSINESS APPLICATIONS

NESS
-ICATIONS
anagement
formation System
IIS)
anning
erforming
valuating
ommunicating

EVANT
RNING OBJECTIVE

Describe a
management
mation system, and
ain how it enhances
agement decision
ng.

LO5 The Role of Management Information Systems in Quality Management

Many traditional management information systems contain only financial data. However, in today's competitive business environment, the information system should identify, monitor, and maintain continuous, detailed analyses of a company's activities, use social media and mobile technologies, and provide managers with timely measures of operating results. This kind of **management information system (MIS)** is designed to support such philosophies as lean operations, activity-based management (ABM), and total quality management (TQM).

By focusing on activities, rather than costs, an MIS provides managers with information that is needed to increase responsiveness to customers and reduce processing time. More accurate product and service costs lead to improved pricing decisions. Nonvalue-adding activities are highlighted, and managers can work to reduce or eliminate them. An MIS can also analyze the profitability of individual customers or users and look at all aspects of serving them. Overall, the MIS identifies resource usage and cost for each activity and fosters managerial decisions that lead to continuous improvement throughout the organization.

Enterprise Resource Planning Systems and Software as a Service

An MIS can be designed as a fully integrated database system known as an **enterprise resource planning (ERP) system**. An ERP system combines the management of all major business activities (e.g., purchasing, manufacturing, marketing, sales, logistics, and order fulfillment) with support activities (e.g., accounting and human resources) to form one easy-to-access, centralized data warehouse. Advantages of an ERP system are its integration and ability to communicate within an organization and with other businesses' databases. But an ERP system is costly to implement and maintain, can be less than user friendly, and leave many frustrated.

The emerging alternative is **software as a service (SaaS)**. SaaS utilizes the Internet, social media, and mobile technologies to manage all business activities on demand. Advantages of SaaS include low acquisition costs, quick implementations, predictable pricing, reduced internal support staff, and a potentially more agile ability to innovate. Currently, its primary disadvantage is data security and internal controls as multiple company data may co-exist on a shared web infrastructure as multi-tenants. One of the fastest growing companies that provides SaaS is **Workday, Inc.**

Managers' Use of MIS

Managers today use their management information systems' detailed, real-time financial and nonfinancial information about customers, inventory, resources, and the supply chain to manage quality. Without the flexibility and power of database and management information systems like ERP or SaaS, managers would be at a disadvantage in today's rapidly changing and highly competitive business environment.

Planning Managers use the MIS database to obtain relevant and reliable information for formulating strategic plans, making forecasts, and preparing budgets. For example, managers at **Amazon.com** use their MIS to develop forecasts and budgets for existing operations and to create plans for new value-adding products and services.

Performing Managers use the financial and nonfinancial information in the MIS database to implement decisions about personnel, resources, and activities that will minimize waste and improve the quality of their organization's products or services. At **Amazon.com**, managers use their supply-chain and value-chain software to manage operations in ways that ensure accurate order fulfillment and timely delivery.

Evaluating Managers identify and track financial and nonfinancial performance measures to evaluate all major business functions. By enabling the timely comparison of actual performance with expected performance, **Amazon.com**'s MIS allows managers to reward good performance promptly, take speedy corrective actions, and analyze and revise performance measurement plans.

Communicating Managers can use an MIS to generate customized reports that evaluate performance and provide useful information for decision making. For example, managers at **Amazon.com** can consolidate customer profiles from their company's sophisticated database into a real-time report available on their desktops to continuously monitor the changing buying habits of their customers.

MIS and the Management Process The steps managers take during the management process for quality management and measurement are summarized in Exhibit 6.

Exhibit 6
Management Information Systems and The Management Process

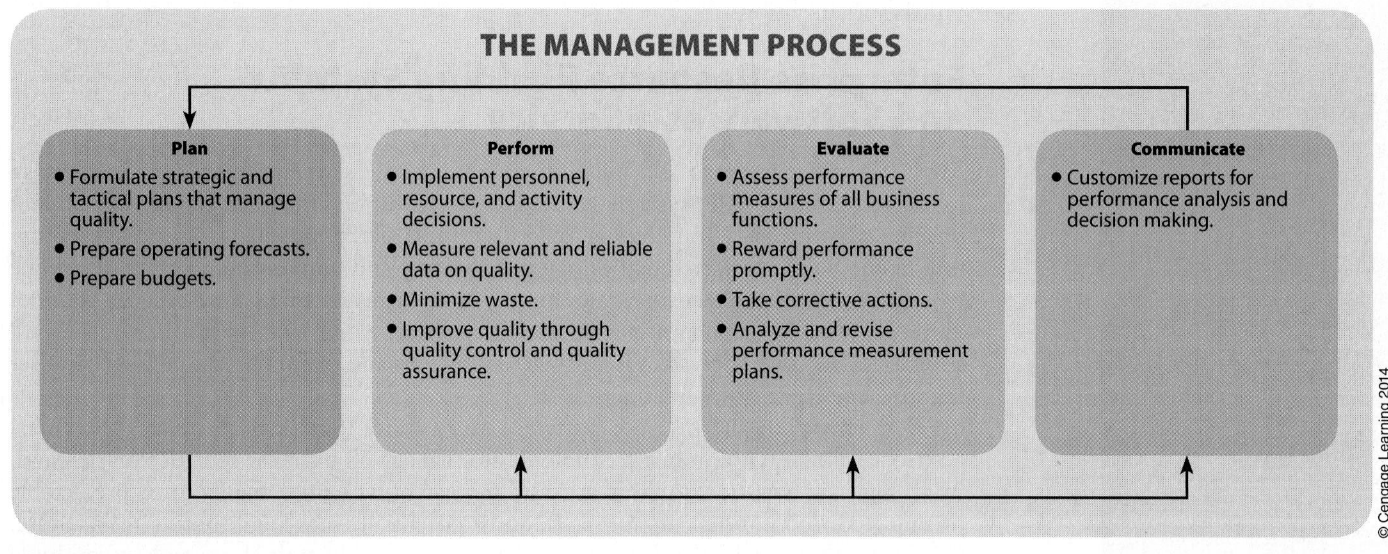

APPLY IT!

Match the four stages of the management process with the examples that follow.

1. Plan
2. Perform
3. Evaluate
4. Communicate

a. Databases can be used to develop forecasts and budgets for existing operations and to create plans for new value-adding products and services.
b. Timely comparison of actual performance with expected performance can be made by managers to reward good performance promptly, take speedy corrective actions, and analyze and revise performance measurement plans.
c. Managers can use supply-chain and value-chain information to manage operations in ways that ensure accurate order fulfillment and timely delivery.
d. Managers can consolidate customer profiles from their company's database into a real-time report available on their desktops to continuously monitor the changing buying habits of their customers.

SOLUTION
1. a; 2. c; 3. b; 4. d

TRY IT! SE9, SE10, E14A, E14B

TriLevel Problem

Facebook

The beginning of this chapter focused on **Facebook**, a social utilities company. Complete the following requirements in order to answer the questions posed at the beginning of the chapter.

Section 1: Concepts

What underlying accounting concepts support quality management and measurement?

Section 2: Accounting Applications

What measures of quality can be used to evaluate operating performance?

Suppose that, three months ago, one of Facebook's application developers installed a new production system in its New Apps Division. A lean approach is now followed for everything from ordering supplies to the delivery of apps. The division's manager is very interested in the initial results of the venture. The following data have been collected for your analysis:

	A	B	C	D	E	F	G	H	I
1					**Week**				
2		**1**	**2**	**3**	**4**	**5**	**6**	**7**	**8**
3	Warranty claims	2	4	1	1	–	5	7	11
4	Average setup time								
5	(hours)	0.30	0.25	0.25	0.30	0.25	0.20	0.20	0.15
6	Purchase-order lead								
7	time (hours)	2.4	2.3	2.2	2.3	2.4	2.4	2.4	2.5
8	Production cycle time								
9	(minutes)	2.7	2.6	2.5	2.6	2.6	2.6	2.6	2.7
10	Average process time								
11	(minutes)	1.90	1.90	1.85	1.80	1.90	1.95	1.95	1.90
12	Customer complaints	12	12	10	8	9	7	6	4
13	Production backlog								
14	(units)	9,210	9,350	9,370	9,420	9,410	8,730	8,310	7,950
15	Machine downtime								
16	(hours)	86.5	83.1	76.5	80.1	90.4	100.6	120.2	124.9
17	Equipment utilization								
18	rate (%)	98.2	98.6	98.9	98.5	98.1	97.3	96.6	95.7
19	On-time deliveries (%)	93.2	94.1	96.5	95.4	92.1	90.5	88.4	89.3
20	Machine maintenance								
21	time (hours)	34.6	32.2	28.5	22.1	18.5	12.6	19.7	26.4
22									

1. Analyze the nonfinancial measures of quality of the division for the eight-week period. Focus on the following areas of performance:
    a. Production performance
    b. Delivery cycle time
    c. Customer satisfaction
2. Summarize your findings in a report to the division's manager.

Section 3: Business Applications

Why does quality help managers improve company performance and maintain a competitive edge?

To answer this question, match this chapter's manager responsibilities with when they occur within the management process.

a. Plan	1. Customize reports for performance analysis and decision making.
b. Perform	2. Assess performance measures of all business functions.
c. Evaluate	3. Implement personnel, resource, and activity decisions.
d. Communicate	4. Formulate strategic and tactical plans that manage quality.
	5. Reward performance promptly.
	6. Measure relevant and reliable data on quality.
	7. Prepare operating forecasts.
	8. Take corrective actions.
	9. Minimize waste.
	10. Prepare budgets.
	11. Analyze and revise performance measurement plans.
	12. Improve quality through quality control and quality assurance.

SOLUTION

Section 1: Concepts

The concepts of *relevance* and *understandability* underlie quality. Doing business over the Internet has added a rich dimension to quality as managers try to understand the ever-changing e-business environment. Managers need on-demand quality performance measures to support their decision making as they strive to satisfy users today and create innovative products and services for tomorrow. At **Facebook**, the quality of a user's experience is enhanced by the company's management information system. By maintaining user profiles based on previous visits and activities, Facebook can greet users as they return to the site with a web page customized to their preferences. Facebook's managers also use their information system's highly developed infrastructure to meet the changing expectations of a diverse customer base. In understanding its users and the responsiveness of the company's value chain, these managers use relevant nonfinancial and financial quality measures for decision making and performance management.

Section 2: Accounting Application

1. (*Note*: The data given were reorganized as shown below, and one additional piece of information, average waste time, was calculated from the data.)

	A	B	C	D	E	F	G	H	I	J	K
1						Week					Weekly
2			1	2	3	4	5	6	7	8	Average
3	a.	**Production Performance**									
4		Machine downtime (hours)	86.5	83.1	76.5	80.1	90.4	100.6	120.2	124.9	95.3
5		Equipment utilization rate (%)	98.2	98.6	98.9	98.5	98.1	97.3	96.6	95.7	97.7
6		Machine maintenance time (hours)	34.6	32.2	28.5	22.1	18.5	12.6	19.7	26.4	24.3
7	b.	**Delivery Cycle Time**									
8		On-time deliveries (%)	93.2	94.1	96.5	95.4	92.1	90.5	88.4	89.3	92.4
9		Average setup time (hours)	0.30	0.25	0.25	0.30	0.25	0.20	0.20	0.15	0.24
10		Purchase-order lead time (hours)	2.4	2.3	2.2	2.3	2.4	2.4	2.4	2.5	2.4
11		Production cycle time (minutes)	2.7	2.6	2.5	2.5	2.5	2.6	2.6	2.7	2.6
12		Average process time (minutes)	1.90	1.90	1.85	1.80	1.90	1.95	1.95	1.90	1.89
13		Production backlog (units)	9,210	9,350	9,370	9,420	9,410	8,730	8,310	7,950	8,969
14		Average waste time (hours)	0.50	0.45	0.40	0.50	0.45	0.45	0.45	0.65	0.48
15	c.	**Customer Satisfaction**									
16		Customer complaints	12	12	10	8	9	7	6	4	8.5
17		Warrantly claims	2	4	1	1	—	5	7	11	3.9
18											

2. The analysis of the operating data for the division for the last eight weeks revealed the following:
   - **Production Performance:** Machine downtime is increasing. Also, the equipment utilization rate is down. Machine maintenance time originally decreased, but it has increased in the past two weeks. Department managers should be aware of these potential problem areas.
   - **Delivery Cycle Time:** The company is having trouble maintaining the averages for delivery cycle time established eight weeks ago. On-time delivery percentages are slipping. Waste time is increasing, which is contrary to goals. Backlogged orders are decreasing, which is a good sign from a lean viewpoint, but could spell problems in the future. On the positive side, setup time seems to be under control. Emphasis needs to be placed on reducing lead time, cycle time, and process time.
   - **Customer Satisfaction:** Customer satisfaction seems to be improving, as the number of complaints is decreasing rapidly. However, warranty claims have risen significantly in the past three weeks, which may be a signal of quality problems.

Overall, the company can see good signs from the new equipment, but needs to pay special attention to all potential problem areas.

Section 3: Business Applications

1. d
2. c
3. b
4. a
5. c
6. b
7. a
8. c
9. b
10. a
11. c
12. b

Chapter Review

Discuss quality and how it relates to the accounting concepts of relevance and understandability. LO 1

Quality is the result of an operating environment in which a product or service meets or conforms to a customer's specifications the first time it is produced or delivered. Quality has many dimensions that extend beyond the mere creation and delivery of a product or service. Quality performance measures help support decision making as managers try to satisfy customers today and create innovative products and services for tomorrow. Total quality management is an organizational environment in which all business functions work together to build quality into a firm's products or services.

Identify the awards and organizations that promote quality. LO 2

The importance of quality has been acknowledged worldwide through the granting of numerous awards, certificates, and prizes for quality. Three of the most prestigious awards are the Deming Prizes, the EFQM Excellence Award, and the Malcolm Baldrige Quality Award. In addition, the International Organization for Standardization promotes quality management through standards like the ISO 9000 and 14000 series of standards.

Describe total quality management (TQM), and identify financial and nonfinancial measures of quality. LO 3

The costs of quality are measures of the costs that are specifically related to the achievement or non-achievement of product or service quality. The costs of quality have two components. One is the cost of conforming to a customer's product or service standards by preventing defects and failures and by appraising quality and performance. The other is the cost of nonconformance—the costs incurred when defects are discovered before a product is shipped and the costs incurred after a defective product or faulty service is delivered to the customer. The objective of TQM is to reduce or eliminate the costs of nonconformance, the internal and external failure costs that are associated with customer dissatisfaction.

Use measures of quality to evaluate operating performance. LO 4

Nonfinancial measures of quality are related to product design, vendor performance, production performance, delivery cycle time, and customer satisfaction. Those measures, together with the costs of quality, help a firm meet its goal of continuously improving product or service quality and the production process.

Describe a management information system, and explain how it enhances management decision making. LO 5

A management information system (MIS) focuses on the management of activities, not on costs. Thus, an MIS provides managers with improved knowledge of the internal and external processes for which they are responsible or access. The MIS can integrate a company as a company-based ERP system or be Internet-based like SaaS, where data are available on demand and support social media and mobile technologies.

As managers plan, they use the MIS database to obtain relevant and reliable information for formulating strategic plans, making forecasts, and preparing budgets. They use financial and nonfinancial information in the MIS database to implement decisions about personnel, resources, and activities that will minimize waste and improve the quality of their organization's products or services. By enabling the timely comparison of actual to expected performance, the MIS allows managers to reward performance promptly, take speedy corrective actions, and analyze and revise performance measurement plans.

Key Terms

appraisal costs 1148 (LO3)
benchmarking 1144 (LO1)
computer-aided design (CAD) 1150 (LO3)
computer-integrated manufacturing (CIM) systems 1151 (LO3)
costs of conformance 1148 (LO3)
costs of nonconformance 1148 (LO3)
costs of quality 1148 (LO3)
delivery cycle time 1151 (LO3)
delivery time 1151 (LO3)
Deming Prize 1145 (LO2)
EFQM Excellence Award 1145 (LO2)
enterprise resource planning (ERP) system 1157 (LO5)
external failure costs 1148 (LO3)
internal failure costs 1148 (LO3)
ISO 9000 1146 (LO2)
ISO 14000 1147 (LO2)
ISO 26000 1147 (LO2)
ISO 31000 1147 (LO2)
kaizen 1144 (LO1)
Malcolm Baldrige National Quality Award 1146 (LO2)
management information system (MIS) 1157 (LO5)
prevention costs 1148 (LO3)
process mapping 1145 (LO1)
production cycle time 1151 (LO3)
purchase-order lead time 1151 (LO3)
quality 1144 (LO1)
return on quality (ROQ) 1144 (LO1)
Six Sigma 1144 (LO1)
software as a service (SaaS) 1157 (LO5)
total quality management (TQM) 1144 (LO31)

Chapter Assignments

DISCUSSION QUESTIONS

LO 1, 5 **DQ1. CONCEPT ▶ BUSINESS APPLICATION ▶** How do managers use the concept of relevance during the management process?

LO 1, 5 **DQ2. CONCEPT ▶ BUSINESS APPLICATION ▶** How do managers use the concept of understandability during the management process?

LO 1, 5 **DQ3. BUSINESS APPLICATION ▶** How do companies continue to anticipate customer needs now that e-commerce has changed the way goods and services are obtained?

LO 1, 5 **DQ4. BUSINESS APPLICATION ▶** You have been asked to develop a plan for installing a management information system in your company. What kind of information will you need to gather to make an informed decision about all aspects of the management process?

SHORT EXERCISES

LO 1 **Return on Quality**

SE1. For many years, Greg Pirolo has used return on quality (ROQ) to evaluate quality. What assumptions about quality did he make?

LO 1 **Quality and Cycle Time**

SE2. Motorola's Finance Department has adapted the concept of delivery cycle time to include the measurement of cycle times for processing customer credit memos, invoices, and orders. Why would such performance measures contribute to Motorola's quest for Six Sigma quality?

LO 2 **Quality Award Recipients**

SE3. What types of organizations are represented by recent recipients of the Malcolm Baldrige Award? Consult the website at www.nist.gov/baldrige/.

LO 3 **Costs of Quality in a Service Business**

SE4. ABC Insurance Agency incurred the following activity costs related to service quality. Identify those that are costs of conformance (CC) and those that are costs of nonconformance (NC).

Policy processing improvements	$76,400
Customer complaints response	34,100
Policy writer training	12,300
Policy error losses	82,700
Policy proofing	39,500

LO 3 **Measures of Quality**

SE5. Internal reports on quality at Lakelawn Press Company generated the following information for the School Division for the first three months of the year:

Total sales	$50,000,000
Costs of quality:	
Prevention	$ 523,000
Appraisal	77,000
Internal failure	860,000
External failure	640,000

Compute the following. (Round to two decimal places.)

1. Total costs of quality as a percentage of sales
2. Ratio of costs of conformance to total costs of quality
3. Ratio of costs of nonconformance to total costs of quality
4. Costs of nonconformance as a percentage of total sales

LO 3 **Nonfinancial Measures of Quality**

SE6. ACCOUNTING CONNECTION ▶ For a fast-food restaurant that specializes in deluxe hamburgers, identify two nonfinancial measures of good product quality and two nonfinancial measures of poor product quality.

LO 3 **Vendor Quality**

SE7. ACCOUNTING CONNECTION ▶ Cite some specific measures of vendor quality that Nikki Mile could use when she installs a quality-certification program for the vendors that supply her company, Emboss It, Inc., with direct materials.

LO 4 **Measures of Delivery Cycle Time**

SE8. ACCOUNTING CONNECTION ▶ Quality Products, Inc., has developed a set of nonfinancial measures to evaluate on-time product delivery for one of its best-selling cosmetics. The following data have been generated for the past four weeks:

Week	Purchase-Order Lead Time	Production Cycle Time	Delivery Time
1	3.0 days	3.5 days	4.0 days
2	2.3 days	3.5 days	3.5 days
3	2.4 days	3.3 days	3.4 days
4	2.5 days	3.2 days	3.3 days

Compute the total delivery cycle time for each week. Evaluate the delivery performance. Is there an area that needs management's attention?

LO 5 **Traits of a Management Information System**

SE9. BUSINESS APPLICATION ▶ What kinds of information does a management information system capture? How do managers use such information?

LO 5 **Continuous Improvement**

SE10. BUSINESS APPLICATION ▶ May Patt is the controller for Patt Industries. She has been asked to develop a plan for installing a management information system in her company. The president has already approved the concept and has given Patt the go-ahead. What kind of information will Patt need to give managers to help them with their decision making?

EXERCISES: SET A

LO 2 **Awards for Quality**

E1A. The International Organization for Standardization facilitates international exchange. List at least two examples of their more popular standards.

LO 3 **Costs of Conformance in a Service Business**

E2A. Hollis Home Health Care, LLP, incurred the service-related activity costs for the month that follow.

Total sales	$50,000
Quality training of employees	400
Vendor audits	200
Quality-certified vendors	200
Preventive maintenance	300
Quality sampling of services	400
Field testing of new services	250
Quality circles	50
Quality improvement projects	150
Technical service support	75
Inspection of services rendered	175

Prepare an analysis of the costs of conformance by identifying the prevention costs and appraisal costs, and compute the percentage of sales represented by prevention costs, appraisal costs, and total costs of conformance.

LO 3 **Costs of Nonconformance in a Service Business**

E3A. Home Health Care, LLP, incurred the service-related activity costs for the month that follow.

Total sales	$24,000
Reinspection of rework	50
Investigation of service defects	300
Lawsuits	100
Quality-related downtime	75
Failure analysis	50
Customer complaint processing	500
Retesting of service scheduling	25
Restoration of reputation	0
Lost sales	100
Replacement services	500

Prepare an analysis of the costs of nonconformance by identifying the internal failure costs and external failure costs, and compute the percentage of sales represented by internal failure costs, external failure costs, and total costs of nonconformance. (Round percentages to two decimal places.)

LO 3 **Measures of Quality in a Service Business**

E4A. Rehab Health Care, LLC, incurred the service-related activity costs for the month that follow.

Total sales	$40,000
Customer complaint processing	1,000
Employee training	400
Reinspection and retesting	500
Design review of service procedures	300
Technical support	200
Investigation of service defects	800
Sample testing of vendors	100
Inspection of supplies	150
Quality audits	250
Quality-related downtime	300

Prepare an analysis of the costs of quality for Rehab Health Care. Categorize the costs as (a) costs of conformance, with subsets of prevention costs and appraisal costs, or (b) costs of nonconformance, with subsets of internal failure costs and external failure costs. Compute the percentage of sales represented by prevention costs, appraisal costs, total costs of conformance, internal failure costs, external failure costs, total costs of nonconformance, and total costs of quality. Also compute the ratio of costs of conformance to total costs of quality and the ratio of costs of nonconformance to total costs of quality.

LO 3 **Costs of Quality**

E5A. La Coupe Corporation produces and supplies automotive manufacturers with the mechanisms used to adjust the positions of front seating units. Several competitors have recently entered the market, and management is concerned that the quality of the company's current products may be surpassed by the quality of the new competitors'

(Continued)

products. The controller was asked to conduct an analysis of the efforts in January to improve product quality. His analysis generated the following costs of quality:

Training of employees	$50,400
Customer service	13,600
Reinspection of rework	28,000
Quality audits	30,300
Design review	49,500
Warranty claims	7,100
Sample testing of materials	26,400
Returned goods	98,700
Preventive maintenance	45,700
Quality engineering	41,800
Setup for testing new products	41,100
Scrap and rework	44,200
Losses caused by vendor scrap	65,800
Product simulation	29,400

1. Prepare a detailed analysis of the costs of quality.
2. **ACCOUNTING CONNECTION** ▶ Comment on the company's current efforts to improve product quality.

LO 3

Measuring Costs of Quality

E6A. Lola Corporation has two departments that produce two separate product lines. The company has been implementing total quality management over the past year. Revenue and costs of quality for that year follow.

	Dept. R	Dept. Q	Totals
Annual sales	$10,200,000	$10,000,000	$20,200,000
Costs of quality:			
Prevention costs	$ 106,000	$ 204,500	$ 310,500
Appraisal costs	104,001	99,999	204,000
Internal failure costs	194,000	97,500	291,500
External failure costs	144,000	60,000	204,000
Totals	$ 548,001	$ 461,999	$ 1,010,000

Which department is taking a more serious approach to implementing TQM? Base your answer on the following computations. (Round to two decimal places.)

1. Total costs of quality as a percentage of sales
2. Ratio of costs of conformance to total costs of quality
3. Ratio of costs of nonconformance to total costs of quality
4. Costs of nonconformance as a percentage of sales

LO 4

Measures of Product Design Quality

E7A. ACCOUNTING CONNECTION ▶ Vu It, Inc.'s management's goal was to be the first to market with its newest product, TV sunglasses. Comment on how the company's measures of product design quality, which follow, compare with the industry benchmarks.

Measures of Product Design Quality	Vu It, Inc.	Industry Benchmark
Number of design defects detected	20	20
Unresolved design defects at time of product introduction	5	2
Average time between defect detection and correction (hours)	2	4
Time to market (time from design idea to market) (days)	50	80

LO 4

Measures of Vendor Performance

E8A. ACCOUNTING CONNECTION ▶ Howe Curtin, the manager of a hotel that caters to traveling businesspeople, is reviewing the nonfinancial measures of quality for the hotel's dry-cleaning service. Six months ago, he contracted with a local dry-cleaning company to provide the service to hotel guests. The cleaner promised a four-hour turnaround on all dry-cleaning orders. Comment on the following measures for the last six months:

	January	February	March	April	May	June
Percentage of complaints	2%	3%	2%	3%	3%	2%
Percentage of on-time deliveries	100%	85%	100%	90%	80%	100%
Number of orders	500	600	600	700	800	800

LO 4

Measures of Production Performance

E9A. Analyze the following nonfinancial measures of quality for Sweet Express, Inc., a supplier of novelty candy boxes, for a recent four-week period. Focus specifically on measures of production performance.

Measures of Quality	Week 1	Week 2	Week 3	Week 4
Percentage of defective products per million produced	0.9%	0.7%	0.5%	0.4%
Equipment utilization rate	89%	90%	89%	90%
Machine downtime (hours)	11	9	12	11
Machine maintenance time (hours)	9	8	8	9
Machine setup time (hours)	3	4	5	3

LO 4

Measures of Delivery Cycle Time

E10A. Compute the missing numbers for **a**, **b**, **c**, and **d** for the delivery cycle time for Companies M, N, Q, and P.

Company	Purchase-Order Lead Time	Production Cycle Time	Delivery Time	Total Delivery Cycle Time
M	**a**	2	1	5
N	2	5	**b**	10
Q	10	**c**	15	32
P	2	7	3	**d**

LO 4

Analysis of Waste Time

E11A. ACCOUNTING CONNECTION ▶ Calculate the missing numbers for **a**, **b**, **c**, and **d** to analyze the waste time for the following orders. Comment on your findings.

Name of Order	Production Cycle Time	Average Process Time	Average Setup Time	Waste Time
Jones	6	**a**	2	1
Huang	**b**	8	4	3
Gonzales	8	4	**c**	2
Poon	7	3	1	**d**

LO 4

Nonfinancial Measures of Quality and TQM

E12A. ACCOUNTING CONNECTION ▶ "A satisfied customer is the most important goal of this company!" was the opening remark of the corporate president, Alicia Les, at Wonder Tube Company's monthly executive committee meeting. The company manufactures tube products for customers in 16 western states. It has four divisions, each

(Continued)

producing a different type of tubing material. Les, a proponent of total quality management, was reacting to the latest measures of quality from the four divisions. The data for the four divisions follow.

	Brass Division	Plastics Division	Aluminum Division	Copper Division	Company Averages
Vendor on-time delivery	96.30%	90.50%	97.20%	87.10%	92.61%
Production quality rates (defective parts per million)	1,300	2,600	1,200	4,300	2,400
On-time shipments	87.10%	76.30%	89.70%	73.50%	81.65%
Returned orders	1.00%	4.00%	0.75%	6.00%	3.00%
Number of customer complaints	20	52	6	58	34
Number of warranty claims	6	11	3	13	9

Why was Les upset? Which division or divisions do not appear to have satisfied customers? What criteria did you use to make your decision?

LO 4 **Nonfinancial Data Analysis**

E13A. Strong Company makes racing bicycles. Its Lightspeed model is considered the top of the line in the industry. Three months ago, to improve quality and reduce production time, Strong purchased and installed a computer-integrated manufacturing system for the Lightspeed model. Management is interested in cutting time in all phases of the delivery cycle. The controller's office gathered the following data for the past four-week period:

	Week			
	1	2	3	4
Average process time (hours)	23.6	23.4	22.8	22.2
Average setup time (hours)	1.5	1.4	1.3	1.2
Customer complaints	8	7	9	9
Delivery time (hours)	34.0	35.0	36.0	38.0
On-time deliveries (%)	97.1	96.7	96.2	95.3
Production backlog (units)	8,030	8,040	8,020	8,030
Production cycle time (hours)	28.5	27.9	27.2	26.4
Purchase-order lead time (hours)	38.5	36.2	35.5	34.1
Warranty claims	3	4	3	2

Analyze the performance of the Lightspeed model for the four-week period, focusing specifically on product delivery cycle time and on customer satisfaction. (Round the weekly averages to two decimal places.)

LO 5 **Adapting to Changing Information Needs**

E14A. BUSINESS APPLICATION ▶ "What's all the fuss about managers needing to focus on activities instead of costs?" demanded Lucy LaVern, the controller of Wishes, Inc. "The bottom line is all that matters, and our company's current management information system is just fine for figuring that out. I know that our system is eight years old, but if it isn't broken, why should we fix it?" How would you respond to Lucy?

EXERCISE: SET B

Visit the textbook companion website at www.cengagebrain.com to access Exercise Set B for this chapter.

PROBLEMS

LO 3

Costs and Nonfinancial Measures of Quality

SPREADSHEET

✓1 and 2: Kenicott Company: Total prevention costs: $678,000
✓1 and 2: Total appraisal costs: $445,000
✓1 and 2: Total internal failure costs: $319,200
✓1 and 2: Total external failure costs: $538,650

P1. Inturn Enterprises, Inc., operates as three autonomous companies, each with a chief executive officer who oversees its operations. At a recent corporate meeting, the company CEOs agreed to adopt total quality management and to track, record, and analyze their costs and nonfinancial measures of quality. All three companies are operating in highly competitive markets. Sales and quality-related data for September follow.

	Avondale Company	Kenicott Company	Silvertone Company
Annual sales	$11,000,000	$13,000,000	$10,553,800
Costs of quality:			
Vendor audits	$ 69,000	$ 184,800	$ 130,800
Quality audits	58,000	115,000	141,500
Failure analysis	188,500	92,400	16,350
Design review of products	80,500	176,700	218,000
Scrap and rework	207,000	160,800	21,200
Quality-certified suppliers	48,000	105,000	231,000
Preventive maintenance	92,000	158,400	163,500
Warranty adjustments	149,000	105,600	49,050
Product recalls	201,250	198,000	80,050
Quality training of employees	149,500	237,900	272,500
End-of-process sampling and testing	34,500	145,200	202,700
Reinspection of rework	126,500	66,000	27,250
Returned goods	163,103	72,600	16,350
Customer complaint processing	109,250	162,450	38,150
Total costs of quality	$ 1, 676,103	$ 1,980,850	$ 1,608,400
Nonfinancial measures of quality:			
Number of warranty claims	60	32	10
Customer complaints	107	52	18
Defective parts per million	4,610	2,190	1,012
Returned orders	9.20%	4.10%	0.90%

REQUIRED

1. Prepare an analysis of the costs of quality for the three divisions. Categorize the costs as (a) costs of conformance, with subsets of prevention costs and appraisal costs, or (b) costs of nonconformance, with subsets of internal failure costs and external failure costs. Compute the total costs in each category for each company.
2. For each company compute the percentage of sales represented by prevention costs, appraisal costs, total costs of conformance, internal failure costs, external failure costs, total costs of nonconformance, and total costs of quality. (Round to two decimal places.)
3. **ACCOUNTING CONNECTION ▶** Interpret the cost-of-quality data for each company. Is its product of high or low quality? Why? Is each company headed in the right direction to be competitive?
4. **ACCOUNTING CONNECTION ▶** Evaluate the nonfinancial measures of quality in terms of customer satisfaction. Are the results consistent with your analysis in requirement 3? Explain your answer.

LO 3, 4

SPREADSHEET

✔1: Weekly average for equipment utilization rate: 97.98%
✔1: Weekly average for process time: 7.14 hours
✔1: Delivery cycle time for week one: 74.60 hours
✔1: Weekly average for delivery cycle time: 73.43 hours
✔1: Waste time for week one: 2.8 hours
✔1: Weekly average for waste time: 2.63 hours
✔1: Weekly average for warranty claims: 2.75 claims

Analysis of Nonfinancial Data

P2. Convenience Enterprises, Inc., manufactures several lines of small machinery. Before the company installed automated equipment, the total delivery cycle time for its Coin machine models averaged about three weeks. Last year, management decided to purchase a new computer-integrated manufacturing system for the Coin line. A summary of operating data for the past eight weeks for the Coin line follows.

	Week							
	1	2	3	4	5	6	7	8
Average process time (hours)	7.20	7.20	7.10	7.40	7.60	7.20	6.80	6.60
Average setup time (hours)	2.20	2.20	2.10	1.90	1.90	1.80	2.00	1.90
Customer complaints	5	6	4	7	6	8	9	9
Delivery time (hours)	36.20	37.40	37.20	36.40	35.90	35.80	34.80	34.20
Equipment utilization rate (%)	98.10	98.20	98.40	98.10	97.80	97.60	97.80	97.80
Machine downtime (hours)	82.30	84.20	85.90	84.30	83.40	82.20	82.80	80.40
Machine maintenance time (hours)	50.40	52.80	49.50	46.40	47.20	45.80	44.80	42.90
On-time deliveries (%)	92.40	92.50	93.20	94.20	94.40	94.10	95.80	94.60
Production backlog (units)	15,230	15,440	15,200	16,100	14,890	13,560	13,980	13,440
Production cycle time (hours)	12.20	12.60	11.90	11.80	12.20	11.60	11.20	10.60
Purchase-order lead time (hours)	26.20	26.80	26.50	25.90	25.70	25.30	24.80	24.20
Warranty claims	2	2	3	2	3	4	3	3

REQUIRED

1. Analyze the performance of the Coin machine line for the eight-week period. Focus on performance in the following areas. (Round to two decimal places.)
   a. Production performance
   b. Delivery cycle time, including computations of delivery cycle time and waste time
   c. Customer satisfaction
2. **ACCOUNTING CONNECTION ▶** Summarize your findings in a report to the company's president, Deborah Shimon.

LO 3

✔1: Alta's total costs of conformance: $74,000
✔1: Alta's total costs of nonconformance: $57,000
✔2: Alta's ratio of costs of conformance to costs of quality: 0.56 to 1
✔2: Alta's ratio of costs of nonconformance to costs of quality: 0.44 to 1

Costs of Quality

P3. Barbara Speiss, regional manager of Candy Heaven, is evaluating the performance of four candy kitchens in her region. In accordance with the company's costs-of-quality standards of performance, the four locations provided the following data for the past six months:

	Alta	Provo	Snowbird	Copper
Sales	$1,800,000	$1,500,000	$1,400,000	$1,200,000
Prevention costs	$ 32,000	$ 48,000	$ 16,000	$ 20,000
Appraisal costs	42,000	32,000	18,000	25,000
Internal failure costs	24,000	21,000	42,000	30,000
External failure costs	33,000	16,000	45,000	25,000
Total costs of quality	$ 131,000	$ 117,000	$ 121,000	$ 100,000

REQUIRED

1. For each location, compute the percentages of sales represented by prevention costs, appraisal costs, total costs of conformance, internal failure costs, external failure costs, total costs of nonconformance, and total costs of quality. (Round to two decimal places.)
2. For each location, calculate the ratio of costs of conformance to costs of quality and the ratio of costs of nonconformance to costs of quality. (Round to two decimal places.)
3. **ACCOUNTING CONNECTION ▶** Interpret the cost-of-quality data for each location. Rank the locations in terms of quality.

LO 3, 4

Interpreting Measures of Quality

P4. ACCOUNTING CONNECTION ▶ Circuit Corporation supplies integrated circuitry to major appliance manufacturers in all parts of the world. Producing a high-quality product in each of the company's four divisions is the mission of management. Each division is required to record and report its efforts to achieve quality in all of its primary product lines. The following information for the most recent three-month period was submitted to the chief financial officer:

	Macon Division		Dothan Division		Valdosta Division		Columbia Division	
	Amount	% of Revenue	Amount	% of Revenue	Amount	% of Revenue	Amount	% of Revenue
Costs of Conformance								
Prevention costs:								
Quality training of employees	$ 4,400		$ 15,600		$ 23,600		$ 8,900	
Process engineering	3,100		19,700		45,900		9,400	
Preventive maintenance	5,800		14,400		13,800		11,100	
Total prevention costs	$ 13,300	0.95%	$ 49,700	3.11%	$ 83,300	5.55%	$ 29,400	1.73%
Appraisal costs:								
End-of-process sampling and testing	$ 3,500		$ 19,500		$ 21,400		$ 6,900	
Quality audits of products	6,100		11,900		17,600		8,700	
Vendor audits	4,100		10,100		9,800		7,300	
Total appraisal costs	$ 13,700	0.98%	$ 41,500	2.59%	$ 48,800	3.25%	$ 22,900	1.35%
Total costs of conformance	$ 27,000	1.93%	$ 91,200	5.70%	$132,100	8.80%	$ 52,300	3.08%
Costs of Nonconformance								
Internal failure costs:								
Quality-related downtime	$ 26,800		$ 8,300		$ 6,500		$ 22,600	
Scrap and rework	17,500		9,100		7,800		16,200	
Scrap disposal losses	31,200		7,200		3,600		19,900	
Total internal failure costs	$ 75,500	5.39%	$ 24,600	1.54%	$ 17,900	1.19%	$ 58,700	3.45%
External failure costs:								
Warranty claims	$ 22,600		$ 4,400		$ 2,500		$ 17,100	
Customer complaint processing	31,600		8,100		6,400		22,300	
Returned goods	29,900		5,600		3,100		19,800	
Total external failure costs	$ 84,100	6.01%	$ 18,100	1.13%	$ 12,000	0.80%	$ 59,200	3.48%
Total costs of nonconformance	$159,600	11.40%	$ 42,700	2.67%	$ 29,900	1.99%	$117,900	6.93%
Total costs of quality	$186,600	13.33%	$133,900	8.37%	$162,000	10.79%	$170,200	10.01%
Ratios of Nonfinancial Measures:								
Number of sales to number of warranty claims	168 to 1		372 to 1		996 to 1		225 to 1	
Number of products produced to number of products reworked	1,420 to 1		3,257 to 1		6,430 to 1		2,140 to 1	
Change in throughput time (positive amount means time reduction)	(−4.615%)		2.163%		5.600%		(−1.241%)	
Total number of deliveries to number of late deliveries	86 to 1		168 to 1		290 to 1		128 to 1	

REQUIRED

1. Rank the divisions in order of their apparent product quality.
2. What three measures were most important in your rankings in **1**? Why?
3. Which division is most successful in its bid to improve quality? What measures illustrate its high-quality rating?
4. Consider the two divisions producing the lowest-quality products. What actions would you recommend to the management of each division? Where should their quality dollars be spent?

ALTERNATE PROBLEMS

LO 3

SPREADSHEET

✔1 and 2: West Division's total prevention costs: $665,000
✔1 and 2: West Division's total appraisal costs: $370,500
✔1 and 2: West Division's total internal failure costs: $57,000
✔1 and 2: West Division's total external failure costs: $199,500

Costs and Nonfinancial Measures of Quality

P5. Stainless Company operates as three autonomous divisions. Each division has a general manager in charge of product development, production, and distribution. Management recently adopted total quality management, and the divisions now track, record, and analyze their costs and nonfinancial measures of quality. All three divisions are operating in highly competitive marketplaces. Sales and quality-related data for April follow.

	North Division	West Division	South Division
Annual sales	$8,500,000	$9,500,000	$13,000,000
Costs of quality:			
Field testing	$ 51,600	$ 112,800	$ 183,950
Quality audits	17,200	79,100	109,650
Failure analysis	103,100	14,700	92,700
Quality training of employees	60,200	188,000	167,700
Scrap and rework	151,000	18,800	154,800
Quality-certified suppliers	34,400	94,000	108,200
Preventive maintenance	65,800	148,000	141,900
Warranty claims	107,500	42,300	106,050
Customer complaint processing	151,500	108,100	154,800
Process engineering	94,600	235,000	232,200
End-of-process sampling and testing	24,700	178,600	141,900
Scrap disposal losses	77,400	23,500	64,500
Returned goods	152,500	16,200	45,150
Product recalls	64,500	32,900	64,500
Total costs of quality	$1,156,000	$1,292,000	$ 1,768,000
Nonfinancial measures of quality:			
Defective parts per million	3,410	1,104	1,940
Returned orders	7.40%	1.10%	3.20%
Customer complaints	62	12	30
Number of warranty claims	74	16	52

REQUIRED

1. Prepare an analysis of the costs of quality for the three divisions. Categorize the costs as (a) costs of conformance, with subsets of prevention costs and appraisal costs, or (b) costs of nonconformance, with subsets of internal failure costs and external failure costs. Compute the total costs for each category for each division.
2. For each division, compute the percentage of sales represented by prevention costs, appraisal costs, total costs of conformance, internal failure costs, external failure costs, total costs of nonconformance, and total costs of quality.
3. **ACCOUNTING CONNECTION ▶** Interpret the cost-of-quality data for each division. Is each division's product of high or low quality? Explain your answers. Are the divisions headed in the right direction to be competitive?
4. **ACCOUNTING CONNECTION ▶** Evaluate the nonfinancial measures of quality in terms of customer satisfaction. Are the results consistent with your analysis in requirement **3**? Explain your answers.

LO 3, 4

SPREADSHEET

✔1: Weekly average for equipment utilization rate: 96.39%
✔1: Weekly average for process time: 11.53 hours
✔1: Delivery cycle time for week one: 57.90 hours
✔1: Weekly average for delivery cycle time: 58.04 hours
✔1: Waste time for week one: 3.10 hours
✔1: Weekly average for waste time: 3.58 hours
✔1: Weekly average for warranty claims: 3.75 claims

Analysis of Nonfinancial Data

P6. Electronics Company is known for its high-quality products and on-time deliveries. Six months ago, it installed a computer-integrated manufacturing system in its Small Components Department. The new equipment produces the entire component, so the finished product is ready to be shipped when needed. During the past eight-week period, the controller's staff gathered the data that follow.

	Week							
	1	2	3	4	5	6	7	8
Average process time (hours)	10.90	11.10	10.60	10.80	11.20	11.80	12.20	13.60
Average setup time (hours)	2.50	2.60	2.60	2.80	2.70	2.40	2.20	2.20
Customer complaints	11	10	23	15	9	7	5	6
Delivery time (hours)	26.20	26.40	26.10	25.90	26.20	26.60	27.10	26.40
Equipment utilization rate (%)	96.20	96.10	96.30	97.20	97.40	96.20	96.40	95.30
Machine downtime (hours)	106.40	108.10	120.20	110.40	112.80	102.20	124.60	136.20
Machine maintenance time (hours)	64.80	66.70	72.60	74.20	76.80	66.60	80.40	88.20
On-time deliveries (%)	97.20	97.50	97.60	98.20	98.40	96.40	94.80	92.60
Production backlog (units)	10,246	10,288	10,450	10,680	10,880	11,280	11,350	12,100
Production cycle time (hours)	16.50	16.40	16.30	16.10	16.30	17.60	19.80	21.80
Purchase-order lead time (hours)	15.20	15.10	14.90	14.60	14.60	13.20	12.40	12.60
Warranty claims	4	8	2	1	6	4	2	3

REQUIRED

1. Analyze the performance of the Small Components Department for the eight-week period. Focus on performance in the following areas: (a) production performance, (b) delivery cycle time (include computations of delivery cycle time and waste time), and (c) customer satisfaction. (Round to two decimal places.)
2. **ACCOUNTING CONNECTION ▶** Summarize your findings in a report to the department's superintendent, Pierre Jour.

LO **3**

Costs of Quality

✓1: Subchapter S Portal percentage of sales represented by prevention costs: 0.20%
✓1: Subchapter S Portal appraisal costs: 0.35%
✓1: Subchapter S Portal total internal failure costs: 0.40%
✓1: Subchapter S Portal total external failure costs: 0.69%
✓2: Ratio of costs of conformance to costs of quality, Subchapter S Portal: 0.34 to 1
✓2: Ratio of costs of nonconformance to costs of quality, Subchapter S Portal: 0.66 to 1

P7. Charles Caroll, the regional manager of Quik File, Inc., is evaluating the performance of four ecommerce tax preparation sites in his region. The following data for the past six months were presented to him by each site in accordance with the company's costs-of-quality standards of performance:

	Partnership Portal	Corporation Portal	Subchapter S Portal	Sole Proprietorship Portal
Sales	$5,000,000	$10,000,000	$8,000,000	$6,000,000
Prevention costs	$ 62,000	$ 58,000	$ 16,000	$ 20,000
Appraisal costs	32,000	42,000	28,000	15,000
Internal failure costs	54,000	31,000	32,000	40,000
External failure costs	23,000	26,000	55,000	35,000
Total costs of quality	$ 171,000	$ 157,000	$ 131,000	$ 110,000

REQUIRED

1. For each site, compute the percentages of sales represented by prevention costs, appraisal costs, total costs of conformance, internal failure costs, external failure costs, total costs of nonconformance, and total costs of quality. (Round to two decimal places.)
2. For each site, calculate the ratio of costs of conformance to costs of quality and the ratio of costs of nonconformance to costs of quality. (Round to two decimal places.)
3. **ACCOUNTING CONNECTION ▶** Interpret the cost-of-quality data for each site. Rank the sites in terms of quality.

LO **3, 4**

Interpreting Measures of Quality

✓1 and 2: Division A total prevention costs: $20,200
✓1 and 2: Division A total appraisal costs: $26,100
✓1 and 2: Division A total internal failure costs: $61,600
✓1 and 2: Division A total external failure costs: $50,200
✓1 and 2: Division A number of sales to number of warranty claims: 295 to 1

P8. Salmon Corporation has five divisions, each manufacturing a product line that competes in the global marketplace. The company is planning to compete for the Malcolm Baldrige Award, so management requires that each division record and report its efforts to achieve quality in its product line. The information below was submitted to the company's controller for the most recent six-month period.

(Continued)

	A	B	C	D	E	F
1		Division A	Division B	Division C	Division D	Division E
2	**Total Revenue**	$886,000	$1,040,000	$956,000	$1,225,000	$1,540,000
3	**Costs of Quality**					
4	Customer complaint processing	$10,400	$12,600	$12,300	$10,100	$15,600
5	Scrap and rework	26,800	13,500	38,700	11,900	34,800
6	Quality audit of products	13,600	28,400	6,300	25,600	11,700
7	Returned goods	18,700	11,400	38,400	11,300	36,000
8	Warranty claims	21,100	6,400	36,200	6,500	42,600
9	Quality training of employees	8,900	12,600	4,600	11,400	4,200
10	Preventive maintenance	11,300	18,700	8,300	13,600	6,300
11	Failure analysis	34,800	9,800	46,900	10,200	56,900
12	Inspection of materials	12,500	18,700	7,800	17,500	5,600
13	**Nonfinancial Measure of Quality**					
14	Number of warrantly claims versus	22	12	46	12	62
15	number of sales	6,500	8,900	7,200	9,800	9,600
16	Number of products reworked versus	150	140	870	70	900
17	number of products manufactured	325,000	456,000	365,000	450,000	315,600

REQUIRED

1. Prepare an analysis of the costs of quality for each division. Categorize the costs as costs of conformance or costs of nonconformance. (Round to two decimal places.)
2. For each division, compute the percentage of total revenue for each of the four cost-of-quality categories and the ratios for the nonfinancial data. (Round percentages to two decimal places.)
3. Rank the divisions in order of their apparent product quality.
4. **ACCOUNTING CONNECTION ▶** What three measures were most important in your rankings in requirement 3? Why?
5. **ACCOUNTING CONNECTION ▶** Which division has been most successful in its bid to improve quality? What measures illustrate its high quality rating?
6. **ACCOUNTING CONNECTION ▶** Consider the two divisions producing the lowest-quality products. What actions would you recommend to the management of each division? Where should their quality dollars be spent?

CASES

LO 1

Conceptual Understanding: Quality Measures and Techniques

C1. Motorola's Total Customer Satisfaction (TCS) Teams are cross-functional teams that use customer-focused methods to solve quality and process problems. According to Motorola's website, one TCS Team success story involved an international supplier with quality and delivery problems. These problems required additional order expediting and rework and were causing customer dissatisfaction. The TCS Team's report to management disclosed the following:

- By evaluating and revising the product's design with input from the international supplier, the team created a more robust finished product.
- The team's adoption of process capability studies, together with continuous monitoring, resulted in improved quality for the international supplier.
- When sourcing was moved to a local supplier, the number of times the inventory turned over annually improved. It went from 26 to 52 times a year.
- Over the three-year life of the product, the team's changes resulted in $831,438 in cost savings.

1. From the TCS Team's report, identify the key issues involved in solving the international supplier's quality and process problems.
2. How could the team have applied the process-based techniques of benchmarking and process mapping to improve quality?

LO 3, 4

Conceptual Understanding: Evaluating Performance Measures

C2. Harn Company and Ocala Company compete in the same industry. Each company is located in a large western city, and each employs between 300 and 350 people. Both companies have adopted a total quality management approach, and both want to improve their ability to compete in the marketplace. They have installed common performance measures to help track their quest for quality and a competitive advantage.

During the most recent three-month period, Harn and Ocala generated the data that follow.

	Harn Company		Ocala Company	
Performance Measures	**Financial**	**Nonfinancial**	**Financial**	**Nonfinancial**
Production performance:				
Equipment utilization rate		89.4%		92.1%
Machine downtime (in machine hours)		720		490
Delivery cycle time:				
On-time deliveries		92.1%		96.5%
Purchase-order lead time (hours)		17		18
Production cycle time (hours)		14		16
Waste time (hours)		3		2
Customer satisfaction:				
Customer complaints		28		24
Scrap and rework costs	$14,390		$13,680	
Field service costs	9,240		7,700	

1. For each measure, indicate which company has the better performance.
2. Which company is more successful in achieving a total quality environment and an improved competitive position? Explain your answer.

LO 3, 4

Interpreting Management Reports: Reports on Quality Data

C3. Jack Knome is chief executive officer of Red Tundra Machinery, Inc. The company adopted a JIT operating environment five years ago. Since then, each segment of the company has been converted, and a complete computer-integrated manufacturing system operates in all parts of the company's five plants. Processing of Red Tundra's products now averages less than four days once the materials have been put into production.

Knome is worried about customer satisfaction and has asked you, as the controller, for some advice and help. He has also asked the Marketing Department to perform a quick survey of customers to determine weak areas in customer relations. A summary of four customers' replies follows.

- **Customer A:** Customer for five years; waits an average of six weeks for delivery; located 1,200 miles from plant; returns an average of 3 percent of products; receives 90 percent on-time deliveries; never hears from salesperson after placing order; likes quality or would go with competitor.
- **Customer B:** Customer for seven years; waits an average of five weeks for delivery; orders usually sit in backlog for at least three weeks; located 50 miles from plant; returns about 5 percent of products; receives 95 percent on-time deliveries; has great rapport with salesperson; salesperson is why this customer is loyal.

(Continued)

- **Customer C:** Customer for twelve years; waits an average of seven weeks for delivery; located 1,500 miles from plant; returns about 4 percent of products; receives 92 percent on-time deliveries; salesperson is available but of little help in getting faster delivery; customer is thinking about dealing with another source for its product needs.
- **Customer D:** Customer for fifteen years; very pleased with company's product; waits almost five weeks for delivery; located 120 miles from plant; returns only 2 percent of goods received; rapport with salesperson is very good; follow-up service of salesperson is excellent; would like delivery cycle time reduced to equal that of competitors; usually deals with three-week backlog.

1. Identify the areas of concern, and give at least three examples of reports that will help managers improve the company's response to customer needs.
2. Assume that you are asked to write a report that will provide information about customer satisfaction. In preparation for writing the report, answer the following questions:
   a. What kinds of information do you need to prepare this report?
   b. Why is this information relevant?
   c. Where would you find this information (i.e., what sources would you use)?
   d. When would you want to obtain this information?

LO 5

Ethical Dilemma: MIS and Ethics

C4. BUSINESS APPLICATION ▶ Three months ago, Max Enterprises hired a consultant, Stacy Stone, to assist in the design and installation of a new management information system for the company. Mike Carney, one of Max's systems design engineers, was assigned to work with Stone on the project. During the three-month period, Stone and Carney met six times and developed a tentative design and installation plan for the MIS. Before the plan was to be unveiled to top management, Carney asked his supervisor, Toby Bohoven, to look it over and comment on the design.

Included in the plan was the consolidation of three engineering functions into one. Both of the supervisors of the other two functions had seniority over Bohoven, so he believed that the design would lead to his losing his management position. He communicated this to Carney and ended his comments with the following statement: "If you don't redesign the system to accommodate all three of the existing engineering functions, I will give you an unsatisfactory performance evaluation for this year!"

How should Carney respond to Bohoven's assertion? Should he handle the problem alone, keeping it inside the company, or communicate the comment to Stone? Outline Carney's options, and be prepared to discuss them in class.

Continuing Case: Cookie Company

C5. In this chapter, in preparation for developing a website for your company, you will compare the quality of cookie manufacturers' websites. Visit three sites from the following list:

- www.cheryls.com
- www.davidscookies.com
- www.famous-amos.com
- www.mrsfields.com

What features does each site offer its customers? Do the sites offer both pre- and post-sale assistance? In your opinion, how have these websites affected the way cookies are sold? What features will your company's website have?

APPENDIX A

Accounting for Unincorporated Businesses

Throughout the book, we have focused on accounting for the corporate form of business. In this appendix, our focus is on accounting for sole proprietorships and partnerships.

Accounting for Sole Proprietorships

A **sole proprietorship** is a business owned by one person. For the individual, this business form can be a convenient way of separating business activities from personal interests. Legally, however, the proprietorship is the same economic unit as the individual. The sole proprietor receives all the profits or losses and is liable for all the obligations of the business. Proprietorships represent the largest number of businesses in the United States, but typically they are the smallest in size. The life of a proprietorship ends when the owner wishes it to or at the owner's death or incapacity.

When someone invests in his or her own company, the amount of the investment is recorded in that person's Capital account. For example, the journal entry to record the initial investment of $10,000 by Eleani Melas in her new mail-order business would be a debit to the Cash account for $10,000 and a credit to the Eleani Melas, Capital account for $10,000.

During the period, Melas will probably withdraw assets from the business for personal living expenses. Because there is no legal separation between the owner and the sole proprietorship, it is not necessary to make a formal declaration of a withdrawal, as would be required in the case of corporate dividends. The withdrawal of $500 by Melas is recorded as a debit to the Eleani Melas, Withdrawals account for $500 and a credit to the Cash account for $500.

Revenue and expense accounts for sole proprietorships are closed out to Income Summary in the same way they are for corporations. Income Summary, however, is closed to the Capital account instead of to Retained Earnings. For example, the closing entries that follow assume a net income of $1,000 and a withdrawal of $500.

Income Summary	1,000	
Eleani Melas, Capital		1,000
To close Income Summary		
Eleani Melas, Capital	500	
Eleani Melas, Withdrawals		500
To close Withdrawals		

Accounting for Partnerships

The Uniform Partnership Act, which has been adopted by most states, defines a **partnership** as "an association of two or more persons to carry on as co-owners of a business for profit." Normally, partnerships are formed when owners of small businesses wish to combine capital or managerial talents for some common business purpose. Partnerships are treated as *separate entities,* with their own accounting records and financial statements. However, legally there is no economic separation between a partnership and its owners. Note that corporations are legal entities (whereas partnerships and sole proprietorships are not), but all three are considered separate accounting entities.

Characteristics of Partnerships

Some of the important characteristics of partnerships follow.

Voluntary Association A partnership is a voluntary association of individuals. Therefore, a partner is responsible under the law for his or her partners' actions within the scope of the business. Therefore, a partner must be allowed to choose the people who join the partnership.

Partnership Agreement To form a partnership, two or more people simply agree to partner in a business enterprise. Their **partnership agreement** does not have to be in writing. However, it is good business practice to have a written document that clearly states the details of the partnership, including:

- Name, location, and purpose of the business
- Names of the partners and their respective duties
- Investments of each partner
- Method of distributing income and losses
- Procedures for the admission and withdrawal of partners, the withdrawal of assets allowed each partner, and the liquidation (termination) of the business

Limited Life Because a partnership is formed by an agreement, it has a **limited life**. It may be dissolved when (a) a new partner is admitted; (b) when a partner withdraws, goes bankrupt, is incapacitated (to the point that he or she cannot perform as obligated), retires, or dies; or (c) when the terms of the partnership agreement are met (e.g., when the project for which the partnership was formed is completed). The partnership agreement can be written to cover each of these situations, thus allowing the partnership to continue legally.

Mutual Agency Each partner is an agent of the partnership within the scope of the business. Because of this **mutual agency**, any partner can bind the partnership to a business agreement as long as he or she acts within the scope of the company's normal operations. For example, a partner in a used-car business can bind the partnership through the purchase or sale of used cars. But this partner cannot bind the partnership to a contract for buying men's clothing or any other goods that are not related to the used-car business.

Unlimited Liability Each partner has personal **unlimited liability** for all the debts of the partnership. If a partnership cannot pay its debts, creditors must first satisfy their claims from the assets of the business. If these assets are not enough to pay all debts, the creditors can seek payment from the personal assets of each partner. If a partner's personal assets are used up before the debts are paid, the creditors can claim additional assets from the remaining partners who are able to pay. Each partner, then, can be required by law to pay all the debts of the partnership.

Co-Ownership of Partnership Property When individuals invest property in a partnership, they give up the right to their separate use of the property. The property becomes an asset of the partnership and is owned jointly by the partners.

Participation in Partnership Income Each partner has the right to share in the company's income and the responsibility to share in its losses. The partnership agreement should state the method of distributing income and losses to each partner. If the agreement describes how income should be shared but does not mention losses, losses are distributed in the same way as income. If the agreement does not describe the method of income and loss distribution, the partners must share income and losses equally.

Advantages of Partnerships

Partnership has the following advantages:

- It can be easy to form, change, and dissolve.
- It facilitates the pooling of capital resources and individual talents.
- It has no corporate tax burden. Because a partnership is not a legal entity for tax purposes, it does not have to pay a federal income tax, as do corporations, but must file an informational return.
- It gives the partners a certain amount of freedom and flexibility.

STUDY NOTE: *There is no federal income tax on partnerships. Partners are taxed at their personal rates. However, partnerships must file an informational return with the IRS, and some state and local governments levy a tax on them. An example of this is the Michigan Single Business Tax.*

Disadvantages of Partnerships

On the other hand, partnership has the following disadvantages:

- The life of a partnership is limited.
- One partner can bind the partnership to a contract (mutual agency).
- The partners have unlimited personal liability.
- It is more difficult for a partnership to raise large amounts of capital and to transfer ownership interests than it is for a corporation.

Accounting for Partners' Equity

The owner's equity in a partnership is called **partners' equity**. In accounting for partners' equity, it is necessary to maintain separate Capital and Withdrawals accounts for each partner and to divide the income of the company among the partners. In the partners' equity section of the balance sheet, the balance of each partner's Capital account is listed separately:

Liabilities and Partners' Equity		
	Dr.	*Cr.*
Total liabilities		$28,000
Partners' equity:		
Sand, capital	$25,000	
Kira, capital	34,000	
Total partners' equity		59,000
Total liabilities and partners' equity		$87,000

Each partner invests cash or other assets or both in the partnership, according to the partnership agreement. Noncash assets should be *valued* at their fair market value on the date they are transferred to the partnership. The assets invested by a partner are debited to the proper account, and the total amount is credited to the partner's Capital account.

To illustrate, we will use Lori Mind and Rose Padilla, who have agreed to combine their capital and equipment in a partnership to operate a jewelry store.

Recording Partners' Investments

Transaction According to their partnership agreement, Mind will invest $28,000 in cash and $37,000 worth of furniture and displays, and Padilla will invest $40,000 in cash and $30,000 worth of equipment. Related to the equipment is a note payable for $10,000, which the partnership assumes.

Analysis The journal entry to record Mind and Padilla's initial investments

▲ *increases Cash* and other assets with debits for their value

▲ *increases* each partner's capital with a credit for the amount of the partner's contribution to the partnership

A	=	L	+	OE
+28,000				+65,000
+37,000				

A	=	L	+	OE
+30,000		+10,000		+60,000
+40,000				

Journal Entries

2014		Dr.	Cr.
July 1	Cash	28,000	
	Furniture and Displays	37,000	
	Lori Mind, Capital		65,000
	Initial investment of Lori Mind in Mind and Padilla		
1	Cash	40,000	
	Equipment	30,000	
	Notes Payable		10,000
	Rose Padilla, Capital		60,000
	Initial investment of Rose Padilla in Mind and Padilla		

STUDY NOTE: *Padilla's noncash contribution is equal to the fair market value of the equipment less the amount owed on the equipment because the partnership assumed the liability.*

Comment The *values* assigned to the assets would be included in the partnership agreement. These values can differ from those carried on the partners' personal books. For example, the equipment that Rose Padilla contributed had a value of only $22,000 on her books, but its market value had increased considerably after she purchased it. The book value of Padilla's equipment is not important. The fair market value of the equipment at the time of transfer *is* important, however, because it represents the amount of money Padilla has invested in the partnership. Later investments are recorded in the same way.

Distribution of Partnership Income

A partnership's income can be distributed according to whatever method the partners specify in the partnership agreement. If the agreement says nothing about the distribution of income, the partners share it equally. Income in this form of business normally has three components:

- Return to the partners for the use of their capital (called *interest on partners' capital*)
- Compensation for services the partners have rendered (partners' salaries)
- Other income for any special contributions individual partners may make to the partnership or for risks they may take

The breakdown of total income into its three components helps clarify how much each partner has contributed to the firm.

STUDY NOTE: *The division of income is one area in which a partnership differs from a corporation. In corporations, each common share receives an equal dividend. Partners can use any method they agree on to divide partnership income.*

Distributing income among partners can be accomplished by using stated ratios or capital balance ratios or by paying the partners' salaries and interest on their capital and sharing the remaining income according to stated ratios. Salaries and interest here are not salaries expense or interest expense in the ordinary sense of the terms. They do not affect the amount of reported net income. Instead, they refer to ways of determining each partner's share of net income on the basis of time the partner spends and the money he or she invests in the partnership. The computations of each partner's share of net income are relevant to the closing entries in which the Income Summary account is closed to the partners' capital accounts.

Stated Ratios

One method of distributing income is to give each partner a stated ratio of the total income. If each partner is making an equal contribution to the firm, each can assume the same share of income. It is important to understand that an equal contribution to the firm does not necessarily mean an equal capital investment in the firm.

One partner may be devoting more time and talent to the firm, whereas another may have made a larger capital investment. If the partners contribute unequally to the firm, unequal stated ratios can be appropriate.

Distributing Income Using Stated Ratios

Transaction Mind and Padilla had a net income last year of $140,000. The stated ratio is 60 percent for Mind and 40 percent for Padilla.

Computation The computation of each partner's share of the income is computed as follows.

Mind ($140,000 × 0.60)	$ 84,000
Padilla ($140,000 × 0.40)	56,000
Net income	$140,000

Analysis The journal entry to record each partner's share of the income

- *closes Income Summary* with a debit for the amount of net income
- ▲ *increases* each partner's capital account with a credit for their share of net income

Journal Entry

A	=	L	+	OE
				−140,000
				+84,000
				+56,000

2015		Dr.	Cr.
July 30	Income Summary	140,000	
	Lori Mind, Capital		84,000
	Rose Padilla, Capital		56,000
	Distribution of income for the year to the partners' Capital accounts		

Comment This entry illustrates the *separate entity* concept that the partners as individuals are separate from the partnership entity.

Salaries, Interest, and Stated Ratios

STUDY NOTE: *Partnership income cannot be divided solely on the basis of salaries or interest. An additional component, such as stated ratios, is needed.*

Partners generally do not contribute equally to a firm. To make up for unequal contributions, a partnership agreement can allow for partners' salaries, interest on partners' capital balances, or both in the distribution of income. Again, salaries and interest of this kind are not deducted as expenses before the partnership income is determined.

To illustrate an allowance for partners' salaries, assume that Mind and Padilla agree to annual salaries of $8,000 and $7,000, respectively, and to divide any remaining income equally between them. Each salary is charged to the appropriate partner's Withdrawals account when paid. Assuming the same $140,000 income for the first year, the calculations for Mind and Padilla follow.

	Income of Partner		Income
	Mind	Padilla	Distributed
Total income for distribution			$ 140,000
Distribution of salaries:			
Mind	$ 8,000		
Padilla		$ 7,000	(15,000)
Remaining income after salaries			$ 125,000
Equal distribution of remaining income:			
Mind ($125,000 × 0.50)	62,500		
Padilla ($125,000 × 0.50)		62,500	(125,000)
Remaining income			—
Income of partners	$70,500	$69,500	$ 140,000

Salaries allow for differences in the services that partners provide the business. However, they do not take into account the differences in invested capital. To allow for capital differences, each partner can receive, in addition to salary, a stated interest on his or her invested capital. Suppose that Lori Mind and Rose Padilla agree to annual salaries of $8,000 and $7,000, respectively, as well as 10 percent interest on their beginning capital balances. They also agreed to share any remaining income equally. The calculations for Mind and Padilla, assuming income of $140,000, follow.

	Income of Partner		Income Distributed
	Mind	Padilla	
Total income for distribution			$ 140,000
Distribution of salaries:			
Mind	$ 8,000		
Padilla		$ 7,000	(15,000)
Remaining income after salaries			$ 125,000
Distribution of interest:			
Mind ($65,000 × 0.10)	6,500		
Padilla ($60,000 × 0.10)		6,000	(12,500)
Remaining income after salaries and interest			$ 112,500
Equal distribution of remaining income:			
Mind ($112,500 × 0.50)	56,250		
Padilla ($112,500 × 0.50)		56,250	(112,500)
Remaining income			—
Income of partners	$70,750	$69,250	$ 140,000

Dissolution of a Partnership

Dissolution of a partnership occurs whenever there is a change in the original association of partners. When a partnership is dissolved, the partners lose their authority to continue the business as a *going concern*. This does not mean that the business operation necessarily is ended or interrupted. However, from a legal and accounting standpoint, the *separate entity* ceases to exist. The remaining partners can act for the partnership in finishing the affairs of the business or in forming a new partnership that will be a new accounting entity. The dissolution of a partnership takes place through, among other events, the admission of a new partner, the withdrawal of a partner, or the death of a partner.

Admission of a New Partner

The admission of a new partner dissolves the old partnership because a new association has been formed. Dissolving the old partnership and creating a new one requires the consent of all the original partners and the ratification of a new agreement.

An individual can be admitted to a partnership in one of two ways:

- Purchasing an interest in the partnership from one or more of the original partners
- Investing assets in the partnership

Purchasing an Interest from a Partner When a person purchases an interest in a partnership from an original partner, the transaction is personal between these two people. However, the interest purchased must be transferred from the Capital account of the selling partner to the Capital account of the new partner.

Purchasing All Interest from a Partner

Transaction Lori Mind decides to sell her interest of $70,000 in Mind and Padilla to Adam Novak for $100,000 on August 31, 2016. Rose Padilla agrees to the sale.

Analysis The journal entry to record this sale

▼ *decreases Lori Mind, Capital* with a debit

▲ *increases Adam Novak, Capital* with a credit

Journal Entry

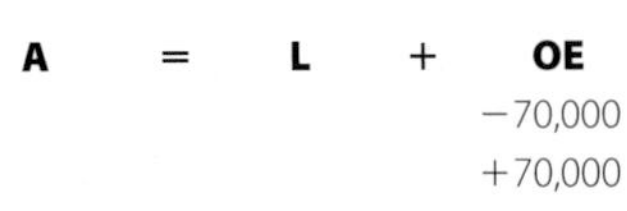

A	=	L	+	OE
				−70,000
				+70,000

2016		Dr.	Cr.
Aug. 31	Lori Mind, Capital	70,000	
	Adam Novak, Capital		70,000
	Transfer of Lori Mind's equity to Adam Novak		

Comment Notice that the entry records the book value of the equity, not the amount Novak pays. The amount Novak pays is a personal matter between Novak and Mind. Because the amount paid does not affect the assets or liabilities of the firm, it is not entered in the records.

Purchasing Partial Interest from Partners

Transaction Adam Novak purchases half of Lori Mind's $70,000 interest in the partnership and half of Rose Padilla's $80,000 interest by paying a total of $100,000 to the two partners on August 31, 2016. The assets of the firm are valued correctly.

Analysis The journal entry to record this sale

▼ *decreases Lori Mind, Capital* and *Rose Padilla, Capital* with debits

▲ *increases Adam Novak, Capital* with a credit

Journal Entry

A	=	L	+	OE
				−35,000
				−40,000
				+75,000

2012		Dr.	Cr.
Aug. 31	Lori Mind, Capital	35,000	
	Rose Padilla, Capital	40,000	
	Adam Novak, Capital		75,000
	Transfer of half of Lori Mind's and Rose Padilla's equity to Adam Novak		

Comment If the asset accounts did not reflect their current values, the asset accounts (and Capital accounts) would need to be adjusted before admitting the new partner. A new partnership *entity separate* from its partners has now been formed with three partners instead of two.

Investing Assets in a Partnership When a new partner is admitted through an investment in the partnership, both the assets and the partners' equity in the firm increase. This is because the assets the new partner invests become partnership assets, and as partnership assets increase, partners' equity increases.

New Partner Investing Assets in a Partnership

Transaction Adam Novak wants to invest $75,000 for a one-third interest in the partnership of Mind and Padilla. The Capital accounts of Lori Mind and Rose Padilla are $70,000 and $80,000, respectively. The assets of the firm are valued correctly. The partners agree to admit Novak.

Computation Novak's $75,000 investment equals a one-third interest after it is added to the previously existing capital of the partnership:

Lori Mind, Capital	$ 70,000
Rose Padilla, Capital	80,000
Novak's investment	75,000
Total capital after Novak's investment	$225,000
One-third interest = $225,000 ÷ 3 =	$ 75,000

Analysis The journal entry to record the admission of a new partner

▲ *increases Cash* with a debit

▲ *increases Adam Novak, Capital* with a credit

Journal Entry

A	=	L	+	OE
+75,000				+75,000

2016		Dr.	Cr.
Aug. 31	Cash	75,000	
	Adam Novak, Capital		75,000
	Admission of Adam Novak for a one-third interest in the company		

Comment A new partnership *entity separate* from its partners has now been formed. The cash from the new partner, Adam Novak, goes to the partnership and not to the partners. The partnership assets and partnership equity have grown by $75,000.

STUDY NOTE: *The original partners receive a bonus because the entity is worth more as a going concern than the fair market value of the net assets would otherwise indicate. That is, the new partner is paying for unrecorded partnership value.*

Bonus to the Old Partners A partnership is sometimes so profitable or otherwise advantageous that a new investor is willing to pay more than the actual dollar interest he or she receives in the partnership. For instance, suppose an individual pays $100,000 for an $80,000 interest in a partnership. The $20,000 excess of the payment over the interest purchased is a **bonus** to the original partners. The bonus must be distributed to the original partners according to the partnership agreement. When the agreement does not cover the distribution of bonuses, it should be distributed to the original partners in accordance with the method for distributing income.

Bonus to the Old Partners

Transaction Assume that Mind and Padilla's firm has operated for several years and that the partners' capital balances and the stated ratios for distribution of income are as follows.

Partners	Capital Balances	Stated Ratios
Mind	$160,000	55%
Padilla	140,000	45
	$300,000	100%

Adam Novak wants to join the firm. He offers to invest $100,000 on December 1 for a one-fifth interest in the business and income. The original partners agree to the offer.

Computation The computation of the bonus to the original partners follows.

Partners' equity in the original partnership		$300,000
Cash investment by Adam Novak		100,000
Partners' equity in the new partnership		$400,000
Partners' equity assigned to Adam Novak ($400,000 × ⅕)		$ 80,000
Bonus to the original partners:		
Investment by Adam Novak	$100,000	
Less equity assigned to Adam Novak	80,000	$ 20,000
Distribution of bonus to original partners:		
Lori Mind ($20,000 × 0.55)	$ 11,000	
Rose Padilla ($20,000 × 0.45)	9,000	$ 20,000

Analysis The journal entry to record the bonus for the existing partners

▲ *increases Cash* by $100,000 with a debit

▲ *increases* each partner's capital account with a credit

Journal Entry

A	=	L	+	OE
+100,000				+11,000
				+9,000
				+80,000

2016		Dr.	Cr.
Dec. 1	Cash	100,000	
	Lori Mind, Capital		11,000
	Rose Padilla, Capital		9,000
	Adam Novak, Capital		80,000
	Investment by Adam Novak for a one-fifth interest in the firm, and the bonus distributed to the original partners		

Comment A new partnership *entity separate* from its partners has now been formed. The partners, Lori Mind and Rose Padilla, receive an increase in their capital accounts for part of Adam Novak's contribution to the partnership. Novak's desire to join the partnership makes him willing to accept less than the share would have been if he had not paid a bonus to the other partners.

Bonus to the New Partner A partnership might want a new partner for several reasons. A partnership in financial trouble might need additional cash, or the partners might want to expand the firm's markets and need more capital. Also, the partners might know a person who would bring a unique talent to the firm. Under these conditions, a new partner may be admitted to the partnership with the understanding that part of the original partners' capital will be transferred (credited) to the new partner's Capital account as a bonus.

Bonus to the New Partner

Transaction Suppose that Lori Mind and Rose Padilla have invited Adam Novak to join the firm. Novak is going to invest $60,000 on December 1 for a one-fourth interest in the company. The stated ratios for distribution of income or loss for Mind and Padilla are 55 percent and 45 percent, respectively. If Novak is to receive a one-fourth interest in the firm, the interest of the original partners represents a three-fourths interest in the business.

Computation The computation of Novak's bonus follows.

Total equity in partnership:		
Lori Mind, Capital		$160,000
Rose Padilla, Capital		140,000
Investment by Adam Novak		60,000
Partners' equity in the new partnership		$360,000
Partners' equity assigned to Adam Novak ($360,000 × ¼)		$ 90,000
Bonus to new partner:		
Equity assigned to Adam Novak	$90,000	
Less cash investment by Adam Novak	60,000	$ 30,000
Distribution of bonus from original partners:		
Lori Mind ($30,000 × 0.55)	$16,500	
Rose Padilla ($30,000 × 0.45)	13,500	$ 30,000

Analysis The journal entry to record the bonus to the new partner

▲ *increases Cash* with a debit

▼ *decreases Lori Mind, Capital* and *Rose Padilla, Capital* with debits

▲ *increases Adam Novak, Capital* with a credit

A	=	L	+	OE
+60,000				−16,500
				−13,500
				+90,000

Journal Entry

2016		Dr.	Cr.
Dec. 1	Cash	60,000	
	Lori Mind, Capital	16,500	
	Rose Padilla, Capital	13,500	
	Adam Novak, Capital		90,000
	To record the investment by Adam Novak of cash and a bonus from Mind and Padilla		

Comment A new partnership *entity separate* from its partners has now been formed. The partners, Lori Mind and Rose Padilla, were willing to accept a decrease in their capital accounts to get Adam Novak to join the new partnership.

Withdrawal of a Partner

STUDY NOTE: *There is no impact on the income statement when a partner withdraws. The only change is on the balance sheet.*

Generally, a partner has the right to withdraw from a partnership in accord with legal requirements. However, to avoid disputes when a partner does decide to withdraw or retire from the firm, the partnership agreement should describe the procedures to be followed. The agreement should specify:

- Whether an audit will be performed
- How the assets will be reappraised
- How a bonus will be determined
- By what method the withdrawing partner will be paid

A partner who wants to withdraw from a partnership can do so in one of several ways. The partner can sell his or her interest to another partner or to an outsider, with the consent of the remaining partners, or the partner can withdraw assets equal to his or her capital balance, less than his or her capital balance (with a bonus to the remaining partners), or greater than his or her capital balance (with a bonus to the withdrawing partner). These alternatives are illustrated in Exhibit 1. Techniques of accounting for partner withdrawals are reserved for more advanced courses.

Exhibit 1
Alternative Ways for a Partner to Withdraw

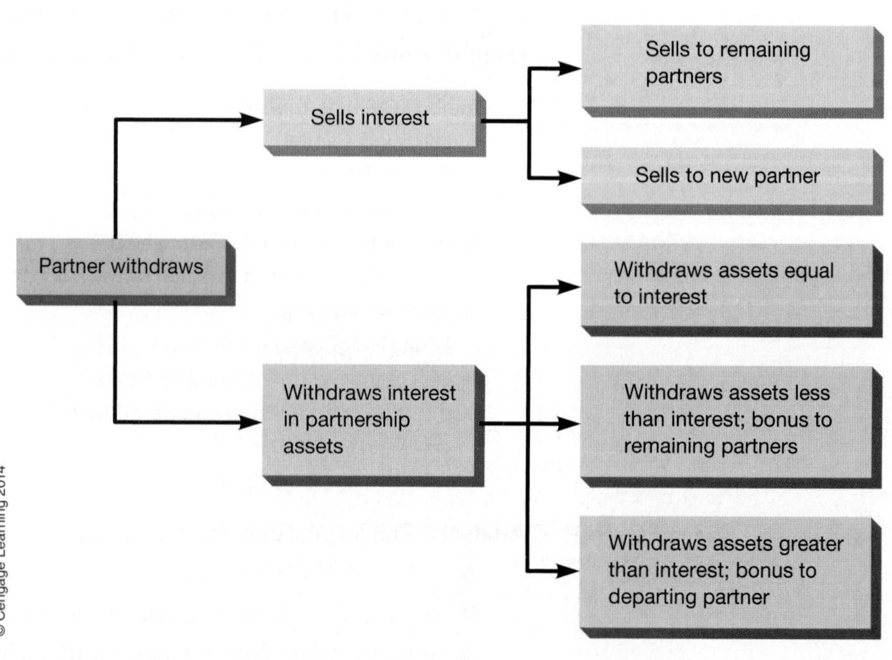

Death of a Partner

When a partner dies, the partnership is dissolved because the original association has changed. The partnership agreement should state the actions to be taken. Normally, the books are closed, and financial statements are prepared. These actions are necessary to determine the capital balance of each partner on the date of the death. The agreement may also indicate whether an audit should be conducted, assets appraised, and a bonus recorded, as well as what procedures have been established for settling with the deceased partner's heirs. The remaining partners may purchase the deceased's equity, sell it to outsiders, or deliver certain business assets to the estate. If the firm intends to continue, a new partnership must be formed.

Liquidation of a Partnership

The **liquidation** of a partnership is the process of selling enough assets to pay the partnership's liabilities and distributing any remaining assets among the partners. Liquidation is a special form of dissolution. When a partnership is liquidated, the business will not continue. As the assets of the business are sold, any gain should be distributed to the partners according to the stated ratios. As cash becomes available, it must be applied first to outside creditors, then to loans from partners, and finally to the partners' capital balances.

Key Terms

bonus 1184
dissolution 1182
limited life 1178
liquidation 1187
mutual agency 1178
partnership 1177
partnership agreement 1178
partners' equity 1179
sole proprietorship 1177
unlimited liability 1178

Assignments

DISCUSSION QUESTIONS

DQ1. How does the accounting concept of sole proprietorship differ from the legal concept?

DQ2. Even though, from an accounting standpoint, partnerships are separate entities from the partners, why is it important for people to form partnerships with people they can trust?

DQ3. When accounts receivable are transferred into a partnership, at what amount should they be recorded?

DQ4. What is a disadvantage of receiving a large salary as part of a partner's distribution?

DQ5. If the value of a partnership is worth far more than the book value of the assets on the balance sheet, would a new partner entering the partnership be more likely to pay a bonus to the old partners or receive a bonus from the old partners?

SHORT EXERCISES

Sole Proprietorship Transactions

SE1. Prepare journal entries to record the transactions for Matt Ing's sole proprietorship that follow.

1. Ing invests $5,000 in his business.
2. Ing closed his Income Summary account's credit balance of $800.
3. Ing closed his Withdrawals account's debit balance of $300.

Partnership Characteristics

SE2. Indicate whether each statement below is a reflection of (a) voluntary association, (b) a partnership agreement, (c) limited life, (d) mutual agency, or (e) unlimited liability.

1. A written contract among partners.
2. Any partner can sign a contract obligating the partnership.
3. A partner may be liable for the debts of the partnership.
4. A partnership ends when a partner is admitted, withdraws, retires, or dies.
5. A partner may leave a partnership if he or she wants to.

Partnership Formation

SE3. Martin contributes cash of $24,000, and Steven contributes office equipment that cost $20,000 but is valued at $16,000 to the formation of a new partnership. Prepare the journal entry to form the partnership.

Distribution of Partnership Income

SE4. During the first year, the Martin and Steven partnership in **SE3** earned an income of $10,000. Assume the partners agreed to share income in the ratio of the beginning balances of their capital accounts. How much income should be transferred to each Capital account?

Distribution of Partnership Income

SE5. During the first year, the Martin and Steven partnership in **SE3** earned an income of $10,000. Assume the partners agreed to share income by figuring interest on the beginning capital balances at 10 percent and dividing the remainder equally. How much income should be transferred to each Capital account?

Admission of a New Partner

SE6. After the partnership has been operating for a year, the Capital accounts of Martin and Steven are $15,000 and $10,000, respectively. Sania buys a one-fourth interest in the partnership by investing cash of $5,000. What will be the Capital account balances of the partners in the new Martin, Steven, and Sania partnership, assuming that the new partner receives a bonus and that Martin and Steven share income equally? Prepare the journal entry to record the transfer of ownership on the partnership books.

EXERCISES: SET A

Partnership Characteristics

E1A. Indicate whether each action that follows is a reflection of (a) voluntary association, (b) a partnership agreement, (c) limited life, (d) mutual agency, or (e) unlimited liability.

1. A partner signs an contract obligating the partnership.
2. A partner leaves a partnership for personal reasons.
3. A partner has to pay some of the debts of the partnership.

4. The partners write a contract among themselves.
5. A partner leaves the partnership ending the partnership.

Partnership Advantages and Disadvantages

E2A. Indicate whether each statement below is a reflection of an (a) advantage or a (b) disadvantage of the partnership form of business.

1. It is easy to form, change, and dissolve.
2. The life of a partnership is limited.
3. It gives the partners a certain amount of freedom and flexibility.
4. It is more difficult for a partnership to raise large amounts of capital and to transfer ownership interests than it is for a corporation.

Partnership Formation

E3A. Hanna Hark and Jamie Rice are watch repairmen who want to form a partnership and open a jewelry store. An attorney prepares their partnership agreement, which indicates that assets invested in the partnership will be recorded at their fair market value and that liabilities will be assumed at book value.

The assets contributed by each partner and the liabilities assumed by the partnership follow.

Assets	**Hanna Hark**	**Jamie Rice**	**Total**
Cash	$ 80,000	$60,000	$140,000
Accounts receivable	104,000	40,000	144,000
Allowance for uncollectible accounts	8,000	6,000	14,000
Supplies	2,000	1,000	3,000
Equipment	40,000	20,000	60,000
Liabilities			
Accounts payable	64,000	18,000	82,000

Prepare the journal entries necessary to record the original investments of Hark and Rice in the partnership.

Distribution of Income

E4A. Isha Shah and Brian Ruben agreed to form a partnership. Shah contributed $400,000 in cash, and Ruben contributed assets with a fair market value of $800,000. The partnership, in its initial year, reported net income of $240,000. Calculate the distribution of the first year's income to the partners under each of the following conditions:

1. Shah and Ruben failed to include stated ratios in the partnership agreement.
2. Shah and Ruben agreed to share income in a 3:2 ratio.
3. Shah and Ruben agreed to share income in the ratio of their original investments.
4. Shah and Ruben agreed to share income by allowing 10 percent interest on original investments and sharing any remainder equally.

Distribution of Income: Salaries and Interest

E5A. Assume that the partnership agreement of Shah and Ruben in **E4A** states that Shah and Ruben are to receive salaries of $40,000 and $48,000, respectively; that Shah is to receive 6 percent interest on his capital balance at the beginning of the year; and that the remainder of income and losses are to be shared equally. Calculate the distribution of the income under the following conditions:

1. Income totaled $240,000 before deductions for salaries and interest.
2. Income totaled $96,000 before deductions for salaries and interest.

Admission of a New Partner: Recording a Bonus

E6A. Gamine, Ronald, and Fenny have equity in a partnership of $80,000, $80,000, and $120,000, respectively, and they share income in a ratio of 1:1:3. The partners have agreed to admit Amit to the partnership. Prepare journal entries to record the admission of Amit to the partnership under the following conditions:

1. Amit invests $120,000 for a 20 percent interest in the partnership, and a bonus is recorded for the original partners.
2. Amit invests $120,000 for a 40 percent interest in the partnership, and a bonus is recorded for Amit.

EXERCISES: SET B

Visit the textbook companion website at www.cengagebrain.com to access Exercise Set B for this chapter.

PROBLEMS

Partnership Formation and Distribution of Income

✔ 2c: Thomas 2013 income: $67,200; Thomas 2014 income: $32,000
✔ 2d: Thomas 2013 income: $72,000; Thomas 2014 income: $28,000
✔ 2f: Thomas 2013 income: $85,200; Thomas 2014 income: $41,200

P1. In January 2013, Edi Thomas and George Lopez agreed to produce and sell chocolate candies. Thomas contributed $480,000 in cash to the business. Lopez contributed the building and equipment, valued at $440,000 and $280,000, respectively. The partnership had an income of $168,000 during 2013 but was less successful during 2014, when income was only $80,000.

REQUIRED

1. Prepare the journal entry to record the investment of both partners in the partnership.
2. Determine the share of income for each partner in 2013 and 2014 under each of the following conditions:
   a. The partners agreed to share income equally.
   b. The partners failed to agree on an income-sharing arrangement.
   c. The partners agreed to share income according to the ratio of their original investments.
   d. The partners agreed to share income by allowing interest of 10 percent on their original investments and dividing the remainder equally.
   e. The partners agreed to share income by allowing salaries of $80,000 for Thomas and $56,000 for Lopez, and dividing the remainder equally.
   f. The partners agreed to share income by paying salaries of $80,000 to Thomas and $56,000 to Lopez, allowing interest of 9 percent on their original investments, and dividing the remainder equally.
3. **ACCOUNTING CONNECTION ▶** What are some of the factors that need to be considered in choosing the plan of partners' income sharing among the options shown in requirement 2?

Distribution of Income: Salaries and Interest

SPREADSHEET

✔ 1: Chevron income: $58,400

P2. Wilkes and Chevron are partners in a tennis shop. They have agreed that Wilkes will operate the store and receive a salary of $104,000 per year. Chevron will receive 10 percent interest on his average capital balance during the year of $500,000. The remaining income or losses are to be shared by Wilkes and Chevron in a 2:3 ratio.

REQUIRED

Determine each partner's share of income under each of the following conditions. In each case, the income is stated before the distribution of salary and interest.

1. Income was $168,000.
2. Income was $88,000.

Distribution of Income: Salaries and Interest

SPREADSHEET

✔ 2: Jan income: $60,400; Pat income: $178,640; Misa income: $72,160

P3. Jan, Pat, and Misa are partners in South Central Company. The partnership agreement states that Jan is to receive 8 percent interest on his capital balance at the beginning of the year, Pat is to receive a salary of $200,000 a year, and Misa will be paid interest of 6 percent on his average capital balance during the year. Jan, Pat, and Misa will share any income or loss after salary and interest in a 5:3:2 ratio. Jan's capital balance at the beginning of the year was $1,200,000, and Misa's average capital balance for the year was $1,440,000.

REQUIRED

Determine each partner's share of income under the following conditions. In each case, the income is stated before the distribution of salary and interest.

1. Income was $1,090,400.
2. Income was $311,200.

APPENDIX B

Accounting for Investments

A company invests in the stock or debt securities of other firms for one or more of the following reasons:

- A company may temporarily have excess funds on which it can earn a return.
- Investments may be an integral part of the company's business, as in the case of a bank.
- A company may invest in other firms for the purpose of partnering with or controlling them.

Concepts and Management Issues Related to Investments

Recognition, *valuation*, *classification*, *disclosure*, and *ethics* apply to accounting for investments.

Recognition

Recognition of investments as assets follows the general rule for recording transactions described earlier in the text. Purchases of investments are recorded on the date on which they are made, and sales of investments are reported on the date of sale. At the time of the transaction, there is either a transfer of funds or a definite obligation to pay. Income from investments is reported as other income on the income statement. Any gains or losses on investments are also reported on the income statement. Gains and losses appear as adjustments in the operating activities section of the statement of cash flows. The cash amounts of purchases and sales of investments appear in the investing activities section of the statement of cash flows.

Valuation

Like other purchase transactions, investments are *valued* according to the *cost principle*—that is, their cost at the time they are purchased. This cost includes any commissions or fees. However, after the purchase, the value of investments on the balance sheet is adjusted to reflect subsequent conditions, including the following:

- Changes in the market value or fair value of the investments
- Changes caused by the passage of time (as in amortization)
- Changes in the operations of the investee companies

Long-term investments must be evaluated annually for any impairment or decline in value that is more than temporary. If such an impairment exists, a loss on the investment must be recorded.

IFRS

Under certain conditions, companies are required to measure investments at fair value. Recall that *fair value* is defined as the *exchange price* associated with an actual or potential business transaction between market participants. This requirement applies to all types of investments, except an investment in a subsidiary that is consolidated with the parent's financial statements. Fair value is not difficult to determine when there is a ready market in which there are buyers and sellers for an asset. However, if a ready market does not exist, another valuation technique must be used. For example, valuation might be determined by referring to the current fair value of another investment that is substantially the same. If that option is not available, valuation might be determined through discounted cash flow analysis.[1] Through the convergence project of the FASB and IASB, valuation practices under GAAP have come more in line with international financial reporting standards (IFRS).

Classification

Investments in debt and equity securities are *classified* as either short-term or long-term. **Short-term investments** (or *marketable securities*) have a maturity of more than 90 days but are intended to be held only until cash is needed for current operations. (As pointed out in an earlier chapter, investments with a maturity of *less* than 90 days are classified as cash equivalents.) **Long-term investments**, which are intended to be held for more than one year, are reported in the investments section of the balance sheet. Although long-term investments may be just as marketable as short-term assets, management intends to hold them for an indefinite time.

Short-term and long-term investments must be further classified as trading securities, available-for-sale securities, or held-to-maturity securities.[2]

- **Trading securities** are debt or equity securities bought and held principally for the purpose of being sold in the near term.
- **Available-for-sale securities** are debt or equity securities that do not meet the criteria for either trading or held-to-maturity securities. They may be short- or long-term, depending on what management intends to do with them.
- **Held-to-maturity securities** are debt securities that management intends to hold until their maturity date.

Exhibit 1 illustrates the classification of short- and long-term investments.

Exhibit 1
Classification of Equity Investments

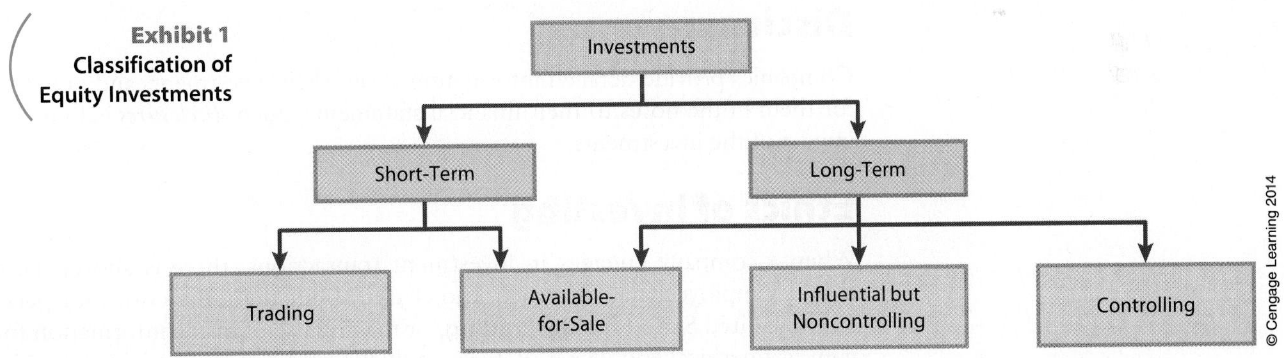

Exhibit 2 shows the accounting treatment of various levels of equity investments, that is, ownership of another company's stock. It also shows the relationship between the percentage of ownership in a company's stock and the investing company's level of control.

In general, the percentage of ownership in another company's stock has the following effects:

- **Noninfluential and noncontrolling investment:** A firm that owns less than 20 percent of the stock of another company has no influence on the other company's operations.
- **Influential but noncontrolling investment:** A firm that owns between 20 to 50 percent of another company's stock can exercise *significant influence* over that company's operating and financial policies, even though it holds 50 percent or less of

Exhibit 2
Accounting for Equity Investments

Level of Control	Percentage of Ownership	Classification	Accounting Treatment
Noninfluential and noncontrolling	Less than 20%	Short-term investments—trading securities	Recorded at cost initially; cost adjusted after purchase for changes in market value; unrealized gains and losses reported on income statement
		Short-term or long-term investments—available-for- sale securities	Recorded at cost initially; cost adjusted for changes in market value with unrealized gains and losses to other comprehensive income
Influential but noncontrolling	Between 20% and 50%	Long-term investments	Equity method: recorded at cost initially; cost subsequently adjusted for investor's share of net income or loss and for dividends received
Controlling	More than 50%	Long-term investments	Financial statements consolidated

the voting stock. Indications of significant influence include representation on the board of directors, participation in policymaking, exchange of managerial personnel, and technological dependency between the two companies.

- **Controlling investment:** A firm that owns more than 50 percent of another company's stock.

Disclosure

Companies provide detailed information about their investments and how they account for them in the notes to their financial statements. Such *disclosures* help users assess the impact of the investments.

Ethics of Investing

When a company engages in investment transactions, there is always the possibility that its employees may use their knowledge about the transactions for personal gain. In the United States, **insider trading**, or making use of inside information for personal gain, is unethical and illegal. Before a publicly held company releases significant information about an investment to its stockholders and the general public, its officers and employees are not allowed to buy or sell stock in the company or in the firm whose shares the company is buying. Only after the information is released to the public can insiders engage in such trading. The Securities and Exchange Commission vigorously prosecutes any individual, whether employed by the company in question or not, who buys or sells shares of a publicly held company based on information not yet available to the public.

Not all countries prohibit insider trading. Until recently, insider trading was legal in Germany; but with the goal of expanding its securities markets, that country reformed its securities laws. It established the Federal Authority for Securities Trading (FAST), in part to oversee insider trading. However, historically, FAST devotes few staff members to investigations of insider trading, whereas the SEC has a much larger staff for these types of investigations.[3] Other countries continue to permit insider trading.

Short-Term Investments in Trading Securities

As pointed out earlier, all trading securities are short-term investments, while available-for-sale securities may be either short-term or long-term.

Trading Securities

Trading securities are always short-term investments and are frequently bought and sold to generate profits on short-term changes in their prices. They are *classified* as current assets on the balance sheet and are *valued* at fair value, which is usually the same as market value. An increase or decrease in the fair value of a company's total trading portfolio (the group of securities it holds for trading purposes) is included in net income in the period in which the increase or decrease occurs.

Purchase of Trading Securities

Transaction Jackson Company buys 10,000 shares of **IBM** for $900,000 ($90 per share) and 10,000 shares of **Microsoft** for $300,000 ($30 per share) on October 25, 2014. The purchase is made for trading purposes—that is, Jackson's management intends to realize a gain by holding the shares for only a short period.

Analysis The journal entry to record the investment at cost

▲ *increases Short-Term Investments* with a debit for the cost of $1,200,000 ($900,000 + $300,000)

▼ *decreases Cash* with a credit of $1,200,000

Journal Entry

A	=	L	+	SE
+1,200,000				
−1,200,000				

2014			
Oct. 25	Short-Term Investments	1,200,000	
	Cash		1,200,000
	To record investment in stocks for trading ($900,000 + $300,000 = $1,200,000)		

Comment This investment is *classified* as short-term, because the intent is to resell the securities in the near future rather than to hold them for more than one year.

Year-End Valuation and Adjustment

Transaction At year-end, **IBM**'s stock price has decreased to $80 per share and **Microsoft**'s has risen to $32 per share. The trading portfolio is now *valued* at $1,120,000:

Security	Market Value	Cost	Gain (Loss)
IBM (10,000 shares)	$ 800,000	$ 900,000	$(100,000)
Microsoft (10,000 shares)	320,000	300,000	20,000
Totals	$1,120,000	$1,200,000	$ (80,000)

Analysis Because the current fair value of the portfolio is $80,000 less than the original cost of $1,200,000, an *unrealized loss* has occurred. The journal entry to record the year-end adjustment

▲ *increases Unrealized Loss on Short-Term Investments* with a debit for the cost of $80,000

▲ *increases Allowance to Adjust Short-Term Investments to Market* with a credit of $80,000

Journal Entry

A	=	L	+	SE
−80,000				−80,000

2014			
Dec. 31	Unrealized Loss on Short-Term Investments	80,000	
	Allowance to Adjust Short-Term Investments to Market		80,000
	To record unrealized loss on trading portfolio		

STUDY NOTE: *The Allowance to Adjust Short-Term Investments to Market account is never changed when securities are sold. It changes only when an adjusting entry is made at year-end.*

Comment The unrealized loss will appear on the income statement as a reduction in income. The loss is unrealized because the securities have not been sold. If unrealized gains occur due to the increase in *value* of the portfolio, they are treated the same way.

The Allowance to Adjust Short-Term Investments to Market account appears on the balance sheet as a contra-asset, as follows.

Short-term investments (at cost)	$1,200,000
Less allowance to adjust short-term investments to market	80,000
Short-term investments (at market)	$1,120,000

Or, more simply:

Short-term investments (at market value, cost is $1,200,000)	$1,120,000

Sale of Trading Securities

Transaction Jackson sells its 10,000 shares of **Microsoft** for $35 per share on March 2, 2015.

Analysis The journal entry to record a realized gain on trading securities

- ▲ *increases Cash* with a debit for the selling price of $350,000
- ▼ *decreases Short-Term Investments* with a credit of $300,000
- ▲ *increases Gain on Sale of Investments* with a credit for the difference of $50,000

Journal Entry

A	=	L	+	SE
+350,000				+50,000
−300,000				

2015			
Mar. 2	Cash	350,000	
	Short-Term Investments		300,000
	Gain on Sale of Investments		50,000
	To record sale of 10,000 shares of Microsoft for $35 per share; cost was $30 per share		

Comment The realized gain will appear on the income statement. The realized gain is unaffected by the adjustment for the unrealized loss at the end of 2014. The two transactions are treated independently. If the stock had been sold for less than cost, a realized loss on investments would have been recorded. Realized losses also appear on the income statement.

Year-End Valuation and Adjustment

Transaction During 2015, Jackson buys 4,000 shares of **Apple** at $32 per share and has no transactions involving its shares of **IBM**. By December 31, 2015, the price of IBM's stock has risen to $95 per share, or $5 per share more than the original cost, and Apple's stock price has fallen to $29, or $3 less than the original cost. We can now analyze Jackson's trading portfolio as follows.

Security	Market Value	Cost	Gain (Loss)
IBM (10,000 shares)	$ 950,000	$ 900,000	$ 50,000
Apple (4,000 shares)	116,000	128,000	(12,000)
Totals	$1,066,000	$1,028,000	$ 38,000

Analysis The market value of Jackson's trading portfolio now exceeds the cost by \$38,000 (\$1,066,000 − \$1,028,000). This amount represents the targeted ending balance for the Allowance to Adjust Short-Term Investments to Market account. Recall that at the end of 2014, that account had a credit balance of \$80,000, meaning that the market value of the trading portfolio was less than the cost. Because no entries are made to the account during 2015, it retains its balance until adjusting entries are made at the end of the year. The adjustment for 2015 must be \$118,000—enough to result in a debit balance of \$38,000 in the allowance account. The journal entry to record the year-end adjustment

▼ *decreases Allowance to Adjust Short-Term Investments to Market* with a debit of \$118,000

▲ *increases Unrealized Gain on Short-Term Investments* with a credit of \$118,000

Journal Entry

A	=	L	+	SE
+118,000				+118,000

		Dr.	Cr.
2015			
Dec. 31	Allowance to Adjust Short-Term Investments to Market	118,000	
	Unrealized Gain on Short-Term Investments		118,000
	To record unrealized gain on trading portfolio (\$80,000 + \$38,000 = \$118,000)		

Comment The 2015 ending balance of Jackson's allowance account can be determined as follows.

Allowance to Adjust Short-Term Investments to Market			
Dec. 31, 2015 Adj.	118,000	Dec. 31, 2014 Bal.	80,000
Dec. 31, 2015 Bal.	38,000		

Short-term investments are presented on the balance sheet as follows.

Short-term investments (at cost)	\$1,028,000
Plus allowance to adjust short-term investments to market	38,000
Short-term investments (at market)	\$1,066,000

Or, more simply:

Short-term investments (at market value, cost is \$1,028,000)	\$1,066,000

Available-for-Sale Securities

Short-term available-for-sale securities are accounted for in the same way as trading securities, with two exceptions:

- An unrealized gain or loss is reported as other comprehensive income (loss).
- If a decline in the value of a security is considered permanent, it is charged as a loss on the income statement.

Long-Term Investments in Equity Securities

The accounting treatment of long-term investments in equity securities, such as common stock, depends on the extent to which the investing company can exercise control over the other company.

Noninfluential and Noncontrolling Investment

As noted earlier, available-for-sale securities are debt or equity securities that cannot be *classified* as trading or held-to-maturity securities. When long-term equity securities are involved, a further criterion for classifying them as available for sale is that they be non-influential and noncontrolling investments of less than 20 percent of the voting stock. Accounting for long-term available-for-sale securities requires using the **cost-adjusted-to-market method**. With this method, the securities are initially recorded at cost and are thereafter adjusted periodically for changes in market value by using an allowance account.[4]

Available-for-sale securities are *classified* as long term if management *intends* to hold them for more than one year. When accounting for long-term available-for-sale securities, the unrealized gain or loss resulting from the adjustment is reported as other comprehensive income (loss).

At the end of each accounting period, the total cost and the total market value of these long-term investments must be determined. If the total market value is less than the total cost, the difference must be credited to a contra-asset account called Allowance to Adjust Long-Term Investments to Market. Because of the long-term nature of the investment, the debit part of the entry, which represents a decrease in value below cost, is treated as a temporary decrease and does not appear as a loss on the income statement. It is shown in an account called Unrealized Loss on Long-Term Investments.* This account is reported on a statement of other comprehensive income. If the market value exceeds the cost, the allowance account is added to Long-Term Investments, and the unrealized gain appears on the statement of other comprehensive income.

When a company sells its long-term investments in stock, the difference between the sale price and the cost of the stock is recorded and reported as a realized gain or loss on the income statement. Dividend income from such investments is recorded by a debit to Cash and a credit to Dividend Income.

In the sections that follow, we show how to account for Nardini Corporation's purchase and sale of long-term investments in equity securities of two corporations—Herald and Taza.

Purchase of a Long-Term Investment

Transaction On June 1, 2014, Nardini Corporation paid cash for the following long-term investments: 10,000 shares of Herald Corporation common stock (representing 2 percent of outstanding stock) at $25 per share; 5,000 shares of Taza Corporation common stock (representing 3 percent of outstanding stock) at $15 per share.

Analysis The journal entry to record the investment at cost

▲ *increases Long-Term Investments* with a debit of $325,000

▼ *decreases Cash* with a credit of $325,000

Journal Entry

A	=	L	+	SE
+325,000				
−325,000				

2014			
June 1	Long-Term Investments	325,000	
	Cash		325,000
	To record investments in Herald common stock (10,000 shares × $25 = $250,000) and Taza common stock (5,000 shares × $15 = $75,000)		

* If the decrease in market value of a long-term investment is deemed permanent or if the investment is deemed impaired, the decline or impairment is recorded by debiting a loss account that will affect the income statement instead of the Unrealized Loss account.

Comment These investments are *classified* as long term because of management's intent to hold them more than one year.

Year-End Adjustment

Transaction At the end of 2014, the market price of Herald's common stock is $21; the market price of Taza's is $17.

Analysis Nardini Corporation's trading portfolio is now *valued* at $295,000:

Company	Shares	Market Price	Total Market	Total Cost
Herald	10,000	$21	$210,000	$250,000
Taza	5,000	17	85,000	75,000
			$295,000	$325,000

Because the current fair value of the portfolio is $30,000 less than the original cost of $325,000, an *unrealized* loss has occurred. The journal entry to record the year-end adjustment

▲ *increases Unrealized Loss on Long-Term Investments* with a debit of $30,000

▲ *increases Allowance to Adjust Long-Term Investments to Market* with a credit of $30,000

Journal Entry

A	=	L	+	SE
−30,000				−30,000

		Debit	Credit
2014			
Dec. 31	Unrealized Loss on Long-Term Investments	30,000	
	Allowance to Adjust Long-Term Investments to Market		30,000
	To record reduction of long-term investment to market		

Comment As noted previously, the Unrealized Loss on Long-Term Investments does not appear on the income statement but appears on the statement of other comprehensive income. The Allowance to Adjust Long-Term Investments to Market is a contra-asset account that reduces investments on the balance sheet.

Sale of a Long-Term Investment

Transaction On April 1, 2015, a change in policy required the sale of 2,000 shares of Herald common stock at $23.

Analysis The journal entry to record this sale

▲ *increases Cash* with a debit for the selling price of $46,000

▲ *increases Loss on Sale of Investments* with a debit of $4,000

▼ *decreases Long-Term Investments* with a credit of $50,000

Journal Entry

A	=	L	+	SE
+46,000				−4,000
−50,000				

		Debit	Credit
2015			
Apr. 1	Cash	46,000	
	Loss on Sale of Investments	4,000	
	Long-Term Investments*		50,000
	To record sale of 2,000 shares of Herald common stock		

*2,000 × $23 =	$46,000
2,000 × $25 =	50,000
Loss	$ 4,000

Comment Nardini's sale of stock was the result of a change in policy. This illustrates that *intent* is often the only difference between long-term investments and short-term investments.

Cash Dividend Received

Transaction On July 1, 2015, Nardini received a cash dividend from Taza equal to $0.20 per share.

Analysis The journal entry to record the cash dividend received

▲ *increases Cash* with a debit of $1,000 ($0.20 × 5,000 shares)

▲ *increases Dividend Income* with a credit of $1,000

Journal Entry

A	=	L	+	SE
+1,000				+1,000

2015			
July 1	Cash	1,000	
	Dividend Income		1,000
	To record receipt of cash dividend from Taza stock (5,000 × $0.20 = $1,000)		

Comment Dividend Income is *classified* on the income statement as other income below operating income.

Year-End Adjustment

Transaction At the end of 2015, the market price of Herald's common stock was $24; the market price of Taza's was $13.

Analysis The trading portfolio is now *valued* at $257,000:

Company	Shares	Market Price	Total Market	Total Cost
Herald	8,000	$24	$192,000	$200,000
Taza	5,000	13	65,000	75,000
			$257,000	$275,000

The adjustment will equal the previous balance ($30,000 from the December 31, 2014, entry) minus the new balance ($18,000), or $12,000. The new balance of $18,000 is the difference at the present time between the total market value and the total cost of all investments ($257,000). The journal entry to record the year-end adjustment

▲ *increases Allowance to Adjust Long-Term Investments to Market* with a debit of $12,000

▼ *decreases Unrealized Loss on Long-Term Investments* with a credit of $12,000

Journal Entry

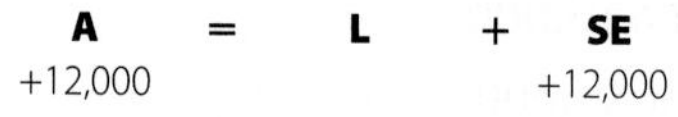

2015			
Dec. 31	Allowance to Adjust Long-Term Investments to Market	12,000	
	Unrealized Loss on Long-Term Investments		12,000
	To record the adjustment in long-term investment so it is reported at market		

Comment Even though the portfolio increased in value from last year, it did not result in a credit to unrealized gain. It reduced the unrealized loss from last year. Only if the entire unrealized loss had been eliminated would an unrealized gain be recorded for the difference.

Also, the Allowance to Adjust Long-Term Investments to Market and the Unrealized Loss on Long-Term Investments are reciprocal accounts, each with the same dollar balance:

▼ The *Allowance* account *reduces* long-term investments by the amount by which the cost of the investments exceeds market.

▼ The *Unrealized Loss* account *reduces* other comprehensive income by a similar amount.

The effects of these transactions on T accounts are as follows.

Allowance to Adjust Long-Term Investments to Market (A Contra-Asset Account)

Dec. 31, 2015 Adj.	12,000	Dec. 31, 2014 Bal.	30,000
		Dec. 31, 2015 Bal.	18,000

Unrealized Loss on Long-Term Investments (A Contra-Equity Account)

Dec. 31, 2014 Bal.	30,000	Dec. 31, 2015 Adj.	12,000
Dec. 31, 2015 Bal.	18,000		

The opposite effects will exist if market value exceeds cost, resulting in an unrealized gain.

An Influential but Noncontrolling Investment

As noted, ownership of 20 percent or more of a company's voting stock is considered sufficient to influence the company's operations. When that is the case, the **equity method** should be used to account for the stock investment. The equity method presumes that an investment of 20 percent or more is not a passive investment and that the investor should therefore share proportionately in the success or failure of the company. The three main features of this method are as follows.

- The investor records the original purchase of the stock at cost.
- The investor records its share of the company's periodic net income as an increase in the Investment account, with a corresponding credit to an income account. Similarly, it records its share of a periodic loss as a decrease in the Investment account, with a corresponding debit to a loss account.
- When the investor receives a cash dividend, the Cash account is increased, and the Investment account is decreased.

In the sections that follow, we use the equity method to account for ITO Corporation's purchase and sale of long-term investments in equity securities.

Purchase of an Equity Investment

Transaction On January 1 2014, ITO Corporation acquired 40 percent of Quay Corporation's voting common stock for $180,000.

Analysis The journal entry to record the investment at cost

▲ *increases Investment in Quay Corporation* with a debit of $180,000

▼ *decreases Cash* with a credit of $180,000

Journal Entry

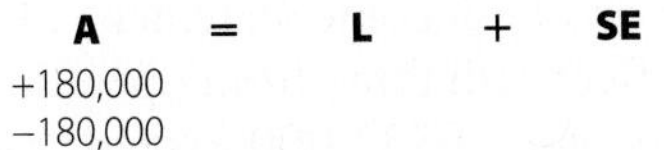

2014			
Jan. 1	Investment in Quay Corporation	180,000	
	Cash		180,000
	To record investment in Quay Corporation common stock for a 40 percent ownership		

Comment This entry is similar to the entries made for other investments, but note that with a 40 percent share of ownership, ITO can exert significant influence over Quay's operations.

Recognition of Income

Transaction On December 31, 2014, Quay reported income of $80,000.

Analysis Because ITO can exert significant influence over Quay, 40 percent of Quay's earnings, or $32,000 (40% × $80,000), is considered to be ITO's. The journal entry to recognize income

▲ *increases Investment in Quay Corporation* with a debit of $32,000

▲ *increases Income, Quay Corporation Investment* with a credit of $32,000

Journal Entry

A	=	L	+	SE
+32,000				+32,000

2014			
Dec. 31	Investment in Quay Corporation	32,000	
	Income, Quay Corporation Investment		32,000
	To record 40% of income reported by Quay Corporation (40% × $80,000 = $32,000)		

Comment Note that ITO's share of Quay's income will appear on ITO's income statement.

Receipt of Cash Dividend

Transaction Quay paid cash dividends of $8,000 on December 31, 2014.

Analysis Because ITO can exert significant influence over Quay, the amount of the cash dividend, or $8,000 (40% × $20,000), received from Quay is considered a reduction of ITO's investment in Quay. The journal entry to record the dividend

▲ *increases Cash* with a debit of $8,000

▼ *decreases Investment in Quay Corporation* with a credit of $8,000

Journal Entry

A	=	L	+	SE
+8,000				
−8,000				

2014			
Dec. 31	Cash	8,000	
	Investment in Quay Corporation		8,000
	To record cash dividend from Quay Corporation (40% × $20,000 = $8,000)		

Comment The balance of the Investment in Quay Corporation account after these transactions is $204,000, as follows.

Investment in Quay Corporation			
Jan. 1, 2014 Investment	180,000	Dec. 31, 2014 Dividend received	8,000
Dec. 31, 2014 Share of income	32,000		
Dec. 31, 2014 Balance	204,000		

The share of income is reported as a separate line item on the income statement as a part of income from operations. The dividends received affect cash flows from operating activities on the statement of cash flows. The reported income of $32,000 exceeds the cash received by $24,000.

A Controlling Investment

Some firms that own less than 50 percent of another company's voting stock exercise such powerful influence that, for all practical purposes, they control the other company's policies. Nevertheless, ownership of more than 50 percent of the voting stock is required for accounting recognition of control. When a firm has a controlling interest in another company, a parent-subsidiary relationship is said to exist. The investing company is the **parent company**; the other company is a **subsidiary**.

Because a parent company and its subsidiaries are separate legal entities, each prepares separate financial statements. However, because of their special relationship, they are viewed for external financial reporting purposes as a single economic entity. For this reason, the FASB requires that they combine their financial statements into a single set of statements called **consolidated financial statements**.**

Investments in Debt Securities

As noted in previous chapters, debt securities are considered financial instruments because they are claims that will be paid in cash. When a company purchases debt securities, it records them at cost plus any commissions and fees. Like investments in equity securities, short-term investments in debt securities are *valued* at fair value at the end of the period and are accounted for as trading securities or available-for-sale securities. However, the accounting treatment is different if they qualify as held-to-maturity securities.

Held-to-Maturity Securities

As noted earlier, held-to-maturity securities are debt securities that management intends to hold to their maturity date. Such securities are recorded at cost and are *valued* on the balance sheet at cost adjusted for the effects of interest. In the sections that follow, we show how to account for the purchase and sale of investments in debt securities for Webber Company.

Purchase of Held-to-Maturity Securities

Transaction On December 1, 2014, Webber Company pays $97,000 for U.S. Treasury bills, which are short-term debt of the federal government. The bills will mature in 120 days at $100,000.

Analysis Webber would record the purchase much as it would other short-term investments. Thus, the journal entry to record the investment at cost

▲ *increases Short-Term Investments* with a debit for the cost of $97,000

▼ *decreases Cash* with a credit for $97,000

Journal Entry

A	=	L	+	SE
+97,000				
−97,000				

2014			
Dec. 1	Short-Term Investments	97,000	
	Cash		97,000
	To record purchase of U.S. Treasury bills that mature in 120 days		

Comment If the maturity date of the treasury bills were less than 90 days, they would be *classified* as cash equivalents, rather than short-term investments.

Year-End Accrual of Interest

Transaction At Webber's year-end on December 31, the interest income earned to date must be accrued in an adjusting entry.

Analysis The journal entry to record the year-end adjustment

▲ *increases Short-Term Investments* with a debit for the accrued interest of $750 ($3,000 × 30/120)

▲ *increases Interest Income* with a credit for $750

**The concepts and procedures related to the preparation of consolidated financial statements are the subject of more advanced courses.

Journal Entry

A	=	L	+	SE
+750				+750

2014			
Dec. 31	Short-Term Investments	750	
	Interest Income		750
	To record accrual of interest on U.S. Treasury bills ($3,000 × 30/120 = $750)		

Comment On December 31, the U.S. Treasury bills would be shown on the balance sheet as a short-term investment at their amortized cost of $97,750 ($97,000 + $750). The market *value* of the investment is ignored.

Receipt of Interest

Transaction On March 31, 2015, Webber receives the maturity value of the treasury notes.

Analysis The journal entry to record the receipt of interest

- ▲ *increases Cash* with a debit for the maturity value of $100,000
- ▼ *decreases Short-Term Investments* with a credit for $97,750
- ▲ *increases Interest Income* by a credit of the difference of $2,250

Journal Entry

A	=	L	+	SE
+100,000				+2,250
−97,750				

2015			
Mar. 31	Cash	100,000	
	Short-Term Investments		97,750
	Interest Income		2,250
	To record receipt of cash at maturity of U.S. Treasury bills and recognition of related income		

Comment Note that the total interest income of $3,000 has been divided into the amount earned in 2014 ($750) and the amount earned in 2015 ($2,250). There is no gain or loss on the transaction.

Long-Term Investments in Bonds

Like all investments, investments in bonds are recorded at cost, which, in this case, is the price of the bonds plus the broker's commission. When bonds are purchased between interest payment dates, the purchaser must also pay an amount equal to the interest that has accrued on the bonds since the last interest payment date. Then, on the next interest payment date, the purchaser receives an interest payment for the whole period. The payment for accrued interest should be recorded as a debit to Interest Income, which will be offset by a credit to Interest Income when the semiannual interest is received.

Subsequent accounting for a corporation's long-term bond investments depends on the *classification* of the bonds. If the company plans to hold the bonds until they are paid off on their maturity date, they are considered held-to-maturity securities. Except in industries like insurance and banking, it is unusual for companies to buy the bonds of other companies with the express purpose of holding them until they mature, which can be in 10 to 30 years. Thus, most long-term bond investments are classified as available-for-sale securities, meaning that the company plans to sell them at some point before their maturity date. Such bonds are accounted for at fair value, much as equity or stock investments are. Fair value is usually the market value. When bonds are intended to be held to maturity, they are accounted for not at fair value but at cost, adjusted for the amortization of their discount or premium. The procedure is similar to accounting for long-term bond liabilities, except that separate accounts for discounts and premiums are not used.

Key Terms

available-for-sale securities 1193
consolidated financial statements 1203
controlling investment 1194
cost-adjusted-to-market method 1198
equity method 1201
held-to-maturity securities 1193
influential but noncontrolling investment 1193
insider trading 1194
long-term investments 1193
noninfluential and noncontrolling investment 1193
parent company 1203
short-term investments 1193
subsidiary 1203
trading securities 1193

Chapter Assignments

DISCUSSION QUESTIONS

1. What is the role of fair value in accounting for investments?

2. What are the differences between trading securities, available-for-sale securities, and held-to-maturity securities?

3. Why are the level and percentage of ownership important in accounting for equity investments?

4. How are trading securities valued at the balance sheet date?

5. What are unrealized gains and losses on trading securities? On what statement are they reported?

6. How does accounting for available-for-sale securities differ from accounting for trading securities?

7. At what value are held-to-maturity securities shown on the balance sheet?

PROBLEMS

Trading Securities

✔ 2: Total cost: $408,000
✔ 2: Total market: $442,000

P1. Omar Corporation, which has begun investing in trading securities, engaged in the following transactions:

Jan. 6 Purchased 7,000 shares of Quaker Oats stock, $30 per share.
Feb. 15 Purchased 9,000 shares of EG&G, $22 per share.

At year-end on June 30, Quaker Oats was trading at $40 per share, and EG&G was trading at $18 per share.

REQUIRED

1. Prepare journal entries to record the purchases.
2. Record the necessary year-end adjusting entry. (Include a schedule of the trading portfolio cost and market in the explanation.)
3. Prepare the journal entry to record the sale of all the EG&G shares on August 20 for $16 per share. Is this entry affected by the June 30 adjustment?

Methods of Accounting for Long-Term Investments

P2. L Teague Corporation has the following long-term investments:

Investment	Percentage of Ownership
1. Ariel Corporation common stock	60%
2. Copper, Inc., common stock	13%
3. Staffordshire Corporation nonvoting preferred stock	50%
4. EQ, Inc., common stock	100%
5. Rue de le Brasseur (of France) common stock	35%
6. Nova Scotia Cannery (of Canada) common stock	70%

REQUIRED

For each of these investments, tell which of the following methods should be used for external financial reporting, and why:

a. Cost-adjusted-to-market method
b. Equity method
c. Consolidation of parent and subsidiary financial statements

Long-Term Investments

✔ Total unrealized loss: $60,000

P3. Fulco Corporation has the following portfolio of long-term available-for-sale securities at year-end, December 31, 2014:

Company	Percentage of Voting Stock Held	Cost	Year-End Market Value
A Corporation	4%	$ 80,000	$ 95,000
B Corporation	12%	375,000	275,000
C Corporation	5%	30,000	55,000
Total		$485,000	$425,000

Both the Unrealized Loss on Long-Term Investments account and the Allowance to Adjust Long-Term Investments to Market account currently have a balance of $40,000 from the last accounting period.

REQUIRED

Prepare T accounts with a beginning balance for each of these accounts. Record the effects of the above information on the accounts, and determine the ending balances.

Long-Term Investments: Cost-Adjusted-to-Market and Equity Methods

✔ Value of Curry: $2,045,000

P4. On January 1, Rourke Corporation purchased, as long-term investments, 8 percent of the voting stock of Taglia Corporation for $250,000 and 45 percent of the voting stock of Curry Corporation for $2 million. During the year, Taglia had earnings of $100,000 and paid dividends of $40,000. Curry had earnings of $300,000 and paid dividends of $200,000. The market value did not change for either investment during the year.

REQUIRED

Which of these investments should be accounted for using the cost-adjusted-to-market method? Which should be accounted for using the equity method? At what amount should each investment be carried on the balance sheet at year-end? Give your reasoning for each choice.

Held-to-Maturity Securities

SPREADSHEET

✔ 2014 Interest Income: $2,000

P5. Dale Company experiences heavy sales in the summer and early fall, after which time it has excess cash to invest until the next spring. On November 1, 2014, the company invested $194,000 in U.S. Treasury bills. The bills mature in 180 days at $200,000.

REQUIRED

Prepare journal entries to record the purchase on November 1; the adjustment to accrue interest on December 31, which is the end of the fiscal year; and the receipt of cash at the maturity date of April 30, 2015.

Comprehensive: Accounting for Investments

SPREADSHEET

✔ 2: Adjustment to decrease investments: $7,200,000

P6. Gulf Coast Corporation is a successful oil and gas exploration business in the southwestern United States. At the beginning of 2014, the company made investments in three companies that perform services in the oil and gas industry. The details of each of these investments follow.

Gulf Coast purchased 100,000 shares of Marsh Service Corporation at a cost of $16 per share. Marsh has 1.5 million shares outstanding and, during 2014, paid dividends of $0.80 per share on earnings of $1.60 per share. At the end of the year, Marsh's shares were selling for $24 per share.

Gulf Coast also purchased 2 million shares of Crescent Drilling Company at $8 per share. Crescent has 10 million shares outstanding. In 2014, Crescent paid a dividend of $0.40 per share on earnings of $0.80 per share. During the year, the president of Gulf Coast was appointed to Crescent's board of directors. At the end of the year, Crescent's stock was selling for $12 per share.

In another action, Gulf Coast purchased 1 million shares of Logan Oil Field Supplies Company's 5 million outstanding shares at $12 per share. The president of Gulf Coast sought membership on Logan's board of directors but was rebuffed when a majority of shareholders stated they did not want to be associated with Gulf Coast. Logan paid a dividend of $0.80 per share and reported a net income of only $0.40 per share for the year. By the end of the year, its stock price had dropped to $4 per share.

REQUIRED

1. For each investment, prepare journal entries to record the (a) initial investment, (b) receipt of cash dividend, and (c) recognition of income (if appropriate).
2. What adjusting entry (if any) is required at the end of the year?
3. Assuming that Gulf Coast sells its investment in Logan after the first of the year for $6 per share, what journal entry would be made?
4. Assuming no other transactions occur and that the market value of Gulf Coast's investment in Marsh exceeds cost by $2,400,000 at the end of the second year, what adjusting entry (if any) would be required?
5. What principal factors were considered in determining how to account for Gulf Coast's investments? Should they be shown on the balance sheet as short-term or long-term investments? What factors affect this decision?

Long-Term Investments: Equity Method

✔ 1: Ending balance: $734,000

P7. Rylander Corporation owns 35 percent of the voting stock of Waters Corporation. The Investment account on Rylander's books as of January 1, 2014, was $720,000. During 2014, Waters reported the following quarterly earnings and dividends:

Quarter	Earnings	Dividends Paid
1	$160,000	$100,000
2	240,000	100,000
3	120,000	100,000
4	(80,000)	100,000
	$440,000	$400,000

Because of the percentage of voting shares Rylander owns, it can exercise significant influence over Waters' operations. Therefore, Rylander must account for the investment using the equity method.

REQUIRED

1. Prepare a T account for Rylander's investment in Waters, and enter the beginning balance, the relevant entries for the year in total, and the ending balance.
2. What is the effect and placement of the entries in requirement 1 on Rylander's earnings as reported on the income statement?
3. What is the effect and placement of the entries in requirement 1 on the statement of cash flows?
4. How would the effects on the statements differ if Rylander's ownership represented only a 15 percent share of Waters?

APPENDIX C

The Time Value of Money

The **time value of money** is the concept that cash flows of equal dollar amounts separated by an interval of time have different present values because of the effect of compound interest. The notions of interest, present value, present value of an ordinary annuity, and annuity due are all related to the time value of money.

Interest

STUDY NOTE: Interest is a cost associated with the passage of time, whether or not there is a stated interest rate.

Interest is the cost associated with the use of money for a specific period of time.

Simple Interest

Measure **Simple interest** is the interest cost for one or more periods when the amount on which the interest is computed stays the same from period to period.

Example If you accept an 8 percent, $30,000 note due in 90 days, how much will you receive in total when the note comes due?

$$\begin{aligned}\text{Interest Expense} &= \text{Principal} \times \text{Rate} \times \text{Time}\\ &= \$30{,}000 \times 8/100 \times 90/360\\ &= \underline{\underline{\$600}}\end{aligned}$$

The total that you will receive is computed as follows.

$$\begin{aligned}\text{Total} &= \text{Principal} + \text{Interest}\\ &= \$30{,}000 + \$600\\ &= \underline{\underline{\$30{,}600}}\end{aligned}$$

Compound Interest

Measure **Compound interest** is the interest cost for two or more periods when the amount on which interest is computed includes all interest paid in previous periods.

Example You make a deposit of $5,000 in a savings account that pays 6 percent interest. You expect to leave the principal and accumulated interest in the account for three years. What will be your account balance at the end of the three years? Assuming that the interest is paid at the end of the year, that the interest is added to the principal at that time, and that this total in turn earns interest, the amount at the end of three years is computed as follows.

(1) Year	(2) Principal Amount at Beginning of Year	(3) Annual Amount of Interest (Col. 2 × 0.06)	(4) Accumulated Amount at End of Year (Col. 2 + Col. 3)
1	$5,000.00	$300.00	$5,300.00
2	5,300.00	318.00	5,618.00
3	5,618.00	337.08	5,955.08

At the end of three years, you will have $5,955.08 in your savings account.

Present Value

Present Value

Measure **Present value** is the amount that must be invested today at a given rate of compound interest to produce a given value at a future date.

Example Home State Bank needs $1,000 one year from now. How much should it invest today to achieve that goal if the interest rate is 5 percent?

Present Value × (1.0 + Interest Rate) = Future Value
Present Value × 1.05 = $1,000.00
Present Value = $1,000.00 ÷ 1.05
= $952.38*

*Rounded

Thus, to achieve a future value of $1,000.00, a present value of $952.38 must be invested. Interest of 5 percent on $952.38 for one year equals $47.62, and the two amounts added together equal $1,000.00.

Present Value of a Single Sum Due in the Future

Measure Present value that must be invested today at a given rate of compound interest to produce a given value at a date multiple time periods in the future.

Example Home State Bank wants to be sure of having $4,000 at the end of three years. How much must the company invest today in a 5 percent savings account to achieve that goal?

Manual Computation By adapting the preceding equation, the present value of $4,000 at compound interest of 5 percent for three years in the future may be computed as follows.

Year	Amount at End of Year	÷	1.0 + Interest Rate	=	Present Value at Beginning of Year
3	$4,000.00	÷	1.05	=	$3,809.52
2	3,809.52	÷	1.05	=	3,628.11
1	3,628.11	÷	1.05	=	3,455.34

Home State Bank must invest a present value of $3,455.34 to achieve a future value of $4,000 in three years.

Table Computation Table 1 is used to compute the value today of a single amount of cash to be received sometime in the future. To use Table 1, you must first know (1) the time period in years until funds will be received, (2) the stated annual rate of interest, and (3) the dollar amount to be received at the end of the time period.

In Table 1, look down the 5 percent column, finding the row for period 3. The factor there is 0.864. Multiplied by $1, this factor gives the present value of $1 to be received three years from now at 5 percent interest. For Home State Bank, the present value would be solved as follows.

Present Value = Future Value × Present Value Factor
= $4,000 × 0.864
= $3,456

Except for a rounding difference of $0.66, this gives the same result as the previous calculation.

The factor values for Table 1 are:

$$\text{PV Factor} = (1 + r)^{-n}$$

Where r is the rate of interest and n is the number of time periods.

Present Value of an Ordinary Annuity

STUDY NOTE: *The first payment of an ordinary annuity is always made at the end of the first year.*

Measure When we calculate the present value of equal amounts equally spaced over a period of time, we are computing the present value of an ordinary annuity. An **ordinary annuity** is a series of equal payments or receipts that will begin one time period from the current date.

Example Home State Bank has sold a piece of property and is to receive $15,000 in three equal annual cash payments of $5,000, beginning one year from today. What is the present value of this sale, assuming a current interest rate of 5 percent?

Manual Computation This present value can be determined by calculating a separate present value for each of the three payments (using Table 1) and summing the results, as follows.

Future Cash Receipts (Annuity)

Year 1	Year 2	Year 3		Present Value Factor at 5 Percent (from Table 1)		Present Value
$5,000			×	0.952	=	$ 4,760
	$5,000		×	0.907	=	4,535
		$5,000	×	0.864	=	4,320
Total present value						$13,615

The present value of this sale is $13,615. Thus, there is an implied interest cost (given the 5 percent rate) of $1,385 associated with the payment plan that allows the purchaser to pay in three installments.

Table Computation Table 2 is used to compute the present value of a *series* of *equal* annual cash flows. Using Table 2, look down the 5 percent column, finding the row for period 3. The factor there is 2.723. That factor, when multiplied by $1, gives the present value of a series of three $1 payments, spaced one year apart, at compound interest of 5 percent. For Home State Bank, the present value would be solved as follows.

Present Value = Periodic Payment × Present Value Factor
= $5,000 × 2.723
= $13,615

This result is the same as the one computed earlier.

The factor values for Table 2 are:

$$\text{PV Factor} = \frac{1-(1+r)^{-n}}{r}$$

Where r is the rate of interest and n is the number of time periods.

To summarize, if Home State Bank is willing to accept a 5 percent rate of return, management will be equally satisfied to receive a single cash payment of $13,615 today or three equal annual cash payments of $5,000 spread over the next three years.

Present Value of an Annuity Due

Measure An **annuity due** is a series of equal cash flows for N time periods, but the first payment occurs immediately. The present value of the first payment equals the face value of the cash flow; Table 2 then is used to measure the present value of N − 1 remaining cash flows.

Table Computation Home State Bank will make 20 lease payments; each payment of $10,000 is due on January 1, beginning in 2014. Determine the present value on January 1, 2014, assuming an interest rate of 8 percent.

Present Value = Immediate Payment + Present Value of 19 Subsequent Payments at 8%
= $10,000 + ($10,000 × 9.604)
= $106,040

For each of the following situations, identify the correct factor(s) to use from Table 1 or 2. Then use the factor(s) to compute the appropriate present value.

1. Annual net cash inflows of $35,000 for five years, discounted at 16 percent
2. An amount of $25,000 to be received at the end of ten years, discounted at 12 percent
3. The amount of $28,000 to be received at the end of two years, and $15,000 to be received at the end of years 4, 5, and 6, discounted at 10 percent.
4. The amount of 10 payments of $5,000 due on January 1, beginning immediately in 2014. Assume an interest rate of 10 percent.

SOLUTION

1. From Table 2, use factor 3.274, as follows.

   $35,000 × 3.274 = $114,590 present value

TABLE 1
Present Value of $1 to Be Received at the End of a Given Number of Time Periods

Periods	1%	2%	3%	4%	5%	6%	7%	8%	9%	10%	12%
1	0.990	0.980	0.971	0.962	0.952	0.943	0.935	0.926	0.917	0.909	0.893
2	0.980	0.961	0.943	0.925	0.907	0.890	0.873	0.857	0.842	0.826	0.797
3	0.971	0.942	0.915	0.889	0.864	0.840	0.816	0.794	0.772	0.751	0.712
4	0.961	0.924	0.888	0.855	0.823	0.792	0.763	0.735	0.708	0.683	0.636
5	0.951	0.906	0.883	0.822	0.784	0.747	0.713	0.681	0.650	0.621	0.567
6	0.942	0.888	0.837	0.790	0.746	0.705	0.666	0.630	0.596	0.564	0.507
7	0.933	0.871	0.813	0.760	0.711	0.665	0.623	0.583	0.547	0.513	0.452
8	0.923	0.853	0.789	0.731	0.677	0.627	0.582	0.540	0.502	0.467	0.404
9	0.914	0.837	0.766	0.703	0.645	0.592	0.544	0.500	0.460	0.424	0.361
10	0.905	0.820	0.744	0.676	0.614	0.558	0.508	0.463	0.422	0.386	0.322
11	0.896	0.804	0.722	0.650	0.585	0.527	0.475	0.429	0.388	0.350	0.287
12	0.887	0.788	0.701	0.625	0.557	0.497	0.444	0.397	0.356	0.319	0.257
13	0.879	0.773	0.681	0.601	0.530	0.469	0.415	0.368	0.326	0.290	0.229
14	0.870	0.758	0.661	0.577	0.505	0.442	0.388	0.340	0.299	0.263	0.205
15	0.861	0.743	0.642	0.555	0.481	0.417	0.362	0.315	0.275	0.239	0.183
16	0.853	0.728	0.623	0.534	0.458	0.394	0.339	0.292	0.252	0.218	0.163
17	0.844	0.714	0.605	0.513	0.436	0.371	0.317	0.270	0.231	0.198	0.146
18	0.836	0.700	0.587	0.494	0.416	0.350	0.296	0.250	0.212	0.180	0.130
19	0.828	0.686	0.570	0.475	0.396	0.331	0.277	0.232	0.194	0.164	0.116
20	0.820	0.673	0.554	0.456	0.377	0.312	0.258	0.215	0.178	0.149	0.104
21	0.811	0.660	0.538	0.439	0.359	0.294	0.242	0.199	0.164	0.135	0.093
22	0.803	0.647	0.522	0.422	0.342	0.278	0.226	0.184	0.150	0.123	0.083
23	0.795	0.634	0.507	0.406	0.326	0.262	0.211	0.170	0.138	0.112	0.074
24	0.788	0.622	0.492	0.390	0.310	0.247	0.197	0.158	0.126	0.102	0.066
25	0.780	0.610	0.478	0.375	0.295	0.233	0.184	0.146	0.116	0.092	0.059
26	0.772	0.598	0.464	0.361	0.281	0.220	0.172	0.135	0.106	0.084	0.053
27	0.764	0.586	0.450	0.347	0.268	0.207	0.161	0.125	0.098	0.076	0.047
28	0.757	0.574	0.437	0.333	0.255	0.196	0.150	0.116	0.090	0.069	0.042
29	0.749	0.563	0.424	0.321	0.243	0.185	0.141	0.107	0.082	0.063	0.037
30	0.742	0.552	0.412	0.308	0.231	0.174	0.131	0.099	0.075	0.057	0.033
40	0.672	0.453	0.307	0.208	0.142	0.097	0.067	0.046	0.032	0.022	0.011
50	0.608	0.372	0.228	0.141	0.087	0.054	0.034	0.021	0.013	0.009	0.003

2. From Table 1, use factor 0.322, as follows.
   $25,000 × 0.322 = $8,050 present value
3. From Table 1, use the factors indicated in the table below.

Amount to Be Received	×	Present Value Factor	=	Present Value
$28,000	×	0.826	=	$23,128
15,000	×	0.683	=	10,245
15,000	×	0.621	=	9,315
15,000	×	0.564	=	8,460
Total				$51,148

4. From Table 2, use factor 5.759 as follows.
   $5,000 + ($5,000 × 5.759) = $33,795

TABLE 1
Present Value of $1 to Be Received at the End of a Given Number of Time Periods (*Continued*)

14%	15%	16%	18%	20%	25%	30%	35%	40%	45%	50%	Periods
0.877	0.870	0.862	0.847	0.833	0.800	0.769	0.741	0.714	0.690	0.667	1
0.769	0.756	0.743	0.718	0.694	0.640	0.592	0.549	0.510	0.476	0.444	2
0.675	0.658	0.641	0.609	0.579	0.512	0.455	0.406	0.364	0.328	0.296	3
0.592	0.572	0.552	0.516	0.482	0.410	0.350	0.301	0.260	0.226	0.198	4
0.519	0.497	0.476	0.437	0.402	0.328	0.269	0.223	0.186	0.156	0.132	5
0.456	0.432	0.410	0.370	0.335	0.262	0.207	0.165	0.133	0.108	0.088	6
0.400	0.376	0.354	0.314	0.279	0.210	0.159	0.122	0.095	0.074	0.059	7
0.351	0.327	0.305	0.266	0.233	0.168	0.123	0.091	0.068	0.051	0.039	8
0.308	0.284	0.263	0.225	0.194	0.134	0.094	0.067	0.048	0.035	0.026	9
0.270	0.247	0.227	0.191	0.162	0.107	0.073	0.050	0.035	0.024	0.017	10
0.237	0.215	0.195	0.162	0.135	0.086	0.056	0.037	0.025	0.017	0.012	11
0.208	0.187	0.168	0.137	0.112	0.069	0.043	0.027	0.018	0.012	0.008	12
0.182	0.163	0.145	0.116	0.093	0.055	0.033	0.020	0.013	0.008	0.005	13
0.160	0.141	0.125	0.099	0.078	0.044	0.025	0.015	0.009	0.006	0.003	14
0.140	0.123	0.108	0.084	0.065	0.035	0.020	0.011	0.006	0.004	0.002	15
0.123	0.107	0.093	0.071	0.054	0.028	0.015	0.008	0.005	0.003	0.002	16
0.108	0.093	0.080	0.060	0.045	0.023	0.012	0.006	0.003	0.002	0.001	17
0.095	0.081	0.069	0.051	0.038	0.018	0.009	0.005	0.002	0.001	0.001	18
0.083	0.070	0.060	0.043	0.031	0.014	0.007	0.003	0.002	0.001		19
0.073	0.061	0.051	0.037	0.026	0.012	0.005	0.002	0.001	0.001		20
0.064	0.053	0.044	0.031	0.022	0.009	0.004	0.002	0.001			21
0.056	0.046	0.038	0.026	0.018	0.007	0.003	0.001	0.001			22
0.049	0.040	0.033	0.022	0.015	0.006	0.002	0.001				23
0.043	0.035	0.028	0.019	0.013	0.005	0.002	0.001				24
0.038	0.030	0.024	0.016	0.010	0.004	0.001	0.001				25
0.033	0.026	0.021	0.014	0.009	0.003	0.001					26
0.029	0.023	0.018	0.011	0.007	0.002	0.001					27
0.026	0.020	0.016	0.010	0.006	0.002	0.001					28
0.022	0.017	0.014	0.008	0.005	0.002						29
0.020	0.015	0.012	0.007	0.004	0.001						30
0.005	0.004	0.003	0.001	0.001							40
0.001	0.001	0.001									50

TABLE 2
Present Value of $1 Received Each Period for a Given Number of Time Periods

Periods	1%	2%	3%	4%	5%	6%	7%	8%	9%	10%	12%
1	0.990	0.980	0.971	0.962	0.952	0.943	0.935	0.926	0.917	0.909	0.893
2	1.970	1.942	1.913	1.886	1.859	1.833	1.808	1.783	1.759	1.736	1.690
3	2.941	2.884	2.829	2.775	2.723	2.673	2.624	2.577	2.531	2.487	2.402
4	3.902	3.808	3.717	3.630	3.546	3.465	3.387	3.312	3.240	3.170	3.037
5	4.853	4.713	4.580	4.452	4.329	4.212	4.100	3.993	3.890	3.791	3.605
6	5.795	5.601	5.417	5.242	5.076	4.917	4.767	4.623	4.486	4.355	4.111
7	6.728	6.472	6.230	6.002	5.786	5.582	5.389	5.206	5.033	4.868	4.564
8	7.652	7.325	7.020	6.733	6.463	6.210	5.971	5.747	5.535	5.335	4.968
9	8.566	8.162	7.786	7.435	7.108	6.802	6.515	6.247	5.995	5.759	5.328
10	9.471	8.983	8.530	8.111	7.722	7.360	7.024	6.710	6.418	6.145	5.650
11	10.368	9.787	9.253	8.760	8.306	7.887	7.499	7.139	6.805	6.495	5.938
12	11.255	10.575	9.954	9.385	8.863	8.384	7.943	7.536	7.161	6.814	6.194
13	12.134	11.348	10.635	9.986	9.394	8.853	8.358	7.904	7.487	7.103	6.424
14	13.004	12.106	11.296	10.563	9.899	9.295	8.745	8.244	7.786	7.367	6.628
15	13.865	12.849	11.938	11.118	10.380	9.712	9.108	8.559	8.061	7.606	6.811
16	14.718	13.578	12.561	11.652	10.838	10.106	9.447	8.851	8.313	7.824	6.974
17	15.562	14.292	13.166	12.166	11.274	10.477	9.763	9.122	8.544	8.022	7.120
18	16.398	14.992	13.754	12.659	11.690	10.828	10.059	9.372	8.756	8.201	7.250
19	17.226	15.678	14.324	13.134	12.085	11.158	10.336	9.604	8.950	8.365	7.366
20	18.046	16.351	14.878	13.590	12.462	11.470	10.594	9.818	9.129	8.514	7.469
21	18.857	17.011	15.415	14.029	12.821	11.764	10.836	10.017	9.292	8.649	7.562
22	19.660	17.658	15.937	14.451	13.163	12.042	11.061	10.201	9.442	8.772	7.645
23	20.456	18.292	16.444	14.857	13.489	12.303	11.272	10.371	9.580	8.883	7.718
24	21.243	18.914	16.936	15.247	13.799	12.550	11.469	10.529	9.707	8.985	7.784
25	22.023	19.523	17.413	15.622	14.094	12.783	11.654	10.675	9.823	9.077	7.843
26	22.795	20.121	17.877	15.983	14.375	13.003	11.826	10.810	9.929	9.161	7.896
27	23.560	20.707	18.327	16.330	14.643	13.211	11.987	10.935	10.027	9.237	7.943
28	24.316	21.281	18.764	16.663	14.898	13.406	12.137	11.051	10.116	9.307	7.984
29	25.066	21.844	19.189	16.984	15.141	13.591	12.278	11.158	10.198	9.370	8.022
30	25.808	22.396	19.600	17.292	15.373	13.765	12.409	11.258	10.274	9.427	8.055
40	32.835	27.355	23.115	19.793	17.159	15.046	13.332	11.925	10.757	9.779	8.244
50	39.196	31.424	25.730	21.482	18.256	15.762	13.801	12.234	10.962	9.915	8.305

TABLE 2

Present Value of $1 Received Each Period for a Given Number of Time Periods (*Continued*)

14%	15%	16%	18%	20%	25%	30%	35%	40%	45%	50%	Periods
0.877	0.870	0.862	0.847	0.833	0.800	0.769	0.741	0.714	0.690	0.667	1
1.647	1.626	1.605	1.566	1.528	1.440	1.361	1.289	1.224	1.165	1.111	2
2.322	2.283	2.246	2.174	2.106	1.952	1.816	1.696	1.589	1.493	1.407	3
2.914	2.855	2.798	2.690	2.589	2.362	2.166	1.997	1.849	1.720	1.605	4
3.433	3.352	3.274	3.127	2.991	2.689	2.436	2.220	2.035	1.876	1.737	5
3.889	3.784	3.685	3.498	3.326	2.951	2.643	2.385	2.168	1.983	1.824	6
4.288	4.160	4.039	3.812	3.605	3.161	2.802	2.508	2.263	2.057	1.883	7
4.639	4.487	4.344	4.078	3.837	3.329	2.925	2.598	2.331	2.109	1.922	8
4.946	4.772	4.607	4.303	4.031	3.463	3.019	2.665	2.379	2.144	1.948	9
5.216	5.019	4.833	4.494	4.192	3.571	3.092	2.715	2.414	2.168	1.965	10
5.453	5.234	5.029	4.656	4.327	3.656	3.147	2.752	2.438	2.185	1.977	11
5.660	5.421	5.197	4.793	4.439	3.725	3.190	2.779	2.456	2.197	1.985	12
5.842	5.583	5.342	4.910	4.533	3.780	3.223	2.799	2.469	2.204	1.990	13
6.002	5.724	5.468	5.008	4.611	3.824	3.249	2.814	2.478	2.210	1.993	14
6.142	5.847	5.575	5.092	4.675	3.859	3.268	2.825	2.484	2.214	1.995	15
6.265	5.954	5.669	5.162	4.730	3.887	3.283	2.834	2.489	2.216	1.997	16
6.373	6.047	5.749	5.222	4.775	3.910	3.295	2.840	2.492	2.218	1.998	17
6.467	6.128	5.818	5.273	4.812	3.928	3.304	2.844	2.494	2.219	1.999	18
6.550	6.198	5.877	5.316	4.844	3.942	3.311	2.848	2.496	2.220	1.999	19
6.623	6.259	5.929	5.353	4.870	3.954	3.316	2.850	2.497	2.221	1.999	20
6.687	6.312	5.973	5.384	4.891	3.963	3.320	2.852	2.498	2.221	2.000	21
6.743	6.359	6.011	5.410	4.909	3.970	3.323	2.853	2.498	2.222	2.000	22
6.792	6.399	6.044	5.432	4.925	3.976	3.325	2.854	2.499	2.222	2.000	23
6.835	6.434	6.073	5.451	4.973	3.981	3.327	2.855	2.499	2.222	2.000	24
6.873	6.464	6.097	5.467	4.948	3.985	3.329	2.856	2.499	2.222	2.000	25
6.906	6.491	6.118	5.480	4.956	3.988	3.330	2.856	2.500	2.222	2.000	26
6.935	6.514	6.136	5.492	4.964	3.990	3.331	2.856	2.500	2.222	2.000	27
6.961	6.534	6.152	5.502	4.970	3.992	3.331	2.857	2.500	2.222	2.000	28
6.983	6.551	6.166	5.510	4.975	3.994	3.332	2.857	2.500	2.222	2.000	29
7.003	6.566	6.177	5.517	4.979	3.995	3.332	2.857	2.500	2.222	2.000	30
7.105	6.642	6.234	5.548	4.997	3.999	3.333	2.857	2.500	2.222	2.000	40
7.133	6.661	6.246	5.554	4.999	4.000	3.333	2.857	2.500	2.222	2.000	50

ENDNOTES

Chapter 1

1 Based on *Statement of Financial Accounting Concepts No.1*, "Objectives of Financial Reporting by Business Enterprises" (Norwalk, Conn.: Financial Accounting Standards Board, 1978), par. 9.
2 Ibid.
3 Information based on ExxonMobil, Form 10-K, For the Fiscal Year Ended December 31, 2011, and International Monetary Fund's World Economic Outlook Database.
4 We assume in the early chapters of this book that common stock is listed at par value.
5 *Accounting Principles Board Statement No. 4*, "Basic Concepts and Accounting Principles Underlying Financial Statements of Business Enterprises" (New York: AICPA, 1970), par. 138.
6 Based on Securities and Exchange Commission, *Roadmap for the Potential Use of Financial Statements Prepared in Accordance with International Financial Reporting Standards by US Issuers*, August 2008.
7 Based on "Brand Research Shows CPAs Viewed Positively in Marketplace," *AICPA News Update*, October 20, 2008.
8 Based on *Statement Number 1C*, "Standards of Ethical Conduct for Management Accountants" (Montvale, N.J.: Institute of Management Accountants, 1983; revised 1997).
9 CVS Corporation, *Annual Report*, 2011.
10 Based on National Commission on Fraudulent Financial Reporting, *Report of the National Commission on Fraudulent Financial Reporting* (Washington, D.C.: 1987), p. 2.
11 Target Corporation, Form 10-K, For the Fiscal Year Ended January 29, 2011.
12 Costco Wholesale Corporation, *Annual Report*, 2011.
13 Southwest Airlines Co., *Annual Report*, 1996.

Chapter 2

1 Based on "Boeing, Singapore Airlines Finalize Order for Eight 777-300ERs," *Press Release*, Boeing, November 17, 2011.
2 Based on "Boeing Finalizes 787 Order," *HeraldNet*, April 17, 2010.
3 ASC 820 and IFRS 13.
4 Based on *Statement of Financial Accounting Standards No. 157*, "Fair Value Measurements" (Norwalk, Conn.: Financial Accounting Standards Board, 2007).
5 The Boeing Company, Form 10-K, For the Fiscal Year Ended December 31, 2011.
6 Ibid.
7 Ibid.
8 Data from The Bank of New York Mellon Corporation, Form 10-K, For the Fiscal Year Ended December 31, 2011.

Chapter 3

1 Data from Netflix, Inc., Form 10-K, For the Fiscal Year Ended December 31, 2011.
2 Netflix, Inc., Form 10-K, For the Fiscal Year Ended December 31, 2011.
3 Based on Securities and Exchange Commission, *Staff Accounting Bulletin No. 10*, 1999.
4 In our discussion, we assume that the amount of depreciation has been established.
5 Based on Netflix, Inc., Form 10-K, For the Fiscal Year Ended December 31, 2011.
6 Based on Ken Brown, "Wall Street Plays Numbers Games with Savings, Despite Reforms," *The Wall Street Journal*, July 22, 2003.
7 Based on Mark S. Beasley and others, "Fraudulent Financial Reporting 1998–2007: An Analysis of U.S. Companies," *Committee of Sponsoring Organizations*, 2010, p. 3.
8 Based on "Microsoft Settles with SEC," *CBSNews.com*, June 5, 2002.
9 Data from Lyric Opera of Chicago, Financial Statements, April 30, 2011.
10 Data from The Walt Disney Company, Form 10-K, For the Fiscal Year Ended October 1, 2011.

Chapter 4

1 Data from McDonald's Corporation, Form 10-K, For the Fiscal Year Ended December 31, 2011.
2 http://www.fasb.org, July 12, 2008.
3 *Statement of Financial Accounting Concepts No. 1*, "Objectives of Financial Reporting by Business Enterprises" (Norwalk, Conn.: Financial Accounting Standards Board, 1978), pars. 32–54.
4 *Statement of Financial Accounting Concepts No. 2*, "Qualitative Characteristics of Accounting Information" (Norwalk, Conn.: Financial Accounting Standards Board, 1980), par. 20.
5 Based on L. Todd Johnson, "Relevance and Reliability," *The FASB Report*, February 28, 2005.
6 Based on Securities and Exchange Commission, *Staff Accounting Bulletin No. 99*, 1999.
7 *Accounting Principles Board, Opinion No. 20*, "Accounting Changes" (New York: AICPA, 1971), par. 17.
8 Based on Ray J. Groves, "Here's the Annual Report. Got a Few Hours?" *The Wall Street Journal Europe*, August 26–27, 1994.
9 Roger Lowenstein, "Intrinsic Value: Investors Will Fish for Footnotes in 'Abbreviated' Annual Reports," *The Wall Street Journal*, September 14, 1995.
10 Dell Computer Corporation, Form 10-K, For the Fiscal Year Ended March 13, 2012.
11 Based on "Ex-Chief of WorldCom Is Found Guilty in $11 Billion Fraud," *The New York Times*, March 16, 2005.
12 Based on Roger Lowenstein, "Intrinsic Value: The '20% Club' No Longer Is Exclusive," *The Wall Street Journal*, May 4, 1995.
13 Based on Securities and Exchange Commission, *Staff Accounting Bulletin No. 99*, 1999.
14 Data from The Gap, Inc., Form 10-K, For the Fiscal Year Ended January 29, 2011, and Abercrombie & Fitch Co., Form 10-K, For the Fiscal Year Ended January 29, 2011.

Chapter 5

1 Wal-Mart Stores, Inc., Form 10-K, For the Fiscal Year Ended January 31, 2012.
2 Based on "Credit Card Statistics," *CreditCards.com*, April 21, 2012.
3 For a comparison of complete journal entries made under the perpetual and periodic inventory systems, see the Review Problem in this chapter.
4 Based on Rafael Solorzano, "Forecast of E-Commerce Sales for 2011 and Beyond," www.fortune3.com, January 27, 2011.
5 Based on Joel Millman, "Here's What Happens to Many Lovely Gifts After Santa Rides Off," *The Wall Street Journal*, December 26, 2001.
6 Based on Matthew Rose, "Magazine Revenue at Newsstands Falls in Worst Year Ever," *The Wall Street Journal*, May 15, 2001.
7 Helpful ratios for calculating the three components of the financing period will be covered in subsequent chapters on inventories, receivables, and current liabilities.

Chapter 6

1 Data from Cisco Systems, Form 10-K, For the Fiscal Year Ended July 30, 2011.
2 Ibid.
3 Based on American Institute of Certified Public Accountants, *Accounting Trends & Techniques* (New York: AICPA, 2011).
4 Cisco Systems, Form 10-K, For the Fiscal Year Ended July 30, 2011.
5 Based on Ernst & Young, *U.S. GAAP vs. IFRS: The Basics*, 2007.
6 Based on American Institute of Certified Public Accountants, *Accounting Trends & Techniques* (New York: AICPA, 2011).
7 Based on Dell Computer, Form 10-K, For the Fiscal Year Ended February 3, 2012.
8 Based on Securities and Exchange Commission, SEC Announces Fraud Charges Against Former Rite Aid Senior Management, June 21, 2002.
9 Based on Highbeam Research, "Former Rent-Way Executive Gets Prison, Fine in Fraud Case," November 23, 2003.
10 Based on American Institute of Certified Public Accountants, *Accounting Trends & Techniques* (New York: AICPA, 2008).
11 Data from ExxonMobil Corporation, Form 10-K, For the Fiscal Year Ended December 31, 2006.

12 Data from ExxonMobil Corporation, Form 10-K, For the Fiscal Year Ended Decmber 31, 2011.
13 Data from Walgreen Co., Form 10-K, For the Fiscal Year Ended August 31, 2011.

Chapter 7

1 Based on Committee of Sponsoring Organizations of the Treadway Commission (COSO), *Internal Control—Integrated Framework, 1985–2012.*
2 Based on *Professional Standards*, vol. 1, Sec. AU 325.16.
3 Based on Elizabeth Woyke, "Attention Shoplifters," *BusinessWeek*, September 11, 2006.
4 Based on Grant Thornton, "Understanding and Preventing Retail Fraud," National Retail Federation, April 2009.
5 Based on Tom Lauricella, Shafali Anand, and Valerie Bauerlein, "A $34 Billion Cash Fund to Close Up," *The Wall Street Journal*, December 11, 2007.
6 Nike, Inc., Form 10-K, For the Fiscal Year Ended May 31, 2012.
7 Based on American Institute of Certified Public Accountants, *Accounting Trends & Techniques* (New York: AICPA, 2011).
8 Based on "Credit Card Statistics," *creditcards.com*, April 21, 2011.
9 Costco Wholesale Corporation, Form 10-K, For the Fiscal Year Ended August 28, 2011.
10 Ibid.
11 Based on Committee of Sponsoring Organizations of the Treadway Commission, "Press Release: Financial Fraud at U.S. Public Companies, May 20, 2010."
12 Based on Amy Merrick, "Starbucks Accuses Employee, Husband of Embezzling $3.7 Million from Firm," *The Wall Street Journal*, November 20, 2000.

Chapter 8

1 Data from Hewlett-Packard Company, Form 10-K, For the Fiscal Year Ended October 31, 2011.
2 Based on Jesse Drucker, "Sprint Expects Loss of Subscribers," *The Wall Street Journal*, September 24, 2002.
3 Based on International Accounting Standards Board, *Framework for the Preparation and Presentation of Financial Statements* (October 2008).
4 Based on American Institute of Certified Public Accountants, *Accounting Trends & Techniques* (New York: AICPA, 2010).
5 Based on "Bad Loans Rattle Telecom Vendors," *BusinessWeek*, February 19, 2001.
6 Based on Scott Thurm, "Better Debt Bolsters Bottom Lines," *The Wall Street Journal*, August 18, 2003.
7 Based on Circuit City Stores, Inc., Form 10-K, For the Fiscal Year Ended February 28, 2005.
8 Based on Deborah Solomon and Damian Paletta, "U.S. Drafts Sweeping Plans to Fight Crisis as Turmoil Worsens in Credit Markets," *The Wall Street Journal*, September 19, 2008.
9 Based on Heather Timmons, "Do Household's Numbers Add Up?" *BusinessWeek*, December 10, 2001.
10 Based on Steve Daniels, "Bank One Reserves Feed Earnings," *Crain's Chicago Business*, December 15, 2003.
11 Based on Jonathon Weil, "Accounting Scheme Was Straightforward but Hard to Detect," *The Wall Street Journal*, March 20, 2003.
12 Hewlett Packard Company, Form 10-K, For the Fiscal Year Ended October 31, 2011.
13 Information based on promotional brochures of Mitsubishi Corp.
14 Based on Elizabeth McDonald, "Unhatched Chickens," *Forbes*, February 19, 2001.
15 Based on CompuCredit Holdings Corporation, Form 10-K, For the Fiscal Year Ended December 31, 2009.
16 Data from Walgreen Co., Form 10-K, For the Fiscal Year Ended August 31, 2011.

Chapter 9

1 Data from Apple Inc., Form 10-K, For the Fiscal Year Ended September 24, 2011.
2. Based on *Statement of Financial Accounting Standard No. 144,* "Accounting for the Impairment or Disposal of Long-Lived Assets" (Norwalk, Conn.: Financial Accounting Standards Board, 2001).
3 Based on Edward J. Riedl, "An Examination of Long-lived Asset Impairments," *The Accounting Review*, Vol. 79, No. 3, pp. 823–852.
4 Based on *Statement of Financial Accounting Standards No. 34,* "Capitalization of Interest Cost" (Norwalk, Conn.: Financial Accounting Standards Board, 1979), pars. 9–11.
5 Leasehold improvements are sometimes included in the intangible assets section because they revert to the lessor and are therefore more of a right than a physical asset.
6 Based on American Institute of Certified Public Accountants, *Accounting Trends & Techniques* (New York: AICPA, 2011).
7 Ibid.
8 This method of revising depreciation is used widely in industry and is supported by *Opinion No. 9* and *Opinion No. 20* of the Accounting Principles Board.
9 Some special rules apply and are addressed in more advanced courses.
10 If the useful life of a plant asset is less than the expected life of the resource, the shorter life should be used to compute depreciation, using straight-line or declining-balance methods.
11 Based on *Statement of Financial Accounting Standards No. 25,* "Suspension of Certain Accounting Requirements for Oil and Gas Producing Companies" (Norwalk, Conn.: Financial Accounting Standards Board, 1979).
12 Based on Jonathan Weil, "Oil Reserves Can Sure Be Slick," *The Wall Street Journal*, March 11, 2004.
13 Based on *Statement of Financial Accounting Standards No. 142,* "Goodwill and Other Intangible Assets" (Norwalk, Conn.: Financial Accounting Standards Board, 2001), pars. 11–17.
14 Based on "BrandZ Top 100 Most Valuable Global Brands 2011," *www.millardbrown.com*, 2011.
15 Note that if the company developed the bottle cap internally instead of purchasing the patent, the costs of developing the cap—such as researchers' salaries and the costs of supplies and equipment used in testing—would be expensed as incurred.
16 Data from General Motors Company, Form 10-K, For the Fiscal Year Ended December 31, 2011.
17 Data from Abbott Laboratories, Form 10-K, For the Fiscal Year Ended December 31, 2011.
18 Based on *Statement of Financial Accounting Standards No. 2,* "Accounting for Research and Development Costs" (Norwalk, Conn.: Financial Accounting Standards Board, 1974), par. 12.
19 Based on *Statement of Financial Accounting Standards No. 86,* "Accounting for the Costs of Computer Software to Be Sold, Leased, or Otherwise Marketed" (Norwalk, Conn.: Financial Accounting Standards Board, 1985).
20 Based on *Statement of Financial Accounting Standards No. 142,* "Goodwill and Other Intangible Assets" (Norwalk, Conn.: Financial Accounting Standards Board, 2001), pars. 11–17.
21 Based on American Institute of Certified Public Accountants, *Accounting Trends & Techniques* (New York: AICPA, 2011).
22 Data from General Mills, Inc., *Quarterly Report*, 2012; H.J. Heinz Company, Form 10-K, For the Fiscal Year Ended April 29, 2012; Cisco Systems, *Quarterly Report*, 2012.
23 Based on Southwest Airlines Co., *Annual Report*, 2002.
24 Costco Wholesale Corporation, Form 10-K, For the Fiscal Year Ended August 28, 2011.
25 International Business Machines Corporation, Form 10-K, For the Fiscal Year Ended December 31, 2011.
26 Data from Starwood Hotel & Resorts Worldwide, Inc. Form 10-K, For the Fiscal Year Ended December 21, 2011; Marriot International, Inc., Form 10-K, For the Fiscal Year Ended December 30, 2011.

Chapter 10

1 Data from Microsoft Corporation, Form 10-K, For the Fiscal Year Ended June 30, 2011.
2 The Hershey Company, Form 10-K, For the Fiscal Year Ended December 31, 2011.
3 Based on "Small Business Poll on Compensating Employees," quoted on sbinformation.about.com, June 6, 2010.
4 The Hershey Company, Form 10-K, For the Fiscal Year Ended December 31, 2011.
5 Based on "Press Room," www.webfyer.com, January 4, 2010.
6 Based on "Overview of U.S. Coupon Distribution and Redemption Trends," March 29, 2012, NCH Marketing Services, www.nchmarketing.com.
7 Based on *Statement of Financial Accounting Standards No. 5,* "Accounting for Contingencies" (Norwalk, Conn.: Financial Accounting Standards Board, 1975).
8 Based on American Institute of Certified Public Accountants, *Accounting Trends & Techniques* (New York: AICPA, 2012).
9 Data from Microsoft Corporation, *Annual Report,* 2011.
10 Based on American Institute of Certified Public Accountants, *Accounting Trends & Techniques* (New York: AICPA, 2012).

11 Data from Microsoft Corporation, Form 10-K, For the Fiscal Year Ended June 30, 2011.
12 Based on *Accounting Standards Codification (ASC) 820*, "Fair Value Measurements and Disclosures (Norwalk, Conn.: Financial Accounting Standards Board, revised by Accounting Standards Update (ASU 2011-04 in 2011)).
13 Based on *Accounting Standards Codification (ASC) 820*, "Fair Value Measurements and Disclosures [Norwalk, Conn.: Financial Accounting Standards Board, revised by Accounting Standards Update (ASU 2011-04 in 2011)] and IFRS 13, "Fair Value Measurement," International Accounting Standards Board, (2011).
14 Based on "Clarifications on Fair-Value Accounting," U.S. Securities and Exchange Commission, *Release 2008-234*, October 1, 2008.
15 Data from WorldCom (MCI, Inc.), Form 10-K, For the Fiscal Year Ended December 31, 2004.
16 Advertisement, *Chicago Tribune*, December 2007.
17 Data from Oracle Corporation, Form 10-K, For the Fiscal Year Ended May 31, 2011; Cisco Systems, Inc., Form 10-K, For the Fiscal Year Ended July 30, 2011.

Chapter 11

1 Data from McDonald's Corporation, Form 10-K, For the Fiscal Year Ended December 31, 2011.
2 Data from Southwest Airlines, Form 10-K, For the Fiscal Year Ended December 31, 2011. We cover deferred income taxes in greater detail in a later chapter.
3 Based on Mary Williams Walsh, "$53 Billion Shortfall for New Jersey Retiree Care," *The New York Times*, July 25, 2007.
4 Based on *www.morningstar.com*, May 9, 2012.
5 Based on Accounting Principles Board, *Opinion No. 21*, "Interest on Receivables and Payables" (New York: AICPA, 1971), par. 15.
6 Based on *Statement of Financial Accounting Standards No. 13*, "Accounting for Leases" (Norwalk, Conn.: Financial Accounting Standards Board, 1976), par. 10.
7 Based on *Statement of Financial Accounting Standards No. 158*, "Employers' Accounting for Defined Benefit Pension and Other Postretirement Plans" (Norwalk, Conn.: Financial Accounting Standards Board, 2007).
8 Based on Lee Hawkins, Jr., "S&P Cuts Rating on GM and Ford to Junk Status," *The Wall Street Journal*, May 6, 2005.
9 Data from McDonald's, Inc., Form 10-K, For the Fiscal Year Ended December 31, 2011.
10 Based on Tom Sullivan and Sonia Ryst, "Kodak $1Billion Issue Draws Crowds," *The Wall Street Journal*, October 8, 2003.
11 Adapted from quotations in *The Wall Street Journal Online*, December 18, 2007.
12 Data from Intel Corporation, Form 10-K, For the Fiscal Year Ended December 31, 2011.

Chapter 12

1 Data from Google, Inc., Form 10-K, For the Fiscal Year Ended December 31, 2011.
2 Based on "Key Stats," Securities Industry and Financial Markets Association, April 2012.
3 Based on "The FASB's Basic Ownership Approach and a Reclassification of Preferred Stock as a Liability," *www.cfo.com*, July 18, 2008.
4 Based on Amir Efrati, "Google Preserves Cash and Control," *The Wall Street Journal*, April 13, 2012.
5 Based on Michael Rapaport and Jonathan Weil, "More Truth-in-Labeling for Accounting Carries Liabilities," *The Wall Street Journal*, August 23, 2003.
6 Based on American Institute of Certified Public Accountants, *Accounting Trends & Techniques* (New York: AICPA, 2011).
7 Data from Abbott Laboratories, Form 10-K, For the Fiscal Year Ended December 31, 2011.
8 Based on American Institute of Certified Public Accountants, *Accounting Research Bulletin No. 43* (New York: AICPA, 1953), chap. 7, sec. B, par. 10.
9 Based on American Institute of Certified Public Accountants, *Accounting Research Bulletin No. 43* (New York: AICPA, 1953), chap. 7, sec. B, par. 13.
10 Based on Nike, Inc., Form 10-K, For the Fiscal Year Ended May 31, 2007.
11 Based on Yahoo! Finance.com, June 3, 2012.
12 Based on "General Mills Declares Two-for-One Stock Split," *MarketWatch.com*, May 3, 2010.
13 Data from Microsoft Corporation, Form 10-K, For the Fiscal Year Ended June 30, 2011.
14 Ibid.
15 Based on American Institute of Certified Public Accountants, *Accounting Trends & Techniques* (New York: AICPA, 2011).
16 Data from Google, Inc., Form 10-K, For the Fiscal Year Ended December 31, 2011.
17 Based on "Spotlight on Stock Options Backdating," *www.sec.gov*, 2010.
18 Based on Mariss Marr, "Dreamworks Shares Rise 38% on First Day," *The Wall Street Journal*, October 10, 2004; Yahoo! Finance.com, December 26, 2007.
19 Data from IBM Corporation, Form 10-K, For the Fiscal Year Ended December 31, 2009; Based on "IBM Board Approves $5 Billion for Stock Repurchase," *www.wopular.com*, June 17, 2010.
20 Based on Yahoo! Finance.com, 2007.

Chapter 13

1 Data from Amazon.com, Inc., Form 10-K, For the Fiscal Year Ended December 31, 2011.
2 Based on American Institute of Certified Public Accountants, *Accounting Trends & Techniques* (New York: AICPA, 2011).
3 Based on Martin Peers and Robin Sidel, "WorldCom Causes Analysts to Evaluate EBITDA's Role," *The Wall Street Journal*, July 15, 2002.
4 Based on Ian McDonald, "Companies Are Rolling in Cash. Too Bad," *The Wall Street Journal*, August 20, 2006; Justin Lahart, "U.S. Firms Build Up Record Cash Piles," *The Wall Street Journal*, June 11, 2010.
5 Based on Lulu Chang, "Companies Hoarding Cash," *CNBC*, July 19, 2010.
6 Based on "Free Cash Flow Standouts," *Upside Newsletter*, October 3, 2005.
7 Amazon.com, *Form 10-K*, For the Fiscal Year Ended December 31, 2011.
8 Gary Slutsker, "Look at the Birdie and Say: 'Cash Flow'," *Forbes*, October 25, 1993.
9 Jonathan Clements, "Yacktman Fund Is Bloodied but Unbowed," *The Wall Street Journal*, November 8, 1993.
10 Jeffery Laderman, "Earnings, Schmearnings—Look at the Cash," *BusinessWeek*, July 24, 1989.
11 Amazon.com, *Form 10-K*, For the Fiscal Year Ended December 31, 2011.
12 Data from Fleetwood Enterprises, Inc., *10Q*, July 29, 2001.
13 Enron Corporation, *Press Release*, October 16, 2001.

Chapter 14

1 Data from Starbucks Corporation, Form 10-K, For the Fiscal Year Ended October 2, 2011.
2 Based on "Fourteen Key Business Ratios," *dnb.com*, 2012.
3 Based on *Statement of Financial Accounting Standards No. 131*, "Segment Disclosures" (Norwalk, Conn.: Financial Accounting Standards Board, 1997).
4 Based on Belverd E. Needles, Jr., Anton Shigaev, Marian Powers, and Mark L. Frigo, "Strategy and Integrated Financial Ratio Performance Measures: A Longitudinal Multi-Country Study of High Performance Companies," in *Studies in Financial and Managerial Accounting*, vol. 20, edited by Marc Epstein and Jean-Francois Manzoni (London: JAI Elsevier Science Ltd., 2010), pp. 211–252.
5 Based on Belverd E. Needles, Jr., Marian Powers, and Mark L. Frigo, "Performance Measurement and Executive Compensation: Practices of High Performance Companies," in *Studies in Financial and Managerial Accounting*, vol. 18, edited by Marc Epstein and Jean-Francois Manzoni (London: JAI Elsevier Science Ltd., 2008).
6 Based on Starbucks Corporation, Form 10-K, For the Fiscal Year Ended October 2, 2011.
7 Ibid.
8 Based on "After Charge for Licensing, McDonald's Posts a Record Loss," *The New York Times*, July 25, 2007; Christina Cheddar Berk, "Campbell's Profit Jumps 31 Percent," *The Wall Street Journal*, November 22, 2005.
9 Based on American Institute of Certified Public Accountants, *Accounting Trends & Techniques* (New York: AICPA, 2011); Starbucks Corporation, Form 10-K, For the Fiscal Year Ended October 2, 2011; Starbucks Corporation, Form 10-K, For the Fiscal Year Ended September 27, 2009.
10 Based on Jonathan Weil, "Pro Forma in Earnings Reports?... As If," *The Wall Street Journal*, April 24, 2003.
11 Based on David Henry, "The Numbers Game," *BusinessWeek*, May 14, 2001.
12 Starbucks Corporation, *Proxy Statement*, 2011.
13 Ibid.
14 Ibid.
15 Based on "Technology Firms Post Strong Earnings but Stock Prices Decline Sharply," *The Wall Street Journal*, January 21, 1988; Donald R. Seace, "Industrials Plunge 57.2 Points—Technology Stocks' Woes Cited," *The Wall Street Journal*, January 21, 1988.

Chapter 15

1 http://imanet.org/about_ethics_statement.asp.
2 Based on Andrew Ross Sorkin, "Albertsons Nears Deal, Yet Again, To Sell Itself," *The New York Times*, January 23, 2006.
3 Based on Karen Lundebaard, "Bumpy Ride," *The Wall Street Journal*, May 21, 2001.
4 Based on Curtis C. Verschoor, "Economic Crime Results from Unethical Culture," *Strategic Finance*, March 2009.
5 *Statement No. 1A* (New York: Institute of Management Accountants, 1982).

Chapter 18

1 Adapted from "Just In Time, Toyota Production System & Lean Manufacturing," http://www.strategosinc.com/just_in_time.htm.

Chapter 20

1 Based on Omar Aguilar, "How Strategic Performance Management Is Helping Companies Create Business Value," *Strategic Finance,* January 2003.
2 Jeremy Hope and Robin Frase, "Who Needs Budgets?" *Harvard Business Review*, February 2003.

Chapter 21

1 EVA is a registered trademark of the consulting firm Stern Stewart & Company.

Chapter 22

1 www.irobot.com

Chapter 23

1 Based on Alan Fuhrman, "Your e-Banking Future," *Strategic Finance*, April 2002.

Chapter 25

1 Based on Christopher Lawton, "Anheuser-Busch Rolls Out the Price Jump," *The Wall Street Journal*, October 23, 2002.

Chapter 26

1 www.nist.gov/baldrige
2 www.iso.org

GLOSSARY

A

Accelerated method A method of depreciation that allocates relatively large amounts of the depreciable cost of an asset to earlier years and smaller amounts to later years. (p. 407)

Account balance The difference in dollars between the total debit footing and the total credit footing of an account. (p. 92)

Accounting An information system that measures, processes, and communicates financial information about an economic entity. (p. 4)

Accounting conventions Rules of thumb, or general principles, for recording transactions and preparing financial statements. Also called *constraints.* (p. 206)

Accounting cycle A series of steps whose basic purpose is to produce financial statements for decision makers. (p. 94)

Accounting equation Assets = Liabilities + Stockholders' Equity. (p. 9)

Accounting rate-of-return method A method of evaluating capital investments designed to measure the estimated performance of a potential capital project. It is calculated by dividing the project's average annual net income by the average cost of the investment. (p. 1082)

Accounts Basic units for accumulating and storing accounting data from similar transactions. (p. 90)

Accounts payable Short-term obligations to suppliers for goods and services. Also called *trade accounts payable.* (p. 444)

Accounts receivable Short-term financial assets that arise from sales on credit at the wholesale or retail level. (p. 364)

Accounts receivable aging method A method of estimating uncollectible accounts based on the assumption that a predictable proportion of each dollar of accounts receivable outstanding will not be collected. (p. 369)

Accrual The recognition of an expense or revenue that has arisen but has not yet been recorded. (p. 143)

Accrual accounting Recording transactions in the periods in which they occur, rather than in the periods in which cash is received or paid. Also called the *matching rule.* (p. 139)

Accrued expenses Expenses incurred but not recorded in the accounts; unrecorded expenses. (p. 146)

Accrued liabilities Liabilities that are not already in the accounting records. (p. 446)

Accrued revenues Revenues for which a service has been performed or goods delivered but for which no entry has been made; unrecorded revenues. (p. 150)

Accumulated Depreciation Contra-asset accounts used to accumulate depreciation on specific long-term assets. (p. 145)

Activity base The activity for which relationships are established. Also called *denominator activity* or *cost driver.* (p. 874)

Activity-based costing (ABC) A method of assigning costs that calculates a more accurate product cost than traditional methods by categorizing all indirect costs by activity, tracing the indirect costs to those activities, and assigning those costs to products using a cost driver related to the cause of the cost. (pp. 767, 835)

Activity-based management (ABM) An approach to managing an organization that identifies all major operating activities, determines the resources consumed by each activity and the cause of the resource usage, categorizes the activities as either adding value to a product or service or not adding value, and seeks to reduce or eliminate non-value-adding activities. (p. 835)

Actual costing method A method of cost measurement that uses the actual costs of direct materials, direct labor, and overhead to calculate a product or service unit cost. (p. 725)

Additional paid-in capital The amount investors pay for a corporation's stock above the stated par value. (p. 10)

Additions Enlargements to the physical layout of a plant asset. (p. 400)

Adjusted trial balance A trial balance prepared after all adjusting entries have been recorded and posted to the accounts. (p. 152)

Adjusting entries Entries made to apply accrual accounting to transactions that span accounting periods. (p. 142)

Aging of accounts receivable The process of listing each customer's receivable account according to the due date of the account. (p. 369)

Allowance for Uncollectible Accounts A contra-asset account that reduces accounts receivable to the amount expected to be collected in cash. Also called *Allowance for Doubtful Accounts* and *Allowance for Bad Debts.* (p. 367)

Allowance method A method of accounting for uncollectible accounts by expensing estimated uncollectible accounts in the period in which the related sales take place. (p. 366)

American Institute of Certified Public Accountants (AICPA) The professional association of certified public accountants. (p. 17)

Amortization The periodic allocation of the cost of an intangible asset to the periods it benefits. (p. 398)

Appraisal costs The costs of activities that measure, evaluate, or audit products, processes, or services to ensure their conformance to quality standards and performance requirements. (p. 1148)

Articles of incorporation An official document filed with and approved by a state that authorizes the incorporators to do business as a corporation. (p. 8)

Asset impairment Loss of revenue-generating potential of a long-lived asset before the end of its useful life; the difference between an asset's carrying value and its fair value, as measured by the present value of the expected cash flows. (p. 399)

Asset turnover A measure of profitability that shows how efficiently assets are used to produce sales; calculated as Net Revenue ÷ Average Total Assets. (pp. 216, 965, 665)

Assets The economic resources of a company that are expected to benefit future operations. (p. 10)

Auction-based pricing Occurs when sellers post what they have for sale, ask for price bids, and accept the buyer's offer to purchase at a certain price; also occurs when buyers post what they want, ask for prices, and accept a seller's offer to sell at a certain price. (p. 1106)

Audit An examination of a company's financial statements and the accounting systems, controls, and records that produced them in order to render an independent professional opinion about whether they have been presented fairly, in all material respects, in conformity with GAAP. (p. 17)

Audit committee A group of independent directors with financial expertise who objectively evaluate management's performance; established by the board of directors as required by the Sarbanes-Oxley Act. (p. 8)

Authorization The approval of transactions or activities. (p. 329)

Authorized shares The maximum number of shares a corporation can issue without a change in its state charter. (p. 546)

Average-cost method An inventory costing method in which inventory is priced at the average cost of the goods available for sale during the period. Also called *weighted average method*. (p. 293)

Average costing method A process costing method that assigns an average cost to all products made during an accounting period. (p. 796)

Avoidable costs Costs that can be eliminated by dropping a segment. (p. 1046)

B

Backflush costing A product costing approach in which all product costs are first accumulated in the Cost of Goods Sold account and at the end of the period are "flushed back," or worked backward, into the appropriate inventory accounts. (p. 843)

Balance sheet The financial statement that shows a business's assets, liabilities, and stockholders' equity as of a specific date. Also called the *statement of financial position*. (p. 12)

Balanced scorecard A framework that links the perspectives of an organization's four basic stakeholder groups—financial (investors), learning and growth (employees), internal business processes, and customers—with the organization's mission and vision, performance measures, strategic and tactical plans, and resources. (p. 968)

Bank reconciliation The process of accounting for the difference between the balance appearing on a company's bank statement and the balance in its Cash account. (p. 338)

Bank statement A printed or electronic record of the balance in a bank account and the amounts that have been paid into it and withdrawn from it over a given period of time. (p. 336)

Base year In financial analysis, the first year to be considered in any set of data. (p. 658)

Batch-level activities Activities performed each time a batch of goods is produced. (p. 836)

Benchmarking A technique for determining a company's competitive advantage by comparing its performance with that of its closest competitors. (pp. 970, 1144)

Benchmarks Measures of the best practices in an industry. (p. 970)

Betterments Improvements that do not add to the physical layout of a plant asset. (p. 400)

Bill of activities A list of activities and related costs that is used to compute the costs assigned to activities and the product unit cost. (p. 837)

Board of directors A group of individuals that are elected or appointed to oversee the activities of a corporation. (p. 8)

Bond A security, usually long term, representing money that a corporation or other entity borrows from the investing public. (p. 489)

Bond certificate Evidence of an organization's debt to a bondholder. (p. 489)

Bond indenture A contract that defines the terms of a bond issue. (p. 489)

Bond issue The total value of bonds issued at one time. (p. 489)

Bonding The process of carefully checking an employee's background and insuring the company against theft by that person. (p. 330)

Bonds payable The most common type of long-term debt for companies. (p. 486)

Book value A company's total assets less its liabilities; stockholders' equity or net assets. (p. 567)

Book value per share The equity of the owner of one share of stock in a corporation's net assets. (p. 567)

Bookkeeping The process of recording financial transactions and keeping financial records. (p. 5)

Brand name A registered name that can be used only by its owner to identify a product or service. (p. 417)

Breakeven point The point at which total revenues equal total costs. (p. 881)

Budget(s) Plan of action based on forecasted transactions, activities, and events; includes a forecasted income statement, statement of cash flows, and balance sheet. (pp. 728, 908)

Budget committee A committee made up of top management that has overall responsibility for budget implementation. (p. 928)

Budgeted balance sheet A statement that projects an organization's financial position at the end of an accounting period. (p. 924)

Budgeted income statement A projection of an organization's net income for an accounting period based on the revenues and expenses estimated for that accounting period. (p. 920)

Budgeting The process of identifying, gathering, summarizing, and communicating financial and nonfinancial information about an organization's future activities. (p. 908)

Business An economic unit that aims to sell goods and services to customers at prices that will provide an adequate return to its owners. (p. 21)

Business plan A comprehensive statement of how a company will achieve its strategic, tactical, and operating objectives. (p. 728)

Business transactions Economic events that affect a business's financial position and that should be recorded in the accounting records. (pp. 5, 88)

C

Call price A specified price, usually above face value, at which a corporation can buy back its bonds before maturity. (p. 490)

Callable bonds Bonds that the issuing corporation can buy back and retire at a call price before their maturity dates. (p. 490)

Callable preferred stock Preferred stock that the issuing corporation can redeem or retire at a stated price. (p. 549)

Capital expenditure An expenditure for the purchase or expansion of a long-term asset, which is recorded in an asset account. (p. 400)

Capital expenditures budget A detailed plan outlining the anticipated amount and timing of capital outlays for long-term assets during an accounting period. (p. 921)

Capital investment analysis The process of making decisions about capital investments. It includes identifying the need for a capital investment, analyzing courses of action to meet that need, preparing reports for managers, choosing the best alternative, and dividing funds among competing needs. Also called *capital budgeting*. (p. 1074)

Capital investment decisions Management decisions about when and how much to spend on capital facilities and other long-term projects. (p. 1074)

Capital lease A long-term lease that resembles a purchase or sale on installment and in which the lessee assumes the risk of ownership. (p. 488)

Carrying value The unexpired portion of an asset's cost. Also called *book value*. (pp. 145, 399, 1077)

Cash Coins and currency on hand, checks and money orders from customers, and deposits in checking and savings accounts; for purposes of the statement of cash flows, both cash and cash equivalents. (p. 596)

Cash basis of accounting Accounting for revenues and expenses on a cash-received and cash-paid basis. (p. 140)

Cash budget A projection of the cash that an organization will receive and the cash that it will pay out during an accounting period. (p. 921)

Cash dividends A distribution of earnings to a corporation's stockholders; a corporation's board of directors has the sole authority to declare them. (p. 446)

Cash equivalents Short-term investments that will revert to cash in 90 days or less from the time they are purchased; examples include money market accounts, commercial paper, and U.S. Treasury bills. (pp. 337, 596)

Cash flow yield A measure of a company's ability to generate operating cash flows in relation to net income; calculated as Net Cash Flows from Operating Activities ÷ Net Income. (pp. 616, 667)

Cash flows The inflows and outflows of cash into and out of a business. (p. 14)

Cash flows to assets A measure of the ability of assets to generate operating cash flows; calculated as Net Cash Flows from Operating Activities ÷ Average Total Assets. (pp. 618, 668)

Cash flows to sales A measure of the ability of sales to generate operating cash flows; calculated as Net Cash Flows from Operating Activities ÷ Net Sales. (pp. 617, 667)

Cash-generating efficiency A company's ability to generate cash from its current or continuing operations. (p. 616)

Certified public accountant (CPA) A public accountant who has met stringent state licensing requirements. (p. 16)

Chart of accounts A list of account numbers and titles that facilitates finding accounts in the ledger. (p. 90)

Check An authorization for the bank to pay the vendor in the amount of the invoice less any applicable discount. (p. 336)

Check authorization A form that an accounting department prepares after it has compared a receiving report with a purchase order and invoice and that authorizes the issuance of a check to pay the invoice. (p. 336)

Classification The process of assigning transactions to the appropriate accounts. (p. 89)

Classified financial statements General-purpose external financial statements that are divided into subcategories. (p. 209)

Commercial paper Unsecured loans sold to the public, usually through professionally managed investment firms, as a means of borrowing short-term funds. (p. 445)

Commitment A legal obligation that does not meet the technical requirements for recognition as a liability. (p. 457)

Committed costs The costs of design, development, engineering, testing, and production that are engineered into a product or service at the design stage of development. (p. 1113)

Common-size statement A financial statement in which the components are expressed as percentages of a total figure in the statement. (p. 661)

Common stock Shares of stock that carry voting rights but that rank below preferred stock in terms of dividends and the distribution of assets. (pp. 8, 546)

Comparability The convention of presenting information in a way that enables decision makers to recognize similarities, differences, and trends over different periods in the same company and among different companies. (p. 206)

Compensation committee A committee of independent directors appointed by a public corporation's board of directors to determine how top executives will be compensated. (p. 681)

Complete information All the information necessary for a reliable decision. (p. 206)

Compound entry A journal entry in which more than two accounts are involved. (p. 98)

Compound interest The interest cost for two or more periods when, after each period, the interest of that period is added to the amount on which interest is computed in future periods. (p. 458)

Computer-aided design (CAD) A computer-based engineering system with a built-in program to identify poorly designed parts or manufacturing processes, which means that engineers can correct these problems before production begins. (p. 1150)

Computer-integrated manufacturing (CIM) systems The use of computers to coordinate the production and its support operations. (p. 1151)

Confirmative value Information that confirms or changes previous evaluations. (p. 205)

Conservatism The convention that when faced with two equally acceptable alternatives, the accountant chooses the one least likely to overstate assets and income. (p. 207)

Consignment Merchandise that its owner (the consignor) places on the premises of another company (the consignee) with the understanding that payment is expected only when the merchandise is sold and that unsold items may be returned to the consignor. (p. 289)

Consistency The convention requiring that once a company has adopted an accounting procedure, it must use it from one period to the next unless a note to the financial statements informs users of a change in procedure. (pp. 206, 678)

Contingent liability A potential liability that arises from a past transaction and is dependent on a future event. (pp. 379, 456)

Continuity The difficulty associated with not knowing how long a business will survive. (p. 139)

Continuous budget A rolling 12-month budget that summarizes budgets for the next 12 months. Each month managers prepare a budget for that month, 12 months hence. (p. 928)

Continuous improvement The management concept that one should never be satisfied with what is, but should instead constantly seek improved efficiency and lower cost through better methods, products, services, processes, or resources. (p. 846)

Contra account An account whose balance is subtracted from an associated account in the financial statements. (p. 145)

Contributed Capital Assets that stockholders have invested in a corporation. Also called *Paid-in Capital.* (pp. 10, 212, 542)

Contribution margin (CM) The amount that remains after all variable costs are subtracted from sales. (p. 879)

Contribution margin income statement An income statement that is formatted to emphasize cost behavior rather than organizational functions (sometimes referred to as a variable costing income statement). (p. 879)

Control activities Policies and procedures that management establishes to ensure that the objectives of internal control are met. (p. 329)

Control environment A company's ethics, philosophy and operating style, organizational structure, method of assigning authority and responsibility, and personnel policies and practices. (p. 329)

Controllable costs and revenues Costs and revenues that are the result of a manager's actions, influence, or decisions. (p. 957)

Conversion costs The costs of converting direct materials into a finished product; the sum of direct labor costs and overhead costs. Also called *processing costs.* (pp. 714, 797, 844)

Convertible bonds Bonds that can be exchanged for the issuing corporation's common stock. (p. 490)

Convertible preferred stock Preferred stock that the owner can exchange for common stock. (p. 548)

Copyright An exclusive right granted by the federal government to reproduce and sell literary, musical, and other artistic materials and computer programs for a period of the author's life plus 70 years. (p. 417)

Core competency The activity that a company does best and that gives it an advantage over its competitors. (p. 832)

Corporate governance The oversight of a corporation's management and ethics by its board of directors. (p. 8)

Corporation A business unit granted a state charter recognizing it as a separate legal entity having its own rights, privileges, and liabilities distinct from those of its owners. (p. 7)

Cost The net purchase price of an asset plus all reasonable and necessary expenditures to get it in place and ready for use. (p. 405)

Cost allocation The process of assigning a collection of indirect costs to a specific cost object using an allocation base known as a cost driver. (p. 763)

Cost behavior The way costs respond to changes in volume or activity. (p. 872)

Cost-benefit The convention that the benefits gained from providing accounting information should be greater than the costs of providing that information. Also called *cost constraint.* (p. 206)

Cost center A responsibility center whose manager is accountable only for controllable costs that have well-defined relationships between the center's resources and certain products or services. (p. 958)

Cost constraint The convention that the benefits gained from providing accounting information should be greater than the costs of providing that information. Also called *cost-benefit.* (p. 206)

Cost driver An activity base that causes a cost pool to increase in amount as the cost driver increases in volume. (p. 763)

Cost flow The association of costs with their assumed flow versus their actual goods flow in the operations of a company. (p. 289)

Cost hierarchy A framework for classifying activities according to the level at which their costs are incurred. (p. 836)

Cost object The destination of an assigned, or allocated, cost. (p. 763)

Cost of capital The minimum desired rate of return on an investment, such as assets invested in an investment center. (p. 967)

Cost of goods available for sale The sum of beginning inventory and the net cost of purchases during an accounting period. (p. 257)

Cost of goods manufactured The cost of all units completed and moved to Finished Goods Inventory during an accounting period. (p. 720)

Cost of goods manufactured budget A detailed plan that summarizes the estimated costs of production during an accounting period. (p. 918)

Cost of goods sold The amount a merchandiser paid for the merchandise it sold during an accounting period or the cost to a manufacturer of making the products it sold during an accounting period. Also called *cost of sales* or *cost of revenue.* (pp. 245, 720)

Cost-plus contracts Job contracts that require the customer to pay all costs incurred in performing the job plus a predetermined amount of profit. (p. 761)

Cost-plus transfer price A price based on either the full cost or the variable costs incurred by the producing division plus an agreed-on profit percentage. (p. 1116)

Cost pool The collection of overhead costs assigned to a cost object. (p. 763)

Cost principle The practice of recording transactions at the exchange price at the point of recognition. (p. 89)

Cost savings The decrease in operating costs that will result from the proposed capital investments. (p. 1077)

Cost-volume-profit (CVP) analysis An examination of the cost behavior patterns that underlie the relationships among cost, volume of output, and profit. (p. 881)

Costs of conformance The costs of good quality that are incurred to ensure the successful development of a product or service. (p. 1148)

Costs of nonconformance The costs of poor quality that are incurred to correct defects in a product or service. (p. 1148)

Costs of quality Both the costs of achieving quality and the costs of poor quality in the manufacture of a product or the delivery of a service. (pp. 846, 1148)

Coupon bonds Bonds not registered with the issuing organization that bear coupons stating the amount of interest due and the payment date. (p. 491)

Credit The right side of an account. (p. 92)

Creditors Those who lend money or deliver goods and services to a company before being paid. (p. 20)

Crossfooting Adding and subtracting numbers across a row. (p. 194)

Cumulative preferred stock Preferred stock on which unpaid dividends accumulate over time and that must be satisfied before a dividend can be paid to common stockholders. (p. 547)

Current assets Cash and other assets that a company can reasonably expect to convert to cash, sell, or consume within one year or its normal operating cycle, whichever is longer. (p. 209)

Current liabilities Obligations due to be paid or performed within one year or within the normal operating cycle, whichever is longer. (pp. 211, 442)

Current ratio A measure of liquidity, or short-term debt-paying ability; calculated as Current Assets ÷ Current Liabilities. (pp. 214, 673)

Customer list A list of customers or subscribers. (p. 417)

D

Days' inventory on hand A measure that shows the average number of days taken to sell inventory; calculated as Days in Accounting Period ÷ Inventory Turnover. (pp. 305, 671)

Days' payable A measure that shows the average number of days a company takes to pay its accounts payable; calculated as Days in Accounting Period ÷ Payables Turnover. (pp. 466, 673)

Days' sales uncollected A measure that shows the number of days, on average, that a company must wait to receive payment for credit sales; calculated as Days in Accounting Period ÷ Receivables Turnover. (pp. 378, 672)

Debit The left side of an account. (p. 92)

Debt to equity ratio A measure of profitability that shows the proportion of a company's assets that is financed by creditors and the proportion financed by the stockholders; calculated as Total Liabilities ÷ Total Stockholders' Equity. (pp. 219, 519, 669)

Decentralized organization A business that is organized into divisions or operating segments with a separate manager assigned to each segment. (p. 1116)

Declaration date The date on which a board of directors declares a dividend. (p. 560)

Declining-balance method An accelerated method of depreciation in which depreciation is computed by applying a fixed rate to the carrying value (the declining balance) of a tangible long-lived asset. (p. 407)

Deferral The postponement of the recognition of an expense already paid or of revenue received in advance. (p. 143)

Deferred income taxes A postponement in paying taxes as the result of using different methods to calculate income taxes for financial reporting and tax purposes. (p. 488)

Defined benefit plan A pension plan in which the employer contributes an amount annually to fund estimated future pension liability. (p. 516)

Defined contribution plan A pension plan in which the employer makes a fixed annual contribution, usually a percentage of the employee's gross pay. (p. 516)

Definitely determinable liabilities Current liabilities that are set by contract or statute and that can be measured exactly. (p. 444)

Delivery cycle time The time between the acceptance of an order and the final delivery of the product or service to the customer. (p. 1151)

Delivery expense The transportation cost of delivering merchandise incurred by the seller. Also called *freight-out.* (p. 250)

Delivery time The time between the completion of a product and its receipt by the customer. (p. 1151)

Deming Prize A prize created by the Japanese Union of Scientists and Engineers that honors individuals or groups who have contributed to the development and dissemination of total quality control. (p. 1145)

Depletion The exhaustion of a natural resource through mining, cutting, pumping, or other extraction, and the way in which the cost is allocated. (p. 398)

Deposits in transit Deposits a company has sent to its bank but that the bank did not receive in time to enter on the bank statement. (p. 338)

Depreciable cost The cost of an asset less its residual value. (p. 405)

Depreciation The portion of the cost of a long-term asset allocated to any one accounting period. Also called *depreciation expense.* (pp. 145, 398)

Differential cost A cost that changes among alternatives. Also called an *incremental cost.* (p. 1040)

Direct charge-off method A method of accounting for uncollectible accounts by directly debiting an expense account when bad debts are discovered; it violates the matching rule but is required for computing federal income tax. (p. 365)

Direct costs Costs that can be conveniently and economically traced to a cost object. (p. 712)

Direct labor budget A detailed plan that estimates the direct labor hours needed during an accounting period and the associated costs. (pp. 713, 916)

Direct labor costs The costs of the labor needed to make a product or perform a service that can be conveniently and economically traced to specific units of the product or service. (p. 713)

Direct labor efficiency variance The difference between the standard direct labor hours allowed for good units produced and the actual direct labor hours worked multiplied by the standard direct labor rate. Also called *direct labor quantity* or *usage variance.* (p. 1007)

Direct labor rate standard The hourly direct labor rate that is expected to prevail during the next accounting period for each function or job classification. (p. 1000)

Direct labor rate variance The difference between the standard direct labor rate and the actual direct labor rate multiplied by the actual direct labor hours worked. Also called *direct labor spending variance.* (p. 1007)

Direct labor time standard The expected labor time required for each department, machine, or process to complete the production of one unit or one batch of output. (p. 1000)

Direct materials costs The costs of the materials used in making a product that can be conveniently and economically traced to specific units of the product. (p. 713)

Direct materials price standard A careful estimate of the cost of a specific direct material in the next accounting period. (p. 999)

Direct materials price variance The difference between the standard price and the actual price per unit multiplied by the actual quantity purchased. Also called *direct materials spending* or *rate variance.* (p. 1004)

Direct materials purchases budget A detailed plan that identifies the quantity of purchases required to meet budgeted production and inventory needs and the costs associated with those purchases. (p. 914)

Direct materials quantity standard An estimate of the amount of direct materials, including scrap and waste, that will be used in an accounting period. (p. 999)

Direct materials quantity variance The difference between the standard quantity allowed and the actual quantity used multiplied by the standard price. Also called *direct materials efficiency* or *usage variance.* (p. 1004)

Direct method The procedure for converting the income statement from an accrual basis to a cash basis by adjusting each item on the income statement. (p. 599)

Discontinued operations Segments that are no longer part of a company's operations. (p. 680)

Discount The amount by which a bond's face value exceeds its issue price, which occurs when the market interest rate is higher than the face interest rate. (p. 490)

Discounting A method of selling notes receivable to a bank in which the bank derives its profit by deducting the interest from the maturity value of the note. (p. 380)

Discretionary cost center A responsibility center whose manager is accountable for costs only and in which the relationship between resources and the products or services produced is not well defined. (p. 958)

Dishonored note A promissory note that the maker cannot or will not pay at the maturity date. (p. 375)

Diversified companies Companies that operate in more than one industry. Also called *conglomerates.* (p. 655)

Dividend yield A measure of a stock's current return to an investor in the form of dividends; calculated as Dividends per Share ÷ Market Price per Share. (pp. 569, 675)

Dividends A distribution of a corporation's assets (usually cash generated by past earnings) to its stockholders. (pp. 11, 213, 559)

Dividends in arrears Past dividends on cumulative preferred stock that remain unpaid. (p. 547)

Double-declining-balance method An accelerated method of depreciation in which a fixed rate equal to twice the straight-line percentage is applied to the carrying value (the declining balance) of a tangible long-lived asset. (p. 407)

Double-entry system The accounting system in which each transaction is recorded with at least one debit and one credit so that the total amount of debits equals the total amount of credits. (p. 90)

Double taxation Taxation of corporate earnings twice—once as income of the corporation and once as income to the stockholders in the form of dividends. (p. 543)

Due care Competence and diligence in carrying out professional responsibilities. (p. 18)

Duration of a note The time between a promissory note's issue date and its maturity date. (p. 374)

E

Early extinguishment of debt The retirement of a bond issue before its maturity date. (p. 490)

Earnings management The manipulation of revenues and expenses to achieve a specific outcome. (p. 155)

Economic entity A unit that exists independently, such as a business, hospital, or a governmental body. (p. 4)

Economic Stimulus Act of 2008 A federal income tax law that allows a small company to expense the first $250,000 of equipment expenditures. (p. 409)

Economic value added (EVA) The shareholder wealth created by an investment center; calculated as After-Tax Operating Income − [Cost of Capital in Dollars × (Total Assets − Current Liabilities)]. (p. 967)

Effective interest method A method of amortizing bond discounts or premiums that applies a constant interest rate (the market rate when the bonds were issued) to the bonds' carrying value at the beginning of each interest period. (p. 499)

EFQM Excellence Award An annual award presented by the European Foundation for Quality Management to businesses and organizations operating in Europe that excel in quality management. (p. 1145)

Electronic funds transfer (EFT) The transfer of funds from one bank to another through electronic communication. (p. 338)

Employee A worker who is paid a wage or salary and who is under the organization's direct supervision and control. (p. 448)

Engineering method A method that separates costs into their fixed and variable components by performing a step-by-step analysis of the tasks, costs, and processes involved in completing an activity or product. (p. 879)

Enterprise resource planning (ERP) system A database system that combines the management of all major business activities with support activities to form one easy-to-access, centralized data warehouse. (p. 1157)

Equivalent production A measure that applies a percentage-of-completion factor to partially completed units to compute the equivalent number of whole units produced during a period for each type of input. Also called *equivalent units.* (p. 797)

Estimated liabilities Definite debts or obligations whose exact amounts cannot be known until a later date. (p. 452)

Estimated useful life The total number of service units expected from a long-term asset. (p. 405)

Ethics A code of conduct that addresses whether actions are right or wrong. (p. 23)

Exchange gain or loss A gain or loss due to exchange rate fluctuation between the date of sale and the date of payment; it is reported on the income statement. (p. 266)

Exchange rate The value of one currency in terms of another. (p. 6)

Ex-dividend A description of stock between the record date and the date of payment, during which the right to the dividend remains with the person who owned the stock on the record date. (p. 560)

Expenditure A payment or an obligation to make future payment for an asset or a service. (p. 400)

Expenses Decreases in stockholders' equity resulting from the costs of goods and services used in the course of earning revenues. (pp. 10, 138)

External failure costs The costs incurred to correct mistakes discovered by customers after the delivery of a defective product or service. (p. 1148)

Extraordinary repairs Repairs that significantly enhance a plant asset's estimated useful life or residual value and thereby increase its carrying value. (p. 400)

F

Face interest rate The fixed rate of interest paid to bondholders based on the face value of the bonds. (p. 489)

Face value The principal amount of each share of stock; also called *par value.* (p. 489)

Facility-level activities Activities performed to support a facility's general manufacturing process. (p. 836)

Factor An entity that buys accounts receivable. (p. 379)

Factoring The sale or transfer of accounts receivable. (p. 379)

Fair value The exchange price of an actual or potential business transaction between market participants. (p. 89)

Faithful representation The qualitative characteristic of information that financial information must be complete, neutral, and free from material error. (p. 206)

Financial accounting The process of generating and communicating accounting information in the form of financial statements to those outside the organization. (p. 4)

Financial Accounting Standards Board (FASB) The most important body for developing rules on accounting practice; it issues Statements of Financial Accounting Standards. (p. 17)

Financial analysis The evaluation and interpretation of financial statements and related performance measures to determine whether a business is well managed and achieving its goals. (p. 22)

Financial budgets Budget projections of the financial results for an accounting period. (p. 908)

Financial leverage A corporation's ability to increase earnings for stockholders by earning more on assets than it pays in interest on the debt it incurred to finance the assets. Also called *trading on equity.* (p. 518)

Financial position The economic resources that belong to a company and the claims (equities) against those resources at a particular time. (p. 9)

Financial ratio analysis A technique of financial performance evaluation that identifies key relationships between components of the financial statements. (p. 664)

Financial ratios Comparisons between the elements on financial statements from one period to another and from one company to another. (p. 22)

Financial statement analysis An evaluation method that shows how items in a company's financial statements relate to the company's financial performance objectives. Also called *financial performance measurement.* (p. 654)

Financial statements The primary means of communicating important accounting information to users. They include the income statement, statement of stockholders' equity, balance sheet, and statement of cash flows. (p. 4)

Financing activities Activities undertaken by management to obtain adequate funds (as from stockholders and creditors) to begin and to continue operating a business. (pp. 21, 597)

Financing period The amount of time from the purchase of inventory until it is sold and payment is collected, less the amount of time creditors give the company to pay for the inventory. (pp. 264, 671)

Finished Goods Inventory account An inventory account that shows the costs assigned to all completed products that have not been sold. (p. 718)

First-in, first-out (FIFO) costing method A process costing method in which the cost flow follows the actual flow of production so that the costs assigned to the first products processed are the first costs transferred out when those products flow to the next process, department, or work cell. (p. 795)

First-in, first-out (FIFO) method An inventory costing method based on the assumption that the costs of the first items acquired should be assigned to the first items sold. (p. 293)

Fiscal year Any 12-month accounting period. (p. 139)

Fixed cost(s) A cost that remains constant within a defined range of activity or time period. (pp. 714, 874)

Fixed cost formula A horizontal line in the relevant range, $Y = b$, where Y is total fixed cost and b is the fixed cost in the relevant range. (p. 874)

Fixed overhead budget variance The difference between budgeted and actual fixed overhead costs. Also called *budgeted fixed overhead variance.* (p. 1014)

Fixed overhead volume variance The difference between budgeted fixed overhead costs and the overhead costs that are applied to production using the standard fixed overhead rate. (p. 1014)

Flexible budget A summary of expected costs for a range of activity levels. Also called a *variable budget.* (p. 961)

Flexible budget formula An equation that determines the expected, or budgeted, cost for any level of output; calculated as (Variable Cost per Unit × Number of Units Produced) + Budgeted Fixed Costs. (p. 961)

FOB destination A term indicating that the seller retains title to the merchandise until it reaches its destination and that the seller bears the shipping costs. (p. 249)

FOB shipping point A term indicating that the buyer assumes title to the merchandise at the shipping point and bears the shipping costs. (p. 249)

Footings Working totals of columns of numbers. To foot means to total a column of numbers. (p. 92)

Form 8-K Current reports filed by U.S. public corporations with the Securities and Exchange Commission. (p. 656)

Form 10-K An annual report filed by U.S. public corporations with the Securities and Exchange Commission. (p. 656)

Form 10-Q A quarterly report filed by U.S. public corporations with the Securities and Exchange Commission. (p. 656)

Franchise The right to an exclusive territory or market. (p. 417)

Fraudulent financial reporting The intentional preparation of misleading financial statements. (p. 23)

Free cash flow The amount of cash that remains after deducting the funds a company must commit to continue operating at its planned level; calculated as Net Cash Flows from Operating Activities – Dividends – Purchases of Plant Assets + Sales of Plant Assets. (pp. 422, 618, 668)

Free from material error Information that meets a minimum level of accuracy so it does not distort what is being reported. (p. 206)

Freight-in The transportation cost of receiving merchandise incurred by the buyer. (p. 250)

Full-costing method A method of accounting for the costs of exploring and developing oil and gas resources in which all costs are recorded as assets and depleted over the estimated life of the producing resources. (p. 416)

Full disclosure The convention requiring that a company's financial statements and the accompanying notes present all information relevant to the users' understanding of the statements. Also called *transparency.* (pp. 207, 678)

Full product cost A cost that includes not only the costs of direct materials and direct labor but also the costs of all production and nonproduction activities required to satisfy the customer. (p. 832)

Future value The amount an investment will be worth at a future date if invested at simple interest or compound interest. (p. 458)

G

General and administrative expenses Expenses for accounting, personnel, credit checking, collections, and any other expenses that apply to overall operations. (p. 246)

General journal The simplest and most flexible type of journal. (p. 106)

General ledger A book or file that contains all of a company's accounts arranged in the order of the chart of accounts. Also called the *ledger.* (p. 90)

Generally accepted accounting principles (GAAP) The conventions, rules, and procedures that define accepted accounting practice at a particular time. (p. 16)

Goal/vision The overriding objective of a business to increase the value of the stakeholders' interest in the business. (p. 727)

Going concern The assumption that unless there is evidence to the contrary, a business will continue to operate indefinitely. (p. 139)

Goods flow The actual physical movement of goods in the operations of a company. (p. 289)

Goodwill The excess of the amount paid for a business over the fair market value of the business's net assets. (pp. 211, 417)

Governmental Accounting Standards Board (GASB) The board responsible for issuing accounting standards for state and local governments. (p. 18)

Gross margin The difference between net sales and cost of goods sold. Also called *gross profit.* (p. 245)

Gross margin pricing method Emphasizes the use of income statement information to determine a selling price; also called the *income statement method.* (p. 1107)

Gross profit method A method of inventory estimation based on the assumption that the ratio of gross margin for a business remains relatively stable from year to year. Also called *gross margin method.* (p. 302)

Gross sales Total revenue from cash and credit sales during an accounting period. (p. 245)

Group depreciation The grouping of similar items to calculate depreciation. (p. 408)

H

High-low method A three-step approach to separating a mixed cost into its variable and fixed components. (p. 878)

Horizontal analysis A technique for analyzing financial statements in which changes from the previous year to the current year are computed in both dollar amounts and percentages. (p. 658)

I

Imprest system A system for controlling small cash disbursements by establishing a fund at a fixed amount and periodically reimbursing the fund by the amount necessary to restore the original cash balance. (p. 338)

Income before income taxes The amount on which income taxes will be determined; calculated as Income from Operations +/– Other Revenues and Expenses. (p. 247)

Income from operations Gross margin minus operating expenses. Also called *operating income.* (p. 246)

Income statement A financial statement that summarizes the revenues earned and expenses incurred by a business over an accounting period. (p. 12)

Incremental analysis A technique used in decision analysis that compares alternatives by focusing on the differences in their projected revenues and costs. Also called *differential analysis.* (p. 1040)

Incremental revenue Total revenue if product/service is sold at split-off point minus total revenue if product/service is sold after further processing. (p. 1051)

Incurred costs The actual costs incurred in making a product. (p. 1113)

Independence The avoidance of all relationships that impair or appear to impair an accountant's objectivity. (p. 18)

Independent contractor An individual who offers services for a fee but who is not under the organization's direct control or supervision. (p. 448)

Index number In trend analysis, a number that shows changes in related items over time and that is calculated by setting the base year equal to 100 percent. (p. 660)

Indirect costs Costs that cannot be conveniently or economically traced to a cost object. (p. 712)

Indirect labor costs The costs of labor for production-related activities that cannot be conveniently or economically traced to a unit of the product or service. (p. 713)

Indirect materials costs The costs of materials that cannot be conveniently and economically traced to a unit of the product or service. (p. 713)

Indirect method The procedure for converting the income statement from an accrual basis to a cash basis by adjusting net income for items that do not affect cash flows, including depreciation, amortization, depletion, gains, losses, and changes in current assets and current liabilities. (p. 600)

Information and communication A component of internal control that refers to the way in which the accounting system gathers and treats information and how it communicates individual responsibilities within the system. (p. 329)

Initial public offering (IPO) A company's first issue of capital stock to the public. (p. 541)

Inspection time The time spent looking for product flaws or reworking defective units. (p. 841)

Institute of Management Accountants (IMA) A professional organization made up primarily of managerial accountants. (p. 18)

Intangible assets Long-term assets with no physical substance whose value stems from the rights or privileges accruing to their owners. (pp. 211, 398)

Integrity Honesty, candidness, and the subordination of personal gain to service and the public trust. (p. 18)

Interest The cost of borrowing money or the return on lending money, depending on whether one is the borrower or the lender. (pp. 374, 458)

Interest coverage ratio A measure of the degree of protection a company has from default on interest payments; calculated as (Income Before Income Taxes + Interest Expense) ÷ Interest Expense. (pp. 519, 670)

Interest receivable Any interest accrued on promissory notes. (p. 367)

Interim financial statements Financial statements issued for a period of less than one year, usually a quarter or a month. (p. 656)

Interim periods Accounting periods of less than one year. (p. 139)

Internal control A process designed by a company to establish the reliability of the accounting records and financial statements in accordance with generally accepted accounting principles (GAAP) and to ensure that the company's assets are protected. (p. 328)

Internal failure costs The costs incurred to correct mistakes found by the company when defects are discovered before a product or service is delivered to a customer. (p. 1148)

Internal Revenue Service (IRS) The agency that interprets and enforces the tax laws governing the assessment and collection of revenue for operating the federal government. (p. 18)

International Accounting Standards Board (IASB) An organization that encourages worldwide cooperation in the development of accounting principles; it has approved more than 40 international standards of accounting. (p. 17)

International financial reporting standards (IFRS) Accounting standards set by the IASB that are used in many parts of the world, including Europe, and by foreign companies registered in the United States. (p. 17)

Inventory accounting An accounting system in which the primary objective is to apply accrual accounting to the determination of cost of inventory sold during the accounting period. (p. 288)

Inventory cost The invoice price of an asset less purchases discounts, plus freight-in, plus applicable taxes and tariffs. (p. 288)

Inventory turnover A ratio indicating the number of times a company's average inventory is sold during an accounting period; calculated as Cost of Goods Sold ÷ Average Inventory. (pp. 304, 671)

Investing activities Activities undertaken by management to spend capital in productive ways that will help a business achieve its goals. (pp. 21, 597)

Investment center A responsibility center whose manager is accountable for profit generation and who can also make significant decisions about the resources the center uses. (p. 958)

Investments Assets, usually long-term, that are not used in the normal operation of a business and that management does not intend to convert to cash within the next year. (p. 211)

Investors Stockholders who have a direct financial interest in the success of the company in which they have invested. (p. 20)

Invoice A form that a vendor sends to a purchaser describing the goods delivered and the quantity, price, and terms of payment. (p. 336)

ISO 9000 Guidelines created by the International Organization for Standardization (ISO) that cover the design, development, production, final inspection and testing, installation, and servicing of products, processes, and services. (p. 1146)

ISO 14000 Guidelines created by the International Organization for Standardization (ISO) that provide a management framework to minimize the harmful environmental effects of business activities and continually improve environmental performance. (p. 1147)

ISO 26000 Guidelines created by the International Organization for Standardization (ISO) that provide social responsibility guidance. (p. 1147)

ISO 31000 Guidelines created by the International Organization for Standardization (ISO) that outline risk management principles and guidelines. (p. 1147)

Issued shares The shares of stock sold or otherwise transferred to stockholders. (p. 546)

J

Job order A customer order for a specific number of specially designed, made-to-order products. (p. 754)

Job order cost card A document on which all costs incurred in the production of a particular job order are recorded; part of the subsidiary ledger for the Work in Process Inventory account. (p. 754)

Job order costing system A product costing system that traces the costs of direct materials, direct labor, and overhead to a specific batch of products or a specific job order; used by companies that make unique or special-order products. (p. 754)

Joint costs The common costs shared by two or more products before they are split off. Also called *common costs.* (p. 1051)

Joint products Two or more products made from a common material or process that cannot be identified as separate products or services during some or all of the production process. (p. 1051)

Journal A chronological record of all transactions; the place where transactions first enter the accounting records. Also called *book of original entry.* (p. 96)

Journal entry A journal notation that records a single transaction. (p. 96)

Journal form A way of recording a transaction in which the date, debit account, and debit amount appear on one line and the credit account and credit amount appear on the next line. (p. 96)

Just-in-time (JIT) operating environment A method of reducing levels of inventory by working closely with suppliers to coordinate and schedule deliveries so that goods arrive just at the time they are needed. (p. 305)

Just-in-time (JIT) operating philosophy A system that requires that all resources—materials, personnel, and facilities—be acquired and used only as needed; it focuses on eliminating or reducing waste in the production of products and services. (p. 839)

K

Kaizen Suggestions from employees for improvements to the production process. (pp. 841, 1144)

L

Last-in, first-out (LIFO) method An inventory costing method based on the assumption that the costs of the last items purchased should be assigned to the first items sold. (p. 294)

Lean operation An operating philosophy that requires that all resources—materials, personnel, and facilities—be acquired and used only as needed to create value for customers; its objective is to reduce costs by eliminating waste. (p. 839)

Leasehold A right to occupy land or buildings under a long-term rental contract. (p. 417)

Leasehold improvements Improvements to leased property that become the property of the lessor at the end of the lease. (p. 403)

Ledger account form An account form that has four dollar amount columns: one column for debit entries, one column for credit entries, and two columns (debit and credit) for showing the balance of the account. (p. 107)

Legal capital The number of shares of stock issued times the par value; the minimum amount a corporation can report as contributed capital. (p. 543)

Liabilities A business's present obligations to pay cash, transfer assets, or provide services to other entities in the future. (p. 10)

License The right to use a formula, technique, process, or design. (p. 417)

LIFO liquidation The reduction of inventory below previous levels because sales of older, lower-priced units have exceeded the purchases of units for the current period. (p. 297)

Limited liability The limited risk of loss that applies to stockholders' investments in corporations. It is limited to the amount stockholders paid for their shares of stock. (p. 7)

Line of credit An arrangement with a bank that allows a company to borrow funds as needed. (p. 443)

Liquidating dividend A dividend that exceeds retained earnings and that a corporation usually pays only when it is going out of business or reducing its operations. (p. 559)

Liquidity Having enough cash available to pay debts when they are due and to take care of unexpected needs for cash. (pp. 21, 214)

Long-term assets Assets that have a useful life of more than one year, are used in the operation of a business, and are not intended for resale. Less commonly called fixed assets. (p. 398)

Long-term liabilities Debts and obligations due beyond one year or beyond the normal operating cycle. (pp. 212, 442, 486)

Lower-of-cost-or-market (LCM) rule A method of valuing inventory at an amount less than cost when the replacement cost falls below historical cost. (p. 290)

M

Make-or-buy decisions Decisions about whether to make a part internally or buy it from an external supplier. (p. 1043)

Malcolm Baldrige National Quality Award An award created by the U.S. Congress that recognizes U.S. organizations for their achievements in quality and business performance. (p. 1146)

Management The people who have overall responsibility for operating a business and meeting its goals of profitability and liquidity. (p. 19)

Management information systems (MIS) The interconnected subsystems that provide the information needed to run a business. (pp. 5, 1157)

Managerial accounting The process of generating and communicating accounting information about operating, investing, and financing activities for internal use by managers. (pp. 5, 710)

Manufacturing company A company that makes and sells products. (p. 245)

Manufacturing cost flow The flow of manufacturing costs (direct materials, direct labor, and overhead) through the Materials Inventory, Work in Process Inventory, and Finished Goods Inventory accounts into the Cost of Goods Sold account. (p. 718)

Margin of safety The number of sales units or amount of sales dollars by which actual sales can fall below planned sales without resulting in a loss. (p. 881)

Marginal cost The change in total cost caused by a one-unit change in output. (p. 1105)

Marginal revenue The change in total revenue caused by a one-unit change in output. (p. 1105)

Market Current replacement cost of inventory. (p. 290)

Market interest rate The rate of interest paid in the market on bonds of similar risk. Also called *effective interest rate.* (p. 489)

Market transfer price Based on the price that could be charged if a segment could buy from or sell to an external party; also called *external market price.* (p. 1116)

Marketable securities Short-term investments that have a maturity of more than 90 days but are intended to be held only until cash is needed for current operations. (p. 596)

Master budget A set of operating budgets and a set of financial budgets that detail an organization's financial plans for a specific accounting period. (p. 908)

Material Information that if omitted or misstated could influence economic decisions made by users of financial statements. (p. 205)

Materiality The convention that refers to the relative importance of an item or event in a financial statement and its influence on the decisions of the users of financial statements. (p. 205)

Materials Inventory account An inventory account that shows the balance of the cost of unused materials. (p. 718)

Maturity date The date on which a promissory note must be paid. (p. 374)

Maturity value The total proceeds of a promissory note—face value plus interest—at the maturity date. (p. 375)

Merchandise inventory The goods on hand at any one time that are available for sale to customers. (p. 242)

Merchandising company A business that earns income by buying and selling goods. (p. 242)

Minimum rate of return The rate of return that must be exceeded to ensure profitability. Also called the *hurdle rate.* (p. 1075)

Mission statement A description of the fundamental way in which a company will achieve the goal of increasing stakeholders' value. (p. 728)

Mixed cost formula A linear equation, Y = a(X) + b, where *Y* is total mixed cost, *a* is the variable rate per unit, *X* is the units produced, and *b* is the fixed cost for the period. (p. 875)

Mixed costs Costs that have both variable and fixed components. (p. 875)

Money measure The recording of all business transactions in terms of money. (p. 5)

Monitoring Management's regular assessment of the quality of internal control. (p. 329)

Mortgage A debt secured by real property. (p. 487)

Moving time The time spent moving a product from one operation or department to another. (p. 841)

Multistep income statement An income statement that goes through a series of steps to arrive at net income. (p. 244)

N

Natural resources Long-term assets purchased for the economic value that can be taken from the land and used up. (p. 398)

Negotiated transfer price A price arrived at through bargaining between the managers of the buying and selling divisions or segments. (p. 1116)

Net assets Assets minus liabilities; stockholders' equity. Also called *net worth.* (p. 10)

Net cash inflows The balance of increases in projected cash receipts over increases in projected cash payments resulting from a capital investment. (p. 1077)

Net cost of purchases Total purchases plus freight-in less any deductions such as purchases returns and allowances and discounts from suppliers for early payment. (p. 257)

Net income The difference between revenues and expenses when revenues exceed expenses. Also called *net earnings.* (pp. 11, 138, 247)

Net loss The difference between expenses and revenues when expenses exceed revenues. (pp. 11, 138)

Net present value method A method of evaluating capital investments in which all future cash flows for each proposed project are discounted to their present values and the amount of the initial investment is subtracted from their sum. The projects with the highest positive net present value—the amount that exceeds the initial investment—are selected for implementation. (p. 1079)

Net sales The gross proceeds from sales of merchandise (gross sales) less sales returns and allowances and any discounts allowed. Also called *net revenue.* (p. 245)

Neutral information Information that is free from bias intended to achieve a certain result or to bring about a particular behavior. (p. 206)

No-par stock Capital stock that does not have a par value. (p. 550)

Non-value-adding activity An activity that adds cost to a product or service but does not increase its market value. (p. 834)

Non-value-adding cost The cost of an activity that adds cost to a product or service but does not increase its market value. (p. 715)

Noncash investing and financing transactions Significant investing and financing transactions involving only long-term assets, long-term liabilities, or stockholders' equity that do not affect current cash inflows or outflows. (p. 599)

Noncompete covenant A contract limiting the rights of others to compete in a specific industry or line of business for a specified period. (p. 417)

Noncumulative preferred stock Preferred stock that does not oblige the issuer to make up a missed dividend in a subsequent year. (p. 547)

Normal balance The usual balance of an account; the side (debit or credit) that increases the account. (p. 93)

Normal capacity The average annual level of operating capacity needed to meet expected sales demand. (p. 874)

Normal costing method A method of cost measurement that combines the actual direct costs of materials and labor with estimated overhead costs to determine a product or service unit cost. (p. 726)

Normal operating cycle The average time a company needs to go from spending cash to receiving cash. (p. 209)

Notes payable A promissory note that represents a loan from a bank or other creditor; a long-term debt when due in more than one year. (p. 487)
Notes receivable Collective term for promissory notes held by the entity to which payment is promised (payee). (p. 365)
NSF (nonsufficient funds) checks Checks that a company has deposited but that are not paid when the bank presents them to the issuer's bank. (p. 338)

O

Objectivity Impartiality and intellectual honesty. (p. 18)
Obsolescence The process of becoming out of date, which is a factor in the limited useful life of tangible assets. (p. 404)
Off-balance-sheet financing Structuring long-term debts in such a way that they do not appear as liabilities on the balance sheet. (p. 519)
Operating activities Activities undertaken by management in the course of running a business. (pp. 21, 597)
Operating budgets Budget plans used in daily operations. (p. 908)
Operating capacity The upper limit of an organization's productive output capability, given its existing resources. (p. 873)
Operating cycle The time it takes to sell products and collect payment for them. (pp. 242, 671)
Operating expenses Expenses other than cost of goods sold incurred in running a business. (p. 246)
Operating lease A short-term lease in which the risks of ownership remain with the lessor and for which payments are recorded as rent expense. (p. 513)
Operating objectives Short-term goals that outline expectations for the performance of day-to-day operations. (p. 728)
Operations costing system A product costing system that combines parts of job order costing and process costing to create a hybrid system designed specifically for an organization's production process. (p. 754)
Opportunity costs The benefits that are forfeited or lost when one alternative is chosen over another. (p. 1042)
Ordinary annuity A series of equal payments made at the end of equal intervals of time, with compound interest on the payments. (p. 461)
Organization chart A visual representation of an organization's hierarchy of responsibility for the purposes of management control. (p. 959)
Other assets A balance sheet category that some companies use to group all assets other than current assets and property, plant, and equipment. (p. 209)
Other revenues and expenses The section of a multistep income statement that includes revenues and expenses not related to a company's operating activities. Also called *nonoperating revenues and expenses.* (p. 247)
Outsourcing The use of other companies to perform a process or service in the value chain that is not among an organization's core competencies. (pp. 832, 1043)
Outstanding checks Checks that a company has issued and recorded but that do not yet appear on its bank statement. (p. 338)
Outstanding shares Shares that have been issued and that are still in circulation. (p. 546)
Overapplied overhead costs The amount by which overhead costs applied using the predetermined overhead rate exceed the actual overhead costs for the accounting period. (p. 764)
Overhead budget A detailed plan of anticipated manufacturing costs, other than direct materials and direct labor costs, that must be incurred to meet budgeted production needs. (p. 916)
Overhead costs Production-related costs that cannot be practically or conveniently traced to an end product or service. Also called *factory overhead*, *factory burden*, *manufacturing overhead*, *service overhead*, or *indirect production costs.* (p. 713)

P

Par value An arbitrary amount assigned to each share of stock; constitutes a corporation's legal capital. (pp. 10, 543)
Participative budgeting A process in which personnel at all levels of an organization actively engage in making decisions about a budget. (p. 927)
Partners' equity The equity section of a partnership's balance sheet. (p. 212)
Partnership A business that is owned by two or more people and that is not incorporated. (p. 6)
Patent An exclusive right granted by the federal government for a period of 20 years to make a particular product or use a specific process. (p. 417)
Payables turnover The number of times, on average, that a company pays its accounts payable in an accounting period; calculated as (Cost of Goods Sold +/− Change in Merchandise Inventory) ÷ Average Accounts Payable (pp. 465, 672)
Payback period method A method of evaluating capital investments that bases the decision to invest in a capital project on the minimum length of time it will take to get back the amount of the initial investment in cash. The payback period is calculated by dividing the cost of investment by the annual net cash inflows. (p. 1081)
Payment date The date on which a dividend is paid. (p. 560)
Pension fund A fund established by the contributions of an employer and often of employees from which payments are made to employees after retirement or upon disability or death. (p. 516)
Pension plan A contract requiring a company to pay benefits to its employees after they retire. (p. 516)
Percentage of gross margin The gross margin divided by net sales. (p. 246)
Percentage of net sales method A method of estimating uncollectible accounts based on the assumption that a predictable proportion of each dollar of sales will not be collected. (p. 368)
Performance-based pay The linking of employee compensation to the achievement of measurable business targets. (p. 972)
Performance management and evaluation system A set of procedures that account for and report on both financial and nonfinancial performance so that a company can identify how well it is doing, where it is going, and what improvements will make it more profitable. (p. 956)

Performance measurement The use of quantitative tools to gauge an organization's performance in relation to a specific goal or an expected outcome. (p. 956)

Performance measures Quantitative tools that gauge and compare an organization's performance in relation to a specific goal or an expected outcome. (pp. 22, 956)

Period costs The costs of resources used during an accounting period that are not assigned to products or services. Also called *noninventoriable costs* or *selling, administrative, and general expenses.* (p. 713)

Periodic independent verification A periodic check of records against assets by someone other than the person responsible for accounting records and assets. (p. 330)

Periodic inventory system A system for determining inventory on hand by periodically taking a physical count. (p. 242)

Periodicity The assumption that although the lifetime of a business is uncertain, it is still useful to estimate its net income in terms of accounting periods. (p. 139)

Perpetual inventory system A system for determining inventory on hand by keeping continuous records of the quantity and, usually, the cost of individual items as they are bought and sold. (p. 242)

Petty cash fund A fund for making small payments of cash when it is inconvenient to pay by check. (p. 340)

Petty cash voucher A form signed by a person who receives cash from a petty cash fund; lists the date, amount, and purpose of the expenditure. (p. 341)

Physical controls Controls that limit access to assets. (p. 330)

Physical deterioration A decline in the useful life of a depreciable asset resulting from use and from exposure to the elements. (p. 404)

Physical inventory An actual count of all merchandise on hand. (pp. 242, 328)

Post-closing trial balance A trial balance prepared after all adjusting and closing entries have been posted to ensure that all temporary accounts have zero balances and that total debits equal total credits. (p. 191)

Posting The process of transferring journal entry information from the journal to the ledger. (p. 108)

Practical capacity Theoretical capacity reduced by normal and expected work stoppages. Also called *engineering capacity.* (p. 874)

Predetermined overhead rate The rate calculated before an accounting period begins by dividing the cost pool of total estimated overhead costs by the total estimated cost driver for that pool. (p. 764)

Predictive value Information that helps capital providers make decisions about future actions. (p. 205)

Preferred stock Stock that has preference over common stock, usually in terms of dividends and the distribution of assets. (p. 546)

Premium The amount by which a bond's issue price exceeds its face value, which occurs when the market interest rate is lower than the face interest rate. (p. 490)

Prepaid expenses Expenses paid in advance that have not yet expired; an asset account. (p. 143)

Present value The amount that must be invested today at a given rate of interest to produce a given future value. (p. 459)

Prevention costs The costs associated with the prevention of defects and failures in products and services. (p. 1148)

Price/earnings (P/E) ratio A measure of confidence in a company's future; calculated as Market Price per Share ÷ Earnings per Share. (pp. 570, 674)

Primary processes Components of the value chain that add value to a product or service. (p. 832)

Prime costs The primary costs of production; the sum of direct materials costs and direct labor costs. (p. 714)

Pro forma financial statements Financial statements that show projections rather than actual results and that are often used to communicate business plans to external parties. (p. 909)

Process cost report A report that managers use to track and analyze costs in a process costing system. (pp. 754, 795)

Process costing system A product costing system that traces the costs of direct materials, direct labor, and overhead to processes, departments, or work cells and then assigns the costs to the products manufactured by those processes, departments, or work cells; used by companies that produce large amounts of similar products or liquid products or that have long, continuous production runs of identical products. (pp. 754, 794)

Process mapping A method of using a visual diagram to indicate process inputs, outputs, constraints, and flows to help managers to identify unnecessary efforts and inefficiencies in a business process. (p. 1145)

Process value analysis (PVA) A technique that analyzes business processes by relating activities to the events that prompt those activities and to the resources that the activities consume. (p. 833)

Processing time The actual amount of time spent working on a product. (p. 841)

Product costing system A set of procedures that is used to account for an organization's product costs and to provide timely and accurate unit cost information for pricing, cost planning and control, inventory valuation, and financial statement preparation. (p. 754)

Product costs The costs assigned to inventory, which include the costs of direct materials, direct labor, and overhead. Also called *inventoriable costs.* (p. 713)

Product-level activities Activities performed to support a particular product line. (p. 836)

Product unit cost The cost of manufacturing a single unit of a product, computed either by dividing the total cost of direct materials, direct labor, and overhead by the total number of units produced, or by determining the cost per unit for each element of the product cost and summing those per unit costs. (p. 713)

Production budget A detailed plan showing the number of units that a company must produce to meet budgeted sales and inventory needs. (p. 913)

Production cycle time The time it takes to make a product. (p. 1151)

Production method A method of depreciation that assumes depreciation is solely the result of use and that allocates depreciation based on the units of use or output during each period of an asset's useful life. Also called the *units of production method.* (p. 406)

Profit center A responsibility center whose manager is accountable for both revenue and costs and for the resulting operating income. (p. 958)

Profit margin A measure of profitability that shows the percentage of each sales dollar that results in net income; calculated as Net Income ÷ Net Revenues (or Net Sales). (pp. 215, 665, 965)

Profitability The ability to earn enough income to attract and hold investment capital. (pp. 21, 215)

Promissory note(s) An unconditional promise to pay a definite sum of money on demand or at a future date. (pp. 365, 444)

Property, plant, and equipment Tangible long-term assets used in the day-to-day operations of a business. Also called *operating assets, fixed assets, tangible assets, long-lived assets*, or *plant assets*. (pp. 211, 398)

Public Company Accounting Oversight Board (PCAOB) A governmental body created by the Sarbanes-Oxley Act to regulate the accounting profession. It has the power to determine the standards that auditors must follow. (p. 17)

Pull-through production A production system in which a customer's order triggers the purchase of materials and the scheduling of production for the required products. (p. 840)

Purchase discounts Discounts that buyers take for early payment of merchandise; the Purchases Discounts account is a contra-purchases account used under the periodic inventory system. (p. 249)

Purchase order A form that a company's purchasing department sends to a vendor describing the items ordered and the quantity, price, terms, and shipping date. (p. 336)

Purchase-order lead time The time it takes a company to take and process an order and organize so that production can begin. (p. 1151)

Purchase requisition A formal written request for a purchase that a company's credit office (requesting department) sends to the purchasing department. (p. 336)

Purchases account A temporary account used under the periodic inventory system to accumulate the cost of merchandise purchased for resale during an accounting period. (p. 258)

Purchases Returns and Allowances account A contra-purchases account used under the periodic inventory system to accumulate cash refunds, credits on account, and other allowances made by suppliers. (p. 259)

Push-through production A production system in which products are manufactured in long production runs and stored in anticipation of customers' orders. (p. 840)

Q

Qualitative characteristics Standards for judging accounting information. (p. 205)

Quality The result of an operating environment in which a product or service meets or conforms to a customer's specifications the first time it is produced or delivered. (p. 1144)

Quality of earnings The substance of earnings and their sustainability into future periods. (p. 677)

Queue time The time a product spends waiting to be worked on once it enters a new operation or department. (p. 841)

Quick ratio A measure of short-term debt-paying ability; calculated as (Cash + Marketable Securities + Receivables) ÷ Current Liabilities. (p. 674)

R

Receivables turnover A ratio for measuring the average number of times receivables are turned into cash during an accounting period; calculated as Net Sales ÷ Average Accounts Receivable. (pp. 377, 672)

Receiving report A form on which an employee in a company's receiving department notes the quantity, type of goods, and their condition upon delivery from the vendor. (p. 336)

Recognition The determination of when a business transaction should be recorded. (p. 88)

Recognition point The predetermined time at which a transaction should be recorded; usually, the point at which title passes to the buyer. (p. 111)

Record date The date on which ownership of stock, and thus the right to receive a dividend, is determined. (p. 560)

Registered bonds Bonds that the issuing company registers in the names of the bondholders. (p. 491)

Registrar An official responsible for keeping a register or official records of stock transfers for a corporation. (p. 543)

Regression analysis A mathematical approach to separating a mixed cost into its variable and fixed components. (p. 879)

Relevance The qualitative characteristic of information that has a direct effect on a decision. (p. 205)

Relevant range The span of activity in which a company expects to operate. (p. 874)

Residual income (RI) The operating income that an investment center earns above a minimum desired return on invested assets; calculated as Investment Center's Operating Income − (Desired ROI × Assets Invested). (p. 966)

Residual value The portion of an asset's acquisition cost expected to be recovered at the date of its disposal. Also called *salvage value, disposal value*, or *trade-in value*. (p. 405)

Responsibility accounting An information system that classifies data according to areas of responsibility and reports each area's activities by including only the categories that the assigned manager can control. (p. 956)

Responsibility center An organizational unit whose manager has been assigned the responsibility of managing a portion of the organization's resources. The five types of responsibility centers are a cost center, discretionary cost center, revenue center, profit center, and investment center. (p. 956)

Restructuring The estimated cost of a change in a company's operations, usually involving the closing of facilities and the laying off of personnel. (p. 680)

Retail method A method of inventory estimation, used in retail merchandising businesses, in which inventory at retail value is reduced by the ratio of cost to retail price. (p. 301)

Retained earnings Stockholders' claims to assets arising from the earnings of the business; the accumulated earnings of a corporation since its inception, minus any losses, dividends, or transfers to contributed capital. Also called *Earned Capital*. (pp. 10, 213)

Return on assets A measure of profitability that shows how efficiently a company uses its assets to produce income; calculated as Net Income ÷ Average Total Assets. (pp. 217, 666)

Return on assets pricing method Focuses on earning a specified rate of return on the assets employed in the operation; also called the *balance sheet method*. (p. 1108)

Return on equity A measure of how much income is earned on each dollar invested by the company's owners/stockholders; calculated as Net Income ÷ Average Stockholders' Equity. (pp. 220, 569, 670)

Return on investment (ROI) A traditional performance measure that takes into account both operating income and the assets invested to produce that income; calculated as Operating Income ÷ Assets Invested. (p. 964)

Return on quality (ROQ) The result that occurs when the marginal revenues possible from a higher-quality good or service exceed the marginal costs of providing that higher quality. (p. 1144)

Revenue center A responsibility center whose manager is accountable primarily for revenue and whose success is based on its ability to generate revenue. (p. 958)

Revenue expenditure An expenditure for ordinary repairs and maintenance of a long-term asset, which is recorded by a debit to an expense account. (p. 400)

Revenue recognition The process of determining when revenue should be recorded. (p. 140)

Revenues Increases in stockholders' equity resulting from operating a business. (pp. 10, 138)

Risk assessment The identification of areas in which risk of loss of assets or inaccuracies in accounting records is high. (p. 329)

S

Salaries Compensation of employees at a monthly or yearly rate. (p. 447)

Sales budget A detailed plan, expressed in both units and dollars, that identifies the product (or service) sales expected during an accounting period. (p. 912)

Sales discount A discount given to a buyer for early payment of a sale made on credit; the Sales Discounts account is a contra-revenue account. (p. 249)

Sales forecast A projection of the estimated sales in units based on an analysis of external and internal factors. (p. 913)

Sales mix The proportion of each product's unit sales relative to the company's total unit sales. (p. 884)

Sales mix decision A decision to select the alternative that maximizes the contribution margin per constrained resource. (p. 1048)

Sales returns and allowances Refunds, credits, and discounts given to customers who have received defective goods. (p. 245)

Sales Returns and Allowances account A contra-revenue account used to accumulate cash refunds, credits on account, and other allowances made to customers who have received defective or otherwise unsatisfactory products. (p. 254)

Sarbanes-Oxley Act An act of Congress that regulates financial reporting in public corporations. (p. 23)

Scatter diagram A chart of plotted points that helps determine whether a linear relationship exists between a cost item and its related activity measure. (p. 877)

Secured bonds Bonds that carry a pledge of certain assets as a guarantee of repayment. (p. 490)

Securities and Exchange Commission (SEC) A governmental agency that regulates the issuing, buying, and selling of stocks. It has the legal power to set and enforce accounting practices for firms whose securities are sold to the general public. (p. 18)

Securitization The grouping of receivables into batches for sale at a discount to companies and investors. (p. 379)

Segment margin A segment's sales revenue minus its direct costs (direct variable costs and direct fixed costs traceable to the segment). (p. 1046)

Sell-or-process-further decision A decision about whether to sell a joint product at the split-off point or sell it after further processing. (p. 1051)

Selling and administrative expenses budget A detailed plan of operating expenses, other than those related to production, that are needed to support sales and overall operations during an accounting period. (p. 917)

Selling expenses The costs of storing goods and preparing them for sale; preparing displays, advertising, and otherwise promoting sales; and delivering goods to a buyer if the seller has agreed to pay the cost of delivery. (p. 246)

Separate entity A business that is treated as distinct from its creditors, customers, and owners. (p. 6)

Separation of duties No one person can authorize transactions, handle assets, or keep records of assets. (p. 330)

Serial bonds Bonds in one issue that mature on different dates. (p. 490)

Service unit cost The cost to perform one service. (p. 713)

Share of stock A unit of ownership in a corporation. (p. 8)

Short-run decision analysis The systematic examination of any decision whose effects will have the greatest impact within the next year. (p. 1040)

Short-term notes payable Promissory notes issued by companies to meet their short-term funding needs. (p. 444)

Simple interest The interest cost for one or more periods when the amount on which the interest is computed stays the same from period to period. (p. 458)

Single-step income statement An income statement that arrives at net income in a single step. (p. 247)

Six Sigma A level of quality by which customers would perceive a company's products and services as perfect. (p. 1144)

Software Capitalized costs associated with computer programs developed for sale, lease, or internal use and amortized over the estimated economic life of the programs. (p. 417)

Software as a service (SaaS) A database system that utilizes the Internet, social media, and mobile technologies to manage all business activities on demand. (p. 1157)

Sole proprietorship A business that is owned by one person and that is not incorporated. (p. 6)

Source documents Invoices, checks, receipts, or contracts that support the details of a transaction. (p. 96)

Special order decisions Decisions about whether to accept or reject special orders at prices below the normal market prices. (p. 1044)

Specific identification method An inventory costing method in which the cost of each item in ending inventory is identified as coming from a specific purchase. (p. 292)

Split-off point A specific point in the production process at which two or more joint products become separate and identifiable. At that point, a company may choose to sell the product as is or process it into another form for sale to a different market. (p. 1051)

Standard costing A method of cost control with three components: a standard, or predetermined, performance level; a measure of actual performance; and a measure of the difference, or variance, between standard and actual performance. (p. 998)

Standard costing method A method of cost measurement that uses the estimated or standard costs of direct materials, direct labor, and overhead to calculate a product or service unit cost. (p. 726)

Standard costs Realistic estimates of costs based on analyses of both past and projected operating costs and conditions. (p. 998)

Standard direct labor cost The standard wage for direct labor multiplied by the standard hours of direct labor. (p. 1000)

Standard direct materials cost The standard price for direct materials multiplied by the standard quantity for direct materials. (p. 999)

Standard fixed overhead rate Total budgeted fixed overhead costs divided by an expression of capacity, usually normal capacity in terms of standard direct labor hours or units. (p. 1000)

Standard overhead cost The sum of the estimates of variable and fixed overhead costs in the next accounting period. (p. 1000)

Standard variable overhead rate Total budgeted variable overhead costs divided by an expression of capacity, such as the expected number of standard machine hours or standard direct labor hours. (p. 1000)

Start-up and organization costs The costs of forming a corporation. (p. 544)

Stated value The value of each share of stock issued by a corporation as set by the board of directors; some states specify a minimum amount. (p. 551)

Statement of cash flows A financial statement that shows the inflows and outflows of cash from operating activities, investing activities, and financing activities over an accounting period. (pp. 14, 596)

Statement of cost of goods manufactured A formal statement summarizing the flow of all manufacturing costs incurred during an accounting period. (p. 723)

Statement of retained earnings A financial statement that shows the changes in retained earnings over an accounting period. (p. 12)

Statement of stockholders' equity A financial statement that summarizes changes in the components of the stockholders' equity section of the balance sheet. Also called the *statement of changes in stockholders' equity*. (p. 545)

Static budgets Budgets that are prepared once a year and do not change during the annual budget period. (p. 927)

Step cost A cost that remains constant in a relevant range of activity and increases/decreases in a stairstep-like manner when activity is outside the relevant range. (p. 874)

Stock dividend A proportional distribution of shares among a corporation's stockholders. (p. 562)

Stock option plans Plans that give employees the right to purchase their companies' stock under specified terms. (p. 571)

Stock split An increase in the number of outstanding shares of stock accompanied by a proportionate reduction in the par or stated value. (p. 564)

Stockholders The owners of a corporation whose ownership is represented by shares of stock but who do not directly control the corporation's operations. (p. 7)

Stockholders' equity The equity section of a balance sheet for a corporation; the owners' claims to the business. Also called *shareholders' equity*. (pp. 10, 212)

Storage time The time a product spends in materials storage, work in process inventory, or finished goods inventory. (p. 841)

Straight-line method A method of depreciation that assumes depreciation depends only on the passage of time and that allocates an equal amount of depreciation to each accounting period in an asset's useful life. (pp. 405, 498)

Strategic objectives Broad, long-term goals that determine the fundamental nature and direction of a business and that serve as a guide for decision making. (p. 728)

Strategic planning The process by which management establishes an organization's long-term goals. (p. 926)

Successful efforts accounting A method of accounting for the costs of exploring and developing oil and gas resources in which successful exploration is recorded as an asset and depleted over the estimated life of the resource and all unsuccessful efforts are immediately written off as losses. (p. 415)

Sunk cost A cost that was incurred because of a previous decision and that cannot be recovered through the current decision. (p. 1041)

Supply chain The path that leads from the suppliers of the materials from which a product is made to the final consumer. Also called the *supply network*. (pp. 728, 832)

Supply-chain management A system of ordering and tracking inventory conducted over the Internet. (p. 305)

Support services Components of the value chain that facilitate the primary processes but do not add value to a product or service. (p. 832)

T

T account The simplest form of account, which is used to analyze transactions. (p. 92)

Tactical objectives Mid-term goals that position an organization to achieve its long-term strategies. (p. 728)

Target costing A pricing method designed to enhance a company's ability to compete, especially in markets for new and emerging products; calculated as Target Price – Desired Profit. (p. 1112)

Term bonds Bonds in one issue that mature at the same time. (p. 490)
Theoretical capacity The maximum productive output for a given period in which all machinery and equipment are operating at optimum speed, without interruption. Also called *ideal capacity.* (p. 874)
Theory of constraints (TOC) A management theory that contends that limiting factors, or bottlenecks, occur during the production of any product or service, but that once managers identify such a constraint, they can focus their attention and resources on it and achieve significant improvements. (p. 843)
Throughput time The time it takes to move a product through the entire production process. (p. 841)
Time and materials pricing A pricing method used by service companies by which they use two computations: one for direct labor and one for materials and parts; also called parts and labor pricing. (p. 1110)
Time value of money The costs or benefits derived from holding or not holding money over time. (p. 458)
Timeliness The qualitative characteristic of information that enables users to receive information in time to influence a decision. (p. 206)
Total direct labor cost variance The difference between the standard direct labor cost for good units produced and actual direct labor costs. (p. 1007)
Total direct materials cost variance The difference between the standard cost and actual cost of direct materials. Also called *good units produced.* (p. 1004)
Total fixed overhead cost variance The difference between actual fixed overhead costs and the standard fixed overhead costs that are applied to good units produced using the standard fixed overhead rate. (p. 1012)
Total manufacturing costs The total costs of direct materials, direct labor, and overhead incurred and transferred to Work in Process Inventory account during an accounting period. Also called *current manufacturing costs.* (p. 719)
Total overhead cost variance The difference between actual overhead costs and standard overhead costs applied. (p. 1010)
Total quality management (TQM) A management tool that requires that all parts of a business work together to build quality into the business's product or service. (pp. 846, 1144)
Total variable overhead cost variance The difference between actual variable overhead costs and the standard variable overhead costs that are applied to good units produced using the standard variable overhead rate. (p. 1011)
Trade credit Credit granted to customers by wholesalers or retailers. (p. 364)
Trade discount A deduction (usually 30 percent or more) off a list or catalogue price, which is not recorded in the accounting records. (p. 248)
Trademark A registered symbol that can be used only by its owner to identify a product or service. (p. 417)
Trading securities A type of marketable security that a company buys and sells for making a profit in the near term as opposed to holding it indefinitely for investment purposes. (p. 597)
Transfer agents A trust company, bank, or similar financial institution assigned by a corporation to maintain records of investors and account balances and transactions. (p. 543)
Transfer price The price at which goods and services are charged and exchanged between a company's divisions or segments. (p. 1116)
Treasury stock Shares of the corporation's own stock that it has bought back on the open market, which reduces the ownership of the business. (p. 545)
Trend analysis A variation of horizontal analysis in which percentage changes are calculated for several successive years instead of for two years. (p. 660)
Trial balance A comparison of the total of debit and credit balances in the accounts to check that they are equal. (p. 104)

U

Uncollectible accounts Accounts receivable owed by customers who cannot or will not pay. Also called *bad debts.* (p. 365)
Underapplied overhead costs The amount by which actual overhead costs exceed the overhead costs applied using the predetermined overhead rate for the accounting period. (p. 765)
Understandability The qualitative characteristic of information that enables users to comprehend the meaning of the information they receive. (p. 206)
Underwriter An intermediary between the corporation and the investing public who facilitates an issue of stock or other securities for a fee. (p. 543)
Unearned revenues Revenues received in advance for which the goods have not yet been delivered or the services performed; a liability account. (pp. 148, 450)
Unit-level activities Activities performed each time a unit is produced. (p. 836)
Unsecured bonds Bonds issued on an corporation's general credit. Also called *debenture bonds.* (p. 490)

V

Valuation The process of assigning a monetary value to a business transaction and the resulting assets and liabilities. (p. 89)
Value-adding activity An activity that adds value to a product or service as perceived by the customer. (p. 834)
Value-adding cost The cost of an activity that increases the market value of a product or service. (p. 715)
Value-based systems An accounting system that provides better customer-related, activity-based information than does the traditional cost-based system. (p. 832)
Value chain A sequence of activities, or primary processes, that add value to a product or service; also includes support services that facilitate these activities. (p. 832)
Variable cost(s) A cost that changes in direct proportion to a change in productive output (or some other measure of volume). (pp. 714, 872)
Variable cost formula A straight line equation, $Y = a(X)$, where Y is total variable cost, a is the variable rate per unit, and X is the units produced. (p. 873)
Variable costing A method of preparing profit center performance reports that classifies a manager's controllable costs as either fixed or variable and produces a variable costing income statement. (p. 962)

Variable overhead efficiency variance The difference between the standard direct labor hours allowed for good units produced and the actual hours worked multiplied by the standard variable overhead rate per hour. (p. 1012)

Variable overhead spending variance The difference between actual variable overhead costs and the standard variable overhead rate multiplied by the actual hours used. Also called the *variable overhead rate variance.* (p. 1012)

Variance The difference between a standard cost and an actual cost. (p. 998)

Variance analysis The process of computing the differences between standard costs and actual costs and identifying the causes of those differences. (p. 999)

Verifiability The qualitative characteristic of information that helps assure users that information faithfully represents what it purports to depict. (p. 206)

Vertical analysis A technique for analyzing financial statements that uses percentages to show how the different components of a statement relate to a total figure in the statement. (p. 661)

W

Wages Compensation of employees at an hourly rate. (p. 447)

Work cell An autonomous production line that can perform all required operations efficiently and continuously. (p. 840)

Work in Process Inventory account An inventory account used to record the manufacturing costs incurred and assigned to partially completed units of product. (p. 718)

Work sheet A type of working paper used as a preliminary step in recording adjusting and closing entries and that is used in preparing the financial statements. (p. 192)

Working capital A measure of liquidity that shows the net current assets on hand to continue business operations; calculated as Total Current Assets – Total Current Liabilities. (p. 214)

Working papers Documents that accountants use to organize their work and that support the information in the financial statements. (p. 192)

Write-down A reduction in the value of an asset below its carrying value on the balance sheet. Also called a *write-off.* (p. 680)

Z

Zero-based budgeting Budgets that are prepared anew each period. All budget items must be justified; nothing is taken for granted. (p. 928)

Zero coupon bonds Bonds that do not pay periodic interest but that pay a fixed amount on the maturity date. (p. 498)

COMPANY NAME INDEX

SUBJECT INDEX

C